CASES

ON

LABOR LAW

By

JAMES M. LANDIS

PROFESSOR OF LAW, HARVARD UNIVERSITY
MEMBER OF SECURITIES AND EXCHANGE COMMISSION

CHICAGO
THE FOUNDATION PRESS, INC.
1934

34-31604

TO

LOUIS D. BRANDEIS
ASSOCIATE JUSTICE
OF THE
SUPREME COURT OF THE UNITED STATES

PREFACE

As a term "labor law" is capable of embracing those instances where the law is concerned either directly with the welfare of workers or with the relations between employers and employees. Hardly a branch of our legal order does not regard as a circumstance material to the fashioning of a rule of law the fact that a party litigant is one of that group of workers generically described as "labor." Thus contracts of employment are governed by a different rule as to the implication of conditions precedent to counter-performance upon the other side; non-performance by the employee has, again, consequences different from that attendant upon default by other contractors. Special considerations have led to the development of a law of master and servant, differing considerably from that of principal and agent, and supplanted in recent years because of its inadequacies by the workmen's compensation acts. Equitable doctrines governing the specific performance of contracts depending for their application upon the character of the service to be rendered distinguish "labor" contracts from other agreements calling for personal service. Judicial enforcement of money claims, through exemptions, by permitting resort on occasion to the criminal law, by limitations upon the power of assignment, by restrictions upon the right of garnishment and otherwise, takes account of the fact of the status of employment. Constitutional law bristles with issues that concern labor relations. The power of the state to impose special liabilities upon groups because of the fact that they are laborers or to confer special privileges upon them for a like reason is and promises to continue to be a battleground of constitutional adjudication. The regulation of various industries, in behalf of a class of workers, deemed incapable under modern industrial conditions of adequately safeguarding their interests, takes innumerable forms and presents varying occasions for invoking constitutional guaranties.

These and other like aspects of law may with right claim shelter under such a term as labor law. An excuse for excluding them must rest not on logical but practical pedagogical grounds. Labor law, broadly defined in this fashion, already runs through the law-school curriculum. No sufficient reason exists for clustering these divergent subjects about the employer-employee relationship and divorcing them from the governing legal conceptions, which already take account in their application of the fact that "labor" is concerned. A narrower conception of labor law must therefore be found, one which will not only bridge a gap in current legal training but will also deal with matters likely to be of vital concern to modern industrial society. A conception which seems to meet

vii

these two requirements centers about the legal treatment accorded to the right of combination by employers and employees and its exercise. The problems of labor law, as popularly conceived today, apart from such issues as group themselves about the constitutionality of social legislation, at bottom resolve themselves into a consideration of the extent to which combinations may pursue variant policies. The element of concerted effort as distinguished from individual action dominates the field, and requires for exploration of its basis knowledge of the conditions of modern industry and the rise of combinations to grapple with its problems. This phase of labor law finds practically no treatment in the traditional legal curriculum. On the other hand, it presses upon practice and theory for consideration.

This conception has dominated the collection of materials in this book. It has, of course, necessitated the sacrificing of much that is pertinent to a fuller conception of the labor problem. No account, for example, is taken of factory legislation and of the multitudinous devices, such as arbitration, employee representation, unemployment insurance, and the like, which seek to furnish means either for a better adjustment of employer-employee conflicts or to provide the employee a securer livelihood. These problems might, perhaps, be said to concern the labor economist more than the labor lawyer, though no labor lawyer, worthy of his salt, dare be ignorant of the larger aspects of his field. Nor is much emphasis placed upon trade union law, in so far as that may concern itself with the rights of an individual member of the association as against the union. This is simply one branch of the law dealing generally with unincorporated associations and, as such, is best taught about the source from which it stems. Obviously no single volume can hope to produce the "compleat" labor lawyer. This seeks only to acquaint him by a lawyer-like concern for details with certain aspects of law, fundamental to any approach to the labor problem as a whole.

Some apology is necessary for the cumulative citations contained in the footnotes. On occasion, the collections of cases have been exhaustive, either with the purpose of illustrating the extent of a particular doctrine or of affording a convenient collection of authorities in a field where neither digest nor standard treatises perform that function. Cases from inferior courts are also cited with little hesitation because of their novelty or because they show a wider application of appellate doctrine. Only rarely is reference made to continental authorities, for the basic assumptions of continental law are generally so foreign that comparison of detailed applications is frequently fruitless.

No general bibliography has been included. To do so would make for unnecessary volume. Instead, reference is made to the relevant social and economic materials in the footnotes with the purpose of pointing to the student access to whatever has a bearing upon the legal problems involved. No references are made to the standard treatises—some of which are noted in the margin ¹—for these have adequate indices. Nor has this volume been planned to afford the basis of a course of thirty-six, seventy-two or a hundred and forty-four lecture hours. Upon its adaptability to programs differing in their demands must rest its claim for publication.

Cambridge, Mass.

JAMES M. LANDIS.

---

¹ Books starred are deemed of special value. American: Andrews, Labor Problems and Labor Legislation (4th ed. 1932); Beckner, History of Labor Legislation in Illinois (1929); *Berman, Labor and the Sherman Act (1930); Blum, Labor Economics (1925); Clark, Law of the Employment of Labor (1911); Cogley, Law of Strikes, Lockouts and Labor Organizations (1894); Commons, Trade Unionism and Labor Problems (1921); Commons and Andrews, Principles of Labor Legislation (Rev. ed. 1927); Commons and Others, History of Labor in the United States (1918); *Commons and Others, Documentary History of American Industrial Society (1910); Cooke, Law of Trade and Labor Combinations (2d ed. 1909); Downey, History of Labor Legislation in Iowa (1910); Eaves, History of California Labor Legislation (1910); *Frankfurter and Greene, The Labor Injunction (1930); Frey, The Labor Injunction (n.d.); Groat, Attitude of American Courts in Labor Cases (1911); Lauchheimer, The Labor of Maryland (1917); Lauck and Watts, The Industrial Code (1922); Martin, Modern Law of Labor Unions (1910); Mason, Organized Labor and the Law (1925); *Oakes, Organized Labor and Industrial Conflicts (1927); Ryan, History of Labor Legislation in Oklahoma (1932); Steever, Control of Labor through Union Discipline (1931); Stimson, Handbook to the Labor Law of the United States (1896); *Witte, The Government in Labor Disputes (1932).

English: Assinder, Legal Position of Trade Unions (1912); Cohen, Trade Union Law (3rd ed. 1913); *Cole, A Short History of the British Working Class Movement (1925); Erle, The Law Relating to Trade Unions (1869); Ferguson, Trade Disputes and the Trade Unions Act (1927); Greenwood, Law Relating to Trade Unions (1911); Hammond, The Village Labourer (1919); Hammond, The Town Labourer (1919); Hammond, The Skilled Labourer (1919); *Hammond, The Rise of Modern Industry (1925); Haslam, The Law Relating to Trade Combinations (1931); *Hedges and Winterbottom, The Legal History of Trade Unionism (1930); Henderson, Trade Unions and the Law (1927); Hewitt, Trade Unions and the Law (1927); Pennant, Trade Unions and the Law (1905); Schloesser and Clark, Legal Position of Trade Unions (1913); *Slesser and Baker, Trade Union Law (3rd ed. 1927); Slesser and Henderson, Industrial Law (1924); Sophian, Trade Union Law and Practice (1927); Webb, Industrial Democracy (1920); *Webb, History of Trade Unionism (Rev. ed. 1920).

TABLE OF CONTENTS

PREFACE vii

TABLE OF CASES xiii

CHAPTER

    I. HISTORICAL INTRODUCTION 1

    II. GENERAL THEORIES 38

    III. INTERFERENCE WITH ADVANTAGEOUS RELATIONS 77

        Section 1. Inducing Breach of Contract 77

        Section 2. Inducing Termination of a Relationship..... 101

        Section 3. Legislative Interference with Anti-Union
                Contracts 167

    IV. THE CONDUCT OF A STRIKER 190

    V. THE ENDS FOR WHICH MEN MAY STRIKE 300

    VI. THE TRADE AGREEMENT 358

    VII. THE BOYCOTT 403

    VIII. THE UNION LABEL 483

    IX. FEDERAL INTERVENTION IN LABOR CONTROVERSIES 495

    X. EMPLOYER INTERFERENCE WITH THE "RIGHT" TO WORK.... 655

    XI. EMPLOYER INTERFERENCE WITH THE "RIGHT" TO TRADE.... 688

INDEX 695

TABLE OF CASES

(Reference is to pages)

Adair v. United States, 167
Ælolian Company v. Fischer, 605, 611
Allen v. Flood, 49
American Steel Foundries v. Tri-City Central Trades Council, 131, 211
Anderson v. Shipowners Ass'n of the Pacific Coast, 680
Armentrout, People v., 194
Auburn Draying Co. v. Wardell, 453

Barker Painting Co. v. Brotherhood of Painters, Decorators, and Paperhangers of America, 336
Barnes v. Typographical Union No. 16, 207
Bayer v. Brotherhood of Painters, Decorators and Paperhangers of America, Local 301, 347
Bayonne Textile Corporation v. American Federation of Silk Workers, 629
Bedford Cut Stone Co. v. Journeymen Stone Cutters' Association, 593
Berry v. Donovan, 370
Bomes v. Providence Local No. 223, 245
Bossert v. Dhuy, 445
Bricklayers', Masons' & Plasterers' International Union v. Seymour Ruff & Sons, 467
Brimelow v. Casson, 82
Brims, United States v., 591

Carew v. Rutherford, 328
Carlson v. Carpenter Contractors' Association of Chicago, 425
Central Metal Products Corp. v. O'Brien, 87
Cohn & Roth Electric Co. v. Bricklayers', Masons' and Plasterers' Local Union No. 1, 472
Coppage v. Kansas, 174
Cornellier v. Haverhill Shoe Manufacturers' Ass'n, 669
Coronado Coal Company v. United Mine Workers of America, 575
Cote v. Murphy, 419
Curran v. Galen, 385

Debs, Petitioner, In re, 496
Denver Tramway Corporation and Amalgamated Ass'n of Street and Electric Railway Employees of America, Div. 1001, In the matter of, 643

Deon v. Kirby Lumber Co., 688
Dick v. Northern Pacific Ry. Co., 655
Duplex Printing Co. v. Deering, 532

Edward F. Caldwell & Co. and Lighting Equipment Workers' Local Union No. 19427, In the matter of, 640
Empire Theatre Co. v. Cloke, 430
Exchange Bakery & Restaurant, Inc. v. Rifkin, 145

Fink & Son v. Butchers' Union No. 422, 433
Fryns v. Fair Lawn Fur Dressing Co., 624

Garret v. Taylor, 38
Gasaway v. Borderland Coal Corporation, 132
General Cigar Company and Cigar Makers International Union of America, In the matter of, 639
Gevas v. Greek Restaurant Workers' Club, 237
Gill Engraving Co. v. Doerr, 458
Goldman v. Cohen, 396
Great Northern Ry. Co. v. Brosseau, 223
Great Northern Ry. Co. v. Local Great Falls Lodge of I. A. of M., 515

Hackney v. Fordson Coal Company, 692
Hilton v. Sheridan Coal Co., 657
Hitchman Coal Co. v. Mitchell, 110
Hoban v. Dempsey, 375

Industrial Association of San Francisco v. United States, 583
Interborough Rapid Transit Co. v. Green, 159
Interborough Rapid Transit Co. v. Lavin, 150
International Organization, U. M. W. A. v. Red Jacket Consolidated Coal & Coke Co., 134
Iron Molders' Union v. Allis-Chalmers Co., 438

Jacobs v. Cohen, 388
Johnson v. American Railway Express Co., 361
Johnson v. Oregon Stevedoring Co., 684
Jonas Glass Co. v. Glass Bottle Blowers' Association, 103

xiii

Keeble v. Hickeringill, 38
Kemp v. Division No. 241, 320

Lawlor v. Loewe, 529
Levering & Garrigues Co. v. Morrin, 184
Loewe v. Lawlor, 522
Lundoff-Bicknell Co. v. Smith, 341

McCarter v. Chamber of Commerce, 414
McCord v. Thompson-Starrett Company, 393
Mogul Steamship Co. v. McGregor, Gow & Co., 42
Moody v. Model Window Glass Co., 358

Nann v. Raimist, 250
National Aniline & Chemical Co. and Allied Chemical Workers' Local No. 18705, In the matter of, 645
National Fireproofing Co. v. Mason Builders' Ass'n, 476
New York, Chicago & St. Louis R. R. Co. v. Schaffer, 662
Nixon, People of State of New York v., 190
Nolan v. Farmington Shoe-Mfg. Co., 164

Parker, Judge, Rejection of, 141
People v. Armentrout, 194
People of the State of New York v. Nixon, 190
Peoples Pharmacies, Inc. and Maryland Ass'n of Employee Pharmacists, Inc., In the matter of, 650
Pickett v. Walsh, 311
Pittsburgh Terminal Coal Corporation v. United Mine Workers of America, 258
Plant v. Woods, 300
Prudential Insurance Company of America v. Cheek, 672

Quinn v. Leathem, 61

R An W Hat Shop, Inc. v. Scully, 91
Railway Employees' Dept., A. F. of L., United States v., 262
Rutan, C. B., Company v. Local Union, No. 4, Hatters' Union of America, 340

Schwartz v. Wayne Circuit Judge, 399
Scott-Stafford Opera House Company v. Minneapolis Musicians Association, 333
Seattle Brewing & Malting Co. v. Hansen, 409
Sheehan v. Levy, 352
Shinsky v. O'Neil, 381
Shinsky v. Tracey, 378
Sorrell v. Smith, 69
South Wales Miners' Federation v. Glamorgan Coal Co., 77
Steffes v. Motion Picture Machine Operators' Union of Minneapolis, 405
Stillwell Theatre, Inc. v. Kaplan, 97
Strasser v. Moonelis, 488

Tamaqua Underwear Co. and Amalgamated Clothing Workers of America, In the matter of, 652
Tarleton v. M'Gawley, 40
Thacker Coal Co. v. Burke, 106
Tracy v. Banker, 491
Truax v. Corrigan, 266

United Leather Workers' International Union v. Herkert & Meisel Trunk Co., 571
United Mine Workers of America v. Coronado Coal Company, 549
United States v. Brims, 591
United States v. Railway Employees' Dept., A. F. of L., 262
United States Gypsum Co. v. Heslop, 439

Vegelahn v. Guntner, 199

Weener v. Brayton, 483
Western Powder Mfg. Co. v. Interstate Coal Co., 620
White Mountain Freezer Co. v. Murphy, 209
Williams v. United States, 511
Willis v. Muscogee Manufacturing Co., 665

Young v. Canadian Northern Ry. Co., 365

CHAPTER I.

HISTORICAL INTRODUCTION.

An approach to labor law can be given a beginning only for pedagogical purposes. Such a beginning must necessarily be an arbitrary one,
but nevertheless far enough back to give both breadth and perspective to
the subject. It is best, perhaps, to take the period of the Black Death
as a starting point, inasmuch as one major consequence of that catastrophe
was to accelerate the process that had already begun, namely the movement
away from an essentially feudalistic economy.

Little common or national law dealing with the labor contract and
its incidents is to be found prior to 1348. The problems were, in the main,
still local. Though industrial enterprise was developing on a small scale
in the towns, the control that the master had over his journeymen or his
apprentices was shaped primarily by regulations of the numerous gilds,
here and there supplemented by the by-laws of the municipalities.[1] In
agriculture, though the labor services attending the institution of villeinage
were fast being commuted for wage payments, thus implying a shift from
the relationship of lord and villein to that of master and servant,[2] such
little mobility attended the laborer that the sanctions necessary for the
enforcement of the relationship needed only to be of a local and not a
national character.

This economy was shaken by the Black Death. The depopulation
that ensued brought with it labor scarcity, and thus created such a disturbing bargaining power in the individual artisan and laborer as to provoke
national intervention.[3] Thus in 1349 came the emergency Ordinance of
Laborers,[4] which was confirmed in 1351 by the Statute of Laborers.[5]
The central feature of these statutes consisted of their introducing into
national law the conception of the duty to labor as well as the conception
of the duty to perform that labor according to fixed and defined standards.
Inasmuch as English legal treatment of the labor contract was to be dominated for centuries by the legal conceptions embodied in these statutes,
their provisions demand some detailed examination.

---

[1] Villeinage seems practically to have disappeared by the end of the fourteenth
century. Cassidy, "The Emergence of the Free Labor Contract," 18 Am. Econ. Rev.
201, 210 (1928).

[2] By the end of the fourteenth century the greater part of town industry was
organized on the gild basis. Few artisans remained outside the forty thousand craft
and social gilds then in existence. Cassidy, *supra* at 211. Municipal regulations seem
first to have been confined to dealing with controversies, but later took over many
of the regulatory functions theretofore exercised by the gilds. *Id.* 212.

[3] Lipson, Economic History of England, The Middle Ages, 82-98 (1929).

[4] 23 Edw. 3.

[5] 25 Edw. 3, st. 1.

They aimed to strike at the individual bargaining power that the Black Death had released. The means employed were to compel persons to labor [6] and to fix the wages of all labor, first at pre-plague prices [7] and later according to a schedule of wages.[8] The taking of excess wages was punished with severity.[9] Moreover, the details of the labor contract were minutely regulated. Day-by-day employment was largely abolished and term engagements substituted.[10] The hiring of certain classes of laborers was required to be done openly and not in private.[11] Of especial importance are the provisions of these statutes that made the labor contract legally enforceable by imposing penalties for its violation. These were utilized by the courts as a basis for devising civil remedies for effectively enforcing labor contracts.[12] The Ordinance of Laborers also imposed liability, both civil and criminal, upon the master who enticed a servant away from another or retained a servant in his employ who had broken his contract of service with another master.[13]

Basic to an understanding of labor law is a realization that these statutes initiated a policy whereby the labor contract and the labor relationship were accorded a different status by the law than that given other contracts and other relationships. With wages fixed, demanding or taking wages in excess of those established by law or custom was criminal. To the civil liability that the law generally attached to the violation of a contract, these statutes thus added a criminal liability if the contract was one that called for labor. The right to employ one's economic bargain-

---

[6] 23 Edw. 3, c. 1.

[7] *Id.*

[8] 25 Edw. 3, st. 1, cc. 1-3.

[9] Under the Ordinance, the laborer taking excessive wages was subject to a penalty of double the sum taken, and the artificer or workman taking more than he was entitled to under the Ordinance, was subject to imprisonment. The latter type of penalty was generally extended to all laborers under the Statute. See Putnam, Enforcement of the Statute of Laborers, 82 (1908).

[10] 25 Edw. 3, st. 1, c. 1. Contracts calling for several days employment, where the statute stipulated a longer term, were commonly held invalid. Brooke Abr. Lab. 51.

[11] 25 Edw. 3, st. 1, c. 1.

[12] See Putnam, op. cit., 189-199; 2 Holdsworth, History of English Law, 462 (3d ed. 1923).

[13] The Ordinance itself provided for no civil liability, but simply a criminal penalty. 23 Edw. 3, c. 2. The civil action, however, was developed out of the Ordinance. Some authorities assume that such an action existed at common law before the Ordinance. See Culpeper, J., in Y.B. 11 Henry 4, f. 23, pl. 46 (1409); 1 Traver's Bolton's Justice, 308 (1750). At common law the master only had an action where the second master took the servant *vi et armis* out of his service. Putnam, *op. cit.*, 195. But under the Ordinance the master had a right against the second master where the latter simply persuaded the servant to leave the first master's service or not to enter into the first master's service when the servant had agreed to do so, and also where the second master took into his service a servant that he knew had broken his engagement with the first master. Brooke Abr. Lab. 33; Fitz. Na. Br. fol. 168b. These provisions of the Ordinance were extended to all classes of laborers and not restricted to manual laborers. School teachers, seneschals, merchants and others fell within the scope of the section. Putnam, *op. cit.* 186-188. The only established exception was that of the chaplain. Brooke Abr. Lab. 16.

ing power, otherwise commonly recognized,[14] was denied to the laborer seeking to dispose of his labor.

The actual enforcement of these statutes is shrouded with considerable doubt. Though later Parliaments piously protested that the statutes were deliberately flouted and thus tried to correct this situation by increasing the penalties for violation, the records are quite replete with attempts to punish offenders.[15] But in the perspective of centuries the actual enforcement of these statutes is of little consequence as compared with their effect in molding the outlines of the law generally concerned with their subject matter. From the Statutes of Laborers sprang the conceptions which were to move courts in the next few centuries in creating a law to govern the relationship of master and servant. Such judge-made law could not, if it were at all true to the ideals of the legislation of Edward III, look with favor upon laborers using either individually or collectively their economic bargaining power; nor could it do otherwise than regard as punishable, breach of the labor contract or interference with the master-servant relationship.

The policy set forth in the Statutes of Laborers was reiterated and amplified by later Parliaments. Though no emergency now pressed for the passage of such legislation, the earlier statutes were re-enacted upon numerous occasions [16] with changes in detail but without deviation from their original purpose of rigidly controling the labor bargain.[17]

The problem of collectivity also appears upon the economic stage of that time. Combinations of artisans and laborers seeking to get higher wages and improve their labor conditions were frequent during the fourteenth century. Much confusion exists as to the attitude that the law took towards these combinations. Writers of repute of the nineteenth and twentieth centuries have sought to deny the existence of any doctrine that the common law regarded a combination of laborers to better their

---

[14] The assizes of bread and ale, as well as the specific provisions of the Ordinance and the Statute limiting the retail prices of articles of necessity, together with similar regulations adopted by various municipalities controlling victuallers, operated to limit the area of bargaining power in other fields. The prohibitions against regrating, forestalling and engrossing must also be noted. See Lipson, *op. cit.*, 270. Nevertheless the restrictions imposed upon bargaining in the labor field must be regarded as exceptional.

[15] See, generally, Putnam, *op. cit., passim.*

[16] For statutes confirming and supplementing the policy of the Statute of Laborers, see 34 Edw. 3, cc. 9 and 10 (1360) ; 42 Edw. 3, c. 6 (1368) ; 2 Rich. 2, st. 1, c. 8 (1378) ; 12 Rich. 2, cc. 3, 4, 5, 7 (1388) ; 13 Rich. 2, st. 1, c. 7 (1389) ; 4 Hen. 4, c. 14 (1402) ; 7 Hen. 4, c. 17 (1405) ; 2 Hen. 5, st. 1, c. 4 (1414) ; 4 Hen. 5, c. 4 (1416) ; 2 Hen. 6, c. 14 (1423) ; 3 Hen. 6, c. 1 (1424) ; 6 Hen. 6, c. 3 (1427) ; 8 Hen. 6, cc. 8 and 11 (1429) ; 11 Hen. 7, c. 22 (1494) ; 12 Hen. 7, c. 3 (1496) ; 4 Hen. 8, c. 5 (1512) ; 6 Hen. 8, c. 3 (1514) ; 2 and 3 Edw. 6, c. 15 (1548).

[17] See Rogers, Six Centuries of Work and Wages, *229 et seq.* (1884). For the thesis that the later legislation cannot be regarded as emergency legislation, but that its proponents employed the debacle of the Black Death as an excuse for introducing a policy of wage regulation deemed advantageous to their own interests, see Robo, "The Black Death in the Hundred of Farnham," 44 Eng. Hist. Rev. 560 (1929). It is of interest to note that the plague was followed by legislation in France, applicable to the county of Paris, substantially similar to the Statute of Laborers. See Robbins, "A Comparison of the Effects of the Black Death on the Economic Organization of France and England," 36 Jour. Pol. Econ. 446, 474 (1928).

condition as criminal.[18] Their insistence begins with the assumption that
all legal treatment of the right of combination must derive from the Ordinance of Conspirators of 1304.[19] This in terms dealt only with abuses
of legal process. True, it was extended to embrace conspiracies to defraud
in later years [20] and the courts were permitted to reach the conspiracy
prior to the commission of any act in pursuance of it, the very conspiracy
being regarded as a sufficiently overt act to be punishable.[21] But, it is
contended, that so far as conspiracies to raise wages were concerned, they
were not punishable at "common law," even though on occasion statutes
expressly made them criminal. The judicial declarations in the seventeenth century which treated such conspiracies as common law crimes [22]
are regarded by these writers either as "not law" or as being based upon
an erroneous statement in Hawkins' Pleas of the Crown.[23] The Combination Acts of 1799 and 1800 are therefore contended by them to be the
introduction of a new policy rather than, like most legislation, authentic
confirmation of existing legal conceptions.[24]

So runs the argument that has been widely accepted by lawyers and
judges. It rests at bottom on a narrow conception of "common law,"
which regards that system as being composed exclusively of reported
judicial decisions with a penumbra of dicta. Such an approach over-
looks the significance of trial court judgments which may never have
reached the higher courts to be authenticated by opinions but represent,
nevertheless, a system of political sanctions which should appropriately
be called law. The approach also neglects to search for the aims of a
society as they may be indicated by the policies expressed in statutes—
statutes which are of themselves the germinating source of "common
law." It would be odd, indeed, for a civilization which sought by law
to repress individual bargaining by the laborer to permit him freely
to engage in collective bargaining. It would be more than odd for a court
to punish a laborer for terminating his relationship with his master, and
to punish him for demanding more than the customary wages, and at
the same time refuse to treat as criminal a combination of laborers seeking
to use their combined bargaining power to bring about an increase in

---

[18] See, e.g., Wright, Law of Criminal Conspiracies (1873) passim; Webb, History of Trade Unionism, c. 2 (1920). For an extended exposition of this viewpoint,
see Sayre, "Criminal Conspiracy," 35 Harv. Law Rev. 393 (1922).

[19] 33 Edw. 1, st. 2. This ordinance, known as the Third Ordinance of Conspirators, summed up the earlier legislation upon conspiracy. See 13 Edw. 1, c. 12
(1285); 28 Edw. 1, c. 10 (1200). See also 4 Edw. 3, c. 11 (1330).

[20] Wright, op. cit., 33.

[21] Anon. 27 Ass. f. 138, pl. 44 (1354); Sydenham v. Keilaway, Cro. Jac. 8
(1574); Poulterers' Case, 9 Co. 55b (1611).

[22] Chief among these cases are Rex v. Journeymen Tailors, 8 Mod. 10 (1721);
Rex v. Eccles, Leach C.C. 274 (1783); Rex v. Hammond, 2 Esp. 719 (1799).

[23] "There can be no doubt, but that all Confederacies whatsoever, wrongfully
to prejudice a third Person, are highly criminal at Common Law, as where divers
Persons confederate together by indirect Means to impoverish a third Person. . ."
Hawkins, Pleas of the Crown, bk. 1, c. 72, §2 (1716).

[24] A brilliant essay taking a different viewpoint and picturing the Combination
Acts as carrying forth the existing policy of the law, is George, "The Combination
Laws Reconsidered," 1 Econ. Hist. 214 (1927). See also 2 Holdsworth, op. cit., 470.

wage rates. And even a cursory examination of the records of four-teenth and fifteenth century legal proceedings will reveal that collective bargaining for advantages to labor was regarded by the law as conduct which could not be tolerated but must be punished.

There is an abundance of evidence from which this legal attitude towards combinations of workingmen is discoverable. Confederacies of artisans seeking to alter wages or laboring conditions, that were established either by law or custom, were a matter of increasing concern, both legis-lative and judicial. As the distinction between masters and journeymen became more marked, journeymen gilds sought to use the power of com-bination to improve their laboring conditions. The reverse was also true, for combinations of masters are to be found seeking to use their powers to resist change and trying to drive wages to the level that they thought appropriate. Illustrations of this legal attitude towards efforts at col-lective bargaining will serve to make more concrete the early fashioning of law to deal with the problems of combination.

As early as 1299 the records disclose the prosecution of a carpenter for combining with others of his trade to bind themselves not to observe an ordinance of the City of London fixing their daily wages.[25] In 1339 a jury found five carpenters guilty of combining to prevent other car-penters who were not "free" of the city from accepting less than a stip-ulated daily wage.[26] In 1349 a group of bakers were indicted for agreeing among themselves not to work except at wages in excess of the customary rate.[27] In the same year a number of cordwainers were prosecuted for much the same offense.[28] In 1360 parliamentary disapproval of com-binations on the part of masons and carpenters was manifested by a statute which provided that "all alliances and covines of masons and carpenters, and congregations, chapters, ordinances and oaths betwixt them made, shall be from henceforth void and wholly annulled: so that every mason and carpenter of what condition that he be, shall be compelled by his master to whom he serveth, to do every work that to him pertaineth to do, or of free stone, or of rough stone."[29] In 1365 we find an attach-ment against several cordwainers for "rebelling against the masters of the mistery," and their liberation after payment of a fine with a warning by the court "not to join in covins and confederacies in future."[30] The next year one jury finds several fullers guilty "of forming a confederacy, calling out the working fullers and committing assault by contumelious words,"[31] while another jury returns a verdict against Flemish weavers for pursuing a similar course of conduct.[32] In 1381 a group of spur-riers were convicted of conspiring to raise wages and determine the con-

---

[25] See George, *supra*, 223.
[26] *Ibid.*
[27] *Ibid.*
[28] *Ibid.*
[29] 34 Edw. 3, c. 9.
[30] Calendar of Plea and Memoranda Rolls of the City of London, 1364-1381 (Thomas ed. 1929) 22-23.
[31] *Id.* 54.
[32] *Id.* 65.

ditions of their labor. A chief count in this complaint set forth an attempt to collect dues from the members of their craft to provide a fund for pursuing their common design.[33] In 1396 one finds the master saddlers of London complaining that their journeymen "had formed covins thereon with the object of raising their wages to an excess."[34] With the turn of the century, a second legislative attack on labor combination is made, a statute in 1424 proscribing the holding of congregations and chapters of masons aimed at defeating the policy of the Statute of Laborers. Offenders against its provisions were to be punished as felons.[35]

Such a sampling is enough to give a picture of the legal treatment of the right of combination. The attitude made manifest is one repressive of collective bargaining by workingmen and, as such, it continues throughout the fifteenth century, featured by occasional judicial condemnations of confederacies, and more often by municipal and gild ordinances aimed directly at combinations of their journeymen.[36] Parliamentary disapproval of collective action was forthcoming again in 1548.

The Bill of Conspiracies of Victuallers and Craftsmen,[37] enacted that year, imposed heavy penalties upon "any artificers, workmen or labourers [who] do conspire, covenant, or promise together, or make any oaths, that they shall not make or do their works but at a certain price of rate, or shall not enterprize or take upon them to finish that another hath become, or shall do but a certain work in a day, or shall not work but at certain hours and times." A statute such as this, general in its application, and expressive of a policy already more than two centuries old, leaves little doubt of the basic attitude of the older English law towards the right of combination.

That judicial pronouncements from the higher courts are lacking during this period, is immaterial. Two centuries were to elapse before judges of higher courts were to be called upon to make "common law" to deal with combinations of workingmen striving to improve their conditions. When that occasion arrived, it would have been inconceivable for judges in making law to turn their backs to economic postulates common then to some four centuries of law-making, namely, those that regarded as unlawful combinations of workingmen to dictate or effect the labor bargain.

In 1562 the Elizabethan Statute of Laborers was enacted.[38] This, as distinguished from the intermediate legislation, was a comprehensive labor code. It repeated much of the earlier legislation and sought to reconcile the conflicts that had been developed. In its main outlines it intro-

---

[33] *Id.* 291-294.

[34] See Cassidy, *supra*, 212.

[35] 3 Hen. 6, c. 1.

[36] For additional material on this period, see Lipson, *op. cit.*, 349-363; Bonnett, "The Origin of the Labor Injunction," 5 So. Cal. Law Rev. 105, 109 (1931).

[37] 2 and 3 Edw. 6, c. 15.

[38] 5 Eliz., c. 4.

duced no novel principles but simply reaffirmed the policies developed by the earlier statutes. It dealt with three major problems.[39] By a series of provisions, most of them concerned with the questions raised by the system of apprenticeship, it aimed at the improvement of the technical performance of artisans.[40] Its second objective was to effect an appropriate distribution of the existing labor supply as between industry and agriculture, by placing restrictions upon the mobility of town and country laborers [41] and by insisting upon certain qualifications as a condition for exemption from the necessity of serving at husbandry.[42] Its third and chief concern was more accurately to define the relationship of master and servant.

In dealing with the problems arising out of the labor contract, the Statute of Elizabeth made few departures from the earlier law. It reenforced the idea of the obligation to labor, compelling certain classes of individuals, both men and women,[43] to engage either in industry [44] or agriculture.[45] It retained the conception of a duty to work at a fixed wage, but provided administrative machinery for determining periodically and for different industries what that wage should be.[46] Taking and giving excessive wages were made punishable by fine and imprisonment.[47] Breach of the labor contract by master or servant was made a penal offence,[48] and imprisonment of a servant until he should be willing to work at the prescribed wage was authorized.[49] Hours of service and the term for which the contract should run were also fixed by the Statute.[50]

The Statute of Elizabeth neglected to make any special provision dealing with the enticement of servants. But the action for enticement

---

[39] See 2 Holdsworth, History of English Law, 380 (1924).

[40] §§ 25-36, 41, 42. These clauses of the Statute were repealed in 1809 so far as they affected the wool manufacturers and were completely repealed in 1814. See Perry, "The Repeal of the Apprenticeship Clauses of the Statute of Apprentices," 3 Econ. Hist. Rev. 67 (1931).

[41] By § 7 persons who had neither worked nor had any training in the crafts. nor had insufficient independent means of subsistence were compellable to perform agricultural labor. By § 22 justices of the peace and constables were authorized to get together a *posse comitatus* of artificers and laborers to prevent a loss of a harvest.

[42] 5 Eliz. c. 4.

[43] By § 24 unmarried women over twelve and under forty years could be compelled to serve.

[44] § 4.

[45] § 7.

[46] § 15.

[47] §§ 18-19.

[48] §§ 5, 9, 13.

[49] § 9.

[50] §§ 2, 12. These sections are the source of the common law rule holding that when a master hires a servant without mentioning any time of service, the term is for a year. Co. Litt. 42b; Fawcett v. Cash, 5 B. & Ad. 907 (1834). See Holdsworth, "A Neglected Aspect of the Relations between Economic and Legal History," 1 Econ. Hist. Rev. 114 (1927).

survived this neglect, being recognized as late as 1795 as still having as wide a scope as was originally given it.[51]   Not only was enticement still actionable, but the mere employment of a servant who had broken his first contract of service sufficed to make the second master liable if he knew of the servant's having fled from his first master.[52]

The Statute of Elizabeth thus again reaffirmed the tenor of legal treatment theretofore given the labor contract.   In some aspects it indicates a less repressive attitude towards industrial and agricultural labor than had prevailed during the earlier centuries.   The administrative machinery that it set up for wage determination afforded some play to the growing needs of the laborer.   Then, too, industrial activity had a considerable expansion during the later Elizabethan era and the consequent dependence upon the artisan led to some further favorable consideration of his position.   But no recognition had yet been afforded by the law to any right on the part of the laborer either individually or collectively to use his economic bargaining power to further his interests as a laborer.

The seventeenth century was barren in the development of labor law.   The disturbed condition of England during the major portion of that century operated as a check upon such industrial activity as had been begun under Elizabeth.   The Cromwellian rebellion, however much it furthered the interests of the gentry, had no spokesman or champion for the artisan.   Thus no relaxation in the rigor of the law is ascertainable,[53] nor is there any fundamental change in the general attitude of the ruling classes toward the laborer.

The Revolution of 1688 and the growth of responsible government that ensued brought back a degree of economic stability that meant fairly rapid development of manufactures.   The beginning of the eighteenth century thus brings the labor problem to the forefront.   The advantages of combination both to employers and workingmen were soon realized by them, whereas the general social order remained convinced of the potential dangers incipient in such concerted action.   It is thus only natural that combinations of employers to raise prices were regarded as punishable.   The economic power latent in such combination and the uses to which it could be put could hardly expect to receive sympathetic treat-

---

51 Hart v. Aldridge, 1 Cowp. 54 (1774).

52 In Adams and Bafeald's case, 1 Leo. 240 (1591), a divided court held that actual enticement had to be shown, but the King's Bench in Blake v. Lanyon, 6 T.R. 221 (1795), held that mere employment of a servant known to be under contract with another was actionable. See 4 Holdsworth, History of English Law, 383 (1924).

53 The attitude manifested by the courts continued intensely paternalistic in character and still regarded individual attempts to disturb existing economic conditions as wrongs to the body politic. Cf. James Bigg's case, 11 Co. 93b, 98a (1616) ; Rex v. Sidley, 1 Sid. 168 (1664).

ment from a judiciary or a government still dominated by a land-owning gentry.[54]

In the field of labor relations the attitude of government towards combinations of laborers is made evident by a series of statutes condemning concerted activity of all kinds directed towards the alteration of existing labor relationships. Thus in 1720 Parliament, reciting that the journeymen tailors of London and Westminster "have entered into combinations to advance their wages to unreasonable prices, and lessen their usual hours of work, which is of evil example, and manifestly tends to the prejudice of trade, to the encouragement of idleness, and to the great necessity of the poor, decreed that all such contracts, covenants or agreements be null and void, and that all persons entering into them should be condemned to hard labor or the common gaol without bail or mainprize."[55] In 1725 the weavers, accused by Parliament of having "presumed, contrary to law, to enter into Combinations," were directed not to enter into such combinations under pain of imprisonment.[56] In 1749 the provisions of this statute were extended to cover journeymen dyers and persons engaged in the manufacture of felts and hats, as well as to other textile trades.[57] In 1773 the journeymen weavers in silk manufacture were forbidden to enter into any combination to raise their wages and also to assemble in any numbers exeeeding ten with the intent to frame or deliver petitions touching their wages or prices of work unless such petitions were for presentation to the justices of peace, who had been invested with the right to fix the wages.[58] In 1793 riotous conduct by seamen, keelmen, casters and ship carpenters of the type that would commonly occur during labor difficulties was made highly penal.[59] In 1796 employees in the paper manufactories were forbidden to combine to raise their wages and all as-

---

[54] Thus in Anon., 12 Mod. 248 (1698), Holt, C.J., granted leave to file an information against several plate-button workers for combining by covenants not to sell under a set rate, saying: "It is fit that all confederacies, by those of trade to raise their rates, should be suppressed." The effort to explain cases of this character on the ground that they violated the engrossing statutes. See Wright, Criminal Conspiracies, (Am. ed. 1887) 35, and Nelles, "The First American Labor Case," 41 Yale Law Jour. 165, 196 (1931)), cannot be justified. The act of refusing to sell except at a certain price was not in itself a violation of the engrossing statutes. The court thus had to find that the illegality resided in the fact of combination. Similarly in Rex v. Norris, 2 Ken. 300 (1758), an information was filed against salt proprietors for agreeing under a penalty of £200 not to sell salt under a certain price. "Lord Mansfield declared, that if any agreement was made to fix the price of salt, or any other necessary of life (which salt emphatically was), by people dealing in that commodity, the court would be glad to lay hold of an opportunity, *from what quarter soever the complaint came*, to show their sense of the crime; and that at what rate soever the price was fixed, high or low, made no difference, for all such agreements were of bad consequence, and ought to be discountenanced. He mentioned an indictment, upon one of the last home-circuits, against the bakers of the town of Farnham, for such an agreement." See also 12 Geo. 1, c. 35 (1725); 2 Geo. 2, c. 15, (1729).

[55] 7 Geo. 1, st. 1, c. 13.

[56] 12 Geo. 1, c. 34, amended by 29 Geo. 2, c. 33 (1756), and 30 Geo. 2, c. 12 (1759). See Hammond, The Skilled Labourer, 157 (1919).

[57] 22 Geo. 2, c. 27, amended by 17 Geo. 3, c. 55 and c. 56 (1777).

[58] 13 Geo. 3, c. 68.

[59] 33 Geo. 3, c. 67.

semblages for such a purpose were declared illegal.[60] The very existence of a society was looked upon with suspicion and, if secret or if the members were bound together by oaths, such societies were regarded as unlawful and their members subjected to criminal penalties.[61]

The course of English legislation for Ireland is essentially similar. In 1727 combinations to enhance the price of coals were specifically proscribed.[62] In 1729 a statute was passed generally making criminal all combinations which sought to control the pursuit of a trade, affect the price of goods, raise wages or lessen the hours of work.[63] In 1743 a complementary statute was enacted seeking to make the provisions of the former statute more effectual by treating congregations of persons for the ends mentioned as unlawful assemblies.[64] In 1755 combinations of miners were legislated against.[65] In 1763 another comprehensive anti-combination statute was passed which made it criminal for any person to summon "any manufacturer, artificer, weaver, journeyman, apprentice, or labourer, usually employed in any branch of the linen, hempsen, or cotton manufacture, or . . . in any other trade or manufacture, to appear at any meeting in order to consult upon, or to enter into any rule, agreement, or combination to ascertain or fix the price of labour or workmanship . . . or . . . by force, menaces, or otherwise, hinder or attempt to hinder any such manufacturer, artificer, weaver, journeyman, apprentice, or labourer as aforesaid, to work at his or their respective trade or trades, at such prices as he or they shall agree for with his or their respective employers . . ."[66] In 1771 combinations of the journeymen tailors and journeymen shipwrights of Dublin designed to raise their wages were outlawed.[67] In 1779 Parliament decreed that all such combinations among manufacturers as well as journeymen were "publick nuisances," and elaborately cataloged what acts antecedent to the actual carrying out of the conspiracy were sufficient to support a conviction.[68]

The development of the treatment of combinations of laborers by the courts during this period parallels the legislative attitude. The records disclose several instances when the magistrates dealt rigorously with combinations of employees seeking to raise their wages.[69] In 1721 in *Rex v. Journeymen-Tailors of Cambridge*,[70] an indictment of journeymen tailors for conspiracy to raise their wages was considered by the King's Bench. The case, inasmuch as later authorities regarded it as a land-

---

[60] 36 Geo. 3, c. 111.

[61] 39 Geo. 3, c. 79 (1799).

[62] 1 Geo. 2, c. 21, § 1.

[63] 3 Geo. 2, c. 14.

[64] 17 Geo. 2, c. 8, § 3.

[65] 29 Geo. 2, c. 12, § 11. This Act was made perpetual by 1 Geo. 3, c. 17, § 15 (1761).

[66] 3 Geo. 3, c. 34, §§ 23, 24.

[67] 11 and 12 Geo. 3, c. 33.

[68] 19 and 20 Geo. 3, c. 19, amended by 25 Geo. 3, c. 48, § 18 (1785). See also 27 Geo. 3, c. 15 (1787).

[69] See Heaton, "The Assignment of Wages in the West Riding of Yorkshire in the Seventeenth and Eighteenth Centuries," 24 Econ. Jour. 210.

[70] 8 Mod. 10 (1721).

mark in labor law, deserves special notice. The court held that the indictment set forth a crime saying that "a conspiracy of any kind is illegal although the matter about which they conspired might have been lawful for them, or any of them to do, if they had not conspired to do it, as appears in the case of *The Tubwomen v. The Brewers of London.*"[71] The authority of this case as accurately setting forth the common-law doctrine 'of conspiracy as applied to combinations of laborers was to be disputed at later periods and is disputed today. It is said not to be an instance of the application of the common law inasmuch as the conduct complained of was made criminal by the statute of 7 Geo. 1, c. 13.[72] To this, however, there are two conclusive answers. The statute of 7 Geo. 1, c. 13, by its terms applied only to the journeymen tailors of London and Westminster, whereas the defendants were journeymen tailors of Cambridge. Furthermore the indictment was brought not under the statute but under common law, the court replying to the contention that the indictment was faulty by not concluding *contra forman statuti,* by saying that the indictment need not so conclude inasmuch as it was "for a *conspiracy,* which is an offense at common law." A further attack upon the case has been made on the ground that the reporter could not be relied upon.[73] But though the Modern Reports may be justly so criticized in general terms, more evidence of their fallaciousness in this instance is demanded in order to substantiate such an assault. Finally the case is disputed upon the thesis that it has no foundation at "common law."[74] The answer to such a charge is not to be made by merely counting the few authorities that may antedate the case. "Common law" must be made to meet the occasions that arise, and a review of the antecedent social trends demonstrates how inescapably, from the viewpoint of that society, the court was driven to its conclusion that combinations of employees to raise wages were criminal conspiracies. As Recorder Levy of the Mayor's Court in Philadelphia about a hundred years later succinctly described the common law attitude towards collective labor action: "A combination of workmen to raise their wages may be considered in a two fold point of view: one is to benefit themselves . . . the other is to injure those who do not join their society. The rule of law condemns both."[75]

---

[71] The case of The Tubwomen v. The Brewers of London, referred to as a precedent by the court, has never been definitely placed. It is generally supposed to be the case of Rex v. Starling, 1 Leo. 125, 1 Sid. 174, 1 Keb. 650 (1665). See Pennington, "The Tubwomen v. The Brewers of London," 3 Col. Law Rev. 447 (1903).

[72] For the terms of the statute, see *supra* p. 9. For the contention that the case is no authority because based on statute, see Sayre, "Criminal Conspiracy", 35 Harv. Law Rev. 339, 403 (1922); Nelles, "The First American Labor Case," 41 Yale Law Jour. 165, 197 (1931).

[73] See, *e.g.,* Sampson *arguendo* in People v. Melvin, 3 Common and Andrews, Doc. Hist. of Am. Ind. Soc. 284 (1910).

[74] See Hedges and Winterbottom, The Legal History of Trade Unionism, 17 (1930); Wright, Criminal Conspiracies, § 1 (1873); Sayre, *supra;* Nelles, *supra,* at 199.

[75] Case of the Philadelphia Cordwainers (1806), 3 Commons and Andrews, Doc. Hist. of Am. Ind. Soc. 59. 233 (1910).

The decision in the *Journeymen Tailors* case was followed in *Rex v. Eccles*,[76] where the indictment set forth conduct on the part of journeymen tailors designed to impoverish an employer. In that case Lord Mansfield took occasion to state that "the illegal combination is the gist of the offense, persons in possession of any articles of trade may sell them at such prices as they may individually please, but if they confederate and agree not to sell them under certain prices, it is conspiracy; so every man may work at what price he pleases, but a combination not to work under certain prices is an indictable offense."[77] It is true that these two decisions are the only pronouncements upon this subject made during that century by the greater courts. But evidence exists that prosecutions of striking workmen for conspiracy were not uncommon in the inferior courts. In 1761 indictments were returned against journeymen cabinetmakers for combining to raise their wages and lessen their hours of work.[78] In 1765 and 1770 London tailors were indicted for conspiracy at the Old Bailey without any particular regard to the statutes affecting the pursuit of their trade.[79] In 1786 five London bookbinders were convicted of conspiracy for leading a strike to reduce their working hours from twelve to eleven.[80] In 1798 five journeymen printers were indicted for conspiracy at the Old Bailey,[81] and in 1799 two London shoemakers were prosecuted for picketing and two York shoemakers were convicted of combining to raise the price of their labor.[82]

Secondary authorities uniformly concur in this view that the general crime of conspiracy embraced all the common collective activities of employees.[83] Indeed, the conception that there was no such common law crime capable of making illegal the ordinary employee combination, seems not to have been seriously argued until in a later era, men sought a legal justification for their humanitarian impulses and a defense for their avowal of the desirability of trade unionism.[84] The philosophical

---

[76] Leach C.C. 274 (1783).

[77] See also Grose, J., in Rex v. Mawbey, 6 T.R. 619, 636 (1796): "As in the case of journeymen conspiring to raise their wages: each may insist on raising his wages if he can; but if several meet for the same purpose, it is illegal, and the parties may be indicted for a conspiracy."

[78] See George, "The Combination Law Reconsidered," 1 Econ. Hist. 214, 220 (1927).

[79] *Ibid.* It is probable that indictments for the common law crime of conspiracy were resorted to rather than prosecutions under the statute because of the more severe penalties attached to the former crime.

[80] Webb, History of Trade Unionism, 79 (1920 ed.).

[81] *Id.* 78.

[82] *Id.* 79, 80.

[83] See *e.g.*, Traver's Bolton's Justice, c. 57 (1750); Crown Circ. Com. 169 (Stubbs and Talmasch ed. 1749), 249 (6th ed. 1790), 134 (1st Am. ed. 1816); M'Nally, Justice of the Peace, 503 (10th ed. 1820); East, Pleas of the Crown, 462 (1803).

[84] This method of legal argument is common to writers trained in the viewpoint of the historical school. Instead of attacking existing doctrine as being socially unjustifiable, their method of approach is to demonstrate by historical research that the true legal doctrine is that which they deem socially justifiable. An example of the same phenomenon in legal writing is to be found in those American scholars who, disliking the American constitutional doctrine of judicial supremacy, seek to demonstrate that Marbury v. Madison, was wrong as a matter of "law."

difficulty involved in the conclusion that conspiracy was the gist of the offense and that two or more could not combine to do what each of them acting individually could lawfully do disturbed none of the judges during this period.[85]   Instead they reacted to the inevitable impulse of trying to protect their economic society against the thrust of collective action by both employers and employees, trying either to retain the earlier concept of governmental determination of wages and hours or the later assumption that as to these and other conditions of labor only individual bargaining was to be allowed.   They perceived concretely enough the dangers to their traditional economy involved by any recognition of the legality of collective action and, in seeking for an appropriate legal instrument with which to avert that danger, naturally enough seized upon the convenient and flexible device of conspiracy.   By making the legality of combination depend upon the test of "illegal purposes" or "unlawful means,"[86] they were enabled to mould a legal doctrine that would serve the end of keeping their civilization true to what they conceived to be its objectives.

The Combination Acts of 1799 and 1800 are thus not to be regarded as ushering in any new or unusual legal concepts but rather as confirm-

---

[85] Sergeant Talfourd seems alone to have been bothered with the question of just what constituted the offense. Thus he says: "It is not easy to understand on what principle conspiracies have been holden indictable where neither the end nor the means are, in themselves, regarded by the law as criminal, however reprehensible in point of morals. Mere concert is not in itself a crime. . . . If, then, there be no indictable offence in the object; no indictable offence in the means; and no indictable offence in the concert, in what part of the conduct of the conspirators is the offence to be found? Can several circumstances, each perfectly lawful, make up an unlawful act? And yet such is the general language held on this subject, that at one time the immorality of the object is relied on; at another, the evidence of the means; while, at all times, the concert is stated to be the essence of the charge; and yet that concert, independent of an illegal object or illegal means, is admitted to be blameless." Dickinson, A Practical Guide to the Quarter Sessions, 201 (Talfourd's ed. 1829). *Cf.* also Holmes, J., dissenting in Vegelahn v. Guntner, 167 Mass. 92 (1896) : "But there is a notion which latterly has been insisted on a good deal, that a combination of person to do what any one of them lawfully might do by himself will make the otherwise lawful conduct unlawful. It would be rash to say that some as yet unformulated truth may not be hidden under this proposition. But in the general form in which it has been presented and accepted by many courts, I think it plainly untrue, both on authority and on principle." Similarly Professor Sayre, following Sergeant Talfourd's line of thought, can find nothing in the addition of the element of concert, in itself not criminal, to other acts admittedly not criminal which can logically support the conclusion that the result should be regarded as criminal. Sayre, Criminal Conspiracy, 35 Harv. Law Rev. 393, 411 (1922). Dicey's answer to this contention is that the element of concert so remakes the other elements as to result in a new and different thing. Dicey, Law and Opinion in England, 154 (2d ed. 1926). Obviously an economic society relegated to individual bargaining is a wholly different society from one that recognizes the validity of collective action. To judges, opposed to such a latter society, concert of action for ends individually lawful to attain would naturally be regarded as unlawful.

[86] The most succinct statement of this doctrine was made by Lord Denman in Jones' Case, 4 B. & Ad. 345, 349 (1832) : "An indictment for a conspiracy ought to show, either that it was for an unlawful purpose, or to effect a lawful purpose by unlawful means."

ing a viewpoint towards labor centuries old in its origin and application.[87]
True, back of the urge of these statutes was the growing fear of combination, engendered largely by the impregnation of English workingmen with Jacobean doctrines and accelerated by a growing realization
on the part of labor that collectivity was the only means whereby it could
hope to compete with the economic power of the employer. Legislation
is frequently resorted to to confirm existing legal doctrine with the hope
that public enunciation of its character and a renewed public avowal to
enforce it will lead to greater general public obedience. Motives of this
type lay behind these enactments.

The Act of 1799 [88] was in itself largely accidental. It resulted from
a petition of the master millwrights for leave to bring in a bill to deal in
a more summary fashion with combinations among their workmen, which
on Wilberforce's suggestion was extended into a general combination
law.[89] The Act made "illegal, null, and void . . . all contracts, covenants
and agreements whatsoever, in writing or not in writing, at any time or
times heretofore made or entered into by or between any journeymen
manufacturers or other workmen, or other persons within this kingdom,
for obtaining an advance of wages of them, or any of them, or any other
journeymen manufacturers or workmen, or other persons in any manufacture, trade, or business, or for lessening or altering their or any of
their usual hours of time or working, or for decreasing the quantity of
work, or for preventing or hindering any person or persons from employing whomsoever he, she, or they shall think proper to employ in his, her,
or their manufacture, trade or business, or for controlling or in any way
affecting any person or persons carrying on any manufacture, trade, or
business, in the conduct or management thereof."[90] Persons concerned
in the making of such contracts or persons entering into them were made
criminally liable.[91] Furthermore, every journeyman or workman who
should "by giving money, or by persuasion, solicitation or intimidation,
or any other means, directly or indirectly, endeavour to prevent any unhired
or unemployed journeyman, or workman, or other person in any manufacture, trade, or business, or any other person wanting employment in
such manufacture, trade, or business, from hiring himself to any manufacturer or tradesman, or person conducting any manufacture, trade, or
business, or who shall, for the purpose of obtaining an advance of wages
or for any other purpose contrary to the provision of this act by any
means whatsoever, directly or indirectly, decoy, persuade, solicit, intimi-

---

[87] Most legal writing on this subject has followed the lead of the Webbs in
treating these Acts as inaugurating a "far-reaching change of policy." See Webb,
The History of Trade Unionism. 64 (1920 ed.); Hedges and Winterbottom, The
Legal History of Trade Unionism, c. 3 (1930); Hammond, The Town Labourer,
112 (1919). The contrary viewpoint is effectively presented in George, "The Combination Laws Reconsidered," 1 Econ. Hist. 214 (1927).

[88] 39 Geo. 3, c. 81.

[89] The parliamentary history of the Act of 1799 as well as of the Act of 1800
is fully set forth in Hammond, The Town Labourer, c. 7 (1919).

[90] § 1.

[91] § 2.

date, influence, or prevail, or attempt or endeavour to prevail, on any journeyman or workman, or other person hired or employed, or to be hired or employed in any such manufacture, trade or business, to quit or leave his work, service or employment, or who shall hinder or prevent, or attempt to hinder or prevent, any manufacturer or tradesman, or other person, from employing in his or her manufacture, trade, or business, such journeymen, workmen, and other persons as he or she shall think proper, or who, being hired or employed shall refuse to work with any other journeyman or workman employed or hired to work therein," should be guilty of a criminal offense.[92] Other sections of the Act made criminal attending a meeting for the purposes declared illegal by the statute, and soliciting funds or making subscriptions for effectuating such ends.[93] Trials under the Act were before a single justice of the peace without the intervention of a jury.

The Act of 1799 brought forth some protests from the workmen,[94] and the next Parliament alleviated a little, but only a little, its rigor. The Act of 1800 [95] substituted two magistrates for the one magistrate theretofore set up as the court to try offenses under the Act. It eliminated the vague phraseology of "directly or indirectly" in the anti-picketing section of the Act, substituting therefor the words "wilfully and maliciously." The most important change, however, was the addition of certain arbitration clauses, giving a judicial remedy in those situations where objection was made to wages, hours or the conditions of labor. But the anti-combination features of the Act of 1799 were kept intact.

The period from 1800 to 1824 is replete with persecutions of collective labor tactics of all kinds. Many of these were prosecutions brought under the Combination Act of 1800;[96] but many, generally more severe in character, were still prosecutions at common law for conspiracy.[97] The Act of 1800, however, demonstrated the ruling viewpoint that combinations of workmen were not to be tolerated and for a time there were efforts to make the statute more drastic rather than to relax its rigor.[98] Meanwhile, however, trade union activities were being carried on even though occasionally the leaders were caught and severely punished. Industrial unrest furthered the general resentment of the working class to this

---

[92] § 3.

[93] §§ 4, 5.

[94] See Hammond, The Town Labourer, 124 (1919).

[95] 40 Geo. 3, c. 106.

[96] See Hammond, op. cit., 129-134. The Webbs in their History of Trade Unionism (1920 ed.) 71-93, give numerous instances of the prosecution of striking workmen, but they do not make clear whether these prosecutions are under the Combination Acts or at common law.

[97] "But what the inquiry [the evidence given to the parliamentary Committee on Artisans and Machinery in 1824] does show is that the Act of 1800 was a far less potent instrument of oppression than a prosecution for conspiracy at common law. . . . For instance, the prosecution of The Times compositors in 1810 which started Place on his campaign against the Combination Laws, was under an indictment for conspiracy, sentences of from nine months to two years' imprisonment being given." George, "The Combination Laws Reconsidered," 1 Econ. Hist. 214, 216 (1927).

[98] See Hammond, op. cit., 134.

denial of the right of collective action. The introduction of machinery
resulted in repeated reductions of wages, and the substitution of women
and children for the skilled adult male worker that the alterations of
processes made possible meant continued degradation of the standard
of living.

The movement for the repeal of the Combination Act of 1800 springs
largely from a general reaction to the severe treatment accorded combinations of workers during this period. More particularly it is attributable
to the efforts of two men, Francis Place and Joseph Hume.[99] The former,
a tailor and an employer, who had recoiled from the judicial handling
of combinations of workmen seeking to improve their unfortunate circumstances, was abetted in Parliament by the able radical Hume. In
1824 they succeeded in getting a parliamentary committee appointed to
consider the combination laws, and so adroitly managed both the committee and the evidence presented to it, that the declaratory resolutions
of the committee were enacted with scarcely any debate by Parliament.

Such was the genesis of the Combination Act of 1824.[100] It repealed
all the earlier combination laws and provided further that workmen combining to obtain an advance in wages, to lessen their hours of work or to
decrease the quantity of work, to induce others to depart from their
work, or to regulate the mode of carrying on the trade, should not be
subject to indictment or prosecution for conspiracy under common law
or under statute. Similar liberty was accorded combinations of masters.
Persons, however, who used violence or threats or intimidation wilfully
and maliciously to induce others to leave their work or not to accept
work or to accomplish other similar ends were still to be criminally
punishable. Conspiracies to effect these ends by such means were also
outlawed.

The victory of Place and Hume in the Combination Act of 1824 was
short-lived. Not only had Parliament failed adequately to recognize the
import of this legislation when it passed the statute, but workmen, taking
advantage of its provisions, organized a series of strikes that made public
opinion recoil from the grant of these liberties.[101] Thus the employers
in the next Parliament insisted upon its repeal. Place and Hume fought
a brilliant rear-guard action but could only win for the workmen upon
minor details. The Combination Act of 1825 [102] had few positive provisions of great significance. It elaborated somewhat the anti-picketing
provisions of the Act of 1824 making it a crime if "any person shall by
violence to the person or property, or by threats or intimidation or by
molesting or in any way obstructing another, or endeavour to force any
journeyman, manufacturer, workman or other person hired or employed in
any manufacture, trade or business, to depart from his hiring, employment or work, or to return his work before the same shall be finished,

---

[99] The full story of Place's efforts is to be found in Wallace, Life of Francis
Place, c. 8 (1898).
[100] 5 Geo. 4, c. 95.
[101] See Webb, *op. cit.*, 104.
[102] 6 Geo. 4, c. 129.

or prevent or endeavour to prevent any journeyman, manufacturer, work-man or other person not being hired or employed from hiring himself to, or from accepting work or employment from any person or per-sons . . ."[103]   Employees were expressly permitted to meet together for "consulting upon and determining" the rate of wages or hours, and agreements fixing wages and hours were legalized.[104] The great impor-tance of the Act of 1825, however, lies in its repeal of the Act of 1824 thus restoring the common law of conspiracy as applied to collective labor action.[105]

The common law of conspiracy was not, however, restored to its full extent. The Act of 1825 had legalized voluntary collective action in the form of trade agreements when dealing with wages and hours of labor. The legalization of these ends when attempted by such "vol-untary" means, had a tendency to make the pursuit of those ends by the ordinary peaceful strike not punishable as a criminal conspiracy.[106] No cases thereafter, like *Rex v. Journeyman Tailors of Cambridge,* hold in-dictable the mere combination to raise wages or lessen hours of work.[107] This judicial attitude had the effect of permitting the existence of trade unions; but, at the same time, activities of workmen deemed oppressive of employers were still punished by emphasizing the illegality of the means that they employed. Though the strike *per se* might not be unlaw-ful, not only were its ordinary incidents unlawful, but when directed towards ends deemed undesirable by the judges, the strike was regarded as that type of an unlawful "threat" which made its participants guilty of criminal conspiracy. Thus any strike which sought the discharge of certain persons obnoxious to the striking workers was illegal, either as a matter of common law or as the sort of "threat" made illegal under section 3 of the Act of 1825.[108] Furthermore any type of picketing was

---

103 § 3.

104 § 4.

105 For an analysis and comparison between the Combination Acts of 1824 and 1825, see Dicey, Law and Opinion in England, 191-202 (1926).

106 See Erle, The Law Relating to Trade Unions, 57 (1869) ; Crompton, J., in Walsby v. Anley, 3 E. & E. 516, 523 (1861) ; Cockburn, C.J. in Regina v. Stainer, 11 Cox C.C. 483, 486 (1870).

107 Thus in Regina v. Selsby, 5 Cox C.C. 495n, 498 (1847), Rolfe, B., says: "It is doubtless lawful for people to agree among themselves not to work except on certain terms." See also Cockburn, C.J., in Wood v. Bowson, 2 Q.B. 21, 25 (1866) : ". . . we ought, as long as nothing is done contrary to the law, to leave it open to labour on the one hand and capital on the other to make the best terms they can for themselves. Large numbers of men, who have not the advantage of wealth, very often can protect their own interests only by means of association and co-operation, and we ought not to strain the law against men who have only their labour and their association by which they can act in the assistance of one another."

108 Thus in Walsby v. Anley, 3 E. & E. 516 (1861), an employer in the building trades refused to employ any person unless he signed a declaration recognizing the right of the employer and the employee to make any individual bargain that they chose and also promising not to join a trade union. Other employees threatened to strike unless two employees who had signed this declaration should be discharged. These employees were then prosecuted under section 3 of the Act of 1825 and their conviction was affirmed by the Queen's Bench. The court agreed that the conduct of the workmen amounted to a "threat" and a "molesting" of the master. In Regina v. Rowlands, 5 Cox C.C. 436, 462-463 (1851), Erle, J., instructed the jury: ". . . and

unlawful.[109] Not only was it unlawful to persuade workmen to break their contracts of employment, but to pay them not to work was equally illegal, as well as merely to persuade them to leave the employment of their master.[110]

An effort to give striking workmen a little more leeway was made by the Molestation of Workmen Act of 1859,[111] which sought to legalize peaceful persuasion if indulged in during a strike for shorter hours or higher wages, provided that no inducement of a breach of contract was made. It defined peaceful persuasion as "endeavoring peaceably, and in a reasonable manner, and without threat or intimidation, direct or indirect, to persuade others to cease or abstain from work." But the apparent legislative victory here gained was destroyed by the amplification of "threats" and "intimidation" by Baron Bramwell in *Regina v. Druitt*.[112] There, though the strike was merely for higher wages, the actions of pickets were practically made impossible by the test laid down

---

you should still be of the opinion that the combination was for the purpose of obstructing Messrs. Perry in carrying on their business, and so to force them to consent to this book of prices, and in pursuance of that concert, they persuaded the free men and gave money to the free men to leave the employ of Messrs. Perry, the purpose being to obstruct him in his manufacture, and to injure him in his business, and so to force his consent, I am of opinion that that also would be a violation in point of law. . . . I think, with respect to any intimidation of Mr. Perry, there does not seem to be anything like a direct threat of personal violence, or anything like a direct threat of actual violence to his property; but if a powerful body intimate that his lawful freedom of action will be interfered with unless he consents to certain terms, it will be for you to consider whether he might not be reasonably said to be intimidated if such matters occurred to him." The same instructions were given in Regina v. Duffield, 5 Cox C.C. 404 (1851). In Skinner v. Keitch, 10 Cox C.C. 493 (1867), a secretary of a union informed an employer that the union men would quit work unless the non-union men were discharged. The court held that not only was this a violation of section 3 of the Act of 1825 but also that the end of the closed shop made the combination an illegal conspiracy. The unreal position to which this doctrine led the courts is demonstrated by Wood v. Bowson, 2 Q.B. 21 (1866). There union men left work in pursuance of a union resolution because the employer would not limit his apprentices, but the reason for their leaving work was not communicated to the employer prior to their having done so. It was held that this conduct did not amount to a threat, though the court intimated that it would have been a threat if the union had told the employer that the men would quit work unless apprentices were limited.

[109] A different attitude was originally taken in Regina v. Selsby, 5 Cox C.C. 495n (1847). There Baron Rolfe sought to limit illegal picketing to cases where threats of bodily harm were made to workers. The test he applied to the words of the pickets was "whether the fair result of it (the words) was to intimate to the person to whom it was addressed, that some bodily harm would happen to him if he persevered in his intention of working. . . . It is doubtless lawful for people to agree among themselves not to work except on certain terms; that being so, I am not aware of any illegality in their peaceably trying to persuade others to adopt the same view. . . . My opinion is, that if there was no other object than to persuade people that it was in their interest not to work except for certain wages, and not to work unless certain regulations were complied with in a peaceable way, that it was not illegal. If I am wrong, I am sorry for it, but my opinion is, that that is the law." Pp. 497, 498.

[110] Regina v. Duffield, 5 Cox C.C. 404 (1851); Regina v. Rowlands, 5 Cox C.C. 436, 466 (1851). A threat to blacklist a non-conforming workman was illegal. O'Neill and Galbraith v. Longman, 9 Cox C.C. 360 (1863). See Hedges and Winterbottom, The Legal History of Trade Unionism, 50 (1930).

[111] 22 Vict. c. 34.

[112] 10 Cox C.C. 592 (1869).

"It was perfectly lawful," said Baron Bramwell, "to endeavour to persuade persons who had not hitherto acted with them to do so, provided that
persuasion did not take the shape of compulsion or coercion . . . Even
if the jury should be of the opinion that the picket did nothing more
than his duty as a picket, and if that duty did not extend to abusive language and gestures such as had been described, still, if that was calculated to have a deterring effect on the minds of ordinary persons, by
exposing them to having their actions watched, and to encounter black
looks, that would not be permitted by the law of the land."[113]

Following the Act of 1825 the common law of restraint of trade
assumed a new significance. Prior thereto an objective that might make
criminal a combination might, indeed, be in restraint of trade. Most of
the objectives of combinations of workmen were in restraint of individual bargaining power in the sense that they sought by collective action
to create a bargaining power of their own which would have some
opportunity to compete with that of the employer on equal terms. But
because the instrument of conspiracy was so flexible, permitting judges
to designate as unlawful and hence illegal any end whose pursuit by
workmen they disapproved, there was no need to find that the objective
was also in restraint of trade. True, philosophical individualists objected
to trade unionism on the ground that it sought to interfere with liberty
of contract,[114] failing to discern that inequality of bargaining power
negatives the possibility of freedom in contracting. Because of the restrictions that were gradually placed upon the extent of criminal conspiracy, the applicability of the doctrine of restraint of trade to combinations of workmen became of practical legal importance.

No differentiation between restraint of trade and criminal conspiracy
had been made in the cases decided prior to 1800. Dicta supporting the
identity of these two concepts were uttered in the Exchequer Chamber in
Hilton v. Eckersley.[115] But the dicta did not endure. Judges soon inclined to the conclusion that the mere fact that a combination was in
restraint of trade was insufficient to make the combination criminal.[116]
But the fact that conduct was in restraint of trade had serious civil consequences. An agreement so tainted was unenforceable.[117] Thus all legal

---

[113] P. 601. W. P. Roberts, the leading Chartist lawyer of the time, advised
his clients, the stonemasons, in order to avoid this decision "not under any circumstances to act together, but one by one to approach the foreman and give notice of
their leaving, offering no reasons. Any remarks or persuasion to be addressed to the
scab should be done exclusively by a letter posted in a distant town by a friend not
connected with the dispute." Postgate, The Builders' History, 279 (1924).

[114] See, *e.g.,* the opposition of Richard Cobden and Miss Martineau to trade
unionism as furthering monopoly and destroying freedom of contract. Dicey, Law
and Opinion in England, 199 (1926). Francis Place himself held no particular
brief for trade unionism but abetted collective action by employees as a defensive
measure against the combinations of employers. He seems to have envisaged a
return to true individual bargaining. *Id.* 198.

[115] 6 El. & Bl. 47 (1856). See the criticism of this decision by Erle, J., who
dissented, in Erle, The Law Relating to Trade Unions, 38 (1869).

[116] See Cockburn, C.J., in Regina v. Stainer, 11 Cox C.C. 483, 486 (1870);
Bowen, L.J., in Mogul S.S. Co. v. McGregor, Gow & Co., 23 Q.B.D. 598 (1889).

[117] Hilton v. Eckersley, *supra.*

validity was withdrawn from such obligations as workmen might place
upon each other in furtherance of their common ends. Another effect of
the doctrine that combinations in restraint of trade were unlawful, was
seriously to cripple the activities of trade unions by placing their funds
beyond the pale of the protection ordinarily afforded by the criminal
law. Their property being jointly owned by their members, larceny or
embezzlement of that property by one of the joint owners was no crime
at common law.[118] The Friendly Societies Act of 1855 [119] was supposed
to have afforded trade unions the necessary protection against dishonesty
on the part of their officers by abrogating the common law that larceny
by a joint owner was not criminal. But the Act by its terms was limited
to societies established for no illegal purpose. In *Hornby v. Close*,[120]
a trade union was held to be excluded from the provisions of this Act
inasmuch as it had among its purposes the illegal, though not criminal,
one of men binding "themselves not to work except under certain
conditions, and to support one another, in the event of being thrown out
of employment, in carrying out the views of the majority." Such a viewpoint, which made of trade unionism "something like betting and gam-
bling, public nuisances and immoral considerations—things condemned and
suppressed by the law"[121] could hardly be expected to survive. By the
Larceny and Embezzlement Act of 1868 and the Trades Unions Funds
Protection Act of 1869 [122] the bar that this judicial doctrine imposed
against prosecuting trade union officials for their dishonesty was removed.[123]

During the period from 1825 to 1870 judicial and legislative relaxation of the severe common law attitude towards combinations of work-

----

[118] Regina v. Blackburn, 11 Cox. C.C. 159 (1868).
[119] 18 & 19 Vict. c. 63.
[120] L.R. 2 Q.B. 153 (1867). A similar conclusion was reached in Farrer v.
Close, L.R. 4 Q.B. 602 (1869). *Cf.* Regina v. Hunt, 8 C. & P. 642 (1838). These
decisions were a shock to trade unionism which had fancied its legal status secure
after the passage of the Act of 1855. See Webb, The History of Trade Unionism,
262 (1920 ed.).
[121] Frederic Harrison in 1867, quoted in Webb, *op. cit.*, 262.
[122] 31 & 32 Vict. c. 116; 32 & 33 Vict. c. 61.
[123] See, *e.g.*, Regina v. Stainer, 11 Cox C.C. 483 (1870) ; Regina v. Tankard,
[1894] 1 Q.B. 548. Another application of this general doctrine of restraint of trade
to hamper the activities of trade unions was made by virtue of the legislation against
the taking of oaths. In 1797 a statute was passed (37 Geo. 3, c. 23) making it
highly criminal for any illegal society to require its members to take an oath.
Though the statute was not aimed at trade unions, being concerned with the
seditious societies that revolution in France had generated, it was applied in 1802
to punish certain journeymen shearmen who had united to raise their wages and
exacted oaths of their members. Rex v. Marks, 3 East 157. In 1817 this statute was
further extended (57 Geo. 3, c. 19, § 25), still, however, directed towards the spread
of seditious societies. In 1834 the statute was used to suppress the oath-bound confederacy of the Grand National Consolidated Trades Union. Leaders in the Dorchester laborers' agitation were tried under its terms, found guilty and transported,
despite an impressive labor protest against such action by the government. Rex v.
Lovelass, 6 C. & P. 596 (1834). See also Rex v. Dixon, 6 C. & P. 601 (1834). For
the full story of the Dorchester laborers, see Webb, The History of Trade Unionism, 144-148 (1920 ed.). These prosecutions had the effect of causing the oath to be
dropped from trade union ceremonies.

men was of such a character as to permit trade unionism to exist, but every effective action of trade unionism ran into the danger of being judicially denounced as illegal. The Reform Act of 1832 can hardly be deemed to have worked to the benefit of labor. After a few years it elevated to power the industrial employing class. Magistrates seem generally to have been imbued with the prejudices of this class against organized labor,[124] and after 1850 prosecutions of striking laborers increased rather than declined. As one writer puts it: "There was no change in the law, but the change in the application of the law had been immense. Wherever a conviction could be by any fiction sustained, the Bench lent itself gladly to the process. Sentences were increased, bullying grew worse, prosecutions more frequent. The government assisted by sending soldiers to break strikes and did not consider the relief of cases of oppression."[125]

The old master and servant acts were also employed during this period to work intolerable hardship upon employees. Under them, though a master could only be sued civilly for a breach of contract, a workman who committed the same offense could be proceeded against criminally and imprisoned for three months. Furthermore, the servant could not take the stand in his own defense, and could be summarily arrested and tried before a single justice of the peace from whose decision there was no appeal.[126] These inequalities and injustices were not removed until the passage of the Master and Servant Act of 1867.[127]

Trade union agitation against the existing law resulted in the appointment of a Royal Commission of Inquiry in 1867 with terms of reference that permitted it to embrace the entire subject.[128] Its report, inconclusive in character, argued against the advantages of trade unionism but recommended the legalization of certain aspects of union activity. To the agitation thus aroused can be ascribed the Trade Union Act of 1871[129] and the Criminal Law Amendment Act[130] of the same year. The former act expressly provided that "the purposes of any trade union shall not by reason merely that they are in restraint of trade, be deemed to be unlawful so as to render any member of such trade union liable to criminal prosecution for conspiracy or otherwise."[131] It also specified that "the purposes of any trade union shall not, by reason merely that they are in restraint of trade, be unlawful so as to render void or voidable

---

[124] In 1861 workmen of Cockfield were arrested for combining to get higher wages and were imprisoned and sentenced without being given the opportunity to make their defense through a lawyer. In 1865 picketing masons were similarly treated by a Lord Mayor who remarked in the trial, "We know nothing about societies here, and if you knew less of them it would be better for you." See Postgate, The Builders' History, 160-162 (1924).
[125] Postgate, op. cit., 276.
[126] See Webb, op. cit., 249.
[127] 30 & 31 Vict. c. 141.
[128] For the origin and history of this Commission, see Webb, op. cit., 260-269.
[129] 34 and 35 Vict. c. 31.
[130] 34 and 35 Vict. c. 32. The parliamentary history of this legislation is to be found in Webb, op. cit., 274-282.
[131] § 2.

any agreement or trust."[132] Other sections of the Act provided remedies for the enforcement of the newly legalized types of agreements, and established a system for the registry of trade unions. The Act of 1871 is important in all its many aspects as the source of much English trade union law.[133] These features of the Act, however, are of little general concern. But it is of major importance in that it removed from trade union activity the judicial harassments placed thereon by the application of the common law of restraint of trade.

The Criminal Law Amendment Act of 1871 is of interest in its effort further to define the limits of picketing and the nature of illegal threats and intimidation. Violence to person or property was expressly banned. So also threats or intimidation to any person in a "manner as would justify a justice of the peace, on complaint made to him, to bind over the person so threatening or intimidating, to keep the peace." Molestation or obstruction was made illegal when done with a view to coerce either an employer to dismiss a workman or not to offer him employment, a workman to cease work or not to accept employment, employees or workmen to belong or not to belong to particular associations or to pay fines imposed by any association, or an employer "to alter the mode of carrying on his business, or the number or description of any persons employed by him." Molestation or obstruction was defined to consist in persistently following a person from place to place, hiding tools or other property owned by such person or hindering him in the use thereof, or watching or besetting the house where such person resides or works or carries on business or happens to be, or the approach to such house or place, or if with two or more other persons following such person in a disorderly manner in or through any street or road.

The Act did not repeal any earlier legislation nor legalize any type of conduct theretofore regarded as criminal. Its inability to meet the growing complaints of trade unionists was soon to be made manifest. Petty prosecutions continued, and imprisonment threatened practically any activity designed to induce men to leave work and join a group of strikers. In 1872 twelve gas-stokers were sentenced to imprisonment for conducting a strike in the London gas works. They agreed simultaneously to break their contracts and for this were convicted of conspiracy.[134] The basis of the decision is again that of molestation consisting in compelling the[ir] employer to conduct his business in a fashion other than that which pleased him.[135] In 1875 the allowable areas of picketing were again

---

[132] § 3.

[133] See Hedges and Winterbottom, The Legal History of Trade Unionism, 65-90 (1930).

[134] Regina v. Bunn, 12 Cox C.C. 316 (1872).

[135] Thus, Brett, J., in his charge to the jury says: "I will tell you that there is an improper molestation if there is anything done with an improper intent, which you shall think is annoyance or an unjustifiable interference and which in your judgment would have the effect of annoying or interfering with the minds of the persons carrying on such a business as this Gas Company is conducting. And I tell you that the breach without just cause of such contracts as have been proved in this case is an illegal act by the servant who does it. It is an illegal act, and what

sharply confined by the decision of Baron Cleasby in *Regina v. Hilbert*.[136] Though to be guilty of unlawful conduct, the jury had to find a watching and besetting with the intention of coercing workmen to quit the employment, coercion need only be such as would "operate upon the mind so as to take liberty of will, by giving rise to a fear of violence by threats, or to some apprehension of loss or ruin, or to feelings of annoyance." [137]

With the fall of Gladstone in 1874, who had consistently resisted any further change in the legislation affecting trade unions, trade unionists [138] succeeded in pressing to enactment the Conspiracy and Protection Act of 1875,[139] which repealed the Criminal Law Amendment Act of 1871. Section 3 of the Act of 1875 expressly provided that "an agreement or combination by two or more persons to do or procure to be done any act in contemplation or furtherance of a trade dispute between employees and workmen shall not be indictable as a conspiracy if such act committed by one person would not be punishable as a crime." It further sought more accurately to define the allowable limits of picketing by making it criminal for any "person who, with a view to compel any other person to abstain from doing or to do any act which such other person has a legal right to do or to abstain from doing, wrongfully and without authority, (1) Uses violence to or intimidates such other person or his wife or children or injures his property; or (2) Persistently follows such other person about from place to place; or (3) Hides any tools, clothes or other property owned or used by such person or deprives him of or hinders him in the use thereof; or (4) Watches or besets the house or other place where such person resides or works, or carries on business or happens to be, or the approach to such house or place; or (5) Follows such other person with two or more other persons in a disorderly manner in or through any street or road." [140] But "attending at or near the house or place where a person resides, or works, or carries on business, or happens to be, or the

---

[136] is more it is a criminal act, that is to say, it is an act which makes each of them liable to the criminal law and therefore if they did agree to interfere with the exercise of their employers' business by simultaneously breaking such contracts even if you were to suppose that to interfere with their employers' business was a lawful thing for them to do—yet if they agreed and combined to do that lawful act by the unlawful means of simultaneously breaking all these contracts, they were then agreeing to do that which may be assumed to be a lawful act by unlawful means and that would bring them within the definition of conspiracy." Regina v. Bunn, *supra*, at 339-340.

[136] 13 Cox C.C. 82.

[137] *Id.* 87.

[138] Trade unionism was an active political force in the election of 1874 and the Conservative leaders were alive to this new political power. See Webb, *op. cit.*, 290. That election returned to the House of Commons its first labor members, Alexander McDonald and Thomas Burt, two officials of the National Union of Miners.

[139] 38 and 39 Vict. c. 86. Another victory for the trade union movement consisted in the passage of the Employees and Workmen Act of 1875, 38 and 39 Vict. c. 90.

[140] § 7.

approach to such house or place in order merely to obtain or communicate information" was not to be deemed an illegal watching or besetting.[141]

The Act of 1875 finally abolished the loose common law doctrine of conspiracy as applied to labor combinations. As earlier applied, it was never again to raise its head in the courts. But in other respects, judges soon found ways and means to impose severe restrictions upon labor activities. Though it was the obvious purpose of the Act of 1875 to legalize that type of conduct loosely described as peaceful picketing,[142] in 1876 Baron Huddleston found it to be criminal to watch and beset for the purpose of persuading men to quit work even though no truly intimidatory means were employed.[143] This situation was to remain uncorrected until 1906.

More serious, however, was the development of the tort of civil conspiracy. Unable to regard collective action directed towards ends not independently criminal as a criminal conspiracy, the judges inclined to the view that where such action resulted in temporal damage it remained actionable as a civil wrong. Considerable uncertainty existed as to the boundaries of this doctrine but its enunciation first by implication in *Allen v. Flood*[144] and then by decision in *Quinn v. Leatham*[145] made of the doctrine a reality that had a potency to trade unionism almost equal to that of the older doctrine of criminal conspiracy.[146] The threat of such a doctrine was immensely increased by the decision in *Taff Vale Railway Co. v. Amalgamated Society of Railway Servants,*[147] holding trade union funds liable for torts committed by trade unionists. The decision, after some thirty years of immunity assumed to have been possessed by trade unions under the Acts of 1871 and 1876, came as a surprise to the legal profession as well as trade unionists.[148]

---

[141] *Ibid.* Other sections of the Act made it criminal for employees in gas or water works to break a contract of service when the probable consequences of their doing so would be to deprive inhabitants of their gas or water, or for any employees to break contracts of service where the probable consequences of such action would be to "endanger human life, or cause serious bodily injury, or to expose valuable property whether real or personal to destruction or serious injury." §§ 4, 5.

[142] See G. R. Askwith in Minutes of Evidence before the Royal Commission on Trade Disputes and Trade Combinations, Cd. 2826 (1906) p. 9.

[143] Regina v. Bauld, 13 Cox C.C. 282 (1876). Accord: Lyons v. Wilking [1899] 1 Ch. 255; Walters v. Green [1899] 2 Ch. 696; Charnock v. Court [1899] 2 Ch. 35. *Cf.* Ward. Lock & Company v. Printers' Assistants' Society, 22 T.L.R. 327 (1906).

[144] [1898] A.C. 1.

[145] [1901] A.C. 495. See also Giblan v. National Amalgamated Labourers' Union [1903] 2 K.B. 600.

[146] "The danger to Trade Unions consists not so much in the judgement by the application of the dicta of certain Law-lords who took part in it. In Quinn v. Leatham there was the element of procuring to break contract. But the dicta of Quinn v. Leatham show clearly that there might be an action of damages based on any conspiracy to injure or to do harm, and it is obvious the very essence of a strike is in one sense injury to those against whom it is directed." Report of the Royal Commission on Trade Disputes and Trade Combinations, 1906, Cd. 2825, pp. 14-15.

[147] [1901] A.C. 426.

[148] For intimations as to such a ruling, see Trollope v. London Bldg. Trades Federation, 11 T.L.R. 280 (1895); Pink v. Federation of Trades, 8 T.L.R. 216, 711 (1893).

The first years of the twentieth century also saw an application of the doctrine of inducing breach of contract in a way that was deemed inimical to trade union interests. Ordinary trade union objectives were not deemed by the House of Lords in *South Wales Miners' Federation v. Glamorgan Coal Company* [149] and *Danaby Collieries Co. v. Yorkshire Miners' Association*,[150] to have enough justification to induce the breach of contracts of service without consequent liability. Advantage was taken of this legal doctrine to make tortious practically all efforts by striking workmen to induce those who took their places to quit their work and join the strikers.

These discontents—the Taff Vale doctrine, the tort of civil conspiracy, the tort of inducing breach of a labor contract, and the abridgment of peaceful picketing—led finally to the Trade Disputes Act of 1906.[151] It was preceded by prolonged and vociferous agitation directed primarily against the Taff Vale doctrine.[152] In 1903 a Royal Commission was appointed but its report made three years later was unacceptable to the trade unionists for the amendments it suggested to the law were deemed inadequate to cure what were regarded to be its outstanding defects. In the general election of 1906 trade unionists were especially active, electing twenty-nine candidates to Parliament and supporting strongly those Liberal candidates that sponsored their suggested changes in trade union law

The Trade Disputes Act of 1906 dealt with all the questions that had been mooted.[153] It confined civil conspiracy to the same narrow limits as the Act of 1875 had confined criminal conspiracy, by providing that "an act done in pursuance of an agreement or combination by two or more persons shall, if done in contemplation or furtherance of a trade dispute, not be actionable unless the act, if done without any such agreement or combination, would be actionable."[154] Courts were forbidden to entertain any action against a trade union in respect of any tortious act alleged to have been committed by or on behalf of the trade union.[155] It was also provided that "an act done by a person in contemplation or furtherance of a trade dispute shall not be actionable on the ground only that it induces some other person to break a contract of employment or that it is an interference with the trade, business or employment of some other person, or with the right of some other person to dispose of his capital or his labour as he wills."[156] Finally it was made "lawful for one or more

149 [1905] A.C. 239.
150 [1906] A.C. 239.
151 6 Edw. 7, c. 47.
152 See Webb, *op. cit.*, 604.
153 See Geldart, "The Present Law of Trade Disputes and Trade Unions," 2 Pol. Quar. 17 (1914); Posner, "English Trade Disputes Act of 1906," 10 Cal. Law Rev. 395 (1922).
154 § 2. On the nature and meaning of a "trade dispute" see § 5(3) and Conway v. Wade [1909] A.C. 506; Larkin v. Long [1915] A.C. 814; Hodges v. Webb [1920] 2 Ch. 129.
155 § 4. See Vacher & Sons v. London Society of Compositors [1913] A.C. 107; Bussey v. Amalgamated Society of Railway Servants, 24 T.L.R. 437 (1908).
156 § 3. On the legislative history of this section see Landis, A Note on "Statutory Interpretation," 43 Harv. Law Rev. 889 n. 12 (1930).

persons, acting on their own behalf or on behalf of a trade union or of
an individual employer or firm in contemplation or furtherance of a trade
dispute to attend at or near a house or place where a person resides or
works or carries on business or happens to be, if they so attend merely
for the purpose of peacefully obtaining or communicating information, or
of peacefully persuading any person to work or abstain from working."[157]

Trade unionism, as a political force, shortly thereafter received a
severe blow in the decision of the House of Lords in *Amalgamated Society
of Railway Servants v. Osborne*.[158] The effect of that judgment was to
restrain a trade union from using its funds for the support of any political
party, in this case the new Labor Party that had counted so heavily in
the general election of 1906.[159] With some hesitation and reluctance,
inasmuch as the judgment received considerable support in Liberal as well
as Conservative circles, the Trade Union Act of 1913 [160] finally corrected
this limitation imposed upon trade union activities. Trade unions thereafter could devote their funds to the furtherance of political objectives if
they had received authority for that purpose from the members of the
union. Any member could, however, claim exemption from any levy if
the funds were to be devoted to political purposes.

During the period of the World War no significant changes in the
legal status of trade unionism took place, though the circumstances of the
times made for greater growth of the trade union movement. Legislation
looking toward the betterment of specific conditions and further revising
and supplementing the existing systems of arbitration, was enacted together
with several temporary measures restricting the right to strike and
the right of collective bargaining.[161] The General Strike of 1926, however, brought about, in part, the overthrow of the Labor Government and
the passage in the following year of the Trade Disputes and Trade Unions
Act of 1927.[162] This Act declared illegal any strike or lock-out which

---

[157] § 2. The Royal Commission had strenuously opposed any legalization of
peaceful picketing contending that any picketing "must savour of compulsion" and
that peaceful picketing "is really a contradiction in terms." Report of the Royal
Commission on Trade Disputes and Trade Combinations, Cd. 2825 (1906) pp. 11, 76.
[158] [1910] A.C. 87.
[159] For a discussion of the Osborne judgment, see Webb, *op. cit.*, 608-631;
Geldart, The Osborne Judgment and After (1910); Hedges and Winterbottom,
op. cit., 102. On the incidence of the same problem in Scotland, see Carmont, The
Scottish "Osborne Case," 22 Jurid. Rev. 329 (1922).
[160] 2 and 3 Geo. 5, c. 30.
[161] See Cole, Labour in War Time (1915); Cole, Self-Government in Industry
(1919); Webb, *op. cit.*, 639; Milne-Bailey, Trade Union Documents, 30 (1929);
Amulree, Industrial Arbitration in Great Britain, 121-192 (1929). See also 7 and 8
Geo. 5, c. 45; 9 and 10 Geo. 5, cc. 42, 69; 10 and 11 Geo. 5, c. 55.
[162] The General Strike brought forth a judgment from Mr. Justice Astbury, not
essential however to the decision, that the General Strike was contrary to law.
National Sailors' & Firemen's Union v. Reed [1926] 1 Ch. 536. The same view had
been taken by Sir John Simon in a series of political speeches. See Simon, The
General Strike (1928). Mr. Justice Astbury based his conclusion upon the ground
that the strike was not in furtherance of a trade dispute and thus was beyond the
pale of the protection afforded by the Acts of 1875 and 1906. For criticism of this
decision, see Goodhart, "The Legality of the General Strike in England," 36 Yale
Law Jour. 464 (1927).

had "any object other than, or in addition to, the furtherance of a trade dispute within the trade or industry in which the strikers" or the employers locking-out were engaged, or any strike or lock-out which was "designed or calculated to coerce the Government either directly or by inflicting hardship upon the community."[163] By narrowing the definition of trade dispute,[164] this section had the effect of making illegal not only the general strike as such but all "sympathetic strikes."[165] Engaging in such a strike, except merely quitting work or refusing to accept employment, was made illegal and subjected the offender on summary conviction to fine and imprisonment. Trade unions were forbidden to take disciplinary measures against members engaging in strikes made illegal by the Act.[166] Mass picketing of any kind was declared illegal[167] and any picketing of a person at his residence was similarly penalized.[168] The

---

[163] § 1.

[164] It was provided that "a trade dispute shall not be deemed to be within a trade or industry unless it is a dispute between employers and workmen, or between workmen and workmen, in that trade or industry, which is connected with the employment or non-employment or the terms of the employment, or with the conditions of labour, of persons in that trade or industry." Workmen were to be deemed to be within the same "trade or industry if their wages or conditions of employment are determined in accordance with the conclusions of the same joint industrial council, conciliation board or other similar body, or in accordance with agreements made with the same employer or group of employees."

[165] The general language of this section was one of the chief points of opposition of labor leaders to the Act, their contention being that it enabled unsympathetic judges to make impossible unified trade union activity. See e.g. the speech of the Marquis of Reading, 68 Hans. Deb. (H.L. 1927) 67. For a bibliography of trade union literature critical of the Act, see Witte, "British Trade Union Law since the Trade Disputes and Trade Union Act of 1927," 26 Am. Pol. Sci. Rev. 345, 346 (1932). Compare the following from the Report of the Royal Commission on Trade Disputes and Trade Combinations, Cd. 2825, p. 15 (1906): "We are of the opinion that the Act of 1875 should be made to extend to so-called secondary strikes, and we state this with greater confidence because the majority of those examined by us, whose opinion was of the greatest weight, agreed that there was no valid reason for drawing a distinction between secondary and other strikes." No cases have arisen since 1927 in which any attempt has been made to invoke this provision. See Witte, *supra*, 346.

[166] § 2.

[167] The Act provided in section 3: "(1) It is hereby declared that it is unlawful for one or more persons (whether acting on their own behalf or on behalf of a trade union or of an individual employer or firm, and notwithstanding that they may be acting in contemplation or furtherance of a trade dispute) to attend at or near a house or place where a person resides or works or carries on business or happens to be, for the purpose of obtaining or communicating information or of persuading or inducing any person to work or abstain from working, if they so attend in such numbers or otherwise in such manner as to be calculated to intimidate any person in that house or place, or to obstruct the approach thereto or egress therefrom, or to lead to a breach of the peace; and attending at or near any house or place in such numbers or in such manner as is by this subsection declared to be unlawful shall be deemed to be a watching or besetting of that house or place within the meaning of section seven of the Conspiracy and Protection of Property Act, 1875. (2) In this section the expression 'to intimidate' means to cause in the mind of a person a reasonable apprehension of injury to him or to any member of his family or to any of his dependents or of violence or damage to any person or property, and the expression 'injury' includes injury to a person in respect of his business, occupation, employment or the source of income, and includes any actionable wrong."

[168] § 3 (4).

Act of 1913 was stringently curtailed by requiring an assent from each trade union member as a condition precedent to the legality of a levy upon him for funds for political purposes.[169]

The return of the MacDonald government to power witnessed an attempt to modify the provisions of the Act of 1927.[170] Liberal members, however, still fearful of legalizing activity of the nature of a general strike, succeeded in blocking the attempt.[171] No cases of significance have arisen under the Act, nor has it had as yet an important effect in altering ordinary collective labor activity despite the re-ordering of the legal boundaries that it brought about.[172]

It is necessary now to return to the development of labor in the United States during the period from 1800 to 1890,[173] for it contrasts basically with the English development.[174] To go back into the colonial period is not possible in the present state of knowledge. No extended examination of the material in our colonial records dealing with the position of the wage-earner has been made.[175] No gilds as such flourished

---

[169] §§ 4, 7. A further section prohibited civil servants from belonging to any organization whose membership was not confined to civil servants. The purpose of this section was to compel various civil service organizations, comprising some 160,000 individuals, to give up their affiliation with the Trade Union Congress. See Bowen, "Civil Service Unions in Trade Disputes Bill," 9 Labor Mag. 494 (1931); Macrae-Gibson, "The British Civil Service and the Trade Union Act of 1927," 23 Am. Pol. Sci. Rev. 922 (1929). Section 6 of the Act made it illegal for local and public authorities to exact anti-union contracts of their employees or to require their sub-contractors to pursue union or anti-union policies. For general discussions of the Act of 1927, see Millis, "The British Trade Disputes and Trade Unions Act, 1927," 36 Jour. Pol. Econ. 305 (1928); Mason, "The British Trades Disputes Act of 1927," 22 Am. Pol. Sci. Rev. 143 (1928).

[170] In 1929, Sir W. A. Jowitt, the Attorney-General, gave notice that he would present on behalf of the Government a bill to amend the Act of 1927. 229 Hans. Deb. 45 (H.C. 1929). In 1931 such a bill was introduced, which had been indorsed by the Trade Union Congress. See Memorandum on the Trade Disputes and Trade Unions Bill, Cd. 3749 (1930).

[171] See Witte, "British Trade Union Law since the Trade Disputes and Trade Union Act of 1927," 26 Am. Pol. Sci. Rev. 345, 349 (1932).

[172] See Witte, supra.

[173] No effort is made in this introduction to carry the development beyond 1890, inasmuch as the materials of its latter day history are contained in this book. Though many of the recent English cases are also to be found in the book, the legislative development in England is both so continuous and so seamless that it is necessary to trace the earlier conceptions down to the present date. On the other hand, 1890, the period of the Sherman Act, affords a convenient terminus for the beginnings of labor law in America.

[174] ". . . Broadly speaking, the political genius of our people has evolved this system—that we have not sought to make strikes illegal, but we have sought to control, and vigorously control, what was done during the strike. The American policy has been exactly the opposite. The Americans have sought to make strikes illegal, and it is an interesting reflection to the student of comparative history that just at the time when we are abandoning our old policy and having recourse to the American policy—that is the very time when the Americans are abandoning their policy and adopting ours." Sir W. A. Jowitt, the Attorney-General, during the second reading of the bill to amend the Trade Disputes Act of 1927, 247 Hans. Deb. 392 (H.C. 1931), quoted in Frankfurter and Greene, "Congressional Power over the Labor Injunction," 31 Col. Law Rev. 385, 410 (1931).

[175] Some scattered materials on this early period are to be found in 1 Commons and Associates, History of Labour in the United States, 25, 50, 110 (1926).

in the Colonies,[176] and though instances of collective labor action for the benefit of workmen are to be found,[177] the legal attitude towards such activity has not been explored. Our first contact with the labor problem thus arises out of a case decided in the Mayor's Court of Philadelphia in 1806. Recurring difficulties in the shoe industry, alternating between lock-outs by the masters and strikes by the workmen,[178] finally precipitated an indictment for conspiracy of several journeymen cordwainers. The charge embraced not only a combination to raise wages but the pursuit of this end by intimadatory means as well as a combination not to work for any employer who might hire a cordwainer at wages less than those the combination demanded.[179] In disposing of the case, however, the judge, Recorder Levy, applied the older accepted English doctrine that a combination of employees to raise their wages was a criminal conspiracy. Such a conclusion need hardly occasion surprise. From an industrial standpoint, there is little reason to suppose that American conditions differed radically from those in England. The judiciary of the country was generally dominated by men of a Federalist stamp who would be inclined readily to accept the attitude displayed by English judges. Nor was there much in the movement that had gained political independence for the Colonies or in the new democratic dogmas of the Jeffersonian party, that would make strenuously for deeming such English law as existed as inapplicable to this country because of its antipathy to American conditions.[180]

The following decades were to see general acquiescence in the doctrine of the *Cordwainers' Case*.[181] In 1810 in the Court of General. Sessions in New York City in *People v. Melvin*,[182] certain striking cordwainers

---

[176] Only two instances of trade gilds are known. See 1 *id.* 46.

[177] See Seyboldt, "Trade Agreements in Colonial Boston," 2 New Eng. Quar. 307 (1929).

[178] See Gabster, The Labor Movement in the Shoe Industry, 11-15 (1924).

[179] The case, known as the Case of the Philadelphia Cordwainers, was reported and printed in pamphlet form. The most accessible report, however, is in 3 Commons & Gilmore, Doc. Hist. Am. Soc. 59-248 (1910).

[180] Professor Nelles in "The First American Labor Case," 41 Yale Law Jour. 165 (1931)—a lengthy review of the Cordwainers' Case—argues strongly for the proposition that the decision is indicative of a Hamiltonian victory over Jeffersonian conceptions. But little is to be found in the contemporaneous writings of the period, apart from the argument of counsel for the defendants in this and similar cases, to the effect that the common law of conspiracy was particularly offensive to Jeffersonian ideals. One searches pre-Civil War American political and philosophical writing vainly for any justification or adequate weighing of collective labor action. But this again is not surprising. English thought upon the subject, though the question had been thoroughly aired in the English political arena, was until the fifties confused by the enigma of reconciling individual liberty with collective activity. Even Francis Place, it will be remembered, whose concern with this subject was not only concrete but persistent, failed to find any better basis than a purely defensive one for the justification of collective labor activity.

[181] In 1809 a number of cordwainers were tried for compelling a master to discharge a workman and one was found guilty. Baltimore Cordwainers' Case, 3 Commons & Gilmore, *op. cit.*, 249. A catalogue of twenty cases decided between 1806 and 1845 is to be found in Nelles, "Commonwealth v. Hunt," 32 Col. Law Rev. 1128, 1166 (1932).

[182] 2 Wheeler C. C. (N.Y.) 262 (1810).

were again indicted for conspiracy. The character of the Mayor's instructions to the jury, which found the defendants guilty, vary little from those either of the English judges or of Recorder Levy. A combination "to do an act, unlawful in itself, to the prejudice of other persons," or to accomplish a lawful end by unlawful means, is to be deemed a criminal conspiracy"; "the common law of England . . . must be deemed to be applicable." Emphasis in this case, however, was laid upon the unlawfulness of the strike as a means to accomplish the end, rather than upon the end of higher wages as being unlawful in and of itself.[183]

In the *Pittsburgh Cordwainers' Case* [184] in 1815, striking cordwainers again were convicted of conspiracy. Though no specific mention is there made that the pursuit of higher wages by united action is of itself unlawful, among ends denounced as illegal by the court are efforts "to compel men to work, at certain prices," "to compel an employer to hire a certain description of persons," "to compel men to become members of a particular society, or to contribute towards it." Again, following *People v. Melvin,* the strike as a means of accomplishing ends is stated to be illegal inasmuch as it is a menacing of employers with a total destruction of their trade.

Equality of application of this general doctrine, at least, characterized the courts, for in 1821 the Supreme Court of Pennsylvania expressed the view that combinations of masters to depress wages are criminal if their effort is to decrease wages "below what they would be, if there was no recurrence to artificial means by either side."[185] In 1824 journeymen tailors in Buffalo striking for higher wages are again convicted of conspiracy.[186] In 1827, however, a slight alleviation in the application of the law becomes discernible.[187] In that year journeymen tailors were again hailed before the Mayor's Court of Philadelphia for conspiracy to

---

[183] Mr. Witte contends that the doctrine of the Cordwainers' Case never "attained the status of generally accepted law" in this country. He points out that in most of the cases, except the Cordwainers' Case and People v. Fisher, 14 Wend. 9 (N.Y. 1835), the instances in which workmen were found guilty of conspiracy presented indictments containing counts charging violence, picketing, closed shop rules, and the like, besides counts merely alleging a combination to raise wages. See Witte, "Early American Labor Cases," 35 Yale Law Jour. 825, 826 (1926). A legalistic view of "law," of course, supports this contention; but if law is to be derived from the expressions of judges and the temper of courts in which indictments for conspiracy were pressed, such a thesis is difficult to sustain.

[184] 4 Commons & Gilmore, *op. cit.*, 15.

[185] Commonwealth v. Carlisle, Bright 36 (Pa. 1821).

[186] 4 Commons & Gilmore, *op. cit.*, 93. In People v. Trequier, 1 Wheeler C. C. 142 (1823), defendant hatters were found guilty of conspiracy for combining not to work with employees who were not members of their organization.

[187] Though in the earlier cases the defendants were found guilty, negligible punishments were visited upon them. In the Philadelphia Cordwainers' Case, the defendants were fined eight dollars. In People v. Melvin and the Pittsburgh Cordwainers' Case the fines were one dollar. In the Buffalo Tailors' Case the fine was two dollars. These punishments contrast strongly with the severe sentences meted out by English judges in similar cases, and indicate more toleration on the part of American judges to collective action by employees. Also in the American trials eminent counsel came to the defense of indicted workmen, counsel who sought by such action to attain political preferment. No similar conduct characterized the British Bar.

raise their wages.[188]   But on this occasion the Recorder refused to accept the doctrines laid down in the *Philadelphia* and the *Pittsburgh Cordwainers' Cases.*   A combination merely "by indirect means to prejudice a third person" was said not to be illegal because such a standard was too indefinite.   And as to the legality of the strike as such, the Recorder stated that "the defendants had as much right to leave the service of their employers, as the employers had to discharge them."   He went on: "If they had the right individually, I can see no reason, why the same right might not be exercised by them collectively and simultaneously, nor can I conceive a case, where if the object be legal, that which is done by one becomes illegal only when done by many, provided the means are not criminal."[189]   The Recorder expressly refused to declare that a combination seeking merely to raise wages was criminal, observing that this "has never been decided on in the United States, and for this I have the authority of the present Chief Justice of the state."[190]   The defendants, however, were found to have committed indictable offenses in that they assembled by their employer's store in a turbulent and disorderly manner, and had by "promises and threats" induced men to leave the service of their employer.

Though two years later striking shoemakers were again found guilty in a Pennsylvania court of combining to raise their wages,[191] a Baltimore court refused to regard as criminal conspirators weavers who had agreed not to work for an employer because he had reduced their wages.[192]   But before the recession from the doctrine of the *Philadelphia Cordwainers' Case* began definitely, it was once again to find judicial affirmance.   An inferior New York court had quashed an indictment of journeymen shoemakers for combining to raise their wages.   By threat of a strike they had compelled an employer to discharge a workman because he was willing to work for less than they had stipulated.   On appeal to the Supreme Court of New York, this decision was reversed.[193]   Chief Justice Savage relied upon the earlier common law cases and expressly declared that combinations to raise wages were criminal under the law of the state.[194]

---

[188] Commonwealth v. Moore, 4 Commons & Gilmore, *op. cit.,* 99.

[189] *Id.* 255.

[190] *Id.* 261.

[191] Case of the Chambersburg Shoemakers, 4 *id.* 273.   In 1829 three Philadelphia spinners were bound ever to keep the peace during a strike. 4 *id.* 265.

[192] Case of the Baltimore Weavers, 4 *id.* 269.   A distinctly liberal note was also struck in the Case of the Hartford Carpet Weavers tried before a Connecticut Court in 1833.   See Niles' Register, Sept. 27, 1834. See also 4 Commons & Gilmore, *op. cit.,* Supp., 15.

[193] People v. Fisher, 14 Wend. 1 (N.Y. 1835).

[194] "It is important," said the Chief Justice, "to the best interests of society that the price of labor be left to regulate itself, or rather be limited by the demand for it. Combinations and confederacies to *enhance* or *reduce* the prices of labor, or of any articles of trade or commerce, are injurious."   Inasmuch as the criminal common law of England had been abrogated by the legislature, the indictment in this case was for violation of 2 Rev. Stat. 726, sec. 42, which made it criminal "to commit any act injurious to the public health, to public morals, or to trade or commerce."   This statute, in the opinion of the court, substantially reincorporated common law doctrines of criminal conspiracy with regard to activities of the type alleged.

A year later, upon the strength of this doctrine, twenty tailors were convicted of conspiracy in New York and heavily fined by Judge Edwards.[195]

This action of Judge Edwards and the decision of Chief Justice Savage in *People v. Fisher* were not quietly received. In New York and in Washington mass protests were made and the figures of the two judges burned in effigy.[196] Shortly thereafter shoemakers who had struck to compel a master to pay a fine for having employed a non-union workman were acquitted by a jury in Hudson, New York, despite a charge by the court almost directing a verdict of guilty.[197] A similar result followed an attempt in the same year to indict two Philadelphia plasterers for refusing to work for an employer because he had employed a workman who refused to maintain the wage-scale demanded by the plasterers.[198] Four years later began the prosecution of the seven leaders of the Boston Journeymen Bootmakers' Society [199] that was to result in the significant decision of *Commonwealth v. Hunt*.[200]

The indictment in *Commonwealth v. Hunt* set forth a combination of the defendants not to work for any employer who should employ a person not a member of the defendants' society, a combination to effect the discharge of one Horne from the employ of Wait, and a combination to prevent Horne from following his trade as a bootmaker. After the defendants had been found guilty in the lower court of conspiracy, exceptions were taken which, in substance, raised the issue of whether the indictment set forth a criminal offense. The exception on this score was sustained by Chief Justice Shaw in an opinion which has been aptly characterized as "a consummate fusion of considerations of social advantage with technicality."[201] Shaw refused to find anything illegal in the mere fact of a combination not to work if persons were employed who were not members of the organization sponsored by the combination. He based this conclusion upon the fact that such a combination might have a worthy, as well as an unworthy objective, and no particular unworthy objective had been set forth in the indictment. Shaw applied the same reasoning to the second substantive charge, saying again that the legality of effecting the discharge of a workman depended also upon the end sought thereby and no unsocial end was set forth in the indictment. Shaw refused to allow these lacks in the indictment to be supplied by such evidence as was adduced at the trial as to the objects of the defendants' society. In answer to the contention that the combination to impoverish Horne was criminal, Shaw again conceived the possibilty of such con-

---

[195] See 4 Commons & Gilmore, *op. cit.*, 315.
[196] See Witte, *supra*, 827.
[197] 4 Commons & Gilmore, *op. cit.*, 277.
[198] 4 *id.* 335.
[199] For the report of the proceedings in the Municipal Court of Boston, see Thacher's Crim. Cas. 609 (1840).
[200] 4 Metc. 111 (Mass. 1842). A full discussion of this case, drawing for the first time upon notes of the testimony at the trial taken by the defendants' counsel is to be found in Nelles, "Commonwealth v. Hunt," 32 Col. Law Rev. 1128 (1932).
[201] Nelles, *supra*, at 1148.

duct being directed towards a worthy end, and no unworthy end having been set forth in the indictment nor illegal means to accomplish the purpose having been averred, this charge must also fail. In dealing with the act of quitting work, Shaw refused to regard this as illegal in itself, concluding that its illegality must depend upon the end to be sought thereby.

Analysis of Chief Justice Shaw's opinion reveals little in substantive legal doctrine contained in the decision.[202] True, he foreshadows clearly the doctrine of a later day that the legality of a strike is to be made to depend upon the end sought to be attained. But his demolition of the indictment pursues a highly technical course, and he avoids carefully any characterization of the true activity of the strikers as sanctioned by law. Nowhere in his judgment is there any indication that the earlier common law authorities are being rejected; instead, even though they be accepted, technical construction of the indictment fails to disclose a case within their ambit—the pursuit by a combination of an unlawful end or of a lawful end by unlawful means.[203] But despite the obviously intentional lack of substantive doctrine in *Commonwealth v. Hunt,* the case is still outstanding. Primarily, it demonstrated the attitude of, perhaps, the leading American court under a recognizedly great Chief Justice towards combinations of employees. That attitude is in marked contrast to that earlier displayed by Recorder Levy and only lately re-affirmed by Chief Justice Savage. Though legalistic to the extreme in his defense of the particular defendants, Shaw could hardly have failed to be aware of the growing demand for the recognition of the legality of the common objectives of trade unions.[204] Nor would other judges be likely to be unaware of such considerations as they could easily subsume beneath the legalism of *Commonwealth v. Hunt.* Certainly, from 1842 to the Civil War prosecutions for conspiracy upon the theory of the earlier cases languished. Only three conspiracy cases involving labor matters are known to have

---

[202] The case has been regarded by many writers as overthrowing the "archaic" doctrines of the earlier cases and beginning the modern law of labor combinations. Thus Dr. Witte says of the case: "Today, such a strike [a strike to procure the discharge of a non-union workman] is illegal in Massachusetts; but in this case in 1842 the Supreme Court of that state in a unanimous decision written by Chief Justice Shaw held the conduct of these strikers to have been entirely lawful." "Early American Labor Cases," 35 Yale Law Jour. 825, 828 (1926). Deriving such a conclusion from the case neglects wholly the technical basis of Shaw's decision. Thus Professor Nelles rightly says: "Shaw was careful, it will have been noted, to leave open various doors through which, should occasions arise, law could move to break effective labor organizations." Nelles, *supra,* at 1151. Curiously enough, however, he goes on to say: "Yet the main points which earlier counsel in American labor cases had pressed in vain seemed established for good and all: that special unlawfulnesses peculiar to labor organizations were not to be transplanted from England, and that whatever one person may lawfully do, any number may lawfully undertake, even if the result is to maintain the closed shop." *Ibid.*

[203] Shaw used the term "criminal" rather than "unlawful," but the occasion for the use of this term seems due to the form in which the defendant's exception was presented to the court rather than a determined rejection of the looseness implicit in the accepted common law formula.

[204] For an analysis of the political and social considerations that may well have moved Chief Justice Shaw, see Nelles, *supra,* 1151-1162.

occurred during these twenty years and none of these seems to have been pressed to a conclusion.[205] Furthermore, these years mark a decided growth in the numbers and activities of trade unions.

The intrinsic weakness of *Commonwealth v. Hunt* was to be made manifest after the Civil War, when with the surge of industrial development that the War launched antagonistic considerations came boldly to the front. The first indications of attempts to contract the allowable area of trade union activity are to be found in anti-strike and anti-union legislation that beginning in 1863 was quite frequently pressed upon and enacted by state legislatures. Outstanding among these was the La Salle Black Law passed by Illinois in 1863 [206] which not only prohibited preventing by threats, intimidation or other means, persons from working at any lawful business on any terms that they might see fit, but also made illegal all combinations seeking to deprive possessors of property of its lawful use or management or seeking to keep persons from being employed by such possessors of property.[207] Connecticut passed a similar statute in 1864, and Minnesota followed in 1867.[208]

The attitude reflected by these statutes soon found its counterpart in judicial decisions. In 1867 in *State v. Donaldson*,[209] the Supreme Court of New Jersey held certain defendants guilty of criminal conspiracy for having combined to compel the discharge of several workers who were not members of their organization. So far as the conduct of the defendants was concerned, it did not differ from that of the indicted shoemakers in *Commonwealth v. Hunt*. But the court was able on technical grounds to find that the decision of Chief Justice Shaw in the Massachusetts case was not a governing precedent,[210] and concluded that the aim of the combination was unlawful because "the effort was to dictate to this employer whom he should discharge from his employ."[211] The doc-

---

[205] See Witte, *supra*, at 829; Nelles, *supra*, at 1163.

[206] Ill. Laws 1863, p. 70.

[207] See Beckner, History of Labor Legislation in Illinois, 9 (1929).

[208] Minn. Stat. (Mason, 1927) §§ 10055-56.

[209] 32 N.J.L. 151 (1867).

[210] Unlike the indictment in Commonwealth v. Hunt, the indictment in State v. Donaldson specifically alleged that the defendants combined to compel the employer to dismiss Charles Beggan and William Prendergast "without having any lawful cause of objection to said Charles and William." Thus Beasley, C.J., was technically entitled to say: "As to the case of The Commonwealth v. Hunt, 4 Met. 111, it is clearly distinguishable, and I concur entirely, as well with the principles embodied in the opinion which was read in the case, as in the result which was attained. The foundation of the indictment in that case, was the formation of a club by journeymen boot-makers, one of the regulations of which was, that no person belonging to it should work for any master workmen who should employ any journeyman or other workman who should not be a member of such club. Such a combination does not appear to possess any feature of illegality, for the law will not intend, without proof, that it was formed for the accomplishment of any illegal end."

[211] As to the present status of State v. Donaldson, see Pitney, C., in Jonas Glass Co. v. Glass Bottle Blowers Ass'n., 77 N.J.Eq. 219, 224 (1908): "The Act of 1883 (P.L. p. 36) is, as we think, properly to be treated as merely rendering the combination no longer indictable; in effect, as repealing the rule laid down by the Supreme Court of this state in State v. Donaldson. . . ." See also Jersey Printing Co. v. Cassidy, 63 N.J.Eq. 759, 762 (1902).

trine of the *Donaldson case* found practically unanimous application [212] in a series of cases that featured the growing labor unrest of the early seventies,[213] an unrest that was to culminate in the Railway Strike of 1877. Indeed, so serious was the menace of this judicial doctrine that in several states legislation attempting to legalize types of collective labor action was enacted.[214]

The "Molly Maguire" episode of the seventies [215] and the Railway Strike of 1877[216] again raised the issue of the allowable extent of concerted action by employees. In the Railway Strike not only were the state militia employed, but for the first time federal troops were called out to suppress peace-time strikes. One reaction to the failure of this wide-spread strike was legislation aimed at strikes and their conduct.[217] On the other hand, wide sympathy for the cause of the strikers was expressed, and in the ranks of labor it inculcated the need for even stronger cooperation among employees.[218] It is true that in the decade that followed, further prosecutions for criminal conspiracy took place.[219]

---

[212] In Master Stevedores Ass'n v. Walsh, 2 Daly 5 (N.Y. 1867), C.J. Daly held valid a by-law of an association imposing a penalty upon any member who should work for less than the prices fixed by the association. Chief Justice Daly held that the objects of such an association were not in restraint of trade and contended that the doctrine that it was a criminal conspiracy to combine to raise wages was not part of the common law.

[213] People v. Van Nostrand (N.Y. 1867), reported in Wright, Criminal Conspiracies, 164 (Carson's Am. ed. 1887); Commonwealth v. Curren, 3 Pitts. 143 (1869). Dr. Witte also lists the following cases that arose during this period: Pennsylvania-Hunters' Point R.R. Car-drivers, 1869 (American Workman, Aug. 7, 1869); Erie printers, 1873 (Typographical Union Convention Proceedings, 1870); Pittsburgh printers, 1873 (Pittsburgh Commercial, Nov. 21 and 29. 1873; Pittsburgh Nat'l Labor Tribune, Mar. 14, 1874); New York—Keyes case, 1863 (N.Y. Sun, Apr. 10 and 23, 1863); New York bricklayers, 1868 (Workingmen's Advocate, Dec. 9, 1868); Morrisiana bricklayers and Kingston cigar makers, 1868 (Nat'l Labor Union Convention Proc. 1868, p. 12); New York Crispins, 1876 (N.Y. Herald, Mar. 10 and 30, Apr. 1, 1876); Connecticut, New Haven printers, 1871 (New Haven Journeyman Printer. June 20, July 6 and 11, 1871); Newark bricklayers, 1868: Paterson molders, 1868 (Molders' Journ. 1868, p. 40); Chicago molders, 1873 (Workingmen's Advocate, Apr. 5, 1873). See "Early American Labor Cases," 35 Yale Law Jour. 825, 829 (1926). See also Carew v. Rutherford. 106 Mass. 1 (1870).

[214] See e.g. N.Y. Laws, 1870, c. 18; Ill. Laws. 1873, c. 76; N.J. Laws, 1877. c. 142. See, especially Pennsylvania Acts of May 8, 1869, June 14, 1872, and April 20, 1876, as detailed in Witte, *supra,* 830-831.

[215] See 2 Commons and Associates, *op. cit.*, 181-185.

[216] See 2 *id.* 185-191.

[217] See e.g. Kan. Laws, 1879, c. 134; Mich. Acts, 1877, c. 11. See also Connecticut Act of 1878. Wright, *op. cit.*, 172. And see Stimson, Handbook to the Labor Law of the United States, 304 n. 1 (1895).

[218] See Gompers, Seventy Years of Life and Labor, 140 (1925).

[219] Commonwealth ex rel. Vallette v. Sheriff, 15 Phila. 393 (1881); People v. Wilzig, 4 N.Y. Cr. 403 (1886); People v. Kostka, 5 N.Y. Cr. 429 (1886); State v. Schilling, 1885 Rep. Wis. Labor Stat. 275 (1886); State v. Stewart, 59 Vt. 273, 9 Atl. 559 (1887); State v. Glidden, 55 Conn. 47. 8 Atl. 890 (1887); Callan v. Wilson, 127 U.S. 540 (1888); Crump v. Commonwealth, 84 Va. 927, 6 S.E. 620 (1888); People ex rel. Gill v. Walsh, 110 N.Y. 633, 17 N.E. 871 (1888). See Cheyney, "Decisions of the Courts in Conspiracy and Boycott Cases," 4 Pol. Sci. Quar. 261 (1889).

For later cases, see State v. Dyer, 67 Vt. 690, 32 Atl. 814 (1895); State v. Stockford, 77 Conn. 227, 58 Atl. 769 (1904). Cf. People v. Commerford, 233 App. Div. 2, 251 N.Y.S. 132 (1931); People v. Makvista, 224 App. Div. 419, 231 N.Y.S. 279 (1928).

But this legal instrument had, in the main, spent itself. A broader consciousness of the need for collective action to combat the swift rise of corporate power was afoot.[220] Juries might incline too sympathetically towards workers seeking to use the only effective means available to them to improve their conditions. But, principally, the new remedy of the injunction makes resort to the more ponderous means of indictment for criminal conspiracy unnecessary and less efficacious.[221]

The earliest precedent for the use of the injunction in labor controversies occurred in England in the case of *Springhead Spinning Co. v. Riley* in 1868,[222] but the basis there set forth for the issuance of the injunction was the restraint of conduct amounting to the destruction of property rather than mere "intimidation" of fellow-workmen or of an employer. In this country the origin of the injunction dates back to the Railway Strike of 1877.[223] In that year Judge Drummond, Circuit Judge for the Seventh Circuit, found strikers in Indiana and Illinois guilty of contempt for interfering with the general orders of the court directing the receivers of the railroads to operate their trains.[224] The judicial power summarily to punish for disorders occasioned by strikers thus invoked found rapid expansion in the next decade. It was sought to be employed independently of the fact of receivership in New York in 1880.[225] In 1883 injunctions were issued against glass workers in Baltimore and in Ohio.[226] In 1884 in Iowa an injunction was issued in a coal miners' strike,[227] and in 1885 in the same State a boycott and unfair list was enjoined.[228] During the railway strike of 1886, five injunctions were issued in Chicago by Judge Gresham, who had been active in this respect in the Strike of 1877; eight more federal injunctions were issued in Missouri, two in Kansas, and others in Arkansas and Texas.[229] In the same year in Virginia and in New York injunc-

---

[220] "The power wielded by the great corporations in this country is almost incredible, and in their treatment of their subordinates they ignore entirely the principle that property has its duties as well as its privileges." Great Britain, Foreign Office, Commercial Reports, Vol. 84, No. 22, Reports Respecting the Late Industrial Conflicts in the United States, Report No. 3 (1877) quoted in Nelles, "A Strike and its Legal Consequences," 40 Yale Law Jour. 507, 527 (1931).

[221] See *e.g.*, the public sympathy aroused in behalf of the strikers during the street-car strike of 1886 in New York City. Peck, Twenty Years of the Republic, 127 (1917).

[222] L.R. 6 Eq. 551 (1868).

[223] See Nelles, "A Strike and its Legal Consequences," 40 Yale Law Jour. 507 (1931). See also Frankfurter and Greene, The Labor Injunction, 21 (1930); Witte, "Early American Labor Cases," 35 Yale Law Jour. 825, 832 (1926); Bonnett, "The Origin of the Labor Injunction," 5 So. Cal. Law Rev. 105 (1931).

[224] King v. Ohio & Miss. Ry., 14 Fed. Cas. 539 (C.C. Ind. 1877); Secor v. Toledo, Peoria & Warsaw Ry., 21 Fed. Cas. 968, 971 (C.C.N.D. Ill. 1877). These cases and their background are fully discussed in Nelles, *supra*. Similar orders in receivership cases were made in the Wabash strike of 1885 and the strike of 1886. See Stimson, *op. cit.*, 326-334.

[225] See Johnston Harvester Co. v. Meinhardt, 60 How. Pr. 168 (N.Y. 1880), aff'd in 24 Hun 289 (N.Y. 1881).

[226] Powderly, Thirty Years of Labor, 442.

[227] Rep. Iowa Bur. Lab. Stat. 155 (1885).

[228] Bradstreets, Dec. 19, 1885.

[229] See Witte, *supra*, 833.

tions were issued in state courts.[230]   In 1888 the use of the injunction to restrain picketing was expressly approved by the Supreme Judical Court of Massachusetts in *Sherry v. Perkins*.[231]   This together with the affirmance of the action of the Circuit Court for the Northern District of Illinois [232] in enjoining Debs and his associates in the Pullman Strike of 1894 by the Supreme Court of the United States [233] set a final seal of approval upon the use of injunctions in labor controversies.[234]

Upon such a background as this must the anti-trust and anti-combination statutes of the United States, especially the Sherman Act of 1890,[235] be considered.   They proscribed in sweeping terms "every contract, combination in the form of trust or otherwise, or conspiracy, in restraint of trade or commerce," imposed penalties for engaging in such conduct and authorized government to sue to enjoin the forbidden practices.   Some contemporaneous evidence indicates that labor combinations were not included in their terms,[236] but doubt must attend such a conjecture for the possibilities implicit in the broad legislative generalizations were more patent than latent.   The courts, at least, failed to curtail their application to combinations of capital as distinguished from combinations of labor.[237]   But their development, the use and scope of the injunction, the determination of the legality of collective labor action by reference to its aims, the allowable limits of conduct by strikers, these are all subjects that demand the type of careful scrutiny possible only by examination of the materials themselves.

---

[230] *Ibid.*

[231] 147 Mass. 212, 17 N.E. 307 (1888).

[232] United States v. Debs, 64 Fed. 724 (C.C.N.D. Ill. 1894).

[233] Debs v. United States, 158 U.S. 564 (1895)

[234] Other early cases involving the use of the injunction are Casey v. Cincinnati Typographical Union No. 3, 45 Fed. 135 (S.D. Ohio 1891) ; Coeur d'Alene Consolidated & Mining Co. v. Miners' Union, 51 Fed. 260 (C.C.D. Idaho 1892) ; Blindell v. Hagan, 54 Fed. 40 (E.D. La. 1893) ; Brace Bros. v. Evans, 5 Pa. Co. Ct. 163 (1888) ; Murdock v. Walker, 152 Pa. 595, 25 Atl. 492 (1893) ; Barr v. Essex Trades Council, 53 N.J. Eq. 101, 30 Atl. 885 (1894). See Stimson *op. cit.*, c. 9.

[235] 26 Stat. 209. On the effect of the Interstate Commerce Act of 1887 on labor combinations, see Frankfurter and Greene, *op. cit.*, 6.

[236] The available evidence in behalf of this contention is fully set forth in Berman, Labor and the Sherman Act, Pt. 1 (1930). See also Frankfurter and Greene, *op. cit.*, 139.

[237] United States v. Workingmen's Amalgamated Council, 54 Fed. 994 (E.D. Iowa 1893), aff'd in 57 Fed. 85 (C.C.A. 5th, 1893).

CHAPTER II.

GENERAL THEORIES.

GARRET v. TAYLOR.

King's Bench [1621]. Cro. Jac. 567.

Action on the case. Whereas he was a free mason, and used to sell stones, and to make stone-buildings, and was possessed of a lease for divers years to come of a stone-pit in *Hedington,* in the county of *Oxford,* and digged divers stones there, as well to sell as to build withal; that the defendant, to discredit and to deprive him of the commodity of the said mine, imposed so many and so great threats upon his workmen, and all comers disturbed, threatening to mayhem and vex them with suits if they bought any stones; whereupon they all desisted from buying, and the others from working, &c.

After judgment by *nihil dicit* for the plaintiff, and damages found by inquisition to fifteen pounds, it was moved in arrest of judgment, That this action lay not; for nothing is alledged but only words, and no act nor insult; and causeless suits on fear are no cause of action.

Sed non allocatur: for the threatening to mayhem, and suits, whereby they durst not work or buy, is a great damage to the plaintiff, and his losing the benefit of his quarries a good cause of action: and although it be not shewn how he was possessed for years, by what title, &c. yet that being but a conveyance to this action, was held to be well enough. And adjudged for the plaintiff.[1]

KEEBLE v. HICKERINGILL.

Queen's Bench [1706]. 11 East 574n.

Action upon the case. Plaintiff declares that he was, 8th *November* in the second year of the Queen, lawfully possessed of a close of land called *Minott's Meadow, et de quodam vivario, vicato a decoy pond,* to which divers wildfowl used to resort and come: and the plaintiff had at his own costs and charges prepared and procured divers decoy ducks, nets, machines and other engines for the decoying and taking of the wild-

---

[1] For a review of the early authorities dealing with kindred situations, see: Wigmore, "The Boycott and Kindred Practices as Ground for Damages," 21 Am. Law Rev. 509 (1887).

fowl, and enjoyed the benefit in taking them: the defendant, knowing which, and *intending to damnify the plaintiff in his vivary,* and *to fright and drive away the wildfowl used to resort thither, and deprive him of his profit,* did, on the 8th of *November,* resort to the head of the said pond and vivary, and did discharge six guns laden with gunpowder, and with the noise and stink of the gunpowder did drive away the wildfowl then being in the pond: and on the 11th and 12th days of *November* the defendant, *with design to damnify the plaintiff, and fright away the wildfowl,* did place himself with a gun near the vivary, and there did discharge the said gun several times that was then charged with the gunpowder against the said decoy pond, whereby the wildfowl were frighted away, and did forsake the said pond. Upon not guilty pleaded, a verdict was found for the plaintiff and 20 *l.* damages.

HOLT, C.J. I am of opinion that this action doth lie. It seems to be new in its instance, but is not new in the reason or principle of it. For, 1st, this using or making a decoy is lawful. 2dly, This employment of his ground to that use is profitable to the plaintiff, as is the skill and management of that employment. As to the first, Every man that hath a property may employ it for his pleasure and profit, as for alluring and procuring decoy ducks to come to his pond. To learn the trade of seducing other ducks to come there in order to be taken is not prohibited either by the law of the land or the moral law; but it is as lawful to use art to seduce them, to catch them, and destroy them for the use of mankind, as to kill and destroy wildfowl or tame cattle. Then when a man useth his art or his skill to take them, to sell and dispose of for his profit; this is his trade; and he that hinders another in his trade or livelihood is liable to an action for so hindering him. Why otherwise are scandalous words spoken of a man in his profession actionable, when without his profession they are not so? Though they do not affect any damage, yet are they mischievous in themselves; and therefore in their own nature productive of damage; and therefore an action lies against him. Such are all words that are spoken of a man to disparage him in his trade, that may bring damage to him; though they do not charge him with any crime that may make him obnoxious to punishment; as to say a merchant is broken, or that he is failing, or is not able to pay his debts, 1 *Roll.* 60.1; all the cases there put. How much more, when the defendant doth an actual and real damage to another when he is in the very act of receiving profit by his employment. Now there are two sorts of acts for doing damage to a man's employment, for which an action lies; the one is in respect of a man's privilege; the other is in respect of his property. In that of a man's franchise or privilege whereby he hath a fair, market, or ferry, if another shall use the like liberty, though out of his limits, he shall be liable to an action; though by grant from the king. But therein is the difference to be taken between a liberty in which the public hath a benefit, and that wherein the public is not concerned. 22 *H.*6.14, 15. The other is where a violent or malicious act is done to a man's occupation, profession, or way of getting a livelihood; there an action lies in all cases.

But if a man doth him damage by using the same employment; as if
Mr. *Hickeringill* had set up another decoy on his own ground near the
plaintiff's, and that had spoiled the custom of the plaintiff, no action would
lie, because he had as much liberty to make and use a decoy as the plaintiff. This is like the case of 11 *H*.4.47. One schoolmaster sets up a new
school to the damage of an ancient school, and thereby the scholars are
allured from the old school to come to his new. (The action was held
there not to lie.) But suppose Mr. *Hickeringill* should lie in the way with
his guns, and fright the boys from going to school, and their parents
would not let them go thither; sure that schoolmaster might have an action for the loss of his scholars. 29 *E*.3.18. A man hath a market, to
which he hath toll for horses sold: a man is bringing his horse to market
to sell: a stranger hinders and obstructs him from going thither to the
market: an action lies, because it imports damage. Action upon the case
lies against one that shall by threats fright away his tenants at will.
9 *H*.7.8. 21 *H*.6.31. 9 *H*.7.7. 14 *Ed*. 4.7. *Vide Rastal*. 662. 2 *Cro*. 423.
Trespass was brought for beating his servant, whereby he was hindered
from taking his toll; the obstruction is a damage, though not the loss of
his service. ² * * *

TARLETON v. M'GAWLEY.

Nisi Prius 1794. Peake N.P. Cas. 270.

This was a special action on the case. The declaration stated that
the Plaintiffs were possessed and owners of a certain ship called the
Tarleton, which at the time of committing the grievance was lying at
Calabar on the coast of *Africa,* under the command of ....
Fairweather. That the ship had been fitted out at *Liverpool* with goods
proper for trading with the natives of that coast for slaves and other
goods. That also before the committing the grievance *Fairweather* had
sent a smaller vessel called the *Bannister* with a crew on board, under the
command of one *Thomas Smith,* and loaded with goods proper for trading with the natives, to another part of the said coast called *Cameroon,*
to trade with the natives there. That while the last-mentioned ship was

² Accord: Carrington v. Taylor, 11 East 571 (1809); Ibottson v. Peat, 3 Hurl.
& C. 644 (1865); Whittaker v. Stangvick, 100 Minn. 386, 111 N. W. 295 (1907);
Prince de Wagram v. Marais, Cour de Paris, Dec. 2, 1871, Dalloz 73, 2, 185; *Cf.*
Emack v. Kane, 34 Fed. 46 (1888).
    "As regards Keeble v. Hickeringill, Carrington v. Taylor, and Bowen v. Hall,
I venture to assert that those cases were distinctly overruled by the majority of the
Lords, if or so far as they decided that to obstruct a person in his trade by any act
not in itself unlawful was an actionable tort. The correctness of this assertion can,
of course, be tested in no other way than by a careful perusal of the judgments of
the majority of the Lords who took part in the decision." Memorandum on Allen
v. Flood, [1898] A.C. 1, by Arthur Cohen, in Report of the Royal Commission
on Trade Disputes and Trade Combinations, Cd. 2825, p. 25 (1906).
    On the malicious use of property to injure a neighbor, see: Holbrook v. Mor-
rison, 214 Mass. 209, 100 N.E. 1111 (1913); Kuzniak v. Kozminski, 107 Mich. 444,
65 N.W. 275 (1895); and cases collected in Ames & Smith, Cases on Torts (Pound's
ed.) 927, note.

lying off *Cameroon,* a canoe with some natives on board came to the same for the purpose of establishing a trade, and went back to the shore, of which Defendant had notice. And that he well knowing the premises, but *contriving and maliciously intending to hinder and deter the natives from trading* with the said *Thomas Smith,* for the benefit of the Plaintiffs, with force and arms, fired from a certain ship called the *Othello,* of which he was master and commander, a certain cannon loaded with gunpowder and shot at the said canoe, and killed one of the natives on board the same. *Whereby the natives of the said coast were deterred and hindered from trading with the said* T. Smith *for the benefit, &c. and Plaintiffs lost their trade.* * * *

The Plaintiffs called *Thomas Smith,* who proved the facts stated in the declaration; and further, that the Defendant had declared the natives owed him a debt, and that he would not suffer any ship to trade with them until that was paid; in pursuance of which declaration he committed the act complained of by the Plaintiffs. On his cross examination he admitted that by the custom of that coast no *Europeans* can trade until a certain duty has been paid to the king of the country for his licence, and that no such duty had been paid, or licence obtained by the captain of the Plaintiffs' vessel. * * *

LORD KENYON: This action is brought by the Plaintiffs to recover a satisfaction for a civil injury which they have sustained. The injury complained of is, that by the improper conduct of the Defendant the natives were prevented from trading with the Plaintiffs. The whole of the case is stated on the record, and if the parties desire it, the opinion of the Court may hereafter be taken whether it will support an action. I am of opinion it will. This case has been likened to cases which it does not at all resemble. It has been said that a person engaged in a trade violating the law of the country cannot support an action against another for hindering him in that illegal traffick. That I entirely accede to, but it does not apply to this case. This is a foreign law; the act of trading is not itself immoral, and a *jus positivum* is not binding on foreigners. The king of the country and not the Defendant should have executed that law. Had this been an accidental thing, no action could have been maintained, but it is proved that the Defendant had expressed an intention not to permit any to trade, until a debt due from the natives to himself was satisfied. If there was any court in that country to which he could have applied for justice he might have done so, but he had no right to take the law into his own hands.

The Plaintiffs had a verdict, and the parties agreed to refer the damages to arbitration. [3]

---

[3] Accord: St. Johnsbury & Lake Champlain R.R. Co. v. Hunt, 55 Vt. 570 (1882). In Rex v. Kerr, a *nisi prius* case reported in the *London Times* for Dec. 17, 18, and 19, 1931, the court ruled that a person would be guilty of an intent to extort "if—although he honestly believes a debt is due—he threatens to employ discreditable means [in the instant case threatening to tell a true but otherwise slanderous statement concerning the debtor] whereby to injure his debtor, either physically or morally."

MOGUL STEAMSHIP CO. v. McGREGOR, GOW & CO.

Court of Appeal [1899]. L.R. 23 Q.B.D. 598.

Appeal from the judgment of Lord Coleridge, C.J., in an action tried without a jury, reported 21 Q.B.D. 544.

The plaintiffs claimed damages for a conspiracy to prevent them from carrying on their trade between London and China, and an injunction against the continuance of the alleged wrongful acts. * * *

BOWEN, L.J. We are presented in this case with an apparent conflict or antinomy between two rights that are equally regarded by the law—the right of the plaintiffs to be protected in the legitimate exercise of their trade, and the right of the defendants to carry on their business as seems best to them, provided they commit no wrong to others. The plaintiffs complain that the defendants have crossed the line which the common law permits; and inasmuch as, for the purposes of the present case, we are to assume some possible damage to the plaintiffs, the real question to be decided is whether, on such an assumption, the defendants in the conduct of their commercial affairs have done anything that is unjustifiable in law. The defendants are a number of shipowners who formed themselves into a league or conference for the purpose of ultimately keeping in their own hands the control of the tea carriage from certain Chinese ports, and for the purpose of driving the plaintiffs and other competitors from the field. In order to succeed in this object, and to discourage the plaintiffs' vessels from resorting to those ports, the defendants during the "tea harvest" of 1885 combined to offer to the local shippers very low freights, with a view of generally reducing or "smashing" rates, and thus rendering it unprofitable for the plaintiffs to send their ships thither. They offered, moreover, a rebate of 5 per cent. to all local shippers and agents who would deal exclusively with vessels belonging to the Conference, and any agent who broke the condition was to forfeit the entire rebate on all shipments made on behalf of any and every one of his principals during the whole year—a forfeiture of rebate or allowance which was denominated as "penal" by the plaintiffs' counsel. It must, however, be taken as established that the rebate was one which the defendants need never have allowed at all to their customers. It must also be taken that the defendants had no personal ill-will to the plaintiffs, nor any desire to harm them except such as is involved in the wish and intention to discourage by such measures the plaintiffs from sending rival vessels to such ports. The acts of which the plaintiffs particularly complained were as follows:—First, a circular of May 10, 1885, by which the defendants offered to the local shippers and their agents a benefit by way of rebate if they would not deal with the plaintiffs, which was to be lost if this condition was not fulfilled. Secondly, the sending of special ships to Hankow in order by competition to deprive the plaintiffs' vessels of profitable freight. Thirdly, the offer at Hankow of freights at a level which would not repay a shipowner for his adventure, in order to "smash" freights and frighten the plaintiffs from the field. Fourthly, pressure put on the defendants' own agents to induce them to ship only by the defendants' vessels, and not by those of the plaintiffs. It is to be observed with regard to all these acts of which complaint is made that they were acts that in themselves could not be said to be illegal unless made so by the object with which, or the combination in the course of which, they were done; and that in reality what is complained of is the pursuing of trade competition to a length which the plaintiffs consider oppressive and prejudicial to themselves. We were invited by the plaintiffs' counsel to accept the position from which their argument started—that an action will lie if a man maliciously and wrongfully conducts himself so as to injure another in that other's trade. Obscurity resides in the language used to state this proposition. The terms "maliciously," "wrongfully," and "injure" are words all of which have accurate meanings, well known to the law, but which also have a popular and less precise signification, into which it is necessary to see that the argument does not imperceptibly slide. An intent to "injure" in strictness means more than an intent to harm. It connotes an intent to do wrongful harm. "Maliciously," in like manner, means and implies an intention to do an act which is wrongful, to the detriment of another. The term "wrongful" imports in its turn the infringement of some right. The ambiguous proposition to which we were invited by the plaintiffs' counsel still, therefore, leaves unsolved the question of what, as between the plaintiffs and defendants, are the rights of trade. For the purpose of clearness, I desire, as far as possible, to avoid terms in their popular use so slippery, and to translate them into less fallacious language wherever possible.

The English law, which in its earlier stages began with but an imperfect line of demarcation between torts and breaches of contract, presents us with no scientific analysis of the degree to which the intent to harm, or, in the language of the civil law, the *animus vicino nocendi,* may enter into or affect the conception of a personal wrong; see *Chasemore v. Richards.* (7 H.L.C. 349, at p. 388.) All personal wrong means the infringement of some personal right. "It is essential to an action in tort," say the Privy Council in *Rogers v. Rajendro Dutt,* (13 Moore, P.C. 209) "that the act complained of should under the circumstances be legally wrongful as regards the party complaining; that is, it must prejudicially affect him in some legal right; merely that it will, however directly, do a man harm in his interests, is not enough." What, then, were the rights of the plaintiffs as traders as against the defendants? The plaintiffs had a right to be protected against certain kind of conduct; and we have to consider what conduct would pass this legal line or boundary. Now, intentionally to do that which is calculated in the ordinary course of events to damage, and which does, in fact, damage another in that other person's property or trade, is actionable if done without just cause or excuse. Such intentional action when done without just cause or excuse is what the law calls a malicious wrong (see *Bromage v. Prosser* (4 B. &

C. 247) ; *Capital and Counties Bank v. Henty,* per Lord Blackburn. (7 App. Cas. 741, at p. 772)). The acts of the defendants which are complained of here were intentional, and were also calculated, no doubt, to do the plaintiffs damage in their trade. But in order to see whether they were wrongful we have still to discuss the question whether they were done without any just cause or excuse. Such just cause or excuse the defendants on their side assert to be found in their own positive right (subject to certain limitations) to carry on their own trade freely in the mode and manner that best suits them, and which they think best calculated to secure their own advantage.

What, then, are the limitations which the law imposes on a trader in the conduct of his business as between himself and other traders? There seem to be no burdens or restrictions in law upon a trader which arise merely from the fact that he is a trader, and which are not equally laid on all other subjects of the Crown. His right to trade freely is a right which the law recognises and encourages, but it is one which places him at no special disadvantage as compared with others. No man, whether trader or not, can, however, justify damaging another in his commercial business by fraud or misrepresentation. Intimidation, obstruction, and molestation are forbidden; so is the intentional procurement of a violation of individual rights, contractual or other, assuming always that there is no just cause for it. The intentional driving away of customers by shew of violence: *Tarleton v. M'Gawley* (Peak, N.P.C. 270) ; the obstruction of actors on the stage by preconcerted hissing: *Clifford v. Brandon* (2 Camp. 358) ; *Gregory v. Brunswick* (6 Man. & G. 205) ; the disturbance of wild fowl in decoys by the firing of guns: *Carrington v. Taylor* (11 East, 571), and *Keeble v. Hickeringill* (11 East, 574, n.) ; the impeding or threatening servants or workmen: *Garret v. Taylor* (Cro. Jac. 567) ; the inducing persons under personal contracts to break their contracts: *Bowen v. Hall* (6 Q.B.D. 333) ; *Lumley v. Gye* (2 E. & B. 216) ; all are instances of such forbidden acts. But the defendants have been guilty of none of these acts. They have done nothing more against the plaintiffs than pursue to the bitter end a war of competition waged in the interest of their own trade. To the argument that a competition so pursued ceases to have a just cause or excuse when there is ill-will or a personal intention to harm, it is sufficient to reply (as I have already pointed out) that there was here no personal intention to do any other or greater harm to the plaintiffs than such as was necessarily involved in the desire to attract to the defendants' ships the entire tea freights of the ports, a portion of which would otherwise have fallen to the plaintiffs' share. I can find no authority for the doctrine that such a commercial motive deprives of "just cause or excuse" acts done in the course of trade which would but for such a motive be justifiable. So to hold would be to convert into an illegal motive the instinct of self-advancement and self-protection, which is the very incentive to all trade. To say that a man is to trade freely, but that he is to stop short at any act which is calculated to harm other tradesmen, and which is designed to attract business to his own shop, would be a strange and impossible counsel of perfection. But we were told that competition ceases to be the lawful exercise of trade, and so to be a lawful excuse for what will harm another, if carried to a length which is not fair or reasonable. The offering of reduced rates by the defendants in the present case is said to have been "unfair." This seems to assume that, apart from fraud, intimidation, molestation, or obstruction, of some other personal right *in rem* or *in personam,* there is some natural standard of "fairness" or "reasonableness" (to be determined by the internal consciousness of judges and juries) beyond which competition ought not in law to go. There seems to be no authority, and I think, with submission, that there is no sufficient reason for such a proposition. It would impose a novel fetter upon trade. The defendants, we are told by the plaintiffs' counsel, might lawfully lower rates provided they did not lower them beyond a "fair freight," whatever that may mean. But where is it established that there is any such restriction upon commerce? And what is to be the definition of a "fair freight"? It is said that it ought to be a normal rate of freight, such as is reasonably remunerative to the shipowner. But over what period of time is the average of this reasonable remunerativeness to be calculated? All commercial men with capital are acquainted with the ordinary expedient of sowing one year a crop of apparently unfruitful prices, in order by driving competition away to reap a fuller harvest of profit in the future; and until the present argument at the bar it may be doubted whether shipowners or merchants were ever deemed to be bound by law to conform to some imaginary "normal" standard of freights or prices, or that Law Courts had a right to say to them in respect of their competitive tariffs, "Thus far shalt thou go and no further." To attempt to limit English competition in this way would probably be as hopeless an endeavour as the experiment of King Canute. But on ordinary principles of law no such fetter on freedom of trade can in my opinion be warranted. A man is bound not to use his property so as to infringe upon another's right. *Sic utere tuo ut alienum non laedas.* If engaged in actions which may involve danger to others, he ought, speaking generally, to take reasonable care to avoid endangering them. But there is surely no doctrine of law which compels him to use his property in a way that judges and juries may consider reasonable: see *Chasemore v. Richards* (7 H.L.C. 349.) If there is no such fetter upon the use of property known to the English law, why should there be any such a fetter upon trade?

It is urged, however, on the part of the plaintiffs, that even if the acts complained of would not be wrongful had they been committed by a single individual, they become actionable when they are the result of concerted action among several. In other words, the plaintiffs, it is contended, have been injured by an illegal conspiracy. Of the general proposition, that certain kinds of conduct not criminal in any one individual may become criminal if done by combination among several, there can be no doubt. The distinction is based on sound reason, for a combination may make oppressive or dangerous that which if it proceeded only from a single person would be otherwise, and the very fact of the combination may shew that the object is simply to do harm, and not to exercise one's own just rights. In the application of this undoubted principle it is necessary to be very careful not to press the doctrine of illegal conspiracy beyond that which is necessary for the protection of individuals or of the public; and it may be observed in passing that as a rule it is the damage wrongfully done, and not the conspiracy, that is the gist of actions on the case for conspiracy: see *Skinner v. Gunton* (1 Wms. Saund. 229); *Hutchins v. Hutchins* (7 Hill's New York Cases, 104; Bigelow's Leading Cases on Torts, 207). But what is the definition of an illegal combination? It is an agreement by one or more to do an unlawful act, or to do a lawful act by unlawful means: *O'Connell v. The Queen* (11 Cl. & F. 155); *Reg. v. Parnell* (14 Cox, Criminal Cases, 508); and the question to be solved is whether there has been any such agreement here. Have the defendants combined to do an unlawful act? Have they combined to do a lawful act by unlawful means? A moment's consideration will be sufficient to shew that this new inquiry only drives us back to the circle of definitions and legal propositions which I have already traversed in the previous part of this judgment. The unlawful act agreed to, if any, between the defendants must have been the intentional doing of some act to the detriment of the plaintiffs' business without just cause or excuse. Whether there was any such justification or excuse for the defendants is the old question over again, which, so far as regards an individual trader, has been already solved. The only differentia that can exist must arise, if at all, out of the fact that the acts done are the joint acts of several capitalists, and not of one capitalist only. The next point is whether the means adopted were unlawful. The means adopted were competition carried to a bitter end. Whether such means were unlawful is in like manner nothing but the old discussion which I have gone through, and which is now revived under a second head of inquiry, except so far as a combination of capitalists differentiates the case of acts jointly done by them from similar acts done by a single man of capital. But I find it impossible myself to acquiesce in the view that the English law places any such restriction on the combination of capital as would be involved in the recognition of such a distinction. If so, one rich capitalist may innocently carry competition to a length which would become unlawful in the case of a syndicate with a joint capital no larger than his own, and one individual merchant may lawfully do that which a firm or a partnership may not. What limits, on such a theory, would be imposed by law on the competitive action of a joint-stock company limited, is a problem which might well puzzle a casuist. The truth is, that the combination of capital for purposes of trade and competition is a very different thing from such a combination of several persons against one, with a view to harm him, as falls under the head of an indictable conspiracy. There is no just cause or excuse in the latter class of cases. There is such a just cause or excuse in the former. There are cases in which the very fact of a combination is evidence of a design to do that which is hurtful without just cause—is evidence—to use a technical expression—of malice. But it is perfectly legitimate, as it seems to me, to combine capital for all the mere purposes of trade for which capital may, apart from combination, be legitimately used in trade. To limit combinations of capital, when used for purposes of competition, in the manner proposed by the argument of the plaintiffs, would, in the present day, be impossible—would be only another method of attempting to set boundaries to the tides. Legal puzzles which might well distract a theorist may easily be conceived of imaginary conflicts between the selfishness of a group of individuals and the obvious well-being of other members of the community. Would it be an indictable conspiracy to agree to drink up all the water from a common spring in a time of drought; to buy up by preconcerted action all the provisions in a market or district in times of scarcity: see *Rex v. Waddington* (1 East, 143); to combine to purchase all the shares of a company against a coming settling-day; or to agree to give away articles of trade gratis in order to withdraw custom from a trader? May two itinerant match-vendors combine to sell matches below their value in order by competition to drive a third match-vendor from the street? In cases like these, where the elements of intimidation, molestation, or the other kinds of illegality to which I have alluded are not present, the question must be decided by the application of the test I have indicated. Assume that what is done is intentional, and that it is calculated to do harm to others. Then comes the question, Was it done with or without "just cause or excuse"? If it was *bonâ fide* done in the use of a man's own property, in the exercise of a man's own trade, such legal justification would, I think, exist not the less because what was done might seem to others to be selfish or unreasonable: see the summing-up of Erle, J., and the judgment of the Queen's Bench in *Reg. v. Rowlands*. (17 Q.B. 671.) But such legal justification would not exist when the act was merely done with the intention of causing temporal harm, without reference to one's own lawful gain, or the lawful enjoyment of one's own rights. The good sense of the tribunal which had to decide would have to analyse the circumstances and to discover on which side of the line each case fell. But if the real object were to enjoy what was one's own, or to acquire for one's self some advantage in one's property or trade, and what was done was done honestly, peaceably, and without any of the illegal acts above referred to, it could not, in my opinion, properly be said that it was done without just cause or excuse. One may with advantage borrow for the benefit of traders what was said by Erle, J., in *Reg. v. Rowlands* (17 Q.B. 671, at p. 687, n.), of workmen and of masters: "The intention of the law is at present to allow either of them to follow the dictates of their own will, with respect to their own actions, and their own property; and either, I believe, has a right to study to promote his own advantage, or to combine with others to promote their mutual advantage."

Lastly, we are asked to hold the defendants' Conference or association illegal, as being in restraint of trade. The term "illegal" here is a misleading one. Contracts, as they are called, in restraint of trade, are

not, in my opinion, illegal in any sense, except that the law will not enforce them. It does not prohibit the making of such contracts; it merely
declines, after they have been made, to recognise their validity. The law
considers the disadvantage so imposed upon the contract a sufficient shelter
to the public. The language of Crompton, J., in *Hilton v. Eckersley* (6
E. & B. 47), is, I think, not to be supported. No action at common law
will lie or ever has lain against any individual or individuals for entering
into a contract merely because it is in restraint of trade. Lord Eldon's
equity decision in *Cousins v. Smith* (13 Ves. 542) is not very intelligible,
even if it be not open to the somewhat personal criticism passed on it by
Lord Campbell in his Lives of the Chancellors. If indeed it could be
plainly proved that the mere formation of "conferences," "trusts," or
"associations" such as these were always necessarily injurious to the public—a view which involves, perhaps, the disputable assumption that, in a
country of free trade, and one which is not under the iron régime of statutory monopolies, such confederations can ever be really successful—and
if the evil of them were not sufficiently dealt with by the common law
rule, which held such agreements to be void as distinct from holding them
to be criminal, there might be some reason for thinking that the common
law ought to discover within its arsenal of sound common-sense principles some further remedy commensurate with the mischief. Neither of
these assumptions are, to my mind, at all evident, nor it is the province
of judges to mould and stretch the law of conspiracy in order to keep pace
with the calculations of political economy. If peaceable and honest combinations of capital for purposes of trade competition are to be struck
at, it must, I think, be by legislation, for I do not see that they are under
the ban of the common law.

In the result, I agree with Lord Coleridge, C.J., and differ, with regret,
from the Master of the Rolls. The substance of my view is this, that
competition, however severe and egotistical, if unattended by circumstances of dishonesty, intimidation, molestation, or such illegalities as I
have above referred to, gives rise to no cause of action at common law.
I myself should deem it to be a misfortune if we were to attempt to prescribe to the business world how honest and peaceable trade was to be
carried on in a case where no such illegal elements as I have mentioned
exist, or were to adopt some standard of judicial "reasonableness," or of
"normal" prices, or "fair freights," to which commercial adventurers,
otherwise innocent, were bound to conform.

In my opinion, accordingly, this appeal ought to be dismissed with
costs. [4] * * *

Appeal dismissed.[5]

---

[4] The concurring opinion of Fry, L.J., and the dissenting opinion of Lord Esher,
M.R., are omitted. The decision of the Court of Appeal was affirmed by the House of
Lords [1892] A.C. 25.

[5] "The ground of decision really comes down to a proposition of policy of rather
a delicate nature concerning the merit of the particular benefit to themselves intended
by the defendants, and suggests a doubt whether judges with different economic sympathies might not decide such a case differently when brought face to face with the

ALLEN v. FLOOD.

House of Lords. [1898] A.C. 1.

The facts material to this appeal (omitting matters not now in question) were as follows: In April 1894 about forty boiler-makers, or "iron-men," were employed by the Glengall Iron Company in repairing a ship at the company's Regent Dock in Millwall. They were members of the boiler-makers' society, a trade union, which objected to the employment of shipwrights on ironwork. On April 12 the respondents Flood and Taylor, who were shipwrights, were engaged by the company in repairing the woodwork of the same ship, but were not doing ironwork. The boiler-makers, on discovering that the respondents had shortly before been employed by another firm (Mills & Knight) on the Thames in doing ironwork on a ship, became much excited and began to talk of leaving their employment. One of them, Elliott, telegraphed for the appellant Allen, the London delegate of the boiler-makers' society. Allen came up on the 13th, and being told by Elliott that the iron-men, or some of them, would leave at dinner-time, replied that if they took the law into their own hands he would use his influence with the council of the society that they should be deprived of all benefit from the society and be fined, and that they must wait and see how things settled. Allen then had an interview with Halkett, the Glengall Company's manager, and Edmonds the foreman, and the result was that the respondents were discharged at the end of the day by Halkett. An action was then brought by the respondents against Allen for maliciously and wrongfully and with intent to injure the plaintiffs procuring and inducing the Glengall Company to break their contract with the plaintiffs and not to enter into new contracts with them, and also maliciously, &c., intimidating and coercing the plaintiffs to break, &c., and also unlawfully and maliciously conspiring with others to do the above acts.

At the trial before Kennedy J. and a common jury Halkett and Edmonds were called for the plaintiffs, and gave their account of the interview with Allen. In substance it was this: Allen told them that he had been sent for because Flood and Taylor were known to have done ironwork in Mills & Knight's yard, and that unless Flood and Taylor were discharged all the members of the boiler-makers' society would be "called out" or "knock off" work that day: they could not be sure which expres-

---

issue. * * * I make these suggestions, not as criticisms of the decisions, but to call attention to the very serious legislative considerations which have to be weighed. The danger is that such considerations should have their weight in an inarticulate form as unconscious prejudice or half conscious inclination. To measure them justly needs not only the highest powers of a judge and a training which the practice of the law does not insure, but also a freedom from prepossessions which is very hard to attain." Holmes, "Privilege, Malice and Intent," 8 Harv. Law Rev. 1, 8-9, (1894), reprinted in Holmes, Collected Legal Papers, 117. See also: Bowen v. Matheson, 14 Allen, 499 (Mass. 1867); Bohn Mfg. Co. v. Hollis, 54 Minn. 223, 55 N.W. 1119 (1893); Scottish Coop. Wholesale Society v. Glasgow Fleshers' Trade Defense Ass'n, 35 Scot. L.R. 645 (1898).

sion was used; that Halkett had no option; that the iron-men were doing their best to put an end to the practice of shipwrights doing ironwork, and whenever these men were employed, or other shipwrights who had done ironwork, the boiler-makers would cease work—in every yard on the Thames. Halkett said that if the boiler-makers (about 100 in all were employed) had been called out it would have stopped the company's business, and that in fear of the threat being carried out he told Edmonds to discharge Flood and Taylor that day, and that if he knew of any shipwrights having worked on ironwork elsewhere, when he was engaging men, for the sake of peace and quietness for themselves he was not to employ them. Allen was called for the defence. His account of the interview is discussed in the judgment of Lord Halsbury L.C.

Kennedy J. ruled that there was no evidence of conspiracy, or of intimidation or coercion, or of breach of contract, Flood and Taylor having been engaged on the terms that they might be discharged at any time. In the ordinary course their employment would have continued till the repairs were finished or the work slackened.

In reply to question put by Kennedy J. the jury found that Allen maliciously induced the Glengall Company (1.) to discharge Flood and Taylor from their employment; (2.) not to engage them; that each plaintiff had suffered 20l. damages; and that the settlement of the dispute was a matter within Allen's discretion. After consideration Kennedy J. entered judgment for the plaintiffs for 40l. This decision was affirmed by the Court of Appeal (Lord Esher M.R., Lopes and Rigby L.JJ.). [1895] 2 Q.B. 21. Against these decisions Allen brought the present appeal. It was argued first before Lord Halsbury L.C. and Lords Watson, Herschell, Macnaghten, Morris, Shand, and Davey on December 10, 12, 16, 17, 1895, and again (the following judges having been summoned to attend—Hawkins, Mathew, Cave, North, Wills, Grantham, Lawrance and Wright JJ.) on March 25, 26, 29, 30, April 1, 2, 1897 before the same noble and learned Lords, with the addition of Lords Ashbourne, and James of Hereford. * * *

Dec. 14. LORD HALSBURY L.C. * * * As I have said, in the face of this evidence, how any one can doubt that it was the communications made by Allen that caused the dismissal of these two men, I am not able to understand; and in what I have to say hereafter I shall assume as proved, or, at all events, as established by evidence proper to be submitted to a jury, that it was Allen who caused the dismissal of the plaintiffs.

The first objection made to the plaintiffs' right to recover for the loss which they thus undoubtedly suffered is that no right of the plaintiffs was infringed, and that the right contended for on their behalf is not a right recognised by law, or, at all events, only such a right as everyone else is entitled to deprive them of if they stop short of physical violence or obstruction. I think the right to employ their labour as they will is a right both recognised by the law and sufficiently guarded by its provisions to make any undue interference with that right an actionable wrong.

Very early authorities in the law have recognised the right; and, in my view, no authority can be found which questions or qualifies it. The schoolmaster who complained that his scholars were being assaulted and brought an action, the quarry owner who complained that his servants were being menaced and molested, were both held to have a right of action. And it appears to me that the importance of those cases, and the principle established by them, have not been sufficiently considered. It is said that threats of violence or actual violence were unlawful means: the lawfulness of the means I will discuss hereafter. But the point on which these cases are important is the existence of the right. It was not the schoolmaster who was assaulted; it was not the quarry owner who was assaulted or threatened; but, nevertheless, the schoolmaster was held entitled to bring an action in respect of the loss of scholars attending his school, and the quarry owner in respect of the loss of workmen to his quarry. They were third persons; no violence or threats were applied to them, and the cause of action, which they had a right to insist on, was the indirect effect upon themselves of violence and threats applied to others.

My Lords, in my view these are binding authorities to shew that the preliminary question, namely, whether there was any right of the plaintiffs to pursue their calling unmolested, must be answered in the affirmative. The question of what is the right invaded would seem to be reasonably answered, and the universality of the right to all Her Majesty's subjects seems to me to be no argument against its existence. It is, indeed, part of that freedom from restraint, that liberty of action, which, in my view, may be found running through the principles of our law.

As I have said, I will deal separately both with the remedy for the infringement of that right, if it has been infringed, and with the means by which it is alleged to have been infringed * * *.

First it is said that the company were acting within their legal rights in discharging the plaintiffs. So they were; but does that affect the question of the responsibility of the person who caused them so to act by the means he used? The scholars who went away from the school were entitled to do so. The miners were entitled to cease working at the quarry. The natives were entitled to avoid running the risk of being shot; but the question is, What was the cause of their thus exercising their legal right? * * *

My Lords, I do not think that the case of *Keeble* v. *Hickeringill* (11 East, 574, n.) stands alone, though if it did, considering who decided it, and that certainly in later years it has been much quoted and commented on, and never until now, so far as I am aware, criticised or questioned, I should be quite content to rely upon the authority of so profound a lawyer as Sir John Holt, and such an expositor as he was of the spirit of freedom which runs through the English law: but it will be also observed that in this House Lords Bramwell and Field, and in the Court of Appeal Bowen L.J., assume it to be good law. * * *

But, referring to Bowen, L.J.'s observation, which to my mind is exactly accurate, "in order to justify the intentional doing of that which is calculated in the ordinary course of events to damage, and which does, in fact, damage another in that other person's property or trade," you must have some just cause or excuse.

Now, the word "malicious" appears to me to negative just cause or excuse; and without attempting an exhaustive exposition of the word itself, it appears to me that, if I apply the language of Bowen L.J., it is enough to shew that this was within the meaning of the law "malicious."

It appears to me that no better illustration can be given of the distinction on which I am insisting between an act which can be legally done and an act which cannot be so done because tainted with malice, than such a colloquy between the representative of the master and the representative of the men as might have been held on the occasion which has given rise to this action. If the representative of the men had in good faith and without indirect motive pointed out the inconvenience that might result from having two sets of men working together on the same ship, whose views upon the particular question were so diverse that it would be inexpedient to bring them together, no one could have complained; but if his object was to punish the men belonging to another union because on some former occasion they had worked on an iron ship, it seems to me that the difference of motive may make the whole difference between the lawfulness or unlawfulness of what he did. * * *

If concerted collective action to enforce, by ruining the men's employment, the will of a large number of men upon a minority, whether the minority consists of a small or of a large number, be a cause of action where the actual damage is produced, it would seem to be a very singular result that an individual who falsely assumes the character of representing a large body, uses the name of that large body to give force and support to the threat which he utters, and so produces the injury to the individual, or to the minority, could shield himself from responsibility by proving that the body whose power and influence he had falsely invoked as his supporters had given him no authority for his threats; so that, if they in truth authorized him, he and they might all have been responsible, while the false statement that he made, though acting upon the employer by the same pressure because it was believed and producing the same mischief to the person against whom it was directed, could establish no cause of action against himself because it was false. * * *

My Lords, I regret that I am compelled to differ so widely with some of your Lordships; but my difference is founded on the belief that in denying these plaintiffs a remedy we are departing from the principles which have hitherto guided our Courts in the preservation of individual liberty to all. I am encouraged, however, by the consideration that the adverse views appear to me to overrule the views of most distinguished judges, going back now for certainly 200 years, and that up to the period when this case reached your Lordships' House there was an unanimous consensus of opinion; and that of eight judges who have given us the benefit of their opinions, six have concurred in the judgments which your Lordships are now asked to overrule.

Lord Watson: * * * The appellant contends that judgment ought to be entered in his favour, inasmuch as the findings of the jury, when rightly interpreted, do not disclose any cause of action against him; and, alternatively, that these findings being against the weight of evidence, the case ought to be sent back for new trial. I have not found it necessary to consider the second of these propositions, having arrived at the conclusion that the first of them is well founded.

The substance of the verdict may be resolved into these three findings: first, that the Glengall Iron Company discharged the respondents from their employment and did not re-engage them; secondly, that the company were induced to do so by the appellant; and, thirdly, that the appellant maliciously induced the action of the company. There is no expression in the verdict which can be held, either directly or by implication, to impeach the legality of the company's conduct in discharging the respondents. The mere fact of an employer discharging or refusing to engage a workman does not imply or even suggest the absence of his legal right to do either as he may choose. It is true that the company is not a party to this suit; but it is also obvious that the character of the act induced, whether legal or illegal, may have a bearing upon the liability in law of the person who procured it. The whole pith of the verdict, in so far as it directly concerns the appellant, is contained in the word "maliciously" —a word which is susceptible of many different meanings. The expression "maliciously induce," as it occurs upon the face of the verdict, is ambiguous: it is capable of signifying that the appellant knowingly induced an act which of itself constituted a civil wrong, or it may simply mean that the appellant procured, with intent to injure the respondents, an act which, apart from motive, would not have amounted to a civil wrong; and it is, in my opinion, material to ascertain in which of these senses it was used by the jury.

Although the rule may be otherwise with regard to crimes, the law of England does not, according to my apprehension, take into account motive as constituting an element of civil wrong. Any invasion of the civil rights of another person is in itself a legal wrong, carrying with it liability to repair its necessary or natural consequences, in so far as these are injurious to the person whose right is infringed, whether the motive which prompted it be good, bad, or indifferent. But the existence of a bad motive, in the case of an act which is not in itself illegal, will not convert that act into a civil wrong for which reparation is due. A wrongful act, done knowingly and with a view to its injurious consequences, may, in the sense of law, be malicious; but such malice derives its essential character from the circumstance that the act done constitutes a violation of the law. There is a class of cases which have sometimes been referred to as evidencing that a bad motive may be an element in the composition of civil wrong; but in these cases the wrong must have its root in an act which the law generally regards as illegal, but excuses its perpetration in certain exceptional circumstances from considerations of public policy. These are well known as cases of privilege, in which the protection which the law gives to an individual who is within the scope of these considerations consists in this—that he may with immunity commit an act which is a legal wrong and but for his privilege would afford a good cause of action against him, all that is required in order to raise the privilege and entitle him to protection being that he shall act honestly in the discharge of some duty which the law recognises, and shall not be prompted by a desire to injure the person who is affected by his act. Accordingly, in a suit brought by that person, it is usual for him to allege and necessary for him to prove an intent to injure in order to destroy the privilege of the defendant. But none of these cases tend to establish that an act which does not amount to a legal wrong, and therefore needs no protection, can have privilege attached to it; and still less than an act in itself lawful is converted into a legal wrong if it was done from a bad motive. * * *

It does not appear to me to admit of doubt that the jury, in finding the action of the company to have been maliciously induced by the appellant, simply meant to affirm that the appellant was influenced by a bad motive, namely, an intention to injure the respondents in their trade or calling of shipwrights. * * *

Assuming that the Glengall Iron Company, in dispensing with the further services of the respondents, were guilty of no wrong, I am willing to take it that any person who procured their act might incur responsibility to those who were injuriously affected by it, if he employed unlawful means of inducement directed against him. * * *

It is, in my opinion, the absolute right of every workman to exercise his own option with regard to the persons in whose society he will agree or continue to work. It may be deplorable that feelings of rivalry between different associations of working men should ever run so high as to make members of one union seriously object to continue their labour in company with members of another trade union; but so long as they commit no legal wrong, and use no means which are illegal, they are at perfect liberty to act upon their own views. That the boilermakers who were employed at the Regent Dock, Millwall, did seriously resent the presence among them of the respondents very plainly appears from the evidence of the respondents themselves; and that they would certainly have left the dock had the respondents continued to be employed appears to me to be an undoubted fact in the case. They were not under any continuing engagement to their employers, and, if they had left their work and gone out on strike, they would have been acting within their right, whatever might be thought of the propriety of the proceeding. Not only so; they were, in my opinion, entitled to inform the Glengall Iron Company of the step which they contemplated, as well as of the reasons by which they were influenced, and that either by their own mouth, or, as they preferred, by the appellant as their representative. If the workmen had made the communication themselves, and had been influenced by bad motives towards the respondents, then, according to the law which has been generally accepted by the Courts below, they would each and all of them have incurred responsibility to the respondents. * * *

I am quite alive to the fact that the question which we have to decide is one of importance, and also that it has never been previously considered by this House. Having come to the conclusion, with the majority of your Lordships who have heard the appeal, that the doctrine advanced by the respondents is neither sound in principle nor supported by authority, I move that the order appealed from be reversed, and judgment entered for the appellant, and that the appellant have his costs of this appeal, and costs in both Courts below, including the costs of the trial.

LORD ASHBOURNE: * * * The plaintiffs had, in my opinion, a clear right to pursue their lawful calling, to have the full benefit of their employment, and the right to enjoy the legitimate, reasonable, and probable expectation of a continuance of their employment. It would be, I think, an unsatisfactory state of the law that allowed the wilful invader of such a right without lawful cause or justification to escape from the consequences of his action—that would not hold him liable for maliciously inducing men being denied their accustomed employment, and that would not afford to those he had injured legal grounds of action. * * *

* * * To intimidate an employer into breaking a contract with a particular workman, and to coerce or maliciously induce an otherwise willing employer not to give him future employment, alike does that workman serious damage in his trade and prevents him from earning his wages. The object of the wrongdoer is the same in each case. Here the motive of the defendant was founded on the determination to inflict punishment on the plaintiffs for their past action by driving them out of their employment.

In my opinion there was evidence that the defendant acted without legal excuse or justification in invading the right of the plaintiffs to exercise their calling without hindrance; and there was evidence to go to the jury that the defendant intimidated and coerced or maliciously induced the Glengall Iron Company not to enter into new contracts with the plaintiffs.

I entirely concur in the conclusion of the Lord Chancellor, and think that the appeal should be dismissed.

LORD HERSCHELL: * * * It is to be observed, in the first place, that the company in declining to employ the plaintiffs were violating no contract—they were doing nothing wrongful in the eye of the law. The course which they took was dictated by self-interest: they were anxious to avoid the inconvenience to their business which would ensue from a cessation of work on behalf of the ironworkers. It was not contended at the bar that merely to induce them to take this course would constitute a legal wrong, but it was said to do so because the person inducing them acted maliciously. The Master of the Rolls declined in the present case to define what was meant by "maliciously": he considered this a question to be determined by a jury. But if acts are, or are not, unlawful and actionable, according as this element of malice be present or absent, I think it is essential to determine what is meant by it. I can imagine no greater danger to the community than that a jury should be at liberty to impose the penalty of paying damages for acts which are otherwise lawful, because they choose, without any legal definition of the term, to say that they are malicious. No one would know what his rights were. The result would be to put all our actions at the mercy of a particular tribunal whose view of their propriety might differ from our own. However malice may be defined, if motive be an ingredient of it, my sense of the danger would not be diminished.

The danger is, I think, emphasised by the opinions of some of the learned judges. * * * The malice depends on the means used and the disregard of one's neighbour, and the test of its existence is whether these are such as no honest and fair-minded man ought to resort to. There is here room for infinite differences of opinion. Some, I dare say, applying this test would consider that a strike by workmen at a time damaging to the employer, or a "lock-out" by an employer at a time of special hardship to the workmen, were such means, and exhibited such a disregard of his neighbour as an honest and fair-minded man ought not to resort to. Others would be of the contrary opinion. The truth is, this suggested test makes men's responsibility for their actions depend on the fluctuating opinions of the tribunal before whom the case may chance to come as to what a right-minded man ought or ought not to do in pursuing his own interests. * * *

It is certainly a general rule of our law that an act *primâ facie* is not unlawful and actionable on account of the motive which dictated it. I put aside the case of conspiracy, which is anomalous in more than one respect. * * *

If, then, the men had ceased to work for the company either of their own motion or because they were "called out," and the company in order to secure their return had thought it expedient no longer to employ the plaintiffs, they could certainly have maintained no action. Yet the damage to them would have been just the same. * * * I am quite unable to conceive how the plaintiffs can have a cause for action, because, instead of the ironworkers leaving, either of their own motion or because they were called out, there was an intimation beforehand that either the one or the other of these courses would be pursued. * * *

The object which the appellant and the ironworkers had in view was that they should be freed from the presence of men with whom they disliked working, or to prevent what they deemed an unfair interference with their rights by men who did not belong to their craft doing the work to which they had been trained. Whether we approve or disapprove of such attempted trade restrictions, it was entirely within the right of the ironworkers to take any steps, not unlawful, to prevent any of the work which they regarded as legitimately theirs being entrusted to other hands. * * *

In the present case it was admitted that the defendant had no personal spite against the plaintiffs. His object was, at the utmost, to prevent them in the future from doing work which he thought was not within their province, but within that of the ironworkers. If he had acted in exactly the same manner as he did at a time when the plaintiffs were engaged upon ironwork, his motive would have been precisely the same as it was in the present case, and the result to the plaintiffs would have been in nowise different. I am unable to see, then, that there is any difference either in point of ethics or law between the two cases. The ironworkers were no more bound to work with those whose presence was disagreeable to them than the plaintiffs were bound to refuse to work because they found that this was the case. The object which the defendant, and those whom he represented, had in view throughout was what they believed to be the interest of the class to which they belonged; the step taken was a means to that end. The act which caused the damage to the plaintiffs was that of the iron company in refusing to employ them. The company would not subordinate their own interests to the plaintiffs. It is conceded that they could take this course with impunity. Why, then, should the defendant be liable because he did not subordinate the interests of those he represented to the plaintiffs'? Self interest dictated alike the act of those who caused the damage, and the act which is found to have induced them to cause it. * * *

For the reasons I have given I think the judgment should be reversed, and judgment entered in the action for the defendant with costs. * * *

LORD MACNAGHTEN: My Lords, I am sorry to say that I must begin by recapitulating the facts of the case. For the findings of the jury, taken by themselves, do not convey to my mind any definite meaning. The jury have found that the appellant Allen "maliciously induced" the Glengall Iron Company to discharge the respondents from their service, and they have awarded damages in consequence. I do not know what the jury meant by the word "induced"; I am not sure that I know what they meant by the word "maliciously." Sometimes, indeed, I rather doubt whether I quite understand that unhappy expression myself. I am therefore compelled to turn for help to the evidence at the trial, accepting, as I suppose the jury must have accepted, the account given by the respondents in preference to that offered by the appellant wherever there may be any shadow of difference between them. * * *

So we see now, I think, what the findings of the jury come to if they are to be treated as being in accordance with the evidence. They must mean that Allen induced the company to discharge the plaintiffs, by representing to the manager, not otherwise than in accordance with the truth, the state of feeling in the yard, and the intentions of the workmen, and that he did so "maliciously," because he must have known what the issue of his communication to the manager would be, and naturally perhaps he was not sorry to see an example made of persons obnoxious to his union. But is his conduct actionable? It would be very singular if it were. No action would lie against the company for discharging the two shipwrights. No action would lie against the iron-men for striking against them. No action would lie against the officers of the union for sanctioning such a strike. But if the respondents are right the person to answer in damages is the man who happened to be the medium of communication between the iron-men and the company—the most innocent of the three parties concerned, for he neither set the "agitation" on foot, nor did he do anything to increase it, nor was his the order that put an end to the connection between employer and employed. * * *

But if the immediate agent cannot be made liable, though he knows what he is about and what the consequences of his action will be, it is difficult to see on what principle a person less directly connected with the affair can be made responsible unless malice has the effect of converting an act not in itself illegal or improper into an actionable wrong. But if that is the effect of malice, why is the immediate agent to escape? Above all, why is he to escape when there is no one else to blame and no one else answerable? And yet many cases may be put of harm done out of malice without any remedy being available at law. Suppose a man takes a transfer of a debt with which he has no concern for the purpose of ruining the debtor, and then makes him bankrupt out of spite, and so intentionally causes him to lose some benefit under a will or settlement—suppose a man declines to give a servant a character because he is offended with the servant for leaving—suppose a person of position takes away his custom from a country tradesman in a small village merely to injure him on account of some fancied grievance not connected with their dealings in the way of buying and selling—no one, I think, would suggest that there could be any remedy at law in any of those cases. But suppose a customer, not content with taking away his own custom, says something not slanderous or otherwise actionable or even improper in itself to induce a friend of his not to employ the tradesman any more. Neither the one nor the other is liable for taking away his own custom. Is it possible that the one can be made liable for inducing the other not to employ the person against whom he has a grudge? If so, a fashionable dressmaker might now and then, I fancy, be plaintiff in a very interesting suit. The truth is that questions of this sort belong to the province of morals rather than to the province of law. Against spite and malice the best safeguards are to be found in self-interest and public opinion. Much more harm than good would be done by encouraging or permitting inquiries into motives when the immediate act alleged to have caused the loss for which redress is sought is in itself innocent or neutral in character, and one which anybody may do or leave undone without fear of legal consequences. Such an inquisition would, I think, be intolerable, to say nothing of the probability of injustice being done by juries in a class of cases in which there would be ample room for speculation and wide scope for prejudice. * * *

I am of opinion that judgment should be entered for the appellant. * * *

Lord Shand: My Lords, I am of opinion that the judgment complained of should be reversed, and judgment entered for the defendant with costs. * * *

The jury has, however, found expressly by their verdict that the defendant did "maliciously induce the Glengall Iron Company not to engage the plaintiffs," and under the direction of the learned judge assessed damages, for which his Lordship granted a decree. * * *

I confess that, even if the direction given were sound in law, as I think it was not, the facts of the case were such as I should have thought should have precluded such a verdict being given, if these, with the assistance of the learned judge, had received the weight to which they were entitled at the hands of the jury. If anything is clear on the evidence, it seems to me to be this—that the defendant was bent, and bent exclusively, on the object of furthering the interests of those he represented in all he did—that this was his motive of action, and not a desire, to use the words of the learned judge, "to do mischief to the plaintiffs in their lawful calling."

The case was one of competition in labour, which, in my opinion, is in all essentials analogous to competition in trade, and to which the same principles must apply; and I ask myself what would be the thought of the application of the word "malicious" to the conduct of a tradesman who induces the customer of another tradesman to cease making purchases from one with whom he had long dealt, and instead to deal with him, a rival in trade. The case before the jury was, in my view, in no way different, except that in the one case there was competition in labour—in the other there would be competition in trade.

Some of the learned consulted judges speak of Allen's conduct as having been caused by a desire to inflict "punishment" on the shipwrights for past acts, and indicate that, if the shipwrights had been actually working at ironwork on the vessel at the time, the case would have been different. I cannot agree in any such view. "Punishment" in a wide and popular sense may possibly be used, though incorrectly, to describe the boiler-makers' action; but it is quite clear that what they were resolved to do, and really did, was, while marking their sense of the injury which they thought (rightly or wrongly is not the question) the shipwrights were doing to them in trenching on their proper line of business, to take a practical measure in their own defense. Their object was to benefit themselves in their own business as working boiler-makers, and to prevent a recurrence in the future of what they considered an improper invasion on their special department of work. How this could possibly be regarded as "malicious," even in any secondary sense that can reasonably be attributed to that term, I cannot see. * * *

Coming now directly to the merits of the question in controversy in the case, the argument of the plaintiffs and the reasons for the opinions of the majority of the consulted judges seem to me to fail, because, although it is no doubt true that the plaintiffs were entitled to pursue their trade as workmen "without hindrance," their right to do so was qualified by an equal right, and indeed the same right, on the part of other workmen. The hindrance must not be of an unlawful character. It must not be by unlawful action. Amongst the rights of all workmen is the right of competition. In the like manner and to the same extent as a workman has a right to pursue his work or labour without hindrance, a trader has a right to trade without hindrance. That right is subject to the right of others to trade also, and to subject him to competition—competition which is in itself lawful, and which cannot be complained of where no unlawful means (in the sense I have already explained) have been employed. The matter has been settled in so far as competition in trade is concerned by the judgment of his House in the *Mogul Steamship Co.* Case ([1892] A.C. 25). I can see no reason for saying that a different principle should apply to competition in labour. In the course of such competition, and with a view to secure an advantage to himself, I can find no reason for saying that a workman is not within his legal rights in resolving that he will decline to work in the same employment with certain other persons, and in intimating that resolution to his employers. * * *

As already fully explained, there was no case of malice in the ordinary sense of the term, as meaning personal ill-will, presented to the jury; but I agree with those of your Lordships who hold that, even if such a motive had existed in the mind of the defendant, this would not have created liability in damages. On the grounds already stated, I think the defendant only exercised a legal right in intimating that the boilermakers would leave work if the plaintiffs were continued; he used no fraud or illegal means in the assertion of that right; and the exercise by a person of a legal right does not become illegal because the motive of action is improper or malicious: *Bradford Corporation v. Pickles* ([1895] A.C. 587) and the *Mogul Steamship Co.* Case ([1892] A.C. 25) already cited. * * * 6

*Order of the Court of Appeal reversed and judgment entered for the appellant with costs here and below including the costs of the trial; cause remitted to the Queen's Bench Division.*7

---

6 The opinions of the judges, summoned to attend the House of Lords are omitted. Of these, Hawkins, Cave, North, Wills, Grantham and Lawrance, JJ., were of the opinion that the judgment of the Court of Appeal should be affirmed, whereas Mathew and Wright, JJ., were of the contrary opinion.

The opinion of Lord Morris for affirmance of the judgment of the Court of Appeal and the opinions of Lord Davey and Lord James of Hereford for the reversal of the judgment of the Court of Appeal are omitted.

7 For comment on this case, see: Freund, "Malice and Unlawful Interference," 11 Harv. Law Rev. 449 (1898); Wilgus, "The Authority of Allen v. Flood," 1 Mich. Law Rev. 28 (1902); "Memorandum on Allen v. Flood," by Arthur Cohen in Report of the Royal Commission on Trade Disputes and Trade Combinations, (1906) Cd. 2825, p. 24; 11 Harv. Law Rev. 405 (1898).

For discussion as to the theoretical bases of the case, see: Ames, "How Far an Act May Be a Tort Because of Wrongful Motive of Actor," 18 Harv. Law Rev. 411 (1905); Walton, "Motive as an Element in Torts in the Common and in the Civil Law," 22 Harv. Law Rev. 501 (1909); Lewis, "Should the Motive of the Defendant Affect the Question of his Liability," 5 Col. Law Rev. 107 (1905); 26 Harv. Law Rev. 740 (1913).

Cf. May v. Wood, 172 Mass. 11, 51 N.E. 191 (1898); Moran v. Dunphy, 177 Mass. 485, 59 N.E. 125 (1901); Tuttle v. Buck, 107 Minn. 145, 119 N.W. 946 (1909); Beardsley v. Kilmer, 200 App. Div. 378, 193 N.Y.S. 285; Glendon Iron Co. v. Uhler, 75 Pa. 467 (1874); Arnold v. Moffit, 30 R.I. 310, 75 Atl. 502 (1910); Lancaster v. Hamburger, 70 Ohio St. 156, 71 N.E. 289 (1904).

"No doubt a legal system may exist, or might be constructed, in which the law of tort was founded on the principle, that intentionally to cause damage to another person, is in the absence of reasonable cause, an actionable tort, it being left to the

QUINN v. LEATHEM.

House of Lords. [1901] A.C. 495.

The respondent brought an action in Ireland against five defendants, Craig, Davey, Quinn (the appellant), Dornan and Shaw, alleging causes of action which are summarised in the judgment of Lord Brampton. At the trial before Fitz-Gibbon L.J. and a special jury at Belfast in July, 1896, evidence was given for the plaintiff to the following effect. Craig was president, Quinn treasurer, and Davey secretary of a trade union registered as the Belfast Journeymen Butchers' and Assistants' Association. By rule 11 of the association it was the duty of all members to assist their fellow unionists to obtain employment in preference to non-society men.

The plaintiff, a flesher at Lisburn for more than twenty years, in July, 1895, was employing Dickie and other assistants who were not members of the union. At a meeting of the association at which Craig, Quinn, Dornan and Shaw were present, and which the plaintiff attended by Davey's invitation, the plaintiff offered to pay all fines, debts and demands against his men, and asked to have them admitted to the society. This was refused, and a resolution was passed that the plaintiff's assistants should be called out. Craig told the plaintiff that his meat would be stopped at Munce's if he did not comply with their wishes. Munce, a butcher, had been getting about 30 l. worth weekly of meat from the plaintiff for twenty years.

The plaintiff in his evidence said: "For the last four years Munce has had an agreement with me to take my fine meat at so much a pound. He expected me to send it to him every week, and there was no week he did not get it. I had no written agreement with him. Whenever I killed I sent it, but I was not bound—only by word of mouth. It was only that if I sent it he would take it." What this meant did not clearly appear, but Munce's clerk who was called said, "Munce had no contract with the plaintiff: if he wanted his meat he could take it or reject it if he chose; it came weekly and was never refused. Neither was bound either to take or supply it."

In September Davey wrote to the plaintiff that if he continued to employ non-union labour the society would be obliged to adopt extreme measures. After some negotiations with Munce Davey wrote to him that having failed to make a satisfactory arrangement with the plaintiff,

---

judge to decide whether there is or is not a reasonable cause. It is, however, impossible, since the decision in Allen v. Flood, to mantain that such a principle is recognised in our existing legal system; for it would be evidently inconsistent with the legal proposition which, to use Lord Lindley's words, was so fully and authoritatively established by that case; and which his Lordship stated in the following words: 'An act otherwise lawful although harmful does not become actionable by being done from a bad motive and with intent to annoy or harm another.' Nor is it less evident that to introduce such a fundamental principle would be in the highest degree unwise and inexpedient, inasmuch as it would make the whole law of torts vague and uncertain, until a great quantity of new judge-made law had determined in what cases there is and in what cases there is not reasonble cause or justification." Royal Commission on Trade Disputes, Cd. 2825, p. 30 (1906).

they had no other alternative but to instruct Munce's employees to cease work immediately the plaintiff's beef arrived. On September 20 Munce sent a telegram to the plaintiff, "Unless you arrange with society you need not send any beef this week as men are ordered to quit work," and Munce ceased to deal with the plaintiff. The plaintiff said that in consequence of this he was put to great loss, a quantity of fine meat having been killed for Munce.

Dickie, who had been ten years in the plaintiff's employ, was called and said that he was employed by the week, that he was called out by the society, that he gave the plaintiff no notice when he left, that he left in the middle of the week, and that the plaintiff did not pay him for the broken week. There was no evidence of damage to the plaintiff, pecuniary or otherwise, caused by Dickie's breach of contract.

Evidence was given that "black lists" were issued by the society, containing (*inter alia*) the names of tradesmen who had dealings with the plaintiff, and one of whom was induced not to deal with him, but there was no evidence connecting Quinn with these lists.

The learned judge's notes of the evidence proceeded thus:—

At the close of the plaintiff's case "O'Shaughnessy, Q.C., asked for a non-suit or direction for the defendants on the grounds: 1st. That to sustain the action a contract made with Leathem must be proved to have been made and broken through the acts of the defendants, and that there was no evidence of such contract or breach. 2nd. That there was no evidence of pecuniary damage to the plaintiff through the acts of the defendants. 3rd. That the ends of the defendants and the means taken by them to promote those ends as appearing in evidence were legitimate, and there was no evidence of actual damage to the plaintiff.

"I declined to withdraw the case from the jury. O'Shaughnessy, Q.C., then stated that he called no evidence for the defendants. Chambers addressed the jury for the plaintiff. O'Shaughnessy, Q.C., replied for the defendants. I charged the jury, leaving them the following questions, to which I append their findings: 1. Did the defendants or any of them wrongfully and maliciously induce the customers or servants of the plaintiff named in the evidence to refuse to deal with the plaintiff? —Answer: Yes. 2. Did the defendants or any two or more of them maliciously conspire to induce the plaintiff's customers or servants named in the evidence or any of them not to deal with the plaintiffs or not to continue in his employment, and were such persons so induced not so to do?—Answer: Yes. 3. Did the defendants Davey, Dornan and Shaw, or any of them, publish the 'black list' with intent to injure the plaintiff in his business, and if so did the publication so injure him?—Answer: Yes.

"The jury found for the plaintiff, with 250 *l.* damages, of which 50 *l.* was for damages on the cause of action relating to the 'black lists,' and 200 *l.* was for damages on the other causes of action. I directed the jury that there was no evidence against the defendants Craig and Quinn upon the cause of action relating to the 'black lists,' and I directed them to assess the damages (if any) on that cause of action separately. On the above findings, on the application of Serjeant Dodd, I gave judgment for the plaintiff upon the other causes of action against all the defendants, with 200 *l.* damages, and against the defendants Davey, Dornan and Shaw upon the cause of action relating to the 'black lists' for the further sum of 50 *l.* damages.

"* * * Upon the meaning of the words 'wrongfully and maliciously' in the questions, I told the jury that they had to consider whether the intent and actions of the defendants went beyond the limits which would not be actionable, namely, securing or advancing their own interests or those of their trade by reasonable means, including lawful combination, or whether their acts, as proved, were intended and calculated to injure the plaintiff in his trade through a combination and with a common purpose to prevent the free action of his customers and servants in dealing with him, and with the effect of actually injuring him, as distinguished from acts legitimately done to secure or advance their own interests. * * * Finally, I told the jury that acts done with the object of increasing the profits or raising the wages of any combination of persons, such as the society to which the defendants belonged, whether employers or employed, by reasonable and legitimate means, were perfectly lawful, and were not actionable so long as no wrongful act was maliciously—that is to say, intentionally—done to injure a third party. To constitute such a wrongful act for the purposes of this case, I told the jury that they must be satisfied that there had been a conspiracy, a common intention and a combination on the part of the defendants to injure the plaintiff in his business, and that acts must be proved to have been done by the defendants in furtherance of that intention which had inflicted actual money loss upon the plaintiff in his trade. Whether the acts of the defendants were or were not in that sense actionable was the question which I told the jury they had to try upon the evidence. At the conclusion of my charge, at the request of O'Shaughnessy, Q.C., for the defendants, I divided this single question into the written questions which I submitted to the jury as above stated. * * *"

A motion was made "to set aside the verdict and judgment and enter a verdict for the defendants, or, in the alternative, for a new trial on the ground of misdirection of the learned judge in refusing to direct for the defendants; leaving to the jury the case as against all the defendants on the evidence; and in that on the evidence no actionable wrong was shewn; * * *"

In the Irish Court of Appeal (Lord Ashbourne L.C., Porter M.R., Walker and Holmes L.JJ.) the decision below was affirmed with costs, the judgment for the plaintiff being amended by omitting the part as to the recovery of 50 *l.* damages. (*Leathem v. Craig,* [1899] 2 I.R. 667.) Quinn alone brought the present appeal. * * *

EARL OF HALSBURY L.C.: My Lords, in this case the plaintiff has by a properly framed statement of claim complained of the defendants,

and proved to the satisfaction of a jury that the defendants have wrongfully and maliciously induced customers and servants to cease to deal
with the plaintiff, that the defendants did this in pursuance of a conspiracy
framed among them, that in pursuance of the same conspiracy they
induced servants of the plaintiff not to continue in the plaintiff's employment, and that all this was done with malice in order to injure the plaintiff, and that it did injure the plaintiff. If upon these facts so found the
plaintiff could have no remedy against those who had thus injured him,
it could hardly be said that our jurisprudence was that of a civilized community, nor indeed do I understand that any one has doubted that, before the decision in *Allen v. Flood* in this House, such fact would have
established a cause of action against the defendants. Now, before dis-
cusing the case of *Allen v. Flood* and what was decided therein, there
are two observations of a general character which I wish to make,
and one is to repeat what I have very often said before, that every judgment must be read as applicable to the particular facts proved, or assumed
to be proved, since the generality of the expressions which may be found
there are not intended to be expositions of the whole law, but governed
and qualified by the particular facts of the case in which such expressions are to be found. The other is that a case is only an authority for
what it actually decides. I entirely deny that it can be quoted for a
proposition that may seem to follow logically from it. Such a mode of
reasoning assumes that the law is necessarily a logical code, whereas
every lawyer must acknowledge that the law is not always logical at all.
My Lords, I think the application of these two propositions renders the
decision of this case perfectly plain, notwithstanding the decision of the
case of *Allen v. Flood*.

Now, the hypothesis of fact upon which *Allen v. Flood* was decided
by a majority in this House was that the defendant there neither uttered
nor carried into effect any threat at all: he simply warned the plaintiff's
employers of what the men themselves, without his persuasion or influence, had determined to do, and it was certainly proved that no resolution
of the trade union had been arrived at at all, and that the trade union official had no authority himself to call out the men, which in that case was
argued to be the threat which coerced the employers to discharge the
plaintiff. It was further an element in the decision that there was no
case of conspiracy or even combination. What was alleged to be done
was only the independent and single action of the defendant, actuated in
what he did by the desire to express his own views in favour of his fellow members. It is true that I personally did not believe that was the
true view of the facts, but, as I have said, we must look at the hypothesis
of fact upon which the case was decided by the majority of those who
took part in the decision. My Lords, in my view what has been said already is enough to decide this case without going further into the facts
of *Allen v. Flood;* but I cannot forbear accepting with cordiality the
statement of them prepared by two of your Lordships, Lord Brampton
and Lord Lindley, with so much care and precision.

Now, in this case it cannot be denied that if the verdict stands there was conspiracy, threats, and threats carried into execution, so that loss of business and interference with the plaintiff's legal rights are abundantly proved, and I do not understand the very learned judge who dissented to have doubted any one of these propositions, but his view was grounded on the belief that *Allen v. Flood* had altered the law in these respects, and made that lawful which would have clearly been actionable before the decision of that case. My Lords, for the reasons I have given I cannot agree with that conclusion. I do not deny that if some of the observations made in that case were to be pushed to their logical conclusion it would be very difficult to resist the Chief Baron's inflexible logic; but, with all the respect which any view of that learned judge is entitled to command and which I unfeignedly entertain, I cannot concur. This case is distinguished in its facts from those which were the essentially important facts in *Allen v. Flood*. Rightly or wrongly, the theory upon which judgment was pronounced in that case is one whereby the present is shewn to be one which the majority of your Lordships would have held to be a case of actionable injury inflicted without any excuse whatever. * * *

LORD MACNAGHTEN * * * Precisely the same questions arise in this case as arose in *Temperton* v. *Russell.* ([1893] 1 Q.B. 715.) The answers, I think, must depend on precisely the same considerations. Was *Lumley* v. *Gye,* (2 E. & B. 216) rightly decided? I think it was. *Lumley v. Gye* was much considered in *Allen v. Flood*. But as it was not directly in question, some of your Lordships thought it better to suspend their judgment. In this case the question arises directly, and it is necessary to express an opinion on the point. Speaking for myself, I have no hesitation in saying that I think the decision was right, not on the ground of malicious intention—that was not, I think, the gist of the action—but on the ground that a violation of legal right committed knowingly is a cause of action, and that it is a violation of legal right to interfere with contractual relations recognised by law if there be no sufficient justification for the interference.

The only other question is this: Does a conspiracy to injure, resulting in damage, give rise to civil liability? It seems to me that there is authority for that proposition, and that it is founded in good sense. * * * That a conspiracy to injure—an oppressive combination—differs widely from an invasion of civil rights by a single individual cannot be doubted. I agree in substance with the remarks of Bowen L.J. and Lords Bramwell and Hannen in the *Mogul* Case. A man may resist without much difficulty the wrongful act of an individual. He would probably have at least the moral support of his friends and neighbours; but it is a very different thing (as Lord FitzGerald observes) when one man has to defend himself against many combined to do him wrong.

* * * I do not think that the acts done by the defendants were done "in contemplation or furtherance of a trade dispute between employers

and workmen." So far as I can see, there was no trade dispute at all. Leathem had no difference with his men. They had no quarrel with him. For his part he was quite willing that all his men should join the union. He offered to pay their fines and entrance moneys. What he objected to was a cruel punishment proposed to be inflicted on some of his men for not having joined the union sooner. There was certainly no trade dispute in the case of Munce. But the defendants conspired to do harm to Munce in order to compel him to do harm to Leathem, and so enable them to wreak their vengeance on Leathem's servants who were not members of the union.

I also think that the provision in the Conspiracy and Protection of Property Act, 1875, which says that in certain cases an agreement or combination is not to be "indictable as a conspiracy," has nothing to do with civil remedies.

LORD SHAND: My Lords, after the able and full opinions of the learned judges of the Court of Appeal in Ireland holding that the verdict and judgment for the plaintiff ought to stand, the grounds of my opinion that the judgment ought to be affirmed and the appeal dismissed may be shortly stated. I refrain from any detailed reference to the numerous cases cited in the argument. These have been considered and discussed by the judges of the Court of Appeal, and I concur in the reasoning of the majority of their Lordships, and they have been already dealt with in my judgment in the case of *Allen v. Flood.*

In that case I expressed my opinion that while combination of different persons in pursuit of a trade object was lawful, although resulting in such injury to others as may be caused by legitimate competition in labour, yet that combination for no such object, but in pursuit merely of a malicious purpose to injure another, would be clearly unlawful; and, having considered the arguments in this case, my opinion has only been confirmed.

The learned judge before whom the case was tried, with reference to the words "wrongfully and maliciously" in the first question, told the jury that the questions to be answered by them were matters of fact only to be determined on the evidence, and in particular involved the question whether the intention of the defendants was to injure the plaintiff in his trade, as distinguished from the intention of legitimately advancing their own interests. The verdict affirms that this was the fact, for after the direction of the learned judge no other interpretation can be given to the finding that the acts complained of were done by the defendants "wrongfully and maliciously."

This being clearly so, the question now raised is really whether, in consequence of the decision of this House in the case of *Allen v. Flood,* and of the grounds on which that case was decided, it is now the law that where the acts complained of are in pursuance of a combination or conspiracy to injure or ruin another, and not to advance the parties' own trade interests, and injury has resulted, no action will lie, or, to put the question in a popular form, whether the decision in *Allen v. Flood* has made boycotting lawful. * * *

As to the vital distinction between *Allen v. Flood,* and the present case, it may be stated in a single sentence. In *Allen v. Flood* the purpose of the defendant was by the acts complained of to promote his own trade interest, which it was held he was entitled to do, although injurious to his competitors, whereas in the present case, while it is clear there was combination, the purpose of the defendants was "to injure the plaintiff in his trade as distinguished from the intention of legitimately advancing their own interests."

It is unnecessary to quote from the judgments of the majority of the learned judges in *Allen v. Flood* to shew their opinions on the importance of this essential point. * * *

The ground of judgment of the majority of the House, however varied in expression by their Lordships, was, as it appears to me, that Allen in what he said and did was only exercising the right of himself and his fellow workmen as competitors in the labour market, and the effect of injury thus caused to others from such competition, which was legitimate, was not a legal wrong.

It is only necessary to add that the defendants here have no such defence as legitimate trade competition. Their acts were wrongful and malicious in the sense found by the jury—that is to say, they acted by conspiracy, not for any purpose of advancing their own interests as workmen, but for the sole purpose of injuring the plaintiff in his trade. I am of opinion that the law prohibits such acts as unjustifiable and illegal; that by so acting the defendants were guilty of a clear violation of the rights of the plaintiff, with the result of causing serious injury to him, and that the case of *Allen v. Flood,* as a case of legitimate competition in the labour market, is essentially different, and gives no ground for the defendant's argument. * * *

LORD BRAMPTON: * * * In this case the alleged cause of action is very different from that in *Allen v. Flood.* It is not dependent upon coercion to break any particular contract or contracts, though such causes of action are introduced into the claim; but the real and substantial cause of action is an unlawful conspiracy to molest the plaintiff, a trader in carrying on his business, and by so doing to invade his undoubted right, thus described by Alderson B. in delivering the judgment of the Exchequer Chamber in *Hilton* v. *Eckersley* (6 E. & B. 74) : "*Primâ facie* it is the privilege of a trader in a free country in all matters not contrary to law to regulate his own mode of carrying it on according to his own discretion and choice. If the law has in any matter regulated or restrained his mode of doing this, the law must be obeyed. But no power short of the general law ought to restrain his free discretion." * * *

I will deal now with the conspiracy part of the claim, respecting which much confusion and uncertainty seems somehow to have arisen, which I find it difficult to understand. * * *

I will endeavour briefly to state how I view the matter practically, so far as it concerns this case.

A conspiracy consists of an unlawful combination of two or more persons to do that which is contrary to law, or to do that which is wrongful and harmful towards another person. It may be punished criminally by indictment, or civilly by an action on the case in the nature of conspiracy if damage has been occasioned to the person against whom it is directed. It may also consist of an unlawful combination to carry out an object not in itself unlawful by unlawful means. The essential elements, whether of a criminal or of an actionable conspiracy, are, in my opinion, the same, though to sustain an action special damage must be proved * * *

It has often been debated whether, assuming the existence of a conspiracy to do a wrongful and harmful act towards another and to carry it out by a number of overt acts, no one of which taken singly and alone would, if done by one individual acting alone and apart from any conspiracy, constitute a cause of action, such acts would become unlawful or actionable if done by the conspirators acting jointly or severally in pursuance of their conspiracy, and if by those acts substantial damage was caused to the person against whom the conspiracy was directed: my own opinion is that they would.

* * * It is at all times a painful thing for any individual to be the object of the hatred, spite, and ill-will of any one who seeks to do him harm. But that is as nothing compared to the danger and alarm created by a conspiracy formed by a number of unscrupulous enemies acting under an illegal compact, together and separately, as often as opportunity occurs regardless of law, and actuated by malevolence, to injure him and all who stand by him. Such a conspiracy is a powerful and dangerous engine, which in this case has, I think, been employed by the defendants for the perpetration of organized and ruinous oppression.[8] * * *

Order appealed from affirmed and appeal dismissed with costs.[9]

---

[8] The concurring opinions of Lords Robertson and Lindley are omitted.

[9] The relationship of Quinn v. Leathem to the Trade Disputes Act of 1906 is illustrated by the following passages from the Report of the Royal Commission on Trade Disputes of 1906: "The danger to Trade Unions consists not so much in the judgment of Quinn v. Leathem as in the possible expansion of the judgment by the application of the dicta of certain of the Law-lords who took part in it. In Quinn v. Leathem there was the element of procuring to break contract. But to break a contract is to involve liability for damages, and the procuring to break a contract is itself a tortious act. Lumley v. Gye, 2 E & B 216. We are aware that Lumley v. Gye has been much discussed, but we consider it has been authoritatively affirmed as good law by the recent judgment of the House of Lords in The Glamorgan Coal Co. (Ltd.) and others v. The South Wales Miners' Federation and others, [1905] A.C. 239. But the dicta of Quinn v. Leathem show clearly that there might be an action of damages based on any conspiracy to injure or to do harm, and it is obvious the very essence of a strike is in one sense injury to those against whom it is directed. Thus, procuring to strike might by the law of Quinn v. Leathem, coupled with that of Taff Vale, involve Trade Union funds in liability, even where there had been no procuring to break existing contracts. * * *

"The indefiniteness of the law of conspiracy to injure prevents it from being a practical guide of conduct to workmen as to what they may do in times of strike and what they must avoid. The mere fact that two make a conspiracy is enough in the

SORRELL v. SMITH.

House of Lords. [1925] A.C. 700.

Appeal from an order of the Court of Appeal, [1924] 1 Ch. 506, reversing a judgment of Russell J., [1923] 2 Ch. 32, in an action brought by the appellant against the respondents. * * * Russell J. granted an injunction, but his judgment was reversed by the Court of Appeal (Bankes, Warrington and Scrutton L.JJ.) and judgment was entered for the respondents. * * *

VISCOUNT CAVE L.C.: My Lords, the facts of this case are clearly stated in the judgment of Russell J., and for present purposes they may be very briefly summarized. The publishers of the London daily newspapers supply their papers to wholesale newsagents, who in their turn supply them to retail newsagents for sale to the public. The retail newsagents have a trade union known as the National Federation of Retail Newsagents, Booksellers and Stationers, and that federation has for some time advocated a policy which they call the "distance limit policy," and which is described by the learned judge as a policy for preventing newcomers from opening shops for the retail sale of newspapers in any area where the supply of newspapers is, in the opinion of the federation, already sufficiently provided for. The interests of the publishers as regards the circulation of their newspapers are looked after by the respondents, who are a committee of the circulation managers of the London dailies, and the "distance limit policy" of the retail federation does

---

case of unwritten law to produce confusion, where unspecified acts, lawful for individuals, are to be made unlawful when done in combination. But the law itself is unintelligible to workmen. The defendants in Quinn v. Leathem, after judgment had been given against them, must presumably have been at loss to understand which in particular of the acts done by them it was that, though not unlawful for individuals, was condemned as unlawful to be done in combination, or in what respect their strike differed from an ordinary strike against individual non-Unionists. They could only know that, reviewing their conduct as a whole, the House of Lords had pronounced their combination to be an oppressive combination, a conspiracy to injure.

"The perplexity as to the scope of the law is not confined to workmen. I believe it is no exaggeration to say that a lawyer is unable to advise a Trade Union with any confidence on elementary points connected with a strike and with public order—as, for instance, whether it is actionable for a committee or for two or more workmen acting together to organise a strike against non-Unionists at all; or to threaten an employer with a strike; or to prompt a strike to workmen not predisposed to strike; or when the strike has been once started to persuade other workmen to join it, and especially to persuade men in the service of the employer to leave that service, or workmen in the service of employers in other trades to strike in sympathy.

"For these reasons it appears to me that the law of conspiracy to injure is a law unfitted for workmen in case of Trade Disputes." Cd. 2825, pp. 14-15, 89 [1906].

See also: Dicey in 18 Law Quar. Rev. 1 (1902); Chalmers-Hunt, "Labour Competition and the Law," 19 Law Quar. Rev. 37, 182 (1903); Lewis, "Some Leading English Cases on Trade and Labor Disputes," 48 Am. Law Reg. 125 (1903); Charlesworth, "Conspiracy as a Ground of Liability in Tort," 36 Law Quar. Rev. 38 (1920); Pollock, Law of Torts, 321-337 (12th ed. 1923).

Cf. Federal Trade Comm. v. Raymond Bros. Clark Co., 263 U.S. 565 (1924), and Locker v. American Tobacco Co., 195 N.Y. 565, 88 N.E. 289 (1909), with Eastern States Retail Lumber Dealers' Ass'n v. United States, 234 U.S. 600 (1914); Arkansas Wholesale Grocers Ass'n v. Federal Trade Comm., 18 Fed.(2d) 866 (8th cir. 1927), certiorari denied in 275 U.S. 533 (1927).

not commend itself to the respondents, who probably look to free competition among newsagents as tending to increase sales.

Early in the year 1922 some newcomers commenced selling papers in a London area which, in the opinion of the London district council of the retail federation, was already sufficiently equipped with retail newsagents, and these newcomers obtained their supplies of papers from a firm of wholesale newsagents called Ritchie Brothers, of Shoe Lane. Thereupon the London district council took action in support of their policy. Having failed to persuade Messrs. Ritchie to stop supplies to the newcomers, they, on February 15, 1922, held a special meeting of the branch presidents and secretaries of their London district, at which a resolution was passed in the following terms: "That we ask one member from each branch to volunteer to withdraw his supply from Ritchie on any of the ground he covers, and further action be taken to draw him into line with other wholesalers on the distance limit policy." On the same day a meeting of the Shoreditch branch of the federation was held, and the secretary of that branch, who had attended the meeting of presidents and secretaries held by the district council, explained what had occurred at that meeting and asked for volunteers to take action against Ritchie Brothers in the manner described in the above resolution. The appellant, Mr. Sorrell, who was a retail newsagent at Hoxton and was obtaining his supplies from Ritchie Brothers, was a member of the Shoreditch branch, and was present at the branch meeting, and after a number of speeches had been delivered he volunteered to take the action desired. Accordingly, on February 20, the appellant gave notice to Ritchie Brothers that he would not require papers from them after February 27, and on the latter date he transferred his custom to other wholesale newsagents—Messrs. Watson, of Dalston Lane. It is suggested that it was convenient to the appellant to deal with Watson's rather than with Ritchie's because Watson's were nearer to his shop and gave him slightly better terms; but it was found by the learned judge that what decided the appellant to leave Ritchie was the call for volunteers at his branch. None of the newcomers who had been supplied by Ritchie were within the area of the appellant's trade.

On receiving the appellant's notice, Ritchie Brothers, who were apparently aware of the purpose of the move, asked the respondent committee to take the matter up, and thereupon the committee (to put it shortly) told Watson's that, unless they ceased to supply the appellant with newspapers, the supply of papers to them would be stopped. They also communicated with Messrs. W. H. Smith & Son, through whom some of the papers were being supplied to Watson's, and requested them to stop the supply to Watson's unless Watson's ceased to supply the appellant. This pressure proved effective, and on March 24 Watson's wrote to the committee stating that they would discontinue the appellant's supplies of daily newspapers after March 25. A question arose as to the appellant being entitled to a longer notice of discontinuance, and on March 25

Watson's gave to the appellant a notice of discontinuance expiring on April 1. On March 28 the appellant issued the writ in this action, claiming an injunction restraining the respondents in combination or otherwise from procuring or attempting to procure a breach of contract between the appellant and Watson's, or from interfering or attempting to interfere with the right of the appellant to enter into or continue such contracts or contractual relations with Watson's as he willed or generally with his right to carry on his business as he willed and claiming damages.

The action was heard by Russell J., who after reciting the above events, summed up his conclusions of fact as follows ([1923] 2 Ch. 41): "From the above recital the following facts emerge: (1.) The plaintiff at the request of his branch ceased to deal with Ritchie's, because Ritchie's were supplying newcomers who, in the opinion of the retail federation, were persons to whom the distance limit policy should be applied. (2.) The defendants at the request of Ritchie's and in combination intervened, and for the purpose of securing that the plaintiff should return to Ritchie's as a customer brought pressure to bear on Watson's to discontinue their supplies to the plaintiff. (3.) This pressure was exerted on Watson's in part directly, by threatening to discontinue supplies to Watson's, and in part indirectly, through W. H. Smith & Son, by threatening to discontinue supplies to W. H. Smith & Son if they did not discontinue supplies to Watson's so long as Watson's continued to supply the plaintiff. In other words, the defendants combined to bring it about by threats that Watson's should refuse to deal with the plaintiff—that is, they combined to interfere, by coercion of Watson's, with the trade of the plaintiff, with his right to carry on his business as he would, and to deal with such people as he thought fit. I will add this additional fact, of which I am upon the evidence satisfied, that in acting as they did the defendants were not actuated by any spite against the plaintiff, or by any intention or desire to injure him. They desired that he should take back his custom to Ritchie's; they were quite unaware of the fact, if it be the fact, that it was to the plaintiff's advantage, pecuniarily and otherwise, to deal with Watson's rather than with Ritchie's."

He added that in his view of the evidence no case arose of the defendants combining to procure a breach of any contract between the plaintiff and Watson's, and that no breach of contract had in fact taken place. Under an undertaking given to the Court, Messrs. Watson had continued to supply the plaintiff, and accordingly no question of damages arose at the trial and the application was for an injunction only. Russell J., in a careful judgment, expressed the opinion that the case of *Quinn v. Leathem* ([1901] A.C. 495) had decided that a combination of two or more to induce by threats a man's customers not to deal with him was, if damage resulted, actionable, unless justification existed, and that the decision did not, in his opinion, depend upon the existence in the combination of an intent to injure; and, holding that there was no sufficient justification for the action of the defendants, which he attributed solely to their desire to have the final voice in each case as to the application of the "distance limit policy" of the retail federation, he granted an injunction.

On appeal from this judgment the Court of Appeal (Bankes, Warrington and Scrutton L.JJ.), following the decision of the same Court in *Ware and De Freville v. Motor Trade Association* ([1921] 3 K.B. 40), held that an intent to injure was an essential part of the offence charged, and being of opinion that the defendants had taken action, not for the mere purpose of obtaining control of the "distance limit policy," but in order to protect their trade interests by securing a free sale of newspapers, they held this to be a sufficient justification for the defendants' action. They accordingly reversed the judgment given for the plaintiff, and ordered judgment to be entered for the defendants with costs. The plaintiff thereupon appealed to this House.

My Lords, the argument on this appeal ranged over a wide field and involved the examination of a large number of authorities, including the famous trilogy of cases in your Lordships' House: *Mogul S.S. Co. v. McGregor, Gow & Co.* [1892] A.C. 25; *Allen v. Flood* [1898] A.C. 1; and *Quinn v. Leathem* [1901] A.C. 495. Such an examination is of no value, unless it yields some general principle or test which may be of service in deciding other cases; and from these authorities, which I have carefully read and considered, I deduce as material for the decision of the present case two propositions of law, which may be stated as follows:—

(1.) A combination of two or more persons wilfully to injure a man in his trade is unlawful and, if it results in damage to him, is actionable.

(2.) If the real purpose of the combination is, not to injure another, but to forward or defend the trade of those who enter into it, then no wrong is committed and no action will lie, although damage to another ensues.

The distinction between the two classes of cases is sometimes expressed by saying that in cases of the former class there is not, while in cases of the latter class there is, just cause or excuse for the action taken.

To quote the material parts of the long series of judgments upon which the above conclusions are based would be an endless task, but an attempt to classify the more important of them may be of service. The first proposition is at least as old as *Garret v. Taylor* (1620) Cro. Jac. 567, and appears in many later cases; and although it seemed for a moment to be obscured by some observations made in the judgments in *Allen v. Flood*, [1898] A.C. 1, it was (I think) fully re-established in *Quinn v. Leathem*, [1901] A.C. 495, where Lord Halsbury said that, if upon the facts there found (which fell within the above definition) the plaintiff could have no remedy against those who had thus injured him, it could hardly be said that our jurisprudence was that of a civilised community. The first proposition is further illustrated by

the cases of *Gregory v. Duke of Brunswick* (1843) 6 Man. & G.
205; *Temperton v. Russell* [1893] 1 Q.B. 715; and *Giblan v. National Amalgamated Labourers' Union of Great Britain and Ireland*,
[1903] 2 K.B. 600. The second proposition was fully established in the
Mogul case [1892] A.C. 25 and in *Allen v. Flood* [1898] A.C. 1; and effect
was given to it in *Scottish Co-operative Wholesale Society v. Glasgow
Fleshers' Trade Defence Association*, 35 S.L.R. 645; *Mackenzie v. Iron
Trades Employers' Insurance Association* [1910] S.C. 79; *Ware and De
Freville v. Motor Trade Association* [1921] 3 K.B. 40; and *Reynolds v.
Shipping Federation* [1924] 1 Ch. 28. Both propositions were stated by
Bowen L.J. with characteristic lucidity in the *Mogul Steamship* case
(1889) 23 Q.B.D. 598, 612, and were summarised by Lord Parker in
Attorney-General for Australia v. Adelaide Steamship Co. [1913] A.C.
781, 793. In enumerating these authorities I have not included cases where
the defendants had procured a breach of contract, as those cases stand on a
special footing, and in the present case no such breach was procured.
Among these cases are *Lumley v. Gye* (1853) 2 E. & B. 216; *South Wales
Miners' Federation v. Glamorgan Coal Co.* [1905] A.C. 239; *Conway v.
Wade* [1909] A.C. 506; and *Larkin v. Long* [1915] A.C. 814.

To the text of the above general propositions I would add the following footnotes:—

(a)   Although the first proposition is confined to a combination of two
or more, it does not necessarily follow that the existence of a combination
is essential to the commission of the offence. There is some authority
for the view that what is unlawful in two is not lawful in one, and that
the circumstance that two or more persons combine to cause the injury,
while it may be very relevant as evidence of the purpose and as an aggravation of the damage, is not itself an essential element in the cause of
action: see the opinions expressed by Palles C.B. in *Kearney v. Lloyd*
(1890) 26 L.R.Ir. 268, 280 and by Romer L.J. in the *Giblan* case [1903]
2 K.B. 600, 619; and see also *Huttley v. Simmons* [1898] 1 Q.B. 181.
But in the present case, where a combination clearly existed, this question
does not arise; and accordingly I express no opinion upon it.

(b)   In some cases "malice" is postulated as an element in the tort
which I am considering. If the word means only that the act complained
of is wilfully and knowingly done, or that it is done for the purpose of
injuring another, then it is rightly used in this connection. But there
is a tendency to interpret "malice" as connoting personal enmity or spite
or some other evil motive; and as such a motive is neither an essential
element in the offence nor conclusive of the offence having been committed, it seems better to forego the use of the word.

(c)   The second proposition, of course, assumes the absence of means
which are in themselves unlawful, such as violence or the threat of violence or fraud. Your Lordships were asked to say that a threat to withdraw custom or supplies falls within this category, and of itself introduces
an element of illegality; but although there are passages in the books
which appear to support that contention, it did not appear to me that the

contention was made good. If a trader may withdraw his custom without breaking any law, he may with equal legality express his intention of withdrawing it unless his wishes are met, subject always to the condition that the purpose of the threat is to forward his trade interests and not wilfully and ultroneously to injure the trade of another: see, on this point, *Hodges v. Webb* [1920] 2 Ch. 70 and *White v. Riley* [1921] 1 Ch. 1 and the observations of Holmes J. in the American case of *Vegelahn v. Guntner* (1896) 167 Mass. 92.

(d) There is here no question of a "trade dispute" within the meaning of the Trade Disputes Act, 1906. The quarrel here is not between employer and workman or between workman and workman, but between trader and trader. The above observations, therefore, are not directed to such a case.

My Lords, if these conclusions are applied to the present case, it is not difficult to arrive at a decision upon this appeal. That the defendants combined in a proceeding, the necessary effect of which would have been to injure the plaintiff in his trade unless he submitted to their conditions, may be assumed; but did they do so for the purpose of injuring the plaintiff in his trade, or was it their purpose and object to forward or defend their own trade? I am satisfied that the latter is the true view. The learned trial judge found as a fact that the defendants were not actuated by any spite against the plaintiff or by any intention or desire to injure him. Their purpose was to defeat the "distance limit policy" of the retail federation, which they considered injurious to the free sale of their newspapers; and because the plaintiff, at the instance of the retail federation and in concert with them, was endeavoring to forward that policy by withdrawing his custom from Ritchie's, the defendants, as a counter move, declined to supply Watson's with papers which they could hand on to the plaintiff. Both moves were episodes in a trade war which was being waged between the retailers of newspapers on the one hand and the producers and wholesalers on the other, and were adopted in the supposed interests of one or the other side. Stroke and counter stroke, whether wise or not, were equally prompted by a desire to forward or protect trade interests. The plaintiff struck the first blow, and when it was countered by a similar blow struck by the defendants ran to the Court for protection. His attitude recalls the saying of a French author: *"Cet animal est très méchant; quand on l'attaque, il se défend."* Apparently he forgot that if the defendants were acting illegally then so was he, and that if he was acting illegally a Court of equity would hardly be disposed to help him. I think that in this case it was proved that the defendants took action for the sole purpose of protecting their own trade, and accordingly that they have not committed or threatened to commit any wrong and are not liable to any proceedings.

For these reasons, which substantially agree with those given by the learned Lords Justices in the Court of Appeal, I am of the opinion that this appeal fails, and I move your Lordships that it be dismissed with costs.

LORD DUNEDIN: * * * I have read and reread the judgment in *Quinn v. Leathem,* ([1901] A.C. 479, 500), and I confess I found it very hard to understand how any one could come to the conclusion that conspiracy was only a side issue instead of being, as I think it clearly was, the very gist and essence of the decision. * * *

When it comes to judgment, Lord Halsbury C. in his very opening sentences puts it as a case of conspiracy. Lord Halsbury had been in the minority in *Allen v. Flood,* and he protests against *Allen v. Flood* being carried beyond its own facts. Lord Macnaghten explained with great clearness the import of *Allen v. Flood.* It had, he explained, laid down no new law, but he said the headnote might have been taken from the words of Parke B. in *Stevenson v. Newnham* (13 C.B. 285, 297) (1853): "An act which does not amount to a legal injury cannot be actionable because it is done with a bad intent." And then he explains that what *Allen v. Flood* had done was to sweep away the erroneous proposition laid down by Brett L.J. in *Bowen v. Hall* (6 Q.B.D. 333) and *Temperton v. Russell* ([1893] 1 Q.B. 715), the very proposition on which, as I have above remarked, the first question and finding viewed as not being a conspiracy could be founded. That view, therefore, really leaves the conspiracy finding No. 2 as the only finding remaining. Speaking of Lord Watson's judgment in *Allen v. Flood,* he says: "Obviously Lord Watson was convinced in his own mind that a conspiracy to injure might give rise to civil liability even though the end were brought about by conduct and acts which by themselves and apart from the element of combination or concerted action could not be regarded as a legal wrong." Applying this to the facts of *Quinn v. Leathem,* it is obvious that as a mere question of an act by itself Munce might at any moment have refused to take Leathem's beef and no wrong would have been perpetrated. Further on Lord Macnaghten says: "That a conspiracy to injure—an oppressive combination—differs widely from an invasion of civil rights by a single individual cannot be doubted. I agree in substance with the remarks of Bowen L.J. and Lords Bramwell and Hannen in the *Mogul* case. A man may resist, without much difficulty, the wrongful act of an individual * * * but it is a very different thing (as Lord FitzGerald observes) when one man has to defend himself against many combined to do him wrong."

All this is right in the teeth of the argument for the appellant quoted above.

My Lords, I need not multiply citations. Lord Shand goes on combination and conspiracy alone, so does Lord Brampton. I cite only one sentence ([1901] A.C. 522): "I note, in confirmation of this, that the Lord Justice pointedly told the jury that proof of a conspiracy was essential to the support of the action."

To sum up. There are some observations in Lord Lindley's judgment which might seem to point to another ground of action, and Lord Halsbury proceeds on the ground of threats, which in that case he regarded as illegal means or, in other words, tortious acts, as well as a conspiracy to injure. But as regards the others, Lord Macnaghten demolished in terms every finding as the basis of the verdict except the finding of the conspiracy, and in the judgments of all the others, all, save conspiracy, has passed out of sight.   In fact, I indorse what was said by Atkin L.J. in *Ware and De Freville* ([1921] 3 K.B. 90). "The case seems to me not to turn in any degree on the evidence as to threats. The foundation of the decision was the principle, expressly reserved in the decision in *Allen v. Flood,* that a combination to injure may be unlawful where the intention by one is not."

My Lords, it may seem self confident to be positive when so many learned persons have expressed other views, but candidly I never held a clearer opinion than the one I now express, that the effect of *Allen* v. *Flood* and *Quinn v. Leathem* is to settle beyond dispute that in an action against an individual for injury he has caused to the plaintiff by his action, the whole question is whether the act complained of was legal, and motive or intent is immaterial; but that in an action against a set of persons in combination, a conspiracy to injure, followed by actual injury, will give a good cause for action, and motive or intent when the act itself is not illegal is of the essence of the conspiracy.[10] * * *

---

[10] The concurring opinions of Lords Sumner and Buckmaster are omitted.   For comment on this case, see 37 Harv. Law Rev. 143 (1923).

CHAPTER III.

INTERFERENCE WITH ADVANTAGEOUS RELATIONS.

Section 1. Inducing Breach of Contract.

SOUTH WALES MINERS' FEDERATION v. GLAMORGAN COAL CO.

House of Lords. [1905] A.C. 239.

The Glamorgan Coal Company, Limited, and seventy-three other plaintiffs, owners of collieries in South Wales, brought this action against the South Wales Miners' Federation, its trustees and officers, and several members of its executive council, claiming damages for wrongfully and maliciously procuring and inducing workmen in the collieries to break their contracts of service with the plaintiffs, and alternatively for wrongfully and maliciously conspiring to do so. Evidence of the facts proved at the trial before Bigham J. without a jury is set forth in the report of his judgment [1903] 2. K.B. 546-58, and the principal facts are stated by Lord James in this House. Briefly the case was as follows. The federation (which was registered as a trade union) was formed (*inter alia*) to consider trade and wages, to protect the workmen and regulate the relation between them and employers, and to call conferences. The wages were paid upon a sliding scale agreement, rising and falling with the price of coal. In November, 1900, the council of the federation, fearing that the action of merchants and middlemen would reduce the price of coal and consequently the rate of wages, resolved to order a "stop-day" on November 9, and informed the workmen. This order was obeyed by over 100,000 men, who took a holiday and thereby broke their contracts of service. At a conference held on November 12 between delegates of the men and the council a resolution was passed authorizing the council to declare a general holiday at any time they might think it necessary for the protection of wages and of the industry generally. In October and November, 1901, the council (as Bigham J. found) ordered four stop-days for the same reason as before, and the men took a holiday on each of those days in breach of their contracts. Bigham J. found that the action of the federation was dictated by an honest desire to forward the interest of the workmen and was not in any sense prompted by a wish to injure the masters, between whom and the men there was no quarrel or ill-will; that having been requested by the men by the resolution of November 12, 1900, to advise and direct them as to when to stop work, the federation and its officers did to the best of their ability advise and direct the men honestly and without malice of any kind against the plaintiffs, and therefore had lawful justification or excuse for what they did. The learned judge gave judgment for the defendants. This decision was reversed by the Court of Appeal (Romer and Stirling L.JJ., Vaughan Williams L.J. dissenting), who entered judgment for the plaintiffs, the damages to be assessed [1903] 2 K.B. 545. * * *

EARL OF HALSBURY L.C. (read by Lord Macnaghten). My Lords, I cannot think that in this case there is anything to be determined except the question of fact. I say so because the questions of law discussed are so well settled by authority, and by authority in this House.

To combine to procure a number of persons to break contracts is manifestly unlawful. This is found as a fact to have been done here, and is also found to have caused serious damage to the persons who were entitled to have these contracts performed.

It is, further, a principle of the law, applicable even to the criminal law, that people are presumed to intend the reasonable consequences of their acts. It is not, perhaps, necessary to have recourse to such a presumption where, as upon the facts stated, it is apparent that what they were doing must necessarily cause injury to the employers. We start, then, with the infliction of an unlawful injury upon the persons entitled to have the services of their workmen. It follows that this is an actionable wrong unless it can be justified.

Now it is sought to be justified, first, because it is said that the men were acting in their own interest, and that they were sincerely under the belief that the employers would themselves benefit by their collieries being interrupted in their work; but what sort of excuse is this for breaking a contract when the co-contractor refuses to allow the breach? It seems to me to be absurd to suppose that a benefit which he refuses to accept justified an intentional breach of contractual rights. It may, indeed, be urged in proof of the allegation that there was no ill-will against the employers. I assume this to be true, but I have no conception what can be meant by an excuse for breaking a contract because you really think it will not harm your co-contractor.

I absolutely refuse to discuss the cases which have been suggested widely apart from the question of what pecuniary advantage may be reaped from breaking a contract, where, upon moral or religious grounds, people may be justly advised to refuse to perform what they have agreed to do.

Some cases may be suggested when higher and deeper considerations may, in a moral point of view, justify the refusal to do what has been agreed to be done. Such cases may give rise to the consideration whether, in a moral or religious point of view, you are not bound to indemnify the person whom your refusal injures; but a Court of law has only to decide whether there is a legal justification.

Again, I refuse to go into a discussion of the duty or the moral right to tender advice. The facts in this case shew nothing in the nature of advice, even if the supposed duty could be created by people who made them their official advisers who were to advise them even to break the law. But, as I have said, these are peremptory orders given by the official superiors of the body, and it has been found by the learned judge who tried the case that the body sued was responsible for the interference with the workmen.

I think the appeal should be dismissed.

Lord Macnaghten: * * * It was argued—and that was the only argument—that although the thing done was *primâ facie* an actionable wrong, it was justifiable under the circumstances. That there may be a justification for that which in itself is an actionable wrong I do not for a moment doubt. And I do not think it would be difficult to give instances putting aside altogether cases complicated by the introduction of moral considerations. But what is the alleged justification in the present case? It was said that the council—the executive of the federation—had a duty cast upon them to protect the interests of the members of the union, and that they could not be made legally responsible for the consequences of their action if they acted honestly in good faith and without any sinister or indirect motive. The case was argued with equal candour and ability. But it seems to me that the argument may be disposed of by two simple questions. How was the duty created? What in fact was the alleged duty? The alleged duty was created by the members of the union themselves, who elected or appointed the officials of the union to guide and direct their action; and then it was contended that the body to whom the members of the union have thus committed their individual freedom of action are not responsible for what they do if they act according to their honest judgment in furtherance of what they consider to be the interest of their constituents. It seems to me that if that plea were admitted there would be an end of all responsibility. It would be idle to sue the workmen, the individual wrong-doers, even if it were practicable to do so. Their counsellors and protectors, the real authors of the mischief, would be safe from legal proceedings. The only other question is, What is the alleged duty set up by the federation? I do not think it can be better described than it was by Mr. Lush. It comes to this—it is the duty on all proper occasions, of which the federation or their officials are to be the sole judges, to counsel and procure a breach of duty.

I agree with Romer and Stirling L.JJ., and I think the appeal must be dismissed.

LORD JAMES: * * * The judgment of Bigham J. proceeds on the
ground that "to support an action for procuring a breach of contract it
is essential to prove actual malice."

I cannot concur in this view of the law. * * *

But a further question has to be disposed of. At the trial and at the
bar of your Lordship's House the counsel for the appellants contended
that their clients had good cause and excuse for the alleged unlawful act
they committed. That such justification—such "good cause and excuse"
—may exist is, I think, a sound proposition. The above words of Lord
Macnaghten and of Bowen L.J. so declare. The facts upon which this attempted justification in this case is based are fully before your Lordships
and need not be recapitulated. I take the results of them to be that in
one sense the defendants acted in good faith. They, I think, honestly
believed that the stoppage of work they resolved upon would increase the
price of coal and so benefit both the workmen and the employers. Towards their employers the defendants entertained no malice. * * * The
intention of the defendants was directly to procure the breach of contracts. The fact that their motives were good in the interests of those
they moved to action does not form any answer to those who have suffered
from the unlawful act. During the arguments that have been addressed
to your Lordships I do not think quite sufficient distinction was drawn
between the intention and the motives of the defendants. Their intention
clearly was that the workmen should break their contracts. The defen-
ants' motives, no doubt, were that by so doing wages should be raised.
But if in carrying out the intention the defendants purposely procured
an unlawful act to be committed, the wrong that is thereby inflicted cannot be obliterated by the existence of a motive to secure a money benefit
to the wrong-doers.

For these reasons I think the judgment of the Court of Appeal should
be affirmed.

LORD LINDLEY: * * * The appellants' counsel did not deny that, in
his view of the case, the defendants' conduct required justification, and
it was contended (1) that all which the officials did was to advise the
men, and (2) that the officials owed a duty to the men to advise and
assist them as they did.

As regards advice, it is not necessary to consider when, if ever, mere
advice to do an unlawful act is actionable when the advice is not libellous or slanderous. Nor is it necessary to consider those cases in which
a person, whose rights will be violated if a contract is performed, is
justified in endeavouring to procure a breach of such contract. Nor
is it necessary to consider what a parent or guardian may do to protect
his child or ward. That there are cases in which it is not actionable
to exhort a person to break a contract may be admitted; and it is very
difficult to draw a sharp line separating all such cases from all others.
But the so-called advice here was much more than counsel; it was
accompanied by orders to stop, which could not be disobeyed with
impunity. A refusal to stop work as ordered would have been regarded

as disloyal to the federation. This is plain from the speeches given in evidence on the trial; and in my opinion it is a very important element in the case which cannot be ignored. * * *

Then your Lordships were invited to say that there was a moral or social duty on the part of the officials to do what they did, and that, as they acted *bonâ fide* in the interest of the men and without any ill-will to the employers, their conduct was justifiable; and your Lordships were asked to treat this case as if it were like a case of libel or slander on a privileged occasion. My Lords, this contention was not based on authority, and its only merits are its novelty and ingenuity. The analogy is, in my opinion, misleading, and to give effect to this contention would be to legislate and introduce an entirely new law, and not to expound the law as it is at present. It would be to render many acts lawful which, as the law stands, are clearly unlawful. * * *

*Order of the Court of Appeal affirmed
and appeal dismissed with costs.*[1]

---

[1] Accord: Patterson Glass Co. v. Thomas, 28 Cal. App. Dec. 1385 (1919); Burgess v. Georgia, F. & A. Ry. Co., 148 Ga. 415, 96 S.E. 864 (1918); Brost Pattern Works v. Reid, 24 Ohio N.P. (N.S.) 864 (1918); Best Service Wet Wash Laundry Co. v. Dickson, 121 Misc. 416, 201 N.Y.S. 173 (1923). For consequences of such a breach of contract upon the employee's right to recover for services rendered, see: Ressig v. Waldorf-Astoria Hotel Co., 185 App. Div. 4, 172 N.Y.S. 616 (1918), aff'd in 229 N.Y. 553, 129 N.E. 912 (1920).

Cf. Legris v. Marcotte, 129 Ill. App. 67 (1906); Denaby & Cadeby Main Collieries v. Yorkshire Miners Ass'n [1906] A.C. 384.

The Glamorgan case has an obvious relationship to § 3 of the Trade Disputes Act of 1906, which provided that "an act done by a person in contemplation or furtherance of a trade dispute shall not be actionable on the ground only that it induces some other person to break a contract of employment * * *." The moving considerations that underlay this provision can be gathered from the following excerpts from the debate in Parliament on the Trade Disputes Bill. "Sir John Walton [the Attorney-General in charge of the bill] said that cases which had been described by the hon. Member for Clitheroe [Mr. Shackleton] would, he feared, be held by a court of law to be cases of malicious persuasion * * *. Take the illustration given by the hon. Member from Derby, who went down into the country to explain the merits of his strike to a large number of men imported by the railway company whom he wished to join the men who had struck. He was enjoined by injunction by the High Court on the ground that he was maliciously inducing them to break their contracts. Under these circumstances the conduct of a strike was exceedingly difficult." 162 Parl. Deb. 1685-86 (Aug. 3, 1906). The Lord Chancellor (Lord Loreburn): "There was the case of a strike where some Irishmen had been induced by the employers to come over to Whitehaven for the purpose of taking the places of the men who were out on strike. These Irishmen did not know that a strike was going on, and one of the officials of the trade union met them at the station and said to them—'My men, do you know what you are coming for? You are coming to replace your comrades who are on strike. I will pay your fares back again to Ireland. Will you go back?' Not wishing to injure their comrades these men went back; but the trade union was held responsible and had to pay damages because it was an interference with a contract." 166 Parl. Deb. 694-5 (Dec. 4, 1906). "Mr. Clement Edwards said he * * * would give one or two further examples. It constantly happened that a client went to a solicitor and pointed out that he had entered into a contract which to the solicitor might appear to be rather an unconscionable one. In consequence of the advice of the solicitor the client broke the contract, but no one had ever suggested that the solicitor was also liable for damages for inducing the breach. Or there was the case of a man who entered into a contract to go out to work for three or five years on the West Coast of Africa. His health broke down and he came home and consulted a doctor. The doctor advised him on the ground of health to sacrifice everything, and to throw up his employment in West

BRIMELOW v. CASSON.

Chancery Division [1924] 1 Ch. 302.

Witness Action. The plaintiff was the manager of a touring theatrical company. From Christmas, 1922, until March, 1923, he ran a touring pantomime, which ended at Maidenhead. His company was then reconstituted on a co-operative basis, under which profits were to be equally divided, the chorus girls receiving a minimum salary of 1*l.* a week. Under this régime the plaintiff ceased to be the employer of members of the company. It came to an end on June 23, 1923. The plaintiff then began to run the company, and still ran it, as an employer, but on a percentage basis, with minimum guarantees. In the case of chorus girls, their contracts provided for a weekly wage of 3 per cent. of the net takings, with a guaranteed minimum of 1*l.* 10*s.* weekly, for one week's rehearsal without pay, and for "no play, no pay." The contracts were for no fixed duration; they ran from week to week. No tour was booked for any fixed period or for any appreciable time ahead. The plaintiff admitted that under this new arrangement the chorus girls never got beyond their guarantee—that is to say, they never received more than their 30*s.* a week. His opinion was that a girl could live comfortably on 1*l.* a week if two or three of them lived together. Under this new arrangement the company played at Dorking, Burton, Kettering, Plymouth, Coventry, and Cannock. It was due to play at Dudley for the week beginning August 13, 1923, and at West Bromwich for the week beginning August 20, by virtue of two contracts made between the plaintiff and the defendant Kennedy, who owned theatres at those two towns. Before the contracts were signed the plaintiff was asked by Kennedy's agent how he stood with the association,

---

Africa. There was a breach of contract there for which the man was responsible, but no one had suggested that the doctor should also be liable in damages for the breach. And why? Because it was held in all these cases that there was just cause and excuse on the part of the person advising or inducing the breach. That was exactly the position which, it was understood, prevailed in regard to the trade union official, the expert adviser of the men. Because he was an expert in the matter of industrial conditions and in the matter of economic relations the duty was placed upon him to advise. It was not a new principle they were laying down. They were asking that the principle should apply as to just cause and excuse for interference to the trade unionists on whom was placed the duty of advising, and that they should be placed in the category of those who could plead just cause and excuse." 164 Parl. Deb. 153-4 (Nov. 5, 1906).

See, generally, Carpenter, "Interference with Contract Relations," 41 Harv. Law Rev. 728 (1928); Chapin, "Interfering with Contractual Rights as Constituting a Tort," 1 N.J. Law Rev. 144 (1916); Hodge, "Wrongful Interference by Third Parties with the Rights of Employers and Employed," 28 Am. Law Rev. 47 (1894); Sayre, "Inducing Breach of Contract," 36 Harv. Law Rev. 663 (1923); Schofield, "The Principle of Lumley v. Gye and its Application," 2 Harv. Law Rev. 19 (1888); Solinger, "Pre-Contractual Interference by a Third Party," 6 Cin. Law Rev. 322 (1932); 24 Col. Law Rev. 185 (1924).

In those states, where no right of action lies for inducing a breach of contract, inducing the breach of an employer-employee contract is generally regarded as actionable. *Cf.* Esswell v. Ford, 208 Ala. 101, 94 So. 67 (1922); Patterson Glass Co. v. Thomas, 41 Cal. App. 559, 183 Pac. 190 (1919).

and replied: "Quite all right. I have never been approached by any of the association ever since I have been on the road." This statement was false, and the plaintiff knew it to be so.

Five associations represented the respective interests of the different classes of persons engaged in the theatrical calling—namely, the Association of Touring Managers, the Variety Artists' Federation, the Actors' Association, the Musicians' Union, and the National Association of Theatrical Employees. The four last were registered trade unions, the first named was not. In March, 1923, a committee was formed by these five associations composed of representatives of each association, and was called the Joint Protection Committee, the J.P.C. The defendant Casson was a member of it, and was one of the representatives of the Association of Touring Managers; he was until recently chairman of the committee. * * *

For some considerable time past the Actors' Association (which included all the leading actors and actresses among its members) had been struggling to secure a living wage for chorus girls. Experience had shown in the past that in a very large number of cases the absence of a living wage drove such girls to prostitution. The minimum wage stipulated for by the Actors' Association, and embodied in what was known as the Valentine contract, was in the case of chorus girls 2l. 10s. a week. Another feature obnoxious to the Actors' Association was the sharing system or commonwealth company, not because it was bad *per se,* but because experience had shown that in most cases most of the money went to the manager and the others were paid too little or not at all. It was a system obviously capable of abuse, and one in which failure would hit hardest those least able to afford it. The Actors' Association had for some time past occupied itself in dealing with the question of "the bogus manager"—that is, a manager who recurrently failed to meet his obligations to his company or who paid them so little that they could not afford to live decently. The Actors' Association, or the Joint Protection Committee, had from time to time received reports about the plaintiff.

In 1920 the secretary of the Actors' Association wrote to the plaintiff and pointed out that he was breaking their rules in paying his chorus girls only 1l. 15s. a week, out of which they had to provide for tights, shoes, and washing. In March, 1923, the plaintiff informed an organizer of the Actors' Association that he was paying his chorus girls 2l. 5s. a week when he was only paying 1l.

In July, 1923, a lady who was a member of the plaintiff's company came to see Mr. Lugg, the secretary of the Actors' Association, with reference to the case of a young unmarried girl, a member of the plaintiff's company and aged about eighteen, who was living in immorality with another member of the company, a tiny, deformed creature, a dwarf. He was an abnormal man. Mr. Lugg brought the complaints against the plaintiff before the Joint Protection Committee, which, on July 25, passed a resolution "that Jack Arnold's show be proscribed as from

August 6, it being operated on sharing contracts for performers." The J.P.C. also sent to the various managers of theatres a printed form: "It having been proved to the satisfaction of the J.P.C. that J. B. Arnold of the King Wu Tut Tut Revue is an undesirable person every step will be taken by the said committee to prevent his appearance at any place of entertainment. Signed, Louis Casson (chairman), Albert Voyce (secretary)." The J.P.C. wrote to the plaintiff that they had notified all managerial associations that on and after August 6 he would not be allowed to present his company. Mr. Lugg, in accordance with his instructions, went to Plymouth on July 27, and saw the girl, who admitted to him that the only reason she was living with the dwarf was that she had not enough money to live on. On August 2 the J.P.C. wrote to the plaintiff: "Mr. Lugg's report on his interview with you and some of your company at Plymouth last week was considered by the J.P.C. yesterday, and the J.P.C. adheres to their resolution, the contents of which were conveyed to you by the J.P.C. last week."

When the plaintiff engaged this couple on a joint contract he was aware that they were then living together. On August 10, 1923, the defendant Fry had an interview with the plaintiff, and told him that the J.P.C. had received complaints that he was not paying the minimum wage agreed between the Actors' Association and the Association of Touring Managers. The plaintiff replied that he cared nothing for any of the associations. Fry told the plaintiff he must consider himself in dispute with the Actors' Association. The company went to Dudley to open on August 13. Fry was there, and informed Kennedy, the proprietor of the theatre, that the Actors' Association was in dispute with Arnold and that the J.P.C. had proscribed him. Fry induced Kennedy to sign an undertaking not to allow Arnold to appear. The result was that the company neither played at Dudley that week nor at West Bromwich in the following week.

No threats were made to Kennedy to induce him to break his contract, but Fry, acting on the instructions of the J.P.C. and the Actors' Association, induced him to do so in order to further the dispute which existed between the plaintiff and the Actors' Association, which was supported by the other bodies by reason of the J.P.C. having taken the matter up. The defendants Casson, Voyce, and Fry admitted that they intended to induce theatre proprietors to break their contracts with the plaintiff and to abstain from entering into contracts with him, with the avowed object of driving him off the road, unless and until he paid the minimum wage of 2l. 10s. a week.

The writ was issued on August 22, 1923. An interim injunction until the trial having been refused by the vacation judge, the campaign against the plaintiff was vigorously pursued.

The plaintiff asked for an injunction to restrain the defendants Casson, Voyce, and Fry, their servants and agents, from inducing, or procuring, or conspiring, or combining, or attempting to induce or procure any person to break any contract or abstain from entering into a contract with him. The plaintiff asked for damages for breach of contract against the defendant Kennedy. * * *

RUSSELL J. stated the facts and continued: It is difficult to speak of this condition of things with restraint. A young girl, almost a child, forced by underpayment to continue in sexual association with this abnormal man is, to my mind, a terrible and revolting tragedy, but the question which I have to decide is whether the acts of the defendants make them liable to an action at the suit of the plaintiff, or whether in the circumstances of this case there exists a sufficient justification for the acts which in the absence of such justification would be actionable. Before discussing the law let me say something further about the facts of this particular case. A multitude of matters and incidents in connection with his companies, and the members thereof, were put to the plaintiff in cross-examination, but as to most of these no affirmative evidence was given. Mr. Hastings deliberately refrained from calling such evidence, being content to rest his case as to specific incidents on the incident of the girl and the dwarf, and on the evidence as to another young girl in the company, whose wage was only 1*l*. 10*s*. a week, which shows there are reasons for believing that she was resorting to immorality. The evidence further reveals cases of unpaid landladies' bills. There can be no doubt that the company and its members were leading a hand to mouth existence.

In my opinion, it is true to say that the evils which the Joint Protection Committee and the associations represented by it anticipate as the result of a company being run by a manager paying insufficient salaries are to be found in the plaintiff's company. *Prima facie* interference with a man's contractual rights and with his right to carry on his business as he wills is actionable; but it is clear on the authorities that interference with contractual rights may be justified; *a fortiori* the inducing of others not to contract with a person may be justified. * * *

My task here is to decide whether, in the circumstances of this case, justification existed for the acts done. Let me summarize the salient facts of the present case. * * * In these circumstances, have the defendants justification for their acts? That they would have the sympathy and support of decent men and women I can have no doubt. But have they in law justification for those acts? As has been pointed out, no general rule can be laid down as a general guide in such cases, but I confess that if justification does not exist here I can hardly conceive the case in which it would be present. These defendants, as it seems to me, owed a duty to their calling and to its members, and, I am tempted to add, to the public, to take all necessary peaceful steps to terminate the payment of this insufficient wage, which in the plaintiff's company had apparently been in fact productive of those results which their past experience had led them to anticipate. "The good sense" of this tribunal leads me to decide that in the circumstances of the present case justification did exist.

The result on this part of the case is that the defendants, Casson, Vovce, and Fry, have established a good defence to the plaintiff's action. This decision renders it unnecessary to consider the defence raised by them under s. 3 of the Trade Disputes Act, 1906, but in case the opinion of a higher Court is sought, it may be convenient to indicate shortly my views thereon. The plaintiff urged various points against this defence. He said that the case of actors was not within the section at all, because by the definition section the words "trade dispute" mean a dispute in which workmen are concerned, that is, "persons employed in trade or industry," and that acting is neither a trade nor an industry. This appears to me a narrow view of the section. There is no definition of "trade or industry" in the Act, but it seems to me that the business of presenting histrionic performances to the public for profit may fairly be described as a trade or industry in which many persons, including actors, are employed. It was further said that there was no trade dispute in fact. I do not agree. There was a dispute between the Actors' Association and the plaintiff upon the question that the plaintiff was employing actors at wages below the minimum wage. Another point urged was that this could not be a trade dispute within the Act, because certain employers—namely, the Association of Touring Managers—were represented on the Joint Protection Committee. This fact does not, in my opinion, alter the nature of the dispute or the parties to it. It was essentially a dispute which concerned the general body of actors represented by the Actors' Association on the one hand and an employer of actors on the other. Finally, it was said that the Act could afford no defence to the action, so far as it related to the inducement of Kennedy to break his contracts, because those contracts were not contracts of employment. As at present advised, this appears to me a good point. The protection of the section only extends to the grounds of actionability there specified. If the act is actionable on other grounds it is still actionable on those grounds. The section appears to me to afford no defence to an action brought in respect of the procurement of breach of a contract not being a contract of employment.

The remainder of the case—namely, the action against the defendant Kennedy—may be disposed of shortly. In ordinary circumstances Kennedy would be responsible for such damages, if any, as the plaintiff suffered by reason of Kennedy's breaches of contract. But the contracts were brought about by reason of a representation made by the plaintiff which was false, and known by the plaintiff to be false. Before the contracts were signed the plaintiff was asked how he stood with the association, and he replied: "Quite all right. I have never been approached by any of the association ever since I have been on the road." The statement was false, and false to the plaintiff's knowledge. If this be so, it is admitted by his counsel that he cannot recover.

The result is that the action is dismissed with costs. [2]

---

[2] *Cf.* Cook v. Wilson, 108 Misc. 438, 178 N.Y.S. 463 (1919) ; Read v. Friendly Society of Operative Stonemasons [1902] 2 K.B. 732.

CENTRAL METAL PRODUCTS CORP. v. O'BRIEN.

United States District Court for the Northern District of Ohio (1922). 278 Fed. 827.

WESTENHAVER, District Judge: This cause has been heard, argued, and submitted on plaintiff's application for a preliminary injunction. The affidavits, exhibits, and the briefs of counsel and authorities therein cited have been fully and carefully examined and considered. Press of business prevents the preparation and filing of an extended opinion at this time, and the urgency of the matter is such that it should be disposed of without delay; hence my conclusion only will be briefly stated.

Plaintiff is, and for a long time past has been, engaged in the business of manufacturing, erecting, and installing metal doors, metal frames, transoms, and sash. It has two factories and places of business, one at Canton, Ohio, and the other at College Point, Long Island. Its method of doing business is to manufacture its product at one or the other of its plants, ship it to the buildings where the same is to be installed, and personally, by means of its agents and other employees, to erect and install. On June 30, 1921, it duly entered into a contract in writing with the defendant the city of Cleveland, through its duly authorized agents, to furnish, deliver, set up, and install certain interior metal doors, metal sash, metal frames, and casings for the City Hospital of the city of Cleveland, then and since under construction. The amount of this contract aggregates the sum of $224,000. That this contract was duly and legally entered into, that the city of Cleveland has not any right to cancel or terminate it, and that the plaintiff is free to select and employ any competent labor to perform this work of installation, are matters not in dispute. It follows, therefore, that plaintiff's right to this contract, to perform the same, and to reap the profits resulting to it from such performance, is a right of property standing upon the same legal basis and entitled to the same legal protection as is any person's right to full possession and ownership of his private dwelling.

The defendant William O'Brien is vice president of the Amalgamated Sheet Metal Workers' International Alliance and secretary of Local Union No. 65 of that Alliance; J. T. Nester is business agent of Local No. 65, and the defendants Frank Vancourt, Glenn B. Lockwood, William Kerver, David Kahn, and J. Thompson are members of Local No. 65. The Amalgamated Sheet Metal Workers' International Alliance and Local Union No. 65 are both unincorporated, voluntary associations, and these individuals are made defendants as members of Local No. 65 representing the total membership, which it is alleged exceeds 30 in number and are too numerous to be made defendants. The defendant J. Harold MacDowell is architect of the city of Cleveland, having supervision on behalf of the city over the construction of the said City Hospital, and Dudley Blossom, at the time this bill was filed and the case heard, was director of public welfare of said city, and either had or assumed charge of supervising and directing the construction work on said hospital.

The plaintiff fabricated the material at one of its plants, shipped it to and delivered it upon the City Hospital premises, and began the work of installation some time early in October, 1921. The plaintiff sent its supervisory staff to said hospital and employed union carpenters at the union wage scale and on union terms and conditions, and members of the United Brotherhood of Carpenters and Joiners of America to perform the actual work of erection and installation. William O'Brien and J. T. Nester, acting on behalf of Local No. 65 and the Amalgamated Sheet Metal Workers' International Alliance, demanded that this work of installation should be done by the members of their sheet metal workers' union. Complainant refused to comply with this request, for reasons immaterial to mention, because entirely within its legal rights. Upon this refusal, said O'Brien and Nester then demanded of the architect and director of public welfare that plaintiff be required to discharge its union carpenters and employ members of its sheet metal workers' union to perform this labor or to break the contract of the city with plaintiff and take over the work and do it itself with employees, members of the sheet metal workers' union. This demand not having been acceded to with sufficient promptness, defendants O'Brien and Nester called a strike by withdrawing union sheet metal workers who were working for other contractors on the City Hospital, about the latter part of October, 1921, and, the officials of the city still not acceding to the demand, later, the latter part of November, a further strike was called by withdrawing sheet metal workers, members of Local No. 65, from working for contractors who were engaged upon the Auditorium Building under construction on behalf of the city. There is evidence tending to show that threats were also made to call strikes of sheet metal workers, members of Local No. 65, on school buildings under construction on behalf of the board of education, and also of having other strikes called by other sympathetic unions on the City Hospital and the City Auditorium, which evidence, however, is denied by defendants, and is, for the purposes of the present hearing, regarded as not proved.

Later, the latter part of November or the early part of December, the defendant J. H. MacDowell, city architect, and Dudley Blossom, director of public welfare, acceded to the demands of the defendants representing Local No. 65. They directed plaintiff to discontinue further erection work, and upon refusal of plaintiff, through its employees, so to do, police officers of the city of Cleveland, acting under some unknown and undisclosed authority, appeared at the City Hospital building and excluded plaintiff's employees from the premises and prevented further performance, under threat of arrest. The architect and director of public welfare, while assuming to act on behalf of the city of Cleveland, do not appear to have been acting under any other authority than such as was assumed or usurped by them. Upon this hearing, affidavits were filed on behalf of the city, and argument was made by an assistant to the director of law in support of the position taken by the architect and director of public welfare. Early in December, after procuring from said architect and director of public welfare written assurances that plaintiff must employ members of the sheet metal workers' union or that its contract would be broken and further work of installation done by the city, said O'Brien and Nester caused the sheet metal workers to return to work on the City Auditorium and for other contractors on the City Hospital, but plaintiff has since been unable, by reason of the conduct complained of, to proceed further with its work, which is now at a standstill.

Such, in brief, are the main outstanding facts. No other conclusion therefrom can be drawn than that the defendants have entered into a conspiracy to deprive plaintiff of its property and to injure its business. A conspiracy is an agreement of two or more persons to commit an unlawful act, or to commit a lawful act by unlawful means. It is immaterial if the city or its architect and director of public welfare were induced to become members of the conspiracy under coercion or to avoid pecuniary loss or other trouble. See *Aberthaw Construction Co. v. Cameron,* 194 Mass. 209, 80 N.E. 478, 120 Am. St. Rep. 542; *Lehigh Structural Steel Co. v. Atlantic Smelting & Refining Co.* (N.J. Ch.) 111 Atl. 376; *Buyer v. Guillan* (2 C.C.A.) 271 Fed. 65.

The conspiracy here was unlawful in its purpose. Its ultimate object was to prevent performance by plaintiff of its contract and to deprive it of its contract, unless it would comply with terms and conditions contrary to its contract rights, such as neither the city nor the other defendants had any right to impose or exact. In making this statement I am not unmindful of the contention of defendants other than those representing the city that they are members of and acting for a labor union, and were seeking only to obtain an advantage for the members of their respective unions, as to which some observations will be here made. The means resorted to to carry out the conspiracy were unlawful. In the first place, the defendants O'Brien and Nester were attempting to induce the city to break its contract with the plaintiff, and it is settled law that one may not induce or persuade, much less coerce, one to break his contract with another. This rule is so fundamental that it has been held that officers and agents of a union may not induce or persuade employees to break a contract of employment. See *Hitchman Coal & Coke Co. v. Mitchell,* 245 U.S. 249, 38 Sup. Ct. 65, 62 L. Ed. 260, L.R.A. 1918C, 497, Ann. Cas. 1918B, 461. For additional authority, see *Westinghouse Elec. & Mfg. Co. v. Diamond State Fibre Co.* (D.C.) 268 Fed. 121; *Iron Molders' Union v. Allis-Chalmers Co.* (7 C.C.A.) 166 Fed. 45, 91 C.C.A. 631, 20 L.R.A. (N.S.) 315, syllabi 4 and 6.

Defendant's contention that the action herein noted was taken solely in the interests of the union members of the Amalgamated Sheet Metal Workers' International Alliance and its Local Union No. 65, for the purpose of enforcing a jurisdictional award, made by some national board, of this class of work to the sheet metal workers' union, does not justify or protect the defendants. Plaintiff asserts that the bodies joining in, creating, and enforcing the jurisdictional award are a conspiracy or combination in restraint of trade, having for its object the creation of a monopoly in the members of the sheet metal workers' union, in the labor of erecting and installing sheet metal work of this kind and character. I deem it immaterial to consider this last suggestion. * * *

There is no dispute here between any of the labor union defendants and the plaintiff concerning terms or conditions of employment. They are not seeking to compel plaintiff to employ union labor or to conduct its business on union terms and conditions. Plaintiff's employees are members of the United Brotherhood of Carpenters and Joiners of America, having a national membership of 400,000, as compared with a membership of 24,000 of the Amalgamated Sheet Metal Workers' International Alliance. Plaintiff's union employees are satisfied with the terms and conditions of their employment and the rate of pay, which the evidence shows are the same conditions and wage scale as have been adopted by Local No. 65. If plaintiff accedes to the defendants' demand and employs members of the sheet metal workers' union, then the members of the carpenters' and joiners' union might with equal legal right indulge in the same conduct as is here alleged against defendants. If they did so, their legal standing would be precisely the same. It results that all the cases cited on behalf of defendants, even if not in conflict with the decisions of the United States Supreme Court and the greater weight of authority, have no application whatever to the controversy before the court.

The union defendants have a right to obtain business in the way of employment and wages which plaintiff has the power to dispose of, on the same terms and none other, as the plaintiff would have the right to obtain a contract which a competitor was seeking to obtain. In no event does that right include the right to induce or persuade another to break an existing contract, much less to do so by coercion, or by the calling of sympathetic strikes and the institution of secondary boycotts. If plaintiff were employing nonunion laborers and undertaking to perform this contract on an open shop basis, the better considered cases all hold that defendants might not resort to the means to which they are now resorting to prevent the performance by plaintiff of its contract. See *Hitchman Coal & Coke Co. v. Mitchell*, 245 U.S. 249, 38 Sup. Ct. 65, 62 L. Ed. 260, L.R.A. 1918C, 497, Ann. Cas. 1918B, 461; *Aberthaw Construction Co. v. Cameron*, 194 Mass. 209, 80 N.E. 478, 120 Am. St. Rep. 542; *Burnham v. Dowd*, 217 Mass. 351, 104 N.E. 841, 51 L.R.A.(N.S.) 778; *Pickett v. Walsh*, 192 Mass. 572, par. 5 of head notes, 78 N.E. 753, 6 L.R.A.(N.S.) 1067, 116 Am. St. Rep. 272, 7 Ann. Cas. 638; *Buyer v. Guillan* (2 C.C.A.) 271 Fed. 65; *Lehigh Structural Steel Co. v. Atlantic Smelting & Refining Co.* (N.J. Ch.) 111 Atl. 376.

The remedy at law by an action for breach of contract against the city is not adequate. In the first place, it does not appear that the city, through any properly and lawfully constituted authority, is a party to the conspiracy, and no one except the city council could properly commit a legal breach of plaintiff's contract. In the second place, the injury to plaintiff's business, good will, and trade could not be measured or included in determining the damages in an action at law. For this and other reasons, it is settled law that injunction is the proper remedy. See *Lehigh Structural Steel Co. v. Atlantic Smelting & Refining Co.* (N.J.Ch.) 111 Atl. 376; *Aberthaw Construction Co. v. Cameron*, 194 Mass. 209, 80 N.E. 478, 120 Am. St. Rep. 542.

A preliminary injunction will be granted as prayed for in paragraph 1, except as to the last sentence thereof, which does not appear at this time to be justified upon the present state of the record. Bond in the penalty of $2,000 will be required, conditioned to pay such costs and damages, if any, as the defendants or any one of them may sustain, or as may be awarded against plaintiff in the event this injunction shall be held to have been improvidently awarded.[3]

R AN W HAT SHOP, INC. v. SCULLY.

Supreme Court of Errors of Connecticut. 98 Conn. 1 (1922).

Suit to restrain the defendants from combining and conspiring together to injure the plaintiff's business, and for damages, brought to and tried by the Superior Court in Fairfield County, Maltbie, J.; facts found and judgment rendered for the defendants, and appeal by the plaintiff. *Error and judgment reversed.*

The process of the manufacture of fur felt hats is divided into two parts: one, the production of the "hats in the rough," called the "making," the other, the completion of the "hats in the rough" ready for wear, called the "finishing." Many factories carry on both branches of the manufacture, while some confine their business to the "making," and some to the "finishing." The workers employed in these processes are known as "makers," and "finishers," and, in addition, certain women who work in the finishing shops are known as "trimmers;" each of these classes follows what is practically a different craft. The business is largely unionized, and the local unions are made up of those who follow one of these crafts. These crafts are bound together by joint interests, and together make up one trade, and all the unions are affiliated as the "United Hat-

---

[3] An appeal was taken from this decree but dismissed as moot in O'Brien v. Fackenthal, 284 Fed. 850 (6th cir. 1922). After remand a supplemental bill was filed in which it was made to appear that there were issues still alive, whereupon an injunction was ordered, which was sustained upon appeal. O'Brien v. Fackenthal, 5 Fed.(2d) 389 (6th cir. 1925), commented on in 39 Harv. Law Rev. 101 (1925).

Accord: McFarland Co. v. O'Brien, 6 Fed.(2d) 1016 (N.D. Ohio 1925) Moore v. Whitty, 299 Pa. 58, 149 Atl. 93 (1930).

Upon the general question of jurisdictional strikes, see *infra,* p. 319.

ters of North America," a voluntary association, with some ten thousand members and about thirty unions.

The defendant Local No. 10 is a union of "makers" employed in Danbury and vicinity, of which defendant Jeremiah Sculley is president and defendant John O'Hara is secretary. The defendant Local No. 11 is a union of "finishers" employed in Danbury and vicinity, of which defendant Cornelius McCue is president and Hugh Shalvoy is secretary. The defendant Local No. 15 is a union of "makers" employed in Norwalk and vicinity. The defendant Local No. 16 is a union of "finishers" employed in Norwalk and vicinity, of which Charles Lynch is president and the defendant Royal Raymond is secretary. Each of these unions is a voluntary association.

The defendant Michael Green is the national president of the United Hatters of North America, and the defendant Martin Lawlor is the national secretary and treasurer of that organization.

Prior to June, 1919, union manufacturers of "hats in the rough" were not restricted by any rule or custom from selling that product to any finisher whether or not he conducted a union shop, and neither rule nor custom of the unions gave union "finishing" shops any preference. Union workmen in "finishing" shops, however, would not, and by the custom of the unions were forbidden to, work on "hats in the rough" which were produced in nonunion "making" shops. * * *

In the spring of 1919, both union and nonunion shops had difficulty in purchasing sufficient "hats in the rough" to fill their orders. Because of this lack of material, union "finishing" shops were either unable to, or were threatened with inability to, operate full time. Complaints of this were made to the officers of the United Hatters of North America, and these came to the attention of the defendants Green and Lawlor, as president and secretary and treasurer, respectively, of that organization. In the effort to secure an adequate supply of "hats in the rough" for the union "finishing" shops, defendants Green and Lawlor instructed orally and in writing the officers of local unions, including those in Danbury, to visit and inform the union "making" shops that in their judgment union "finishing" shops should be given preference over nonunion "finishing" shops in the matter of supplying "hats in the rough," and that no shipments of these should be made to the latter until the needs of the union "finishing" shops had been satisfied. These instructions came in due course to the officers of Locals Nos. 10 and 11 at Danbury, but these unions never as a body took action thereon.

Defendants Sculley and O'Hara, president and secretary of Local No. 10, singly or together, either in person or by other means of communication, gave these instructions to the officers of six or seven of the union "making" shops in Danbury, and these officers stated to these shops the purport of the instructions they had received. The instructions of Green and Lawlor were not confined to this State and were not directed against any particular manufacturer. Their immediate purpose was to secure sufficient "hats in the rough" for union "finishing" shops, and thereby to secure steady employment for the members of the affiliated unions, the natural effect of these instructions, if carried out, would be to make it more difficult, if not in some instances impossible, for nonunion "finishing" shops to secure sufficient "hats in the rough" with which they could fill their orders and keep their shops open, and to cause breaches of contract between union "making" shops and nonunion "finishing" shops; and all this defendants Green, Lawlor, Sculley and O'Hara knew, or ought as reasonable men to have known. The giving of these instructions was a reasonable means to the end purposed and they were adopted in good faith

On June 24th, 1919, plaintiff had orders for 6,200 dozen hats for fall delivery, their value being between $300,000 and $400,000, and about ninety per cent thereof were from customers outside the State and called for delivery outside the State. It had contracted for substantially enough "hats in the rough" to take care of its needs in filling its own order; its contracts being about equally divided between union and nonunion shops. The plaintiff and its predecessor had for a number of years purchased a considerable number of "hats in the rough" from George McLachlan, who operated a union "making" shop in Danbury. Prior to June 24th, 1919, plaintiff had ordered from McLachlan a very considerable number of these hats, which he had accepted for fall delivery, but delivery for a large part of these orders had not at this time been made. On said day Sculley and O'Hara, pursuant to the instructions received from Green and Lawlor, visited McLachlan and stated to him the purport of the instructions.

At this interview it appeared that McLachlan had a lot of "hats in the rough" ready for shipment to plaintiff. McLachlan inquired if he should deliver these, and Sculley and O'Hara asked if he had any others ready for shipment for plaintiff in the shop, and ascertaining that there were none, told McLachlan that he might deliver the hats ready for shipment. They did not ask him whether he had accepted orders from the plaintiff which were not filled, nor were they informed, nor did they have knowledge as to this, but from the purport of the conversation and McLachlan's conduct they might, as reasonable men, have so inferred.

A few days later McLachlan asked and received permission to deliver to plaintiff a few dozen more of hats which were of a special kind. McLachlan delivered to plaintiff no other hats than these after this time upon its orders.

Sculley and O'Hara used no threats to McLachlan, but he obeyed the instructions and breached his contract with plaintiff because of his knowledge of the power of the unions to embarrass him in the operation of his factory, and his fear that they would do so and exact a penalty from him. McLachlan would, without these instructions, have filled these orders, but he was not sorry to have a reason for breaching his contract with plaintiff, because he could obtain for the undelivered hats a price higher than the contract price. A few days after McLachlan ceased shipments to plaintiff, Wimpfheimer, president and treasurer of plaintiff, secured an interview with Sculley and O'Hara, and asked that McLachlan be permitted to continue filling plaintiff's orders, but they refused to grant this. In the course of the interview, Sculley and O'Hara either learned that McLachlan had in his shop accepted and unfilled orders from the plaintiff, or heard statements which would have indicated to any reasonable person that this was the case. A few days after this action was begun, plaintiff sought to have McLachlan resume shipments to it, and thereupon McLachlan asked O'Hara for such permission, but he refused to give it. By reason of McLachlan's breach of his contract plaintiff suffered a very considerable loss.

The court reached the following conclusions: (1) The purpose of the defendants Green and Lawlor in giving these instructions, and of defendants Sculley, OHara and McCue in carrying them out as they did, was legitimate. (2) The giving and carrying out of these instructions was a reasonable means to accomplish that purpose. (3) Any incidental interference with the contract rights of the plaintiff arising out of the acceptance of its orders by McLachlan was therefore justifiable. (4) The defendants are not then liable to the plaintiff for any damage it may have suffered by reason of that interference. * * *

WHEELER, C.J.: * * * The single remaining question before us is stated in plaintiff's brief as follows: "It is unlawful to knowingly induce a breach of contract either with intent to injure a third party or to secure a benefit for oneself." The facts found show that defendants Sculley and O'Hara were the agents of Green and Lawlor throughout this transaction. They further show that defendants Green, Lawlor, Sculley and O'Hara intentionally procured, by means of these instructions, the breach of McLachlan's contracts with plaintiff, when Sculley and O'Hara had personal knowledge of their existence and Green and Lawlor had knowledge through that of their agents Sculley and O'Hara, for the purpose of securing for union "finishing" shops an adequate supply of "hats in the rough," so as to secure to the members of the affiliated unions steady employment. It thus appears that these defendants, who represented these unions, knew of these contracts when they procured their breach, and that their purpose was to benefit the unions and their members.

The plaintiff was free to make any legal contract with McLachlan, and he with the plaintiff, which did not wrongfully infringe upon the legal rights of others or offend against public rights, and their liberty to so contract was a right which our law gave and guaranteed to each. When the plaintiff and McLachlan entered into their contracts, each acquired the right to have the other fulfil them according to their terms, or to obtain damages for the failure to fulfil. These were the duties which the contracts imposed on each, and these were the rights which they created. Such contract relation gave to each a property right in the contracts, and any intentional interference with the rights of either by a third party was an interference with his rights of property, and if intentionally done by one not having equal or superior rights or by one knowing of this contract relation, it was a wrongful interference subjecting him who procured the breach to an action for the damage resulting from the tort.

When one acting under a right of his own interferes with an existing contract in ignorance of it, he has committed no wrong. The mere fact that his act injures another does not create a liability, for he was acting within his own rights and did not intentionally or wrongfully cause the injuries. And where one acting under an equal or a superior right causes such injury to a contract relation, he will not be liable for resulting damage, for he had a right to do what he did. Procuring the breach of a contract without knowledge of it, or acting in the exercise of an equal or a superior right, is acting with just cause or excuse, and, when this appears, it is a justification for what would otherwise be an actionable wrong.

Sculley and O'Hara acted with personal knowledge of plaintiff's contracts. Green and Lawlor acted with knowledge, because their agents, Sculley and O'Hara, obtained this knowledge while carrying out the instructions of their principals, Green and Lawlor. Their attempted justification is that they acted in the exercise of an equal or superior right to that of the plaintiff, and that the injury to it was incidental to their exercise of their undoubted right, and consequently was *damnum absque injuria*. Their justification is that they sought to benefit those whom they represent by securing for them the means for steady employment. The purpose was legitimate and commendable, but it could not be carried out in disregard of the rights of plaintiff, which were existent before this purpose was conceived. The plaintiff's rights were superior to those of these defendants. A justification for injury to another cannot rest upon the violation of his existing rights which he who justifies knew of. Though the defendants' purpose was commendable, the means used to carry it through cannot be justified. The knowingly procuring McLachlan to breach his contracts with plaintiff were wrongful acts of defendants and done intentionally by them, and for the resulting damage they are liable. "The gist of the action is not the intent to injure, but to interfere without justification with plaintiff's contractual rights with knowledge thereof." *Lamb v. Cheney & Son.* 227 N.Y. 418, 422, 125 N.E. 817; *Quinn v. Leathem,* L.R. [1901] App. Cas. 495.

The trial court held that liability for procuring the breach of these contracts would have arisen had their breach been the end sought, but when the end sought was the securing of work for the members of the union and the breach of the contracts was an incident following the carrying out of this legitimate purpose, no liability would arise. If such a doctrine were law, a third person or combination of persons could compel the breach of any contract and justify by saying to him who had suffered great loss because of the breach of his contract: "We did not do it to cause you injury or to breach your contract, but to improve our financial condition; the breach of your contract was a mere incident to the fulfilment of our purpose." The inviolability of contracts would then be an incident to the self-interest of men. It may be that an occasional authority has announced this doctrine, but an extended examination satisfies us that the authorities generally upon this subject are not in accord with it and are in accord with the conclusions to which we have come.

The intentional procurement of the breach of an existent contract, if done with knowledge of the contract and without just cause or excuse, makes him who causes the breach liable for resulting damage; and this is so even though he acted in promoting his own legitimate interests. * * *

There is error as to Green, Lawlor, Sculley and O'Hara, the judgment as to them is reversed, and the Superior Court is ordered to enter its judgment for $5,139.75, with interest from January 1st, 1920, against defendants Green, Lawlor, Sculley and O'Hara; as to the other defendants there is no error.

In this opinion CURTIS and BURPEE, J.J, concurred. GAGER, J., concurred in the result, but died before the opinion was written.

BEACH J. (dissenting): If the defendants named in the rescript had acted for their personal benefit, and without any better justification than their own rights as individuals to induce McLachlan to break his contract with the plaintiff, I should concur. But in fact they are officers of a trades union comprising makers and finishers of hats, and as such they represented their union finishers who were short of work, and for whose benefit they acted, and they also represented the right of the union makers employed at McLachlan's shop to induce him to give priority of deliveries to union finishing shops.

It seems to me that the fundamental question in the case is whether these union makers had a right to "induce" McLachlan to give priority of deliveries to the shops where their fellow-unionists were employed and in need of work. Practically speaking, McLachlan yielded because of the fear of a contest with the United Hatters, and the prospect of a strike in the background; and the question may be tested by inquiry whether the makers employed in his shop had a legal right to strike in order to compel him to give priority in deliveries to union finishing shops. It must be conceded that if McLachlan had not been under contract to make deliveries elsewhere, the joint interests of the makers and finishers and their joint membership in the United Hatters would have justified such a strike, and the next question is whether the existence of such a contract, coupled with the knowledge of it, takes away the legal right to strike for the purpose stated. I think not, because the duty to refrain from inducing one party to break his contract with the other is purely passive. In the Hohfeldian terminology it is a "no-right" rather than a "duty."

A stranger to a contract may not, for his own benefit and without legal justification, knowingly induce a breach of it, but he is not bound to assist in its performance. And so the union makers employed in Mc-

Lachlan's shop were not bound, in the absence of such an agreement on their part, to continue to make hats in order that the plaintiff might remain undisturbed in the enjoyment of its contract with their employer. Although they knew of the contract, they might strike for any reason for which they might lawfully strike in the absence of such a contract. Otherwise, employers of labor could extinguish the possibility of lawful strikes by posting notices of their outstanding contract obligations.

And since the makers themselves could lawfully strike to compel McLachlan to give priority in deliveries to union finishing shops, whether they knew of his contract with the plaintiff or not, it follows that their representatives could lawfully induce McLachlan to do so, whether they knew of the contract or not.

For this reason it seems clear to me that the defendants' right to induce McLachlan to give priority in deliveries to union finishing shops was in law equal to the plaintiff's right of property in his contract; and I feel compelled to dissent.[4]

STILLWELL THEATRE, INC., v. KAPLAN.

New York Court of Appeals. 259 N.Y. 405, 182 N.E. 63 (1932).

POUND C.J.: These are labor cases in which injunctions have been granted at the suit of proprietors of moving picture theaters, enjoining defendant during the existence of contracts between the Empire State Motion Picture Operators' Union, Inc., and each of the respective plaintiffs from doing any act or acts calculated to induce or cause a breach of such contracts; from picketing and patrolling the streets in front of or near the respective theaters, and from committing any act or acts which are calculated to or apt to harm, harass, or embarrass the respective plaintiffs in the conduct of their business, and which are calculated to cause persons desiring to enter the theaters to refrain from so doing; from exhibiting any sign or signs and distributing any notices in front of or near said theaters; from suggesting to any person or persons the boycotting of plaintiffs' business; from interfering in any manner above set forth or in any other manner or by any other means with the business, custom, or trade of the plaintiffs, or making any false statements respecting the plaintiffs or the plaintiffs' business; from accosting, coercing,

---

[4] For comment on the case, see: 32 Yale Law Jour. 171 (1922); 71 Univ. of Pa. Law Rev. 138 (1923).

Cf. Niles-Bement-Pond Co. v. Iron Moulder's Union. 246 Fed. 851 (S.D. Ohio, 1917), rev'd on other grounds in 258 Fed. 408 (6th cir. 1918); Dail-Overland Co. v. Willys-Overland, 263 Fed. 171 (N.D. Ohio, 1919); Vonnegut Machinery Co. v. Toledo Machine & Tool Co., 263 Fed. 192 (N.D. Ohio, 1920); Carroll v. C. & O. Coal Agency Co., 124 Fed. 305 (4th cir. 1903); Snow Iron Works v. Chadwick, 227 Mass. 382. 116 N.E. 801 (1917).

intimidating, or in any manner interfering with persons employed by the plaintiffs or seeking to enter their employ, from entering or continuing in such employment, or doing any other illegal act in reference thereto.

The word "defendant," as hereinafter used, refers to labor union Local 306.

The real controversy is between Local 306 of the International Alliance of Theatrical Stage Employees and Moving Picture Machine Operators' Union of the United States and Canada, affiliated with the American Federation of Labor, and a member of the State Federation of Labor and of the Central Trades and Labor Council of Greater New York and the Empire State Motion Picture Operators' Union, Incorporated, which is not affiliated with those organizations nor with any other labor union or body. Each plaintiff made a contract with the latter union whereby plaintiff is obliged to employ none other than members of that union as motion picture operators at such plaintiff's theater, which contract ran from September 1, 1930, to August 31, 1931. Defendant picketed plaintiffs' theaters with a sign which read: "Owners of this theatre refuse to employ members of Motion Picture Operators' Union Local 306, affiliated with the American Federation of Labor." The picketing was peaceful; not accompanied by any acts of violence, trespass, or intimidation, and the sign truly stated the fact. Unquestionably defendant in picketing these three theaters was actuated by a desire to improve labor conditions as to wages, hours, number of employees and conditions of work, although incidental disadvantage to the employer might result. "Resulting injury [from lawful picketing] is incidental and must be endured." *(Exchange Bakery & Restaurant, Inc. v. Rifkin,* 245 N.Y. 260, 263.)

While the trial court made findings in all three actions that a sign printed in Jewish characters and carried by the pickets was misleading in that it conveyed the idea that union labor was not employed on the premises and also that the purpose of the picketing was in part to destroy plaintiff's business, the judgment was based solely on the ground that the picketing was illegal because its purpose was to induce or cause a breach of the contract between the plaintiffs respectively and the rival union. The Appellate Division, unanimously affirming the judgment, rested its decision on the same ground. It said: "The evidence amply justified the finding that the Empire State Motion Picture Operators' Union is a *bona fide* labor union; that there were valid, binding, and subsisting contracts of employment for definite periods of time between the plaintiffs and that union at the time the defendant conducted its picketing of the theaters of the plaintiffs, and that this picketing was conducted with knowledge on the part of the defendant of the existence of such contracts. Such orderly picketing with truthful placards was wrongful, although the means employed were otherwise lawful, because such acts were indulged in to attain a wrongful and therefore an unlawful purpose, to wit, the breach of contracts of employment for fixed and definite periods of time." (235 App. Div. 738.)

The Court of Appeals has for many years been disposed to leave the parties to peaceful labor disputes unmolested when economic rather than legal questions were involved. The employer, if threatened in his business life by the violence of the unions or by other wrongful acts, might have the aid of the court to preserve himself from damage threatened by recourse to unlawful means, but the right of the workmen to organize to better their condition has been fully recognized. The fact that such action may result in incidental injury to the employer does not in itself constitute a justification for issuing an injunction against such acts. The interests of capital and labor are at times inimical and the courts may not decide controversies between the parties so long as neither resorts to violence, deceit or misrepresentation to bring about desired results. (*National Protective Ass'n v. Cumming*, 170 N.Y. 315; *Paine Lumber Co. v. Neal*, 244 U.S. 459, 471; *Bossert v. Dhuy*, 221 N.Y. 342.) Acts must be legal but they may be legal or illegal according to circumstances.

The case of *Hitchman Coal & Coke Co. v. Mitchell* (245 U.S. 229) has often been cited as authority for the proposition that inducements of a breach of contract for a definite term of employment are illegal, even in the case of solicitation by groups of laborers, but, as the Supreme Court of the United States said of that case in *American Steel Foundries v. Tri-City Central Trades Council* (257 U.S. 184, 211) "the unlawful and deceitful means used [to molest the plaintiff rather than to better the fortunes of the worker] were quite enough to sustain the decision of the court without more." (*Cf. Lamb v. Cheney & Son*, 227 N.Y. 418.) It has never been held by this court that a labor union is without justification in fairly setting forth its claims in a controversy over terms and conditions of employment by sign, handbill, or newspaper advertisement as a legitimate means of economic coercion, nor does the *Hitchman* case so hold, nor is that case a final authority on this point concerning the laws of New York. *Paine Lumber Co. v. Neal, supra.*

The law of the state of New York, as declared by this court, is perhaps more favorable to the defendant than that of the United States Supreme Court or other jurisdictions. The doctrine of the *Hitchman* case as applied to labor disputes by some of our lower courts has never been accepted here, if it has not been specifically rejected. A review of recent cases establishes this fact.

The question whether union tactics, merely persuasive in character, directed to the inducement of a breach of contract for a term are ever justified was expressly reserved in *Exchange Bakery & Restaurant, Inc. v. Rifkin (supra*, p. 267). The court, per Andrews, J., said: "Here, however, we do not need to decide whether where the object of the act is to aid in a labor dispute, there is just cause or excuse for such interference with existing contracts, and if not how specific the contract must be, nor how substantial the term of employment contained therein to permit equity to intervene."

In *Interborough Rapid Transit Co. v. Lavin* (247 N.Y. 65, 79), the court, per Lehman, J., said: "This court has not yet been called upon to decide whether employees may lawfully be urged to make a choice in breach of a definite contract." Of these cases it has been said: "Thus, the judges of a great tribunal indicate their conviction that when dealing with legal problems enmeshed in dynamic social forces, courts ought to decide only the case before them and to remain open to all the wisdom the future may hold." (The Labor Injunction, by Frankfurter & Greene, p. 42.)

In *Nann v. Raimist* (255 N.Y. 307, 314) it was held that it was within the competency of a labor union to announce to the world its thought that another labor union was not dealing with its members in such a way as to promote the interests of organized labor and to persuade by peaceful picketing the employers of such labor to employ the members of the rival union.

In *Steinkritz Amusement Corp. v. Kaplan* (257 N.Y. 294), which was a companion case to these now before us, no opinion was written on this point. The court was divided. A majority held that a broad injunction restraining not only picketing but other acts as well should be modified by striking out the restraining provisions except as to picketing. By abuse of picketing, it was held that the union had forfeited the right to picket. Cardozo, Ch.J., and Lehman, J., were of the opinion that the injunction should be limited to picketing "with an untruthful sign". The injunction was greatly modified although the contract between employer and rival union existed. It was suggested in support of the injunction, as has been held in the cases now before the court, that the right of the defendant peacefully and truthfully to declare to the world that the business practices of the rival union were unjust and that theaters which patronized that union ought not to be patronized by the public had been lost because the plaintiff had a year's contract with the rival union. The answer was that the public had no contract with the employer; that the union addressed itself to the public and that no one was asked to break any contract. The collateral result of the attempted persuasion of the public not to patronize the theater while it employed the members of the rival union might make it unprofitable for the employer to go on with the contract, but to state fairly and truly to the public that the conduct of the employer is socially objectionable to a labor union is no persuasion to break a contract. This court has never undertaken to restrain such conduct, although it has had the opportunity. It has been at pains to avoid doing so. The cases cited *supra* disclose independence of the *Hitchman* doctrine and of the cases which follow and enlarge upon that doctrine. We would be departing from established precedents if we upheld this injunction. We would thereby give to one labor union an advantage over another by prohibiting the use of peaceful and honest persuasion in matters of economic and social rivalry. This might strike a death blow to legitimate labor activities. It is not within the province of the courts to restrain conduct which is within the allowable area of economic conflict.[5]

> *The judgments should be reversed and the complaint dismissed in each case, with costs in all courts.*[6]

Section 2. Inducing Termination of a Relationship.

TENNESSEE CODE, 1932.

§ 8559. **Unlawful to entice away employees.**—It shall be unlawful for any person, knowingly, to hire, contract with, decoy or entice away, directly or indirectly, any one, who is at the time under contract or in the employ of another; and any person so under contract or employ of another, leaving his employ without good and sufficient cause, before the expiration of the time for which he was employed, shall forfeit to the employer all sums due for service already rendered, and be liable for such other damages the employer may reasonably sustain by such violation of contract. (1875, ch. 93, sec. 1.)

§ 8560. **Penalty and damages.**—Any person violating the provisions of the first clause of the preceding section shall be liable to the party who originally was entitled to the services of said employee, by virtue of a previous contract, for such damages as he may reasonably sustain by the loss of the labor of said employee; and, whether he had knowledge of an existing contract or not, if he fails or refuses to discharge the person so hired, or to pay such damages as the original employer may reasonably claim, after he has been notified that the person is under con-

---

[5] The dissenting opinion of O'Brien, J., is omitted.

[6] For a discussion of the case, see: 46 Harv. Law Rev. (1932). Accord: J. H. & S. Theatres v. Fay, 260 N.Y. 315, 183 N.E. 509 (1932); Pleaters & Stitchers Ass'n v. Taft, 131 Misc. 506, 227 N.Y.S. 185. *Contra:* Goyette v. Watson Co., 245 Mass. 577, 140 N.E. 285 (1923); Wolchak v. Wiseman, 145 Misc. 268, 259 N.Y.S. 225 (1932); Esco Operating Co. v. Kaplan, 144 Misc. 646, 258 N.Y.S. 303 (1932); I. J. Fox, Inc. v. Gold, 87 N.Y. Law Jour. 354 (Sup. Ct. 1932); Winthrop Baking Co. v. Bless, 78 N.Y. Law Jour. 42 (Sup. Ct. 1927). *Cf.* Talbot v. Skerstons, 5 Law & Labor, 7 (Sup. Ct. Mass. 1922); Church Shoe Co. v. Turner, 218 Mo. App. 516, 279 S.W. 232 (1926); United Tailors v. Amalgamated Workers, 29 Ohio N.P. 439 (1926); British Columbia Tel. Co. v. Morrison, 29 Brit. Col. 289 (1921). As to the enforceability of the agreement between the employer and the union, see: Roosevelt Amusement Corp. v. Empire State M. P. O. Union, 231 App. Div. 872, 246 N.Y.S. 855 (1930), and Unity Amusement Co. v. Empire State M. P. O. Union, 231 App. Div. 872, 246 N.Y.S. 854 (1930), affirming 144 Misc. 644, 258 N.Y.S. 240 (1930). Compare, also: Citizens L. H. & P. Co. v. Montgomery L. & W. P. Co., 171 Fed. 553 (D. Ala. 1909).

tract, or has violated the contract with such other person, which amount shall be ascertained, and the collection enforced by action for damages before any court or justice of the peace of the county where said violation occurs, or the party violating said section may reside. (*Ib.*, sec. 2, modified.) [1]

---

[1] For similar legislation see: Alabama Code (1928); §§ 3985-3987; Ark. Stats. (1919, Kirby & Castle), § 5960; Fla. Gen. Laws (1927), §§ 7166, 7167; Ga. Penal Code (1926), §§ 123, 125; La. Crim. Stats. (1929, Marr), § 57; Miss. Code (1930), § 900; N.C. Code (1931), §§ 4469, 4470; S.C. Code (1932), § 1314. See also: Tenn. Code (1932), § 7811; Ky. Stats. (1930, Carroll), § 2601. For the reconstruction origin of these statutes, see: Bryan v. State, 44 Ga. 328, 332 (1871).

In Louisiana the statute creates only a penal offense and gives no civil action. Kline v. Eubanks, 109 La. 241, 33 So. 211 (1902); Wolf & Sons v. New Orleans Tailor-Made Pants Co., 113 La. 388, 37 So. 2 (1904). The North Carolina statute and Georgia statutes were originally only applicable to cases where the contract between master and servant was in writing, but were later amended to include oral contracts. Hightower v. State, 72 Ga. 482 (1884); Hudgins v. State, 126 Ga. 639, 55 S.E. 492 (1906); State v. Rice, 76 N.C. 194 (1877). The North Carolina and Mississippi statutes are inapplicable unless the servant has actually entered into the master's service, even though a valid contract may be in existence. Hendricks v. State, 79 Miss. 368, 30 So. 708 (1901); Alford v. Pegues, 92 Miss. 558, 46 So. 76 (1908); Sears v. Whitaker, 136 N.C. 37, 48 S.E. 517 (1904); State v. Holly, 152 N.C. 839, 67 S.E. 53 (1910).

The statutes as applied to inducing a breach of contract between master and servant are constitutional. State v. Nix, 165 Ala. 126, 51 So. 754 (1910); Johns v. Patterson, 138 Ark. 420, 211 S.W. 387 (1919); Rhoden v. State, 161 Ga. 73, 129 S.E. 640 (1925); State v. Hurdle, 113 Miss. 736, 74 So. 681 (1917). The statutes apply to employees. Abingdon Mills v. Grogan, 167 Ala. 146, 52 So. 596 (1910); Hardie-Tynes Mfg. Co. v. Cruse, 189 Ala. 64, 66 So. 597 (1915). *Cf.* Liberty Warehouse Co. v Burley Tobacco, etc., Ass'n, 276 U.S. 71 (1928); Comm. v. Hodges, 137 Ky. 233, 125 S.W. 689 (1910).

In some states the statutes make criminal knowingly employing a servant who has already broken his contract with his former master, where there is no justifiable excuse for such breach. Tarpley v. State, 79 Ala. 271 (1885); Morris v. Neville, 11 Lea 271 (Tenn. 1881). They are, however, commonly interpreted so as to absolve such a defendant of liability. Tucker v. State. 86 Ark. 436, 111 S.W. 275 (1908); Park v. Depriest, 138 Ark. 86, 210 S.W. 777 (1919); Broughton v. State. 114 Ga. 34, 39 S.E. 866 (1901); McAllister v. State, 122 Ga. 744, 50 S.E. 921 (1905); Evans v. State, 121 Miss. 252, 83 So. 167 (1919); Thompson v. Box, 147 Miss. 1, 112 So. 597 (1927); Waldrup v. State. 154 Miss. 646, 122 So. 771 (1929); Hill v. Duckworth, 155 Miss. 484, 124 So. 641 (1929), overruling Armistead v. Chatters, 71 Miss. 509, 15 So. 39 (1893), and Hoole v. Dorroh, 75 Miss. 257, 22 So. 829 (1897); .State v. Holly, *supra. Cf.* Armstrong v. Bishop, 151 Miss. 353, 117 So. 512 (1928); Shaw v. Fisher, 113 S.C. 287, 102 S.E. 325 (1920) A contrary construction of the statute is regarded by these states as making it unconstitutional. Johns v. Patterson, *supra*; Minton v. Early, 183 N.C. 199, 111 S.E. 347 (1922). The statute is not applicable to situations where the first master has given the servant just cause for breaking the contract. Beale v. Yazoo Yarn Mill, 125 Miss. 807, 88 So. 411 (1921); Jordan v. Lewis, 162 Tenn. 653, 39 S.W.(2d) 743 (1931).

The contract between the first master and his servant need not be enforceable State v. Harwood, 104 N.C. 724, 10 S.E. 171 (1889). *Cf.* State v. Anderson, 104 N.C. 771, 10 S.E. 475 (1889). *Contra:* Poston v. Lyerly, 105 S.C. 37, 89 S.E. 392 (1916).

JONAS GLASS CO. v. GLASS BOTTLE BLOWERS' ASSOCIATION.

New Jersey Court of Errors and Appeals. 77 N.J. Eq. 219, 79 Atl. 262 (1910).

On appeal from a decree of the former chancellor advised by Vice-Chancellor Bergen, whose opinion is reported in 72 N.J.Eq. (2 Buch.) 653.

The opinion of the court was delivered by PITNEY, CHANCELLOR:

* * * The final decree that is now under review awards an injunction restraining the defendants as follows:

First. From knowingly and intentionally causing or attempting to cause, by threats, offers of money, payments of money, offering to pay expenses, or by inducement or persuasion, any employe of the complainant under contract to render service to it to break such contract by quitting such service.

Second. From personal molestation of persons willing to be employed by complainant with intent to coerce such persons to refrain from entering such employment.

Third. From addressing persons willing to be employed by complainant, against their will, and thereby causing them personal annoyance, with a view to persuade them to refrain from such employment.

Fourth. From loitering or picketing in the streets or on the highways or public places near the premises of complainant with intent to procure the personal molestation and annoyance of persons employed or willing to be employed by complainant, and with a view to cause persons so employed to refrain from such employment.

Fifth. From entering the premises of the complainant against its will with intent to interfere with its business.

Sixth. From violence, threats of violence, insults, indecent talk, abusive epithets, annoying language, acts or conduct, practiced upon any persons without their consent, with intent to coerce them to refrain from entering the employment of complainant or to leave its employment.

Seventh. From attempting to cause any persons employed by complainant to leave such employment by intimidating or annoying such employes by annoying language, acts or conduct.

Eighth. From causing persons willing to be employed by complainant to refrain from so doing by annoying language, acts or conduct.

Ninth. From inducing, persuading or causing, or attempting to induce, persuade or cause, the employes of complainant to break their contracts of service with complainant or quit their employment.

Tenth. From threatening to injure the business of any corporation, customer or person dealing or transacting business and willing to deal and transact business with the complainant, by making threats in writing or by words for the purpose of coercing such corporation, customer or person against his or its will so as not to deal with or transact business with the complainant.

Each portion of the injunctive relief thus granted is directed to some manifestation of the strife that was carried on by the combined defendants against the complainant. And in each respect the injunction is justified by the evidence in the case.

The employes of complainant referred to in the decree are those who either refused to join the strike or who entered complainant's employ after the strike. With respect to these, it will be observed that the defendants are restrained from using coercion, inducements or persuasion to bring about a termination of the employment, whether the employe be under contract of service or not.

With respect to other persons, not as yet employed but willing to take employment under the complainant, the defendants are restrained from interfering to prevent this by coercion or personal molestation and annoyance; but are not restrained from using mere persuasion in such a case.

There is a restraint against picketing designed to molest and annoy persons employed or willing to be employed.

And there is a restraint against the continuance of the boycott.

It is clear beyond dispute that the complainant has suffered grievously in its property and business through the acts of the defendants, whose continuance is thus prohibited. That the injury to the complainant is irreparable by action at law is likewise clear.

If, therefore, the acts themselves are unlawful and violative of the property rights of the complainant, the injunction is proper.

The conduct of defendants in using coercion in some cases and persuasion in others in order to bring about breaches of the contracts of personal service existing between complainant and some of its employes—defendants having, of course, full notice of the existing employment—was unlawful and actionable, upon well-settled principles. 3 Bl. Com. 142; *Lumley v. Gye,* 2 El. & Bl. 216, 224; *Bowen v. Hall,* 6 Q. B. Div. 333; *Angle v. Chicago, &c., Railway Co.,* 151 U.S. 13.

And the same is true of conduct whose object and purpose were to bring about a termination of the relation of master and servant between the complainant and its employes in cases where there was no binding contract of service, but a mere service at will. *Noice, Administratrix, v. Brown,* 39 N.J. Law (10 Vr.) 569, 572; *Brennan v. United Hatters,* 73 N.J. Law (44 Vr.) 729, 743.

In *Frank & Dugan v. Herold,* 63 N.J. Eq. (18 Dick.) 443, 450, Vice-Chancellor Pitney said that to create the relation of master and servant it is not necessary that there should be a contract in writing, or even verbal, between them to work for any particular length of time; that the relation exists when the one person is willing from day to day to work for another, and that other person desires the labor and makes his business arrangements accordingly.

Whether an action will lie for interference in the relations existing between employer and employe where there is a mere service at will, and where the interference is the result of fair competition in the labor market, is a question mooted but not necessary to be decided in the present case. The defendants were not competitors in the labor market. Their interference had for its immediate object the crippling of the complainant's business. The only semblance of excuse alleged is that defendants desired to bring about "improved labor conditions" in complainant's works; but this object did not warrant the resort to unlawful measures.

Reliance is placed by the defendants upon the "Act relative to persons combining and encouraging other persons to combine." **P.L.** 1883 p. 36; Gen. Stat. p. 2344 pl. 23. The enactment is:

"That it shall not be unlawful for any two or more persons to unite, combine or bind themselves by oath, covenant, agreement, alliance or otherwise, to persuade, advise, or encourage, by peaceable means, any person or persons to enter into any combination for or against leaving or entering into the employment of any person, persons or corporation."

In *Mayer v. Journeymen Stonecutters' Asso.*, 47 N.J. Eq. (2 Dick.) 519, 531, Vice-Chancellor Green apparently treated this act as legalizing private injuries. And in *Cumberland Glass Manufacturing Co. v. Glass Bottle Blowers' Asso.*, 59 N.J. Eq. (14 Dick.) 49, 53, Vice-Chancellor Reed construed it as permitting the adoption of peaceable measures for inducing workmen to quit or to refuse to enter an employment. Whatever may have been the purpose of its framer, there are, as we think, constitutional obstacles in the way of giving the act so extensive a force. The rights of enjoying and defending life and liberty, acquiring, possessing and protecting property, and pursuing and obtaining safety and happiness, are declared by our constitution to be unalienable. N.J. Const., art. 1 pl. 1. No act of the legislature is to be construed as infringing upon these rights unless its language plainly and clearly requires such a construction. If its language so reads, it is to the extent indicated unconstitutional and void. The act of 1883 is, as we think, properly to be treated as merely rendering the combination no longer indictable; in effect, as repealing the rule laid down by the supreme court of this state in *State v. Donaldson,* 32 N.J. Law (3 Vr.) 151. It does not legitimize an invasion of private rights nor prevent the party injured from having full redress. Its proper scope is indicated in the opinion of Vice-Chancellor Pitney in *Frank & Dugan v. Herold,* 63 N.J. Eq. (18 Dick.) 443, 447, 448.

So much of the decree as awards an injunction to restrain the defendants from using coercive measures to prevent the flow of labor to complainant's works is likewise proper. In *Jersey City Printing Co. v. Cassidy,* 63 N.J. Eq. (18 Dick.) 759, 765, Vice-Chancellor Stevenson recognized and enforced the right of an employer to an injunction to prevent undue interference with those who wish to come to him for employment. It is principally upon this ground that injunctions against what is known as picketing have been sustained in this and other jurisdictions.

So much of the decree as is directed against the continuance of the boycott is plainly justified by the evidence, and accords with the law.

Barr v. Essex Trades Council, 53 N.J. Eq. (8 Dick.) 101; *Martin v. McFall,* 65 N.J. Eq. (20 Dick.) 91; *Temperton v. Russell* (1893), 1 Q.B. Div. 715; *Quinn v. Leathem* (1901), A.C. 495.

> *The decree under review should be affirmed, with costs.*

* * *

GARRISON, J. (dissenting) :

In so far as the decree appealed from directs that the defendants be enjoined from the peaceable persuasion of persons who are not under any contract to serve the complainant, I think the court below was in error, and that to that extent its decree should be reversed.

I am requested by Justice Swayze and by Judge Bogert to say that they concur in the foregoing view.[2]

For affirmance—THE CHANCELLOR, CHIEF-JUSTICE, REED, TRENCHARD, PARKER, VOORHEES, VREDENBURGH, VROOM, GREEN, GRAY—10.

For reversal—GARRISON, SWAYZE, MINTURN, BOGERT—4.[3]

THACKER COAL CO. v. BURKE.

Supreme Court of West Virginia. 59 W. Va. 253, 53 S.E. 161 (1906).

* * *

BRANNON, J.: The Thacker Coal and Coke Company filed a declaration in trespass on the case in the circuit court of Mingo county against Charles Burke and five others for damage for enticing servants from the plaintiff's service, which declaration upon demurrer was dismissed, and the company sued out a writ of error.

Certain legal principles control the case. In *Transportation Co. v. Oil Co.,* 50 W. Va. 611, we find it stated, on authority there given, that "If one wantonly and maliciously, whether for his own benefit or not, induces a person to violate his contract with a third person to the injury of that third person, it is actionable." * * *

The first count of the declaration alleges that the company is owner and operator of a coal mine, and was engaged on the 8th day of August, 1901, in the business of mining coal from the mine; that in order to carry on the business it was necessary for the plaintiff to employ, and it did employ, a large number of men to work in the mine, who were engaged in the company's service in working the mine and loading coal on railroad cars for shipment to parties with whom the plaintiff had contracts to furnish coal; that the defendants well knowing these facts, but contriving and wickedly and maliciously intending to injure the plaintiff

---

[2] The dissenting opinion of Minturn, J., is omitted.

[3] Accord: Haskins v. Royster, 70 N.C. 601 (1874). *Contra:* Rogers v. Evarts, 17 N.Y.S. 264 (1891), aff'd sub. nom. Reynolds v. Everett, 67 Hun. 294, 22 N.Y.S. 306 (1893), aff'd in 144 N.Y. 189, 39 N.E. 72 (1894).

in its business, unlawfully, wrongfully, maliciously, without justifiable cause, without the consent and against the will of the plaintiff, molested, obstructed and hindered the plaintiff in its said business "by wilfully, wrongfully and maliciously persuading, inducing, enticing and procuring said servants of the plaintiff, employed as aforesaid, to absent themselves and depart from the plaintiff's service;" that on pretext and by reason of such persuasion, enticement and procuration the said servants on the date aforesaid, without license and against the will and consent of the plaintiff, wrongfully absented themselves and departed from said service, and continued to do so; that the plaintiff was unable to employ other servants to work in its mine in the place of the servants so enticed away, and was thereby prevented from prosecuting and carrying on its business as extensively and profitably as it could and would have done, had not its servants been induced and enticed by the defendants to quit its service.

The first count does not, in words, state an express contract for service between employer and employee. By the language used in the books a contract must exist. This count says the miners were *"employed"* by the plaintiff and in actual service. Now, if the law gives action for enticement of a servant, it is not conceivable that a third person can maliciously entice away a lot of employes, simply because there was no contract fixing term of service. The relation of master and servant exists. In such case there is a contract recognized by law, an implied contract by which the employee can recover for his service. By entering such service the employee agrees, contracts to work. It is no difference that he can quit when he pleases. In *Walker v. Cronin,* 107 Mass. 555, was such a count and the court held it good. *Frank v. Herold,* 63 N.J. Eq. 443, meets this objection. It says: "To make out the relation of master and servant, it is not necessary that there be any written, or even verbal, contract between the parties to work for any particular length of time, but the relation exists where one person is willing to work for another from day to day, and that other desires the labor and makes his business arrangements accordingly. Employers, where third parties interfere with their employes against the latter's consent, and endeavor by unlawful means to induce them to quit work, have a right to sue for relief." In *Chipley v. Atkinson,* 28 Fla. 206, 11 Am. St. R. 367, it was held that an action for procuring discharge of a servant could be maintained though no time of service was fixed. The court said that so long as the servant chose to continue another person could not interfere, and "neither the fact that the term of service interrupted is not for a fixed period nor the fact that there is not a right of action against the person who is induced or influenced to terminate the service, or who refuses to perform his agreement, is, of itself a bar of action against a third person maliciously and wantonly procuring the termination of or a refusal to perform the agreement." In *Vegelahn v. Guntner,* 167 Mass. 92, 57 Am. St. R. 443, it is held unlawful to conspire to prevent employes from continuing in service though there is no fixed period of service. This count is interpreted as alleging a subsisting contract between the company and its servants in process of execution. Even where there is a full right of competition, where one party does an act hurtful to another, even though it be maliciously done, we held it to be justified and not actionable, except where it produced the breach of a contract. But we said that if there was a contract between a competitor and his customers in trade, any action by a third person causing a breach of that contract, between its parties, was wrongful action, and subject to an action for damages, even though it was done for the benefit of the interfering party in the lawful competition of trade. We held that the advancement of the interest of the third party for self-preservation in trade would not justify his causing one of the parties to that contract to break it. *Transportation Co. v. Oil Co.,* 50 W. Va. 611. A party cannot have a justifiable cause to instigate, to move, the breach of a contract between master and servant. We repeat that the law says that where there is such a contract and a third party causes its violation, he is liable to an action. We do not have to say whether if the interference is without malice it is actionable, since the declaration avers a knowledge by the defendant of the existence of the contract, and avers that they maliciously and wrongfully caused its breach. We do not deny the principle that a man may do an act damaging another, even maliciously, when he has legal excuse or justification therefor; but we say that when his action, with knowledge on his part of a contract, causes, by intention, a breach of that contract, he is liable to damages even though he acts for the promotion of his own interest. But in the present case the declaration avers that the defendants had no justification. It does not intimate that their action was moved by a purpose to benefit their own business, their own trade, their own interest in any shape. On the contrary it avers that their action was characterized by a wilful intent to injure the plaintiff without justifiable cause. If they had justifiable cause for their action the declaration does not speak it, and we are governed, on demurrer, by the declaration. Therefore, we hold that the first count of the declaration states a cause of action. We, however, say that it is defective in not specifying the servants who were enticed.

The second count alleges that the plaintiff to secure miners from other states made special written contracts with certain miners, to-wit: "William Linder and eight others, residents of North Carolina, whereby these miners agree to come to plaintiff and enter into service and engage in digging and shipping coal from its mine at a certain fixed rate per ton," specifying the rate, and that the company paid their fares of $11.50 each from North Carolina to the mine under contract with the miners that the fares were to be repaid the plaintiff out of the wages earned by the miners in mining for the plaintiff; that on the arrival near the mine the defendants, knowing of such contract, wrongfully, maliciously and with unlawful purpose to injure the business of the plaintiff and against the consent of the plaintiff, induced and enticed said miners to break their several contracts of service and refuse to enter the service of the plaintiff according to the written contract, and persuaded and induced and enticed them to depart, and that by reason of said persuasion and enticement said miners, engaged under said written contract, wholly failed and refused to perform their contracts and enter the service of the plaintiff, and immediately departed from the place where they were employed to work without having entered the service of the plaintiff and without having paid the plaintiff the money advanced for said railroad fare, and that none of the miners have returned to work in the said mine. Under the principles stated above this count shows a good cause of action.

A third count alleges that the plaintiff being such operator of a coal mine made a written contract with Samuel Bowean whereby Bowean contracted to mine for the plaintiff five hundred tons of coal, and Bowean had entered upon the performance of the contract, and that the defendants knowing of such contract, unlawfully, wrongfully, maliciously and with unlawful purpose to injure the business of the plaintiff, induced and enticed Bowean to break and disregard the contract, and that Bowean, by reason of such enticement, broke and refused to execute the contract. Under principles above stated this count shows a good cause of action.

A fourth count says that the plaintiff, being owner and operator of such coal mine, made special written contracts with Alvin Hunter and other persons named, whereby each one of them obligated himself to mine for the plaintiff a certain fixed amount of coal at a specified rate per ton; that said Hunter and others had actually started upon the performance of their contracts, that the defendants well knowing thereof, contriving and falsely and maliciously intending to injure, vex, harass, oppress, impoverish and wholly ruin the plaintiff in its business, unlawfully and maliciously did agree, confederate, combine and form themselves into a conspiracy to persuade, entice and procure Hunter and others named to violate, break and wholly disregard their contracts with the plaintiff; that the defendants having so conspired and confederated under the name of the "United Mine Workers of America," contriving and intending as aforesaid, in pursuance and execution of their conspiracy, on a day named, unlawfully, wantonly, wrongfully and maliciously, without justifiable cause, and against the will of the plaintiff, molested, obstructed and hindered the plaintiff in its business of mining and shipping coal by wilfully, wantonly, wrongfully and maliciously persuading, enticing and procuring Hunter and the others named to break, violate and disregard their contracts, and that on pretext and because of such persuasion, Hunter and others, against the will, and without the consent of the plaintiff, without cause, violated their contracts by refusing to continue their work of mining coal as required by their contracts, and have not performed their contracts. Under principles above stated this Count shows a good cause of action. *Employing Club v. Doctor Blosser Co.,* 50 S.E. 353.

The defendants rely on Code of 1899, p. 1053, section 14, reading as follows: "Nor shall any person or persons or combination of persons by force, threats, menace or intimidation of any kind, prevent or attempt to prevent from working in or about any mine, any person or persons who have the lawful right to work in or about the same, and who desire so to work; but this provision shall not be so construed as to prevent any two or more persons from associating themselves together under the name of Knights of Labor, or any other name they may desire, for any lawful purpose, or from using moral suasion or lawful argument, to induce any one not to work on and about any mine." This statute is a penal, criminal statute; for it makes the acts in it specified unlawful, and by section 17 imposes a punishment. This is a criminal act. It does not pretend to create rights between individuals. It prohibits certain acts, and the proviso simply curtails the scope of the enactment by saying that the enacting clause shall not be construed to impair any right, already existing, if existing, to join the organization therein specified or use moral suasion. It is only a curb upon the enactment. It does not affirmatively grant, create or originate those rights. It does not make them lawful, if before unlawful. And could the Legislature authorize any person to violate a contract?

We, therefore, reverse the judgment, overrule the demurrer, except as to the first count, and remand the case to the circuit court for further proceedings, with leave to amend the first count of the declaration.

Reversed.[4]

HITCHMAN COAL CO. v. MITCHELL,

Supreme Court of the United States. 245 U.S. 229 (1917).

MR. JUSTICE PITNEY delivered the opinion of the court.

This was a suit in equity, commenced October 24, 1907, in the United States Circuit (afterwards District) Court for the Northern District of West Virginia, by the Hitchman Coal & Coke Company, a corporation organized under the laws of the State of West Virginia, against certain citizens of the State of Ohio, sued individually and also as officers of the United Mine Workers of America. Other non-citizens of plaintiff's State were named as defendants but not served with process. Those who were served and who answered the bill were T. L. Lewis, Vice President of the U. M. W. A. and of the International Union U. M. W. A.; William Green, D. H. Sullivan, and "George" W. Savage, (his correct Christian name is Gwilym), respectively President, Vice President, and Secretary-Treasurer of District No. 6, U. M. W. A.; and A. R. Watkins, John Zelenka, and Lee Rankin, respectively President, Vice President and Secretary-Treasurer of Sub-district No. 5 of District No. 6.

Plaintiff owns about 5,000 acres of coal lands situate at or near Benwood, in Marshall County, West Virginia, and within what is known as the "Pan Handle District" of that State, and operates a coal mine thereon, employing between 200 and 300 men, and having an annual output, in

---

[4] *Cf.* Baldwin Lumber Co. v. Internat'l Brotherhood, etc., 91 N.J. Eq. 240, 109 Atl. 147 (1920).

and before 1907, of about 300,000 tons. * * * The general object of the bill was to obtain an injunction to restrain defendants from interfering with the relations existing between plaintiff and its employees in order to compel plaintiff to "unionize" the mine. * * *

The District Court based its decision upon two grounds: (1) That the organization known as the United Mine Workers of America, and its branches, as conducted and managed at the time of the suit and for many years before, was a common-law conspiracy in unreasonable restraint of trade, and also and especially a conspiracy against the rights of non-union miners in West Virginia; and (2) That the defendants, in an effort to compel the plaintiff to enter into contractual relations with the Union relating to the employment of labor and the production of coal, although having knowledge of express contracts existing between plaintiff and its employees which excluded relations with the Union, endeavored by unlawful means to procure a breach of these contracts by the employees.

A brief recital of previous transactions between the parties becomes material. The Union is a voluntary and unincorporated association which was organized in the year 1890 in the States of Ohio and Indiana, and afterwards was extended to other States. It is made up of national or "international," district, sub-district, and local unions. District No. 6 comprises the coal districts of Ohio and the Panhandle of West Virginia. Sub-district No. 5 of that district comprises five counties and parts of counties in Ohio, and the Panhandle.

The answering defendants were and are active and influential members—leaders—of the Union, as well as officers. Savage, Lewis, and Sullivan have been members from its formation in 1890, and have held important offices in it and attended the national conventions. The others are long-time members, and possessed an influence indicated by the offices they held, but not limited to the duties of those offices.

From 1897 to 1906 what were known as joint interstate conferences were held annually or biennially between officials of the Union and representatives of the operators in the "Central Competitive Field" (which includes Western Pennsylvania, Ohio, Indiana, and Illinois, but not West Virginia), for the purpose of agreeing upon the scale of wages and the conditions of employment in that field. In addition there were occasional conferences of the same character affecting other States and districts.

Plaintiff's mine is within the territorial limits of Sub-district No. 5 of District No. 6. Coal-mining operations were commenced there in the early part of the year 1902, and the mine was operated "non-union" until April, 1903, when, under threats from the Union officials, including defendants Watkins and Sullivan, that a certain unionized mine in Ohio, owned by the same proprietors, would be closed down if the men at the Hitchman were not allowed to organize, plaintiff consented to the unionization of the latter mine. This went into effect on the 1st of April, 1903, and upon the very next day the men were called out on strike because of a disagreement with the company as to the basis upon which mining should be paid for. The strike continued until May 23, requiring plaintiff to cease operations and preventing it from fulfilling its contracts, the most important of which was one for the daily supply of engine coal to the Baltimore & Ohio Railroad at a coaling station adjoining the mine. The financial loss to plaintiff was serious. The strike was settled and the men resumed work upon the basis of a modification of the official mining scale applicable to the Hitchman mine.

Again, in the spring of 1904, there was difficulty in renewing the scale. A temporary scale, agreed upon between operators and miners for the month of April, 1904, was signed in behalf of the Hitchman Company on the 18th of April. Two days later the men at the Hitchman struck, and the mine remained idle for two months, during which time plaintiff sustained serious losses in business and was put to heavy expense in obtaining coal from other sources to fill its contract with the Baltimore & Ohio Railroad Company. The strike was settled by the adoption of the official scale for the Panhandle District, with amendatory local rules for the Hitchman mine.

After this there was little further trouble until April 1, 1906, when a disagreement arose between the Union and an association of operators with which plaintiff was not connected—the association being in fact made up of its competitors—about arranging the terms of the scale for the ensuing two years. At the same time a similar disagreement arose between the operators and the Union officials in the Central Competitive Field. The result was a termination of the interstate conferences and a failure to establish any official scale for the ensuing two years, followed by a widespread strike, or a number of concurrent strikes, involving the most of the bituminous coal-producing districts. There was absolutely no grievance or ground of disagreement at the Hitchman mine, beyond the fact that the mining scale expired by its own terms on March 31, and the men had not received authority from the Union officials either to renew it or to agree to a new one in its place. Plaintiff came to an understanding with the local union to the effect that if its men would continue at work the company would pay them from April 1st whatever the new scale might be, except that if the new scale should prove to be lower than that which expired on March 31, there should be no reduction in wages, while if the scale was raised the company would pay the increased amount, dating it back to April 1st. This was satisfactory to the men; but as the question of a new scale was then under discussion at a conference between the officials of the Union and the representatives of the Operators' Association, and plaintiff's employees wished to get the sanction of their officers, the manager of the Hitchman mine got into communication with those officials, including defendant Green, President of District No. 6, and endeavored to secure their assent to the temporary arrangement, but without success. Then a committee of the local union, including Daugherty, its President, took up the matter with Green and received permission to mine and load engine coal until further notice from him. Under this arrangement the men remained at work for about two weeks. On April 15th, defendant Zelenka, Vice President of the sub-district, visited the mine, called a meeting of the miners, and addressed them in a foreign tongue, as a result of which they went on strike the next day, and the mine was shut down until the 12th of June, when it resumed as a "non-union" mine, so far as relations with the U. M. W. A. were concerned.

During this strike plaintiff was subjected to heavy losses and extraordinary expenses with respect to its business, of the same kind that had befallen it during the previous strikes.

About the 1st of June a self-appointed committee of employees called upon plaintiff's president, stated in substance that they could not remain longer on strike because they were not receiving benefits from the Union, and asked upon what terms they could return to work. They were told that they could come back, but not as members of the United Mine Workers of America; that thenceforward the mine would be run non-union, and the company would deal with each man individually. They assented to this, and returned to work on a non-union basis. Mr. Pickett, the mine superintendent, had charge of employing the men, then and afterwards, and to each one who applied for employment he explained the conditions, which were that while the company paid the wages demanded by the Union and as much as anybody else, the mine was run non-union and would continue so to run; that the company would not recognize the United Mine Workers of America; that if any man wanted to become a member of that union he was at liberty to do so; but he could not be a member of it and remain in the employ of the Hitchman Company; that if he worked for the company he would have to work as a non-union man. To this each man employed gave his assent, understanding that while he worked for the company he must keep out of the Union.

Since January, 1908 (after the commencement of the suit), in addition to having this verbal understanding, each man has been required to sign an employment card expressing in substance the same terms. This has neither enlarged nor diminished plaintiff's rights, the agreement not being such as is required by law to be in writing.

Under this arrangement as to the terms of employment, plaintiff operated its mine from June 12, 1906, until the commencement of the suit in the fall of the following year. * * *

In fact, all coal mines in the Panhandle and elsewhere in West Virginia, except in a small district known as the Kanawha field, were run "non-union," while the entire industry in Ohio, Indiana, and Illinois was operated on the "closed-shop" basis, so that no man could hold a job about the mines unless he was a member of the United Mine Workers of America. Pennsylvania occupied a middle ground, only a part of it being under the jurisdiction of the Union. Other States need not be particularly mentioned.

The unorganized condition of the mines in the Panhandle and some other districts was recognized as a serious interference with the purposes of the Union in the Central Competitive Field, particularly as it tended to keep the cost of production low, and, through competition with coal produced in the organized field, rendered it more difficult for the operators there to maintain prices high enough to induce them to grant certain concessions demanded by the Union. This was the subject of earnest and protracted discussion in the annual international convention of the U. M. W. A. held at Indianapolis, Indiana, in the month of January, 1907, at which all of the answering defendants were present as delegates and participated in the proceedings. The discussion was based upon statements contained in the annual reports of John Mitchell, as President of the Union (joined as a defendant in the bill but not served with process), and of defendant Lewis, as Vice President, respecting the causes and consequences of the strike of 1906, and the policy to be adopted by the Union for the future. In these reports it was made to appear that the strike had been caused immediately by the failure of the joint convention of operators and miners representing the central and southwestern competitive fields, held in the early part of the year 1906, to come to an agreement for a renewal of the mining scale; that the strike was widespread, involving not less than 400,000 mine workers, was terminated by "district settlements," with variant results in different parts of the territory involved, and had not been followed by a renewal of the former relations between the operators and miners in the Central Competitive Field. Another result of the strike was a large decrease in the membership of the Union. Two measures of relief were proposed: first, that steps be taken to reëstablish the joint interstate conferences; and second, the organization of the hitherto unorganized fields, including the Panhandle District of West Virginia, under closed-shop agreements, with all men about the mines included in the membership of the United Mine Workers of America. In the course of the discussion the purpose of organizing West Virginia in the interest of the unionized mine workers in the Central Competitive Field, and the probability that it could be organized only by means of strikes, were repeatedly declared and were disputed by nobody. All who spoke advocated strikes, differing only as to whether these should be nation-wide or sectional. * * *

The discussion continued during three days, and at the end of it the report of a committee which expressed disagreement with Vice President Lewis' opposition to sectional settlements and recommended "a continuation in the future of the same wise, conservative business-like policies" that had been pursued by President Mitchell, was adopted by a *viva voce* vote.

The plain effect of this action was to approve a policy which, as applied to the concrete case, meant that in order to relieve the union miners of Ohio, Indiana, and Illinois from the competition of the cheaper product of the non-union mines of West Virginia, the West Virginia mines should be "organized" by means of strikes local to West Virginia, the strike benefits to be paid by assessments upon the union mines in the other States mentioned, while they remained at work.

This convention was followed by an annual convention of Sub-district 5 of District 6, held in the month of March, 1907, at which defendants Watkins and Rankin were present as President and Secretary of the sub-district. Defendant Lewis, as National Vice President, occupied the chair during several of the sessions. Defendant Zelenka was present as a delegate, and also Thomas Hughes, who, while named as a defendant in the present suit, was not served with process. Watkins and Rankin in their reports recommended the complete unionization of the mines in the Panhandle counties, with particular reference to the Hitchman, the Glendale, the Richland, and two others; and as a result it was resolved "that the Sub-District officers, together with the District officers, be authorized to take up the work of organizing every mine in the Sub-District as quickly as it can be done."

Evidently in pursuance of this resolution, defendants Green, Zelenka, and Watkins, about July 1, 1907, called at plaintiff's office and laid before its general manager, Mr. Koch, a proposition for the unionization of the mine. He declined to consider it, but at their request laid it before plaintiff's board of directors, who rejected the proposition, and the manager informed Green of this. In one of the interviews Koch informed these defendants of the terms of plaintiff's working agreement with its employees to the effect that the mine was to be run non-union and they were not to become members of the Union. * * *

The evidence renders it clear that Hughes was sent into the Panhandle to organize all the mines there, in accordance with the resolution of the sub-district convention. The bill made a statement of his activities, and alleged that he was acting as an organizer for the Union. Defendants' final answers made a complete denial, but in this are contradicted by admissions made in the earlier answers and by other and undisputed evidence. The only defendant who testified upon the subject declared that Hughes was employed by District No. 6 as an organizer, but denied that he had power or authority to shut down the Hitchman mine. * * *

The evidence shows that he had distinct and timely notice that membership in the Union was inconsistent with the terms of employment at all three mines, and a violation of the express provisions of the agreement at the Hitchman and Glendale.

Having unsuccessfully applied to Koch and McKinley for their coöperation, Hughes proceeded to interview as many of the men as he could reach and to hold public meetings in the interest of the Union. There is clear and uncontradicted evidence that he did not confine himself to mere persuasion, but resorted to deception and abuse. In his public speeches he employed abusive language respecting Mr. Pickett, William Daugherty, and Jim Jarrett.[5] He prophesied, in such a way that ignorant, foreign-born miners, such as he was addressing, naturally might believe him to be speaking with knowledge, that the wages paid by the Hitchman would be reduced unless the mine was unionized. The evidence as to the methods he employed in personally interviewing the miners, while meagre, is significant. Myers, a Hitchman miner, testified: "He told me that he was

[5] Mr. Pickett was superintendent of the Hitchman and Glendale mines, and it was with him that the miners made their agreements to refrain from membership in the Union; Daugherty and Jarrett were miners at the Hitchman, and had been, respectively, President and Financial Secretary of the local union at the time of the 1906 strike, when the local deserted the U. M. W. A.

a good friend of Mr. Koch, and that Mr. Koch had nothing against having the place organized again. He said he was a friend of his, and I made the remark that I would ask Mr. Koch and see if it was so; and he said no, that was of no use because he was telling me the truth." He did not confine his attentions to men who already were in plaintiff's employ, but in addition dissuaded men who had accepted employment from going to work.

A highly significant thing, giving character to Hughes' entire course of conduct, is that while his solicitation of the men was more or less public, as necessarily it had to be, he was careful to keep secret the number and the names of those who agreed to join the Union. Myers, being asked to allow his name to be entered on a book that Hughes carried, tried to see the names already entered, "but he would not show anything; he told me he had it, and I asked him how many names was on it, and he said he had about enough to 'crack off.'" To Stewart, another Hitchman miner, he said "he was forming a kind of secret order among the men; he said he had a few men—he did not state the number of them—and he said each man was supposed to give him so much dues to keep it going, and then he said after he got the majority he would organize the place." * * *

If there be any practical distinction between organizing the miners and organizing the mine, it has no application to this case. Unionizing the miners is but a step in the process of unionizing the mine, followed by the latter almost as a matter of course. Plaintiff is as much entitled to prevent the first step as the second, so far as its own employees are concerned, and to be protected against irreparable injury resulting from either. Besides, the evidence shows, without any dispute, that defendants contemplated no half-way measures, but were bent on organizing the *mine,* the "consent" of plaintiff to be procured through such a control of its employees as would render any further independent operation of the mine out of the question. This is evident from the discussions and resolutions of the international and sub-district conventions, from what was said by defendants Green, Zelenka, and Watkins to plaintiff's manager, and to the operator of the Richland, and from all that was said and done by Hughes in his effort to organize the Hitchman, Glendale, and Richland mines.

In short, at the time the bill was filed, defendants, although having full notice of the terms of employment existing between plaintiff and its miners, were engaged in an earnest effort to subvert those relations without plaintiff's consent, and to alienate a sufficient number of the men to shut down the mine, to the end that the fear of losses through stoppage of operations might coerce plaintiff into "recognizing the union," at the cost of its own independence. The methods resorted to by their "organizer" were such as have been described. The legal consequences remain for discussion. * * *

That the plaintiff was acting within its lawful rights in employing its men only upon terms of continuing non-membership in the United Mine Workers of America is not open to question. Plaintiff's repeated costly experiences of strikes and other interferences while attempting to "run union" were a sufficient explanation of its resolve to run "non-union," if any were needed. But neither explanation nor justification is needed. Whatever may be the advantages of "collective bargaining," it is not bargaining at all, in any just sense, unless it·is voluntary on both sides. The same liberty which enables men to form unions, and through the union to enter into agreements with employers willing to agree, entitles other men to remain independent of the union and other employers to agree with them to employ no man who owes any allegiance or obligation to the union. In the latter case, as in the former, the parties are entitled to be protected by the law in the enjoyment of the benefits of any lawful agreement they may make. This court repeatedly has held that the employer is as free to make non-membership in a union a condition of employment, as the working man is free to join the union, and that this is a part of the constitutional rights of personal liberty and private property, not to be taken away even by legislation, unless through some proper exercise of the paramount police power. *Adair v. United States,* 208 U.S. 161, 174; *Coppage v. Kansas,* 236 U.S. 1, 14. In the present case, needless to say, there is no act of legislation to which defendants may resort for justification.

Plaintiff, having in the exercise of its undoubted rights established a working agreement between it and its employees, with the free assent of the latter, is entitled to be protected in the enjoyment of the resulting status, as in any other legal right. That the employment was "at will," and terminable by either party at any time, is of no consequence. In *Truax v. Raich,* 239 U.S. 33, 38, this court ruled upon the precise question as follows: "It is said that the bill does not show an employment for a term, and that under an employment at will the complainant could be discharged at any time for any reason or for no reason, the motive of the employer being immaterial. The conclusion, however, that is sought to be drawn is too broad. The fact that the employment is at the will of the parties, respectively, does not make it one at the will of others. The employé has manifest interest in the freedom of the employer to exercise his judgment without illegal interference or compulsion, and, by the weight of authority, the unjustified interference of third persons is actionable although the employment is at will." (Citing many cases.)

In short, plaintiff was and is entitled to the good will of its employees, precisely as a merchant is entitled to the good will of his customers although they are under no obligation to continue to deal with him. The value of the relation lies in the reasonable probability that by properly treating its employees, and paying them fair wages, and avoiding reasonable grounds of complaint, it will be able to retain them in its employ, and to fill vacancies occurring from time to time by the employment of other men on the same terms. The pecuniary value of such reasonable probabilities is incalculably great, and is recognized by the law in a variety of relations. See *Brennan v. United Hatters,* (cited with approval in *Truax v. Raich, supra*) 73 N.J.L. 729, 749; *Brown v. Honiss,* 74 N.J.L. 501, 514 *et seq.; Jersey City Printing Co. v. Cassidy,* 63 N.J. Eq. 759, 767; *Walker v. Cronin,* 107 Massachusetts, 555, 565-566; *Moran v.*

Dunphy, 177 Massachusetts, 485, and cases there cited; *L. D. Wilcutt &*
Sons Co. v. Driscoll, 200 Massachuetts, 110, 117, etc.

The right of action for persuading an employee to leave his employer is universally recognized—nowhere more clearly than in West
Virginia—and it rests upon fundamental principles of general application,
not upon the English statute of laborers. *Thacker Coal Co. v. Burke,* 59
W. Va. 253, 255; 8 Ann. Cas. 885, 886; *Walker v. Cronin,* 107 Massachusetts, 555, 567; *Angle v. Chicago, St. Paul &c. Ry. Co.,* 151 U.S. 1,
13; *Noice Adm'x v. Bron,* 39 N.J.L. 569, 572.

We turn to the matters set up by way of justification or excuse for
defendants' interference with the situation existing at plaintiff's mine.

The case involves no question of the rights of employees. Defendants have no agency for plaintiff's employees, nor do they assert any disagreement or grievance in their behalf. In fact, there is none, if there
were, defendants could not, without agency, set up any rights that employees might have. The right of the latter to strike would not give to
defendants the right to instigate a strike. The difference is fundamental.

It is suggested as a ground of criticism that plaintiff endeavored to
secure a closed non-union mine through individual agreements with its
employees, as if this furnished some sort of excuse for the employment of
coercive measures to secure a closed union shop through a collective agreement with the Union. It is a sufficient answer, in law, to repeat that plaintiff had a legal and constitutional right to exclude union men from its employ. But it may be worth while to say, in addition: first, that there was
no middle ground open to plaintiff; no option to have an "open shop" employing union men and non-union men indifferently; it was the Union that
insisted upon closed-shop agreements, requiring even carpenters employed
about a mine to be members of the Union, and making the employment
of any non-union man a ground for a strike; and secondly, plaintiff was in
the reasonable exercise of its rights in excluding all union men from its employ, having learned, from a previous experience, that unless this were
done union organizers might gain access to its mine in the guise of laborers.

Defendants set up, by way of justification or excuse, the right of
workingmen to form unions, and to enlarge their membership by inviting
other workingmen to join. The right is freely conceded, provided the objects of the union be proper and legitimate, which we assume to be true,
in a general sense, with respect to the Union here in question. *Gompers*
v. Bucks Stove & Range Co., 221 U.S. 418, 439. The cardinal error of
defendants' position lies in the assumption that the right is so absolute that
it may be exercised under any circumstances and without any qualification;
whereas in truth, like other rights that exist in civilized society, it must
always be exercised with reasonable regard for the conflicting rights of
others. *Brennan v. United Hatters,* 73 N.J.L. 729, 749. The familiar
maxim, *Sic utere tuo ut alienum non lædas*—literally translated, "So use
your own property as not to injure that of another person," but by more
proper interpretation, "so as not to injure *the rights* of another," (Broom's
Leg. Max., 8th ed., 289)—applies to conflicting rights of every descrip-

tion. For example, where two or more persons are entitled to use the same road or passage, each one in using it is under a duty to exercise care not to interfere with its use by the others, or to damage them while they are using it. And a most familiar application is the action for enticing an employee, in which it never was a justification that defendant wished to retain for himself the services of the employee. 1 Black. Com. 429; 3 *Id*. 142.

Now, assuming defendants were exercising, through Hughes, the right to invite men to join their Union, still they had plain notice that plaintiff's mine was run "non-union," that none of the men had a right to remain at work there after joining the Union, and that observance of this agreement was of great importance and value both to plaintiff and to its men who had voluntarily made the agreement and desired to continue working under it. Yet defendants, far from exercising any care to refrain from unnecessarily injuring plaintiff, deliberately and advisedly selected that method of enlarging their membership which would inflict the greatest injury upon plaintiff and its loyal employees. Every Hitchman miner who joined Hughes' "secret order" and permitted his name to be entered upon Hughes' list was guilty of a breach of his contract of employment and acted a lie whenever thereafter he entered plaintiff's mine to work. Hughes not only connived at this, but must be deemed to have caused and procured it, for it was the main feature of defendants' plan, the *sine qua non* of their programme. Evidently it was deemed to be necessary, in order to "organize the Panhandle by a strike movement," that at the Hitchman, for example, man after man should be persuaded to join the Union, and having done so to remain at work, keeping the employer in ignorance of their number and identity, until so many had joined that by stopping work in a body they could coerce the employer and the remaining miners to "organize the mine," that is, to make an agreement that none but members of the Union should be employed, that terms of employment should be determined by negotiation not with the employees but with union officers—perhaps residents of other States and employees of competing mines—and that all questions in controversy between the mine operator and the miners should likewise be settled with outsiders.

True, it is suggested that under the existing contract an employee was not called upon to leave plaintiff's employ until he actually joined the Union, and that the evidence shows only an attempt by Hughes to induce the men to *agree* to join, but no attempt to induce them to violate their contract by failing to withdraw from plaintiff's employment after *actually joining*. But in a court of equity, which looks to the substance and essence of things and disregards matters of form and technical nicety, it is sufficient to say that to induce men to *agree* to join is but a mode of inducing them to join, and that when defendants "had sixty men who had signed up or agreed to join the organization at Hitchman," and were "going to shut the mine down as soon as they got a few more men," the sixty were for practical purposes, and therefore in the sight of equity, already members of the Union, and it needed no formal ritual or taking of an oath to constitute them such; their uniting with the Union in the plan to subvert the system of employment at the Hitchman mine, to which they had voluntarily agreed and upon which their employer and their fellow employees were relying, was sufficient.

But the facts render it plain that what the defendants were endeavoring to do at the Hitchman mine and neighboring mines cannot be treated as a *bona fide* effort to enlarge the membership of the Union. There is no evidence to show, nor can it be inferred, that defendants intended or desired to have the men at these mines join the Union, *unless they could organize the mines*. Without this, the new members would be added to the number of men competing for jobs in the organized districts, while non-union men would take their places in the Panhandle mines. Except as a means to the end of compelling the owners of these mines to change their method of operation, the defendants were not seeking to enlarge the union membership.

In any aspect of the matter, it cannot be said that defendants were pursuing their object by *lawful* means. The question of their intentions—of their *bona fides*—cannot be ignored. It enters into the question of malice. As Bowen, L.J., justly said, in the *Mogul Steamship Case*, 23 Q.B. Div. 613, "Intentionally to do that which is calculated in the ordinary course of events to damage, and which does, in fact, damage another in that other person's property or trade, is actionable if done without just cause or excuse." And the intentional infliction of such damage upon another, without justification or excuse, is malicious in law. *Bitterman v. Louisville & Nashville R. R. Co.*, 207 U.S. 205, 223; *Brennan v. United Hatters*, 73 N.J.L. 729, 744 *et seq.*, and cases cited. Of course, in a court of equity, when passing upon the right of injunction, damage threatened, irremediable by action at law, is equivalent to damage done. And we cannot deem the proffered excuse to be a "*just* cause or excuse," where it is based, as in this case, upon an assertion of conflicting rights that are sought to be attained by unfair methods, and for the very purpose of interfering with plaintiff's rights, of which defendants have full notice.

Another fundamental error in defendants' position consists in the assumption that all measures that may be resorted to are lawful if they are "peaceable"—that is, if they stop short of physical violence, or coercion through fear of it. In our opinion, any violation of plaintiff's legal rights contrived by defendants for the purpose of inflicting damage, or having that as its necessary effect, is as plainly inhibited by the law as if it involved a breach of the peace. A combination to procure concerted breaches of contract by plaintiff's employees constitutes such a violation. *Flaccus v. Smith*, 199 Pa. St. 128; 54 L.R.A. 640; *South Wales Miners' Federation v. Glamorgan Coal Co.*, [1905] A.C. 239, 244, 250, 253; *Jonas Glass Co. v. Glass Bottle Blowers Association*, 77 N.J. Eq. 219, 223.

The present is not a case of merely withholding from an employer an economic need—as a supply of labor—until he assents to be governed by union regulations. Defendants have no supply of labor of which plaintiff stands in need. By the statement of defendant Lewis himself, made in his formal report to the Indianapolis convention of 1907, out of more than 370,000 coal miners in the States of Pennsylvania, Maryland, Virginia, and West Virginia, less than 80,000 (about 22 per cent.) were members of the Union. Considering the Panhandle separately, doubtless the proportion was even smaller, and the supply of non-union labor ample. There is no reason to doubt that if defendants had been actuated by a genuine desire to increase the membership of the Union without unnecessary injury to the known rights of plaintiff, they would have permitted their proselytes to withdraw from plaintiff's employ when and as they became affiliated with the Union—as their contract of employment required them to do—and that in this event plaintiff would have been able to secure an adequate supply of non-union men to take their places. It was with knowledge of this, and because of it, that defendants, through Hughes as their agent, caused the new members to remain at work in plaintiff's mine until a sufficient number of men should be persuaded to join so as to bring about a strike and render it difficult if not practically impossible for plaintiff to continue to exercise its undoubted legal and constitutional right to run its mine "non-union."

It was one thing for plaintiff to find, from time to time, comparatively small numbers of men to take vacant places in a going mine, another and a much more difficult thing to find a complete gang of new men to start up a mine shut down by a strike, when there might be a reasonable apprehension of violence at the hands of the strikers and their sympathizers. The disordered condition of a mining town in time of strike is matter of common knowledge. It was this kind of intimidation, as well as that resulting from the large organized membership of the Union, that defendants sought to exert upon plaintiff, and it renders pertinent what was said by this court in the *Gompers Case* (221 U.S. 418, 439), immediately following the recognition of the right to form labor unions: "But the very fact that it is lawful to form these bodies, with multitudes of members, means that they have thereby acquired a vast power, in the presence of which the individual may be helpless. This power, when unlawfully used against one, cannot be met, except by his purchasing peace at the cost of submitting to terms which involve the sacrifice of rights protected by the Constitution; or by standing on such rights and appealing to the preventive powers of a court of equity. When such appeal is made it is the duty of government to protect the one against the many as well as the many against the one."

Defendants' acts cannot be justified by any analogy to competition in trade. They are not competitors of plaintiff; and if they were their conduct exceeds the bounds of fair trade. Certainly, if a competing trader should endeavor to draw custom from his rival, not by offering better or cheaper goods, employing more competent salesmen, or displaying more attractive advertisements, but by persuading the rival's clerks to desert him under circumstances rendering it difficult or embarrassing for him to fill their places, any court of equity would grant an injunction to restrain this as unfair competition.

Upon all the facts, we are constrained to hold that the purpose entertained by defendants to bring about a strike at plaintiff's mine in order to compel plaintiff, through fear of financial loss, to consent to the unionization of the mine as the lesser evil, was an unlawful purpose, and that the methods resorted to by Hughes—the inducing of employees to unite with the Union in an effort to subvert the system of employment at the mine by concerted breaches of the contracts of employment known to be in force there, not to mention misrepresentation, deceptive statements, and threats of pecuniary loss communicated by Hughes to the men—were unlawful and malicious methods, and not to be justified as a fair exercise of the right to increase the membership of the Union.

There can be no question that plaintiff was threatened with danger of an immediate strike as a result of the activities of Hughes. The effect of his arguments and representations is not to be judged from the testimony of those witnesses who rejected his overtures. Naturally, it was not easy for plaintiff to find men who would testify that they had agreed with Hughes to break their contract with plaintiff. One such did testify. But the true measure of the extent of his operations and the probability of his carrying them to success are indicated by his declaration to Myers that he had about enough names at the Hitchman to "crack off," by the statement to McKinley that twenty-four men at the Glendale mine had joined the organization, and sixty at the Hitchman, and by the fact that they actually succeeded in shutting down the Richland about the middle of October. The declaration made concerning the Glendale is corroborated by the evidence of what happened at that mine.

That the damage resulting from a strike would be irremediable at law is too plain for discussion.

Therefore, upon the undisputed facts of the case, and the indubitable inferences from them, plaintiff is entitled to relief by injunction. Having become convinced by three costly strikes, occurring within a period of as many years, of the futility of attempting to operate under a closed-shop agreement with the Union, it established the mine on a non-union basis, with the unanimous approval of its employees—in fact upon their suggestion—and under a mutual agreement, assented to by every employee, that plaintiff would continue to run its mine non-union and would not recognize the United Mine Workers of America; that if any man wanted to become a member of that Union he was at liberty to do so, but he could not be a member and remain in plaintiff's employ. Under that agreement plaintiff ran its mine for a year and more, and so far as appears, without the slightest disagreement between it and its men, and without any grievance on their part. Thereupon defendants, having full notice of the working agreement between plaintiff and its men, and acting without any agency for those men, but as representatives of an organization of mine workers in other States, and in order to subject plaintiff to such participation by the Union in the management of the mine as necessarily results from the making of a closed-shop agreement, sent their agent to the mine, who, with full notice of, and for the very purpose of subverting, the status arising from plaintiff's working agreement and subjecting the mine to the Union control, proceeded, without physical violence, indeed, but by persuasion accompanied with threats of a reduction of wages and deceptive statements as to the attitude of the mine management, to induce plaintiff's employees to join the Union and at the same time to break their agreement with plaintiff by remaining in its employ after joining; and this for the purpose not of enlarging the membership of the Union, but of coercing plaintiff, through a strike or the threat of one, into recognition of the Union.

As against the answering defendants, plaintiff's right to an injunction is clear; as to the others named as defendants, but not served with process, the decree is erroneous, as already stated.

Respecting the sweep of the injunction, we differ somewhat from the result reached by the District Court.

So far as it restrains—(1) Interfering or attempting to interfere with plaintiff's employees for the purpose of unionizing plaintiff's mine without its consent, by representing or causing to be represented to any of plaintiff's employees, or to any person who might become an employee of plaintiff, that such person will suffer or is likely to suffer some loss or trouble in continuing in or in entering the employment of plaintiff, by reason of plaintiff not recognizing the Union, or because plaintiff runs a non-union mine; (2) Interfering or attempting to interfere with plaintiff's employees for the purpose of unionizing the mine without plaintiff's consent, and in aid of such purpose knowingly and wilfully bringing about the breaking by plaintiff's employees of contracts of service known at the time to exist with plaintiff's present and future employees; (3) Knowingly and wilfully enticing plaintiff's employees, present or future, to leave plaintiff's service on the ground that plaintiff does not recognize the United Mine Workers of America or runs a non-union mine, etc.; (4) Interfering or attempting to interfere with plaintiff's employees so as knowingly and wilfully to bring about the breaking by plaintiff's employees, present and future, of their contracts of service, known to the defendants to exist, and especially from knowingly and wilfully enticing such employees, present or future, to leave plaintiff's service without plaintiff's consent; (5) Trespassing on or entering upon the grounds and premises of plaintiff or its mine for the purpose of interfering therewith or hindering or obstructing its business, or with the purpose of compelling or inducing, by threats, intimidation, violent or abusive language, or persuasion, any of plaintiff's employees to refuse or fail to perform their duties as such; and (6) Compelling or inducing or attempting to compel or induce, by threats, intimidation, or abusive or violent language, any of plaintiff's employees to leave its service or fail or refuse to perform their duties as such employees, or compelling or at-tempting to compel by like means any person desiring to seek employ-ment in plaintiff's mine and works from so accepting employment therein; the decree is fully supported by the proofs. But it goes further, and awards an injunction against picketing and against acts of physical vio-lence, and we find no evidence that either of these forms of inter-ference was threatened. The decree should be modified by eliminating picketing and physical violence from the sweep of the injunction, but without prejudice to plaintiff's right to obtain an injunction hereafter against these forms of interference if proof shall be produced, either in proceedings supplemental to this action or in an independent action, that such an injunction is needed.

> *The decree of the Circuit Court of Appeals is reversed, and the decree of the District Court is modified as above stated, and as so modified it is affirmed, and the cause is remanded to the District Court for further proceedings in conformity with this opinion.*

MR. JUSTICE BRANDEIS, dissenting.

This suit was begun October 24, 1907. The Hitchman Coal & Coke Company, plaintiff below, is the owner of a coal mine in West Virginia. John Mitchell and nine others, defendants below, were then the chief executive officers of the United Mine Workers of America and of its district and sub-district organizations having "jurisdiction" over the ter-ritory in which plaintiff's mine is situated; and were sued both individu-ally and as such officers. The mine had been "unionized" about three years prior to April 16th, 1906; and until about that date was operated as a "union" mine, under a collective agreement with a local union of the United Mine Workers of America. Then a strike was declared by the union; and a short shut-down followed. While the strike so declared was still in force, as the bill alleges, the company re-opened the mine as a closed non-union mine. Thereafter persons applying for work were required as a condition of obtaining employment to agree that they would not, while in the service of the company, be a member of the union, and if they joined the union would withdraw from the company's employ.[6]

---

[6] About two months *after* the restraining order was issued in this case the plaintiff company began the practice of requiring applicants for work to sign employment cards, in the following terms:

"I am employed by and work for the Hitchman Coal & Coke Company with the express understanding that I am not a member of the United Mine Workers of America, and will not become so while an employee of the Hitchman Coal & Coke Company; that the Hitchman Coal & Coke Company is run non-union and agrees with me that it will run non-union while I am in its employ. If at any time I am employed by the Hitchman Coal & Coke Company I want to become connected with the United Mine Workers of America, or any affiliated organization, I agree to with-draw from the employment of said company, and agree that while I am in the employ of that company I will not make any efforts amongst its employees to bring about the unionizing of that mine against the company's wish. I have either read the above or heard the same read."

Prior to that time, the agreement rested in oral understanding merely. and is

Alleging that efforts were being made illegally to unionize its mine "without its consent," the company brought in the United States Circuit (now District) Court for the Northern District of West Virginia this suit to enjoin such efforts. District Judge Dayton granted a restraining order upon the filing of the bill. An order was entered May 26, 1908, continuing it as a temporary injunction. A motion to modify the same was denied, September 21, 1909. 172 Fed. Rep. 963. An appeal from this order was dismissed by the Circuit Court of Appeals, March 11, 1910. 176 Fed. Rep. 549. The case was then heard on the merits; defendants having denied in their answer all the charges of unlawful conduct set forth in the bill; and on January 18, 1913, a decree was entered for a perpetual injunction substantially in the form of the restraining order. 202 Fed. Rep. 512. This decree was reversed by the Circuit Court of Appeals on June 1, 1914 (214 Fed. Rep. 685) ; but a stay was granted pending an application to this court for a writ of certiorari. The company appealed to this court and also applied for a writ of certiorari. The appeal was dismissed, as the jurisdiction of the Circuit (District) Court was rested wholly upon diversity of citizenship, plaintiff being a corporation organized under the laws of West Virginia and all the defendants citizens and residents of other States. 241 U.S. 644. A writ of certiorari was granted, however, March 13, 1916. The case was argued at that term and a reargument was ordered * * *

The Circuit Court of Appeals, reversing the decree of the District Court, held that the United Mine Workers of America was not an unlawful organization under the laws of West Virginia, that its validity under the Federal Anti-Trust Act could not be considered in this proceeding; that so long as defendants "refrained from resorting to unlawful measures to effectuate" their purpose "they could not be said to be engaged in a conspiracy to unionize plaintiff's mine"; that "the evidence fails to show that any unlawful methods were resorted to by these defendants in this instance"; and specifically that there was nothing in the individual contracts which barred defendants from inducing the employees to join the union. With these conclusions I agree substantially.

*First: The alleged illegality of the United Mine Workers of America under the law of West Virginia. * * **

Second: The alleged illegality of the United Mine Workers of America under the Federal Anti-Trust Act.

---

sufficiently indicated in the following excerpts from the testimony of the mine superintendent as to what he told the men applying for employment:

"I also told them that any man who wanted to become a member of the United Mine Workers—that that was his business—but he could not be a member of the United Mine Workers and be affiliated with the United Mine Workers and be under the employ of the Hitchman Coal & Coke Company, or be under the jurisdiction of the United Mine Workers; that the mine was run non-union so far as the United Mine Workers of America were concerned.

"Q. You mean you made every man understand that while he worked for the Hitchman Company he must keep out of the union?

"A. Yes, sir; or at least they said they understood it."

The District Judge undertook to pass upon the legality of the United Mine Workers of America under the Federal Anti-Trust Act; but the question was not in issue in the case. It had not been raised in the bill or by answer. Evidence bearing upon the issue was properly objected to by defendants and should have been excluded.

Third: The alleged conspiracy against the West Virginia Mines.

It was doubtless the desire of the United Mine Workers to unionize every mine on the American continent and especially those in West Virginia which compete directly with the mines of Western Pennsylvania, Ohio, Indiana, and other States already unionized. That desire and the purpose to effect it were not unlawful. They were part of a reasonable effort to improve the condition of workingmen engaged in the industry by strengthening their bargaining power through unions; and extending the field of union power. No conspiracy to shut down or otherwise injure West Virginia was proved, nor was there any averment in the bill of such conspiracy, or any issue otherwise raised by the pleadings which justified the consideration of that question by the District Court.

Fourth: "Unionizing plaintiff's mine without plaintiff's consent."

The fundamental prohibition of the injunction is against acts done "for the purpose of unionizing plaintiff's mine without plaintiff's consent." Unionizing a shop does not mean, inducing the employees to become members of the union.[7] It means inducing the employer to enter into a collective agreement with the union governing the relations of the employer to the employees. Unionizing implies, therefore, at least *formal* consent of the employer. Both plaintiff and defendants insisted upon ex-

---

[7] A witness for the defendants testified as follows:

"There is a difference between unionizing a mine and unionizing the employees in a mine; unionizing the employees is having the men join the organization; unionizing a mine is creating joint relations between the employers and employees; a mine cannot be unionized unless the employer enters into contractual relations with the union; it is not the policy or purpose of the United Mine Workers as an organization to coerce a man into doing a thing against his will; this distinction between unionizing a mine and unionizing the employees of a mine has existed since the organization came about, and this method of unionizing a mine existed in 1906 and 1907."

A witness for the plaintiff testified that "the term 'union,' when applied to mining, means the United Mine Workers, and a union mine is a mine that is under their jurisdiction and so recognized * * *." The contrary is "non-union or open shop." And further, "The men might be unionized at a mine and the mine owners not recognize the union. That would in effect be an open shop. When I said 'unionize the employees' I meant practically all of the employees; but a union mine, as I understand it, is one wherein the closed shop is practically enforced." In such case, the witness explained, the operator would be practically in contract relation with the organization.

It was also testified: "The difference between organizing the men at the mine and organizing the mine is that when the miners are organized the work of organizing the mine is only just started. They next proceed to meet with the operator who owns the mine, or operates it, for the purpose of making contracts or agreements. Under the constitution and methods of the United Mine Workers a mine cannot be organized without the consent of the owner, and it is not the object or purpose of the United Mine Workers to do so, and never has been; it has never been attempted as far as witness knows. After a mine has been organized, the agreement between the employer and the organization is paramount. The constitution of the organization has nothing to do with the workings afterwards; that agreement does not take away from the operator the control of his men."

ercising the right to secure contracts for a closed shop. The plaintiff sought to secure the *closed non-union shop* through individual agreements with employees. The defendants sought to secure the *closed union shop* through a collective agreement with the union. Since collective bargaining is legal, the fact that the workingmen's agreement is made not by individuals directly with the employer, but by the employees with the union and by it, on their behalf, with the employer, is of no significance in this connection. The end being *lawful*, defendant's efforts to unionize the mine can be illegal, only if the methods or means pursued were unlawful; unless indeed there is some special significance in the expression "unionizing without plaintiff's consent."

It is urged that a union agreement curtails the liberty of the operator. Every agreement curtails the liberty of those who enter into it. The test of legality is not whether an agreement curtails liberty, but whether the parties have agreed upon some thing which the law prohibits or declares otherwise to be inconsistent with the public welfare. The operator by the union agreement binds himself: (1) to employ only members of the union; (2) to negotiate with union officers instead of with employees individually the scale of wages and the hours of work; (3) to treat with the duly constituted representatives of the union to settle disputes concerning the discharge of men and other controversies arising out of the employment. These are the chief features of a "unionizing" by which the employer's liberty is curtailed. Each of them is legal. To obtain any of them or all of them men may lawfully strive and even strike. And, if the union may legally strike to obtain each of the things for which the agreement provides, why may it not strike or use equivalent economic pressure to secure an agreement to provide them?

It is also urged that defendants are seeking to "coerce" plaintiff to "unionize" its mine. But coercion, in a legal sense, is not exerted when a union merely endeavors to induce employees to join a union with the intention thereafter to order a strike unless the employer consents to unionize his shop. Such pressure is not coercion in a legal sense. The employer is free either to accept the agreement or the disadvantage. Indeed, the plaintiff's whole case is rested upon agreements secured under similar pressure of economic necessity or disadvantage. If it is coercion to threaten to strike unless plaintiff consents to a closed union shop, it is coercion also to threaten not to give one employment unless the applicant will consent to a closed non-union shop. The employer may sign the union agreement for fear that *labor* may not be otherwise obtainable; the workman may sign the individual agreement for fear that *employment* may not be otherwise obtainable. But such fear does not imply coercion in a legal sense.

In other words an employer, in order to effectuate the closing of his shop to *union* labor, may exact an agreement to that effect from his employees. The agreement itself being a lawful one, the employer may withhold from the men an economic need—employment—until they assent to make it. Likewise an agreement closing a shop to *non-union* labor being lawful, the union may withhold from an employer an economic need—labor—until he assents to make it. In a legal sense an agreement entered into, under such circumstances, is voluntarily entered into; and as the agreement is in itself legal, no reason appears why the general rule that a legal end may be pursued by legal means should not be applied. Or, putting it in other words, there is nothing in the character of the agreement which should make *unlawful* means used to attain it, which in other connections are recognized as *lawful*.

Fifth: There was no attempt to induce employees to violate their contracts.

The contract created an employment at will; and the employee was free to leave at any time. The contract did not bind the employee *not* to join the union; and he was free to join it at any time. The contract merely bound him to withdraw from plaintiff's employ, if he joined the union. There is evidence of an attempt to induce plaintiff's employees to *agree* to join the union; but none whatever of any attempt to induce them to violate their contract. Until an employee actually joined the union he was not, under the contract, called upon to leave plaintiff's employ. There consequently would be no breach of contract until the employee both joined the union *and* failed to withdraw from plaintiff's employ. There was no evidence that any employee was persuaded to do that or that such a course was contemplated. What perhaps was intended was to secure agreements or assurances from individual employees that they would join the union when a large number of them should have consented to do so; with the purpose, when such time arrived, to have them join the union together and strike—unless plaintiff consented to unionize the mine. Such a course would have been clearly permissible under the contract.

Sixth: Merely persuading employees to leave plaintiff's employ or others not to enter it was not unlawful.

To induce third persons to leave an employment is actionable if done maliciously and without justifiable cause although such persons are free to leave at their own will. *Truax v. Raich,* 239 U.S. 33, 38; *Thacker Coal Co. v. Burke,* 59 W. Va. 253. It is equally actionable so to induce others not to enter the service. The individual contracts of plaintiff with its employees added nothing to its right in this connection, since the employment was terminable at will.

As persuasion, considered merely as a means, is clearly legal, defendants were within their rights if, and only if, their interference with the relation of plaintiff to its employees was for justifiable cause. The purpose of interfering was confessedly in order to strengthen the union, in the belief that thereby the condition of workmen engaged in mining would be improved; the bargaining power of the individual workingman was to be strengthened by collective bargaining; and collective bargaining was to be ensured by obtaining the union agreement. It should not, at this day, be doubted that to induce workingmen to leave or not to enter an employment in order to advance such a purpose is justifiable when the workmen are not bound by contract to remain in such employment.

Seventh: There was no "threat, violence or intimidation."

The decree enjoined "threats, violence or intimidation." Such action would, of course, be unlawful though employed in a justifiable cause. But there is no evidence that any of the defendants have resorted to such means. The propaganda among plaintiff's employees was conducted almost entirely by one man, the defendant Hughes, a District No. 6 organizer. His actions were orderly and peaceable, consisting of informal talks with the men, and a few quietly conducted public meetings,[8] in which he argued the benefits of organization and pointed out to the men that, although the company was then paying them according to the union scale, there would be nothing to prevent a later reduction of wages unless the men united. He also urged upon the men that if they lost their present jobs, membership in the union was requisite to obtaining employment in the union mines of the neighboring States. But there is no suggestion that he exceeded the moderate bounds of peaceful persuasion, and indeed, if plaintiff's witnesses are to be believed, men with whom Hughes had talked, his argument made no impression on them, and they expressed to him their satisfaction with existing conditions at the mine.

When this suit was filed no right of the plaintiff had been infringed and there was no reasonable ground to believe that any of its rights would be interfered with; and, in my opinion, the Circuit Court of Appeals properly reversed the decree of the District Court, and directed that the bill be dismissed.

MR. JUSTICE HOLMES and MR. JUSTICE CLARKE concur in this dissent.[9]

---

[8] Following is a notice of one of Hughes' meetings which was torn from a telegraph pole in the street by the plaintiff's mine superintendent:

"Notice to the miners of the Hitchman mine. There will be a mass meeting Friday evening at 6.30 P.M. at Nick Heil's Base Ball Grounds, for the purpose of discussing the principals of organization. President William Green will be present. All miners are cordially invited to attend."

[9] Accord: Eagle Glass & Mfg. Co. v. Rowe, 245 U.S. 275 (1917); Patton v. United States, 288 Fed. 812 (4th cir. 1923); Keeney v. Borderland Coal Corp., 282 Fed. 269 (4th cir. 1922); Dwyer v. Alpha Pocahontas Coal Co., 282 Fed. 270 (4th cir. 1922); Internat'l Organization, U. M. W. A. v. Leevale Coal Co., 285 Fed. 32 (4th cir. 1922); Internat'l Organization, U. M. W. A. v. Carbon Fuel Co., 288 Fed. 1020 (4th cir. 1923); Clay v. Lewis, 1 Law & Labor, No. 8, p. 8 (U.S.D.C. Ind. 1919); Red Jacket C. & C. Co. v. Lewis (U.S.D.W.Va. 1921), in Hearings before the Committee on Education and Labor pursuant to S. Res. 80, U.S. Senate, 67th Cong. 1st sess. p. 754 (1921); Rice, Barton & Fales Machine, Etc., Co. v. Willard, 242 Mass. 566, 136 N.E. 629 (1922); National Equipment Co. v. Donovan, 1 Law & Labor, No. 10, p. 9 (Mass. 1919); Ellis Co. v. McBride, 3 Law & Labor, 193 (Mass. 1921); Springfield Foundry Co. v. Campbell, 3 Law & Labor, 259 (Mass. 1921); Currier & Sons v. International Moulders' Union of North America, 93 N.J. Eq. 61, 115 Atl. 66 (1921); Third Avenue Ry. Co. v. Shea, 109 Misc. 18, 179 N.Y.S. 43 (1919), aff'd in 191 App. Div. 949, 181 N.Y.S. 956 (1920); Floersheimer v. Schlesinger, 115 Misc. 9, 187 N.Y.S. 891 (1921); Schwartz & Jaffee v. Hillman, 115 Misc. 61, 189 N.Y.S. 21 (1921); Schafer v. Internat'l Pattern Makers' League, 2 Law & Labor, 188 (Sup. Ct. Ohio 1920); Quemahoning Creek Coal Co. v. Brophy, 5 Law & Labor, 274 (Comm.

Pl. Pa. 1923) ; Nashville Ry. & Light Co. v. Lawson, 144 Tenn. 78, 229 S.W. 741 (1921) ; State v. Bittner, 102 W. Va. 677, 136 S.E. 202 (1926) ; Algonquin Coal Co. v. Lewis, 3 Law & Labor 257 (W. Va. 1921) ; Altizer v. Internat'l Organization, U. M. W. A., 5 Law & Labor, 123 (Cir. Ct. W. Va. 1923) ;. Simpson Creek Collieries Co. v. United Mine Workers of America, (Cir. Ct. W. Va. 1924), in Hearings before the Committee on Interstate Commerce pursuant to S. Res. 105, U.S. Senate, 70th Cong., 1st sess., p. 1203 (1928) ; Lorain Coal & Dock Co. v. United Mine Workers of America (Cir. Ct. W. Va. 1924), *ibid.* 1268; Algona Coal & Coke Co. v. Lewis, (Cir. Ct. W. Va. 1921), in Hearings before the Commission on Education and Labor pursuant to S. Res. 80,. U.S. Senate, 67th Cong. 1st sess., p. 757 (1921) ; Trade Press Pub. Co. v. Milwaukee Typographical Union, 180 Wis. 449, 193 N.W. 507 (1923). *Cf.* Piermont v. Schlesinger, 196 App. Div. 658, 188 N.Y.S. 35 (1921) ; Segenfeld v. Friedman, 117 Misc. 731, 193 N.Y.S. 128 (1922).

Upon the necessity of individual contracts between employers and employees for the application of the Hitchman doctrine, see: Callan v. Exposition Cotton Mills, 149. Ga. 119, 99 S.E. 300 (1919) ; McMichael v. Atlanta Envelope Co., 151 Ga. 776, 108 S.E. 226 (1921) ; Diamond Block Coal Co. v. United Mine Workers of America, 188 Ky. 477, 222 S.W. 1079 (1920).

Upon the application of the doctrine to anti-union contracts for a term as distinguished from contracts accompanying employment at will, see: United Shoe Machinery Corp. v. Fitzgerald. 237 Mass. 537, 130 N.E. 86 (1921) ; Reed Co. v. Whiteman, 238 N.Y. 545, 144 N.E. 885 (1924), qualified in Exchange Bakery & Restaurant v. Rifkin, 245 N.Y. 260, 267, 157 N.E. 130 (1927) ; Vail-Ballou Press v. Casey, 125 Misc. 689, 212 N.Y.S. 113 (1925) ; Flaccus v. Smith, 199 Pa. 128, 48 Atl. 894 (1901).

In Montgomery v. Pacific Electric Ry. Co., 253 Fed. 382 (9th cir. 1919), 293 Fed. 680 (9th cir. 1923), the complainant company alleged that "it had been and was the fixed policy of the appellee to prevent unionizing its employees, and that by the terms and conditions of the contract of employment with each of its employees, it was agreed that the latter should deal directly with its employer and not through any union or alleged representative body." Upon this basis the court enjoined the defendants, officers of a union, conducting a strike for the recognition of the union, from persuading plaintiff's employees to become members of their organization, because that organization was to be brought into active relation "between the plaintiff and its employees in all matters relating to employment, thus bringing about a breach of contract between the plaintiff and its employees wherein it had been agreed, and the agreement observed for years, that the plaintiff in all matters relating to such employees should deal directly with them and not through any union or other representative body." P. 687. In Kinloch Telephone Co. v. Local Union No. 2, 275 Fed. 241 (8th cir. 1921), the employer hired both union and non-union employees, and had entered into an agreement between "the employees of said companies who were members of said locals," conceding the open shop policy of the employer, allowing peaceful solicitation of employees to become members of the union outside working hours, and providing for arbitration of controversies and against stoppage of work pending arbitration. The agreement was not signed by the employees but by representatives of the union, but the employees had knowledge of the agreement. A strike having been called, in violation of the agreement, the court enjoined all picketing and persuasion inasmuch as it was an effort to persuade employees to break their contracts against stopping work. A petition for certiorari was denied in 257 U.S. 662 (1921). In Armstrong v. United States, 18 Fed.(2d) 371 (7th cir. 1927), a street car company had entered into contracts with its employees whereby "they, upon consideration passing to them from the company, agreed not to strike or participate in any strike of the employees of said company or enter into any agreement to engage in such strike, or counsel or advise any other employee so to do * * *." P. 372. Defendant employees who had gone on strike were enjoined from "soliciting and persuading its employees to violate and breach their said contract by going upon strike and quitting their employment in a body." *Ibid.* The case does not set forth the contracts themselves nor the nature of the consideration received by the employees. For the terms of the injunction and the background of this case, see: Hearings before a Subcommittee of the Committee on the Judiciary on S. 1482, U.S. Senate, 70th Cong. 1st sess., pp. 227-241 (1928). See also: Day v. United States, 19 Fed.(2d) 21 (7th cir. 1927).

For comment on the Hitchman case, see: Cook. "Privileges of Labor Unions in the Struggle for Life," 27 Yale Law Jour. 779 (1918) ; Powell, "Collective Bargaining in the Supreme Court," 33 Pol. Sci. Quar. 346 (1918) ; Simpson, "Constitutional

AMERICAN STEEL FOUNDRIES v. TRI-CITY CENTRAL TRADES COUNCIL.

Supreme Court of the United States. 257 U.S. 184, 211 (1921).

MR. CHIEF JUSTICE TAFT delivered the opinion of the court.[10]

* * * The principle followed in the *Hitchman Case* can not be invoked here.   There the action was by a coal mining company of West Virginia against the officers of an International Labor Union and others to enjoin them from carrying out a plan to bring the employees of the complainant company and all the West· Virginia mining companies into

---

Rights and the Industrial Struggle," 30 W. Va. Law Quar. 1, 16 (1924) ; 3 Corn. Law Quar. 317 (1918) ; 18 Col. Law Rev. 252 (1918) ; 31 Harv. Law Rev. 648 (1918).

For a contempt proceeding based upon the Hitchman injunction, wherein members of the union were regarded as guilty of violating its terms by approaching miners of the Hitchman Company, working under anti-union contracts, and urging them by argument and persuasion to suspend work and go home, in aid of a general effort to unionize the mine, see: United States ex rel. Hitchman C. & C. Co. v. Lewis (U.S.D.W.Va. 1922) in Hearings before a Subcommittee on the Judiciary on S. 1482, U.S. Senate, 70th Cong. 1st sess., p. 618 (1928).   See also: Hearings before Committee on Interstate Commerce pursuant to Sen. Res. 105, U.S. Senate, 70th Cong., 1st sess., pp. 2122-2133 (1928).

The Hitchman case had an undoubted effect upon the extension of anti-union contracts by non-union operators in the coal industry, as well as in other industries. "A recent labor estimate is that 1,250,000 workingmen are now employed under yellow-dog contracts. This is very likely an overstatement, but there are instances of such contracts in all parts of the country. Their use is general in the non-union coal fields of the eastern states, in the boot and shoe industry in New England, in the full-fashioned hosiery industry, and in several large street-car systems." Witte, The Government in Labor Disputes, 222 (1932).   See also: Report of U.S. Coal Commission, 172, 1331-2 (1923).   For examples of specific types of such anti-union provisions, see the employment contracts of the following West Virginia and Ohio coal companies, reprinted in Hearings before the Committee on Interstate Commerce pursuant to S. Res. 105, U.S. Sen., 70th Cong. 1st sess., (1928) ; Atlantic Contracting Co., p. 3399; Boomer C. & C. Co., p. 704; Brady-Warner Coal Corp., p. 2090; Cabin Creek Consolidated Coal Co., p. 2095; Clarkson Coal· Mining Co., p. 2256; Island Creek Coal Co., p. 1950; New River Co., p. 2110; Pursglove Mining Co.. p. 1253; Warner Colleries Co., p. 2337; West Va. C. & C. Co., p. 2056; Wheeling & Lake Erie Coal Mining Co., p. 2441 ; Youghiogheny & Ohio Coal Co., p. 2418; Seidman, The Yellow-Dog Contract. App'x (1932).. For an early example of such contracts. see: Lloyd, A Strike of Millionaires Against Miners, c. 8 (1890).   For the early history of the employment of such contracts, see: Seidman, *supra*, c. 1.   For the attitude of operators towards the Hitchman case, compare the following excerpt from the brief of the Island Creek Co., in defense of their anti-union policy before the United States Senate: "Open Shop is Legal. 4. Operators of coal mines have a constitutional right to operate their mines either as open shop mines or as closed shop non-union mines without interference by union organizers; they have the constitutional right to discharge a member of the union, and they have the added moral obligation to keep out any United Mine Workers' organizer, because the history of the mine has inevitably been followed by strikes, murder, arson, disjointing of tipples, and shooting up of mines." Hearings before the Committee on Education and Labor pursuant to S. Res. 80, U.S. Sen. 67th Cong., 1st sess., p. 14 (1921).

For the general history of the industrial struggle in the coal industry, see: Report of U.S. Coal Commission (1923) ; Hinrichs, "The United Mine Workers of America and the Non-Union Coal Fields," 110 Col. Studies in History. Economics and Law (1923) ; Lane, Civil War in West Virginia (1921) ; Suffern, Conciliation and Arbitration in the Coal Industry of America (1915) ; Suffern, The Coal Miners' Struggle for Industrial Status (1926).

10 For the full opinion in this case, see *post* p. 211.

the International Union, so that the Union could control, through the union employees, the production and sale of coal in West Virginia, in competition with the mines of Ohio and other States. The plan thus projected was carried out in the case of the complainant company by the use of deception and misrepresentation with its non-union employees, by seeking to induce such employees to become members of the Union contrary to the express term of their contract of employment that they would not remain in complainant's employ if union men, and after enough such employees had been secretly secured, suddenly to declare a strike against complainant and to leave it in a helpless situation in which it would have to consent to be unionized. This court held that the purpose was not lawful, and that the means were not lawful and that the defendants were thus engaged in an unlawful conspiracy which should be enjoined. The unlawful and deceitful means used were quite enough to sustain the decision of the court without more. The statement of the purpose of the plan is sufficient to show the remoteness of the benefit ultimately to be derived by the members of the International Union from its success and the formidable country-wide and dangerous character of the control of interstate commerce sought.

GASAWAY v. BORDERLAND COAL CORPORATION.

United States Circuit Court of Appeals for the Seventh Circuit. 278 Fed. 56 (1921).

Appeal from the District Court of the United States for the District of Indiana. ·

Suit by the Borderland Coal Corporation against Ora Gasaway, W. D. Van Horn, and others. From a decree granting a temporary injunction (275 Fed. 871), the named defendants appeal. Remanded, with directions.[11]

Baker, C.J. " * * * Bill and affidavits show the following trespasses upon appellee's property rights in interstate commerce: Destruction of appellee's property used in operating its mine; interference with and intimidation of appellee's officers, agents, and employees, by armed forces, by assaults, by threatening and abusive language, and by intrusions upon their privacy without invitation or consent; inducing appellee's employees secretly to change from non-union to union men, and to remain in appellee's employment in violation of their contracts, the terms of which were known to the trespassers; and in using money, sent into West Virginia by the United Mine Workers' general or executive officers, to aid in the commission of the foregoing trespasses. All these unlawful acts (none of which was specified in the decree) should be enjoined by the preliminary injunction, with leave to the District Court to restrain

---

[11] The statement of facts and the decree of the district court are omitted.

other specifically threatened trespasses upon appellee's property rights, if any is shown.

But appellee was not satisfied with such a decree * * *.

Appellee sought and obtained a decree restraining "the unionization or attempted unionization of the nonunion mines" in the Williamson district. Appellants, and their agents and representatives in West Virginia, are thus enjoined from publishing lawful union arguments and making lawful union speeches in the closed district; from making lawful appeals to those in the pool of unemployed labor to join the union rather than the nonunion ranks; and from using lawful persuasion to induce any one of appellee's employés to join the union and thereupon instantly and openly to sever his relationship with appellee, not in violation of, but in exact accordance with, his contract with appellee. Manifestly the purpose of such publications, public speeches, and personal persuasions would be to enlarge the membership of the union. * * * In the present state of the law, and without a constitutional exercise of the legislative power of regulation, appellee had no greater right to a decree suppressing lawful action (such as the publications, speeches and personal persuasions heretofore mentioned in this paragraph) in support of the closed union shop program than appellants had to a similar decree suppressing similar lawful action in support of the closed nonunion shop program. Neither side had any such right. * * *

From the record as it now stands we are convinced that the District Court committed substantial errors in exercising its judicial discretion in the following particulars: (1) In not confining the grant of relief to appellee; (2) in not limiting the prohibition of the unionization or attempted unionization of appellee's mine to the threatened direct and immediate interfering acts shown by the bill and affidavits; * * *

The decree should be recast, and for that purpose the cause is remanded, with the direction to the District Court to enter a preliminary injunction decree which shall be in consonance with this opinion.[12]

---

[12] Accord: La France Electrical Const. & Supply Co. v. International Brotherhood of Electrical Workers, 108 Ohio 61, 140 N.E. 899 (1923); Boldt Construction Co. v. United Brotherhood of Carpenters & Joiners, 3 Law & Labor, 227 (Comm. Pleas, Ohio 1921); Kilby Mfg. Co. v. Local No. 218, 5 Law & Labor, 93 (Ohio App. 1922); Kraemer Hosiery Co. v. American Federation of F. F. H. W., 305 Pa. 206, 157 Atl. 588 (1931).

INTERNATIONAL ORGANIZATION, U. M. W. A. v.
RED JACKET CONSOLIDATED COAL & COKE CO.

United States Circuit Court of Appeals for the Fourth Circuit. 18 Fed.(2d) 839 (1927).

These are twelve suits instituted by various owners and operators of coal mines in West Virginia, against the International Organization, United Mine Workers of America, the district and local unions of that organization in West Virginia, and various of its international, district, and local officers and members, who are named as defendants in the several suits. Complainants are 316 in number, embracing most of the coal companies operating on a nonunion basis in what is known as the Southern West Virginia field. The suits are instituted to restrain interference with business of complainants by the union and its members, on the ground that such interference constitutes a restraint of interstate trade and commerce in violation of the Sherman Act (Comp. St. § 8820 *et seq.*).

The International Organization, United Mine Workers of America, is an unincorporated labor organization of the United States and Canada, having a membership of 475,000, or approximately 75 per cent. of all persons working in or around coal mines, coal washeries, and coke ovens on the American continent. It is recognized by a large percentage of the mines of the United States, which are known as Union mines and are operated on the "closed union shop" basis; that is to say, no laborers are employed in or about such mines who are not members of the union. Complainants operate their mines nonunion on the "closed nonunion shop" basis; that is, their employees are notified that the company will not employ union men and accept employment with that understanding, and in the case of most of them the employees have entered into contracts that they will not join the union while remaining in the service of the employer. Complainants operate in what is probably the most important nonunion coal field of the United States. Their combined annual tonnage amounts to over 40,000,000 tons, 90 per cent. or more of which is shipped out of West Virginia in interstate commerce. The controversy involved in the several suits is not a controversy between complainants and their employes over wages, hours of labor, or other cause, but is a controversy between them as nonunion operators and the international union, which is seeking to unionize their mines.

The suit of the Red Jacket Coal Company was instituted September 30, 1920. That company operates in Mingo county, W. Va., in the Williamson-Thacker field, which is and has always been nonunion territory. A strike was declared by the union in this field about July 1, 1920, in an attempt to unionize it, and the suit was instituted to enjoin the union and its officers and members from interfering with the company's employees by violence, threats, intimidation, picketing, and the like, or by procuring them to breach their contracts with plaintiff in the manner enjoined in *Hitchman Coal Co. v. Mitchell*, 245 U.S. 229, 38 S. Ct. 65, 62 L. Ed. 260

L.R.A. 1918C, 497; Ann. Cas. 1918B, 461.   The suit of the Borderland
Coal Company was instituted September 26, 1921.   This company also
operates in Mingo county, and it asks injunctive relief, not only in behalf
of itself, but also in behalf of 62 other companies operating in the same
territory, who were actually made parties to the suit on April 8, 1922.
Shortly prior to the institution of the Borderland suit, armed union miners
to a number variously estimated at between 5,000 and 7,000 had congregated at Marmet, W. Va., had announced their intention of marching
across Logan county and into Mingo county with the avowed purpose of
unionizing that field, and had actually engaged in a pitched battle with
state officers, as a result whereof martial law had been declared and federal troops had been sent into the territory to preserve the peace.   In this
suit practically the same relief is sought as in the Red Jacket suit.

On April 1, 1922, while the strike order of July 1, 1920, in the Williamson-Thacker field was still outstanding and the efforts of the union
in that field were being continued, the union called a nation-wide strike
because of its failure to reach a basic wage agreement with the union
operators of the central competitive field (Illinois, Indiana, Ohio, and
Western Pennsylvania).   This strike was declared to apply to nonunion
as well as to union miners, and measures were taken to make it effective
throughout the Williamson-Thacker, Winding Gulf, and Greenbrier fields
of West Virginia, which had always been nonunion, as well as in the
Kanawha and New River fields, where the union had for a time been recognized, but where operation had been commenced on the "closed non-
union shop" basis under contracts between the operators and their employees.   Violence, threats, intimidation, and interference with contract
were resorted to, and nine suits were instituted by the nonunion operators
to enjoin the union, its officers and members, from interfering with their
employees and the operation of their mines, and asking the same relief
as was asked in the Red Jacket and Borderland suits.   In each of these
suits a number of companies operating in the same general neighborhood
joined as complainants, and, as heretofore stated, 62 companies operating
in the Williamson-Thacker field joined as complainants in the Borderland suit which had been instituted sometime prior thereto.

Temporary injunctions were obtained in all of these suits.   In a
number of them appeals were taken to this court, and the injunctive orders
of the District Court were modified.   *Keeney et al. v. Borderland Coal
Corporation et al.*, 282 F. 269; *Dwyer v. Alpha Pocahontas Coal Co. et
al.* and four other cases, 282 F. 270; *International Organization, United
Mine Workers of America et al. v. Leevale Coal Co. et al.*, 285 F. 32.

The general strike of 1922 was settled by the Cleveland wage agreement of August of that year, but the strike was continued against the
nonunion operators of West Virginia.   Upon the making of the wage
agreement, certain companies, which had joined as complainants in
some of the bills, entered into wage agreements recognizing the union, and
withdrew as complainants.   On September 18, 1922, a bill was filed in

behalf of the Carbon Fuel Company and a number of others against the
defendants in the other cases and the companies who had withdrawn from
the suits as complainants, asking not only that the same relief be awarded
as was asked in the other suits, but also that these companies be enjoined
from paying to the United Mine Workers the "check-off" provided for in
their contract; that is, a certain sum from the wages of each miner employed which the contract provided should be paid to the union. A
preliminary injunction was granted, which, on appeal, was modified by
this court. *International Organization, United Mine Workers of America,
v. Carbon Fuel Co. et al.*, 288 F. 1020.

On May 21, 1923, the District Court entered an order consolidating
all twelve of the cases pending; and the defendants, having already moved
to dismiss in the various cases for misjoinder of parties plaintiff, objected
to the consolidation, and excepted to the order directing same. A great
mass of evidence was then taken, which, with the pleadings and affidavits,
covers 5,000 pages of the printed record. The District Judge, on October
16, 1925, made an extended finding of facts, which was filed as a part of
the record in each case, and in each case entered the same final decree,
from which the defendants have appealed.

The District Judge found, among other things, that defendants
had conspired to restrain interstate trade and commerce in coal, and that
at the time these suits were instituted the United Mine Workers of
America, its officers, agents, representatives, and members were attempting "(a) unlawfully, maliciously, and unreasonably to induce, incite, and
cause the employees of the plaintiffs in said suits, respectively, to violate
their said contracts of employment with said plaintiffs; (b) to compel
said employees of said plaintiffs by use of force, intimidation, threats,
violence, vile epithets, abusive language, and false and fraudulent statements, to cease working for said plaintiffs and to become members of
said union; (c) to compel the plaintiffs to recognize said International
Organization, United Mine Workers of America, and to deal with it
and operate their mines under closed shop contracts with it, including
the 'check-off' provisions, or to close down their mines." He further
found that it was a part of the policy and plan of the union to have members thereof obtain, keep, and hold possession of dwelling houses belonging
to the complainants, which were constructed and maintained by them for
the use of their employees as incidental to such employment, and were
absolutely necessary to the operation of their mines, and that the union
was maintaining persons in the wrongful occupation of such houses for
the purpose of preventing the houses being used by persons who were
willing to work, and for the purpose of harassing complainants' non-
union employees.

Upon these findings a final decree was entered in each case, the
effective provisions of which are those approved by this court in the

Carbon Fuel Case, 288 F. 1020. By this decree defendants are restrained and enjoined:

"(1) From interfering with the employees of the plaintiffs or with men seeking employment at their mines by menaces, threats, violence, or injury to them, their persons, families, or property, or abusing them, or their families, or by doing them violence in any way or manner whatsoever, or by doing any other act or thing that will interfere with the right of such employees and those seeking employment to work upon such terms as to them seem proper, unmolested, and from in any manner injuring or destroying the properties of the plaintiffs, or either of them, or from counseling or advising that these plaintiffs should in any way or manner be injured in the conduct and management of their business and in the enjoyment of their property and property rights.

"(2) From trespassing upon the properties of the plaintiffs, or either of them, or by themselves, or in co-operation with others, from inciting, inducing, or persuading the employees of the plaintiffs to break their contract of employment with the plaintiffs.

"(3) From aiding or assisting any other person or persons to commit or attempt to commit any of the acts herein enjoined.

"(4) From aiding or abetting any person or persons to occupy or hold without right, any house or houses or other property of the plaintiffs, or any of them, by sending money or other assistance to be used by such persons in furtherance of such unlawful occupancy or holding."

The defendants filed twenty-eight assignments of error, which present five principal contentions for consideration by this court: (1) That the evidence does not establish a conspiracy in restraint of interstate trade and commerce in violation of the Sherman Act; (2) that there was misjoinder of parties plaintiff in the several suits and error in the order of consolidation; (3) that the injunctive decree is too broad, in that it forbids peaceful persuasion as well as violence and intimidation; (4) that the court should not have enjoined defendants from rendering assistance to persons to enable them to occupy or hold without right houses belonging to complainants; and (5) that those of complainants who had had wage agreements with the union were *in pari delicto* with defendants and therefore not entitled to relief. * * *

PARKER, Circuit Judge (after stating the facts as above). The first question for our consideration is whether the evidence establishes a conspiracy in restraint of interstate trade and commerce, in violation of the Sherman Act. This inquiry goes not merely to the propriety of the granting of the injunction, but to the very existence of the power to grant it; for, except in the case of the Red Jacket Coal Company, the jurisdiction of the court in all of the cases rests, not upon diversity of citizenship, but upon the fact that they arise under the laws of the United States. Complainants ask an injunction under the Clayton Act (38 Stat. 730) to prevent injuries threatened in the carrying out of a conspiracy violative of the Sherman Act. Unless, therefore, there is shown a conspiracy violative of the Sherman Act, no case is shown arising under the laws of the United States, and the jurisdiction of the court is at an end. * * * [13]

In their criticism of the scope of the injunction, defendants make complaint of the restraints contained in paragraphs 2 and 4. As the language criticised is that approved by this court in *International Organization, United Mine Workers of America et al. v. Carbon Fuel Co. et al.,* 288 F. 1020, we might content ourselves with referring to that decision as the law of the case in the Carbon Fuel Case now before us and as binding authority in the other cases; but we shall go further and say that in the light of the decisions of the Supreme Court we have no doubt as to the correctness of the paragraphs criticised.

With respect to the second paragraph, complaint is made that it restrains defendants "from inciting, inducing, or persuading the employees of the plaintiffs to break their contract of employment with the plaintiffs." This language is certainly not so broad as that of the decree approved by the Supreme Court in *Hitchman Coal & Coke Co. v. Mitchell,* 245 U.S. 229, 261, 38 S. Ct. 65, 62 L. Ed. 260, L.R.A. 1918C, 497, Ann. Cas. 1918B, 461, which also enjoined interference with the contract by means of peaceful persuasion. The doctrine of that case has been approved by the Supreme Court in the later cases of *American Steel Foundries v. Tri-City Central Trades Council,* 257 U.S. 184, 42 S. Ct. 72, 66 L. Ed. 189, 27 A.L.R. 360, and *United Mine Workers v. Coronado Coal Co.,* 259 U.S. 344, 42 S. Ct. 570, 66 L. Ed. 975, 27 A.L.R. 762, and applied by this court in *Bittner v. West Virginia-Pittsburgh Coal Co.,* 15 F.(2d) 652, by the Circuit Court of Appeals of the Eighth Circuit in *Kinloch Telephone Co. v. Local Union,* 275 F. 241, and by the Circuit Court of Appeals of the Ninth Circuit in *Montgomery v. Pacific Electric Ry. Co.,* 293 F. 680.

It is said, however, that the effect of the decree, which, of course, operates indefinitely *in futuro,* is to restrain defendants from attempting to extend their membership among the employees of complainants who are under contract not to join the union while remaining in complainants' service, and to forbid the publishing and circulating of lawful arguments and the making of lawful and proper speeches advocating such union membership. They say that the effect of the decree, therefore, is that, because complainants' employees have agreed to work on the nonunion basis, defendants are forbidden, for an indefinite time in the future, to lay before them any lawful and proper argument in favor of union membership.

If we so understood the decree, we would not hesitate to modify it.

---

[13] The portion of the opinion holding that the defendants were engaged in a conspiracy in violation of the Sherman Act is here omitted. The portion of the opinion holding that there was no misjoinder of parties plaintiff in the several suits nor error in the order of consolidation is also omitted.

As we said in the Bittner Case, there can be no doubt of the right of defendants to use all lawful propaganda to increase their membership.[14] On the other hand, however, this right must be exercised with due regard to the rights of complainants. To make a speech or to circulate an argument under ordinary circumstances dwelling upon the advantages of union membership is one thing. To approach a company's employees, working under a contract not to join the union while remaining in the company's service, and induce them, in violation of their contracts, to join the union and go on a strike for the purpose of forcing the company to recognize the union or of impairing its power of production, is another and very different thing. What the decree forbids is this "inciting, inducing, or persuading the employees of plaintiff to break their contracts of employment"; and what was said in the Hitchman Case with respect to this matter is conclusive of the point involved here. The court there said:

"But the facts render it plain that what the defendants were endeavoring to do at the Hitchman mine and neighboring mines cannot be treated as a *bona fide* effort to enlarge the membership of the union. There is no evidence to show, nor can it be inferred, that defendants intended or desired to have the men at these mines join the union, *unless they could organize the mines*. Without this, the new members would be added to the number of men competing for jobs in the organized districts, while nonunion men would take their places in the Panhandle mines. Except as a means to the end of compelling the owners of these mines to change their method of operation, the defendants were not seeking to enlarge the union membership. * * * Another fundamental error in defendants' position consists in the assumption that all measures that may be resorted to are lawful if they are 'peaceable'—that is, if they stop short of physical violence, or coercion through fear of it. In our opinion, any violation of plaintiff's legal rights contrived by defendants for the purpose of inflicting damage, or having that as its necessary effect, is as plainly inhibited by the law as if it involved a breach of the peace. A

---

[14] In Bittner v. West Virginia-Pittsburgh Coal Co., 15 Fed. (2d) 652 (4th cir. 1926), the injunction awarded followed exactly the terms of the injunction awarded in the Hitchman case. To the contention of the defendants that its scope was too wide, the court replied: "Defendants criticize the scope of the injunction, contending that its effect is to forbid the publishing and circulating of lawful arguments and the making of lawful speeches advocating membership in the union in the neighborhood of plaintiff's mines, but we do not think that this is the proper construction of the order, which is an exact copy of that which was approved by the Supreme Court of the United States in the Hitchman Coal Co. case. In view of what was said by that court in American Foundries Company v. Tri-City Council, there can be no doubt as to the right of defendants to use all lawful propaganda to increase their membership. See: Gasaway v. Borderland Coal Co., 278 Fed. 56. But, that there may be no misunderstanding in the matter, we think that the order should be modified by adding thereto the following provision: 'Provided, that nothing herein contained shall be construed to forbid the advocacy of union membership, in public speeches or circulation of arguments, when such speeches or arguments are free from threats and other devices to intimidate, and from attempts to persuade the complainant's employes or any of them to violate their contracts with it.'" P. 659.—Ed.

combination to procure concerted breaches of contract by plaintiff's employees constitutes such a violation."

The inhibition of section 20 of the Clayton Act (Comp. St. § 1243d) against enjoining peaceful persuasion does not apply, as this is not a case growing out of a dispute concerning terms or conditions of employment, between an employer and employee, between employers and employees, or between employees, or between persons employed and persons seeking employment; but is a case growing out of a dispute between employers and persons who are neither ex-employees nor seeking employment. In such cases, section 20 of the Clayton Act has no application. *American Foundries v. Tri-City Council,* 257 U.S. 184, 202, 42 S. Ct. 72, 66 L. Ed. 189, 27 A.L.R. 360; *Duplex Printing Press Co. v. Deering,* 254 U.S. 443, 471, 41 S. Ct. 172, 65 L. Ed. 349, 16 A.L.R. 196; *Bittner v. West Virginia-Pittsburgh Coal Co.* (C.C.A. 4th) 15 F.(2d) 652, 658.

The principal criticism of paragraph 4 of the decree is that it violates paragraph 20 of the Clayton Act, but, as we have seen above, that section has no application to a case such as this. We see no other reason why paragraph 4 of the decree is not proper. Under the law of West Virginia, when the employees of complainants quit work and refuse to surrender the houses of complainants occupied by them, they become trespassers on complainants' property. *Angel v. Black Band Consol. Coal Co.,* 96 W. Va. 47, 122 S.E. 274, 35 A.L.R. 568. The effect of the fourth paragraph of the decree is to enjoin defendants from aiding and abetting such persons in occupying or holding without right houses belonging to complainants, or in other words, from aiding and abetting in trespasses committed on complainants' property in furtherance of the design of the conspiracy. It is clear that no more effective way of shutting down the mines could be devised than to get the houses of the mine villages in possession of persons who refuse to work in the mines and withhold possession of the houses from persons who are willing to work.

The basis of the contention that certain of the complainants are *in pari delicto* with the defendants and therefore not entitled to relief, as we understand the contention, is that those complainants operated on the union basis for a number of years and paid the "check-off" to the union. This contention assumes two propositions, (1) that the "check-off" is illegal and in furtherance of the conspiracy; and (2) that, once having been parties to the conspiracy, complainants cannot withdraw therefrom and be protected against it when it is directed against them. Without following this argument into all of its ramifications, it is sufficient to say that we see nothing to connect these complainants with the conspiracy except their payment of the "check-off," and we see nothing of itself illegal in the "check-off," nor do we think that, by agreeing to the "check-off," they became parties to the conspiracy of defendants. As said in *Gasaway v. Borderland Coal Co.* (C.C.A. 7th) 278 F. 56, 65:

"So far as the contracts themselves and this record disclose, the check-off is the voluntary assignment by the employee of so much of his wages as may be necessary to meet his union dues, and his direction to his employer to pay the amount to the treasurer of his union. In that aspect the contract provision is legal, and quite evidently there are many lawful purposes for which dues may be used."

It follows that, while we do not approve of all of the findings of fact made by the District Court, we think that the decree entered in the several cases was sustained by the evidence and same is accordingly affirmed.

Affirmed.[15]

These cases were heard by the three Circuit Judges. The late Judge Rose concurred in the decision that the decrees of the District Court should be affirmed. He expressed a desire, however, to examine the record with a view of satisfying himself whether jurisdiction existed as to the defendants Lewis, Green, and Murray. He died before the opinion could be submitted to him.

EXTRACTS FROM THE PROCEEDINGS RELATIVE TO THE REJECTION BY THE UNITED STATES SENATE OF THE NOMINATION OF JUDGE JOHN J. PARKER AS ASSOCIATE JUSTICE OF THE SUPREME COURT OF THE UNITED STATES.

Excerpt from a letter of Judge Parker to Hon. Lee S. Overman, dated April 24, 1930:

"On the appeal in the *Red Jacket* case the validity of the contracts and the scope of the injunction, as a matter of fact, were not seriously contested, as counsel doubtless realized that we were bound by the Supreme Court's decision in the *Hitchman* case. The principal point pressed before us related to the jurisdiction of the court; but this was clearly

---

[15] Certiorari was denied in this case in 275 U.S. 536 (1927). Upon the effect of such a denial of review, compare the following comments: "Mr. Borah: The Senator does not mean to say that by reason of the fact that the Supreme Court denied the writ, therefore they affirmed the holding of Judge Parker? Mr. Jones: It seems to me that if they thought there was error in Judge Parker's holding they should have granted the writ and brought the case up to them for review. Mr. Borah: The Supreme Court has said many times that in the refusal of a writ they do not pass upon the merits of the controversy at all. Mr. Jones: I do not think that excuses the Supreme Court in its responsibility in denying the writ asked for in a case where the decision of the court below was based on a decision rendered by the Supreme Court." 72 Cong. Rec. 8439-9 (1930). "What would have been the fate of a decision by Judge Parker in the Red Jacket case, contrary to that which he rendered, is indicated by the fact that the United Mine Workers filed a petition for a writ of certiorari with the Supreme Court of the United States, asking that court to review Judge Parker's decision, and the petition for certiorari was denied." Memorandum of Att'y-Gen'l Mitchell to President Hoover, New York Times, April 14, 1930.

See. generally: Carey and Oliphant, "The Present Status of the Hitchman Case," 29 Col. Law Rev. 441 (1929).

controlled by the decision in the second *Coronado* case (268 U.S. 295).
In passing, I would call attention to the fact that the *Red Jacket* case seems
to be much misunderstood. The injunction therein did not prevent
employees from quitting work or joining a union.[16]   In fact, it was not
a suit between employers and employees at all, but between mine owners,
on the one hand, who had made contracts with their employees not to
join the union and the union, on the other, which sought not only by inducement and persuasion, but also by violence and intimidation, to induce
the employees, in violation of their contracts, to join the union and go
on a strike. The Supreme Court had held in the *Hitchman* case that this
might not lawfully be done, and reversed the circuit court of appeals
of this circuit for not enjoining under similar circumstances peaceful
persuasion as well as violence and intimidation." (72 Cong. Rec. 7793)

Excerpts from the speech of Senator Borah, of Idaho, who opposed
confirmation:

"I am willing to concede that the *Hitchman* case in its original delivery restrained the employees from breaching the contract or restrained
the union from persuading them to breach the contract; but it was only
when it was accompanied, in my opinion, with deceit and misrepresentation—in other words, a scheme and a plan by which the employer was
to be misled. That was restrained; and the court would restrain that
if there had been no contract. Such acts, such conduct, would have been
subject to restraint, if they had been injurious to the employer's property, without a contract. * * * I am very frank to admit that if the
Hitchman case had stood alone, without the construction placed upon it
by the *Tri-City* case, such inference as was made by the Fourth Circuit Court of Appeals might have been justified, but 10 years elapsed between the holding in the *Hitchman* case and the decision in the *Red
Jacket* case, and in those 10 years a vast amount of criticism from law-

---

[16] Upon the question of what the injunction in the Red Jacket case did or did not
restrain, compare, besides the statements above, the following comments: "* * * and
I would like to ask you, Senator, what, after an injunction of that kind has been
granted, after it has been illuminated by this decision of the circuit court of appeals,
and a review of it denied by the Supreme Court of the United States, what you could
say to your clients, were they mine workers, if they asked you what further efforts
they could make to organize this pool of nonunion labor. I say they have been insulated against any attempt, any fair attempt, any real effective attempt on the part
of the union to organize them by fair reasoning or persuasion." Henry Warrum,
attorney for the United Mine Workers of America, in Hearings before a Subcommittee of the Committee on the Judiciary on S. 1482, U.S. Sen., 70th Cong. 1st sess.,
pp. 627-8 (1928). "That the defendants [in the Red Jacket case] were permitted to
carry on unionization activities among complainant's employees by peaceful means
so long as they did not urge recruits to remain at work seems clear." Carey & Oliphant, "The Present Status of the Hitchman Case," 29 Col. Law Rev. 441, 452
(1929). "Mr. Lewis [President of the United Mine Workers of America]: That
injunction was issued in perpetuity against posterity. The Chairman: Against peaceful interference? Mr. Lewis: Against any kind of persuasion to have any one of
those 40,000 men join the United Mine Workers. I can not legally say to any one
of those 40,000 men, and the United Mine Workers may not employ any man in
America to say to them, 'Come and join our union; it will better your condition';
because I would be in contempt of that writ." Hearings before the Committee on
Interstate Commerce pursuant to S. Res. 105, U.S. Sen., 70th Cong. 1st sess., pp.
408-9 (1928).—Ed.

yer and layman alike had been leveled at the *Hitchman* case. It seems perfectly clear to me that, upon reconsideration of the principle involved in the *Hitchman* case, the court clearly intended to hold that labor unions were lawful, that union members had a right to solicit membership, that if that solicitation were not accompanied by threats, intimidation, or deceit it was within their right, and that they could not be restrained from such solicitation." (72 Cong. Rec. 7933, 7936, April 9, 1930.)

Excerpt from the speech of Senator Wagner, of New York, who opposed confirmation:

"Now, we come to the final question: Did the *Hitchman* case actually foreclose Judge Parker's judgment in the *Red Jacket* case? Let us compare the two cases: In the *Hitchman* case the court found the following facts: First. An antiunion promise. Second. A union actuated by malicious purpose. Third. Deception and abuse in the methods employed by the union organizers. Fourth. The employees persuaded to join the union and stay at work secretly. In the *Red Jacket* case the court found the following facts: First. An antiunion promise. Second. A conspiracy in restraint of interstate commerce. Third. No evidence of deception or fraud. Fourth. Men persuaded to join the union and quit. On their very fact the two cases are far apart. Let us continue the analysis of each of the four groups of facts: First. The only factor they have in common is the antiunion contract. But had not Chief Justice Taft already stated in the later *Tri-City* case that the fraud and deceit, rather than the contract, explained the decision in the *Hitchman* case? Second. Judge Parker approved a finding that the union was engaged in a conspiracy in restraint of trade. He could not have approved this finding unless he believed and held that it was unlawful for a union to extend its membership and its influence in order to improve the conditions of the workers in the industry. Is that the law in the United States? There is not a lawyer in this Chamber who would agree that such is the law. The notion that a union was an unlawful conspiracy has been dead and buried too long to be disinterred at this late day. There was no finding of conspiracy in the *Hitchman* case. Had Judge Parker rejected the conspiracy finding the court would have been entirely without jurisdiction in the case and the injunction could not have issued. Yet, we are told that Judge Parker was constrained to follow the *Hitchman* case! Third. There was no fraud and deceit in the methods of the organizers in the *Red Jacket* case. In the *Hitchman* case the court based its decision upon these facts. Yet we are told that Judge Parker but followed the precedent of the *Hitchman* case! Fourth. In the *Hitchman* case the court found that the men were persuaded to join the union and secretly continue at work in violation of their understanding with their employer. No such fact was present in the *Red Jacket* case. Quite to the contrary, the court specifically found that the men were persuaded to join and quit. That was not violative of the terms of the employment arrangement. That was not in breach of any possible contract. That was perfectly lawful. Yet we are told that Judge Parker but followed the *Hitchman* case!" (*72 Cong. Rec. 8037, April 30, 1930.*)

Excerpt from the speech of Senator Hebert, of Rhode Island, who favored confirmation:

"On the other question, as to whether any actionable wrong justifying an injunction was committed by the union men in attempting by peaceable means to induce nonunion employees to violate their contracts of employment by joining the union, Judge Parker again bases his decision on the *Hitchman* case where substantially similar contracts were involved, and the Supreme Court held that peaceful efforts by the strikers to induce the company employees to agree to join the union while remaining in plaintiff's employ were properly enjoined. There does not appear to be a point decided in the *Red Jacket* case on which Judge Parker assumed to exercise any independent judgment or opinion. He and his associates felt bound by the Supreme Court decisions. In holding the contracts valid and that peaceable efforts to induce the nonunion men to break them were properly enjoined, he merely quoted rulings to that effect in the *Hitchman* case." (*72 Cong. Rec. 8100, May 1, 1930*)

Excerpt from the speech of Senator Jones, of Washington, who favored confirmation:

"Judge Parker followed what he thought was the law as laid down by the highest court in the land. He could not overthrow the decision of the Supreme Court. That court, however, could have overthrown his decision. It did not do it. Hence I say in all humility that blame, if blame there is, for the decision in the *Red Jacket* case, rests upon the Supreme Court of the United States. But this is not all. I join with the Senators who condemn the scope of the injunction issued in the *Red Jacket* case and affirmed by the Supreme Court. It went too far. It enjoined the doing of that which ought not to be enjoined. Every citizen should have the right to talk peacefully with other citizens, and seek in a peaceful way to have them take peaceful action. The Supreme Court evidently felt that under the law as it now exists such acts should be enjoined and should have been enjoined in the *Red Jacket* case." (*72 Cong. Rec. 8439, May 6, 1930.*)

Excerpt from the memorandum submitted on April 13, 1930, by Attorney General Mitchell to President Hoover *re* the nomination of Judge Parker:

"On the other question, as to whether any questionable wrong, justifying an injunction, was committed by the union men in attempting by peaceable means to induce non-union employes to violate their contracts of employment by joining the union, Judge Parker again bases his decision on the *Hitchman* case, where substantially similar contracts were involved and the Supreme Court held that peaceful efforts by the strikers to induce the company employes to agree to join the union while remaining in plaintiff's employ were properly enjoined. There does not appear to be a point decided in the *Red Jacket* case on which Judge

Parker assumed to exercise any independent judgment or opinion. He and his associates felt bound by the Supreme Court decisions. In holding the contracts valid and that peaceable efforts to induce the non-union men to break them were properly enjoined, he merely quoted rulings to that effect in the *Hitchman* case." (New York Times, April 14, 1930, p. 2.)"[17]

* * *

EXCHANGE BAKERY & RESTAURANT, INC. v. RIFKIN.

New York Court of Appeals. 245 N.Y. 260, 157 N.E. 130 (1927).

ANDREWS, J.: A workman may leave his work for any cause whatever. He need make no defense, give no explanations. Whether in good or bad faith, whether with malice or without, no one can question his action. What one man may do, two may do or a dozen, so long as they act independently. If, however, any action taken is concerted; if it is planned to produce some result, it is subject to control. As always, what is done, if legal, must be to effect some lawful result by lawful means, but both a result and a means lawful in the case of an individual may be unlawful if the joint action of a number.

A combination to strike or to picket an employer's factory to the end of coercing him to commit a crime, or to pay a stale or disputed claim would be unlawful in itself although for an individual, his intent in leaving work does not make wrongful the act otherwise lawful. His wrong, if wrong there be, would consist of some threat, of something beyond the mere termination of his contract with his employer. Likewise a combination to effect many other results would be wrongful. Among them would be one to strike or picket a factory where the intent to injure rests solely on malice or ill will. Another's business may not be so injured or ruined. It may be attacked only to attain some purpose in the eye of the law thought sufficient to justify the harm that may be done to others.

The purpose of a labor union to improve the conditions under which its members do their work; to increase their wages; to assist them in other ways may justify what would otherwise be a wrong. So would an effort to increase its numbers and to unionize an entire trade or business. It may be as interested in the wages of those not members, or in the conditions under which they work as in its own members because of the in-

---

[17] On May 7, 1930, by a vote of 41 to 39, with 16 senators not voting, the Senate of the United States after extended debate refused to advise and consent to the nomination of Judge John J. Parker of the United States Circuit Court of Appeals for the Fourth Circuit, to be Associate Justice of the Supreme Court of the United States. (72 Cong. Rec. 8487.)

fluence of one upon the other. All engaged in a trade are affected by the prevailing rate of wages. All, by the principle of collective bargaining. Economic organization to-day is not based on the single shop. Unions believe that wages may be increased, collective bargaining maintained only if union conditions prevail, not in some single factory but generally. That they may prevail it may call a strike and picket the premises of an employer with the intent of inducing him to employ only union labor. And it may adopt either method separately. Picketing without a strike is no more unlawful than a strike without picketing. Both are based upon a lawful purpose. Resulting injury is incidental and must be endured.

Even if the end sought is lawful, the means used must be also. "Picketing" connotes no evil. It may not be accompanied, however, by violence, trespass, threats or intimidation express or implied. No crowds may be collected on or near the employer's property. The free entrance of strangers, customers or employees may not be impeded. There may be no threats—no statements oral or written, false in fact, yet tending to injure the employer's business. We here make no attempt to enumerate all the acts that might make picketing illegal. Doubtless there are others. When the situation in a particular case comes to be reviewed by the courts there will be no difficulty in drawing the line between acts permissible and acts forbidden.

We have been speaking in terms of the workman. We might equally have spoken in terms of the employer. The rule that applies to the one also applies to the other. The latter may hire and discharge men when and where he chooses and for any reason. But again any combination must be for lawful ends secured by lawful means. If believed to be for their interests employers may agree to employ non-union men only. By proper persuasion they may induce union men to resign from their unions. They may not, however, because of mere malice or ill will, combine to limit the opportunities of any one to obtain employment. The means adopted must be lawful. No violence or intimidation, no threats, no trespass, no harmful false statements, no means that would be improper were the workman the actor.

In writing as we have done, we have in mind cases where the strike, the picketing or the lockout is made use of by associates in the same trade or business; where the end sought, therefore, directly affects those, masters or men, engaged therein. We do not consider so-called sympathetic strikes, boycotts or lockouts where interest is more remote. Questions that may arise under such circumstances are not before us. Neither do we consider strikes or lockouts not connected with labor disputes, but designed to enforce political action.

Where the end or the means are unlawful and the damage has already been done the remedy is given by a criminal prosecution or by a recovery of damages at law. Equity is to be invoked only to give protection for the future. To prevent repeated violations, threatened or probable, of the complainant's property rights, an injunction may be granted. This is no novel assumption of jurisdiction. For many years, while leaving to the law redress for single or isolated wrongs to property rights, where there is danger of their repetition, the chancellor has used this weapon to protect the innocent. The theoretical basis of this power has been said to be the avoidance of a multiplicity of actions. Whatever the basis, however, the power is undoubted. It has been exercised in many ways. Repeated trespasses have been prevented; the continued pollution of streams; the maintenance of nuisances; the misuse of a trade name. Other instances might be cited. The rule is not different where behind the facts presented to the court lies a labor dispute. Freedom to conduct a business, freedom to engage in labor, each is like a property right. Threatened and unjustified interference with either will be prevented. But the basis of permissible action by the court is the probability of such interference in the future, a conclusion only to be reached through proof contained in the record. Unless the need for protection appears, equity should decline jurisdiction.

In the case before us findings of fact were made by the Special Term resulting in a judgment for the defendants. Most of such findings were reversed by the Appellate Division. As a substitute new findings were made by that court and a sweeping injunction was granted to the plaintiff. It, therefore, becomes our duty to review these findings and to determine for ourselves whether they are sustained by the weight of the evidence. (Civ. Prac. Act, sec. 589.)

In 1918 the plaintiff corporation was formed. From the first its intention was to employ only non-union waitresses in its restaurant. Always, with one exception, an applicant for employment was questioned as to her membership in any union and only those who denied such a connection were engaged. No contract as to this matter was then made but the applicant was hired at the rate of $8 per week for full time or $5 for half time. This hiring was at will and might be ended at any time by either party. (*Cuppy v. Stollwerck Brothers,* 216 N.Y. 591.) Thereafter the waitresses were asked repeatedly if they had joined a union. They always denied it. If it had been discovered that their denials were untrue they would have been at once discharged. Also after beginning work each waitress signed a paper stating that it was the understanding that she was not a member of any union, pledging herself not to join one or if she did to withdraw from her employment. She further promised to make no efforts to unionize the restaurant, and says that she will attempt to adjust by individual bargaining any dispute that may arise. This paper was not a contract. It was merely a promise based upon no consideration on the part of the plaintiff. From fourteen to sixteen waitresses were employed and so far as appears the conditions of their work was satisfactory to them.

The three defendants are members of a waiters' union. Its schedule of wages is $15 a week for full time and $10 for half time. Apparently at their instigation four waitresses joined the union after employment was obtained. They had not been members on the date when they were originally engaged. The fact that they had done so was not known to the plaintiff. Efforts were also made to induce other employees to take the same course. At the same time the plaintiff was asked to unionize its restaurant, but it refused.

The Appellate Division has based its decision in part upon the theory that the defendants wrongfully attempted to persuade the plaintiff's employees to break this alleged contract. Even had it been a valid subsisting contract, however, it should be noticed that whatever rule we may finally adopt, there is as yet no precedent in this court for the conclusion that a union may not persuade its members or others to end contracts of employment where the final intent lying behind the attempt is to extend its influence. In *Lamb v. Cheney & Son* (227 N.Y. 418) we said that where a specific contract of employment for a definite time exists another may not intentionally, without just cause or excuse, interfere therewith. In *Posner Co. v. Jackson* (223 N.Y. 325) an employee, having made an express contract to perform specific, unique and extraordinary services for a fixed period, was induced to break it by a rival manufacturer. She might herself have been enjoined from violating her negative covenants. So he who persuaded her to do so might be held in damages. Finally in *Reed Co. v. Whiteman* (238 N.Y. 545) it was sought to use these cases as authority to support an injunction against a labor union which was persuading employees who were engaged under a written contract from week to week, to strike. In that case, however, there was a finding, binding upon us, to the effect that the action of the union was "with the intent and purpose solely of preventing plaintiff from doing any business and of ruining plaintiff in its business, and bringing disorder into plaintiff's business." Contract or no contract such an act, induced solely by malice, was wrongful. Here, however, we do not need to decide whether where the object of the act is to aid in a labor dispute, there is just cause or excuse for such interference with existing contracts, and if not how specific the contract must be, nor how substantial the term of employment contained therein to permit equity to intervene. Nor need we discuss the correlative question as to how far contracts made by unions with their members, providing that they are to work only in union shops, are to be protected.

On April 22, 1925, some of the defendants representing the union entered the plaintiff's restaurant as ordinary customers. They did this, however, with the preconceived design of causing a strike by blowing a whistle at a time inconvenient to the plaintiff when many patrons were present. In so acting they were clearly trespassers and if such trespasses were to be continued in the future they might be enjoined. It was an isolated wrong, however, and adequate compensation might be recovered in an action at law. When the strike was declared the four waitresses who had joined the union at once stopped work and left the premises. In so doing one of them threatened an officer of the plaintiff and she interfered with the access of a patron of the restaurant. A crowd collected but was soon dispersed. Again we have an isolated instance of intimidation occuring at the outset of the strike. Thereafter there was picketing which consisted of two women walking in the street close to the curb but near the premises, having placards ten by sixteen inches in size pinned to their dresses and bearing the legend: "Waitresses Strike Picket. Waiters Union Local No. 1. Affiliated with the American Federation of Labor and the United Hebrew Trades." There was no violence; no intimidation; no obstruction of entrances to the premises; no collection of crowds. This course of conduct continued for four days until it was ended by a temporary injunction.

Under such a state of facts the defendants have been enjoined from "patrolling the sidewalk and street in front of and near the plaintiff's premises, from approaching, accosting, threatening, assaulting or intimidating any person desiring to enter the premises, from blockading the entrance thereto, from collecting crowds, from exhibiting any signs or notices in the vicinity, from suggesting a boycott, and from coercing or intimidating any person seeking to enter the employment of the plaintiff." In this we think the Appellate Division has erred.

As we have indicated, the action of those defendants who entered the restaurant when the strike was called was a trespass. There is, however, no indication that such acts will be repeated. There was no contract between the plaintiff and its waitresses in regard to the union with which the defendants can be said to have interfered. There is nothing untruthful in the placards carried by the pickets, even assuming that the word "strike" is to be confined to cases where some of those who have become employees of the plaintiff have left its employment to obtain relief in a labor dispute. Such was the case here. Three of these four waitresses were employed by the plaintiff long before they became members of the union. Their reply to inquiries then made was entirely truthful. To the fourth, no questions were put. If they subsequently joined the union they might have been discharged; but until they were discharged they remained in the plaintiff's employment. Except on the one occasion the picketing was entirely lawful and for a lawful object, although the plaintiff's business might be injured thereby. It is said that the strike was not properly called because of the neglect of some preliminaries which the union rules required in such a case, and that the four waitresses referred to were not properly members of the union because their dues had not been paid. This is a question as to which the plaintiff is not interested.

It is quite true that where unlawful picketing has been continued; where violence and intimidation have been used and where misstatements as to the employers' business have been distributed, a broad injunction prohibiting all picketing may be granted. The course of conduct of the strikers has been such as to indicate the danger of injury to property if any picketing whatever is allowed. Such is not this case. Nor should a court of equity intervene where there is no evidence that wrongs have been committed or threatened on the theory that the defendant is not harmed by the prohibition of such unlawful acts.

> *The judgment of the Appellate Division should be reversed and that of the Special Term affirmed, with costs in this court and in the Appellate Division.*[18]

INTERBOROUGH RAPID TRANSIT CO. v. LAVIN.

New York Court of Appeals. 247 N.Y. 65, 159 N E. 863 (1928).

LEHMAN, J.: The plaintiff is a public service corporation. It operates a system of rapid transit railroads in the city of New York consisting of approximately one hundred and thirty-eight miles of elevated railroad and two hundred and forty-four miles of subway railroad. It is said that it transports over three million passengers daily on approximately nine thousand trains. It is evident that the general public of the city of New York is interested in the safe, efficient and unbroken operation of this great instrument for the transportation of passengers.

In 1916 there was a general strike of the employees operating the subway and elevated lines of the plaintiff. After the strike was ended a voluntary unincorporated association was formed under the name of the "Brotherhood of Interborough Rapid Transit Company Employees." Substantially the whole body of employees of the plaintiff joined the brotherhood. The members of the brotherhood adopted a constitution which was submitted to and approved by the board of directors of the plaintiff at a meeting held on August 30th, 1916. Thereafter the brotherhood prepared a new constitution which was submitted to and approved by the board of directors of the plaintiff at a meeting held on April 6th, 1920. That constitution is now in full force and effect. By its terms the constitution may be amended by a two-thirds vote of the members of the general committee at a regular meeting, provided that certain preliminary formalities have been complied with.

The constitution provides (section 9): "The General Committee shall be vested with the power at all times to promote the welfare of the members of the Brotherhood and of the Company by amicable adjustment of all questions as to wages and working conditions that may arise from time to time. Section 10: The decision of the General Com-

---

[18] The dissenting opinion of Crane, J., is omitted.

For comment on the case, see 38 Yale Law Jour. 249 (1927) ; 12 Minn. Law Rev. 81 (1927).

For comment upon the picketing aspects of the case, see *infra*, pp. 152, 156, 163.

mittee in all controversies between the Brotherhood and the Company shall be final."

On June 30th the secretary of the brotherhood sent to Mr. Frank Hedley, the plaintiff's president and general manager, a letter: "I am instructed by the general committee to confirm in writing, the understanding arrived at at the conference held at our office, Wednesday, June 30th, at which conference it was agreed by the committee on behalf of our members, to allow wages and working conditions to remain 'As Is' for one year beginning July 1st, 1926." Mr. Hedley acknowledged this communication in a letter dated the same day stating: "I am in receipt of your letter of June 30th, 1926, confirming by direction of the General Committee, the understanding reached at a conference held at this office on Wednesday, June 30th, 1926, to the effect that wages and working conditions would remain as then existing for one year, beginning July 1st, 1926. This will confirm such understanding on the part of the management of the Company."

At that time the defendants Lavin, Bark, Phelan and Walsh were employees of the plaintiff and members of the general committee of the brotherhood. Under the constitution of the brotherhood the employees of the plaintiff company were grouped according to the nature of their work and the place the work was performed. Each group constituted a local of the brotherhood. On July 1st, 1926, at the instigation of the defendants Lavin, Bark and Phelan, a meeting of the members of Local No. 7 of the transportation department, consisting of motormen and switchmen employed in the subway division of plaintiff's railroad system, was held. By a vote of 579 against 7 the members rejected a proposal that the wages and working conditions of the plaintiff's employees should remain unchanged. The defendants Lavin, Bark and Phelan made speeches at that meeting urging that those present should withdraw from the brotherhood and should form a new organization called by these defendants the Consolidated Railroad Workers Union of Greater New York. On the following day the defendants Lavin, Bark and Phelan, purporting to represent the men present at the meeting, delivered to Hedley, plaintiff's president and general manager, a written communication containing a demand for recognition of the Consolidated Railroad Workers of Greater New York and for a wage increase to one dollar per hour for motormen and seventy-five cents per hour for switchmen. It concluded with the words: "In the event that the above is not agreed to by you representing the I. R. T. Company by six (6) P. M. Saturday July 3d, 1926, these men will cease work at 12:01 A. M. on Tuesday, July 6th, 1926." On July 6th a strike on plaintiff's railroad lines, induced by Lavin, Bark and Phelan began and lasted till July 30th, 1926, causing a large financial loss to the plaintiff. The four individual defendants were leaders in the strike. After the strike was ended they were not employed by the defendant. By various means they have urged and are urging employees of the plaintiff corporation to become members of the Amalgamated Association of Street and Electric Railway Employees of America. They are trying to induce these employees to believe that they will be able to secure better pay and conditions of employment through demands made on their behalf by the Amalgamated Association than under the present system of bargaining by the brotherhood.

The plaintiff has brought this action to secure an injunction which would in effect prohibit the defendants from inducing the plaintiff's employees by lawful or unlawful means from leaving the plaintiff's employ. The complaint also asks damages for past acts. Upon motion by the plaintiff an injunction in broadest terms has been granted *pendente lite.* Leave to appeal has been granted by the Appellate Division and the question certified: "Do the facts pleaded and the facts stated in the moving papers, and the public interest, justify, in the exercise of judicial discretion, an injunction *pendente lite* as prayed for or any part thereof?"

Some of the "facts pleaded and the facts stated in the moving papers" are denied by defendants. Upon a motion for an injunction *pendente lite,* a substantial denial of a material allegation in the moving papers may become a decisive factor in the exercise of judicial discretion. In view, however, of the form of the question certified, we shall disregard all denials, at least until we have determined whether the allegations contained in the moving papers are in law sufficient to sustain the injunction.

Where there is proof of threatened wrong which the courts have power to enjoin, there may be room for the exercise of a sound judicial discretion in the determination of whether that power should be exercised. If the moving papers show that the defendants have done and are threatening to do acts which constitute a wrongful interference with, and disturbance of the relations existing between the plaintiff and its employees, doubtless the public interest in the safe, efficient and uninterrupted operation of the plaintiff's railway system might be a consideration of some weight in determining whether an injunction should issue. In the recent case of *Exchange Bakery & Restaurant, Inc. v. Rifkin* (245 N.Y. 260), we have pointed out that the basis of permissible action by the court in labor disputes, as in other situations, is the probability of threatened and unjustified interference with rights of the plaintiff. That basis must be shown even where the public has an interest in the outcome.

The relations of the plaintiff and its employees are based on consent. Each has freedom of contract. The plaintiff has not entered into any contracts with the individual workers which binds the plaintiff to employ them for any definite period. The employees are not bound to continue in the plaintiff's employ longer than they desire. Employment is terminable at the will of either party at a moment's notice. We speak now only of those relations which according to the allegations of the moving papers existed at the time the injunction was granted. We do not pass upon the effect of new arrangements which, the plaintiff's brief suggests, have been made since that time. Possibly they might present other questions than those which may be raised upon the present record.

The operation of the plaintiff's railway requires a great organization. The affidavits show that it employs about fourteen thousand men.

Some of these employees require peculiar skill and training. If they leave the plaintiff's employ it may be difficult for the plaintiff to replace them. If the workers leave simultaneously in large numbers, doubtless this difficulty in finding others to fill their places would interfere, at least for a time, with the operation of plaintiff's railways and cause the plaintiff great loss.

The plaintiff may doubtless determine for itself the conditions of employment upon its railways which will in its opinion best assure its own interests and the interests of the public, provided it can induce sufficient workers to accept these conditions. It may refuse to employ workers who will not accept a condition or make an agreement that they will not join a particular union or combination of workers while in the plaintiff's employ. Doubtless such a condition, if imposed and accepted, lessens the power of the workmen to compel an employer to meet demands of the workers. The workmen may refuse to accept employment based on such conditions or on any other conditions which the employer chooses to impose. Demands of workmen may sometimes be fair and sometimes unfair. Combinations give the workmen a power of compulsion which may work harm to their employer, the public and even to themselves. Where the workmen do not combine they may be compelled by force of economic circumstances to accept unfair terms of employment. Such conflicting considerations of economic policy are not primarily the concern of the courts. Freedom of contract gives to workers and employers the right to fix by individual or collective bargaining the terms of employment acceptable to both. Unless the workers have by agreement, freely made, given up such rights, they may without breach of contract leave an employment at any time separately or in combination, and may demand new terms of employment which in turn must be fixed by bargain.

In this case the plaintiff claims that its workmen have agreed collectively that they will not join or become identified in any manner with the Amalgamated Association of Street and Electric Railway Employees of America or with any other association of railway or other employees, and that the defendants may not lawfully induce the workmen to break this contract. The assertion in the moving papers that such a contract has been made constitutes only a conclusion. The facts shown must be examined to determine whether the conclusion is justified.

The constitution of the brotherhood provides that employees of the company, except officials and persons having power of discipline, shall be eligible to become members of the brotherhood, and that "Beginning February 1st, 1920, each newly employed person who is eligible for membership in the Brotherhood shall upon appointment and as a condition of employment, agree to join the Brotherhood and to accept its obligations. Such persons, however, shall only be eligible to become members of the Brotherhood after having worked thirty days." In another section, provision is made that all applicants for membership in the brotherhood "shall take the obligation" as appearing in Appendix A "to the constitution." That obligation reads as follows: "In conformity with the policy adopted by the Brotherhood and consented to by the Company, and as a condition of employment, I expressly agree that I will remain a member of the Brotherhood during the time I am employed by the Company and am eligible to membership therein; that I am not, and will not become identified in any manner with the Amalgamated Association of Street and Electric Railway Employees of America, or with any other association of street railway or other employees, with the exception of this Brotherhood, and the Voluntary Relief Department of the Company while a member of the Brotherhood or in the employ of the Company, and that a violation of this agreement or the interference with any member of the Brotherhood in the discharge of his duties or disturbing him in any manner for the purpose of breaking up or interfering with the Brotherhood shall of itself constitute cause for dismissal from the employ of the Company."

Here we have a clearly expressed contractual obligation between the brotherhood and each of its members. True, that contractual obligation may be terminated by any member by withdrawal from the plaintiff's employ, with consequent separation of the company brotherhood. That circumstance does not, however, detract from its binding force, as long as membership in the brotherhood continues. We are here not concerned with the rights of the brotherhood, but with rights asserted by the employer. Question still remains whether the workers have assumed similar obligation to the plaintiff.

That question is not free from doubt. The constitution of the brotherhood was submitted to the approval of the directors of the plaintiff corporation before it became effective. That circumstance suggests that it was intended that the terms of the constitution should become a binding contract between the plaintiff and the brotherhood and its members. Some of the provisions of the constitution too give apparent force to the suggestion. On the other hand, the provision of the constitution that it may be amended by a two-thirds vote of the general committee of the brotherhood, and the absence of provision that changes so made must be approved by the plaintiff, tends to negative any conclusion that the constitution was intended as a contract with plaintiff, and there are other provisions of the constitution which it is difficult to believe that the company intended should be binding upon it.

Undoubtedly the primary purpose of the constitution was to create a form of combination of workmen which would be acceptable to the plaintiff and with which it would be willing to deal in arranging wages and terms of employment. The constitution must be submitted to plaintiff's approval so that the plaintiff should be able to determine whether it would accept the combination so formed. The plaintiff's officers perhaps had their own views as to the nature of the combination which would effect the best results. These views may be reflected in the constitution of the brotherhood. So long as the members of the brotherhood abided by its terms and joined no outside union or combination, the plaintiff might rest secure that collective demands of its workers would be formulated by them alone and that in collective bargaining the workers would be represented by members of the general committee of the brotherhood who were themselves in the plaintiff's pay and employ. Perhaps the plaintiff preferred that the brotherhood should have real or apparent independence rather than be bound to it by contract or other ties than mutual advantage. The constitution of the brotherhood is not in terms or effect a contract between the plaintiff and the brotherhood or its members, but a factor recognized by both sides in the relations of the employer and employed.

The plaintiff might ban from its employ all who would not abandon, as a condition of employment, their privilege of joining any union or combination of workmen. It preferred to employ men who would become members of a company brotherhood whose constitution had been approved by it. The record does not show that the plaintiff exacted any express promise from any worker at the time he entered its employ to join the brotherhood and no other combination of labor while in its employ. Undoubtedly it was understood that all workers must join the brotherhood and abide by its constitution if they remained in plaintiff's employ. The distinction is a close one between such an understanding and an actual contract. In this case such distinction has, perhaps, no practical effect. All knew that failure to abide by the understanding must result in discharge and that, as long as the employment continued, the brotherhood was the only association which might voice the collective demands of the employees.

The organization of a working force of 14,000 men to operate the plaintiff's great railway system is a considerable accomplishment. It constitutes a significant factor in the value of the plaintiff's going business. The plaintiff's employees may have the right to leave that organization singly or in combination, yet interference with that organization by an officious outsider, merely for the purpose of injuring the plaintiff, or inducement maliciously held out to the employees to leave the organization might constitute a wrong which the courts would have power to remedy. (*Beardsley v. Kilmer*, 236 N.Y. 80.) The defendants do not contend otherwise. They maintain that in the present case they are endeavoring to accomplish a lawful purpose by lawful means, and that they are not acting maliciously.

The individual defendants are former employees of the plaintiff whose employment has been terminated because they instigated a concerted demand for change of conditions of employment. A combination of employees for such purpose is not unlawful, and even after an employee has left or been discharged he may continue efforts to effect such a combination, for the purpose of regaining employment upon conditions satisfactory to him. The defendants now, apparently, are working in behalf of the Amalgamated Association of Street and Electric Railway Employees of America. Though the plaintiff's employees are prohibited by the plaintiff from joining that association or union, the union may, despite the prohibition, attempt to recruit its membership from those employees, at least where the prohibition is not part of a contract of employment for a definite term. "It may be as interested in the wages of those not members, or in the conditions under which they work as in its own members because of the influence of one upon the other." (*Exchange Bakery & Restaurant, Inc. v. Rifkin, supra.*) Collective bargaining by an association limited to employees of one company; prohibition by an employer against joining other labor associations may weaken or indeed threaten the existence of a general labor union. The union may argue the greater effectiveness of its own methods, the validity of its own principles. Where employees have freedom of choice, a labor union may not be accused of malicious interference when it urges the employees to make that choice in its favor, even though that choice may involve termination of present employment and consequent disruption of a business organization. This court has not yet been called upon to decide whether employees may lawfully be urged to make a choice in breach of a definite contract. We do not decide that now. At least so far as the injunction prohibits the defendants from inducing the plaintiff's employees to leave their positions and to terminate their employment, it is not justified upon this record.

The defendants have, however, gone farther. They have urged the plaintiff's employees to join the Amalgamated Association secretly, and to conceal their new affiliations from their employer while remaining in its employ. It may be that such action on their part goes beyond the limits of permissible interference by an outsider in the relations between employer and employee. The plaintiff has made its choice to employ none who are members of other labor associations than the brotherhood. The defendants have the right to induce the plaintiff's employees to join the Amalgamated Association though that may involve termination of their employment. They are under no obligation to the plaintiff to inform it that some of the plaintiff's employees are joining the union, so that the plaintiff may exercise its choice of retaining or discharging the new members. They are not under any obligation even to urge or compel their new members to give their employer such information. The defendants are acting for themselves or the Amalgamated Association; and in taking lawful action to advance the interests of the members of that union they are under no affirmative duty of protecting the privileges or even rights of the plaintiff.

A more doubtful question is whether the defendants may not be under a duty to refrain from urging the plaintiff's employees to *conceal* from their employer that they are acting contrary to their employer's expressed wish, if not command. Employment by the plaintiff is based upon the understanding that its employees are members of the brotherhood and abide by its rules. Membership in that association is not merely an inducement to employment; it constitutes an important factor in the relationship of employer and employed. The advice by the defendants to the employees to conceal their membership in the Amalgamated Association can have but one purpose: to induce the plaintiff through such concealment to continue an employment it would otherwise terminate. Exercise by the plaintiff of the privilege of freedom to discharge is to be nullified by concealment of the fact that the employees are acting contrary to the understanding upon which they were originally employed, though if such fact were known it would result in discharge by the plaintiff. Continuation of employment induced by such concealment is calculated to result in undermining the company brotherhood and in the substitution for it of another association of workers with power to compel the plaintiff to accept its demands. Even though we should assume, without deciding, that the plaintiff's employees are themselves not under a contractual or other legal obligation to court discharge by information to the plaintiff that they are joining the Amalgamated Association, the question would still remain whether the defendants are justified in urging the employees to *conceal* facts which, if disclosed, would lead inevitably to their discharge. That question has not been argued on this appeal. We do not answer it now. Many factors must enter into its solution. Not all appear in this record. We merely state the question to point out that we are in no wise determining it.

Though we have decided that the defendants may not be enjoined from inducement by lawful means to leave the service of the plaintiff or to join an organization of employees other than the brotherhood or to make demands upon the plaintiff for increased wages, yet even such purposes may not be effected by unlawful means. In labor disputes, as in all other disputes, the courts may and should restrain acts which are themselves unlawful, regardless of the purpose of the acts. The defendants may not without the permission of the plaintiff enter upon the plaintiff's property or place any signs thereon for the purpose of inducing even lawful action on the part of the employees. That would constitute a trespass. The defendants may not achieve their purpose through malicious falsehood and deceit. They may not use force or intimidation. They may not injure or deface the plaintiff's property. The injunction includes prohibition of all such acts, and to that extent it is justified if the record shows that such acts are threatened. We shall not extend this opinion by analysis of the record upon that point. There is some evidence of threatened trespass; perhaps there is also some evidence even though slight, of other threatened wrongs. Though the court at Special Term would have been justified in issuing an injunction against any threatened use of unlawful means even to achieve a lawful end, and though we leave open the question of whether the defendants may be enjoined from inducing the plaintiff's employees to conceal from the plaintiff that they had joined the Amalgamated Association, the injunction as issued, in its broad scope, was beyond the power of the court. Under these circumstances the orders should be reversed and the motion remitted to the Special Term in order that it may exercise its discretion as to whether an injunction of more limited scope should issue, upon the facts contained in this record.

Both parties have upon this appeal cited decisions, most of them from other jurisdictions, which they urge support certain of their contentions. Some of the opinions in these cases are of great weight because of the strength of the reasoning and the authority of the tribunals. The law that should be applied in this jurisdiction to the circumstances disclosed by the record has been established by repeated decisions of this court. Difficulty, if any, lies in the application of established rules of law to particular facts. Attempt by analysis to reconcile or distinguish decisions where other courts have passed upon a state of facts in which analogy is more or less complete would be futile. It might even tend to confusion or deduction of rules which are rigid or arbitrary. In this State the courts may interpose their mandates between contesting parties only where there is attempt to effectuate an unlawful purpose, or to effectuate a lawful purpose by unlawful means. The privilege of freedom of contract may not be destroyed by force or fraud. Against the threatened use of such means the courts must exercise their full powers unflinchingly. Business and property rights in their broadest sense should be immune from malicious interference. They rest upon established principles of law; they are subject to attack within limits fixed by law. The plaintiff in the exercise of its lawful rights and to accomplish a lawful purpose has built up a great organization of workers who are willing to remain at work as long as the conditions of their work are satisfactory to them. No outsider may maliciously destroy the plaintiff's freedom of choice of the men it will employ and of the conditions of employment. No outsider may maliciously destroy the workers' freedom of choice whether they will accept and continue the employment offered to them. Wrong may not be imputed to the defendants if they seek to further their own lawful interests and purposes by argument and persuasion intended to induce the plaintiff's workers to quit their employment or to join a union or association of other workers and through such union make collective demand for other terms of employment. Wrong begins, if at all, if the defendants use unlawful means to carry out their purpose or perhaps if they attempt to induce the plaintiff's workers to conceal facts where concealment constitutes in effect deception, or to do other acts which contravene express or implied obligation to their employer upon which the employer has legal and equitable right to insist.

The question certified should be answered to the effect that an injunction for some part of the relief prayed for is justified by the record and the order of the Appellate Division and that of Special Term should be reversed, without costs to either party, and the motion remitted to Special Term to proceed in accordance with this opinion.

CARDOZO, Ch. J., POUND, CRANE, ANDREWS, KELLOGG and O'BRIEN, JJ., concur.

Ordered accordingly.[19]

---

[19] For comment on the case, see: 13 Corn. Law Quar. 447 (1928) ; 41 Harv. Law Rev. 770 (1928).

INTERBOROUGH RAPID TRANSIT CO. v. GREEN.

Supreme Court of New York. 131 Misc. 682, 227 N.Y.S. 258 (1928).

WASSERVOGEL, J.: Plaintiff, upon notice duly given to defendants, seeks to enjoin them *pendente lite* from various acts claimed to be illegal and in violation of an alleged contract between the Brotherhood of the Interborough Rapid Transit Company and the individual members thereof, employees of plaintiff. Plaintiff is a common carrier of passengers, operating its system of rapid transit railroads in the city of New York. The Brotherhood of Interborough Rapid Transit Company Employees was organized in 1916, after a strike of plaintiff's employees. The present membership of the Brotherhood is approximately 14,000 persons, all employees of plaintiff. The Brotherhood, otherwise referred to by the parties as the "company union," adopted a constitution which was submitted to and approved by plaintiff's board of directors. On June 30, 1927, a contract was entered into between plaintiff and the Brotherhood "acting by and through the general committee thereof on behalf of the members of the Brotherhood now employed and hereafter to be employed by the company during the term of this agreement." By the terms of this contract the company agreed to employ the members of the Brotherhood, and the Brotherhood, in behalf of such members, agreed that they would work for the company for a period of two years from April 30, 1927, upon certain conditions therein set forth. Each of plaintiff's employees was required to and did sign an instrument in form as follows:

"I hereby declare that I have read, or heard read, the collective bargaining and arbitration agreement entered into between Interborough Rapid Transit Company and the Brotherhood of Interborough Rapid Transit Company employees, dated the 30th day of June, 1927, and I hereby ratify and approve the same and each and every provision thereof; and in consideration of my employment by the company until and including the 30th day of April, 1929, upon the terms and conditions therein set forth, I hereby covenant and agree with said company and Brotherhood that I will remain in the employ of said company until and including the 30th day of April, 1929, unless in the meantime by mutual consent my employment is sooner terminated; and, as a conditon of my said employment, I further covenant and agree that I will remain a member of the Brotherhood and faithfully observe the constitution, rules, and obligations thereof during the period of my employment, and that I am not now and during the period of my employment I will not become a member of or identified in any manner with the Amalgamated Association of Street and Electric Railway Employees of America, or with any other organization of street railway or other employees, or with any other labor organization, excepting the said Brotherhood and except as provided in said agreement dated June 30, 1927, between the company and the Brotherhood.

"I agree further to and with the company and the Brotherhood that the constitution as now amended, which I hereby ratify and approve, or as it may hereafter be amended, with the consent of the company, shall constitute a contract between the Interborough Rapid Transit Company and the Brotherhood, binding upon me and that my employment and performance of services hereunder shall be deemed to be sufficient evidence of the acceptance of this agreement by the Interborough Rapid Transit Company as a binding contract between the company and myself.

"Dated this 30th day of June, 1927."

The complaint alleges that defendants Coleman and Shea, with notice of the aforesaid two-year contract of employment and arbitration, willfully and maliciously began to serve upon the plaintiff demands for recognition of the Amalgamated; that they continued their campaign to organize the plaintiff's employees; that they planned to call a strike on July 26, 1927, but after conferring with the mayor of the city of New York announced an abandonment of the strike; and that since that time, by various methods set forth in the complaint, the defendants have been continuing their efforts to organize the employees of the plaintiff as members of the Amalgamated.

The complaint also alleges that the defendants agreed among themselves to destroy company unions and the contractual relations existing between them and employers; that defendant Phelan and others instigated and carried on an unlawful strike among the employees of plaintiff; that in August and September, 1926, the defendant Mahon and others conspired among themselves to destroy the Brotherhood and induced plaintiff's employees to become members of the Amalgamated; that in September, 1926, the defendants created Division No. 977 of the Amalgamated and have since been engaged in carrying on a campaign to induce plaintiff's employees to break their contracts of employment and obligations to the Brotherhood and to become members of the Amalgamated by various means, including personal interviews, the use of threatening and abusive language, the circulation of scurrilous and defamatory reports and by inducing plaintiff's employees to secretly violate their contracts of employment and become members of the Amalgamated while continuing in the service of the plaintiff and ostensibly remaining faithful to their obligations as members of the Brotherhood.

It is further alleged that the plaintiff has already been damaged to the extent of $130,000; that the plaintiff has property rights protected by the Federal and State Constitutions that are being threatened by the defendants, and the complaint asks for a judgment restraining defendants from persuading the employees of the plaintiff to break their contracts of employment and committing various acts therein set forth, and also awarding plaintiff damages.

Defendants in their amended answer substantially deny all the material allegations of the complaint and set up certain defenses, largely to the effect that the two-year contract of employment is void and unenforcible by reason of alleged fraud, deception, duress, and overreaching conduct on the part of plaintiff. The material allegations in affidavits submitted in support of the complaint are also denied.

Upon the argument of this motion it appeared that the situation here presented is substantially the same as was that in the *Lavin* case recently decided by the Court of Appeals (*Interborough Rapid Transit Co. v. Lavin,* 247 N.Y. 65), *except* that in the *Lavin* case the contract involved was one "at will," whereas in the instant case the contract is claimed to have a definite term of two years, and is otherwise different in form.

While plaintiff claims that the present contract involves mutual rights and obligations and was, therefore, made upon ample consideration, it is the contention of defendants that it is without consideration and because of the conditions to which it was made subject, should fail in equity. Defendants call attention to the fact that the separate ratifying instrument (*supra*) is signed by the employees, and does not contain any promise by the company to employ the men for any period of time; that it was not executed by the company, and any promise of the company to employ the men for a period of two years must come through the general committee of the Brotherhood, which by the terms of the constitution of the Brotherhood had the power to bind the men. Assuming, however, that the promise contained in clause 1 of the contract between the company and the Brotherhood with respect to an employment of two years was actually made by the company to the men, it seems to me that such promise is practically made valueless to the employees by clauses 5 and 6 of this contract which provide:

"5.   Anything herein to the contrary notwithstanding the company may discharge and terminate the employment of any employee for the following reasons:

"(a) For joining or being a member, or agreeing to join in the future, or becoming identified with in any manner, or agreeing to become identified in any manner in the future with the Amalgamated Association of Street and Electric Railway Employees of America or any other labor organization other than the Brotherhood, except as provided in paragraph 7 hereof.

"(b)   In case any member shall be expelled from the Brotherhood for violating any of the terms of this agreement, or for violating any provisions of the constitution or obligations of the Brotherhood, or any agreement contained in said constitution of the Brotherhood, provided the company is satisfied that he was so expelled for such cause.

"(c)   For incompetency, inefficiency, or carelessness in the performance of duty, or for intoxication or the use of alcoholic beverages, or for dishonesty, insubordination, or refusal or neglect or physical incapacity to perform his duty.

"Except as to questions of discharge provided in subdivisions (a) and (b) of this paragraph 5, and questions of discharge for dishonesty, insubordination, or refusal or neglect or physical incapacity to perform his duty, *of which the management of the company shall be the sole judge,* the general committee of the Brotherhood, or its officers, shall be entitled to take up and confer with the management respecting such discharge.

and in case of disagreement the provisions of the constitution of the Brotherhood as to arbitration shall apply to such discharge.

"6. Notwithstanding any provision herein contained, the company retains the right, at any time, to suspend or terminate the employment of any member of the Brotherhood, whenever his services shall be rendered unnecessary by reason of the adoption of any new device or the extension of the use of any existing device or whenever his services shall be rendered unnecessary by reason of any change in economic conditions or the seasonal requirements of the company. The company agrees, however, in all cases before suspending or terminating the employment of any member of the Brotherhood, whenever it may be reasonably possible, to transfer any such employee to some other department of the service, providing he is competent to do the work; and, in the event that such suspension or termination shall be found necessary, any such employee shall be placed automatically upon a preferred list for re-employment whenever the needs of the company shall require additional employees of his class. Any such suspension or termination of employment, however, shall be the subject of conference and review as provided in the constitution of the Brotherhood, and, in case of disagreement, of arbitration as therein provided."

Unlimited and practically unhampered power to discharge employees is given to the company. Even as regards the causes of discharge listed as arbitrable, as, whenever the services of the employee "shall be rendered unnecessary by reason of any change in economic conditions or the seasonal requirements of the company," or "by reason of the adoption of any new device or the extension of the use of any existing device," arbitration here would merely establish that the causes exist and that, therefore, the company may discharge. The contract purports to bind the employee for two years, while the employer is not in substance subject to a reciprocal obligation. Where an employee abandons all right to leave the service of his employer, whereas the employer reserves practically entire freedom to discharge him, there is no compensating consideration.

Whatever the status of the contract at law, the provisions above referred to are, to say the least, inequitable. The term of the contract is, in effect, controlled by the will of the employer and plaintiff is, therefore, in no better position than it was in the *Lavin* case. Not only the employees, but also the third parties made defendants in this case may, in a court of equity, avail themselves of the defense interposed.

In the view that I have taken of the contract it only remains to determine whether the commission of, or threat to commit, such acts on the part of defendants has been established as would justify a court of equity to intervene.

Plaintiff claims that the allegations of the complaint and the affidavits submitted in its behalf are sufficient to show threatened wrong and irreparable injury to warrant the issuance of the restraining order here sought. Its learned counsel has properly urged, and as a matter of fact it was held in the *Lavin* case, LEHMAN, J., writing, that "Where there is proof of threatened wrong which the courts have power to enjoin, there

may be room for the exercise of a sound judicial discretion in the determination of whether that power should be exercised. If the moving papers
show that the defendants have done and are threatening to do acts which
constitute a wrongful interference with, and a disturbance of the relations
existing between the plaintiff and its employees, doubtless the public interest in the safe, efficient and uninterrupted operation of the plaintiff's
railway system might be a consideration of some weight in determining
whether an injunction should issue."

Upon the record before me I do not find such conditions to exist.
Inducing the breach of promise to work is not involved. It has not been
established that violence, threats, fraud or overreaching conduct have
been used to induce plaintiff's employees to become members of the Amalgamated Association, nor that other acts have been committed or threatened which would warrant the issuance of a restraining order.

The Court of Appeals has held, ANDREWS, J., writing (*Exchange
Bakery & Restaurant, Inc. v. Rifkin,* 245 N.Y. 260), that "The purpose
of a labor union to improve the conditions under which its members do
their work; to increase their wages; to assist them in other ways may
justify what would otherwise be a wrong. *So would an effort to increase
its numbers* and to unionize an entire trade or business. It may be as interested in the wages of those not members, * * * as in its own members
because of the influence of one upon the other. All engaged in a trade are
affected by the prevailing rate of wages. All, by the principle of collective
bargaining.* * * Where the end or the means are unlawful and the damage has already been done the remedy is given by a criminal prosecution
or by a recovery of damages at law. Equity is to be invoked only to give
protection for the future. To prevent repeated violations, threatened or
probable, of the complainant's property rights, an injunction may be
granted."

Plaintiff in support of its contention lays stress upon decisions in
Hitchman Coal & Coke Co. v. Mitchell (245 U.S. 229) and *International
Organization, United Mine Workers of America v. Red Jacket Consolidated Coal & Coke Co.* ([C.C.A.] 18 F.[2d] 839). Upon the argument of this motion it was conceded, however, that these decisions were
called to the attention of the Court of Appeals in the *Lavin* case and that
court stated: "Both parties have upon this appeal cited decisions, most of
them from other jurisdictions, which they urge support certain of their
contentions. Some of the opinions in these cases are of great weight because of the strength of the reasoning and the authority of the tribunals.
The law that should be applied in this jurisdiction to the circumstances
disclosed by the record has been established by repeated decisions of this
court."

The court at Special Term is bound to follow the decisions of the
Court of Appeals. In the *Lavin* case the Court of Appeals held: "The defendants have the right to induce the plaintiff's employees to join the
Amalgamated Association though that may involve termination of their
employment. They are under no obligation to the plaintiff to inform it

that some of the plaintiff's employees are joining the union, so that the plaintiff may exercise its choice of retaining or discharging the new members. They are not under any obligation even to urge or compel their new members to give their employer such information. The defendants are acting for themselves or the Amalgamated Association, and in taking lawful action to advance the interests of the members of that union they are under no affirmative duty of protecting the privileges or even rights of the plaintiff."

Plaintiff has not established that defendants urged its employees "to conceal from their employer that they are acting contrary to the employer's express wish." Upon the record before me I have reached the conclusion that the intervention of a court of equity at this time is not warranted.

Motion denied.[20]

NOLAN v. FARMINGTON SHOE-MFG. CO.

United States District Court for the District of Massachusetts.
25 Fed.(2d) 906 (1928).

BREWSTER, District Judge: This is a bill of complaint, brought by the plaintiff, on behalf of the Shoe Workers' Protective Union, a labor union of persons engaged in the various branches of the trade in the making of boots and shoes.

The fourth paragraph of the bill of complaint contains the following allegations:

"4. The plaintiff humbly complains and says that each member of the aforesaid Shoe Workers' Protective Union has, by contract with every member thereof and with the Shoe Workers' Protective Union, assumed certain obligations, among which is a contract that no member of said association will sign or enter into individual contracts of employment with any person, firm, association, or corporation, or any contract which provides that he will not become or remain a member of the Shoe Workers' Protective Union or any local union thereof."

As to this paragraph of plaintiff's bill of complaint, I find that a member of the union in his application promises to obey and abide by the constitution of the union. The constitution (article I, section 3) provides in substance that the approval of the application for membership constitutes a contract between the applicant and the union, and between him and every member of the union, "whereby, in consideration of the benefits and advantages secured to him by reason of his membership therein, he

---

20 The brief of defendants in this case has been published by the Workers' Education Bureau (1928). See also: Carey and Oliphant, "The Present Status of the Hitchman case." 29 Col. Law Rev. 441 (1929). *Cf.* Altman v. Schlesinger, 24 App. Div. 513, 198 N.Y.S. 128 (1922); Mitchell Bros. Co. v. Internat'l Ladies Garment Workers, 5 Law & Labor, 251 (U.S.D.C. 1923).

agrees (1) that he will remain a member of the Shoe Workers' Protective Union until he is expelled; (2) that he will not violate any of the provisions of this constitution; * * * (3) that he will not enter into or sign any individual contract of employment with any person, firm, association, or corporation, or any contract or agreement, which provides that he will not become or remain a member of the Shoe Workers' Protective Union or any local union thereof."

For the purposes of this case, I am prepared to assume, without deciding, that a member of the union has undertaken certain valid contractual obligations by virtue of his application and the approval thereof by the union.

In the fifth paragraph the plaintiff alleged in substance that the defendant employed a large number of members of the union with knowledge that they were members, and with knowledge of the obligation which the members had assumed with the union; that on November 8, 1927, the defendant was formally notified of the existence of the contract, but had disregarded the same, and that it had endeavored, and was endeavoring, to induce the members to violate the contract by entering into individual contract, one of the provisions of which was that the person signing the contract would not become, or remain, a member of any labor or trade union, and in order to induce members to violate the contract the defendant had threatened to discharge any who refused to sign the individual agreement with the defendant, and that, as a result of this malicious interference, many members of the union had been induced to violate the contract; that the defendant purposes to continue with the malicious interference.

The plaintiff has failed to establish by his evidence the allegations of this paragraph. I entertain some doubts whether, if the allegations had been proved, there would have been a sufficient showing of irreparable injury to entitle the plaintiff to relief in equity, but the evidence falls so far short of the allegations that it becomes unnecessary to decide this question. It also becomes unnecessary to consider the defense, raised by the defendant, involving the validity of the contract between the union and its members, if that defense were open to it.

The facts established by the evidence are that members of the union were employed by the defendant corporation in its shoe factory at Dover, N. H. Prior to the 8th day of November, 1927, the defendant called its employees together and asked them to sign a contract, which read as follows:

"In consideration of my employment by the Farmington Shoe-Manufacturing Company, with full knowledge that it operates as an open shop, I voluntarily agree that I shall do nothing directly or indirectly to change that status of the operation of the company; that I will do nothing to change the status of my fellow workmen, nor will I aid or assist in any manner any person to make said Farmington Shoe-Manufacturing Company or its employees conduct work under other than an open shop basis."

It was intimated at the time that any employee refusing to sign would be asked to terminate his employment, and two of the employees who refused to sign were discharged. Two of the employees at first refused to sign, stating that they were members of the union. They were given time to think the matter over, and on the following day, but before the defendant had received the notice, hereafter referred to, indicated an intention to sign and later did sign.

On November 8, 1927, the general counsel for the union sent a written notice to the defendant, notifying it that a number of its employees were members of the union, and that their membership obligated them not to enter into or sign any individual contract of employment with any person, firm, association, or corporation. This notice was not received until about noon of the following day. It might be noted in passing that the notice did not contain an accurate statement of the contract between the employees and the union, set out in plaintiff's bill of complaint. The article of the constitution, already quoted, provides that a member shall not enter into any individual contract that he will not become or remain a member of the union. The language of the contract which was omitted in the notice is of vital importance. It will appear from the contract, which the defendant required of its employee, that the individual contract which it was exacting was not a contract which provided that the employee should not be a member of the union. No employee was discharged because of his membership in the union. To at least two of the employees the representative of the defendant expressly disclaimed any intention of interfering with the employees' membership in the union. He stated in substance that, if the employee signed the agreement, the defendant had no objection to his retaining his union membership.

The defendant did not require its employees, as a condition of employment, to sever their connection with the union. All the defendant sought in the individual contract was the right to continue as a open shop, and this demand was not necessarily incompatible with membership in a trade union.

The evidence fails to disclose that the defendant was aware of the provisions of the constitution of the union, upon which the alleged contract is based, until receipt of the notice, nor does it disclose that, subsequent to the receipt of the notice, the defendant did anything tending to induce its employees to violate or disregard their obligations to the union.

The plaintiff has altogether failed to bring this case within the doctrine of *Hitchman Coal & Coke Co. v. Mitchell*, 245 U.S. 229, 38 S. Ct. 65, 62 L. Ed. 260, L.R.A. 1918C, 497, Ann. Cas. 1918B, 461. There is nothing in the case to warrant the inference that the defendant entered into any unlawful conspiracy to work injury to the union. Its rights to conduct an open shop; and to employ labor only upon the condition that the employee will do nothing to interfere with that right, must be deemed beyond controversy, in view of *Hitchman Coal & Coke Co. v. Mitchell, supra*, and numerous other decisions in both the state and federal courts.

The Shoe Workers' Protective Union cannot, by incorporating inconsistent provisions into its constitution, or by contract with its members, curtail or abridge this right of the employer. It is only when an employer enters into an unlawful conspiracy for the purpose of working injury to the union, and adopts unlawful means to that end, that the doctrine of *Hitchman Coal & Coke Co. v. Mitchell, supra,* can be invoked. There is no evidence before me to warrant the finding that the defendant purposely and maliciously entered upon its line of conduct, in order to prevent the performance of any valid contract that may have existed between the union and its members who were in the employ of the defendant. Whatever it did to induce its employees to sign the agreement with it was done before it was aware of the provisions contained in the by-laws and constitution of the union. Obviously the defendant was actuated by a desire to promote harmony and stability in its own manufactory, by reducing the possibilities of labor disturbances, and whatever was done to that end was done in furtherance of a lawful purpose, and not designed or intended to work injury to others. There has been no invasion of the rights of the plaintiff's organization which would justify a court of equity in granting relief.

Bill may be dismissed.[21]

Section 3. Legislative Interference with Anti-Union Contracts.

ADAIR v. UNITED STATES.

Supreme Court of the United States. 208 U.S. 161 (1908).

MR. JUSTICE HARLAN delivered the opinion of the court.

This case involves the constitutionality of certain provisions of the act of Congress of June 1, 1898, 30 Stat. 424, c. 370, concerning carriers engaged in interstate commerce and their employés.[1] * * *

---

[21] *Cf.* New England Wood Heel Co. v. Nolan, 268 Mass. 191, 167 N.E. 323 (1929); Internat'l Stereotypers & Electrotypers Union v. Meyer, 6 Law & Labor, 244 (Super. Ct. Ohio 1923). See: Stern, "A New Legal Problem in the Relations of Capital and Labor," 74 Univ. of Pa. Law Rev. 523 (1926).

---

[1] The sections of the opinion setting forth the other provisions of the Act of 1898, commonly known as the Erdman Act, which concern the scheme for arbitration set up by that Act are omitted. Section 10 was in aid of the general arbitration scheme. The relationship between that section and the other provisions of the Act plays no part in the majority opinion. Mr. Justice McKenna in his dissent, however, emphasizes this characteristic of Section 10, saying "the inquiry must be whether § 10 of the act of Congress has relation to the purpose which induced the act and which it was enacted to accomplish, and whether such purpose is in aid of interstate commerce and not a mere restriction upon the liberty of carriers to employ whom they please, or to have business relations with whom they please." P. 182.

The 10th section, upon which the present prosecution is based, is in these words:

"That any employer subject to the provisions of this act and any officer, agent, or receiver of such employer, who shall require any employé, or any person seeking employment, as a condition of such employment, to enter into an agreement, either written or verbal, not to become or remain a member of any labor corporation, association, or organization; *or shall threaten any employé with loss of employment, or shall unjustly discriminate against any employé because of his membership in such a labor corporation, association, or organization;* or who shall require any employé or any person seeking employment, as a condition of such employment, to enter into a contract whereby such employé or applicant for employment shall agree to contribute to any fund for charitable, social, or beneficial purposes; to release such employer from legal liability for any personal injury by reason of any benefit received from such fund beyond the proportion of the benefit arising from the employer's contribution to such fund; or who shall, after having discharged an employé, attempt or conspire to prevent such employé from obtaining employment, or who shall, after the quitting of an employé, attempt or conspire to prevent such employé from obtaining employment, is hereby declared to be guilty of a misdemeanor, and, upon conviction thereof in any court of the United States of competent jurisdiction in the district in which such offense was committed, shall be punished for each offense by a fine of not less than one hundred dollars and not more than one thousand dollars."

It may be observed in passing that while that section makes it a crime against the United States to unjustly discriminate against an employé of an interstate carrier because of his being a member of a labor organization, it does not make it a crime to unjustly discriminate against an employé of the carrier because of his *not* being a member of such an organization.

The present indictment was in the District Court of the United States for the Eastern District of Kentucky against the defendant Adair. * * *

It thus appears that the criminal offense charged in the count of the indictment upon which the defendant was convicted was, in substance and effect, that being an agent of a railroad company engaged in interstate commerce and subject to the provisions of the above act of June 1, 1898, he discharged one Coppage from its service *because of his membership in a labor organization*—no other ground for such discharge being alleged.

May Congress make it a criminal offense against the United States—as by the tenth section of the act of 1898 it does—for an agent or officer of an interstate carrier, having full authority in the premises from the carrier, to discharge an employé from service simply because of his membership in a labor organization?

This question is admittedly one of importance, and has been examined with care and deliberation. And the court has reached a conclusion which, in its judgment, is consistent with both the words and spirit of the Constitution and is sustained as well by sound reason.

The first inquiry is whether the part of the tenth section of the act of 1898 upon which the first count of the indictment was based is repugnant to the Fifth Amendment of the Constitution declaring that no person shall be deprived of liberty or property without due process of law. In our opinion that section, in the particular mentioned, is an invasion of the personal liberty, as well as of the right of property, guaranteed by that Amendment. Such liberty and right embraces the right to make contracts for the purchase of the labor of others and equally the right to make contracts for the sale of one's own labor; each right, however, being subject to the fundamental condition that no contract, whatever its subject matter, can be sustained which the law, upon reasonable grounds, forbids as inconsistent with the public interests or as hurtful to the public order or as detrimental to the common good. This court has said that "in every well-ordered society, charged with the duty of conserving the safety of its members, the rights of the individual in respect of his liberty may, at times, under the pressure of great dangers, be subjected to such restraint, to be enforced by reasonable regulations, as the safety of the general public may demand." *Jacobson v. Massachusetts,* 197 U.S. 11, 29, and authorities there cited. Without stopping to consider what would have been the rights of the railroad company under the Fifth Amendment, had it been indicted under the act of Congress, it is sufficient in this case to say that as agent of the railroad company and as such responsible for the conduct of the business of one of its departments, it was the defendant Adair's right—and that right inhered in his personal liberty, and was also a right of property—to serve his employer as best he could, so long as he did nothing that was reasonably forbidden by law as injurious to the public interests. It was the right of the defendant to prescribe the terms upon which the services of Coppage would be accepted, and it was the right of Coppage to become or not, as he chose, an employé of the railroad company upon the terms offered to him. Mr. Cooley, in his treatise on Torts, p. 278, well says: "It is a part of every man's civil rights that he be left at liberty to refuse business relations with any person whomsoever, whether the refusal rests upon reason, or is the result of whim, caprice, prejudice or malice. With his reasons neither the public nor third persons have any legal concern. It is also his right to have business relations with any one with whom he can make contracts, and if he is wrongfully deprived of this right by others, he is entitled to redress." * * *

While, as already suggested, the rights of liberty and property guaranteed by the Constitution against deprivation without due process of law, is subject to such reasonable restraints as the common good or the general welfare may require, it is not within the functions of government—at least in the absence of contract between the parties—to compel any person in the course of his business and against his will to accept or retain the personal services of another, or to compel any person, against his will, to perform personal services for another. The right of a person to sell his labor upon such terms as he deems proper is, in its essence, the same as the right of the purchaser of labor to prescribe the conditions upon which he will accept such labor from the person offering to sell it. So the right of the employé to quit the service of the employer, for whatever reason, is the same as the right of the employer, for whatever reason, to dispense with the services of such employé. It was the legal right of the defendant Adair—however unwise such a course might have been—to discharge Coppage because of his being a member of a labor organization, as it was the legal right of Coppage, if he saw fit to do so—however unwise such a course on his part might have been—to quit the service in which he was engaged, because the defendant employed some persons who were not members of a labor organization. In all such particulars the employer and the employé have equality of right, and any legislation that disturbs that equality is an arbitrary interference with the liberty of contract which no government can legally justify in a free land. These views find support in adjudged cases, some of which are cited in the margin.[2] Of course, if the parties by contract fix the period of service, and prescribe the conditions upon which the contract may be terminated, such contract would control the rights of the parties as between themselves, and for any violation of those provisions the party wronged would have his appropriate civil action. And it may be—but upon that point we express no opinion—that in the case of a labor contract between an employer engaged in interstate commerce and his employé, Congress could make it a crime for either party without sufficient or just excuse or notice to disregard the terms of such contract or to refuse to perform it. In the absence, however, of a valid contract between the parties controlling their conduct towards each other and fixing a period of service, it cannot be, we repeat, that an employer is under any legal obligation, against his will, to retain an employé in his personal service any more than an employé can be compelled, against his will, to remain in the personal service of another. So far as this record discloses the facts the defendant, who seemed to have authority in the premises, did not agree to keep Coppage in service for any particular time, nor did Coppage agree to remain in such service a moment longer than he chose. The latter was at liberty to quit the service without assigning any reason for his leaving. And the defendant was at liberty, in his discretion, to discharge Coppage from service without giving any reason for so doing.

As the relations and the conduct of the parties towards each other was not controlled by any contract other than a general agreement on one side to accept the services of the employé and a general agreement on the other side to render services to the employer—no term being fixed for the continuance of the employment—Congress could not, consistently with the Fifth Amendment, make it a crime against the United States to discharge the employé because of his being a member of a labor organization.

[2] People v. Marcus, 185 N.Y. 257; National Protection Ass'n v. Cummings, 170 N.Y. 315; Jacobs v. Cohen, 183 N.Y. 207; State v. Julow, 129 Mo. 163; State v. Goodwill, 33 W. Va. 179; Gillespie v. People, 188 Ill. 176; State v. Kreutzberg, 114 Wis. 530; Wallace v. Georgia, C. & N. Ry. Co., 94 Ga. 732; Hundley v. L. & N. R. R. Co., 105 Ky. 162; Brewster v. Miller's Sons & Co., 101 Ky. 268; N. Y. &c. R. R. Co. v. Schaffer, 65 Ohio St. 414; Arthur v. Oakes, 63 Fed. 310.

But it is suggested that the authority to make it a crime for an agent or officer of an interstate carrier, having authority in the premises from his principal, to discharge an employé from service to such carrier, simply because of his membership in a labor organization, can be referred to the power of Congress to regulate interstate commerce, without regard to any question of personal liberty or right of property arising under the Fifth Amendment. This suggestion can have no bearing in the present discussion unless the statute, in the particular just stated, is within the meaning of the Constitution a regulation of commerce among the States. If it be not, then clearly the Government cannot invoke the commerce clause of the Constitution as sustaining the indictment against Adair.

* * * Manifestly, any rule prescribed for the conduct of interstate commerce, in order to be within the competency of Congress under its power to regulate commerce among the States, must have some real or substantial relation to or connection with the commerce regulated. But what possible legal or logical connection is there' between an employé's membership in a labor organization and the carrying on of interstate commerce? Such relation to a labor organization cannot have, *in itself* and in the eye of the law, any bearing upon the commerce with which the employé is connected by his labor and services. Labor associations, we assume, are organized for the general purpose of improving or bettering the conditions and conserving the interests of its members as wage-earners—an object entirely legitimate and to be commended rather than condemned. But surely those associations as labor organizations have nothing to do with interstate commerce as such. One who engages in the service of an interstate carrier will, it must be assumed, faithfully perform his duty, whether he be a member or not a member of a labor organization. His fitness for the position in which he labors and his diligence in the discharge of his duties cannot in law or sound reason depend in any degree upon his being or not being a member of a labor organization. It cannot be assumed that his fitness is assured, or his diligence increased, by such membership, or that he is less fit or less diligent because of his not being a member of such an organization. It is the employé as a man and not as a member of a labor organization who labors in the service of an interstate carrier. * * *

Looking alone at the words of the statute for the purpose of ascertaining in scope and effect, and of determining its validity, we hold that there is no such connection between interstate commerce and membership in a labor organization as to authorize Congress to make it a crime against the United States for an agent of an interstate carrier to discharge an employé because of such membership on his part. If such a power exists in Congress it is difficult to perceive why it might not, by absolute regulation, require interstate carriers, under penalties, to employ in the conduct of its interstate business *only* members of labor organizations, or *only* those who are *not* members of such organizations—a power which could not be recognized as existing under the Constitution of the United States. No such rule of criminal liability as that to which we have referred can be regarded as, in any just sense, a regulation of interstate commerce. We need scarcely repeat what this court has more than once said, that the power to regulate interstate commerce, great and paramount as that power is, cannot be exerted in violation of any fundamental right secured by other provisions of the constitution. *Gibbons v. Ogden,* 9 Wheat. 1, 196; *Lottery case,* 188 U.S. 321, 353. * * *

The judgment must be reversed, with directions to set aside the verdict and judgment of conviction, sustain the demurrer to the indictment, and dismiss the case.

It is so ordered.

MR. JUSTICE HOLMES, dissenting.[3]

I also think that the statute is constitutional, and but for the decision of my brethren I should have felt pretty clear about it.

As we all know, there are special labor unions of men engaged in the service of carriers. These unions exercise a direct influence upon the employment of labor in that business, upon the terms of such employment and upon the business itself. Their very existence is directed specifically to the business, and their connection with it is at least as intimate and important as that of safety couplers, and, I should think, as the liability of master to servant, matters which, it is admitted, Congress might regulate, so far as they concern commerce among the States. I suppose that it hardly would be denied that some of the relations of railroads with unions of railroad employés are closely enough connected with commerce to justify legislation by Congress. If so, legislation to prevent the exclusion of such unions from employment is sufficiently near.

The ground on which this particular law is held bad is not so much that it deals with matters remote from commerce among the States, as that it interferes with the paramount individual rights, secured by the Fifth Amendment. The section is, in substance, a very limited interference with freedom of contract, no more. It does not require the carriers to employ any one. It does not forbid them to refuse to employ any one, for any reason they deem good, even where the notion of a choice of persons is a fiction and wholesale employment is necessary upon general principles that it might be proper to control. The section simply prohibits the more powerful party to exact certain undertakings, or to threaten dismissal or unjustly discriminate on certain grounds against those already employed. I hardly can suppose that the grounds on which a contract lawfully may be made to end are less open to regulation than other terms. So I turn to the general question whether the employment can be regulated at all. I confess that I think that the right to make contracts at will that has been derived from the word liberty in the amendments has been stretched to its extreme by the decisions; but they agree that sometimes the right may be restrained. Where there is, or generally is believed to be, an important ground of public policy for restraint the Constitution does not forbid it, whether this court agrees or disagrees with the policy pursued. It cannot be doubted that to prevent strikes, and,

---

[3] The dissenting opinion of Mr. Justice McKenna is omitted. Mr. Justice Moody did not participate in the decision of the case.

so far as possible, to foster its scheme of arbitration, might be deemed by Congress an important point of policy, and I think it impossible to say that Congress might not reasonably think that the provision in question would help a good deal to carry its policy along. But suppose the only effect really were to tend to bring about the complete unionizing of such railroad laborers as Congress can deal with, I think that object alone would justify the act. I quite agree that the question what and how much good labor unions do, is one on which intelligent people may differ,—I think that laboring men sometimes attribute to them advantages, as many attribute to combinations of capital disadvantages, that really are due to economic conditions of a far wider and deeper kind—but I could not pronounce it unwarranted if Congress should decide that to foster a strong union was for the best interest, not only of the men, but of the railroads and the country at large.[4]

---

[4] *Cf.* Texas & N. O. R. R. Co. v. Brotherhood of Ry. & S. S. Clerks, 281 U.S. 548 (1930). In this case the Brotherhood sought to enjoin the Railroad from influencing or coercing its employees from designating representatives of its own choosing for the purposes of an arbitration under the Railway Labor Act of 1926. Section 3 of that Act provided that the respective parties to a proceeding should select representatives "as may be provided in their corporate organization or unincorporated association, or by other means of collective action, without interference, influence or coercing exercised by either party over the self-organization or designation of representatives by the other." The Brotherhood had been the designated agent of the railway clerks in the employ of the Railroad to represent them in all matters relating to employment. Pending a controversy over wages which had been referred to the United States Board of Mediation, the Railroad sought to instigate the formation of a union among its clerks, and endeavored to intimidate its employees into joining this union and withdrawing from the Brotherhood, and thus prevent the employees from freely designating their representatives by collective action. The "intimidation" consisted mainly of threats to discharge those employees from its service who refused to join the union and withdraw from the Brotherhood. An injunction against this and other means of interference was awarded. In affirming the action of the lower court, Chief Justice Hughes, speaking for the Supreme Court, said: "We entertain no doubt of the constitutional authority of Congress to enact the prohibition. The power to regulate commerce is the power to enact 'all appropriate legislation' for its 'protection and advancement' (The Daniel Ball, 10 Wall. 557, 564); to adopt measures 'to promote its growth and insure its safety' (County of Mobile v. Kimball, 102 U.S. 691, 696, 697); to 'foster, protect, control and restrain' (Second Employers' Liability Cases, 223 U.S. 1, 47). Exercising this authority, Congress may facilitate the amicable settlement of disputes which threaten the service of the necessary agencies of interstate transportation. In shaping its legislation to this end, Congress was entitled to take cognizance of actual conditions and to address itself to practicable measures. The legality of collective action on the part of employees in order to safeguard their proper interests is not to be disputed. It has long been recognized that employees are entitled to organize for the purpose of securing the redress of grievances and to promote agreements with employers relating to rates of pay and conditions of work. American Steel Foundries v. Tri-City Central Trades Council, 257 U.S. 184, 209. Congress was not required to ignore this right of the employees but could safeguard it and seek to make their appropriate collective action an instrument of peace rather than of strife. Such collective action would be a mockery if representation were made futile by interferences with freedom of choice. Thus the prohibition by Congress of interference with the selection of representatives for the purpose of negotiation and conference between employers and employees, instead of being an invasion of the constitutional right of either, was based on the recognition of the rights of both. The petitioners invoke the principle declared in Adair v. United States, 208 U.S. 161, and Coppage v. Kansas, 236 U.S. 1, but these decisions are inapplicable. The Railway Labor Act of 1926 does not interfere with the normal exercise of the right of the carrier to select its employees or to

COPPAGE v. KANSAS.

Supreme Court of the United States. 236 U.S. 1 (1915).

MR. JUSTICE PITNEY delivered the opinion of the court.

In a local court in one of the counties of Kansas, plaintiff in error was found guilty and adjudged to pay a fine, with imprisonment as the alternative, upon an information charging him with a violation of an act of the legislature of that State, approved March 13, 1903, being Chap. 222 of the session laws of that year, found also as §§ 4674 and 4675, Gen. Stat. Kansas 1909. The act reads as follows:

"AN ACT to provide a penalty for coercing or influencing or making demands upon or requirements of employés, servants, laborers, and persons seeking employment.

"Be it Enacted, etc.:

"SECTION 1. That it shall be unlawful for any individual or member of any firm, or any agent, officer or employé of any company or corporation, to coerce, require, demand or influence any person or persons to enter into any agreement, either written or verbal, not to join or become or remain a member of any labor organization or association, as a condition of such person or persons securing employment, or continuing in the employment of such individual, firm, or corporation.

"SEC. 2. Any individual or member of any firm or any agent, officer or employé of any company or corporation violating the provisions of this act shall be deemed guilty of a misdemeanor, and upon conviction thereof shall be fined in a sum not less than fifty dollars or imprisoned in the county jail not less than thirty days."

The judgment was affirmed by the Supreme Court of the State, two justices dissenting (87 Kansas, 752), and the case is brought here upon the ground that the statute, as construed and applied in this case, is in conflict with that provision of the Fourteenth Amendment of the Constitution of the United States which declares that no State shall deprive any person of liberty or property without due process of law.

---

discharge them. The statute is not aimed at this right of the employers but at the interference with the right of employees to have representatives of their own choosing. As the carriers subject to the Act have no constitutional right to interfere with the freedom of the employees in making their selections, they cannot complain of the statute on constitutional grounds." Pp. 570-571. See Berman, "The Supreme Court and the Railway Labor Act," 20 Am. Econ. Rev. 619 (1930) ; 40 Yale Law Jour. 92 (1930) ; 25 Ill. Law Rev. 310 (1931) ; 42 Harv. Law Rev. 108 (1929).

For criticism of the Adair case, see: Olney, "Discrimination against Union Labor—Legal?," 42 Am. Law Rev. 161 (1908). For Attorney General Olney's position upon the attitude of railroads discharging their employees because of membership in a union, see the brief filed by him in Platt v. Phila. & Reading R. R. Co., (Cir. Ct. Pa. 1894), reprinted in Publications Church Social Union, Ser. B. No. 9 (Dec. 15, 1895). For Attorney General Olney's part in the framing of the Erdman Act, especially § 10 thereof, see James, Richard Olney and his Public Service, c. VI (1923). See also: Darling, "The Adair Case," 42 Am. Law Rev. 884 (1908).

Cf. Railway Employees' Dept. v. Nashville, C. & St. L. Ry. Co., U.S. R.R. Labor Bd. Dec. No. 2305 (1924) ; Division No. 807 v. Omaha & Council Bluffs St. Ry. Co., Nat'l. War Labor Bd. Docket No. 154 (1919).

The facts, as recited in the opinion of the Supreme Court, are as follows: About July 1, 1911, one Hedges was employed as a switchman by the St. Louis & San Francisco Railway Company, and was a member of a labor organization called the Switchmen's Union of North America. Plaintiff in error was employed by the railway company as superintendent, and as such he requested Hedges to sign an agreement, which he presented to him in writing, at the same time informing him that if he did not sign it he could not remain in the employ of the company. The following is a copy of the paper thus presented:

Fort Scott, Kansas, ...1911.

Mr. T. B. Coppage, Superintendent Frisco Lines, Fort Scott:

We, the undersigned, have agreed to abide by your request, that is, to withdraw from the Switchmen's Union, while in the service of the Frisco Company.

(Signed)   ....

Hedges refused to sign this, and refused to withdraw from the labor organization. Thereupon plaintiff in error, as such superintendent, discharged him from the service of the company.

* * * We have to deal, therefore, with a statute that, as construed and applied, makes it a criminal offense punishable with fine or imprisonment for an employer or his agent to merely prescribe, as a condition upon which one may secure certain employment or remain in such employment (the employment being terminable at will), that the employé shall enter into an agreement not to become or remain a member of any labor organization while so employed; the employé being subject to no incapacity or disability, but on the contrary free to exercise a voluntary choice.

In *Adair v. United States,* 208 U.S. 161, this court had to deal with a question not distinguishable in principle from the one now presented. * * *

Unless it is to be overruled, this decision is controlling upon the present controversy; for if Congress is prevented from arbitrary interference with the liberty of contract because of the "due process" provision of the Fifth Amendment, it is too clear for argument that the States are prevented from the like interference by virtue of the corresponding clause of the Fourteenth Amendment; and hence if it be unconstitutional for Congress to deprive an employer of liberty or property for threatening an employé with loss of employment or discriminating against him because of his membership in a labor organization, it is unconstitutional for a State to similarly punish an employer for requiring his employé, as a condition of securing or retaining employment, to agree not to become or remain a member of such an organization while so employed.

It is true that, while the statute that was dealt with in the *Adair Case* contained a clause substantially identical with the Kansas act now under consideration—a clause making it a misdemeanor for an employer to require an employé or applicant for employment, as a condition of such employment, to agree not to become or remain a member of a labor organization,—the conviction was based upon another clause, which related to discharging an employé because of his membership in such an organization; and the decision, naturally, was confined to the case actually presented for decision. In the present case, the Kansas Supreme Court sought to distinguish the *Adair* decision upon this ground. The distinction, if any there be, has not previously been recognized as substantial, so far as we have been able to find. The opinion in the *Adair Case,* while carefully restricting the decision to the precise matter involved, cited (208 U.S. on page 175), as the first in order of a number of decisions supporting the conclusion of the court, a case (*People v. Marcus,* 185 N.Y. 257), in which the statute denounced as unconstitutional was in substance the counterpart of the one with which we are now dealing.

But, irrespective of whether it has received judicial recognition, is there any real distinction? The constitutional right of the employer to discharge an employé because of his membership in a labor union being granted, can the employer be compelled to resort to this extreme measure? May he not offer to the employé an option, such as was offered in the instant case, to remain in the employment if he will retire from the union; to sever the former relationship only if he prefers the latter? Granted the equal freedom of both parties to the contract of employment, has not each party the right to stipulate upon what terms only he will consent to the inception, or to the continuance, of that relationship? And may he not insist upon an express agreement, instead of leaving the terms of the employment to be implied? Can the legislature in effect require either party at the beginning to act covertly; concealing essential terms of the employment—terms to which, perhaps, the other would not willingly consent—and revealing them only when it is proposed to insist upon them as a ground for terminating the relationship? Supposing an employer is unwilling to have in his employ one holding membership in a labor union, and has reason to suppose that the man may prefer membership in the union to the given employment without it—we ask, can the legislature oblige the employer in such case to refrain from dealing frankly at the outset? And is not the employer entitled to insist upon equal frankness in return? Approaching the matter from a somewhat different standpoint, is the employé's right to be free to join a labor union any more sacred, or more securely founded upon the Constitution, than his right to work for whom he will, or to be idle if he will? And does not the ordinary contract of employment include an insistence by the employer that the employé shall agree, as a condition of the employment, that he will not be idle and will not work for whom he pleases but will serve his present employer, and him only, so long as the relation between them shall continue? Can the right of making contracts be enjoyed at all, except by parties coming together in an agreement that requires each party to forego, during the time and for the purpose covered by the agreement, any inconsistent exercise of his constitutional rights?

These queries answer themselves. The answers, as we think, lead to a single conclusion: Under constitutional freedom of contract, whatever either party has the right to treat as sufficient ground for terminating the employment, where there is no stipulation on the subject, he has the right to provide against by insisting that a stipulation respecting it shall be a *sine qua non* of the inception of the employment, or of its continuance if it be terminable at will. It follows that this case cannot be distinguished from *Adair v. United States.*

The decision in that case was reached as the result of elaborate argument and full consideration. The opinion states (208 U.S. 171): "This question is admittedly one of importance, and has been examined with care and deliberation. And the court has reached a conclusion which, in its judgment, is consistent with both the words and spirit of the Constitution and is sustained as well by sound reason." We are now asked, in effect, to overrule it; and in view of the importance of the issue we have re-examined the question from the standpoint of both reason and authority. As a result, we are constrained to re-affirm the doctrine there applied. Neither the doctrine nor this application of it is novel; we will endeavor to re-state some of the grounds upon which it rests. The principle is fundamental and vital. Included in the right of personal liberty and the right of private property—partaking of the nature of each—is the right to make contracts for the acquisition of property. Chief among such contracts is that of personal employment, by which labor and other services are exchanged for money or other forms of property. If this right be struck down or arbitrarily interfered with, there is a substantial impairment of liberty in the long-established constitutional sense. The right is as essential to the laborer as to the capitalist, to the poor as to the rich; for the vast majority of persons have no other honest way to begin to acquire property, save by working for money.

And interference with this liberty so serious as that now under consideration, and so disturbing of equality of right, must be deemed to be arbitrary, unless it be supportable as a reasonable exercise of the police power of the State. But, notwithstanding the strong general presumption in favor of the validity of state laws, we do not think the statute in question, as construed and applied in this case, can be sustained as a legitimate exercise of that power. * * *

Laying aside, therefore, as immaterial for present purposes, so much of the statute as indicates a purpose to repress coercive practices, what possible relation has the residue of the Act to the public health, safety, morals or general welfare? None is suggested, and we are unable to conceive of any. The Act, as the construction given to it by the state court shows, is intended to deprive employers of a part of their liberty of contract, to the corresponding advantage of the employed and the upbuilding of the labor organizations. But no attempt is made, or could reasonably be made, to sustain the purpose to strengthen these voluntary organizations, any more than other voluntary associations of persons, as a legitimate object for the exercise of the police power. They are not public institutions, charged by law with public or governmental duties, such as would render the maintenance of their membership a matter of direct concern to the general welfare. If they were, a different question would be presented.

As to the interest of the employed, it is said by the Kansas Supreme Court (87 Kansas, p. 759) to be a matter of common knowledge that "employés, as a rule, are not financially able to be as independent in making contracts for the sale of their labor as are employers in making contracts of purchase thereof." No doubt, wherever the right of private property exists, there must and will be inequalities of fortune; and thus it naturally happens that parties negotiating about a contract are not equally unhampered by circumstances. This applies to all contracts, and not merely to that between employer and employé. Indeed a little reflection will show that wherever the right of private property and the right of free contract co-exist, each party when contracting is inevitably more or less influenced by the question whether he has much property, or little, or none; for the contract is made to the very end that each may gain something that he needs or desires more urgently than that which he proposes to give in exchange. And, since it is self-evident that, unless all things are held in common, some persons must have more property than others, it is from the nature of things impossible to uphold freedom of contract and the right of private property without at the same time recognizing as legitimate those inequalities of fortune that are the necessary result of the exercise of those rights. But the Fourteenth Amendment, in declaring that a State shall not "deprive any person of life, liberty or property without due process of law," gives to each of these an equal sanction; it recognizes "liberty" and "property" as co-existent human rights, and debars the States from any unwarranted interference with either.

And since a State may not strike them down directly it is clear that it may not do so indirectly, as by declaring in effect that the public good requires the removal of those inequalities that are but the normal and inevitable result of their exercise, and then invoking the police power in order to remove the inequalities, without other object in view. The police power is broad, and not easily defined, but it cannot be given the wide scope that is here asserted for it, without in effect nullifying the constitutional guaranty. * * *

It is said in the opinion of the state court that membership in a labor organization does not necessarily affect a man's duty to his employer; that the employer has no right, by virtue of the relation, "to dominate the life nor to interfere with the liberty of the employé in matters that do not lessen or deteriorate the service"; and that "the statute implies that labor unions are lawful and not inimical to the rights of employers." The same view is presented in the brief of counsel for the State, where it is said that membership in a labor organization is the "personal and private affair" of the employé. To this line of argument it is sufficient to say that it cannot be judicially declared that membership in such an organization has no relation to a member's duty to his employer; and therefore, if freedom of contract is to be preserved, the employer must be left at liberty to decide for himself whether such membership by his employé is consistent with the satisfactory performance of the duties of the employment.

Of course we do not intend to say, nor to intimate, anything inconsistent with the right of individuals to join labor unions, or do we question the legitimacy of such organizations so long as they conform to the laws of the land as others are required to do. Conceding the full right of the individual to join the union, he has no inherent right to do this and still remain in the employ of one who is unwilling to employ a union man, any more than the same individual has a right to join the union without the consent of that organization. Can it be doubted that a labor organization —a voluntary association of working men—has the inherent and constitutional right to deny membership to any man who will not agree that during such membership he will not accept or retain employment in company with non-union men? Or that a union man has the constitutional right to decline proffered employment unless the employer will agree not to employ any non-union man? (In all cases we refer, of course, to agreements made voluntarily, and without coercion or duress as between the parties. And we have no reference to questions of monopoly, or interference with the rights of third parties or the general public. These involve other considerations, respecting which we intend to intimate no opinion. See *Curran v. Galen,* 152 N.Y. 33; 46 N.E. Rep. 297; *Jacobs v. Cohen,* 183 N.Y. 207, 213, 214; 76 N.E. Rep. 5; *Plant v. Woods,* 176 Massachusetts, 492; 57 N.E. Rep. 101; *Berry v. Donovan,* 188 Massachusetts, 353; 74 N.E. Rep. 603; 3 A. & E. Ann. Cas. 738; *Brennan v. United Hatters,* 73 N.J. Law, 729, 738; 65 Atl. Rep. 165, 169; 9 A. & E. Ann. Cas. 698, 702.) And can there be one rule of liberty for the labor organization and its members, and a different and more restrictive rule for employers? We think not; and since the relation of employer and employé is a voluntary relation, as clearly as is that between the members of a labor organization, the employer has the same inherent right to prescribe the terms upon which he will consent to the relationship, and to have them fairly understood and expressed in advance.

When a man is called upon to agree not to become or remain a member of the union while working for a particular employer, he is in effect only asked to deal openly and frankly with his employer, so as not to retain the employment upon terms to which the latter is not willing to agree. And the liberty of making contracts does not include a liberty to procure employment from an unwilling employer, or without a fair understanding. Nor may the employer be foreclosed by legislation from exercising the same freedom of choice that is the right of the employé.

To ask a man to agree, in advance, to refrain from affiliation with the union while retaining a certain position of employment, is not to ask him to give up any part of his constitutional freedom. He is free to decline the employment on those terms, just as the employer may decline to offer employment on any other; for "It takes two to make a bargain." Having accepted employment on those terms, the man is still free to join the union when the period of employment expires; or, if employed at will, then at any time upon simply quitting the employment. And, if bound by his own agreement to refrain from joining during a stated period of em ployment, he is in no different situation from that which is necessarily incident to term contracts in general. For constitutional freedom of contract does not mean that a party is to be as free after making a contract as before; he is not free to break it without accountability. Freedom of contract, from the very nature of the thing, can be enjoyed only by being exercised; and each particular exercise of it involves making an engagement which, if fulfilled, prevents for the time any inconsistent course of conduct.

So much for the reason of the matter; let us turn again to the adjudicated cases.

The decision in the *Adair* case is in accord with the almost unbroken current of authorities in the state courts.[5] * * *

Upon both principle and authority, therefore, we are constrained to hold that the Kansas act of March 13, 1903, as construed and applied so as to punish with fine or imprisonment an employer or his agent for merely prescribing, as a condition upon which one may secure employment under or remain in the service of such employer, that the employé shall enter into an agreement not to become or remain a member of any labor organization while so employed, is repugnant to the "due process" clause of the Fourteenth Amendment, and therefore void.

Judgment reversed, and the cause remanded for further proceedings not inconsistent with this opinion.

MR. JUSTICE HOLMES, dissenting.[6]

I think the judgment should be affirmed. In present conditions a workman not unnaturally may believe that only by belonging to a union can he secure a contract that shall be fair to him. *Holden v. Hardy,* 169 U.S. 366, 397. *Chicago, Burlington & Quincy R. R. v. McGuire,* 219 U.S. 549, 570. If that belief, whether right or wrong, may be held by a reasonable man, it seems to me that it may be enforced by law in order to establish the equality of position between the parties in which liberty of contract begins. Whether in the long run it is wise for the workingmen to enact legislation of this sort is not my concern, but I am strongly of opinion that there is nothing in the Constitution of the United Sates to prevent it, and that *Adair v. United States,* 208 U.S. 161, and *Lochner v. New York,* 198 U.S. 45, should be overruled. I have stated my grounds

---

[5] Mr. Justice Pitney here reviews the state decisions, which held similar laws unconstitutional. State v. Julow, 129 Mo. 163, 31 S.W. 781 (1895); Gillespie v. People, 188 Ill. 176, 58 N.E. 1007 (1900), State ex rel. Zillmer v. Kreutzberg, 114 Wis. 530, 90 N.W. 1098 (1902); People v. Marcus, 185 N.Y. 257, 77 N.E. 1073 (1906); State ex rel. Smith v. Daniels, 118 Minn. 155, 136 N.W. 584 (1912). See also, Jackson v. Berger, 92 Ohio St. 130, 110 N.E. 732 (1915).

[6] The dissenting opinion of Mr. Justice Day, with whom Mr. Justice Hughes concurred, is omitted.

in those cases and think it unnecessary to add others that I think exist. See further *Vegelahn v. Guntner,* 167 Massachusetts, 92, 104, 108. *Plant v. Woods,* 176 Massachusetts, 492, 505. I still entertain the opinions expressed by me in Massachusetts.[7]

MATERIAL UPON THE POLICY OF EXACTING ANTI-UNION CONTRACTS.

Report of the United States Coal Commission, (1923) Pt. 1, p. 179: "Notwithstanding the decisions of the Supreme Court of the United States that the so-called 'yellow-dog' contract is legal, the commission is of the opinion that it is a source of economic irritation, and is no more justifiable than any other form of contract which debars the individual from employment solely because of membership or nonmembership in any organization. The right of an employer to discharge for disloyalty, dishonesty, and incompetency or other unlawful conduct should not be abridged, but he should not be permitted to blacklist a discharged laborer for any other reason than disloyalty, dishonesty, or unlawful conduct." [8]

League for Industrial Rights, 2 Law & Labor, 166 (1920): * * * "Recently, anti-union contracts, so offensive in character as to call for unqualified condemnation, have come to our attention. One of them, entitled

---

[7] For criticism of the decision, see: Powell, "Collective Bargaining," 33 Pol. Sci. Quar. 396 (1918) ; 28 Harv. Law Rev. 496 (1915) ; 24 Yale Law Jour. 677 (1915) ; 13 Mich. Law Rev. 497 (1915) ; 63 Univ. of Pa. Law Rev. 566 (1915) ; 2 Va. Law Rev. 540 (1915). For statutory developments antagonistic to the underlying concepts of the case, see: 44 Harv. Law Rev. 1287 (1931).

Cf. Owen v. Westwood Lumber Co., 22 Fed.(2d) 992 (D. Ore. 1927) (holding unconstitutional a state statute making it criminal to threaten the discharge of an employee unless he trades at a particular place). Ex parte Messer, 87 Fla. 92, 99 So. 330 (1924) (holding unconstitutional a state statute placing restrictions upon the employment of laborers in a county other than that of their residence) ; In re Opinion of the Justices, 267 Mass. 607, 166 N.E. 401 (1929) (advising against the constitutionality of a state statute invalidating contracts of employment whereby the employer requires as a consideration for the employment that the employee purchase some capital stock in the employer's business) ; In re Opinion of the Justices, 220 Mass. 627, 108 N.E. 807 (1915) (advising against the constitutionality of a statute forbidding the discharge of railroad employees upon information touching their conduct until such employee is given the opportunity to make a statement in the presence of persons furnishing such information) ; Poye v. Texas, 89 Texas Cr. 225, 230 S.W. 161 (1921) (upholding the constitutionality of a state statute forbidding discharge of an employee because of testimony given by him before a state industrial commission). See, generally, Harper, "Due Process of Law in State Labor Legislation," 26 Mich. Law Rev. 599, 763, 888 (1928).

Cf. Prudential Ins. Co. v. Cheek, *infra,* p. 672.

See also: Schwemming, "Protection of Employees against Abrupt Discharge," 30 Mich. Law Rev. 666 (1932) ; Molitor, "The Protection of the Workers against Unfair Dismissal in Continental Legislation," 15 Internat'l Lab. Rev. 230 (1925) ; Picard, "French Legislation on the Dismissal of Workers," 23 Internat'l Lab. Rev. 1 (1931).

[8] The National War Labor Board prescribed the use of anti-union contracts in the industries over which it had jurisdiction. See: Employees v. Gen'l Electric Co., Nat'l War Labor Bd. Docket No. 19 (1918) ; Employees v. Wash. Ry. & Elec. Co., *id.* No. 1049 (1919).

'Independent Employe Contract,' contains the following: 'That during his employment, said employe will not become a member of any labor union and will have no dealings, communications or interviews with the officers, agents or members of any labor union, in relation to membership by such employe in a labor union, or in relation to the employment of such employe.'

"Under the terms of this agreement, a man agrees to speak to no union man or woman, whether it be his wife, brother, sister, father or mother, concerning his conditions of employment or union membership. Shall employes be thus driven to sell their birthright for a mess of pottage? Can the resourcefulness of radical leadership devise any means better calculated to influence the workers and the public against the employing class? In the name of justice—in the name of public policy— in the name of many other considerations—let us have an end of this."

MAXEY J., dissenting in *Kraemer Hosiery Co. v. American Federation of F. F. H. W.,* 305 Pa. 206, 237-238, 157 Atl. 588 (1931): "These essentially coercive anti-union contracts are socially wrong and legally indefensible. * * * Those employers who frankly recognize the right of employees to unite and to make their united voices heard in matters affecting the conditions of their employment are, according to my view, not only in harmony with the spirit of the age but are showing farsighted self-interest, for reactionism always begets radicalism.

"These anti-union contracts contravene sound public policy for the further reason that they are provocative of violence. Millions of people in the United States, both within and without labor unions, detest these contracts as illegitimate weapons in contests between capital and labor. The very name by which these contracts are commonly known, to wit, 'yellow dog contract,' indicates the public appraisal of them. Yet, according to the decree before us, these contracts are so sacrosanct that equity should shield them even from public discussion.

"These anti-union contracts are not regarded by employers as contracts whose breach gives rise to actions at law. There is no record of any employer ever suing an employee for violating them. This anti-union contract has never served any purpose except as an emplacement for equity's longest range injunction gun. It is a verbal contrivance to inveigle a court of equity into an alliance with the opponents of labor unions in the battle of ideas between unionism and nonunionism."

Senator Borah closing the debate upon the confirmation of Judge J. J. Parker's nomination as Supreme Court Justice, 72 Cong. Rec. 8487 (1930): "In all this debate no Senator has soiled his lips by defending the justice of the contract which is involved in this controversy. No Senator has undertaken to say that it is sound or humane; and, in my opinion, that of itself ought to weigh heavily in determining this question. We are asked in effect to approve and commend that which we are unwilling openly to justify." [9]

[9] For a collection of opinion evidence as to the social justifiability of anti-union contracts, see: 75 Cong. Rec. 4694-4696 (1932).

ACT OF MARCH 23, 1932.

47 U.S. Stat. 70, c. 90.

SEC. 1. * * * That no court of the United States, as herein defined, shall have jurisdiction to issue any restraining order or temporary or permanent injunction in a case involving or growing out of a labor dispute, except in a strict conformity with the provisions of this Act; nor shall any such restraining order or temporary or permanent injunction be issued contrary to the public policy declared in this Act.

SEC. 2.   In the interpretation of this Act and in determining the jurisdiction and authority of the courts of the United States, as such jurisdiction and authority are herein defined and limited, the public policy of the United States is hereby declared as follows:

Whereas under prevailing economic conditions, developed with the aid of governmental authority for owners of property to organize in the corporate and other forms of ownership association, the individual unorganized worker is commonly helpless to exercise actual liberty of contract and to protect his freedom of labor, and thereby to obtain acceptable terms and conditions of employment, wherefore, though he should be free to decline to associate with his fellows, it is necessary that he have full freedom of association, self-organization, and designation of representatives of his own choosing, to negotiate the terms and conditions of his employment, and that he shall be free from the interference, restraint, or coercion of employers of labor, or their agents, in the designation of such representatives or in self-organization or in other concerted activities for the purpose of collective bargaining or other mutual aid or protection; therefore, the following definitions of, and limitations upon, the jurisdiction and authority of the courts of the United States are hereby enacted.

SEC. 3. Any undertaking or promise, such as is described in this section, or any other undertaking or promise in conflict with the public policy declared in section 2 of this Act, is hereby declared to be contrary to the public policy of the United States, shall not be enforceable in any court of the United States and shall not afford any basis for the granting of legal or equitable relief by any such court, including specifically the following:

Every undertaking or promise hereafter made, whether written or oral, express or implied, constituting or contained in any contract or agreement or hiring or employment between any individual, firm, company, association, or corporation, and any employee or prospective employee of the same, whereby

(a) Either party to such contract or agreement undertakes or promises not to join, become, or remain a member of any labor organization or of any employer organization; or

(b) Either party to such contract or agreement undertakes or promises that he will withdraw from an employment relation in the event that he joins, becomes, or remains a member of any labor organization or of any employer organization. * * * [10]

LEVERING & GARRIGUES CO. v. MORRIN

Circuit Court of Appeals for the Second Circuit, 1934. 71 F.(2d) 284.

Manton, C.J.

Appeal from a final decree. The decree, as entered, is alleged to be in violation of the labor law (29 U.S.C.A. Sec. 104 (a, e, g-i)). The case was here before (61 F.(2d) 115), where we reversed the lower court, and that reversal was affirmed by the Supreme Court (289 U.S. 103, 53 S. Ct. 549, 77 L. Ed. 1062). We directed that the bill be dismissed, without prejudice, for lack of jurisdiction unless the appellees amended so as to correct the jurisdictional defect by striking from the bill a number of defendants. Below, the court permitted the amendment and enjoined the present appellants.

These appellants, by the decree made October 14, 1933, amended January 8, 1934, are restrained and enjoined, with their agents or servants or those in active concert with them, "from inducing or attempting to induce owners, architects or general contractors to let no subcontracts to plaintiffs for the erection of structural iron and steel on buildings now being or to be erected in the Metropolitan District of New York, by sending to them circulars or other writing, stating, threatening, warning or intimating * * * that members of the unions associated with the International may or will refuse to work on buildings upon which plaintiffs

---

[10] For the remaining sections of this Act, see *infra* p. 186.

For similar legislation, see: 1931 Ariz. Laws, c. 19; 1931 Colo. Laws, c. 112; 1932 N. J. Laws, c. 244; 1931 Ohio Laws, p. 562; 1931 Ore. Laws, c. 247; 1931 Wis. Laws, c. 376. See: Doscow, "Statutes Outlawing Yellow-Dog Contracts," 17 Am. Bar Assn. Jour. 516 (1931).

Upon the constitutionality of such legislation, see: Opinion of the Justices, 271 Mass. 598, 171 N.E. 234 (1930), criticized in 44 Harv. Law Rev. 293 (1930) and 25 Ill. Law Rev. 307 (1931); Opinion of the Justices, 275 Mass. 580, 176 N.E. 649 (1931), criticized in Corn. Law Quar. 472 (1932); and 17 Iowa Law Rev. 110 (1931). See also: Frankfurter and Greene, "Congressional Power over the Labor Injunction," 31 Col. Law Rev. 385 (1931); Witte, "Yellow Dog Contracts" 6 Wis. Law Rev. 21 (1930); MacDonald, "The Constitutionality of Wisconsin's Statute Invalidating 'Yellow Dog' Contracts," 6 Wis. Law Rev. 86 (1931); Cochrane, "Attacking the 'Yellow Dog' in Labor Contracts," 15 Am. Law Rev. 151 (1925); Cochrane, "Labor's Campaign Against 'Yellow Dog' Contracts Makes Notable Gains," 17 Am. Labor Leg. Rev. 142 (1927); Christ, "The Federal Anti-Injunction Bill," 26 Ill. Law Rev. 516 (1932); Daugherty, "Anti-Union Contracts," 9 Harv. Bus. Rev. 191 (1931).

For the Congressional history of the Act of 1932, see: Witte, "The Federal Anti-Injunction Act," 16 Minn. Law Rev. 638 (1932).

have or may have subcontracts, or by ordering, instigating, carrying on or supporting sympathetic strikes, on buildings upon which plaintiffs have or may have subcontracts, or from otherwise attempting by coercive pressure, threats or intimidation, or such other unlawful means, to compel or influence owners, architects and general contractors not to patronize the plaintiffs."

After issue was joined, the matter was referred to a master, who found that, at the time of the occurrences involved, the building industry in the metropolitan district of New York was completely organized, excepting as to appellants and other members of the Iron League. Unions had been recognized and were operating under union conditions including a closed shop. The appellees and other members of the Iron League were operating on an open shop basis, the effect of this being that, in the construction of large buildings, members of unions operating closed shop and working on the same building at trades other than steel erection would have to work side by side with nonunion men who might be employed by members of the League. This gave rise to a controversy resulting in continuous strife between the Iron League and the International Union for a number of years. The League insisted on operating on an open shop plan, employing both union and nonunion men. The International's policy has been to cause the League to recognize the union and work under union conditions, including the closed shop. As a result, strikes and labor troubles occurred from time to time during the years, some of which were sympathetic strikes.

The master found that the controversy and dispute between the union and the appellees arose because of this difference of opinion and purposes; that the purpose of the appellants was to obtain a closed shop condition, and the purpose of the appellees to obtain an open shop condition in their employment of labor; that, by making public, notifying, advising and urging owners, architects, and contractors engaged in the building business that members of the unions would cease and refuse to perform any work or to remain in any relation of employment with them if the subcontracts let for the erection of steel did not provide for the closed shop; that the appellants did give publicity to the existence of their complaint against the appellees by advertising, speaking, and patrolling and they did so advise and notify the contractors that, unless their requests were granted, they would advise, urge, and get the agreement of others to cease to perform any work or to remain in any relation of employment with them; that appellants, appellees, the owners, architects, and contractors, were all engaged in the same industry; that the dispute was not attended by fraud or violence; and that the defendants did not stand in direct relationship of employer and employee with the appellees.

The present appellants, Paul Morrin, William J. McGinn, Charles Massey, and Earl Calvert, are members of the International Association of Bridge, Structural and Ornamental Iron Workers and are now the sole defendants, for, after the reversal on the former appeal, permission was granted by the District Court to discontinue the suit as to the other named defendants.

In reversing the lower court, we stated that the District Court was to determine whether recent legislation (29 U.S.C.A. Secs. 101-115) had any application to further proceedings in this cause. The applicable provision of the statute is section 104, which reads:

"Sec. 104. *Enumeration of specific acts not subject to restraining orders or injunctions.* No court of the United States shall have jurisdiction to issue any restraining order or temporary or permanent injunction in any case involving or growing out of any labor dispute to prohibit any person or persons participating or interested in such dispute (as these terms are herein defined) from doing, whether singly or in concert, any of the following acts:

"(a) Ceasing or refusing to perform any work or to remain in any relation of employment; * * *

"(e) Giving publicity to the existence of, or the facts involved in, any labor dispute, whether by advertising, speaking, patrolling, or by any other method not involving fraud or violence; * * *

"(g) Advising or notifying any person of an intention to do any of the acts heretofore specified;

"(h) Agreeing with other persons to do or not to do any of the acts heretofore specified; and

"(i) Advising, urging, or otherwise causing or inducing without fraud or violence the acts heretofore specified, regardless of any such undertaking or promise as is described in section 103 of this chapter."

No court of the United States may grant a restraining order, temporary or permanent, in a labor dispute because of doing in concert the acts enumerated in section 104. Section 113 provides:

"Sec. 113. *Definitions of terms and words used in chapter.* When used in this chapter, and for the purposes of this chapter—

"(a) A case shall be held to involve or to grow out of a labor dispute when the case involves persons who are engaged in the same industry, trade, craft, or occupation; or have direct or indirect interests therein; or who are employees of the same employer; or who are members of the same or an affiliated organization of employers or employees; whether such dispute is (1) between one or more employers or associations of employers and one or more employees or associations of employees; (2) between one or more employers or associations of employers and one or more employers or associations of employers; or (3) between one or more employees or associations of employees and one or more employees or associations of employees; or when the case involves any conflicting or competing interests in a 'labor dispute' (as hereinafter defined) of 'persons participating or interested' therein (as hereinafter defined).

"(b) A person or association shall be held to be a person participating or interested in a labor dispute if relief is sought against him or it, and if he or it is engaged in the same industry, trade, craft, or occupation in which such dispute occurs, or has a direct or indirect interest therein, or is a member, officer, or agent of any association composed in whole or in part of employers or employees engaged in such industry, trade, craft, or occupation.

"(c)   The term 'labor dispute' includes any controversy concerning terms or conditions of employment, or concerning the association or representation of persons in negotiating, fixing, maintaining, changing, or seeking to arrange terms or conditions of employment, regardless of whether or not the disputants stand in the proximate relation of employer and employee.

"(d)   The term 'court of the United States' means any court of the United States whose jurisdiction has been or may be conferred or defined or limited by Act of Congress, including the courts of the District of Columbia."

We think that the relief granted in the decree appealed from is in violation of the above statute. The cause grows out of a labor dispute, as defined in section 113 (c), and is a controversy between members of an association of employers and members of an association of employees engaged in the same industry (section 113 (a, c)). The appellees were seeking to arrange terms or conditions of employment.

Now, under the statute, a District Court cannot restrain the notifying of parties by interested individuals (section 104 (g))' of an intention to refuse to work; nor can the court prevent, in the absence of fraud or violence, the giving of publicity to the facts in the controversy (section 104 (e)) or encouraging others to refuse to work (section 104 (i)). The fact that the notification and the publicity will result in coercing the parties informed and cause them to refrain from contracting with the appellees cannot be taken into consideration, for the court is without the power to prevent such notification. The court has not the power or authority to issue an injunction against these appellants who are engaged in a controversy arising out of an attempt to establish a closed shop by notifying general contractors and architects of an intention of members of a union to refuse to work, nor can these appellees prevent these appellants from refusing to work or inciting sympathetic strikes.

It is argued, however, that the deprivation of the District Court of its power to issue an injunction in a case which does not involve interstate commerce and where the jurisdiction of the court is based upon diversity of citizenship is tantamount to a grant of jurisdiction with a concurrent withholding of the power to properly administer the causes over which the jurisdiction has been granted, and therefore the statute is unconstitutional within the rule announced in *Michaelson v. United States*, 266 U.S. 42, 45 S. Ct. 18, 69 L. Ed. 162, 35 A.L.R. 451. However, Congress has the power, as now exercised, of withdrawing this jurisdiction from the District Court. Congress may give either whole or restricted jurisdiction at its discretion provided there is no extension beyond the boundaries fixed by the Constitution (*Kline v. Burke Construction Co.*, 260 U.S. 226, 43 S. Ct. 79, 67 L. Ed. 226, 24 A.L.R. 1077), and Congress has the power to regulate the power which it grants (*Ex parte Robinson,* 19 Wall. 505, 22 L. Ed. 205; *Michaelson v. United States, supra*).

It has been said that the attributes which inhere on a grant of power over a subject and which are inseparable from it, cannot be rendered practically inoperative. But the power to issue an injunction is not necessarily within the class of inherent attributes. *Smith v. Apple,* 264 U.S. 274, 44 S. Ct. 311, 68 L. Ed. 678. Congress has not exceeded its powers in this legislation.

We think it unnecessary to consider here whether this statute denying injunctive relief differs from statutes regarded as valid athough they curtailed remedies. In *Duplex Printing Press v. Deering,* 254 U.S. 443, 41 S. Ct. 172, 65 L. Ed. 349, 16 A.L.R. 196, the statute limited the power to grant injunctions where the relationship of employer and employee existed. The constitutionality of the enactment was raised but not discussed. The court, however, recognized the limitation, by acknowledging that the statute imposed restrictions upon the powers of the federal equity court, and in fact stated that the restriction was in the nature of a special privilege or immunity to a particular class. But the sole effect of the restriction was the subjection of the statute to a strict construction. In *Truax v. Corrigan,* 257 U.S. 312, 42 S. Ct. 124, 128, 66 L. Ed. 254, 27 A.L.R. 375, upon which the appellees rely, the Supreme Court held unconstitutional a state statute which prohibited the issuance of injunctions in all cases, but those in which the acts complained of were accompanied by violence. But the *Truax* Case involved the power of a state Legislature and is to be further distinguished on the basis of the different effects of the respective statutes upon property rights. The Supreme Court stated: "The opinion of the State Supreme Court (20 Ariz. 7, 176 P. 570) in this case, if taken alone, seems to show that the statute grants complete immunity from any civil or criminal action to the defendants, for it pronounces their acts lawful."

In the instant case, the statute considered grants no such complete immunity. Therefore a case is not presented calling for the invocation of the due process clause, since the present statute is in effect nothing more than a limitation affecting remedy rather than property rights. The right of a litigant, as stated in *Kline v. Burke Construction Co., supra,* at page 233 of 260 U.S., 43 S. Ct. 79, 82, "to maintain an action in a federal court on the ground that there is a controversy between citizens of different states is not one derived from the Constitution of the United States, unless in a very indirect sense. * * * The Constitution simply gives to the inferior courts the capacity to take jurisdiction in the enumerated cases' but it requires an act of Congress to confer it. * * * A right which thus comes into existence only by virtue of an act of Congress, and which may be withdrawn by an act of Congress after its exercise has begun, cannot well be described as a constitutional right."

Since Congress may curtail this remedy or withdraw the jurisdiction of the District Court, no constitutional rights based upon the withdrawal of remedial rights can be successfully raised, since the litigant never had an absolute constitutional right to have a federal court take jurisdiction. While we held on the former appeal that there was no jurisdiction, we did permit the District Court leave to allow appellees to amend the complaint. Although the complaint was amended, a new decree could not be entered, for the court had not the power to grant the injunction. The statute was applicable and binding on the lower court at the time of the entry of the decree. *Duplex Printing Press Co. v. Deering, supra.*

Decree reversed.[11]

---

[11] See also Cinderella Theatre Co. v. Sign Writers' Local Union, 6 F. Supp. 164 (E.D. Mich. 1934). Upon the necessity of a showing of inability of county and city officials to afford necessary protection, as a condition precedent to issuance of an injunction, see Laclede Steel Co. v. Newton, 6 F. Supp. 625 (S.D. Ill. 1934) ; Knapp-Monarch Co. v. Anderson, 104 C.C.H. 5495 (E.D. Ill. 1934). Upon the necessity of a hearing in open court prior to issuance of a temporary injunction, see United States v. Weirton Steel Co., 6 F. Supp. 255 (D. Del. 1934). Upon the damages assessable against plaintiff on its bond as a consequence of dismissal of temporary injunction, see Cinderella Theatre Co. v. Sign Writers' Local Union, 6 F. Supp. 830 (E.D. Mich. 1934).

See also National Industrial Recovery Act, *post* p. 616, and cases collected thereunder.

CHAPTER IV.

THE CONDUCT OF A STRIKER.

PEOPLE OF THE STATE OF NEW YORK v. NIXON.

New York Court of Appeals.   248 N.Y. 182, 161 N.E. 463 (1928).

Appeal, by permission, from a judgment of the Appellate Term of the Court of Special Sessions of the city of New York, entered September 27, 1927, which affirmed a judgment of a Magistrate's Court of the city of New York convicting the defendants of the crime of disorderly conduct.

LEHMAN, J.: Twenty persons, named as defendants in this case, were arrested in the early morning of May 27th, 1927, while walking on the sidewalk on the southerly side of West Twenty-ninth street. The police officer, who arrested them, charged in the sworn complaint that they were in "West 29th Street using threatening, abusive and insulting behavior, with intent to provoke a breach of the peace, and whereby a breach of the peace might be occasioned, that said defendants at the hour of 7:30 A. M. did then and there while picketing with a number of others parade up and down in mass formation, thereby obstructing the sidewalk and causing pedestrians to use the roadway." Nineteen of the defendants have been convicted upon this charge, after a trial before a magistrate, and have been sentenced to terms of imprisonment in the workhouse.

This appeal is one of six appeals from judgments of conviction of about one hundred and twenty people, of whom about fifty are women. All the appeals were argued together. The complaints in all the cases are similar. The alleged offenses all occurred at the same place and within the space of a few days. They were all tried before the same magistrate, and it is evident that the magistrate assumed that the defendants, found guilty in all these cases, were walking on this street as part of some tactics adopted to further the interests of a party to a strike or labor dispute in the fur industry. In some cases there is vague evidence which perhaps supports this assumption.

Though the evidence in the six cases is not identical, and the differences may produce varying consequences, yet the determination of the questions involved in the instant case, which the parties chose as the basis of the oral argument in this court, will dictate the answer to most of the questions presented in the remaining cases on appeal. In this case the police officer who made the arrest testified that he had

190

the defendants under observation for ten minutes. They were walking on the south side of Twenty-ninth street between Sixth and Seventh avenues. They were "parading" four abreast. The sidewalk was about twelve feet wide. The defendants in walking four abreast occupied about six feet of the sidewalk. "The regular amount of traffic was just barely getting through." Some persons were "caused" to enter the roadway. The officer stated: "I fell in line with them and walked up to the south-west corner of 29th Street and Sixth Avenue. When they got to the corner they turned around and they marched back again on the same side and a few persons were caused to enter the roadway again. I then placed them under arrest." Another officer assisted in the arrest. Neither officer warned the defendants before the arrest. The defendants apparently submitted to arrest without protest.

We have set forth the entire testimony almost verbatim. There is no suggestion in the record that the defendants' march up and down the street was not quiet and orderly. There is no suggestion that the defendants' demeanor was threatening, abusive or insulting or that any person on the street or elsewhere believed that he was being threatened, insulted or abused. Nineteen or twenty persons walked up and down a busy street four abreast. They were guilty, we may well concede, of atrociously bad manners, and they discommoded some other persons lawfully using the street, to the extent that a few pedestrians were caused to enter the roadway. There is no evidence that the persons discommoded showed any particular annoyance. Perhaps bad manners are too usual to evoke unusual irritation or annoyance. As yet bad manners have not been made punishable by imprisonment. The question presented here is whether the defendants' conduct went beyond mere bad manners and tended towards a breach of the peace.

It is difficult to define exactly and comprehensively the kind of conduct which "tends to a breach of the peace," though a "breach of the peace" was punishable at common law. A definition has been essayed by the Legislature in section 722 of the Penal Law. "In cities of five hundred thousand inhabitants or over any person who, with intent to provoke a breach of the peace, or whereby a breach of the peace may be occasioned, * * * (2) acts in such a manner as to annoy, disturb, interfere with, obstruct, or be offensive to others; (3) congregates with others on a public street and refuses to move on when ordered by the police." We do not now decide whether under sections 1458 and 1459 of the Consolidation Act, a magistrate has discretion to find that conduct which does not fall strictly within the offense defined by the Legislature may nevertheless constitute disorderly conduct which tends to a breach of the peace. At least the discretion confided to a magistrate cannot be without limits. The act complained of must at least be one which reasonably does tend to a breach of the peace, and it is not without significance that the Legislature has made "congregating on the street" a criminal offense only when the offender refuses to move on when ordered by the police.

Though the charge recites that the offense charged was committed while the defendants were picketing, no evidence was produced to sustain this allegation. Doubtless both the magistrate and the defendants assumed, even without proof, that a labor dispute existed in the fur trade at that time, and that the defendants were walking in the street in pursuance of some tactics intended to advance the interest of a party or parties to that dispute. Even if we, also, should assume the existence of such facts without proof, the question before us would remain unaffected by such facts. It has been said at times that picketing in large numbers near a place of business where a strike is in progress is in itself a threat of violence, and invites counter-violence. Circumstances may in particular cases justify a finding to that effect. Here we are not informed of the nature or extent of the labor dispute, if such there was. If there was a strike on the block where the defendants were walking, it may, for aught that appears, have been in connection with a business conducted on the top floor of one of the loft buildings along the street. There is nothing to show that any other person could have regarded the defendants' conduct as a threat or as calculated to coerce or impede any one. In the absence of evidence, we may not infer that the conduct of the defendants was intended as a threat, or could be so construed, or was an incentive to violence by others. Even if the defendants were parties to a labor dispute, no circumstances are shown which, it is even claimed, might possibly be considered as an excuse for or palliation of conduct constituting an invasion of the rights of the public. On the other hand, no circumstances have been shown which would give the color of disorder and violence to conduct which is otherwise colorless. Upon this record no question is presented of the rights of parties to a labor dispute to the use of the streets for their own purposes—or of any abuse by them of such rights. The sole question is whether a number of pedestrians walking, quietly, four abreast, on the sidewalk, creating no excitement or disturbance, may without warning by the police be arrested for disorderly conduct and sentenced to a term of imprisonment.

To us it seems that there should be no doubt of the answer to that question. Men and women constantly congregate or walk upon the streets in groups, quite oblivious of the fact that in some degree they are thereby causing inconvenience to others using the street. A public meeting may have aroused such interest that groups of men and women continue the discussion while walking up and down the street. Groups linger in quiet social converse after the religious edifice where services have been held is emptied. School children and college youths, laborers, athletic "fans" and church members, perhaps even judges, do at times congregate or walk upon the streets in numbers sufficient to cause other pedestrians to stand aside or step into the roadway. Surely such conduct is not always "disorderly" and does not always tend to a breach of the peace. The magistrate may draw distinction between innocent and wrongful conduct, but finding of guilt must be based upon logical inference from the circumstances of the case. Of course, no one urges that distinction may be based merely upon difference of social or economic position. Here the fact, if it be a fact, that the defendants are participants or sympathizers in a labor dispute, is immaterial, since there is no evidence from which any inference may be drawn that their quiet presence in numbers at this particular place was in some way calculated to make the labor dispute disorderly. In the absence of evidence that the defendants caused substantial annoyance to others, or persisted in their conduct after protest from others or warning from a police officer, we find the evidence insufficient to sustain the conviction of the defendants in this case.

In the case of *People v. Friedman* (248 N.Y. 531) the evidence produced to sustain the charge is in all material respects similar to the evidence produced in the instant cases. We find that it does not sustain the judgment of conviction. In the other four cases the circumstances are different. There the evidence, though meagre and unsatisfactory, yet seems to us sufficient to support a finding that the defendants acted recklessly of the rights and convenience of others, and that their conduct tended to a breach of the peace.

In all these four cases there is evidence that before the defendants were arrested they were warned by police officers that they must not persist in marching up and down the street in large groups. Police officers are guardians of the public order. Their duty is not merely to arrest offenders but to protect persons from threatened wrong and to prevent disorder. In the performance of their duties they may give reasonable directions. Present at the point where the defendants were congregating they might early sense the possibility of disorder. Even a protest from pedestrians who were annoyed by the defendants' conduct might be a significant element in determining whether persistence in such conduct was wrongful. Enough has been shown in these cases to justify the officers in warning the defendants. Refusal to heed the warning so given; persistence in parading the street in groups thereafter, is, perhaps, so significant of a contumacious disregard of the rights of others that it supports the finding of guilt of the defendants. In these cases the judgments must be affirmed.[1]

---

[1] Accord: People v. Friedman, 248 N.Y. 531, 162 N.E. 513 (1928); People v. Phillips, 245 N.Y. 401, 157 N.E. 153 (1927); People v. Arko, 40 N.Y. Crim. Rep. 149, 199 N.Y.S. 402 (1922); People v Schroedeman, 133 Misc. 557, 232 N.Y.S. 302 (1929); People v. Wecker, 246 N.Y.S. 708 (Spec. Sess. 1930). *Cf.* People v. Squires. 135 Misc. 214, 238 N Y S. 151 (1929); People v. Jenkins. 255 N.Y. 637, 175 N.E. 348 (1931), aff'g 138 Misc. 498, 247 N.Y.S. 444 (1930) (upholding a conviction for disorderly conduct of picketers parading with misleading signs). *Cf., contra,* State v. Christie, 97 Vt. 461, 123 Atl. 849 (1924); Comm. v. Silvers, 11 Pa. Co. Ct. 481 (1892); Comm. v. Redshaw, 12 Pa. Co. Ct. 91 (1892); State v. Dehan, 3 Law & Labor, 208 (La. City Ct. 1921).

For picketing as the crime of unlawful assembly, see: State v. Butterworth, 104 N.J.L. 579, 142 Atl. 57 (1928), rev'g 104 N.J.L. 43, 139 Atl. 161 (1927); McGehee

PEOPLE v. ARMENTROUT.

Appellate Department, Superior Court, California. 118 Cal. App. 761, 1 Pac.(2d) 556.

YANKWICH, J., *pro tem.*   In three complaints the five defendants were charged with the violation of two sections of what is known as the Los Angeles city "anti-picketing" ordinance. (Ord. No. 20586 N.S.) The first count of each of these complaints charged violation of section 1 through the making of loud and unusual noises for the purpose of inducing, influencing and attempting to induce and influence, persons to refrain from entering the Rialto Theater at 812 South Broadway, in the city of Los Angeles. Defendants Thomas W. Armentrout, Joseph P. Dufrane, and James Doyle are charged with the commission of the offense on December 3, 1930. (No. 19535.) In another complaint, Ernest Apac and Joe Hough are charged with the commission of the offense on December 4, 1930. (No. 19537.) In a third complaint, Joe Hough and James Doyle are charged with the commission of the offense on December 11, 1930. (No. 19735.) As to the second count which charged loitering and picketing, the trial court granted a new trial. The defendants were found guilty by a jury and judgment was pronounced by the court on March 24, 1931. The defendant Armentrout was fined two hundred and fifty ($250) dollars; Dufrane was fined fifty ($50) dollars; the others were fined twenty-five ($25) dollars, upon count I of the complaint. As to count II the trial court granted a new trial.

The determination of the sufficiency of the evidence to sustain the conviction requires a discussion of section 1 of the anti-picketing ordinance under which the prosecution was had. Before doing so, however, it is well to state briefly that the defendant Armentrout was the assistant business manager of the Projectionists' Union, consisting of motion picture machine operators. The union was engaged in a controversy with the proprietor of the Rialto Theater, who had locked out the members of the union, whom he had previously employed. For several weeks prior to the dates covered by the complaints, newsboys had been stationed by Dufrane, acting as circulation manager, upon the street at the north and south property lines of the theater to sell copies of the "Los Angeles Citizen," a newspaper of general circulation, published by the labor movement in Los Angeles, and to cry the headlines of the newspaper. On November 28, 1930, the editor of the newspaper issued, at the request of T. H. Eckerson, business manager of the union, a special edition of 500 copies which contained all the material published in the regular edition except that the front page had been changed by printing thereon

---

v. State, 23 Tex. App. 330 (1887). *Cf.* Bolin v. State, 193 Ind. 302, 139 N.E. 659 (1923).

    For picketing as a nuisance, see: Iverson v. Dilno, 44 Mont. 270, 119 Pac. 719 (1911).

    For the use of the criminal law to suppress picketing, see: Witte, The Government in Labor Disputes, c. 8 (1932); Claghorn, The Immigrant's Day in Court, 244-297 (1923).

    For the use of the Post Office Department's power to exclude as non-mailable matter propaganda in aid of a closed shop campaign, see the San Antonio decision in 4 Law & Labor, 233 (1922).

in large type headlines: "Trade unionists and their families and friends will need no further information to have them decide that they do not patronize the Rialto Theatre because it is on the unfair list of organized labor. By T. H. Eckerson, business representative of the Moving Picture Projectionists Union No. 150." The front page also carried a banner line in large type: "Rialto, Broadway are yet on the unfair list." On page three of this edition was the article relating to the controversy which appeared also in the regular edition.

For crying out loud certain words claimed to be the headlines of this special edition the prosecution was instituted. And it is the contention of the defendants that they were merely selling newspapers, and that, assuming they were making loud and unusual noises in so doing, these were not unusual, but such as are made by newsboys everywhere, and are clearly recognized and legalized by the exception to what is known as the "ballyhoo" or street advertising ordinance of the city of Los Angeles. (Ord. No. 6859 N.S.)

In passing upon this contention it is well to consider the anti-picketing ordinance in the light of certain rights of laboring men which are recognized by law, and the right of every citizen to speak freely in peace time, without being subjected to legislative or administrative restrictions, not covered by the law of libel, contempt, and/or regulatory measures passed pursuant to the police power. Section 1 of the ordinance reads:

"It shall be unlawful for any person, in or upon any public street, alley or public place in the city of Los Angeles, to make any loud or unusual noise, or to speak in a loud or unusual tone, or to cry out or proclaim, for the purposes of inducing or influencing, or attempting to induce or influence, any person to refrain from entering any works or factory or any place of business or employment, or for the purpose of inducing or influencing, or attempting to induce or influence, any person to refrain from purchasing or using any goods, wares, merchandise or other article or articles, or for the purpose of inducing or influencing, or attempting to induce or influence, any person to refrain from doing or performing any service or labor in any works, factory, place of business or employment, or for the purpose of intimidating, threatening or coercing any person who is performing, seeking or obtaining service or labor in any works, factory, place of business or employment."

The ordinance has been declared a valid exercise of the police power. (*Matter of Williams*, 158 Cal. 550, [111 Pac. 1035].) Similar ordinances have been upheld elsewhere. (*Thomas v. Indianapolis*, 195 Ind. 440 [35 A.L.R. 1194, 45 N.E. 550]; *Ex parte Stout*, 82 Tex. Cr. Rep. 183, [L.R.A. 1918C, 277, 198 S.W. 967]; *Watters v. Indianapolis*, 191 Ind. 671 [134 N.E. 482]; see note, "The boycott as a weapon in industrial dispute," 6 A.L.R. 909; 16 A.L.R. 230; 27 A.L.R. 651.)

[1] In interpreting the ordinance it is well to bear in mind that courts have recognized the right of workmen engaged in industrial dis-

putes to appeal to others in sympathy with their cause by spreading the news of this dispute. Whatever be the loss the employer may suffer from the social pressure resulting from this appeal, he cannot complain. (16 R.C.L. 457.) To make this appeal effective the working man may—as it has been pithily put in one case—"hire a hall or print a paper." * * *

[2] The right of free speech and of a free press is guaranteed by the Constitution of California (art. I, sec. 9.)

"Liberty of circulation is as essential to that freedom as liberty of publishing; indeed, without the circulation the publication would be of little value." (*Ex parte Jackson,* 96 U.S. 727 [24 L. Ed. 877, 879].)

"The word 'publish' ordinarily means to disclose, reveal, proclaim, *circulate* or make public." (*In re Monrovia Morning Post,* 199 Cal. 263, 266 [248 Pac. 1017].)

The constitutional guaranty against the abridgment of the freedom of the press means, first of all, immunity from restraint *previous* to publication. No general restraint previous to publication has been exercised in the English-speaking world since the licensing-of-printing act of the Long Parliament against which John Milton's Areopagitica was directed. The guaranty is also a positive injunction against the curtailment of the right of expression after it is made, subject, of course, to war-time restrictions or to such restrictions as may be imposed upon expressions in advocacy of violence. (*Schenck v. United States,* 249 U.S. 47 [63 L. Ed. 470, 39 Sup. Ct. Rep. 261]; *Stromberg v. United States,* 283 U.S. 359 [75 L. Ed. 1117]; *Near v. Minnesota ex rel. Olson,* 283 U.S. 696 [75 L. Ed. 1357]; *People v. Steelik,* 187 Cal. 361 [203 Pac. 78].) In California, injunctive relief against the publication of what (upon publication) might be libel or contempt is denied. (*Goldberg, Bowen & Co. v. Stablemen's Union,* 149 Cal. 429, [117 Am. St. Rep. 145, 9 Ann. Cas. 1219, 8 L.R.A. (N.S.) 460, 86 Pac. 806]; *In re Wood,* 194 Cal. 49 [227 Pac. 908]; *Dailey v. Superior Court,* 112 Cal. 94 [53 Am. St. Rep. 160, 32 L.R.A. 273, 44 Pac. 458]. See, *In re Shortridge,* 99 Cal. 526 [37 Am. St. Rep. 78, 21 L.R.A. 755, 34 Pac. 227].)

The portion of the ordinance under which the defendants stand convicted was aimed more at boycotting than at picketing. It was aimed at *oral* means of inducing persons not to enter the premises or to trade or work upon them. The use of *printed* means is covered by section 2. The Supreme Court has expressed doubts about the constitutionality of that section, particularly as it applies to "loitering." (*Matter of Williams, supra.*) We take it that even that section, in so far as it prohibits the use of banners, signs and other similar physical means of persuasion, was aimed at banners or signs or circulars which are exhibited or offered *free* and not those which are, like a newspaper, offered for sale. The persuasion at which the section is directed is the direct persuasion not to patronize or work, and not the indirect persuasion, which comes from adhering to a cause by being convinced of its justness. Were it otherwise, if a labor union should induce a newspaper of general circulation to

ublish an article in advocacy of its cause, in the course of a labor difficulty, the circulation of the newspaper in the vicinity of another's place
of business might be entirely prohibited upon the ground that the reader
might, by reading it, be convinced of the rightness of the union's cause and
be induced to refuse to patronize or work. At the oral argument counsel
or the people contended for such power. But we know of no decision
which would recognize it. The statement in *Crouch v. Central Labor
Council,* 134 Or. 612, [293 Pac. 729], to the effect that the display of a
newspaper is "equivalent to carrying a banner or wearing a sash with
objectionable reference" and that such display might be prohibited was
not made in an action under a statute or ordinance prohibiting the doing
of the act. It arose in a proceeding in equity. The same court, in interpreting an anti-picketing ordinance, has held that such an ordinance
cannot be sustained if it denies the lawful doing of a lawful act, such as
the right to strike. (*Hall v. Johnson,* 87 Or. 21 [Ann. Cas. 1918E, 49, 169
Pac. 515].) And while courts have upheld laws aimed at the suppression
of particular issues of indecent publications, we doubt if any constitutional authority or principle could be found which would sustain an
ordinance which sought to suppress the circulation of a newspaper in
the vicinity of a place of business merely because its purchase by prospective patrons *might* result in the withdrawal of patronage or work.
The freedom of the press would become illusory if it hung on so slight
a thread. What precedes relates more to section 2 of the ordinance. It
may seem beyond the issues here involved, because the trial court granted
a new trial as to the counts based upon it. It is referred to because a
good portion of the argument of counsel for the people is directed to the
point that the acts of the defendants amounted to picketing. "Picketing"
proper is denounced by section 2 of the ordinance. The first part of section 1, under which count 1 of the three complaints was drawn, is directed at boycotting. The purpose alleged in the complaint is "inducing,
influencing and attempting to induce and influence persons to refrain
from entering a certain place of business; and for the purpose of inducing,
influencing and attempting to induce and influence persons to refrain
from purchasing tickets from a certain place of business, to-wit: Rialto
Theatre, located at 812 South Broadway in the city of Los Angeles."

[3] We conclude that neither the sale of the newspaper nor its
display would constitute a violation of the ordinance. Nor would it be
a violation of the ordinance to cry out the headlines, *as a part of an appeal to buy the newspaper,* whatever form that appeal might take. If
the evidence in the record indicated that the defendants confined themselves to announcing *"Extra. Read the Citizen. All about the Rialto
Theatre being unfair,"* or words to similar effect, the judgment could not
be upheld. For, aside from the general constitutional considerations
heretofore adverted to, the news vendors would come clearly within the
exception of Ordinance No. 6859 N.S., the more so as the evidence shows
that the manner of calling did not differ from that used by newsboys in
ordinary cases.

[4] However, there is evidence in the record which shows clearly that the newsboys in calling out did not always use the phrase "Rialto Theatre unfair to labor" *in conjunction with an appeal to* read or buy "The Los Angeles Citizen." There is evidence in the record that the reference to the newspaper was omitted altogether. The words "Rialto Theatre unfair to labor" thus became words intended to achieve the result denounced in the ordinance, and charged in count 1 of the complaints. And the mere fact that, at the same time, the newspaper may have been exhibited does not change the character of the words. A careful examination of the record shows that this occurred upon all the dates charged in the complaints—December 3, 4 and 11. The charge as to December 17th against the defendant Dufrane is not supported by the evidence. This is conceded by the people. There was no calling out on that day. But while evidence was directed to this date we find no count in the complaints based upon it. [5] As to other days, the evidence is clear that he placed the newsboys (Doyle, Hough and Apac) upon the north and south property line of the theater, told them what to say, and that, when he did not himself participate in calling out, he directed their actions in such a manner as to be held responsible for the words used, even though he may have testified that his instructions to them were to mention the newspaper in conjunction with what they called out. (*People v. Wilson,* 93 Cal. App. 632, 636 [269 Pac. 951].) The judgment as to him and Apac, Doyle and Hough is sustained by the evidence. However, the judgment cannot be sustained as to the defendant Armentrout. * * *[1]

> *The judgment as to Armentrout should be reversed. As to the other defendants the judgments are affirmed.*[2]

---

[1] A portion of the opinion, dealing with Armentrout's criminal liability as principal for the acts of those actually violating the ordinances in question, is omitted. McLucas, P.J., and Shaw, J., in a separate opinion, which is omitted, disagreed with Yankwich, J., on this issue, and, being in a majority the judgments against all of the appellants were affirmed.

[2] For picketing as a violation of anti-picketing ordinances, see: Ferguson v. Peake, 18 Fed.(2d) 166 (D.C. App. 1927); Ex parte Williams, 158 Cal. 550, 111 Pac. 1035 (1910); Thomas v. City of Indianapolis, 195 Ind. 440, 145 N.E. 550 (1924); Ex parte Stout, 82 Texas Cr. 183, 198 S.W. 967 (1917). *Cf.* Hall v. Johnson, 87 Ore. 21, 169 Pac. 515 (1917). Such ordinances were held invalid in St. Louis v. Gloner, 210 Mo. 502, 109 S.W. 30 (1908); St. Louis v. Caplan, 109 S.W. 33 (Mo. 1908); St. Louis v. Sagan, 109 S.W. 33 (Mo. 1908); St. Louis v. Abramovitz, 109 S.W. 33 (Mo. 1908); In re Sweitzer, 13 Okla. Cr. 154, 162 Pac. 1134 (1917).

For picketing as a violation of ordinances aimed at unlicensed street advertising, see: Watters v. City of Indianapolis, 191 Ind. 671, 134 N.E. 482 (1922); Comm. v. Haffner, 279 Mass. 73, 180 N.E. 615 (1932).

For picketing as a violation of ordinances forbidding unlicensed street meetings, see: City of Duquesne v. Fincke, 269 Pa. 112, 112 Atl. 130 (1921).

VEGELAHN v. GUNTNER.

Supreme Judicial Court of Massachusetts. 167 Mass. 92, 44 N.E. 1077 (1896).

* * * The [1] following decree was entered at a preliminary hearing
upon the bill: "This cause came on to be heard upon the plaintiff's motion for a temporary injunction; and after due hearing, at which the
several defendants were represented by counsel, it is ordered, adjudged,
and decreed that an injunction issue *pendente lite,* to remain in force
until the further order of this court, or of some justice thereof, restraining the respondents and each and every of them, their agents and servants, from interfering with the plaintiff's business by patrolling the
sidewalk or street in front or in the vicinity of the premises occupied
by him, for the purpose of preventing any person or persons who now are
or may hereafter be in his employment, or desirous of entering the same,
from entering it, or continuing in it; or by obstructing or interfering with
such persons, or any others, in entering or leaving the plaintiff's said
premises; or by intimidating, by threats or otherwise, any person or persons who now are or may hereafter be in the employment of the plaintiff,
or desirous of entering the same, from entering it, or continuing in it;
or by any scheme or conspiracy among themselves or with others, organized for the purpose of annoying, hindering, interfering with, or preventing any person or persons who now are or may hereafter be in the
employment of the plaintiff, or desirous of entering the same, from entering it, or from continuing therein."

Hearing upon the bill and answers before *Holmes,* J., who reported
the case for the consideration of the full court, as follows:

"The facts admitted or proved are that, following upon a strike of
the plaintiff's workmen, the defendants have conspired to prevent the
plaintiff from getting workmen, and thereby to prevent him from carrying
on his business unless and until he will adopt a schedule of prices which
has been exhibited to him, and for the purpose of compelling him to accede
to that schedule, but for no other purpose. If he adopts that schedule
he will not be interfered with further. The means adopted for preventing the plaintiff from getting workmen are, (1) in the first place, persuasion and social pressure. And these means are sufficient to affect the
plaintiff disadvantageously, although it does not appear, if that be material, that they are sufficient to crush him. I ruled that the employment
of these means for the said purpose was lawful, and for that reason refused an injunction against the employment of them. If the ruling was
wrong, I find that an injunction ought to be granted.

"(2) I find also, that, as a further means for accomplishing the desired end, threats of personal injury or unlawful harm were conveyed to
persons seeking employment or employed, although no actual violence was
used beyond a technical battery, and although the threats were a good deal
disguised, and express words were avoided. It appeared to me that there

---

[1] The allegations of the bill are omitted.—Ed.

was danger of similar acts in the future. I ruled that conduct of this kind should be enjoined.

"The defendants established a patrol of two men in front of the plaintiff's factory, as one of the instrumentalities of their plan. The patrol was changed every hour, and continued from half-past six in the morning until half-past five in the afternoon, on one of the busy streets of Boston. The number of men was greater at times, and at times showed some little inclination to stop the plaintiff's door, which was not serious, but seemed to me proper to be enjoined. The patrol proper at times went further than simple advice, not obtruded beyond the point where the other person was willing to listen, and conduct of that sort is covered by (2) above, but its main purpose was in aid of the plan held lawful in (1) above. I was satisfied that there was probability of the patrol being continued if not enjoined. I ruled that the patrol, so far as it confined itself to persuasion and giving notice of the strike, was not unlawful, and limited the injunction accordingly.

"There was some evidence of persuasion to break existing contracts. I ruled that this was unlawful, and should be enjoined.

"I made the final decree appended hereto. If, on the foregoing facts, it ought to be reversed or modified, such decree is to be entered as the full court may think proper; otherwise, the decree is to stand."

The final decree was as follows: "This cause came on to be heard, and was argued by counsel; and thereupon, on consideration thereof, it is ordered, adjudged, and decreed that the defendants, and each and every of them, their agents and servants, be restrained and enjoined from interfering with the plaintiff's business by obstructing or physically interfering with any persons in entering or leaving the plaintiff's premises numbered 141, 143, 145, 147 North Street in said Boston, or by intimidating, by threats, express or implied, of violence or physical harm to body or property, any person or persons who now are or hereafter may be in the employment of the plaintiff, or desirous of entering the same, from entering or continuing in it, or by in any way hindering, interfering with, or preventing any person or persons who now are in the employment of the plaintiff from continuing therein, so long as they may be bound so to do by lawful contract." * * *

ALLEN, J.: The principal question in this case is whether the defendants should be enjoined against maintaining the patrol. The report shows that, following upon a strike of the plaintiff's workmen, the defendants conspired to prevent him from getting workmen, and thereby to prevent him from carrying on his business, unless and until he should adopt a certain schedule of prices. The means adopted were persuasion and social pressure, threats of personal injury or unlawful harm conveyed to persons employed or seeking employment, and a patrol of two men in front of the plaintiff's factory, maintained from half past six in the morning till half past five in the afternoon, on one of the busiest streets of Boston. The number of men was greater at times, and at times showed some little disposition to stop the plaintiff's door. The patrol proper at times went further than simple advice, not obtruded beyond the point where the other person was willing to listen; and it was found that the patrol would probably be continued, if not enjoined. There was also some evidence of persuasion to break existing contracts.

The patrol was maintained as one of the means of carrying out the defendants' plan, and it was used in combination with social pressure, threats of personal injury or unlawful harm, and persuasion to break existing contracts. It was thus one means of intimidation indirectly to the plaintiff, and directly to persons actually employed, or seeking to be employed, by the plaintiff, and of rendering such employment unpleasant or intolerable to such persons. Such an act is an unlawful interference with the rights both of employer and of employed. An employer has a right to engage all persons who are willing to work for him, at such prices as may be mutually agreed upon; and persons employed or seeking employment have a corresponding right to enter into or remain in the employment of any person or corporation willing to employ them. These rights are secured by the Constitution itself. *Commonwealth v. Perry,* 155 Mass. 117. *People v. Gillson,* 109 N.Y. 389. *Braceville Coal Co. v. People,* 147 Ill. 66, 71. *Ritchie v. People,* 155 Ill. 98. *Low v. Rees Printing Co.,* 41 Neb. 127. No one can lawfully interfere by force or intimidation to prevent employers or persons employed or wishing to be employed from the exercise of these rights. In Massachusetts, as in some other States, it is even made a criminal offence for one by intimidation or force to prevent or seek to prevent a person from entering into or continuing in the employment of a person or corporation. Pub. Sts. c. 74, § 2.[2] Intimidation is not limited to threats of violence or of physical injury to person or property. It has a broader signification, and there also may be a moral intimidation which is illegal. Patrolling or picketing, under the circumstances stated in the report, has elements of intimidation like those which were found to exist in *Sherry v. Perkins,* 147 Mass. 212. It was declared to be unlawful in *Regina v. Druitt,* 10 Cox C.C. 592; *Regina v. Hibbert,* 13 Cox C.C. 82; and *Regina v. Bauld,* 13 Cox C.C. 282.[3] It was assumed to be unlawful in *Trollope v. London Building Trades Federation,* 11 T.L.R. 228, though in that case the pickets were withdrawn before the bringing of the bill. The patrol was an unlawful interference both with the plaintiff and with the workmen, within the principle of many cases, and, when instituted for the purpose of interfering with his busi-

[2] For a collection of such statutes and a discussion of their effect upon the legal limits of picketing, see: Hallerstein, "Picketing Legislation and the Courts," 10 N.C. Law Rev. 158, 168 (1932).—Ed.

[3] "Our resulting contempt for statutes means, at bottom, that as lawyers, judges and law-teachers, we are ignorant of the directions that law is taking. It allows us to be complacent toward a judicial logic still building with materials that legislation has repudiated. Even the knowledge that the materials are outdated may be lacking. (*Cf.* * * * the attitude of the Supreme Judicial Court of Massachusetts in Vegelahn v. Guntner, 167 Mass. 92, 44 N.E. 1077 (1896), relying for authority upon the English decisions of Reg. v. Druitt, 10 Cox C.C. 592 (1867) ; Reg. v. Hibbert, 13 Cox C.C. 82 (1875), then repudiated by the Criminal Law Amendment Act, 1871, 34 & 35 Vict. c. 31, and the Conspiracy and Protection of Property Act, 1875, 38 & 39 Vict. c. 86.)" Landis, "Book Review," 45 Harv. Law Rev. 953 (1932).—Ed.

ness, it became a private nuisance. See *Carew v. Rutherford*, 106 Mass. 1; *Walker v. Cronin*, 107 Mass. 555; *Barr v. Essex Trades Council*, 8 Dick. 101; *Murdock v. Walker*, 152 Penn. St. 595; *Wick China Co. v. Brown*, 164 Penn. St. 449; *Cœur d'Alene Consolidated & Mining Co. v. Miners' Union*, 51 Fed. Rep. 260; *Temperton v. Russell*, [1893] 1 Q.B. 715; *Flood v. Jackson*, 11 T.L.R. 276; *Wright v. Hennessey*, a case before Baron Pollock, 52 Alb. L. J. 104; *Judge v. Bennett*, 36 W.R. 103; *Lyons v. Wilkins*, [1896] 1 Ch. 811.

The defendants contend that these acts were justifiable, because they were only seeking to secure better wages for themselves by compelling the plaintiff to accept their schedule of wages. This motive or purpose does not justify maintaining a patrol in front of the plaintiff's premises, as a means of carrying out their conspiracy. A combination among persons merely to regulate their own conduct is within allowable competition, and is lawful, although others may be indirectly affected thereby. But a combination to do injurious acts expressly directed to another, by way of intimidation or constraint, either of himself or of persons employed or seeking to be employed by him, is outside of allowable competition, and is unlawful. Various decided cases fall within the former class, for example: *Worthington v. Waring*, 157 Mass. 421; *Snow v. Wheeler*, 113 Mass. 179; *Bowen v. Matheson*, 14 Allen, 499; *Commonwealth v. Hunt*, 4 Met. 111; *Heywood v. Tillson*, 75 Maine, 225; *Cote v. Murphy*, 159 Penn. St. 420; *Bohn Manuf. Co. v. Hollis*, 54 Minn. 223; *Mogul Steamship Co. v. McGregor*, [1892] A.C. 25; *Curran v. Treleaven*, [1891] 2 Q.B. 545, 561. The present case falls within the latter class.

Nor does the fact that the defendants' acts might subject them to an indictment prevent a court of equity from issuing an injunction. It is true that ordinarily a court of equity will decline to issue an injunction to restrain the commission of a crime; but a continuing injury to property or business may be enjoined, although it may also be punishable as a nuisance or other crime. *Sherry v. Perkins*, 147 Mass. 212. *In re Debs*, 158 U.S. 564, 593, 599. *Baltimore & Potomac Railroad v. Fifth Baptist Church*, 108 U.S. 317, 329. *Cranford v. Tyrrell*, 128 N.Y. 341, 344. *Gilbert v. Mickle*, 4 Sandf. Ch. 357. *Mobile v. Louisville & Nashville Railroad*, 84 Ala. 115, 126. *Arthur v. Oakes*, 63 Fed. Rep. 310. *Toledo, Ann Arbor, & North Michigan Railway v. Pennsylvania Co.*, 54 Fed. Rep. 730, 744. *Emperor of Austria v. Day*, 3 DeG., F. & J. 217, 239, 240, 253. *Hermann Loog v. Bean*, 26 Ch. D. 306, 314, 316, 317. *Monson v. Tussaud*, [1894] 1 Q.B. 671, 689, 690, 698.

A question is also presented whether the court should enjoin such interference with persons in the employment of the plaintiff who are not bound by contract to remain with him, or with persons who are not under any existing contract, but who are seeking or intending to enter into his employment. A conspiracy to interfere with the plaintiff's business by means of threats and intimidation, and by maintaining a patrol in front of his premises in order to prevent persons from entering his employment, or in order to prevent persons who are in his employment from continuing

therein, is unlawful, even though such persons are not bound by contract
to enter into or to continue in his employment; and the injunction should
not be so limited as to relate only to persons who are bound by existing
contracts. *Walker v. Cronin,* 107 Mass. 555, 565. *Carew v. Rutherford,*
106 Mass. 1. *Sherry v. Perkins,* 147 Mass. 212. *Temperton v. Russell.*
[1893] 1 Q.B. 715, 728, 731. *Flood v. Jackson,* 11 L.T.R. 276.

In the opinion of a majority of the court the injunction should be
in the form originally issued.

So ordered.[4]

HOLMES, J.: In a case like the present, it seems to me that, whatever
the true result may be, it will be of advantage to sound thinking to have the
less popular view of the law stated, and therefore, although when I have
been unable to bring my brethren to share my convictions my almost in-
variable practice is to defer to them in silence, I depart from that practice
in this case, notwithstanding my unwillingness to do so in support of an
already rendered judgment of my own.

In the first place, a word or two should be said as to the meaning of
the report. I assume that my brethren construe it as I meant it to be construed, and that, if they were not prepared to do so, they would give an
opportunity to the defendants to have it amended in accordance with what
I state my meaning to be. There was no proof of any threat or danger of
a patrol exceeding two men, and as of course an injunction is not granted
except with reference to what there is reason to expect in its absence, the
question on that point is whether a patrol of two men should be enjoined.
Again, the defendants are enjoined by the final decree from intimidating
by threats, express or implied, of physical harm to body or property, any
person who may be desirous of entering into the employment of the plaintiff so far as to prevent him from entering the same. In order to test the
correctness of the refusal to go further, it must be assumed that the defendants obey the express prohibition of the decree. If they do not, they
fall within the injunction as it now stands, and are liable to summary punishment. The important difference between the preliminary and the final
injunction is that the former goes further, and forbids the defendants to
interfere with the plaintiff's business "by any scheme * * * organized for
the purpose of * * * preventing any person or persons who now are or
may hereafter be * * * desirous of entering the [plaintiff's employment]
from entering it." I quote only a part, and the part which seems to me
most objectionable. This includes refusal of social intercourse, and even
organized persuasion or argument, although free from any threat of
violence, either express or implied. And this is with reference to persons
who have a legal right to contract or not to contract with the plaintiff, as
they may see fit. Interference with existing contracts is forbidden by the
final decree. I wish to insist a little that the only point of difference which
involves a difference of principle between the final decree and the preliminary injunction which it is proposed to restore, is what I have men-

---

[4] The dissenting opinion of Field, C.J., is omitted.—Ed.

tioned, in order that it may be seen exactly what we are to discuss. It appears to me that the judgment of the majority turns in part on the assumption that the patrol necessarily carries with it a threat of bodily harm. That assumption I think unwarranted, for the reasons which I have given. Furthermore, it cannot be said, I think, that two men walking together up and down a sidewalk and speaking to those who enter a certain shop do necessarily and always thereby convey a threat of force. I do not think it possible to discriminate, and to say that two workmen, or even two representatives of an organization of workmen, do,—especially when they are, and are known to be, under the injunction of this court not to do so. See Stimson, Handbook to Labor Law, § 60, esp. pp. 290, 298, 299, 300; *Regina v. Shepherd,* 11 Cox C.C. 325. I may add, that I think the more intelligent workingmen believe as fully as I do that they no more can be permitted to usurp the State's prerogative of force than can their opponents in their controversies. But if I am wrong, then the decree as it stands reaches the patrol, since it applies to all threats of force. With this I pass to the real difference between the interlocutory and the final decree.

I agree, whatever may be the law in the case of a single defendant, *Rice v. Albee,* 164 Mass. 88, that when a plaintiff proves that several persons have combined and conspired to injure his business, and have done acts producing that effect, he shows temporal damage and a cause of action, unless the facts disclose, or the defendants prove, some ground of excuse or justification. And I take it to be settled, and rightly settled, that doing that damage by combined persuasion is actionable, as well as doing it by falsehood or by force. *Walker v. Cronin,* 107 Mass. 555. *Morasse v. Brochu,* 151 Mass. 567. *Tasker v. Stanley,* 153 Mass. 148.

Nevertheless, in numberless instances the law warrants the intentional infliction of temporal damage because it regards it as justified. It is on the question of what shall amount to a justification, and more especially on the nature of the considerations which really determine or ought to determine the answer to that question, that judicial reasoning seems to me often to be inadequate. The true grounds of decision are considerations of policy and of social advantage, and it is vain to suppose that solutions can be attained merely by logic and the general propositions of law which nobody disputes. Propositions as to public policy rarely are unanimously accepted, and still more rarely, if ever, are capable of unanswerable proof. They require a special training to enable any one even to form an intelligent opinion about them. In the early stages of law, at least, they generally are acted on rather as inarticulate instincts than as definite ideas for which a rational defence is ready.

To illustrate what I have said in the last paragraph, it has been the law for centuries that a man may set up a business in a country town too small to support more than one, although he expects and intends thereby to ruin some one already there, and succeeds in his intent. In such a case he is not held to act "unlawfully and without justifiable cause," as was alleged in *Walker v. Cronin* and *Rice v. Albee.* The reason, of course, is that the doctrine generally has been accepted that free competition is worth more to society than it costs, and that on this ground the infliction of the damage is privileged. *Commonwealth v. Hunt,* 4 Met. 111, 134. Yet even this proposition nowadays is disputed by a considerable body of persons, including many whose intelligence is not to be denied, little as we may agree with them.

I have chosen this illustration partly with reference to what I have to say next. It shows without the need of further authority that the policy of allowing free competition justifies the intentional inflicting of temporal damage, including the damage of interference with a man's business, by some means, when the damage is done not for its own sake, but as an instrumentality in reaching the end of victory in the battle of trade. In such a case it cannot matter whether the plaintiff is the only rival of the defendant, and so is aimed at specifically, or is one of a class all of whom are hit. The only debatable ground is the nature of the means by which such damage may be inflicted. We all agree that it cannot be done by force or threats of force. We all agree, I presume, that it may be done by persuasion to leave a rival's shop and come to the defendant's. It may be done by the refusal or withdrawal of various pecuniary advantages which, apart from this consequence, are within the defendant's lawful control. It may be done by the withdrawal, or threat to withdraw, such advantages from third persons who have a right to deal or not to deal with the plaintiff, as a means of inducing them not to deal with him either as customers or servants. *Commonwealth v. Hunt,* 4 Met. 111, 132, 133. *Bowen v. Matheson,* 14 Allen, 499. *Heywood v. Tillson,* 75 Maine, 225. *Mogul Steamship Co. v. McGregor* [1892] A.C. 25.

I pause here to remark that the word "threats" often is used as if, when it appeared that threats had been made, it appeared that unlawful conduct had begun. But it depends on what you threaten. As a general rule, even if subject to some exceptions, what you may do in a certain event you may threaten to do, that is, give warning of your intention to do in that event, and thus allow the other person the chance of avoiding the consequences. So as to "compulsion," it depends on how you "compel." *Commonwealth v. Hunt,* 4 Met. 111, 133. So as to "annoyance" or "intimidation." *Connor v. Kent, Curran v. Treleaven,* 17 Cox C.C. 354, 367, 368, 370. In *Sherry v. Perkins,* 147 Mass. 212, it was found as a fact that the display of banners which was enjoined was part of a scheme to prevent workmen from entering or remaining in the plaintiff's employment, "by threats and intimidation." The context showed that the words as there used meant threats of personal violence, and intimidation by causing fear of it.

I have seen the suggestion made that the conflict between employers and employed is not competition. But I venture to assume that none of my brethren would rely on that suggestion. If the policy on which our law is founded is too narrowly expressed in the term free competition, we may substitute free struggle for life. Certainly the policy is not limited to struggles between persons of the same class competing for the same end. It applies to all conflicts of temporal interests.

So far, I suppose, we are agreed. But there is a notion which latterly has been insisted on a good deal, that a combination of persons to do what any one of them lawfully might do by himself will make the otherwise lawful conduct unlawful. It would be rash to say that some as yet unformulated truth may not be hidden under this proposition. But in the general form in which it has been presented and accepted by many courts, I think it plainly untrue, both on authority and on principle. *Commonwealth v. Hunt,* 4 Met. 111. *Randall v. Hazelton,* 12 Allen, 412, 414. There was combination of the most flagrant and dominant kind in *Bowen v. Matheson* and in the *Mogul Steamship Company's* case, and combination was essential to the success achieved. But it is not necessary to cite cases; it is plain from the slightest consideration of practical affairs, or the most superficial reading of industrial history, that free competition means combination, and that the organization of the world, now going on so fast, means an ever increasing might and scope of combination. It seems to me futile to set our faces against this tendency. Whether beneficial on the whole, as I think it, or detrimental, it is inevitable, unless the fundamental axioms of society, and even the fundamental conditions of life, are to be changed.

One of the eternal conflicts out of which life is made up is that between the effort of every man to get the most he can for his services, and that of society, disguised under the name of capital, to get his services for the least possible return. Combination on the one side is patent and powerful. Combination on the other is the necessary and desirable counterpart, if the battle is to be carried on in a fair and equal way. I am unable to reconcile *Temperton v. Russell,* [1893] 1 Q.B. 715, and the cases which follow it, with the *Mogul Steamship Company* case. But *Temperton v. Russell* is not a binding authority here, and therefore I do not think it necessary to discuss it.

If it be true that workingmen may combine with a view, among other things, to getting as much as they can for their labor, just as capital may combine with a view to getting the greatest possible return, it must be true that when combined they have the same liberty that combined capital has to support their interests by argument, persuasion, and the bestowal or refusal of those advantages which they otherwise lawfully control. I can remember when many people thought that, apart from violence or breach of contract, strikes were wicked, as organized refusals to work. I suppose that intelligent economists and legislators have given up that notion to-day. I feel pretty confident that they equally will abandon the idea that an organized refusal by workmen of social intercourse with a man who shall enter their antagonist's employ is wrong, if it is dissociated from any threat of violence, and is made for the sole object of prevailing if possible in a contest with their employer about the rate of wages. The fact, that the immediate object of the act by which the benefit to themselves is to be gained is to injure their antagonist, does not necessarily make it unlawful, any more than when a great house lowers the price of certain goods for the purpose, and with the effect, of driving a smaller antagonist from the business. Indeed, the question seems to me to have been decided as long ago as 1842 by the good sense of Chief Justice Shaw, in *Commonwealth v. Hunt,* 4 Met. 111. I repeat at the end, as I said at the beginning, that this is the point of difference in principle, and the only one, between the interlocutory and the final decree. See *Regina v. Shepherd,* 11 Cox C.C. 325; *Connor v. Kent, Gibson v. Lawson, Curran v. Treleaven,* 17 Cox C.C. 354.

The general question of the propriety of dealing with this kind of case by injunction I say nothing about, because I understand that the defendants have no objection to the final decree if it goes no further, and that both parties wish a decision upon the matters which I have discussed.

BARNES v. TYPOGRAPHICAL UNION NO. 16.

Supreme Court of Illinois.   232 Ill. 424, 83 N.E. 940 (1908).

MR. JUSTICE CARTWRIGHT delivered the opinion of the court: * * * It is next contended that if any injunction was authorized, the injunction granted was too broad in enjoining appellants from peaceful picketing of complainants' premises and from congregating about or near their places of business for the purpose of inducing or soliciting employees to leave the employment. It is contended that a peaceful picket line around a shop is entirely lawful. But this court has held otherwise in *Franklin Union v. People,* 220 Ill. 355, where endorsement was given to the doctrine of *Beck v. Railway Teamsters' Protective Union,* 118 Mich. 497, by quoting therefrom, as follows: "To picket complainants' premises in order to intercept their teamsters or persons going there to trade is unlawful. It, itself, is an act of intimidation and an unwarrantable interference with the right of free trade. The highways and public streets must be free to all for the purposes of trade, commerce and labor. The law protects the buyer, the seller, the merchant, the manufacturer and the laborer in the right to walk the streets unmolested. It is no respecter of persons, and it makes no difference, in effect, whether the picketing is done ten or ten hundred feet away." The court also gave its approval to the decision in *Vegelahn v. Guntner,* 167 Mass. 92. In that case a patrol of two men in front of the plaintiff's factory, maintained as one of the means of carrying out the defendants' plan, was held to be an unlawful interference with the rights of the employer and the employed. The patroling or picketing of the premises was considered to have elements of intimidation, and the court decided that the motive of obtaining better wages for themselves on the part of the defendants did not justify maintaining a patrol in front of the complainant's premises as a means of carrying out their conspiracy. The very fact of establishing a picket line is evidence of an intention to annoy, embarrass and intimidate, whether physical violence is resorted to or not. There have been a few cases where it was held that picketing, by a labor union, of a place of business is not necessarily unlawful if the pickets are peaceful and well behaved, but if the watching and besetting of the workmen is carried to such a length as to constitute an annoyance to them or their employer it becomes unlawful. But manifestly that is not a safe rule and furnishes no fixed or certain standard of what is lawful or unlawful. Any picket line must result in annoyance both to the employer and the workmen, no matter what is said or done, and to say that the court is to determine by the degree of annoyance whether it shall be stopped or not would furnish no guide, but leave the question to the individual notions or bias of the particular judge.[1] To picket the complainants' premises was in itself an act of intimidation and an unwarrantable interference with their rights. Pickets were, in fact, guilty of actual intimidation and threats, but if they had not been, the complainants were entitled to be protected from the annoyance.

Another supposed right of the defendants asserted by counsel is the exercise of the power of persuasion, and it must be conceded that argument and persuasion are lawful if not directed to the accomplishment of an illegal and unlawful purpose. The object of the defendants as set forth in the bill was illegal, and if there is a malevolent intent to produce an illegal result, and it is produced, it makes no difference whether it is accomplished by mere persuasion or by physical violence.[2] (*Curran v. Galen*, 152 N.Y. 33.) An act which is naturally innocent, when done with actual malice for the purpose of injuring another, and followed by

---

[1] "There is and can be no such thing as peaceful picketing, any more than there can be chaste vulgarity, or peaceful mobbing, or lawful lynching. When men want to converse or persuade, they do not organize a picket line. When they only want to see who are at work, they go and see, and then leave, and disturb no one physically or mentally." McPherson, J., in Atchison, T. & S. F. Ry. Co., v. Gee, 139 Fed. 582, 584 (Cir. Ct. Iowa 1905).

"The evidence on this matter laid before us is on this point overwhelming, and is evidence which the Trade Unions have made no attempt to contradict. What it comes to is this, that *watching and besetting* for the purpose of peaceably persuading is really a contradiction in terms. The truth is that picketing—however conducted—when it consists of watching and besetting the house, etc., and it is to be observed that the statute [Conspiracy and Protection of Property Act, 1875] places no limit to the number of persons attending for the purpose only of obtaining or communicating information or to the length of time during which such attendance may be maintained —is always and of necessity in the nature of an annoyance to the person picketed. As such, it must savour of compulsion, and it cannot be doubted that it is because it is found 'to compel that Trade Unions systematically resort to it. It is obvious how easy it must be to pass from the language of persuasion into that of abuse, and from words of abuse to threats and acts of violence." Report of the Royal Commission on Trade Disputes of 1906, Cd. 2825, 11.

For a collection of cases in accord with the Barnes case, see: Hallerstein, "Picketing Legislation and the Courts," 10 N.C. Law Rev. 158, 171-3 (1932) ; Sayre, "Labor and the Courts," 39 Yale Law Jour. 682, 702 (1930).—Ed.

[2] Where the purpose of the strike is itself illegal, all picketing, whether or not otherwise illegal, can be enjoined. Sarros v. Nouris, 15 Del. Ch. 391, 138 Atl. 607 (1927) ; Beckerman v. Bakery Union, 28 Ohio N.P.(N.S.) 550 (1931).—Ed.

such injury, is not excused because the act might be innocent under other conditions. It would be no excuse, in law, for a defendant to say: "It is true, I have interfered with an absolute legal right of the plaintiff to his injury and with a malicious intent to inflict such injury; but my act was not a legal wrong, because I did not commit any breach of the peace or any act of violence, or threaten to do so." The law allows laborers to combine for the purpose of obtaining lawful benefits for themselves, but it gives no sanction to combinations, either of employers or employed, which have for their immediate purpose the injury of another. * * *[3]

WHITE MOUNTAIN FREEZER CO. v. MURPHY.

Supreme Court of New Hampshire. 78 N.H. 398, 101 Atl. 357 (1917).

PARSONS, C.J. * * * The second question raised relates to the conduct of the strike. The plaintiffs' counsel asked the court to rule that all organized picketing is unlawful. The court declined to so rule, but did rule that reasonable picketing was lawful; unreasonable, unlawful; and the plaintiffs excepted. The term picketing is new in the law of the state. The only definition in the case is "picketing * * * by twos, who parade the streets, observe who are entering and leaving the plaintiffs' shops in order that they may argue and persuade them to join the strike." The allegations of the bill lead to the inference that picketing may mean something more than peaceful parading, whatever that may mean. The dictionary defines picketing as "to post watchers at the approaches to a place of employment affected by a strike in order to ascertain those who work there and persuade them, or otherwise influence them, to give up the work." Webst. Dict. Picket; R. & L. Law Dict. Picketing. The cases cited in the notes, 4 L.R.A.(N.S.) 302 and 50 L.R.A.(N.S.) 412, indicate that the term may include a wide range of action. The material question is whether the acts done in prosecution of the strike are lawful or unlawful, whether properly described as picketing or by some other term.[1] Although the term is not found in the law of the state, Public

---

[3] The dissenting opinion of Scott and Farmer, J.J., is omitted.

[1] For a collection of cases stating that picketing is not necessarily illegal, see: Hallerstein, "Picketing Legislation and the Courts," 10 N.C. Law Rev. 158, 173-4 (1932); Sayre, "Labor and the Courts," 39 Yale Law Jour. 682, 701 (1930). See also: Southern California I. & S. Co. v. Amalgamated Ass'n of Iron, etc., Workers, 186 Cal. 604, 200 Pac. 1 (1921); Paramount Enterprises v. Mitchell, 104 Fla. 407, 140 So. 328 (1932); Church Shoe Co. v. Turner, 218 Mo. App. 516, 279 S.W. 232 (1926).

Upon the question of how near a picket must be stationed to the employer's place of business in order to be a "picket", see: Sterling Chain Theatres v. Central

Statutes, *c.* 266, *s.* 12, as amended by *c.* 211, Laws 1913, and P.S., *c.* 264, *ss.* 1, 2, may be aimed at some acts included within the term or naturally resulting from the proceeding so called. The substance of the court's ruling was the application of the test of reasonable conduct under all the circumstances. Whether when the facts are found the acts of which the plaintiffs complain can be found to be reasonable in fact cannot be determined until the facts are found. If one may interfere with another's lawful business when it is a reasonable thing to do, it follows that he may do so in a manner not unreasonable in fact or because forbidden by legislative mandate.

Case discharged.

THE CLAYTON ACT OF OCTOBER 15, 1914.

38 U.S. Stat. c. 323, 730.

SEC. 6. That the labor of a human being is not a commodity or article of commerce. Nothing contained in the antitrust laws shall be construed to forbid the existence and operation of labor, agricultural, or horticultural organizations, instituted for the purposes of mutual help, and not having capital stock or conducted for profit, or to forbid or restrain individual members of such organizations from lawfully carrying out the legitimate objects thereof; nor shall such organizations, or the members thereof, be held or construed to be illegal combinations or conspiracies in restraint of trade, under the antitrust laws.

Sec. 20. That no restraining order or injunction shall be granted by any court of the United States, or a judge or the judges thereof, in any case between an employer and employees, or between employers and employees, or between employees, or between persons employed and persons seeking employment, involving, or growing out of, a dispute concerning terms or conditions of employment, unless necessary to prevent irreparable injury to property, or to a property right, of the party making the application, for which injury there is no adequate remedy at law, and such property or property right must be described with particularity in

---

Labor Council of Seattle, 155 Wash. 217, 283 Pac. 1081 (1930); Adams v. Local No. 400, 124 Wash. 564, 215 Pac. 19 (1923).

Upon the legality of picketing an employee's residence as distinguished from the employer's place of business, see: Davis v. State, 200 Ind. 88, 161 N.E. 375 (1928).

Upon the question as to how far constitutional guarantees of free speech restrain the issuance of injunctions against utterances in the course of picketing, see: Coeur D'Alene Mining Co. v. Miners Union, 51 Fed. 26 (Cir. Ct. Idaho 1892); Truax v. Bisbee Local, 19 Ariz. 379, 171 Pac. 121 (1918); Robison v. Hotel & Restaurant Employees, 35 Idaho 418, 207 Pac. 132 (1922); Vulcan Detinning Co. v. St. Clair, 315 Ill. 40, 145 N.E. 657 (1924); Ex parte Tucker, 110 Texas 335, 220 S.W. 75 (1920); Hughes v. Motion Picture Machine Operators, 282 Mo. 384, 221 S.W. 95 (1920).

For adumbrations of what type of conduct is "intimidating" under unusual circumstances, see: King v. Weiss & Lesh Mfg. Co., 266 Fed. 257 (6th cir. 1920).

the application, which must be in writing and sworn to by the applicant or by his agent or attorney.

And no such restraining order or injunction shall prohibit any person or persons, whether singly or in concert, from terminating any relation of employment, or from ceasing to perform any work or labor, or from recommending, advising, or persuading others by peaceful means so to do; or from attending at any place where any such person or persons may lawfully be, for the purpose of peacefully obtaining or communicating information, or from peacefully persuading any person to work or to abstain from working; or from ceasing to patronize or to employ any party to such dispute, or from recommending, advising, or persuading others by peaceful and lawful means so to do; or from paying or giving to, or withholding from, any person engaged in such dispute, any strike benefits or other moneys or things of value; or from peaceably assembling in a lawful manner, and for lawful purposes; or from doing any act or thing which might lawfully be done in the absence of such dispute by any party thereto; nor shall any of the acts specified in this paragraph be considered or held to be violations of any law of the United States.

AMERICAN STEEL FOUNDRIES v. TRI-CITY CENTRAL TRADES COUNCIL.

Supreme Court of the United States. 257 U.S. 184 (1921).

MR. CHIEF JUSTICE TAFT delivered the opinion of the court.

The American Steel Foundries is a New Jersey corporation operating a large plant for the manufacture of steel products in Granite City, Illinois. In May, 1914, it filed a bill in the District Court for the Southern District of Illinois to enjoin the defendants, the Tri-City Central Trades Council, and fourteen individual defendants, some of them officers of the Council, all of them citizens of other States than New Jersey, from carrying on a conspiracy to prevent complainant from retaining and obtaining skilled laborers to operate its plant. The bill charged that the conspiracy was being executed by organized picketing, accompanied by threats, intimidation and violence toward persons employed or seeking employment there. The defendants in their answer admitted that the Central Trades Council had established a picket upon streets leading to the plant, with instructions to notify all persons entering it that a strike had been called because of reduction of wages, and to use all honorable means to persuade such persons not to take the places of the men on the strike; admitted the participation of individual defendants in the picketing, but denied threats of injury or violence or responsibility for the violence that admittedly had occurred. After replication was filed, the cause was heard.

A restraining order issued on filing of the bill, and a final decree was entered by which defendants were "perpetually restrained and enjoined from in any way or manner whatsoever by use of *persuasion*, threats, or personal injury, intimidation, suggestion of danger or threats of violence of any kind, from interfering with, hindering, obstructing or stopping, any person engaged in the employ of the American Steel Foundries in connection with its business or its foundry in the City of Granite City, County of Madison, State of Illinois, or elsewhere; and from interfering by *persuasion*, violence or threats of violence in any manner with any person desiring to be employed by said American Steel Foundries in its said foundry or plant; and from inducing or attempting to compel or induce by *persuasion*, threats, intimidation, force or violence or putting in fear or suggestions of danger any of the employees of the American Steel Foundries or persons seeking employment with it so as to cause them to refuse to perform any of their duties as employees of the American Steel Foundries; and from preventing any person by *persuasion*, threats, intimidation, force or violence, or suggestion of danger or violence, from entering into the employ of said American Steel Foundries; and from protecting, aiding or assisting any person, or persons in committing any of said acts; and from assembling, loitering or congregating about or in proximity of the said plant or factory of the American Steel Foundries for the purpose of doing, or aiding or encouraging others in doing, any of the said unlawful or forbidden acts or things; *and from picketing or maintaining at or near the premises of the complainant, or on the streets leading to the premises of said complainant, any picket or pickets,* and from doing any acts or things whatever in furtherance of any conspiracy or combination among them, or any of them, to obstruct, or interfere with said American Steel Foundries, its officers, agents or employees, in the free and unrestrained control and operation of its plant, foundry and property and the operation of its business; and also from ordering, directing, aiding, assisting or in any manner abetting any person committing any or either of the acts aforesaid; and also from entering upon the grounds, foundry or premises of the American Steel Foundries without first obtaining its consent; and from injuring or destroying any of the property of the said American Steel Foundries." * * *

The Circuit Court of Appeals modified the final decree by striking out the word "persuasion" in the four places in which it occurred, and by inserting after the clause restraining picketing the following: "in a threatening or intimidating manner." 238 Fed. 728.[1]

---

[1] The restraining order in this case was granted on May 18, 1914. A temporary injunction was granted on May 28, 1914, and the final decree entered on June 9, 1914. This was reversed with directions to modify by the Seventh Circuit Court of Appeals on December 6, 1916. The case then went by certiorari to the Supreme Court of the United States where it was argued on January 17, 1919; restored to the docket for reargument on June 1, 1920; reargued on October 5, 1920; again restored to the docket for reargument on June 6, 1921; again reargued on October 4, 5, 1921, and decided on December 5, 1921.—Ed.

The Tri-City Central Trades Council is a labor organization composed of representatives of thirty-seven trade unions of Granite City, Madison and Venice, adjoining towns in Illinois, including among them electricians, cranemen, mill hands, machinists, and stationary engineers. In April, 1914, the complainant, which ordinarily in full operation employed 1600 men, and whose plant had been shut down since November of the previous year, resumed operations with about 350 of its regular men, 150 of whom belonged to the skilled trades, electricians, cranemen, mill hands, machinists and blacksmiths. At this trial, the works manager testified: "When we opened April 6th we employed whoever we saw fit, whoever applied for employment at the gate. We only had called for in round numbers 300 men, and laid off approximately 1300 men. Eighty or ninety per cent of the employees were old men. I assume these men were members of various organizations; I can't state definitely as to that." When business was resumed in April, half of the skilled workmen were given wages at rates from two cents to ten cents an hour below those paid before the plant had shut down. The Trades Council was advised of this about April 15th, and appointed a committee to secure reinstatement of the previous wages. The manager of the complainant told them that he ran an open shop, did not recognize organized labor and would not deal with the committee, but would entertain any complaint by an employee. The Council thereupon, on April 22nd, declared a strike on complainant's plant and displayed outside of the entrance to the plant a printed notice announcing that a strike was on at the plant and calling on union men and all labor to remain away from the works in order that an increase in wages might be secured. Only two men, defendants Churchill and Cook, acted upon the order to strike. Churchill was a member of the Machinist's Union. Cook was not a member of any union. The Council then established a picket, which was carried on for three or four weeks without intermission until the bill was filed on May 18th, and a restraining order issued. * * *[2]

It is clear from the evidence that from the outset, violent methods were pursued from time to time in such a way as to characterize the attitude of the pickets as continuously threatening. A number of employees, sometimes fifteen or more, slept in the plant for a week during the trouble, because they could not safely go to their homes. The result of the campaign was to put employees and would-be employees in such fear that many abandoned work and this seriously interfered with the complainant in operating the plant until the issue of the restraining order.

The first question in the case is whether § 20 of the Clayton Act, October 15, 1914, c. 323, 38 Stat. 738, is to be applied in this case. The act was passed while this case was pending in the Circuit Court of Appeals. In *Duplex Printing Press Co. v. Deering*, 254 U.S. 443, 464, a suit to restrain a secondary boycott had been brought before the passage of

---

[2] A portion of the opinion reviewing the conflicting evidence upon the violent character of the picketing is omitted.—Ed.

the act, but did not come to hearing until after its passage. It was held that, because relief by injunction operates *in futuro* and the right to it must be determined as of the time of the hearing, § 20 of the act, relating to injunctions, was controlling in so far that decrees entered after its passage should conform to its provisions. The decree here appealed from in the District Court had been entered before the Clayton Act passed. But the whole cause was taken up by the appeal. The complaint had no vested right in the decree of the District Court while it was subject to review. *Rafferty v. Smith, Bell & Co.*, this day announced, *post, 226.* The Circuit Court of Appeals was called upon to approve or to change the decree and was obliged, therefore, to regard the new statute in its conclusion, and so are we.

Section 20 is as follows:

"That no restraining order or injunction shall be granted by any court of the United States, or a judge or the judges thereof, in any case between an employer and employees, or between employers and employees, or between employees, or between persons employed and persons seeking employment, involving, or growing out of, a dispute concerning terms or conditions of employment, unless necessary to prevent irreparable injury to property, or to a property right, of the party making the application, for which injury there is no adequate remedy at law, and such property or property right must be described with particularity in the application, which must be in writing and sworn to by the applicant or by his agent or attorney.

"And no such restraining order or injunction shall prohibit any person or persons, whether singly or in concert, from terminating any relation of employment, or from ceasing to perform any work or labor, or from recommending, advising, or persuading others by peaceful means so to do; or from attending at any place where any such person or persons may lawfully be, for the purpose of peacefully obtaining or communicating information, or from peacefully persuading any person to work or to abstain from working; or from ceasing to patronize or to employ any party to such dispute, or from recommending, advising, or persuading others by peaceful and lawful means so to do; or from paying or giving to, or withholding from, any person engaged in such dispute, any strike benefits or other moneys or things of value; or from peaceably assembling in a lawful manner, and for lawful purposes; or from doing any act or thing which might lawfully be done in the absence of such dispute by any party thereto; nor shall any of the acts specified in this paragraph be considered or held to be violations of any law of the United States."

It has been determined by this court that the irreparable injury to property or to a property right, in the first paragraph of § 20, includes injury to the business of an employer, and that the second paragraph applies only in cases growing out of a dispute concerning terms or conditions of employment, between an employer and employee, between employers and employees, or between employees, or between persons employed and persons seeking employment, and not to such dispute between an employer and persons who are neither ex-employees nor seeking employment. *Duplex Printing Press Co. v. Deering,* 254 U.S. 443. Only two of the defendants, Cook and Churchill, who left at the time of the strike, can invoke in their behalf § 20. We must, therefore, first consider the propriety of the decree as against them, and then as against the other defendants.[8]

The prohibitions of § 20, material here, are those which forbid an injunction against, first, recommending, advising or persuading others by peaceful means to cease employment and labor; second, attending at any place where such person or persons may lawfully be for the purpose of peacefully obtaining or communicating information, or peacefully persuading any person to work or to abstain from working; third, peaceably assembling in a lawful manner and for lawful purposes. This court has already called attention in the *Duplex Case* to the emphasis upon the words "peaceful" and "lawful" in this section. 254 U.S. 443, 473. It is clear that Congress wished to forbid the use by the federal courts of their equity arm to prevent peaceable persuasion by employees, discharged or expectant, in promotion of their side of the dispute, and to secure them against judicial restraint in obtaining or communicating information in any place where they might lawfully be. This introduces no new principle into the equity jurisprudence of those courts. It is merely declaratory of what was the best practice always. Congress thought it wise to stabilize this rule of action and render it uniform.[4]

The object and problem of Congress in § 20, and indeed of courts of equity before its enactment, was to reconcile the rights of the employer in his business and in the access of his employees to his place of business and egress therefrom without intimidation or obstruction, on the one hand, and the right of the employees, recent or expectant, to use peaceable and lawful means to induce present employees and

---

[3] Upon the question of who are "employees" within the terms of statutes framing the extent of their operation in terms similar to the Clayton Act, see: 37 Harv. Law Rev. 486 (1924). See also: Duplex Printing Co. v. Deering, *post,* p. 532; Bull v. Internat'l Alliance of Theatrical Stage Employees, 119 Kan. 713, 241 Pac. 459 (1925); Giltner v. Beckner, 133 Kan. 170; 298 Pac. 780 (1931); Comm. v. Hoffman, 103 Pa. Sup. Ct. 433, 157 Atl. 221 (1931). Upon the question of what is a dispute "concerning terms or conditions of employment," see: Heitkemper v. Central Labor Council of Portland, 99 Ore. 1, 192 Pac. 765 (1920); Monday Co. v. Automobile, Aircraft & Vehicle Workers, 171 Wis. 532, 177 N.W. 867 (1920). Compare the abandonment of these tests in favor of the broader conception of a "trade dispute" in The Trade Disputes Act of 1906, 6 Edw. VII, c. 47. § 5; U.S. Act of March 23. 1932, § 13, *post,* p. 294; Pa. Act of June 23, 1931, § 1, L. 1931, No. 311. See also the abandonment of the employer-employee test in favor of "persons" in Act of June 19, 1925, Ill. Laws, p. 378; Act of March 29, 1926, N.J. Laws, c. 207.—Ed.

[4] Compare the following statement from the presidential address of W. H. Taft before the American Bar Association shortly after the passage of the Clayton Act: "All these provisions have been called the charter of liberty of labor. We have seen that the changes from existing law they make are not broadly radical and that most of them are declaratory merely of what would be the law without the statute. This is a useful statute in definitely regulating procedure in injunctions and in express definition of what may be done in labor disputes. But what I fear is that when the statute is construed by the courts it will keep the promise of the labor leaders to the ear and break it to the hope of the ranks of labor." Am. Bar Ass'n Rep. 359, 380 (1914). For the legislative history of the Clayton Act, see: Frankfurter and Greene, The Labor Injunction, c. 4 (1930).—Ed.

would-be employees to join their ranks, on the other. If, in their attempts at persuasion or communication with those whom they would enlist with them, those of the labor side adopt methods which however lawful in their announced purpose inevitably lead to intimidation and obstruction, then it is the court's duty which the terms of § 20 do not modify, so to limit what the propagandists do as to time, manner and place as shall prevent infractions of the law and violations of the right of the employees, and of the employer for whom they wish to work.

How far may men go in persuasion and communication and still not violate the right of those whom they would influence? In going to and from work, men have a right to as free a passage without obstruction as the streets afford, consistent with the right of others to enjoy the same privilege. We are a social people and the accosting by one of another in an inoffensive way and an offer by one to communicate and discuss information with a view to influencing the other's action are not regarded as aggression or a violation of that other's rights. If, however, the offer is declined, as it may rightfully be, then persistence, importunity, following and dogging become unjustifiable annoyance and obstruction which is likely soon to savor of intimidation. From all of this the person sought to be influenced has a right to be free and his employer has a right to have him free.[5]

The nearer this importunate intercepting of employees or would-be employees is to the place of business, the greater the obstruction and interference with the business and especially with the property right of access of the employer. Attempted discussion and argument of this kind in such proximity is certain to attract attention and congregation of the curious, or, it may be, interested bystanders, and thus to increase the obstruction as well as the aspect of intimidation which the situation quickly assumes. In the present case the three or four groups of picketers, were made up of from four to twelve in a group. They constituted the picket lines. Each union interested, electricians, cranemen, machinists and blacksmiths, had several representatives on the picket line, and assaults and violence ensued. They began early and continued from time to time during the three weeks of the strike after the picketing began. All information tendered, all arguments advanced and all persua-

---

[5] Attempts have been made to translate this principle into action by embodying in injunctions provisions against such "importunate intercepting of employees." Thus in Pittsburgh Terminal Corp. v. United Mine Workers of America (U.S.D.C.Pa. 1927), the injunction specified: "(e) The peaceful persuasion herein referred to * * * does not include talking to any person after having been notified or advised by him of his unwillingness to be talked with, or pursuing or following such person for any such purpose." See: Hearings before a Subcommittee of the Committee on the Judiciary, U.S. Senate, 70th Cong. 1st sess., on S. 1482, p. 73 (1928). In New York Trust Co., Trustee v. Amalgamated Ass'n of Street & Electric Ry. Employees (U.S. D.C. La. 1929), the injunction required the pickets "in their single efforts at communication or persuasion, [not to] obstruct an unwilling listener by importunate following or dogging his steps." See: 11 Law & Labor, 176. In United Brotherhood of Miners v. United Mine Workers of America, Dist. No. 13 (U.S.D.C. Iowa 1927), the pickets were enjoined "from obstructing any unwilling listener by persistently following or accompanying him." See: Hearings, supra, at 115.—Ed.

sion used under such circumstances were intimidation. They could not
be otherwise. It is idle to talk of peaceful communication in such a
place and under such conditions. The numbers of the pickets in the
groups constituted intimidation. The name "picket" indicated a militant
purpose, inconsistent with peaceful persuasion. The crowds they drew
made the passage of the employees to and from the place of work, one
of running the gauntlet. Persuasion or communication attempted in such
a presence and under such conditions was anything but peaceable and
lawful. When one or more assaults or disturbances ensued, they characterized the whole campaign, which became effective because of its intimidating character, in spite of the admonitions given by the leaders to
their followers as to lawful methods to be pursued, however sincere.
Our conclusion is that picketing thus instituted is unlawful and can not
be peaceable and may be properly enjoined by the specific term because
its meaning is clearly understood in the sphere of the controversy by
those who are parties to it. We are supported in that view by many well
reasoned authorities, although there has been contrariety of view. *Barnes
& Co. v. Typographical Union*, 232 Ill. 424; *Franklin Union v. People*,
220 Ill. 355; *Philip Henrici Co. v. Alexander*, 198 Ill. App. 568; *Vegelahn
v. Guntner*, 167 Mass. 92; *Jonas Glass Co. v. Glass Association*, 72 N.J.
Eq. 653, s.c. 77 N.J. Eq. 219; *Jersey City Printing Co. v. Cassidy*, 63 N.J.
Eq. 759; *Frank & Dugan v. Herold*, 63 N.J. Eq. 443; *Goldberg, Bowen, &
Co. v. Stablemen's Union*, 149 Cal. 429; *Pierce v. Stablemen's Union*, 156
Cal. 70; *Local Union No. 313 v. Stathakis*, 135 Ark. 86; *Beck v. Teamsters'
Union*, 118 Mich. 497; *In re Langell*, 178 Mich. 305; *Jensen v. Cooks' &
Waiters' Union*, 39 Wash. 531; *St. Germain v. Bakery & Confectionery
Workers' Union*, 97 Wash. 282; *Jones v. Van Winkle Gin & Machine
Works*, 131 Ga. 336; *Union Pacific R. R. Co. v. Ruef*, 120 Fed. 102; *Atchi-
son, Topeka & Santa Fe Ry. Co. v. Gee*, 139 Fed. 582; *Stephens v. Ohio
State Telephone Co.*, 240 Fed. 759.

A restraining order against picketing will advise earnest advocates
of labor's cause that the law does not look with favor on an enforced
discussion of the merits of the issue between individuals who wish to
work, and groups of those who do not, under conditions which subject
the individuals who wish to work to a severe test of their nerve and
physical strength and courage. But while this is so, we must have every
regard to the congressional intention manifested in the act and to the
principle of existing law which it declared, that ex-employees and others
properly acting with them shall have an opportunity, so far as is consistent with peace and law, to observe who are still working for the
employer, to communicate with them and to persuade them to join the
ranks of his opponents in a lawful economic struggle. Regarding as
primary the rights of the employees to work for whom they will, and,
undisturbed by annoying importunity or intimidation of numbers, to go
freely to and from their place of labor, and keeping in mind the right
of the employer incident to his property and business to free access of
such employees, what can be done to reconcile the conflicting interests?

Each case must turn on its own circumstances. It is a case for the flexible remedial power of a court of equity which may try one mode of restraint, and if it fails or proves to be too drastic, may change it. We think that the strikers and their sympathizers engaged in the economic struggle should be limited to one representative for each point of ingress and egress in the plant or place of business and that all others be enjoined from congregating or loitering at the plant or in the neighboring street by which access is had to the plant, that such representatives should have the right of observation, communication and persuasion but with special admonition that their communication, arguments and appeals shall not be abusive, libelous or threatening, and that they shall not approach individuals together but singly, and shall not in their single efforts at communication or persuasion obstruct an unwilling listener by importunate following or dogging his steps.[6] This is not laid down as a rigid rule, but only as one which should apply to this case under the circumstances disclosed by the evidence and which may be varied in other cases. It becomes a question for the judgment of the Chancellor who has heard the witnesses, familiarized himself with the *locus in quo* and observed the tendencies to disturbance and conflict. The purpose should be to prevent the inevitable intimidation of the presence of groups of pickets, but to allow missionaries.[7]

---

[6] In Greenfield v. Central Labor Council, 104 Ore. 236, 192 Pac. 783 (1920), the court said: "The decree of the circuit court will be modified, and one will be entered here permitting the defendants during business hours to place and maintain one picket only, on the outer edge of the sidewalk, at each public entrance to plaintiff's stores, with authority to each picket to wear a banner or scarf inscribed with the words, 'Unfair to Organized Labor. Local Union No. 1257,' and in the usual, ordinary tone of voice used by one individual in addressing another on the public street to say to any prospective customer: 'This place is unfair to organized labor. Please do not patronize it. Friends of union labor and all workingmen will not patronize this place'— but not in any manner to impede or interfere with the right of any one to enter or depart from the said stores, or any passer-by." See, also: Greenfield v. Central Labor Council, 104 Ore. 259, 207 Pac. 168 (1922).—Ed.

[7] The practice, since the Tri-City case, of limiting the number of pickets and specifying their activities, has become common. Thus in E. H. Scott Transportation Co. v. Murphy (U.S.D.C. Ohio 1929), a proviso was attached to the injunction reading: "Provided, however, that nothing herein contained shall be held to restrain the defendants from stationing upon the sidewalk adjacent to the entrance to the complainant's Cleveland terminal and one of the sidewalk adjacent to its Ashtabula station, who may quietly and peaceably solicit any of the complainant's employes to become a member of said Truck Drivers' Local Union No. 407, and persuade any employe to quit complainant's employ, but said representative shall not annoy or intimidate anyone in either access to or egress from complainant's property, nor use abusive or threatening language; and provided further that such persons so stationed at the entrance shall be selected by the defendants and at all times wear conspicuously a number to readily identify each of them as the persons stationed in accordance with this order; and the name of each such person, together with his identification number, shall be first filed with the clerk of this court." See: 11 Law & Labor, 254. Provisions of the injunction order in Clarkson Coal Co. v. United Mine Workers of America (U.S.D.C. Ohio, 1927) read: "7 * * * Persuasion in the presence of three or more persons congregated with the persuader is not peaceful persuasion, and is hereby prohibited * * * 10. * * * (b) Not more than three persons at a time shall be stationed at any picket post, and no other person shall be permitted to stand or loiter at any place within One Hundred feet (100) from the limits of any picket post for any purpose whatsoever. * * * (d) A list containing the names of picket details as soon as chosen, will be

With these views, it is apparent that we can not sustain the qualification of the order of the District Court which the Circuit Court of Appeals made. That court followed the case of *Iron Molders' Union v. Allis-Chalmers Co.*, 166 Fed. 45, and modified the order of the District Court which enjoins defendants "from picketing or maintaining at or near the premises of the complainant, or on the streets leading to the premises of said complainant, any picket or pickets" by adding the words "in a threat-

---

delivered to the United States Marshal, Southern District of Ohio, accompanied by a rough plat or plats showing the designation and location of each picket post. * * * (e) Each picket shall be a citizen of the United States, and shall be able to speak the English language." See: 9 Law & Labor, 290. Concerning the last clause of this injunction, President Green made the following comment: "Now, the significance of that prohibition must impress you when I explain that more than 90 per cent of the workers in these mines in eastern Ohio were foreign-speaking men. * * * These Italians [the strikebreakers] come in, Senator; the picket must be an English-speaking person, he must be a citizen of the United States. He cannot speak to the Italians in their own language, and the Italian member of the unions is prohibited from doing so by court order." See: Hearings before a Subcommittee of the Committee on the Judiciary, U.S. Senate, 70th Cong. 1st sess., on S. 1482, 70-71 (1928). The following defense of this provision was made by R. L. Ireland, Jr., general manager of the Pittsburgh & Eastern Coal Company: "It seems strange to me that these paragraphs have been criticized in view of the fact that the men who worked at our mines under union conditions were also able to converse with their foremen in English. Further it seems that, in view of the fact Mr. Lewis consistently claims that the United Mine Workers of America as an organization is typically American, he would insist that his subordinates use only as pickets American citizens who are familiar with laws of the State of Ohio and the United States and the rights of citizens. Furthermore, as Judge Hough stated himself, the United States marshals are all citizens who speak English and therefore could not converse with the pickets if they also could not speak English." Hearings before the Committee on Interstate Commerce, U.S. Senate, 70th Cong. 1st sess., pursuant to S. Res. 105, 2457 (1928). See also: Hearings before a Subcommittee of the Committee on the Judiciary, U.S. Senate, 70th Cong. 1st sess., on S. 1482, 527-556 (1928).

For cases limiting the number and activity of pickets, see: United Chain Theatres v. Philadelphia M. P. M. O. Union, 50 Fed.(2d) 189 (E.D. Pa. 1931); Great Northern Ry. Co. v. Brosseau, *post*, p. 223; Goldfield Cons. Mines Co. v. Goldfield Miners Union, 159 Fed. 500 (Cir. Ct. Nev. 1908); Forstmann & Huffman Co. v. United Front Committee, 99 N.J. Eq. 230, 133 Atl. 202 (1926); Snead & Co. v. Internat'l Molders' Union, 103 N.J. Eq. 332, 143 Atl. 331 (1928); Reed Co. v. Whiteman, 238 N.Y. 545, 144 N.E. 885 (1923); Bloomfield Co. v. Joint Board of Cloak, Suit, Skirt & Dressmakers' Union, 12 Law & Labor, 90 (Comm. Pl. Ohio 1930); La France Elec. & Const. Supply Co. v. Internat'l Brotherhood of Electrical Workers, 108 Ohio St. 61, 140 N.E. 899 (1923). *Cf.* Internat'l Pocketbook Workers v. Orlove, 158 Md. 496, 148 Atl. 826 (1929).

"Since the Tri-City case, however, it is almost universal practice carefully to limit the number of pickets. The device of requiring the persons stationed to be registered and to wear distinguishing bands or numbers is now being frequently resorted to; and the distance which the 'representatives' must constantly keep between each other is sometimes prescribed in the injunction. One court has even placed a limitation upon the hours when the workers may maintain the patrol. The treatment of the matter by the courts takes on a ludicrous aspect. It is industrial struggle with which the courts are dealing. If strikers observe the law under the rules which have been laid down, the picket line must be carried on with the decorum of a college debate, with one or two men at each entrance representing the workers, registered, and even limited in the hours in which they may exhort, the tone of voice they may use, and the gestures they may make in addressing workers in a plant which may employ a thousand workers. The irony which labor has often experienced in the courts, is reflected in these results, for the outlawry of group appeal on the picket line, one of labor's most effective weapons, has grown out of the construction of organized labor's Magna Charta at the hands of a court eloquently praising trade unionism." Hallerstein, "Picketing Legislation and the Courts," 10 N.C. Law Rev. 158, 183 (1932).—Ed.

ening or intimidating manner." This qualification seems to us to be inadequate. In actual result, it leaves compliance largely to the discretion of the pickets. It ignores the necessary element of intimidation in the presence of groups as pickets. It does not secure practically that which the court must secure and to which the complainant and his workmen are entitled. The phrase really recognizes as legal that which bears the sinister name of "picketing" which it is to be observed Congress carefully refrained from using in § 20.

There remains to consider, so far as defendants Churchill and Cook, the ex-employees, are concerned, the part of the decree of the District Court which forbade them by persuasion to induce employees, or would-be employees to leave, or stay out of, complainant's employ. The effect of it is to enjoin persuasion by them at any time or place. This certainly conflicts with § 20 of the Clayton Act. The decree must be modified as to these two defendants by striking out the word "persuasion."

The second important question in the case is as to the form of decree against the Tri-City Trades Council and the other defendants. What has been said as to picketing applies to them, of course, as fully as to the ex-employees, but how as to the injunction against persuasion?

The argument made on behalf of the American Foundries in support of enjoining persuasion is that the Tri-City Central Trades Council and the other defendants being neither employees nor strikers were intruders into the controversy, and were engaged without excuse in an unlawful conspiracy to injure the American Foundries by enticing its employees, and, therefore, should be enjoined.

It is to be noted, that while there was only one member of the unions of the Trades Council who went out in the strike, the number of skilled employees then engaged by the Foundries was not one-quarter of the whole number of men who would be engaged when it was in full operation. The works manager said that eighty or ninety per cent of the employees were old men and that he assumed these men were members of various organizations. Other witnesses, members of the unions, testified that they had been employees of complainant in the previous fall. It is thus probable that members of the local unions were looking forward to employment when complainant should resume full operation and even though they were not ex-employees within the Clayton Act, they were directly interested in the wages which were to be paid.

Is interference of a labor organization by persuasion and appeal to induce a strike against low wages under such circumstances without lawful excuse and malicious? We think not. Labor unions are recognized by the Clayton Act as legal when instituted for mutual help and lawfully carrying out their legitimate objects. They have long been thus recognized by the courts. They were organized out of the necessities of the situation. A single employee was helpless in dealing with an employer. He was dependent ordinarily on his daily wage for the maintenance of himself and family. If the employer refused to pay him the wages that he thought fair, he was nevertheless unable to leave the employ and to resist arbitrary and unfair treatment. Union was essential to give laborers an opportunity to deal on equality with their employer. They united to exert influence upon him and to leave him in a body in order by this inconvenience to induce him to make better terms with them. They were withholding their labor of economic value to make him pay what they thought it was worth. The right to combine for such a lawful purpose has in many years not been denied by any court. The strike became a lawful instrument in a lawful economic struggle or competition between employer and employees as to the share or division between them of the joint product of labor and capital. To render this combination at all effective, employees must make their combination extend beyond one shop. It is helpful to have as many as may be in the same trade in the same community united, because in the competition between employers they are bound to be affected by the standard of wages of their trade in the neighborhood. Therefore, they may use all lawful propaganda to enlarge their membership and especially among those whose labor at lower wages will injure their whole guild. It is impossible to hold such persuasion and propaganda without more, to be without excuse and malicious. The principle of the unlawfulness of maliciously enticing laborers still remains and action may be maintained therefore in proper cases, but to make it applicable to local labor unions, in such a case as this, seems to us to be unreasonable.

The elements essential to sustain actions for persuading employees to leave an employer are first, the malice or absence of lawful excuse, and, second, the actual injury. The effect of cases cited as authority must be determined by an examination of the pleadings and facts to see how the malice or lack of lawful excuse was established, and whether there was not illegality present in the means used. Thus *Walker v. Cronin,* 107 Mass. 55, and *Thacker Coal Co. v. Burke,* 59 W. Va. 253, suits by an employer against members of a labor union in which the right of action for persuading was sustained, were heard on demurrer to the complaint. The element of malice was supplied by averment of the complaint, and was, of course, admitted by the demurrer. There are other cases in which the persuasion was accompanied by the intent to secure a breach of contract, or was part of a secondary boycott or had elements of fraud, misrepresentation or intimidation in it. *Perkins v. Pendleton,* 90 Me. 166, was a case of the latter kind. In *Lucke v. Clothing Cutters,* 77 Md. 396, it was held unlawful in a labor union to seek to compel an employer to discharge the plaintiff by intimidation, and it was said that the state law authorizing formation of trade unions to secure most favorable conditions for labor of their members was not a warrant for making war upon the non-union man or for illegal interference with his rights and privileges. A suit by an employee who seeks to hold a labor union liable for seeking his discharge by threatening to strike unless his employer discharges him, stands on a different footing from a mere effort by a labor union to persuade employees to leave their employment. There are in such a combination against an employee the suggestions of coercion, attempted monopoly, deprivation of livelihood and remoteness of the legal purpose of the union to better its members' condition, not present in a case like the present. Without entering into a discussion of those cases which include *Brennan v. United Hatters of North America,* 73 N.J.L. 729; *Curran v. Galen,* 152 N.Y. 33; *Berry v. Donovan,* 188 Mass. 354, and *Plant v. Woods,* 176 Mass. 492, it is sufficient to say they do not apply here.

The counsel for the Steel Foundries rely on two cases in this court to support their contention. The first is that of *Hitchman Coal & Coke Co. v. Mitchell,* 245 U.S. 229. The principle followed in the *Hitchman Case* can not be invoked here. There the action was by a coal mining company of West Virginia against the officers of an International Labor Union and others to enjoin them from carrying out a plan to bring the employees of the complainant company and all the West Virginia mining companies into the International Union, so that the Union could control, through the union employees, the production and sale of coal in West Virginia, in competition with the mines of Ohio and other States. The plan thus projected was carried out in the case of the complainant company by the use of deception and misrepresentation with its non-union employees, by seeking to induce such employees to become members of the Union contrary to the express term of their contract of employment that they would not remain in complainant's employ if union men, and after enough such employees had been secretly secured, suddenly to declare a strike against complainant and to leave it in a helpless situation in which it would have to consent to be unionized. This court held that the purpose was not lawful, and that the means were not lawful and that the defendants were thus engaged in an unlawful conspiracy which should be enjoined. The unlawful and deceitful means used were quite enough to sustain the decision of the court without more. The statement 'of the purpose of the plan is sufficient to show the remoteness of the benefit ultimately to be derived by the members of the International Union from its success and the formidable country-wide and dangerous character of the control of interstate commerce sought. The circumstances of the case make it no authority for the contention here.

Duplex Printing Press Co. v. Deering, 254 U.S. 443, also cited, can have no bearing here. In that case, the International Association of Machinists, an unincorporated association, having a membership of more than 60,000, united in a combination to compel the complainant to unionize its factory, enforce the closed shop, the eight-hour day and the union scale of wages by boycotting the interstate trade of the company. They conducted in the City of New York a campaign of threatening the customers of the Printing Press Company, the trucking companies that carried its presses, and those who were engaged in the work of setting up such presses, with injury to them in their business, if they continued to deal with the Duplex Company or its presses. It was a palpable effort on the part of the International Association of Machinists to institute a secondary boycott, that is, by coercion, to use the right of trade of persons having nothing to do with the controversy between the Duplex Company and the Machinist's Union, and having no interest in it, to injure the Duplex Company in its interstate trade. This was decided not to be within § 20 of the Clayton Act, but was held, following the case of *Loewe v. Lawlor*, 208 U.S. 274, to be an unlawful combination in restraint of interstate trade. The *Hitchman Case* was cited in the *Duplex Case*, but there is nothing in the *ratio decidendi* of either which limits our conclusion here or which requires us to hold that the members of a local labor union and the union itself do not have sufficient interest in the wages paid to the employees of any employer in the community to justify their use of lawful and peaceable persuasion to induce those employees to refuse to accept such reduced wages and to quit their employment. For this reason, we think that the restraint from persuasion included within the injunction of the District Court was improper, and in that regard the decree must also be modified. In this we agree with the Circuit Court of Appeals.

> The decree of the Circuit Court of Appeals is reversed in part and affirmed in part and the case is remanded to the District Court for modification of its decree in conformity with this opinion.

MR. JUSTICE BRANDEIS concurs in substance in the opinion and the judgment of the court.

MR. JUSTICE CLARKE dissents.[8]

GREAT NORTHERN RY. CO. v. BROSSEAU.

United States District Court for the District of North Dakota. 286 Fed. 414 (1923).

AMIDON, District Judge: This is a suit brought by plaintiff against defendants to restrain them from threats and acts of violence in connection with the strike of the railway shop crafts which was started on July 1, 1922. A temporary restraining order was issued, and has been continued in force after a full hearing until quite recently, when a preliminary injunction was issued. A large number of affidavits and a considerable body of oral evidence has been introduced upon the question of plaintiff's right to a preliminary injunction, and upon the several

---

[8] For comment on the case, see: Univ. of Pa. Law Rev. 101 (1922); 8 Va. Law Reg. N.S. 401 (1922).

Compare as to the construction of similar state statutes, Truax v. Corrigan, 20 Ariz. 7, 176 Pac. 570 (1918); Ossey v. Retail Clerks Union, 326 Ill 405, 158 N.E. 162 (1927); Roesch Enamel Range Co. v. Carbine, 247 Ill. App. 248 (1928); Greenfield v. Central Labor Council, 104 Ore. 236, 207 Pac. 168 (1922).

Upon the enactment of similar state legislation, see: Chamberlain. "The Legislature and Labor Injunctions," 11 Am. Bar Ass'n Jour. 815 (1925); Donovan, "Legislation Affecting Labor Injunctions," 16 Am. Bar Ass'n Jour. 561 (1930); 22 Ill. Law Rev. 888 (1928).

hearings in contempt proceedings for violations of the temporary restraining order. During the three months the case has been pending, and the different proceedings have been taken, the court has been called upon to investigate the law applicable to such a case, and a few matters that I have learned are of sufficient importance to justify their statement.

Neither the restraining order nor the preliminary injunction prepared by counsel was signed by the court. During the 30 years that courts have been dealing with strikes by means of injunctions, these orders have steadily grown in length, complexity, and the vehemence of their rhetoric. They are full of the rich vocabulary of synonyms which is a part of our English language. They are also replete with superlative words and the superlative phrases of which the legal mind is fond. The result has been that such writs have steadily become more and more complex and prolix. All of this, it seems to me, is foreign to their legitimate purpose. They, like the proper bill in such cases, ought to arise out of the facts of each specific case. Injunctions are addressed to laymen.[1] They ought to be so brief and plain that laymen can understand them. They ought to be framed in the fewest possible words. The order should not express the bias or violence of a party to such a controversy or his attorney. I therefore framed the orders in this case with these objects in view. The purpose ought to be to state the specific acts that are forbidden. It also helps to show where the line separating wrong from right conduct lies, to state what acts are not forbidden. So I attempted to do that in the orders that were issued. A copy of the restraining part of the injunction will be found in the margin.[2] The result has been that the strikers have been able to understand the orders, and have shown a keen desire to do so and obey them. The officers of the union in charge of the strike, and a great majority of the men, have joined with the peace officers in a sincere effort to conduct the strike in a lawful and orderly manner. A few cases of alleged disobedience have been brought to the attention of the court, but many of these upon a hearing have been found to be without merit. I have been informed from time to time by deputy marshals who are stationed at each of the terminal points, that the strikers, with rare exceptions, were sincerely desirous of obeying the orders of the court and conducting the strike in a lawful manner.

---

[1] In International Tailoring Co. v. Amalgamated Clothing Workers of America, 7 Law & Labor, 237 (Sup. Ct. Ill. 1925), the court after considering how far an anti-injunction statute of Illinois restricted the issuance of injunctions against picketing, issued an injunction which forbade the defendants "from picketing or maintaining any picket or pickets at or near the premises of the complainant * * * in a manner that is intimating or unlawful; but this does not, however, restrain in any way or prevent the defendants from maintaining pickets or persuading employes of the complainant, or from following or calling upon the employes of the complainant or from congregating in a peaceable manner, as provided in the Act of the Legislature of the State of Illinois, entitled 'An Act Relating to Disputes Concerning Terms and Conditions of Employment.' "—Ed.

[2] See note at end of case.

The experience both upon the hearings as to whether a preliminary injunction should issue, and upon the contempt proceedings, have convinced me that affidavits are an untrustworthy guide for judicial action.[3] That is the case in all legal proceedings, but it is peculiarly true of litigation growing out of a strike, where feelings on both sides are necessarily wrought up, and the desire for victory is likely to obscure nice moral questions and poison the minds of men by prejudice. Many of the affidavits submitted on behalf of plaintiffs have been made by private detectives or guards. As a class they are overzealous, through their desire to prove to the detective bureaus that they are efficient, and to the railway company that they are indispensable. Speaking generally, such detectives are mostly drawn from a class of people in large cities which would cause little credence to be given to their statements in ordinary litigation. The evidence that has come to me from wholly trustworthy sources in the present case satisfies me that the sooner public police officers are substituted for such private detectives, the better it will be for all parties concerned in strikes.[4]

Early after the suit was brought, one or more deputy marshals were stationed at each of the terminal points of railway companies in the state. They were selected from civil life, and were wholly disconnected from either of the parties to the strike. They were men of mature years, good sense, and courage. I am satisfied that these officers have done more to maintain law and order than any other single influence. These public officers have been of great service to the court, in giving it disinterested reports as to all conflicts that have arisen.

Experience, as I have stated, has caused me to be so incredulous of affidavits that I have required in all important matters the presence of the chief witnesses upon each side at the hearing. These witnesses have been subjected to oral examination. The court has had a chance to observe their demeanor. A comparison of the picture produced by their testimony with that produced by their affidavits has proven the utter untrustworthiness of affidavits. Such documents are packed with falsehoods,

[3] See: Holcomb, J., in Pacific Coast Coal Co. v. District No. 10, U. M. W. A., 122 Wash. 423, 435, 210 Pac. 953 (1922) ; Frankfurter & Greene, The Labor Injunction. 66-81 (1930).—Ed.

[4] "It was widely said at the time that this [the mob violence in the Pullman strike of 1894] was partly the work of *agents provocateurs* acting for the railways. Undeniably the railroads had employed many queer characters. The Federal marshals had appointed some 3,600 deputies who were selected by the General Managers' Association [representing the railroads involved], were armed and paid for by the railroads, and acted in the double capacity of railway employees and United States officers. The press described them as 'toughs' and Marshal Donnelly as in part 'worthless' and drunken." Nevins, Grover Cleveland, 622 (1932).

On the power of the state to prevent importation by employers of lawless strikebreakers, see: Arkansas v. Kansas & T. Coal Co., 96 Fed. 353 (Cir. Ct. W.D. Ark. 1899). See, also: Tobias, "The Newport Dock Dispute," 26 Law Quar. Rev. 377 (1910). On the power of municipal authorities to prevent such importation, see: American Steel & Wire Co. v. Davis, 2 Law & Labor, 41 (U.S.D.C Ohio, 1920) ; Mullins Body Corp. v. Internat'l Ass'n of Machinists, 3 Law & Labor, 149 (U.S.D.C. Ohio, 1921).—Ed.

or with half-truths, which in such a matter are more deceptive than deliberate falsehoods.[5]

The most serious complaint that can be made against injunctions, which have become so prominent a part of the law in dealing with strikes in the United States, is the fact that courts have become accustomed to decide the most important questions of fact, often involving the citizen's liberty, upon this wholly untrustworthy class of proof.

In England, the acts which American courts are accustomed to restrain have been made crimes in the Conspiracy Statute of 1875 and its amendments. There injunctions have completely ceased in the theater of strikes. The acts having been made criminal, any party who is guilty of doing them is promptly arrested, tried, and, if found guilty, punished. If either party seeks an appeal in such a case, the appeal is heard inside of 30 days. The evidence is never printed, but a typewritten copy of it is certified up to the appellate court. The controverted questions of fact, if there be any, are usually reduced to a single point or two by experienced counsel, and the evidence itself is only looked at by the court in case counsel are unable to agree upon the facts. As a rule these criminal appeals are there disposed of in a few days after a judgment of guilty has been pronounced. In the most important cases the appeal is heard within 30 days, and final judgment rendered. There is no reason why a similarly prompt practice should not be established in our courts.

The Great Northern and Northern Pacific Railroads are both transcontinental lines passing entirely across this state. They both have numerous branch lines. The Northern Pacific has three terminal yards and repair points, and the Great Northern five. The Great Northern brought the present suit, and has had injunctive relief restraining the defendants in accordance with the provisions that are usually employed in such writs. The Northern Pacific has brought no suit, and has no injunctions. I have been kept as well informed by deputy marshals in the case of the Northern Pacific as in that of the Great Northern. I think, on the whole, there has been no material difference as to violation of the railway company's rights on the two lines. This experience convinces me that the injunction is a much less potent factor in maintaining good order than is usually believed.[6]

I have had occasion to make a careful study of section 20 of the Clayton Act (Comp. St. §1243d) and section 2 of the English Trades Dispute Act of 1906. The reports of the judicial committee both of the House and the Senate state that the section of our statute referred to was copied from the English section. The form in which they are

---

5 See Fuller. J., in Long v. Bricklayers' & Masons' International Union, 17 Pa. Dist. Ct. 985 (1908). See also: 41 Harv. Law Rev. 909 (1928).—Ed.

6 See: McCracken, Strike Injunctions in the New South (1931) *passim*; Witte, "Value of Injunctions in Labor Disputes." 32 Jour. Pol. Econ. 335 (1924); Witte, "Results of Injunctions in Labor Disputes." 12 Am. Lab. Leg. Rev. 197 (1922); Witte, "Social Consequences of Injunctions in Labor Disputes," 24 Ill. Law Rev. 772 (1930); Frankfurter and Greene, The Labor Injunction, App. viii (1930).—Ed.

framed differs, but their legal effect is the same. The English statute says that "it shall be lawful" to do the specific acts mentioned in each of the statutes. This, as a necessary inference, forbade the courts to issue injunctions restraining workmen from doing those acts. The American statute reverses this order. It expressly forbids courts to issue injunctions or restraining orders forbidding workmen to do the acts specified in section 20, and then in its last clause declares as follows:

"Nor shall any of the acts specified in this paragraph be considered or held to be violations of any law of the United States."

Our statute forbids expressly the issuing of injunctions against the doing of the acts, and also declares that the doing of the same shall not be construed or held to be a violation of federal Law. The English act, without expressly dealing with the subject by forbidding injunctions, does so impliedly by conferring upon employés in the case of a trade dispute the right to do the acts. The only difference in the two statutes is that our law is express on the subject of forbidding injunctions in the cases specified, while the English statute accomplishes the same result by implication.

I am convinced that the American statute does not authorize strikers to go upon the property of the company without its consent for the purpose "of attending at any place" where new employés may be, "for the purpose of peacefully obtaining or communicating information, or peacefully persuading such new employés to abstain from working." That is the natural interpretation of the statute, and had been placed upon it before its adoption here. Slesser & Baker, "The Law of Trade Unions," p. 217.

The difference in the civil life habits of England and the United States results in widely different effects from the same statute in the two countries. In Great Britain strikers and the new employés are a part of the common life of the community. They mingle freely with one another. The opportunities for peaceful persuasion are a part of the daily intercourse. There the private armed detective is unknown. Nobody carries arms in England, but members of the army and navy; even policemen carry nothing but their sticks, and soldiers, in the rare cases in which they are called out to repress riots in connection with strikes, use nothing but their hand arms. In such a field the right of peaceful persuasion is natural and easy. It results sometimes in violent words, occasionally in violent acts with fists, and more rarely with bricks. The policemen, however, are quite equal to coping with such a situation. Guilty parties are promptly arrested, tried, and, if found guilty, promptly punished. The writ of injunction in strike cases has been unknown in England during the period when it has attained such universal use with us.

In the United States new workmen are recruited from fields remote from the strike. They are brought into the company's yards in cars. They sleep and eat on the ground, and are surrounded by a cordon of private detectives. This practice in no small degree nullifies the provisions of the Clayton Act (38 Stat. 730). There are no opportunities for peaceful persuasion.[7] The new employés are schooled in the notion that if they leave the stockade they will be in imminent danger. The contrast between the situations in England and America presents an impressive example of how differently the same statute works in countries whose habits of life are different.

In American Steel Foundries Co. v. Tri-State Central Trades Council, 257 U.S. 184, 42 Sup. Ct. 72, 66 L. Ed. 189, the number of pickets at any single point was limited to one. The court, however, is careful to state that no mathematical formula was intended for the purpose of all cases. Each case must depend to some extent upon the local situation. The danger of intimidation and attack is not confined to aggressions by strikers.[8] The impartial history of strikes teaches that

---

[7] "Mr. Lewis [President of the United Mine Workers of America]: You are familiar with the policy in effect there that whenever union pickets attempt to engage in conversation with any of the strike breakers, that the company has mounted near the picket line, two sirens which they blow at those times.

"Mr. Jones [President of the Ohio Collieries Company]: Yes, sir. And the pickets have some megaphones that bother our men. We try to counteract the noise by the use of sirens.

"Mr. Lewis: Has the use of sirens been fairly effective for that purpose?

"Mr. Jones: I understand that they have.

"Mr. Lewis: Because megaphones can hardly compete with your steam or electric sirens.

"Mr. Jones: We hope not."

Hearings before the Committee on Interstate Commerce pursuant to Sen. Res. 105, 70th Cong. 1st sess., p. 2235 (1928).—Ed.

[8] For instances of violence by employers' agents or representatives, see: Kusnir v. Pressed Steel Car Co., 201 Fed. 146 (S.D.N.Y. 1912) (assault by armed guard); Pennsylvania Mining Co. v. Jarnigan, 222 Fed. 889 (8th cir., 1915) (assaults by armed guards); United Mine Workers of America, Dist. No. 17 v. Chapin, 286 Fed. 959 (S.D.W.Va. 1923) (attempt to enjoin sheriff and coal operators from using intimidatory means to keep union organizers out of Logan county); Scipio v. Pioneer Mining & Mfg. Co., 166 Ala. 666, 52 So. 43 (1910) (assault by deputy sheriff appointed at request of company, but company held not liable); State v. Payne, 127 Minn. 445, 149 N.W. 945 (1914) (kidnapping of member of strikers' committee); Fagan v. Pittsburgh Terminal Coal Corp., 299 Pa. 109, 149 Atl. 159 (1930) (false imprisonment by coal and iron police, but company not held liable); Ruffner v. Jamison Coal & C. Co., 247 Pa. 34, 92 Atl. 1075 (1915) (assaults by armed guards, but company held not liable); Welsh v. Vinton Colliery Co., 5 Law & Labor, 36 (Comm. Pl. Pa. 1923) (attempt to enjoin coal company from using intimidatory means to prevent meetings of United Mine Workers); Hudson v. St. Louis S. W. Ry. Co., 293 S.W. 811 (Texas Comm. App. 1927), 295 S.W. 577 (Texas Comm. App. 1927), 17 S.W.(2d) 793 (Texas Comm. App. 1929) (unprovoked killing of picketer by state ranger paid by railroad); Howitz v. Dickinson, 25 S.W.(2d) 966 (Texas Civ. App. 1930) (employer throwing eggs at picket). Cf. Williams v. Gt. Southern Lumber Co., 279 U.S. 19 (1928); State v. Meese, 200 Wis. 454, 225 N.W. 746 (1929). See: 39 Yale Law Jour. 1214 (1930).

For descriptions of the activities of armed guards and state police in industrial disputes, see: Material on Pennsylvania Coal and Iron Police in Hearings before the Committee on Interstate Commerce, U.S. Senate, 70th Cong. 1st sess., pursuant to Sen. Res. 105 (1928); Woltman and Nunn, "Cossacks," 15 Am. Mercury, 399 (1928); Shalloo, "The Private Police of Pennsylvania," 146 Am. Acad. Pol. Sci. 55 (1929); Witte, Government in Labor Disputes, 190-194 (1932); National Committee for the Defense of Political Prisoners, Harlan Miners Speak (1932).

For condemnation of the practice of employing armed guards, see: Final Report of Commission on Industrial Relations, 96 (1916); Final Report of the Industrial Commission, H.R. Doc. 380, 57th Cong. 1st sess., 891 (1902); Report of the United

there is as much danger to strikers on the picket line from private detectives and sometimes from new employés, as there is of the same kind of wrong on the part of strikers against new employés. My experience in the present strike clearly confirms that view. The strikers on the picket line are entitled to have enough present to shield them against the temptation of their adversaries to resort to violent methods. They also need the same protection against trumped-up charges or unfair evidence relative to any assaults that may occur on either side. At the beginning of the present strike the pickets had large tents at important points of ingress to the company's property, and were accustomed to assemble there, especially in the nighttime, in large numbers. I became convinced from the evidence that such tents, or the assembling of large numbers at or near the company's property, was a serious intimidation to workmen going about the yards in the necessary performance of their duties. I therefore required all such tents to be removed. The place for union men to meet for conference or in any considerable numbers is at their union hall. I limited the number of pickets at points of ingress and egress to three, and experience has justified that limitation as fair to both sides.

The Clayton Act, in both sections 17 and 20 (Comp. St. §§ 1243a, 1243d), uses the words "irreparable injury," and declares that such injury is necessary to support injunctive relief. What is the meaning of these words as used in the statute? Every strike as its natural consequence causes irreparable injury to the employer, and if the employment is quasi public, it causes the same kind of injury to the public. That is the purpose of the strike, and the only sanction which gives it

___

States Coal Commission, 156 (1923); Senator Kenyon in Sen. Rep. 457, 67th Cong. 2d sess., (1922); E. T. England, Att'y-Gen'l of West Virginia, in Hearings before the Committee on Education and Labor pursuant to Sen. Res. 80, 67th Cong. 1st sess., 720 (1921).

See also: Max Ams Machine Co. v. Internat'l Ass'n of Machinists, 92 Conn. 297, 102 Atl. 706 (1917) (no recovery for cost of keeping armed guards in the absence of threatening conduct by strikers); Ex parte Reilly, 2 Law & Labor, 40 (Comm. Pl. Ohio, 1920) (anti-armed guard ordinance invalid). *Cf.* Glasbrook Bros., Ltd. v. Glamorgan City Council [1925] A.C. 270. For legislation aimed at the employment of armed guards and authorizing the employment of industrial police, see: U. S. Dept. Labor, Bureau of Labor Statistics, Bull. No. 370, 109-112 (1925).

Upon the use of martial law to control activities of strikers, see: authorities and references collected in Witte, The Government in Labor Disputes, 198-201 (1932). In addition thereto, see: Brewer, "Use of Military to Restrain Industrial Tumults and Disorders," 20 Case & Comm. 108 (1913); Shumaker, "Martial Law to Suppress Disorder," 26 Law Notes, 225 (1923); Cullen, "The Decline of Personal Liberty in America," 48 Am. Law Rev. 345 (1914); "Military Strike Duty," 73 New Republic 113 (1932).

Upon the practice of industrial espionage, see Howard, The Labor Spy (1924); Witte, The Government in Labor Disputes, 183-190 (1932); Report of the United States Coal Commission, 1331 (1923); testimony of C. E. Lesher, president of Pittsburgh Coal Company, re subsidizing of National Labor Tribune, a purported labor paper, in Hearings before the Committee on Interstate Commerce pursuant to Sen. Res. 105, U.S. Senate, 70th Cong. 1st sess., 484-490 (1928); Hearings before a Subcommittee of the Committee on the Judiciary on S. 1482, 70th Cong. 1st sess., 129-130, 236 (1928); Grant, The National Erectors' Association and International Association of Bridge and Structural Ironworkers, c. 15 (1915); Wood Mowing & Reaping Machine Co. v. Toohey, 114 Misc. 185, 192-195, 186 N.Y.S. 95, 100-101 (1921).—Ed.

force. Notwithstanding this injury, Congress in express terms grants
to employés the right to strike and to inflict such injuries. The Clayton Act was passed in 1914. Congress acted with a full knowledge of
the disastrous consequences resulting from strikes, particularly in the
case of coal mining and transportation. Notwithstanding these natural
and inevitable injuries, the right of laboring men to strike has been
fully maintained in statutes, and is a part of our equity jurisprudence,
where that is not misinterpreted by the courts. That was the direct
issue in the famous Jenkins injunction case. *Farmers' Loan & Trust Co.
v. Northern Pacific R. Co.* (C.C.) 60 Fed. 803. There were special
circumstances in that case for restraining a strike. The Northern Pacific
Railroad Company was in the hands of receivers appointed by Judge
Jenkins. As a result of the panic of 1893, those receivers reported to
Judge Jenkins that it was necessary to reduce the wages of the railroad
employés. A full hearing was had upon their petition, in which the
railroad employés had participated and were represented by able counsel.
After this hearing Judge Jenkins made an order directing that the
wage scale of workmen on the road should be reduced. It was against
that order, and the reduction in wages which it authorized, that the
employés of the road threatened to strike. Judge Jenkins believed that
the disastrous consequences of the strike to interstate commerce, and
the carriage of mails, would be such that it was his duty to restrain the
workmen from resorting to that method of redress, and issued an injunction forbidding them to strike. But the Circuit Court of Appeals,
speaking by Mr. Justice Harlan of the Supreme Court, held this view
to be wrong, and decided that in the economic struggle the right to
strike was a weapon, a last and desperate weapon, which laboring men
had the right to use for the purpose of securing what they believed to be
just wages and wholesome conditions. *Arthur v. Oakes,* 63 Fed. 310, 11
C.C.A. 209, 25 L.R.A. 414.

The same considerations were present in the mind of Congress, as is
shown by the reports of both the House of Representatives and the
Senate, when the Clayton Act was passed. The whole subject had been
dramatically presented in the railroad strike of 1894, and other similar
strikes, and also in the great coal strike of 1902. Both strikes, even if
the strikers and those professing to act with them had refrained from
every act of violence, would have caused the most appalling injuries,
threatening not only the comfort, but the life, of vast numbers of people. The light in which Congress acted, and the numerous investigations which it had made, are fully referred to in the dissenting opinion
of Mr. Justice Brandeis in *Truax v. Corrigan,* 257 U.S. 312, 368, 42 Sup.
Ct. 124, 66 L. Ed. 254.

The constitutionality of the Clayton Act has not, so far as I know,
been questioned in the Supreme Court. That court, on the contrary, in
American Steel Foundries Co. v. Tri-State Central Trades Council, 257
U.S. 184, 42 Sup. Ct. 72, 66 L. Ed. 189, clearly indicates that it regards
the statute, when properly construed, as constitutional. It reversed the

decision of the trial court, because it issued an injunction "forbidding the ex-employés from persuading employés and would-be employés to leave or stay out of employment," on the ground that the decision of the trial court was in conflict with the Clayton Act. See 257 U.S. 208, 42 Sup. Ct. 78 (66 L. Ed. 189). There are several other features of this decision which by implication sustain its constitutionality.

Duplex Printing Co. v. Deering, 254 U.S. 443, 41 Sup. Ct. 172, 65 L. Ed. 349, 16 A.L.R. 196, by its whole course of reasoning, holds that the Clayton Act is constitutional, and, while the court decides that the statute does not legalize the secondary boycott, it does hold (1) that the last paragraph of section 20 forbids federal courts to enjoin the doing of any of the acts therein specified; (2) that the doing of any of those acts shall not be held to violate any law of the United States, such, for instance, as the Conspiracy Act or the Sherman Anti-Trust Law (Comp. St. §§ 8820-8823, 8827-8830).

Notwithstanding the legislative history of the statute, and its highly remedial character, as indicated by its history and the reports of the committees having it in charge, many lower federal courts have studiously striven to disregard its plain language, as well as the actual intent of Congress, as disclosed by the history of the statute. Some have held that all strikes cause irreparable injury, and therefore the employer is entitled to an injunction to prevent such injury.[9] Other courts have gone so far as to hold that the entire statute was a trick by Congress to so frame the measure that one part of it would nullify the other.[10] Other courts have said there was no such thing as peaceful picketing, and hence no such thing as peaceful persuasion, and therefore the plain language of the statute must be disregarded by the court, and all picketing and all attempts by strikers to exercise their rights of peaceful persuasion were to be restrained, and injunctions have been accordingly issued.[11] Other courts, notwithstanding the specific language of the last clause of section 20 that the doing of the acts which it permits should not be held to be in conflict with any federal law, have restrained strikes upon the ground that they violated the Sherman Anti-Trust Law and statutes forbidding the obstruction of the United States mails.[12]

In my judgment, all such action by courts is a gross abuse of judicial power, and a direct refusal on their part to obey a statute which was intended to limit their powers. It may be that the statute is economically and socially unwise, because of the vast injuries which strikes

---

[9] *Cf.* King v. Weiss & Lesh Mfg. Co., 266 Fed. 257 (6th cir. 1920).—Ed.

[10] See: Taft, "Presidential Address," 39 Am. Bar Ass'n Rep. 359 (1914); Davenport, "An Analysis of the Labor Sections of the Clayton Anti-Trust Bill," 80 Cent. Law Jour. 46 (1915); Mason, "The Labor Clauses of the Clayton Act," 18 Am. Pol. Sci. Rev. 489 (1924).—Ed.

[11] *Cf.* Stephens v. Ohio State Tel. Co., 240 Fed. 759 (N.D. Ohio 1917); Kroger Grocery & B. Co. v. Retail Clerks' I. P. Ass'n, 250 Fed. 890 (D. Mo., 1918); Dail-Overland Co. v. Willys-Overland, 263 Fed. 171 (N.D. Ohio, 1920); Vonnegut Machinery Co. v. Toledo Machine & Tool Co., 263 Fed. 192 (N.D. Ohio, 1920).—Ed.

[12] *Cf.* Alaska S. S. Co. v. Internat'l Longshoremen's Ass'n, 236 Fed. 964 (D. Wash. 1916).—Ed.

inflict upon society. Those considerations, however, are for Congress and not for the courts. There is no reason that a just court can assign why American courts should not have as cheerfully obeyed the Clayton Act as the English courts obeyed the Trades Disputes Act of 1906.

The capital objection to restraining workmen from striking is the futility of such injunctions. Even if the workmen obeyed the injunction, it would be possible and likely that they would perform their services in such a manner as would not promote the interest of their employers. Americans cannot be held permanently by an injunction in a state of peonage. This was the capital consideration that actuated the Circuit Court of Appeals in reversing the order of Judge Jenkins. It was one of the important motives which led Congress to pass the Clayton Act. There were other motives equally potent, as is shown by the legislative history referred to by Mr. Justice Brandeis in the *Truax* Case, which Congress thought justified them in granting to workmen all rights specified in the Clayton Act.

It must result from the foregoing that the irreparable injury referred to in the Clayton Act is something other and different from the irreparable injury to which I have referred above, and which is the natural result of a strike, and the sanction which gives it force. The history of trade disputes shows that these words are intended to embrace direct injuries to new employés, or to the property of the employer, by acts of trespass or violence, and also obstruction of the employer in obtaining new employés by means of threats, abuse, or violence—in a word, conduct which prevents by means of violence or duress the employer from carrying on his business.

These are the only legitimate fields for injunctive relief, and to gather up the natural and inevitable consequences of the strike, and use them as the basis of injunctive relief, is simply to proceed in a mental circle.

The injunction recently issued in Chicago, and the earlier one issued at Indianapolis, in connection with the bituminous coal strike, were not only in direct violation of the Clayton Act, as thus interpreted, but they carry government by injunction into new fields.[13] They virtually hold that the power of courts to issue injunctions in strike cases, not only has no limits in equity jurisprudence, but that Congress cannot frame a law to limit this power which courts may not nullify by skillful construction.

The Transportation Act of 1920 (41 Stat. 456) begins the discussion of labor disputes at page 469. Section 313, at page 473, seems to be the only section as to violations of the board's decision, and a fair interpretation of the language there used makes the decisions of the board only advisory. That has been the holding of the courts. Section 402, subsections 10, 11 and 15, pp. 476 and 477, require car service to be safe and

---

[13] The reference is to the injunctions awarded by Judge Anderson in United States v. Hayes (D.C. Ind. 1919) (bill of complaint and temporary restraining order reprinted in Hearings before a Subcommittee of the Committee on the Judiciary, U.S. Senate, 7th Cong. 1st sess., on S. 1482, 516-525 (1928)), and by Judge Wilkerson in United States v. Railway Employees' Dept., A. F. of L., 283 Fed. 479 (N.D. Ill. 1922). For the injunction in the latter case, see, *post*, p. 262.—Ed.

adequate, and the law provides in subsection 17 a penalty upon the carrier for failure to provide such service.

So far as I can discover, there is at the present time no statute in force, except the Sherman Anti-Trust Act, making interference with interstate commerce a criminal offense. Such a statute was passed and approved August 10, 1917 (Comp. St. 1918, Comp. St. Ann. Supp. 1919, § 8536 [9]), two months after we entered the Great War. It was a war measure. It provides that:

"Any person * * * who shall, during the war in which the United States is now engaged, knowingly and willfully, by physical force or intimidation by threats of physical force obstruct or retard * * * the orderly conduct or movement in the United States of interstate or foreign commerce, or the orderly makeup or movement or disposition of any train, or the movement or disposition of any locomotive car, or other vehicle on any railroad or elsewhere in the United States engaged in interstate or foreign commerce shall be deemed guilty of a misdemeanor, and for every such offense shall be punishable by a fine of not exceeding $100 or by imprisonment for not exceeding six months, or by both such fine and imprisonment."

Two things are noteworthy in this statute: (1) It is confined to the period of the war. (2) It is narrowly limited to "physical force or intimidation by threats of physical force."

These limitations, both as to time and the character of the act, throw a clear light upon the intent of Congress not to interfere with the Clayton Act, save to the extent thus narrowly limited by the language of the statute. There is also a proviso attached for the purpose of removing all doubt, stating that nothing in the section "shall be construed to repeal, modify or affect either section 6 or section 20" of the Clayton Act.

This caution of Congress shows a wide difference between the view of Congress with respect to the Clayton Act and the views that have recently been expressed by courts.

The right to do the acts specified in section 20 of the Clayton Law is conditioned upon the existence of such a controversy as the statute mentions. If railway employés quit the service in the absence of such controversy, and with the malevolent purpose of obstructing interstate commerce or the mails, this would be a violation of the Anti-Trust Act, and the conspiracy statute. Such a malevolent purpose, however, would have to be shown to be the primary intent of the strike. Given the existence of such a controversy as the law specifies, then the doing of the acts named in it is rightful, notwithstanding such conduct causes obstruction to commerce and the mails, and inflicts irreparable injury upon the company and the public. This must be true; otherwise, the right to do the acts would be wholly taken away as to employés on interstate railways. It is also true that, when such a controversy exists, the doing of the acts mentioned in section 20 ought to be presumed to have as their primary purpose the promotion of the employés' side of the controversy, and not the obstruction of the mails and interstate commerce. Nor can the doing of wrongful or criminal acts by single members or local groups be used to show a conspiracy on the part of the union or its officers to carry on the strike by such unlawful means. Such a conspiracy could only be shown either by clear proof of an agreement on the part of the union or its officers to use such means, or the abetting by them of those who were guilty of the unlawful conduct. In the absence of such proof, such unlawful deeds should be treated as showing the intent only of those using such wrongful means. Any other reasoning belies human experience, and nullifies the presumption against tortious or criminal conduct.

The present shopmen's strike affords conclusive proof of these views. No disinterested person who has come into immediate touch with the officers and members of the union has failed to be impressed with their purpose neither to use nor permit the use of wrongful means in carrying on the strike. The entire marshal's force in this district has repeatedly borne testimony to that effect. I cite a single instance. The city of Marmarth is the shop town on the main line of the Milwaukee road in this state. It is located on the extreme western boundary, in what is known as the "Bad Lands." On the return to the order to show cause why a preliminary injunction should not be issued, and after the strike had been going on for weeks, disinterested men of all classes, ministers, bankers, merchants, professional men, peace officers, and justices, gave affidavits that the period of the strike had been characterized by unusually good order, and that they knew, from their daily intercourse with union men and their officers, that such was their policy in carrying on the strike. And why should this not be true? It was the policy, not only of good citizenship, but of good sense. Any resort to violence would have stripped the union of all moral support from the public, and placed the strike under the ban of all good citizens. Of course, it is true that in national unions, like those in the railway service, having a membership running up into thousands and drawn from all sections of the country with our varying notions of law and order, a great variety in character and sense will be shown. There will be some hotheads, and a few who may be believers in dynamite and the dagger as a means of furthering the cause of working men.

I cannot conceive, however, of a graver injustice than to treat the acts of such individuals or groups as an index of the character or intent of any union in the railway service. Any person who is acquainted with these men will resent such an imputation. It is false to the creative influence of the great responsibilities which is the weft and woof of the railway service. It is likewise true that the underworld of our cities takes advantage of periods of public excitement, such as results from our large strikes, to resort to incendiarism and violence, because this creates the atmosphere in which they can plunder and pillage. Why should wrongs and crimes, whether done by hotheads in the union or by vicious outsiders, who claim to be their friends, be seized upon as an index of the character of the union or its officers? Why not deal with such wrongs and crimes as we do in other fields of life?

Why not treat them as the acts of those who do them, or aid and abet such doers? Why not hunt down the guilty persons and punish them, and not impute their misdeeds to the striking union and its officers by a presumption which belies the known facts as well as the policy which common sense would dictate to the union and its officers as the only course for them to pursue? Just legal administration can give but one answer to these questions.

NOTE

The restraining part of the injunction order is as follows:

"Ordered and adjudged that the defendants and all persons acting with them be and they are hereby enjoined and restrained as follows:

"1. From using threats or vulgar or abusive epithets or language towards plaintiff's employés, agents or officers, or towards persons about to become such.

"2. From injuring plaintiff's employés, agents or officers, or persons about to become such, or their families, or their property.

"3. From injuring plaintiff's property, personal or real, or any property or passengers in plaintiff's care, or being transported upon any of its lines.

"4. From trespassing upon plaintiff's property.

"5. From warning plaintiff's employés, agents or officers, or persons about to become such, or the families of either, that they will suffer or be likely to suffer any of the wrongs or injuries enjoined in this order, if they enter plaintiff's employment or continue therein.

"6. From aiding or advising any person to commit any of said wrongs or injuries.

"7. From going upon or near plaintiff's said properties, or the homes of plaintiff's employés, agents or officers, for the purpose of doing any of said wrongs or injuries.

"8. From having and keeping at or near any point of ingress or egress to or from plaintiff's property more than three pickets, all other defendants and persons acting with them being restrained and enjoined from being present, and from assembling or loitering at or about any of said points or at or near plaintiff's property. If other persons desire to confer with pickets, they must choose occasions when they are not acting as pickets.

"A small tent may be erected at or near any point at which such pickets are stationed to protect them from the weather while they are on duty; but there must not be present at any such tent at any single time any one but the pickets who are there on duty. It is to be used by them and not by others.

"The defendants and those acting with them are enjoined from erecting or maintaining at or near plaintiff's property any other tents than those permitted by this section. If any other tents have been heretofore erected, they must be promptly removed.

"9. From attempting to do any of the acts above forbidden.

"This order does not enjoin or restrain the defendants, or persons acting with them, from using towards plaintiff's employés, or persons about to become such, language of peaceable persuasion or entreaty, for the purpose of inducing them not to enter plaintiff's employment or to cease therefrom; nor does it restrain or enjoin the defendants or persons acting with them from peacefully imparting information to such employés of plaintiff or persons about to become such, for the purpose just specified; but this order is intended to and does enjoin and restrain the defendants and persons acting with them from doing any of the things hereinbefore forbidden in this order under the claim or pretense of using peaceful persuasion or entreaty, or peacefully imparting information. So long as the defendants and those acting with them confine themselves to a peaceful and orderly exercise of their rights specified in this section, the plaintiff, its officers, agents, employés and guards are enjoined from interfering with them, and particularly—

"1. From using towards them threatening or abusive language or epithets.

"2. From inflicting upon them any personal injuries or attempting to do so.

"3. The armed guards of plaintiff are enjoined specifically from drawing or exhibiting firearms or other dangerous weapons, for the purpose of intimidating such pickets, and from using firearms or other dangerous weapons at all except in the presence of imminent peril such as threatens very serious injury to the person of the party using such weapons, or others in the employ of the company, or to resist the imminent and immediate danger of the destruction of personal property or injury to engines or switches, or any other similar property that would imperil the public in using the company's railway, or the employés of plaintiff in the prosecution of its business, and on such occasions from using said firearms or other dangerous weapons when there is any other reasonable means of preventing the aforesaid wrongful acts.

"It is further ordered that a copy of this preliminary injunction shall be mailed to each of the defendants and to all persons known to be acting with them, at his present address, in so far as such address can reasonably be ascertained, and that ten copies of said order be posted in conspicuous public places in the vicinity of the roundhouse, shops, yards and other property of the Great Northern Railway Company, in each of the following places in North Dakota, namely, New Rockford, Devils Lake, Grand Forks, Minot and Williston, and that a copy of this preliminary injunction be also mailed to the principal officers and agents of the plaintiff, and each of the special guards employed by plaintiff, at the points above mentioned; that such mailing and posting be done by the United States marshal for the district of North Dakota.

"That a copy of this preliminary injunction may also be published in a newspaper published in the places above specified, which publication shall be attended to by said Great Northern Railway Company or its representative.

"It is further ordered, that any person who shall tear down, deface, destroy, or in any manner interfere with any of the copies of this preliminary injunction that shall be posted pursuant to this order, shall be held in contempt of this court, and shall be punished accordingly."

GEVAS v. GREEK RESTAURANT WORKERS' CLUB.

New Jersey Court of Chancery. 99 N.J. Eq. 770, 134 Atl. 309 (1926).

BERRY, V.C.: This bill is filed to obtain an injunction against the Greek Restaurant Workers' Club and certain individuals, some of whom are members of that organization, restraining them from unlawfully interfering with complainant's business, intimidating the complainant's employes, loitering and picketing upon the street in front of complainant's restaurant, and generally from hindering or interfering with or obstructing complainant's business, either by inducing or attempting to induce or compelling by threats, intimidation, force or violence, any of complainant's employes to leave his service, or otherwise, or by interfering with the customers' peaceful patronage of that restaurant. The complainant conducts the Essex Restaurant at 919 Broad street, Newark, New Jersey, and has done so for six years last past. He has built up a substantial business there, the average annual gross receipts of which amount to $100,000. He employs sixteen persons, including cooks, waitresses, &c. The defendants are the Greek Restaurant Workers' Club, sometimes known as "The Lunch Room-Cafeteria-Delicatessen Workers' Club"; David Stein, an organizer and representative of the American Federation of Labor; Costas Dritsas, a member of the executive committee of the Greek Restaurant Workers' Club, and twenty other persons who are either members of said club or were participants in the acts complained of in the bill.

I deem it important, as having a direct bearing on the activities of the defendant club which are here complained of, to now say that in April of this year seven other cases in which bills had been filed in this court, by proprietors of Greek restaurants in and near Newark, against exactly the same defendants as are here named, and in which the acts complained of were of exactly the same character, came before me in the same manner as the instant case. In six of these cases, after hearing on return of the orders to show cause, I advised preliminary injunctions, denying an injunction in the seventh because of lack of proof.

The bill alleges that no strike exists in complainant's restaurant; that there has not been any strike in that establishment; that no employes had been discharged or left complainant's employ during the month preceding the filing of the bill; that none of the present employes of complainant are members of the defendant club; that prior to the acts complained of in the bill representatives of this club called on the complainant's employes and demanded that they join this club on pain of physical violence; that on July 9th, 1926, a representative of the defendant club called on the complainant and tried to induce him to sign an agreement which provided that complainant would not employ anyone in his business not a member of the defendant club; that he declined to do so; that immediately thereafter, members of the club appeared in front of the complainant's restaurant with placards on their breasts and backs on which were printed in bold type the following words: "Strike— the workers at Essex Lunch are on strike; we are striking to reduce our hours from twelve to ten and one day off a week"; that these men began parading back and forth on the sidewalks in front of the restaurant and so close to the entrance thereof as to interfere with the ingress and egress of the patrons; that the defendants have threatened physical violence against the complainant's employes if they continue to work for complainant and do not strike; the elbowing of patrons, frightening and intimidating them and threats of physical violence against them, and the use of indecent and abusive language; that all of complainant's employes are satisfied with the conditions of their employment, have made no complaint, are not desirous of quitting their employment and do not want to strike.

I think it can be fairly stated that substantially all of the material allegations of the bill are amply supported by complainant's affidavits. * * *

It clearly appears, also, that there is no strike of the employes of complainant's restaurant. It is true that many of the affidavits submitted on behalf of the defendants claim that a "walkout" occurred on July 9th, but a careful analysis of these affidavits discloses the fact that only four of complainant's employes, namely, Vergos, Papaines, Agapitos and T. Gevas, left at that time. * * *

* * * The facts in this case are substantially the same as those shown in the other six cases in which injunctions were advised, the only difference being that there is perhaps a little less of threatening by word of mouth and less violence here, due, in my judgment, to the fact that prompter application for relief was made to this court in the instant case than in the former cases. The defendants vigorously deny any acts of violence and allege that their picketing has been conducted in a peaceable manner without molestation of either employes or patrons of complainant's restaurant. Defendants' own affidavits show, however, that the picketing was continued from six A. M. until one A. M. of the following day, during the period in which it was carried on, and until stopped by the restraining order of this court. These affidavits show that the pickets paraded up and down continuously in front of the complainant's restaurant wearing the placards referred to. Defendants claim that the pickets have not even spoken to the employes in complainant's restaurant, and they claim that the picketing is a peaceful, persuasive measure only. But if, as defendants say, the pickets have not communicated with any of complainant's employes, I am at a loss to understand the object or purpose of

this picketing unless it is the coercion, by intimidation, of the complainant and his employes into a recognition of the union, coupled, perhaps, with the idea of boycotting the complainant and injuring him in the conduct of his business, by inducing complainant's patrons to withdraw their patronage. No other purpose could possibly be advanced for a continuous parade of pickets, although only two in number, in front of complainant's restaurant for a period of eighteen hours at a stretch. Defendants' affidavits show that there were eight of these pickets working in relays. Complainant alleges that a continuance of the activities of the defendants complained of will irreparably injure his business, and this is obviously so. The defendants claim that their actions are entirely peaceful and that they are therefore within their legal rights, citing, in support of this contention, numerous decisions of the courts of this and other states and of the United States supreme court, among which may be mentioned *Keuffel & Esser v. International Association of Machinists,* 93 N.J. Eq. 429; *Forstmann & Huffman Co. v. United Front, &c., Committee, &c.,* 99 N.J. Eq. 230, and *American Steel Foundries v. Tri-City General Trades Council,* 257 U.S. 184; 66 L. Ed. 189. They further contend that even if the activities of defendants were not permissible under the cases cited, they have now been legalized by the legislature of this state, and cite P. L. 1926 p. 348 ch. 207, in support of this contention. That act is entitled, "An act relating to disputes concerning terms or conditions of employment, the communicating of information and limiting the issue of restraining orders and injunctions in certain cases."

In the view I take of this issue, the first point to be determined is whether or not the picketing and other acts complained of are such as can be justified under our decisions irrespective of the statute referred to; and second, if not, whether that statute is applicable and they can be justified under its provisions.

It has long been recognized in this state that picketing in labor disputes may be legal or illegal depending upon its purpose or the manner of its conduct, the question of the legality or illegality being one of fact to be determined according to the circumstances of each particular case. *Fletcher Co. v. International Association of Machinists,* 55 Atl. Rep. 1077; *Frank & Dugan v. Herold,* 63 N.J. Eq. 443; *Jonas Glass Co. v. Glass Bottle Blowers' Assn.,* 72 N.J. Eq. 653; affirmed, 77 N.J. Eq. 219; *Keuffel & Esser v. International Association of Machinists, supra; Forstmann & Huffman Co. v. United, &c., Workers, supra,* although in *Baldwin Lumber Co. v. International Brotherhood, &c.,* 91 N.J. Eq. 241, Vice-Chancellor Foster held that "peaceful picketing engaged in for the purpose of persuasion, regardless of whether the persuasion was addressed to present or prospective employes of complainant" would be enjoined. The *Baldwin Case* was decided in 1920, prior to the decision of the United States supreme court in *American Steel Foundries v. Tri-City G. T. Council, supra,* which was decided in 1922. In the *Tri-City Case,* it is said that Chief-Justice Taft held that peaceful (?) picketing was lawful. This decision was followed by the *Keuffel & Esser Case,* decided by our court of errors and appeals in January, 1922. That court, in commenting on the *Tri-City Case,* said:

"It decided that the employer had the right to the access of his employes to his place of business and egress therefrom without intimidation or obstruction, and the employes recent or expectant had the right to use peaceable and lawful means to induce present employes and would-be employes to join their ranks. The legality of any particular conduct depends on the facts of the particular case. Picketing may or may not be lawful, depending on whether or not it has an immediate tendency to intimidation of the other party to the controversy [to which we add, 'if he has ordinary firmness of mind'], or an immediate tendency to obstruct free passage such as the streets afford, consistent with the right of others to enjoy the same privilege. Thus, men may accost one another with a view of influencing action but may not resort to persistent importunity, following and dogging. The number of pickets may of itself make the picketing unlawful, since it may amount to intimidation. Every one knows that threats of bodily harm may be made by a mere show of force without violence of language or breach of the peace, and that mere numbers may intimidate. The real question is, Does the conduct under existing facts amount to intimidation?"

The results of these decisions are tersely summed up by Vice-Chancellor Bentley in *Forstmann & Huffman Co. v. United, &c., Workers, supra,* as follows:

"Under these opinions, I take it, picketing in itself, for all its militant name, may be legal or illegal in a dispute between employer and employe, according to the manner in which it is carried on." And further: "If, however, this privilege is abused by violence, persistence against the other's wish, annoyance or otherwise, then the employer is entitled to have the striker enjoined from such illegal practice. This shows that it is the opinion of the supreme court of the United States and of the court of errors and appeals of this state that picketing, as such, may not amount to a trespass upon another's rights." * * *

Obviously, the line of demarcation between peaceful picketing, if there is any such thing, and that which is threatening, intimidating or coercive, is so finely drawn as to be almost imperceptible. While the great weight of authority is to the effect that "peaceful picketing" for a lawful purpose is legal, I have found no case in which the term has been so defined that it may be universally applied. * * *

There is respectable authority to the effect that "there is and can be no such thing as peaceable picketing any more than there can be chaste vulgarity, or peaceful mobbing or lawful lynching" (*Atchison, Topeka and Santa Fe Railway Co. v. Gee,* 139 Fed. Rep. 582), and as the highest court in the land has held that "peaceful picketing" is a "contradiction in terms" (*per* Chief-Justice Taft, in *Truax v. Corrigan, supra*), this statement would seem to have ample support. However, even in our own state "picketing in its mildest form" is said to be "a nuisance." *Jonas Glass Co. v. Glass Bottle Blowers' Association, supra.* Nor have I been able to find any reported New Jersey case where picketing has been the subject of the complaint and where an injunction has not issued. Whether or not this is because the statement of the court in *Atchison, Topeka & Santa Fe Railway Co. v. Gee, supra,* is correct, is not necessary for me to suggest. But in determining whether picketing in a given cause is or is not peaceable, "the real question is, Does the conduct under existing facts amount to intimidation?" *Keuffel & Esser v. International Association, &c., supra.* Picketing has been said to be "a pretense for persuasion, but is intended for intimidation," and that while neither intimidation nor fraud can be defined "every person knows whether his acts are fraudulent and he also knows whether his acts are intimidating." *Union Pacific R. Co. v. Ruef,* 120 Fed. Rep. 102. It is obvious, however, that intimidation does not necessarily depend upon numbers, and numbers are always comparative. In the *Keuffel & Esser Case,* Mr. Justice Swayze said that "twenty-five or fifty pickets might be intimidating where a single picket probably would not;" but the reverse may also be true. Where the massing of twenty-five or fifty pickets might not intimidate the employer or employes of a plant employing thousands of workers, two or three, or even one, might be intimidating where the number of employees is small, as here. *Harvey v. Chapman,* 226 Mass. 191; 115 N.E. Rep. 304. Nor is it necessary that the picket or pickets intimidate by word of mouth or by actual physical violence. *Barr v. Essex Trades Council,* 53 N. J. Eq. 101; *Keuffel & Esser v. International Assn., supra.* Restraint of the mind is just as potent as a threat of physical violence. *Webb v. Cooks' and Waiters' Union* (Texas Civil Appeals), 205 S.W. Rep. 465. A single sentinel, constantly parading in front of a place of employment for any extended length of time may be just as effective in striking terror to the souls of the employes, bound there by their duty, as was the swinging pendulum in Poe's famous story "The Pit and the Pendulum" to the victim chained in its ultimate path. In fact, silence is sometimes more striking and impressive than the loud mouthings of the mob. It is the show of force back of the demonstration, or the inevitableness of the impending disaster, which tries men's souls and drives them to desperation. It is admitted that back of the present demonstration is the full force and power of the American Federation of Labor, of which the pickets are mere sentinels or scouts. In *Gompers v. Bucks Stove and Range Co.,* 221 U.S. 418, 439; 55 L. Ed. 797, 805; 34 L.R.A.(N.S.) 874, the court said:

"But the very fact that it is lawful to form these bodies, with multitudes of members, means that they have thereby acquired a vast power, in the presence of which the individual may be helpless This power, when unlawfully used against one, cannot be met, except by his purchasing peace at the cost of submitting to terms which involve the sacrifice of rights protected by the constitution, or by standing on such rights and appealing to the preventive powers of a court of equity. When such appeal is made, it is the duty of the government to protect the one against the many as well as the many against the one."

With the knowledge of this force back of the movement, one picket may well strike terror to the employer or his small band of employes. The fact that the pickets in this case paraded continuously, soldier-like, in front of the complainant's place of business, for a period of eighteen hours at a stretch, gave this picketing a sinister aspect, irrespective of whether or not threats by word of mouth were made, or acts of violence indulged in. Coupled with the fact that the pickets remained silent, as is alleged by the defendants, and communicated with no one, this constant parading was intimidating in itself.

But the proof here goes further. Threats of physical violence, dogging, and persistence in the acts of the defendants against the will of the complainant and his employes is shown. These are especially mentioned as inhibited in the *Tri-City* and in the *Keuffel & Esser Cases;* but aside from this, what is the object of the acts complained of? Is the picketing pursued in quest of information? Obviously not, as the defendants say the pickets communicated with no one. Whatever information is available to the eye is just as available *sans* pickets and placards. I have already said that the apparent purpose of the defendants was to unionize the Greek restaurants in Newark and vicinity, of which the complainant's restaurant is one, and this against the will of both employer and employes. The instant case is only part and parcel of the general plan. The demands of the defendant club, the union, are that the restaurant proprietors employ only club members and pay them wages and fix hours of work to be determined by the club. There is here no real dispute between employes and employer concerning the terms or conditions of the employment, nor are the defendants acting in behalf of dissatisfied and complaining employes. * * *

It should be borne in mind that there is no strike in the complainant's place of business, and that his employes are not members of the defendant club. True, the defendants have attempted to call a strike, but they have been unsuccessful, and in this attempt they have support neither in law nor in reason. That employes may strike of their own volition does not justify the conduct of members of a labor organization, to which such employes do not belong, in instigating a strike. *Ruddy v. United Assn.,* 79 N.J. Law 467; *Eagle Glass Co. v. Rowe,* 245 U.S. 275; 62 L. Ed. 286; *Hitchman Coal Co. v. Mitchell,* 245 U.S. 229; 62 L. Ed. 260; *W. H. Snow Iron Works v. Chadwick,* 227 Mass. 382; 116 N.E. Rep. 801; Note 6 A.L.R. 918; *Harvey v. Chapman,* 226 Mass. 191; 115 N. E. Rep. 304.

Picketing, the object of which is unlawful, irrespective of its militant or intimidating character, may be restrained whether peaceable in fact or not. Even peaceful acts, if unlawful and resulting in irreparable injury, may be enjoined.

It, of course, appears that the four employes of the complainant who exercised their right to quit his employment on July 9th, were members of the defendant club; but even admitting, for the purpose of argument, that there were four of complainant's employes who quit on July

9th, which, as I have stated before, is not sufficiently supported by the answering affidavits, and is denied by the complainant, it seems to me that this is merely proof of the suggested plan of these defendants to accomplish an illegal object by the process which has been graphically described as "boring from within" (note 26 A.L.R. 158), examples of which are shown in *Cyrus Currier & Sons v. International Molders' Union*, 93 N.J. Eq. 61, and *Hitchman Coal Co. v. Mitchell, supra.* In the latter case, Mr. Justice Pitney, speaking for the United States supreme court, said:

"This court repeatedly has held that the employer is as free to make non-membership in a union a condition of employment as the working man is free to join the union, and that this is a part of the constitutional rights of personal liberty and private property, not to be taken away even by legislation, unless through some proper exercise of the paramount police power."

The instant case is similar in principle and facts to *Harvey v. Chapman, supra,* where the union was restrained from maintaining a single picket in front of complainant's store, and where it was found that no strike existed and that the statements used on the placards were false, and that the parading and picketing and boycotting was designed merely to compel complainant to discharge employes who had refused to pay union dues.

It is clear that the acts of the defendant complained of constitute an unlawful interference with complainant's business, and cannot be justified under our decisions, and should be restrained unless justifiable under P. L. 1926 ch. 207. That act became effective on July 4th, 1926, and so far as pertinent to the issue reads as follows:

"No restraining order or writ of injunction shall be granted or issued out of any court of this state in any case involving or growing out of a dispute concerning terms or conditions of employment, enjoining or restraining any person or persons, either singly or in concert, from terminating any relation of employment, or from ceasing to perform any work or labor, or from peaceably and without threats or intimidation recommending, advising or persuading others so to do; or from peaceably and without threats or intimidation being upon any public street or highway or thoroughfare for the purpose of obtaining or communicating information, or to peaceably and without threats or intimidation persuade any person or persons to work or abstain from working, or to employ or to cease to employ, any party to a labor dispute, or to peaceably and without threats or intimidation recommend, advise or persuade others so to do, provided said persons remain separated one from the other at intervals of ten paces or more."

It is contended by the complainant that this act is unconstitutional and that, therefore, the acts of the defendants cannot be justified thereunder. But before considering that question it must first be determined that that act, assuming its constitutionality, is applicable to the present controversy. If not, then the constitutional question is not in issue and cannot be passed upon here. Legislation of this kind has generally been held to be declaratory of, and not as changing, the laws theretofore in force. Note, 27 A.L.R. 360, 413. Accordingly, such statutes do not render lawful any act or acts which were unlawful at the time the statutes were enacted, and the existence of a dispute is a condition of the immunity to injunction declared by the statute; nor is it enough that such a controversy formerly existed where the employer has been successful in filling the places of the strikers. *Quinlivan v. Dail-Overland Co.*, 274 Fed. Rep. 56; note, 27 A.L.R. 415. Such statutes have also been held not to apply in the case of strikes for a wrongful purpose. *Ibid.* I have already held that here no strike, in fact, exists, and that the acts of the defendants complained of are in furtherance of a wrongful and illegal purpose. This statute, therefore, has no application to the present controversy, the constitutionality of the act is not involved, and a consideration of that question is unnecessary.

It is argued that no preliminary injunction should issue in this case because the allegations of the bill and the accompanying affidavits are met by a full and complete denial in the affidavits of the defense. This objection is completely answered by Vice-Chancellor Bentley in the *Forstmann & Huffman Co. Case, supra.*

It is also urged that irrespective of the application of P. L. 1926 ch. 207, the defendants are entitled to a substantial modification of the restraint already imposed in the order to show cause, and motion to that end was made by counsel for the defendant on the return of the order. This motion is denied. This being, as I view it, a case of unlawful interference with a lawful business lawfully conducted, the restraint originally advised is none too sweeping in its scope and effect.

I will advise a decree in accordance with these conclusions.[1]

---

[1] For comment on the case, see: 12 Corn. Law Quar. 226 (1927).

On the legality of picketing in the absence of a strike, and the meaning of "strike" in such a connection, see: 40 Harv. Law Rev. 896 (1927) ; 27 Col. Law Rev. 190 (1927).

Accord: as to the proposition that picketing in the absence of a strike is unlawful, Waitresses' Union, Local No. 249 v. Benish Restaurant, 6 Fed.(2d) 568 (8th cir. 1925) ; Missouri Pants Co. v. Amalgamated Clothing Workers of America, 2 Law & Labor, 222 (U.S.D.C. Mo. 1920) ; Snead & Co. v. Local No. 7, Internat'l Molders Union, 103 N.J. Eq. 332, 143 Atl. 331 (1928) ; Steinberg v. International Alliance Theatrical Stage Employees, 13 Law & Labor, 66 (Ohio App. 1930) ; United Tailors v. Amalgamated Workers, 26 Ohio N.P. 439 (1927) ; Crouch v. Central Labor Council, 134 Ore. 612, 293 Pac. 729 (1930) ; Mechanic v. Hoffman, 10 Law & Labor, 83 (Cir. Ct. Wis. 1928). Prior to the abrogation of this doctrine by Exchange Bakery Co. v. Rifkin, *supra*, p. 145, the same rule prevailed in the lower New York courts, Daitch & Co. v. Retail Grocery & D. C. Union, 129 Misc. 343, 221 N.Y.S. 446 (1927) ; Yates Hotel Co. v. Meyers, 195 N.Y.S. 558 (1922) ; Stuyvesant L. & B. Corp. v. Reiner, 192 App. Div. 939, 182 N.Y.S. 953 (1920), aff'g 110 Misc. 357, 181 N.Y.S. 212 (1920); Tapley Co. v. Rivera, N.Y.L.J., July 15, 1921; American Lithographic Co. v. Castro, N.Y.L.J., March 3, 1922; Tuchband v. Rogel, N.Y.L.J., October 28, 1922; Cushman's Sons v. Amalgamated Food Workers, N.Y.L.J., April 19, 1926; Wicke Ribbon Co. v. Korn, 2 Law & Labor, 273 (N.Y. Sup. Ct. 1920) ; C. & S. Amusement Co. v. Sherman, 3 Law & Labor, 66 (N.Y. Sup. Ct. 1921) ; Hampton Restaurant v. Morris, 3 Law & Labor, 187 (N.Y. Sup. Ct. 1921).

As to whether picketing is lawful to compel an employer not to operate his own plant but to employ members of the union, see: Roraback v. Moving Picture Machine Operators Union, 140 Minn. 481, 168 N.W. 766 (1918) ; Campbell v. Moving Picture

BOMES v. PROVIDENCE LOCAL NO. 223.

Supreme Court of Rhode Island. 51 R.I. 500, 155 Atl. 581 (1931).

STEARNS, C.J.: This is a bill in equity brought by complainant, the owner and operator of the Liberty Theatre on Broad street in Providence, praying for an injunction to restrain the respondents from interfering with complainant's business by picketing or patrolling the sidewalk or street in front of or near said theatre for the purpose of interfering with any persons entering or leaving the theatre.

The respondents are Local No. 223, an unincorporated organization of motion picture machine operators, and Philip F. Suparman, Herbert F. Slater and Abraham Kroll, members of said organization.

The cause was heard by a justice of the Superior Court upon bill, answer, replication and oral proof. The decision was for the complainant. By the decree of the court, respondents were enjoined "from picketing or patrolling the sidewalk or street in front of or near complainant's

---

Machine Operators, 151 Minn. 220, 186 N.W. 781 (1922) ; Hughes v. Kansas City Motion Picture Machine Operators, 282 Mo. 304, 221 S.W. 95 (1920).

The distinction between picketing to dissuade employees from entering or continuing an employment relationship, and picketing to persuade customers from entering or continuing a relationship with the employer is rarely enunciated in the cases. The courts, however, are unquestionably more ready to enjoin picketing directed against customers than picketing directed against employees. See : e.g. the following cases dealing with customer picketing: Local Union No. 313 v. Stathakis, 135 Ark. 86, 205 S.W. 450 (1918) ; Bull v. Internat'l Alliance of Theatrical Stage Employees, 119 Kan. 713, 241 Pac. 459 (1925) ; Grimes v. Durnin, 80 N.H. 145, 114 Atl. 273 (1921) ; Yablonowitz v. Korn, 205 App. Div. 440, 199 N.Y.S. 769 (1923) ; Clark Lunch Co. v. Cleveland Waiters & Beverage Dispensers, 8 Law & Labor, 181 (Ohio App. 1926) ; Park v. Locals 106, etc., 22 Ohio N.P. (N.S.) 257 (1920) ; Moreland Theatres Corp. v. Portland M. P. O. Protective Union, 140 Ore. 35, 12 Pac.(2d) 333 (1932) ; Webb v. Cooks', Waiters' & Waitresses' Union, 205 S.W. 465 (Texas Civ. App. 1918) ; Cooks', Waiters' & Waitresses' Local Union v. Papageorge, 230 S.W. 1086 (Texas Civ. App. 1921) ; Jensen v. Cooks' & Waiters' Union of Seattle, 39 Wash. 531, 81 Pac. 1069 (1905) ; St. Germain v. Bakery & C. Workers' Union, 97 Wash. 282, 166 Pac. 665 (1917) ; Schuberg v. Local Internat'l Alliance Theatrical Stage Employees, [1926] 2 W.W.R. 254 (Brit. Col.). In a few cases, however, the distinction between these two types of picketing is expressly taken. Thus in Robison v. Hotel & Restaurant Employees, Local Union No. 782, 35 Idaho 418, 207 Pac. 132 (1922), the court refused to allow the picketing of a restaurant, saying: "We confine our decision to the facts presented by the case at bar. We are not dealing in this case with questions which might arise in a case where a manufacturing or other plant, having no direct dealings with the general public, is involved, nor with any question relating to secondary boycott. We conclude that the stationing of pickets in front of or near to respondents' places of business in this case was necessarily intimidating in character, and was properly enjoined." In United Chain Theatres v. Philadelphia M. P. M. O. Union, 50 Fed.(2d) 189 (E.D. Pa. 1931), the court upheld a limited degree of picketing intended to dissuade the public from patronizing complainant's theatre, specifically making the point that the conditions were such that the calling of strikes would be futile, and therefore to deny picketing would be to "deny to employees in cases like the present resort to their only practicable weapon."

The question as to what is a "strike" is also raised by the statutes making it penal to advertise for help during a strike without specifically mentioning the existence of the strike. See : West Allis Foundry Co. v. State, 186 Wis. 24, 202 N.W. 302 (1925) ; 3 Wis. Law Rev. 316 (1925). Upon the constitutionality of such legislation, see : Comm. v. Libbey, 216 Mass. 356, 103 N.E. 923 (1914) ; Riter-Conley Mfg. Co. v. Wryn, 70 Okla. 247, 174 Pac. 280 (1918) ; Biersach & Niedermeyer Co. v. State, 177 Wis. 388, 188 N.W. 650 (1922).

theatre for the purpose of preventing or persuading any person or persons from entering said theatre; and from annoying, hindering, obstructing or interfering with any person or persons who may be entering or leaving or about to enter or leave said theatre while in the employment of the complainant at said theatre, or who may desire to enter such employment, and from intimidating or coercing by threats or otherwise any such person or persons." The cause is in this court on respondents' appeal the reason of which is that said decree is against the law and the evidence.

The trial justice found the facts as follows: Complainant has in his employ two operators of his motion picture machine; the respondents attempted to force complainant to make a contract with the union to employ only members of the union; to accomplish their purpose, respondents began proceedings in the nature of a boycott against the theatre; at such times as the theatre was open for business, two members of the union paraded back and forth on the sidewalk in front of the theatre with paper placards on their hats upon which, conspicuously printed were the words, "This theatre does not employ union moving picture machine operators affiliated with the American Federation of Labor." This picketing was done under instructions from the union; one of these pickets pushed against a young woman who was about to enter the theatre and told her not to enter, that it was dangerous to go inside; other patrons who were about to enter the theatre were also approached by the pickets and told it was dangerous to enter; one patron was stopped on the sidewalk near the entrance by a picket who said: "I know you won't go into a scab place, a non-union place."

Since the institution of the picketing complainant's receipts from his business have fallen off. It appears in evidence that a contract between the respondent union and the complainant had expired in June, 1927, and the union, in June, 1928, had withdrawn the union operators from the theatre. A short time before the acts complained of occurred, an agent of the international association, with which the local union is affiliated, went with Mr. Slade to complainant's theatre and tried to get him to make a contract with the union. After he refused to make such a contract, respondents, in January, 1930, organized and established a systematic picketing of the theatre and the present proceedings were then begun.

The entrance from the sidewalk to the lobby of the theatre is 30 feet wide. On each side of this entrance there is a small store not connected with the theatre. The proprietor of one of the stores objected to the presence of the pickets in front of his store. Thereafter the two pickets walked, either together or singly, back and forth on the sidewalk in front of the theatre entrance usually at times when a performance was beginning or ending.

The respondent Slade, who is the president and business manager of the local union, was appointed by the executive board of the union to direct the picketing. Mr. Slade assigned and relieved the pickets every two hours and supervised their method of operation. He parked his automobile on the side of the street opposite the theatre entrance. When he wished to instruct or change the pickets he blew his automobile horn. This was a summons to the pickets who crossed the street to his automobile, received his instructions and then returned to the theatre entrance.

Complainant's machine operators work singly, by reliefs. They enter and leave the theatre by a side door on the south side and do not use the front entrance at all.

Respondents claim their picketing was lawful and that any coercion or intimidation of the patrons of the theatre was unauthorized and forbidden. The findings of fact by the trial justice are to the contrary and the evidence sustains such findings. Respondents ask that the injunction decree be modified so as to permit picketing without coercion or intimidation. The question raised, as thus appears, is limited by the facts of this particular case. It is not a question of the right to picket in a strike or in a labor controversy between an employer and his employees. Complainant's employees are satisfied with their wages and the conditions under which they work. There has been no intent nor attempt by respondents to persuade these employees·to join the union or to refuse to work for less than the union rate of wages.

The primary and plain object of the picketing was to injure complainant's business and thereby to force him, not merely to employ union men, but to make a contract to do so for a considerable period of time.

The respondents have the right to persuade the public by any lawful means to patronize or to refuse to patronize complainant's theatre. But this right is not superior to the right of complainant to conduct his business free from unlawful interference. The attempt to unionize complainant's theatre may result in actual injury to complainant but it is not a legal injury unless the damage resulting therefrom is caused by a violation of a legal right of the complainant. There is a violation of such a legal right when the methods used are coercive. This principle was recognized and approved in *Macauley Bros. v. Tierney,* 19 R.I. 255.

This is the first time that the question of picketing has arisen in this court. The decisions on that question in the State and Federal courts and the reasons therefor are many and conflicting. See 6 A.L.R., p. 894 and pp. 916-981. We think that much of the uncertainty and confusion in the reported decisions results from the attempt to establish a general rule of law which shall govern in every labor controversy; but no such general rule has yet been established and each case must be decided upon consideration of the facts and of the rights of the opposing parties.

Picketing, if it is peaceful and unaccompanied by coercion, duress or intimidation, is lawful. See *American Foundries v. Tri-City Council,* 257 U.S. 184. The difficulty is in deciding in a particular case whether the methods·actually used are lawful or unlawful. The trial justice was of the opinion that the action of the respondents was in the nature of a secondary boycott. This has been defined as a combination to influence A. by exerting some sort of economic or social pressure against persons who deal

with A. See Labor Injunction, Frankfurter & Greene, p. 43 and cases
cited. To affix a name to particular actions complained of is a matter
of description; it does not help materially in the decision of the question
of the lawfulness of the acts.

It is unnecessary in the instant case to attempt to define the limits
within which persons, combining for their own advantage to do acts injurious to the business of another, may legally proceed to accomplish that
result. Granting that peaceful picketing is lawful and the display of
placards of the kind in question on the public street is lawful, all the
authorities agree that such actions are unlawful when accompanied by coercion or intimidation. *Goldberg &c. Co. v. Stablemen's Union,* 149 Cal.
429; *St. Germain v. Bakery & C. Workers' Union,* 97 Wash. 282; *Bull v.
International Alliance,* 119 Kan. 713; *Steffes v. Motion Picture M. O. U.,*
136 Minn. 200.

The respondents have been enjoined from picketing only in front of
or near the theatre for the purpose of preventing or persuading persons
from entering the theatre and from obstructing or interfering with employees who may be entering or leaving the theatre. The only restraint
imposed on the giving of information to or the persuasion of the public is
upon picketing in a very limited area which is filled with traffic. The
course of conduct of the respondents has been such as to demonstrate the
danger of injury to complainant's business if picketing near the theatre
entrance is now authorized by the court.

In the circumstances and in view of the deliberate violation by respondents of the rights of complainants, we think that to now permit any
picketing in the limited space near the theatre would inevitably result in the
obstruction of the public use of the street and sidewalk and an added injury
to complainant. For the reasons stated we are of the opinion that the injunction was warranted in this case.

The decree of the Superior Court is affirmed and the appeal therefrom is denied and dismissed. The cause is remanded to the Superior
Court for further proceedings.

HAHN, J., dissenting. In a labor dispute it is lawful and proper to
bring to the attention of the public the fact that a particular business or
industry does not employ union labor. *Exchange Bakery v. Rifkin,* 245
N.Y. 260. If the business or industry be a theatre or moving picture house
which employs comparatively few persons, it is lawful and proper for a
labor organization to notify the public that the particular theatre does
not employ union labor in order that the public may be made acquainted
with this fact and withhold their patronage therefrom if they desire so to
do. Such a notice may be given in several ways and a common and usual
method is by having men walk on the sidewalk in front of the place of
business carrying a placard or banner on which is printed the information
desired to be made public. In the instant case a moving picture theatre
employed two operators of the picture machines. Originally union men
were employed in the theatre and thereafter the owner refused to deal
with the union and employed non-union men. This he had a legal right to

do. The respondent Local No. 223, being a branch of the Union of Motion Picture Operators, had two men patrol the sidewalk in front of the complainant's theatre. These two men had upon their hats placards, which are exhibits in this case, having printed thereon the following words: "This Theatre Does Not Employ Union Moving Picture Machine Operators Affiliated with the American Federation of Labor." This was a true statement of fact.

The evidence shows that the two men were there for some time and walked up and down the sidewalk before the theatre and that they used no intimidation, duress or physical force to prevent patrons from entering the theatre other than in certain specific cases in which they are charged with conduct which will be hereinafter discussed. While it has been held, and is undoubtedly the law, that if picketing is accompanied by violence, intimidation, duress or physical force to such an extent as to interfere with the conduct of a business, an injunction should be entered restraining future picketing on the basis that by doing such acts it has been shown that peaceful picketing will not accomplish the purpose desired but the evidence of this fact should be clear and convincing. In the instant case, however, there is no substantial evidence of intimidation, duress, physical force or coercion.

It is alleged that one of the men named Kroll by his acts and words prevented prospective patrons from entering the complainant's theatre. The testimony is that he spoke to four people; one of them, a brother-in-law of the complainant, who had been known to Kroll personally for twenty years and as brother-in-law of the complainant for many years; another, a man who had been engaged in many business transactions with said complainant and the third, two women, one of whom was well enough acquainted with said complainant as to be authorized to enter the theatre without tickets in order to escort a child therein from the theatre to her home. In each of these cases it is alleged that Mr. Kroll said: "Don't go in there, it's dangerous." The making of such statements is denied by Mr. Kroll. It does not appear in evidence what effect these words had upon the brother-in-law and the business associate of the proprietor. The alleged use of such words in addressing these two men would have had so little weight with them that Mr. Kroll's denial of the use of the words is undoubtedly true. As to the two women it appears that they sought to get into a conversation with Kroll before entering the theatre. In my opinion the evidence in this case utterly fails to show an abuse of the right of the respondents to notify the public that the theatre did not employ union help.

The record leads strongly to the conclusion that the real basis of this complaint arises from the fact that complainant's business was affected by the publicity given to his position in regard to labor. Had there been any substantial interference with his business by threats or otherwise he would have had little difficulty in establishing the same much more convincingly by disinterested witnesses.

The Superior Court found that the respondent Kroll had spoken to
the four persons above mentioned and entered a restraining order enjoining all respondents, its employees, agents and servants from picketing or
patrolling the sidewalk or- street in front of or near complainant's theatre
for the purpose of preventing or persuading any person or persons from
entering said theatre.

On the evidence presented an injunction absolutely prohibiting all
picketing in front of this theatre is not warranted and the appeal should
be sustained and the decree reversed.

SWEENEY, J., concurs in the dissenting opinion of HAHN, J.[1]

NANN v. RAIMIST.

New York Court of Appeals. 255 N.Y. 307, 174 N.E. 690 (1931).

CARDOZO, CH.J.: The controversy is one between rival labor unions
competing for supremacy.

The trade represented by the two unions is that of bakers and con-
fectioners. The plaintiff association is a local union of the Amalgamated
Food Workers; the defendant association, which is affiliated with the
American Federation of Labor, is a local union of the Bakery and Confectionery Workers' International Union of America. Each union is accustomed to make contracts with employers in the trade whereby the employers so contracting agree to employ the members of the chosen union
to the exclusion of all others. The contracts are not for a fixed period,
but are terminable at will. They prescribe the conditions of service for
the workers, and in particular the wages. The schedule of wages fixed by
the Amalgamated is considerably lower than that fixed by the International. The International, however, has established what is described as
the "substitute system" for the benefit of its members. According to this
system, known also as the "stagger system," a member employed by the
week must give up part of his time to a member out of a job, when the
supply of union labor is in excess of the demand. The result is to shorten
the week for some members, but to make it impossible for others to be
idle altogether. The substitution is one to which a proprietor contracting

----

[1] Accord: Vaughan v. Kansas City M. P. O. U., 36 Fed.(2d) 78 (W.D. Mo. 1929);
Levy & Delaney v. International Pocketbook Workers' Union, 114 Conn. 319, 158 Atl.
795 (1932). *Contra:* International Pocketbook Workers' Union v. Orlove, 158 Md.
496, 148 Atl. 826 (1930). For other cases where, like the principal case, on the basis
of prior illegal acts, all picketing whether legal or illegal was enjoined, see: 44 Harv.
Law Rev. 971 (1931).

Upon the legality of mass picketing, see: Langenberg v. United Cloth & Cap
Makers, 266 Fed. 127 (E.D. Mo. 1920); Beaton v. Tarrant, 102 Ill. App. 124 (1902);
Forstman & Hoffman Co. v. United Front Committee, 99 N.J. Eq. 230, 133 Atl. 202
(1926); Jefferson & Indiana Coal Co. v. Marks, 287 Pa. 171, 134 Atl. 430 (1926).

with the union is required to submit. The Amalgamated, on the other
hand, has refused to apply this system to the shops subject to its control.
Its members, if employed at all, work more days in the week, but at a lower
wage by the day. Their weekly earnings are sometimes higher and sometimes lower than the earnings of their rivals.

For some years the two unions worked in harmony, each acting within
its own sphere of influence, and not encroaching on the other. Gradually,
however, the Amalgamated began to draw away employers who had given
allegiance to the International. There was attraction in the lower wages
and in escape from the inconvenience and perhaps the loss of efficiency
occasioned at times by the employment of substitutes. Trouble soon
developed.

The International, menaced by defections, made demand on the Amalgamated that it merge or surrender. A blunt refusal followed. Upon this
the International threatened to drive the Amalgamated out of existence.
It would go from shop to shop, would make the methods of its rival
manifest to the world, and in the words of a witness "wipe it off the map."
The campaign had its beginnings in August, 1927. In that month the
Winthrop Baking Company, allied with the Amalgamated, opened a new
shop. Members of the International spoke from wagons at the street
corner, and others bearing signs paraded up and down the street. They
denounced the Amalgamated as a "fake" union, a union made up of
"scabs," asserted that theirs was the only regular or genuine union, and
told passers-by that a strike was going on and that by encouraging their
rival they would be giving aid and comfort to the bosses. This happened on August 30 and again the following day. The Winthrop Company sued for an injunction, and obtained an order restraining interference with its business, but the order was narrower in scope than the one
demanded. The International was restrained from marching up and down
in front of the bakery with false or misleading signs, and from making
false and misleading statements, but it was not restrained from picketing.
The bakery, dissatisfied with the scope of the restraint, appealed to the
Appellate Division, and there on December 7, 1927, the order was affirmed.

Picketing, if there had been any in the meantime, had been peaceful
and without disorder. A change came about toward the end of 1927 and
the beginning of 1928. The evidence as to what happened is conflicting.
In view of the findings of the trial court we state the version of the testimony adverse to the defendant.

On January 3, 1928, there was disorder at the Winthrop bakery. Two
men walked up and down the street telling every customer that "the place
was on strike," and not to patronize it till the strike was over. Ten other
men, members of the union, were hanging about the street corners. When
the day's work was over, an employee of the bakery, coming out of the
shop, was set upon and beaten.

On January 4 the pickets were on hand again. Once more the customers were notified that a strike was in progress, and most of them

walked by and did their shopping elsewhere. About noon some one was heard to telephone the International headquarters to send as many men as possible. In response to this message three taxicabs drew up. A fight ensued between the occupants and men from the Amalgamated who were already on the scene. One of the workers at the bakery was set upon and beaten. The police were notified, and thereafter, till the commencement of this action, an officer was posted at the scene of trouble.

Disorder occurred also at another bakery about the same time. On December 28, 1927, Scheffer & Edelstein opened a new shop. They had formerly been members of the International, but had gone over to the Amalgamated. Pickets informed the customers that the shop was not a union one, and that a strike was going on. Some one told a picket that he had no right to do such things, and that he must go away from the bakery. At this there was a fight, the picket striking the first blow. Only a few days before, the proprietors of the bakery had refused to give up their alliance with the plaintiff union or cancel their existing contract. A few days later, terrified by the interference with their business, they signed a contract with the defendant.

On January 12, 1928, the Amalgamated began the present action to enjoin the International from destroying its existence by violent or illegal acts, the suit previously brought by the Winthrop bakery being discontinued soon thereafter. The Court at Special Term granted an injunction in the form stated below,* and the Appellate Division unanimously affirmed.

---

* "Ordered, adjudged and decreed that the defendant, Lasar Raimist, as Treasurer of Local No. 500 of the Bakery and Confectionery Workers' International Union of America, an unincorporated association, consisting of seven or more persons, his agents, servants, associates, confederates and all persons combining and conspiring with him or them or any of them, be and they hereby are perpetually enjoined and restrained and prohibited from interfering with the conduct of the business of any store, bakery or shop having a contract with the plaintiff union and/or where any members of plaintiff union are employed; from threatening or intimidating, directly or indirectly, by placard or sign or other writing or by word of mouth or by force or otherwise, any member of the plaintiff union, and/or any employer of any member or members of plaintiff union or any person or persons having a contract with plaintiff union, and from picketing or marching or loitering in front of the premises of any employer of any member of the plaintiff union or of any person having a contract with the plaintiff union, or in the vicinity of such premises, or gathering or causing any crowd to collect there, from asserting or representing orally or in writing that plaintiff union is a 'scab' union or is not a regular union, and/or asserting or representing that any bakery or shop having a contract with plaintiff union or employing any member thereof is a 'scab' shop, and/or that the label of the defendant union is the only union label and/or that the label of the plaintiff union is not a union label, or is a scab label, or that the bread or other food baked in any shop or bakery having a contract with the plaintiff union or employing any member of plaintiff union is not union bread or food; and/or from persuading or inducing any employer of labor having a contract with the plaintiff and/or employing any member of the plaintiff, to breach or terminate such contract or to discharge or terminate the employment of any member of plaintiff union, and/or from persuading or inducing any member of plaintiff union to leave his employ or withdraw or resign from such union, and/or from interfering in any manner above set forth or in any other manner, or by any other means, with the business, custom or trade of any employer having a contract with the plaintiff or employing any member of the plaintiff, or making any false statements respecting any such employer or the plaintiff union or any members thereof, or the products of any such shop or employer or doing any other illegal act in reference thereto."

The plaintiff, if threatened in its business life by the violence of the defendant or by other wrongful acts, may have the aid of the court to preserve itself from disruption through recourse to these unlawful means. The remedy is not lost because the controversy is one between the members of rival unions, and not, as happens oftener, between unions and employers (*Tracey v. Osborne*, 226 Mass. 25; *Goyette v. Watson Co.*, 245 Mass. 577). On the other hand, the legality of the defendant's conduct is not affected by the fact that no strike is in progress in any of the plaintiff's shops (*Exchange Bakery & Restaurant, Inc. v. Rifkin*, 245 N.Y. 260.) If the defendant believes in good faith that the policy pursued by the plaintiff and by the shops united with the plaintiff is hostile to the interests of organized labor, and is likely, if not suppressed, to lower the standards of living for workers in the trade, it has the privilege by the pressure of notoriety and persuasion to bring its own policy to triumph (*Exchange Bakery & Restaurant, Inc., v. Rifkin, supra; Bossert v. Dhuy*, 221 N.Y. 342).

Upon the facts exhibited in this record the defendant went beyond the bounds of lawful conduct in conducting its campaign for the suppression of its rival. These acts were of such a nature as to justify some of the restraints imposed by the courts below, though they are insufficient to give support to others. The defendant does not complain of the injunction against acts of violence or intimidation or against causing crowds to gather or loitering in groups. Those provisions of the judgment may stand as they were written. What the defendant complains of is the injunction against picketing, against false and misleading signs and statements, and against peaceable persuasion.

(1) "Where unlawful picketing has been continued; where violence and intimidation have been used and where misstatements as to the employers' business have been distributed, a broad injunction prohibiting all picketing may be granted" (*Exchange Bakery & Restaurant, Inc., v. Rifkin, supra*, at p. 145). "The course of conduct of the strikers" is then "such as to indicate the danger of injury to property if any picketing whatever is allowed" (*Ibid*).

Before this action was begun, the defendant had already been restrained in the suit by the Winthrop bakery from acts of violence or disorder, from picketing with false and misleading signs and from other false and misleading statements. These prohibitions it had violated, or so the trier of the facts has found. It had set upon and beaten innocent workmen. It had falsely asserted that a strike was in progress. By such falsehoods it had driven customers to other bakeries, had forced unwilling proprietors to succumb to its demands, and in so doing had threatened the prosperity and indeed the very existence of its rival.

Whether the trial court in view of this record of defiance, would give the defendant still another chance to picket peacefully and in order, was something to be determined in the exercise of a wise discretion. This court may not interfere except for manifest abuse. "It becomes a question for the judgment of the Chancellor who has heard the witnesses, familiarized himself with the *locus in quo* and observed the tendencies to disturbance and conflict" (*American Steel Foundries v. Tri-City C. T. Council,* 257 U.S. 184, 207). One chance the defendant had already been given. It had defied the mandate and abused the privilege. How many more chances was it to have before the court could intervene? An injunction does not issue in such circumstances as punishment for the past (*Iron Molders Union v. Allis-Chalmers Co.,* 166 Fed. Rep. 45, 49; Frankfurter & Greene, The Labor Injunction, p. 116). Its only legitimate end is protection for the future. Not improbably a writ could have been framed whereby the desired end would have been attained by prohibitions less complete. We might have preferred such restraints if we had been exercising the powers of a chancellor. Sitting in this court we deal solely with defect of power or with abuse of discretion so gross as to be equivalent to defect of power. The injunction in this aspect is not to be sustained upon any theory that picketing *per se* is to be condemned as an illegal act. This court is committed to a contrary doctrine (*Exchange Bakery & Restaurant, Inc., v. Rifkin, supra*). The injunction is sustained upon the theory that the defendant having been permitted to picket subject to conditions, violated those conditions, and in contempt of the existing mandate picketed with violence and with falsehood, spreading terror with a strong hand and a multitude of people. In the judgment of the trial court, "the [defendant's] course of conduct * * * has been such as to indicate the danger of injury to property if any picketing whatever is allowed" (*Exchange Bakery & Restaurant, Inc., v. Rifkin, supra*). We cannot say that a basis for that belief is lacking altogether.

The injunction as written is not limited to the shops that had been the scenes of violence and intimidation, but extends to any others connected with the plaintiff's union. The defendant had threatened to go from one shop to another. A saving clause is necessary, however, to avoid misapprehension. The decree, perpetual in its operation, is broad enough to prohibit picketing for all time at any bakery or shop in alliance with the plaintiff, no matter what the grievance or the occasion of the controversy. This is too far-reaching. At some time in the future, a controversy unrelated to the dispute between the plaintiff and the defendant may arise between the defendant and a bakery or shop now protected by the judgment. The evidence is that 370 shops or bakeries are within the terms of the injunction. The restraint is to be interpreted as limited to acts done by the defendant in furtherance of its plan to exterminate the plaintiff union or in the course of the controversy that is the subject of the pending action.

(2) The injunction as to false and misleading statements should be limited to one prohibiting the false announcement of a strike (*Wilner v. Bless,* 243 N.Y. 544).

With picketing restrained, the plaintiff is in little need of protection by an injunction against words. The remedy when so applied is an exceptional one at best, and is to be reserved for those cases where the exigency is clear (*Wilner v. Bless, supra; Beck v. Railway Teamsters' Pro-*

tective Union, 118 Mich. 497). Equity does not intervene to restrain the publication of words on a mere showing of their falsity (*Marlin Fire Arms Co. v. Shields,* 171 N.Y. 384). It intervenes in those cases where restraint becomes essential to the preservation of a business or of other property interests threatened with impairment by illegal combinations or by other tortious acts, the publication of the words being merely an instrument and incident (*Beck v. Railway Teamsters' Protective Union, supra; Gompers v. Bucks Stove & Range Co.,* 221 U.S. 418, 431; *Steinert & Sons Co. v. Tagen,* 207 Mass. 394, 397; *Hotel & R. R. News Co. v. Clark,* 243 Mass. 317, 323; *Allen Mfg. Co. v. Smith,* 224 App. Div. 187, 191; Pound, Equitable Relief against Defamation, etc., 29 Harv. L.R. 640, 666; Pound, Chafee's Cases on Equitable Relief against Defamation [2d ed.], 1930, collating the authorities).

In the case at hand most of the statements imputed to the defendant were well within its rights. This is true, for example, of the circulars and handbills. They amount to nothing more than praise of its own achievements, and criticism of the methods of its rival, with an appeal to the public for sympathy and preference. Warning is given that the International "is the only union that is on the look-out that its members should work under union conditions, which means like human beings and not like mules." Warning is given that "this Amalgamated organization, which calls itself a 'union,' is such a union that it is willing to ruin our conditions which were gained with your support." For those reasons and others the appeal is made to consumers to buy only "with this union label," a phrase followed by a reproduction of the label in use by the defendant. There is argument and entreaty, over-colored and hectic, involving perhaps at times the deduction from meagre facts of debatable conclusions. There is no such malevolent distortion as to justify repression. Courts have enough to do in restraining physical disorder without busying themselves with logomachies in which the embattled words are the expression of the opinion of the writer or the speaker.[1] If there is redress for such a wrong, unassociated with wrongful acts, the remedy is not in equity.

---

[1] The following cases are illuminating upon the attitude taken by other courts toward the policing of strikers' language. "We think it is clear that the words 'This house is unfair to organized labor,' printed upon a placard, are permissible * * *. Neither do we think legitimate objection can be made to the words, 'This house is unfair to organized labor; why patronize an unfair house; why not patronize a house with organized labor.' The expression, 'This house is unfair to organized labor; why not patronize a union house; go where they have all white help,' is legitimate or not according to the truthfulness or falsity of the implication that the house is employing other than white help. The expression, 'This beanery is on the bum' cannot be upheld. Although it may not have been intended seriously, it carried with it an implication of deterioration of service and is not permissible. The expression, 'Why not patronize a union house and you won't have to turn your back to the public and you will not be ashamed,' is not permissible, because this evidently was intended to cause moral intimidation upon the patrons of the place and doubtless with many people would have that effect. Neither do we think justifiable the expression 'This house is unfair and will be unfair to you.' This was addressed to the patrons of the restaurants, and when addressed to the public generally carried an implication of dishonesty or lack of integrity." Robison v. Hotel and Restaurant Employees Local

Other statements, not in the circulars and handbills, but testified to by witnesses, are closer to the border line. This is true of declarations that the plaintiff is a "scab" and not a regular union, and that any one dealing with its bakeries will not be buying union bread. Even these statements, however, are in essence expressions of opinion, dependent, in the main, upon an appraisal of methods and motives, and gaining much of their significance from context and occasion. Standing by themselves, the statements may be unduly broad. Heard or read in the light of the context or in the setting of the occasion, they may wear another aspect.· They are then seen to be opinions merely. The opinion may be erroneous, but it does not follow that the defendant will be required to withdraw it under penalty of contempt. Indeed, there is a near approach to the ludicrous when a member of one union debating an industrial dispute with a member of another, is restrained by the solemn mandate of an injunction from stating his belief that the rival union is a "scab." [2] An injunction might draw a distinction between one context and another, yet the dividing line is one that it would be hard to make manifest by words. Perhaps an attempt to draw it would be necessary if picketing were to continue. With picketing out, the danger, if any, is too slight, the zone of demarcation too nebu-

---

No. 782, 35 Idaho 418, 430-431, 207 Pac. 132 (1922). In Hotel & Railroad News Co. v. Leventhal, 243 Mass. 317, 137 N.E. 534 (1922), girls who were discharged for an unspecified cause organized to compel their reinstatement and the recognition of the union, and published a circular entitled the "Story of the News Stand Girls." Upon a finding by the master that the publication was "inaccurate, misleading and unwarranted in many material particulars, that it was intended to disparage the plaintiff by charging the company with unjust treatment of its employees, and with having acted arbitrarily and without justification in refusing to take them back, or to negotiate for their return as members of the union", the court ordered an injunction to issue prohibiting defendants "from publishing and circulating any statement in whole or in part of the nature and character of the 'Story of the News Stand Girls' as set forth in the record, for the purpose of coercing the plaintiff to reinstate its discharged employees and to employ only union labor." In Olympia Operating Co. v. Costello, 278 Mass. 125, 179 N.E. 804 (1932), the court enjoined the defendants from carrying a placard declaring "Union Billposters Locked Out" on the ground that such a statement was false, inasmuch as the defendants who had been doing outside billposting struck because of the refusal of the plaintiff to permit them to do inside billposting. In Martin v. Francke, 227 Mass. 272, 116 N.E. 404 (1917), the court said: "The second exception is to the finding of the master upon uncontradicted evidence 'that the usual and ordinary meaning and significance of the word "unfair" among labor men is practically the same as that of the word "scab" among labor men.' If and in so far as the meaning of the word 'unfair' was material to any issue involved at the hearing, it was a question to be decided upon the evidence. If the defendants believed that the word 'unfair' did not have the significance of the word 'scab' they were entitled to introduce evidence to the contrary; if they did not see fit to do so we cannot say that the finding of the master, which was in accordance with the uncontradicted evidence, was not warranted. The exception to this finding cannot be sustained." Cf. Godin v. Niebuhr, 236 Mass. 350, 128 N.E. 406 (1920). —Ed.

[2] "Much importance is attached to the fact, if it be a fact, that some of the defendants on a few occasions used the word 'scab'. I cannot feel myself shocked by that word. The law, although, perhaps, deprecating its use, is not so sensitive as to be outraged by it. The word is coarse and offensive, to be sure, but it carries with it no import of infamy or crime. Its meaning is perfectly well known and its use is

lous, to turn the attempt into a duty. Equity does not act for every shadowy or unsubstantial wrong.

A genuine controversy exists between two competing groups as to the effectiveness and sincerity of the methods of one of them. By concession the form of a union has been adopted by each of the two bodies. Whether the spirit also is there, the spirit, that is to say, for which unions are created, is a question not susceptible of answer without heed being given to many imponderable elements. The plaintiff does not prevail

---

common. Webster gives this definition of the word: 'A workng man who works for lower wages than, or under conditions contrary to, those prescribed by the trade union; also, one who takes the place of a working man on a strike.' This definition embraces no thought of violence, no infraction of the law, no threat, no menace. Why should this word be especially tabooed? It is offensive, beyond question, and perhaps opprobrious. It would be better unsaid, but why should the court enjoin strikers from using this particular word, or enjoin them from anything because they have used it? There is no reason, as I comprehend the rules of equity." Howard, J., in Wood Mowing & Reaping Machine Co. v. Toohey, 114 Misc. 185, 190-191, 186 N.Y.S. 95 (1921). Accord: People v. Radt, 71 N.Y.S. 846 (Gen. Sess. 1900). "It is a matter of common knowledge that the word 'scab', as a designation of a human being, is one of the most opprobrious and insulting in the English language. One of the common literal meanings is (Webster's Internat'l Dict., Ed. 1922): 'An incrustation over a sore or pustule formed by the drying up of the discharge from the diseased part.' Other and less literal, but (in times of strike) extremely common, meanings are: 'A dirty, paltry fellow. A workman who works for lower wages than, or under conditions contrary to, those prescribed by the trade union; also, one who takes the place of a workman on a strike; a rat; used opprobriously by trade unionists.' Webster's Dict. 1922. No man can be called a scab without thought of the putrescent and loathsome object which the term applied to himself suggests. Testimony from any one or more of the employees that being publicly excluded from a public place by a most highly offensive designation was annoying and insulting would have been supererogatory. Even judges are not justified in refusing to act on knowledge which is common to practically all sane and adult inhabitants of the United States." United States v. Taliaferro, 290 Fed. 214, 218 (W.D. Va. 1922), aff'd in 290 Fed. 906 (4th cir. 1923), holding defendant guilty of contempt for displaying in his barber shop during a strike a sign saying "No Scabs Wanted in Here." *Contra:* Illinois Malleable Iron Co. v. Michalek, 279 Ill. 221, 116 N.E. 714 (1917); Cohen v. United States, 295 Fed. 633 (6th cir. 1924). "Mr. Vinson: The cry of 'scab' has a deterrent and a frightful effect upon men that want to work in a non-union plant, has it not, Colonel? Mr. Wiley: [President of Boone County Coal Corp., W. Va.] Yes, sir; and it is not the cry of 'scab' as applied to himself. He can stand that without any trouble; but when his wife comes in and says, 'I cannot live here. They call me a scab wife.' And his children come in crying and saying, 'I am miserable because the other fellows will not play with me. They call me scab.' It is more than a man can be expected to stand, and he takes the easiest way and gives up his principles and does what he is told to do." Hearings before the Committee on Education and Labor pursuant to Sen. Res. 80, U.S. Senate, 67th Cong. 1st sess. 989 (1921). "They may have a right to work, but by the eternal gods they haven't any right to your jobs. It has been entirely too healthy for scabs around Blocton; that has been the trouble with you. What would you do with a rattlesnake if one of them would start crawling into this meeting now? (A Voice. Kill him.) A rattlesnake never did you half as much harm as a scab did. I have not said that the scabs should be driven out. But you know what Christ did with those money lenders in the temple at Jerusalem * * *. That is what Christ did with these fellows that were not any good; these money lenders were saints compared with these scabs who are around in these mines. There you have Christ's law. God's law, rather, laid down through our Savior, as an example to go by here in Alabama. I like to see men who are Christians be Christians through and through, practical Christians, men who are willing to put Christianity into their every day life." Speech of Van Bittner at Blocton, Ala. *ibid.* at 1030. *Cf.* Prince v. Socialistic Pub. Ass'n. 31 Misc. 234, 64 N.Y.S. 285 (1900) (holding "scab" libellous *per se*).—Ed.

by showing that the defendant's criticism is wrong, though even this it
fails to do. What is wrong must be so clearly wrong that only "disinterested malevolence" (*American Bank & Trust Co. v. Federal Reserve Bank,*
256 U.S. 350, 358), or something close akin thereto, can have supplied the
motive power (*Steinert & Sons Co. v. Tagen, supra*). If less than this
appears, a court of equity will stand aside.

(3) The other prohibitions are an impairment of the defendant's
indubitable right to win converts over to its fold by recourse to peaceable
persuasion, and to induce them by like methods to renounce allegiance to
its rival. Recent decisions of this court have established that fundamental
right too emphatically and forcefully to make further vindication needful
(*Exchange Bakery & Restaurant, Inc., v. Rifkin, supra; Interborough
R. T. Co. v. Lavin,* 247 N.Y. 65). All these provisions must be expunged
from the decree.

The judgment of the Appellate Division and that of the Special Term
should be modified in accordance with this opinion, and as modified affirmed, without costs.

If the parties are unable to agree upon the form of the judgment, the
form may be settled upon an application to the court.

POUND, CRANE, LEHMAN, KELLOGG, O'BRIEN and HUBBS, JJ., concur.

Judgment accordingly.[3]

PITTSBURGH TERMINAL COAL CORPORATION v. UNITED MINE WORKERS OF AMERICA.

District Court of the United States for the Western District of Pennsylvania.

This cause came on to be heard upon the application of the plaintiff
for a preliminary injunction and was heard upon the verified bill of complaint, the affidavits submitted by plaintiff in support thereof, the affidavits
submitted by certain defendants in opposition thereto, and the rebuttal af-

---

[3] For comment on the case, see: 44 Harv. Law Rev. 971 (1931); 31 Col. Law
Rev. 717 (1931); 16 Minn. Law Rev. 118 (1931).

For the further application of the doctrine in the case, see: Steinkritz Amusement Corp. v. Kaplan, 257 N.Y. 294, 178 N.E. 11 (1931); Brooklyn United Theatre
v. Internat'l Alliance of Stage Employees etc. Union, 257 N.Y. 555, 178 N.E. 793
(1931); J. H. & S. Theatres v. Fay, 260 N.Y. 315, 183 N.E. 509 (1932); Aberon
Bakery Co. v. Raimist, 141 Misc. 774. 254 N.Y.S. 38 (1931); Tree-Mark Shoe Co. v.
Schwartz, 139 Misc. 136, 248 N.Y.S. 56 (1931). See: 45 Harv. Law Rev. 936 (1932).

Cf. Herzog v. Cline, 131 Misc. 816, 819, 227 N.Y.S. 462 (1927): "Where there
are several unions in a trade and an employer exercises his right to hire members of
one of them rather than of the others, he should not be subject to strikes solely
because of his choice. If he were to be subject thereto for such reason alone, there
might be continuous strikes against him, with no object other than to determine the
survival of the 'strongest' union. The employer himself might not survive. Such
strikes in my opinion would be deemed in law to be based on malice, and malicious
strikes are unlawful."

fidavits submitted by plaintiff, and was fully argued by counsel for the respective parties. Upon consideration whereof, the court finds:

That all of the defendants have been duly served with summons by subpoena and with the order to show cause heretofore issued herein as appears from the record of this cause, except: John L. Lewis, Joe Vujnovic, William J. Patton, Edward Snyder, Frank J. Hayes, Thomas W. Hughes, Fred Gollick, William Hynes, William Cadman, and Stanley Davis.

That the plaintiff is entitled to a preliminary injunction as prayed for (except as modified herein) for the reason that it clearly appears from the specific facts contained in the verified bill of complaint and by the evidence submitted that immediate and irreparable damage and loss will result to plaintiff unless a preliminary injunction be granted and that for such damage and loss the plaintiff is without any adequate remedy at law.

IT IS THEREFORE ORDERED, ADJUDGED, AND DECREED that the defendants, the United Mine Workers of America, and all officers, committees, boards, and members thereof; the defendant District No. 5 of the United Mine Workers of America and all officers, committees, boards, and members thereof; the defendants Local Unions Nos. 820, 1339, 2363, 2500, 5085, and 5157, and all officers, committees, boards, and members thereof; the defendants, Philip Murray, Thomas Kennedy, P. T. Fagan, William Hargest, John O'Leary, and James Flood, individually and as incumbents of the offices and stations indicated in the bill of complaint, together with all other individual defendants named herein, and all members of said bodies or associations whether served with process or not, and all persons acting in combination or concert with them or who aid, assist, or abet said defendants or any of them in the acts hereinafter referred to, are collectively and severally and in their associated and organized capacity, as well as individually, enjoined from doing or attempting to do any of the following acts:

(1) From assaulting, beating, coercing, threatening, intimidating, insulting, molesting, or in any way interfering with plaintiff's employees or their families; or the officers, foremen, agents, or the persons in the employ of plaintiff; or any person transacting any business with, or rendering any service to or for plaintiff or entering, approaching or leaving plaintiff's properties or any of them in connection with such transaction, business, or service; or any person applying for or seeking employment with plaintiff, or any former employee of plaintiff seeking, intending, or desiring to resume employment with plaintiff, including the families of such applicants.

(2) From interfering by violence, threats, intimidation, insult, calling of names or epithets, or in any like manner interfering with any actual or proposed contractual relationship between plaintiff and his employees, or interfering in any way, except as provided in section 6 hereof, with the right of plaintiff and such employees or intending employees or persons desiring or seeking employment to agree unmolested upon such terms of employment as plaintiff and such persons may regard proper.

(3) From exploding dynamite, powder, or other explosives upon or near any property of plaintiff, or injuring, defacing, destroying, or interfering with any property, real or personal, of plaintiff, or of any of plaintiff's employees or intending employees; or shooting at or toward any property of plaintiff or at or toward any employee of plaintiff or any vehicle or conveyance owned by or engaged in any service for plaintiff; throwing rocks, stones, or other missiles at or toward plaintiff's employees, property, or vehicles or at vehicles or automobiles engaged in any service for plaintiff's benefit.

(4) From obstructing, impeding, hindering, preventing, or interfering with the operation of plaintiff's mines, or any of them, or the doing of any act connected with such operation, or obstructing, impeding, hindering, preventing, or interfering with the production, mining, transportation, or shipment of coal by plaintiff from its mines described in the bill of complaint.

(5) From trespassing upon plaintiff's property, mines, tipples, or cars for any purpose, or upon any other lands, places, highways, or property (except entering voting places, post offices, or physicians' offices), with the intent or purpose of committing any act forbidden by this decree.

(6) From congregating, loitering, parading, or gathering about or near plaintiff's properties or from picketing the same except as follows:

(a) One picket post may be maintained upon or immediately adjacent to each public highway leading to each mine of plaintiff, but not upon its property, and not closer than 100 feet to any building or structure (not including company houses) used by plaintiff as an office or in its operations.

(b) Not more than three persons at a time shall be stationed at any picket post, and no other person shall be permitted to stand or loiter at any place within 100 feet from the limits of any picket post for any purpose whatsoever.

(c) Each picket post established shall be not to exceed 100 feet in length along the highway, and its limits shall be indicated by a sign, flag, or marker.

(d) Relief pickets shall not stay in the vicinity of picket posts when not on duty.

(e) Pickets on duty at their respective posts may peacefully observe, communicate with, and persuade persons, but shall not make use of abusive or threatening language. The peaceful persuasion herein referred to is peaceful persuasion directed toward one who is not known to be an employee, in the effort to keep him from becoming an employee, or directed toward one who is an employee, in the effort to induce him to terminate his relation of employment; it does not include talking to any person after having been notified or advised by him of his unwillingness to be talked with, or pursuing, or following any such person for any such purpose. Nothing contained in this section shall be construed to prevent defendants from meeting in ordinary neighborhood or social gatherings or from attending meetings of their unions in their union halls, provided that such gatherings or meetings shall not be conducted with the purpose or effect of violating the provisions or the spirit of this injunction, and the respective officers of such defendant unions as well as the persons taking part in such gatherings or meetings are charged with the responsibility of carrying this provision completely into effect.

(7) From hereafter detaining or occupying any mining house or houses of plaintiff by causing the same to be occupied against plaintiff's will by persons not employed by plaintiff; excepting that this decree shall not affect any cause now instituted and pending in the State courts of Pennsylvania, at the time of the commencement of this action and affecting the possession of such houses.

(8) From disbursing any funds for any further appeal bonds, attorney services, court costs, or otherwise for the purpose of enabling, aiding, encouraging, or procuring any person to occupy against the plaintiff's will any such mining houses of plaintiff; from signing any further appeal bond or depositing, providing, or furnishing security for such appeal bond to prolong or aid in litigation respecting the possession of said houses; but nothing herein shall prevent Oliver K. Eaton and William H. Coleman, or either of them, representing as attorneys and counsel the individual occupants of miners' houses in the appeals in the Superior Court of Pennsylvania

(9) From interfering with plaintiff in the exercise of any right reserved to it under its leases of said miners' houses to secure repossession of the same and to remove the effect of any occupant thereof: *Provided;* That nothing herein contained shall interfere with the individual right of any tenant or tenants of any such house or houses to interpose in any court of competent jurisdiction any legal defense which he may have.

(10) Such defendants as are still occupying plaintiff's houses are enjoined from annoying, disturbing, insulting, interfering with, or threatening the families of plaintiff's employees and from encouraging members of defendant unions from using their occupancy of plaintiff's homes as a means of disturbing, annoying, or interfering with plaintiff's employees in neighboring houses or doing any other kind of injury to plaintiff's employees or property.

(11) This injunction shall become effective upon the plaintiff giving bond conditioned according to law in the sum of $50,000; said bond has this day been filed and approved.

F. P. Schoonmaker,
United States District Judge.

Dated at Pittsburgh, Pa., this 11th day of October, 1927.

UNITED STATES v. RAILWAY EMPLOYEES' DEPT., A. F. OF L.

This cause [1] having come on for final hearing upon pleadings and proofs, and the pleadings and proofs having been considered, it is now, this 12th day of July, 1923, ORDERED, ADJUDGED and DECREED; * * *

Third. That said defendants, and each of them, and each and all of their officers, attorneys, servants, agents, associates, members, employees, and all persons acting in aid of or in conjunction with them, be, and they hereby are, permanently restrained and enjoined from—

(a) In any manner interfering with, hindering or obstructing said railway companies, or any of them, their officers, agents, servants or employees in the operation of their respective railroads and systems of transportation or the performance of their public duties and obligations in the transportation of passengers and property in interstate commerce and the carriage of the mail, and from in any manner interfering with, hindering or obstructing the officers, agents, servants or employees of said railway companies, or any of them, engaged in its construction, inspection, repair, operation or use of trains, locomotives, cars, or other equipment of said railway companies, or any of them, and from prevent-

---

[1] For opinions at various stages of this case, see: United States v. Railway Employees' Dept., A. F. of L. 283 Fed. 479 (N.D. Ill. 1922) (opinion granting preliminary injunction); 286 Fed. 228 (N.D. Ill. 1923) (opinion denying motion for dissolution of temporary injunction and dismissal of bill); 290 Fed. 978 (N.D. Ill. 1923) (on final hearing).

For an analysis of the terms of the injunction, comparing it with the Debs injunction, see: Frankfurter and Landis, 37 Harv. Law Rev. 1101 (1924); reprinted in Frankfurter and Greene, The Labor Injunction, App. IV (1930).

For comment favorable to the issuance of the injunction, see: 8 Am. Bar Ass'n Jour. 624 (1922); 17 Ill. Law Rev. 440 (1923); 21 Mich. Law. Rev. 90 (1922); 71 Univ. of Pa. Law Rev. 83 (1922). For comment critical of its issuance, see 32 Yale Law Jour. 166 (1922). See also: McGuire, "The Injunction and the Railway Strike," 11 Geo. Law Jour. No. 4, 1 (1923). For a collection of contemporary newspaper comment on its issuance, see 12 Am. Labor Leg. Rev. 157 (1922). For the "inside" story surrounding the issuance of the injunction, see: Daugherty and Dixon, The Inside Story of the Harding Tragedy, 132-153 (1932).

"I was led recently to make such a review of our industrial history by my desire to account for the growing bitterness of organized labor toward the federal courts * * *. I accordingly addressed a letter to every United States district attorney asking him to secure from the clerk's office in his district a copy of all such injunction orders made by the United States Court in his district during the last few years. Courteous attention to my request has supplied me with a most interesting mass of material. The study of these orders discloses an evolution mildly comparable with the growth of the corporate mortgage. The injunction orders have become more and more comprehensive and far-reaching in their provisions until they culminate in the Shopmen's Injunction order already referred to. Every thoughtful lawyer who has not already done so should read that order and meditate upon its significance. In so doing he should have in mind that during the shopmen's strike in 1922 nearly every one of the 261 'Class 1' railroads and a number of short-line railroads applied for injunctions in the various federal courts. No applications were denied. In all nearly 300 were issued." Pepper, "Injunctions in Labor Disputes" 49 Am. Bar Ass'n Rep. 174, 178-179 (1924), reprinted in 30 Pa. Bar Ass'n Rep. 291 (1924). See also: Bonney, "Federal Intervention in Labor Disputes", 7 Minn. Law Rev. 467, 550 (1923).

ing or attempting to prevent any person or persons from freely entering into or continuing in the employment of said railway companies, or any of them, for the construction, inspection, repair, operation or use of locomotives, cars, rolling stock,.or other equipment;

(*b*) In any manner conspiring, combining, confederating, agreeing and arranging with each other or with any other person or persons, organizations or associations to injure or interfere with or hinder said railway companies, or any of them, in the conduct of their lawful business of transportation of passengers and property in interstate commerce and the carriage of the mail; or to injure, interfere with, hinder or annoy any officer or employee of said railway companies, or any of them, in connection with the performance of their duties as such officers or employees, or while going to or returning from the premises of said railway companies in connection with their said employment, or at any time or place, by displays of force or numbers, the making of threats, intimidation, acts of violence, opprobrious epithets, jeers, suggestions of danger, taunts, entreaties, or other unlawful acts or conduct, or to injure, interfere with, hinder, or annoy by any such acts any persons or person desirous of, contemplating or intending to enter into such employment;

(*c*) Loitering or being unnecessarily in the vicinity of the points and places of ingress or egress of the employees of said railway companies, or any of them, to and from such premises in connection with their said employment for the purpose of doing any of the things herein prohibited; or aiding, abetting, directing or encouraging any person or persons, organization, or association, by letters, telegrams, telephone, word of mouth, or otherwise, to do any of the acts heretofore described in this and preceding paragraphs; trespassing, entering or going upon the premises of the said railway companies, or any of them, without their consent, at any place or in the vicinity of any place where the employees of said companies, or any of them, are engaged in constructing, inspecting, overhauling, or repairing locomotives, cars, or other equipment, or where such employees customarily perform such duties or at any other place on the premises of said railway companies, or any of them, except where the public generally are invited to come to transact business with said railway companies as common carriers of passengers and property in interstate commerce;

(*d*) Inducing or attempting to induce with intent to further said conspiracy by the use of threats, violent or abusive language, opprobrious epithets, physical violence or threats thereof, intimidation, displays of force or numbers, or jeers, any person or persons to abandon the employment of said railway companies, or any of them, or to refrain from entering such employment;

(*e*) Engaging, directing or procuring others to engage in the practice commonly known as picketing, that is to say, assembling or causing to be assembled numbers of the members of said Federated Shop Crafts, or others in sympathy with them, in the vicinity of where the employees of said railway companies, or any of them, are required to work and perform their duties, or at or near the places of ingress or egress, or along the ways traveled by said employees thereto or therefrom, and by threats, jeers, violent or abusive language, violence or threats of violence, taunts, entreaties or argument, or by any similar acts preventing or attempting to prevent any of the employees of said railway companies, or any of them, from entering upon or continuing in their duties as such employees, or so preventing or attempting to prevent, any other person or persons from entering or continuing in the employment of said railway companies, or any of them; and aiding, abetting, ordering, assisting, directing, or encouraging in any way any person or persons in the commission of any of said acts;

(*f*) Congregating or maintaining, or directing, aiding, or encouraging the congregating or maintaining upon, at or near any of the yards, shops, depots, terminals, tracks, waylands, roadbeds, or premises of said railway companies, or any of them, of any guards, pickets, or persons to perform any act of guarding, picketing, or patrolling any such yards, shops, depots, terminals or other premises of said railway companies, or any of them; or in any manner threatening or intimidating, by suggestions of danger or by personal violence towards any servant or employee of said railway companies, or any of them, or towards persons contemplating the entering of their employment; or aiding, encouraging, directing, or causing any other person or persons so to do;

(*g*) Doing or causing, or in any manner conspiring, combining, directing, commanding or encouraging the doing or causing the doing by any person or persons of any injury or bodily harm to any of the servants, agents or employees of said railway companies, or any of them; going singly or collectively to the home, abode, or place of residence of any employee of the said railway companies, or any of them, for the purpose of intimidating, threatening, or coercing such employee or member of his family, or in any manner by violence or threats of violence, intimidation, opprobrious epithets, or other acts of like character, directed towards any said employee or member of his family, for the purpose of inducing or attempting to induce such employee to refuse to perform his duties as an employee of said railway companies, or any of them; or so attempting to prevent any person or persons from entering the employ of any of said railway companies, or aiding, encouraging, directing, commanding or causing any person or persons so to do;

(*h*) In any manner directly or indirectly hindering, obstructing, or impeding the operation of any train or trains of said railway companies, or any of them, in the movement and transportation of passengers and property in interstate commerce or in the carriage of the United States mail, or in the performance of any other duty as common carriers, or aiding, abetting, causing, encouraging or directing any person or persons, association or organization to do or cause to be done any of the matters or things aforesaid;

(*i*) In any manner, with intent to further said conspiracy, by letters, printed or other circulars, telegrams, telephones, word of mouth, oral persuasion, or communication, or through interviews published in newspapers, or other similar acts, encouraging, directing or commanding any person, whether a member of any or either of said labor organizations or associations defendants herein, to abandon the employment of said railway companies, or any of them, or to refrain from entering the service of said railway companies, or any of them;

Fourth. The said defendants, Bert M. Jewell, J. F. McGrath, John Scott, James W. Kline, J. J. Hunes, J. A. Franklin, Martin F. Ryan, William H. Johnston, E. C. Davison and James P. Noonan, and each of them, as officers as aforesaid and as individuals, be and they hereby are permanently restrained and enjoined from—

(*a*) Issuing any instructions, or making any requests, public statements or communications heretofore enjoined and restrained in this decree to any defendant herein, or to any officer or member of any said labor organizations constituting the said Federated Shop Crafts, or to any officer or member of any system federation thereof, with intent to further said conspiracy, for the purpose of inducing or calculated to induce any such officer or member, or any other persons whomsoever, to do or say anything intended or calculated to cause any employee of said railway companies, or any of them, to abandon the employment thereof, or any persons to refrain from entering the employment thereof to aid in the movement and transportation of passengers and property in interstate commerce and the carriage of the United States mail;

(*b*) Using, or causing to be used, or consenting to the use of any of the funds or moneys of said labor organizations in aid of or to promote or encourage the doing of any of the matters or things hereinbefore restrained and enjoined.

But nothing herein contained shall be construed to prohibit the use of the funds or moneys of any of said labor organizations for any lawful purpose, and nothing contained in this decree shall be contrued to prohibit the expression of an opinion or argument not intended to aid or encourage the doing of any of the acts hereinbefore enjoined, or not calculated to maintain or prolong a conspiracy to restrain interstate commerce or the carriage of the United States mail.

Fifth. That the United States shall recover its costs herein to be taxed by the clerk of the court and shall have execution therefor.

Enter:

JAMES H. WILKERSON.

10 o'clock a. m.
July twelfth, 1923.

TRUAX v. CORRIGAN.

Supreme Court of the United States. 257 U.S. 312 (1921).

MR. CHIEF JUSTICE TAFT delivered the opinion of the court.

The plaintiffs in error, who were plaintiffs below, and will be so called, own, maintain and operate, on Main Street, in the City of Bisbee, Arizona, a restaurant, known as the "English Kitchen." The defendants are cooks and waiters formerly in the employ of the plaintiffs, together with the labor union and the trades assembly of which they were members. All parties are residents of the State of Arizona.

The complaint set out the following case:

In April, 1916, a dispute arose between the plaintiffs and the defendants' union concerning the terms and conditions of employment of the members of the union. The plaintiffs refused to yield to the terms of the union, which thereupon ordered a strike of those of its members who were in plaintiffs' employ. To win the strike and to coerce and compel the plaintiffs to comply with the demands of the union, the defendants and others unknown to the plaintiffs entered into a conspiracy and boycott to injure plaintiffs in their restaurant and restaurant business, by inducing plaintiffs' customers and others theretofore well and favorably disposed, to cease to patronize or trade with the plaintiffs. The method of inducing was set out at length and included picketing, displaying banners, advertising the strike, denouncing plaintiffs as "unfair" to the union and appealing to customers to stay away from the "English Kitchen," and the circulation of handbills containing abusive and libelous charges against plaintiffs, their employees and their patrons, and intimations of injury to future patrons. Copies of the handbills were set forth in exhibits made part of the complaint.

In consequence of defendants' acts, many customers were induced to cease from patronizing plaintiffs, and their daily receipts, which had been in excess of the sum of $156 were reduced to $75. The complaint averred that if the acts were continued, the business would be entirely destroyed, and that the plaintiffs woud suffer great and irreparable injury; that for the plaintiffs to seek to recover damages would involve a multiplicity of suits; that all the defendants were insolvent, and would be unable to respond in damages for any injury resulting from their acts and the plaintiffs were therefore without any adequate remedy at law.

The complaint further averred that the defendants were relying for immunity on Paragraph 1464 of the Revised Statutes of Arizona, 1913, which is in part as follows:

"No restraining order or injunction shall be granted by any court of this state, or a judge or the judges thereof, in any case between an employer and employees, or between employers and employees, or between employees, or between persons employed and persons seeking employment, involving or growing out of a dispute concerning terms or conditions of employment, unless necessary to prevent irreparable injury to property or to a property right of the party making the application, for which injury there is no adequate remedy at law, and such property or property right must be described with particularity in the application, which must be in writing and sworn to by the applicant or by his agent or attorney.

"And no such restraining order or injunction shall prohibit any person or persons from terminating any relation of employment, or from ceasing to perform any work or labor, or from recommending, advising, or persuading others by peaceful means so to do; or from attending at or near a house or place where any person resides or works, or carries on business, or happens to be for the purpose of peacefully obtaining or communicating information, or of peacefully persuading any person to work or to abstain from working; or from ceasing to patronize or to employ any party to such dispute; or from recommending, advising, or persuading others by peaceful means so to do; * * *"

The plaintiffs alleged that this paragraph if it made lawful defendants' acts contravened the Fourteenth Amendment to the Constitution of the United States by depriving plaintiffs of their property without due process of law, and by denying to plaintiffs the equal protection of the laws, and was, therefore, void and of no effect. Upon the case thus stated the plaintiffs asked a temporary, and a permanent, injunction.

The defendants filed a demurrer, on two grounds: First, that the complaint did not state facts sufficient to constitute a cause of action, in that the property rights asserted therein were not, under Paragraph 1464, Revised Statutes of Arizona, 1913, of such character that their irreparable injury might be enjoined, and secondly, that upon its face the complaint showed a want of equity.

The Superior Court for Cochise County sustained the demurrer and dismissed the complaint, and this judgment was affirmed by the Supreme Court of Arizona.

The ruling of the Supreme Court proceeded first on the assumption that the gravamen of the complaint was that the defendants were merely inducing patrons to cease their patronage by making public the fact of the dispute and the attitude of plaintiffs in it, and, secondly, on the proposition that, while good will is a valuable factor in business success, "no man * * * has a vested property right in the esteem of the public," that, while the plaintiff had a clear right to refuse the demand of the union, the union had a right to advertise the cause of the strike. The court held that the purpose of Paragraph 1464 was to recognize the right of workmen on a strike to use peaceable means to accomplish the lawful ends for which the strike was called; that picketing, if peaceably carried on for a lawful purpose, was no violation of the rights of the person whose place of business was picketed; that, prior to the enactment of Paragraph 1464, picketing was unlawful in Arizona because it was presumed to induce breaches of the peace, but that plaintiffs had no vested right to have such a rule of law continue in that State; that under Paragraph 1464 picketing was no longer conclusively presumed to be unlawful; that the paragraph simply dealt with a rule of evidence requiring the courts to substitute evidence of the nature of the act for the presumption otherwise arising; that the plaintiffs' property rights were not invaded by picketing unless the picketing interfered with the free conduct of the business; that plaintiffs did not claim that defendants had by violent means invaded their rights, and that if that kind of picketing were charged and established by proof plaintiffs would be entitled to relief to the extent of prohibiting violence in any form.

The effect of this ruling is that, under the statute, loss may be inflicted upon the plaintiffs' property and business by "picketing" in any form if violence be not used, and that, because no violence was shown or claimed, the campaign carried on, as described in the complaint and exhibits, did not unlawfully invade complainants' rights.

The facts alleged are admitted by the demurrer, and in determining their legal effect as a deprivation of plaintiffs' legal rights under the Fourteenth Amendment, we are at as full liberty to consider them as was the State Supreme Court. *Mackay v. Dillon,* 4 How. 421; *Dower v. Richards,* 151 U.S. 658, 667. Nor does the court's declaration that the statute is a rule of evidence bind us in such an investigation. *Bailey v. Alabama,* 219 U.S. 219, 238, 239; *Chicago, Milwaukee & St. Paul Ry. Co. v. Minnesota,* 134 U.S. 418; *Mugler v. Kansas,* 123 U.S. 623, 661; *Corn Products Refining Co. v. Eddy,* 249 U.S. 427, 432. In cases brought to this court from state courts for review, on the ground that a federal right set up in the state court has been wrongly denied, and in which the state court has put its decision on a finding that the asserted federal right has no basis in point of fact or has been waived or lost, this court as an incident of its power to determine whether a federal right has been wrongly denied, may go behind the finding to see whether it is without substantial support. If the rule were otherwise, it almost always would be within the power of a state court practically to prevent a review here. *Kansas City Southern Ry. Co. v. Albers Commission Co.,* 223 U.S. 573, 591, 593; *Cedar Rapids Gas Light Co. v. Cedar Rapids,* 223 U.S. 655, 668, 669; *Southern Pacific Co. v. Schuyler,* 227 U.S. 601, 611. Another class of cases in which this court will review the finding of the court as to the facts is when the conclusion of law and findings of fact are so intermingled as to make it necessary, in order to pass upon the question to analyze the facts. *Northern Pacific Ry. Co. v. North Dakota,* 236 U.S. 585, 593; *Jones National Bank v. Yates,* 240 U.S. 541, 552, 553. In view of these decisions and the grounds upon which they proceed, it is clear that in a case like the present, where the issue is whether a state statute in its application to facts which are set out in detail in the pleadings and are admitted by demurrer, violates the Federal Constitution, this court must analyze the facts as averred and draw its own inferences as to their ultimate effect, and is not bound by the conclusion of the State Supreme Court in this regard. The only respect in such a case in which this court is bound by the judgment of the State Supreme Court is in the construction which that court puts upon the statute.

The complaint and its exhibits make this case:

The defendants conspired to injure and destroy plaintiffs' business by inducing their theretofore willing patrons and would-be patrons not to patronize them and they influenced these to withdraw or withhold their patronage:

(1) By having the agents of the union walk forward and back constantly during all the business hours in front of plaintiffs' restaurant and within five feet thereof, displaying a banner announcing in large letters that the restaurant was unfair to cooks and waiters and their union.

(2) By having agents attend at or near the entrance of the restaurant during all business hours and continuously announce in a loud voice, audible for a great distance, that the restaurant was unfair to the labor union.

(3) By characterizing the employees of the plaintiffs as scab Mexican labor, and using opprobrious epithets concerning them in handbills continuously distributed in front of the restaurant to would-be customers.

(4) By applying in such handbills abusive epithets to Truax, the senior member of plaintiffs' firm, and making libelous charges against him, to the effect that he was tyrannical with his help, and chased them down the street with a butcher knife, that he broke his contract and repudiated his pledged word; that he had made attempts to force cooks and waiters to return to work by attacks on men and women; that a friend of Truax assaulted a woman and pleaded guilty; that plaintiff was known by his friends, and that Truax's treatment of his employees was explained by his friend's assault; that he was a "bad actor."

(5) By seeking to disparage plaintiffs' restaurant, charging that the prices were higher and the food worse than in any other restaurant, and that assaults and slugging were a regular part of the bill of fare, with police indifferent.

(6) By attacking the character of those who did patronize, saying that their mental calibre and moral fibre fell far below the American average, and enquiring of the would-be patrons—Can you patronize such a place and look the world in the face?

(7) By threats of similar injury to the would-be patrons—by such expressions as "All ye who enter here leave all hope behind." "Don't be a traitor to humanity"; by offering a reward for any of the ex-members of the union caught eating in the restaurant; by saying in the handbills: "We are also aware that handbills and banners in front of a business house on the main street give the town a bad name, but they are permanent institutions until William Truax agrees to the eight-hour day."

(8) By warning any person wishing to purchase the business from the Truax firm that a donation would be necessary, amount to be fixed by the District Trades Assembly, before the picketing and boycotting would be given up.

The result of this campaign was to reduce the business of the plaintiffs from more than $55,000 a year to one of $12,000.

Plaintiffs' business is a property right (*Duplex Printing Press Co. v. Deering,* 254 U.S. 443, 465) and free access for employees, owner and customers to his place of business is incident to such right. Intentional injury caused to either right or both by a conspiracy is a tort. Concert of action is a conspiracy if its object is unlawful or if the means used are unlawful. *Pettibone v. United States,* 148 U.S. 197, 203; *Duplex Printing Press Co. v. Deering, supra.* Intention to inflict the loss and the actual loss caused are clear. The real question here is, were the means used illegal? The above recital of what the defendants did, can leave no doubt of that. The libelous attacks upon the plaintiffs, their business, their employees, and their customers, and the abusive epithets applied to them were palpable wrongs. They were uttered in aid of the plan to induce plaintiffs' customers and would-be customers to refrain from patronizing the plaintiffs. The patrolling of defendants immediately in front of the restaurant on the main street and within five feet of plaintiffs' premises continuously during business hours, with the banners announcing plaintiffs' unfairness; the attendance by the picketers at the entrance to the restaurant and their insistent and loud appeals all day long, the constant circulation by them of the libels and epithets applied to employees, plaintiffs and customers, and the threats of injurious consequences to future customers, all linked together in a campaign, were an unlawful annoyance and a hurtful nuisance in respect of the free access to the plaintiffs' place of business. It was not lawful persuasion or inducing. It was not a mere appeal to the sympathetic aid of would-be customers by a simple statement of the fact of the strike and a request to withhold patronage. It was compelling every customer or would-be customer to run the gauntlet of most uncomfortable publicity, aggressive and annoying importunity, libelous attacks and fear of injurious consequences, illegally inflicted, to his reputation and standing in the community. No wonder that a business of $50,000 was reduced to only one-fourth of its former extent. Violence could not have been more effective. It was moral coercion by illegal annoyance and obstruction and it thus was plainly a conspiracy.

It would consume too great space to refer to the mass of authority which sustains this conclusion. It is sufficient to cite the general discussion of the subject in *Gompers v. Bucks Stove & Range Co.,* 221 U.S. 418, 439. Well known decisions on similar facts are *Sherry v. Perkins,* 147 Mass. 212; *Barr v. Essex Trades Council,* 53 N.J. Eq. 101; *Purvis v. Local No. 500,* 214 Pa. St. 348; *Wilson v. Hey,* 232 Ill. 389; *Casey v. Cincinnati Typographical Union,* 45 Fed. 135; *Pierce v. Stablemen's Union,* 156 Cal. 70.

A law which operates to make lawful such a wrong as is described in plaintiffs' complaint deprives the owner of the business and the premises of his property without due process, and can not be held valid under the Fourteenth Amendment.

The opinion of the State Supreme Court in this case if taken alone seems to show that the statute grants complete immunity from any civil or criminal action to the defendants, for it pronounces their acts lawful. If, however, we are to assume that the criminal laws of Arizona do provide prosecution for such libels against the plaintiffs though committed by this particular class of tort feasors, (*Truax v. Bisbee Local No. 380,* 19 Ariz. 379), still the tort here committed was not a mere libel of plaintiffs. That would not have had any such serious consequences. The libel of the plaintiffs here was not the cause of the injury; it was only one step or link in a conspiracy, unlawfully to influence customers.

It is argued that, while the right to conduct a lawful business is property, the conditions surrounding that business, such as regulations of the State for maintaining peace, good order, and protection against disorder, are matters in which no person has a vested right. The conclusion to which this inevitably leads in this case is that the State may withdraw all protection to a property right by civil or criminal action for its wrongful injury if the injury is not caused by violence. This doctrine is supposed to find support in the case of *New York Central R. R. Co. v. White,* 243 U.S. 188, 198, and cases there cited. These cases, all of them, relate to the liabilities of employers to employees growing out of the relation of employment for injuries received in the course of employment. They concern legislation as to the incidents of that relation. They affirm the power of the State to vary the rules of the common law as to the fellow servant doctrine, assumption of risk, and negligence, in that relation. They hold that employers have no vested right in those rules of the common law. The broad distinction between one's right to protection against a direct injury to one's fundamental property right by another who has no special relation to him, and one's liability to another with whom he establishes a voluntary relation under a statute is manifest upon its statement. It is true that no one has a vested right in any particular rule of the common law, but it is also true that the legislative power of a State can only be exerted in subordination to the fundamental principles of right and justice which the guaranty of due process in the Fourteenth Amendment is intended to preserve, and that a purely arbitrary or capricious exercise of that power whereby a wrongful and highly injurious invasion of property rights, as here, is practically sanctioned and the owner stripped of all real remedy, is wholly at variance with those principles.

It is to be observed that this is not the mere case of a peaceful secondary boycott as to the illegality of which courts have differed and States have adopted different statutory provisions. A secondary boycott of this kind is where many combine to injure one in his business by coercing third persons against their will to cease patronizing him by threats of similar injury. In such a case the many have a legal right to withdraw their trade from the one, they have the legal right to withdraw their trade from third persons, and they have the right to advise third persons of their intention to do so when each act is considered singly. The question in such cases is whether the moral coercion exercised over a stranger to the original controversy by steps in themselves legal becomes a legal wrong. But here the illegality of the means used is without doubt and fundamental. The means used are the libelous and abusive attacks on the plaintiffs' reputation, like attacks on their employees and customers, threats of such attacks on would-be customers, picketing and patrolling of the entrance to their place of business, and the consequent obstruction of free access thereto—all with the purpose of depriving the plaintiffs of their business. To give operation to a statute whereby serious losses inflicted by such unlawful means are in effect made remediless, is, we think, to disregard fundamental rights of liberty and property and to deprive the person suffering the loss of due process of law.

If, however, contrary to the construction which we put on the opinion of the Supreme Court of Arizona, it does not withhold from the plaintiffs all remedy for the wrongs they suffered but only the equitable relief of injunction, there still remains the question whether they are thus denied the equal protection of the laws.

The Arizona constitution provides that the superior court shall have jurisdiction in all cases of equity and, in pursuance of this provision, Paragraph 1456 of the Revised Statutes of Arizona, 1913, declares:

"Judges of the superior courts may grant writs of injunction, returnable to said courts, in the following cases:

"1. Where it shall appear that the party applying for such writ is entitled to the relief demanded, and such relief or any part thereof requires the restraint of some act prejudicial to the applicant.

"2. Where, pending litigation, it shall be made to appear that a party is doing some act respecting the subject of litigation, or threatens, or is about to do some act, or is procuring or suffering the same to be done, in violation of the rights of the applicant, which act would tend to render the judgment ineffectual.

"3. In all other cases where the applicant for such writ may show himself entitled thereto under the principles of equity."

The necessary effect of these provisions and of Paragraph 1464 is that the plaintiffs in error would have had the right to an injunction against such a campaign as that conducted by the defendants in error, if it had been directed against the plaintiffs' business and property in any kind of a controversy which was not a dispute between employer and former employees. If the competing restaurant keepers in Bisbee had inaugurated such a campaign against the plaintiffs in error and conducted it with banners and handbills of a similar character, an injunction would necessarily have issued to protect the plaintiffs in the enjoyment of their property and business.

This brings us to consider the effect in this case of that provision of the Fourteenth Amendment which forbids any State to deny to any person the equal protection of the laws. The clause is associated in the Amendment with the due process clause and it is customary to consider them together. It may be that they overlap, that a violation of one may involve at times the violation of the other, but the spheres of the protection they offer are not coterminous. The due process clause, brought down from Magna Charta, was found in the early state constitutions, and later in the Fifth Amendment to the Federal Constitution as a limitation upon the executive, legislative and judicial powers of the Federal Government, while the equality clause does not appear in the Fifth Amendment and so does not apply to congressional legislation. The due process clause requires that every man shall have the protection of his day in court, and the benefit of the general law, a law which hears before it condemns, which proceeds not arbitrarily or capriciously but upon inquiry, and renders judgment only after trial, so that every citizen shall hold his life, liberty, property and immunities under the protection of the general rules which govern society. *Hurtado v. California,* 110 U.S. 516, 535. It, of course, tends to secure equality of law in the sense that it makes a required minimum of protection for every one's right of life, liberty and property, which the Congress or the legislature may not withhold. Our whole system of law is predicated on the general, fundamental principle of equality of application of the law. "All men are equal before the law," "This is a government of laws and not of men," "No man is above the law," are all maxims showing the spirit in which legislatures, executives and courts are expected to make, execute and apply laws. But the framers and adopters of this Amendment were not content to depend on a mere minimum secured by the due process clause, or upon the spirit of equality which might not be insisted on by local public opinion. They therefore embodied that spirit in a specific guaranty.

The guaranty was aimed at undue favor and individual or class privilege, on the one hand, and at hostile discrimination or the oppression of inequality, on the other. It sought an equality of treatment of all persons, even though all enjoyed the protection of due process. Mr. Justice Field, delivering the opinion of this court in *Barbier v. Connolly,* 113 U.S. 27, 32, of the equality clause, said—"Class legislation, discriminating against some and favoring others, is prohibited, but legislation which, in carrying out a public purpose, is limited in its application, if within the sphere of its operation it affects alike all persons similarly situated, is not within the amendment." In *Hayes v. Missouri,* 120 U.S. 68, the court speaking through the same Justice said the Fourteenth Amendment "does not prohibit legislation which is limited either in the objects to which it is directed, or by the territory within which it is to operate. It merely requires that all persons subjected to such legislation shall be treated alike, under like circumstances and conditions, both in the privileges conferred and in the liabilities imposed." Thus the guaranty was intended to secure equality of protection not only for all but against all similarly situated. Indeed, protection is not protection unless it does so. Immunity granted to a class however limited, having the effect to deprive another class, however limited, of a personal or property right, is just as clearly a denial of equal protection of the laws to the latter class as if the immunity were in favor of, or the deprivation of right permitted worked against, a larger class.

Mr. Justice Matthews, in *Yick Wo v. Hopkins,* 118 U.S. 356, 369, speaking for the court of both the due process and the equality clause of the Fourteenth Amendment said:

"These provisions are universal in their application, to all persons within the territorial jurisdiction, without regard to any differences of race, of color, or of nationality; *and the equal protection of the laws is a pledge of the protection of equal laws.*"

The accuracy and comprehensive felicity of this description of the effect of the equality clause are shown by the frequency with which it has been quoted in the decisions of this court. It emphasizes the additional guaranty of a right which the clause has conferred beyond the requirement of due process.

With these views of the meaning of the equality clause, it does not seem possible to escape the conclusion that by the clauses of Paragraph 1464 of the Revised Statutes of Arizona, here relied on by the defendants, as construed by its Supreme Court, the plaintiffs have been deprived of the equal protection of the law.

It is beside the point to say that plaintiffs had no vested right in equity relief and that taking it away does not deprive them of due process of law. If, as is asserted, the granting of equitable remedies falls within the police power and is a matter which the legislature may vary as its judgment and discretion shall dictate, this does not meet the objection under the equality clause which forbids the granting of equitable relief to one man and the denying of it to another under like circumstances and in the same territorial jurisdiction. The Fourteenth Amendment, as this court said in *Barbier v. Connolly,* already cited, intended "not only that there should be no arbitrary deprivation of life or liberty, or arbitrary spoliation of property, but that equal protection and security should be given to all under like circumstances in the enjoyment of their personal and civil rights; that all persons should be equally entitled to pursue their happiness and acquire and enjoy property; *that they should have like access to the courts of the country for the protection of their persons and property, the prevention and redress of wrongs, and the enforcement of contracts;* that no impediment should be interposed to the pursuits of any one except as applied to the same pursuits by others under like circumstances; that no greater burdens should be laid upon one than are laid upon others in the same calling and condition, and that in the administration of criminal justice no different or higher punishment should be imposed upon one than such as is prescribed to all for like offences."

If, as claimed, the legislature has full discretion to grant or withhold equitable relief in any class of cases, indeed to take away from its courts all equity jurisdiction and leave those who are wronged to suits at law or to protection by the criminal law, the legislature has the same power in respect to the declaration of crimes. Suppose the legislature of the State were to provide that such acts as were here committed by defendants, to wit, the picketing or patrolling of the sidewalk and street in front of the store or business house of any person and the use of handbills of an abusive and libelous character against the owner and present and future customers with intent to injure the business of the owner, should be a public nuisance and be punishable by fine and imprisonment, and were to except ex-employees from its penal provisions. Is it not clear that any defendant could escape punishment under it on the ground that the statute violated the equality clause of the Fourteenth Amendment? That is the necessary effect of *Connolly v. Union Sewer Pipe Co.*, 184 U.S. 540, where an anti-trust act was held invalid under this same clause because it contained the excepting provision that it should "not apply to agricultural products or live stock while in the hands of the producer or raiser." That was a stronger case than this because there the whole statute was one dealing with economic policy and was a declaration of *mala prohibita* that had theretofore been lawful, from which it was strongly argued that the exception was justified in the interest of agriculture, and was a proper exception by permissible classification. Here is a direct invasion of the ordinary business and property rights of a person, unlawful when committed by any one, and remediable because of its otherwise irreparable character by equitable process, except when committed by ex-employees of the injured person. If this is not a denial of the equal protection of the laws, then it is hard to conceive what would be. To hold it not to be, would be, to use the expression of Mr. Justice Brewer in *Gulf, Colorado & Santa Fe Ry. Co. v. Ellis,* 165 U.S. 150, 154, to make the guaranty of the equality clause "a rope of sand."

In *Missouri v. Lewis,* 101 U.S. 22, we find one of the earlier and one of the most helpful discussions of the application of the equality clause to judicial procedure by Mr. Justice Bradley speaking for this court. In that case one who had been disbarred by the Court of Appeals of St. Louis sought to avoid the effect of this action by the contention that he was denied the equal protection of the laws because he was not given the right of appeal to the Supreme Court of the State, granted to litigants in the State, except in St. Louis and three other counties. It was held that the equality clause did not apply because the state legislature had the right to vary the system of courts and procedure in various parts of the State. Mr. Justice Bradley said (p. 30) :

"The last restriction, as to the equal protection of the laws, is not violated by any diversity in the jurisdiction of the several courts as to subject-matter, amount, or finality of decision, if all persons within the territorial limits of their respective jurisdictions have an equal right, in like cases and under like circumstances, to resort to them for redress." Again (p. 31) :

"For, as before said, it [i. e., the equality clause] has respect to persons and classes of persons. It means that no person or class of persons shall be denied the same protection of the laws which is enjoyed by other persons or other classes in the same place and under like circumstances."

To sustain the distinction here between the ex-employees and other tort feasors in the matter of remedies against them, it is contended that the legislature may establish a class of such ex-employees for special legislative treatment. In adjusting legislation to the need of the people of a State, the legislature has a wide discretion and it may be fully conceded that perfect uniformity of treatment of all persons is neither practical nor desirable, that classification of persons is constantly necessary and that questions of proper classification are not free from difficulty. But we venture to think that not in any of the cases in this court has classification of persons of sound mind and full responsibility, having no special relation to each other, in respect of remedial procedure for an admitted tort been sustained. Classification must be reasonable. As was said in *Gulf, Colorado & Santa Fe Ry. Co. v. Ellis,* 165 U.S. 155, classification "must always rest upon some difference which bears a reasonable and just relation to the act in respect to which the classification is proposed, and can never be made arbitrarily and without such basis." As was said in *Magoun v. Illinois Trust & Savings Bank,* 170 U.S. 283, 293: "The rule [i. e., of the equality clause] is not a substitute for municipal law; it only prescribes that that law have the attribute of equality of operation, and equality of operation does not mean indiscriminate operation on persons merely as such, but on persons according to their relations." The same principle is repeated and enforced in *Southern Ry. Co. v. Greene,* 216 U.S. 400, 417: "While reasonable classification is permitted, without doing violence to the equal protection of the laws, such classification must be based upon some real and substantial distinction, bearing a reasonable and just relation to the things in respect to which such classification is imposed; and classification cannot be arbitrarily made without any substantial basis." Classification is the most inveterate of our reasoning processes. We can scarcely think or speak without consciously or unconsciously exercising it. It must therefore obtain in and determine legislation; but it must regard real resemblances and real differences between things, and persons, and class them in accordance with their pertinence to the purpose in hand. Classification like the one with which we are here dealing is said to be the development of the philosophic thought of the world and is opening the door to legalized experiment. When fundamental rights are thus attempted to be taken away, however, we may well subject such experiment to attentive judgment. The Constitution was intended, its very purpose was, to prevent experimentation with the fundamental rights of the individual. We said through Mr. Justice Brewer, in *Muller v. Oregon,* 208 U.S. 412, that "it is the peculiar value of a written constitution that it places in unchanging form limitations upon legislative action, and thus gives a permanence and stability to popular government which otherwise would be lacking."

It is urged that this court has frequently recognized the special classification of the relations of employees and employers as proper and necessary for the welfare of the community and requiring special treatment. This is undoubtedly true, but those cases, the *Second Employers' Liability Cases,* 223 U.S. 1; *New York Central R. R. Co. v. White,*

243 U.S. 188; *Hawkins v. Bleakly,* 243 U.S. 210; *Mountain Timber Co. v. Washington,* 243 U.S. 219; *Middleton v. Texas Power & Light Co.,* 249 U.S. 152 and *Arizona Employers' Liability Cases,* 250 U.S. 400, as we have already pointed out in discussing the due process clause, were cases of the responsibility of the employer for injuries sustained by employees in the course of their employment. The general end of such legislation is that the employer shall become the insurer of the employee against injuries from the employment without regard to the negligence, if any, through which it occurred, leaving to the employer to protect himself by insurance and to compensate himself for the additional cost of production by adding to the prices he charges for his products. It seems a far cry from classification on the basis of the relation of employer and employee in respect of injuries received in course of employment to classification based on the relation of an employer, not· to an employee, but to one who has ceased to be so, in respect of torts thereafter committed by such ex-employee on the business and property right of the employer. It is really a little difficult to say, if such classification can be sustained, why special legislative treatment of assaults upon an employer or his employees by ex-employees may not be sustained with equal reason. It is said the State may deal separately with such disputes because such controversies are a frequent and characteristic outgrowth of disputes over terms and conditions of employment. Violence of ex-employees toward present employees is also a characteristic of such disputes. Would this justify a legislature in excepting ex-employees from criminal prosecution for such assaults and leaving the assaulted persons to suits for damages at common law?

Our conclusion, that plaintiffs are denied the equal protection of the laws, is sustained by the decisions in this court in *Truax v. Raich,* 239 U.S. 33; *Atchison, Topeka & Santa Fe Ry. Co. v. Vosburg,* 238 U.S. 56; *Southern Ry. Co. v. Greene,* 216 U.S. 400; *Connolly v. Union Sewer Pipe Co.,* 184 U.S. 540; *Cotting v. Kansas City Stock Yards Co.,* 183 U.S. 79; *Gulf, Colorado & Santa Fe Ry. Co. v. Ellis,* 165 U.S. 150. In the state courts, we find equal support for it. *Bogni v. Perotti,* 224 Mass. 152; *Pearson v. Portland,* 69 Me. 278; *Goldberg, Bowen & Co. v. Stablemen's Union,* 149 Cal. 429, 434; *Pierce v. Stablemen's Union,* 156 Cal. 70, 74; *Funkhouser v. Randolph,* 287 Ill. 94; *Houston v. Pulitzer Publishing Co.,* 249 Mo. 332; *Phipps v. Wisconsin Central Ry. Co.,* 133 Wisc. 153; *Park v. Detroit Free Press Co.,* 72 Mich. 560; *C., N. O. & T. P. Ry. Co. v. Clark & Bennett,* 11 Ky. Law Rep. 286.

It is urged that in holding Paragraph 1464 invalid, we are in effect holding invalid § 20 of the Clayton Act. Of course, we are not doing so. In the first place, the equality clause of the Fourteenth Amendment does not apply to congressional but only to state action. In the second place, § 20 of the Clayton Act never has been construed or applied as the Supreme Court of Arizona has construed and applied Paragraph 1464 in this case.

We have but recently considered the clauses of § 20 of the Clayton Act, sometimes erroneously called the "picketing" clauses. *American Steel Foundries v. Tri-City Central Trades Council, ante,* 184. They forbid an injunction in labor controversies prohibiting any person "from attending at any place where any such person or persons may lawfully be, for the purpose of peacefully obtaining or communicating information, or from peacefully persuading any person to work or to abstain from working; or from ceasing to patronize or to employ any party to such dispute, or from recommending, advising, or persuading others by peaceful and lawful means so to do."

We held that under these clauses picketing was unlawful, and that it might be enjoined as such, and that peaceful picketing was a contradiction in terms which the statute sedulously avoided, but that, subject to the primary right of the employer and his employees and would-be employees to free access to his premises without obstruction by violence, intimidation, annoyance, importunity or dogging, it was lawful for ex-employees on a strike and their fellows in a labor union to have a single representative at each entrance to the plant of the employer to announce the strike and peaceably to persuade the employees and would-be employees to join them in it. We held that these clauses were merely declaratory of what had always been the law and the best practice in equity, and we thus applied them. The construction put upon the same words by the Arizona Supreme Court makes these clauses of Paragraph 1464 as far from those of § 20 of the Clayton Act in meaning as if they were in wholly different language.

We conclude that the demurrer in this case should have been overruled, the defendants required to answer, and that if the evidence sustained the averments of the complaint, an injunction should issue as prayed.

Objection is made to this conclusion on the ground that as we hold certain clauses of Paragraph 1464 of the Arizona Code, as construed, invalid, they can not be separated from Paragraph 1456 which must also be held invalid and then there is no law in Arizona authorizing an injunction in this or any case. *Connolly* v. *Union Sewer Pipe Co.,* 184 U. S. 540, is cited to sustain this view. There a new anti-trust statute was enacted making criminal and subject to injunction what before had not been so. The exception from its operation of products of the farm in the hands of the producers, contained in the law as enacted, was declared to be a denial of equal protection of the laws, and the whole law was declared invalid because the court in view of the exception could not assume that the legislature would have enacted the law, had it known that the producers of farm products would have come within its terms. But here the case is quite different. Paragraph 1456 has been the statute law of Arizona, State and Territory, since 1901. It was first adopted in the Code of the Territory of 1901. It was continued in force, by virtue of the new constitution of Arizona adopted by the people in 1912, which merely changed the name of the court, upon which general equity jurisdiction was conferred, from the District Court to the

Superior Court, and which provided that the authority, jurisdiction, practice and procedure of the district courts should continue in force and apply and govern superior courts until altered or repealed. Arizona came into the Union with this constitution February 14, 1912. At the session of 1912 provision was made for revision and codification of the laws. The present Code was adopted by the legislature at its third special session of 1913. Paragraph 1464 was passed, as the Code itself states, at the second session of 1913. Thus Paragraph 1464 was an amendment to Paragraph 1456, and was included with the original section in the code revision of 1913. To invalidate Paragraph 1456 we must assume that had the legislature known that the clauses of Paragraph 1464 here involved, construed as the Arizona Supreme Court has construed them, were unconstitutional, it would have repealed all the existing law conferring the equitable power of injunction on its first instance courts of general jurisdiction. We can not make this assumption. The exception introduced by amendment to Paragraph 1456 proving invalid, the original law stands without the amendatory exception.

The judgment of the Supreme Court of Arizona is reversed and the case remanded for further proceedings not inconsistent with this opinion.

MR. JUSTICE HOLMES, dissenting.

The dangers of a delusive exactness in the application of the Fourteenth Amendment have been adverted to before now. *Louisville & Nashville R. R. Co. v. Barber Asphalt Paving Co.,* 197 U.S. 430, 434. Delusive exactness is a source of fallacy throughout the law. By calling a business "property" you make it seem like land, and lead up to the conclusion that a statute cannot substantially cut down the advantages of ownership existing before the statute was passed. An established business no doubt may have pecuniary value and commonly is protected by law against various unjustified injuries. But you cannot give it definiteness of contour by calling it a thing. It is a course of conduct and like other conduct is subject to substantial modification according to time and circumstances both in itself and in regard to what shall justify doing it a harm. I cannot understand the notion that it would be unconsitutional to authorize boycotts and the like in aid of the employees' or the employers' interest by statute when the same result has been reached constitutionally without statute by Courts with whom I agree. See *The Hamilton,* 207 U.S. 398, 404. In this case it does not even appear that the business was not created under the laws as they now are. *Denny v. Bennett,* 128 U.S. 489.

I think further that the selection of the class of employers and employees for special treatment, dealing with both sides alike, is beyond criticism on principles often asserted by this Court. And especially I think that without legalizing the conduct complained of the extraordinary relief by injunction may be denied to the class. Legislation may begin where an evil begins. If, as many intelligent people believe, there is more danger that the injunction will be abused in labor cases than elsewhere I 'can feel no doubt of the power of the legislature to deny it in such cases. I refer to two decisions in which I have stated what I understand to be the law sanctioned by many other decisions. *Carroll v. Greenwich Insurance Co.*, 199 U.S. 401, 411. *Quong Wing v. Kirkendall*, 223 U.S. 59.

In a matter like this I dislike to turn attention to anything but the fundamental question of the merits, but *Connolly v. Union Sewer Pipe Co.*, 184 U.S. 540, raises at least a doubt in my mind of another sort. The exception and the rule as to granting injunctions are both part of the same code, enacted at the same time. If the exception fails, according to the *Connolly Case* the statute is bad as a whole. It is true that here the exception came in later than the rule, but after they had been amalgamated in a single act I cannot know that the later legislature would have kept the rule if the exception could not be allowed. If labor had the ascendancy that the exception seems to indicate, I think that probably it would have declined to allow injunctions in any case if that was the only way of reaching its end. But this is a matter upon which the State Court has the last word, and if it takes this view its decision must prevail. I need not press further the difficulty of requiring a State Court to issue an injunction that it never has been empowered to issue by the quasi-sovereign that created the Court.

I must add one general consideration. There is nothing that I more deprecate than the use of the Fourteenth Amendment beyond the absolute compulsion of its words to prevent the making of social experiments that an important part of the community desires, in the insulated chambers afforded by the several States, even though the experiments may seem futile or even noxious to me and to those whose judgment I most respect. I agree with the more elaborate expositions of my brothers Pitney and Brandeis and in their conclusion that the judgment should be affirmed.

MR. JUSTICE BRANDEIS, dissenting.

The first legislature of the State of Arizona adopted in 1913 a Civil Code. By Title 6, c. III, it sets forth conditions and circumstances under which the courts of the State may or may not grant injunctions. Paragraph 1464 contains, among other things, a prohibition against interfering by injunction between employers and employees, in any case growing out of a dispute concerning terms or conditions of employment, unless interposition by injunction is necessary to protect property from injury through violence. Its main purpose was doubtless to prohibit the courts from enjoining peaceful picketing and the boycott. With the wisdom of the statute we have no concern. Whether Arizona in enacting this statute transgressed limitations imposed upon the power of the States by the Fourteenth Amendment is the question presented for decision.

The employer has, of course, a legal right to carry on his business for profit; and incidentally the subsidiary rights to secure and retain customers, to fix such prices for his product as he deems proper, and to buy merchandise and labor at such prices as he chooses to pay. This right to carry on business—be it called liberty or property—has value; and, he who interferes with the right without cause renders himself liable. But for cause the right may be interfered with and even be destroyed. Such cause exists when, in the pursuit of an equal right to further their several interests, his competitors make inroads upon his trade, or when suppliers of merchandise or of labor make inroads upon his profits. What methods and means are permissible in this struggle of contending forces is determined in part by decisions of the courts, in part by acts of the legislatures. The rules governing the contest necessarily change from time to time. For conditions change; and, furthermore, the rules evolved, being merely experiments in government, must be discarded when they prove to be failures.

Practically every change in the law governing the relation of employer and employee must abridge, in some respect, the liberty or property of one of the parties—if liberty and property be measured by the standard of the law theretofore prevailing. If such changes are made by acts of the legislature, we call the modification an exercise of the police power. And, although the change may involve interference with existing liberty or property of individuals, the statute will not be declared a violation of the due process clause, unless the court finds that the interference is arbitrary or unreasonable or that, considered as a means, the measure has no real or substantial relation of cause to a permissible end.[1] Nor will such changes in the law governing contests between employer and employee be held to be violative of the equal protection clause, merely because the liberty or property of individuals in other relations to each other (for instance, as competitors in trade or as vendor and purchaser) would not, under similar circumstances, be subject to like abridgement. Few laws are of universal application. It is of the nature of our law that it has dealt not with man in general but with him in relationships. That a peculiar relationship of individuals may furnish legal basis for the classification which satisfies the requirement of the Fourteenth Amendment[2] is clear. That the relation of employer and employee affords a constitutional basis for legislation applicable only to persons standing

---

[1] Muller v. Oregon, 208 U.S. 412; Dominion Hotel v. Arizona, 249 U.S. 265.

[2] "The rule, therefore, is not a substitute for municipal law; it only prescribes that that law have the attribute of equality of operation, and equality of operation does not mean indiscriminate operation on persons merely as such, but on persons according to their relations." Mr. Justice McKenna in Magoun v. Illinois Trust & Savings Bank, 170 U.S. 283, 293.

In Fidelity Mutual Life Association v. Mettler, 185 U.S. 308, and Northwestern National Life Insurance Co. v. Riggs, 203 U.S. 243, the relation of insurer and insured was made the subject of regulation; in Western Union Telegraph Co. v. Commercial Milling Co., 218 U.S. 406; Seaboard Air Line Ry. v. Seegers, 207 U.S. 73; Yazoo & Mississippi Valley R. R. Co. v. Jackson Vinegar Co., 226 U.S. 217, that of public utility and patron; in Noble State Bank v. Haskell, 219 U.S. 104, that of banker and depositor; in St. Louis & San Francisco Ry. Co. v. Mathews, 165 U.S. 1; Missouri, Kansas & Texas Ry. Co. v. May, 194 U.S. 267; and Minneapolis & St. Louis Ry. Co. v. Emmons, 149 U.S. 364, that of railway and adjoining landowner.

in that relation has been repeatedly held by this court.[3] The questions submitted are whether this statutory prohibition of the remedy by injunction is in itself arbitrary and so unreasonable as to deprive the employer of liberty or property without due process of law;—and whether limitation of this prohibition to controversies involving employment denies him equal protection of the laws.

Whether a law enacted in the exercise of the police power is justly subject to the charge of being unreasonable or arbitrary, can ordinarily be determined only by a consideration of the contemporary conditions, social, industrial and political, of the community to be affected thereby. Resort to such facts is necessary, among other things, in order to appreciate the evils sought to be remedied and the possible effects of the remedy proposed. Nearly all legislation involves a weighing of public needs as against private desires; and likewise a weighing of relative social values. Since government is not an exact science, prevailing public opinion concerning the evils and the remedy is among the important facts deserving consideration; particularly, when the public conviction is both deep-seated and widespread and has been reached after deliberation.[4] What, at any particular time, is the paramount public need is, necessarily, largely a matter of judgment. Hence, in passing upon the validity of a law challenged as being unreasonable, aid may be derived from the experience of other countries and of the several States of our Union in which the common law and its conceptions of liberty and of property prevail. The history of the rules governing contests between employer and employed in the several English-speaking countries illustrates both the susceptibility of such rules to change and the variety of contemporary opinion as to what rules will best serve the public interest. The divergence of opinion in this difficult field of governmental action should admonish us not to declare a rule arbitrary and unreasonable merely because we are convinced that it is fraught with danger to the public weal, and thus to close the door to experiment within the law.

In England a workingman struggling to improve his condition, even when acting singly, was confronted until 1813 with laws limiting the amount of wages which he might demand.[5] Until 1824 he was punishable as a criminal if he combined with his fellow workmen to raise wages or shorten hours or to affect the business in any way, even if there

---

[3] Holden v. Hardy, 169 U.S. 366; St. Louis, Iron Mountain & St. Paul Ry. Co. v. Paul, 173 U.S. 404; Tullis v. Lake Erie & Western R. R. Co., 175 U.S. 348; Knoxville Iron Co. v. Harbison, 183 U.S. 13; Atkin v. Kansas, 191 U.S. 207; Great Southern Hotel Co. v. Jones, 193 U.S. 532; Minnesota Iron Co. v. Kline, 199 U.S. 593; Wilmington Star Mining Co. v. Fulton, 205 U.S. 60; Muller v. Oregon, 208 U.S. 412; McLean v. Arkansas, 211 U.S. 539; Louisville & Nashville R. R. Co. v. Melton, 218 U. S. 36; Mobile, Jackson & Kansas City R. R. Co. v. Turnipseed, 219 U.S. 35; Chicago, Rock Island & Pacific Ry. Co. v. Arkansas, 219 U.S. 453; Arizona Employers' Liability Cases, 250 U.S. 400. Compare: Second Employers' Liability Cases, 223 U.S. 1.

[4] Muller v. Oregon, 208 U.S. 412, 420.

[5] 53 Geo. 3, c. 40. For the earlier law see, for instance, 23 Edw. 3, c. 1-8; 25 Edw. 3, c. 1-7, The Statutes of Laborers; 5 Eliz., c. 4; 1 Jac. 1, c. 6.

was no resort to a strike.[6] Until 1871 members of a union who joined in persuading employees to leave work were liable criminally, although the employees were not under contract and the persuasion was both peaceful and unattended by picketing.[7] Until 1871 threatening a strike, whatever the cause, was also a criminal act.[8] Not until 1875 was the right of workers to combine in order to attain their ends conceded fully. In that year Parliament declared that workmen combining in furtherance of a trade dispute should not be indictable for criminal conspiracy unless the act if done by one person would be indictable as a crime.[9] After that statute a combination of workmen to effect the ordinary objects of a strike was no longer a criminal offense. But picketing, though peaceful, in aid of a strike, remained illegal;[10] and likewise the boycott.[11] Not until 1906 was the ban on peaceful picketing and the bringing of pressure upon an employer by means of a secondary strike or a boycott removed.[12] In 1906, also, the act of inducing workers to break their contract of employment (previously held an actionable wrong)[13] was expressly declared legal.[14] In England improvement of the condition of workingmen and their emancipation appear to have been deemed recently the paramount public need.

---

[6] 5 Geo. 4, c. 95, (replaced by 6 Geo. 4, c. 129). For the earlier law see, for instance, 34 Edw. 3, c. 9; The King v. Journeymen Tailors of Cambridge, 8 Modern, 10; Wright, The Law of Criminal Conspiracies.

[7] Criminal Law Amendment Act (1871), 34 & 35 Vic., c. 32, § 1, last paragraph. For the earlier law see Regina v. Rowlands, 2 Den. 363.

[8] Criminal Law Amendment Act (1871), 34 & 35 Vic., c. 32, § 1, sub-sec. 2. For the earlier law see Walsby v. Anley, 3 E. & E. 516; Skinner v. Kitch, 10 Cox C.C. 493; L.R. 2 Q.B. 393 (1867).

[9] The Conspiracy and Protection of Property Act (1875), 38 & 39 Vic., c. 86, § 3. But see Rigby v. Connol, L.R. 14 Ch. D. 482, 491.

[10] 38 & 39 Vic., c. 86, § 7; Regina v. Bauld, 13 Cox C.C. 282; Lyons v. Wilkins, [1896] 1 Ch. 811, 826, 831; [1899] 1 Ch. 255; Taff Vale Ry. Co. v. Amalgamated Society of Railway Servants, [1901] A.C. 426.

[11] Temperton v. Russell, [1893] 1 Q. B. 715; Quinn v. Leathem, [1901] A. C. 495. But compare with these cases Boots v. Grundy, 82 L. T. R. 769; Scottish Co-operative Society v. Glasgow Fleshers, 35 Scottish L. R. 645; Bulcock v. St. Anne's Master Builders' Federation, 19 T. L. R. 27; a distinction between these and the two former is pointed out in Quinn v. Leathem, *supra*, p. 61. The Royal Commission on Trade Disputes and Trade Combinations, whose recommendations were the basis of the Trade Disputes Act, 1906, 6 Edw. 7, c. 47, recommended, Report, p. 16, "that an act should be passed for the following objects:—* * * (2) To declare strikes from whatever motive or for whatever purposes (including sympathetic or secondary strikes), apart from crime or breach of contract, legal * * *." It is probable that §§ 1 and 3 of the Act of 1906 make the secondary strike or boycott in the course of a trade dispute legal. But see note 14, par. 2.

[12] The Trade Disputes Act (1906), 6 Edw. 7, c. 47, § 2.

[13] Read v. Friendly Society of Stonemasons, [1902] 2 K.B. 88; *id.*, 732; South Wales Miners' Federation v. Glamorgan Coal Co., [1905] A.C. 239.

[14] 6 Edw. 7, c. 47, § 3, "An act done by a person in contemplation or furtherance of a trade dispute shall not be actionable on the ground only that it induces some other person to break a contract of employment or that it is an interference with the trade, business, or employment of some other person, or with the right of some other person to dispose of his capital or his labour as he wills." But the employee who breaks his contract remains personally liable in damages.

The law of England still prohibits certain practices which might prove effective in the struggle between employer and employee. Thus the Trade Disputes Act, *supra,*

In the British Dominions the .rules governing the struggle between employer and employed were likewise subjected to many modifications; but the trend of social experiment took a direction very different from that followed in the mother country. Instead of enabling the worker to pursue such methods as he might deem effective in the contest, statutes were enacted in some of the Dominions which forbade the boycott, peaceful picketing, and even the simple strike and the lockout;[15] use of the injunction to enforce compliance with these prohibitions was expressly sanctioned;[16] and violation of the statute was also made punishable by criminal proceedings.[17] These prohibitions were the concomitants of prescribed industrial arbitration through administrative tribunals by which the right of both employer and employee to liberty and property were seriously abridged in the public interest. Australia[18] and New Zealand[19] made compulsory both arbitration and compliance with the award.[20] Canada limited the compulsion to a postponement of the right

does not sanction some threats or coercion, Conway v. Wade, [1909] A. C. 506, 511. It does not permit a strike to force the discharge of a member of the union who has not paid a fine, Conway v. Wade, *supra*. Nor does it permit inducing an employer's men to break their contracts in order to force him to join an employers' association, since this is not a trade dispute within the meaning of the act, Larkin v. Long, [1915] A. C. 814. The judges are by no means agreed as to what constitutes coercion. Compare: Hodges v. Webb, [1920] 2 Ch. 70; Valentine v. Hyde, [1919] 2 Ch. 129; Pratt v. British Medical Association, [1919] 1 K. B. 244; and Davies v. Thomas, [1920] 1 Ch. 217.

[15] Australia: Commonwealth Conciliation and Arbitration Act, 1904-15, §§ 6-9; New South Wales, Industrial Arbitration Act, 1912-1918, §§ 48D and 48E; compare Queensland, Industrial Arbitration Act, 1916, § 65. New Zealand: Industrial Conciliation and Arbitration Act, 1908, § 108; Industrial Conciliation and Arbitration Amendment Act, 1908, Part I.

[16] The Industrial Disputes Act of New South Wales, 1908, § 60, made strikes and lockouts illegal and the Industrial Arbitration Act, 1912, which replaced it, continued their outlawry, §§ 44-48, and expressly provided that they might be enjoined by the Court of Industrial Arbitration; but by the Act of 1918, § 15, §§ 45 to 48 inclusive of the earlier act, dealing with strikes, were amended:

"45. The following strikes and no others shall be illegal:—

"(a) Any strike by employees of the crown, etc.

"(b) Any strike by the employees in an industry the conditions of which are for the time being wholly or partially regulated by an award or by an industrial agreement: etc.

"(c) Any strike which has been commenced prior to the expiry of fourteen clear days notice in writing of intention to commence the same or of the existence of such conditions as would be likely to lead to the same given the Minister, etc.

"46. In the event of an illegal strike occurring in any industry, the court may order any trade union, whose executive or members are taking part in or aiding or abetting the strike, to pay a penalty not exceeding five hundred pounds."

The Commonwealth Conciliation and Arbitration Act, 1904, § 38(e), provides that the Court of Arbitration and Conciliation shall have power "to enjoin any organization or person from committing or continuing any contravention of this Act."

[17] See note 15, *supra.*

[18] The Commonwealth Conciliation and Arbitration Act, 1904-1915, §§ 19-31. (Printed as Appendix A to Commonwealth Acts 1914-1915.) See Henry B .Higgins, "A New Province for Law and Order," 29 Harv. Law Rev. 13; 32 Harv. Law Rev. 189; 34 Harv. Law Rev. 105.

[19] Industrial Conciliation and Arbitration Act, 1908, *supra*, §§ 53-104, as amended by Acts 1908, No. 239, Part II; Acts 1911, No. 33; Acts 1913, No. 7.

[20] Compare Kansas act creating a court of industrial relations, Laws 1920, c. 29. State v. Howat, 107 Kan. 423; State v. Howat, 109 Kan. 376; Court of Industrial Relations v. Charles Wolff Packing Co., 109 Kan. 629.

to strike until the dispute should have been officially investigated and re-ported upon.[21] In these Dominions the uninterrupted pursuit of indus-try and the prevention of the arbitrary use of power appear to be deemed the paramount public needs.

In the United States the rules of the common law governing the struggle between employer and employee have likewise been subjected to modifications. These have been made mainly through judicial decisions. The legal right of workingmen to combine and to strike in order to secure for themselves higher wages, shorter hours and better working conditions received early general recognition.[22] But there developed great diversity of opinion as to the means by which,[23] and also as to the persons through whom,[24] and upon whom [25] pressure might permissibly be exerted in order

---

[21] Industrial Disputes Investigation Act, 1907, 6-7 Edw. 7, c. 20, §§ 56, 57. Rex v. McGuire, 16 O.L.R. 522. 9-10 Edw. 7, c. 29. 8-9 Geo. 5, c. 27. 10-11 Geo. 5, c. 29.
   Picketing is illegal. Criminal Code, Canada, § 501; Krug Furniture Co. v. Union of Woodworkers, 5 O.L.R. 463; Cotter v. Osborne, 18 Man. 471; Vulcan Iron Works v. Winnipeg Lodge, 21 Man. 473; Le Roi Mining Co. v. Rossland Miners Union, 8 B.C. 370. But see Rev. Stats., B.C., c. 228.

[22] Commonwealth v. Hunt, 4 Met. 111; for earlier common law and statutory provisions see Carew v. Rutherford, 106 Mass. 1, 14; 1 Weeden, Economic and Social History of New England, pp. 173, 334. Freund, Police Power, § 331; 1 Com-mons, History of Labor in the United States, c. 5.

[23] For the boycott see note 28, infra, p. 286; and for peaceful picketing, note 29, infra, p. 287.
   In some jurisdictions the strike was considered an unlawful means of procuring the unionization of the shop,—see Plant v. Woods, 176 Mass. 492; Pickett v. Walsh, 192 Mass. 572, 585; Lucke v. Clothing Cutters' Assembly, 77 Md. 396; Erdman v. Mitchell, 207 Pa. St. 79; Freund, Police Power, § 331;—while in others it was re-garded as permissible,—National Protective Association v. Cumming, 170 N.Y. 315; Kemp v. Division No. 241, 255 Ill. 213; Grant Construction Co. v. St. Paul Building Trades Council, 136 Minn. 167; State v. Van Pelt, 136 N. Car. 633; Jetton-Dekle Lumber Co. v. Mather, 53 Fla. 969; Cohn & Roth Electric Co. v. Bricklayers Union, 92 Conn. 161.

[24] In some jurisdictions the officers of the national union, not being employees, are regarded as outsiders with no justification for their acts,—Booth v. Burgess, 72 N.J. Eq. 181; Jonas Glass Co. v. Glass Bottle Blowers' Association, 72 N.J. Eq. 653; 77 N.J. Eq. 219. In other jurisdictions it is held that they are furthering a legitimate interest,—see Allen v. Flood, [1898] A. C. 1; Jose v. Metallic Roofing Co., [1908] A. C. 514, rev'g 14 O.L.R. 156; Gill Engraving Co. v. Doerr, 214 Fed. 111; Lindsay & Co. v. Montana Federation of Labor, 37 Mont. 264. See American Steel Foundries v. Tri-City Central Trades Council, ante, 131.

[25] In some jurisdictions the courts seek to localize the conflict by making it illegal to bring in any party beyond those between whom the original dispute arose,—Burnham v. Dowd, 217 Mass. 351; Booth v. Burgess, 72 N.J. Eq. 181; Purvis v. United Brotherhood, 214 Pa. St. 348;—in other jurisdictions it is considered that anyone having business relations with either party which bear on the matter in controversy has violated his neutrality and is subject to reprisal from the union which is carrying on the struggle,—Bossert v. Dhuy, 221 N.Y. 342; Master Build-ers' Association v. Domascio, 16 Colo. App. 25; Pierce v. Stablemen's Union, 156 Cal. 70, 76; Cohn & Roth Electric Co. v. Bricklayers Union, 92 Conn. 161; Gill Engraving Co. v. Doerr, 214 Fed. 111; Grant Construction Co. v. St. Paul Building Trades Council, 136 Minn. 167. See 31 Harv. Law Rev. 482, and Auburn Draying Co. v. Wardell, 227 N.Y. 1, for limitations.
   Again, in some states it is unlawful to resort to the method of notifying persons that a strike will occur if a non-union employer or his product is employed,—Booth v. Burgess, 72 N.J. Eq. 181; Gray v. Building Trades Council, 91 Minn. 171;—while in other states it is lawful,—Cohn & Roth Electric Co. v. Bricklayers Union, 92 Conn. 161, 167; Bossert v. Dhuy, 221 N.Y. 342.

to induce the employer to yield to the demands of the workingmen.
Courts were required, in the absence of legislation, to determine what
the public welfare demanded;—whether it would not be best subserved
by leaving the contestants free to resort to any means not involving a
breach of the peace or injury to tangible property; whether it was consistent with the public interest that the contestants should be permitted
to invoke the aid of others not directly interested in the matter in
controversy; and to what extent incidental injury to persons not parties
to the controversy should be held justifiable.

The earliest reported American decision on peaceful picketing appears to have been rendered in 1888;[26] the earliest on boycotting in
1886.[27] By no great majority the prevailing judicial opinion in America
declares the boycott as commonly practiced an illegal means[28] (see *Duplex Printing Press Co. v. Deering,* 254 U.S. 443), while it inclines towards

---

[26] Sherry v. Perkins, 147 Mass. 212; but the doctrine was not established until
eight years later, Vegelahn v. Guntner, 167 Mass. 92.

[27] The earliest reported cases seem to be People v. Wilzig, 4 N.Y. Crim. 403; and
People v. Kostka, 4 N.Y. Crim. 429, both of which occurred in June, 1886; the leading
case of State v. Glidden, 55 Conn. 46, came the next year. Laidler, however, speaks of
an unreported case in 1840; see Laidler, Boycotts and the Labor Struggle, p. 70;
see also 2 Commons, History of Labor in the United States, 267, 317, 364.

[28] Some of the difference of opinion results from a difference in definition. A boycott is sometimes defined so as to entail violence or malicious oppression, State v.
Glidden, 55 Conn. 46; while in other cases it is simply pressure exerted by abstention
from business relations, Mills v. United States Printing Co., 99 App. Div. 605, aff'd
199 N.Y. 76. The terms primary and secondary as describing the boycott are also of
uncertain content. Only a boycott that is free of violence or malevolence is anywhere
held to be lawful. This peaceful boycott in support of a bona fide industrial conflict,
however, is not everywhere held lawful, and its lawfulness often is held to depend on
whether it is used against the industrial antagonist directly (primary boycott) or
against an outsider because of his influence on or connection with the industrial
antagonist (secondary boycott). Holding the boycott, primary and secondary, illegal:
Wilson v. Hey, 232 Ill. 389; Beck v. Railway Teamsters' Union, 118 Mich. 497; Gray v.
Building Trades Council, 91 Minn. 171; Booth v. Burgess, 72 N.J. Eq. 181; Purvis v.
United Brotherhood, 214 Pa. St. 348; Patch Manufacturing Co. v. Protection Lodge,
77 Vt. 294; State v. Glidden, 55 Conn. 46; Crump v. Commonwealth, 84 Va. 927, 939;
Jensen v. Cooks', etc. Union, 39 Wash. 531; Webb v. Cooks', etc. Union, (Texas)
205 S.W. 465; Seubert v. Reiff, 164 N.Y.S. 522; American Federation of Labor v.
Buck's Stove & Range Co., 33 App. D.C. 83; Burnham v. Dowd, 217 Mass. 351; My
Maryland Lodge v. Adt, 100 Md. 238.

Holding primary boycott legal: Foster v. Retail Clerks' Association, 78 N.Y.S.
860, 867; Butterick Publishing Co. v. Typographical Union, 100 N.Y.S. 292; Gill En-
graving Co. v. Doerr, 214 Fed. 111; Empire Theatre Co. v. Cloke, 53 Mont. 183;
Steffes v. Motion Picture Union, 136 Minn. 200; Stoner v. Robert, 43 Wash. (D.C.)
L. Rep. 437; Guethler v. Altman, 26 Ind. App. 587; Pierce v. Stablemen's Union, 156
Cal. 70; Riggs v. Cincinnati Waiters, 5 Ohio N.P., 386; McCormick v. Local Union,
13 Ohio Cir. Ct. (N.S.) 545; Ex parte Sweitzer, 13 Okla. Cr. 154. See Laws of
Utah, 1917, c. 68; Root v. Anderson, (Mo.) 207 S.W. 255.

Holding secondary boycott legal: Bossert v. Dhuy, 221 N.Y. 342—though compare Auburn Draying Co. v. Wardell, 227 N.Y. 1; Stoner v. Robert, 43 Wash. (D.C.)
L. Rep. 437; Lindsay & Co. v. Montana Federation of Labor, 37 Mont. 264; Pierce v.
Stablemen's Union, 156 Cal. 70, 76; Parkinson Co. v. Building Trades Council, 154 Cal.
581; see Marx & Haas Jeans Clothing Co. v. Watson, 168 Mo. 133.

the legality of peaceful picketing.[29] See *American Steel Foundries v. Tri-City Central Trades Council, ante,* 184. But in some of the States, notably New York, both peaceful picketing and the boycott are declared permissible.[30] Judges, being thus called upon to exercise a quasi-legislative function and weigh relative social values, naturally differed in their conclusions on such questions.[31]

In England, observance of the rules of the contest has been enforced by the courts almost wholly through the criminal law or through actions at law for compensation. An injunction was granted in a labor dispute as early as 1868.[32] But in England resort to the injunction has not been frequent and it has played no appreciable part there in the conflict between capital and labor. In America the injunction did not secure recognition as a possible remedy until 1888.[33] When a few years later its use became extensive and conspicuous, the controversy over the remedy overshadowed in bitterness the question of the relative substantive rights of the parties. In the storms of protest against this use many thoughtful lawyers joined.[34] The equitable remedy, although applied in accordance with established practice, involved incidents which, it was asserted, endangered the personal

[29] Holding picketing in itself illegal: Vegelahn v. Guntner, 167 Mass. 92; Pierce v. Stablemen's Union, 156 Cal. 70; Barnes & Co. v. Chicago Typographical Union, 232 Ill. 424; Lyon & Healy v. Piano, etc. Workers' Union, 289 Ill. 176; Beck v. Railway Teamsters' Union, 118 Mich. 497; Clarage v. Luphringer, 202 Mich. 612; Baldwin Lumber Co. v. Brotherhood of Teamsters, etc., 91 N.J. Eq. 240; Baasch v. Cooks Union, 99 Wash. 378; Webb v. Cooks', etc. Union, (Texas) 205 S.W. 465; the Washington Act, 1915, c. 181, declaring picketing to be unlawful, was defeated on referendum in 1916; Atchison, Topeka & Santa Fe Ry. Co. v. Gee, 139 Fed. 582.
  Stating that peaceful picketing is lawful: Riggs v. Cincinnati Waiters, 5 Ohio N.P. 386; McCormick v. Local Union, 13 Ohio Cir. Ct. (N.S.) 545; Jones v. Van Winkle Machine Works, 131 Ga. 336, 340; Karges Furniture Co. v. Amalgamated, etc., Union, 165 Ind. 421, 430, 431; Everett Waddey Co. v. Richmond Typographical Union, 105 Va. 188, 197; Steffes v. Motion Picture Union, 136 Minn. 200,—see also Laws 1917, c. 493; Stoner v. Robert, 43 Wash. (D.C.) L. Rep. 437; Empire Theatre Co. v. Cloke, 53 Mont. 183; Mills v. United States Printing Co., 99 App. Div. 605, affd. 199 N.Y. 76; Ex parte Sweitzer, 13 Okla. Cr. 154; White Mountain Freezer Co. v. Murphy, 78 N.H. 398; see Utah, Laws of 1917, c. 68; American Engineering Co. v. International Moulders Union, 25 Pa. Dist. 564; Iron Molders' Union v. Allis-Chalmers Co., 166 Fed. 45; St. Louis v. Gloner, 210 Mo. 502.
[30] Mills v. United States Printing Co., 99 App. Div. 605, affd. 199 N.Y. 76; see also cases in note 29, *supra,* from Ohio, Minnesota, Montana, and Oklahoma.
[31] Compare: Plant v. Woods, 176 Mass. 492, 502, last paragraph, with Cohn & Roth Electric Co. v. Bricklayers Union, 92 Conn. 161, 167, and, Bossert v. Dhuy, 221 N.Y. 342, 359. See Geldart, The Present Law of Trade Unions and Trade Disputes, p. 24; Hoxie, Trade Unionism in the United States, p. 231; "Strikes and Boycotts," 34 Harv. Law Rev. 880.
[32] Springhead Spinning Co. v. Riley, L.R. 6 Eq. 551.
[33] The earliest case of importance was Sherry v. Perkins, 147 Mass. 212 (1888). But injunctions were granted four or five years earlier. 2 Commons, History of Labor in the United States, 504.
[34] "Government by Injunction," by W. H. Dunbar, 13 Law Quar. Rev. 347; "Government by Injunction," by Charles Noble Gregory, 11 Harv. Law Rev. 487; "Injunction and Organized Labor," by Charles C. Allen, 28 Am. Law Rev. 828; "The Modern Use of Injunctions," by F. J. Stimson, 10 Pol. Sci. Quar. 189; "Strikes and Courts of Equity," by William Draper Lewis, 46 Am. Law Reg. 1; "Government by Injunction," by Percy L. Edwards, 57 Albany Law Jour. 8; "The Abuses of Injunction," by Samuel Seabury, 29 Arena 561; "Government by Injunction," by Cornelius H. Fauntleroy, 69 Cent. Law Jour. 129; "Government by Injunction," by Thomas F. Hargis, 4 Amer. Fed. 227. See Report of U. S. Industrial Commission (1901) vol. XVII, p. 611.

liberty of wage-earners. The acts enjoined were frequently, perhaps usually, acts which were already crimes at common law or had been made so by statutes. The issues in litigation arising out of trade disputes related largely to questions of fact. But in equity issues of fact as of law were tried by a single judge, sitting without a jury. Charges of violating an injunction were often heard on affidavits merely, without the opportunity of confronting or cross-examining witnesses.[35] Men found guilty of contempt were committed in the judge's discretion, without either a statutory limit upon the length of the imprisonment, or the opportunity of effective review on appeal, or the right to release on bail pending possible revisory proceedings.[36] The effect of the proceeding upon the individual was substantially the same as if he had been successfully prosecuted for a crime; but he was denied, in the course of the equity proceedings, those rights which by the Constitution are commonly secured to persons charged with a crime.

It was asserted that in these proceedings an alleged danger to property, always incidental and at times insignificant, was often laid hold of to enable the penalties of the criminal law to be enforced expeditiously without that protection to the liberty of the individual which the Bill of Rights was designed to afford; that through such proceedings a single judge often usurped the functions not only of the jury but of the police department; that, in prescribing the conditions under which strikes were permissible and how they might be carried out, he usurped also the powers of the legislature; and that incidentally he abridged the constitutional rights of individuals to free speech, to a free press and to peaceful assembly.

It was urged that the real motive in seeking the injunction was not ordinarily to prevent property from being injured nor to protect the owner in its use, but to endow property with active, militant power which would make it dominant over men. In other words, that, under the guise of protecting property rights, the employer was seeking sovereign power. And many disinterested men, solicitous only for the public welfare, believed that the law of property was not appropriate for dealing with the forces beneath social unrest; that in this vast struggle it was unwise to throw the power of the State on one side or the other according to principles deduced from that law; that the problem of the control and con-

---

[35] In Long v. Bricklayers, etc. Union, 17 Pa. Dist. 984, the judge prefaced his opinion as follows, "Hardly anything of greater private or public gravity is ever presented to the court, and yet these matters are constantly receiving adjudication without a single witness brought before the judge. It is a bad practice. I confess my inability to determine with any satisfaction from an inspection of inanimate manuscript, questions of veracity. In disposing of the present rule, I am compelled to find, as best I may from perusing two hundred and thirty-five lifeless typewritten pages of conflicting evidence, the facts which must determine respondent's guilt or innocence on the quasi-criminal charge of contempt."

[36] Hake v. People, 230 Ill. 174, 196, discretion of judge; Tinsley v. Anderson, 171 U.S. 101, 107-108, unlimited commitment; State v. Erickson, 66 Wash. 639, 641; State v. Chouteau County Court, 51 Mont. 337, 342; Scoric v. United States, 217 Fed. 871, scope of review; People v. Tefft, 3 Cow. (N.Y.) 340; Matter of Vanderbilt, 4 Johns. Ch. (N.Y.) 57, admission to bail within discretion of judge.

duct of industry demanded a solution of its own; and that, pending the ascertainment of new principles to govern industry, it was wiser for the State not to interfere in industrial struggles by the issuance of an injunction.[37]

After the constitutionality and the propriety of the use of the injunction in labor disputes was established judicially, those who opposed the practice sought the aid of Congress and of state legislatures. The bills introduced varied in character and in scope. Many dealt merely with rights; and, of these, some declared, in effect, that no act done in furtherance of a labor dispute by a combination of workingmen should be held illegal, unless it would have been so if done by a single individual; while others purported to legalize specific practices, like boycotting or picketing. Other bills dealt merely with the remedy; and of these, some undertook practically to abolish the use of the injunction in labor disputes, while some merely limited its use either by prohibiting its issue under certain conditions or by denying power to restrain certain acts. Some bills undertook to modify both rights and remedies.[38] These legislative proposals occupied the attention of Congress during every session but one in the twenty years between 1894 and 1914.[39] Reports recommending such legislation were repeatedly made by the Judiciary Committee of the House or that of the Senate; and at some sessions by both.[40] Prior to 1914, legislation of this character had at several sessions passed the House;[41] and in that year Congress passed and the President approved

---

[37] See Final Report of the (U.S.) Industrial Commission (1902); Final Report of the (U.S.) Commission on Industrial Relations (1915), (Sen. Doc. 415, 64th Cong., 1st sess.), vol. 1, pp. 52-53, 90-92, vol. 11, testimony of Mr. Gilbert E. Roe, p. 10477; testimony of Mr. Arthur Woods, p. 10550; testimony of Dr. Frank Goodnow, p. 10599. American Federationist. vol. 7, p. 350; vol. 9, p. 685; vol. 15, p. 976.

[38] 53rd Cong.: S. 1563, S. 1898, S. 2253, H.R. 7362, H.R. 7363; 54th Cong.: S. 237, S. 1750, S. 2984, H.R. 319; 56th Cong.: S. 4233, H.R. 8917; 57th Cong.: S. 1118, S. 4553, H.R. 9678, H.R. 11060; 58th Cong.: H.R. 89, H.R.1234, H.R. 4063, H.R. 6782, H.R. 8136, H.R. 18327; 59th Cong.: S. 2829. H.R. 4445, H.R. 9328, H.R. 17976, H.R. 18171, H.R. 18446, H.R. 18752; 60th Cong.: S. 4533, S. 4727, S. 5888, H.R. 69, H.R. 94, H.R. 17137, H.R. 21358, H.R. 21359, H.R. 21454, H.R. 21489, H.R. 21539, H.R. 21629, H.R. 21991, H.R. 22010, H.R. 22032, H.R. 22298, H.R. 26300, H.R. 24781, H.R. 36609; 61st Cong.: S. 3291, S. 4481, H.R. 3058, H.R. 9766, H.R. 10890, H.R. 16026, H.R. 18410, H.R. 20486, H.R. 20680, H.R. 20827, H.R. 21334, H.R. 22566; 62nd Cong.: S. 6266, H.R. 4015, H.R. 4651, H.R. 5328, H.R. 5606, H.R. 9435, H.R. 11032, H.R. 23189, H.R. 21486, H.R. 21595, H.R. 22208, H.R. 22349, H.R. 22354, H.R. 22355, H.R. 23635; 63rd Cong.: S. 927, H.R. 1873, H.R. 4659, H.R. 5484, H.R. 15657—which became the Clayton Act.

[39] See note 38, supra. Also 53rd Cong.: resolutions to investigate the use of the injunction in certain cases, 26 Cong. Rec. 2466; 56th Cong.: debate, 34 Cong. Rec. 2589; 60th Cong.: hearings, Sen. Doc. 525; special message of the President, Sen. Doc. 213. 42 Cong. Rec. 1347; papers relating to injunctions in labor cases, Sen. Docs. 504 and 524; 61st Cong.: debate, 45 Cong. Rec. 343; 62nd Cong.: debate, 48 Cong. Rec. 6415-6470; hearings, Sen. Doc. 944; petitions, Sen. Doc. 440; hearings before the House Committee on the Judiciary, Jan. 11, 17-19, February 8, 14, 1912; hearings before a subcommittee of Senate Committee on the Judiciary, 62nd Cong., 2nd sess.; 63rd Cong., see debates on H.R. 15657 (the Clayton Act).

[40] 54th Cong., H.R. No. 2471; 56th Cong. H.R. No. 1987, 2007; 57th Cong. S.R. No. 1650, H.R. No. 1522; 62nd Cong. H.R. No. 612; 63rd Cong. S.R. No. 698, H.R. No. 627, Conference Report, Sen. Doc. 585.

[41] In the 57th Cong., H.R. 11060 passed the House, 35 Cong. Rec. 4995. In the 62nd Cong., H.R. 23635 passed the House, 48 Cong. Rec. 6470, 6471.

the Clayton Act, § 20 of which is substantially the same as Paragraph 1464 of the Arizona Civil Code. Act of October 15, 1914, c. 323, 38 Stat. 730, 738.

Such was the diversity of view concerning peaceful picketing and the boycott expressed in judicial decisions and legislation in English-speaking countries when in 1913 the new State of Arizona, in establishing its judicial system, limited the use of the injunction and when in 1918 its Supreme Court was called upon to declare for the first time the law of Arizona on these subjects. The case of *Truax v. Bisbee Local No. 380*, 19 Ariz. 379, presented facts identical with those of the case at bar.[42] In that case the Supreme Court made its decision on four controverted points of law. In the first place, it held that the officials of the union were not outsiders with no justification for their acts (19 Ariz. 379, 390).[43] In the second place, rejecting the view held by the federal courts and the majority of the state courts on the illegality of the boycott, it specifically accepted the law of New York, Montana and California, citing the decisions of those States (19 Ariz. 379, 388, 390).[44] In the third place, it rejected the law of New Jersey, Minnesota and Pennsylvania that it is illegal to circularize an employer's customers, and again adopted the rule declared in the decisions of the courts of New York, Montana, California and Connecticut (19 Ariz. 379, 389).[45] In deciding these three points the Supreme Court of Arizona made a choice between well-established precedents laid down on either side by some of the strongest courts in the country. Can this court say that thereby it deprived the plaintiff of his property without due process of law?

The fourth question requiring decision was whether peaceful picketing should be deemed legal. Here, too, each of the opposing views had the support of decisions of strong courts.[46] If the Arizona court had decided that by the common law of the State the defendants might peacefully picket the plaintiffs, its decision, like those of the courts of Ohio, Minnesota, Montana, New York, Oklahoma and New Hampshire, would surely not have been open to objection under the Federal Constitution; for this court has recently held that peaceful picketing is not unlawful. *American Steel Foundries v. Tri-City Central Trades Council, supra*. The Supreme Court of Arizona found it unnecessary to determine what was

---

[42] In this case the Supreme Court of Arizona said: "This action is founded upon the identical facts upon which the case of Truax v. Bisbee Local No. 380, 19 Ariz. 379, was founded. * * * The questions presented in this record were necessarily decided by this court in the former hearing of the matter." Truax v. Corrigan, 20 Ariz. 7, 8.

[43] See note 24, p. 285, *supra*.

[44] See note 28, p. 286, *supra*.

[45] See note 25, p. 285, *supra*, 2nd paragraph; also Lindsay & Co. v. Montana Federation of Labor, 37 Mont. 264; Parkinson Co. v. Building Trades Council, 154 Cal. 581.

[46] See note 29, p. 287, *supra*.

the common law of the State on that subject, because it construed Paragraph 1464 of the Civil Code as declaring peaceful picketing to be legal. In the case at bar, commenting on the earlier case, the court said: "The statute adopts the view of a number of courts which have held 'picketing,' if peaceably carried on for a lawful purpose, to be no violation of any legal right of the party whose place of business is 'picketed,' and whether as a fact the picketing is carried on by peaceful means, as against the other view, taken by the federal courts and many of the state courts, that picketing is *per se* unlawful." Shortly before that decision the Criminal Court of Appeals of Oklahoma had placed a similar construction upon a statute of that State, declaring that "the doctrine [that picketing is not *per se* unlawful] represents the trend of legal thought of modern times, and is specifically reflected in the statute above construed." *Ex parte Sweitzer,* 13 Okl. Cr. 154, 160. See *St. Louis v. Gloner,* 210 Mo. 502. A State, which despite the Fourteenth Amendment possesses the power to impose on employers without fault unlimited liability for injuries suffered by employees,[47] and to limit the freedom of contract of some employers and not of others,[48] surely does not lack the power to select for its citizens that one of conflicting views on boycott by peaceful picketing which its legislature and highest court consider will best meet its conditions and secure the public welfare.

The Supreme Court of Arizona, having held as a rule of substantive law that the boycott as here practiced was legal at common law; and that the picketing was peaceful and, hence, legal under the statute (whether or not it was legal at common law), necessarily denied the injunction, since, in its opinion, the defendants had committed no legal wrong and were threatening none. But even if this court should hold that an employer has a constitutional right to be free from interference by such a boycott or that the picketing practiced was not in fact peaceful, it does not follow that Arizona would lack the power to refuse to protect that right by injunction. For it is clear that the refusal of an equitable remedy for a tort is not necessarily a denial of due process of law. And it seems to be equally clear that such refusal is not necessarily arbitrary and unreasonable when applied to incidents of the relation of employer and employee. The considerations which show that the refusal is not arbitrary or unreasonable show likewise that such refusal does not necessarily constitute a denial of equal protection of the laws merely because some, or even the same, property rights which are excluded by this statute from protection by injunction, receive such protection under other circumstances or between persons standing in different relations. The acknowledged legislative discretion exerted in classification, so frequently applied in

---

[47] Arizona Employers' Liability Cases, 250 U.S. 400.
[48] Dominion Hotel v. Arizona, 249 U.S. 265.

defining rights, extends equally to the grant of remedies.[49] It is for the legislature to say—within the broad limits of the discretion which it possesses—whether or not the remedy for a wrong shall be both criminal and civil and whether or not it shall be both at law and in equity.

A State is free since the adoption of the Fourteenth Amendment, as it was before, not only to determine what system of law shall prevail in it, but, also, by what processes legal rights may be asserted, and in what courts they may be enforced. *Missouri v. Lewis,* 101 U.S. 22, 31; *Iowa v. Iowa Central Ry. Co.,* 160 U.S. 389. As a State may adopt or reject trial by jury, *Walker v. Sauvinet,* 92 U.S. 90; or adopting it may retain or discard its customary incidents, *Hayes v. Missouri,* 120 U.S. 68; *Brown v. New Jersey,* 175 U.S. 172; *Maxwell v. Dow,* 176 U.S. 581; as a State may grant or withhold review of a decision by appeal, *Reetz v. Michigan,* 188 U.S. 505; so it may determine for itself, from time to time, whether the protection which it affords to property rights through its courts shall be given by means of the preventive remedy or exclusively by an action at law for compensation.

Nor is a State obliged to protect all property rights by injunction merely because it protects some, even if the attending circumstances are in some respects similar. The restraining power of equity might conceivably be applied to every intended violation of a legal right. On grounds of expediency its application is commonly denied in cases where there is a remedy at law which is deemed legally adequate. But an injunction has been denied on grounds of expediency in many cases where the remedy at law is confessedly not adequate. This occurs whenever a dominant public interest is deemed to require that the preventive remedy, otherwise available for the protection of private rights, be refused and the injured party left to such remedy as courts of law may afford. Thus, courts ordinarily refuse, perhaps in the interest of free speech, to restrain actionable libels. *Boston Diatite Co. v. Florence Manufacturing Co.,* 114 Mass. 69; *Prudential Assurance Co. v. Knott,* L.R. 10 Ch. App. 142. In the interest of personal liberty they ordinarily refuse to enforce specifically, by mandatory injunction or otherwise, obligations involving personal service. *Arthur v. Oakes,* 63 Fed. 310, 318; *Davis v. Foreman,* [1894] 3 Ch. 654, 657; *Gossard v. Crosby.* 132 Ia. 155, 163, 164. In the desire to preserve the separation of governmental powers they have declined to protect by injunction mere political rights, *Giles v. Harris,* 189 U.S. 475; and have refused to interfere with the

---

[49] In Gooch v. Stephenson, 1 Shepley (Me.) 371 (1836), the plaintiff attacked as unconstitutional a statute declaring that no action of trespass should be brought against an owner of cattle breaking through an insufficient fence. The court, *inter alia,* said:

"It has been insisted that justice and the security of rights is best promoted by maintaining the remedy as it before existed; but that is an argument which addresses itself to the legislative power, and not to the judicial. * * * It was for the legislature to determine what protection should be thrown around this species of property; * * * and where he [the owner] might invoke the aid of courts of justice. They have no power to take away vested rights; but they may regulate their enjoyment."

In this case the public importance of good fences was held to justify the denial of an existing remedy for injuries to property or a curtailment of the right.

operations of the police department. *Davis v. American Society for the Prevention of Cruelty to Animals,* 75 N.Y. 362; *Delaney v. Flood,* 183 N.Y. 323; compare *Bisbee v. Arizona Insurance Agency,* 14 Ariz. 313. Instances are numerous where protection to property by way of injunction has been refused solely on the ground that serious public inconvenience would result from restraining the act complained of. Such, for example, was the case where a neighboring land owner sought to restrain a smelter from polluting the air, but that relief, if granted would have necessitated shutting down the plant and this would have destroyed the business and impaired the means of livelihood of a large community.[50] There are also numerous instances where the circumstances would, according to general equity practice, have justified the issue of an injunction, but it was refused solely because the right sought to be enforced was created by statute, and the courts, applying a familiar rule, held that the remedy provided by the statute was exclusive.[51]

Such limitations upon the use of the injunction for the protection of private rights have ordinarily been imposed in the interest of the public by the court acting in the exercise of its broad discretion. But, in some instances, the denial of the preventive remedy because of a public interest deemed paramount, has been expressly commanded by statute. Thus, the courts of the United States have been prohibited from staying proceedings in any court of a State, Judicial Code, § 265; and also from enjoining the illegal assessment and collection of taxes. Revised Statutes, § 3224; *Snyder v. Marks,* 109 U.S. 189; *Dodge v. Osborn,* 240 U.S. 118. What Congress can do in curtailing the equity power of the federal courts, state legislatures may do in curtailing equity powers of the state court; unless prevented by the constitution of the State. In other words States are free since the adoption of the Fourteenth Amendment as they were before, either to expand or to contract their equity jurisdiction. The denial of the more adequate equitable remedy for private wrongs is in essence an exercise of the police power, by which, in the interest of the public and in order to preserve the liberty and the property of the great majority of the citizens of a State, rights of property and the liberty of the individual must be remoulded, from time to time, to meet the changing needs of society.

For these reasons, as well as for others stated by Mr. Justice Holmes and Mr. Justice Pitney, in which I concur, the judgment of the Supreme Court of Arizona should, in my opinion, be affirmed:—first, because in

---

[50] See McCarthy v. Bunker Hill & Sullivan Mining Co., 164 Fed. 927; Bliss v. Anaconda Copper Mining Co., 167 Fed. 342; 186 Fed. 789; Cameron Furnace Co. v. Pennsylvania Canal Co., 2 Pearson (Pa.) 208; Johnson v. United Railways Co., 227 Mo. 423, 450; Conger v. New York, W. S. & B. R. R. Co., 120 N.Y. 29; Wilkins v. Diven, 106 Kan. 283; Marconi Wireless Telegraph Co. v. Simon, 227 Fed. 906; 231 Fed. 1021.

[51] Dimmick v. Delaware, Lackawanna & Western R. R. Co., 180 Pa. St. 468; Curran v. Delano, 235 Pa. St. 478; Janney v. Buell, 55 Ala. 408; the mechanics' lien, for instance, is not protected by equitable remedies but only by statutory provisions, Chandler v. Hanna, 73 Ala. 390; Walker v. Daimwood, 80 Ala. 245; Phillips on Mechanics Liens, §§ 307, 308.

permitting damage to be inflicted by means of boycott and peaceful picketing Arizona did not deprive the plaintiffs of property without due process of law or deny them equal protection of the laws; and secondly, because, if Arizona was constitutionally prohibited from adopting this rule of substantive law, it was still free to restrict the extraordinary remedies of equity where it considered their exercise to be detrimental to the public welfare, since such restriction was not a denial to the employer either of due process of law or of equal protection of the laws.[52]

ACT OF MARCH 23, 1932.

47 U.S. Stat. 70, c. 90.

* * * SEC. 4.[1] No court of the United States shall have jurisdiction to issue any restraining order or temporary or permanent injunction in any case involving or growing out of any labor dispute to prohibit any person or persons participating or interested in such dispute (as these terms are herein defined) from doing, whether singly or in concert, any of the following acts:

(a) Ceasing or refusing to perform any work or to remain in any relation of employment;

(b) Becoming or remaining a member of any labor organization or of any employer organization, regardless of any such undertaking or promise as is described in section 3 of this Act;

(c) Paying or giving to, or withholding from, any person participating or interested in such labor dispute, any strike or unemployment benefits or insurance, or other moneys or things of value;[2]

-----

[52] The dissenting opinion of Mr. Justice Pitney, with which Mr. Justice Clarke concurred, is omitted.

For comment on the case, see: 10 Cal. Law Rev. 237 (1922); 22 Col. Law Rev. 252 (1922); 7 Corn. Law Quar. 251 (1922); W. Va. Law Quar. 144 (1922); 31 Yale Law Jour. 408 (1922). See also: Powell, "The Supreme Court's Control over the Issue of Injunctions in Labor Disputes," 12 Proc. Acad. Pol. Sci. 37 (1928); Mason, "The Labor Decisions of Chief Justice Taft," 78 Univ. of Pa. Law Rev. 585 (1930); 30 Harv. Law Rev. 75 (1916).

Accord: Bogni v. Perotti, 203 Mass. 25, 112 N.E. 853 (1916).

-----

[1] For §§ 1 to 3 of the act, see, *ante*, p. 183.

[2] *Cf.* Borderland Coal Corp. v. Internat'l U. M. Workers, 275 Fed. 871 (D. Ind. 1921), as modified in Gasaway v. Borderland Coal Corp., 278 Fed. 56 (7th cir. 1921). In United States v. Hayes (D. Ind. 1919), defendant officials of the United Mine Workers of America were enjoined "from issuing any messages of encouragement or exhortation to striking miners or mine workers or unions thereof to abstain from work and not to return to the mines in pursuance of such strike; and from issuing and distributing, or taking any steps to procure the issuance or distribution, to miners and mine workers striking and abstaining from work in pursuance of such strike, of so-called strike benefits or sums of money previously accumulated or subsequently acquired to assist such striking miners and mine workers to subsist while striking or to aid them in any way by reason of or with reference to such strike and abstaining from work. * * *" See: Hearings before a Subcommittee of the Committee on the Judiciary, U.S. Senate, 70th Cong. 1st sess., on S. 1482, 525 (1928).

(d) By all lawful means aiding any person participating or interested in any labor dispute who is being proceeded against in, or is prosecuting, any action or suit in any court of the United States or of any State;[3]

(e) Giving publicity to the existence of, or the facts involved in, any labor dispute, whether by advertising, speaking, patrolling, or by any other method not involving fraud or violence;

(f) Assembling peaceably to act or to organize to act in promotion of their interests in a labor dispute;[4]

(g) Advising or notifying any person of an intention to do any of the acts heretofore specified;

(h) Agreeing with other persons to do or not to do any of the acts heretofore specified; and

(i) Advising, urging, or otherwise causing or inducing without fraud or violence the acts heretofore specified, regardless of any such undertaking or promise as is described in section 3 of this Act.

SEC. 5. No court of the United States shall have jurisdiction to issue a restraining order or temporary or permanent injunction upon the ground that any of the persons participating or interested in a labor dispute constitute or are engaged in an unlawful combination or conspiracy because of the doing in concert of the acts enumerated in section 4 of this Act.

SEC. 6. No officer or member of any association or organization, and no association or organization participating or interested in a labor dispute, shall be held responsible or liable in any court of the United States for the unlawful acts of individual officers, members, or agents, except upon clear proof of actual participation in, or actual authorization of, such acts, or of ratification of such acts after actual knowledge thereof.

SEC. 7. No court of the United States shall have jurisdiction to issue a temporary or permanent injunction in any case involving or growing out of a labor dispute, as herein defined, except after hearing the testimony of witnesses in open court (with opportunity for cross-examination) in support of the allegations of a complaint made under oath, and testimony in opposition thereto, if offered, and except after findings of fact by the court, to the effect—

(a) That unlawful acts have been threatened and will be committed unless restrained or have been committed and will be continued

---

[3] Compare § 8 of the decree in Pittsburgh Terminal Coal Corp. v. United Mine Workers of America, *ante*, p. 258.

[4] In Clearfield Bituminous Coal Corp. v. Phillips (Comm. Pl. Pa. 1927), the defendants were enjoined "from congregating about or near the town of Rossiter where the employees and their families go, from operating and maintaining automobile patrols on the streets and roads of Rossiter, from erecting or causing to be erected or maintaining billboards for purpose of displaying signs warning men to stay away from Rossiter, from congregating on the Magyar Presbyterian Church lot, or any other lot, lots, place, or places at the time the employees of the plaintiff enter the mine and at the time the employees of the plaintiff come out of the mine, from singing song or songs in hearing of the employees of the plaintiff of a threatening or hostile nature." See: Hearings on S. 1482, *supra*.

unless restrained,[5] but no injunction or temporary restraining order shall be issued on account of any threat or unlawful act excepting against the person or persons, association, or organization making the threat or committing the unlawful act or actually authorizing or ratifying the same after actual knowledge thereof;

(b) That substantial and irreparable injury to complainant's property will follow;

(c) That as to each item of relief granted greater injury will be inflicted upon complainant by the denial of relief than will be inflicted upon defendants by the granting of relief;

(d) That complainant has no adequate remedy at law; and

(e) That the public officers charged with the duty to protect complainant's property are unable or unwilling to furnish adequate protection.[6]

Such hearing shall be held after due and personal notice thereof has been given, in such manner as the court shall direct, to all known persons against whom relief is sought, and also to the chief of those public officials of the county and city within which the unlawful acts have been threatened or committed charged with the duty to protect complainant's property: *Provided, however,* That if a complainant shall also allege that, unless a temporary restraining order shall be issued without notice, a substantial and irreparable injury to complainant's property will be unavoidable, such a temporary restraining order may be issued upon testimony under oath, sufficient, if sustained, to justify the court in issuing a temporary injunction upon a hearing after notice. Such a temporary restraining order shall be effective for no longer than five days and shall become void at the expiration of said five days. No temporary restraining order or temporary injunction shall be issued except on condition that complainant shall first file an undertaking with adequate security in an amount to be fixed by the court sufficient to recompense those enjoined for any loss, expense, or damage caused by the improvident or erroneous issuance of such order or injunction, including all reasonable costs (together with a reasonable attorney's fee) and expense of defense against the order or against the granting of any injunctive relief sought in the same proceeding and subsequently denied by the court.

The undertaking herein mentioned shall be understood to signify an agreement entered into by the complainant and the surety upon which a decree may be rendered in the same suit or proceeding against said complainant and surety, upon a hearing to assess damages of which hearing complainant and surety shall have reasonable notice, the said complainant and surety submitting themselves to the jurisdiction of the court for that purpose. But nothing herein contained shall deprive any

---

[5] That threatened future injury rather than past illegal acts is the basis for injunctive relief, see: Exchange Bakery & Restaurant v. Rifkin, *ante*, p. 145; Commercial Binding & Printing Co. v. Tacoma Typographical Union, 85 Wash. 234, 147 Pac. 1143 (1915). But compare: Baasch v. Cooks Union, Local No. 33, 99 Wash. 378, 169 Pac. 843 (1918).

[6] *Cf.* Manker v. Bakers' Internat'l Union, 220 Misc. 516, 221 N.Y.S. 106 (1927).

party having a claim or cause of action under or upon such undertaking from electing to pursue his ordinary remedy by suit at law or in equity.

SEC. 8. No restraining order or injunctive relief shall be granted to any complainant who has failed to comply with any obligation imposed by law which is involved in the labor dispute in question, or who has failed to make every reasonable effort to settle such dispute either by negotiation or with the aid of any available governmental machinery of mediation or voluntary arbitration.[7]

SEC. 9. No restraining order or temporary or permanent injunction shall be granted in a case involving or growing out of a labor dispute, except on the basis of findings of fact made and filed by the court in the record of the case prior to the issuance of such restraining order or injunction; and every restraining order or injunction granted in a case involving or growing out of a labor dispute shall include only a prohibition of such specific act or acts as may be expressly complained of in the bill of complaint or petition filed in such case and as shall be expressly included in said findings of fact made and filed by the court as provided herein.

SEC. 10. Whenever any court of the United States shall issue or deny any temporary injunction in a case involving or growing out of a labor dispute, the court shall, upon the request of any party to the proceedings and on his filing the usual bond for costs, forthwith certify as in ordinary cases the record of the case to the circuit court of appeals for its review. Upon the filing of such record in the circuit court of appeals, the appeal shall be heard and the temporary injunctive order affirmed, modified, or set aside with the greatest possible expedition, giving the proceedings precedence over all other matters except older matters of the same character.

SEC. 11. In all cases arising under this Act in which a person shall be charged with contempt in a court of the United States (as herein defined), the accused shall enjoy the right to a speedy and public trial by an impartial jury of the State and district wherein the contempt shall have been committed: *Provided*, That this right shall not apply to contempts committed in the presence of the court or so near thereto as to interfere directly with the administration of justice or to apply

---

[7] *Cf. contra:* Thomson Machine Co. v. Brown, 89 N.J. Eq. 326, 104 Atl. 129, 108 Atl. 116 (1918) ; Berg Auto Trunk & Specialty Co. v. Wiener, 121 Misc. 796, 200 N.Y.S. 745 (1923). Upon the application of the equitable doctrine of clean hands to the issuance of injunctions in labor disputes, see: Carpenters' Union v. Citizens' Committee to Enforce the Landis Award, 333 Ill. 225, 164 N.E. 393 (1928) ; Sinsheimer v. United Garment Workers, 77 Hun 215, 28 N.Y.S. 321 (1894) ; Segenfeld v. Friedman, 117 Misc. 731, 193 N.Y.S. 128 (1922) ; McGrath v. Norman, 221 App. Div. 804, 223 N.Y.S. 288 (1927) ; Schwartz & Benjamin v. Alexanderson, 138 Misc. 919, 246 N.Y.S. 422 (1930) ; David Adler & Sons Co. v. Maglio, 198 Wis. 24, 228 N.W. 123 (1929). See: 43 Harv. Law Rev. 1120 (1930). *Cf.* Moore Drop Forging Co. v. Fisher, 239 Mass. 434, 132 N.E. 169 (1921).

to the misbehavior, misconduct, or disobedience of any officer of the court in respect to the writs, orders, or process of the court.[8]

SEC. 12. The defendant in any proceeding for contempt of court may file with the court a demand for the retirement of the judge sitting in the proceeding, if the contempt arises from an attack upon the character or conduct of such judge and if the attack occurred elsewhere than in the presence of the court or so near thereto as to interfere directly with the administration of justice. Upon the filing of any such demand the judge shall thereupon proceed no further, but another judge shall be designated in the same manner as is provided by law. The demand shall be filed prior to the hearing in the contempt proceeding.

SEC. 13. When used in this Act, and for the purposes of this Act—

(a) A case shall be held to involve or to grow out of a labor dispute when the case involves persons who are engaged in the same industry, trade, craft, or occupation; or have direct or indirect interests therein; or who are employees of the same employer; or who are members of the same or an affiliated organization of employers or employees; whether such dispute is (1) between one or more employers or associations of employers and one or more employees or associations of employees; (2) between one or more employers or associations of employers and one or more employers or associations of employers; or (3) between one or more employees or associations of employeees and one or more employees or associations of employees; or when the case involves any conflicting or competing interests in a "labor dispute" (as hereinafter defined) of "persons participating or interested" therein (as hereinafter defined).

(b) A person or association shall be held to be a person participating or interested in a labor dispute if relief is sought against him or it, and if he or it is engaged in the same industry, trade, craft, or occupation in which such dispute occurs, or has a direct or indirect interest therein, or is a member, officer, or agent of any association composed in whole or in part of employers or employees engaged in such industry, trade, craft, or occupation.

(c) The term "labor dispute" includes any controversy concerning terms or conditions of employment, or concerning the association or representation of persons in negotiating, fixing, maintaining, changing, or seeking to arrange terms or conditions of employment, regardless of whether or not the disputants stand in the proximate relation of employer and employee.

(d) The term "court of the United States" means any court of the United States whose jurisdiction has been or may be conferred or

---

[8] *Cf.* Michaelson v. United States, 266 U.S. 42 (1924). See: Frankfurter and Landis, "Power of Congress over Procedure in Criminal Contempts in 'Inferior' Federal Courts," 37 Harv. Law Rev. 1010 (1924); 36 Harv. Law Rev. 1012 (1923); Frankfurter and Greene, The Labor Injunction, 189-198 (1930).

defined or limited by Act of Congress, including the courts of the District of Columbia.

Sec. 14. If any provision of this Act or the application thereof to any person or circumstance is held unconstitutional or otherwise invalid, the remaining provisions of the Act and the application of such provisions to other persons or circumstances shall not be affected thereby.

Sec. 15. All Acts and parts of Acts in conflict with the provisions of this Act are hereby repealed.

CHAPTER V.

THE ENDS FOR WHICH MEN MAY STRIKE.

PLANT v. WOODS.

Supreme Judicial Court of Massachusetts. 176 Mass. 492, 57 N.E. 1011 (1900).

BILL IN EQUITY, filed in the Superior Court, by the officers and members "of the voluntary association known as Union 257, Painters and Decorators of America of Springfield, Massachusetts, which Union is affiliated with a national organization of the same name, with headquarters at Lafayette in the State of Indiana," against the officers and members "of the voluntary association known as Union 257, Painters and Decorators of America, which Union is affiliated with a national organization of the same name, with headquarters at Baltimore in the State of Maryland," to restrain the defendants from any acts or the use of any methods tending to prevent the members of the plaintiff association from securing employment or continuing in their employment. Hearing before DEWEY, J., who entered the following decree:

"This cause came on to be heard, and was argued by counsel; and thereupon, on consideration thereof, it is ordered, adjudged, and decreed that the defendant association, the defendants, and each and every of them, their committees, agents, and servants, be restrained and strictly enjoined from interfering and from combining, conspiring, or attempting to interfere, with the employment of members of the plaintiffs' said association, by representing or causing to be represented in express or implied terms, to any employer of said members of plaintiffs' association, or to any person or persons or corporation who might become employers of any of the plaintiffs, that such employers will suffer or are likely to suffer some loss or trouble in their business for employing or continuing to employ said members of plaintiffs' said association; or by representing, directly or indirectly, for the purpose of interfering with the employment of members of the plantiffs' said association, to any who have contracts or may have contracts for services to be performed by employers of members of plaintiffs' said association, that such persons will or are likely to suffer some loss or trouble in their business for allowing such employers of members of plaintiffs' said association (and because they are such employers) to obtain or perform such contracts; or by intimidating, or attempting to intimidate, by threats, direct or indirect, express or implied, of loss or trouble in business, or otherwise, any person or persons or corporation who now are employing or may hereafter employ or desire to employ any of the members of the plaintiffs' said association; or by attempting by any scheme or conspiracy, among themselves or with others, to annoy, hinder, or interfere with, or prevent any person or persons or corporation from employing or continuing to employ a member or members of plaintiffs' said association; or by causing, or attempting to cause, any person to discriminate against any employer of members of plaintiffs' said association (because he is such employer) in giving or allowing the performance of contracts to or by such employer; and from any and all acts, or the use of any methods, which by putting or attempting to put any person or persons or corporation in fear of loss or trouble, will tend to hinder, impede, or obstruct members, or any member, of the plaintiffs' said association from securing employment or continuing in employment. And that the plaintiffs recover their costs, taxed as in an action of law."

The case was reported, at the request of both parties, for the determination of this court. The facts appear in the opinion.

* * *

HAMMOND, J.: This case arises out of a contest for supremacy between two labor unions of the same craft, having substantially the same constitution and by-laws. The chief difference between them is that the plaintiff union is affiliated with a national organization having its headquarters in Lafayette in the State of Indiana, while the defendant union is affiliated with a similar organization having its headquarters in Baltimore in the State of Maryland. The plaintiff union was composed of workmen who in 1897 withdrew from the defendant union.

There does not appear to be anything illegal in the object of either union as expressed in its constitution and by-laws. The defendant union is also represented by delegates in the Central Labor Union, which is an organization composed of five delegates from each trade union in the city of Springfield, and had in its constitution a provision for levying a boycott upon a complaint made by any union.

The case is before us upon a report after a final decree in favor of the plaintiffs, based upon the findings stated in the report of the master.

The contest became active early in the fall of 1898. In September of that year, the members of the defendant union declared "all painters not affiliated with the Baltimore headquarters to be non-union men," and voted to "notify the bosses" of that declaration. The manifest object of the defendants was to have all the members of the craft subjected to the rules and discipline of their particular union, in order that they might have better control over the whole business, and to that end they combined and conspired to get the plaintiffs and each of them to join the defendant association, peaceably if possible, but by threat and intimidation if necessary. Accordingly, on October 7, they voted that "if our demands are not complied with, all men working in shops where Lafayette people are employed refuse to go to work." The plaintiffs resisting whatever persuasive measures, if any, were used by the defendants, the latter proceeded to carry out their plan in the manner fully set forth in the master's report. Without rehearsing the circumstances in detail it is sufficient to say here that the general method of operations was substantially as follows.

A duly authorized agent of the defendants would visit a shop where one or more of the plaintiffs were at work and inform the employer of the action of the defendant union with reference to the plaintiffs, and ask him to induce such of the plaintiffs as were in his employ to sign applications for reinstatement in the defendant union. As to the general nature of these interviews the master finds that the defendants have been courteous in manner, have made no threats of personal violence, have referred to the plaintiffs as non-union men, but have not otherwise represented them as men lacking good standing in their craft; that they have not asked that the Lafayette men be discharged, and in some cases have expressly stated that they did not wish to have them discharged, but only that they sign the blanks for reinstatement in the defendant union. The master, however, further finds, from all the circumstances under which those requests were made, that the defendants intended that employers of Lafayette men should fear trouble in their business if they continued to employ such men, and that employers to whom these requests were made were justified in believing that a failure on the part of their employees who were Lafayette men to sign such reinstatement blanks, and a failure on the part of the employers to discharge them for not doing so, would lead to trouble in the business of the employers in the nature of strikes or a boycott, and the employers to whom these requests were made did believe that such results would follow, and did suggest their belief to the defendants, and the defendants did not deny that such results might occur; that the strikes which did occur appear to have been steps taken by the defendants to obtain the discharge of such employees as were Lafayette men who declined to sign application blanks for reinstatement; that these defendants did not in all cases threaten a boycott of the employers' business, but did threaten that the place of business of at least one such employer would be left off from a so-called "fair list" to be published by the Baltimore Union. The master also found that, from all the evidence presented, the object which the Baltimore men and the defendant association sought to accomplish in all the acts which were testified to was to compel the members of the Lafayette Union to join the Baltimore Union, and as a means to this end they caused strikes to be instituted in the shops where strikes would seriously interfere with the business of the shops, and in all other shops they made such representations as would lead the proprietors thereof to expect trouble in their business.

We have, therefore, a case where the defendants have conspired to compel the members of the plaintiff union to join the defendant union, and to carry out their purpose have resolved upon such coercion and intimidation as naturally may be caused by threats of loss of property by strikes and boycotts, to induce the employers either to get the plaintiffs to ask for reinstatement in the defendant union, or, that failing, then to discharge them. It matters not that this request to discharge has not been expressly made. There can be no doubt, upon the findings of the master and the facts stated in his report, that the compulsory discharge of the plaintiffs in case of non-compliance with the demands of the defendant union is one of the prominent features of the plan agreed upon.

It is well to see what is the meaning of this threat to strike, when taken in connection with the intimation that the employer may "expect trouble in his business." It means more than that the strikers will cease to work. That is only the preliminary skirmish. It means that those who have ceased to work will, by strong, persistent, and organized persuasion and social pressure of every description, do all they can to prevent the employer from procuring workmen to take their places. It means much more. It means that, if these peaceful measures fail, the employer may reasonably expect that unlawful physical injury may be done to his property; that attempts in all the ways practised by organized labor will be made to injure him in his business, even to his ruin, if possible; and that, by the use of vile and opprobrious epithets and other annoying conduct, and actual and threatened personal violence, attempts will be made to intimidate those who enter or desire to enter his employ; and that whether or not all this be done by the strikers or only by their sympathizers, or with the open sanction and approval of the former, he will have no help from them in his efforts to protect himself.

However mild the language or suave the manner in which the threat to strike is made under such circumstances as are disclosed in this case, the employer knows that he is in danger of passing through such an ordeal as that above described, and those who make the threat know that as well as he does. Even if the intent of the strikers, so far as respects their own conduct and influence, be to discountenance all actual or threatened injury to person or property or business, except that which is the direct necessary result of the interruption of the work, and even if their connection with the injurious and violent conduct of the turbulent among them or of their sympathizers be not such as to make them liable criminally or even answerable civilly in damages to those who suffer, still with full knowledge of what is to be expected they give the signal, and in so doing must be held to avail themselves of the degree of fear and dread which the knowledge of such consequences will cause in the mind of those—whether their employer or fellow workmen—against whom the strike is directed; and the measure of coercion and intimidation imposed upon those against whom the strike is threatened or directed is not fully realized until all those probable consequences are considered.

Such is the nature of the threat, and such the degree of coercion and intimidation involved in it.

If the defendants can lawfully perform the acts complained of in the city of Springfield, they can pursue the plaintiffs all over the State in the same manner, and compel them to abandon their trade or bow to the behests of their pursuers.

It is to be observed that this is not a case between the employer and employed, or, to use a hackneyed expression, between capital and labor, but between laborers all of the same craft, and each having the same right as any one of the others to pursue his calling. In this, as in every other case of equal rights, the right of each individual is to be exercised with due regard to the similar right of all others, and the right of one be said to end where that of another begins.

The right involved is the right to dispose of one's labor with full freedom. This is a legal right, and it is entitled to legal protection. Sir William Erle in his book on Trade Unions, page 12, has stated this in the following language, which has been several times quoted with approval by judges in England: "Every person has a right under the law, as between him and his fellow subjects, to full freedom in disposing of his own labor or his own capital according to his own will. It follows that every other person is subject to the correlative duty arising therefrom, and is prohibited from any obstruction to the fullest exercise of this right which can be made compatible with the exercise of similar rights by others. Every act causing an obstruction to another in the exercise of the right comprised within this description—done, not in the exercise of the actor's own right, but for the purpose of obstruction—would, if damage should be caused thereby to the party obstructed, be a violation of this prohibition."

The same rule is stated with care and discrimination by Wells, J. in *Walker v. Cronin,* 107 Mass. 555, 564: "Every one has a right to enjoy the fruits and advantages of his own enterprise, industry, skill and credit. He has no right to be protected against competition; but he has a right to be free from malicious and wanton interference, disturbance or annoyance. If disturbance, or loss, come as a result of competition, or the exercise of like rights by others, it is *damnum absque injuria,* unless some superior right by contract or otherwise is interfered with. But if it come from the merely wanton or malicious acts of others, without the justification of competition or the service of any interest or lawful purpose, it then stands upon a different footing."

In this case the acts complained of were calculated to cause damage to the plaintiffs, and did actually cause such damage; and they were intentionally done for that purpose. Unless, therefore, there was justifiable cause, the acts were malicious and unlawful. *Walker v. Cronin, ubi supra. Carew v. Rutherford,* 106 Mass. 1, and cases cited therein.

The defendants contend that they have done nothing unlawful, and, in support of that contention, they say that a person may work for whom he pleases; and, in the absence of any contract to the contrary, may cease to work when he pleases, and for any reason whatever, whether the same be good or bad; that he may give notice of his intention in advance, with or without stating the reason; that what one man may do several men acting in concert may do, and may agree beforehand that they will do, and may give notice of the agreement; and that all this may be lawfully done notwithstanding such concerted action may, by reason of the consequent interruption of the work, result in great loss to the employer and his other employees, and that such a result was intended. In a general sense, and without reference to exceptions arising out of conflicting public and private interests, all this may be true.

It is said also that, where one has the lawful right to do a thing, the motive by which he is actuated is immaterial. One form of this statement appears in the first head-note in *Allen v. Flood,* as reported in [1898] A.C. 1, as follows: "An act lawful in itself is not converted by a malicious or bad motive into an unlawful act so as to make the doer of the act liable to a civil action." If the meaning of this and similar expressions is that where a person has the lawful right to do a thing irrespective of his motive, his motive is immaterial, the proposition is a mere truism. If, however, the meaning is that where a person, if actuated by one kind of a motive, has a lawful right to do a thing, the act is lawful when done under any conceivable motive, or that an act lawful under one set of circumstances is therefore lawful under every conceivable set of circumstances, the proposition does not commend itself to us as either logically or legally accurate.

In so far as a right is lawful, it is lawful, and in many cases the right is so far absolute as to be lawful whatever may be the motive of the actor, as where one digs upon his own land for water, (*Greenleaf v. Francis,* 18 Pick. 117,) or makes a written lease of his land for the purpose of terminating a tenancy at will, (*Groustra v. Bourges,* 141 Mass. 7,) but in many cases the lawfulness of an act which causes damage to another may depend upon whether the act is for justifiable cause; and this justification may be found sometimes in the circumstances under which it is done irrespective of motive, sometimes in the motive alone, and sometimes in the circumstances and motive combined.

This principle is of very general application in criminal law, and also is illustrated in many branches of the civil law, as in cases of libel and of procuring a wife to leave her husband. *Tasker v. Stanley,* 153 Mass. 148, and cases therein cited. Indeed the principle is a prominent feature underlying the whole doctrine of privilege, malice, and intent. See on this an instructive article in 8 Harvard Law Review, 1, where the subject is considered at some length.

It is manifest that not much progress is made by such general statements as those quoted above from *Allen v. Flood,* whatever may be their meaning.

Still standing for solution is the question, Under what circumstances, including the motive of the actor, is the act complained of lawful, and to what extent?

In cases somewhat akin to the one at bar this court has had occasion to consider the question how far acts, manifestly coercive and intimidating in their nature, which cause damage and injury to the business or property of another, and are done with intent to cause such injury and partly in reliance upon such coercion, are justifiable.

In *Bowen v. Matheson,* 14 Allen, 499, it was held to be lawful for persons engaged in the business of shipping seamen to combine together into a society for the purpose of competing with other persons engaged in the same business, and it was held lawful for them, in pursuance of that purpose, to take men out of a ship, if men shipped by a non-member were in that ship; to refuse to furnish seamen through a non-member; to notify the public that they had combined against non-members, and had "laid the plaintiff on the shelf"; to notify the plaintiff's customers and friends that the plaintiff could not ship seamen for them; and to interfere in all these ways with the business of the plaintiff as a shipping agent, and compel him to abandon the same. The justification for these acts, so injurious to the business of the plaintiff and so intimidating in their nature, is to be found in the law of competition. No legal right of the plaintiff was infringed upon, and, as stated by Chapman, J., in giving the opinion of the court (p. 503), "if their effect is to destroy the business of shipping-masters who are not members of the association, it is such a result as in the competition of business often follows from a course of proceeding that the law permits." The primary object of the defendants was to build up their own business, and this they might lawfully do to the extent disclosed in that case, even to the injury of their rivals.

Similar decisions have been made in other courts where acts somewhat coercive in their nature and effect have been held justifiable under the law of competition. *Mogul Steamship Co. v. McGregor,* [1892] A.C. 25. *Bohn Manuf. Co. v. Hollis,* 54 Minn. 223. *Macauley v. Tierney,* 19 R.I. 255.

On the other hand, it was held in *Carew v. Rutherford,* 106 Mass. 1, that a conspiracy against a mechanic,—who is under the necessity of employing workmen in order to carry on his business,—to obtain a sum of money from him which he is under no legal obligation to pay, by inducing his workmen to leave him, or by deterring others from entering into his employ, or by threatening to do this so that he is induced to pay the money demanded, under a reasonable apprehension that he cannot carry on his business without yielding to the demands, is an illegal, if not a criminal, conspiracy; that the acts done under it are illegal, and that the money thus obtained may be recovered back. Chapman, C.J. speaking for the court, says that there is no doubt that, if the parties under such circumstances succeed in injuring the business of the mechanic, they are liable to pay all the damages done to him.

That case bears a close analogy to the one at bar. The acts there threatened were like those in this case, and the purpose was, in substance, to force the plaintiff to give his work to the defendants, and to extort from him a fine because he had given some of his work to other persons.

Without now indicating to what extent workmen may combine and in pursuance of an agreement may act by means of strikes and boycotts to get the hours of labor reduced or their wages increased, or to procure from their employers any other concession directly and immediately affecting their own interests, or to help themselves in competition with their fellow-workmen, we think this case must be governed by the principles laid down in *Carew v. Rutherford, ubi supra*. The purpose of these defendants was to force the plaintiffs to join the defendant association, and to that end they injured the plaintiffs in their business, and molested and disturbed them in their efforts to work at their trade. It is true they committed no acts of personal violence, or of physical injury to property, although they threatened to do something which might reasonably be expected to lead to such results. In their threat, however, there was plainly that which was coercive in its effect upon the will. It is not necessary that the liberty of the body should be restrained. Restraint of the mind, provided it would be such as would be likely to force a man against his will to grant the thing demanded, and actually has that effect, is sufficient in cases like this. As stated by Lord Bramwell in *Regina v. Druitt,* 10 Cox C.C. 592, 600, "No right of property, or capital, * * * was so sacred, or so carefully guarded by the law of this land, as that of personal liberty. * * * That liberty was not liberty of the body only. It was also a liberty of the mind and will; and the liberty of a man's mind and will, to say how he should bestow himself and his means, his talents, and his industry, was as much a subject of the law's protection as was that of his body."

It was not the intention of the defendants to give fairly to the employer the option to employ them or the plaintiffs, but to compel the latter against their will to join the association, and to that end to molest and interfere with them in their efforts to procure work by acts and threats well calculated by their coercive and intimidating nature to overcome the will.

The defendants might make such lawful rules as they please for the regulation of their own conduct, but they had no right to force other persons to join them.

The necessity that the plaintiffs should join this association is not so great, nor is its relation to the rights of the defendants, as compared with the right of the plaintiffs to be free from molestation, such as to bring the acts of the defendants under the shelter of the principles of trade competition. Such acts are without justification, and therefore are malicious and unlawful, and the conspiracy thus to force the plaintiffs was unlawful. Such conduct is intolerable, and inconsistent with the spirit of our laws.

The language used by this court in *Carew v. Rutherford,* 106 Mass. 1, 15, may be repeated here with emphasis, as applicable to this case: "The acts alleged and proved in this case are peculiarly offensive to the free principles which prevail in this country; and if such practices could enjoy impunity, they would tend to establish a tyranny of irresponsible persons over labor and mechanical business which would be extremely injurious to both." See, in addition to the authorities above cited, *Commonwealth v. Hunt,* 4 Met. 111; *Sherry v. Perkins,* 147 Mass. 212, 214; *Vegelahn v. Guntner,* 167 Mass. 92, 97; St. 1894, c. 508, § 2;[1] *State v. Donaldson,* 3

Vroom, 151; *State v. Stewart,* 59 Vt. 273; *State v. Glidden,* 55 Conn. 46; *State v. Dyer,* 67 Vt. 690; *Lucke v. Clothing Cutters & Trimmers' Assembly,* 77 Md. 396.

As the plaintiffs have been injured by these acts, and there is reason to believe that the defendants contemplate further proceedings of the same kind which will be likely still more to injure the plaintiffs, a bill in equity lies to enjoin the defendants. *Vegelahn v. Guntner, ubi supra.*

Some phases of the labor question have recently been discussed in the very elaborately considered case of *Allen v. Flood, ubi supra.* Whether or not the decision made therein is inconsistent with the propositions upon which we base our decision in this case, we are not disposed, in view of the circumstances under which that decision was made, to follow it. We prefer the view expressed by the dissenting judges, which view, it may be remarked, was entertained not only by three of the nine lords who sat in the case, but also by the great majority of the common law judges who had occasion officially to express an opinion.

There must be, therefore, a decree for the plaintiffs. We think, however, that the clause, "or by causing or attempting to cause, any person to discriminate against any employer of members of plaintiffs' said association (because he is such employer) in giving or allowing the performance of contracts to or by such employer," is too broad and indefinite, inasmuch as it might seem to include mere lawful persuasion and other similar and peaceful acts; and for that reason, and also because so far as respects unlawful acts it seems to cover only such acts as are prohibited by other parts of the decree, we think it should be omitted.

Inasmuch as the association of the defendants is not a corporation, an injunction cannot be issued against it as such, but only against its members, their agents and servants.

As thus modified, in the opinion of the majority of the court, the decree should stand.   *Decree accordingly.*

HOLMES, C.J. When a question has been decided by the court, I think it proper, as a general rule, that a dissenting judge, however strong his convictions may be, should thereafter accept the law from the majority and leave the remedy to the Legislature, if that body sees fit to interfere. If the decision in the present case simply had relied upon *Vegelahn v. Guntner,* 167 Mass. 92, I should have hesitated to say anything, although I might have stated that my personal opinion had not been weakened by the substantial agreement with my views to be found in the judgments of the majority of the House of Lords in *Allen v. Flood,* [1898] A.C. 1.

---

[1] This section is as follows: "No person shall, by intimidation or force, prevent or seek to prevent a person from entering into or continuing in the employment of any person or corporation." For similar legislation, see: Hallerstein, "Picketing Legislation and the Courts," 10 N.C. Law Rev. 158, 168 (1932). Compare the conclusion of the Court of Criminal Appeal in Rex v. Jones, London Times, Dec. 18, 1928, that a representation by a union official that his men would quit unless a non-union man was discharged was "intimidation" within the meaning of Section 3 of the Trade Disputes and Trade Unions Act, 1927, and as such criminal.—Ed.

But much to my satisfaction, if I may say so, the court has seen fit to adopt the mode of approaching the question which I believe to be the correct one, and to open an issue which otherwise I might have thought closed. The difference between my brethren and me now seems to be a difference of degree, and the line of reasoning followed makes it proper for me to explain where the difference lies.

I agree that the conduct of the defendants is actionable unless justified. *May v. Wood,* 172 Mass. 11, 14, and cases cited. I agree that the presence or absence of justification may depend upon the object of their conduct, that is, upon the motive with which they acted. *Vegelahn v. Guntner,* 167 Mass. 92, 105, 106. I agree, for instance, that if a boycott or a strike is intended to override the jurisdiction of the courts by the action of a private association, it may be illegal. *Weston v. Barnicoat,* 175 Mass. 454. On the other hand, I infer that a majority of my brethren would admit that a boycott or strike intended to raise wages directly might be lawful, if it did not embrace in its scheme or intent violence, breach of contract, or other conduct unlawful on grounds independent of the mere fact that the action of the defendants was combined. A sensible workingman would not contend that the courts should sanction a combination for the purpose of inflicting or threatening violence or the infraction of admitted rights. To come directly to the point, the isssue is narrowed to the question whether, assuming that some purposes would be a justification, the purpose in this case of the threatened boycotts and strikes was such as to justify the threats. That purpose was not directly concerned with wages. It was one degree more remote. The immediate object and motive was to strengthen the defendants' society as a preliminary and means to enable it to make a better fight on questions of wages or other matters of clashing interests. I differ from my brethren in thinking that the threats were as lawful for this preliminary purpose as for the final one to which strengthening the union was a means. I think that unity of organization is necessary to make the contest of labor effectual, and that societies of laborers lawfully may employ in their preparation the means which they might use in the final contest.

Although this is not the place for extended economic discussion, and although the law may not always reach ultimate economic conceptions, I think it well to add that I cherish no illusions as to the meaning and effect of strikes. While I think the strike a lawful instrument in the universal struggle of life, I think it pure phantasy to suppose that there is a body of capital of which labor as a whole secures a larger share by that means. The annual product, subject to an infinitesimal deduction for the luxuries of the few, is directed to consumption by the multitude, and is consumed by the multitude, always. Organization and strikes may get a larger share for the members of an organization, but, if they do, they get it at the expense of the less organized and less powerful portion of the laboring mass. They do not create something out of nothing. It is only by divesting our minds of questions of ownership and other machinery of distribution, and by looking solely at the question of consumption,—asking ourselves what is

the annual product, who consumes it, and what changes would or could
we make,—that we can keep in the world of realities.   But, subject to the
qualifications which I have expressed, I think it lawful for a body of workmen to try by combination to get more than they now are getting, although
they do it at the expense of their fellows, and to that end to strengthen
their union by the boycott and the strike.[2]

_____

[2] The decision in Plant v. Woods has led to a firm substantive rule in Massachusetts that the strike for the recognition of the union or for the closed shop is
illegal. Aberthaw Construction Co. v. Cameron, 194 Mass. 208, 80 N.E. 478 (1907);
Folsom v. Lewis, 208 Mass. 336, 94 N.E. 316 (1911), where the court remarked that
the purpose of the union was "to compel the employers * * * to submit to an attempt
to obtain for the union a complete monopoly of the labor market in this line of business. * * * This has been held to go beyond the limit of justifiable competition. * * *
Strengthening the forces of a labor union, to put it in a better condition to enforce
its claims in controversies that may afterwards arise with employers, is not enough to
justify an attack upon the business of an employer by inducing his employees to
strike"; Hanson v. Innis, 211 Mass. 301, 97 N.E. 756 (1912); Snow Iron Works v.
Chadwick, 227 Mass. 382, 116 N.E. 801 (1917); Harvey v. Chapman, 226 Mass. 191,
115 N.E. 304 (1917); Baush Machine Tool Co. v. Hill, 231 Mass. 30, 120 N.E. 188
(1918): Smith v. Bowen, 232 Mass. 106, 121 N.E. 814 (1919); Folsom Engraving Co.
v. McNeil, 235 Mass. 269, 126 N.E. 479 (1920); Goyette v. Watson Co., 245 Mass. 577,
140 N.E. 285 (1923); Stearns Lumber Co. v. Howlett, 260 Mass. 45, 157 N.E. 82 (1927)
semble; Alden Bros. v. Dunn, 264 Mass. 355, 162 N.E. 773 (1928). In New England
Wood Heel Co. v. Nolan, 268 Mass. 191, 167 N.E. 323 (1929), though the court admitted that the closed shop was not the end sought by the defendant union, it held the
strike illegal because it sought "(1) to prevent the recalcitrant union members from
demoralizing the entire personnel of the union by working for a less rate than they
themselves had participated in adopting as proper; (2) to prevent the plaintiff from
aiding and abetting those members from carrying out that design; or (3) to compel
the plaintiff to restore to the union members the standard union rates." For a collection of Massachusetts precedents and consideration of the rationale underlying them,
see: 45 Harv. Law Rev. 1226 (1932).

   Accord: Sarros v. Nouris, 15 Del. Ch. 391, 138 Atl. 607 (1927); Ruddy v. United
Ass'n Journeymen Plumbers, 79 N.J.L. 467, 75 Atl. 742 (1910); Baldwin Lumber Co.
v. Internat'l Brotherhood, etc., 91 N.J. Eq. 240, 109 Atl. 147 (1920); Prospect Garage
v. Funeral Car Operators, 12 Law & Labor 178 (N.J. Ch. 1930); Erdman v. Mitchell,
207 Pa. 79, 56 Atl. 327 (1903); Bausbach v. Reiff, 244 Pa. 559, 91 Atl. 224 (1914);
Moreland Theatres Corp. v. Portland M. P. O. Protective Union, 140 Ore. 35, 12
Pac.(2d) 333 (1932); State v. Dyer, 67 Vt. 690, 32 Atl. 514 (1894). Cf. White Mountain Freezer Co. v. Murphy, _supra_, p. 209. .

   See: Lewis, "The Closed Market, the Union Shop, and the Common Law," 18
Harv. Law Rev. 444 (1905); Lewis, "The Modern American Cases Arising out of
Trade and Labor Disputes," 53 Am. Law Reg. 465 (1905); Ballard, "The Strike for
the Closed Shop," 59 Univ. of Pa. Law Rev. 340 (1911); Darling, "The Closed Shop
Controversy," 18 Green Bag 339 (1906); McLennon, "Some of the Rights of Traders
and Laborers," 16 Harv. Law Rev. 237 (1903); Sayre, "Labor and the Courts," 39
Yale Law Jour. 682 (1930); Smith, "Crucial Issues in Labor Litigation," 20 Harv.
Law Rev. 253, 345, 429 (1907); Wyman, "The Maintenance of the Open Shop," 17
Green Bag 21 (1905).

   See also: Merritt, "The Closed Shop," 195 N. Am. Rev. 66 (1912); Neal, "The
'Open' Shop," 195 N. Am. Rev. 618 (1912). For a bibliography upon the open and
closed shop controversy, see: Beman, The Closed Shop, xxxiii-lxxi (2d ed. 1922).

   For a brief survey of comparative law on this issue, see: "Freedom of Association," Int. Lab. Office, Ser. A, No. 28, 83-88 (1927). See also: Mathis v. Syndicat des
Musiciens, Moniteur judiciare de Lyon, No. 27 (Cour d'Appel de Lyon, 1927), abstracted in 1927 Intern'l Survey of Leg. Dec. on Labour Law, 88; Judgment of the
Landgericht of Dresden, Feb. 5, 1927, Hanseatische Gerichtszeitung (Arbeitsrecht)
p. 75, abstracted in 1927 _id._ 198; Judgment of the Kammergericht of Berlin, 1924,
Jurist. Wochenshrift, 1925, No. 5, 269, abstracted in 1925 _id._ 164; Judgment of the
Oberlandesgericht of Jena in 1925, Gewerkschaftszeitung, Supplement Arbeiterrecht
and Arbeiterversicherung, 1926, p. 85, abstracted in 1926 _id._ 169; Maran's Case, Droit
Ouvrier 1927. 214 (Cour de Cassation, 1926), abstracted in 1927 _id._ 79.

PICKETT v. WALSH.

Supreme Judicial Court of Massachusetts. 192 Mass. 572, 78 N.E. 753 (1906).

Loring, J.: This suit in equity comes before us on an appeal from a final decree, where the evidence was taken by a commissioner and where no findings of fact were made in the lower court.

The bill was brought to enjoin the defendants from combining and conspiring to interfere with the plaintiffs in pursuing their trade of brick and stone pointers. The purpose of the bill as stated in the prayers for relief was to enjoin the defendants (1) from combining and conspiring in any way to compel L. P. Soule and Son Company, or any other person, firm or corporation, by force, threats, intimidation or coercion, to discharge the complainants in the bill of complaint, to wit: Robert H. Pickett, Charles A. Pickett, Thomas J. Lally and Walter H. Wilkins, or to refrain from further employing them in and about their trade and occupation; (2) from combining and conspiring to compel the owners of the so-called Ford Building on Ashburton Place in the City of Boston to break or decline to carry out their said contract with the complainant Robert H. Pickett; and (3) from combining and conspiring to interfere with the said complainants, or any of them, in the practice of their trade and occupation, or to prevent them from obtaining further employment thereat.

The defendants were the officers of two unincorporated bricklayers' unions, to wit, Unions No. 3 and No. 27, and of one stone masons' union, to wit, Union No. 9. The plaintiffs also undertook to make each one of the three unincorporated unions parties defendant. The Bricklayers' Union No. 27 seems from the evidence not to have been concerned in the matters in dispute. For this reason we shall not refer to it again except to show later on that there is no evidence that it took part in the matters here in question. The individual defendants were one Driscoll, the walking delegate of the Bricklayers' Union No. 3, one Walsh, the walking delegate of the Stone Masons' Union No. 9, and other persons who were officers of those two unions.

It appears from the evidence that the trade of brick and stone pointing is a trade which, in the neighborhood of the city of Boston at any rate, has been carried on to some extent as a separate trade for nearly if not quite one hundred years. It further appears that there are now some forty-five men engaged in that trade in the vicinity of that city.

The trade of a brick or a stone pointer consists in going over a building (generally when it is first erected) to clean it and to put a finish on the mortar of the joints. Apparently in the city of Worcester, and to some extent in the city of Boston, this work of pointing is done by bricklayers and stone masons.

The dispute which gave rise to the suit now before us had its origin in a set of rules adopted in January, 1905, by the Bricklayers' and Masons' International Union of America, to which the two unions here in question were subordinate. This set of rules contained a provision that bricklaying masonry should consist (*inter alia*) of "all pointing and cleaning brick walls," and that stone masonry should consist (*inter alia*) of the "cleaning and pointing of stone work." The practical working of the principles of brick and stone masonry as defined in these rules was left to the subordinate unions.

By the Constitution, By-Laws and Rules of Order of the Bricklayers' Union No. 3, it is provided that members shall not accept employment "where a difficulty exists in consequence of questions involving the rules which govern the Union," and that any member violating a law of the union shall on conviction "be reprimanded, suspended or fined at the discretion of the Union." No similar provision appears in the extract from the Constitution of the Stone Masons' Union which was in evidence, but it is not a violent assumption from the action of the masons and from the testimony of Walsh, the walking delegate of the Stone Masons' Union, that the members of the Masons' Union stood on the same footing as the members of the Bricklayers' Union in this respect.

In other words, the make-up of the two unions was such that any member of a subordinate union (which had adopted a working rule containing in substance the provisions of the working rules of the International Union as to cleaning and pointing buildings) who continued to work on a job on which a pointer was at work was liable to be reprimanded, fined or suspended.

This brings us to the action taken by the unions here in question.

There was an executive committee of the two unions. On July 28, 1905, this executive committee voted "that beginning September 18, 1905, no member of the Bricklayers' and Masons' unions of Boston and vicinity, will work on any building where the contractor will not agree to have the pointing done by bricklayers or masons."

This action of the executive committee was formally adopted by the Bricklayers' Union No. 3, and seems to have been informally adopted by the Stone Masons' Union No. 9. In pursuance thereof the following circular letter was issued: "The Bricklayers' and Masons' Unions of Boston and vicinity have voted that no bricklayer or mason will work for any firm or contractor who will not employ bricklayers or masons to do the pointing of brick, terra cottta and stone masonry. This action to go into effect September 18, 1905."

In September, 1905, L. D. Willcutt and Son as general contractors were erecting (among other buildings) a stone building on the corner of Massachusetts Avenue and Boylston Street in Boston. On the eighteenth day of that month, Mr. L. D. Willcutt of that firm was notified that if he did not discharge the pointers who were working for his firm in pointing that building all the masons and bricklayers working for his firm on other buildings in Boston (all of whom were union men) would strike. Thereupon he suspended the work which was being done by the pointers on the building on the corner of Massachusetts Avenue and Boylston Street. This evidence was admitted to show that there was a general scheme that where pointing was given to any one beside union bricklayers and stone masons there would be a strike. * * *

It further appeared from the evidence that the brick and stone pointers of Boston applied to the Building Trades Council for a charter. It is stated in the record of the Brick Masons' Union No. 3, that "the said pointers about a year ago applied to the A. F. of L. for a charter, which was denied them, the American Federation of Labor taking the stand that brick and stone pointing was a part of the bricklayers' and masons' trade." On September 11, 1905, the Brick Masons' Union No. 3 voted to "file a protest to the B. T. C. against their granting a charter to the brick and stone pointers of Boston," and on September 18 it was voted "that this Committee [sic] send communication to B. T. C. requesting that body not to grant a charter to the so-called brick and stone pointers." It was admitted that the men engaged in the business of brick and stone pointers were not qualified for the business of bricklayers and stone masons.

There was evidence that at the interview between Driscoll and Mr. Willcutt, Mr. Willcutt told Driscoll that he did not believe that, when there were twelve hundred men in the union and thirty pointers outside, all this fuss was being made to get the pointers' work for the union men; that he thought it was "simply a question of dictation to us;" and on Mr. Willcutt's asking him (Driscoll) "Do you really want it or do you want to drive the men out of business?" Driscoll smiled and said: "That is a charitable way of looking at it."

There seem to be three causes of action upheld by the decree.

In the first place, Robert H. Pickett, one of the plaintiffs, had a contract with the owners of the Ford Building and was at work under it when the defendants struck. He seeks protection from a strike on L. P. Soule and Son Company to force the owners of the Ford Building to give this work to the unions and to take it away from him. Except for the fact of this contract, in which the plaintiff Robert H. Pickett alone was concerned, the first and second causes of action are alike.

The second cause of action consists in the effort of all the plaintiffs to be protected from being discharged or not employed by the L. P. Soule and Son Company because the defendant struck work for that corporation so long as that corporation worked on a building on which Robert H. Pickett was employed by the owners of that building.[1]

Finally, the plaintiffs sought to be protected against a strike by the defendants in order to get the work of pointing for the members of their unions.

No objection has been taken to the bill on the ground of multifariousness. We therefore shall consider all three causes of action.

We will consider first the last of the three causes of action.

The question, so far as this the third cause of action goes (apart from a question of fact which we will deal with later on), is whether

---

[1] The portion of the opinion dealing with the disposition of the first and second causes of action, which the court held entitled the plaintiff to relief, are omitted.—Ed.

the defendant unions have a right to strike for the purpose for which
they struck; or, to put it more accurately and more narrowly, it is this:
Is a union of bricklayers and stone masons justified in striking to force
a contractor to employ them by the day to do cleaning and pointing at
higher wages than pointers are paid, where the contractors wish to make
contracts with the pointers for such work to be done by the piece because they think they get better work at less cost with no liability for
accidents, and where the pointers wish to make contracts for that work
with the contractors on terms satisfactory to them?

In other words, we have to deal with one of the great and pressing
questions growing out of the existence of the powerful combinations,
sometimes of capital and sometimes of labor, which have been instituted
in recent years where their actions come into conflict with the interests
of individuals. The combination in the case at bar is a combination of
workmen, and the conflict is between a labor union on the one hand
and several unorganized laborers on the other hand.

It is only in recent years that these great and powerful combinations
have made their appearance, and the limits to which they may go in
enforcing their demands are far from being settled.

It is settled however that laborers have a right to organize as labor
unions to promote their welfare.

Further, there is no question of the general right of a labor union
to strike.

On the other hand it is settled that some strikes by labor unions are
illegal. It was held in *Carew v. Rutherford,* 106 Mass. 1, that a strike
by the members of a labor union was illegal when set on foot to force
their employer to pay a fine imposed upon him by the union of which
he was not a member, for not giving the union all his work. To the same
effect see *March v. Bricklayers' & Plasterers' Union No. 1,* 79 Conn. 7.
Again, it was held in *Plant v. Woods,* 176 Mass. 492, that a labor union
could not force other workmen to join it by refusing to work if workmen
were employed who were not members of that union. To the same effect
see *Erdman v. Mitchell,* 207 Penn. St. 79; *O'Brien v. People,* 216 Ill.
354; *Loewe v. California State Federation of Labor,* 139 Fed. Rep. 71.
And see in this connection *Giblan v. National Amalgamated Labourers'
Union,* [1903] 2 K.B. 600.

When and for what end this power of coercion and compulsion commonly known as a strike may be legally used is the question which this
case calls upon us to decide. In the present state of the authorities it
becomes necessary to consider the general principles governing labor
unions and strikes by labor unions.

The right of laborers to organize unions and to utilize such organizations by instituting a strike is an exercise of the common law right of
every citizen to pursue his calling, whether of labor or business, as he in
his judgment thinks fit. It is pointed out in *Carew v. Rutherford,* 106
Mass. 1, 14, that in the earlier days of the colony the government undertook
to control the conduct of labor and business to some extent, but that

later this policy of regulation was abandoned and all citizens were left free to pursue their calling, whether of labor or business, as seemed to them best. This common law right was raised to the dignity of a constitutional right by being incorporated in the Constitution of the Commonwealth. So far as the question now before us goes it is of no consequence whether the right to pursue one's calling (whether it be of labor or of business) is a common law right or a constitutional right, since the violation of it here complained of is on the part of individuals and not on the part of the Legislature. What is of consequence here is that such a right exists. In Article I of the Declaration of Rights it is declared that "All men are born free and equal, and have certain natural, essential, and unalienable rights; among which may be reckoned the right of * * * acquiring, possessing, and protecting property; in fine, that of seeking and obtaining their safety and happiness." It is in the exercise of this right that laborers can legally combine together in what are called labor unions.

This right of one or more citizens to pursue his or their calling as he or they see fit is limited by the existence of the same right in all other citizens. The right and the result are accurately stated by Sir William Erle in his book on Trade Unions in these words: "Every person has a right under the law, as between him and his fellow subjects, to full freedom in disposing of his own labor or his own capital according to his own will. It follows that every other person is subject to the correlative duty arising therefrom, and is prohibited from any obstruction to the fullest exercise of this right which can be made compatible with the exercise of similar rights by others": cited by this court in *Plant v. Woods*, 176 Mass. 492, 498.

We now have arrived at the point where a labor union, being an organization brought about by the exercise on the part of its members of the right of every citizen to pursue his calling as he thinks best, is limited in what it can do by the existence of the same right in each and every other citizen to pursue his and their calling as he or they think best.

In addition to the limitation thus put on labor unions there is a fact which puts a further limitation on what acts a labor union can legally do. That is the increase of power which a combination of citizens has over the individual citizen. Take for example the power of a labor union to compel by a strike compliance with its demands. Speaking generally a strike to be successful means not only coercion and compulsion but coercion and compulsion which, for practical purposes, are irresistible. A successful strike by laborers means, in many if not in most cases, that for practical purposes the strikers have such a control of the labor which the employer must have that he has to yield to their demands. A single individual may well be left to take his chances in a struggle with another individual. But in a struggle with a number of persons combined together to fight an individual the individual's chance is small, if it exists at all.

It is plain that a strike by a combination of persons has a power of coercion which an individual does not have.

The result of this greater power of coercion on the part of a combination of individuals is that what is lawful for an individual is not the test of what is lawful for a combination of individuals; or to state it in another way, there are things which it is lawful for an individual to do which it is not lawful for a combination of individuals to do. Take for example the example put in *Allen v. Flood,* [1898] A.C. 1, 165, of a butler refusing to renew a contract of service because the cook was personally distasteful to him, whereupon, in order to secure the services of the butler, the master refrains from reengaging the cook whose term of service also had expired. We have no doubt that it is within the legal rights of a single person to refuse to work with another for the reason that the other person is distasteful to him, or for any other reason however arbitrary. But it is established in this Commonwealth that it is not legal (even where he wishes to do so) for an employer to agree with a union to discharge a non-union workman for an arbitrary cause at the request of the union. *Berry v. Donovan,* 188 Mass. 353. *A fortiori* the members of a labor union cannot by a strike refuse to work with another workman for an arbitrary cause. For the general proposition that what is lawful for an individual is not necessarily lawful for a combination of individuals see *Quinn v. Leathem,* [1901] A.C. 495, 511; *Mogul Steamship Co. v. McGregor,* 23 Q.B.D. 598, 616; *S.C.* on appeal, [1892] A.C. 25, 45; *Gregory v. Brunswick,* 6 M. & G. 205; *S.C.* on appeal, 3 C.B. 481. It is in effect concluded by *Plant v. Woods,* 176 Mass. 492.

These being the general principles, we are brought to the question of the legality of the strike in the case at bar, namely, a strike of bricklayers and masons to get the work of pointing, or, to put it more accurately, a combination by the defendants, who are bricklayers and masons, to refuse to lay bricks and stone where the pointing of them is given to others. The defendants in effect say we want the work of pointing the bricks and stone laid by us, and you must give us all or none of the work.

The case is one of competition between the defendant unions and the individual plaintiffs for the work of pointing. The work of pointing for which these two sets of workmen are competing is work which the contractors are obliged to have. One peculiarity of the case therefore is that the fight here is necessarily a triangular one. It necessarily involves the two sets of competing workmen and the contractor, and is not confined to the two parties to the contract, as is the case where workmen strike to get better wages from their employer or other conditions which are better for them. In this respect the case is like *Mogul Steamship Co. v. McGregor,* 23 Q.B.D. 598; *S.C.* on appeal [1892] A.C. 25.

The right which the defendant unions claim to exercise in carrying their point in the course of this competition is a trade advantage, namely, that they have labor which the contractors want, or, if you please, cannot get elsewhere; and they insist upon using this trade advantage to get additional work, namely, the work of pointing the bricks and stone which they lay. It is somewhat like the advantage which the owner of back land has when he has bought the front lot. He is not bound to sell them separately. To be sure the right of an individual owner to sell both or none is not decisive of the right of a labor union to combine to refuse to lay bricks or stone unless they are given the job of pointing the bricks laid by them. There are things which an individual can do which a combination of individuals cannot do. But having regard to the right on which the defendants' organization as a labor union rests, the correlative duty owed by it to others, and the limitation of the defendants' rights coming from the increased power of organizations, we are of opinion that it was within the rights of these unions to compete for the work of doing the pointing and, in the exercise of their right of competition, to refuse to lay bricks and set stone unless they were given the work of pointing them when laid. See in this connection *Plant v. Woods,* 176 Mass. 492, 502; *Berry v. Donovan,* 188 Mass. 353, 357.

The result to which that conclusion brings us in the case at bar ought not to be passed by without consideration.

The result is harsh on the contractors, who prefer to give the work to the pointers because (1) the pointers do it by contract (in which case the contractors escape the liability incident to the relation of employer and employee); because (2) the contractors think that the pointers do the work better, and if not well done the buildings may be permanently injured by acid; and finally (3) because they get from the pointers better work with less liability at a smaller cost. Again, so far as the pointers (who cannot lay brick or stone) are concerned, the result is disastrous. But all that the labor unions have done is to say you must employ us for all the work or none of it. They have not said that if you employ the pointers you must pay us a fine, as they did in *Carew v. Rutherford,* 106 Mass. 1. They have not undertaken to forbid the contractors employing pointers, as they did in *Plant v. Woods,* 176 Mass. 492.[2] So far as the

---

[2] "In Plant v. Woods the Supreme Judicial Court enjoined threats to strike on the ground that the purpose of forcing other workmen into the union was unlawful. Six years later in Pickett v. Walsh the same court decided that a strike to secure more work for union men, even though it might result in the discharge of non-union workers, was lawful. The court succinctly pointed out that it was not rejecting its previous view, stating, 'All that the labor unions have done is to say, you must employ us for all the work or none of it. * * * They have not undertaken to forbid the contractors employing pointers as they did in Plant v. Woods.' Only further elucidation is needed to make the distinction palpable. If the employer had accepted the option offered in Pickett v. Walsh, he would, of course, have discharged the non-union workers; if he had not, he would be free to find others to fill the places of the union men. But if the employer had accepted the demands in Plant v. Woods, he would have been forced to discharge the competing workers; and if he had not, he would have been compelled to find others to fill the places of the union men." 45 Harv. Law Rev. 1227 (1932). "Damaging interference should be permitted only where it may contribute directly to the result which the defendants are entitled to attain. It should not be enough that some possible benefit may come to them at some future time. They should be permitted to interfere for the purpose of procuring the plaintiffs' discharge in order to obtain their places, of procuring others to refuse to work for the defendants'

labor unions are concerned the contractors can employ pointers if they choose, but if the contractors choose to give the work of pointing the bricks and stones to others the unions take the stand that the contractors will have to get some one else to lay them. The effect of this in the case at bar appears to be that the contractors are forced against their will to give the work of pointing to the masons and bricklayers. But the fact that the contractors are forced to do what they do not want to do is not decisive of the legality of the labor union's acts. That is true wherever a strike is successful. The contractors doubtless would have liked it better if there had been no competition between the bricklayers' and masons' unions on the one hand and the individual pointers on the other hand. But there is competition. There being competition, they prefer the course they have taken. They prefer to give all the work to the unions rather than get non-union men to lay bricks and stone to be pointed by the plaintiffs.

Further, the effect of complying with the labor unions' demands apparently will be the destruction of the plaintiffs' business. But the fact that the business of a plaintiff is destroyed by the acts of the defendants done in pursuance of their right of competition is not decisive of the illegality of the acts. It was well said by Hammond, J. in *Martell v. White,* 185 Mass. 255, 260, in regard to the right of a citizen to pursue his business without interference by a combination to destroy it: "Speaking generally, however, competition in business is permitted, although frequently disastrous to those engaged in it. It is always selfish, often sharp, and sometimes deadly."

We cannot say on the evidence that pointing is something foreign to the work of a bricklayer or a stone mason and therefore something which a union of bricklayers and stone masons have no right to compete for or insist upon, and so bring the case within *Carew v. Rutherford,* 106 Mass. 1; *March v. Bricklayers & Plasterers Union No. 1,* 79 Conn. 7; and *Giblan v. National Amalgamated Labourers' Union,* [1903] 2 K.B. 600. On the contrary the evidence shows that in Boston the pointing is done to some extent by bricklayers and stone masons, and there is no evidence that the trade of pointers exists outside that city.

The protest of the defendant unions against the plaintiffs being allowed to organize a pointers' union is not an act of oppression. It is not like the refusal of the union in *Quinn v. Leathem,* [1901] A.C. 495, to work with the non-union men or to admit the non-union men to their union. The defendants' unions are not shown to be unwilling to admit the plaintiffs to membership if they are qualified as bricklayers or stone masons. But the difficulty is that the plaintiffs are not so qualified. They are not bricklayers or masons. The unions have a right to determine

employer at lower wages than the defendants are willing to accept, or of procuring others not to buy of the plaintiffs is these others will thereupon naturally buy of the defendants. They should not be permitted to interfere for the purpose of extorting money which there is no obligation to pay, of inducing men to join the union, or prescribing them for disobedience to its rules." McLennon, "Some of the Rights of Traders and Laborers," 16 Harv. Law Rev. 237, 249 (1903).—Ed.

what kind of workmen shall compose the union, and to insist that pointing shall not be a separate trade so far as union work is concerned. They have not undertaken to say that the contractors shall not treat the two trades as distinct. What they insist upon is that if the contractors employ them they shall employ them to do both kinds of work.

The application of the right of the defendant unions, who are composed of bricklayers and stone masons, to compete with the individual plaintiffs, who can do nothing but pointing (as we have said,) is in the case at bar disastrous to the pointers and hard on the contractors. But this is not the first case where the exercise of the right of competition ends in such a result. The case at bar is an instance where the evils which are or may be incident to competition bear very harshly on those interested, but in spite of such evils competition is necessary to the welfare of the community. * * *

It follows that the third clause of the decree, which follows the third prayer of the bill, must be stricken out. * * * [3]

---

[3] "Neither the Massachusetts courts nor any one else has been able to reconcile or adequately to explain such conflicting decisions as Plant v. Woods. * * * Pickett v. Walsh * * *" Sayre, "Labor and the Courts," 39 Yale Law Jour. 682, 697 (1930). But see: 45 Harv. Law Rev. 1226 (1932).

Cf. Wills v. Restaurant Employees, 26 Ohio N.P. (N.S.) 435 (1927) (strike to compel the discharge of colored waiters and the employment of union men, the union not being willing to admit colored waiters into the union) ; Armstrong Cork & Insulation Co. v. Walsh, 276 Mass. 263, 177 N.E. 2 (1931).

Masters in reporting upon the facts of labor controversies have found difficulty in fitting them into the category of the Pickett v. Walsh conception. Smith v. Bowen, 232 Mass. 106, 121 N.E. 814 (1919), the court dealt with the findings below as follows: "In addition he [the lower judge] made these findings: 'I further find that there were other members of the union ready and willing to do the work for which the plaintiff was employed. * * * I further find that the refusal to admit the plaintiff to membership in the union, although justified, because he did not comply with the provisions of the constitution, was not upon that ground, but because the union desired to secure the work which the plaintiff did for its own members, said position being a profitable and a desirable one.' The defendants' first contention is that the case is brought within Pickett v. Walsh, 192 Mass. 572, by the finding that 'the refusal to admit the plaintiff to membership in the union * * * [was] to secure the work which the plaintiff did for its own members.' But this was a finding as to the reason why the union did not admit the plaintiff to membership. It was not a finding as to the purpose of the strike." In Snow Iron Works v. Chadwick, 227 Mass. 382, 116 N.E. 801 (1917), the court said: "If the master's subsidiary findings were only to be considered, it is settled that a strike would not be unlawful if upon ascertaining that they could not have all, they declined to take part of the work. Pickett v. Walsh, 192 Mass. 572. But these findings as they appear in the report are made subordinate to the express findings, 'that the purposes of this strike were primarily to compel the plaintiff to sign the agreement * * * which among other things * * * would have required it to unionize its outside work."

The cases do not raise the issue of the pure jurisdictional strike, apart from breach of contract or pressure directed by the strike upon an employer other than the employer of the objectionable employees. For cases of this character, see O'Brien v. Fackenthal, 5 Fed. (2d) 389 (6th cir. 1925) ; Local No. 65, Amalgamated Sheet Workers v. Fackenthal, 11 Law & Labor, 244 (6th cir. 1929) ; Selden Breck Co. v. Blair, 7 Law & Labor, 255 (U.S.D.C. Mo. 1925) ; Selden Breck Co. v. Local Union No. 253, 7 Law & Labor, 302 (U.S.D.C. Mo. 1925) ; Metal Door & Trim Co. v. Booth, 11 Law & Labor, 25 (U.S.D.C. Ind. 1929) ; Metal Door & Trim Co. v. Local No. 5, 12 Law & Labor, 183 (Sup. Ct. D.C. 1930) ; Dahlstrom Metallic Door Co. v. Local No. 5, 11 Law & Labor, 79, 87

KEMP v. DIVISION NO. 241.

Supreme Court of Illinois. 255 Ill. 213, 99 N.E. 389 (1912).

MR. JUSTICE COOKE delivered the opinion of the court: * * *

The bill was filed by eight employees of the Chicago Railways Company against Division 241 of the Amalgamated Association of Street and Electric Railway Employees of America, a corporation, and the officers and the members of the executive board of Division 241. Its purpose was to obtain an injunction restraining the appellants, their agents, servants and attorneys, from attempting to procure, by means of threats, the discharge of the appellees from the service of the Chicago Railways Company because of the fact that the appellees are not members of said Division 241. * * *

The only reasonable conclusion to be deduced from the allegations and prayer of the bill is, that appellees by this proceeding seek to restrain the union and its officers from calling a strike of its members, the obvious purpose of the injunction sought being to prevent the union employees of the Railways Company from quitting their employment in accordance with the vote previously taken, by which those employees, as members of the union, declared that they would "cease to work with men who after receiving benefits through our organization refuse to continue members," appellees belonging to the class of men with which the union employees had thus declared they would no longer work. The question presented for our determination therefore is, whether a court of equity is authorized, upon application by the non-union employees, to restrain the union and its officers from calling a strike of the union employees in accordance with the vote previously taken by the union employees as members of the union, where the purpose of the proposed strike is to compel the employer to discharge the non-union employees who are engaged in the same class of work. In order to decide this question in the affirmative it would be necessary to hold that had the threatened act been completed, appellees

---

(Sup. Ct. D.C. 1929). See: Davis, "Jurisdictional Disputes," 21 Monthly Lab. Rev. 907 (1925); Cummins, "Jurisdictional Disputes in Carpenters' Unions," 40 Quar. Jour. Econ. 463 (1926); Montgomery, "Jurisdictional Disputes," 35 Jour. Pol. Econ. 91 (1927); Stanley, "Jurisdictional Strikes," 8 Law & Labor, 101 (1926); Barnett, "The Causes of Jurisdictional Disputes in American Trade Unions," 9 Harv. Bus. Rev. 400 (1931); 39 Harv. Law Rev. 101 (1925). See also: Tucker, Decisions of the General Arbitration Board of the New York Building Trades Affecting Jurisdiction of Trade (1910); Winslow, "Conciliation and Arbitration in the Building Trades of Greater New York," U.S. Dept. of Labor, Bur. Lab. Stat. Bull. No. 124 (1913); Whitney, "Jurisdiction in American Building Trades Unions," Johns Hopkins, Stud. Ser. 32 No. 1 (1914); Haber, Industrial Relations in the Building Industry, c. 6 (1930); Bullard, The Public Refuses to Pay, 17 et seq. (1921); Final Report of Joint Legislative Committee on Housing, N.Y. Legis. Doc. No. 48, 47-59 (1923); "Plan for Settlement of Jurisdictional Claims in the Building Industry," 11 Monthly Lab. Rev. 248 (1920); "Agreement between Masons' & Plasterers' Internat'l Union and Operative Plasterers and Cement Finishers' Internat'l Union," 21 Monthly Lab. Rev. 1185 (1925); Report of Proceedings of the Twenty-Second Annual Convention of the American Federation of Labor, Building Trades Department (1928).

would have been entitled to maintain an action for damages against the union and its officers for accomplishing their discharge from the service of the Railways Company, and that such action at law would not afford an adequate remedy because of the financial inability of appellants to respond in adequate damages for the injuries which appellees would suffer by reason of their discharge. The inadequacy of the remedy at law sufficiently appears from the bill, and it will only be necessary to determine whether the appellees would have been entitled to maintain the action for damages had their discharge been accomplished by appellants.

That appellees would sustain damages if discharged by the Railways Company, and that such discharge and consequent damages would be occasioned by the acts of the appellants, acting for and on behalf of the union employees, clearly appears from the bill. The mere fact that one person sustains damage by reason of some act of another is not, however, sufficient to render the latter liable to an action by the former for such damage, but it must further appear that the act which occasioned the damage was a wrongful act and not one performed in the exercise of a legal right, otherwise it is *damnum absque injuria*. * * *

Every employee has a right to protection in his employment from the wrongful and malicious interference of another resulting in damage to the employee, but if such interference is but the consequence of the exercise of some legal right by another it is not wrongful, and cannot, therefore, be made the basis for an action to recover the consequent damages. It is the right of every workman, for any reason which may seem sufficient to him, or for no reason, to quit the service of another, unless bound by contract. This right cannot be abridged or taken away by any act of the legislature, nor is it subject to any control by the courts, it being guaranteed to every person under the jurisdiction of our government by the thirteenth amendment to the Federal constitution, which declares that involuntary servitude, except as a punishment for crime, shall not exist within the United States or any place subject to their jurisdiction. Incident to this constitutional right is the right of every workman to refuse to work with any co-employee who is for any reason objectionable to him, provided his refusal does not violate his contract with his employer; and there is no more foundation for the contention that the employee commits an actionable wrong by informing the employer, before he leaves the service, that he will not work with the objectionable co-employee, and thereby occasioning his discharge, than there would be for the contention that the employee would commit an actionable wrong by quitting the service and afterward stating to the employer his reason therefor, if as a result thereof the employer should choose to discharge the objectionable co-employee. In either case the employee is exercising a legal right, and although it results in damage to the objectionable co-employee, the latter has no cause of action against the former for causing his discharge. In the case at bar, had the union employees, as individuals and without any pre-arranged concert of action, each informed the Railways Company that they would no longer work with appellees because appellees were not members of the union, and had appellees, in consequence thereof, been discharged because the Railways Company chose to retain the services of the union employees, appellees would have had no cause of action against the union employees for thus causing their discharge. Does the fact that the union, its officers and committees, acted as an intermediary between the union employees and the Railways Company, and under the circumstances and for the purposes disclosed by the bill, render unlawful the action by it or them which would have been lawful if performed by the union employees individually?

Labor unions have long since been recognized by the courts of this country as a legitimate part of the industrial system of this nation. The ultimate purpose of such organizations is, through combination, to advance the interests of the members by obtaining for them adequate compensation for their labor, and it has been frequently decided by the American courts that the fact that this purpose is sought to be obtained through combination or concerted action of employees does not render the means unlawful. * * *

The purpose of organizing labor unions is to enable those employees who become members to negotiate matters arising between them and their employers through the intermediation of officers and committees of the union and to accomplish their ends through concerted action. If duly authorized by the employees to adjust any controversy arising between them and their employer, the union, its officers and committees are merely acting as agents of the employees in the matter. If the union employees had the legal right to inform their employer of their refusal to work with appellees, they had the legal right to convey that information to the employer through an agent or agents, and the agent or agents would not commit an actionable wrong thereby nor by reporting back to the union employees the result of the conference with the employer. The demand that appellees be discharged, and the threat that unless the Railways Company complied with the demand the members of the union would call a strike of the employees of the Railways Company, in effect meant no more than the mere statement that the union employees of the Railways Company would no longer work with the non-union employees, and if the Railways Company chose to retain in its employ the non-union men the union employees would quit the service of the Railways Company.

A strike is "the act of a party of workmen employed by the same master in stopping work all together at a preconcerted time, and refusing to continue until higher wages or shorter time, or some other concession, is granted to them by the employer." (Black's Law Dict.) It is "a combined effort of workmen to obtain higher wages or other concessions from their employers by stopping work at a preconcerted time." (Bouvier's Law Dict.) The threat made by the committee that the members of the union would call a strike of the employees of the Railways Company unless their demands were complied with, meant no more than that the union employees would be notified to quit work in a body at a definite time if the non-union employees were retained in the service. This action of the committee, if not then authorized, was ratified by an almost unanimous vote of the union employees, and the union employees thereby authorized and instructed the union, its officers and members, to call the strike which it is sought by this proceeding to prevent. The contemplated action of the union employees is not the result of the dictation of any officer or officers of the union or of any person not interested in the employment, but is the voluntary action of the union employees of the Railways Company. The threatened act of the union and its members is therefore, in effect, the act of the union employees themselves, and if those employees have the right to perform the act by concerted action and for the purposes alleged, their authorized agents commit no actionable wrong in the performance thereof.

As has been pointed out, had the union employees, as individuals and without pre-arrangement, each informed the Railways Company that they would no longer work with appellees, and had the employer voluntarily chosen to discharge appellees rather than lose the services of the union employees, they would have no cause of action against the union employees. No contract rights being involved, the union employees had a right to quit the service of the Railways Company, either singly or in a body, for any reason they chose or for no reason at all. If the only purpose of the union employees was to quit the service and permanently sever their connections with their employer, appellees would in nowise be damaged and could have no grounds for injunctive relief. The bill discloses, however, that this was not the only purpose of the members of the union. They did not propose absolutely to sever their connection with their employer, but by means of a strike to withdraw temporarily their services, and then, by such means as might be proper and permissible, seek to induce their employer to accede to their demands and reinstate them in the service under the conditions they sought to impose. By thus combining it becomes necessary to inquire whether the purpose of the combination was a lawful one.

Ordinarily it is true that what one individual may rightfully do he may do in combination with others. In some jurisdictions the question of the purpose or motive in such cases as this is not inquired into. But in other jurisdictions the opposite view is held, for the very apparent reason that acts done by a combination of individuals may be made much more potent and effective than the same acts done by an individual, and we believe the greater weight of authority to be, that what one individual may lawfully do a combination of individuals has the same right to do, provided they have no unlawful purpose in view. Would the calling of a strike, and the inducing of an employer thereby to accede to the demands of the union employees and to discharge appellees under the circumstances disclosed, be such an interference with the rights of appellees as to be wrongful and malicious?

It has been comparatively but a short time since it was unlawful for workmen to associate themselves together under such organizations as are now known as trades unions, for the purposes of improving the conditions of labor. Such an organization was formerly held to be a criminal conspiracy, and it required statutory enactment in England to permit workmen legally to combine for the purpose of maintaining satisfactory wages and for mutual protection. The right of labor to organize, and to strike, if necessary, without resort to violence or other unlawful conduct, for the betterment of the condition of labor, is now generally recognized by the courts of this country. As was said in *Iron Molders' Union v. Allis-Chalmers Co.,* 166 Fed. Rep. 45: "To organize for the purpose of securing improvement in the terms and condition of labor, and to quit work and to threaten to quit work as a means of compelling or attempting to compel employers to accede to their demands for better terms and conditions, are rights of workmen so well and so thoroughly established in law, (*Thomas v. Railroad Co.,* 62 Fed. Rep. 803; *Arthur v. Oakes,* 63 *id.* 320; *Wabash Railroad Co. v. Hannahan,* 121 *id.* 563;) that nothing remains except to determine in successive cases, as they arise, whether the means used in the endeavor to make the strike effective are lawful or unlawful."

While it cannot be successfully contended that every strike is lawful, it is generally conceded by our courts that workmen may quit in a body, or strike, in order to maintain wages, secure advancement in wages, procure shorter hours of employment or attain any other legitimate object. An agreement by a combination of individuals to strike or quit work for the purpose of advancing their own interests or the interests of the union of which they are members, and not having for its primary object the purpose of injuring others in their business or employment, is lawful. As to whether the object which this bill discloses was sought to be attained by the members of the union was a lawful one or a valid justification of the threat to strike, the authorities in this country are clearly in conflict. Among the cases in other jurisdictions upon which appellees rely in support of their contentions on this point are *Berry v. Donovan,* 188 Mass. 353, *Erdman v. Mitchell,* 207 Pa. 79, *Lucke v. Clothing Cutters,* 77 Md. 396, *Plant v. Woods,* 176 Mass. 492, and *Curran v. Galen,* 152 N.Y. 33, that some of the cases cited by appellees support their contention cannot be denied. A contrary result has been reached, however, by the courts of some of the other States. This precise question has never been passed upon in this State, and were the position of appellees to be sustained it would be a long step in advance of any decision of this court. In the unsettled condition of the law on this question we are not disposed to follow the cases cited by appellees. We are of the opinion that the cases holding the contrary view are supported by the better reasoning.

It does not follow from a consideration of all the material allegations of the bill that the primary object of the union employees, or of the union officers in carrying out the wishes of the members, was to injure appellees. Neither can it be said that any actual malice has been disclosed toward the appellees or an intent to commit a wrongful or harmful act against them. No threats are made and no violence is threatened. The members of the union have simply said to their employer that they will not longer

work with men who are not members of their organization, and that they
will withdraw from their employment and use such proper means as they
may to secure employment under the desired conditions. While this is not
a combination on the part of the union employees to maintain their present
scale of wages, to secure an advance in the rate of wages or to procure
shorter hours of employment, all of which have been universally held to
be proper and lawful objects of a strike, it cannot be said that this is not a
demand for better conditions and a legitimate object for them to seek to
attain by means of a strike.

It is insisted that a strike is lawful only in a case of direct competition, and as it cannot be said that the union employees are in any sense
competing with appellees, their acts cannot be justified. It is true, as has
been stated, that the proposed strike was not to be called for the direct
purpose of securing better wages or shorter hours or to prevent a reduction of wages, any one of which would have been a proper object. The
motive was more remote than that, but it was kindred to it. The purpose
was to strengthen and preserve the organization itself. Without organization the workmen would be utterly unable to make a successful effort to
maintain or increase their wages or to enforce such demands as have been
held to be proper. The following view expressed by Mr. Chief Justice
Holmes in his dissenting opinion in *Plant v. Woods, supra,* in discussing
facts similar to those here involved, is in our opinion a correct statement of
the law and is applicable here: "That purpose was not directly concerned
with wages. It was one degree more remote. The immediate object and motive was to strengthen the defendants' society as a preliminary and means to
enable it to make a better fight on questions of wages or other matters of
clashing interests. I differ from my brethren in thinking that the threats
were as lawful for this preliminary purpose as for the final one to which
strengthening the union was a means. I think that unity of organization is
necessary to make the contest of labor effectual, and that societies of laborers lawfully may employ in their preparation the means which they
might use in the final contest."

If it is proper for workmen to organize themselves into such combinations as labor unions, it must necessarily follow that it is proper for them
to adopt any proper means to preserve that organization. If the securing
of the closed shop is deemed by the members of a labor union of the utmost importance and necessary for the preservation of their organization,
through which, alone, they have been enabled to secure better wages and
better working conditions, and if to secure that is the primary object of the
threat to strike, even though in the successful prosecution of the object of
the combination injury may result incidentally to non-union men through
the loss of their positions, that object does not become unlawful. It is apparent that in this case the sole purpose was to insure employment by the
Railways Company of union men, only. The appellees had the right to retain their membership in the union or not, as they saw fit. On the other
hand, if the members of the union honestly believed that it was to their
best interests to be engaged in the same employment with union men only,

and that it was a detriment and a menace to their organization to associate in the same employment with non-members, it was their right to inform the common employer that they would withdraw from its service and strike unless members of the union, only, were employed, even though an acquiescence in their demands would incidentally result in the loss of employment on the part of the non-union men. It was only incumbent upon them to act in a peaceful and lawful manner in carrying out their plans. * * *

In *Gillespie v. People,* 188 Ill. 176, a statute making it a misdemeanor for an employer to prevent an employee, by threats, from joining a labor organization, or to discharge an employee because of membership in a labor organization, was held to be unconstitutional, and the right of an employer to discharge his employee solely because he would not resign from his union was upheld. That employees might suffer by remaining members of their unions, or that they might through necessity be compelled to disband the organizations they had built up and maintained for their own proper benefit, could not affect the right of the employer. He has the right to manage his business as he sees fit. It would seem that labor organizations should be accorded the same right to manage their affairs and to determine what is best for their own interests. To deny them the right to determine whether their best interests required that they should be associated in their work only with members of their organization would imperil their very existence. If they have the right to make such a requirement, then when their employer procures non-union labor they have the right to strike to enforce that requirement, as that is the only peaceable method available to compel an adjustment of their controversies and to preserve the integrity of their organizations. From the facts as disclosed by the bill it can only be said that the members of the union, upon deliberation, concluded that their own welfare and business interests required that they cease working with those who were not members of their organization. This being their primary object, they have the right to quit the employment and go upon a strike and to use all proper means to secure their re-instatement upon the conditions desired. * * *

The case of *Doremus v. Hennessy,* 176 Ill. 608, and *Wilson v. Hey,* 232 *id.* 389, also relied upon by appellees, and the case of *Purington v. Hinchliff,* 219 *id.* 159, were all boycott cases. The courts are practically unanimous in holding that the acts done and proposed to be done in each of those cases are unlawful, for the reason that they are done with a wrongful motive and for the immediate purpose of inflicting an injury upon another. What was said in those cases applies only to the existence of a boycott or of a threat to boycott. This case partakes of none of the elements of a boycott. The primary object of a boycott being to inflict injury upon another, has universally been held to be illegal. Here the primary object of the combination is to further the interests of the organization and improve and better the condition of its members. Whatever injury may follow to others is merely incidental.

The judgment of the Appellate Court is reversed and the decree of the circuit court is affirmed.

Judgment reversed.[1]

---

[1] The concurring opinion of Carter, J., and the dissenting opinion of Cartwright, Dunn and Hand, J.J., are omitted.

For comment on the case, see: 7 Ill. Law Rev. 320, 323 (1912) ; 8 Ill. Law Rev. 126 (1913) ; 13 Col. Law Rev. 66 (1913) ; 26 Harv. Law Rev. 259 (1913); 61 Univ. of Pa. Law Rev. 255 (1913).

Accord: Parkinson v. Building Trades Council, 154 Cal. 581, 98 Pac. 1027 (1908) *semble;* Jetton-Dekle Lumber Co. v. Mather, 53 Fla. 969, 43 So. 590 (1907) ; Gray v. Building Trades Council, 91 Minn. 171, 97 N.W. 663 (1903) ; National Protective Ass'n v. Cumming, 170 N.Y. 315, 63 N.E. 369 (1902) ; Exchange Bakery & Restaurant Co. v. Rifkin, *supra,* p. 145; Roddy v. United Mine Workers, 41 Okla. 621, 139 Pac. 126 (1914) ; White v. Riley, [1921] 1 Ch. 1; Hodges v. Webb, [1920] 2 Ch. 70; Wolstenholme v. Ariss, [1920] 2 Ch. 403. But *cf.* Hodges v. Webb, [1919] 2 Ch. 129; Rex. v. Jones, London Times, Dec. 18, 1928 (Ct. Crim. App.).

Difficulties have arisen over the question whether, apart from the legality of the end sought by striking, the threat to strike is a "threat" which of itself involves the employment of illegal means and thereby of itself makes the strike illegal. The decision in Valentine v. Hyde, *supra,* largely rests upon this basis. *Cf.* also: Rex. v. Jones, *supra.* Compare Holmes, J., dissenting in Vegelahn v. Guntner, *supra,* p. 199: "I pause here to remark that the word 'threats' often is used as if, when it appeared that threats had been made, it appeared that unlawful conduct had begun. But it depends on what you threaten. As a general rule, even if subject to some exceptions, what you may do in a certain event you may threaten to do, that is, give warning of your intention to do in that event, and thus allow the other person the chance of avoiding the consequences."

The issue of the legality of concerted action to secure a closed shop is also raised indirectly by strikes to compel the discharge of an employee who has been ejected from a union for refusing to pay a fine, following upon his breach of union regulations. The attitude of courts toward the legality of such a strike may depend upon their conclusion as to the right of the union to assess the disputed fine. *Cf.* Brennan v. United Hatters, 73 N.J.L. 729, 65 Atl. 165 (1906) ; Blanchard v. Newark Council, 77 N.J.L. 389, 71 Atl. 1131 (1909), aff'd in 78 N.J.L. 737, 76 Atl. 1087 (1910) ; Giblan v. Nat'l Amalgamated Laborers' Union, [1903] 2 K.B. 300. See also: Schneider v. Local Union No. 60, 116 La. 270, 40 So. 700 (1905) ; Campbell v. Johnson, 167 Fed. 102 (9th cir. 1909) ; Connell v. Stalker, 21 Misc. 609, 48 N.Y.S. 77 (1897). Other courts, however, have regarded such action by the union as illegal, without inquiry as the justice of the union's disciplinary action, erecting either a concept that strikes to compel the payment of fines are illegal, or forbidding to the union the use of such disciplinary pressure. Willcutt & Sons Co. v. Driscoll, 200 Mass. 110, 85 N.E. 897 (1908) ; Martell v. White, 185 Mass. 255, 69 N.E. 1085 (1904) ; Boutwell v. Marr, 71 Vt. 1, 42 Atl. 607 (1899) ; Slenter v. Scott, 16 D.L.R. 659 (1914). For a criticism of this line of approach, see: Martin, Modern Law of Labor Unions, § 149 (1910). See also Blakemore, "Intimidation of Fines in Labor Disputes," 20 Green Bag 620 (1908) ; Martin, "Right of Labor Union to Compel Member to Aid in Strike by Imposing or Threatening to Impose Penalties," 21 Green Bag 445 (1909) ; Steever, "Control of Labor through Union Discipline," 16 Corn. Law Quar. 212 (1931).

CAREW v. RUTHERFORD.

Supreme Judicial Court of Massachusetts. 106 Mass. 1 (1870).

Contract against Alexander Rutherford, Joseph Wagner, Edward Shea, William Cooney, and the "Journeymen Freestone Cutters' Association of Boston and vicinity, an unincorporated association composed of the defendants personally named and other persons to the plaintiff unknown," to recover back $500 as money had and received by the defendants to the plaintiff's use; with the following alternative count in tort: * * *

At the trial in the superior court, before *Brigham*, C. J., without a jury, the judge found these facts:

"The plaintiff in August 1868 was a freestone cutter at South Boston, and had contracted to furnish cut freestone for various buildings, among which was the Roman Catholic cathedral in Boston, in large quantity and at a contract price of $80,000. The defendants, and sixteen other persons, all journeymen freestone cutters, and members of an unincorporated association called the Journeymen Freestone Cutters' Association of Boston, Charlestown, Roxbury, and their vicinities, (of which association the plaintiff was not a member,) together with eight or ten laborers, who were not journeymen stonecutters or skilled laborers, and four apprentices to the freestone cutting trade, constituted the stonecutting force relied upon by the plaintiff to fulfil his said freestone contracts. * * * On the morning of August 18, 1868, the defendant William Cooney, president of said association, who was foreman in the plaintiff's establishment, notified the plaintiff that on the evening of the day before, at a special meeting of the association, it was voted that the plaintiff should pay to the association the sum of $500 as a penalty imposed upon him by the association because he had sent to New York to be executed some of the freestone cutting to be done under his contract for the cathedral; and upon the plaintiff's refusal to make such payment, all the journeymen freestone cutters employed by him (among them, the defendants) left the plaintiff's service in a body, agreeably to said vote and the rules of said association. At his request, the plaintiff was permitted to appear at a meeting of the association and explain the circumstances which induced him to send a part of the stonecutting work required for the cathedral to New York to be executed; and, after explaining that his action in that matter was because of his not having the proper stock for that part of the work when he could procure journeymen to work upon it, and when, having procured such stock, he could not procure a sufficient force of journeymen to work it, there was a motion made and debated in the association, that the previous vote, to the effect that members should withdraw from the plaintiff's service unless he paid $500 as aforesaid, should be reconsidered and rescinded; but the association refused to reconsider or rescind the vote. At this meeting, said vote was read to the plaintiff by the secretary of the association. On the same night or the next morning, the defendants Cooney and Shea, and others, told the plaintiff that all the association men in his shop would desert him at once unless he paid the $500, and that the association refused to rescind the vote. The plaintiff refused to pay, and all his men left his shop at once and in a body, under the lead of Cooney and Shea; and the plaintiff was without men for a week or ten days, and until after he had made the payment of $500 as hereinafter stated. Previously to the payment of the money, and after the men had left him, Cooney and others of the defendants told the plaintiff that neither these men, nor any association men, would be allowed to work in his shop, if he refused to pay the money demanded. In consequence of the withdrawal of the defendants and the other journeymen, the freestone cutting which the plaintiff had contracted to do was stopped, because it was impossible for the plaintiff to procure journeymen or other freestone cutters, who were not members of said association, and who had such skill as was required for the fulfilment of his contracts. Several days after the defendants and the other journeymen had withdrawn from the plaintiff's service, the plaintiff, induced by the necessity of doing so to fulfil said contracts and continue his other stonecutting work, paid to the defendants, to the use of said association, the sum of $500, on August 26, 1868; and the defendants and other journeymen, who had withdrawn as aforesaid, returned to the service and employment of the plaintiff. Said payment was made by the plaintiff as follows: He first made a check payable to the order of the association. This the defendants Cooney and Wagner refused to take, on the ground that no one of those active in procuring it was willing to indorse it. The plaintiff then made a check payable to Wagner or bearer, and gave this check to Cooney, and he, Wagner and others went with the plaintiff to the bank, when the money was passed to Wagner's credit as treasurer of the association. No receipt was given to the plaintiff for this money."

The judge further found as a fact "that the money demanded of the plaintiff was demanded without right, and not under any contract or agreement between him and the defendants."

Upon these findings the judge ruled that the facts would not sustain the action, and ordered judgment for the defendants. The plaintiff alleged exceptions. * * *

CHAPMAN, C. J.: The declaration contains a count in tort, and a count for money had and received. The count in tort alleges, in substance, that the plaintiff was engaged in carrying on the business of cutting freestone in Boston, and employed a great many workmen, and had entered into a contract with builders to furnish them with such stone in large quantities; and the defendants, conspiring and confederating together to oppress and extort money from him, and pretending that he had allowed some of said builders, with whom he had made contracts, to withdraw from his shop a part of the work he had contracted to do, and to procure the same to be done out of the state, caused a vote of the Journeymen Freestone Cutters' Association of Boston to be passed, to the effect that a fine of five hundred dollars was levied upon the plaintiff, and read the vote to him, and threatened him that unless he paid the fine they would, by the power of the association, cause a great number of the workmen employed by him to leave his service; that he refused to pay it, and the defendants caused twelve of his workmen to leave his service for that reason, at their instigation. They further threatened him that, unless he paid the fine, they would, by the power of the association, prevent him from obtaining suitable workmen for carrying on his business, and did so prevent him till he paid the fine, and thus extorted from him the sum of five hundred dollars.

Trial by jury was waived, and the facts found by the judge are reported. It appeared that the plaintiff had made a contract to furnish stone for the Roman Catholic cathedral in Boston, and had employed journeymen to do the work, and relied upon them to fulfill his contracts; and the facts stated in the declaration were substantially proved. The plaintiff was not a member of the association. He had sent some of his work to be done in New York because he could not obtain a sufficient force to do it in Boston, and had not proper stock for the work. If the action can be maintained, it is on the ground that the defendants have done the acts alleged, in violation of the legal rights of the plaintiff.

By the Gen. Sts. c. 160, § 28, which is cited by the plaintiff's counsel, "whoever, either verbally or by a written or printed communication," "maliciously threatens an injury to the person or property of another, with intent thereby to extort money or any pecuniary advantage whatever, or with intent to compel the person so threatened to do any act against his will, shall be punished" as the section prescribes. As this is a penal statute, perhaps it does not extend to a threat to injure one's business by preventing people from assisting him to prosecute it, whereby he loses his profits and is compelled to pay a large sum of money to those who make the threat, though the threat is quite analogous to those specified in the statute, and may be not less injurious. We shall therefore consider, not whether the acts alleged and proved against the defendants were unlawful within the statute, but whether they were so at common law. * * *

There are many cases where money has been wrongfully obtained by fraud, oppression or taking undue advantage of another, without doing him any other injury. This, being tortious, would sustain an action expressly alleging the tort. But an action for money had and received has been maintained in many cases where money has been received tortiously without any color of contract. 1 Chit. Pl. (6th ed.) 352. This class of cases is referred to, because they discuss the question what constitutes an unlawful obtaining of money, such as will subject the party obtaining it to an action for damages. * * *[1]

---

[1] The court here cites and discusses the cases of Shaw v. Woodcock, 7 B. & C. 73 (1827); Morgan v. Palmer, 4 D. & R. 283 (1824); Cadadal v. Collins, 4 Ad. & El. 858 (1836); Wakefield v. Newbon, 6 Q.B. 276 (1844); Sortwell v. Horton, 28 Vt. 370 (1856); Chase v. Dwinal, 7 Greenl. 134 (1830); Harmony v. Bingham, 2 Kernan 99 (1854); Maxwell v. Griswold, 10 How. 242 (1850); Cobb v. Charter, 32 Conn. 358 (1865); James v. Roberts, 18 Ohio 548 (1849); Evans v. Huey, 1 Bay 13 (1784); Marriot v. Hampton, 2 Smith Lead. Cas. (6th Am. Ed.) 453 (1866); Benson v. Munroe, 7 Cush. 125 (1851).—Ed.

Without undertaking to lay down a precise rule applicable to all cases, we think it clear that the principle which is established by all the authorities cited above, whether they are actions of tort for disturbing a man in the exercise of his rights and privileges, or to recover back money tortiously obtained, extends to a case like the present. We have no doubt that a conspiracy against a mechanic, who is under the necessity of employing workmen in order to carry on his business, to obtain a sum of money from him, which he is under no legal liability to pay, by inducing his workmen to leave him, and by deterring others from entering into his employment, or by threatening to do this, so that he is induced to pay the money demanded, under a reasonable apprehension that he cannot carry on his business without yielding to the illegal demand, is an illegal, if not a criminal, conspiracy; that the acts done under it are illegal; and that the money thus obtained may be recovered back, and, if the parties succeed in injuring his business, they are liable to pay all the damage thus done to him. It is a species of annoyance and extortion which the common law has never tolerated.

This principle does not interfere with the freedom of business, but protects it. Every man has a right to determine what branch of business he will pursue, and to make his own contracts with whom he pleases and on the best terms he can. He may change from one occupation to another, and pursue as many different occupations as he pleases, and competition in business is lawful. He may refuse to deal with any man or class of men. And it is no crime for any number of persons, without an unlawful object in view, to associate themselves together and agree that they will not work for or deal with certain men or classes of men, or work under a certain price, or without certain conditions. *Commonwealth v. Hunt,* 4 Met. 111, cited above. *Boston Glass Manufactory v. Binney,* 4 Pick. 425. *Bowen v. Matheson,* 14 Allen, 499.

This freedom of labor and business has not always existed. When our ancestors came here, many branches of labor and business were hampered by legal retrictions created by English statutes; and it was a long time before the community fully undertood the importance of freedom in this respect. Some of our early legislation is of this character. One of the colonial acts, entitled "An act against oppression," punished by fine and imprisonment such indisposed persons as may take the liberty to oppress and wrong their neighbors by taking excessive wages for their work, or unreasonable prices for merchandises or other necessary commodities as may pass from man to man. Anc. Chart. 172. Another required artificers, or handicraftmen meet to labor, to work by the day for their neighbors, in mowing, reaping of corn and the inning thereof. *Ib,* 210. Another act regulated the price of bread. *Ib.* 752. Some of our town records show that, under the power to make by-laws, the towns fixed the prices of labor, provisions and several articles of merchandise, as late as the time of the Revolutionary War. But experience and increasing intelligence led to the abolition of all such restrictions, and to the establishment of freedom for all branches of labor and business; and all persons who have been born and educated here, and are obliged to begin life without property, know that freedom to choose their own occupation and to make their own contracts not only elevates their condition, but secures to skill and industry and economy their appropriate advantages.

Freedom is the policy of this country. But freedom does not imply a right in one person, either alone or in combination with others, to disturb or annoy another, either directly or indirectly, in his lawful business or occupation, or to threaten him with annoyance or injury, for the sake of compelling him to buy his peace; or, in the language of the statute cited above, "with intent to extort money or any pecuniary advantage whatever, or to compel him to do any act against his will." The acts alleged and proved in this case are peculiarly offensive to the free principles which prevail in this country; and if such practices could enjoy impunity, they would tend to establish a tyranny of irresponsible persons over labor and mechanical business which would be extremely injurious to both.

Exceptions sustained.

After this decision, the case was settled by the parties, without another trial.[2]

---

[2] Accord: March v. Bricklayers' Union, 79 Conn. 7, 63 Atl. 291 (1906); Burke v. Fay, 128 Mo. App. 690, 107 S.W. 408 (1908); Goldblatt v. Brindell, N.Y.L.J., May 12, 1925; Dorchy v. Kansas, 272 U.S. 306 (1926) *semble.* Cf. Grassi Contracting Co. v. Bennett, 174 App. Div. 244, 160 N.Y.S. 279 (1916). Contrariwise, the exaction of payment of a claim, irrespective of its legal validity, from an employee under threats of discharge is not recoverable. Day v. Studebaker Bros. Mfg. Co., 13 Misc. 320, 34 N.Y.S. 463 (1895). *Quaere,* whether the introduction of the conspiracy element would alter the result.

The exaction of fines by labor leaders under threats of strikes has been frequently punished by the criminal law either as the crime of extortion or the crime of conspiracy. People v. Curran, 286 Ill. 302, 121 N.E. 637 (1918); People v. Seefeldt, 310 Ill. 441, 141 N.E. 829 (1933); People v. Quesse, 310 Ill. 467, 142 N.E. 187 (1923); People v. Mader, 313 Ill. 277, 145 N.E. 137 (1924); People v. Walczak, 315 Ill. 49, 145 N.E. 660 (1924); People v. Walsh, 322 Ill. 195, 153 N.E. 357 (1926); State v. Dalton, 134 Mo. App. 517, 114 S.W. 1132 (1908); People v. Barondess, 133 N.Y. 649, 31 N.E. 240 (1892).

For "racketeering" of this character by trade union leaders, see: Mintz, "Trade Union Abuses," 6 St. Johns Law Rev. 272 (1932); Budenz, "Racketeers of Organized Labor," 1 Common Sense, No. 4, 27 (1933); Intermediate Report of Joint Legislative Committee on Housing, N.Y. Leg. Doc. No. 60, c. 4 (1922); "Union Abuses in the Building Trades Disclosed by Legislative Inquiry," 9 Law & Labor 248 (1927). See: Adamic, Dynamite (1931) *passim.*

SCOTT-STAFFORD OPERA HOUSE COMPANY v. MINNEAPOLIS MUSICIANS ASSOCIATION.

Supreme Court of Minnesota. 118 Minn. 410, 136 N.W. 1092 (1912).

PHILIP E. BROWN, J.:

The plaintiffs are in the theatrical business in the city of Minneapolis. The defendants are, respectively, a corporation having only musicians as members and the officers thereof. The object of the action is to restrain the defendants from enforcing a certain rule adopted by the defendant corporation relative to acceptance by its members of employment by the plaintiffs. This is an appeal from an order sustaining a general demurrer to the complaint.

The complaint, after alleging the character, business, and residence of the several plaintiffs, proceeds, in substance, as follows: The purpose of the defendant corporation, as indicated by its articles of incorporation, is "to unite the instrumental portions of the musical profession for the better protection of its interests in general and the establishment of a minimum rate of prices to be charged by members of said association for their professional services and the enforcement of good faith and fair dealings among its members; to promote the cultivation of the art, and to create a fund for the erection of a suitable building for musical and other purposes of the association." Practically all the musicians available or qualified for the employment by any of the plaintiffs are members of the defendant corporation, and subject to its rules as interpreted by the officers thereof. Each of the plaintiffs, for a number of years past, has been engaged in the business of giving public entertainments and charging admission thereto; and properly to give the same it has been necessary for each of the plaintiffs to invest large sums of money in permanent equipment, such investment having in fact been made by each of the plaintiffs, and being useless for any purpose other than public entertainments. A necessary part of such entertainments is instrumental music, which has been furnished by the members of the defendant corporation; it being impossible for the plaintiffs to obtain satisfactory music for their entertainments except from such members.

Such being the alleged state of affairs, and the relations between the plaintiffs and the members of the defendant corporation, the complaint further alleges that on June 1, 1911, the defendant corporation "adopted, and threatens to, and will, unless restrained by this court, enforce a rule which prohibits any and all members of defendant corporation from accepting employment or playing in the orchestra of any of the plaintiffs, unless at least a certain number of persons, all members of defendant corporation, are included in such orchestra;" that the number of persons required to make up the orchestra for the different entertainments given by each of the plaintiffs varies with the nature of the entertainment to be given; that in many of the entertainments that are given by each plaintiff an orchestra made up of a less number of persons than is required by the said rule would be entirely satisfactory and sufficient, and that a compliance with the said rule in such entertainments would be and is a useless and needless burden and expense upon such plaintiff; that the officers and members of the board of directors of the defendant corporation propose and plan to, and will, unless restrained, avail themselves of the said rule for the purpose of interfering with each of the above-named plaintiffs and with their business, and will prohibit and prevent each plaintiff from securing musicians who are qualified to perform the parts that are necessary to the proper conduct of such orchestra, and will prevent each and all of plaintiffs from furnishing competent orchestras at their said entertainments, and from properly and successfully conducting their said business; that if the defendant corporation, or its said officers, should attempt to enforce the said rule, all of its members, under the rules and by-laws thereof, would be compelled to, and would in fact, comply with its direction, and would refuse to, and would not in fact, accept employment in the orchestras of any of the plaintiffs, if such plaintiffs, or any of them, did not employ the number of musicians required under the said minimum rule; that there is no disagreement or cause of complaint between any of the plaintiffs and any of the said musicians, and that the only cause of complaint is between the plaintiffs on the one side and the defendant corporation and its officers on the other side, on account of the said rule and its enforcement; and that the plaintiffs are without adequate or any remedy at law. The prayer is for a judgment forever restraining the defendants, and each of them, from in any way interfering with the business of the plaintiffs, or any of them, and from enforcing or attempting to enforce said rule, and for general relief.

1. The plaintiffs' first contention is that the rule complained of is *ultra vires,* and that the "corporation has no right to enforce this *ultra vires* rule to the damage of these plaintiffs, and the officers of the corporation have no right to use the corporation for this purpose as against these plaintiffs." * * *

The plaintiffs in the instant case are in no position to challenge the rules of the defendant corporation as being ultra vires; and, even if they had any standing to make such an attack, we are satisfied that the rule under consideration is not *ultra vires.*

2. Unless, therefore, the acts complained of constitute a breach of some legal or equitable duty, without regard to whether or not they were *ultra vires,* the sustaining of the demurrer was proper. This brings us to the plaintiffs' second and only remaining contention, viz., that "the rule complained of, if not subject to the objection that it is *ultra vires* under the articles of incorporation, is not legally enforceable against these plaintiffs in any event." In connection with this contention the plaintiffs practically admit that it is contrary to *Bohn Mnfg. Co. v. Hollis,* 54 Minn. 223, 55 N. W. 1119, 21 L.R.A. 337, 40 Am. St. 319, and seek to show that the rule established by that case has been repudiated, or at least so modified as not to be determinative of the instant case; *Ertz v. Produce Exchange of Minneapolis,* 79 Minn. 140, 81 N.W. 737, 48 L.R.A. 90, 79 Am. St. 433, and *Tuttle v. Buck,* 107 Minn. 145, 119 N.W. 946, 22 L.R.A. (N.S.) 599,

131 Am. St. 446, 16 An. Cas. 807, being cited in this connection. We think, however, that the instant case is controlled by the *Bohn* case, *supra.* Says the syllabus of that case:

"Any man, unless under contract obligation, or unless his employment charges him with some public duty, has a right to refuse to work for or deal with any class of men, as he sees fit."

This proposition is not attacked in the instant case, nor is it assailable. Hence it follows that any one of the members of the defendant corporation would have had the right to refuse to work for any one of the plaintiffs, except upon such terms and conditions as such member might have seen fit to impose.

"And this right," continues the syllabus in the *Bohn* case, "which one man may exercise singly, any number may agree to exercise jointly."

Again, at page 234, this same case, Mitchell, J., says: "What one man may lawfully do singly, two or more may lawfully agree to do jointly. The number who unite to do the act cannot change its character from lawful to unlawful."

Unquestionably this is the law in this state, and it has never been repudiated or modified by this court. See *State v. Daniels, supra,* page 155, 136 N.W. 584. The cases of *Tuttle v. Buck, supra,* and *Ertz v. Produce Exchange of Minneapolis, supra,* merely stand for a converse rule, which, as stated by Chief Justice Start in the *Ertz* case, page 145, is that "one man singly, or any number of men jointly, having no legitimate interests to protect, may not lawfully ruin the business of another by maliciously inducing his patrons and third parties not to deal with him. * * * This is just what the complaint in this case charges the defendants with doing, and we hold that it states a cause of action." This is equally the settled law; but we do not agree with the plaintiffs in their contention that it applies to the instant case. Paraphrasing the concluding sentence of the *Ertz* case, "This is just what the complaint in this case did *not* charge." There is no allegation of any contractual relation between the plaintiffs, or any of them, and any of the defendants, or any of the members of the defendant corporation. There is no allegation of conspiracy, malice, or ulterior motive. No question of strike, violence, wage, boycott, or violation of contractual relations or public duty, is involved; and no allegation is made that the rule complained of is not beneficial to the members of the defendant corporation.

The plaintiffs' argument is largely based upon the assumption of lack of benefit to such members; but, in the absence of any allegation of such lack of benefit, we think it may fairly be inferred from the facts and circumstances alleged, and from the very nature of the rule recited, that the rule was designed to benefit the members of the defendant corporation. Certainly the rule does not appear to be so manifestly nonadapted to produce benefit as to raise an inference of malice or evil motive. As said in the *Ertz* case, *supra,* in distinguishing the *Bohn* case, *supra:* "It is to be noted that the defendants in the *Bohn* case had similar legitimate interests to protect * * * and that the defendants' efforts to induce parties not to deal * * * were limited to members of the association having similar interests to conserve, and that there was no agreement or combination or attempt to induce other persons not members of the association to withhold their patronage," etc. The rule established by the *Bohn* case was reiterated, though not applied, in the *Ertz* case, and there is nothing in the *Tuttle* case, *supra,* to the contrary.

We think it applies to the instant case, and the order sustaining the demurrer to the complaint is therefore affirmed.[1]

BARKER PAINTING CO. v. BROTHERHOOD OF PAINTERS, DECORATORS, AND PAPERHANGERS OF AMERICA.

Court of Appeals of the District of Columbia. 57 D.C. App. 322,
23 Fed.(2d) 743 (1927).

MARTIN, Chief Justice: This is an appeal from a decree of the lower court, dismissing a bill of complaint filed by appellant for an injunction to prevent the enforcement against it of certain union labor regulations with reference to the employment of union labor by appellant.

It appears from the record that appellant is a corporation located in New York City, and that it takes contracts for inside and outside painting and decorating throughout the United States. When performing such contracts in cities other than New York, appellant employs union painters procured in New York City, together with others procured at the place where the contract is to be performed. The Brotherhood of Painters, Decorators, and Paperhangers of America, Inc., is a union labor organization affiliated with the American Federation of Labor, and is composed of various local unions throughout the country. The latter severally exercise local jurisdiction within certain prescribed areas, and only members of such local unions are eligible to be members of the incorporated organization. The Brotherhood has adopted certain rules and regulations relating to union labor throughout the country, and any infraction of these regulations by a member of a local union may be punished by fine, suspension, or expulsion from the union.

Among the regulations adopted and thus enforced by the Brotherhood are those commonly known as the "higher wage," "shorter week," and "fifty per cent." rules. These provide that, where a contractor undertakes a painting job "outside his home city or town, and in a locality where a district council or local council exists," he shall pay union painters the

---

[1] Accord: Empire Theatre Co. v. Cloke, 53 Mont. 183, 163 Pac. 107 (1917). *Contra:* Haverhill Strand Theatre v. Gillen, 229 Mass. 413, 118 N.E. 671 (1918); Folsom Engraving Co. v. McNeil, 235 Mass. 269, 126 N.E. 479 (1920). *Cf.* Des Moines City Ry. Co. v. Amalgamated Ass'n of St. & Elec. Ry. Employees, 204 Iowa 1195, 213 N.W. 264 (1927); Edelman, Edelman & Berrie v. Retail Grocery & Dairy Clerks' Union, 119 Misc. 618, 198 N.Y.S. 70; Longshore Printing Co. v. Howell, 26 Ore. 527, 38 Pac. 547 (1894).

higher rate of pay and give them the shorter working week prevailing as between the several localities, and shall also employ at least 50 per cent. of the painters engaged upon the local contract from among the members of the local union. The rules also provide that no union authority shall have power to grant exclusive or special privileges to any local union belonging to the Brotherhood, that all local conditions shall be strictly adhered to, and that the shorter workday and the higher wage scale of either locality, as well as the 50 per cent. employment regulation, shall prevail in all cases.

In the year 1923 the appellant entered into a contract to do the painting work for the Walker Hotel in the city of Washington, District of Columbia, for the sum of $70,000, the work to be performed under penalties within a specified time. The New York rate of pay for union painters was $10.50 per day of 8 hours, working 5 days a week, while the Washington rate was $9 per day of 8 hours, working 5½ days a week. Accordingly the enforcement of the higher wage rule under these circumstances would compel appellant, if employing union painters, to pay $10.50 a day for those employed upon the contract, whereas any contractor located in Washington would be able to employ union painters for the same work at $9 per day. Appellant was fully informed concerning these union regulations before it entered into the contract with the hotel company, but it intended to protest against their observance or enforcement in relation to this contract. Accordingly, after taking the contract it conferred with officers of the local union for the purpose of inducing them to waive the higher wage and shorter time requirements; but this request was refused, and appellant was informed that the members of the local union would not be permitted to work upon the contract except in accordance with all of the union rules.

Appellant nevertheless sought to secure union painters by inserting advertisements in the local newspapers, and in answer thereto a number of local union painters appeared at appellant's office at the place of work. These were met there, however, by officers of the union, who informed them that appellant intended to disregard the aforesaid union rules, whereupon the union painters refused to accept the employment and left the place. Appellant then filed its complaint in the lower court, claiming that the rules were discriminatory, unreasonable, arbitrary, and tending to create a monopoly, and that the enforcement thereof by the Brotherhood and the local union, under threat of fine, suspension, or expulsion, constituted a conspiracy, and was a violation of the anti-trust laws of the United States, and, if permitted, would result in irreparable injury to appellant and to appellant's property. Appellant therefore prayed for a temporary restraining order, and for a perpetual injunction against the enforcement thereof. A temporary restraining order was accordingly granted by the court, but upon final hearing the court entered a decree against appellant. This appeal followed.

We think that the decree of the lower court was right. It is clear that the union painters were free either to accept or reject employment upon the terms offered by appellant, and correspondingly that appellant was free to accept or reject the terms of employment offered by the men. In this instance there was no strike or intimidation, nor any threat of disorder or interference with appellant's right to employ nonunion painters. It cannot be claimed that there was any breach of contract by the men; the latter simply refused to enter into any contract of employment upon the terms offered by appellant. It is certain that appellant could not compel the union painters to work for it upon its own terms, regardless of their consent. *Adair v. United States,* 208 U.S. 174, 28 S. Ct. 277, 52 L. Ed. 436, 13 Ann. Cas. 764; National Protective Association v. Cumming, 170 N.Y. 315, 63 N.E. 369, 58 L.R.A. 135, 88 Am. St. Rep. 648; Jersey City Printing Co. v. Cassidy, 63 N.J. Eq. 759, 53 A. 230. And if the refusal of the union painters to work under these circumstances resulted in pecuniary loss to appellant, such loss would be *damnum absque injuria. My Maryland Lodge v. Adt,* 100 Md. 238, 59 A. 721, 68 L.R.A. 752; *Purvis v. United Brotherhood,* 214 Pa. 348, 354, 358, 63 A. 585, 12 L.R.A. (N.S.) 642, 112 Am. St. Rep. 757, 6 Ann. Cas. 275.

As for appellant's charge that the enforcement of the contested rules by the unions under penalty of fine or expulsion constitutes a conspiracy in violation of the anti-trust laws, we think this charge is answered by section 6 of the Clayton Act, which provides that the labor of a human being is not a commodity or article of commerce, and that nothing contained in the Anti-Trust Act shall be construed to forbid the existence and operation of labor organizations, instituted for the purpose of mutual help, and not having capital stock or conducted for profit, or to forbid or restrain individual members of such organziations from lawfully carrying out the legitimate objects thereof; nor shall such organizations, or the members thereof, be held or construed to be illegal combinations or conspiracies in restraint of trade, under the anti-trust laws. 38 Stat. 731, c. 323, § 6 (15 U.S.C.A. § 17). Under these provisions the painters' unions, and the individual members thereof, are entitled to carry out the legitimate objects of their organizations, provided no unlawful means be employed to that end. The adoption of regulations fixing the wages of union labor, together with provisions restricting the number of hours of labor per day and of days per week, are within "the legitimate objects" of such unions within the sense of the Clayton Act. Otherwise the provisions of the act regarding labor unions would be futile.

Moreover, it is not unlawful for such unions to punish a member by fine, suspension, or expulsion for an infraction of the union rules, since membership in the union is purely voluntary. 24 Cyc. 824. Nor do we think that the regulations now in question are discriminatory, unreasonable, arbitrary, or oppressive. The higher wage and shorter week rules were adopted by the Brotherhood prior to the year 1913; the 50 per cent. rule in 1922; and they have been in force ever since. They are designed to meet a situation which without regulation would be productive of confusion and disorder for union labor. The cost of living is higher in some places than in others; therefore union wages vary in different localities. If a contractor employs union labor upon work in his own city, he must pay the union wages of that locality; but, if he moves his force of local labor to another city, he may meet there with a higher or lower union wage scale, as well as with different limitations as to periods of labor. It was to meet these contingencies that the rules now in question were adopted; and this case does not involve their wisdom, but only their legality. The rules do not discriminate against any particular person or place, and are uniform in their operation throughout the country. As far as appears, they were regularly adopted in good faith by the Brotherhood, they govern the conduct of its members only, and the members are lawfully entitled to obey them by abstaining from work in applicable cases if they so desire. *Jersey City Printing Co. v. Cassidy,* 63 N.J. Eq. 759, 53 A. 230.

The present issue has been before the courts in various cases, and the weight of authority is decidedly adverse to appellant's claim. *Barker Painting Co. v. Local Union, etc.* (D.C.) 12 F.(2d) 945; *Barker Painting Co. v. Brotherhood of Painters* (C.C.A.) 15 F.(2d) 16; *New Jersey Painting Co. v. Local Union No. 26,* 96 N.J. Eq. 632, 126 A. 399, 47 A.L.R. 384.

Various arguments are presented by appellant, which we have considered, but have not set out specifically in this opinion; for we consider it sufficient to say that in our judgment appellant's case is without support in law.

The decree of the lower court is affirmed, with costs, and the cause is remanded, for such further orders as are necessary with reference to the injunction *pendente lite* entered in the case below.[1]

---

[1] Certiorari denied in 276 U.S. 631 (1928). Accord: Barker Painting Co. v. Local No. 734, 34 Fed. (2d) 3 (1929), decree affirmed as moot in 281 U.S. 462 (1930); Barker Painting Co. v. Brotherhood, 15 Fed.(2d) 16 (1926), certiorari denied in 273 U.S. 748 (1927); New Jersey Painting Co. v. Local No. 26, 96 N.J. Eq. 632, 126 Atl. 399 (1924); Marshall v. Brotherhood Painters (Pa. Comm. Pl. 1925) (unreported but published in briefs accompanying 281 U.S. 748); Douglas & Bros. Inc. v. Malette (R.I. Sup. Ct.) (unreported but published *ibid.*). *Contra:* Hass Inc. v. Local Union No. 17, 300 Fed. 894 (1924). For comment on these decisions, see: 38 Harv. Law Rev. 400 (1925). *Cf.* Glieman v. Barker Painting Co., 227 App. Div. 585, 238 N.Y.S. 419 (1930). See: Intermediate Report Joint Legislative Committee on Housing, N.Y. Leg. Doc. No. 60, 60 (1922).

C. B. RUTAN COMPANY v. LOCAL UNION, NO. 4, HATTERS' UNION OF AMERICA.

New Jersey Court of Chancery. 97 N.J. Eq. 77, 128 Atl. 622 (1925).

BACKES, V.C.: This bill is to restrain a union labor strike. The complainant is a hat manufacturer. Its factory is divided into three shops—making, finishing and trimming, each employing about twenty-five hands. Finding that the making shop was unprofitable, and that hat bodies could be bought cheaper, the complainant shut it down and discharged the hat makers. Thereupon the finishers quit work. The complainant charges that they struck to compel it to re-establish the making shop. The defendants, finishers, say they quit—struck—because their fellow-unionists were thrown out of work, and because they do not regard it to the interest of union labor to work for an employer who has a making shop and refuses to operate it, and that the policy of the union in this respect is expressed by its by-laws that "no manufacturer shall be allowed the union label who has a plank [making] shop and buys his hats in the rough, unless the plank shop is running at full capacity." That they had the right to, singly or in concert, refuse to work, out of sympathy for their fellow-employes, or because they regarded it as not of advantage to organized labor to work for this complainant under the circumstances, or for no explained reason at all, is beyond question. *New Jersey Painting Co. v. Local No. 26*, 96 N.J. Eq. 632, where many of the leading cases are cited. See, also, *Maisel v. Sigman*, 205 N.Y. Supp. 807; *Saulsbery v. Coopers' International Union*, 147 Ky. 170; *Union Pacific Railroad Co. v. Ruef*, 120 Fed. Rep. 114. Organized labor has the same right to choose its employers as employers have to select their labor, and so long as they confine their activities to advancing their own welfare, whatever the ramifications may be, the other has no cause for complaint, and when these activities, lawfully carried on, conflict, and, as sometimes happens, labor, because of its ascendancy, is powerful enough to dictate terms within the scope indicated, judicial interference is unjustified. If, however, the purpose of a strike is, and as the complainant contends it is here, to compel an employer to run his shop against his will, and to his injury re-employ his discharged hands, for whom he has no use, then the strike is unlawful, for the union has no right to prevent employers of labor from profitably prosecuting their businesses. *Folsom Engraving Co. v. McNeil*, 235 Mass. 269; *Roraback v. Motion Picture Machine Operatives Union*, 140 Minn. 481; *Haverhill Strand Theatre v. Gillen*, L.R.A. 1918 c. 813. The *New Jersey Painting Co. Case, supra,* is in line with accepted authority, that the strike weapon may be used if the object is to advance the interest of organized labor, provided the object be otherwise not unlawful. The act of 1883 (*Comp. Stat.* p. 3051) was there regarded as of greater force than heretofore entertained, but the case does not countenance the strike, to advance the interest of organized labor, if the purpose is to impinge upon the constitutional rights of employers, to pursue their callings unmolested. This court enjoined the strike there involved because it was sought to enforce a rule relating to the wage scale which was thought to discriminate between employers of labor upon an illusory and harmful basis, and was in unfair restraint of trade, but the court of errors and appeals was of the opinion that, although discriminatory, inasmuch as the rule operated alike on all employers similarly fixed, and as its prime object was to establish a standard of wages, it was within the province of the union to make, and a strike to enforce it was not unlawful. The act of 1883 had theretofore been regarded as relieving organized labor only from liability to criminal prosecution (*Jonas Glass Co. v. Glass Bottle Blowers Assn.*, 77 N.J. Eq. 219; *Erdman v. Mitchell*, 207 Pa. 79), but the court of errors and appeals declared the statute to be much broader in its scope. How much, or in what respect, was not indicated. It surely does not extend immunity for invasion of private rights, for that is beyond the power of the legislature to grant. *Adair v. United States*, 208 U.S. 161; *Coppage v. Kansas*, 236 U.S. 1.

The proofs fall short of showing the unlawful purpose charged, although in the circumstances the complainant may have to re-establish its plank shop or go out of business altogether. For such misfortune the members of the union disclaim responsibility, and rightly. They were not under contract to work; they have done nothing more than refrain from working; they have not prevented the complainant from procuring other hands, and none of the usual strike tactics has been resorted to to deter others from taking their places, nor have they in any way interfered with the complainant in the carrying on of its business in its own way. In fine, their attitude has been simply one of hands off and let the complainant get along as best it may without them. This attitude is not open to judicial criticism.

Injunction denied and bill dismissed.[1]

THE LUNDOFF-BICKNELL CO. v. SMITH.

Ohio Court of Appeals for Cuyahoga County. 24 Ohio App. 294, 156 N.E. 243 (1927).

WASHBURN, J.: There are more than a dozen crafts in the building trades industry in Cleveland. In each craft there is an organization of employes and a corresponding organization of employers. There are existing contracts between the employers' organization and the employes' organization in all of the crafts, except that of the painters and glaziers.

---

[1] *Contra:* Welinsky v. Hillman, 185 N.Y.S. 257 (Sup. Ct. 1920); Benito Rovira Inc. v. Yampolsky. 187 N.Y.S. 894 (Sup. Ct. 1921). *Cf.* Jaeckel v. Kaufman, 187 N.Y.S. 889 (Sup. Ct. 1920); Wood Mowing & Mach. Co. v. Toohey, 114 Misc. 185, 186 N.Y.S. 95 (1921); Mechanics Foundry & Machine Co. v. Lynch, 236 Mass. 504, 128 N.E. 877 (1920).

These are entirely separate contracts, and each relates entirely to the craft in reference to which the contract was made, and in said contracts there is no attempt made to cover or agree upon working conditions in crafts other than the one to which the particular contract relates. No two of the contracts are identical, and all combined they cover 150 pages. We cannot attempt to make even a summarization of all of them, but so far as the questions involved in this case are concerned a general idea of them may be obtained from a statement of some of the provisions of one of them, the laborers' contract.

The parties to that contract jointly and severally agreed and covenanted that they would be governed and bound thereby. It provides that the "workmen are at liberty to work for whomsoever they see fit," and that the "employers are at liberty to employ and discharge whomsoever they see fit," and provides:

"It is expressly understood that there shall be no strikes or lockouts of any kind ordered or permitted against the members of either party hereto, pending a decision in accordance with the arbitration plan as outlined in Article XIX. Such decision shall be final and binding on the parties to the dispute. It is understood, however, that union men shall not be compelled to work with nonunion men *in the same trade in or on the same building.*"

It also provides that, in the event members of such workmen's organization cannot be secured with reasonable effort, the employer shall be permitted to hire workmen in that craft who are not members of that organization, provided they signify their willingness to join such organization, and then provides in Article XIX as follows:

"For the purpose of administering this agreement a joint arbitration committee shall be established by the appointment of five members of the party of the first part and an equal number of members of the party of the second part. In case *any* dispute or disagreement shall arise between such parties, the same shall be reported at once, and before any action is taken, to the chairman of such joint committee, who shall call a meeting of the entire committee within twenty-four hours of receipt of such information. There shall be no cessation of work pending such decision."

Many of the other contracts contain provisions similar to the foregoing, providing for an arbitration committee for the purpose of settling disputes between the employers and employes, and providing that there shall be no cessation of work while the parties are attempting to settle their differences, and in most of those that do not contain express provisions to that effect such provisions are fairly implied from the whole contract, considered in the light of all the facts and circumstances.

As has been said, all of the crafts in the building industry were covered by these contracts except the painters and glaziers, whose contract had expired and who had been engaged in a strike during the summer.

The plaintiff company, having the general contract to construct the Bell Telephone building, was a member of several of these contractors' organizations, and each of said company's subcontractors was a member of the contractors' organization in his particular craft.

All of the men working upon the building were union men, being members of said organizations, and on September 13, 1926, the subcontractor for the painting and glazing put four nonunion glaziers to work on the building, and the workmen in the other crafts, through their agents, objected to the employment of said nonunion glaziers on the job, and after some negotiations, not being able to have said nonunion glaziers discharged, all of the men on the job quit work at the same time, and thereupon this action was begun by the plaintiff, the company having the general contract for the construction of the building, and in the court below plaintiff obtained an order requiring the officers of the union organizations to rescind an order to strike, found to have been made by them, and enjoining them from doing anything to induce or influence the men not to go back to work.

On appeal the case has been heard *de novo* in this court.

No strike was called in accordance with and in the manner provided by the constitutions and by-laws of the union organizations, and on the important disputed question of fact in the case we find that the plaintiff has not established by a preponderance of the evidence that the men quit work in obedience to any order made by the officers and agents of said unions; but we do find that the men quit by concerted action and that the officers and agents of said unions were in sympathy with the men's quitting, and took no action to prevent the strike after the contractors had refused to remove the nonunion glaziers from the job, or to have the men go back to work after the strike, or to have the dispute arbitrated in accordance with said contracts.

It should be kept in mind that this is an action in equity, and we are not attempting to determine the rights of the parties at law.

It is the claim of the men who quit, and of the organizations of which they are members, that the quitting of the men was not a violation of their contracts, and it is the claim of the contractor that, even if under each contract the presence of nonunion men in a particular craft justified the workmen in such craft in collectively quitting without violating their contract, none of said contracts gave to the workmen in one craft the right to quit because nonunion men were employed in another craft, and that that matter, not being covered by any express provision of the contracts, was a matter which the workmen were required by the contracts to arbitrate, and that a strike without any attempt to arbitrate was a violation of the contracts.

As has been said, the provisions of these contracts vary. Some of them contain the express provision that matters expressly agreed to in the contracts shall not be subject to arbitration, and in others, where such an express provision is not made, it is implied, and, except as to such matters, the contracts usually provide that *any* dispute or disagreement arising between the parties shall be referred to an arbitration committee.

We are of the opinion that, considering the expressed objects and purposes of these agreements and all the facts and circumstances, the disagreement as to whether or not nonunion glaziers should be permitted to work upon the building was a dispute which the workmen in crafts other than painting and glazing were required to attempt to settle and adjust under the provisions of the contracts, and that the collective quitting of the men without such attempt was a violation of their contracts.

The claim of secondary boycott is inconsistent with the claim that the men had a trade dispute with plaintiff as to whether said contracts covered the situation in which the contracting parties found themselves to be, and which they were bound to arbitrate under said contracts, and we find that the men did have a trade dispute with their employers, and that the facts do not warrant a finding that there was a secondary boycott.

There is no claim that the defendants acted maliciously, with the purpose of merely injuring the plaintiff, and there is no evidence of violence or destruction of property; and we find that the men had a trade dispute with their employers, with whom they had contracts, and that the situation was such that, except for the claimed breach of said contracts, the evidence does not establish an unlawful conspiracy. On the part of the men there was an honest, though untenable, claim as to the proper construction of said contract, and they did not quit their employment for the purpose and with the intention of wronging and injuring the plaintiff; they had a right to quit as they did, unless the contracts made such action wrongful, so the basis of the plaintiff's cause of action is the claimed violation of the contracts.

As we construe said contracts, almost all of them, either by express provision or by implication, bound the men not to strike, but to submit their dispute with their employer concerning the presence of the four nonunion glaziers on the job to arbitration in the manner provided in said contracts, but we recognize the fact that there might have been an honest difference of opinion as to whether or not the contracts required the men to arbitrate the dispute growing out of the presence on the job of said nonunion glaziers—that is, as to whether our construction is the true and proper construction of said contracts.

We find above to be the true and proper construction of said contracts, and that the men violated their contracts by quitting as they did; but we are unable to find that the men were not honest in their contention as to the meaning of said contracts, or that they were guilty of any wrong except the mere violation of their contracts.

The wrong that they did was to quit work in a body, and that was wrong only because they had agreed not to do so.

Plaintiff, the general contractor, was a party to only five of said contracts. The subcontractors who were parties to the other contracts are not parties to this suit. But, assuming that the situation is such that plaintiff's rights were invaded by the violation of all of said contracts, and assuming that said contracts do not contravene public policy, and as to that there is not sufficient evidence to enable us to express an opinion, what relief can a court of equity afford plaintiff, after its men have quit in violation of their contracts?

It has long been settled that, if an individual employe quits work in violation of his express contract, a court of equity will not, indirectly or negatively, by means of an injunction restraining a violation of the contract, compel the employe to perform his contract by performing the personal service he agreed to perform.

Relief of that character has always been regarded as impracticable, and as an invasion of one's natural liberty, involuntary servitude being prohibited by the Constitution. * * *

We conclude that, treating them as individuals, we are without power to make an order that the men, who quit work shall go back to work, or that other members of the defendant unions shall go to work on said building.

As to our power as a court of equity to afford relief to plaintiff, what effect has the fact that the men combined and acted in concert in committing the wrong or violating their contracts?

Men may combine to do a lawful act by lawful means, and their agreement to so act in concert does not constitute a conspiracy and is not illegal. In this case there was no unlawful means employed. Was the violation of their contract unlawful? The mere breaching of a contract is not unlawful; it may be wrong, and may render the wrongdoer liable, but it is not prohibited by law. If one contracts to build a house, he may change his mind and refuse to build it, paying the damages; but he does not commit an unlawful act by such breach of his contract. There are well-considered cases which support the proposition that if two or more whose individual breach of a contract would not be unlawful act together in breaching such contract, and do no wrong except the mere breach of the contract, their acting in concert is not unlawful.

Accordingly, it has been held, and we think properly, that workmen, who are bound by contract not to strike, may, by concerted action, leave the service of their employer and their act in so doing will not constitute an illegal strike, if they have a *bona fide* dispute with their employer, and act honestly and peaceably, and not simply to do injury and wrong, and do not interfere with the free action of others, or molest the property of their employer; in other words, the *mere* violation of a contract not to strike does not render a strike illegal.

But if the view expressed in other cases be adopted, and the collective quitting of the men did constitute an illegal strike in this case, we can find no satisfactory reason for holding that a court of equity can compel them to return to work collectively, any more than individually, and we are of the opinion that the facts of this case do not warrant any such action.

Only a comparatively few of the members of the defendant unions were working on the building in question, and, as has been said, we do not find that the defendant officers and agents of the unions ordered or caused the men to quit; therefore we can make no order requiring them to take any affirmative action to rescind anything done by them.

It is urged, however, by counsel for plaintiff, that this court should issue a mandatory injunction ordering the officers and agents of defendant unions to use their alleged disciplinary power under the constitutions and by-laws of their respective organizations to make the men who struck return to work.

This, too, we do not feel we have the power to do.

A court of equity should not make a *mandatory* order, which is to be enforced by the extraordinary remedy of contempt, unless the ultimate purpose to be accomplished by such order is one which such court is empowered to accomplish. If we cannot order the men themselves, who are parties to this suit, to perform personal services, we ought not to make an order the only purpose of which is to indirectly accomplish that result. * * *

During the hearing of the case, at the suggestion of this court, work was resumed on the building, with the exception of the painting and glazing, and no painting and glazing have been done since then; the men went back to work with the understanding that their doing so would not prejudice their rights in this suit, and hence the decision and order must be based upon the situation as it was at the time said truce was agreed to by the parties. Therefore, for the purposes of this case, the men are not now working, they having quit on September 18; we have found that so quitting was a breach of their contracts, but that, for reasons already given, a court of equity should make no order designed, directly or indirectly, to compel them to go back to work. Ought we to make any order preventing third parties interfering with the contract relations of plaintiff as to the five contracts to which plaintiff was a party? These contracts do not provide for the services of any particular persons, nor is there an *express* stipulation that a particular class of persons should perform the work on said building; if, at the beginning of the construction of said building, plaintiff had determined not to make use of any union labor, or the unions had determined not to do any work on said building, neither of the parties would have violated any *express* provision of the contracts; if a third party, desiring plaintiff to build a building and knowing of said contracts, had required the plaintiff to agree not to employ union men in the construction of the building, would such owner have thereby become liable to the unions for causing plaintiff to breach said contracts? It is no answer to say that these contracts were so made indefinite and uncertain because of a fear that, if they expressed what the parties intended, they would probably violate public policy and be unenforceable.

The contracts established the terms of an employment, and the working conditions when an employer hired a given worker, and expressly provided that there should be no lockouts or strikes; after the contracts have been completely breached, and the situation is such that a court of equity does not have power to compel the parties to resume operations and carry out the contracts, and there is no evidence that the men desire to carry out their contracts by working with nonunion glaziers or submitting that question to arbitration, is there such a contract relation as will justify a court in enjoining third parties from interfering with it?

The glaziers had no contract, and we do not find in the contracts as to the other trades any express or implied provision as to whether non-union glaziers could or could not be employed on the building, and considering the indefiniteness of the contracts and the character of the controversy, and the fact that the men did not quit in obedience to any order of their superiors, and that they have shown no desire to discontinue their breach of said contracts, we do not find, under the facts and circumstances of the case, that plaintiff is entitled to an order protecting its contractual relations from the disruptive influence of third parties.

A decree may be drawn dismissing plaintiff's petition, and in the exercise of our discretion we refuse to punish defendants for contempt of court in not obeying the order of the common pleas court, which we find should not have been made.

FARR, J., concurs.[1]

BAYER v. BROTHERHOOD OF PAINTERS, DECORATORS AND PAPERHANGERS OF AMERICA, LOCAL 301.

New Jersey Court of Errors and Appeals. 108 N.J. Eq. 257, 154 Atl. 759 (1931).

The opinion of the court was delivered by DONGES, J.

The complainant-respondent is a painting contractor operating in the vicinity of the city of Trenton. The defendants-appellants are Brotherhood of Painters, Decorators and Paperhangers of America, Local 301, its principals, agents, officers and servants, and Arthur W. McConnell, who is the business agent of the aforesaid local union.

The difficulty between the parties arises from the alleged interest of complainant in a concern which uses machines to apply paint. Complain-

---

[1] The concurring opinion of Sayre, J., is omitted.
The strike in violation of a trade agreement is generally regarded as illegal without inquiry into the motives of the strikers. Barnes & Co. v. Berry, 156 Fed. 72 (C.C.S.D. Ohio 1907); Preble v. Architectural Iron Workers Union, 260 Ill. App. 435 (1931); Meltzer v. Kaminer, 131 Misc. 813, 227 N.Y.S. 459 (1927); Moran v. Lasette, 221 App. Div. 118, 222 N.Y.S. 283 (1927); M'Grath v. Norman, 221 App. Div. 804, 223 N.Y.S. 288 (1927); Gilchrist Co. v. Metal Polishers, etc., Union, 113 Atl. 320 (N.J. Ch. 1919); Beckerman v. Bakery Union, 28 Ohio N.P. (N.S.) 550 (1931).
Contrariwise, the strike to enforce a trade agreement, unless the agreement itself is illegal, is regarded as legal. Rhodes Bros. Co. v. Musicians Protective Union, 37 R.I. 281, 92 Atl. 641 (1915).
See also: decision of the Landgericht, Hamburg, of May 5, 1927, Hanseatische Gerichtszeitung (Arbeitsrecht), 1927, p. 129, abstracted in 1927 Internat'l Survey of Legal Decisions in Labour Law, 194; decision of the Kammergericht, Berlin, 1924, Juristische Wochenschrift, 1925, No. 5, 269, abstracted in 1925 id. 164.

ant denied that he used such machines in his own business but admitted that he advanced the money for the purchase of such a machine for a corporation in which he is a stockholder and that such corporation uses such machines.

The bill of complaint prays for an injunction restraining defendants and all persons whomsoever associated with them from placing complainant on the unfair list of the defendant union; from proceeding to attempt to collect fines levied upon complainant or his employes; from doing anything whatsoever to keep union men from working for complainant; from injuring the business of complainant in any manner, shape or form; from suggesting, promoting, encouraging or participating in any manner in sympathetic strikes against complainant; from addressing persons willing to be employed by complainant with a view to persuading them or any of them to refrain from working for complainant.

The vice-chancellor found that the union and McConnell, its business agent, had "collectively conspired and by threats and intimidation [of being fined and disciplined by the union] kept others who were willing and desirous of working for complainant, from so doing." He found that the appellants had adopted unlawful means of preventing members of the union from working for the respondent. He further found that it was not against the by-laws or rules of the union for an employer to own stock in a paint-spraying machine, and that the only justification was a paragraph in the minutes of the regular meeting of defendant local, under date of August 13th, 1928, that "a lengthy discussion was held on the spraying machine * * * Local Union 301 again went on record as refusing to recognize the spray machine by prohibiting its use by their members or the recognition of any employer using said machine or associated in any way with the use of one."

The order complained of is very broad, and includes restraint from attempting to collect a fine imposed upon complainant or the fines imposed upon complainant's workmen, members of the local union, "and from threatening or doing anything whatsoever unlawful to prevent or keep union men from working for complainant, and from injuring the business of complainant in any manner, shape or form by any unlawful acts or conduct; and from suggesting, permitting, encouraging or participating in any manner in sympathetic strikes against complainant on account of, or because of any matter or thing heretofore set up in this cause by said defendants, in justification of their acts in this behalf complained of herein by said complainant."

The language of the order just quoted is vague and uncertain as to the acts sought to be restrained. The order restrains the threatening or doing of things "unlawful" to prevent union men from working for complainant, and restrains defendants from acting in any manner in sympathetic strikes against complainant by reason of any matter or thing set up by defendants in justification of their acts. The order restrains *unlawful* acts but does not point out what specific acts defendants are to refrain from performing, and, in the last clause referred to, requires interpretation by defendants of the pleadings and proofs to determine what acts are restrained.

The vice-chancellor concluded that complainant had been declared to be "unfair" to union labor, and that the union had imposed a fine upon him.

If complainant had been declared to be "unfair," no harm could result unless such declaration was followed by the refusal of employes to work for him and by efforts of defendants to induce others to refrain from working for him.

The fragments of minutes of the defendant union as printed in the record do not disclose that any action was taken by the local union against the complainant. It is denied that any fine was assessed against him. As stated in the conclusions of the vice-chancellor, no fine could be collected from complainant, if it had been assessed.

The question to be decided, then, is as to the right of employes to combine, and, by peaceable means, to refuse to work for an employer who does not conform to the rules of the union, and to persuade others to leave such employment or to refuse to enter such employment.

The court below appears to have concluded that efforts to persuade their members not to work or to discipline them for breaking the union rules were unlawful because the conduct of the complainant was not unlawful.

The finding of the court of chancery in this case is in direct conflict with the legislative policy as declared in the act of 1883, page 36 (3 Comp. Stat. p. 3051), which provides "that it shall not be unlawful for any two or more persons to unite, combine or bind themselves by oath, covenant, agreement, alliance or otherwise, to persuade, advise or encourage, by peaceable means, any person or persons to enter into any combination for or against leaving or entering into the employment of any person, persons or corporation."

This act was passed upon by this court in *New Jersey Painting Co. v. Local No. 26, Brotherhood of Painters, &c.,* 96 N.J. Eq. 632, which involved an application to the court of chancery to enjoin a strike called by the business agent of the union to enforce the demand of the union with respect to wages. In that case Mr. Justice Black, speaking for the court, said:

"The law gives the defendants a right to sell their labor to whom they please, when and under such conditions as they may fix, individually or in combinations. They may make rules and regulations, passed in good faith, providing for what they deem to be an economic advantage to themselves. If, in the enforcement of such rules and regulations, they violate no law, but act solely for the declared purpose, the courts ought not and cannot legally enjoin them from such concerted action, simply because such action may affect some employers. How can it be said that such rules and regulations create an unfair restraint of trade? If the law gives the workers such rights, it must protect them in their enjoyment. They cannot be enjoined from their use or interfered with by the courts. Employers have no vested interest in the labor of workers. We think the defendants, by the terms of the statute of 1882, both its letter and spirit, are within its protection."

In the *Painting Company Case* the controversy arose over wages. In the instant case the difference arose over the alleged conduct of complainant in encouraging the use of machines instead of manual labor to apply paint, which practice the defendants regard as inimical to their economic welfare. If, as was said in the *Painting Company Case,* "the union may arbitrarily fix a uniform scale of wage applicable to all its members and strike to enforce its demands," it may likewise arbitrarily fix conditions of labor, and strike to enforce such demands.

Since the case above referred to was decided, the legislature has adopted the act of 1926 (P.L. 1926 p. 348), which provides:

"No restraining order or writ of injunction shall be granted or issued out of any court of this state in any case involving or growing out of a dispute concerning terms or conditions of employment, enjoining or restraining any person or persons, either singly or in concert, from terminating any relation of employment, or from ceasing to perform any work or labor, or from peaceably and without threats or intimidation recommending, advising or persuading others so to do; or from peaceably and without threats or intimidation being upon any public street or highway, or thoroughfare for the purpose of obtaining or communicating information, or to peaceably and without threats or intimidation persuade any person or persons to work or abstain from working, or to employ or to cease to employ any party to a labor dispute, or to peaceably and without threats or intimidation recommend, advise or persuade others so to do, provided said persons remain separated one from the other at intervals of ten paces or more."

Nothing has been proved in this case to warrant a finding that the defendants have done or threatened anything that is not legalized by the acts of the legislature.

It seems clear from the statutes and the decisions of the courts of our own state, as well as of other jurisdictions, that employes may combine for their mutual protection; that they may for themselves conclude what acts and things are for their economic welfare; that they may enforce their demands by strikes, if they thereby violate no contracts of employment; that they may peaceably and without threats or intimidation, induce others to do so, if no contractual rights are violated thereby. None of these acts is unlawful, and the fact that complainant may be affected unfavorably by the regulations of the union established to further their own interests does not render them unlawful.

They have a right to make rules for their guidance and may impose penalties on their members for infractions of their rules. Complainant has no status to complain of the fines imposed upon members of the union and none such are complaining in this suit. The association is a voluntary one and the workmen may decline to become members or withdraw from membership, if dissatisfied with the conduct of its affairs, as some who were in complainant's employ did withdraw from the union.

In the case of *Toledo, A. A. & N. M. Railway Co. v. Pennsylvania Co.*, 54 Fed. Rep. 746, the late Chief-Justice Taft, then a circuit judge, said:

"Ordinarily, when such a combination of persons does not use violence, actual or threatened, to accomplish their purpose, it is difficult to point out with clearness the illegal means or end which makes the combination an unlawful conspiracy; for it is generally lawful for the combiners to withdraw their intercourse and its benefits from any person and to announce their intention of doing so, and it is equally lawful for the others, of their own motion, to do that, which the combiners seek to compel them to do."

In the instant case, there is no charge that defendants have resorted to violence or threatened violence. They have merely determined that complainant's conduct was such as to make it desirable for the union, as a group of employes, to decline to work for him, and, without threats or intimidation, have sought to enforce their demands. Nowhere is there evidence of any act not within the provisions of the statutes, as interpreted by this court.

These considerations result in the conclusion that the record before us does not support the order appealed from, and that the bill should be dismissed. The order of the court of chancery is in all respects, reversed, with costs.

For affirmance—None.

For reversal—THE CHIEF-JUSTICE, CAMPBELL, LLOYD, CASE, BODINE, DALY, DONGES, VAN BUSKIRK, KAYS, HETFIELD, WELLS, JJ. 11.[1]

---

[1] *Cf.* Hopkins v. Oxley Stave Co., 83 Fed. 912 (1897); Minasian v. Osborne, 210 Mass. 250, 96 N.E. 1036 (1911); Davis Machine Co. v. Robinson, 41 Misc. 329, 84 N.Y.S. 837 (1903). See also: Martin, "Do Trade Unions Limit Output," 17 Pol. Sci. Quar. 369 (1902); National Bureau of Economic Research, Recent Economic Changes 92-93 (1929); Cooper, "Recent National Trade Agreements in the Silk Hosiery Industry" 39 Jour. Pol. Econ. 69 (1931); Haber, "Workers' Rights and the Introduction of Machinery in the Men's Clothing Industry," 33 Jour. Pol. Econ. 388 (1925); Barnett, Chapters on Machinery and Labor, c. 6 (1926); Hansen, "Institutional Frictions and Technological Unemployment," 45 Quar. Jour. Econ. 684 (1931); Kaldor, "A Case against Technical Progress," Economica, No. 36, p. 180 (1932). Compare: S. 6 introduced in Wisconsin legislature in 1933 taxing all labor saving machinery introduced by any public utility since 1920 at 50% of the reduction in the labor costs resulting from the use of such machinery, the proceeds to be and for unemployment relief.

SHEEHAN v. LEVY.

Texas Commission of Appeals. 238 S.W. 900 (1922).

POWELL, J.: P. J. Sheehan was a plumbing contractor in the city of
Dallas in the year 1918. At that time he was installing fixtures in one
of the buildings of the Southern Methodist University and in the Texas
& Pacific Railway building. He had other contracts on hand of very
minor importance. He was working plumbers in the summer of 1918,
who were members of Local Union No. 100 of Journeymen Plumbers.
These laborers were employed from week to week, and there is no contention that they were under contract to work for any specific length of
time.

Certain controversies arose from time to time in the latter part of
that summer, between Royse, the business agent of the Local Union, representing his men, and Sheehan. Finally, early in August, Royse advised
Sheehan that the Local Union had a working agreement with the Master
Plumbers' Association, under which many benefits were conserved to the
workmen, and that, for that reason, Sheehan should join the Master
Plumbers' Association and subscribe to the working agreement aforesaid.
In fact, Royse told him that his men could not afford to work for him
after October 1st, that year, unless he did join the Association aforesaid.

Sheehan, for reasons satisfactory to himself, declined to join the Association of Master Plumbers, and, about the middle of October, 1918,
the Local Union withdrew its men who were working for Sheehan. The
latter was paying union wages and observing union hours at the time, but
he did not, at any time, offer to sign a contract giving to the laborers all
the rights which the members of the plumbers' association accorded to
them.

Sheehan filed his petition in the district court of Dallas county, alleging
that the Master Plumbers' Association and the Local Union had conspired
together and agreed that the latter should "pull" Sheehan's men; that
the Master Plumbers' Association required the Local Union to prevent
its members from working for anyone except a member of their association; that the Local Union withdrew its men from Sheehan with malice aforethought, and for the sole purpose of injuring him; that he could
not get others outside of the Local Union who were competent to do his
work; that he was about to suffer irreparable injury; that the Master
Plumbers' Association and the Local Union should both be enjoined from
"pulling" his men or interfering with them in any way; that he should
have judgment for damages he had already sustained.

The Master Plumbers' Association members and the Local Union
all answered, denying the allegations *in toto,* and the latter pleaded that
it took the action in question for a lawful purpose, in a peaceful way, and
solely for the betterment of its members and the serving of a legitimate
purpose of their own. The district court gave a prompt hearing on the
injunction phase of the case, and a great deal of testimony was intro-

duced by all the parties. The record is very lengthy. The trial court refused to enjoin either the Master Plumbers or the Local Union as prayed for. Its judgment, refusing the injunctions, upon appeal by Sheehan, was affirmed by the Court of Civil Appeals at Dallas. See 215 S.W. 229.

The cause is now before us upon writ of error granted by the Supreme Court, upon application therefor by Sheehan.

The evidence was conflicting on Sheehan's allegations that the Master Plumbers' Association had conspired with the Local Union to withdraw Sheehan's laborers and injure him. The district court and the Court of Civil Appeals decided the conflict against Sheehan's contention. For instance, we quote as follows from the opinion of the Court of Civil Appeals:

"In other words, the testimony of the members of the Master Plumbers' Association, if true, fully and completely exonerates them and said association from any connection with or complicity in the action of said Local Union No. 100, in causing any of its members to cease working for appellant, and from any interference on their part of the free exercise by appellant of his right to retain in his employ the men working for him, or to engage whomsoever he pleased in the conduct of his business. It was the peculiar province of the trial court, in view of the conflicting state of the evidence, to determine whether or not appellant was entitled to the injunctive relief asked as against the Master Plumbers' Association and its members, and, having determined that issue against him, we are not authorized to reverse and set aside his action, even though the law applicable to the evidence adduced by appellant would have entitled him to the relief sought."

When the record upon any point contains conflicting evidence, and the district court and Court of Civil Appeals makes the same determination of the conflict, the result is binding upon the Supreme Court. See *Electric Express & Baggage Co. v. Ablon,* 110 Tex. 235, 218 S.W. 1030. Therefore, we hold that Sheehan was not entitled to an injunction, under the facts in this case, as against the Master Plumbers' Association, or its members, also named defendant.

This brings us to the determination of the contention by Sheehan, that he was entitled to an injunction against the Local Union preventing its members from ceasing work for him. We think the Court of Civil Appeals also correctly decided that this injunction was properly denied by the district court. We have reached this conclusion after a most careful reading of the statement of facts.

The law upon this point is well settled in Texas, as well as in other jurisdictions. The Supreme Court of Texas, in the case of *Delz v. Winfree,* 80 Tex. 400, 16 S.W. 111, 26 Am. St. Rep. 755, speaks as follows:

"Plaintiff's petition goes further than to charge that each of the defendants refused to sell to him. It charges that they not only did that, but that they induced a third person to refuse to sell to him. It does not appear from the petition that their interference with the business of plaintiff was done to serve some legitimate purpose of their own, but that it was done wantonly and maliciously, and that it caused, as they intended it should, pecuniary loss to him.

"We think the petition stated a cause of action and that the demurrer should have been overruled."

In the very recent case of *Griffin v. Insurance Co.*, 235 S.W. 202, the Commission of Appeals inserted in its opinion the notation made by our Supreme Court in granting the writ of error therein. We quote from said notation as follows:

"A man may lawfully refuse to have business relations with another for any reason—on account of whim, caprice, prejudice, or ill will. He may lawfully induce others to refrain from having business relations with such third person, though it injuriously affects such person, provided his action be to serve some legitimate interest of his own."

The Commission of Appeals, in the *Griffin* case, *supra*, followed the quoted notation and applied said rule to a determination of the case in hand.

The same rules are announced by the United States Circuit Court in a very able opinion in the case of *Railway Co. v. Pennsylvania Co.*, 54 Fed. 730, 19 L.R.A. 387. The opinion in that case was written by Justice Taft.

In granting the writ of error in the case at bar, our Supreme Court says that, if the Sheehan workers were withdrawn for no other purpose than to injure his business, the withdrawal was wrongful and therefore actionable. So the law is well settled, and we come now to a consideration of the statement of facts to determine whether the Local Union withdrew its men from Sheehan, for the sole purpose of injuring his business, or whether they did so in order that they might serve some legitimate interest of their own. What are the facts?

Arts. 5244 and 5245 of Vernon's Sayles' Revised Civil Statutes of Texas authorize organizations such as labor unions, and give them the right, within certain bounds, to act together to promote their general welfare. Not only does the law of Texas so permit, but other authorities hold that laboring people may "organize for the purpose of promoting their common welfare, elevating their standard of skill, advancing and maintaining their wages, fixing the hours of labor and the rate of wages paid, obtaining employment for their members." See Cyc. vol. 24, p. 819.

After a thorough consideration of the statement of facts in the case at bar, we conclude that the action of the Local Union in question was well within its rights under Texas statutes and the rule just quoted from Cyc.

Before proceeding further, we will say that this case does not involve boycotts or picketing. There is no evidence in the record to bring this case within the condemnation of the rule so ably announced by Chief Justice Taft of the United States Supreme Court in the case of *Truax v. Corrigan*, decided some 90 days since and published in 257 U.S. 312, 42 Sup. Ct. 124, 66 L. Ed. 132. In the case at bar, the Local Union did not interfere in any way with Sheehan in the continuance of his contracts. They did not picket his place of business. They made no threats. They spread no damaging reports about him. They did not ask any others to refrain from working for him. The only thing done was to withdraw from him, after 60 days' prior notice, its members who were then at work for him.

There is absolutely no evidence in this record showing any malice or ill will on the part of the Local Union toward Sheehan. On the contrary, it is full of testimony showing that their relations were at all times of the most friendly character. In the first place, the rule of the Local Union requiring its members to work only for contractors who were members of the Master Plumbers' Association was entirely impersonal. It was not directed toward Sheehan alone. It was a general rule. The record tends to show that all individual plumbing contractors in Dallas joined the association after the promulgation of the rule in question except Sheehan. It further shows that the Local Union did everything in its power in a friendly and proper way to induce Sheehan to join the association and come within the rule. Sheehan offered certain trivial objections to becoming a member of the association. For instance, he said he had not been invited to join. The Local Union then saw to it that the invitation was extended. Not only so, but the initiation fee was reduced from $250 to $125, that he might be the more able financially to join. The entire record is teeming with evidence that Sheehan would have been most cordially admitted to membership in the association. It would be difficult to find a fact case showing more effort on the part of a union to protect a contractor than was shown by the Local Union in question in the case at bar. As already stated, Sheehan was given 60 days' notice of the consequences which would follow his failure to join the association.

But counsel for Sheehan insists that the latter should not be deprived of his liberty as an American citizen. No one made any effort to so deprive him. He had the right to decide whether he would join the association and subscribe to its working agreement with this Local Union, and thereby continue to work the Local's members, or would refuse to do so and employ other laborers. This union contained 40 or 50 members at the time. There is much evidence in the record that Dallas has many other plumbers. There were nonunion plumbing firms and other plumbers not connected with any firm or union. Sheehan could have worked them and exercised his option not to join the association. We see no reason why he should be permitted to say he will not work any one except members of Local Union No. 100 and at the same time dictate the terms of his contract with the members of that union. If he wants to work them and them only, and is unwilling to subscribe to their terms, which they can obtain from other contractors, Sheehan can blame no one but himself. Certainly, men cannot be censured for working where they feel that their general welfare is better subserved.

The district court may have very well concluded that the withdrawal of the men was not damaging Sheehan. The testimony showed he had only two contracts of any moment on hand at the time. He needed one plumber for 7 or 8 days to finish his work at Southern Methodist University, and one for about 20 days to finish at the T. & P. building. If Sheehan had bestirred himself at all, we feel warranted in saying, from the record, that his work could have been promptly completed and no damage would have been incurred. Therefore, the trial court may have concluded that these facts did not authorize an injunction. Sheehan admitted that he made no effort whatever to get any one to replace the men who had been withdrawn.

We are not prepared to say that the withdrawal of the men could have been justified had Sheehan tendered them a contract containing the 21 sections which are included in the working agreement entered into July 22, 1918, between the Local Union in question and the Master Plumbers' Association. If the members of the Local Union could have gotten exactly the same contract with Sheehan that the Master Plumbers offered them, we doubt if they would have had the right to quit working for him just because he would not join the association. The Local Union should not be permitted to dictate membership in some outside organization as a condition precedent to their working for a given individual, where the Local Union would not reap any additional benefits by reason of its demand. We think, in the case at bar, the Local Union was not interested primarily in building up the Master Plumbers' Association. Its increase in membership was only an incident to their chief purpose to better the working conditions of the men. The fact that Sheehan did not join the association and avoid all this litigation is strong evidence, to our minds, that he was unwilling to accede to the 21 conditions embodied in the working agreement aforesaid. That being true, he has no right to complain. Certainly, no one can, in any wise, be censured for choosing to work where he fares better. Sheehan paid union wages and observed union hours, as hereinbefore stated, but there is no pretense that he was willing to accede to the 21 rules in question.

We do not think it necessary to go into the rules of the working agreement. They are in the record. They speak for themselves.

A few reasons for the rule adopted by the Local Union are mentioned by its business agent, Royse, as follows:

"The benefit we received by having a man belong to the Master Plumbers' Association is that we can notify the Master Plumbers' Association, through its secretary or conference board, that certain members are not living up to these agreements or requirements, and have them correct it, which method is easier and less expensive to our union. I have had to furnish the Department of Labor in Washington with reports with reference to our strength. * * * Our board, that is the conference board of the Journeymen Plumbers' Local Union, reached an agreement among themselves and adopted that agreement that we would prohibit our men from working for any one who is not a member of the Master Plumbers' Association, for the reason that, with the proposition handled that way, it would lessen the need for a business agent, and in case of any trouble the two conference boards could just get together and settle any difficulties that might arise, and if we worked for none other than Master Plumbers, they could handle their men and we handle ours, and complaint can be made to the association, whereas, men working for these outside shops there is something always coming up that requires the service of the business agent all the time. * * * I had no malice against Mr. Sheehan in taking the action I took, but I took such action because it was one of our rules; I thought it was for the best interest of the union." (Statement of facts, pp. 83-85.)

From the testimony above quoted, it will be seen that the rule in question obtained at least two advantages for the men. It reduced the expense of operating the union and thereby lessened the dues of its members. It greatly facilitated the settlement of disputes between the contractor and the laborers. These are concededly valuable rights. They are undisputed in the record.

The Court of Civil Appeals, in the instant case, has given us the benefit of a very able opinion by the late Justice Talbot. On pages 232 and 233 of 215 S.W. he shows some of the benefits to the men, flowing from the rule adopted. He concludes his survey of the facts with the following statement:

"It is fair to conclude from the record now before us that the purpose of appellees, in taking the action complained of, was to promote the interest of the members of their organizations, and not for the purpose of maliciously working injury and damage to appellant, and does not come under the condemnation of the rules of law and decisions which firmly prohibit all combinations and conspiracies formed in restraint of trade, or to injure and damage the business of the person or persons at whom they are directed."

The trial court found that the union, in taking its action, was serving a legitimate purpose of its own. The Court of Civil Appeals so found. We think there is evidence to support such finding. In fact, we think there is an abundance of testimony in support thereof. Therefore, we think the Supreme Court is bound by that finding of fact. As said before, the law is clear. We think the Court of Civil Appeals correctly affirmed the judgment of the trial court.

Therefore, we recommend that the judgments of the district court and the Court of Civil Appeals be affirmed.

CURETON, C. J. The judgment recommended in the report of the Commission of Appeals is adopted, and will be entered as the judgment of the Supreme Court.[1]

----

[1] Cf. Overland Pub. Co. v. Union Lithograph Co., 57 Cal. App. 366, 207 Pac. 412 (1922); Employing Printers Club v. Doctor Blosser Co., 122 Ga. 509, 50 S.E. 353 (1905); Brescia Const. Co. v. Stone Masons Contractors' Ass'n, 195 App. Div. 647, 187 N.Y.S. 77 (1921); Coons v. Chrystie, 24 Misc. 296, 53 N.Y.S. 668 (1898); Larkin v. Long, [1915] A.C. 814. See also: Reynolds v. Davis, 198 Mass. 294, 84 N.E. 457 (1908).

CHAPTER VI.

THE TRADE AGREEMENT.

MOODY v. MODEL WINDOW GLASS CO.

Arkansas Supreme Court. 145 Ark. 197, 224 S.W. 436 (1920).

SMITH, J.: This cause was heard by the court below sitting as a jury, and the parties now agree that the sufficiency of the testimony to support the court's finding presents the only question in the case.

According to the undisputed testimony, it appears that appellee operated its window glass factory during the year 1917 at Fort Smith under what was known as the national agreement, this being a general contract entered into between the Window Glass Manufacturers of the United States and the National Window Glass Workers. Article 5 of this agreement reads as follows: "Article 5. Any company hiring a member and said member upon arriving and reporting for duty, finding no vacancy existing or plant not ready to operate, as per notification, shall pay said member at the rate of $20 per week until place is vacant or plant in operation, or, at the option of the member, said company shall defray all expenses incurred by said member from the time he left his home or place of starting until his return to destination."

Appellee's manager, whose name was Zenor, had, prior to becoming manager, been a member of the Glass Workers' Union, and was familiar with this article 5, and knew that it entered into and was a part of the contract of employment between members of the Glass Workers' Union and companies operating, as appellee did, under this national agreement.

Appellants had been employed at appellee's plant during the year 1917, but went to California when the plant closed down, and were at work there when appellant Gerard received from appellee the following letter:

"Fort Smith, Ark., Sept. 6, 1918.

"Mr. John Gerard, Stockton, Calif.

"Friend John: Yours of the 25th of July at hand, and in reply to same will say I am depending on you and Moody in your old places this coming season. Please advise me by return mail if you will be on hand. I can not say just what time we will get started. But will let you know in time.

358

"I hope you are having a good time. Kindest regards to yourself and all the boys there.

"Very truly."

Gerard answered this letter and inquired when he should report, and in reply received the following letter:

"Fort Smith, Ark., Nov. 19, 1918.

Mr. John Gerard, G. D., Stockton, Cal.

"Dear Sir: Replying to yours of July 25th, would say we expect to start on December 9 if nothing happens to prevent same.

"Kindly advise us by return mail if we can depend on your being here at the start.

"Yours very truly,
"Model Window Glass Company."

Gerard answered this letter on the 22d, advising that he would be on hand when the plant resumed operations.

Thereafter appellants left California for Fort Smith on December 3, and sent appellee a telegram on that day announcing their departure. They arrived in Fort Smith on December 7, and reported for duty on December 9, and found that appellee's plant was not in operation. According to appellants, Zenor told them that he would take care of them as usual, and would pay them the $20 per week as provided in the national agreement, and this payment of $20 per week was made to each of them for two weeks, but at the end of the third week payment of the $20 was refused, whereupon appellants gave the two weeks' notice required by another article of the national agreement that they would quit appellee's services unless the payments were made.

Zenor testified that it was customary to advise men when to report, and that the letters sent out above were written pursuant to that custom, and that it was also customary for the men to write when they would report; but appellants gave him no notification of the time when they would report except in the telegram dated December 3. But on December 4th the company wrote the following letter:

"Dec. 4, 1918.
"Mr. John Gerard, Stockton, California.

"Dear Sir: Replying to yours of the 22d inst., would say we are sorry to say start has been delayed for some reason unknown to us. We will therefore have to advise you further; will send transportation if you are in need of same.

"Yours very truly,
"Model Window Glass Company."

Attached to this letter was a postscript dated December 20, containing the statement that the wage committee had disagreed, and that, "We are going to blow December 31 and are going to demand a scale." This letter would have informed its recipient that its blowers were not expected to report until December 31, and that the previously existing wage scale between employer and employee was no longer effective. Zenor testified that the wage scale between appellee and the union, of which appellants were members, expired December 8, and that he did not know why it was not renewed on that day.

It is undisputed that the letter of December 4 was not sent appellants; and it is also undisputed that appellants left California on December 3, relying upon appellee's letter of November 19 that the plant would start on December 9; and it is undisputed that the plant had, during appellants' previous employment, been run as a union plant, and therefore operated under the national agreement; and it is undenied that appellants supposed the wage scale was in effect when they left California. But it is not contended that the expiration of the wage scale abrogated other provisions of the national agreement, and the binding effect of article 5, set out above, was not impaired because the wage scale had expired.

Zenor admitted that he told appellants, when they reported to him, that he would take care of them, and he admits that two payments of $20 each were made to appellants; but he says these payments were mere loans, and that the first advance was made in order that appellants might send the money to their homes as Christmas gifts.

Appellee was plaintiff below, and recovered judgment against each of the appellants for the $40 paid them; and the counterclaims of appellants, for the five weeks' pay, at $20 per week, less the $40 advanced, were dismissed; and this appeal is from that judgment.

We think the court below erred in its judgment. The facts stated constituted an implied contract, if not an express contract, to settle with appellants according to the terms of the national agreement. The correspondence set out above warranted appellants in believing, under the circumstances of the case, that they would be given employment, or be paid in accordance with the provisions of the national agreement, with reference to which the parties must be held to have contracted. Appellants paid their own transportation and expenses from California, and remained unemployed for five weeks; yet they ask no recovery on that account. They ask judgment only for the money coming to them under the agreement, with reference to which they contracted; and we think an erroneous judgment was entered by the court below, and that judgment will, therefore, be reversed and the cause remanded for a new trial.[1]

---

[1] Accord: United States Daily Corp. v. Nichols, 32 Fed. (2d) 834 (D.C. App. 1929) (defendant not a member of publishers' association with which trade agreement was made); Gregg v. Starks, 188 Ky. 834, 224 S.W. 459 (1920) (plaintiff not a member of union with which trade agreement was made); Piercy v. Louisville & Nashville Ry. Co., 198 Ky. 477, 248 S.W. 1042 (1923); Keysaw v. Dotterweich Brewing Co., 121 App. Div. 58, 105 N.Y.S. 562 (1907); Langmade v. Olean Brewing Co., 137 App. Div. 355, 121 N.Y.S. 388 (1910); Cross Mountain Coal Co v. Ault, 157 Tenn. 461, 9 S.W. 692 (1928).

In some cases enforcement of the rights of the individual under the trade agreement is made to depend upon whether he has actually ratified or accepted the agreement, the court regarding the union in the capacity of an agent nego-

JOHNSON v. AMERICAN RAILWAY EXPRESS CO.

South Carolina Supreme Court. 163 S.C. 198, 161 S.E. 473 (1931).

Per Curiam.

Upon consideration of the petition of the appellant in this cause, it is ordered that the opinion filed herein on April 1, 1931, be withdrawn; that the following opinion be substituted for the same; and that the petition for rehearing be dismissed.

This is an action by the plaintiff, formerly an employee as an express messenger, of the defendant company, for damages resulting as alleged, from his wrongful discharge. The ground of his complaint is that he was discharged without just cause or excuse, and in violation of the provisions of an agreement entered into between the company and the union of express messengers, of which the plaintiff was a member, guaranteeing to an employee, before his discharge, an investigation of the grounds of complaint against him. Issues being joined, the case was tried at the November, 1928, term of said Court before his Honor, Judge T. S. Sease, and a jury. At the conclusion of the testimony offered on behalf of the plain-

tiating an agreement subsequently to be ratified by individuals. Gary v. Central of Ga. Ry. Co., 44 Ga. App. 120, 160 S.E. 716 (1931); Burnetta v. Marceline Coal Co., 180 Mo. 241, 79 S.W. 136 (1904); West v. Baltimore & Ohio R. R. Co., 103 W. Va. 417, 137 S.E. 654 (1927).

In many cases the agreement is regarded as the measure of the individual's right without inquiry as to its nature. Mastell v. Salo, 140 Ark. 408, 215 S.W. 583 (1919); George v. Chicago, R.I. & P. Ry. Co., 183 Minn. 610, 235 N.W. 673 (1931); St. Louis, B. & M. Ry. Co. v. Booker, 287 S.W. 130 (Tex. Civ. App. 1926).

"The process of collective bargaining results, not in a labor contract, but in a trade agreement. This imposes no obligation upon the employer to offer or upon the laborers to accept work; it guarantees neither to the employers workmen nor to the laborers jobs. It is nothing more than a statement of the conditions upon which such work as is offered and accepted is to be done. The contract of employment is still between the individual employer and the individual employee, though the provision of the order in which men are to be taken on and laid off may give to or withhold from laborers a chance to dispose of their services." Hamilton, "Collective Bargaining," Ency. Soc. Sciences (1930).

See: Rice, "Collective Labor Agreements in American Law," 44 Harv. Law Rev. 572 (1931); Fuchs, "Collective Labor Agreements in American Law," 10 St. Louis Law Rev. 1 (1925); 24 Col. Law Rev. 409 (1924); 10 N.C. Law Rev. 394 (1932); 31 Col. Law Rev. 1156 (1931); 41 Yale Law Jour. 1221 (1932).

See also: Fuchs, "Collective Labor Agreements in German Law," 15 St. Louis Law Rev. 1 (1929); Fuchs, "The French Law of Collective Labor Agreements," 41 Yale Law Jour. 1005 (1932); Pirou, "The Theory of the Collective Labor Contract in France," 5 Internat'l Lab. Rev. 35 (1922); Pic, "Judicial Remedies in Recent French Legislation for the Enforcement of Agreements of Trade Associations," 12 Internat'l Lab. Rev. 23 (1925); Sitzler, "The Law of Collective Bargaining in Germany," 6 Internat'l Lab. Rev. 511 (1922); Woytinsky, "New Statistics of Collective Agreements in Germany," 23 Internat'l Lab. Rev. 506 (1931); Duguit, "Collective Acts as Distinguished from Contracts," 27 Yale Law Jour. 753 (1918).

See also: Trade Agreements, U.S. Dept. of Labor, Bureau of Lab. Stat. Bull. No. 468 (1928); Phillips, "Trade Agreements: An Outline of Their Contents," (unpub. thesis, Harv. School Bus. Admin.) (1929); "Industrial Stability," 90 Ann. Am. Acad. Pol. Sci. (1920); Phillips, "Arbitration Clauses; An Outline of their Contents as Found in Trade Agreements," (unpub. thesis, Harv. School Bus. Admin.) (1930); Clark, "Collective Bargaining in the United States," 15 Internat'l Lab. Rev 197 (1925); Bloch, "Labor Agreements in the Coal Mines" (1931).

tiff, the defendant made a motion for a nonsuit upon grounds hereinafter referred to, which motion his Honor granted, and, after granting defendant's motion for a nonsuit, his Honor directed a verdict for the plaintiff for nominal damages in the sum of $8 from all of which (according to the agreed statement contained in the transcript of record) this appeal is taken by the plaintiff.

From the testimony of the plaintiff, which for the purpose of this appeal is to be taken as true, the following facts appear:

The plaintiff had been in the employment of the defendant as an express messenger on trains since February, 1924, upon an indefinite term of service. On June 23, 1927, he was on his run from Florence to Washington; when the train arrived at Richmond, about 8:30 p. m., he was met by one McConnell, route agent of the defendant, taken off of his run and carried to a hotel where he met two special agents, Smith and Hughes, and the superintendent, May, in a room of the hotel; after an interview lasting about two hours, the conference broke up without any definite communication to the plaintiff; he was furnished with transportation back to Florence where he was again met by McConnell who informed him that he would be notified later in the day the conclusion reached as to his case; in the evening he was called to the hotel by McConnell and told that the company requested his resignation; the plaintiff did not comply with the suggestion and was told by McConnell to come down to the office the next day and he would have a voucher fixed up and pay him off; the plaintiff went; McConnell had a voucher fixed up for his time up to the time he reached Richmond, but not for the deadhead time from Richmond back to Florence. The ground of complaint against the plaintiff, which he learned after his discharge, was not reporting a messenger seen by him to be handling liquor, supposed to have been abstracted from a shipment, in violation of a stipulation admitted by the plaintiff to have been signed by him: "Q. Will you aid in ridding the service of employees whose honesty is in the least questionable? A. Yes, sir."

On June 28, 1927, the plaintiff wrote to McConnell, route agent, asking for a statement of the grounds of his suspension from service, to which he had no reply.

On June 29, 1927, the plaintiff wrote to the superintendent, May, asking for an investigation of the charges against him. No reply was received thereto until August 5, 1927, after the present action had been begun on July 26th, offering an investigation. The plaintiff was out of employment for six weeks, and thereafter has not earned more than $100.00 per month, about half of his wages as messenger.

Rule 29 of the agreement between the company and the employees thereof represented by the American Federation of Express Workers, is as follows: "An employee who has been in the service for more than ninety days or whose application has been formerly approved shall not be disciplined or dismissed without investigation, at which investigation he may be represented by an employee of his choice or one representative (as per rule 84) of an organization of which he may be a member. He may, however, be held out of the service pending such investigation. He shall have at least twenty-four hours advance notice of such investigation, which shall be held within seven days of the date when charged with the offense or held from service. A decision will be rendered within seven days after completion of investigation."

Rule 37 provides: "If the final decision decrees that charges against the employee were not sustained, the record shall be cleared of the charge; if suspended or dismissed, the employee shall be reinstated and paid for the time lost."

The defendant's motion for a nonsuit was based on the following grounds:

"1. There is no testimony to the effect that the plaintiff was employed for any specified period of time and the only reasonable inference from the testimony is that the contract was terminable at the will of either party and the plaintiff under such circumstances is not entitled to recover because there is no breach of contract which would give rise to an action for damages.

"2. All of the testimony shows that the plaintiff's term of employment was indefinite and the plaintiff cannot maintain an action in tort for a wrongful discharge from employment because such a discharge becomes the basis of an action in tort only when accompanied by a wrongful act which amounts to a trespass with actual or constructive force. A malicious notice disconnected with the infringement of a legal right, even if there were evidence in this case to disclose it, cannot be the subject of a civil action, and there is no testimony to the effect that any trespass was committed or force used in the discharge of the plaintiff.

"3. The working rules of the defendant formed no part of his contract of employment but are incidents thereof and even if there is testimony to the effect that plaintiff was not accorded a hearing provided for in said rules they constitute the sole and exclusive remedies available to the plaintiff, and in addition it appears from the testimony that the plaintiff had not exhausted his remedies under said rules in that he has made no appeal to the final authority of the defendant to whom he has the right to appeal. * * *"

There is no doubt of the correctness of the general proposition that if an employment is for an indefinite term, and each party may terminate it at his pleasure, the discharge even without cause will afford the employee no ground of complaint.

While the term of service of the plaintiff was clearly indefinite, it appears that the clause in the agreement between the union and the express company had the effect of limiting the indefiniteness of the term and the consequent right of the company to discharge an employee, with or without cause, by providing, in effect, that the company could not discharge an employee without cause, at all, and that it could not discharge one with cause until an investigation establishing the alleged charge against him had been formally made after due notice to the employee and an opportunity to appear personally and with a representative. We think that this view is sustained by the further provision in the agreement that if the charge should not be sustained the employee should be restored to his position (quoted above).

The question then is to be decided, not upon the issue whether the term was definite or indefinite, but whether an employee who is a member of the union is in a position to enforce the provisions of an agreement entered into between the carrier and the union, to which he was not a party, but which plainly was made for his benefit.

It has been held by this Court in numerous cases that where a contract is made between two persons, and there is in it a provision that enures to the benefit of a third person not a party to the contract, and perhaps ignorant of its execution, he acquires an enforceable interest in the contract so far as the provision of his interest is concerned. * * *

So that the question in its final analysis turns upon the issue whether an agreement between the employer and the union, of which the employee is a member, which purports to confer certain rights upon the members relating to rates or pay, or conditions of work, is a legal valid contract; for it is plain that if the contract be legal and valid, and secures a benefit to the members, each would be entitled to enforce such benefit.

No legal objection to the legality or validity of such an agreement has been urged by the employer or has occurred to the Court. On the contrary, in the present case, it has been signed by the employer, promulgated and acted upon by it; it must be assumed that it was known to the employees and was an inducement to them to enter or continue in the service; the employer would be estopped to deny its binding force.

As a matter of public policy, to ensure a, friendly spirit between capital and labor, which in these days is severely strained, it should be sustained. Its fairness and reasonableness must appeal to every one; it concedes no more than a fair-minded corporation would not only allow but insist upon, and no less than an honest laborer is entitled to.

In *Texas & N. O. R. Co. v. Brotherhood*, 281 U.S., 548, 50 S. Ct. 427, 434, 74 L. Ed., 1034, the Supreme Court of the United States said in an opinion filed May 26, 1930: "It has long been recognized that employees are entitled to organize for the purpose of securing the redress of grievances and to promote agreements with employers relating to rates of pay and conditions of work. *American Steel Foundries v. Tri-City Cent. Trades Counsel*, 257 U.S., 184, 209, 66 L. Ed., 189, 199, 27 A.L.R., 360, 42 S. Ct., 72. Congress was not required to ignore this right of the employees but could safeguard it and seek to make their appropriate collective action an instrument of peace rather than of strife."

In the case of *Gary v. R. Co.*, 37 Ga. App., 744, 141 S.E., 819, 821, the Court said: "If the contract of employment had contained no provision as to when or how it might be terminated, the defendant might have discharged the plaintiff at will; but since, under specific stipulations, the relation could be severed only in a particular way or on the happening of a certain event, the act of the defendant in dismissing the plaintiff without a compliance with these conditions would constitute a breach of the contract. * * * The clear intent and purpose of the agreement was that the plaintiff could only be dismissed after a hearing which involved the question of the right of the defendant to dismiss him upon some ground." * * *

It must be conceded that other Courts have reached the conclusion that such a stipulation cannot be enforced by the beneficiary employee, unless he has expressly ratified the agreement between the union and the employer. We are not disposed to follow them, in view of our decisions hereinbefore cited. Among the contrary authorities are these: *Hudson v. R. Co.,* 152 Ky., 711, 154 S.W., 47, 45 L.R.A. (N.S.), 184 Ann. Cas., 1915B, 98; *Burnetta v. Marceline Coal Co.,* 180 Mo., 241, 79 S.W., 136, 24 Cyc., 824, 16 R.C.L., 425; *West v. R. Co.,* 103 W. Va., 417, 137 S.E., 654. Cyc. and R.C.L. both rely upon the *Hudson* and *Burnetta cases* and the *West case* upon all four authorities.

As to the suggestion that the matter may be controlled by the provisions of the Railway Labor Act, 45 U.S.C.A., title Railroads, section 151, *et seq.,* we deem it sufficient to state that question is not raised in this appeal. It was not made a ground for a nonsuit, and his Honor, the trial Judge, in no way considered the same.

It therefore follows, that so far as the *Gantt case* [125 S.C. 518, 118 S.E. 920] is irreconcilable with the views herein expressed and conclusions announced, it can no longer be considered authoritative; and it further follows that, under the testimony in this case, his Honor, the trial Judge, was in error in granting the defendant's motion for a nonsuit.[1]

YOUNG v. CANADIAN NORTHERN RY. CO.

Judicial Committee of the Privy Council. [1931] A.C. 83.

The judgment of their Lordships was delivered by LORD RUSSELL OF KILLOWEN. In this case the appellant, who had been in the employ of the respondents (hereinafter called "the railway company") as a machinist, sued the railway company for damages for wrongful dismissal and for other relief. His action was tried in the Court of King's Bench for Manitoba by Dysart J. and was dismissed. An appeal from that judg-

---

[1] For comment on the case, see 31 Mich. Law Rev. 124 (1932).

Accord: Yazoo & M. V. R. Co. v. Sideboard, 161 Miss. 4, 133 So. 669 (1931), commented on in 16 Minn. Law Rev. 100 (1931); Hall v. St. Louis-San Francisco Ry. Co., 224 Mo. App. 431, 28 S.W.(2d) 687 (1930); Gulla v. Barton, 164 App. Div. 293, 149 N.Y.S. 952 (1914); Blum & Co. v. Landau, 23 Ohio App. 426, 155 N.E. 154 (1926); Marshall v. Charlestown & W. C. Ry. Co., 164 S.C. 283, 162 S.E. 348 (1931).

ment to the Court of Appeal for Manitoba was also dismissed. The appellant has now, with the leave of the Court of Appeal, appealed to His Majesty in Council.

The appellant entered the service of the railway company in June, 1920, having a few days before arrived in Canada from England. He left its employ on June 13, 1927, pursuant to a notice dated June 9, 1927, in the following terms: "Your services will not be required after 5 P.M. on June 13, 1927, on account of reduction of staff."

The appellant's claim that this notice operated as a wrongful dismissal was founded upon the allegations: (1.) That the railway company was bound contractually to him not to reduce staff by dismissing him while retaining in its service men junior to him, (2.) that men junior to him had been retained, and (3.) that his "seniority rights" had thereby been violated.

A considerable number of other points were raised, and some of them were argued before the Board; but all are, in their Lordships' view, subsidiary to the question, whether or not the railway company had bound itself to the appellant in the manner indicated. If in truth there was no such contractual obligation between the parties to this action, none of the other questions call for consideration or decision.

According to the evidence, all that passed when the appellant was engaged was this: The appellant saw a Mr. Hough and signed a form of application for employment. He was told to start the following morning. He then asked what wages he was going to receive. "Hough's reply was I would receive the going rate, the machinist's rate." There was no written agreement between the appellant and the railway company. It is evident that the suggested contractual obligation is not capable of being established merely from what happened on that occasion.

The appellant, however, in support of his claim relies on other matters, to which reference must now be made.

There was in existence a document dated November 12, 1919, called Wage Agreement No. 4. The parties to it were, on the one hand the Canadian Railway War Board, on the other hand a body called Division No. 4, Railway Employees' Department, American Federation of Labour. The document describes itself as an agreement "in respect to rates of pay, work hours, and conditions of service for employees in the locomotive and car department of the several railways as specified herein": it further states "This agreement shall be effective on the following railways": the railway company being included under Canadian National Railways. Then follow "rules" to the number of 188.

At the date of this agreement, the Canadian War Board represented the railways of Canada, and when the War Board, in course of time, ceased to exist, the railways of Canada had as their representative in negotiations with representatives of the men, a voluntary association called the Railway Association of Canada. Division No. 4, Railway Employees' Department, American Federation of Labour (hereinafter called "Division No. 4"), was a territorial division of a labour organization, whose headquarters were in the United States. Division No. 4 covered the whole of Canada.

At different times variations of the Wage Agreement No. 4 were agreed to between the Railway Association of Canada and Division No. 4, but for the purposes of this appeal these variations are not material, and Wage Agreement No. 4 need alone be considered.

The appellant alleges that the railway company was contractually bound to him in the terms of Wage Agreement No. 4, and that his dismissal was made in such circumstances that it amounted to a breach by the railway company of certain provisions of Wage Agreement No. 4, more particularly rules 27, 31, 35, 36 and 37, which he says secured to him his seniority rights and other rights. It does not appear to their Lordships necessary to discuss the question whether the railway company in dismissing the appellant did or did not act in violation of those provisions. For the purposes of this appeal they are prepared to assume this point in the appellant's favour, and to consider this appeal upon the footing that the railway company did, in dismissing the appellant, act in violation of the provisions of Wage Agreement No. 4, assuming them to apply.

The outstanding question for decision is whether the railway company was contractually bound to the appellant in the terms of Wage Agreement No. 4, i.e., whether the contract subsisting between the appellant and the railway company included provisions similar to the provisions of Wage Agreement No. 4. Unless that position can be established the appellant is not in a position to sue the railway company for any alleged breach of those provisions.

The trial judge dismissed the appellant's action upon the ground that, because he was not a member of Division No. 4, he could not claim the benefit of Wage Agreement No. 4.

In the Court of Appeal a variety of opinions combined to defeat the appellant.

FULLERTON J.A. (with whom the Chief Justice of Manitoba and Dennistoun J.A. concurred) held that there was no evidence to show that the appellant agreed to work under the conditions fixed by Wage Agreement No. 4, and that any such agreement, if proved, would be unenforceable for want of mutuality.

TRUEMAN J.A. held that the appellant was entitled to enforce against the railway company the provisions of Wage Agreement No. 4, but that under those provisions he had no right at the date of his writ to resort to the law Courts.

ROBSON J.A. assumed, without deciding the point, that the appellant could enforce against the railway company the provisions of Wage Agreement No. 4. Upon that assumption, he agreed with TRUEMAN J.A. that the appellant had appealed to the wrong tribunal.

Their Lordships feel a doubt whether the true question has really been considered by all the learned judges in the Courts below—namely, whether the appellant has established that the contract for service which existed between himself and the railway company included terms by which the railway company either bound itself to the appellant to observe the provisions of Wage Agreement No. 4, or bound itself to the appellant to observe provisions similar to those contained therein.

If that question be answered in the affirmative, it is immaterial whether the appellant was or was not a member of Division No. 4 or of any other or of no labour organization. Further, if that question be answered in the affirmative, there can be no question of the contract being unenforceable for want of mutuality or otherwise. It is simply a contract of employment which embodies special terms. On the other hand, if the question be answered in the negative, the action, so far as it depends upon the existence of that contractual obligation on the part of the railway company, must of necessity fail, and no further question can arise.

Before their Lordships' Board the appellant's counsel sought to establish the existence of the necessary contractual obligation from the following facts which, as he claimed, the evidence proved: That the railway company (whose shops were open shops) treated all its employees alike, whether members of Division No. 4 or not; that when the appellant was hired he was promised "the going rate" and was placed as regards salary under "schedule," which meant the Wage Agreement No. 4; that he was placed on the seniority list referred to in rule 31; that when he was dismissed the railway company gave him the number of days' notice required by rule 27; that when he complained to various officials of the railway company he was referred to the committee, as provided by rule 35. From these facts their Lordships were invited to hold that the necessary contractual obligation had been established.

There can be no doubt upon the evidence that in fact, the provisions of Wage Agreement No. 4 were applied by the railway company to all its employees in its locomotive and car department. One extract from the evidence of the general manager (Mr. Tisdale) makes this clear: "(A.) I understand your question to be this: Is the agreement that was negotiated between the railway companies and Division 4 applicable to all the men in the shop? (Q.) Yes? (A.) The answer is Yes."

Their Lordships, however, are unable to treat these matters as establishing contractual liability by the railway company to the appellant. The fact that the railway company applied the agreement to the appellant, is equally consistent with the view that it did so, not because it was bound contractually to apply it to him, but because as a matter of policy it deemed it expedient to apply it to all.

If the conduct of the railway company in applying the provisions of the agreement to the appellant could be explained only by the existence of a contractual obligation to the appellant so to do, it would be not only permissible, but necessary to hold that the existence of the contractual obligation had been established. In the circumstances, however, of the present case, their Lordships find themselves unable so to decide.

But the matter does not quite rest there. When Wage Agreement No. 4 is examined, it does not appear to their Lordships to be a document adapted for conversion into or incorporation with a service agreement, so as to entitle master and servant to enforce *inter se* the terms thereof. It consists of some 188 "rules," which the railway companies contract with Division No. 4 to observe. It appears to their Lordships to be intended merely to operate as an agreement between a body of employers and a labour organization by which the employers undertake that as regards their workmen, certain rules beneficial to the workmen shall be observed. By itself it constitutes no contract between any individual employee and the company which employs him. If an employer refused to observe the rules, the effective sequel would be, not an action by any employee, not even an action by Division No. 4 against the employer for specific performance or damages, but the calling of a strike until the grievance was remedied.

If, in the present case, the appellant has suffered any injustice at the hands of the railway company, it was in the power of Division No. 4 to obtain justice for him had they chosen so to do. It is suggested that Division No. 4 chose not so to do, because the appellant was a member of a rival organization. Assuming the suggestion to be well founded, the moral thereby pointed would appear to be that in the case of an "open" shop, the protection which an agreement such as Wage Agreement No. 4 affords to a workman who is not a member of the contracting labour organization, is to be measured by the willingness of that body to enforce it on his behalf.

One more observation remains to be made. Their Lordships have dealt with the case as one in which the wrongfulness of the dismissal depended solely upon the alleged violation of provisions contained in Wage Agreement No. 4. No foundation was laid by the evidence for any claim for damages upon the footing that the length of notice given was insufficient under the actual contract of service which existed between the appellant and the railway company.

In the result their Lordships are of opinion that this appeal should fail and be dismissed with costs; as they have already humbly advised His Majesty.[1]

---

[1] The decisions below are to be found in [1929] 4 D.L.R. 452 (Man. K.B.); [1930] 3 D.L.R. 352 (Man. C.A.). The decision should also be contrasted with the earlier decision of the Judicial Committee of the Privy Council in Caven v. Canadian Pac. R. Co., [1925] 3 D.L.R. 841. For comment on the case, see: 31 Col. Law Rev. 1156 (1931); 26 Ill. Law Rev. 922 (1932).

Accord: Kessell v. Great Northern Ry. Co., 51 Fed.(2d) 304 (W.D. Wash. 1931); St. Louis, I. M. & So. Ry. Co. v. Matthews, 64 Ark. 398, 42 S.W. 902 (1897). *Contra:* Nederlandsch Amerikaansche Stoomvart Maatschappij v Stevedores & Longshoremens Benev. Soc., 265 Fed. 397 (E.D. La. 1920); Gilchrist Co. v. Metal Polishers, etc., Union, 113 Atl. 320 (N.J. Ch. 1919); Meltzer v. Kaminer, 131 Misc. 813, 227 N.Y.S. 459 (1927); St. Louis, B. & M. Ry. Co. v. Booker, 5 S.W.(2d) 856 (Texas Civ. App. 1928).

BERRY v. DONOVAN.

Massachusetts Supreme Judicial Court. 188 Mass. 353, 74 N.E. 603 (1905).

KNOWLTON, C. J.: This is an action of tort brought to recover damages sustained by reason of the defendant's malicious interference with the plaintiff's contract of employment. The plaintiff was a shoemaker, employed by the firm of Hazen B. Goodrich and Company at Haverhill, Massachusetts, under a contract terminable at will. At the time of the interference complained of he had been so employed nearly four years. The defendant was the representative at Haverhill of a national organization of shoe workers, called the Boot and Shoe Workers' Union, of which he was also a member. The evidence showed that he induced Goodrich and Company to discharge the plaintiff, greatly to his damage. A few days before the plaintiff's discharge, a contract was entered into between the Boot and Shoe Workers' Union and the firm of Goodrich and Company, which was signed by the defendant for the union, the second clause of which was as follows: "In consideration of the foregoing valuable privileges, the employer agrees to hire as shoe workers, only members of the Boot and Shoe Workers' Union, in good standing, and further agrees not to retain any shoe worker in his employment after receiving notice from the union that such shoe worker is objectionable to the union, either on account of being in arrears for dues, or disobedience of union rules or laws, or from any other cause." The contract contained various other provisions in regard to the employment of members of the union by the firm, and the rights of the firm and of the union in reference to the services of these employees, and the use of the union's stamp upon goods to be manufactured.

The plaintiff was not a member of this union. Soon after the execution of this contract, the defendant demanded of Goodrich and Company that the plaintiff be discharged, and the evidence tended to show that the sole ground for the demand was that the plaintiff was not a member of the union, and that he persistently declined to join it, after repeated suggestions that he should do so.

At the close of the evidence the defendant asked for the following instructions which the judge declined to give:

"1. Upon all the evidence in the case, the plaintiff is not entitled to recover.

"2. Upon all the evidence in the case, the defendant was acting as the legal representative of the Boot and Shoe Workers' Union and not in his personal capacity, and therefore the plaintiff cannot recover.

"3. The contract between the Boot and Shoe Workers' Union and Hazen B. Goodrich and Company was a valid contract, and the defendant, as the legal representative of the Boot and Shoe Workers' Union, had a right to call the attention of Hazen B. Goodrich and Company, or any member of the firm, to the fact that they were violating the terms of the contract in keeping the plaintiff in their employment after the contract was signed, and insisting upon an observance of the terms of the contract, even if the defendant knew that the observance of the terms of the contract would result in the discharge of the plaintiff from their employment.

"4. The contract referred to was a legal contract, and a justification of the acts of the defendant, as shown by the evidence in this case."

"6. The defendant cannot be held responsible in this action, unless it appears that the defendant used threats, or some act of intimidation, or some slanderous statements, or some unlawful coercion to or against the employers of the plaintiff, to thereby cause the plaintiff's discharge; and upon all the evidence in the case there is no such evidence, and the plaintiff cannot recover."

The defendant excepted to the refusal, and to the portions of the charge which were inconsistent with the instructions requested. The jury returned a verdict of $1,500 for the plaintiff. These exceptions present the only questions which were argued before us by the defendant.

The primary right of the plaintiff to have the benefit of his contract and to remain undisturbed in the performance of it is universally recognized. The right to dispose of one's labor as he will, and to have the benefit of one's lawful contract, is incident to the freedom of the individual, which lies at the foundation of the government in all countries that maintain the principles of civil liberty. Such a right can lawfully be interfered with only by one who is acting in the exercise of an equal or superior right which comes in conflict with the other. An intentional interference with such a right, without lawful justification, is malicious in law, even if it is from good motives and without express malice. *Walker v. Cronin,* 107 Mass. 555, 562. *Plant v. Woods,* 176 Mass. 492, 498. *Allen v. Flood,* [1898] A.C. 1, 18. *Mogul Steamship Co. v. McGregor,* 23 Q.B.D. 598, 613. *Read v. Friendly Society of Operative Stonemasons,* [1902] 2 K.B. 88, 96. *Giblan v. National Amalgamated Labourers' Union,* [1903] 2 K.B. 600, 617.

In the present case the judge submitted to the jury, first, the question whether the defendant interfered with the plaintiff's rights under his contract with Goodrich and Company, and secondly, the question whether, if he did, the interference was without justifiable cause. The jury were instructed that, unless the defendant's interference directly caused the termination of the plaintiff's employment, there could be no recovery. The substance of the defendant's contention was, that if he acted under the contract between the Boot and Shoe Workers' Union and the employer in procuring the plaintiff's discharge, his interference was lawful.

This contention brings us to an examination of the contract. That part which relates to the persons to be employed contains, first, a provision that the employer will hire only members of the union. This has no application to the plaintiff's case, for it is an agreement only for the future, and the plaintiff had been hired a long time before. The next provision is, that the employer will not retain in his employment a worker, after receiving notice that he is objectionable to the union, "either on account of being in arrears for dues, or disobedience of union rules or laws, or from any other cause." The first two possible causes for objection could not be applied to persons in the situation of the plaintiff, who were not members of the union or amenable to its laws. As to such persons, the only provision applicable was that the firm would not retain a worker who was objectionable to the union from any cause, however arbitrary the objection, or unreasonable the cause might be. This provision purported to authorize the union to interfere and deprive any workman of his employment for no reason whatever, in the arbitrary exercise of its power. Whatever the contracting parties may do if no one but themselves is concerned, it is evident that, as against the workman, a contract of this kind does·not of itself justify interference with his employment, by a third person who made the contract with his employer. *Curran v. Galen,* 152 N.Y. 33. No one can legally interfere with the employment of another, unless in the exercise of some right of his own, which the law respects. His will so to interfere for his own gratification is not such a right.

The judge rightly left to the jury the question whether, in view of all the circumstances, the interference was or was not for a justifiable cause. If the plaintiff's habits, or conduct, or character had been such as to render him an unfit associate, in the shop, for ordinary workmen of good character, that would have been a sufficient reason for interference in behalf of his shopmates. We can conceive of other good reasons. But the evidence tended to show that the only reason for procuring his discharge was his refusal to join the union. The question, therefore, is whether the jury might find that such an interference was unlawful.

The only argument that we have heard in support of interference by labor unions, in cases of this kind, is that it is justifiable as a kind of competition. It is true that fair competition in business brings persons into rivalry, and often justifies action for one's self, which interferes with proper action of another. Such action, on both sides, is the exercise by competing persons of equal conflicting rights. The principle appealed to would justify a member of the union, who was seeking employment for himself, in making an offer to serve on such terms as would result, and as he knew would result, in the discharge of the plaintiff by his employer, to make a place for the new comer. Such an offer, for such a purpose, would be unobjectionable. It would be merely the exercise of a personal right, equal in importance to the plaintiff's right. But an interference by a combination of persons, to obtain the discharge of a workman because he refuses to comply with their wishes, for their advantage, in some matter in which he has a right to act independently, is not competition. In such a case the action taken by the combination is not in the regular course of their business as employees, either in the service in which they are engaged, or in an effort to obtain employment in other service. The result which they seek to obtain cannot come directly from anything that they do within the regular line of their business as workers competing in the labor market. It can come only from action outside of the province of workingmen, intended directly to injure another, for the purpose of compelling him to submit to their dictation.

It is difficult to see how the object to be gained can come within the field of fair competition. If we consider it in reference to the right of employees to compete with one another, inducing a person to join a union has no tendency to aid them in such competition. Indeed the object of organizations of this kind is not to make competition of employees with one another more easy or successful. It is rather, by association, to prevent such competition, to bring all to equality, and to make them act together in a common interest. Plainly then, interference with one working under a contract, with a view to compel him to join a union, cannot be justified as a part of the competition of workmen with one another.

We understand that the attempted justification rests entirely upon another kind of so called competition, namely, competition between employers and the employed, in the attempt of each class to obtain as large a share as possible of the income from their combined efforts in the industrial field. In a strict sense, this is hardly competition. It is a struggle or contention of interests of different kinds, which are in opposition, so far as the division of profits is concerned. In a broad sense, perhaps the contending forces may be called competitors. At all events, we may assume that, as between themselves, the principle which warrants competition permits also reasonable efforts, of a proper kind, which have a direct tendency to benefit one party in his business at the expense of the other. It is no legal objection to action whose direct effect is helpful to one of the parties in the struggle that it is also directly detrimental to the other. But when action is directed against the other, primarily for the purpose of doing him harm and thus compelling him to yield to the demand of the actor, and this action does not directly affect the property, or business, or status of the actor, the case is different, even if the actor expects to derive a remote or indirect benefit from the act.

The gain which a labor union may expect to derive from inducing others to join it, is not an improvement to be obtained directly in the conditions under which the men are working, but only added strength for such contests with employers as may arise in the future. An object of this kind is too remote to be considered a benefit in business, such as to justify the infliction of intentional injury upon a third person for the purpose of obtaining it. If such an object were treated as legitimate, and allowed to be pursued to its complete accomplishment, every employee would be forced into membership in a union, and the unions, by a combination of those in different trades and occupations, would have complete and absolute control of all the industries of the country. Employers would be forced to yield to all their demands, or give up business. The attainment of such an object in the struggle with employers would not be competition, but monopoly. A monopoly, controlling anything which the world must have, is fatal to prosperity and progress. In matters of this kind the law does not tolerate monopolies. The attempt to force all laborers to combine in unions is against the policy of the law, because it aims at monopoly. It therefore does not justify causing the discharge, by his employer, of an individual laborer working under a contract. It is easy to see that, for different reasons, an act which might be done in legitimate competition by one, or two, or three persons, each proceeding independently, might take on an entirely different character, both in its nature and its purposes, if done by hundreds in combination.

We have no desire to put obstacles in the way of employees, who are seeking by combination to obtain better conditions for themselves and their families. We have no doubt that laboring men have derived and may hereafter derive advantages from organization. We only say that, under correct rules of law, and with a proper regard for the rights of individuals, labor unions cannot be permitted to drive men out of employment because they choose to work independently. If disagreements between those who furnish the capital and those who perform the labor employed in industrial enterprises are to be settled only by industrial wars, it would give a great advantage to combinations of employees, if they could be permitted, by force, to obtain a monopoly of the labor market. But we are hopeful that this kind of warfare soon will give way to industrial peace, and that rational methods of settling such controversies will be adopted universally.

The fact that the plaintiff's contract was terminable at will, instead of ending at a stated time, does not affect his right to recover. It only affects the amount that he is to receive as damages. *Moran v. Dunphy,* 177 Mass. 485, 487. *Perkins v. Pendleton,* 90 Maine, 166, 176. *Lucke v. Clothing Cutters & Trimmers' Assembly,* 77 Md. 396. *London Guarantee & Accident Co. v. Horn,* 101 Ill. App. 355; S.C. 206 Ill. 493.

The conclusion which we have reached is well supported by authority. The principle invoked is precisely the same as that which lies at the foundation of the decision in *Plant v. Woods,* 176 Mass. 492. In that case, although the power that lies in combination and the methods often adopted by labor unions in the exercise of it were stated with great clearness and ability, the turning point of the decision is found in this statement on page 502: "The necessity that the plaintiffs should join this association is not so great, nor is its relation to the rights of the defendants, as compared with the right of the plaintiffs to be free from molestation, such as to bring the acts of the defendants under the shelter of the principles of trade competition." *Carew v. Rutherford,* 106 Mass. 1. *Walker v. Cronin,* 107 Mass. 555, and the other cases cited in *Plant v. Woods, ubi supra,* as well as the later case of *Martell v. White,* 185 Mass. 255, all tend to support us in our decision.

We long have had a statute forbidding the coercion or compulsion by any person of any other "person into a written or verbal agreement not to join or become a member of a labor organization as a condition of his securing employment or continuing in the employment of such person." R. L. c. 106, § 12. The same principle would justify a prohibition of the coercion or compulsion of a person into a written or verbal agreement to join such an organization, as a condition of his securing employment, or continuing in the employment of another person. * * *

We hold that the defendant was not justified by the contract with Goodrich and Company, or by his relations to the plaintiff, in interfering with the plaintiff's employment under his contract. How far the principles which we adopt would apply, under different conceivable forms of contract, to an interference with a workman not engaged, but seeking employment, or to different methods of boycotting, we have no occasion in this case to decide. * * *

Exceptions overruled.

HOBAN v. DEMPSEY.

Massachusetts Supreme Judicial Court. 217 Mass. 166, 104 N.E. 717 (1914).

Rugg, C.J.: The plaintiffs are members of a labor union of longshoremen. There are two groups of defendants, the one members of a different labor union of longshoremen, and the other representatives of certain transatlantic steamship companies. The plaintiffs seek to enjoin the defendants from proceeding with an agreement which consists of thirty articles covering most, if not all, of the conditions of labor likely to arise in the course of such employment. One paragraph provides in substance that all longshoremen employed by the contracting transatlantic steamship lines shall be members of the defendant union whenever such men are available, and whenever such men are not available, then other men may be employed until the defendant union can supply men, but in any event men not members of the defendant union may be employed until the end of the day. It is contended that this clause is so illegal that performance of the contract ought to be enjoined at the instance of third parties. A trial was had before a single justice who, at its conclusion, found that the "contract was freely and fairly entered into between the contracting parties without any purpose or motive on the part of the representatives of the International Longshoremen's Association [the defendant union] to injure the plaintiffs or to coerce them into joining its union or unions, although I am satisfied that the legal effect of the contract may deprive the plaintiffs of employment by the transatlantic steamship lines," and ruled as matter of law that the bill could not be maintained and entered a decree dismissing it. The plaintiffs' appeal brings the case here.

It is familiar law that the findings of fact made by a single justice are not to be set aside unless plainly wrong. There was testimony from witnesses from both groups of defendants that their purpose in entering into the contract was not to harm the plaintiffs, but primarily to secure the welfare of each party to it. The steamship agents testified that they previously had dealt with several different organizations or local unions; that the committees representing these bodies were cumbersome in numbers, not small enough to make an effective body, and in consequence, in case of disagreement as to working conditions, there was difficulty in getting an adjustment; and that work was not done expeditiously and well, and it was felt that if an agreement was made with one strong union, under good control and management, it would be easier to get an adequate supply of labor and to settle troubles that might arise; and that no coercion or intimidation was exercised over them by the defendant union, and that they acted voluntarily with a view singly to their own interests in signing the contract. The advantage to the defendant union lay in securing a permanent arrangement covering all labor conditions, with preference in employment for their own members. The uncontradicted direct testimony was to the effect that the dominant motive on the part of both parties was to gain benefits for themselves and in no sense to harm the plaintiffs. Of course the defendants must be presumed to have intended the natural results of their acts, whatever may have been their oral statement respecting their intention. But it is plain from this summary of testimony that the finding that there was no purpose to injure the plaintiffs or to compel them to join the defendant union was supported by evidence. The tortious acts and motives which frequently have been found to exist in cases involving industrial disputes are absent in the case at bar. There has been no violence, threat or intimidation.

The question remains whether upon the facts found the plaintiffs are entitled to relief. There is no allegation or proof of coercion or violence direct or indirect toward the plaintiffs, or that the plaintiffs or any of them have been discharged from employment as a result of the contract. It is uncontroverted that the employment of longshoremen is occasional, work being offered only upon the arrival and departure of vessels. The plaintiffs' complaint is that, having no present contract, there is likelihood that in the future they will not be able to secure employment to the same extent as formerly from the transatlantic steamship lines by reason of this contract. This is a simple case where employers and a union of employees have made an agreement freely and without any kind of constraint, the terms of which do not require the breaking of contractual relations with any one, to the end that all the work of a specified kind be given to the members of a union so far as they are able to do it, for a limited period of time. If a sufficient number of union men are not supplied, the employer may hire whom he chooses. For aught that appears, the contract may have followed competition between rival groups of workmen to secure the work.

The inducements which moved both parties to the making of the contract were those ordinarily accompanying the kind of competition which is within the bounds of law. There was no fraud, intimidation, molestation, threat or coercion, covert or open, acting either upon the body or mind or property interests of the contracting parties. The incitements to the contract were those of business advantage alone. The terms of the contract do not preclude the employers from procuring workmen from any source if the defendant union does not supply them constantly with a sufficient number of competent longshoremen. But on the contrary, they are given this right expressly. The explicit finding of the single justice was to the effect that a desire or intention to harm the plaintiffs by depriving them of the chance of work, or to compel them to join the defendant union, or to do them any other injury, was not a part of the design of the contract nor one of the influences operating upon the minds of the parties in executing it. Whatever loss may come to them is an incidental result and not an essential element of a contract, whose dominant purpose is within the limits of lawful bargaining. No economic pressure, threat of business loss, or interference with absolute freedom of action was exercised in order to procure the making of the contract. There was nothing of the boycott about the contract, for an essential element of the boycott is intentional injury to somebody. An agreement of this sort under the circumstances disclosed is within the protection of *Pickett v. Walsh,* 192 Mass. 572, 584. It is within the lawful principles as to the conduct of business expounded at length and with great clearness in *Martell v. White,* 185 Mass. 255. See also *Mogul Steamship Co. v. McGregor,* 23 Q.B.D. 598; S.C. on appeal, [1892] A.C. 25. See in this connection, *Commonwealth v. Strauss,* 188 Mass. 229; S.C. 191 Mass. 545. Those principles are the law of this Commonwealth. It is not necessary to repeat or restate them. They are decisive against the contentions of the plaintiffs. There is nothing inconsistent or inharmonious with this conclusion, either in the facts or the principles declared in the numerous decisions by this court involving so-called labor disputes, which are collected in *Minasian v. Osborne,* 210 Mass. 250, at 255. The principles on which those cases were decided are reaffirmed now but they do not reach to the facts of the case at bar as found by the single justice. See also *Quinn v. Leathem,* [1901] A.C. 495; *South Wales Miners' Federation v. Glamorgan Coal Co.* [1905] A.C. 239; *Bowen v. Matheson,* 14 Allen, 499. The facts in the case at bar are different from those presented in *Berry v. Donovan,* 188 Mass. 353, where the direct result of the contract between the defendant and the plaintiff's employer was that the plaintiff was discharged. For the same reason, among others, *DeMinico v. Craig,* 207 Mass. 593, and *Hanson v. Innis,* 211 Mass. 301, are to be distinguished. There was no strike or other compulsion to procure a closed shop, conduct which has been held illegal. As was said by Knowlton, C.J., in *Folsom v. Lewis,* 208 Mass. 336, at 338: "Strengthening the forces of a labor union, to put it in a better condition to enforce its claims in controversies that may afterwards arise with employers, is not enough to justify an attack upon the business of an employer by inducing his employees to strike." *Berry v. Donovan,* 188 Mass. 353. *Plant v. Woods,* 176 Mass. 492. *Pickett v. Walsh,* 192 Mass. 572, 582. *Reynolds v. Davis,* 198 Mass. 294, 302. *McCord v. Thompson-Starrett Co.,* 129 App. Div. (N.Y.) 130, affirmed in 198 N.Y. 587. *Brennan v.*

United Hatters of North America, 44 Vroom, 729. But a different situation is presented by a voluntary and unforced agreement, freely made
solely for the mutual advantage of the contracting parties, which does
not effect the discharge from employment of any one. There are decisions in other jurisdictions to the precise point in harmony with the conclusion here reached. *Jacobs v. Cohen,* 183 N.Y. 207. *Kissam v. United
States Printing Co.,* 199 N.Y. 76. *National Fire Proofing Co. v. Mason
Builders' Association,* 94 C.C.A. 535. See *State v. Toole,* 26 Mont. 22,
33.

Although there is evidence which would warrant a finding that the
defendant union represents "practically the whole of the longshoremen
of the port" of Boston, this has not been found as a fact. It is apparent
both from the frame of the bill, the trend of the trial as disclosed on the
record, and the findings of the single justice, that the hearing did not
proceed upon the theory of an unlawful monopoly or a violation of the
Sherman anti-trust act. Those issues were not tried. Such questions
cannot be raised at this stage of the case and they are not passed upon.
Hence, it is not necessary to consider St. 1911, c. 503, *Connors v. Connolly,* 86 Conn. 641, 651, *Loewe v. Lawlor,* 208 U.S. 274, 293, and
United Shoe Machinery Co. v. La Chapelle, 212 Mass. 467, upon which
the plaintiffs now seek to rely. See also *Russell v. Amalgamated Society
of Carpenters & Joiners,* [1910] 1 K.B. 506; S.C. [1912] A.C. 421.

Decree dismissing bill affirmed.[1]

SHINSKY v. TRACEY.

Massachusetts Supreme Judicial Court. 226 Mass. 21, 114 N.E. 957 (1917).

Bill in equity, filed in the Superior Court on October 27, 1915, and
afterwards amended, praying for an injunction restraining the defendants, officers and members of the United Shoe Workers of America, a
voluntary unincorporated association, "from interfering or from combining, conspiring or attempting to interfere with the plaintiff in obtaining and holding employment and from intimidating or threatening persons who might employ or desire to employ the plaintiff and from in
any way hindering the plaintiff in obtaining or continuing in employment;" and for damages.

---

[1] "Berry v. Donovan, 188 Mass. 353, is distinguishable for reasons stated in
Hoban v. Dempsey, *supra.*" Braley, J., in Goyette v. Watson Co., 245 Mass. 577,
593, 140 N. E. 285 (1923). Unions in Massachusetts, acting under legal advice,
according to information received by the editor, when they succeed in negotiating
a trade agreement for the closed shop, have the employer first discharge all his
workers, then negotiate the agreement, and then re-employ the union men.

The suit was referred to a master. The material facts found and reported by the master in a first and a supplemental report are stated in the opinion. Upon a hearing by McLaughlin, J., the reports of the master were confirmed by an interlocutory decree and a final decree was entered dismissing the bill. The plaintiff appealed. * * *

BRALEY, J.: * * * The first paragraph of the amended bill alleges and the answer admits, that when expelled he had been employed at lasting shoes in a local factory for nearly eight years; and the master reports that, his work being satisfactory, he would have been retained except for the concerted action and conduct of the defendants. Their dominant purpose and controlling motive in procuring his discharge shortly after expulsion, as well as his discharge when he subsequently obtained employment with another shoe company which knew that he was no longer a member of the United Shoe Workers is found to have been, "to punish him and hold him up as an example before their membership," and the letters which they caused to be sent were "to induce the plaintiff's employer in each instance to discharge" him. The justification pleaded in the sixth paragraph of the answer is, that the plaintiff "had been a party to an agreement a copy of which is hereto annexed, and that the employers mentioned by him in his bill of complaint were also parties to said agreement; that the plaintiff violated his agreement and that if any action was taken by his employers or any other person which resulted in injury to him, * * * said action was the direct result of his own unlawful acts, in violating and repudiating the agreement."

It is unnecessary to pass on the validity of the agrement, which is an instrument under seal, or to decide whether the manufacturers or the members of the association could have compelled specific performance, for in the light of the findings quoted this defence vanishes.

It is true that the fifth, and in this connection the important article of this agreement or "Peace Pact" entered into by the association when the plaintiff was a member and certain shoe manufacturers including his employers provides, that "* * * so long as these local unions are in a position to furnish help to do the work no other help may be employed." The defendants nevertheless were not seeking its protection for the economic purpose of furnishing work for their own members, where if this were not done there would not be enough work to keep them employed, which was the motive underlying the strike decided to be lawful in *Minasian v. Osborne*, 210 Mass. 250. Nor were they actuated by a desire to conserve and promote the welfare of the plaintiff and his employers through the offer of friendly advice. *Tasker v. Stanley*, 153 Mass. 148, 150. But to preserve and to compel discipline in their own ranks they intended to proscribe the plaintiff who had become a member of a rival organization and business competitor of the association. It may be added, that at the date of the agreement the plaintiff had been employed for many years under a contract at will which does not appear to have been dependent upon a condition that he should be and remain a member of any organization. The plaintiff's expulsion did not automatically terminate this employment, and his continuance at his work until retired solely through their efforts did not as between themselves constitute a breach of the peace pact or agreement for which he would be liable to the defendants in damages. *Warren v. Stearns,* 19 Pick. 73. *Bryne v. Dorey,* 221 Mass. 399, 404. *Moran v. Dunphy,* 177 Mass. 485.

The report, while stating that the plaintiff has lost the benefit of his contracts of employment, goes further. It is specifically found "that by reason of the control which the defendants and their organization exercise over the shoe industry in Lynn, it will be impossible for the plaintiff hereafter to obtain work in at least ninety per cent of the shoe factories of Lynn in which the labor is controlled by the United Shoe Workers of America, and further as a marked man, it is highly improbable that he could obtain and keep employment in the remaining ten per cent of the shoe factories in Lynn."

The plaintiff manifestly is a sufferer from the consequences of an intentional and a successful boycott. If he had ceased to work at his calling and had engaged in trade the attempt to deprive him of his customers and to destroy his business by the methods described would have been under the master's findings an actionable wrong. *Burnham v. Dowd,* 217 Mass. 351. The right to acquire property by labor is coequal with the right to acquire property by contract and, having the same right to sell his labor as he would have had to sell his merchandise to the highest bidder, it is no less an actionable wrong where the right to his handiwork as a means of subsistence has been malevolently taken away or impaired under industrial conditions which the defendants knew would so operate as to make his further employment in the community where he resides extremely precarious if not practically impossible. *Berry v. Donovan,* 188 Mass. 353, 355, and cases cited. *Hoban v. Dempsey,* 217 Mass. 166, 170. *Cornellier v. Haverhill Shoe Manufacturers' Association,* 221 Mass. 554, 561. *Bogni v. Perotti,* 224 Mass. 152. Martin's Modern Law of Labor Unions, § 132.

While it is apparent upon the record that the plaintiff cannot be effectively aided by injunctive relief, he is entitled to damages. *Perry v. Pye,* 215 Mass. 403, 413. *New England Cement Gun Co. v. McGivern,* 218 Mass. 198, 204. The decree dismissing the bill is reversed, and a decree with costs is to be entered for the amount assessed by the master.

Ordered accordingly.[1]

---

[1] Tracey v. Osborne, 226 Mass. 25, 114 N.E. 959 (1917), was decided upon the same day as Shinsky v. Tracey. In the former case officials of the United Shoe Workers of America brought a bill to enjoin the defendants, the Lasters' Protective Union of Lynn, from interfering with the agreements that the complainant union had negotiated with certain shoe manufacturers. The agreements involved were the same Peace Pacts that were involved in Shinsky v. Tracey. In granting the complainants relief Rugg, C.J., said of the agreement: "The contract in its general outlines is similar to that held legal in Hoban v. Dempsey, 217 Mass. 166. In this aspect the case at bar is governed by that decision. It is putting in the form of an agreement a stipulation that one named labor union shall have, so long as it is able to do it, all the work of a partciular employer, a demand held to

SHINSKY v. O'NEIL.

Massachusetts Supreme Judicial Court. 232 Mass. 99, 121 N.E. 790 (1919).

LORING, J.: The plaintiff in this case (the same person who was the plaintiff in *Shinsky v. Tracey,* 226 Mass. 21) is a laster who had been expelled from the association known as the United Shoe Workers of America and from the local union of that association in the city of Lynn. After the decision in *Shinsky v. Tracey,* he applied on February 1, 1917, to the Adams Shoe Company for employment as a laster. One Benson, who had authority to hire and discharge men for that company, refused to employ him, "feeling bound to comply with the peace pact and fearing that there would be a strike if he employed the plaintiff * * * unless he [the plaintiff] had a permit from the union. The plaintiff, feeling that he could not get such a permit, went away." In March, 1917, the plaintiff applied to A. Fisher and Son for employment as a laster. One Daley had authority to hire and discharge men for this firm. The master made the same finding with respect to Daley that he made with respect to Benson. On April 2, 1917, the plaintiff applied to the Johnson and Wright Shoe Company for employment as a laster. Hedlund had authority to hire and discharge men for this company. Hedlund at first employed the plaintiff, but, on finding out who he was, discharged him. The master found that, "in discharging the plaintiff, [Hedlund] was actuated by a desire to carry out the real wishes of Fish and the union and thus avoid trouble with the union." Fish was the business agent of the local union of the United Shoe Workers of America. Hedlund had conferred with him as to the action he had better take on the plaintiff's application for work. The Adams Shoe Company, A. Fisher and Son and the Johnson and Wright Shoe Company were shoe manufacturers in Lynn. Each of the first two had a peace pact agreement with the United Shoe Workers of America, and the other had a price list agreement with them. The peace pact agreement provided that no person should be employed "other than members in good standing of the United Shoe Workers of America so long as the Local Union * * * are able to furnish help to do said work." The price list agreement provided that all the work should "be given to members in good standing with Lasters' Local Number 1, United Shoe Workers of America."

The case came before the Superior Court on the report of a master, to which no exceptions were taken. A decree was entered in the Superior Court dismissing the bill, and the case is here on an appeal from that decree.

---

be within the limits of allowable competition in Pickett v. Walsh, 192 Mass. 572, 584. The contract does not appear to have been made for the purpose of injuring the defendants, who then were members of the plaintiff union, or for any purpose other than the mutual advantage of the contracting parties. It was entered into freely and not under compulsion or coercion. It was not entered into with a purpose to harm anybody. This does not infringe upon the principles established in Berry v. Donovan, 188 Mass. 353, and Shinsky v. Tracey, *ante,* p. 378, for decisive facts there present are not found in the case at bar." P. 29.

The bill in this suit is not founded on the Sherman anti-trust act (26 U.S. Sts. at Large, 209) nor on St. 1911, c. 503. We have no occasion therefore to consider questions under those statutes which might be thought to arise in this case.

The plaintiff has not undertaken to question the validity of a peace pact agreement between an employer and a labor union. The validity of such an agreement was established by the decision of this court in *Hoban v. Dempsey*, 217 Mass. 166. Nor has the plaintiff undertaken to argue against the validity of a clause in an agreement between an employer of labor and a labor union which provides that all work shall be given by the employer to the union. The validity of such an agreement is a necessary corollary of the decision made in *Pickett v. Walsh*, 192 Mass. 572.

What the plaintiff has contended is that this case is taken out of these decisions by the particular findings made by the master.

He relies in the first place on what was found by the master with respect to the general policy of the United Shoe Workers of America. The master begins his report by stating what the general policy of the United Shoe Workers of America is. He found in the first place that "The United Shoe Workers of America * * * seek as part of their general policy to secure all the work possible for their members, rather than to have it go to unaffiliated workers, and to obtain the highest prices possible for their work." After stating that this is "a part of their general policy" he goes on with this finding: "A part of the policy of the union is to secure and increase in number what are sometimes called 'closed shops,' that is, shops where union members and no others are employed, and one of the purposes of this policy is to enlarge and strengthen the union organization." The plaintiff's contention on these findings is that the master has found that a part of the general policy of the union is legal and a part illegal; that it follows from this that the policy as a whole is illegal and for that reason this case is taken out of *Hoban v. Dempsey* and the doctrine of *Pickett v. Walsh*.

We are not able to accede to this contention of the plaintiff. It is established that workmen can combine to get the advantage of bargaining for their common benefit in respect to the terms and conditions upon and under which they should work. It is further established that, if they are successful in getting the bargain they wish, they can insert in the agreement setting forth that bargain a clause providing that all work of the employer shall be given to them or that a preference shall be given to them in the employment of workmen. So much is established. Workmen cannot hope to succeed in securing the advantages of bargaining for the common benefit unless their combination, their organization, their union (call it what you please) is a large and a strong one. If any member of the combination or union were to testify that he did not wish "to enlarge and strengthen the union organization," no one would believe him. No one would believe that a member of a labor union organized to secure the advantages of bargaining for the common benefit could hope to succeed unless all the members of the union did their best "to enlarge and strengthen the union organiza-tion." So far as this finding of the master is concerned we are of opinion that the policy of the United Shoe Workers of America "to enlarge and strengthen the union organization" is an incident and a necessary incident to a successful combination to secure the advantages of bargaining for the common benefit. What we have said with respect to this finding of the master is also true of the other finding relied upon by the plaintiff, namely, "a part of the policy of the union is to secure and increase in number what are sometimes called 'closed shops.' " We understand by this that the mas-ter means that it is a part of the policy of the United Shoe Workers of America "to secure and increase in number" shops where the employer agrees to give all the work to members of the union, or at any rate to make a preference in their favor in employing workmen.

The purposes of the action in question in *Plant v. Woods,* 176 Mass. 492, and in *Berry v. Donovan,* 188 Mass. 353, are quite different from the purposes which are found by the master to have been included in the gen-eral policy of the United Shoe Workers of America set forth above. In both *Plant v. Woods* and in *Berry v. Donovan* the action taken was taken to force in the one case a number of workmen and in the other a single workman to join a particular union. That was the sole purpose of the action taken in those cases. The decisions in those cases are not decisive of the case at bar where there is a general policy to secure the advantages of bargaining for the common benefit or, as the master puts it, "to secure all the work possible for their members, rather than to have it go to un-affiliated workers, and to obtain the highest prices possible for their work," and where as an incident to that general policy it is found by the master that it was the purpose of the union "to secure and increase in number what are sometimes called 'closed shops' * * * and * * * to enlarge and strengthen the union organization." By the true construction of the mas-ter's report it cannot be taken that his statement of the policy of the United Shoe Workers of America is anything more than this.

The plaintiff has insisted that there is another finding of the master which takes this case out of the decision in *Hoban v. Dempsey* and the doctrine of *Pickett v. Walsh.* That finding is this: "It is then a part of the policy of the union to endeavor to induce the workman to become a member of the union or to make himself in good standing in it, and, failing that, to report to the employer that the workman is not a member of the union in good standing. It is not the custom of the union to refuse mem-bership to workmen wishing to join the union, even though there are members of the union out of work who would like employment; but of course the admission of new members is optional with the union." It is the plaintiff's contention that this finding means "that the union tries to induce the workman to join and admits him regardless of whether its own members are out of work and without employment. It is not the work, but the man and the closed shop which the union really seeks, in order to 'en-large and strengthen the union organization.' " A union which has an agreement with an employer providing (*inter alia*) that all the work shall be given to members of the union or that a preference shall be given to members of the union in employing workmen, would open itself to a serious criticism if it refused to admit to membership men qualified to perform the work done by members of the union in question. By having as a part of its policy "the custom" of not refusing membership to workmen who wished to join, such a union avoids subjecting itself to this criticism. We are of opinion that the finding of the master here relied upon cannot be taken to mean anything more than this.

The last finding of the master which is relied upon by the plaintiff to take this case out of *Hoban v. Dempsey* and the doctrine of *Pickett v. Walsh,* is this: "I find that, as a consequence of the case of *Shinsky v. Tracey,* 226 Mass. 21, and the proceedings leading up to that suit, the defendants, other than Daley and Hedlund, and the union generally were and are in a state of business hostility to the plaintiff." It is plain from the master's finding which follows immediately after this finding, that he did not intend by this finding to state that the refusal to employ the plaintiff was based on "hostility to the plaintiff." Immediately after this finding the master made the following finding: "But I do not find that, in the three incidents related in this report, the defendants or the union did anything adverse to the plaintiff that they would not have done had the plaintiff been a non-member of the union against whom no such hostility existed. Whether the plaintiff could have obtained admission into the union, as an ordinary non-member could, must be a matter of conjecture, because he made no application for admission." It is plain, therefore, that the master's finding went no further than a finding that the union insisted upon an enforcement of the clauses in their agreement with the Adams Shoe Company and with A. Fisher and Son which provided that in employing the lasters preference should be given to members of the union, and of the clause in their agreement with the Johnson and Wright Shoe Company, that all the work in the lasters' department should be given to members of the Lasters' Local No. 1 of the United Shoe Workers of America.

For these reasons we are of opinion that there is nothing in the masters' report which takes this case out of the decision made in *Hoban v. Dempsey* and the doctrine of *Pickett v. Walsh,* and that apart from the Sherman anti-trust act and St. 1911, c. 503 (upon which we intimate no opinion) the agreements between the three employers of lasters here in question and the United Shoe Workers of America were valid agreements.

The result is that the decree appealed from must be affirmed with costs, and it is

So ordered.[1]

---

[1] For comment on the case, see: 28 Yale Law Jour. 611 (1919). Accord: Ryan v. Hayes, 243 Mass. 168, 137 N.E. 344 (1922); Goyette v. Watson Co., 245 Mass. 577, 140 N.E. 285 (1924). *Cf.* Harmon v. United Mine Workers, 166 Ark. 255, 266 S.W. 84 (1924).

CURRAN v. GALEN.

New York Court of Appeals. 152 N.Y. 33, 46 N.E. 297 (1897).

Appeal from a judgment of the General Term of the Supreme Court in the fifth judicial department, entered April 14, 1894, which affirmed an interlocutory judgment in favor of plaintiff entered upon a decision of the court at Special Term sustaining a demurrer to the answer.

The plaintiff demands damages against the defendants for having confederated and conspired together to injure him, by taking away his means of earning a livelihood and preventing him from obtaining employment. He sets out in his complaint that he was an engineer by trade, and that, previously to the acts mentioned, he was earning, by reason of his trade, a large income, and had constant employment at remunerative wages. He sets forth the existence of an unincorporated association in the city of Rochester, where he was a resident, called the Brewery Workingmen's Local Assembly, 1796, Knights of Labor; which was composed of workingmen employed in the brewing business in that city and was a branch of a national organization known as the Knights of Labor. He alleges that it assumed to control by its rules and regulations the acts of its members in relation to that trade and employment, and demands and obtains from its members implicit obedience in relation thereto.

Plaintiff then alleges in his complaint that the defendants Grossberger and Watts wrongfully and maliciously conspired and combined together, and with the said local assembly, for the purpose of injuring him and taking away his means of earning a livelihood, in the following manner, to wit: That in the month of November, 1890, Grossberger and Watts threatened the plaintiff that, unless he would join said local assembly, pay the initiation fee and subject himself to its rules and regulations, they and that association would obtain plaintiff's discharge from the employment in which he then was and would make it impossible for him to obtain any employment in the city of Rochester, or elsewhere, unless he became a member of said association. In pursuance of that conspiracy, upon plaintiff's refusing to become a member of said association, Grossberger and Watts and the association made complaint to the plaintiff's employers and forced them to discharge him from their employ, and, by false and malicious reports in regard to him, sought to bring him into ill-repute with members of his trade and employers and to prevent him from prosecuting his trade and earning a livelihood. The answer, in the first place, admitted all that was alleged in respect to the organization of the local assembly, as to how it was composed and as to its being a branch of the national organization of the Kinghts of Labor, and as to its assuming to control the acts of its members and to demand from them implicit obedience. It then denies, generally and specifically, each and every other allegation in the complaint. As a second and separate answer and defense to the complaint, the defendants set up the existence in the city of Rochester of the Ale Brewers' Association and an agreement between that association and the local assembly described in the complaint, to the effect that all employés of the brewery companies belonging to the Ale Brewers' Association "shall be members of the Brewery Workingmen's Local Assembly, 1796, Knights of Labor, and that no employé should work for a longer period than four weeks without becoming a member." They alleged that the plaintiff was retained in the employment of the Miller Brewing Company "for more than four weeks after he was notified of the provisions of said agreement, requiring him to become a member of the local assembly;" that defendants requested plaintiff to become a member and, upon his refusal to comply, "Grossberger and Watts, as members of said assembly, and as a committee duly appointed for that purpose, notified the officers of the Miller Brewing Company that plaintiff, after repeated requests, had refused for more than four weeks to become a member of said assembly," and that "defendants did so solely in pursuance of said agreement, and in accordance with the terms thereof, and without intent or purpose to injure plaintiff in any way." The plaintiff demurred to the matter set up as a separate defense to the complaint, upon the ground that it was insufficient, in law, upon the face thereof. The Special Term and General Term have sustained the demurrer, and the question is whether this matter, set up by way of special defense, is sufficient to exonerate the defendants from the charge, made in the complaint, of a conspiracy to injure the plaintiff and to deprive him of the means of earning his livelihood. * * *

Per Curiam. In the decision of the question before us we have to consider whether the agreement upon which the defendants rely in defense of this action, and to justify their part in the dismissal of the plaintiff from his employment, was one which the law will regard with favor and uphold, when compliance with its requirements is made a test of the individual's right to be employed. If such an agreement is lawful, then it must be conceded that the defendants are entitled to set it up as a defense to the action; forasmuch as they allege that what they did was in accordance with its terms.

In the general consideration of the subject, it must be premised that the organization, or the co-operation, of workingmen is not against any public policy. Indeed, it must be regarded as having the sanction of law, when it is for such legitimate purposes as that of obtaining an advance in the rate of wages or compensation, or of maintaining such rate. (Penal Code, sec. 170.) It is proper and praiseworthy, and, perhaps, falls within that general view of human society, which perceives an underlying law that men should unite to achieve that which each by himself cannot achieve; or can achieve less readily. But the social principle which justifies such organizations is departed from, when they are so extended in their operation as either to intend, or to accomplish, injury to others. Public policy and the interests of society favor the utmost freedom in the citizen to pursue his lawful trade or calling, and if the purpose of an organization or combination of workingmen be to hamper, or to restrict, that freedom, and, through contracts or arrangements with employers, to coerce other workingmen to become members of the organization and to come under its rules and conditions, under the penalty of the loss of their position, and of deprivation of employment, then that purpose seems clearly unlawful and militates against the spirit of our government and the nature of our institutions. The effectuation of such a purpose would conflict with that principle of public policy which prohibits monopolies and exclusive privileges. It would tend to deprive the public of the services of men in useful employments and capacities. It would, to use the language of Mr. Justice BARRETT in *People ex rel. Gill v. Smith* (5 N.Y. Cr. Rep. at p. 513), "impoverish and crush a citizen for no reason connected in the slightest degree with the advancement of wages, or the maintenance of the rate."

Every citizen is deeply interested in the strict maintenance of the constitutional right freely to pursue a lawful avocation, under conditions equal as to all, and to enjoy the fruits of his labor, without the imposition of any conditions not required for the general welfare of the community. The candid mind should shrink from the results of the operation of the principle contended for here; for there would certainly be a compulsion, or a fettering, of the individual, glaringly at variance with that freedom in the pursuit of happiness, which is believed to be guaranteed to all by the provisions of the fundamental law of the state. The sympathies, or the fellow-feeling which, as a social principle, underlies the association of workingmen for their common benefit, are not consistent with a purpose to oppress the individual who prefers by single effort to gain his livelihood. If organization of workingmen is in line with good government, it is because it is intended as a legitimate instrumentality to promote the common good of its members. If it militates against the general public interest, if its powers are directed towards the repression of individual freedom, upon what principle shall it be justified? In *Regina v. Rowlands* (17 Ad. & Ellis [N.S.], 671) the question involved was of the right by combination to prevent certain workingmen from working for their employers and, thereby, to compel the latter to make an alteration in the mode of conducting their business. The Court of Queen's Bench, upon a motion for a new trial for misdirection of the jury by Mr. Justice ERLE below, approved of his charge, and we quote from his remarks. He instructed the jury that "a combination for the purpose of injuring another is a combination of a different nature, directed personally against the party to be injured, and the law allowing them to combine for the purpose of obtaining a lawful benefit to themselves gives no sanction to combinations which have for their immediate purpose the hurt of another. The rights of workmen are conceded; but the exercise of free will and freedom of action, within the limits of the law, is also secured equally to the masters. The intention of the law is, at present, to allow either of them to follow the dictates of their own will, with respect to their own actions, and their own property, and either, I believe, has a right to study to promote his own advantage, or to combine with others to promote their mutual advantage."

The organization of the local assembly in question by the workingmen in the breweries of the city of Rochester may have been perfectly lawful in its general purposes and methods and may, otherwise, wield its power and influence usefully and justly, for all that appears. It is not for us to say, nor do we intend to intimate, to the contrary; but so far as a purpose appears from the defense set up to the complaint that no employé of a brewing company shall be allowed to work for a longer period than four weeks, without becoming a member of the Workingmen's Local Assembly, and that a contract between the local assembly and the Ale Brewers' Association shall be availed of to compel the discharge of the independent employé, it is, in effect, a threat to keep persons from working at the particular trade and to procure their dismissal from employment. While it may be true, as argued, that the contract was entered into, on the part of the Ale Brewers' Association, with the object of avoiding disputes and conflicts with the workingmen's organization, that feature and such an intention cannot aid the defense, nor legalize a plan of compelling workingmen, not in affiliation with the organization, to join it, at the peril of being deprived of their employment and of the means of making a livelihood.

In our judgment, the defense pleaded was insufficient, in law, upon the face thereof, and, therefore, the demurrer thereto was properly sustained.

The judgment appealed from should be affirmed, with costs.

All concur, except HAIGHT, J., not sitting.

Judgment affirmed.[1]

JACOBS v. COHEN.

New York Court of Appeals. 183 N.Y. 207, 76 N.E. 5 (1905).

GRAY, J.: The plaintiff sues the makers and the indorser on a promissory note, payable to the order of the Protective Coat Tailors' Union, of which he is the president, to recover the amount due thereon. The answer of the defendants denied the allegations of the complaint, except as to the making of the note, and set up as a distinct and separate defense that it was given "as collateral security to the plaintiff, to be applied as liquidated damages, for violation by the defendants, of any of the covenants and conditions of a certain contract." The particular part of the contract set forth is as follows: "That the party of the first part [meaning the makers' firm] shall not employ any help whatsoever other than those belonging to, and who are members of the party of the third part, [meaning a 'union' of the firm's employés] and in good standing, and who conform to the rules and regulations of the said party of the third part, and the said party of the first part shall cease to employ any one and all those employés who are not in good standing, and who do not conform to and comply with the rules and regulations of said party of the third part, upon being notified to that effect by its duly credentialed representatives. That the party of the first part

---

[1] *Cf.* Cusumano v. Schlessinger, 152 N.Y.S. 1081 (App. Div. 1915).

shall not engage any help whatsoever, even those who are members of the party of the third part, without their first having produced a pass-card duly executed and signed by the authorized business agent of the party of the third part; said card to show that the bearer thereof is a member in good standing of the party of the third part, and that he has complied with the rules and regulations thereof in force at that time." The answer then alleged "that the said contract is in restraint of trade and the said contract has for its purpose the combination of employers and employees, whereby the freedom of the citizen, in pursuing his lawful trade and calling, is through such contract, combination and arrangement, hampered and restricted, and has also for its purpose the coercing of workingmen, to become members of the said Employees' Organization and come under its rules and its conditions, under the penalty of the loss of their positions and of deprivation of employment, and that such purposes are in restraint of trade, that they hamper and restrict the freedom of a citizen, in pursuing his lawful trade and calling and that they are against public policy and unlawful." To this defense, the plaintiff demurred, for being insufficient in law. The demurrer was sustained at the Special Term; but, upon appeal to the Appellate Division, in the second department, the judgment sustaining the demurrer was reversed and the demurrer was overruled. Permission was given to the defendants to appeal to this court and the following questions were certified for our review, namely:

"I. Is a contract made by an employer of labor, by which he binds himself to employ and to retain in his employ only members in good standing of a single labor union, consonant with public policy, and enforcible in the courts of justice in this state?

"II. Is the 'Second' separate defense, contained in the answer herein of the defendants, Morris Cohen and Louis Cohen, insufficient upon the face thereof to constitute a defense?"

If we refer to the prevailing opinion of the Appellate Division, it appears that the question in this case was there regarded as within our decision in *Curran v. Galen*, (152 N.Y. 33), and, hence, that the contract was unlawful because contrary to public policy. In this view, I think the learned justices below erred. The contract is annexed to, and made part of, the answer and is tripartite, between the defendants, Morris and Louis Cohen, a firm engaged in the tailoring business, their employés, represented by an attorney in fact, and a voluntary association, formed by the latter and called the Protective Coat Tailors' and Pressers' Union, of which the plaintiff is president. It provided for the employment by the Cohens of their employés, in their various skilled capacities, for the term of one year; for a system of work by the week; for the number of hours of work and for the mode of payment of the wages and, generally, for the regulation of the relations between the employers and their employés, including this particular agreement not to employ others than members of their employés' union. Whatever else may be said of it, this is the case of an agreement voluntarily made by an employer with his workmen, which bound the latter to give their skilled services for a

certain period of time, upon certain conditions, regulating the performance of the work to be done, and restricting the class of workmen, who
should be engaged upon it, to such persons as were in affiliation with an
association, organized by the employers' workmen with reference to the
carrying on of the very work. It would seem as though an employer should
be, unquestionably, free to enter into such a contract with his workmen
for the conduct of the business, without its being deemed obnoxious upon
any ground of public policy. If it might operate to prevent some persons
from being employed by the firm, or, possibly, from remaining in the
firm's employment, that is but an incidental feature. Its restrictions
were not of an oppressive nature, operating generally in the community
to prevent such craftsmen from obtaining employment and from earning
their livelihood. It was but a private agreement between an employer and
his employés, concerning the conduct of the business for a year and securing to the latter an absolute right to limit the class of their fellow-workmen
to those persons, who should be in affiliation with an organization entered
into with the design of protecting their interests in carrying on the work;
as, indeed, the agreement recites. Nor does the answer aver that it was
intended, thereby, to injure other workmen; or that it was made with a
malicious motive to coerce any to their injury, through their threatened
deprivation of all opportunity of pursuing their lawful avocation. To coerce workmen to become members of the employés organization, through
such a contract, is not the allegation of something, which the law will,
necessarily, regard as contravening public policy. The allegation that
its "purposes are in restraint of trade," or that "they hamper and restrict
the freedom of a citizen," or "that they are against public policy," is
the mere statement of a legal conclusion.

If the question were more correctly presented by some appropriate
allegation, I, still, would be of the opinion that the agreement is not one
which comes under the condemnation of the law. The right of workingmen to unite and to organize for the protection of their interests and welfare is not denied. It has been, expressly and recently, declared by this
court. (*Curran v. Galen,* 152 N.Y. 33; *National Protective Association
v. Cumming,* 170 *id.* 315, at pp. 320, 334, 338.) The inviolability of the
right of persons to freedom of action may well extend to any concert of
action for legitimate ends, if consistent with the maintenance of law and
order in the community and if not interfering with the enjoyment and the
exercise by others of their constitutional rights. Their right to combine
and to co-operate for the promotion of such ends as the increase of wages,
the curtailment of hours of labor, the regulation of their relations with
their employer, or for the redress of a grievance, is justifiable. Their
combination is lawful, when it does not extend so far as to inflict injury
upon others, or to oppress and crush them by excluding them from all
employment, unless gained through joining the labor organization, or
trades union. This we have decided and this the law of the state sanctions. (*Curran v. Galen, supra; National Protective Association v. Cum-*

ming, supra; Penal Code, § 170.) As it was observed in *Curran v. Galen,* an underlying law of human society moves men to unite for the better achievement of a common aim and this social principle justifies organized action. Organization, or combination, is a law of human society. It is open to all orders of men, who desire to accomplish some lawful purpose through the greater strength and effectiveness, which organization offers over individual effort. If surrender of individual liberty is involved in combination, that is, nevertheless, but an extension of the right of freedom of action. If, therefore, the organization of workingmen is not obnoxious to moral, or to legal, criticism and only the use, or directing, of the power of the organization to injure others, by preventing them from following their trade, is visited by the law with its condemnation, how can it fairly be said that the refusal of a body of men to work with those not in affiliation with them and an agreement with the employer, by which such are excluded from the shop, is acting beyond legally justifiable limits? Whether the reason for the refusal be purely sentimental, or whether based upon more substantial grounds, such as, for instance, an assurance of the character and of the competent skill of their fellow-workmen, is not material.

The case of *Curran v. Galen, (supra),* which stands unaffected as an authority, presented a very different state of facts. There the plaintiff demanded damages of the defendants, who were officers and members of an association of workingmen in the brewing business in the city of Rochester, for having conspired to injure him and to take away his means of earning a livelihood. In substance, he alleged in his complaint that he was threatened by certain of the defendants, members of the association, that, unless he became a member, they would obtain his discharge from employment and would make it impossible for him to obtain any employment in that city or elsewhere; that, upon his refusing to become a member of the association, the defendants forced his employers to discharge him and, by false and malicious reports circulated in regard to him, sought to bring him into ill-repute with members of his trade and employers, and to prevent him from prosecuting his trade and earning a livelihood. The answer to the complaint, among other defenses, set up an agreement between the Ale Brewers' Association in the city of Rochester and the particular association referred to in the complaint, to the effect that all employés of the brewery companies should be members of the association and that no employé should work for a longer period than four weeks without becoming a member; and that, upon the plaintiff's refusal to comply with defendants' request to become a member of the association, his employers were notified thereof in accordance with the terms of the agreement with the Ale Brewers' Association. To this matter set up as a defense the plaintiff demurred and the order sustaining the demurrer was affirmed in this court. I endeavored to point out in the opinion that the agreement could be no justification for the acts charged in the complaint and that it could not legalize a plan for compelling other workingmen to join the defendants' organization, at the peril of being deprived of employment and of making a livelihood. However lawful and legitimate the purposes of the organization of the workingmen may have been, its power and influence were being unlawfully wielded in efforts to keep other persons from working at the particular trade and to procure their dismissal from employment. In the general discussion of the question, I conceded the general right of workingmen to organize for the common good of the members and sought to show how the agreement and acts, there in question, were contrary to public policy and unlawful, because oppressive and restricting the freedom of others to engage in the same line of occupation, or to make a livelihood at their trade, as a penalty for refusing to join the defendants' organization. That was a very different case from the present one. The subsequent case of *National Protective Association v. Cumming, (supra)*, in no wise overruled *Curran v. Galen.* It was not at all within the principle of the prior case. It concerned a dispute between rival labor organizations. The plaintiff organization sought to restrain the defendants from preventing the employment of its members and from procuring their discharge by any employer through threats and strikes, and the reversal of a judgment awarding the relief demanded was affirmed by this court. The right of the defendants, in that case, to refuse to permit their members to work with others, who were members of a rival organization, and to bring about their discharge upon the common work in which they were engaged, if confined to threats to withdraw from the work, or to ordering a strike of their own members, without resort to injurious acts, was admitted. The defendants' effort was not to compel the others to join with their organization as a condition of being allowed to work and, whether it was to secure only the employment of approved workmen, (which was a possible inference from the facts), or whether it was to obtain an exclusive preference in employment, if without resort to force, or the commission of any other unlawful acts, it was not within the condemnation of the law.

Within, even, the view expressed by the minority of the judges of this court in the *Cumming* case, the contract in the present case was not unlawful, which the employer made with his workingmen. Judge VANN asserted the right of every man "to carry on his business in any lawful way that he sees fit. He may employ such men as he pleases and is not obliged to employ those whom, for any reason, he does not wish to have work for him. He has the right to the utmost freedom of contract and choice in this regard." This contract was voluntarily entered into by the Cohens and, if it provided for the performance of the firm's work by those only who were accredited members, in good standing, of an organization of a class of workingmen whom they employed, were they not free to do so? If they regarded it as beneficial for them to do so, (and such is a recital of the contract), does it lie in their mouths, now, to urge its illegality? That, incidentally, it might result in the discharge of some of those employed, for failure to come into affiliation with their fellow-workmen's organization, or that it might prevent others from being engaged upon the work, is neither something of which the employers may complain, nor something with which public policy is concerned.

I think that the questions certified should be answered in the affirmative and, therefore, that the order of the Appellate Division, reversing the interlocutory judgment and overruling the demurrer, should be reversed and that the interlocutory judgment, which sustained the demurrer should be affirmed, with costs in all the courts to the appellants.[1]

McCORD v. THOMPSON-STARRETT COMPANY.

New York Appellate Division, First Department. 129 App. Div. 130, 113 N.Y. 385 (1908).

SCOTT, J.: We would find no difficulty in affirming this judgment if the Building Trades Employers' Association had gone no further than to order a general "lock out" of the members of the Brotherhood of Carpenters.

The communication of September 22, 1904, however, does go further, and instructs the members of the association that no men may be set to work, or retained at work, who do not at once join a particular labor union, the Greater New York Carpenters' Union.

This requirement, if it is to be considered as the act of the association, was against public policy, illegal and void. (*Curran v. Galen,* 152 N.Y. 33; *Jacobs v. Cohen,* 183 *id.* 207.) I see no reason why we are not bound to regard this requirement as the act of the association. By its constitution the board of governors is designated as the body which is authorized to act for the association and to issue orders to the members. The complaint alleges, and the court has found, that the letter containing the objectionable order was "sent to said defendant by the said Board of Governors and certified by its Secretary." It is true that the letter speaks of the emergency committee as directing that all carpenters then in the employ of a member, who are competent, shall become members at once of the Greater New York Carpenters' Union, and it does not appear who constitute the emergency committee or what power it possessed. But

---

[1] The dissenting opinion of Vann, J., concurred in by Bartlett, J., is omitted.

Cf. Birmingham Paint & Roofing Co. v. Crampton & Tharpe, 39 So. 1020 (Ala. 1905); Dyer Bros. Golden West Iron Works v. Central Iron Works, 182 Cal. 588, 189 Pac. 445 (1920); Associated Hat Manufacturers v. Baird-Unteidt Co., 88 Conn. 332, 91 Atl. 373 (1914); American Dental Co. v. Central Dental Laboratory Co., 2256 Ill. App. 279 (1930); Androff v. Building Trade Employers' Ass'n, 83 Ind. App. 294, 148 N.E. 203 (1925); Judgment of Reichsgericht of July 2, 1925, 111 Entscheidungen des Reichsgerichts in Zivilsachen, 199; Chambre Syndicale de la Coutellerie de Thiers v. Etablissement Sabatier, Gaz. Pal. No. 357, Dec. 23, 1926 (Cour de Cassation, 1926).

See: Grinnell, "An Analysis of the Legal Value of a Labor Union Contract," 41 Am. Law Rev. 197 (1927).

the same letter also contains the injunction, not purporting to emanate from the emergency committee, that no brotherhood carpenter, although willing to sign the arbitration plan, may be set to work unless he at once joins the designated union. Whether these instructions originated with the emergency committee or any one else, the board of governors, by causing them to be subscribed by their secretary and by sending them to the members of the association, adopted them and made them their own. In so doing, as it seems to us, they exceeded their lawful authority and undertook to impose upon the Thompson-Starrett Company an obligation which it was not required to assume. The bonds sued upon, although purporting to be given to secure liquidated damages, are in fact given to secure penalties for non-compliance with the order of the association, for it is apparent that the association, as such, could suffer no actual pecuniary damage from the disobedience of an order.

To collect a penalty for the disobedience of an order, it must appear that the order was one which was rightfully and lawfully given, and as it appears that the association exceeded its authority in requiring that no carpenter should be employed unless he joined a particular union, it follows that the penalty cannot be collected. I do not understand that there is any serious difference of opinion between us as to the illegality of the directions to employ only members of one particular union. This seems to be established by the opinion of the Court of Appeals in *Curran v. Galen* (*supra*), reaffirmed and explained in *Jacobs v. Cohen* (*supra*). In the latter case Judge GRAY, writing for the court, makes it quite clear that while an individual employer may lawfully agree with a labor union to employ only its members, because such an agreement is not of an oppressive nature operating generally throughout the community to prevent craftsmen in the trade from obtaining employment and earning their livelihood, yet that such an agreement when participated in by all or by a large proportion of employers in any community becomes oppressive and contrary to public policy because it operates generally upon the craftsmen in the trade and imposes upon them as a penalty for refusing to join the favored union, the practical impossibility of obtaining employment at their trade and thereby gaining a livelihood. The evidence makes it quite clear that the objectionable order of September 22, 1904, was of the latter class, for it is in evidence that the employers' association embraced nearly every prominent building contractor, and that the "lock out" affected practically the whole building trade in the borough of Manhattan. It is suggested, however, that even if the order to employ only members of the Greater New York Carpenters' Union was beyond the authority of the board of governors of the employers' association, still earlier orders which merely forbade the employment of members of the Brotherhood of Carpenters, were authorized and lawful, and that the disobedience of these by defendants constituted a breach of the conditions of their bonds. Hence, it is argued that the illegal order may be ignored and the forfeiture upheld by reason of the disobedience of the earlier orders, which are assumed to

have been lawful. The difficulty with this argument is that the defendants did obey the earlier orders and did lay off their employees in obedience
to them. Indeed, for a long time after the issuance of the obnoxious order they continued to lock out the members of the Brotherhood of Carpenters, and made effort to obtain a sufficient number of carpenters from
outside the membership of that organization. There certainly is no reason
to suppose that if defendants had filled up their working force with carpenters unaffiliated with any labor organization, the employers' association
would have accepted their action as a compliance with its orders for the
violation of the illegal order of September 22, 1904, is expressly included
in the bill of complaint as a reason for forfeiting the bonds sued upon.
The judgment appealed from must, therefore, be reversed and a new trial
granted, with costs to the appellants to abide the event.

PATTERSON, P.J., and LAUGHLIN, J., concurred; INGRAHAM and
CLARKE, JJ., dissented.[1]

---

[1] The dissenting opinion of Ingraham, J., is omitted. The learned justice contended that the order of September 22, 1904, was made without authority by the
Emergency Committee of the Association and thus for its violation the bond would
not be forfeited. But he contended that after the carpenters had been laid off in
accordance with the order of the board of governors of August 4, 1904, they
were to be re-employed only in compliance with the resolution of that board of
August 12, 1904, which required the members to demand as a condition precedent
to the employment of any mechanic that he should sign the arbitration agreement
of the plaintiff association, and that the plaintiff in re-employing members of the
Brotherhood of Carpenters had violated this order. The learned justice agreed
that "if there was any evidence that this association was organized for the purpose
of compelling all workmen to join a particular union before they were employed,
it would be an illegal association under Curran v. Galen * * *" p. 138.

The decision was affirmed in a memorandum opinion in 198 N.Y. 587, 92 N.E.
1090 (1910).

Accord: Connors v. Connolly, 86 Conn. 641, 86 Atl. 600 (1913) ; Brescia Const.
Co. v. Stone Masons' Contractors' Ass'n, 195 App. Div. 647, 187 N.Y.S. 77 (1921) ;
Grassi Contracting Co. v. Bennett, 174 App. Div. 244, 160 N.Y.S. 279 (1916) ; Lehigh Structural Steel Co. v. Atlantic S. & R. Works, 92 N.J.Eq. 131, 111 Atl. 376
(1920) ; Baldwin Lumber Co. v. Local Union No. 560, 91 N.J.Eq. 240, 109 Atl. 147
(1920) ; Polk v. Cleveland Ry. Co., 20 Ohio App. 317, 151 N.E. 808 (1925). Cf.
Campbell v. People, 72 Colo. 213, 210 Pac. 841 (1922) ; Reihing v. Local Union
No. 52, 94 N.J.L. 240, 109 Atl. 367 (1920). Contra: Des Moines City Ry. Co.
v. Amalgamated Ass'n of St. & Elec. Ry. Employees, 204 Iowa 1195, 213 N.W. 264
(1927) ; American Cloak & Suit Mfrs' Ass'n v. Brooklyn Ladies Garment Mfrs'
Ass'n, 255 N.Y.S. 614 (1931).

See: Lasch & Toll, "The Validity of Agreements to Employ Union Labor
Exclusively," 3 Temple Law Quar. 421 (1929) ; 2 Wis. Law Rev. 369 (1924) ; 22
Mich. Law Rev. 376 (1924).

"A bargains with a labor union to employ only union labor. The bargain is
legal, unless the union has such a monopoly as virtually to deprive non-union
workers of any possibility of employment; and even in that case it is not illegal if
a statute legalizes such labor unions." American Law Institute, Restatement of
the Law of Contracts § 515 (18) (1932).

GOLDMAN v. COHEN.

New York Appellate Division, First Department. 222 App. Div. 631,
227 N.Y.S. 311 (1928).

FINCH, J.: Plaintiff is a labor union; the defendants, a partnership engaged in the business of manufacturing pocketbooks. On August 2, 1926, the union, acting for and on behalf of its members, and pursuant to due authority from them, entered into an agreement in writing with defendants, the pertinent terms of which provide for the hours of labor, the wages of employees, the adjustment of disputes between employees and employer, and further, the union agreed for its members that they would work for defendants under said contract, and the defendants agreed to employ only members of the union and the union agreed to furnish the defendants with such operators as they required in their business. Clause 39 of the agreement reads as follows: "39. It is further agreed that there shall be no strike or lockout pending the determination of complaints or grievances hereunder throughout the entire period of this contract."

The agreement was to endure until the 1st day of August, 1929. The plaintiff claims that while the contract was in force the defendants expressed their intention to conduct a non-union shop and to remove their plant from Manhattan to Lynbrook, L. I. The plaintiff offered to furnish such union labor in Lynbrook as the defendants needed, which offer the plaintiff claims was rejected. The plaintiff thereupon commenced an action upon the ground that the defendants were conspiring to violate the terms of the contract by threatening to lock out the union workers employed by the defendants and that, pursuant to this purpose, the defendants intended to shut down their plant in Manhattan and to move the same to Lynbrook. The plaintiff further moved for an injunction restraining the defendants *pendente lite* from transferring their plant to and carrying on their business at Lynbrook, and from locking out any workers employed by the defendants on account of membership or affiliation with the plaintiff. The Special Term first granted the motion to the extent only of enjoining the defendants from locking out, discharging or discontinuing the employment of any workers employed by the defendants on account of membership in or affiliation with the plaintiff union. Upon a motion for resettlement, the following additional provision was added to the order: "Ordered that the defendants are enjoined from in any way breaching the terms of the aforesaid agreement, entered into between the plaintiff union and the defendants, under date of August 2, 1926." From both orders the defendants appeal.

The making of the contract being conceded and upon this record the same subsisting in full force and effect, the plaintiffs are entitled, pending the trial of the action, to injunctive relief for the protection of such of their rights as are threatened and the violation of which will produce irreparable damage. Usually in the past it has been the employer who has sought the help of the courts for the protection of his rights, but obviously the same principles of law apply equally to both employer and labor union. Where a strike is threatened by a labor union in violation of its contract with an employer, the right of a court of equity to issue an injunction to prevent such contractual violation is well settled. In *Grassi Contracting Co. v. Bennett* (174 App. Div. 244) the court said: "Where a strike, or other action, is threatened by a labor union in violation of its contract, or of the contract of its members with their employers, the jurisdiction of a court of equity to issue an injunction is well recognized (*Reynolds v. Davis*, 198 Mass. 294; *Folsom v. Lewis*, 208 *id.* 336; *National Protective Assn. v. Cumming*, 53 App. Div. 227; affd., 170 N.Y. 315; Cooke Combinations, Monopolies, Labor Unions [2d ed.], § 67 and cases cited. See, also, *Hitchman Coal & Coke Co. v. Mitchell*, 202 Fed. Rep. 512) * * *. It is perfectly lawful to organize to advance or to maintain a scheduled rate of wages, and to call a strike for those purposes, where no contract rights are violated."

Likewise where an employer is threatening to order a lockout of his employees in violation of his contract with the labor union in behalf of the employees, the right of a court of equity to prevent such contractual violation is necessarily measured by the same principle. (*Schlesinger v. Quinto*, 201·App. Div. 487.) In both cases an injunction should issue where there is no adequate remedy at law and the damages are irreparable. In the case of the employer seeking the injunction to prevent a strike of his employees in violation of a contract, such inadequacy of his remedy at law is well established. Likewise this court in a recent case has squarely held that where an employer threatens a lockout in violation of a contract between the union and the employer, such union and the employees have not an adequate remedy at law. On behalf of a majority of the court, it was there said: "It is clear that damages to the individual employee would not afford an adequate remedy in the case under consideration." (*Schlesinger v. Quinto, supra.*) In the case at bar there are no individual contracts and the union insists that the employees have no individual actions. Section 26 of the contract in the case at bar provides: "26. No individual contracts shall be entered into by the employer with any of his workers, * * *." Whether the union may collect damages on behalf of the employees and what is the true measure of the damage to the union, it is not necessary to decide since, for the purposes of this decision, it is certain that the union has more at stake to preserve under this contract than the sum of the damages occasioned by the unlawful discharge of all of the members of the union, assuming that such damages may be recovered by the union. If the union has not the right to invoke the aid of a court of equity to prevent the unlawful violation of a contract such as exists in the case at bar, then such a contract loses most of its force and the rights of collective bargaining are narrowed, and the economic benefits to the community from collective bargaining to a great extent lost. The plaintiff, therefore, is entitled to restrain the defendants from breaching their contract in the respects which this record shows is threatened, namely.

from ordering a lockout of the members of the union because of such
membership therein and from refusing to employ in accordance with defendants' needs, such members as are sent by the union pursuant to the
terms of the contract. The plaintiff is clearly not entitled to enjoin the
defendants from removing their factory to Lynbrook. The contract in
no way purports to restrict the defendants as to the location of their
plant.

The order, however, as resettled is much too broad in enjoining the
defendants from breaching any of the terms and provisions of the very
long and complicated agreement between the parties. It is not every
breach of a contract which a court of equity will enjoin. Only in so far
as it is shown that the particular breach has been threatened and that the
remedy at law is inadequate and the damages irreparable, will a court of
equity intervene. This is the rule applied in the case at bar. It follows
that the resettled order must be modified.

The resettled order should, therefore, be modified so that the same
shall enjoin the defendants during the pendency of the action from locking out or threatening to lock out, discharging or discontinuing employment of any workers employed by the defendants on account of membership in or affiliation with the said International Pocketbook Workers
Union and from refusing to employ as needed workers sent by the union
at the defendants' factory in Lynbrook, and as so modified affirmed, without costs. The appeal from the original order of January 12, 1928, should
be dismissed.

DOWLING, P.J., MERRELL, McAVOY and PROSKAUER, JJ., concur.

Order as resettled modified as stated in opinion and as so modified
affirmed, without costs. Appeal from original order of January 12, 1928,
dismissed. Settle order on notice.[1]

---

[1] Accord: Weber v. Nasser, 286 Pac. 1074 Cal. App. (1930), appeal dismissed
as moot in 210 Cal. 607, 292 Pac. 637 (1930); Pearlman v. Millman, 7 Law &
Labor, 286 (Mass. Super. Ct. 1925); Henry v. Century Shoe Co., 12 Law & Labor,
7 (Mass. Super. Ct. 1929); Schlesinger v. Quinto, 201 App. Div. 487, 194 N.Y.S.
401 (1922); Goldman v. Rosenzweig, N.Y.L.J. Aug 9, 1928, aff'd. in 224 App. Div.
817, 225 App. Div. 669 (1928); Goldman v. Wile Importing Co., 10 Law & Labor, 207
(N.Y. Sup. Ct. 1928), aff'd in 225 App. Div. 852, 226 App. Div. 728 (1929); Rifkin
v. Madelbaum, 10 Law & Labor, 142 (N.Y. Sup. Ct. 1928); Ribner v. Rasco Butter
& Egg Co., 135 Misc. 616, 238 N.Y.S. 132 (1929); Weintraub v. Spilke, 142 Misc.
867, 255 N.Y.S. 50 (1931); Suttin v. Unity Button Works, 258 N.Y.S. 863 (Sup. Ct.
1932); Engelking v. Independent Wet Wash Co., 142 Misc. 510, 254 N.Y.S. 87 (1931);
Leveranz v. Home Brewing Co., 24 Ohio N.P. (N.S.) 193 (1922); Harper v. Local
Union No. 520, 48 S.W. (2d) 1033 (Texas Civ. App. 1932). Cf. McAllen & Har-
lingen Local No. 688 v. Publix Theatres Corp., 51 S.W.(2d) 1090 (Texas Civ.
App. 1932). See also: In re Buffalo & Erie Ry. Co., 250 N.Y. 275, 165 N.E. 291
(1929).

See: Witte, "Labor's Resort to Injunctions," 39 Yale Law Jour. 374 (1930);
Mason, "Organized Labor as Party Plaintiff in Injunction Cases," 30 Col. Law
Rev. 466 (1930).

See also: Chaizy v. Chambre Syndicale des bûcherons de la Machine, Gazette
du Palais, 1927, 2, 945 (Tribunal Civil de Nevers, 1927), abstracted in 1927 Internat'l Survey of Legal Decisions in Labour Law, 91.

SCHWARTZ v. WAYNE CIRCUIT JUDGE.

Supreme Court of Michigan. 217 Mich. 384, 186 N.W. 522 (1922).

MOORE, J.: The plaintiffs filed a bill in chancery against a very large number of individuals, and against the Cigar Makers' International Union, and against Local Union No. 22. The plaintiffs are cigar manufacturers. Until this controversy arose they always ran a union shop. For the purposes of this case it is unnecessary to discuss in detail the occasion of the differences which arose between these parties. It is sufficient to state that a controversy between the union and the shop developed and it is claimed was accompanied by picketing, intimidation and like acts that go with labor disturbances. The plaintiffs filed a bill of complaint reciting their alleged grievances and prayed for an injunction in the usual form to restrain picketing, interference, etc. No individual defendant appeared to defend the case and as to such as were served orders *pro confesso* were duly entered. The local and international unions appeared, however, and filed a cross-bill alleging, among other things, that Schwartz & Sons, in consideration of an acceptance by the union of a reduced scale of wages, agreed to furnish employment to their shop capacity for a year; this employment to be furnished to members of the union only. The cross-bill alleged a breach of this contract and prayed for an injunction, mandatory in its nature, to compel Schwartz & Sons to discharge their present force and re-employ only members of the cigar makers' union.

After a trial the court filed an opinion followed by a decree in which Schwartz & Sons are permanently enjoined—

"From continuing in their employ persons who are not members in good standing of Cigar Makers' International Union, Local No. 22; from hiring persons other than members in good standing of Cigar Makers' International Union, Local No. 22, to work for plaintiffs in the place and stead of the members of the Cigar Makers' International Union Local No. 22, who were discharged by plaintiffs in violation of said contract, until after the 17th day of November, 1921; and from hiring any persons other than members of Cigar Makers' International Union, Local No. 22, to work for plaintiffs in their plant, until after the 17th day of November, 1921."

There is attached to the decree a scale of prices, rules and regulations covering three typewritten pages, with which the petitioners are directed to comply.

It is claimed if the decree is given effect that Schwartz & Sons would be compelled to discharge approximately 200 employees doing steady work and employ 300 workers to be furnished by the Cigar Makers' Union and to pay them a rate of wage fixed by decree of the court. This application is to stay proceedings under this decree until the case on its merits shall have been heard and decided. The lower court expressed doubt as to his power to stay proceedings under this mandatory injunction. This court upon the filing of this petition directed it to stay proceedings upon the filing of a bond until this motion was decided.

In the instant case the practical effect of the decree is to control the conduct of the business of the plaintiffs and if the decree is improperly made it should not be given effect until the case can be heard upon its merits. Should the decree of the court below be given immediate effect? The argument of counsel in favor thereof is as follows:

"Thus we have the rule which may be stated as follows:

"A court of equity will upon application of an employer enjoin an employee from working for another employer, in violation of contract where it appears that the employer will be unable to procure a substitute.

"Reversing the condition of affairs, and bearing in mind the principle of mutuality of remedies in a court of equity, we ask this court to apply the reasoning of such cases, and to lay down the converse rule:

"A court of equity will, upon application of an employee, enjoin an employer from hiring another employee, in violation of contract, where it appears that the employee will be unable to procure a substitute.

"In other words, if an employer may say to an employee: 'You cannot work for my competitor, because it is impossible for me to procure a substitute to take your place' we submit that the employee may say to the employer: 'You cannot hire my competitor, because it is impossible for me to procure a substitute to take your place.' We will concede it would take a long search in the books to find a case in which a court has applied the rule for which we contend. But that search will also reveal that it is a rare case where the court has been asked by an employee to do it." Citing *Turner v. Hampton,* 97 S.W. 761 (Ky. 1906).

That case was very short and it was said:

" 'On the facts of the case an injunction was the proper remedy as in no other way could the plaintiff obtain adequate relief.' * * *

"In the case at bar, it appeared that because of the business depression, it was impossible for the employees to procure a substitute employer. This fact brings the case within the universally recognized rule, and entitles the employees to the injunction they prayed for, and which was granted to them by the lower court.

"Cases of this kind where the employees are seeking redress in the courts, are rare. Labor in the past has failed to take advantage of a resort to the courts for redress of its grievances, to the degree which capital has done so. In this case, labor comes into a court of chancery and asks relief analogous to that which has been granted to capital. Courts of equity exist for the very purpose of furnishing relief in cases where the ordinary rules of law have no technical application. And:

" 'It should not be forgotten, however, that in the increasing complexities of modern business relations, equitable remedies have necessarily and steadily been expanded, and no inflexible rule has been permitted to circumscribe them.' 25 R.C.L. p. 227."

A search will be made in vain in R.C.L. for an authority where an injunction in a case like the one before us was issued.

In 14 R.C.L. at p. 385, it is said:

"General Principles as to Breach by Employee.—The courts have shown greater reluctance in reference to enjoining a man from performing personal service or labor than from conducting a business. The general rule in respect to contracts for personal service seems to be that for a breach thereof a party must avail himself of the remedy afforded at law, and that it will not be specifically enforced indirectly by an injunction restraining the employee from leaving the service of his employer, especially where the services to be rendered are not of an individual and peculiar character. The right of an employee engaged to perform personal services to leave that service rests on the same basis as the right of his employer to discharge him from further personal service. If the leaving in the one case, or the discharging in the other, is in violation of the contract between the parties, the one injured by the breach has his action for damages, and a court of equity will not indirectly or negatively, by means of an injunction restraining the violation of the contract, compel the affirmative performance from day to day, or the affirmative acceptance of merely personal services. Relief of that character has always been regarded as impracticable, for if the relation of employer and employee is to be of value or profit to either, it must be marked by some degree of mutual confidence and satisfaction."

At page 390 of the same authority it is said:

"Breach by Employer.—The same principle controls in case of a breach by an employer, the rule being that an injunction will not lie to compel him to refrain from breaking his contract with his employee and to retain the latter in his service when he is not acceptable to him for service of that character, as a court of equity will not by means of an injunction compel the affirmative acceptance by the employer of the personal services of his employee from day to day; besides the remedy of the employee at law for damages is adequate and complete."

See *Reid Ice Cream Co. v. Stephens,* 62 Ill. App. at p. 339; *Southern Bell, etc., Telegraph Co. v. City of Birmingham,* 211 Fed. 709; *Boyer v. Telegraph Co.,* 124 Fed. 246; *Stone Cleaning & Pointing Union v. Russell,* 77 N.Y. Supp. 1049; *Goldfield Consolidated Mines Co. v. Miners' Union,* 159 Fed. at p. 515; *Osius v. Hinchman,* 150 Mich. 603 (16 L.R.A. [N.S.] 393); *H. W. Gossard Co. v. Crosby,* 132 Iowa, 155 (109 N.W. 483, 6 L.R.A. [N.S.] 1115).

The law has been stated as follows:

"Under ordinary circumstances an employee, whether classed as an agent or as a servant, cannot enforce a contract for service by enjoining a breach on the part of his employer. So the employer will not be enjoined from dismissing an employee or from refusing to continue to employ him, even though such action is a direct violation of contract. * * * For reasons similar to those given for refusing to enjoin the dismissal of an employee, the breach of a contract to employ only members of a certain union will not be enjoined." 22 Cyc. p. 856.

We think the injunction issued based upon the record as made should be stayed.

The writ of mandamus will issue as prayed, with costs.

WIEST, STONE, CLARK, BIRD, and STEERE, JJ., concurred with MOORE, J.

SHARPE, J.: I concur in granting the writ of mandamus ordering the stay of proceedings pending the appeal to this court. Until that appeal be heard, I am of the opinion that we should not determine whether the permanent injunction provided for in the decree was properly or improperly granted.

FELLOWS, C. J., concurred with SHARPE, J.[1]

---

[1] Accord: Schwartz v. Cigar Makers Internat'l Union, 219 Mich. 589, 189 N.W. 55 (1922); Mosshamer v. Wabash Ry. Co., 221 Mich. 407, 191 N.W. 210 (1922); Stone Cleaning & Pointing Union v. Russell, 38 Misc. 513, 77 N.Y.S. 1049 (1902); Berkhammer v. Cleveland & Morgantown Coal Co., 8 Law & Labor, 217 (W. Va. Cir. Ct. 1926).

CHAPTER VII.

THE BOYCOTT.

THE TERM "BOYCOTT."

Wolman, The Boycott in American Trade Unions, pp. 10-13, 48-49, 56, 58-59, 62 (1916).

Originally, the term boycott denoted social ostracism. While still employed extensively to characterize expulsion from social intercourse, the term is now most frequently applied to certain forms of economic or industrial pressure, and more particularly to the economic pressure exerted by the members of labor organizations. The boycotting carried on by trade unions has been variously defined. By some writers coercion of disinterested parties is considered an essential element of this trade-union device. Thus Dr. W. A. Martin, deriving his definition from various judicial opinions, defines the boycott as "a combination to cause a loss to one person by coercing others against their will, to withdraw from him their beneficial business intercourse, by threats, that unless those others do so, the combination will cause similar loss to them." While not placing so great an emphasis on the element of coercion, Dr. T. S. Adams and Dr. H. L. Sumner also consider the support of a disinterested party as a *sine qua non* of the boycott. "The boycott, as used in modern labor disputes," they write, "may be defined as a combination to suspend dealings with another party, and to persuade or coerce others to suspend dealings, in order to force this party to comply with some demand, or to punish him for non-compliance in the past."

An analysis of certain forms of pressure to which the term boycott is commonly applied would indicate that neither of the above elements is an essential and universal attribute of the boycott. To use a concrete illustration, when the members of a local union of bakers, who have been locked out by the master bakers of the community, combine to withdraw their patronage from the bakeries, their action is ordinarily regarded as constituting a boycott upon the unfair employers and would be so termed. Yet the act is marked neither by coercion nor by the support of a third party; it is merely a concerted withdrawal of patronage. Similarly Sidney and Beatrice Webb speak of the "boycott of non-unionists," the term being used to describe the device of the closed shop, or the refusal of union members to work with non-unionists, and the consequent inability of the non-union workman to obtain work in a union shop and of the union employer to engage the services of a non-union workman. Here, however, there may be an element of coercion, since the closed shop is often not voluntarily adopted by the employer but is forced upon him by the union. Whether coercion is present in this second illustration or not, it is possible to detect in these two totally dissimilar examples of the boycott a characteristic which will be found to be common to all forms of pressure that are given that name. This common characteristic is the restriction of market; in one case possibly supplemented by the coercion of a third party, the employer, and in the other free from coercion or persuasion. Thus the purpose of the first boycott is to restrict the selling market of the master bakers; the second limits the market of the non-union workman to non-union shops, and likewise limits the labor market of the employer to union workmen. The boycott may, therefore, be defined as a combination formed for the purpose of restricting the markets of an individual or group of individuals.

Thus defined, the boycott of course includes many forms of pressure exerted by both labor organizations and other types of industrial combinations, which because of the presence of certain peculiar characteristics have received distinguishing names. The blacklist, for instance, which is used by combinations of employers, is a boycott upon the blacklisted laborer, since his field of employment is restricted to the extent that he is unable to receive employment from the manufacturers who subscribe to the blacklist. The strike, likewise, constitutes a boycott of the employer by restricting his market for labor; and if the activity of pickets in keeping strike-breakers from the plant be noted, the element of boycott in the strike is still more clearly shown. The identity of the labor boycott and the closed shop has already been discussed. In spite of the logical desirability of assigning to all such forms of pressure the term boycott, the chronological priority of the term strike, closed shop, and blacklist, not to speak of the peculiar connotations of each, would make the substitution a source of confusion rather than of clearness. In order, therefore, so to delimit this study as not to include those forms of the boycott which are in everyday speech called strikes, blacklists, and so on, the term boycott will be used to describe the efforts of labor combinations to restrict the markets of employers in the purchase and sale of economic goods, whether these goods be raw materials, materials in a partial state of completion, or finished products about to be sold to the ultimate consumer. * * *

The classification of boycotts on materials to be employed here rests upon the conception of industry as being of a given complexity and composed of a number of strata, more or less homogeneous. * * * There are accordingly four classes of boycotts that can be distinguished on the basis of this classification; the backward, forward, lateral, and transportation boycotts.

(1) The backward boycott is defined as the refusal by men in the higher processes of manufacture, or in the higher strata of industry, to work on or with material which in the next lower process of manufacture.

or in the next lower stratum of industry, is made by non-union work-men. * * *

(2) The forward boycott is defined as the refusal by union laborers in the lower processes of manufacture to make material that will probably or certainly be used in the next higher process by non-unionists. This form of the boycott and the backward boycott are reciprocal. Usually a union which at one time imposes the backward boycott is at another time the bene-ficiary of the forward boycott. * * *

(3) The lateral boycott is a boycott on materials, not for the purpose of organizing the workers in the lower or higher processes of manufacture, but to force the employment of members of the same union or of co-ordinate unions, that is, of workers in the same stratum of industry. The bricklayers boycott brick, not because it is made by unorganized brick-makers, but in order to force the organization of the bricklayers employed at the brick-yards in building kilns. This form of boycott occurs generally as the sympathetic strike. Where, for example, manufacturers operating in one territorial division of an industry have trouble with their employees and attempt to have the same work done elsewhere by union labor, the workmen in the places to which the materials have been removed, in sym-pathy with the strikers, refuse to handle the material. * * *

* * * Finally, there is the fourth form of the boycott by which em-ployers may become completely cut off from one another and from in-dustry in general. When this boycott is in force, they sometimes cannot have brought to them the materials they buy and at other times cannot have carried from them the products they sell. This state of affairs arises when manufacturers are boycotted as to transportation facilities.

STEFFES v. MOTION PICTURE MACHINE OPERATORS UNION OF MINNEAPOLIS.

Minnesota Supreme Court, 136 Minn. 200, 161 N.W. 524 (1917).

Action in the district court for Hennepin county against Motion Pic-ture Machine Operators Union of Minneapolis, Local 219, International Alliance Theatrical Stage Employees, an unincorporated society, and cer-tain members of defendant association as individuals, and in behalf of all other members of the association, to restrain defendants from displaying a sign "unfair to organized labor" before plaintiff's place of business, and to recover $1,300 damages. From an order, Molyneaux, J., discharging an order to show cause why the court should not grant a temporary injunc-tion until the trial of the action upon its merits, plaintiff appealed.

Affirmed.

Hallam, J.: 1. The facts in this case are very much in dispute. Plaintiff asked for a temporary injunction on a verified complaint and supporting affidavits. He was met by a verified answer and answering affidavits. The court without making findings denied the injunction. We must assume a state of facts as favorable to the defendants as the showing made by defendants will sustain. From defendants' showing the following facts appear:

Plaintiff operates a motion picture theatre on Twentieth avenue north in Minneapolis. He employs one Supple as operator of his motion picture machine. A trade union of motion picture machine operators, seeking to enlarge the possibilities of the organization, besought plaintiff to enter into an agreement to hire a union operator at union wages and further urged that Supple join the union. To do so he would be obliged to enter as a "permit man," and after a year he would become a full member. During this year he would be subject to be displaced by some union member, should there be one unemployed, but this was not probable. While these negotiations were in progress plaintiff remodelled his theatre, and in that work it was claimed he employed nonunion men though union labor was offered. The result of all their negotiations was that plaintiff finally informed defendants that he would not employ any union man as operator and that if Supple joined the union he would be discharged. Defendants' representative then told plaintiff the union would feel obliged to "banner his place as unfair to organized labor." Plaintiff replied that was just the thing he wanted done, that when it was done before it helped his business and he was glad it was about to start again. Thereupon defendants hired one Clausen to carry back and forth on the street in front of the theatre a banner on which was printed: "This theatre is unfair to organized labor." Many other acts are charged, some of them distinctly unlawful, but they are all denied and in view of the order made by the trial court we must assume that he found such charges made by plaintiff, and denied by defendants, not proven.

2. The term "unfair" as used by organized labor has come to have a meaning well understood. It means that the person so designated is unfriendly to organized labor or that he refuses to recognize its rules and regulations. It charges no moral shortcoming and no want of business capacity or integrity. As applied to a theatre it signifies as to the merits of its performances. As a rule one man has no right to interfere in the business affairs of another, but if his act in so doing is in pursuit of a just purpose to further his own interests he may be justified in so doing, and so long as he does not act maliciously and does not unreasonably or unnecessarily interfere with the rights of his neighbor he cannot be charged with actionable wrong. *George J. Grant Construction Co. v. St. Paul Building Trades Council, supra,* page 167, 161 N.W. 520, 1055.

3. In *Gray v. Building Trades Council,* 91 Minn. 171, 97 N.W. 663, 1118, 63 L.R.A. 753, 103 Am. St. 477, 1 Ann. Cas. 172, it was said that whether a publication that an employer of labor is "unfair" is or is not unlawful depends on the circumstances of each case, that a notification to customers that plaintiffs are "unfair" may portend a threat or intimidation, in which case it will constitute a boycott and is unlawful, but that a mere notification of that sort without more is not a threat, is not unlawful and that the trial court was in error in that case in enjoining such conduct. To the same effect is *Foster v. Retail Clerks' Int. Prot. Assn.,* 39 Misc. 48, 78 N.Y. Supp. 860; *Butterick Pub. Co. v. Typographical Union No. 6,* 50 Misc. 1, 100 N.Y. Supp. 292.

4. The decision in the *Gray* case is controlling and in accordance with it we hold that the court did not err in refusing to enjoin the use of the banner used in this case, unless its use upon the public street was unlawful. If the banner itself is lawful we are unable to see how the mere display of it by a pedestrian upon a public street is unlawful. It is plain that one displaying it may easily fall into unlawful practices. If it be accompanied by acts that constitute obstruction of the street or of access to plaintiff's place of business, or if accompanied by any words or acts which constitute intimidation or threats, the whole transaction is unlawful and should be enjoined. There are claims of this kind in plaintiff's complaint and affidavits but they are all denied. The affidavits on the part of defendants negative any acts of this character. They are to the effect that the banner was displayed on the street and not on the sidewalk, that there has been no interference with patrons of the theatre. The trial court has a large measure of discretion in the matter of granting injunctions *pendente lite.* On this showing we are not disposed to override the order of the trial court in refusing a temporary injunction. This is in harmony with the few decisions we find that bear upon this subject. *Beaton v. Tarrant,* 102 Ill. App. 124; *City of St. Louis v. Gloner,* 210 Mo. 502, 109 S.W. 30, 124 Am. St. 750; *Karges Furniture Co. v. Amalgamated W. Union,* 165 Ind. 421, 75 N. E. 877, 2 L.R.A. (N.S.) 788, 6 Ann. Cas. 829; *Foster v. Retail Clerks' International Protective Assn.,* 39 Misc. 48, 78 N.Y. Supp. 860; *Searle Mfg. Co. v. Terry,* 56 Misc. 265, 106 N.Y. Supp. 438. See also dissenting opinion of Holmes, J., in *Vegelahn v. Guntner,* 167 Mass. 92, 44 N.E. 1077, 35 L.R.A. 722, 57 Am. St. 443. In *Beaton v. Tarrant,* 102 Ill. App. 129, it was said: "Workmen may use the streets and highways in a manner not inconsistent with public travel, for the purpose of entreaty, inducement and peaceable persuasion in good faith, and a patrol or picket may not necessarily imply force or a threat of bodily harm; but to accomplish their purpose they may not overstep the bounds and use threats, abusive epithets or intimidation, or congregate in such number or in such manner or with such a show of force, as is calculated to intimidate a reasonable and prudent man,"

If, on a full hearing on the trial on evidence produced by the parties, the court shall find that the charges in the complaint are true, proper relief can then be given, but we are of the opinion that in denying an injunction on the pleadings and affidavits submitted there was no abuse of discretion.

Order affirmed.

Quinn, J., having taken his seat after the case was submitted, took no part.[1]

---

[1] Accord: United Chain Theatres v. Philadelphia Moving Picture Operators Union, 50 Fed.(2d) 189 (E.D. Pa. 1931) Philip Henrici Co. v. Alexander, 198 Ill. App. 568 (1916); Lindsay & Co. v. Montana Federation of Labor, 37 Mont. 264, 96 Pac. 127 (1908); Iverson v. Dilno, 44 Mont. 271, 119 Pac. 719 (1911); Sinsheimer v. United Garment Workers, 77 Hun 215, 28 N.Y.S. 321 (1894); Mills v. United States Printing Co., 99 App. Div. 605, 91 N.Y.S. 185 (1904); People v. Radt, 15 N.Y. Crim. 174, 71 N.Y.S. 846 (1900); Cohen v. United Garment Workers, 35 Misc. 748, 72 N.Y.S. 341 (1901); Foster v. Retail Clerks' Protective Ass'n, 39 Misc. 48, 78 N.Y.S. 860 (1902); Seubert v. Reiff, 98 Misc. 402, 164 N.Y.S. 522 (1917); Heitkamper v. Hoffman, 99 Misc. 543, 164 N.Y.S. 533 (1917); Public Baking Co. v. Stern, 127 Misc. 229, 215 N.Y.S. 537 (1926); Butterick Pub. Co. v. Typographical Union No. 6, 50 Misc. 1, 100 N.Y.S. 292 (1906); Clark Lunch Co. v. Cleveland Waiters & B. D. Local 106, 22 Ohio App. 265, 154 N.E. 362 (1926); Stoner v. Robert, 43 Wash. L. Rep. 437 (Sup. Ct. D.C. 1915); Dick v. Stephenson, [1923] 3 W.W.R. 761 (Alta.)

"The substance of the matters here complained of is an interference with complainant's interstate trade * * * by what is commonly known as a 'secondary boycott,' that is, a combination not merely to refrain from dealing with complainant, or to advise or by peaceful means persuade complainant's customers to refrain ('primary boycott'), but to exercise coercive pressure upon such customers, actual or prospective, in order to cause them to withhold or withdraw patronage from complainant through fear of loss or damage to themselves should they deal with it." Pitney, J., in Duplex Printing Press Co. v. Deering, 254 U.S. 443, 466 (1921). "Another unlawful means in common use to hinder or prevent willing employees in working and to compel employers to accede to terms, which they would not otherwise adopt, is the *boycott* in its various forms. This, in whatever form it assumes, is unlawful. Applying these principles to the present case, it is unlawful for the defendants to attempt to induce or compel complainant to adopt a particular mode of doing his business by persuading or inducing other persons not to deal with him. * * *" Pitney, V.C., in Martin v. McFall, 65 N.J. Eq. 91, 92, 55 Atl. 465 (1903). "The primary boycott, that is the agreement of one or more to refrain from dealing with another without inducing third parties to stop their patronage, has generally received the sanction of the courts." Laidler, Boycotts, 177 (1913). "A distinction is sometimes drawn between what are classed as primary and secondary boycotts. In the former, the action is directly against the offending employer, the members of the organization simply withholding their patronage as laborers or purchasers, and inducing their fellows to do the same." Clark, The Law of the Employment of Labor, 289 (1911). "In some cases an effort is made to distinguish the primary boycott from the secondary boycott, the latter being the boycott of a third party, usually a merchant who sells the product of the employer primarily boycotted. Many courts in fact use the term 'boycott' as embracing only secondary boycott. But this distinction in practice amounts to little. Few employers of labor sell directly to the consumers. * * * It is significant that all of the statements holding primary boycotts legal are *'obiter dicta,'* or incidental remarks delivered in the course of a decision of some other point, and occur in cases in which the courts found an illegal secondary boycott." Commons and Andrews, Principles of Labor Legislation, 107-108 (1920).

See Cooke, "Solidarity of Interest as Basis of Legality of Boycotting," 11 Yale Law Jour. 153 (1902); Macdonald, "Right of Trade Union to Enforce Boycott," 7 Mich. Law Rev. 499 (1909); McWilliams, "Evolution of the Law Relating to Boycotts," 41 Am. Law Rev. 336 (1907); Reed, "Peaceable Boycotting," 5 Am. Acad. Pol. & Soc. Sci. 28 (1894); Selover, "Boycotts as Conspiracies," 2 Minn. Law Jour.

SEATTLE BREWING & MALTING CO. v. HANSEN.

United States Circuit Court for the Northern District of California.
144 Fed. 1011 (1905).

BEATTY, D.J. (orally) : I have examined the affidavits, as well as the authorities, submitted by counsel in this case, and am prepared to announce my conclusion. I believe it is the general practice in this court to reduce such conclusions to writing and file the same for the benefit of those interested. This, however, is a practice in which I indulge but little, and in this case I have nothing prepared not even notes. What I have to say will be orally stated and in such order as occurs to me as I proceed.

In this case, as in most cases of the kind, I find that the defendants, by affidavits and otherwise, deny most of the charges that are made against them. Among those so denied is the allegation that the drivers or employés of Rapp & Sons quit their employment through fear and threatened violence instigated by the defendants. By their denials I think they have met this charge. They show that these employés quit without compulsion and of their own volition. That they all quit at once is at least suggestive that some unusual influence was brought to bear upon them, but it may have been alone by agreement among themselves and without any influence exercised by any commanding authority.

Of other specific acts charged against them, they deny the matters involved in the newspaper publications referred to. One was by complainant, stating its grievances, and the other the reply of the defendants thereto. If the complainant has the right, as it undoubtedly has, to set forth its views and the reasons of the dispute between the parties, there is no reason why the defendant should not have a like privilege of replying thereto. Certainly, in replying, their statements should not be such as reflect upon and tend to injure the complainant's business, unless the truth shall so operate. I think there is nothing in these publications meriting further notice, and they are passed.

Aside from those matters and the special acts which have been denied by the defendants, I think the whole record and some of the admissions made by defendants show that the contest between these parties is over a question of wages and the character of employment. It is one of the objects of the union laborers to have none but their own people engage in these different employments, which is one of the contests here. They desire that the complainant shall employ only union men, while the complainant desires to enforce what is termed the "open shop." That contest is clearly outlined by the record, and not only does it appear that such is the contention of the defendants, but that this originated in a distant part of

---

167 (1894) ; Wigmore, "The Boycott and Kindred Practices as Ground for Damages," 21 Am. Law Rev. 509 (1887) ; Wyman, "The Law of Boycott," 15 Green Bag, 208 (1903).

See also: Stephen, "On the Suppression of Boycotting," 20 Nineteenth Century 765 (1886) ; Hammond, "The Evolution of the Boycott," 1 Forum 369 (1886) ; Burnett, "The Boycott as an Element in Trade Disputes," 1 Econ. Jour. 163 (1891) ; Stote, "What Boycotts Cost the Nation," 7 Moody's Mag. 370 (1909).

the continent, at Cincinnati, where the first orders or promulgations were made against the complainant. It is unnecessary to review the testimony upon this subject, and, without it, such is stated as the ground of contest between these parties. Unquestionably the complainant has the right to say who its laborers shall be and how it shall employ them. It has the right to manage its own business. It cannot compel the defendants to work for it according to its terms; but it has a right to say how its business shall be operated. On the contrary, the defendants have a right to say whether they will accept those terms or not. If they can procure terms of their own that are better for them and can do it in a peaceful way, they have that right. There is no question about that.

There is a statement by one of the affiants in his affidavit on this point—I imagine suggested by counsel—that it is the desire of the defendants to better their condition, and that is what they are aiming to do. He devotes a page or two to that and moralizing on the downtrodden condition of the laboring people and the oppression of the employers, all of which I think is out of place. I do not think that the laborers are downtrodden, nor do I think that the employers aim to be oppressive, but it is a contest between them; each one doing what he can for his own benefit. It must be conceded by everybody that it is commendable in laboring people to endeavor to better their condition, both morally, physically, and financially, and obtain the best prices they can for their labor and upon the most convenient terms for themselves. That is conceded by everybody. But in doing that they too often, I think, forget one thing. They forget that they must attain their objects by legal and proper means. They must not undertake to accomplish what they desire to the injury or at the expense of other people, and there is where the mistake is too often made. It is conceded by all that they have the right to better their condition, but they must not do it in a way to be oppressive of others. I think that is what they have attempted to do in this case. Perhaps they have not so intended, but the question is as to the result of their acts. Beyond any question, what they are trying to do would be oppressive of the business of these complainants.

Aside from these special charges of acts that they have done, there are things I think that are not disputed. They have circulated these different exhibits, or notices, which are made exhibits in this case. Here is one, which calls attention to the fact that certain parties, saloonkeepers, are using or selling or handling this "Rainier" beer. That is not anything apparently oppressive at first sight. It is simply calling attention to the fact that these parties are using this beer; but what is the design of it, and what is the result of it? Why, it is to intimidate these people or prevent them from dealing in complainant's beer. That far it is oppressive of the business of complainant and tends to destroy its business. There is no question about that, in so far as it would intimidate these people. It must be remembered that there are many timid people in this world, who would be much influenced by danger of even small losses. I have no doubt that many of these men who have this notice would fear that by continuing to engage in the selling of the beer there would be some loss to them, and that far it would hurt their business. Here is another one: "Organized Labor and Friends: Don't drink scab beer!" Then it names certain different kinds of beer and says they are "unfair."

The mere use of the word "unfair" has a very distinct meaning in these days; and when a notice like this is put out it is almost in the nature of a command. Of course, it does not say to the laboring people, "You shall not drink" such beer, but it says: "To Organized Labor and Friends: Don't use this beer!" These organizations, in the way they are trained, for they are as well trained as any military force, understand these rules and know what they mean. The very use of that term "unfair" has a distinct meaning to them, and it is in the nature of a direction to the members of these organizations not to use that beer, and it is also an intimidation to those who are dealing in it. It gives them to understand that that beer will be boycotted; that it is unfair and will be boycotted. That would deter parties from using it or dealing in it. There are a number of that kind. Here is another one: "Guard Your Health by Refusing to Drink Unfair Beer!" Then it proceeds to name the beer that is unfair, and it includes among others the beer of the complainant. All those things are what would be termed now under the law "a boycott." I need not go into the definition of that. We generally understand what it means. But those things tend to unfairly obstruct the business of the complainant, and in that far these defendants are wrong, and it is the duty of the court to restrain them from doing anything that will interfere with the complainant's business.

Among the questions raised in this case is as to the form and extent of the restraining order, and its effect. One of the first matters in which I had anything to do with cases of this kind was some 12 years ago in what was known as the Cœur d'Alene strike. All these questions were brought up there and were passed upon. Thus far they have never been overthrown, I believe, and I shall follow the same rule that I did there. In that case the unions were made parties defendant and the members of the unions, of course, were included, and as far as possible their names were given. The injunction in that case went against the organizations and all of their members, and without service of summons upon all of them. That ruling has never been changed, and I find by examining the records here that that has been the practice in this court. I feel, therefore, fully justified in following that practice. If it is wrong, it is for some other court to settle it; but for some reason these cases have never gotten up to any court which has changed that practice, and that stands as the rule today. It is also well settled that any party, knowing of an injunction, who violates it, is liable, whether he has any legal service upon him or not.[1]

---

[1] The usual practice is to name representatives individuals of a particular class, where the class itself is too numerous to allow of naming each of its members. See: Equity Rule 38, 226 U.S. 659. Proper representatives of the class should be named as defendants. Pickett v. Walsh, 192 Mass. 572, 78 N.E. 753 (1906); Reynolds v.

I think the naming of these parties as associations, not as corporations, serves the purpose of identification. These defendants are identified
as members of these associations, and the individual defendants being alleged to be citizens of this state puts the case within the jurisdiction of
this court. Laying aside for the present the consideration of the question

---

Davis, 198 Mass. 294, 84 N.E. 457 (1908). The question of their representative
character should be looked at from the standpoint of reality rather than of formal-
ity, so that it is proper to name strike leaders instead of merely union officials.
American Steel & Wire Co. v. Wire Drawers' & Die Makers' Union, 90 Fed. 598
(C.C.N.D. Ohio, 1898).

Persons who have not been parties to the illegal conduct complained of, should
not be named as defendants. Corcoran v. Nat'l Telephone Co., 175 Fed. 761 (4th
cir., 1909); Escanaba Mfg. Co. v. Labor Council, 160 Mich. 656 (1910). But it is
proper to join as a defendant a person, even though he has as yet been guilty of no
illegality, where there is reasonable ground to believe that he may participate in the
illegality of which complaint is made. Piano & Organ Workers Internat'l Union
v. Piano & Organ Supply Co., 124 Ill. App. 353 (1906). Cf. Kroger Grocery &
Baking Co. v. Retail Clerks' Internat'l Protective Ass'n, 250 Fed. 890 (E.D. Mo.,
1918); Ellis v. Journeymen Barbers' Internat'l Union, 194 Iowa 1179, 191 N.W. 111
(1922). And the injunction can include union members, where the union is responsible for illegal conduct, even though these members may not individually have participated therein. Illinois Central R.R. Co. v. Internat'l Ass'n of Machinists, 190
Fed. 910, (C.C.E.D. Ill. 1911).

In labor cases, it is common not only to enjoin representative defendants, the
members of the class, their agents and all persons aiding or assisting them, but also
all persons whatsoever to whom notice of the injunction shall come. Thus in the
Jenkins Injunction against the strike on the Northern Pacific Railroad, the order
was directed towards "officers, agents, and employes [of the railroad] * * * and all
persons, associations, and combinations, voluntary or otherwise, whether employes
of said receivers or not, and all persons generally, and each and every one of you, in
the penalty which may ensue, are hereby charged and commanded. * * *" Farmers'
Loan & Trust Co. v. Northern Pac. R. R. Co., 60 Fed. 803 (C.C.E.D. Wis. 1894).
The Debs injunction, besides restraining the defendants, their agents, etc., was also
directed towards "all persons combining and conspiring with them and all other
persons generally." In re Debs, 158 U.S. 564 (1895). For other illustrations and
criticism of this practice, see: Frankfurter and Greene, The Labor Injunction, 86-
89 (1930); Kingsley, "Labor Injunctions in Illinois," 23 Ill. Law Rev. 529 (1929);
Allen, "Injunction and Organized Labor," 28 Am. Law Rev. 828 (1894).

Persons bound by the injunction: Members of class, enjoined as such, without
being named save through the device of, representative defendants, have been held
for violation of the injunction even though they had no notice of it. Shaughnessy
v. Jordan, 184 Ind. 499, 111 N.E. 622 (1915). Unless a clear agency relationship
exists, notice is commonly required. Armstrong v. Superior Court, 173 Cal. 341, 159
Pac. 1176 (1916); Toledo, A. A. & N. M. Ry. Co. v. Pennsylvania Co., 54 Fed. 746
(C.C.N.D. Ohio 1893). Compare as to the New York practice, Neal v. Hutcheson,
160 N.Y.S. 1007 (Sup. Ct. 1916); Borden's Farm Products Co. v. Sterbinsky, 117
Misc. 585, 192 N.Y.S. 757 (1922); People ex rel. Stearns v. Marr, 181 N.Y. 463, 74
N.E. 431 (1905). Where the persons violating the injunction are not members of
the class named through representative defendants, they can be held for contempt if
they have actual notice of the injunction. In re Lennon, 166 U.S. 548 (1897); Puget
Sound Traction L. & P. Co. v. Lawrey, 202 Fed. 263 (W.D. Wash. 1913); Stewart
v. United States, 236 Fed. 838 (8th cir. 1916); McCourtney v. United States, 291
Fed. 497 (8th cir. 1923); O'Brien v. People, 216 Ill. 354, 75 N.E. 108 (1905); State
ex rel. Lindsley v. Grady, 114 Wash. 692, 195 Pac. 1049 (1921); State v. Bittner, 102
W.Va. 677, 136 S.E. 202 (1926). It seems that averments that the defendant has
had notice of the injunction must be contained in the information or petition itself.
United States v. Agler, 62 Fed. 824 (C.C.D. Ind. 1894); Garrigan v. United States,
163 Fed. 16 (7th cir. 1908), certiorari denied in 214 U.S. 514 (1909). In some states
the practice is to the contrary, a stranger not being liable for contempt even though
he has had notice of the injunction. Berger v. Superior Court, 175 Cal. 719, 167
Pac. 143 (1917); Rigas v. Livingston, 178 N.Y. 20, 70 N.E. 107 (1904); In re Zim-

whether these alleged associations are incorporated or not, such designation serves the purpose of locating these defendants and their citizenship as citizens of this state; thus creating the diversity of citizenship which is necessary to give this court jurisdiction. Nor do I think, after reflecting over the matter, that these parties who have not been served, who are alleged to be members of this association, can be dismissed from this case. I was asked the other day to dismiss them, and I declined to do so. I do not think they should be dismissed; but I think they are bound by the proceedings had here.

As to the form of the order, gentlemen, I have examined, in addition to the decision of Judge Morrow, in the recent case of *D. E. Loewe and Others v. California State Federation of Labor* (C.C.) 139 Fed. 71, the writ of injunction issued in that case. I think it is as full as the preliminary restraining order issued in this case, and I think that is a precedent which may be followed here.

My conclusion, therefore, is that this restraining order shall be continued as a temporary injunction, pending the action, and that the form of it may be substantially as has already been issued in a temporary re-

---

merman, 134 App. Div. 591, 119 N.Y.S. 275 (1909); Strawberry Island Co. v. Cowles, 79 Misc. 279, 140 N.Y.S. 333 (1912). See 6 Cal. Law Rev. 149 (1918): Chafee, Cases on Equitable Relief against Torts, 502 (1924). The theory upon which such strangers are held to have been guilty of contempt has been expressed as follows: "A motion to commit a man for breach of an injunction, which is technically wrong unless he is bound by the injunction, is one thing; and a motion to commit a man for contempt of court, not because he is bound by the injunction by being a party to the cause, but because he is conducting himself so as to obstruct the course of justice, is another and totally different thing. * * * In the one case the party who is bound by the injunction is proceeded against for the purpose of enforcing the order of the court for the benefit of the person who got it. In the other case the court will not allow its process to be set at naught and treated with contempt." Lindley, L.J., in Seaward v. Patterson [1897] 1 Ch. 545, 555. To this the following answer has been made: "We are entirely at a loss to see how, there being no disobedience of the injunction charged, as we have shown, there can be any conviction of contempt based on the theory that the affidavit or complaint shows acts 'in contempt of the power and dignity of the court, acts * * * constituting an 'interference with or obstruction of the administration of justice.' There was no 'command' of the court addressed to the petitioner in any way, by name or as a member of any class, and it was not charged that he was acting in concert or connection with or in aid of any party to whom the command was addressed. How, then, can it be said that he was acting in defiance of the command of the court, or in any way interfering with the execution of that command against those to whom it was addressed?" Angellotti, C.J., in Berger v. Superior Court, *supra*, 720-721. The distinction made between these two types of contempt has been maintained in the federal practice, so that a contempt proceeding against one not a party to the injunction order is regarded as of the nature of a "criminal contempt" and as such reviewable by writ of error and not appeal. Besette v. W. B. Conkey Co., 194 U.S. 324 (1904); Matter of Christensen Engineering Co., 194 U.S. 458 (1904). *Quaere* as to the effect of the Acts of January 31, 1928, 45 Stat. 54, and April 26, 1928, 45 Stat. 466, on the distinction.

Upon the power of a court that has issued injunction to punish as contempts thereof acts committed without its territorial jurisdiction, see: Myers v. United States, 264 U.S. 95 (1924); Binkley v. United States, 282 Fed. 244 (8th cir. 1922); McGibbony v. Lancaster, 286 Fed. 129 (5th cir. 1923).

Upon the desuetude of an injunction due to the lapse of time between its issuance and that upon which the acts allegedly constituting contempt were committed, see: Tosh v. West Kentucky Coal Co., 252 Fed. 44 (6th cir. 1918).—Ed.

straining order; but I point you to the writ of injunction in the case referred to in the case of *D. E. Loewe et al. v. California State Federation
of Labor.* I notice, too, that that writ, while directed to these organizations and then to different individuals named as members of the organization, also includes their attorneys, agents, employés, and all persons acting
in aid of or in conjunction with them or any of them. That is as strong
and takes as wide a latitude as have the writs and papers in this case. I
feel justified in following the practice as established by this court, and,
as I say, as I did a number of years ago in the case referred to in Northern
Idaho, and so long as that practice is not overthrown by courts having
the authority to do so, I do not see any reason why it should not be followed. I therefore commend to you, in preparing the form of the writ,
to consult the one to which I have referred. I think it is substantially
about what you have already prepared in the present case.[2]

McCARTER v. CHAMBER OF COMMERCE.

Maryland Court of Appeals.   126 Md. 131, 94 Atl. 541 (1915).

CONSTABLE, J., delivered the opinion of the Court.

The only question in this appeal is one of pleading, and involves only
the sufficiency of the averments of the amended declaration. A demurrer
was interposed by the defendant, and upon it being sustained and judgment entered for the defendant for costs, this appeal was taken from
that judgment. It will be necessary for a determination of the question
to set out quite fully the allegations of the declaration.

It avers that the Baltimore Chamber of Commerce, the appellee, was
a corporation, and had extant on the 10th day of February, 1913, and on
the day of the filing of this suit, the following section of its charter:

"Section 5.   And be it enacted, that the purposes of said corporation
shall be to provide and regulate a suitable room or rooms for a produce
exchange in the City of Baltimore; to inculcate just and equitable principles of trade; to establish and maintain uniformity in commercial usage;
to acquire, preserve and disseminate valuable business information; and
to adjust controversies and misunderstandings between its members and
themselves or between them and other persons thereto consenting, which
may arise in the course of business."

There is also set out in full section 6 of Article 9 of the By-Laws of
the corporation, prescribing the duties of the Executive Committee. There

---

[2] *Accord:* Martin v. Francke, 227 Mass. 272, 116 N.E. 404 (1917). *Cf.* My
Maryland Lodge v. Adt, 100 Md. 238, 59 Atl. 721 (1905); State v. Glidden, 55 Conn.
46, 8 Atl. 890 (1887).

was also in effect the third paragraph of section 11 of Article 9 of the By-Laws, and which was as follows:

"Third—Any corporation, joint stock company, firm or individual not a member of the Baltimore Chamber of Commerce, who shall be accused of any proceedings inconsistent with just and equitable principles of trade, in relation to a transaction had through or with any member of the Baltimore Chamber of Commerce, shall on complaint be summoned before the Complaint Committee and given an opportunity to be heard. Should the Committee be unable to induce a settlement, and the circumstances shall seem to the Committee to warrant, the complaint and all proceedings thereunder shall be referred by the Committee to the Board of Directors, who shall consider the evidence produced before the Complaint Committee, and give both plaintiff and defendant an opportunity to be heard again, and to produce additional evidence at such hearing if either shall so desire, prior to final action in the case; and if, in the opinion of the Board, the charge or charges against said defendant be substantiated, it may, by a vote of not less than two-thirds of all the members present, prohibit said defendant representation on the floor of the Chamber, and any member of the Chamber who shall with knowledge of such prohibition represent or transact business with or on behalf of said defendant, after notice of such prohibition shall have been posted on the bulletin during five days, shall be deemed guilty of wilful violation of the By-Laws, and subject to the penalties prescribed in section 5 of Article 7, and such member shall be proceeded against in accordance with the By-Laws for such violation. All complaints under this section shall be in writing and addressed to the Chairman of the Complaint Committee, who shall cause the same to be served on the defendant, with notice of the time of hearing."

It is then averred that "because the plaintiff was indebted unto one of the members of the said corporation in the sum of eighty dollars, which was a balance due on a note which was being gradually liquidated by the plaintiff" the corporation caused to be posted the following notice:

"Robert McCarter, Reisterstown, Maryland. The attention of members is called to Article 9, section 11, paragraph 3 of the By-Laws. This rule will be strictly enforced."

It is then further averred as follows: "And for a long time prior to the date of the promulgation of the aforesaid notice on the 10th of February, 1913, and as of the date of the filing thereof on the 10th day of February, 1913, and since that date, the plaintiff was employed by certain members of this defendant corporation, and the said defendant corporation, through its officials, agents and employees, on or about the 19th of August, 1913, in accordance with the aforesaid sections of the Charter and By-Laws hereinbefore set forth, cited John M. Frisch and Company, H. C. Jones and Company, G. A. Hax and Company and Sinton Brothers and Company, by whom the plaintiff was employed prior to the 10th of February, 1913, and the aforesaid firms were directed to discharge from their employ and to cease further dealings with the plaintiff, and that some of said firms did immediately discharge from their employ the plaintiff, and that certain other of said firms did not, and that thereafter the said board of directors and certain members of the said corporation, did, by intimidation and coercion compel the remaining firms to discharge this plaintiff from their employ and cease further dealings with him, by threatening to reprimand, suspend or expel said firms, who were members of said defendant, in accordance with section 5 of Article 7 of the defendant's By-Laws." Said section clothes the board of directors with the power to reprimand, suspend or expel, with the consent of a two-thirds vote of the members, any member who has been guilty of a breach of the rules, regulations or by-laws.

It is then charged that, as a result of the illegal action upon the part of the defendant, the plaintiff has been deprived of his position and employment and has been "blackballed and boycotted" by the members of the corporation and has suffered malicious injury.

Stripped of its legal phraseology the complaint of the plaintiff is merely that while employed by several of the individual members of the corporation and being indebted to another of said members, the corporation compelled his employers to discharge him and abstain from further dealings with him under threats, by virtue of a by-law, of themselves being denied the privileges of membership in the corporation. That the posting of the notice under the by-laws was not sufficient to bring about the severance of the relations between the plaintiff and some of the members, but in order to accomplish that end it was necessary to cite the unwilling members before a committee and direct them to observe the by-law. That even then there were some members who persisted in refusing to comply with the by-law and continued the employment of the plaintiff until they were threatened by the board of directors with a reprimand, suspension or expulsion.

The contention of the appellant is, in the language of his brief: "The defendant in procuring breaches of the plaintiff's terms of employment with its members through the coercive means of threatening such employing members with the pains and penalties of Article 5, section 7, of its By-Laws—which included expulsion from the organization and consequent exclusion from the floor of the exchange—violated the plaintiff's legal rights without justification and is answerable therefor in Court for damages thus caused the plaintiff."

It will be noticed that the declaration avers no particular nor definite period of time for the termination of the contracts of employment, and, therefore, it is to be assumed that they were terminable at the will or wish of either party without actionable liability upon the part of either. In other words, a case of hiring from day to day. We do not mean to intimate that because of this a third party has the legal right to maliciously interfere so as to terminate an employment, but only to note that it was the legal right of either employer or employee to bring the employment to an end. And when we use the word malicious we use it in its strictly

legal meaning. "Malice," said BAYLEY, J., in *Bromage v. Prosser,* 4 B.
& C. 255, "in common acceptation, means ill will against a person, but in
its legal sense it means a wrongful act done intentionally without just
cause or excuse." Or as was said in *Lucke v. Clothing, etc., Assembly,*
77 Md. 396. "It is not necessary that such interference should have been
malicious in its character. If it be wrongful, it is equally to be condemned,
and just as much in violation of legal right."

"Any malicious interference with the business or occupation of another, if followed by damage, is an actionable wrong." *Willner v. Silverman,* 109 Md. 341. On the other hand: "It is a part of every man's legal
rights, that he be left at liberty to refuse business relations with any person whomsoever, whether the refusal rests upon reason, or is the result
of whim, caprice, prejudice or malice. *Cooley on Torts,* 278. "The exercise by one man of his legal right cannot be a legal wrong to another.
* * * Whatever one has a legal right to do another can have no right to
complain of." *Id.* 688. But the argument of the appellant is that this is
not a case of one voluntarily refusing to continue business with him, but
a case of one, against his will, being forced by threats and intimidations
made by a third party, the appellee, to sever those relations. And this
brings us, to our minds, to the crucial test of the liability of the appellee;
whether the by-law in question was, in law, a coercive threat upon the
minds of the members of the appellee corporation. If the posting of the
appellant by virtue of it did not so amount, then the fact that the corporation directed certain members to observe it under penalty of the enforcement of its provisions, adds nothing to the claim of the appellant.

The question of whether such a by-law is coercive has given rise to
a conflict of the authorities. There have been many cases where associations have had by-laws similar, or practically so, to the one in this case,
and in some jurisdictions Courts have held the associations liable to parties injured through their enforcement; while in others the opposite conclusion has been reached. See *Bohn Manuf. Co. v. Hollis,* 54 Minn. 223;
Delz v. Winfree, 6 Tex. Civil App. 11; *Brewster v. Miller,* 101 Ky. 368;
Schulten v. Bavarian Brew. Co., 96 Ky. 224; *Reynolds v. Plumbers Material Protec. Assn.,* 63 N.Y. Supp. 303; *Jackson v. Stanfield,* 137 Ind. 592;
Martell v. White, 185 Mass. 255; *Boutwell v. Marr,* 71 Ver. 1; *Heim Brew.
Co. v. Belinder,* 97 Mo. App. 64.

Of the above cited cases we think it only necessary to review that of
Bohn Manuf. Co. v. Hollis, for the reason that in a recent case, *Klingel's
Pharm. v. Sharpe & Dohme,* 104 Md. 218, this Court has reviewed the
facts and approved the finding of the Minnesota Court. In that case a
large number of retail lumber dealers formed a voluntary association by
which they mutually agreed that they would not deal with any manufacturer or wholesale dealer who should sell lumber directly to consumers
at a place where a number of the association was engaged in the retail
business, and they provided in their by-laws that whenever any wholesale
dealer or manufacturer made any such sale, their secretary should notify

all the members of the fact. The plaintiff made such a sale and the secretary made demand upon him for the penalty prescribed by the by-laws, but the plaintiff delayed so long in the payment of the penalty the secretary threatened to send notices to all the members. By the provisions of the by-law any members who continued dealings with such wholesale dealer was subject to expulsion from the association. The plaintiff applied for an injunction to restrain the sending of the notices, but it was held no action would lie and that there was no ground for an injunction. On the question as to whether the by-law providing for expulsion was coercive the Court said: "But this involved no element of coercion or intimidation, in the legal sense of those terms. * * * Nor was any coercion proposed to be brought to bear on the members of the association, to prevent them from trading with the plaintiff. After they received the notices, they would be at entire liberty to trade with plaintiff, or not, as they saw fit. By the provisions of the by-laws, if they traded with the plaintiff, they were liable to be "expelled;" but this simply meant to cease to be members. It was wholly a matter of their own free choice, which they preferred, to trade with the plaintiff, or to continue members of the association." Chief Judge McSherry in delivering the opinion in *Klingel's Pharm. v. Sharpe & Dohme, supra,* approved the opinion in the above case and declared: "There was nothing unlawful in this." Under the authority of those cases there was not such an interference with the rights of the appellant by the appellee corporation as to amount in law to a wrongful and malicious interference for which an action will lie.

We are, therefore, of the opinion that the action of the Court below was correct in sustaining the demurrer, because the declaration avers no act which amounts to an unlawful coercion.

Judgment affirmed, with costs.[1]

---

[1] "Comparing these labor boycott cases with the trade boycott cases, we find that the question whether a boycott of one trader by rival traders is legal is a question in which there is a conflict of authority, but a boycott of a trader by laborers or others who are not rival traders has invariably been held illegal. The same line of distinction has been followed in England. The only justification for the distinction lies in the fact that in the labor boycott cases the connection between the acts of the defendants and their own advancement is sometimes one degree more remote than in the boycott by rival traders. In the trade cases the immediate purpose of the defendants is usually to establish a monopoly through which their own economic advancement is to be secured. In the labor cases the immediate purpose is usually to punish the plaintiff, and through the example of his punishment to make him and others adopt certain rules in the conduct of business, which rules will in the end be beneficial to the economic position of the defendants. The connection between the economic advancement and the boycott being less clear to the judges, there is a tendency to regard the defendants in labor boycotts as persons who have intermeddled in the plaintiff's business without excuse. The distinction, in view of the real facts, is a narrow one, and the writer does not believe it will stand analysis. The boycott is an appeal to force, not an appeal to reason. The force is not physical force, but is none the less an attempt to coerce the will of third persons, so that they will act in a way prejudicial to the plaintiff's interests. The purpose of self-advancement in business or trade is one to be encouraged by the law, but it should not be sufficient to excuse harm to others through the coercion of their customers." Lewis, The Modern American Cases Arising out of Trade and Labor Disputes, 465, 491-492 (1905).
For situations similar to those in the McCarter case, see: Master Builders'

COTE v. MURPHY.

Pennsylvania Supreme Court. 159 Pa. 420, 28 Atl. 190 (1894).

OPINION BY MR. JUSTICE DEAN, January 2, 1894:

The defendants were members of the Planing Mill Association of Allegheny county, and Builders' Exchange of Pittsburgh. The different partnerships and individuals, composing these associations, were in the business of contracting and building and furnishing building material of all kinds. On the 1st of May, 1891, there was a strike of the carpenters, masons and bricklayers in the building trades, bringing about, to a large extent, a stoppage of building.

The men demanded an eight hour day, with no reduction in wages theretofore paid, which the employers refused to grant; then a strike by the unions of the different trades was declared. The plaintiff, at the time, was doing business in the city of Pittsburgh as a dealer in building materials. He was not a member of either the "Planing Mill Association," or of the "Builders' Exchange;" there were also contractors and builders, who belonged to neither of these organizations, who conceded the demands of the workmen; they sought to secure building material from dealers wherever they could, and thus go on with their contracts; if they succeeded in purchasing the necessary material, the result would be, that at least some of the striking workmen would have employment at a higher rate of wages than the two associations were willing to pay; the tendency of this was to strengthen the cause of the strikers, for those employed were able to contribute to the support of their fellow workman who were idle. The two associations already named, sought to enlist all concerned as contractors and builders or as dealers in supplies, whether members of the associations or not, in the furtherance of the one object,

Ass'n v. Domascio, 16 Colo. App. 25, 63 Pac. 782 (1901); Booker & Kinnaird v. Louisville Board of Fire Underwriters, 188 Ky. 771, 224 S.W. 451 (1920); Brewster v. Millers' Sons Co., 101 Ky. 368, 41 S.W. 301 (1897); Bowen v. Matheson, 14 Allen 499 (Mass. 1867); Bohn Mfg. Co. v. Hollis, 54 Minn. 223, 55 N.W. 1119 (1893); Collins v. American News Co., 34 Misc. 260, 69 N.Y.S. 638 (1901); Maculey Bros. v. Tierney, 19 R.I. 255, 33 Atl. 1 (1895); McMaster v. Ford Motor Car Co., 122 S.C. 244, 115 S.E. 244 (1921); Ware & De Freville, Ltd. v. Motor Trade Ass'n [1921] 3 K.B. 40; Hardie & Lane Chilton [1928] 2 K.B. 306. Compare as *contra*, Jackson v. Stanfield, 137 Ind. 592, 36 N.E. 345 (1893); Baldwin v. Escanaba Liquor Dealers Ass'n, 165 Mich. 98, 130 N.W. 214 (1911).

For illustrations of the handling of such situations under state and federal anti-trust legislation, see: Eastern States Retail Lumber Ass'n, 234 U.S. 600 (1914); Grenada Lumber Co. v. Mississippi, 217 U.S. 433 (1910); Boyle v. United States, 40 Fed. (2d) 49 (7th cir. 1930); Arkansas Wholesale Grocers Ass'n v. Federal Trade Commission, 18 Fed. (2d) 866 (8th cir. 1927), certiorari denied in 275 U.S. 533 (1927); United States v. Southern California Wholesale Grocers Ass'n, 7 Fed. (2d) 944 (S.D. Cal. 1925); Wholesale Grocers' Ass'n v. Federal Trade Commission, 277 Fed. 657 (5th cir. 1922); Western Sugar Refinery Co. v. Federal Trade Commission, 275 Fed. 725 (9th cir. 1921); United States v. Hollis, 246 Fed. 611 (D. Minn. 1917); Knauer v. United States, 237 Fed. 8 (8th cir. 1916); Walsh v. Ass'n of Master Plumbers, 97 Mo. App. 280, 71 S.W. 455 (1902); Locker v. American Tobacco Co., 195 N.Y. 565, 88 N.E. 289 (1909).

resistance to the demands of the workmen. The plaintiff, and six other individuals or firms engaged in the same business, refused to join them, and undertook to continue sales of building material to those builders who had conceded the eight hour day. The Planing Mill Association and Builders' Exchange tried to limit their ability to carry on work at the advance, by inducing lumber dealers and others to refrain from shipping, or selling them in quantities, the lumber and other material necessary to carrying on the retail business; in several instances, their efforts were successful, and the plaintiff did not succeed in purchasing lumber from certain of the wholesale dealers in Cleveland and Dubois, where he wanted to buy. The defendants were active members of one or other or both of the associations engaged in the contest with the striking workmen. The strike continued about two months; after it was at an end, the plaintiff brought suit against defendants, averring an unlawful and successful conspiracy to injure him in his business, and to interfere with the course of trade generally, to the injury of the public; that the conspiracy was carried out by a refusal to sell to him building materials themselves, and by threats and intimidation preventing other dealers from doing so. Under the instructions of the court upon the evidence, there was a verdict for plaintiff in the sum of $2,500 damages, which the court reduced to $1,500; then judgment, and from that defendants take this appeal.

The plaintiff's case is not one which appeals very strongly to a sense of justice. The mechanics of Pittsburgh, engaged in the different building trades, on 1st of May, 1891, demanded that eight hours should be computed as a day in payment of their wages. Their right to do this is clear. It is one of the indefeasible rights of a mechanic or laborer in this commonwealth to fix such value on his services as he sees proper, and, under the constitution, there is no power lodged anywhere to compel him to work for less than he chooses to accept. But in this case the workmen went further; they agreed that no one of them would work for less than the demand, and by all lawful means, such as reasoning and persuasion, they would prevent other workmen from working for less. Their right to do this is also clear. At common law, this last was a conspiracy and indictable, but under the Acts of 1869, 1872, 1876 and 1891, employees, acting together by agreement, may, with few exceptions, lawfully do all those things which the common law declared a conspiracy. They are still forbidden, in the prosecution of a strike, preventing any one of their number who may desire to labor from doing so, by force or menace of harm to person or property; but the strike here was conducted throughout in an orderly, lawful manner. The employers, contractors and others, engaged in building and furnishing supplies, members of the two associations already mentioned, to which these defendants belonged, refused to concede the demands of the workmen, and there then followed a prolonged and bitter contest. The members of the associations refused to furnish supplies to those engaged in the construction of any building where the contractor had conceded the eight hour day. This, as individual dealers, they had a clear right to do. They could sell and deliver their material to whom they pleased. But they also went further; they agreed among themselves that no member of the association would furnish supplies to those who were in favor of or had conceded the eight hour day, and that they would dissuade other dealers, not members of the associations, from furnishing building material to such contractors or retail dealers; to the extent of their power, this agreement was carried out. This clearly was combination, and the acts of assembly referred to do not, in terms, embrace employers; they only include within their express terms workmen; hence, it is argued by counsel for appellee, these defendants are subject to all the common law liability of conspirators in their attempts to resist the demand for increased wages; that is, there can be a combination among workmen to advance wages, but there can be no such combination of employers to resist the advance; that which by statute is permitted to the one side, the common law still denies to the other. If this position be well taken, we then have this inequality; the plaintiff who is aiding a combination, either directly or indirectly, intentionally or unintentionally, to advance wages, sues for damages members of another combination who resist the advance. Nor is there any difference in the character of the acts or means on both sides in furtherance of their purposes. The workmen will not work themselves, and they use persuasion and reason with their fellows to keep them from going to work until the demand is conceded; the employers will not sell to contractors who concede the demand, and they do their best to dissuade others engaged in the same business from doing so.

Then, the element of real damage to plaintiff is absent; by far the larger number of dealers in the city and county were members of the combination which refused to sell; only the plaintiff and six others refused to enter the combination; the result was that these seven had almost a monopoly of furnishing supplies to all builders who conceded the advance. Plaintiff admits in his own testimony that thereby his business and profits largely increased; in a few instances he paid more to wholesale dealers and put in more time buying than he would have done if the associations had not interfered with those who sold him; but it is not denied that, as a result of the combination, he was individually a large gainer. True, he avers that, if defendants had gone no further than to refuse to sell themselves, he would have made a great deal more money; that is, he did not make as large a sum as he would have made if they had not dissuaded others, not members of the association, from selling to him; but that, by the fact of the combinations and st_ike, he was richer at the end than when they commenced, is not questioned.

We have then these facts, somewhat peculiar in the administration of justice: A plaintiff suing and recovering damages for an alleged unlawful act, of which he himself, in so far as he aided the workmen's combination, is also guilty, and both acts springing from the same source, a contest between employers and employed as to the price of daily wages;

and then the further fact, that this contest, instead of damaging him, resulted largely to his profit.

We assume, so far as concerns defendants, if their agreement was unlawful, or if lawful, it was carried out by unlawful acts to the damage of plaintiff, the judgment should stand. All the authorities of this state go to show that while the act of an individual may not be unlawful, yet the same act, when committed by a combination of two or more, may be unlawful, and therefore be actionable. A dictum of Lord DENMAN, in *R. v. Seward,* 1 A. & E. 711, gives this definition of a conspiracy: "It is either a combination to procure an unlawful object, or to procure a lawful object by unlawful means." This leaves still undetermined the meaning to be given the words lawful and unlawful, in their connection in the antithesis. An agreement may be unlawful in the sense that the law will not aid in its enforcement, or recognize it as binding upon those who have made it, yet not unlawful in the sense that it will punish those who are parties to it, either criminally or by a verdict in damages. Lord DENMAN is reported to have said afterwards in *R. v. Heck,* 9 A. & E. 690, that his definition was not very correct. See note to sec. 2291, Wharton's Criminal Law.

It is conceded, however, in the case in hand, any one of defendants, acting for himself, had a right to refuse to sell to those favoring the eight hour day, and so, acting for himself, had the right to dissuade others from selling. If the act were unlawful at all, it was because of the combination of a number. GIBSON, J., in *Com. v. Carlisle,* Brightly's R. 39 says: "Where the act is lawful for the individual, it can be the subject of conspiracy when done in concert, only where there is a direct intention that injury shall result from it, or where the object is to benefit the conspirators to the prejudice of the public or the oppression of individuals, and where such prejudice or oppression is the natural and necessary consequence."

In the same case it is held: "A combination is criminal, wherever the act to be done has a necessary tendency to prejudice the public, or to oppress individuals by unjustly subjecting them to the power of the confederacy, and giving effect to the purposes of the latter, whether of extortion or mischief. According to this view of the law, a combination of employers to depress the wages of journeymen below what they would be if there was no recurrence to artificial means, on either side, is criminal." This case puts the law against the combination in as strong terms, if not stronger, than any others of our own state. The significant qualification of the general principle, as mentioned in the last three lines, will be noticed: "if there was no recurrence to artificial means, on either side." The prejudice to the public is the use of artificial means to affect prices whereby the public suffers. A combination of stock brokers to corner a stock, of farmers to raise the price of grain, of manufacturers to raise the price of their product, of employers to reduce the price of labor, of workmen to raise the price, were at the date of that decision, at common law, all conspiracies. The fixed theory of courts and legislators then was, that the price of everything ought to be, and in the absence of combination necessarily would be, regulated by supply and demand. The first to deny the justice of this theory, and to break away from it, was labor, and this was soon followed by the legislation already noticed, relieving workmen from the penalties of what, for more than a century, had been declared unlawful combinations, or conspiracies. Wages, it was argued, should be fixed by the fair proportion labor had contributed in production; the market price, determined by supply and demand, might or might not be fair wages, often was not, and as long as workmen were not free by combination to insist on their right to fair wages, oppression by capital, or, which is the same thing, by their employers, followed. It is not our business to pass on the soundness of the theories which prompt the enactment of statutes. One thing, however, is clear; the moment the legislature relieved one and by far the larger number of the citizens of the commonwealth from the common law prohibitions against combinations to raise the price of labor and by a combination the price was raised, down went the foundation on which common law conspiracy was based, as to that particular subject. Before any legislation on the question, it was held that a combination of workmen to raise the price of labor, or of employers to depress it, was unlawful, because such combination interfered with the price which would otherwise be regulated by supply and demand; this interference was in restraint of trade or business, and prejudicial to the public at large. Such combination made an artificial price; workmen, by reason of the combination, were not willing to work for what otherwise they would accept; employers would not pay what otherwise they would consider fair wages. Supply and demand consist in the amount of labor for sale and the needs of the employer who buys. If more men offer to sell labor than are needed, the price goes down and the employer buys cheap; if fewer than required offer, the price goes up and he buys dear; as every seller and buyer is free to bargain for himself, the price is regulated solely by supply and demand. On this reasoning was founded common law conspiracy in this class of cases. But, in this case, the workmen, without regard to the supply of labor or the demand for it, agree upon what in their judgment is a fair price, and then combine in a demand for payment of that price; when refused, in pursuance of the combination, they quit work, and agree not to work until the demand is conceded; further, they agree by lawful means to prevent all others, not members of the combination, from going to work until the employers agree to pay the price fixed by the combination. And this, as long as no force was used or menaces to person or property, they had a lawful right to do. And so far as is known to us, the price demanded by them may have been a fair one. But it is nonsense to say that this was a price fixed by supply and demand; it was fixed by a combination of workmen on their combined judgment as to its fairness; and, that the supply might not lessen it, they combined to prevent all other workmen in the market from accepting less. Then followed the combination of employers, not to lower the wages theretofore paid, but to resist the demand of a combination for an advance; not to resist an advance which would naturally follow a limited supply in the market, for the supply, so far as the workmen belonging to the combination was concerned, was by combination wholly withdrawn, and as to workmen other than members, to the extent of their power, they kept them out of the market; by artificial means, the market supply was almost wholly cut off. The combination of the employers, then, was not to interfere with the price of labor as determined by the common law theory, but to defend themselves against a demand made altogether regardless of the price, as regulated by the supply. The element of an unlawful combination to restrain trade because of greed of profit to themselves, or of malice toward plaintiff or others is lacking, and this is the essential element on which are founded all decisions as to common law conspiracy in this class of cases. And however unchanged may be the law as to combinations of employers to interfere with wages, where such combinations take the initiative, they certainly do not depress a market price when they combine to resist a combination to artificially advance price. * * *

But, if the agreement itself were not unlawful, were the methods to carry it out unlawful? If the employers' combination here had used illegal methods or means to prevent other dealers from selling supplies to plaintiff, the conspiracy might still have been found to exist. The threats referred to, although what are usually termed threats, were not so in a legal sense. To have said they would inflict bodily harm on other dealers, or villify them in the newspapers, or bring on them social ostracism, or similar declarations, these the law would have deemed threats, for they may deter a man of ordinary courage from the prosecution of his business in a way which accords with his own notions; but to say, and even that is inferential from the correspondence, that if they continued to sell to plaintiff the members of the association would not buy from them, is not a threat. It does not interfere with the dealer's free choice; it may have prompted him to a somewhat sordid calculation; he may have considered which custom was most profitable, and have acted accordingly; but this was not such coercion and threats as constituted the acts of the combination unlawful: *Rodgers v. Duff*, 13 Moore, P.C. 209; *Bowen v. Matheson,* 14 Allen, 499; *Bohn Manufacturing Co. v. Hollis et al.*, Supreme Court of Minnesota, manuscript opinion, not yet reported [55 N.W.R. 1119]. * * *

But without regard to whether the general rule be settled by the weight of authority, as claimed by appellants, we hold here that this combination was not unlawful, because: 1. It was not made to lower the price of wages as regulated by the supply and demand, but to resist an artificial price made by a combination which by statute was not unlawful. 2. The methods adopted to further the objects of the combination were not unlawful. * * *

The refusal of the court below to affirm appellant's seventh prayer for instructions, that, "Under all the evidence the verdict must be for defendants," was error, and, being here assigned for error, the appeal is sustained and judgment reversed.[1]

CARLSON v. CARPENTER CONTRACTORS' ASSOCIATION OF CHICAGO.

Illinois Supreme Court. 305 Ill. 331, 137 N.E. 222 (1922).

Mr. CHIEF JUSTICE THOMPSON delivered the opinion of the court:

John Carlson, plaintiff in No. 14776, is a journeyman carpenter and a member of the carpenters' union. July 18, 1919, and for a long time prior thereto, he was in the employ of Simon Hill, a contractor who did not belong to a contractors' organization. Hill had work to be done and desired to retain Carlson in his employ, and Carlson was able and willing to work and desired to continue his employment. Representatives of the union of which Carlson was a member had signed a working agreement with the Carpenter Contractors' Association, one of the defendants, which did not expire until 1921. This agreement provided, among other things, that there should be no strikes or lock-outs without the sanction of a joint conference board composed of members of the contracting parties, and that the minimum rate of wages until May 31, 1921, should be eighty cents an hour. Notwithstanding this agreement the representatives of the carpenters in June, 1919, presented to representatives of the contractors a demand that the minimum rate of wages be increased to one dollar an hour, giving as their reason the increased cost of living. Following this demand the contractors agreed to increase the wages twelve and one-half cents an hour but refused to grant the rate demanded. Thereupon, July 9,

---

[1] Accord: Buchanan v. Kerr, 159 Pa. 433, 28 Atl. 195 (1894). Cf. Associated Hat Manufacturers v. Baird-Unteidt Co., 88 Conn. 332, 91 Atl. 373 (1914); Carpenters' Union v. Citizens' Committee to Enforce Landis Award, 333 Ill. 225, 164 N.E. 393 (1928); American Dental Co. v. Central Dental Co., 256 Ill. App. 279 (1930); State v. Employers of Labor, 102 Neb. 768, 169 N.W. 717 (1918); Trade Press Pub. Co. v. Milwaukee Typographical Union, 180 Wis. 449, 193 N.W. 507 (1923). For cooperation between steel producers to bring about the erection of structural steel under non-union conditions by a concerted refusal to sell steel f.o.b. to owners or builders operating on a union basis, requiring them instead to contract for it erected in place, see testimony of Eugene G. Grace, in Intermediate Report of Joint Legislative Committee on Housing, N.Y. Leg. Doc. No. 60, 128-130 (1922). See also: Gulick, "Labor Policy of the United States Steel Corporation," 116 Col. Stud. in Hist. Econ. & Public Law, 93-137 (1924).

"An association representing nearly all the building contractors in or near a city, bargains with an association representing the building unions that the contractors shall employ only union men. The bargain has for its object the monopolizing of labor on buildings for union laborers. The bargain is illegal where monopoly would thus be obtained so complete as to destroy the possibility of non-union laborers in the building trades obtaining employment." American Law Institute, Restatement of the Law of Contracts, § 515 (19) (1932).

1919, a general strike was called, in violation of the working agreement. Those contractors or members of the public who were willing to pay one dollar an hour to carpenters were allowed by the carpenters' union to proceed with their work without molestation. Hill agreed to pay Carlson one dollar an hour and Carlson continued in his employ. Oscar Carlson, plaintiff in No. 14777, was in July, 1919, engaged in erecting a building for himself. He is not a carpenter nor a carpenter contractor. After the strike was called he continued to employ union carpenters and paid them the wages demanded. A week after the strike was called the Carpenter Contractors' Association and the Building Construction Employers' Association declared a lock-out of all union workmen in the building trades throughout Lake and Cook counties and the members of such contracting associations ceased operations. This lock-out had little, if any, effect on the situation, because all the union workmen had left the employ of the associated contractors before the lock-out was declared. After the associated contractors left the field, independent contractors, who had been operating in Cook and Lake counties continued to employ union carpenters, and new contractors entered the field and employed the striking carpenters at the wage demanded. In order to make the lock-out effective the associated contractors sought and secured the aid of the dealers in building material. After several conferences the material dealers agreed, at the request of these contractors, who had theretofore been their best and largest customers, representing about eighty per cent of their business, to cease selling and delivering materials to any person employing or about to employ union carpenters or other union labor in the building trades. Thereafter independent contractors, private builders and members of the general public were refused material for the purpose of erecting or repairing buildings, and as a result of their inability to obtain building materials they were compelled to discharge workmen, although willing to pay the wages demanded and to comply with all other requirements of the unions. As a result of the refusal of the material dealers to sell and deliver material Simon Hill was forced to discharge John Carlson and Oscar Carlson was not able to complete his building.

John Carlson filed a statement of claim in the municipal court against the unincorporated associations of employers, the officers and certain members of these associations and twenty-two dealers in building material, all of which defendants have their offices in the city of Chicago. After stating the facts substantially as we have stated them, he alleged that the defendants did "unlawfully and maliciously enter into an agreement, combination and conspiracy to injure the employment of such [union] carpenters, including the plaintiff, and to boycott said carpenters, including the plaintiff, and in furtherance of such agreement, combination and conspiracy the defendants conspired to prevent, and did prevent, the sale of lumber and other building materials in said counties of Cook and Lake, Illinois, and particularly in the city of Chicago, to any and all persons employing or about to employ said carpenters, including the plaintiff; and said defendants, without any legal justification or excuse whatsoever, did specifically prevent the sale of lumber and other building material to the said Simon Hill, who was then and there employing plaintiff, for the express purpose of thereby compelling said Simon Hill to discharge the plaintiff and any other carpenters who might then be in the employ of Simon Hill," and that by reason of such conspiracy plaintiff was deprived of employment for a period of nine weeks. Oscar Carlson filed his statement of claim in the municipal court against the same defendants, and after a statement of the facts alleged that said defendants, "without any legal justification or excuse whatsoever, did prevent the sale of lumber and other building material to the plaintiff for the sole purpose of thereby preventing the plaintiff from giving employment to carpenters," and that by reason of such refusal to sell material he was deprived of the use of his building for two months. A trial was had before the court without a jury, and it denied damages to John Carlson and awarded damages in the amount of $340 to Oscar Carlson. On appeal to the Appellate Court for the First District the judgment against John Carlson was reversed and a judgment entered in his favor in the sum of $396. The judgment in favor of Oscar Carlson was affirmed. Certificates of importance were granted and these appeals prosecuted.

Propositions of law and of fact were submitted to the municipal court, and the court's action on these propositions shows that it found as an ultimate fact that the defendants formed their combination and refused to sell and deliver building materials to persons employing union carpenters and to permit building material to be sold and delivered in Chicago, for the purpose of maliciously injuring plaintiffs. The court denied damages to John Carlson because he was a member of the carpenters' union which violated its working agreement, thereby bringing about the condition which caused him to suffer. The Appellate Court found the facts the same as the municipal court, declaring that "defendants not only agreed to but did in fact succeed in establishing a boycott and blacklist against the striking carpenters;" and again, that "the defendants had the intention and the purpose, by the use of peaceful but notwithstanding powerful means, to compel the striking carpenters to accept less than one dollar an hour for their work. That was the primary and ultimate object of their plan." In reversing the judgment against John Carlson the Appellate Court held that the municipal court erred in applying the law, resting its decision upon the maxim that one wrong does not right another. The controverted question of fact as to whether the damage to plaintiffs was caused by the wrongful acts of defendants has been finally settled by the judgments of the Appellate Court. This court is limited to a review of the questions of law involved.

These are simple actions *ex delicto*. We are called upon to decide whether (1) a legal right of plaintiffs (2) has been invaded (3) by defendants (4) to the injury of plaintiffs. The right of employees to organize and to quit their employment singly or as a group; the right of employers to organize and to discharge their employees singly or to lock them out as a body; the right of dealers to organize and to refuse to sell merchandise to a particular individual, to a group of individuals or to the public at large; the presence of a few crooked business agents in the ranks of labor and of a few criminal profiteers in the ranks of employers and dealers; and the obligation of employers and employees to respect their working agreements, are all subjects full of interest but which have no bearing whatever on the issues involved in these cases and a discussion of any of the subjects would be entirely out of place.

Practically all of the briefs filed on behalf of defendants is devoted to a discussion of the primary purpose of defendants in agreeing to do and in doing the acts which they have done. They contend that their primary purpose was to force organized employees to respect their working agreements; to force the unions to prevent the crooked business agent from calling or threatening to call jurisdictional strikes for the purpose of extorting large sums of money from builders; to protect themselves from great losses because of the uncertainties occasioned by the practices of the unions and their officers, and to otherwise stabilize the building industry. Much of defendants' brief is devoted to a discussion of their rights and to the contention that in self-defense they were legally justified in doing what they did. Defendants' rights are not in any respect involved in this litigation and need not be considered except when necessary to a determination of plaintiffs' rights. The apparent confusion that exists in the law as declared in adjudicated cases in the different jurisdictions is due largely to a faulty mode of approach. Whenever a court permits itself to be led afield into a discussion of the rights of the defendant in tort actions and to become entangled in the subtleties connected with the phrases "primary purpose" and "legal justification," it is apt to have its attention diverted from a consideration of the question whether plaintiff's rights have been invaded by the doing of the act charged. To discuss the rights of the defendant is to confuse rather than clarify the issue. To argue that defendant had a legal right to do what it did and that plaintiff cannot complain of the damage incidentally following the exercise of defendant's rights is to approach the question from the rear. Where A by close attention to business, by aggressive business methods and by offering better values takes customers from B and thereby damages B's business, B is not entitled to recover from A for the reason that he had no legal right to have a monopoly of the business in the territory and not for the reason that A had a right to enter the field. If A digs a well on his farm and thereby destroys a well on B's farm by intercepting the source of water, B cannot recover from A because he had no legal right to a continuance of the exclusive use of the source of water and not because A had the right to dig his well. The court should first determine whether plaintiff has a legal right which it is the duty of defendant to respect and then proceed from that point to determine the controversy. We shall therefore approach the consideration of this case from the standpoint of the plaintiffs.

The trial and Appellate Courts having determined the fact that the combination was formed and the acts pursuant thereto were done by the defendants for the purpose of maliciously injuring plaintiffs and that in carrying out this purpose they actually caused direct and immediate injury to each of them, the sole question for this court is whether plaintiffs are, under the law established in this State, entitled to recover. John Carlson has a right, under the law, as between himself and others, to full freedom in disposing of his own labor according to his own will. He had the right to contract with Simon Hill to work for an agreed wage and under agreed conditions. He was under no contractual relations with any of the defendants which limited this right. He had a right to receive for his services one dollar an hour or any other amount to which he and his employer could agree. Oscar Carlson had the right, under the law, to full freedom in investing his capital in the building which he was erecting and in employing any person free to accept employment from him, at a wage and under conditions agreeable to them. He had the right to a free and open market in which to purchase materials with which to complete his building. These rights being clear, anyone who invades them without lawful cause or justification commits a legal wrong, and the wrong being followed by an injury in consequence thereof, plaintiffs have a right of action for such wrong. Damage inflicted by the use of intimidation, obstruction or molestation with malice is without excuse. The law seeks to protect every person against the wrongful acts of others, whether committed alone or by combination, and an action may be had for injuries done which cause another loss in the enjoyment of any right of privilege or property. No persons, individually or by combination, have the right to directly or indirectly interfere with or disturb another in his lawful business or occupation or for the sake of compelling him to do some act which in his own judgment his own interest does not require. Losses willfully caused by another from motives of malice to one who seeks to exercise and enjoy the fruits and advantages of his own enterprise, industry, skill or credit will sustain an action. (*Doremus v. Hennessy,* 176 Ill. 608; *London Guarantee Co. v. Horn,* 206 id. 493; *O'Brien v. People,* 216 id. 354; *Purington v. Hinchliff,* 219 id. 159; *Gibson v. Fidelity and Casualty Co.,* 232 id. 49; *Wilson v. Hey,* 232 id. 389.) In *Kemp v. Division No. 241,* 255 Ill. 213, three separate opinions were filed, and since less than a majority concurred in each opinion the only question judicially determined in that case is that the demurrer to the bill of complaint filed was properly sustained by the circuit court, yet all of the judges agreed to the fundamental proposition of law held in the earlier decisions cited. There is no occasion for going outside this State for authority, because the law applicable to this case has been definitely settled by our own decisions.

The judgments of the Appellate Court are affirmed.

Judgments affirmed.[1]

---

[1] For comment on the case, see 32 Yale Law Jour. 809 (1923). See also: Carpenters' Union v. Citizens' Committee to Enforce Landis Award, 333 Ill. 225, 164 N.E. 393 (1928), commented on in 2 Dak. Law Rev. 454 (1929); 13 Minn. Law Rev. 612 (1929). For the background of the case, see: Report of Ill. Bldg. Investigation Commission to Gov. Small and the Legislature (1923).

EMPIRE THEATRE CO. v. CLOKE.

Montana Supreme Court.   53 Mont. 183, 163 Pac. 107 (1917).

Mr. JUSTICE SANNER delivered the opinion of the court.

The essential facts in this case are as follows: That the plaintiff (appellant here) is a domestic corporation engaged, since November 20, 1914, in conducting a theater and moving-picture show on Montana Street, in the city of Butte, called the Empire Theatre, an enterprise dependent upon patronage of the public for its success; that the defendants consist of the "Musicians Mutual Union, Local No. 241, American Federation of Musicians," with all its members, not specially named, the Silver Bow Trades & Labor Council, with all its members, not specially named, and certain named persons (thirty-nine in number) sued individually and as officers and members of either the Musicians Union or the Trades & Labor Council; that the Musicians Union and the Trades & Labor Council are voluntary, unincorporated associations, the former of the character known as a labor union formed for the purpose of advancing the condition of its members, the latter a sort of central body composed of delegates from the various labor unions of Butte, the purpose of which is to give to them coherence, solidarity and concert of action, with the power and influence which flow therefrom; that the combined membership of the unions affiliated to the Trades & Labor Council is more than 1,000, and such entire membership is affected whenever that body acts, as it is authorized to do, in the ordering, prosecution and furtherance of strikes and boycotts, its activities in that behalf being binding upon all and enforced by means of fines, expulsion and other penalties; that prior to November 17, 1914, the Musicians Union made demand upon the manager of the Empire Theatre that he employ five members of said union, at a wage rate fixed by it, to play at every show or exhibition of pictures given in said theater; that this demand was refused and the union, in order to enforce compliance therewith, declared a boycott against the said theater, and caused to be, from that date until and including November 29, 1914, carried by a man in a conspicuous place on the sidewalk, immediately in front of said theater during the performances therein, a canvas banner about three by four feet in size, on each side of which was printed in large letters the words, "Notice: The Empire Theatre is unfair to organized Labor"; that for the purpose of making its boycott effective, the union solicited and secured the co-operation of the Trades & Labor Council, so that on November 29, said union, said Trades & Labor Council, and their respective members combined to boycott the plaintiff and its business, and thus to prevent it from securing sufficient patronage to successfully carry on the same unless it would yield to said demand; that in furtherance of such combination the said Trades & Labor Council did, on November 29, 1914, order and declare such boycott, and have caused the banner above mentioned to be carried in a conspicuous place, immediately in front of the Empire Theatre and within eight or ten feet of and in front of the entrance thereto every day since the twenty-ninth day of November, 1914, on which a show or exhibition of any kind was produced therein, and have also, on almost every day since November 29, 1914, publicly announced and openly published orally to the public in general in Butte that persons who patronized said theater would be regarded by the labor unions of Butte as unfair to organized labor and have also caused, on every day since November 29, 1914, and until the service of the restraining order herein, one or more men to stand on and walk along the street in front of and near the Empire Theatre to say, and who did say, to persons about to enter said theater and desiring to do so, that the said theater was unfair to organized labor, and to request, and who did request, such persons not to patronize the same; that these things were intended and done by the defendants and understood by the public as a threat that all persons patronizing the said Empire Theatre would be regarded by the defendants as unfair to union labor, would be listed as such, and would be compelled to pay money to the said union as a penalty, or else be themselves boycotted by the respondents; and the respondents propose to continue these acts, save as prevented or restrained by order of court; that the result of these acts has been to prevent many thousands of persons, desiring to patronize said theater, from doing so, to irritate, annoy and vex the plaintiff and its employees, to prevent the profitable conduct of plaintiff's business and almost destroy the same, and to cause the plaintiff great, irreparable and incalculable damage.

Upon these facts, as alleged with much elaboration, the plaintiff sought a decree, perpetually enjoining the defendants and all persons acting for or under them, or any of them, "from further continuing any of the acts" above referred to, "from further boycotting the plaintiff and its business," "from boycotting any person who may hereafter patronize the said Empire Theatre," and "from in any manner interfering with the business of the plaintiff or with any of the employees of the plaintiff in the discharge of their duties"; but the trial court, though finding the facts to be substantially as above stated, held the plaintiff not entitled to any relief, and entered a judgment of dismissal, from which this appeal was taken.

The denial of any relief was expressly based upon the prior decisions of this court in *Lindsay & Co. v. Montana Federation of Labor etc.*, 37 Mont. 264, 127 Am. St. Rep. 722, 18 L.R.A. (N.S.) 707, 96 Pac. 127, and *Iverson v. Dilno,* 44 Mont. 270, 119 Pac. 719, and the plaintiff, contending that the second part of the Lindsay opinion is *obiter,* insists that so much of both decisions as are really effective, as well as the later case of *Peek v. Northern Pacific Ry. Co.,* 51 Mont. 295, L.R.A. 1916B, 835, 152 Pac. 421, command, upon the facts found, a result exactly opposite.

The portion of the Lindsay opinion asserted to be *obiter* holds that injunction does not lie to restrain the publication of a circular denouncing an enterprise as unfair to organized labor, whether such publication emanate from one or from many persons, a conclusion which is assailed as altogether wrong. Considering how that case was presented, we cannot regard the part referred to as *obiter*. * * *

So premising, we come to the result common to both the *Lindsay* and *Dilno Cases,* which is to declare that labor unions are not unlawful in this state; that such unions may publish and pursue a peaceful boycott against any person or enterprise deemed by them to be unfriendly, and that a combination of such unions or their members for such purposes cannot be viewed as a conspiracy. Attention is called to the emphasis laid in the *Dilno Case* upon the want of an allegation that the publication there considered, to-wit, a banner, veiled a threat, whereas the findings here establish that the acts of the defendants did convey, and were intended to convey, a threat; and from this it is deduced that the combination of the defendants became indeed a powerful and far-reaching conspiracy. The force of this depends upon what is meant by the term "threat," or, to put it in another way, upon what is threatened. Generally speaking, what one may do in a certain event, one may give warning of an intention to do in that event; and such a warning is not a threat in the legal sense, whatever may be implied by the term in colloquial usage. (*Payne v. Western etc. Ry. Co.,* 13 Lea (81 Tenn.), 507, 49 Am. Rep. 666, 674; Holmes, J., in *Vegelahn v. Guntner,* 167 Mass. 92, 107, 57 Am. St. Rep. 443, 35 L.R.A. 722, 44 N.E. 1077.) What, then, was the "threat" conveyed by the acts of the defendants according to the findings? In the last analysis it was that all those who patronized the theater in defiance of the boycott would themselves be classed as unfriendly and subjected to boycott in their turn, a warning similar to that conveyed by the Lindsay circular, implicit in the Dilno banner, and necessarily involved in every earnest boycott. We realize that many courts treat this as a threat in the legal sense because of the power of numbers behind it, and have enjoined the execution of it upon the assumption that the person boycotted is, through the intimidation of others, deprived of something to which he has a vested right. As we see it, this position is unwarranted in every particular. There is no intimidation in the legal sense unless there is a threat in the legal sense. Every person has the right, singly and in combination with others, to deal or refuse to deal with whom he chooses; to reach his decision in that, as in all other matters, upon or without good reason; to regard as unfriendly all those who, with or without justification, refuse to co-operate or sympathize. These rights do not depend upon the character, numbers or influence of those who seek to exercise them; nor upon the occasion for their exercise; nor upon the consequences which may follow from their legitimate use. They have been recognized by this court as existing in an incorporated railway benefit society (*Peek v. Northern Pac. Ry. Co., supra*), and it may be said in passing that they likewise belong to merchants' associations, to consumers interested in the cost of living, and, in some measure, to all other persons or groups of persons by whom a boycott may be conceived and practiced. The defendants had these rights, and, having them, could lawfully announce their intention to assert them. The plaintiff, on the other hand, has no vested right

in the patronage of the defendants, or of anyone else who may choose to
withhold it; and, no more than the plaintiff, have the persons who may
choose to patronize it any vested right to such patronage. Such persons
may take such patronage on the' terms imposed, or not, as they see fit,
just as the defendants and their friends may, if they see fit, choose to
regard a rejection of these terms as a rejection of their patronage. In
short, the "threat" conveyed was to do what the defendants lawfully'
could do—a mere warning of their intention, which they could lawfully
give. (Cooke on Combinations, Monopolies and Labor Unions, secs. 77,
et cit.) A combination to do a lawful thing by lawful means is no conspiracy. Counsel for plaintiff point to the occasion for this boycott, and
eloquently denounce the effrontery of labor unions in dictating to those
who are not held to them by any ties as offensive and as dangerous to our
most precious heritage, personal liberty. Offensive such dictation must
certainly be, but not more offensive nor more dangerous, we think, than
when the like is put forward by agencies of quite a different character.
Attempted dictation, more or less disguised, is ever present; but it is not,
in contemplation of the law, an invasion of liberty so long as it amounts
to nothing more than a demand which one party has a legal right to
make, upon the alternative of its displeasure, and the other the legal
right to refuse, braving that displeasure. We see nothing in the *Peek Case*
to interfere with the conclusions announced in the *Lindsay* and *Dilno
Cases,* but much to confirm them, and we are satisfied that these cases
correctly apply the law to present-day conditions. It follows that the judgment must be upheld so far as the boycott and its publication at large are
concerned. * * *[1]

FINK & SON v. BUTCHERS' UNION NO. 422.

New Jersey Court of Chancery. 84 N.J. Eq. 638, 95 Atl. 182 (1915).

On motion for preliminary injunction.

HOWELL, V.C.: The bill in this case is filed to prevent the defendants from maintaining a boycott against the complainant and the wares
and merchandise which it manufactures and deals in. The complainant
is a New Jersey corporation, having its principal office and place of business in Newark. It manufactures and produces provisions of various
kinds, principally meats and sausages, and its customers are widely spread
over that portion of the state which lies adjacent to Newark. It has
about $250,000 invested in the business, and its total sales prior to the

---

[1] Accord: Parkinson v. Building Trades Council, 154 Cal. 581, 98 Pac. 1027
(1908); Pierce v. Stablemen's Union, 156 Cal. 70, 103 Pac. 324 (1909); Gray v.
Building Trades Council, 91 Minn. 171, 97 N.W. 663 (1903); Grant Const. Co. v.
St. Paul Building Trades Council, 136 Minn. 167, 161 N.W. 520 (1917). *Cf.* Meier
v. Speer, 96 Ark. 618, 132 S.W. 988 (1910).

strike of its employes in January last was of the value of about $100,000 a month. The principal stockholders of the company are stockholders of a corporation doing a similar business in the county of Hudson, and up to the early part of January last both the Jersey City factory and the Newark factory were union shops, that is to say, the workmen were all union men and the work was done in accordance with the union rules. Owing to some difficulty between the Hudson county company and its employes, which caused a strike there, the complainant determined that its factory or shop should no longer be conducted as a union shop, but that after the first Monday of January, 1915, it should be conducted as an open shop, that is to say, open to union men and non-union men on equal terms, and as the men left their work at the end of the week they were told to come back on the following Monday to work, at the same wages and under the same conditions as theretofore, but that the shop thereafter would be an open shop. Thereupon nearly all of the men went on a strike, leaving only about twenty-five out of the whole number of seventy-five in the complainant's employ. Shortly after the complainant succeeded in filling the vacancies and has gone on with its business, but the strike, accompanied by a boycott, has continued down to the time of the filing of the bill.

The bill alleges that the defendants, or some of them, have combined together and agreed among themselves and with the officers and delegates of the union, known as local union No. 422 of Newark, New Jersey, and the Essex trades council and its affiliated unions, and with butchers' union local No. 190 of Hudson county, for the purpose of causing all the persons who were purchasing the complainant's products, and dealing with the complainant in the ordinary course of business, to stop making such purchases and to refrain altogether from business dealings with the complainant; that they have agreed and combined together to effectuate this purpose by means of persuasion, intimidation and annoyance, by the use of intimidating, offensive language and threats to boycott the complainant's merchandise and products, by printing and distributing cards, circulars and posters containing threatening and offensive language, by employing or securing persons to go from house to house to call on families of union working men who deal with the complainant's customers, to induce such customers to refrain from dealing with the complainant, by means whereof certain of the persons who were and had been dealing with the complainant and purchasing its goods and merchandise have altogether suspended such dealing, and that others have been obliged to curtail their purchases from the complainant as a result of the unlawful acts of the defendants; that the complainant's business has been greatly damaged, and during the two months next preceding the filing of the bill had fallen off nearly $22,000. Copies of the printed matter used by the defendants in their campaign of persuasion, coercion and intimidation are annexed to the bill. The fact that they have been circulated in the manner set out in the bill is tacitly admitted, or at least is not denied, the denials in relation thereto reaching only to denials that certain named individuals or associations were responsible therefor. The statement that the circulars were not addressed to the public, but were addressed only to members of the union, appear on the face of the exhibits to be untrue. They are a constant appeal to the "consuming public in general" and to business people who purchase or sell meat products. A large number of them contain the statement that the complainant locked out its men, and a sympathetic appeal is addressed to the public generally in their favor on account of having been driven from their work in mid-winter and without warning, a statement which, so far as the papers in this case show, is untrue. The exhibits call upon the public generally to abstain from using the complainant's products, and many instances are shown in which retail dealers who have for years been customers of the complainant have been threatened with ruination of their business; in many cases members of the union and former employes of the complainant have visited the localities of retail dealers who have been in the habit of purchasing goods of the complainant and have there distributed cards and circulars calling upon such retail dealers and the public to refrain from buying complainant's meat, and in some cases men have paraded in front of such retail dealers' places of business for a day at a time with placards suspended from their shoulders advising the public generally not to buy the complainant's products. There was one poster which was quite largely used which was printed in red ink and contained at the top a skull and crossbones in a frame, and under it these words, "A Fink & Son's products are unfair to organized labor," with a union label at the bottom showing that it was printed by a union shop. This is, perhaps, the most distinctive specimen of intimidating matter produced in the case. That it is intimidating and was intended to have that effect is apparent at the slightest glance. Accompanying some of their circulars were lists of retail dealers and others who were regular customers of the complainant, and the appointment of committees was requested to visit these people and induce them to stop patronizing the complainant and to desist from purchasing its goods. In other cases cards, which are called market cards, and which are given by the unions to retail butchers to show that they are in sympathy with organized labor, have been taken from the butchers for the reason that they would not submit to intimidation by the defendants. One of the characteristic cards reads as follows (*Exhibit E*) :

"Notice to the meat buying public. We, the butcher union workmen of the city of Newark are compelled to take the following action against this meat market because our men have been locked out of A. Fink & Sons for over six weeks. O'Connor meat market, 48 Winans avenue, Newark, N. J., conducts a non-union meat market and sells A. Fink & Sons non-union products, which are not under the government inspection, therefore you do not know what you are buying for your money."

Cards of that same sort were printed and distributed, with a mere change of name, against Oscar Leonhardt, O'Connor's meat market, Benedict's meat market and Schlesinger's meat market. Enough has been said to show the general character and nature of the printed matter used

by the defendants in their boycotting campaign against the complainant.
To go further would be superfluous. All these things are universally held
to be unlawful. They constitute together a cause of action based upon a
conspiracy entered into by the defendants for the purpose of ruining the
business of the complainant and its customers, not for the benefit of the
unions or their policies; not because there is in contemplation any sort of
influence on the labor market, but to maliciously interfere with and ruin
the business men and stop their sales in whom and in which they have no
interest whatever, in order to drive the complainant into compliance with
their wishes. I need only cite the cases of *Barr v. Essex Trades Council,*
53 N.J. Eq. 101; *Martin v. McFall,* 65 N.J. Eq. 91; *Jonas Glass Co. v.
Glass Bottle Association,* 72 N.J. Eq. 653; *affirmed,* 77 N.J. Eq. 219;
Quinn v. Leathem (1901), A.C. 495; 7 L.J.P.C. 76; *Bucks Stove and
Range Co. v. Gompers,* 221 U.S. 418. In *Quinn v. Leathem* the decision
makes a distinction which puts actions of the defendants in this class of
cases upon the proper ground. "In *Allen v. Flood* (1898), A.C. 1, 67;
L.J.Q.B. 119, the purpose of the defendant was by the acts complained of
to promote his own trade interests which it was held he was entitled
to do although injurious to his competitors, whereas in the present case,
while it is clear there was combination, the purpose of the defendants was
to injure the plaintiff in his trade as distinguished from the intention of
legitimately advancing their own interests." It is quite clear that in the
case at bar the action of the defendants consisted of a conspiracy or combination to injure not only the complainant but all persons who, as merchants or otherwise, dealt in or puchased the complainant's products. If
it were lawful to go so far as this there is no limit to the mischief to the
public which such combination and confederacy would not reach to. It
would go to the extent of forbidding an absolutely disinterested person
from purchasing or eating meat prepared by the complainant—a most
absurd proposition.

An injunction order should therefore issue restraining the defendants
from instituting or maintaining a boycott against the complainant and
the products of its factories. It appeared at the argument that some of
the defendants were not served with copies of the bill and the order to
show cause. In so far as these persons have not appeared voluntarily
they cannot be held. There are, likewise, some of the individual defendants who have denied all complicity in the unlawful action charged by
the bill. These denials, however, are in a stereotyped form and as such
have very little weight. It is very much the same as if twenty witnesses
should be produced before a court and each one should swear to the same
set of facts in the same words. Suspicion would be at once aroused at
such uniformity of action and a jury could not be criticised if it disregarded the same altogether.

Another defence was set up. In December, 1913, it is alleged,
the complainant made an agreement with Butchers' Union, No. 422, that
it would unionize its shop or factory upon condition that the union would
undertake to advertise the complainant's business and bring in new cus-

tomers; that in pursuance of such agreement the union did so advertise the complainant's business and brought many new customers, whose names are given in the affidavits. This statement, however, is categorically denied by the manager of the complainant's business, who is alleged to have made the agreement, and, further, it was proved that all the persons claimed to have been introduced as new customers of the complainant were, in fact, old customers antedating the proposed agreement. Even if this were not true, the agreement set out in the affidavit of Mr. Fred Meyer is so scrappy and incomplete that no cause of action could be founded on it, nor can it be used for the purpose of exemplifying the maxim, "He who asks equity must do equity."

Upon the settlement of the order I will determine against whom the injunction should issue.[1]

---

[1] Accord: Loewe v. California State Federation of Labor, 139 Fed. 71, 189 Fed. 714 (C.C.N.D. Cal. 1905, 1911); Rocky Mountain Bell Tel. Co. v. Montana Federation of Labor, 156 Fed. 809 (C.C.D. Mont. 1907); Casey v. Cincinnati Typographical Union No. 3, 45 Fed. 135 (C.C.S.D. Ohio 1891); Old Dominion S. S. Co. v. McKenna, 30 Fed. 48 (C.C.S.D. N.Y. 1887); Wilson v. Hey, 232 Ill. 389, 83 N.E. 928 (1908); McCormick v. Local Unions, 216, 32 Ohio C.C. 165 (1911); Moores v. Bricklayers Union, 23 Wkly. Cin. Law Bull. 48, 10 Ohio Dec. Rep. 665 (1889); State v. Glidden, 55 Conn. 46 (1887); Barr v. Essex Trades Council, 53 N.J. Eq. 101, 30 Atl. 881 (1894); Crump v. Commonwealth; 84 Va. 927, 6 S.E. 620 (1888).

See also: Cheyney, "Decisions of the Courts in Conspiracy and Boycott Cases," 4 Pol. Sci. Quar. 261 (1889); Kales, "Coercive and Competitive Methods in Trade and Labor Disputes," 8 Corn. Law. Quar. 1, 128 (1922); Robbins, "Right to Restrain the Right of Free Speech or a Free Press When Necessary to Make Effective the Terms of an Injunction Restraining a Boycott," 68 Cent. Law Jour. 207 (1909).

"But the secondary boycott is generally held illegal because it is an additional boycott placed upon a third party, usually a merchant, who continues to sell the goods of the boycotted employer. As to this third party the boycott is primary, and he can secure an injunction or damages on the ground of conspiracy to injure him without just cause, or to compel him to break a contract, if he considers the damage to himself worth while. But boycott suits are not often brought by third parties, either because the damage to them is usually slight, since they only need to patronize other manufacturers whose goods the boycotters are willing to buy, or because the courts protect them through suits brought by the party originally boycotted. The employer originally boycotted would not secure protection if he depended on a hundred or a thousand boycotted merchants not seriously concerned to bring separate suits. Consequently the vast majority of boycott cases are brought by the person primarily boycotted, in order to prevent the spread of boycotts to other persons who deal with him; in other words, to prevent a secondary boycott against himself. The boycotted employer hides behind the alleged injury done to third parties in order to get damages, not for them, but for himself, as in the case of the Loewe Co. against the hatters' union. The ground of action is not injury to third parties, but interference with the employers' right to have free and uninterrupted business dealings with all who wish to deal with him. This does not seem to be equal treatment of the employers' blacklist which interferes with the unionists' right to have uninterrupted access to all employers, and the employees' boycott which interfers with the employers' right of access to the commodity market.

"The arguments now used to declare the secondary boycott illegal are those formerly used to declare the strike and the primary boycott illegal. Our recommendation simply carries forward another step the effort to secure equality between

IRON MOLDERS' UNION v. ALLIS-CHALMERS CO.

United States Circuit Court of Appeals for the Seventh Circuit. 166 Fed. 45 (1908).

Before GROSSCUP, BAKER, and SEAMAN, C. J.

BAKER, C. J. * * *: We have not found anything in the evidence that justified the decree as to an "illegal boycott." No attempt was made to touch appellee's dealings or relations with customers and users of its goods. *Oxley Stave Co. v. Coopers' International Union* (C.C.) 72 Fed. 695; *Loewe v. Cal. State Federation of Labor* (C.C.) 139 Fed. 71; *Loewe v. Lawlor*, 208 U.S. 274, 28 Sup. Ct. 301, 52 L. Ed. 488. After the strike was on, appellee sent patterns, on which the strikers had been working, to foundries in other cities. The strikers procured the molders in those foundries, who also were members of the Iron Molders' Union of North America, to refuse to make appellee's castings. Those molders notified their employers that they would have to cancel their contracts to make castings for appellee, or they would quit work. Some employers discharged the notifiers, others refused to cancel and the union men struck, and others complied and the union men stayed. In those instances where the foundrymen fulfilled their contracts, appellee was not damaged; in those where foundrymen broke their contracts, there is no proof that appellee has not collected or cannot collect adequate damages. That might be taken as a reason why appellee on this branch of the case is not entitled to the aid of equity. But there is a more important reason. Appellants were aiming to prevent, and appellee to secure, the doing of certain work in which the skill of appellants' trade was necessary. Here was the ground of controversy, and here the test of endurance. If appellee had the right (and we think the right was perfect) to seek the aid of fellow foundrymen to the end that the necessary element of labor should enter into appellee's product, appellant had the reciprocal right of seeking the aid of fellow molders to prevent that end. To whatever extent employers may lawfully combine and co-operate to control the supply and the conditions of work to be done, to the same extent should be recognized the right of workmen to combine and co-operate to control the supply and the conditions of the labor that is necessary to the doing of the work. In the

---

organized capital and organized labor." Final Report of Commission in Industrial Relations 217-218 (1916) (Report of Commissioners Commons and Harriman).

"We dissent from the recommendation that the secondary boycott should be legalized. We regard the secondary boycott as unjust, inequitable, and vicious, in that it subjects third and innocent parties to injury and, at times, to great loss if not ruin." *Id.* 231 (Dissenting report of Commissioners Weinstock, Ballard and Aishton).

"The only valid distinction from the strike cases is that here the struggle often concerns 'neutrals,' involves industrial war to a point one degree removed from the employer-employee relationship. Is then the social interest in keeping the struggle in close limits sufficient to override the social interest in economic progress and the strengthening of the unions?" 34 Harv. Law Rev. 880, 887 (1921).

fullest recognition of the equality and mutuality of their rights and their restrictions lies the peace of capital and labor, for so they, like nations with equally well drilled and equipped armies and navies, will make and keep treaties of peace, in the fear of the cost and consequences of war. * * *[1]

UNITED STATES GYPSUM CO. v. HESLOP.

United States District Court for the Northern District of Iowa.
39 Fed.(2d) 228 (1930).

Scott, D. J.: A suit in equity by United States Gypsum Company, an Illinois corporation, against John Heslop, Fred W. Knigge, John Maddox, William Carlson, Joseph Hayes, E. D. Russell, Gypsum Mill Workers' Union No. 141, and Gypsum Miners' Union No. 158, citizens of Iowa and residents of Ft. Dodge in said state, for an injunction restraining defendants from conspiring together to injure plaintiff's interstate business and to prevent plaintiff from operating its mine and mill at Ft. Dodge, Iowa, on an open shop basis; from publishing and circulating printed and written statements to the effect that plaintiff is or has been declared unfair to organized labor, and that a strike originating in 1921 at plaintiff's mill at Ft. Dodge is still in force; that plaintiff employs convict labor, and employs its labor under "yellow dog" contract; and for a preliminary injunction and temporary restraining order.

Upon issue joined and after hearing, a preliminary injunction issued and remained in force until final hearing. The cause was tried and submitted upon testimony taken in the form of depositions and other testimony taken in open court. From the admitted facts and undisputed testimony it appears:

That United States Gypsum Company, an Illinois corporation, has for many years engaged in manufacturing and selling gypsum products, such as plaster, wall board, building block, and roof tile. That plaintiff has a quarry or mine and mill at Ft. Dodge, Iowa, and also mills located in New York, Oklahoma, Virginia, and other states, from which mills shipments are made to every state in the Union. The products of the Ft. Dodge mine and mill are shipped into twenty-five to thirty states. The products of the company are principally used in the erection and repairing of buildings and structures, and are sold at points in the

---

[1] The concurring opinion of Grosscup, J., is omitted.

The court, in accordance with the above opinion, vacated provisions of the injunction granted below which forbade defendants "From enforcing, maintaining or aiding any illegal boycott against the said company, its agents or employes. (9) From endeavoring to illegally induce people not to deal with said company, its agents and employes. (10) From preventing or attempting to prevent by threats, intimidation, persuasion or in any other maner any person or corporation from performing work for said complainant and from doing business with it."

Contra: York Mfg. Co. v. Oberdick, 10 Pa. Dist. 463 (1901).

various states to dealers, who in turn sell to contractors and builders. The plaintiff's products all contain, either on the product itself or the container thereof, the name of the company in addition to the trade-mark of the particular product. Such name and trade-mark remains on the product or container until used in construction and easily identifies the same. Approximately 90 per cent. of the products sold by plaintiff are erected or used by union labor.

Plaintiff's mine and mill at Ft. Dodge, Iowa, for a period prior to 1921 were operated upon the so-called closed shop or union basis. At Ft. Dodge, there were two labor unions existing and concerned prior to 1921, *viz.*, Gypsum Mill Workers' Union No. 141, and Gypsum Miners' Union No. 142, and during the period of the World War wages increased very greatly. The contracts with the unions expired on June 30, 1921. In March, 1921 plaintiff suggested to the two unions a continuance of the contract for a period of eighteen months at a materially reduced wage scale. Neither party has made the record very clear as to the negotiations between March and June, but it is quite evident that the men were opposed to any reduction in wages, and no agreement was arrived at. A few days before June 30, 1921, the company announced by published and posted notices a new wage scale, and that the company would operate on an open shop basis after June 30th. On July 1, 1921, the members of the two unions declared and put into effect a strike which continued for a number of weeks. By September, however, approximately from 90 to 95 per cent of the striking workmen had returned to work on the adjusted scale of wages and under the open shop plan or basis. The plaintiff's mine and mill continued to operate on the open shop basis over the succeeding eight years and until the time of the trial, and presumably are still so operating. Since September, 1921, there has been no controversy between the plaintiff and its workmen, either over wages or conditions of employment. There are four other gypsum concerns at Ft. Dodge, owning and operating mines and mills and engaged in interstate commerce in competition with the plaintiff. All of these other mills and mines are, and since 1921 have been, operated on an open shop plan or basis, commonly called the American plan.

During the summer of 1925, Gypsum Mill Workers' Union No. 141 surrendered its charter, and Gypsum Miners' Union No. 142 has also ceased to exist.

Defendant John Heslop, at the time of the strike in 1921, was an employee of plaintiff, engaged as repair man in the mill, but was not a regular millwright. Heslop did not return to work, and has not since 1921 been employed by plaintiff or any other gypsum industry. None of the other defendants have been employed by plaintiff or any other gypsum concern since 1921, with the exception of defendant Maddox, who was an employee of plaintiff for some time during the year 1926, but who ceased to be employed during that year. None of the defendants have since 1921 sought employment from plaintiff, and defendant Heslop testifies that he would not accept employment under the open shop plan, but that he would seek employment under the closed shop plan. The defendant Russell is a practicing physician and never has been employed by the plaintiff or any other gypsum concern, and his connection with the case grows out of his intimacy with defendant Heslop.

During the months of May and June, 1926, defendant Heslop and a few others organized and procured a charter to Gypsum Miners' and Mill Workers' Union No. 158. All of these unions exist under charters from the International Union of Mine, Mill and Smelter Workers affiliated with the American Federation of Labor. Union No. 158, organized by Heslop and others in June, 1926, seems to have been used exclusively for propaganda purposes. No member of the union is in the employ of the plaintiff nor of any other gypsum company at Ft. Dodge, so far as appears from the record, and its membership is confined to a few individuals, none of which are in any way engaged in the gypsum industry.

The individual defendants, with the exception of Dr. Russell, beginning with the month of September, 1923, at intervals up to and including 1928, have published and distributed a series of circulars addressed "To All Central Trades Councils, Building Trades Councils, and State Federations of Labor," charging in substance that plaintiff is unfair to organized labor and asking that the contents of the circulars be published. The exact wording of the various circulars varied. The circulars of September 5, 1923, charged that the plaintiff and four other gypsum companies located at Ft. Dodge who manufactured "Universal Hair Fibered Plaster, Plymouth Cement Plaster Fibered, Plymouth Cement Plaster, unfibered, Plymouth Wood Fiber Plaster, Plymouth Stucco, Plymouth Molding Plaster, Plymouth Wood Fiber No. 20, Acolite Wood Fiber Plaster, Reground Stucco, Acolite Cement Plaster, Iowana Cement Plaster fibered, Plymouth Cement Plaster Double Fibered, are unfair to Organized Labor." That these companies started an open shop fight on July 1, 1921, and that they are running nonunion mills, and asked co-operation in advertising the fact that these corporations are unfair and that the strike is indorsed by the Ft. Dodge Trades and Labor Assembly. At the foot of this circular is printed, "Fort Dodge Trades and Labor Assembly," and with the seal thereof. This circular may be said to have had the approval of the Ft. Dodge Trades and Labor Assembly. The testimony shows, however, that no other circular had the approval of that body. At the head of this circular, as at the head of all others, except the last, in large type were the words, "Watch These Materials." The last circular of May, 1928, had the words, "Continue to Watch These Materials." The circular of June 16, 1924, addressed as before, named only the United States Gypsum Company, plaintiff, recited the various products manufactured by that company, that on July 1, 1921, it started a fight for open shop, that it is unfair to organized labor, and that "the strike of the Gypsum Mill Workers' Union and the International Union of Mine, Mill and Smelter Workers is indorsed by the Fort Dodge Trades and Labor Assembly," and asks publications favorable to organized labor to publish the circular. This circular is signed, John Heslop, President Mill Workers, and bears the seal of Gypsum Mill Workers' Union No. 141. Another circular substantially identical was published and sent out under date of November 16, 1924. Another circular substantially identical, but in addition bearing an alleged copy of a contract headed, "Open Shop or American Plan," and referred to in the record as the "yellow dog" contract. Under date of November 25, 1925, another circular was sent in somewhat different language, and as follows:

"The United States Gypsum Co., manufacturing the following gypsum products, Plasterboard, prybar building blocks, domes, rooftile, wood fibre plaster, hair plaster, sand finish and other gypsum products and they are unfair to organized labor. On July 1, 1921, they started a fight for an open shop against the Millworkers Union No. 141 of Fort Dodge, Iowa, and the battle is still on and will so remain until we get a closed shop contract and an eight-hour day. All reasonable means have failed to bring about a settlement, therefore we ask your co-operation in advertising the fact that this corporation is unfair to organized labor. Inasmuch as there have been traitors, who gave out fake circulars, I ask you Brothers to read the 'Yellow Dog' contract as printed below and then use your own judgment as to whether or not the United States Gypsum Co. is unfair to organized labor. And we most earnestly ask your undivided moral support to bring about a closed shop contract and an eight-hour day.

"John Heslop, President,
"Millworkers Union."

In January, 1928, another circular was sent addressed as before, signed "John Heslop, President, Fred W. Knigge, Secretary-Treasurer," bearing the seal of Gypsum Mill Workers, Union No. 141, describing the plaintiff's products, and again referring to the "fight" of July 1, 1921, and stating "the strike is still in effect," and asking co-operation "in advertising the United States Gypsum Company as unfair to organized labor." Under date of May 25, 1928, another circular was sent, somewhat varied in language, but charging that plaintiff still continued the open shop and is working on the principle of the Yellow Dog contract "printed below," and stating: "We have had good results from the former circulars sent out and we again ask your co-operation and moral support in advertising the fact that the United States Gypsum Company is still unfair to organized labor." This circular was signed, "John Heslop, President, Fred Knigge, Secretary, Gypsum Mill Workers Union." Defendant, Heslop testified that as many as eight or nine hundred and twelve hundred copies of each of the circulars had been distributed to organized labor throughout the country, by sending to labor organization officials and to papers and periodicals. He further testified that the purpose was to bring pressure upon the plaintiff through the dealers to whom plaintiff sold; that his hope was that the dealer when approached by local union officials or leaders would cease to patronize plaintiff or handle its materials. The circulars were sent out with the knowledge of all members of the present Union No. 158. In the spring of 1929, Heslop approached the managers of plaintiff at Ft. Dodge and opened a discussion of the subject of unionizing its mine and mill. His suggestion was declined, and he then advised them that his union would have to continue sending the circulars, and a short time thereafter this suit was brought.

It is quite apparent from the testimony and documentary evidence in the case that the purpose of the defendants was to bring such pressure on the plaintiff as would compel plaintiff to abandon the open shop plan and return to a closed shop policy. That the method adopted was to communicate with union officials throughout the country, and particularly wherever the plaintiff sold its products in the course of interstate commerce, and induce such union officials to watch the plaintiff's materials and intimidate the dealers handling them, and thus cause the dealers to cease handling the plaintiff's materials, and to cause union men to refrain from working on the materials. The testimony further shows that in quite a number of states the defendants' effort had the desired effect; that union officials approached dealers and brought to the attention of the dealers the contents of the circulars in such way as to cause the dealers to cease to purchase plaintiff's product. It would serve no purpose to recapitulate the testimony of the various witnesses who testified from the various parts of the country. Suffice it to say, the testimony shows without conflict that plaintiff's interstate sales were diminished by reason of the activities of the defendants in a material amount, and the volume of circulars being sent to so large a number of local unions and labor papers and periodicals as would doubtless result in material restriction of plaintiff's interstate sales, and would hamper and place a burden upon plaintiff's interstate commerce. Without doubt the defendants' plan and activities embrace all of the principles of the secondary boycott.

Respecting the Dr. Russell letter, I do not find that it has any very material effect upon the case. The letter was, of course, aggravating and largely false. It was written by Dr. Russell, a personal friend of the defendant Heslop, in apparent collaboration with Heslop. Dr. Russell first wrote the letter in longhand and delivered it to Heslop. Heslop had it rewritten in typewriting as I recall with some changes, and the typewritten copies were submitted to Dr. Russell. He approved them and signed ten copies. Heslop distributed a number of these copies, but not generally to the trade. He did, however, send some to periodicals, but the plan of their general circulation was not adopted, and if so was abandoned. Dr. Russell appears to have been a mere tool of Heslop and has in all probability passed out of the scene.

The questions presented for determination on the record are:

1. Did the individual defendants as such and through their organizations, Gypsum Mill Workers' Union No. 141, and Gypsum Miners' Union No. 158, combine to restrain plaintiff's interstate trade under a plan involving the principles of the secondary boycott?

2. Did the execution of said plan result in a material direct restraint of trade?

3. Are the defendants immune under section 20 of the Clayton Act?

Respecting the first and second questions, I think there is no room for controversy. The individual defendants were none of them employees of the plaintiff or any other gypsum concern. So far as the record shows the functions and activities of Gypsum Miners' Union No. 158 have been confined to the sending out of these circulars. Gypsum Mill Workers' Union No. 141, if it has any life or existence, only has been such because the individual defendants, exclusive of Russell, have used its name in connection with these circulars. The plan, as stated, was to bring pressure upon the plaintiff to compel it to abandon its open shop policy, and to unionize its mine and mill against its will. The pressure was to be brought by publishing these circulars far and wide, bringing them to the attention of local union labor leaders with the expectation that those organizations and individuals would bring them to the attention of the dealers, customers of the plaintiff, and of the workmen on jobs that used plaintiff's material, and thus intimidate dealers and induce them to refrain from using plaintiff's materials. "Watch These Materials," "Continue to Watch These Materials," were the slogans that were to be proclaimed, and in addition the declaration that the plaintiff was unfair to union labor. One would certainly be blind not to be able to perceive the intent, purpose, and natural effect of such plan if put in execution. I therefore find that the individual defendants, exclusive of Russell, individually and through the organizations named, did combine to restrain plaintiff's interstate trade and commerce by a plan involving the principles of the secondary boycott. I further find that while the restraint and actual damage has probably not been great in volume compared with the total output of plaintiff's mines and mills, yet the plan once under way, considering the great number of labor organizations and labor papers and periodicals in the country to whom such circulars were and were to be sent, a very material restraint of trade would likely be effected, to the plaintiff's irreparable damage.

Were the defendants immune under section 20 of the Clayton Act (29 U.S.C.A. § 52)? None of the defendants were employees, as stated, nor were they seeking employment, nor had they been recently employees. Eight years had elapsed since any but one of them had been employed, and several years had elapsed since he had left its employ. I think section 20 of the Clayton Act has no application in such circumstances. Examination of the following cited decisions of the Supreme Court of the United States, covering a period of approximately twenty years, will disclose the principles applicable to such cases, with any growth or mutations thereof settled during the period stated: *Loewe v. Lawlor*, 208 U.S. 274, 28 S. Ct. 301, 52 L. Ed. 488, 13 Ann. Cas. 815; *Gompers v. Bucks Stove & Range Co.*, 221 U.S. 418, 31 S. Ct. 492, 55 L. Ed. 797, 34 L.R.A. (N.S.) 874; *Eastern States Lumber Ass'n v. United States*, 234 U.S. 600, 34 S. Ct. 951, 58 L. Ed. 1490, L.R.A. 1915A, 788; *Lawlor v. Loewe*, 235 U.S. 522, 35 S. Ct. 170, 59 L. Ed. 341; *Duplex, etc., Co. v. Deering*, 254 U.S. 443, 41 S. Ct. 172, 65 L. Ed. 349, 16 A.L.R. 196; *American Steel Foundries v. Tri-City Council*, 257 U.S. 184, 42 S. Ct. 72, 66 L. Ed. 189, 27

A.L.R. 360; *Truax v. Corrigan*, 257 U.S. 312, 42 S. Ct. 124, 66 L. Ed. 254, 27 A.L.R. 375; *Bedford Cut Stone Co. v. Journeymen Stone Cutters' Ass'n*, 274 U.S. 37, 47 S. Ct. 522, 71 L. Ed. 916, 54 A.L.R. 791.

Finally, I am of opinion that the interlocutory injunction heretofore decreed should be made permanent with such modifications as will make the same conform to this opinion. I think the form of final decree approved by the Supreme Court of the United States in *Bedford Cut Stone Co. et al. v. Journeymen Stone Cutters' Association of North America et al., supra, mutatis mutandis,* sufficient and proper in this case. Counsel for plaintiff will prepare the final decree in conformity with this opinion, and submit the same for approval within ten days.[1]

BOSSERT v. DHUY.

New York Court of Appeals. 221 N.Y. 342, 117 N.E. 582 (1917).

CHASE, J. The plaintiffs are copartners engaged in the borough of Brooklyn, city of New York, in the manufacture, purchase and sale of doors, sash, blinds, trim, lumber and other kinds of woodwork. They employ from five to six hundred persons in their factories in the production of such woodwork, but do not perform any work in the installation of the woodwork so manufactured by them. All of such woodwork is sold to builders. The defendants are officers, representatives and agents of the United Brotherhood of Carpenters and Joiners of America and of its branches in the city of New York and vicinity. The United Brotherhood of Carpenters and Joiners of America, hereinafter called the Brotherhood, is a voluntary unincorporated association of workmen. It has a membership of about 200,000 journeymen carpenters with headquarters at Indianapolis, Indiana, subdivided into about 1,900 local branches, also voluntary unincorporated associations, over seventy of which local associations are within the limits of the city of New York.

All manufacturers of woodwork who do not operate under an agreement with said Brotherhood or one of its branches and do not agree to employ union carpenters exclusively, are known by the defendants as non-union, unfair or open shop manufacturers and their products are known as non-union, unfair or open shop materials.

----

[1] Accord: Irving v. Joint District Council, 180 Fed. 896 (S.D.N.Y. 1910); Irving v. Neal, 209 Fed. 471 (S.D. N.Y. 1913); Anderson & Lind Mfg. Co. v. Carpenters' Council, 308 Ill. 488, 139 N.E. 887 (1923); A. T. Stearns Lumber Co. v. Howlett, 260 Mass. 45, 157 N.E. 82 (1927), 260 Mass. 45, 163 N.E. 193 (1928); Lohse Patent Door Co. v. Fuelle, 215 Mo. 421, 114 S.W. 997 (1908); Loizeaux Lumber Co. v. Carpenters and Joiners Local of Roselle, 5 Law & Labor 250 (N.J. Ch. 1923); Pacific Typesetting Co. v. Internat'l Typographical Union, 125 Wash. 273, 216 Pac. 358 (1923).

See: Wolman, The Boycott in American Trade Unions, c. 3 (1916).

The plaintiffs operate an open shop, selecting their employees without discrimination against any person on the ground that he is or is not a member of the local union, and pursue this policy as a matter of principle and not for mercenary reasons, and for many years the relations between the plaintiffs and their employees were mutually satisfactory. The Brotherhood issues a monthly paper, its official organ, called *The Carpenter* and holds biennial conventions attended by delegates elected from the local unions. Since 1904 the Brotherhood has been engaged in a general combination among other things to prevent the employment of non-union carpenters or woodworkers in woodworking factories, or in erecting certain kinds of woodwork and has adopted rules which forbid its members from working for any employer who employs any so-called non-union carpenters, and from working on or in connection with any building where materials are used which are purchased from any employer who employs non-union carpenters, and the constitution of the Brotherhood provides that it shall be the duty of local unions to prevent its members encouraging the use of any unfair material by handling the same.

From time to time the Brotherhood in connection with the joint district council of the carpenters' union have circulated a letter which in part is as follows:

"*To Owners, Architects, Contractors, and Builders of New York City and Vicinity:*

"GENTLEMEN.—In order to avoid any labor trouble on jobs you are interested in we deem it necessary to request you to stipulate in all your contracts a clause guaranteeing the employment of recognized union men, also a clause requiring in the execution of all contracts for carpenter work the employment of union made trim, mantels, parquet flooring, and other shop made carpenter work. This applies particularly to all classes of kalamein and metal covered work.

"We desire to inform you that unless this material has been constructed under strict union conditions we shall refuse to handle it. It being a well known fact that the agents of unfair and non-union firms resort to mis-statements in order to obtain contracts in this city we recommend that before placing contracts with any firm not on this list you communicate with this organization regarding the union standing of said firm.

"Stipulating in your contract that your trim, etc., must bear this union label (here appears a cut of label) will avoid all complications."

The rules of the Brotherhood provide in substance that if any member is proven guilty of working with non-union carpenters or on material made in a shop where non-union carpenters are employed, he shall be subject to fine or expulsion from the association.

The defendants having attempted to enforce the rules of the Brotherhood against its members handling non-union made woodwork, this action was brought by the plaintiffs to obtain an injunction against the defendants taking (in substance) any action affecting the plaintiffs and the building material made in their mills. * * *

It is unnecessary in the case now under consideration to hold that in all cases and under all circumstances, whatever a man may do alone he may do in combination with others, but it was clearly established in the *National Protective Association* case that workingmen may organize for purposes deemed beneficial to themselves and in that organized capacity may determine that their members shall not work with non-members or upon specified work or kinds of work.

It was not illegal, therefore, for the defendants to refuse to allow members of the Brotherhood to work in the plaintiffs' mill with non-union men. The same reasoning results in holding that the Brotherhood may by voluntary act refuse to allow its members to work in the erection of materials furnished by a non-union shop. Such action has relation to work to be performed by its members and directly affects them. The voluntary adoption of a rule not to work upon non-union made material and its enforcement differs only in degree from such voluntary rule and its enforcement in a particular case. Such a determination also differs entirely from a general boycott of a particular dealer or manufacturer with a malicious intent and purpose to destroy the good will or business of such dealer or manufacturer. An act, when done maliciously and for an illegal purpose, may be restrained; and held to be within the bounds of reasonable business competition when done in good faith and for a legal purpose. (See Ruling Case Law, vol. 16, pp. 431, 432 and 433.)

It appears by findings that are uncontrovertibly established by reason of the unanimous affirmance of the Special Term by the Appellate Division that it was not the intent and purpose of the defendants in this case to injure the good will or business of the plaintiffs as individuals or of non-union manufacturers generally. In refusing to work on non-union made material, they were conserving their interests as individuals and as members of the Brotherhood, and in so doing necessarily interfered to some extent with non-union manufacturers. Such interference necessarily resulted to some extent also in the *National Protective Association* case, and such fact did not prevent the court sustaining the action of the defendants therein. The importance of the facts in each case involving individual or associate action affecting the relations of employers and employees is such that even although it materially increases the length of this opinion, we quote some of the important findings mentioned:

"1. The United Brotherhood of Carpenters and Joiners of America is a voluntary association and trade union of carpenters whose members consist of so-called 'outside carpenters' who work on buildings, and 'inside carpenters' who work in mills.

"7. That the members have adopted rules *antedating any strikes* against plaintiff's material, by which outside members are not to work on mill products not made in mills manned by their inside members.

"8. That said rules were not adopted with the plaintiff in view, but were intended to apply generally to the products of all non-union mills.

"10. The non-union mills, including that of the plaintiff, *compete in their products with the mills manned by the members of said United Brotherhood.*

"11. That the said United Brotherhood has established a union or minimum rate of wages, and fixed certain hours per day for its members to work, but said union rate of wages does not prevent employers from paying a higher rate of wages to any or all members whom they employ.

"14. The more mills that are unionized the more chance have the outside and inside carpenters of said United Brotherhood to obtain work at union wages and under union conditions.

"17. That it conduces to the betterment of the condition of the members of said United Brotherhood not to install the mill products of plaintiff in buildings.

"18. That the defendants believe it would be to their advantage not to handle the mill products of the plaintiff, and in the matters complained of have been actuated by that belief and motive.

"19. That it would tend to increase the sale of union mill products made by the inside carpenters, members of the United Brotherhood and so secure them in work and increase the chances of outside members to obtain work in union mills, for the outside members to refuse to handle the non-union mill products of the plaintiff.

"21. That none of the members of said United Brotherhood who refuse to install any of the mill products of plaintiff were under contract to give their services for any particular period.

"24. There was no violence, nor any threat of violence, on the part of the defendants in connection with any of the acts complained of.

"25. That no threat, coercion or intimidation was used by any of these defendants to induce the union carpenters to quit work where strikes against plaintiff's material occurred, except the enforcement of the by-laws.

"26. That none of the defendants interfered in any way to prevent the different employers herein whose jobs were struck from procuring non-union carpenters to continue their work.

"29. That the members of the United Brotherhood quit work on all the jobs complained of because of their said rules to work only on union material made by their own members, and of *their own volition.*

"30. That in all matters complained of herein the defendants acted without malice towards plaintiff.

"32. The primary motive and purpose the defendants had in view in all the matters complained of regardless of whether their acts would be in furtherance of such motive and purpose—or not—were to benefit their fellow-members in said brotherhood by procuring them work and helping the sale of the union-made mill products of their fellow-members in mills.

"35. The defendants have refused to install the mill products of other non-union mills than that of the plaintiff.

"43. That to compel the members of said United Brotherhood to work on the mill products of the plaintiff limits the sale of the union mill products made by its members, and, to that extent tends to throw them out of work.

"44. That generally the union rate- of wages is higher and the hours of work shorter per day than in non-union mills.

"46. That the union rate of wages and hours tends to a higher and better standard of living than the non-union rates and hours.

"49. That the hours of labor in plaintiff's mill are more than eight hours per day."

The trial court also found "That said Brotherhood has adopted and sought to enforce and in many instances has enforced rules which forbid and prevent its members from working for any employer who employs any so called non-union carpenters and from working on or in connection with any building where materials are used which are purchased from any employer who employs any non-union carpenters."

In considering this finding of the court we must keep in mind the fact that the action of the Brotherhood did not interfere with any contract between employer and employee. Its action was open and clearly defined and its enforcement was not designed to and did not include any force, fraud, threat or defamation. Its action was voluntary and concerned labor competition in which the association and its members are vitally interested.

The voluntary adoption by an association of employees of reasonable rules relating to persons for whom and conditions under which its members shall work is not illegal at common law. (*National Protective Association v. Cumming, supra; Macauley Brothers v. Tierney,* 19 R.I. 255; *Bohn Manufacturing Co. v. Hollis,* 54 Minn. 223; *J. F. Parkinson Co. v. Building Trades Council,* 154 Cal. 581; Martin Modern Law of Labor Unions, 109; *Gill Engraving Co. v. Doerr,* 214 Fed. Rep. 111; *State v. Van Pelt,* 136 N.C. 663; Ruling Case Law, vol. 16, 450.)

Neither is the enforcement of such rules by the association through fines or by expulsion from the association illegal. Members are thus simply required to obey rules of the association so long as they remain members thereof. (*Bohn Manufacturing Co. v. Hollis, supra.*)

An association of individuals may determine that its members shall not work for specified employers of labor. The question ever is as to its purpose in reaching such determination. If the determination is reached in good faith for the purpose of bettering the condition of its members and not through malice or otherwise to injure an employer the fact that such action may result in incidental injury to the employer does not constitute a justification for issuing an injunction against enforcing such action.

Workingmen cannot be compelled to work when by so doing their position as workingmen will be injured, simply because if they do not continue their work a manufacturing employer will not be able to sell as large a quantity of-material as he otherwise would and thus his good will, trade or business may be affected. (See extended discussion in Harvard Law Review, vol. 20, pp. 253, 345, 429.) "The United States Supreme Court has recently had before it the case of *Paine Lumber Company v. Neal*, 244 U.S. 459, 471 (advanced sheets, August 1, 1917) which was an action to enjoin the United Brotherhood of Carpenters and Joiners of America from conspiring to have its members refuse to work upon material made by the plaintiffs in that action because not made by union labor, and also to enjoin them from enforcing bylaws intended to prevent its members from working upon what is called unfair material. The injunction was denied. Justice HOLMES speaking for the court in affirming the judgment appealed from, and referring to the merits of the controversy, said, 'As this Court is not the final authority concerning the laws of New York we say but a word about them. We shall not believe that the ordinary action of a labor union can be made the ground of an injunction under those laws until we are so instructed by the New York Court of Appeals. *National Protective Association of Steam Fitters & Helpers v. Cumming*, 170 N.Y. 315. Certainly the conduct complained of has no tendency to produce a monopoly of manufacture or building since the more successful it is the more competitors are introduced into the trade. Cases like *Kellogg v. Sowerby*, 190 N.Y. 370, concerning conspiracies between railroads and elevator companies to prevent competition, seem to us very clearly not to have been intended to over-rule the authority that we cite, and not to have any bearing on the present point."

The facts in the *Paine Lumber Company Case* were substantially the same as the facts in the case now before us, and we understand the Supreme Court of the United States to assert in substance and effect that an ordinary common law action should not, even considered with the statutes now in force, be sustained in this state upon the facts shown in that case, or in the case now before us. * * *

Notwithstanding the quoted and other conclusions of law found by the court in this case which would seem to preclude a judgment in favor of the plaintiffs the court found as follows:

"That the combination of the defendants to prevent the sale, use and installation of the plaintiff's wood materials by causing all union carpenters to refuse to handle said materials or work upon any building where said materials were being used, is illegal.

"That the combination of the defendants, as set forth in the findings of fact, constitutes an illegal conspiracy.

"That the combination of the defendants, as set forth in the findings of fact, and the acts in furtherance thereof, constitutes an illegal conspiracy to injure the plaintiff contrary to common law."

By reading the opinion of the court at the Special Term, adopted at the Appellate Division (166 App. Div. 251, 256), with the findings and conclusions of law, it appears that it was the intention of the court to hold that the facts found would not justify a judgment in favor of the plaintiffs except so far as the defendants discriminated against the plaintiffs' mill and refused to handle the plaintiffs' material while at the same time continuing to handle material from other non-union mills. * * *

We do not think that the conclusion of the court is sustained by the findings of fact in the case. A judgment was, however, entered, the affirmative provisions of which are quoted herewith, preceding the opinion. The first paragraph thereof adjudges that the defendants shall not send to any customer or prospective customer of the plaintiffs any letter, circular or communication, printed, written or oral, which in terms or by inference suggests that labor troubles will follow the use of materials purchased from plaintiffs or from any person, firm or corporation declared unfair or whose material does not bear the union label. Upon all the findings before us it is clear that the "labor troubles" therein referred to, simply mean that if non-union made materials are used the members of the Brotherhood will refuse to install the same.

The second paragraph thereof adjudges that the defendants shall not direct, require or compel any person by by-law, rule or regulation or any act thereunder to cease working for another because they use material purchased from non-union shops. And the third paragraph thereof enjoins the defendants from inducing any workmen in their trades to quit work on any building because non-union carpenters are there employed to install material which comes from non-union shops. All of the acts enjoined are under the findings of fact in this case lawful acts done for lawful purposes.

We think that the rules laid down by this court in the *National Protective Association* case require a reversal of the judgment in favor of the plaintiffs upon the findings before us. When it is determined that a labor organization can control the body of its members for the purpose of securing to them higher wages, shorter hours of labor and better relations with their employers, and as a part of such control may refuse to allow its members to work under conditions unfavorable to it, or with workingmen not in accord with the sentiments of the labor union, the right to refuse to allow them to install non-union made material follows as a matter of course, subject to there being no malice, fraud, violence, coercion, intimidation or defamation in carrying out their resolutions and orders.

Voluntary orders by a labor organization for the benefit of its members and the enforcement thereof within the organization is not coercion. The members of the organization as we have already stated who are not willing to obey the orders of the organization are at liberty to withdraw therefrom. The bounds beyond which an association of employees may not as a general rule go in controlling its members in their dealings with employers are not easily determined. They cannot at least extend beyond a point where its or their direct interests cease. There is a material difference in the power of an association so far as it affects its primary or secondary interest. Where the acts of an employee or employees in their individual or associate capacity are reasonably and directly calculated to advance lawful objects, they should not be restrained by injunction.

A strike or boycott may be legal or illegal according to the acts involved therein (*Gray v. Building Trades Council,* 91 Minn. 171; *State v.*

Van Pelt, supra; Gill Engraving Co. v. Doerr, 214 Fed. Rep. 111; *Mills v. U. S. Printing Co.,* 99 App. Div. 605; aff'd 199 N.Y. 76. See, also, opinion of ANDREWS, J., in *Seubert, Inc., v. Reiff,* 98 Misc. Rep. 402), so an action for a direct and primary purpose in the interest of individuals or a combination of individuals taken in good faith to advance the interest of the individuals or combination may be lawful, while a remote and secondary action which carries with it a degree of malice as a matter of law is illegal. In the case now before us if the defendants had called upon the public generally to discontinue using the plaintiffs' material and had sought to prevent all persons by communications, written or otherwise, from dealing with the plaintiffs, their acts would have been illegal.

It does not appear from the record that the defendants in any way interfered with the trade or business of the plaintiffs, except that the members of the Brotherhood were by their voluntary action required to decline using material made in non-union shops and announcement was made of such intention that the same might be known by contractors in advance of the contracts to be entered into in connection with the erection of the work. Such action of the defendants did not extend beyond such refusal to install non-union made material and so far as it amounted to either a strike or a boycott, it directly affected the Brotherhood and its members.

An examination of the many cases called to our attention by the plaintiffs will show that in most instances the acts criticized and condemned were not directly connected with the purpose sought to be conserved by the defendants therein. A few of such cases are as follows: *Loewe v. Lawlor* (208 U.S. 274); *Bailey v. Ass'n of Master Plumbers* (103 Tenn. 99; S.C., 52 S.W. Rep. 853); *Rocky Mountain Bell Telephone Co. v. Montana Fed. of Labor* (156 Fed. Rep. 809); *Barnes v. Chic. Typ. Union* (232 Ill. 424); *Iron Moulders Union v. Allis-Chalmers Co.* (166 Fed. Rep. 45.)

The judgment of the Appellate Division should be reversed and the complaint dismissed, with costs in all courts.

COLLIN, HOGAN, CARDOZO, POUND and ANDREWS, JJ., concur; CRANE, J., takes no part.

Judgment reversed, etc.[1]

---

[1] For comment on the case, see: 31 Harv. Law Rev. 482 (1918); 27 Yale Law Jour. 539 (1918). See also: 52 A.L.R. 1144 (1928).

Accord: Reardon, Inc. v. Caton, 189 App. Div. 501, 178 N.Y.S. 713 (1919); Reardon v. Internat'l Merchant Marine Co., 189 App. Div. 515, 178 N.Y.S. 722 (1919). Cf. Burgess Bros. Co. v. Stewart, 114 Misc. 673, 187 N.Y.S. 873 (1921); Willson & Adams Co. v. Pearce, 135 Misc. 426, 237 N.Y.S. 60 (1929); State v. Van Pelt, 136 N.C. 633 (1904). See also: 20 Col. Law Rev. 882 (1920); 30 Yale Law Jour. 280 (1921).

AUBURN DRAYING CO. v. WARDELL.

New York Court of Appeals. 227 N.Y. 1, 124 N.E. 97 (1919).

COLLIN, J.: This is a contest between the plaintiff and the labor unions of the city of Auburn, New York. There is no serious dispute concerning the material facts. In so far as there is a dispute, we have concluded that the findings of the Special Term are supported by the evidence. While there was not unanimity in the decision of the Appellate Division the divergence related to legal conclusions or the applicability of legal principles.

The action was commenced November 29, 1913. The plaintiff, a corporation, was extensively and prosperously engaged in the general trucking business in the city of Auburn, New York. It employed from thirty to forty-five men, the greater number of whom were not members of a labor union. There existed in Auburn, as voluntary unincorporated labor organizations, twenty-two local labor unions, representing the various trades and occupations, with an aggregate membership of about fourteen hundred persons. There existed also the Central Labor Union, an unincorporated association, made up of degelates from the individual unions, and the members of the local unions were members of it and bound by its constitution, rules, regulations and by-laws. It and certain of the local unions are, through representation by officers, defendants in the action. (Code of Civil Procedure, sections 1919-1924.) Expressed objects of the Central Labor Union were to secure united action in defense of the rights and for the protection of the interests of the working classes and to arbitrate and adjust difficulties that might arise between workmen and their employers. Objects of the local unions were increased wages, greater efficiency, employment, and the improvement of working and social conditions through united action.

The defendant Teamsters' Union No. 679 was organized November 9, 1912. The plaintiff neither forbade nor encouraged its employees to join. In July, 1913, representatives of the unions stated to the plaintiff that unless it took the necessary means to get its men to join the union, Teamsters' Union No. 679, it would be placed on the unfair list. The plaintiff refused to so act and Teamsters' Union No. 679 passed a resolution placing the plaintiff on the unfair list, that is, listed it as an employer who refused to employ and discriminated against union labor and refused to give its employees the conditions asked for by labor organizations with respect to hours of labor, shop conditions and other similar working conditions. Union No. 679 reported, in accordance with a standing resolution of the Central Labor Union, the placing of the plaintiff on the unfair list. The Central Union insisted to the plaintiff that all its employees must join the union and the plaintiff replied they were free to join if they so chose. They refused to join. The Central Labor Union indorsed the placing of the plaintiff upon the unfair list, thus making, under its rules, the action final and operative. The declaration of principles of the Central Labor

Union provided, among other things, as follows: "We shall withdraw and use our influence to have others withdraw all patronage from any unfair employer, or any person patronizing such unfair employer, let his calling be what it may." The by-laws and regulations of the unions provided penalties of fines and expulsion for non-conformity. The Central Union and other local unions took the position that they would consider the company unfair toward organized labor until such time as their employees became members of the Teamsters' Union. They withdrew, and used their influence and positions and their members used their influence and positions to have the employers of their members withdraw patronage from the plaintiff. The findings set forth at length their acts and their effects. In summary, it may be stated that dealers, ice deliverers, bakers, butchers, builders, plumbers and contractors, because of the notices, warnings and declarations of the defendants, in varying and serious degrees discontinued business with the plaintiff and refused further to employ it to do carting, hauling or collection work for fear of loss of business and labor troubles on account of the defendants' combination if they continued business with it. Further findings are: "49. The ultimate hope of the defendants was to better the condition of the members of the unions by bringing into said organization all of the craftsmen and laborers in Auburn, so that their united efforts for higher wages, shorter hours and better working conditions might be more persuasive and effectual, and without such motive or ultimate purpose the boycott would not have been inaugurated; but the immediate business in hand, the specific and direct thing which the defendants were then and there devoting their energies to and focusing all of the disciplined power of their organization upon, was the destruction of the plaintiff's business, in order that the plaintiff, through its sufferings, might be forced to yield to the demands of the union. What was threatened, intended, and in part accomplished by the defendants was injury to the business and property of the plaintiff; the acts performed and results accomplished being also necessarily injurious to trade and commerce; which injury to trade and commerce was intended to be brought about by the defendants through the performance of such acts. 50. All of the foregoing acts of the defendants and those acting in conjunction with them were done in furtherance of the combination and conspiracy to compel the plaintiff to employ union men exclusively, and to discharge any employee who refused to join the union. * * * 52. The said combination of the defendants and all acts in furtherance thereof were calculated and intended to injure and destroy the plaintiff's good will, trade and business, and all of the defendants were members of said combination and acting in furtherance thereof. 53. At the time of the commencement of this suit, plaintiff was suffering irreparable loss and damage to its trade, good will and business from the acts of the defendants in furtherance of their said combination. * * * 55. There has been, during the entire trouble, no force or violence used or threatened. There has been no misstatement of facts, unless the use of the word 'unfair,' when applied to the plaintiff, may have been misleading; and it is not charged that there was any intention to misrepresent the facts in this respect. 56. * * * What was feared by the customers (of plaintiff) was not any voluntary, self-initiated movement of their own employees to quit, but that they would quit because ordered to do so by the organizations to which they belonged, which possessed disciplinary powers to enforce obedience. * * * 58. The said combination of defendants originated solely from the refusal of plaintiff's employees to join the union, the demand made by defendants that plaintiff compel them to join the union, and the refusal of the plaintiff to comply with that demand." As conclusions of law the Special Term found that the combination of the defendants constituted an illegal conspiracy to injure the plaintiff's business and property and their acts were illegal as an intended injury to the plaintiff's business and as unreasonably restrictive of and injurious to trade and commerce and the conspiracy was unlawful as designed to prevent the plaintiff from exercising its lawful trade and calling by threats to do illegal acts; the plaintiff had no adequate remedy at law. The plaintiff was entitled to a decree to recover the damages and a reference to ascertain and report the amount of damages and on the incoming and confirmation of said report to a final judgment against all of the defendants for the amount of said damages thus ascertained, and to a further decree for a permanent injunction against the defendants "to prohibit the enforcement of resolutions, rules or orders of the defendant unions requiring their members to quit the service of employers who patronize the plaintiff, and the giving of notices by or on behalf of said organizations or the officers thereof to such employers, or the public, of an intention to quit provided such employers continued to patronize the plaintiff, and any other attempt or effort to use the powers or authority of the defendant unions over their own members for the purpose of inducing or compelling patrons of the plaintiff, or the public generally, against their will, to refrain from dealing with the plaintiff." A final judgment was entered for such relief, upon the confirmation of the report of a referee.

The briefs and arguments of counsel are concerned with a wide range of problems and principles relative to the rights of labor unions and of employers and employees. The determinative facts presented in the case at bar are, however, few, and the decisive principles are established. The defendants, in concerted actions and measures, interfered with the property rights and the property of the plaintiff. As a part of its property was the right to be employed by, to do work for, to transact business with and to receive compensation from all these who voluntarily sought or desired to thus engage with it. Personal liberty or the right of property embraces the right to make contracts for the purchase of the labor of others and equally the right to make contracts for the sale of one's own labor and the employment of one's individual and industrial resources. The right is not and cannot be absolute. It is subject to the condition that its exercise in the particular transaction shall not be inconsistent with the public interests or hurtful to the public order or detrimental to the common good. Moreover, it is common and reciprocal to all citizens. An unrestrained and unlimited exercise on the part of some persons would clash with and encounter the exercise of a similar freedom on the part of others. The question then arises whether the interference with the action of the one is justified by the exercise of some right of the interfering other. The right of the citizen to effectuate his desire or judgment without interference or compulsion must always be exercised with reasonable regard for the conflicting rights of others. The law recognizes the right and holds and enforces that an invasion of it, without a cause or reason which the law deems essential or useful in the existence or betterment of organized society, is a legal and actionable wrong which may be compensated or restrained. (*Adair v. United States,* 208 U.S. 161; *Hitchman Coal & Coke Co. v. Mitchell,* 245 U.S. 229; *Curran v. Galen,* 152 N.Y. 33; *National Protective Association of Steam Fitters v. Cumming,* 170 N.Y. 315; *Matter of Application of Jacobs,* 98 N.Y. 98.) The action and measures initiated and sustained by the defendants worked serious injury to the property of the plaintiff in consequence of which it sustained substantial damages. Unless the findings of the Special Term and the facts present a legal cause or justification for the interference by the defendants with the business and property of the plaintiff the judgment appealed from is right and must be affirmed.

The interference with and depreciation of the business and earnings of the plaintiff by the conjoint action of the defendants was of the nature and effect of a barrier against access to the plaintiff, its office and place of business. Their action towards the destruction of its business was affirmative and aggressive. It was not simply that the members of Union No. 679, from which the defendants insisted the plaintiff must hire its employees, refused to be employed by the plaintiff or its patrons, unless and until it employed members of the union. The unions and their members sought to induce and induced the employers of labor in the various trades and industries and the people generally in that community to discontinue employing and to abstain from business transactions with the plaintiff, by directly and affirmatively causing loss and injury to their business or interests or fear of loss and injury to their business or interests, in case they did not so discontinue and abstain. They sought to compel and did compel those employers and the people to coerce the plaintiff to unionize its business. They thus attempted and intended to create a general exclusion and isolation of the business of the plaintiff, or in other words, its non-existence so long as the plaintiff refused compliance with their demand that it compel its employees to join Union No. 679. The defendants are intentionally attempting to coerce the plaintiff to unionize its business by aggressively inducing its established and potential customers to ignore its existence in order to be free from the loss and injury which the action of the defendants would otherwise bring to those customers.

The rights, in virtue of which the defendants would justify the interference and the injury, are: (*a*) That of laborers to associate; (*b*) to bring within the labor organizations as members all laborers; (*c*) through the coherent and solidified power and influence flowing from association and united efforts to secure for all laborers higher wages, shorter hours, arbitration of labor disputes and better working conditions. Beyond question those rights exist. Labor unions are and for a long time have been recognized by the courts of this country as a legitimate and useful part of the industrial system. Associations of laborers, to accomplish lawful objects by legal means, have been always recognized and protected by the law of this state. The organizations of the defendants were as lawful as the incorporation of the plaintiff. Their members might and should have promoted their strength, welfare and their intelligent and salutary influence and control. Rights that are lawful and purposes that are useful and just cannot, however, be effectuated and accomplished by unlawful means. The individual cannot injure the property rights of another by the means of causing or controlling through duress, coercion, oppression or fraud, the acts of third persons which produce the injury. The individual may do and does many acts which in their effect are or may be coercive as to another. The right to do those acts inheres in the natural freedom and the civil rights which are his. But there is an important and perceptible distinction, in the realms of justice, civil order and law, between the voluntary acts of an individual, done in the right of personal freedom, the right to do or to refrain from doing, and their injurious effects, and the acts of others, undesired by them, initiated and performed in virtue of the deception, compulsion or oppression on the part of that individual, and their injurious effects. The individual may lawfully refuse to be employed to drive from his neighbor's field the stray cattle which are destroying the crop and thus, in effect, coerce the neighbor to drive them himself or permit the destruction; but he cannot lawfully prevent, through fraud or other form of dishonesty or compulsion of any nature, another from becoming the employee for such purpose. He may lawfully do that which he cannot lawfully attempt to compel another to do. The one is the exercise of the fundamental right of individual choice and volition; the other is the negation and destruction of the right. In the latter case the individual annihilates as to the others the right which he asserts and maintains for himself, and causes injuries as positively and aggressively as he would did he intentionally disable the other or his industrial resources. The law does not tolerate inequality in the existence and enforcement of rights or the definition and redress of wrongs, and the first condition of individual freedom and opportunity is servitude to law. In the instant case the contest did not arise because the members of Union No. 679, or members of the same occupation and of other unions, chose not to work for the plaintiff or for or with men who did engage in business with it, or sought to persuade, in an orderly and proper manner, persons generally to abstain from business transactions with it. It did not arise in the ordinary and natural exercise by the unions of the right to control their own labor and of the right of association. It arose because the defendants, constituting the entire union population of the city of Auburn, inaugurated and carried on, affirmatively and aggressively, through the agencies of fear and coercion, a comprehensive exclusion of the plaintiff from the business of the community, in order to compel it to unionize its business. On the part of the defendants there was organized coercion of the plaintiff into compliance with the demand of the unions that it compel its employees to join Union No. 679, by combining to compel third persons to refrain from having any business relations with it. The defendants were an organized combination, with a unified intent and purpose, causing irreparable damage to the business and property of the plaintiff. Financial pressure, loss of business, interference with freedom of action were imposed by them in order to force the unionization. The law should be and is that the means were unjustifiable and unlawful and the defendants should be enjoined from using them. (*Hitchman Coal & Coke Co. v. Mitchell*, 245 U.S. 229; *Burnham v. Dowd*, 217 Mass. 351; *Beck v. Railway Teamsters' Protective Union*, 118 Mich. 497; *Purvis v. United Brotherhood*, 214 Penn. St. 348; *Fink & Son v. Butchers' Union No. 422*, 84 N.J. Eq. 638; *Harvey v. Chapman*, 226 Mass. 191; *W. A. Snow Iron Works, Inc., v. Chadwick*, 227 Mass. 382; *Martell v. White*, 185 Mass. 255; *Cornellier v. Haverhill Shoe Manufacturers Assn.*, 221 Mass. 554; *New England Cement Gun Co. v. McGivern*, 218 Mass. 198; *Baush Mach. Tool Co. v. Hill*, 120 N.E. Rep. 188 [Mass.], July 16, 1918; *Smith v. Bowen*, 121 N.E. Rep. 814 [Mass.], February 4, 1919.)

What we have written declares sufficiently the clear and inescapable distinction between the facts and legal principles involved in this case and those involved in *Bossert v. Dhuy* (221 N.Y. 342).

The right of the plaintiff to a judgment being affirmed, the form or scope of the judgment rendered is not attacked.

The judgment should be affirmed, with costs.

HISCOCK, Ch. J., CHASE, CUDDEBACK, McLAUGHLIN and CRANE, JJ.. concur; HOGAN, J., not voting.

Judgment affirmed.[1]

GILL ENGRAVING CO. v. DOERR.

United States District Court for the Southern District of New York.
214 Fed. 111 (1914).

In Equity. Suit by the Gill Engraving Company against William Doerr, individually and as business agent of the New York Photo-Engravers' Union No. 1, and others. On motion for an injunction *pendente lite*. Motion denied.

HOUGH, D.J.: Complainant (hereinafter called "Gill Company") has long conducted a photo-engraving business; *i.e.* from a photograph or drawing it produces a plate from which a picture or pattern can be

---

[1] For comment on the case, see: 6 Va. Law Rev. 291 (1920); 29 Yale Law Jour. 120 (1920).

printed. The principal use of such engravings is to adorn the pages of books, magazines, and the like. It follows that, when complainant's work is finished, it is not useful, or at any rate not ordinarily used, except in conjunction with the services of printers, electrotypers, bookbinders, etc. The united efforts of all these tradesmen produce the completed volume, toward which complainant has then contributed but one item. To carry on its business and produce its share in the book trade the Gill Company employs photo-engravers; *i.e.*, men whose trade qualifies them for membership in Union No. 1.

The defendants may be said to represent and act for Union No. 1. As officers of that union they or some of them have written and spoken, acted, and induced others to act in a manner which is thought to justify the charge of the bill; that they and others have long been guilty of "a combination and conspiracy to prevent the employment at his trade of any photo-engraver in the city of New York who was not a member of Union No. 1." It is further charged that the same persons have also been engaged for years in another combination and conspiracy (contrary to common law and the statutes of New York) to "restrain trade and commerce in the production and sale of photo-engravings within the state of New York," to injure and destroy the Gill Company's "good will, trade, and business," and to prevent that company from competing with other photo-engraving shops in which the members of Union No. 1 are or have been exclusively employed.

These several objects of conspiracy defendants (and others equally active but not within the jurisdiction) are alleged to have pursued with the assistance and co-operation of the Allied Printing Trades Council, an aggregation for purposes of mutual assistance of the unions of all the trades commonly considered as requisite for the preparation and publication of a printed book. This allegation is not sustained. Union No. 1 and the allied council have some officers in common, and some letters have been written on paper of the allied council, but everything proved or admitted to have been done was the act of the photo-engravers as represented by Union No. 1, and not of any other trade organization. There is no proof that printers, bookbinders, etc., have taken any part in the matters producing this suit.

The principal officers of complainant (who are named Gill), and therefore the company itself, have been admittedly distrustful of, if not hostile to, Union No. 1 since about 1898, but the definite history of contest begins in 1907. In April of that year the Gill Company kept an open shop [1] employing about 120 men. Union No. 1 "ordered a strike of all union men employed by complainant, comprising about one-half of its employés; said strike took place * * * and caused complainant great loss and damage."

---

[1] A shop is "open" if union and nonunion men are therein employed without discrimination; it is "closed" if either unionism or nonunionism excludes an applicant from employment. Irving v. Joint District Council (C.C.) 180 Fed. 896; Sackett, etc., Co. v. Nat. Ass'n, 61 Misc. 150, 113 N.Y.S. 110.

The immediate causes of the strike in 1907 are stated differently by the contending parties. Undoubtedly one Schwartz was the agent of the union in the matter, and Gill says that Schwartz told him the sole question was the "closed" shop.

Schwartz denies that the strike was ordered in an effort to unionize the Gill Company, and alleges that the reason for striking he gave Gill was that his own employés had entered a protest with the union against the employment of an excessive number of apprentices, a number so great that the Gill Company was "looked upon as a school for teaching photo-engraving, a condition that was eminently unfair [2] to organized labor."

As article 4 of the Constitution of Union No. 1 declares that "this union claims the right to regulate the number of persons who may be employed as apprentices," and article 5 of the same document makes the union initiation fee $30 for all who have learned their trade under the jurisdiction of the union and $200 for those who have done so outside said jurisdiction, the difference between Gill's version of the difficulties of 1907 and that of Schwartz would seem to be one of time merely. But the effect of Schwartz's statement (whatever it was) and of the consequent strike on the Gill Company's conduct is thoroughly admitted. From that date to the present the Gill Company has refused to knowingly employ any union worker, has discharged any and every employé who joined the union, and, in short, has refused to recognize, deal with, or encourage Union No. 1 (or any other union) in any way whatever. For seven years the Gill shop has been "closed" in a recognized but unusual sense of that word.

The record is full of reasons for this action on the part of complainant and of assertions by defendants that the Gill Company does not give to its employés the "same scale of wages and the same working conditions as those generally prevailing." This phrase means conditions which respond to the demands of the union, and, when tested by the affidavits submitted, the difference between the Gill shop and a union shop in New York appear to be these: Some of the Gill employés (the most skillful) get more than union wage; the average or ordinary workman gets less; and special time is allowed in union plants for luncheon, which is not the case in the Gill shop. As mediocrity always outnumbers ability, I think it proven that a shop closed to union men has hitherto been cheaper than one exclusively manned by unionists, and that the most obvious result of change is to make mediocrity more expensive.

No change needing comment is shown to have occurred in the relations between these parties from 1907 to 1913. In that year it is admitted that the defendants Doerr and Brady officially addressed communications to customers or persons of influence with customers of the Gill Company, urging that the business of such customers be diverted

---

[2] The words "fair" and "unfair" are frequently used through the pleadings and the affidavits of defendants. The difference between them is the classic distinction between orthodoxy and heterodoxy. "Fair" means what is pleasing to the parties using the word, and "unfair" means whatever they do not like.

from complainant to union shops. Doerr also sent out circular letters to
friends throughout the land indicating methods by which one large customer of complainant (MacMillan Company) might be coerced into withdrawing patronage from the Gill Company "until such time as it was a
union office." MacMillan promptly succumbed, but there is no evidence
to show whether its action was distasteful or gratifying to itself. Mac-
Millan's change of business relations with complainant is evidenced by
the following (from a letter to defendant Brady):

"Our manufacturing department has been instructed to withhold any
further orders from the Gill Engraving Company for the present; and
all future contracts for printing books will contain a proviso that all work
coming under the jurisdiction of International Photo-Engravers' Union[3]
* * * shall be done in accordance with the scale of wages and conditions
of these unions in the locality where the work is done."

Shortly before the defection of MacMillan Company, other fuel, and
of a different kind, was added to the flames of contest and hatred.

The men managing the Gill Company owned stock and held office in
the Colorplate Company, a concern operating a union shop and doing a
special line of engraving work. Mr. Gill deposes that he was told by the
Colorplate's president that, unless the Gills severed all connection with
that corporation and parted with their stock, "the officers" of Union No.
1 would call a strike. Under this threat the Gills retired, to their loss
directly as shareholders and indirectly as owners of the Gill Company;
the Colorplate Company having done for them work the main concern
was not equipped to do.

This tale, as told by defendants, is that the Colorplate employés were
afraid that the Gills would get control and then discharge them, as was
being done in the Gill Company, whereupon said employés "unanimously
voted that they resign," without "an order on the part of any union officials." The difference between a threatened strike and an announced
unanimous intention to resign is that between tweedledum and tweedledee;
but the fact that the managers of the Gill Company were recognized and
acted against as enemies, by even private members of Union No. 1, is
noticeable and admitted.

On the whole, defendants' union seems to have been encouraged by
the results of effort during 1913, for in January, 1914, at the annual meeting where these defendants were elected to office, the following report
was made, according to the "Official Journal of the International Photo-
Engravers Union":

"With the new year this local (i.e., Union No. 1) has taken a pledge
to organize 100 per cent., if possible. The prospects seem good. The Gill
Engraving Company, which has been the only nonunion concern of any
consequence in the past, is dwindling down to such a size as to no longer
be a detriment to the many fair minded employers in the city. Their com-

---

[3] This "union" is a conference or league of many locals like Union No. 1, and
extends over North America.

petent men are seeing the wisdom of joining our ranks and the others are being discharged, as the Gill Engraving Company seems to find it difficult to hold its old customers or to replace them with new ones. The plan as laid down by the officials last April has been studiously followed out and will be continued indefinitely in the future or until such time as an amicable agreement is reached with the Gill Engraving Company."

In March of 1914 the action was taken by defendants, which evidently produced this suit, for the history of contest which has been related is not asserted to be of importance, except as it shows intent and may induce the court to draw from acts and occurrences, otherwise colorless, the same inferences as do complainant's counsel. A meeting was called of representatives of all union shops under the jurisdiction of Union No. 1, and such representatives were instructed that thereafter the shop in which they worked was to do no business for any customer who likewise did business with a nonunion shop. In order to apprise employers as to who were the probable offenders, a list was handed each shop representative, who was to pass it on to his employer. Defendant Doerr reinforced these instructions by sending a letter to each employer running a union shop in New York, stating that after April 1, 1914, their employés would handle the work only of those customers "who will assure us that they will have their engraving done in shops fair to our members. In other words, we will do all of their work or none."

A few days later new lists were furnished of customers who still refused to have all of their photo-engraving work done under "fair" conditions. This list was much smaller than the one first sent out, and it is alleged and not denied that the reduction in size represented a corresponding reduction in the Gill Company's patronage.

It may be important to ascertain whether this weapon of Union No. 1 is or is not leveled directly or especially at the Gill Company. The position of the union has been stated in writing by several defendants, but perhaps the letter of one Volz (not a defendant, but a vice president and acting with defendants) is most instructive. On March 30, 1914, Volz declares that the union is going to carry out certain of its rights. Though he complains of the Gill Company, the rights that are to be enforced consist in refusing "to do any part of the engraving for any magazine, etc., made in whole or in part by any concern where our members are unjustly discriminated against; * * * all photo-engravings for any publication or concern will be produced either under fair conditions or all under unfair conditions. We refuse to assist publications unfair to our members."

Thus (according to Volz) the war declared is on a class, not any one person, unless that person is *sui generis*. This is exactly what the Gill Company says it is, viz., the only considerable nonunion commercial photo-engraving shop in New York, the only concern whose customers would be likely to have more work than one shop could always do, and therefore (by a process of exclusion) the sole object of the union's hostility, and the only business affected by the order apparently leveled against "unfair conditions" generally.

On this point there has been some conflict, and 13 nonunion shops are enumerated by defendants. Several of these are noncommercial (*i.e.*, doing special work only for one customer), and the rest are so small that the substantial correctness of the statement (above quoted) of the union's newspaper seems proved, viz., that the Gill Company is the "only nonunion concern of any consequence."

Defendant Brady has signed an affidavit (probably drawn after a perusal of reported cases) in which he thus states the purpose and intent of the union's order:

"Publishers who have the substantial part of their work done in antiunion shops, which do not conform to the union scale of wages and hours, do not compete on terms of equality with those publishers who have their work done in shops where union labor is employed and which conform to the union scale of wages and hours. The refusal of the members of the union to perform for publishers that portion of the work which they desire to have performed by members of the union, unless said publishers should send the entire job into shops where members of the union are employed and which conform to the union scale of wages and hours, was intended as an effort to obtain for the members of the union the work of the entire job or jobs of such publishers, and the effect, if any, on the Gill Engraving Company is merely incidental."

It is believed the foregoing covers the whole evidence; there is almost no contradiction as to physical facts; in result it stands admitted that defendants have in concert, as the result of premeditation, by agreement with each other and with persons not parties to this suit, as the representatives of Union No. 1 and by and through their power as such representatives, procured and caused the workmen belonging to their union, being 75 per cent. of the journeymen photo-engravers in New York, exclusively manning every considerable commercial shop in that city, to concertedly refuse to do work for any customer of their several employers who will not agree to patronize exclusively union photo-engravers. These acts have destroyed much of complainant's business and threaten the rest.

As to the purpose with which defendants have acted, I am of opinion that hostility to Gill Company is subordinate and incidental. All nonunion businesses are treated alike; naturally the greater the business the greater the aggregate dislike, but the quality of hatred is the same, irrespective of size. That Gill Company is hurt is gratifying but incidental; the procedure would be the same were complainant non-existent. The priest of Juggernaut may be glad that the car rolls over a personal enemy, but the car rolls primarily to glorify the god within. Of course defendants well knew that their plan of campaign would injure Gill Company; they intended to injure anybody who got in their way and they knew complainant was there; nevertheless the ultimate purpose, the *causa causans,* of defendant's action was deeper and more far-reaching than merely to injure one business. Doerr told nearly the whole truth when he wrote, "We will do all of (your customers') work or none." If he had added "and if they can get it done otherwise after this we will think up something else," he would have told the whole truth, because the great and all-absorbing object of defendants' endeavors was and is to get all the work in the trade, or at any rate all the work worth having, for their own members. This finding of ultimate purpose completes my view of the facts. As to the physical acts and words of the parties, it may again be said there is no conflict worthy the name, but as to the mental facts, as to inferences of intent, men will differ widely, just as a jury would probably disagree on such a subject. This renders the study of motive important, for motive begets intent, as has often been observed by writers on criminal law.

What motive incited defendants to injure Gill Company? None, except that it hinders the expansion and aggrandizement of the union, and therefore gives rise to the same kind of objection that the soldier has to the man who prevents his onward march. It can rarely be said that the soldier is moved by a desire to kill his opponent, but he will kill him if necessary.

Before applying the law to the findings of fact, much that was mentioned in argument may be laid aside. It is not shown that any national statute has been violated; nor that any principle peculiar to national law (e.g., interstate commerce) is concerned; nor that the question presented is complicated by disturbance of the peace, physical trespass, or violence; nor that any government function (e.g., mail transportation) has been interfered with. These exclusions make the case purely local. The jurisdiction of this court is an incident, depending on the New Jersey incorporation of a business wholly conducted in New York City. Therefore I think it desirable that the law of New York should be applied so far as I am capable of discovering it, unless the decisions of federal courts superior to this compel different treatment.

It is asserted that the defendant's acts constitute a crime under New York Penal Code, § 580. I decline to consider such violation as ground for injunctive relief *pendente lite*. * * *

It is further urged that the defendants have engaged in a conspiracy or combination in violation of sections 340, 341, General Business Law of New York (the Donnelly Act). It seems plain enough that this is true, but it is settled that for such cause a private party in his own suit is not entitled to injunctive relief. *Irving v. Neal* (D.C.) 209 Fed. 471; *Paine Lumber Co. v. Neal* (U.S.D.C. November, 1913) 212 Fed. 259, affirmed in 214 Fed. 82, April 7, 1914. Therefore this motion is to be decided by what is usually called common law; i.e., the law of New York as evidenced by the decisions of its courts, supplemented only by the inquiry as to whether any controlling divergence of opinion is found in the appellate tribunals to which this court is more directly responsible. There will also be disregarded much argument resting on the statement that defendants have produced a boycott. In common parlance, a boycott has been attempted or created. But the word is of vague signification, and no accurate and exclusive definition has, so far as I know, ever been given.[4]

Nor does it advance matters to call the affair a boycott, for "it cannot be said that to boycott is to offend the law." *Mills v. U. S. Printing Co.,* 99 App. Div. 611, 91 N.Y. Supp. 185, affirmed in 199 N.Y. 76, 92 N.E. 214. This is not thought to mean that every form of boycotting is lawful, but that the word does not necessarily import illegality. I do not perceive any distinction upon which a legal difference of treatment should be based between a lockout, a strike, and a boycott. They often look very unlike, but this litigation illustrates their basic identity. All are voluntary abstentions from acts which normal persons usually perform for mutual benefit; in all the reason for such abstention is a determination to conquer and attain desire by proving that the endurance of the attack will outlast the resistance of the defense; and for all the law of New York provides the same test, viz., to inquire into the legality (1) of the object in view, and (2) of the means of attainment. When courts generally (with some legislative assistance from behind) abandoned the doctrine that any concerted arrangement which hindered the following of a trade or constituted an attempt to change trade conditions (especially wages) amounted to an actionable conspiracy, this judicial position was quite sure to follow, unless it was admitted that the passing of the old doctrine had left the matter political rather than judicial. This has not yet been done.

It was easy to find out whether a man was hindered, if, as matter of law, the court held the hindering criminal (*Rex v. Eccles,* 1 Lea, C.C. 274); it has not been found so easy to fix any responsibility when a mere result is no longer sufficient to warrant judgment.[5] The leading cases in New York (*Curran v. Galen,* 152 N.Y. 33, 46 N.E. 297, 37 L.R.A. 802, 57 Am. St. Rep. 496; *National Protective Ass'n v. Cumming,* 170 N.Y. 315, 63 N.E. 369, 58 L.R.A. 135, 88 Am. St. Rep. 648; *Jacobs v. Cohen,* 183 N.Y. 207, 76 N.E. 5, 2 L.R.A. [N.S.] 292, 111 Am. St. Rep. 730, 5 Ann. Cas. 280; *Park Co. v. National Druggists,* 175 N.Y. 40, 67 N.E. 136, 62 L.R.A. 632, 96 Am. St. Rep. 578; *McCord v. Thompson-Starrett Co.,* 129 App. Div. 130, 113 N.Y. Supp. 385, affirmed in 198 N.Y. 587, 92 N.E. 1090; *Mills v. U. S. Printing Co., supra*) all show that the court

---

[4] See a collection in Joyce on Monopolies, c. 3.

[5] To parade the cases bearing on such controversies as this is useless, for reconciliation is impossible. Very different viewpoints are afforded by the publications below enumerated. The historical development of the law is admirably stated by Mr. James Wallace Bryan in Johns Hopkins University Studies, series 27, Nos. 3-5 (1909). The American cases to 1908 are critically collated by Mr. Walter G. Merritt in his pamphlet entitled "Limitations on the Right to Strike." The University of Wisconsin's Bulletins on Boycotting and Blacklisting (1906) are endeavors to state impartially results to date. "Boycotts and the Labor Struggle" (H. W. Laidler, 1913), while not a conventional law book, tabulates the confusion of cases, and is especially full in respect of New York. I venture to think that Justice Holmes' article on "Privilege, Malice, and Intent" (8 Harv. Law Rev. 1894) is still the clearest exposition of fundamentals.

sits primarily to decide a question of fact, viz.: What is the object of the combination? The conflicting opinions in the *Cumming Case* illustrate this perfectly. PARKER, C.J., for the court, declared:

"There is no pretense that the defendant associations * * * had any other motive than one, which the law justifies of attempting to benefit their members by securing their employment." There is not "even a hint that a strike was ordered or a notification given of the intention to order a strike for the purpose of accomplishing any other result than that of securing the discharge of the members of the plaintiff association and the substitution of members of the defendant associations in their place. Such a purpose is not illegal."

Whereas VANN, J., for the minority, stated:

"The object of the defendants was not to get higher wages, shorter hours, or better terms for themselves, but to prevent others from following their lawful calling."

And this was the point of acute difference in a court which could not make any findings of fact of its own. The learned judges could not even agree as to the meaning of the findings of the lower court.[6] The English courts devote themselves to deciding the same questions of fact, and find it no easier. *Cf.* the opinions of Lord Shand in *Allen v. Flood,* L.R. 1898, A.C. 1, and *Quinn v. Leathem, infra.*

Applying this rule to this case, it is held that the object of defendant's combination is not to injure Gill Company, though such injury has occurred and was foreseen. The object is to increase the power of the union, so as to get more, better, easier, and better paid work for its members; this is now regarded as laudable.

As to the means employed, everything lately done and alleged as ground for present action consists in threatening strikes. This is the exercise of a legal right. If defendants have sought to attain a legal end by legal means, that a motive, or part of a motive, was hate of Gill Company is immaterial. *Roseneau v. Empire Circuit Co.,* 131 App. Div. 435, 115 N.Y. Supp. 511; *Quinn v. Leathem,* L.R. 1901, A.C., at 538.

That wrong and injury are being done in this matter is plain enough. Why does the law refuse or neglect to correct it? ANDREWS, J., has, I think, given the best answer in *Foster v. Retail Clerks' Ass'n,* 39 Misc. Rep. 48, 78 N.Y. Supp. 860:

"Injury * * * is never good, but to suffer it may entail less evil than to attempt to check it by legal means. * * * In the last analysis this freedom to commit injury, and the bounds imposed upon it are regulated by what has been thought to be public policy."

---

[6] Compare: Newton Co. v. Erickson, 70 Misc. 291, 126 N.Y.S. 949, (1911) and Bossert v. United Brotherhood, 77 Misc. 592, 137 N.Y.S. 321 (1912), for similar difference between trial courts. Justice Holmes wrote in 1894: "The ground of decision really comes down to a proposition of policy of rather a delicate nature concerning the merit of the particular benefit to themselves intended by the defendants, and suggests a doubt whether judges with different economic sympathies might not decide such a case differently when brought face to face with the issue." This was prophetic for New York at least.

The cases cited could be used to show that no bounds have been imposed in New York on wrongs quite as great as that wrought upon complainant.

Defendants have called attention to one fact not found in any case known or shown to me. The Gill Company has declared war on the union by discharging all members found in its shop. It is said this should deprive complainant of the aid of equity, and *Sinsheimer v. United Garment Workers, 77* Hun, 215, 28 N.Y. Supp. 321, is relied on. It is not seen why a person otherwise entitled to protection for his business is deprived of it because he will not employ a certain class of workmen; the nonpreferred workmen are not, therefore, given any right to injure the man who does not prefer them.

In the United States Courts for this circuit, *National Fireproofing Co. v. Mason Builders' Ass'n,* 169 Fed. 259, 94 C.C.A. 535, 26 L.R.A. (N.S.) 148, is controlling. It accepts the New York cases fully, piously regrets the injuries committed, and writes the epitaph of litigation such as this by declaring that, when equal legal rights clash, equity is helpless. This is true; it would have been just as true to point out that the result of legalizing strikes, lockouts, and boycotts under any circumstances must be that those who understand the use of such legal tools can always keep within the law and accomplish their main purpose while inflicting all necessary "incidental" injury.

Considering that the rules as laid down in New York have not been shown to be transgressed, motion denied.

BRICKLAYERS', MASONS' & PLASTERERS' INTERNATIONAL UNION v. SEYMOUR RUFF & SONS.

Maryland Court of Appeals. 160 Md. 483, 154 Atl. 52 (1931).

Digges, J., delivered the opinion of the Court.

The principal question for decision in this case is whether an employer, who has entered into a subcontract to perform work on a certain building, may recover damages against the labor unions of which, with his knowledge, his employees are members, because those unions have ordered them to quit work on the building in question for the reason that the general contractor has refused to employ union labor on other jobs in the same locality; there being no contract of employment between the subcontractor and his employees. This question arises in an action on the case brought in the Circuit Court for Frederick County by the appellee against the Bricklayers', Masons' & Plasterers' International Union of America, a voluntary unincorporated association, hereinafter called the International, the Bricklayers' & Masons' Protective & Beneficial Union No. 7 of Maryland, located at Frederick, Md., a voluntary unincorporated association, hereinafter called Union No. 7, and John T. White.

The declaration alleges that the defendant International is a voluntary unincorporated association consisting of more than seven members, has a recognized group name, and is located in the City of Washington, D. C., but doing business in various states throughout the United States, through its duly authorized agents, and, for the purposes thereinafter mentioned, having appointed the defendant White as its duly authorized agent; that the International is composed of elective and appointive officers and the legally elected representatives of subordinate unions, created and acting under its constitution, and these subordinate unions are located in the various cities throughout various states of the United States, and that the government and superintendence of such subordinate unions is vested in the International, as the supreme head of all unions; that the International has the power to determine the customs and usages in regard to all matters relating to the craft, including the power to legalize and govern strikes and lockouts, and included in such power to order strikes and lockouts is the power to punish local unions and any member or members thereof by severe fines and other penalties, and by expulsion from the union, in the event of their failure to obey an order of the International or its officers to go on strike and refuse to work; that the defendant Union No. 7 is a voluntary unincorporated association consisting of more than seven persons, having a recognized group name, and having its principal office and place of business in the City of Frederick, Md., is a member and one of the subordinate unions of the International, and membership of both of said organizations being composed of "union men"; that the persons forming the plaintiff corporation are contracting stone masons and have been engaged in that business in the City of Baltimore, Md., for many years past, first, as a partnership, and since 1928 as a corporation, and during the entire time in which they have been so engaged they have conducted what is known as a union shop, employing union men only, to wit, men affiliated with the International and its subordinate unions in various cities and states, and doing work with such men in various cities and states of the United States, and, at the time of the wrongs and injuries thereinafter complained of, there was no grievance, trouble, or controversy of any kind between the plaintiff and its employees, the said "union men," nor between the plaintiff and the defendants; that on or about January 8th, 1929, the plaintiff entered into a written contract with Lloyd C. Culler of Frederick, Md., a general contractor having a contract for the erection and completion of a church in Frederick, to do all of the stone masonry, brick, and tile work, furnish labor and material, and set the limestone, for the erection and completion of the church, for the sum of $50,000, and, pursuant to its obligation thereunder, the plaintiff began the work required of it to be done under the contract, and employed union labor only in and about the work, and continued said work until the early part of March, 1929, when the defendants wantonly, unlawfully, and maliciously, and with intent to cause a breach of said contract between Culler and the plaintiff, declared a strike upon said job, and ordered all of said union men employed upon the work by the plaintiff to go on a strike and quit work, and, pursuant to this order, the men did go on strike and quit work, and refused to resume work until ordered to do so by the defendants, and subsequently, upon orders of the defendants, but only after an interval of time, the men resumed work and continued for a few days, when the defendants again wantonly, unlawfully, and maliciously, and with intent to cause a breach of the contract between Culler and the plaintiff, ordered a strike on said job and ordered the men to quit work, and said men did go on strike and quit work and refused to resume work until ordered to do so by the defendants; that the defendants maliciously, wantonly, and unlawfully, notwithstanding the requests and demands of the plaintiff, refused to declare the strike off and order the men back to work, and by reason thereof the plaintiff was unable to continue the work it was required to do in and about the church under its contract with Culler, and on account thereof Culler canceled the contract and notified the plaintiff that he was employing others to finish the work at the risk and expense of the plaintiff; that the acts and conduct of the defendants were not caused or influenced by any violation on the part of the plaintiff of any obligation it owed the defendants or either of them, or to the union men employed by it, but said wanton, malicious, and unlawful acts of the defendants were caused solely and entirely by the desire of the defendants to compel Culler to employ union men on work Culler had contracted to do in Frederick and vicinity, other than the work upon said church, and because Culler refused to comply with the demand of the defendants that he employ union men on all of his other work, the defendants wantonly, maliciously and unlawfully did the acts complained of, thereby causing a breach of the contract between Culler and the plaintiff, and all of the acts were done by the defendants with full knowledge that said acts would result in said breach of contract and cause substantial loss and great injury and damage to the plaintiff, for which the plaintiff claimed the sum of $25,000 damages.

Before discussing the principal question as above set forth, we will dispose of the incidental and subsidiary questions arising out of the pleadings. * * *

The main question, heretofore stated, requires a decision as to the powers of organized labor to compel or coerce action for the benefit of its members. Courts, in deciding cases involving this question, recognizing the possible far-reaching effect of any rule or principle enunciated, should and do approach the question with caution, and have generally refrained from doing more than deciding the case upon its peculiar facts, leaving each succeeding case to be determined in like manner, and giving effect to the development of the law as illustrated by the decisions, and also permitting the court to take cognizance of general conditions as they may exist at the time of the decision; thus enabling the courts to maintain an even balance between the rights of workmen, either individually or in combination, and equal rights guaranteed to all individuals under the law. The line of demarcation where one man's rights, natural or legal, may end, because in conflict with the exercise of some right by others, is shadowy, and is not the subject of definement by any general rule. While this is true, it seems to be now definitely settled that there are certain points through which this line must pass, such as that workmen have the undoubted right to organize for the purpose of securing lucrative employment under proper conditions as to working hours and wages; that, in order to enforce such right, they may peaceably strike or quit work, without liability, in cases where there is no contract of employment to the contrary; that what is a legal right of an individual does not become illegal simply because done in combination with others by concerted action. There would seem to be no doubt that laborers working for an employer against whom they had a just or fancied grievance as to hours of work, wages, and the like, about which there was dispute with the employer, and with whom they have no contract as to the term of their employment, are entitled to withdraw, either singly or in combination, for the purpose of coercing their employer into complying with their demands; and even though such quitting results in loss and damage to the employer, it is not an actionable wrong. This must be true, because, when not bound by contract, every free man has a natural right to work for whom he pleases, and to cease to work when he chooses, without liability on his part to the employer. To enforce the opposite view would lead to the establishment of involuntary servitude. Every employer must recognize this right on the part of the employees, and, if by such action loss results, it is *damnum absque injuria*. The employer has the same undoubted right, when not prevented by contract, to discharge the employees, which may, and in many cases does, result in loss and injury to the employee and those dependent upon him; yet this loss and injury, too, must be suffered by the employee without being able to maintain an action therefor against the employer.

The case made out by the declaration here is entirely different from such as above indicated. The allegations of the declaration, which for the purpose of demurrer must be taken as having been established by competent proof, are, that the plaintiff is a subcontractor employing only union men, having no dispute or controversy with them, or any of the defendants, nor the unions with which the employees are affiliated; that the work being done by the subcontractor was under a contract between it and Culler, this contract providing for the furnishing of material and doing the stone, brick, and tile work in the building of a church at Frederick, for which Culler was the general contractor; that Culler had contracts for the erection of other buildings in and around Frederick, and that he did not employ exclusively union men on these other jobs; that, in order to bring pressure to bear on Culler, for the purpose of compelling him to employ union labor only on his other contracts, the defendants ordered a strike of the employees of the plaintiff; that the plaintiff's employees did strike, quit work, and refuse to return to work unless and until ordered by the defendants; that, after repeated requests by the plaintiff, the defendants refused and failed to order the resumption of work on the part of the plaintiff's employees, which prevented the plaintiff from proceeding with its work in accordance with the terms of its contract with Culler, resulting in the cancellation of the contract by Culler and a notification by him to the plaintiff that he would proceed with the work at the cost and expense of the plaintiff, that, by reason of such acts and refusals on the part of the defendants, the plaintiff suffered great damage, for the recovery of which this suit was instituted.

These facts show a competition between the union, on behalf of its members, and the non-union men who were working for Culler. If these non-union men had been working for the plaintiff, and it had been told by the union that its members would not continue to work while non-union labor was employed on the same job, it would have been legitimate and fair competition, and equivalent to saying that "we will do all of the work which you have on this job, or none," leaving it to the plaintiff to determine which of these two alternatives he would accept. In such case, the grievance or dispute would be directly with the party against whom the strike was ordered; and it is settled that, under such circumstances, the plaintiff would have no right of action against the union. But this is not what was done. The injury to the plaintiff which arose from the strike was inflicted upon it, an innocent party, in order to compel it to coerce the general contractor, Culler. The plaintiff may have been in entire sympathy with union labor, and the allegations of the bill indicate that it was; yet it had no power to coerce its general contractor into employing only union men. The real grievance of the union was not with the plaintiff, but with Culler for his not unionizing his work; and the plaintiff is the innocent victim of such action on the part of the defendants. Again, if the plaintiff could have taken such coercive measures as to compel Culler to employ union men, he had the undoubted right to elect not to do so, and that without any right on the part of the defendants to penalize him for such failure. The defendants owed to the plaintiff the duty of non-interference with the conduct of its work or employees, so long as there was no contention or dispute with it. It is an effort by the defendants to obtain a decision in their favor as against Culler, by forcing an innocent third party, the plaintiff, which has no interest in the dispute, to coerce Culler to accede to the defendants' demands. Such a strike is not a justifiable interference with the right of the plaintiff to pursue its calling without entanglement, by reason of the fact that Culler does not employ exclusively union labor. In our opinion, organized labor's right of coercion and compulsion is limited to strikes on persons with whom the organization has a trade dispute; or, as stated by the Supreme Judicial Court of Massachusetts in *Pickett v. Walsh*, 192 Mass. 587, 78 N.E. 753, 760: "A strike on A, with whom the striker has no trade dispute, to compel A to force B to yield to the strikers' demands, is an unjustifiable interference with the right of A to pursue his calling as he thinks best." See *Lucke v. Clothing Cutters' Assembly*, 77 Md. 396, 26 A. 505; *My Maryland Lodge v. Adt*, 100 Md. 238, 59 A. 721; *Klingel's Pharmacy v. Sharp & Dohme*, 104 Md. 218, 64 A. 1929; *Acker, Merrall & C. Co. v. McGaw*, 106 Md. 536, 68 A. 17; *Sumwalt Ice Co. v. Knickerbocker Ice Co.*, 114 Md. 403, 80 A. 48; *Gray v. Building Trades*

Council, 91 Minn. 171; 97 N.W. 663; *Purington v. Hinchliff,* 219 Ill. 159, 76 N.E. 47; *Beck v. Ry. Teamsters' Union,* 118 Mich. 497, 77 N.W. 13; *Crump's Case,* 84 Va. 927, 6 S.E. 620; *State v. Glidden,* 55 Conn. 46, 8 A. 890; *Walker v. Cronin,* 107 Mass. 555; *Martell v. White,* 185 Mass. 255, 69 N.E. 1085; *Burnham v. Dowd,* 217 Mass. 351, 104 N.E. 841; *New England Cement Gun Co. v. McGivern,* 218 Mass. 198, 105 N.E. 885.

It is contended by the appellants that the union employees of the plaintiff had the right to quit work without assigning any reason or being liable for any loss flowing from such action, and, that being true, the defendants International and Union No. 7 are the agents of the individual members, and therefore, when they acted upon the orders of the International, their agent, it was equivalent to their acting upon their own will and pleasure. While this is an ingenious argument, we do not think the position taken is tenable, first, because, if the plaintiff's employees refused to obey the orders of the International and go on strike, they were subject to fines and penalties, or even expulsion; and, second, even if we admit that an unincorporated association is the agent of each of its individual members, which we do not decide, entertaining the views hereinbefore expressed, holding that organized labor's right of coercion and compulsion is limited to strikes on persons with whom the organization has a trade dispute, it would apply to the principals as well as to the agent.

Finding no error, the judgment will be affirmed.

Judgment affirmed, with costs.[1]

COHN & ROTH ELECTRIC CO. v. BRICKLAYERS, MASONS AND PLASTERERS LOCAL UNION NO. 1.

Connecticut Supreme Court of Errors. 92 Conn. 161, 101 Atl. 659 (1917).

WHEELER, J.: The plaintiff has waived its claim for damages and relies upon its claim for injunctive relief, alleging that the defendant labor unions and the members thereof have combined for the purpose of obtaining a monopoly of all the employment for the members of these local unions in the several building trades in which they are engaged, and for the purpose of excluding from such employment all who are not members.

In furtherance of this purpose and to establish this monopoly the defendants are alleged to have agreed: (1) that no nonunion member shall be employed on any building in Hartford or its vicinity; (2) that no open-

---

[1] *Cf.* Ruff & Sons v. Bricklayers, etc., Union, 163 Md. 687, 164 Atl. 752 (1933); New England Cement Gun Co. v. McGivern, 218 Mass. 198, 105 N.E. 805 (1914); Levering & Garrigues Co. v. Morris, 11 Law & Labor 245 (D.C.S.D. N.Y. 1929), rev'd on jurisdictional grounds in 61 Fed.(2d) 115 (2nd cir. 1932); Beckerman v. Bakery Union, 28 Ohio N.P. (N.S.) 550 (1931). See also: In re Starrett, 45 Fed. (2d) 399 (S.D. N.Y. 1930); Trollope & Sons v. London Bldg. Trades Fed., 11 T.L.R. 228, 280 (1895).

shop employer shall be permitted to supply any labor or materials for any such building; (3) that they will compel all owners, employers, and other persons to refuse to purchase supplies from open-shop employers; (4) that they will refuse to work for any owner or employer who shall purchase supplies from any open-shop employer; (5) that they will boycott all nonunion members and open-shop employers and all persons doing business with them. In furtherance of said boycott the defendants are alleged to have agreed: (6) to cause all members of the defendant unions to refuse to work on every building owned by any person who owns any building on which any nonunion member is employed, or on which any open-shop employer is furnishing, or has contracted to furnish, labor or materials; and (7) to refuse to work on each and every job on which a general contractor may be engaged if any nonunion member is working for such general contractor, or if any open-shop contractor is furnishing, or has contracted to furnish, any labor or materials.

The complaint also alleges that in furtherance of these purposes and agreements the defendants have boycotted the plaintiff and all owners for whose buildings the plaintiff has furnished labor or materials, and all contractors or builders by whom the plaintiff has been employed, directly or indirectly, and have threatened to institute strikes of all of these members on all work on which any of the members were engaged for any owner or by any contractor for whom the plaintiff has furnished labor or materials; and the defendants have instituted strikes in accordance with these threats in all cases where their demands have not been promptly complied with.

Comparing the facts found with those alleged in the complaint, we find a marked dissimilarity. We can discover no finding of the illegal purpose of these defendants which the complaint reiterates, nor one of a conspiracy and agreement such as is alleged, save in one particular. That agreement is not specifically found, but it is found that the several defendant local unions have adopted the same or analogous by-laws obligatory upon all of their members. These by-laws prohibit members working with nonunion men under penalty for violation. They provide that "no member shall work for any employer who is employing nonunion * * * workers," nor on any job contracted for by any nonunion contractor, nor on any job sublet to any contractor by any open-shop or nonunion contractor. The Hartford Structural Building Trade Alliance has adopted a by-law, of which Alliance all the defendant unions are members, and by which by-law all defendants are bound, that "no member of this Alliance shall work with any person * * * working at any trade in the Structural Building Trades Alliance who does not hold a working card" from the Alliance.

These by-laws create an agreement on the part of these several unions and all of their members, binding upon them, that their members will not work for any employer employing nonunion men on that job, nor for any nonunion contractor, nor on any job sublet to any contractor by any open-shop or nonunion contractor. Interpreted together, these several by-laws constitute an agreement, which membership imposed upon all members of the defendant unions, that they would not work on any job on which non-union men or employers are at work.

All members of the defendant unions have ceased to work and refused to work on any building when the nonunion employees of the plaintiff have commenced work on such building. In one instance the members of the defendant unions withdrew from work on five buildings being erected by a single general contractor, because the plaintiff's nonunion employees were at work on one of these buildings. The defendants maintain their legal right to do these acts, and threaten and intend to continue in such course unless restrained by injunction.

The case set up in the complaint is not the agreement to cease work for a contractor if nonunion men are employed by him on any of his jobs, no matter where located, upon which the defendants are not at work and to which they have no relation; and if the complaint does rely upon this cause of action the finding does not support it. It recites that, in one instance, the members of the defendant unions ceased work on five buildings in process of erection by one contractor, because plaintiff's nonunion employees were at work on one of these buildings. A single instance of one act done would hardly permit a holding that the trial judge had, in refusing an injunction, exercised his discretion improperly. It is noticeable that the finding does not state that these strikes were instituted for any of the unlawful purposes so frequently reiterated in the complaint.

The trial court could not find the existence of an illegal purpose without proof, and we cannot so hold without a finding to that effect. If the purpose of the strikes were illegal, they were clear deprivations of the right of the plaintiff to work. *State v. Glidden*, 55 Conn. 46, 8 Atl. 890. If the purpose was to better the condition of the defendants, a situation is presented not heretofore considered by us, viz: a determination of whether an agreement to strike in a case in which the striking workmen are not concerned in a trade dispute, or in which their labor has not come in competition with nonunion labor, is lawful. Its decision is practically another phase of the question decided in *Pickett v. Walsh*, 192 Mass. 572, 582, 78 N.E. 753, in the last point treated in that case, and the first and second causes of action set forth in the complaint, pages 579 and 587 of the opinion. We express no opinion upon this point, leaving its decision open until it is fairly raised in the pleadings and in the record on appeal.

The agreement of the defendant unions and their members, that the members would refuse to work with nonunion men, followed by action by the members ceasing to work with the nonunion men of the plaintiff, is the only ground of complaint which the facts found support. Individuals may work for whom they please, and quit work when they please, provided they do not violate their contract of employment. Combinations of individuals have similar rights, but the liability to injury from the concerted action of numbers has placed upon their freedom to quit work these additional qualifications: that their action must be taken for their own interest and not for the primary purpose of injuring another or others, and neither in end sought, nor in means adopted to secure that end, must it be prohibited by law nor in contravention of public policy. *Connors v. Connolly,* 86 Conn. 641, 86 Atl. 600, is an example oɪ an agreement which we held to be contrary to public policy.

The members of a union, acting upon their agreement, may refuse to enter upon employment with nonunion labor, or refuse to continue their employment with nonunion labor, provided their action does not fall within the qualifications of their freedom of action already stated. *Pickett v. Walsh,* 192 Mass. 572, 582, 78 N.E. 753; *Burnham v. Dowd,* 217 Mass. 351, 356, 104 N.E. 841; *Grassi Contracting Co. v. Bennett,* 174 N.Y. App. Div. 244, 160 N.Y. Supp. 279, 284; *Gray v. Building Trades Council,* 91 Minn. 171, 185, 97 N.W. 663. In *State v. Stockford,* 77 Conn. 227, 237, 58 Atl. 769, HALL, J., thus states our law: "Workmen may lawfully combine to accomplish their withdrawal in a body from the service of their employers for the purpose of obtaining an advance in wages, a reduction of the hours of labor, or any other legitimate advantage, even though they may know that such action will necessarily cause injury to the business of their employers, provided such abandonment of work is not in violation of any continuing contract, and is conducted in a lawful manner and not under such circumstances as to wantonly or maliciously inflict injury to person or property."

The facts found show that the plaintiff has suffered damage in its business and that the defendants contemplated this probable effect. A cause of action was thus made out entitling the plaintiff to judgment, unless the defendants have made out, or the facts presented disclose, that the defendants were justified in what they did. *Connors v. Connolly,* 86 Conn. 641, 647, 86 Atl. 600. The finding is not express upon this point, but we are of the opinion that the necessary implication from the subordinate facts found is a justification for the defendants' course.

The end the defendants had in view by their by-laws was the strengthening of their unions. That was a legitimate end. There is no indication that the real purpose of the defendants was injury to the plaintiff or the nonunion men it employed. Whatever injury was done the plaintiff was a consequence of trade competition, and an incident to a course of conduct by the defendants, begun and prosecuted for their own legitimate interests. The means adopted were lawful: no unlawful compulsion in act or word was present. The plaintiff had its option to employ the defendants or not; trade conditions did not convert this legal option into practical compulsion, since over one third of the men working in all of these trades to which the defendants belong in this locality were nonunion men. The cessation of work was not intended to cause a breach of existing contracts, and the cancellation of some of its contracts by the plaintiff is, so far as we know, attributable to the plaintiff's act, rather than to the defendants'. Certainly the finding is too bare of detail to permit the latter conclusion.

The notification by the defendants to the general contractors and owners, of the probability of a strike by them in case the plaintiff was employed on any job on which they were engaged, was no more than a notice that if nonunion labor was employed on jobs on which the defendant union men were employed the defendants would strike. If defendants had the right to contract that they would not work with nonunion labor, and if they might cease work if nonunion men were employed, as we hold in *State v. Stockford,* 77 Conn. 227, 58 Atl. 769, we can see no unlawfulness in their notice to contractors and employers of what would happen if nonunion men were employed on jobs on which they were engaged. The notice was the course of fair dealing. It did not take away the free choice from the contractor or owner; it possessed him of the facts which might affect his decision.

We do not think the notice was an act fairly within the intimidation statute. General Statutes, § 1296. The facts surrounding the giving of such a notice might bring it within the statute: the facts detailed in this finding do not.

There is no error.

In this opinion the other judges concurred.

NATIONAL FIREPROOFING CO. v. MASON BUILDERS' ASS'N.

United States Circuit Court of Appeals for the Second Circuit. 169 Fed. 259 (1909).

This is an appeal from a decree of the Circuit Court for the Southern District of New York dismissing a bill of complaint in a suit in equity.

The complainant is a corporation under the laws of the state of Pennsylvania and is authorized by its charter to manufacture and install fireproofing. Since its organization it has been engaged almost exclusively in the manufacture and installation of what is known as hollow tile fireproofing and produces over 50 per cent. of the entire output of that article in the United States.

The defendant Mason Builders' Association is a corporation under the laws of the state of New York, composed of master mason builders doing business in the city of New York, but comprising less than a majority of the mason builders of that city.

The defendants the various Bricklayers' Unions, with four exceptions which are chartered, are unincorporated associations. Practically every bricklayer in the city of New York and Long Island is a member of one of these unions.

The object of this suit is to restrain the enforcement of, and to have declared void, an agreement entered into between the Mason Builders' Association and the Bricklayers' Unions, upon the ground that it unlawfully interferes with the business and property of the complainant.

The agreement in question between the Mason Builders' Association and the Bricklayers' Unions is a biennial trade agreement covering the years 1906 and 1907 and relating to rates of wages, hours of labor, the settlement of differences by arbitration, and many other matters in the building trade affecting the interests of the parties. The particular clauses to which the complainant objects are the following:

"(5) The members of the Mason Builders' Association must include in their contracts for building all cutting of masonry, interior brickwork, the paving of brick floors, the installing of concrete blocks, the brickwork of the damp-proofing system and all fireproofing-floor arches, slabs, partitions, furring and roof blocks—and they shall not lump or sublet the installation, if the labor in connection therewith is bricklayers' work as recognized by the trade, the men employed upon the construction of the walls to be given the preference."

"(10) No members of these Bricklayers' Unions shall work for any one not complying with all the rules and regulations herein agreed to." * * *

The work of installing tile fireproofing is considered to be bricklayers' work by the trade, and it would be impracticable for the complainant to undertake such work in the city of New York without employing members of the Bricklayers' Unions. Clause 10, however, provides that members of the unions shall only work for persons complying with all the rules and regulations of the agreement. Among them is clause 5, which provides that the work of installing fireproofing shall not be sublet by a contractor, but must be included in the contract for the building. It follows therefore that these two clauses operate to prevent the complainant from installing its fireproofing in New York City unless it takes the entire contract for erecting a building, which it is not authorized by its charter to do.

In actual operation, too, the clauses in question have prevented the complainant from carrying out contracts for the installation of fireproofing. Thus in 1903 the complainant had a contract with the George A. Fuller Company—a general contractor not a member of the Builders' Association—for installing fireproofing in a building which it was erecting under contract in New York City. The association notified the complainant that its agreement with the unions forbade building contractors subletting the installation of fireproofing, and subsequently all the bricklayers employed upon the building—including those engaged upon the fireproofing—struck. Consequently the complainant was obliged to cancel its contract. Other similar instances are shown in the testimony.

It is evident therefore that these clauses affect owners and general contractors as well as a person who, like the complainant, desires to take separate fireproofing contracts. An owner is practically unable to make a contract for fireproofing alone because if he does the bricklayers will not only refuse to do that work, but will decline to do the other work upon the building. A general contractor, whether a member of the association or not, practically cannot sublet the fireproofing because if he does he will violate clause 5, and the bricklayers will refuse to work for him.

The defendants claim that the object of clause 5 is to benefit the bricklayers by giving them inside as well as outside work and by preventing specialization in their trade. This subject is fully considered in the opinion.

The object of clause 10 is, obviously, to make the trade agreement effective by extending its operation to third persons requiring the labor of bricklayers. While members of the unions may work for others than members of the association, they can only work for such employers as follow the rules and regulations of the agreement. Should the complainant obtain the power to make general building contracts and enter into such contracts, it could then obtain the services of members of the unions in setting the fireproofing required. The complainant, however, does not wish to do business in this manner. It desires to take separate contracts for fireproofing installation and is prevented from so doing business by the operation of the clauses in question.

The allegations of the amended complaint with respect to a combination to injure the complainant, accompanied by threats and intimidation— except as they relate to the enforcement against it of these clauses—are not supported by the evidence. Whatever the defendants have done has been for the enforcement of such clauses, and if they are valid, and their execution and enforcement in the manner shown lawful, no independent cause of action is established. * * *

Before LACOMBE, WARD, and NOYES, C.JJ.

NOYES, C.J. (after stating the facts as above): In considering the legal questions arising in this case, it must be borne in mind at the outset that it is not sufficient to show that the agreement in question may create a monopoly, may be in restraint of trade, or may be opposed to public policy. Agreements of that nature are invalid and unenforceable. The law takes them as it finds them, and as it finds them leaves them; but they are not illegal in the sense of giving a right of action to third persons for injury sustained. *Brown v. Jacobs' Pharmacy Co.*, 115 Ga. 433, 41 S.E. 553, 57 L.R.A. 547, 90 Am. St. Rep. 126. And upon similar principles it seems equally clear that they afford such persons no ground for seeking an injunction against injury threatened.

But the complainant asserts that the agreement in this case is positively unlawful and not merely negatively invalid—that it contravenes both national and state statutes against combinations, and thus does give rights of action to injured persons. With respect to the federal statute, it is not obvious in what way a trade agreement between builders and bricklayers, relating to their work in the state of New York, can be said to directly affect interstate commerce; but the consideration of this question is not necessary because a person injured by a violation of the federal act cannot sue for an injunction under it. The injunctive remedy is available to the government only. An individual can only sue for threefold damages. *Greer v. Stoller* (C.C.) 77 Fed. 2; *Southern Indiana Exp. Co. v. United States Exp. Co.* (C.C.) 88 Fed. 663. See, also, *Bement v. National Harrow Co.*, 186 U.S. 87, 22 Sup. Ct. 747, 46 L. Ed. 1058; *Post v. Southern R. Co.*, 103 Tenn.

184, 52 S.W. 301, 55 L.R.A. 481; *Metcalf v. American School-Furniture Co.* (C.C.) 108 Fed. 909; *Block v. Standard Distilling, etc., Co.* (C.C.) 95 Fed. 978; *Gulf, etc., R. Co. v. Miami Steamship Co.*, 86 Fed. 407, 30 C.C.A. 142; *Pidcock v. Harrington* (C.C.) 64 Fed. 821; *Hagan v. Blindell*, 56 Fed. 696, 6 C.C.A. 86 affirming *Blindell v. Hagan* (C.C.) 54 Fed. 40.

The statute of New York which it is claimed that the defendants violate provides in its first section as follows:

"Every contract, agreement, arrangement or combination, whereby a monopoly in the manufacture, production or sale in this state of any article or commodity of common use is or may be created, established or maintained, or whereby competition in this state in the supply or price of any such article or commodity is or may be restrained or prevented, or whereby, for the purpose of creating, establishing or maintaining a monopoly within this state of the manufacture, production or sale of any such article or commodity, the free pursuit in this state of any lawful business, trade or occupation, is or may be restricted or prevented, is hereby declared to be against public policy, illegal and void." Laws 1899, p. 1514, c. 690.

The complainant says that the agreement in question violates this statute because it tends to create a monopoly in the hands of members of the association and other general contractors who comply with its provisions. It may well be doubted, however, whether a combination of employers and employees in the building trade could ever be for the purpose of creating a monopoly "in the manufacture, production or sale in this state of any article or commodity of common use." Be that as it may, the thing which is essential to the existence of a monopoly—the concentration of business in the hands of a few—is not present here. The business of installing fireproofing in the city of New York is open to all who choose to engage in it under existing economic conditions. General contractors cannot be said to have a monopoly when any person can be a general contractor. Members of the unions cannot be said to be monopolists when any qualified bricklayer can join a union. Moreover, while it is probable under the New York decisions (*Rourke v. Elk Drug Co.*, 75 App. Div. 145, 77 N.Y. Supp. 373) that a person specially injured by a violation of this anti-monopoly statute would have a right of action for damages, it seems, upon the principle of the cases cited with respect to the federal statute, that only the Attorney General can sue for an injunction; such a suit being authorized by a section of the statute.

The complainant, thus failing to show any right to an injunction upon the ground that the agreement is contrary to public policy or in contravention of any state or national anti-trust statute, can only establish that it is entitled to such relief by showing that the execution of the agreement amounted to a conspiracy, and that its enforcement threatens injury; and to ascertain whether the complainant has established this requires the examination of a most important phase of the law of conspiracies as affecting combinations of labor and combinations between labor and capital.

A "conspiracy" may be broadly defined as a combination to effect an illegal object as an end or means. And a "civil conspiracy," which we are considering, may be defined as a combination of two or more persons to accomplish by concerted action an unlawful or oppressive object; or a lawful object by unlawful or oppressive means. To sustain an action, damage must have resulted from the combination; to warrant an injunction, damage must be threatened.

And so the inquiry is: (1) Was the object of the agreement unlawful or oppressive? (2) If the object were lawful and free from oppression, were the means unlawful or oppressive?

The direct object or purpose of a combination furnishes the primary test of its legality. It is not every injury inflicted upon third persons in its operation that renders a combination unlawful. It is not enough to establish illegality in an agreement between certain persons to show that it works harm to others. An agreement entered into for the primary purpose of promoting the interests of the parties is not rendered illegal by the fact that it may incidentally injure third persons. Conversely, an agreement entered into for the primary purpose of injuring another is not rendered legal by the fact that it may incidentally benefit the parties. As a general rule it may be stated that, when the chief object of a combination is to injure or oppress third persons, it is a conspiracy; but that when such injury or oppression is merely incidental to the carrying out of a lawful purpose, it is not a conspiracy. Stated in another way: A combination entered into for the real malicious purpose of injuring a third person in his business or property may amount to a conspiracy and furnish a ground of action for the damages sustained, or call for an injunction, even though formed for the ostensible purpose of benefiting its members and actually operating to some extent to their advantage; but a combination without such ulterior oppressive object, entered into merely for the purpose of promoting by lawful means the common interests of its members, is not a conspiracy. A laborer, as well as a builder, trader, or manufacturer, has the right to conduct his affairs in any lawful manner, even though he may thereby injure others. So several laborers and builders may combine for mutual advantage, and, so long as the motive is not malicious, the object not unlawful, nor oppressive and the means neither deceitful nor fraudulent, the result is not a conspiracy, although it may necessarily work injury to other persons. The damage to such persons may be serious—it may even extend to their ruin—but if it is inflicted by a combination in the legitimate pursuit of its own affairs, it is *damnum absque injuria*. The damage is present, but the unlawful object is absent. And so the essential question must always be whether the object of a combination is to do harm to others or to exercise the rights of the parties for their own benefit. * * *

The object of clause 10 manifestly was to make the stipulations of the agreement generally effective. The mason builders joining in the agreement being bound by its stipulations, it was necessary for their protection that competing outside builders should only employ bricklayers upon the same conditions. So it was for the advantage of the bricklayers themselves to have means for enforcing uniformity in terms of employment.

It also seems clear from the testimony that the object of clause 5 was to benefit the bricklayers. Certainly from their point of view substantial benefits accrue from preventing the installation of fireproofing by separate contractors. Through the operation of this clause the men who do the exposed work secure the easier and safer inside work and more continuous employment than would otherwise be the case. The specialization of the bricklayers' trade through the growth of a class of workmen who would devote themselves to setting fire brick and would, in the end, take all that work from the ordinary bricklayer, is prevented.

It is true that the complainant contends that these advantages are fanciful rather than real, and points out that much of the fireproofing is laid before the walls. Still it appears that a very large amount of fireproofing is done after the walls are completed, and the contention of the bricklayers that they obtain advantages through the operation of clause 5 in securing different kinds of work and steady employment seems well founded. The complainant also contends that there would be no danger of specialization in the bricklayers' trade should it take separate contracts for installing fireproofing, but the evidence does not support this contention. On the contrary, it indicates that the apprehensions of the bricklayers, as shown upon the record, are not without foundation.

Considering all the testimony, we are satisfied that the direct object of the adoption of the clauses in question was to benefit the parties and not to injure the complainant or other persons in a similar situation. Any particular or special intention to injure the complainant is, of course, negatived by the fact that the clauses in question were inserted in the trade agreement between the parties long before the complainant undertook to do any business in the city of New York.

The object of the agreement being neither unlawful nor oppressive, the next inquiry is whether the means adopted to make it effective were unlawful or oppressive.

As indicated in the statement of facts, no threats or acts of intimidation except in connection with the enforcement of clause 5 are shown. Instances do appear, however, in which bricklayers struck and ceased to work because they claimed that work was being done in violation of this clause. So, statements were made by members of the Builders' Association and of the unions that the complainant would not be permitted to take separate contracts for the installation of fireproofing. It is unnecessary to review the acts of the defendants in detail. We are not satisfied that if the defendants or their representatives made threats, they threatened to do anything which they had no right to do. The object of the agreement was not unlawful. The defendants had the right to strike to secure its enforcement. They also had the right to notify the complainant and persons with whom it had dealings that it could not take contracts for the installation of fireproofing contrary to the terms of the agreement without incurring its penalties. But a threat to do that which a person has the right to do is not unlawful. * * *

It therefore follows that the defendants have not entered into a combination to accomplish an unlawful or oppressive object, or a lawful object by unlawful or oppressive means, and are not guilty of a common-law conspiracy.

Finally, the complainant contends that the agreement amounts to a conspiracy under the Penal Code of the state of New York (section 168, subds. 5 and 6). But the principles applicable to conspiracies at common law, which we have considered, apply to conspiracies under the statute. The test of the application of the statute is the purpose of the combination, and if the object and means be lawful, there is no conspiracy, even though a third person may be incidentally injured.

And so the conclusion must be that the Circuit Court was right in dismissing the complaint. Nevertheless it cannot be denied that the complainant has ground for complaining. It desires to engage in a lawful and legitimate business in a lawful and legitimate way and is practically prevented from so doing by the acts of the defendants. Its right to do business in the manner it desires is interfered with, and the law affords it no remedy because such interference is only incidental to the exercise by the defendants of their own right to contract for their own benefit. The complainant is injured, but has no remedy. The law could only make it possible for the complainant to do business in the way it chooses by compelling the defendants to do business in the way they do not choose. But, when equal rights clash, the law cannot interfere.

Decree affirmed, with costs.

CHAPTER VIII.

THE UNION LABEL.

WEENER v. BRAYTON.

Massachusetts Supreme Judicial Court. 152 Mass. 101, 25 N.E. 46 (1890).

Bill in equity, by the members and officers of a voluntary association, against a workman to prevent the alleged infringement of a label as a trade-mark. The defendant demurred to the bill for want of equity. C. ALLEN, J., sustained the demurrer, and dismissed the bill; and the plaintiffs appealed to this court. The material allegations of the bill appear in the opinion.

DEVENS, J: This case is before us upon a demurrer, which concedes for the purpose of this hearing the truth of the allegations of the bill. From these it appears that the plaintiffs are officers and members of the Cigar Makers' Union, No. 97; that this union is a member of the Cigar Makers' International Union of America, which is a voluntary association composed wholly of local unions; that the Cigar Makers' International Union has authorized and directed its president to furnish to all local unions a trade-mark label, to be pasted upon the outside of each box containing cigars made by members of the union; that cigars made by such members have acquired a valuable reputation, and that in consequence thé right to the exclusive use of such labels is of great value; that the defendant has caused to be put on boxes containing inferior cigars, and not made by members of the union, a counterfeit label so closely resembling said union label as to deceive purchasers; and that, for the purpose of deceiving the purchasers and of obtaining higher prices from them, he has sold cigars in boxes on which were pasted such counterfeit labels, well knowing the cigars contained therein were not made by members of the union, and were inferior in workmanship and quality to those made by them, which are rightfully sold under the so called union label.

A trade-mark is a peculiar name or device, by which a person dealing in an article designates it as of a peculiar kind, character, or quality, or as manufactured by or for him, or dealt in by him, and of which he is entitled to the exclusive use. *Rogers v. Taintor,* 97 Mass. 291. *Chadwick v. Covell,* 151 Mass. 190. There is no exclusive ownership of the names, devices, symbols, or marks which constitute a trade-mark, apart from the use or application of them; but the word "trade-mark" is the designation of them when applied to a vendible commodity. The exclusive right to make such use or application is rightly treated as property.

While property in these names, devices, etc. for all purposes cannot exist, yet property as applied to particular vendible articles may exist when such articles have gone into the market identified by them, and have thus obtained reputation or currency by them as indicating a special or superior quality, or as the work of a particular manufacturer, or some other circumstance that commends them to the public. Kerr on Injunctions, (3d ed.) 395. The jurisdiction of a court of equity to restrain the wrongful use of such trade-marks by persons not entitled thereto is founded, not upon the imposition upon the public thus practised, but on the wrongful invasion of the right of property therein which has been acquired by others. A remedy is afforded only to the owner of the right of property in such trade-marks on account of the injury which is thus done to him. The wrong done to him consists in misrespresenting the vendible articles sold as being those of the true owner of the trade-mark, and thus to a greater or less extent depriving him of the benefit of the reputation he has given to the articles made or dealt in by him. To the validity of a trade-mark, so as to entitle any one to a remedy for an invasion thereof, three things have been held necessary: that he must show that he has adopted some marks or signs not in use by others to distinguish the goods manufactured or sold by him from those of other manufacturers or traders; that these must be applied to some article of traffic; and that such articles must have been placed on the market. *Schneider v. Williams,* 17 Stew. 391. *Chadwick v. Covell,* 151 Mass. 190. The right to a trade-mark cannot exist as a mere abstract right, independent of and disconnected from a business. It is not property as distinct from, but only as incident to the business. It cannot be transferred except with the business, may be sold with it, and ordinarily passes with it. *Cigar-Makers' Protective Union v. Conhaim,* 40 Minn. 243.

In the case last cited, the allegations of the bill were apparently the same as those in the case at bar, and the bill was brought by certain persons, members of the Cigar Makers' International Union through their membership in one of the local unions which composed the larger body. It appeared from the complaint, that a device claimed to be a trade-mark, but in its form rather an advertisement, had been adopted by the Cigar Makers' International Union, which was furnished to all local unions for use on the boxes of cigars made by their members; that the right to use it would continue as long as they were members, and would cease when they ceased to be members; and that a manufacturer could only use it by employing members of the union, and would have no right so to use it if he ceased to employ its members. It did not there appear, nor is it alleged in the case at bar, that either the plaintiffs or any one of the unions was a business corporation, association, or partnership for the purpose of manufacturing and selling, or engaged in the manufacture or sale, of cigars. It was held that the device in question—which in all substantial respects was the same with that here considered—was not a trade-mark, and the right to use it was not property, but a personal privilege. Its object was simply to indicate membership in the union, and to obtain whatever advantage the fact of membership might give its members. They had agreed on a certain device which might be placed on their productions. The right to use such a device was obtained merely by joining the association, and did not at all depend upon whether the person had earned a reputation for the manufacture of the particular article. It was therefore held that it could not be protected as a trade-mark.

For similar reasons, we are of opinion that the label alleged by the bill in the case at bar to have been counterfeited cannot be treated as a trade-mark. However disreputable and dishonest it may be falsely to represent goods made by other persons to have been made by members of the union, upon which subject there can be but one opinion, those who do not carry on any business to which the use of the label is incident, who have not applied it to any vendible commodity which has been placed upon the market in which they deal, or of which they are the owners or manufacturers, cannot maintain a bill to restrain the use by the defendant of the label as a trade-mark. It wants every essential element of such a mark; it does not indicate by what person articles were made, but only membership in a certain association; there is no exclusive use of it, but many persons not connected in business and unknown to each other may use it; its rightful use is not connected with any business; it cannot be transferred with any business, but such use is dependent only on membership in the association.

Upon the question whether labels of this character are valid trade-marks there has been some contrariety of opinion.[1] In *People v. Fisher,* 50 Hun, 552, under the New York Penal Code, which does not define a trade-mark in essential particulars differently from the definition usually adopted independently of the statute, it was held that the label was a valid trade-mark; but we are of opinion that it cannot be so treated and considered unless a quite different definition is given to this word from that which it has heretofore received, and quite different conditions from those heretofore recognized are held sufficient to justify proceedings for an injunction against one who dishonestly seeks to make a market for his wares by advertisements thereof which are false and unjustifiable. Without discussing the rights which a purchaser may have who has been deceived by such an advertisement or label, it is necessary for those who claim that their right of property in a trade-mark has been invaded to show that they are in some way, by themselves or with others, the owners

[1] A union label was refused registration as a trade mark upon the ground that it sought to discourage the manufacture of similar goods by non-union shops and also because it did not distinguish the goods of one manufacturer from another but simply indicated that the employees of a manufacturer belonged to a certain association. Cigar Makers' Ass'n of the Pacific Coast, 16 Off. Gaz. 958 (1879); Ex parte the Anti-Adulteration League, 86 Off. Gaz. 1803 (1899). Accord: McVey v. Brendell, 144 Pa. 235, 22 Atl. 912 (1891); Cigar Makers' Protective Union v. Conhaim, 40 Minn. 243, 41 N.W. 943 (1889); Carson v. Ury, 39 Fed. 777 (C.C.E.D. Mo. 1889) *semble.* See also: Sachs, "Property Rights in Union Labels," 13 Law Notes, 106 (1909); Meillon, "The Union Label," 3 Comm. Law Rev. 70 (1905).—Ed.

thereof by reason of some business which they are transacting together and to which its use is incident, and that it is not merely a personal privilege, which they possess as members of a particular association of wide extent and embracing many persons of varied interest, to advertise, or have advertised by those by whom they are employed, the articles made by them as being made by members of such association.

It is urged by the plaintiffs, even if the label in question cannot be considered technically a trade-mark, that where trade-marks have not been infringed courts of equity have granted injunctions against the use on various goods of certain marks, wrappers, and labels when there appeared to be a design to deceive the public by concealing the true origin of the goods, and to make it appear that they were the goods of another. *Croft v. Day,* 7 Beav. 84. *McLean v. Fleming,* 96 U.S. 245. *Brown Chemical Co. v. Myer,* 31 Fed. Rep. 453. *Thomson v. Winchester,* 19 Pick. 214. We have no occasion to question this principle, or the authorities by which it has been sustained. It will be found that, where under such circumstances an injunction has been granted or an action maintained, it has been at the instance of one who was himself a manufacturer, dealer in, or owner of the articles which were fraudulently represented by the counterfeited labels, wrappers, or advertisements to be his. In such case, the fraud complained of would have a natural and inevitable tendency to lessen the sales, affect the reputation of the articles manufactured or dealt in, and injure the business of the complainant, and would thus afford him a ground for relief by reason of the special and peculiar damage which he would sustain, or to which he might be exposed.

The plaintiffs show by their bill that they have a right to use the label in question, and that it is a valuable privilege; but although they aver that they have suffered loss by the use of it by the defendant, they do not show that any business which they pursue has been affected, or that they can have sustained any definite loss or any injury, except that which must be extremely remote and purely speculative.

In *Carson v. Ury,* 39 Fed. Rep. 777, it was held that a union label— answering in all respects to the one annexed to the plaintiffs' bill, and there averred to have been counterfeited by the defendant—did not answer to the definition ordinarily given of a technical trade-mark, because it did not indicate with any degree of certainty by what particular person or firm the cigars were manufactured to which it might be affixed, or serve to distinguish the goods of one cigar manufacturer from another, and also because the complainant did not appear to have any vendible interest in the label, but merely a right to use it so long, and only so long, as he might remain a member of the union. In all these respects it lacked the characteristics of a valid trade-mark. In that case, however, the complainant had averred himself to be a manufacturer of cigars entitled to use the union label, who had used and was actually using it on the cigars manufactured by him, thus guaranteeing the character and quality of his cigars, that he had made profits thereby, and that he had been greatly injured and was liable to be greatly injured by the defendant, who had prepared for sale counterfeit labels in the similitude of those which he had used, and was entitled to use. It was there deemed that the cases of *Cigar-Makers' Protective Union v. Conhaim,* and *Schneider v. Williams, ubi supra,* were distinguishable in this: that in those cases the bills were framed upon the theory that the label was a technical trademark, and as such the property of all the members of the union, and that any one or more members of the union might maintain a suit to restrain any unauthorized person from using the label, whether they were themselves engaged in the manufacture and sale of cigars on their own account or not. It was deemed, therefore, properly to have been held in those cases that the plaintiffs could not be considered to have such a property in the label that they could maintain a bill upon the ground that they were injuriously affected by the fraudulent acts complained of, while in the case then before the court the complainant had averred himself to be a manufacturer of cigars, who had built up a profitable trade and business, which business was liable to be and was damaged by the fraudulent acts complained of.

In the case at bar, there is no allegation that the plaintiffs are themselves, on their own account or with others, manufacturers or dealers in cigars as a business, or even persons actually employed by others in their sale or manufacture, or that the union of which they are members and officers is engaged in any business of that description. They do not by their bill show that they apply or have applied this label to any vendible commodity of which they are the owners, or which they manufacture for the market or place thereon for sale, or in which they deal. Where an association such as the Cigar Makers' Union, embracing many members and many divisions as subordinate unions, has adopted a symbol or device to be used on boxes of cigars made by its members, such device or symbol not indicating by whom the cigars are made, but only that they are made by some of the members of the union, and where the right to use the device or symbol belongs equally to all the members, and continues only while they are members, a bill cannot be maintained by individual members or officers of such association to restrain others wrongfully and fraudulently using such device or symbol from so doing. Any injury to such members or officers is not direct or immediate, nor does it affect them in any business which in some form they conduct. It is upon this ground that such invasions of that which has been held to be property have heretofore been restrained.

Whether, if the bill had contained allegations similar to those found in the case of *Carson v. Ury, ubi supra,* it might have been maintained, we have no occasion now to consider.

Bill dismissed.[2]

---

[2] Accord: McVey v. Brendell. 144 Pa. 235, 22 Atl. 912 (1891). *Cf.* Carson v. Ury, 39 Fed. 777 (C.C.E.D. Mo. 1889). See: Martin, Union Labels, 42 Am. Law Rev. 511 (1908).

STRASSER v. MOONELIS.

Superior Court of the City of New York. 55 N.Y.S. 197 (1888).

Before SEDGWICK, Ch. J., FREEDMAN and INGRAHAM, JJ.

Appeal by defendant from an order continuing an injunction order. The motion to continue came on at Special Term, where the following opinion was delivered:

DUGRO, J.: The plaintiffs complaining on behalf of themselves and of all other members of the "Cigar Makers' International Union of America," show that they are cigar makers and members of the "Cigar Makers' International Union of America"; that said union is a voluntary unincorporated association of practical cigar makers, formed for the purposes of promoting the mental, moral and physical welfare of its members, by assisting them to obtain labor at remunerative prices, by affording them pecuniary aid in sickness, and generally to maintain a high standard of workmanship, and fair wages of cigar makers; that for the purpose of designating the articles manufactured by members of the union, the union devised and adopted a trade-mark or label to which they gave the name of "union label," a fac-simile of which label is attached to the complaint.

That prior to the adoption of said label, the same had not been known or in use in this country or elsewhere, and ever since said adoption the members of said union have been, and are, exclusively entitled to the use of said labels, and the same have been conspicuously pasted on the outside of cigar boxes containing the cigars made by the plaintiffs and other members of the union, on whose behalf the action is brought.

That the said label affixed to cigar boxes is intended as a guarantee that the cigars therein contained are manufactured by members of the union, and that fair wages and good workmanship have been thereby secured; and that the cigars were not made in tenement-houses or state prisons; and for those reasons the same command a higher price in the market than cigars of a similar appearance, but without said label; and that the use of the said label is a source of great profit to the plaintiffs and others on whose behalf this action is brought.

Plaintiffs further show that the defendant has been and is infringing the exclusive right of the plaintiffs and the other members of the union to the use of the said label, in that defendant, with intent to defraud plaintiffs and deceive the public, has sold, and is offering for sale in New York city, boxes of cigars bearing labels which falsely purport to have been issued by the Cigar Makers' International Union of America, and which labels are such close imitations of the genuine labels used by plaintiffs, as aforesaid, that they are calculated to and do deceive and mislead the public into the belief that the cigars sold by defendant are manufactured by members of the aforesaid union; and that the labels used by defendant are false and spurious imitations of the genuine labels and trade-mark of the plaintiffs.

Plaintiffs further show that by reason of defendant's wrongful acts, irreparable damage and injury are caused to them, and therefore they pray for an injunction and account, and for damages.

The defendant, answering on information and belief, denies the use by him of counterfeit labels; he further denies that he has sold, or offered to sell, cigars not made by members of the "Cigar Makers' International Union of America" in boxes bearing labels falsely purporting to have been issued by said union; and for a further defense he alleges as follows: that the plaintiffs are not, nor is the alleged union, manufacturers of cigars in a proprietary sense, or in any right of proprietorship; nor do they, or it, have any right of property, possession or control in cigars made by its alleged members or otherwise; nor do they, or it, have any interest in, or ownership in, or control over the product of the labor of the several alleged members of said alleged union, or of any of them; nor do they, or it, have any royalty on the manufacture or sales of any cigars, whether having said alleged label or trade-mark affixed, or otherwise; nor do they, or it, have any share or interest in the profits of any sales made by any of its alleged members. Defendant, however, does not deny the use by him of genuine union labels on boxes containing cigars manufactured by non-union workmen, or others, not members of the said union.

The affidavits presented by plaintiffs, and a comparison of the genuine and spurious labels, compel me to the view that such a state of facts appear herein as calls for—one question conceded—an injunction *pendente lite*. The question to which I refer, is that raised by the defendant in his contention, that the plaintiffs are not the owners or manufacturers of cigars, but merely laborers employed to convert the material provided into the article of trade. The defendant's counsel, on the argument and in his brief, lays great stress on the fact that the label presented in this case does not come within the settled definition of a trade-mark, as he claims it to be.

It is needless to discuss this phase of the case, for the right to the exclusive use of this label may be sustained, although it fail to be a trade-mark in the precise definition of the term as heretofore used. For whether we call the property-right, which I believe the plaintiffs have in the label, a trade-mark, or by another name, is a matter of slight import. It is a right entitled to the protection of a court of equity on the same principle as that upon which courts have based their right to protect trade-marks and good will. It has been accepted as the rule that the court "proceeds upon the ground that a person has a valuable interest in the good will of his trade or business; and that having appropriated to himself a particular label, or sign, or trade-mark, indicating to those who wish to give him their patronage, that the article is manufactured or sold by him, or by his authority, or that he carries on his business at a particular place, he is entitled to protection against any other person who attempts to pirate on the good will of his friends or customers, or the patrons of his trade or business, by sailing under his flag, without his authority or consent."

It needs no deep study to perceive that the laborer has the same valuable interest in the good will of his labor as a manufacturer has in the good will of his trade. Every man has a property right to the result of his labor, and that he has sold this right by a contract for wages, is no reason why he should be deprived of the right to designate the origin of the result of his work. That it is impossible to attach to this result any badge or label indicative of origin or interest, unless with the consent of the owner of the physical property itself, does not affect the principle applicable to the case.

If certain laborers who, through a union, in the adoption of and in compliance with any set of rules which guarantee or purport to insure a certain class of labor, have thereby increased a demand for their particular labor, and if this union sees fit to designate the labor of the members by any particular symbol, label or sign which is descriptive of the origin or ownership of the labor, such a device as may be adopted is entitled to the protection of a court of equity from fraudulent simulation.

The right to the label seems to me to be a valuable one, for it appears that boxes of cigars to which the label is affixed sell in the market for a higher price than the same cigars sell in boxes upon which the label does not appear. It is clear that if this be so, the natural result of the use of a fraudulent simulation of this label on boxes of cigars without the authority of the union, is such an injury as entitles them to the protection of the court.

The label of the plaintiffs, used as the symbol of their labor, does not conflict with the rules applicable to trade-marks, or any analogous rules, and so, for the purpose for which it is used, it can be considered proper and entitled to protection.

The plaintiffs are entitled to be protected in the use and value of their property, and as in this case it can be adequately protected only by an injunction, an injunction *pendente lite* will issue; order to be settled on notice. * * *

BY THE COURT.—SEDGWICK, Ch. J.: I am of opinion that the plaintiffs, being members of the Cigar Makers' International Union, had an interest in the proper use of the labels of the union, which might upon sufficient grounds, be protected by injunction against the inequitable use of those labels.

I also think that it did not appear conclusively, upon the facts presented in the motion below, that the object of the union was illegal or against public policy, and that the finding of the learned judge below on this subject must here be sustained.

There can be no doubt that the defendant had used, and was about to use, counterfeits of the labels.

The order should be affirmed, with $10 costs to the plaintiffs, to abide the event.

FREEDMAN and INGRAHAM, JJ., concurred.[1]

---

[1] Accord: Hetterman Bros. & Co. v. Powers, 102 Ky. 133, 43 S.W. 180 (1897); Cigar Makers Union No. 1 v. Link, 29 L.R.A. 202 (Balt. C. Ct. 1886); Bloete v. Simon, 19 Abb. N.C. 88 (1887). Cf. Cohn v. People, 149 Ill. 486, 37 N.E. 60 (1894); People v. Fisher, 50 Hun 552, 3 N.Y.S. 786 (1889).

TRACY v. BANKER.

Massachusetts Supreme Judicial Court. 170 Mass. 266, 49 N.E. 308 (1898).

BILL IN EQUITY, filed April 29, 1897, in the Superior Court, by the plaintiff as Vice President of the Cigar Makers' International Union of America, to restrain the defendant from using a label on boxes of cigars manufactured by him.

Hearing before SHELDON, J., who found the following facts.

The Cigar Makers' International Union is a voluntary association of cigar makers. The plaintiff is a member and officer thereof. The objects and operations of the association prior to September, 1896, are as stated in its constitution of 1893, and subsequent to that time as stated in its constitution of 1896. In September, 1880, the union adopted for its protection a label or form of advertisement not previously adopted or owned by any other person, firm, association, or union, announcing that the goods to which it was attached were manufactured by members of the union, and on August 22, 1893, filed copies thereof in the office of the Secretary of the Commonwealth, in accordance with the provisions of St. 1893, c. 443, § 4, and received a duly attested certificate of the record thereof.

In January, 1894, the union altered such label by making some changes in the printed matter thereof, and on April 27, 1894, duly filed copies of the label as altered with the Secretary of the Commonwealth, all proper certificates being made and all necessary formalities complied with. Such label has been in use in its original form from September, 1880, to January, 1894, and in its amended form from January, 1894, to the present time, and has been of considerable value and benefit to the union and to its members. These labels are printed upon specially prepared paper for the union in Chicago, Illinois, and are distributed by its officers to the different local unions in the different States, these local unions being branches of the Chicago union, and are distributed by the officers of these local unions to those manufacturers whom the unions allow to receive them, in the following manner. A member of the union in the factory of each such manufacturer is appointed shop collector, and at stated short intervals, usually of a week, receives from the local union just enough labels to supply one for each box of cigars manufactured or to be manufactured during such interval, with the agreement and upon the condition that such labels shall be used only by placing them upon the boxes of cigars manufactured in such factory. Each separate factory or place of business used for the manufacture of cigars has a particular number assigned to it under the revenue laws of the United States; and whenever labels are issued to any one, the local union issuing them stamps upon each label so issued the number of the union issuing the label, and the factory number of the manufacturer to whom the issue is made. The defendant knows, and has known since the last part of

December, 1893, that the labels of the union are distributed and issued in this way, and upon this agreement and condition.

The union itself does not manufacture or sell, and never has manufactured or sold, any cigars, and does not intend to do so, and its sole revenue is from the dues paid to it by its members; and the union itself derives no pecuniary advantage from the use of the label.

The defendant is a manufacturer of cigars, having a factory in Boston. He did not use the labels issued by the union, or labels similar to them, before November, 1893. At that time, he applied to officers of the local union for permission to use the labels, and received such permission, upon condition that he should make certain sanitary improvements in his factory, which he did. Thereupon he received from the local union these labels until about January 4, 1894, when disputes arose between him and the local union, the right to use the label was taken from him by the union, he discharged those employees of his who were members of the union, and since then he has not employed any members of the union, and has had no right to use the labels other than such right, if any, as may belong to each and every manufacturer of cigars. But he is now using, and since a time early in 1894 has been using, upon the cigars made and sold by him, labels which are exact copies of those of the union. He has procured all the labels so used by him by purchasing them from persons to whom he believed they had been issued by local unions, branches of the International Union, in the manner and upon the condition above stated, and he has mutilated them by erasing the stamped number of the factory to which they purported to have been issued. Some of the labels which he has so purchased and used were really issued in this way, and were used by him in intentional violation of the agreement and condition upon which the union had issued them; but the others of the labels were mere counterfeits of the labels of the union. The statements on the labels, as applied to the cigars made by the defendant, are false, and he knows that they are false.

The officers of the union have for more than two years known of the actions of the defendant above stated. The secretary of the local union, on April 23, 1895, sent to the defendant a letter, warning him that he was liable to be prosecuted criminally, and on January 30, 1895, distributed in Boston and the neighborhood circulars stating that certain brands of cigars which were being sold bore a counterfeit or imitation of the label of the International Union. It also appeared that the officers of the union in 1897, shortly before the filing of this bill, distributed extensively in Boston and vicinity another circular, stating that certain cigars were "scab made" and bore "copy of union label."

The officers of the union were aware of the decision in the case of *Weener v. Brayton,* 152 Mass. 101, and until early in 1897, when they consulted new counsel, supposed they could have no remedy in equity against the defendant.

"I find, if the fact is competent to be proved, that though they were aware of the passage of Sts. 1893, c. 443, and 1895, c. 462, their attention had been called merely to the penal provisions of these statutes, and they were not aware that any redress in equity was given by these statutes, or either of them."

Upon these facts, at the request of both parties, the case was reported for the determination of this court; such decree to be entered therein as justice and equity might require. * * *

HOLMES, J.: This is a bill in equity, brought under St. 1895, c. 462, § 3, by the officer of a voluntary association, as authorized by that section, to prevent the defendant from fraudulently using the association's trades union label, and counterfeits of such label. The defences requiring notice are that the statute protects only merchants or manufacturers, that the association is not of a kind that will be protected by the court, and laches.

The label is part of the well known machinery of trades unions, and the use of it is found, if a finding be necessary, to be of value to the union and its members. It would not be travelling too far from the record, perhaps, if we should assume that the use of the label is in fact, as certainly it might be, of far more economic importance to the union than are many or most of the trade-marks, strictly so called, which are protected by the courts. Nevertheless, technical difficulties, which would have been hard to escape from without some subtlety or a statute, prevented the plaintiff from recovering in a case like this. *Weener v. Brayton,* 152 Mass. 101. See *State v. Bishop,* 128 Mo. 373, 381. That was in 1890. Just before the argument of that case there was an attempt at legislation on the subject. St. 1890, c. 104. Three years later a statute was passed, which certainly looks as if it had been intended in part to meet that decision. St. 1893, c. 443. But this act was still somewhat under the influence of the notion that protection of the label was a protection of manufacture, and after an amendment by St. 1894, c. 285, it was repealed by the act of 1895, which still is in force. It is true that the present statute is entitled "An Act to protect manufacturers from the use of counterfeit labels and stamps." But we can see no sufficient room for doubt that it protects the plaintiff. The first section extends to "any person, association, or union." That unincorporated associations or unions were contemplated is shown by § 3, already referred to, which allows suits to be prosecuted by the officers of such associations or unions. It is impossible to believe that when the statute mentions unincorporated unions it does not refer to trade unions. It authorizes such unions to adopt, as well as to record a label. Therefore it creates a right, if the court is unable to recognize one without its aid. If it applies to trade unions, it must be taken to apply to them as they ordinarily are, that is, as associations of workmen, not as manufacturers or vendors of goods. It contemplates that the labels will be applied to merchandise, as of course they must be, and as these labels are. But it carefully abstains from using a word which implies that the protection or wrongful use of labels is confined to manufacturers or vendors. The policy of the statute is shown by the above cited amendment of 1894 to the earlier act, which had for its object to extend the liability to others beside manufacturers.

If, as we think, the statute expressly creates or recognizes the right of trade unions to be protected in the use of labels for trade union purposes, the suggestion that the association represented by the plaintiff is an unlawful association falls of itself. It is too late to make such a contention as to trade unions generally, even apart from the statute under which this suit is brought. But the general purposes of this union are similar, so far as we know, to the general purposes of other unions. The constitution as a whole is not illegal, and the association is not deprived of the protection of the law for what otherwise would be its rights, if in some incident or particular the purposes which it expresses are unlawful, which we do not imply. See *Cohn v. People,* 149 Ill. 486; *Carson v. Ury,* 39 Fed. Rep. 777; *State v. Hagen,* 6 Ind. App. 167, 173; *State v. Bishop.* 128 Mo. 373.

The plaintiff's association had a label registered under the earlier statute of 1893. The defendant has the boldness to urge that, because he began his attempt to defraud the union in 1894, before the act of 1895 was passed, after having been permitted on his application to use the label for a time, therefore the plaintiff's union has no rights under the statute. We do not think the suggestion needs more than a statement.

The plaintiff has lost no rights through laches. *Nudd v. Powers,* 136 Mass. 273, 277, 278. *Menendez v. Holt,* 128 U.S. 514, 523, 524.

Finally, as the plaintiff makes out his right, it is to be protected against one form of swindling as well as another,—against the use of real labels in a fraudulent way, as well as against the use of counterfeits, if indeed the real labels as used by the defendant after mutilation are not counterfeits within the statute.

Decree for the plaintiff.[1]

---

[1] For the protection of union labels under statutes, see: People v. Dantuma, 252 Ill. 561, 96 N.E. 1087 (1911); State v. Hagen, 6 Ind. App. 167, 33 N.E. 223 (1892); State v. Bishop, 128 Mo. 373, 31 S.W. 9 (1895); Schmalz v. Wooley, 57 N.J. Eq. 303, 41 Atl. 939 (1898); United Garment Workers of America v. Davis, 74 Atl. 306 (N.J. Ch. 1909); Perkins v. Heert, 158 N.Y. 306, 53 N.E. 18 (1899); Wetzel v. Clise, 148 Wash. 75, 268 Pac. 161 (1928); Knuth v. Lepp, 180 Wis. 529, 193 N.W. (1923). For narrow restriction of the statutory protection, see: Lawlor v. Merritt, 78 Conn. 630, 63 Atl. 639 (1906), 79 Conn. 399, 65 Atl. 295 (1906).

For a collection of the statutes protecting union labels, see: U. S. Dept. of Labor, Bureau of Labor Statistics, Bull. No. 370, 112-114 (1925).

For a discussion of the effectiveness of the union label and union fair lists, see: Wolman, The Boycott in American Trade Unions, 92-99 (1916); Spedden, The Trade Union Label (1910).

The refusal to handle materials unless they bore a union label has been enjoined. Black & Boyd Mfg. Co. v. Local No. 514, 10 Law & Labor, 260, 267 (U.S.D.C. Mich. 1928).

CHAPTER IX.

FEDERAL INTERVENTION IN LABOR CONTROVERSIES.

SHERMAN ANTI-TRUST ACT.

Act of July 2, 1890. 26 U.S. Stat. 209.

SEC. 1. Every contract, combination in the form of trust or otherwise, or conspiracy, in restraint of trade or commerce among the several States, or with foreign nations, is hereby declared to be illegal. Every person who shall make any such contract or engage in any such combination or conspiracy, shall be deemed guilty of a misdemeanor, and, on conviction thereof, shall be punished by fine not exceeding five thousand dollars, or by imprisonment not exceeding one year, or by both said punishments, in the discretion of the court.

SEC. 2. Every person who shall monopolize, or attempt to monopolize, or combine or conspire with any other person or persons, to monopolize any part of the trade or commerce among the several States, or with foreign nations, shall be deemed guilty of a misdemeanor, and, on conviction thereof, shall be punished by fine not exceeding five thousand dollars, or by imprisonment not exceeding one year, or by both said punishments, in the discretion of the court. * * *

SEC. 4. The several circuit courts of the United States are hereby invested with jurisdiction to prevent and restrain violations of this act; and it shall be the duty of the several district attorneys of the United States, in their respective districts, under the direction of the Attorney-General, to institute proceedings in equity to prevent and restrain such violations. Such proceedings may be by way of petition setting forth the case and praying that such violation shall be enjoined or otherwise prohibited. When the parties complained of shall have been duly notified of such petition the court shall proceed, as soon as may be, to the hearing and determination of the case; and pending such petition and before final decree, the court may at any time make such temporary restraining order or prohibition as shall be deemed just in the premises.

SEC. 5. Whenever it shall appear to the court before which any proceeding under section four of this act may be pending, that the ends of justice require that other parties should be brought before the court, the court may cause them to be summoned, whether they reside in the district in which the court is held or not; and subpoenas to that end may be served in any district by the marshal thereof.

Sec. 6. Any property owned under any contract or by any combination, or pursuant to any conspiracy (and being the subject thereof) mentioned in section one of this act, and being in the course of transportation from one State to another, or to a foreign country, shall be forfeited to the United States, and may be seized and condemned by like proceedings as those provided by law for the forfeiture, seizure, and condemnation of property imported into the United States contrary to law.

Sec. 7. Any person who shall be injured in his business or property by any other person or corporation by reason of anything forbidden or declared to be unlawful by this act, may sue therefor in any circuit court of the United States in the district in which the defendant resides or is found, without respect to the amount in controversy, and shall recover three fold the damages by him sustained, and the costs of suit, including a reasonable attorney's fee.

Sec. 8. That the word "person," or "persons," wherever used in this act shall be deemed to include corporations and associations existing under or authorized by the laws of either the United States, the laws of any of the Territories, the laws of any State, or the laws of any foreign country.[1]

IN RE DEBS, PETITIONER.

Supreme Court of the United States. 158 U.S. 564 (1895).

On July 2, 1894, the United States, by Thomas E. Milchrist, district attorney for the Northern District of Illinois, under the direction of Richard Olney, Attorney General, filed their bill of complaint in the Circuit Court of the United States for the Northern District of Illinois against these petitioners and others. This bill set forth, among other things, the following facts: It named twenty-two railroad companies, and it alleged that they were engaged in the business of interstate commerce and subject to the provisions of the act of Congress of February 4, 1887, known as "the Interstate Commerce Act," and all other laws of the United States relating to interstate transportation of passengers and freight; that the number of passengers annually carried by them into the city of Chicago from other States than Illinois, and out of Chicago into other States than Illinois, was more than twelve millions, and in like manner that the freight so carried into and out of the city of Chicago, from and into other States

---

[1] See, generally, The Federal Anti-trust Laws with Amendments (1931); Shale, Decrees and Judgments in Federal Anti-Trust Cases (1918); Berman, Labor and the Sherman Act (1930); Emery, "Labor Organizations and the Sherman Law," 20 Jour. Pol. Econ. 599 (1912); Powell, "The Supreme Court's Control over the Issuance of Injunctions in Labor Disputes," 13 Proc. Acad. Pol. Sci. 37 (1928); Terborgh, "The Application of the Sherman Law to Trade-Union Activities," 37 Jour. Pol. Econ. 203 (1929).

.han Illinois, amounted to many millions of tons; that each of the roads was under contract to carry, and in fact carrying, the mails of the United States; that all were by statute declared post roads of the government; that many were by special acts of Congress required at any and all times to carry the troops and military forces of the United States, and provisions, munitions, and general supplies therefor; and that two of them were in the hands of receivers appointed by the courts of the United States. It stated at some length the necessity of the continued and uninterrupted running of such interstate railroads for the bringing into the city of Chicago supplies for its citizens and for the carrying on of the varied industries of that city.

The bill further averred that four of the defendants, naming them, were officers of an association known as the American Railway Union; that in the month of May, 1894, there arose a difference or dispute between the Pullman Palace Car Company and its employés, as the result of which a considerable portion of the latter left the service of the car company; that thereafter the four officers of the railway union combined together, and with others, to compel an adjustment of such dispute, by creating a boycott against the cars of the car company; that, to make such boycott effective, they had already prevented certain of the railroads running out of Chicago from operating their trains, and were combining to extend such boycott against Pullman sleeping cars by causing strikes among employés of all railroads attempting to haul the same. It charged knowledge on the part of the defendants of the necessity of the use of sleeping cars in the operation of the business of the railroads as common carriers, of the contracts for such use between the railroad companies and the car company, of the contracts, laws, and regulations binding the railway companies and the receivers to the carrying of the mails; also of the fact that sleeping cars were and of necessity must be carried upon the trains of said carriers with cars containing the mails; that with this knowledge they entered into a combination and conspiracy to prevent the railroad companies and the receivers, and each of them, from performing their duties as common carriers of interstate commerce, and in carrying into execution that conspiracy did induce various employés of the railway companies to leave the service of the companies, and prevent such companies and the receivers from securing other persons to take their places; that they issued orders, notifications, etc., to the members of the railway union to leave the service of the companies and receivers, and to prevent the companies and receivers from operating their trains; that they had asserted that they could and would tie up, paralyze, and break down any and every of said railway companies and receivers which did not accede to their demands; that in pursuance of the instructions, commands, and requests of said officers large numbers of the employés of the railway companies and receivers left their service.

Then followed these allegations:

"And your orator further charges that said defendants aimed and intended and do now aim and intend in and by the said conspiracy and combination, to secure unto themselves the entire control of the inter-state, industrial and commercial business in which the population of the city of Chicago and of the other communities along the lines of road of said railways are engaged with each other, and to restrain any and all other persons from any independent control or management of such interstate, industrial or commercial enterprises save according to the will and with the consent of the defendants.

"Your orator further avers that in pursuance of said combination and conspiracy and to accomplish the purpose thereof as hereinbefore set forth, the said defendants Debs, Howard, Rogers, Keliher and others, officers of said American Railway Union, issued or caused to be issued the orders and directions as above set forth, and that in obedience of such orders and in pursuance of said conspiracy and combination, numer-ous employés of said railroad companies and receivers unitedly refused to obey the orders of said employers or to perform the usual duties of such service, and many others of such employés quit such service with the common purpose, and with the result of preventing said railroad com-panies and receivers from operating their said railroads and from trans-porting the United States mails, and from carrying on or conducting their duties as common carriers of interstate traffic.

"Your orator further avers that, pursuant to said combination and conspiracy, and under the direction as aforesaid of said officers and di-rectors of said American Railway Union, said other defendants and other persons whose names are to your orator unknown, proceeded by collect-ing together in large numbers, by threats, intimidation, force and violence at the station grounds, yards and right of way of said railroad companies, respectively, in the State of Illinois, to prevent said railroad companies from employing other persons to fill the vacancies aforesaid; to compel others still employés of said railroad companies to quit such employment and to refuse to perform the duties of their service, and to prevent the persons remaining in such service and ready and willing to perform the duties of the same, from doing so.

"Your orator further avers that said defendants, in pursuance of said combination and conspiracy, acting under the direction of said officers and directors of said American Railway Union, did with force and violence at divers times and places within said State of Illinois and elsewhere, stop, obstruct and derail and wreck the engines and trains of said railroad companies, both passenger and freight, then and there engaged in inter-state commerce and in transporting United States mails, by locking the switches of the railroad of said railroad companies, by removing the spikes and rails from the track thereof, by turning switches and dis-placing and destroying signals, by assaulting and interfering with and disabling the switchmen and other employés of said railroad companies having charge of the signals, switches and tracks of said companies, and the movement of trains thereon, and in other manners by force and violence, depriving the employés of said railroad companies in charge of such trains of the control and management of the same, and by these and other unlawful means attempted to obtain and exercise absolute control and domination over the entire operations of said railroads."

The bill further set forth that there had become established in the city of Chicago a business conducted under the name of the Union Stock Yards, at which for many years immense numbers of live stock from States and Territories beyond the State of Illinois had been received, slaughtered, and converted into food products, and distributed to all quarters of the globe, and that all the large centres of population in the United States were in a great degree dependent upon those stock yards for their food supply of that character; that for the purpose of handling such live stock and the product thereof the company conducting such business operated certain railroad tracks, and that in pursuance of the combination and conspiracy aforesaid the four defendants, officers of the railway union, issued orders directing all the employés handling such railroad tracks to abandon such service.

To this was added the following:

"And your orator further alleges that in pursuance of the like combination and unlawful conspiracy, the said defendants and others combining and conspiring with them for the purpose of still further restraining and preventing the conduct of such business, have by menaces, threats and intimidation prevented the employment of other persons to take the place of the employés quitting the service of said company so operating said Union Stock Yards.

"And your orator further charges that by reason of said unlawful combination and conspiracy and the acts and doings aforesaid thereunder, the supply of coal and fuel for consumption throughout the different States of the Union and of grain, breadstuffs, vegetables, fruits, meats and other necessaries of life, has been cut off, interrupted and interfered with, and the market therefor made largely unavailable, and dealers in all of said various products and the consumers thereof have been greatly injured, and trade and commerce therein among the States has been restrained, obstructed and largely destroyed."

The bill alleged that the defendants threatened and declared that they would continue to restrain, obstruct, and interfere with interstate commerce, as above set forth, and that they "will if necessary to carry out the said unlawful combination and conspiracy above set forth tie up and paralyze the operations of every railway in the United States, and the business and industries dependent thereon." Following these allegations was a prayer for an injunction. The bill was verified.

On presentation of it to the court an injunction was ordered commanding the defendants "and all persons combining and conspiring with them, and all other persons whomsoever, absolutely to desist and refrain from in any way or manner interfering with, hindering, obstructing or stopping any of the business of any of the following named railroads," (specifically naming the various roads named in the bill,) "as common carriers of passengers and freight between or among any States of the United States, and from in any way or manner interfering with, hindering, obstructing or stopping any mail trains, express trains or other trains, whether freight or passenger, engaged in interstate commerce, or carrying passengers or freight between or among the States; and from in any manner interfering with, hindering or stopping any trains carrying the mail; and from in any manner interfering with, hindering, obstructing or stopping any engines, cars or rolling stock of any of said companies engaged in interstate commerce, or in connection with the carriage of passengers or freight between or among the States; and from in any manner interfering with, injuring or destroying any of the property of any of said railroads engaged in or for the purpose of, or in connection with, interstate commerce or the carriage of the mails of the United States or the transportation of passengers or freight between or among the States; and from entering upon the grounds or premises of any of said railroads for the purpose of interfering with, hindering, obstructing, or stopping any of said mail trains, passenger or freight trains engaged in interstate commerce, or in the transportation of passengers or freight between or among the States, or for the purpose of interfering with, injuring, or destroying any of said property so engaged in or used in connection with interstate commerce or the transportation of passengers or property between or among the States; and from injuring or destroying any part of the tracks, roadbed, or road, or permanent structures of said railroads; and from injuring, destroying, or in any way interfering with any of the signals or switches of any of said railroads; and from displacing or extinguishing any of the signals of any of said railroads, and from spiking, locking, or in any manner fastening any of the switches of any of said railroads, and from uncoupling or in any way hampering or obstructing the control by any of said railroads of any of the cars, engines, or parts of trains of any of said railroads engaged in interstate commerce or in the transportation of passengers or freight between or among the States, or engaged in carrying any of the mails of the United States; and from compelling or inducing or attempting to compel or induce, by threats, intimidation, persuasion, force, or violence, any of the employés of any of said railroads to refuse or fail to perform any of their duties as employés of any of said railroads in connection with the interstate business or commerce of such railroads or the carriage of the United States mail by such railroads, or the transportation of passengers or property between or among the States; and from compelling or inducing or attempting to compel or induce by threats, intimidation, force, or violence any of the employés of any said railroads who are employed by such railroads, and engaged in its service in the conduct of interstate business or in the operation of any of its trains carrying the mail of the United States, or doing interstate business, or the transportation of passengers and freight between and among the States, to leave the service of such railroads; and from preventing any person whatever, by threats, intimidation, force, or violence from entering the service of any of said railroads and doing the work thereof, in the carrying of the mails of the United States, or the transportation of passengers and freight between or among the States; and from doing any act whatever in furtherance of any conspiracy or combination to restrain either of said railroad companies or receivers in the free and unhindered control and handling of interstate commerce over the lines of said railroads, and of transportation of persons and freight between and among the States; and from ordering, directing, aiding, assisting, or abetting in any manner whatever, any person or persons to commit any or either of the acts aforesaid.

"And it is further ordered that the aforesaid injunction and writ of injunction shall be in force and binding upon such of said defendants as are named in said bill from and after the service upon them severally of said writ by delivering to them severally a copy of said writ or by reading the same to them and the service upon them respectively of the writ of subpoena herein, and shall be binding upon said defendants, whose names are alleged to be unknown, from and after the service of such writ upon them respectively by the reading of the same to them or by the publication thereof by posting or printing, and after service of subpoena upon any of said defendants named herein shall be binding upon said defendants and upon all other persons whatsoever who are not named herein from and after the time when they shall severally have knowledge of the entry of such order and the existence of said injunction."[1]

This injunction was served upon the defendants—at least upon those who are here as petitioners. On July 17 the district attorney filed in the office of the clerk of said court an information for an attachment against the four defendants, officers of the railway union, and on August 1 a similar information against the other petitioners. A hearing was had before the Circuit Court, and on December 14 these petitioners were found guilty of contempt, and sentenced to imprisonment in the county jail for terms varying from three to six months. 64 Fed. Rep. 724. Having been committed to jail in pursuance of this order they, on January 14, 1895, applied to this court for a writ of error and also one of *habeas corpus*. The former was, on January 17, denied, on the ground that the order of the Circuit Court was not a final judgment or decree. The latter is now to be considered.[2] * * *

Mr. Justice Brewer, after stating the case, delivered the opinion of the court.

The case presented by the bill is this: The United States, finding that the interstate transportation of persons and property, as well as the carriage of the mails, is forcibly obstructed, and that a combination and conspiracy exists to subject the control of such transportation to

---

[1] For an analysis of the provisions of this injunction, see: Frankfurter and Landis, "Power of Congress over Procedure in Criminal Contempts," 37 Harv. Law Rev. 1010, 1101 (1924): For the text of a similar injunction issued during the same strike against Eugene V. Debs and others by the Circuit Court of Indiana, see: United States Strike Commission, Report on the Chicago Strike, 179 (1895).—Ed.

[2] Counsel for the petitioners consisted of Lyman Trumbull, S. S. Gregory and Clarence S. Darrow. The United States was represented by Attorney General Olney, Assistant Attorney General Whitney, and Edwin Walker.—Ed.

the will of the conspirators, applied to one of their courts, sitting as a court of equity, for an injunction to restrain such obstruction and prevent carrying into effect such conspiracy. Two questions of importance are presented: First. Are the relations of the general government to interstate commerce and the transportation of the mails such as authorize a direct interference to prevent a forcible obstruction thereof? Second. If authority exists, as authority in governmental affairs implies both power and duty, has a court of equity jurisdiction to issue an injunction in aid of the performance of such duty.

First. What are the relations of the general government to interstate commerce and the transportation of the mails? They are those of direct supervision, control, and management. While under the dual system which prevails with us the powers of government are distributed between the State and the Nation, and while the latter is properly styled a government of enumerated powers, yet within the limits of such enumeration it has all the attributes of sovereignty, and, in the exercise of those enumerated powers, acts directly upon the citizen, and not through the intermediate agency of the State. * * *

Among the powers expressly given to the national government are the control of interstate commerce and the creation and management of a post office system for the nation. Article I, section 8, of the Constitution provides that "the Congress shall have power * * * Third, to regulate commerce with foreign nations and among the several States, and with the Indian tribes.* * * Seventh, to establish post offices and post roads."

Congress has exercised the power granted in respect to interstate commerce in a variety of legislative acts. Passing by for the present all that legislation in respect to commerce by water, and considering only that which bears upon railroad interstate transportation, (for this is the specific matter involved in this case) these acts may be noticed: * * * 3

Under the power vested in Congress to establish post offices and post roads, Congress has, by a mass of legislation, established the great post office system of the country, with all its detail of organization, its machinery for the transaction of business, defining what shall be carried and what not, and the prices of carriage, and also prescribing penalties for all offences against it.

Obviously these powers given to the national government over interstate commerce and in respect to the transportation of the mails were not dormant and unused. Congress had taken hold of these two matters, and by various and specific acts had assumed and exercised the powers

---

3 The court here referred to the Act of June 15, 1866, 14 Stat. 66, authorizing steam railroads to carry mails, government supplies and troops; the Act of March 3, 1873, 17 Stat. 584, regulating the transportation of live stock by railroads; the Act of May 29, 1884, 23 Stat. 31, prohibiting railroads from carrying live stock affected with a contagious disease; the Act of February 4, 1887, 24 Stat. 379, as amended, being the interstate commerce act; the Act of October 1, 1888, 25 Stat. 501, providing for arbitration between railroads and their employees; and the Act of March 2, 1893, 27 Stat. 531, providing for automatic couplers on interstate trains. —Ed.

given to it, and was in the full discharge of its duty to regulate interstate commerce and carry the mails. The validity of such exercise and the exclusiveness of its control had been again and again presented to this court for consideration. It is curious to note the fact that in a large proportion of the cases in respect to interstate commerce brought to this court the question presented was of the validity of state legislation in its bearings upon interstate commerce, and the uniform course of decision has been to declare that it is not within the competency of a State to legislate in such a manner as to obstruct interstate commerce. If a State with its recognized powers of sovereignty is impotent to obstruct interstate commerce, can it be that any mere voluntary association of individuals within the limits of that State has a power which the State itself does not possess?

As, under the Constitution, power over interstate commerce and the transportation of the mails is vested in the national government, and Congress by virtue of such grant has assumed actual and direct control, it follows that the national government may prevent any unlawful and forcible interference therewith. But how shall this be accomplished? Doubtless, it is within the competency of Congress to prescribe by legislation that any interference with these matters shall be offences against the United States, and prosecuted and punished by indictment in the proper courts. But is that the only remedy? Have the vast interests of the nation in interstate commerce, and in the transportation of the mails, no other protection than lies in the possible punishment of those who interfere with it? To ask the question is to answer it. By article 3, section 2, clause 3, of the Federal Constitution it is provided: "The trial of all crimes except in cases of impeachment shall be by jury; and such trial shall be held in the State where the said crime shall have been committed." If all the inhabitants of a State, or even a great body of them, should combine to obstruct interstate commerce or the transportation of the mails, prosecutions for such offences had in such a community would be doomed in advance to failure. And if the certainty of such failure was known, and the national government had no other way to enforce the freedom of interstate commerce and the transportation of the mails than by prosecution and punishment for interference therewith, the whole interests of the nation in these respects would be at the absolute mercy of a portion of the inhabitants of that single State.

But there is no such impotency in the national government. The entire strength of the nation may be used to enforce in any part of the land the full and free exercise of all national powers and the security of all rights entrusted by the Constitution to its care. The strong arm of the national government may be put forth to brush away all obstrucions to the freedom of interstate commerce or the transportation of the mails. If the emergency arises, the army of the Nation, and all its militia, are at the service of the Nation to compel obedience to its laws.

But passing to the second question, is there no other alternative than the use of force on the part of the executive authorities whenever obstructions arise to the freedom of interstate commerce or the transportation of the mails? Is the army the only instrument by which rights of the public can be enforced and the peace of the nation preserved? Grant that any public nuisance may be forcibly abated either at the instance of the authorities, or by any individual suffering private damage therefrom, the existence of this right of forcible abatement is not inconsistent with nor does it destroy the right of appeal in an orderly way to the courts for a judicial determination, and an exercise of their powers by writ of injunction and otherwise to accomplish the same result. * * *

So, in the case before us, the right to use force does not exclude the right of appeal to the courts for a judicial determination and for the exercise of all their powers of prevention. Indeed, it is more to the praise than to the blame of the government, that, instead of determining for itself questions of right and wrong on the part of these petitioners and their associates and enforcing that determination by the club of the policeman and the bayonet of the soldier, it submitted all those questions to the peaceful determination of judicial tribunals, and invoked their consideration and judgment as to the measure of its rights and powers and the correlative obligations of those against whom it made complaint. And it is equally to the credit of the latter that the judgment of those tribunals was by the great body of them respected, and the troubles which threatened so much disaster terminated.

Neither can it be doubted that the government has such an interest in the subject-matter as enables it to appear as party plaintiff in this suit. It is said that equity only interferes for the protection of property, and that the government has no property interest. A sufficient reply is that the United States have a property in the mails, the protection of which was one of the purposes of this bill. * * *

We do not care to place our decision upon this ground alone. Every government, entrusted, by the very terms of its being, with powers and duties to be exercised and discharged for the general welfare, has a right to apply to its own courts for any proper assistance in the exercise of the one and the discharge of the other, and it is no sufficient answer to its appeal to one of those courts that it has no pecuniary interest in the matter. The obligations which it is under to promote the interest of all, and to prevent the wrongdoing of one resulting in injury to the general welfare, is often of itself sufficient to give it a standing in court. This proposition in some of its relations has heretofore received the sanction of this court. * * * [4]

It is obvious from these decisions that while it is not the province of the government to interfere in any mere matter of private controversy between individuals, or to use its great powers to enforce the rights of one against another, yet, whenever the wrongs complained of are

---

[4] The court here relied upon United States v. San Jacinto Tin Co., 125 U.S. 273, which permitted the United States to maintain a bill for the cancellation of a land patent on the ground that it was obtained by fraud or mistake, and United States v. Bell Tel. Co., 128 U.S. 315 (1888), where the United States was permitted to maintain a bill for the cancellation of a patent upon similar grounds.—Ed.

such as affect the public at large, and are in respect of matters which by the Constitution are entrusted to the care of the Nation, and concerning which the Nation owes the duty to all the citizens of securing to them their common rights, then the mere fact that the government has no pecuniary interest in the controversy is not sufficient to exclude it from the courts, or prevent it from taking measures therein to fully discharge those constitutional duties.

The national government, given by the Constitution power to regulate interstate commerce, has by express statute assumed jurisdiction over such commerce when carried upon railroads. It is charged, therefore, with the duty of keeping those highways of interstate commerce free from obstruction, for it has always been recognized as one of the powers and duties of a government to remove obstructions from the highways under its control. * * *

It is said that seldom have the courts assumed jurisdiction to restrain by injunction in suits brought by the government, either state or national, obstructions to highways, either artificial or natural. This is undoubtedly true, but the reason is that the necessity for such interference has only been occasional. Ordinarily the local authorities have taken full control over the matter, and by indictment for misdemeanor, or in some kindred way, have secured the removal of the obstruction and the cessation of the nuisance. As said in *Attorney General v. Brown*, 24 N.J. Eq. (9 C.E. Green) 89, 91: "The jurisdiction of courts of equity to redress the grievance of public nuisances by injunction is undoubted and clearly established; but it is well settled that, as a general rule, equity will not interfere, where the object sought can be as well attained in the ordinary tribunals. *Attorney General v. New Jersey Railroad*, 2 C.E. Green, (17 N.J. Eq.,) 136; *Jersey City v. City of Hudson*, 2 Beasley, (13 N.J. Eq.,) 420, 426; *Attorney General v. Heishon*, 3 C.E. Green, (18 N.J. Eq.,) 410; *Morris & Essex Railroad v. Prudden*, 5 C.E. Green, (20 N.J. Eq.,) 530, 532; High on Injunctions, § 521. And because the remedy by indictment is so efficacious, courts of equity entertain jurisdiction in such cases with great reluctance, whether their intervention is invoked at the instance of the attorney general, or of a private individual who suffers some injury therefrom distinct from that of the public, and they will only do so where there appears to be a necessity for their interference. *Rowe v. The Granite Bridge Corporation*, 21 Pick. 340, 347; *Morris & Essex Railroad v. Prudden, supra*. The jurisdiction of the court of chancery with regard to public nuisances is founded on the irreparable damage to individuals, or the great public injury which is likely to ensue. 3 Daniell's Ch. Pr. 3d ed. Perkins's, 1740." Indeed, it may be affirmed that in no well-considered case has the power of a court of equity to interfere by injunction in cases of public nuisance been denied, the only denial ever being that of a necessity for the exercise of that jurisdiction under the circumstances of the particular case. Story's Eq. Jur. §§ 921, 923, 924;

Pomeroy's Eq. Jur. § 1349; High on Injunctions, §§ 745 and 1554; 2 Daniell's Ch. Pl. and Pr. 4th ed. p. 1636.

That the bill filed in this case alleged special facts calling for the exercise of all the powers of the court is not open to question. The picture drawn in it of the vast interests involved, not merely of the city of Chicago and the State of Illinois, but of all the States, and the general confusion into which the interstate commerce of the country was thrown; the forcible interference with that commerce; the attempted exercise by individuals of powers belonging only to government, and the threatened continuance of such invasions of public right, presented a condition of affairs which called for the fullest exercise of all the powers of the courts. If ever there was a special exigency, one which demanded that the court should do all that courts can do, it was disclosed by this bill, and we need not turn to the public history of the day, which only reaffirms with clearest emphasis all its allegations.

The difference between a public nuisance and a private nuisance is that the one affects the people at large and the other simply the individual. The quality of the wrong is the same, and the jurisdiction of the courts over them rests upon the same principles and goes to the same extent. Of course, circumstances may exist in one case, which do not in another, to induce the court to interfere or to refuse to interfere by injunction, but the jurisdiction, the power to interfere, exists in all cases of nuisance. True, many more suits are brought by individuals than by the public to enjoin nuisances, but there are two reasons for this. First, the instances are more numerous of private than of public nuisances; and, second, often that which is in fact a public nuisance is restrained at the suit of a private individual, whose right to relief arises because of special injury resulting therefrom.

Again, it is objected that it is outside of the jurisdiction of a court of equity to enjoin the commission of crimes. This, as a general proposition, is unquestioned. A chancellor has no criminal jurisdiction. Something more than the threatened commission of an offence against the laws of the land is necessary to call into exercise the injunctive powers of the court. There must be some interferences, actual or threatened, with property or rights of a pecuniary nature, but when such interferences appear the jurisdiction of a court of equity arises, and is not destroyed by the fact that they are accompanied by or are themselves violations of the criminal law. * * *

The law is full of instances in which the same act may give rise to a civil action and a criminal prosecution. An assault with intent to kill may be punished criminally, under an indictment therefor, or will support a civil action for damages, and the same is true of all other offences which cause injury to person or property. In such cases the jurisdiction of the civil court is invoked, not to enforce the criminal law and punish the wrongdoer, but to compensate the injured party for the damages which he or his property has suffered, and it is no defence to the civil action that the same act by the defendant exposes him also to indictment and punishment in a court of criminal jurisdiction. So here, the acts of the defendants may or may not have been violations of the criminal law. If they were, that matter is for inquiry in other proceedings. The complaint made against them in this is of disobedience to an order of a civil court, made for the protection of property and the security of rights. If any criminal prosecution be brought against them for the criminal offences alleged in the bill of complaint, of derailing and wrecking engines and trains, assaulting and disabling employés of the railroad companies, it will be no defence to such prosecution that they disobeyed the order of injunction served upon them and have been punished for such disobedience.

Nor is there in this any invasion of the constitutional right of trial by jury. We fully agree with counsel that "it matters not what form the attempt to deny constitutional right may take. It is vain and ineffectual, and must be so declared by the courts," and we reaffirm the declaration made for the court by Mr. Justice Bradley in *Boyd v. United States,* 116 U.S. 616, 635, that "it is the duty of courts to be watchful for the constitutional rights of the citizen, and against any stealthy encroachments thereon. Their motto should be *obsta principiis.*" But the power of a court to make an order carries with it the equal power to punish for a disobedience of that order, and the inquiry as to the question of disobedience has been, from time immemorial, the special function of the court. And this is no technical rule. In order that a court may compel obedience to its orders it must have the right to inquire whether there has been any disobedience thereof. To submit the question of disobedience to another tribunal, be it a jury or another court, would operate to deprive the proceeding of half its efficiency. * * *

In brief, a court, enforcing obedience to its orders by proceedings for contempt, is not executing the criminal laws of the land, but only securing to suitors the rights which it has adjudged them entitled to.

Further, it is said by counsel in their brief:

"No case can be cited where such a bill in behalf of the sovereign has been entertained against riot and mob violence, though occurring on the highway. It is not such fitful and temporary obstruction that constitutes a nuisance. The strong hand of executive power is required to deal with such lawless demonstrations.

"The courts should stand aloof from them and not invade executive prerogative, nor even at the behest or request of the executive travel out of the beaten path of well-settled judicial authority. A mob cannot be suppressed by injunction; nor can its leaders be tried, convicted, and sentenced in equity.

"It is too great a strain upon the judicial branch of the government to impose this essentially executive and military power upon courts of chancery."

We do not perceive that this argument questions the jurisdiction of the court, but only the expediency of the action of the government in applying for its process. It surely cannot be seriously contended that the court has jurisdiction to enjoin the obstruction of a highway by one person, but that its jurisdiction ceases when the obstruction is by a hundred persons. It may be true, as suggested, that in the excitement of passion a mob will pay little heed to processes issued from the courts, and it may be, as said by counsel in argument, that it would savor somewhat of the puerile and ridiculous to have read a writ of injunction to Lee's army during the late civil war. It is doubtless true that *inter arma leges silent,* and in the throes of rebellion or revolution the processes of civil courts are of little avail, for the power of the courts rests on the general support of the people and their recognition of the fact that peaceful remedies are the true resort for the correction of wrongs. But does not counsel's arguments imply too much? Is it to be assumed that these defendants were conducting a rebellion or inaugurating a revolution, and that they and their associates were thus placing themselves beyond the reach of the civil process of the courts? We find in the opinion of the Circuit Court a quotation from the testimony given by one of the defendants before the United States Strike Commission, which is sufficient answer to this suggestion:

"As soon as the employés found that we were arrested, and taken from the scene of action, they became demoralized, and that ended the strike. It was not the soldiers that ended the strike. It was not the old brotherhoods that ended the strike. It was simply the United States courts that ended the strike. Our men were in a position that never would have been shaken, under any circumstances, if we had been permitted to remain upon the field among them. Once we were taken from the scene of action, and restrained from sending telegrams or issuing orders or answering questions, then the minions of the corporations would be put to work. * * * Our headquarters were temporarily demoralized and abandoned, and we could not answer any messages. The men went back to work, and the ranks were broken, and the strike was broken up, * * * not by the army, and not by any other power, but simply and solely by the action of the United States courts in restraining us from discharging our duties as officers and representatives of our employés."

Whatever any single individual may have thought or planned, the great body of those who were engaged in these transactions contemplated neither rebellion nor revolution, and when in the due order of legal proceedings the question of right and wrong was submitted to the courts, and by them decided, they unhesitatingly yielded to their decisions. The outcome, by the very testimony of the defendants, attests the wisdom of the course pursued by the government, and that it was well not to oppose force simply by force, but to invoke the jurisdiction and judgment of those tribunals to whom by the Constitution and in accordance with the settled conviction of all citizens is committed the determination of questions of right and wrong between individuals, masses, and States.

It must be borne in mind that this bill was not simply to enjoin a mob and mob violence. It was not a bill to command a keeping of the peace; much less was its purport to restrain the defendants from abandoning whatever employment they were engaged in. The right of any laborer, or any number of laborers, to quit work was not challenged. The scope and purpose of the bill was only to restrain forcible obstructions of the highways along which interstate commerce travels and the mails are carried. And the facts set forth at length are only those facts which tended to show that the defendants were engaged in such obstructions.

A most earnest and eloquent appeal was made to us in eulogy of the heroic spirit of those who threw up their employment, and gave up their means of earning a livelihood, not in defence of their own rights, but in sympathy for and to assist others whom they believed to be wronged. We yield to none in our admiration of any act of heroism or self-sacrifice, but we may be permitted to add that it is a lesson which cannot be learned too soon or too thoroughly that under this government of and by the people the means of redress of all wrongs are through the courts and at the ballot-box, and that no wrong, real or fancied, carries with it legal warrant to invite as a means of redress the coöperation of a mob, with its accompanying acts of violence.

We have given to this case the most careful and anxious attention, for we realize that it touches closely questions of supreme importance to the people of this country. Summing up our conclusions, we hold that the government of the United States is one having jurisdiction over every foot of soil within its territory, and acting directly upon each citizen; that while it is a government of enumerated powers, it has within the limits of those powers all the attributes of sovereignty; that to it is committed power over interstate commerce and the transmission of the mail; that the powers thus conferred upon the national government are not dormant, but have been assumed and put into practical exercise by the legislation of Congress; that in the exercise of those powers it is competent for the nation to remove all obstructions upon highways, natural or artificial, to the passage of interstate commerce or the carrying of the mail; that while it may be competent for the government (through the executive branch and in the use of the entire executive power of the nation) to forcibly remove all such obstructions, it is equally within its competency to appeal to the civil courts for an inquiry and determination as to the existence and character of any alleged obstructions, and if such are found to exist, or threaten to occur, to invoke the powers of those courts to remove or restrain such obstructions; that the jurisdiction of courts to interfere in such matters by injunction is one recognized from ancient times and by indubitable authority; that such jurisdiction is not ousted by the fact that the obstructions are accompanied by or consist of acts in themselves violations of the criminal law; that the proceeding by injunction is of a civil character, and may be enforced by proceedings in contempt; that such proceedings are not in execution of the criminal laws of the land; that the penalty for a violation of injunction is no substitute for and no defence to a prosecution for any criminal offences committed in the course of such violation; that the complaint filed in this case clearly showed an existing obstruction of artificial highways for the passage of interstate commerce and the transmission of the mail—an obstruction not only temporarily existing, but threatening to continue; that under such complaint the Circuit Court had power to issue its process of injunction; that it having been issued and served on these defendants, the Circuit Court had authority to inquire whether its orders had been disobeyed, and when it found that they had been, then to proceed under section 725, Revised Statutes, which grants power "to punish, by fine or imprisonment, * * * disobedience, * * * by any party * * * or other person, to any awful writ, process, order, rule, decree or command," and enter the order of punishment complained of; and, finally, that, the Circuit Court, having full jurisdiction in the premises, its finding of the fact of disobedience is not open to review on *habeas corpus* in this or any other court. *Ex parte Watkins*, 3 Pet. 193; *Ex parte Yarbrough*, 110 U.S. 651; *Ex parte Terry*, 128 U.S. 289, 305; *In re Swan*, 150 U.S. 637; *United States v. Pridgeon*, 153 U.S. 48.

We enter into no examination of the act of July 2, 1890, c. 647, 26 Stat. 209, upon which the Circuit Court relied mainly to sustain its jurisdiction. It must not be understood from this that we dissent from the conclusions of that court in reference to the scope of the act, but simply that we prefer to rest our judgment on the broader ground which has been discussed in this opinion, believing it of importance that the principles underlying it should be fully stated and affirmed.

The petition for a writ of *habeas corpus* is

Denied.[5]

---

[5] "That injunction was served simultaneously, or practically so, by all of the courts embracing or having jurisdiction in the territory in which the trouble existed. From Michigan to California there seemed to be concerted action on the part of the courts restraining us from exercising any of the functions of our offices. That resulted practically in the demoralization of our ranks. Not only this, but we were organized in a way that this was the center, of course, of operations. * * * As soon as the employees found that we were arrested and taken from the scene of action, they became demoralized, and that ended the strike. It was not the soldiers that ended the strike; it was not the old brotherhoods that ended the strike; it was simply the United States courts that ended the strike. * * * Our headquarters were temporarily demoralized and abandoned, and we could not answer any messages. The men went back to work, and the ranks were broken, and the strike was broken up by the Federal courts of the United States, and not by the Army, and not by any other power, but simply and solely by the action of the United States courts in restraining us from discharging our duties as officers and representatives of the employees." Testimony of Eugene V. Debs, United States Strike Commission, Report on the Chicago Strike, 143-144 (1895).

Debs was also indicted for conspiracy to obstruct the mails, but the proceedings were later dropped. See: United States v. Debs, 63 Fed. 436 (C.C.N.D. Ill. 1894) (charge to grand jury); United States v. Debs, (N.D. Ill. 1895) (denial of motion to quash indictment).

Injunctions, similar to that obtained in In re Debs, were granted against officials of the American Railway Union by the federal courts in other sections of the country, and criminal proceedings were also instituted. Southern Cal. Ry. Co. v. Rutherford, 62 Fed. 796 (C.C.S.D. Cal. 1894); Thomas v. Cincinnati, N. O. & T. P. Ry. Co., 62 Fed. 803 (C.C.S.D. Ohio, 1894); United States v. Agler, 62 Fed. 824 (C.C.D. Ind. 1894); In re Charge to Grand Jury, 62 Fed. 828 (D.N.D. Ill. 1894); In re Grand Jury, 62 Fed. 834 (D.S.D. Cal. 1894); In re Grand Jury, 62 Fed. 840 (D.N.D. Cal. 1894); United States v. Elliott, 64 Fed. 27 (C.C.E.D. Mo. 1894); United States v. Cassidy, 67 Fed. 698 (N.D. Cal. 1895). See also: Laidler, Boycotts

WILLIAMS v. UNITED STATES.

United States Circuit Court of Appeals for the Fifth Circuit. 295 Fed. 302 (1923).

WALKER, C.J.: The plaintiffs in error (herein called defendants) were convicted under an indictment against them and others which, omitting formal parts, charged as follows:

"That heretofore, to wit, on or about the 1st day of September, 1922, at Houston, Tex., one J. E. Williams, one Charles Poe, one C. C. Hanley,

---

106-107 (1913); Woodworth, "The Railroad Strikers' Case in California," 29 Am. Law Rev. 513 (1895).

For accounts of the Pullman Strike and the Debs injunction, see: United States Strike Commission, Report on the Chicago Strike (1895); Browne, Altgeld of Illinois, 116-174 (1924); Coleman, Eugene V. Debs, 122-187 (1930); Darrow, The Story of My Life, 57-73 (1932); Harrison, Clarence Darrow, 62-77 (1931); James, Richard Olney, 42-59 (1923); 2 McElroy, Grover Cleveland, c. 5 (1923); Nevins, Grover Cleveland, c. 33 (1932); 2 Warren, The Supreme Court in United States History, 702-705 (1926).

The Debs case evoked much professional comment, critical and otherwise. For contemporary literature dealing with the general problems raised by the employment of injunctions in labor disputes, which the Debs case made of general moment, see: Aiken, "Legal Restraint of Labor Strikes," 4 Yale Law Jour. 13 (1894); Allen, "Injunction and Organized Labor," 28 Am. Law Rev. 828 (1894); Dean, "Government by Injunction," 9 Green Bag 540 (1897); Dunbar, "Government by Injunction," 13 Law Quar. Rev. 347 (1897); Dunbar, 'Government by Injunction," 57 Alb. Law Jour. 8 (1898); Gregory, "Government by Injunction," 11 Harv. Law Rev. 487 (1898); Lewis, "A Protest against Administering Criminal Law by Injunction—the Debs Case," 33 Am. Law Reg. (N.S.) 879 (1894); Murphy, "The Use of the Writ of Injunction to Prevent Strikes," 1894 Utah Bar Ass'n Rep. 30; Patteson, "Government by Injunction," 3 Va. Law Reg. 625 (1898); Peterkin, "Government by Injunction," 3 Va. Law Reg. 549 (1897); Rogers, "Government by Injunction," Ind. St. Bar Ass'n Rep. 103 (1898); Stimson, "The Modern Use of Injunctions," 10 Pol. Sci. Quar. 189 (1895); 39 Cent. Law Jour. 177 (1894). See also: Watson, "The Ann Arbor Cases," Tenn. Bar Ass'n Rep. 205 (1893); 33 Am. Law Reg. (N.S.) 81, 147 (1896); 32 Am. Law Reg. (N.S.) 481 (1895). "The Democratic national platform for the presidential campaign of 1896 read as follows: 'We denounce arbitrary interference by Federal authorities in local affairs as a violation of the Constitution of the United States and a crime against free institutions, and we especially object to government by injunction as a new and highly dangerous form of oppression by which Federal Judges, in contempt of the laws of the States and rights of citizens, become at once legislators, judges and executioners; and we approve the bill passed by the last session of the United States Senate, and now pending in the House of Representatives, relative to contempt in Federal courts and providing for trials by jury in certain cases of contempt.' Proceedings of the Democratic National Convention, 194-95 (1896)." Frankfurter and Greene, The Labor Injunction, 19 (1930).

For state legislation dealing specifically with strikes on railroads, see 17 Report of the United States Industrial Commission, 601 (1901).

The federal courts have also assumed jurisdiction to deal with labor controversies where they concern a business under the control of a receiver appointed by a federal court. Intimidation of the employees of the business and destruction of its property has been frequently punished as a contempt. King v. Ohio & M. Ry. Co., Fed. Cas. No. 7800 (C.C.D. Ind. 1877); Secor v. Toledo, P. & W. R. Co., Fed. Cas. No. 12,605 (C.C.N.D. Ill. 1877); In re Doolittle, 23 Fed. 544 (C.C.E.D. Mo. 1885); United States v. Kane, 23 Fed. 748 (C.C. Colo. 1885); McGibbony v. Lancaster, 286 Fed. 129 (5th cir. 1923). Even a concerted quitting of work by such employees when done with the intention of embarrassing the operation of the business has been regarded as enjoinable. Arthur v. Oakes, 63 Fed. 310 (7th cir. 1894). Persuasion of employees to quit work has for a like reason been regarded as a contempt. In re Higgins, 27 Fed. 443 (C.C.N.D. Texas 1886). Also, upon the assumption that an effort to unionize an industry under the control of a receiver was in itself illegal, persuasion of employees to join such a union has been regarded as a contempt. United States v. Weber, 114 Fed. 950 (C.C.W.D. Va. 1902).

one John F. Doak, one John B. Yocham, one H. H. Dietz, one J. M. Morgan, one James L. Doak, and one Val Callaway entered into a conspiracy in restraint of trade and commerce among the several states in violation of section 1, chapter 647 of the Act of Congress of July 2, 1890, commonly known as the Anti-Trust Act (26 Stat. 209), that is to say, the said J. E. Williams, the said Charles Poe, the said C. C. Hanley, the said John F. Doak, the said John B. Yocham, the said H. H. Dietz, the said J. M. Morgan, the said James L. Doak, and the said Val Callaway did conspire, combine, confederate and agree together to do certain acts in restraint of trade and commerce among the several states, at Houston, Harris county, at San Antonio, Bexar county, at Del Rio, Val Verde county, and at El Paso, El Paso county, and at various other places in the state of Texas, namely, to injure and disable locomotives engaged and being used in interstate commerce through and by means of the introduction into the boilers of such locomotives of quicksilver and other injurious chemicals and materials to your grand jurors unknown, at what are commonly known as the Southern Pacific shops, Houston, Tex., the "Sap" shops, and the Southern Pacific shops, in the city of San Antonio, Western district of Texas and the Southern Pacific shops in the city of El Paso, in the Western district of Texas, and within the jurisdiction of this court, such locomotives so injured and disabled, and to be injured and disabled as aforesaid, being in service and regularly used for the transportation of interstate commerce on the lines of railroad of the Southern Pacific system and the San Antonio & Aransas Pass system and other railroads operating within the Western district of Texas and engaged in interstate commerce; and said conspiracy so entered into as aforesaid at the time and place mentioned was thereafter and on or about the 6th day of September, 1922, continued and renewed, and put into effect at San Antonio, Tex., in the San Antonio division of the Western district of Texas, and within the jurisdiction of this court; and said conspiracy so entered into as aforesaid at the times and places mentioned was thereafter and on or about the 11th day of September, 1922, continued and renewed and put into effect at El Paso, Tex., in the El Paso division of the Western district of Texas and within the jurisdiction of this court."

Rulings of the court mentioned herein are duly presented for review.

The court ruled to the effect that the conspiracy charged, though it was entered into at Houston, which is in the Southern district of Texas, could be prosecuted in the Western district of Texas, if in pursuance of the conspiracy one or more of the conspirators did in the last-named district some act to further such conspiracy and to effect the object thereof. That ruling was not erroneous. The conspiracy charged, being one which is made a misdemeanor by section 1 of the Sherman Act (26 Stat. 209 [Comp. St. § 8820]), is subject to prosecution upon its being entered into without the doing of an overt act to effect the object of it. *Nash v. United States*, 229 U.S. 373, 33 Sup. Ct. 780, 57 L. Ed. 1232. The common-law rule that the venue in conspiracy could be laid in any county in which it could be proved that an overt act was done by any one of the conspirators in furtherance of their common design was clearly recognized in the opinion in the case of *Hyde v. United States,* 225 U.S. 347, 365, 32 Sup. Ct. 793, 56 L. Ed. 1114, Ann. Cas. 1914A, 614, which cited with approval authorities supporting that rule. Under that rule the conspiracy charged could be prosecuted in the jurisdiction in which indictment was found, allegations and evidence showing that overt acts were committed in that jurisdiction by some of the alleged conspirators.

The charge of the court to the jury contained the following:

"If the necessary effect of the conspiracy when carried into effect is to directly restrain commerce among the several states, it is immaterial and unimportant whether the conspirators intended such conspiracy should have such effect or not, and it is immaterial and unimportant that such conspirators may have had other objects or purposes in view."

As applied to the issues raised by the pleadings and the evidence, that instruction was not erroneous. Evidence disclosed that the transactions relied on to support the charge made grew out of the railroad shopmen's strike, which started in July, 1922. A feature of a plan which evidence tended to prove was agreed on at Houston between some of the striking shopmen and officials of the union to which they belonged was that strikers or members of their union would, under assumed names and concealing their identity, get employment in Southern Pacific Railway Company shops in San Antonio and El Paso, and while so employed would disable engines of the railway company by putting quicksilver in engine boilers; it being contemplated that the quicksilver, by acting on the copper at the joints between the flues and the steel engine walls, would cause the flues to leak. In behalf of the defendants it was contended that the motive of the parties to the agreement was to injure property of the railway company and to promote the success of the strike, and that interference with interstate commerce was not thought of by them. Undisputed evidence showed that the Southern Pacific Railway Company was engaged in interstate commerce by railroad. Engines are indispensable to such commerce. *Pedersen v. Delaware, Lackawanna & Western R. Co.,* 229 U.S. 146, 151, 33 Sup. Ct. 648, 57 L. Ed. 1125, Ann. Cas. 1914C, 153. Evidence adduced supported a finding that a necessary effect of the successful execution of the plan agreed on would be directly to restrain commerce among the several states, by disabling indispensable instrumentalities of such commerce.

Restraint of interstate commerce is a necessary effect of executing a contract or agreement to disable, not engines which may or may not be used or destined to be used in interstate commerce, but engines generally of an interstate carrier by railroad. "The conspirators must be held to have intended the necessary and direct consequences of their acts, and cannot be heard to say the contrary. In other words, by purposely engaging in a conspiracy which necessarily and directly produces the result which the statute is designed to prevent, they are, in legal contemplation, chargeable with intending that result." *United States v. Patten,* 226 U.S. 525, 543, 33 Sup. Ct. 141, 57 L. Ed. 333, 44 L.R.A. (N.S.) 325; *United Leather Workers International Union v. Herkert & Meisel Trunk Co.* (C.C.A.) 284 Fed. 446. That contracts or agreements having the necessary effect of restraining trade or commerce among the several states cannot be taken out of the category by indulging in general reasoning was distinctly recognized in the opinion in the case of *Standard Oil Co. v. United States,* 221 U.S. 1, 65, 31 Sup. Ct. 502, 55 L. Ed. 619, 34 L.R.A. (N.S.) 834, Ann. Cas. 1912D, 734. The fact that the execution of the conspiracy now in question would have the necessary effect of directly, materially, and substantially restraining interstate commerce by disabling indispensable instrumentalities of such commerce clearly distinguishes that conspiracy from the agreement or plot in regard to coal mining which was in question in the case of *United Mine Workers v. Coronado Co.,* 259 U.S. 344, 42 Sup. Ct. 570, 66 L. Ed. 975. As to the relation of coal mining to interstate commerce, the following was said in the opinion in that case (259 U.S. 410, 42 Sup. Ct. 583, 66 L. Ed. 975):

"Coal mining is not interstate commerce, and obstruction of coal mining, though it may prevent coal from going into interstate commerce, is not a restraint of that commerce, unless the obstruction to mining is intended to restrain commerce in it, or has necessarily such a direct, material, and substantial effect to restrain it that the intent reasonably must be inferred."

The just-quoted statement impliedly recognizes the correctness of the above-stated conclusion as to such a conspiracy as the one which is in question in the instant case. The conspiracy now in question being such a one as makes the parties to it chargeable with the intention to produce the result which the statute is designed to prevent, they could not escape the legal consequences of their conduct by showing that in so conspiring they were influenced by other motives or purposes.

The court's charge to the jury contained the following:

"Evidence has been introduced before you tending to show that at the time the quicksilver was introduced into the engines of the locomotives (if it was so introduced therein) such locomotives were in the shops undergoing repairs, and at the time not actually engaged in interstate transportation or commerce. This case is not to be decided upon the question as to whether or not said locomotives were at the time actually engaged in interstate commerce."

That this instruction was not improper we think is manifest when it is considered in the light of evidence adduced as to the way quicksilver would, and was expected by the conspirators to, be effective in disabling locomotives in the boilers of which it was put. There was evidence tending to prove that it was contemplated by the defendants that the putting of quicksilver in the boiler of a locomotive while it was in a shop undergoing repairs would not immediately disable the locomotive, but that the substantial damage would begin to be done after the locomotive was fired up and ready for its run, in consequence of the heat causing the quicksilver to vaporize and to reach the copper at the connections of the flues with the boiler walls, and that such damage would continue to be done for about eight hours after the locomotive was fired up, and until it might be expected to be engaged in its run. If it was contemplated that the doing of what was agreed to be done would result in the disabling of locomotives while they were in use as instrumentalities of interstate commerce, it is not material that at the time of the use of the means intended to accomplish that result the locomotives were not actually engaged in interstate commerce.

Other rulings complained of have been considered. The conclusion is that the record does not show that any reversible error was committed.

The judgment is affirmed.[1]

GREAT NORTHERN RY. CO. v. LOCAL GREAT FALLS LODGE OF I. A. OF M.

United States District Court for the District of Montana. 283 Fed. 557 (1922).

BOURQUIN, D.J.: This is a hearing upon the interstate railway corporation plaintiff's application to restrain, pending suit, alleged activities of the labor union defendants. No restraining order issued, and a situation fraught with possibilities of grave irreparable injury requires prompt decision. This, the temporary nature of the proceedings and relief, and the evidence, admit of brevity, without sacrifice of any necessary detail or of clarity.

The parties are in the throes of the nation-wide railway strike of July 1, 1922. To plaintiff's charge that defendants, in their refusal to abide by the federal Labor Board's wage scale, "strike against the United States," defendants counter that the associated railroads, in their analogous refusals in respect to some of the board's orders, first and likewise strike.

---

[1] Certiorari was denied in 265 U.S. 591 (1924).

Accord: Vandell v. United States, 6 Fed.(2d) 189 (2d cir. 1925); Knudsen v. Benn, 123 Fed. 636 (C.C. Minn. 1903); United States v. Thomas, 55 Fed. 386 (D.W. Va. 1893); United States v. Drylic, 6 Law & Labor, 69 (U.S.D.C. Ohio, 1924). *Contra*, where the equipment at the time was not engaged in interstate transportation, United States v. Hency, 286 Fed. 165 (N.D. Texas 1923).

Illegal interference, in connection with a strike at the place of production, with goods actually transported in interstate commerce, has been regarded as a violation of the Sherman Act. O'Brien v. United States, 290 Fed. 185 (6th cir. 1923); United States v. Norris, 255 Fed. 423 (N.D. Ill. 1918).

Illegal conduct of the type of the Williams case has also been punished as a conspiracy to obstruct the passage of the mails under § 201 of the Criminal Code. Clements v. United States, 297 Fed. 206 (9th cir. 1924), certiorari denied in 266 U.S. 605 (1924); United States v. Lawhead, Fed. Cas. No. 15,570 (N.D. Ohio 1877); United States v. Clark, Fed. Cas. No. 14,805 (D. Pa. 1877). *Cf.* United States v. Stevens, Fed. Cas. No. 16,392 (D. Me. 1877) (holding criminal the abandonment of a mail train in the midst of a run).

Of the board's functions and orders it suffices to say they are advisory only, the teeth having been drawn from the bill for the Transportation Act (41 Stat. 456). Perhaps the strike may be characterized as mutual, in that relations between the parties are severed because plaintiff refuses to sell its opportunities for labor to defendants, save on its terms, and defendants refuse to sell their labor to plaintiff, save on their terms.

Be that as it may, as always in like struggles, the third party in interest, society, the general public, is ground between the upper and nether millstones of what it characterizes as the mutual selfishness of servitors in quasi public employment. It justly suffers, for that it fails to sufficiently control, as it rightfully can, the activities of both parties, and it will pay the price.

The strike hampers and threatens to incidentally stop plaintiff's interstate transportation. This is not unlawful, and warrants no injunction, so long as but an unintended consequence of lawful exercise of defendants' rights. Although in conflict in some particulars, the evidence is clear and undisputed in sufficient others to disclose that plaintiff's efforts to continue train service are virtually nullified by threats, force, and intimidation inflicted upon such employees as it secures.

These evil acts include excessive masses or groups on or too near plaintiff's premises, libelous epithets and names, unpeaceful domiciliary visits, undue restraint, deportation, and threats of bodily injury in part executed, and which are committed by men singly and in concert, at various times and places. Plaintiff alleges all this is in execution of a conspiracy entered into by defendants to coerce plaintiff from applying the wage scale aforesaid, and defendants deny the charge. It is admitted by plaintiff the national organizations, with jurisdiction over defendants, command the use of none but lawful methods, and it is asserted by defendants they obey, but cannot restrain their members, if disposed to disobey. This assertion is supported by the evidence and accepted as true for the purpose of this proceeding.

Taking into consideration the facts and circumstances in evidence, it is beyond reasonable doubt that some of defendants are afflicted with members who, in and about promotion of union interests in the strike, of their own volition at various times and places have perpetrated the threats, force, and intimidation aforesaid, and are reasonably likely to repeat them. These unlawful practices, though not yet of magnitude, are in proportion to plaintiff's immediate efforts to fill vacancies and may grow by what they feed upon. They are like to an incipient blaze in a forest, which, if not controlled, will grow and spread, until it covers the land with smoke and fire, death and destruction. And that is the reason why their continuance must be restrained by a court of equity. If in the emergency defendants cannot restrain their members, it is the duty of the court in law enforcement to do so, therein serving the best interests of defendants no less than those of plaintiff, nor overlooking those of the third party aforesaid.

All voluntary associations, including labor unions, for acts of their members are responsible to some extent on the theory of agency. Acts not authorized may be ratified, expressly or by implication. It is not always enough to repudiate the acts, for, unless the members are disciplined sufficiently to prevent repetition, the inference that the associations approve, even as they profit by, the acts, may be inevitable, despite the most solemn disavowal of them. The associations can preserve their integrity against impairment by rebellious members, for they have power to control, and even expel, the latter, if necessary. In present circumstances, suits are brought against the association by name, and thus against all the members.

The reason is found in the association's responsibility and control aforesaid, in the great number of members, in the sometime difficulty to know names of all proceeding unlawfully, in the necessity to have jurisdiction over all members, so that if those presently law-abiding in turn practice lawlessness, the penalty (of justice, not vengeance) is swift and sure, and in the necessity on occasion to distinguish the innocent from the guilty. In view of the finding that members of some of defendants, by threats, force, and intimidation, inflict and threaten to inflict irreparable injury within the meaning of that term upon plaintiff's property right to carry on interstate transportation, the law is settled and clear, and virtually conceded by defendants, that plaintiff is now entitled to therefrom restrain such defendants and their members.

These are the unions and members of Great Falls, Havre, Whitefish, and Wolf Point. In respect to the third and fourth, service of a short-day notice was not made upon them in time to enable them to appear and defend herein. For that reason, only a temporary restraining order will issue against them, to continue during the suit, unless on notice hereof, to be given by plaintiff forthwith, they fail to show cause otherwise before the court at Butte on August 7, 1922.

In respect to the defendants of Butte, Lewistown, and Judith Gap, there is no evidence of the charge against them. That they are unions, like the others, imposes no liability for what are acts of others only. In respect to the terms of the order, it is proper to observe that they must be within section 20 of the Clayton Act (Comp. St. § 1243d), which provides that in strikes ex-employees shall not be restrained "from recommending, advising, or persuading others by peaceful means" to quit work, or to refuse to work for the employer, nor "from attending at any place where any such person or persons [ex-employees] may lawfully be, for the purpose of peacefully obtaining or communicating information" or to exercise persuasion as aforesaid, nor "from peaceably assembling in a lawful manner, and for lawful purposes." The order must also comply with section 19 of the act (section 1243c), viz.:

"Specific in terms, and shall describe in reasonable detail * * * the act or acts sought to be restrained."

It must be remembered the strike is lawful, and both parties thereto, if so foolish, to put it mildly, as to persist in disagreement, are to have the fullest freedom within the law, each to promote its or their success over the other—that is, plaintiff to secure employees, if it lawfully can; defendants to prevent, if they lawfully can. They are equally entitled to receive from the court protection against intimidation, and any order of restraint, though in terms directed to one party alone, even as any like order in any suit, imposes correlative restraint upon the other. Its office is protection, and not a shelter for aggression. If abused, a pen may unmake it as a pen hath made. The court's order is to restrain defendants from exceeding the bounds of the Clayton Act, but not to intimidate them from enjoying all within those bounds. In the exercise of the rights that the Clayton Act assures to defendants, they may go to the very line between the lawful and the unlawful, carefully avoiding crossing into forbidden territory.

So may any person in the exercise of any right; and all because no right can be maintained, but by its fearless, vigorous, and full enjoyment. By the Clayton Act Congress recognizes the necessity and value of labor unions and labor activities in the matter of conditions of employment; that they have done and are yet capable of a great work; that to the workman and his, a job is life, wherein eternal vigilance is no less the price of a worthy job than of liberty; and that its loss too often changes the current of human lives and spells disaster. Hence the Clayton Act, to aid his last ditch struggle to retain his job against all comers. To that end the act provides the workmen may "recommend, advise and persuade," and by all lawful means fairly within the import of those terms. All art, eloquence, oratory, and logic are open to the workmen to accomplish persuasion.

Fair, vigorous, and repeated argument is legitimate. Repeated, for what fails to convince to-day may succeed on rehearing to-morrow, even in a Supreme Court. No reason appears why workmen may not model after congressional oratory (some expurgated), or after what is fairly inferable in the consultation room of the Supreme Court on occasion, say, of some decision by the odd justice. Human nature is everywhere alike, and every man is or ought to be earnest, enthusiastic, and fearless in his own, if good, cause. It is not believed that the *American Steel Foundries Case*, 257 U.S. 184, 42 Sup. Ct. 72, 66 L. Ed. 189, decided by the Supreme Court on December 5, 1921, imports otherwise. In it is no clear purpose to denature or "weasel" the act, and limit workmen to methods akin to pink teas and scented notes of invitation. They have their own virile vocabulary and manner, and, so long as within the Clayton Act, there is no censor upon their use. Where Congress gives bread, the courts will not convert it to stone.

The principal thing is that workmen conscientiously heed the mandate of the law and its instruments (the courts) that threats and force and their intimidation must not be used to promote success in strikes, and that of necessity, theirs as well as others, such methods always have been and always will be under the ban and criminal. In respect to pickets, defendants will be allowed two at any point of access to plaintiff's premises where men usually or may be expected to enter. If the entrants are numerous, perhaps more may be necessary. The Clayton Act, by "person or persons," intends that the number of agents shall be governed by circumstances. Obviously, not otherwise could the object of the act be attained.

So, too, the cited case recognizes as always the discretion of the chancellor in respect to pickets. Furthermore, it has happened that pickets need the support of numbers, if only for corroboration. Force and violence are strangers to neither party to strikes, and either may give a Herrin for a Ludlow. The parties forget that aggression incites retaliation, and violence breeds violence. Then, too, the pickets of one are generally confronted, if not overawed, by armed guards of the other, and by police, sheriffs, and marshals, who too often forget they are public officers, with duty to protect both parties, and mistakenly assume they are partisans of one party or the other.

Nor is it believed that the act bans the mere name. Labels go for nothing, and still does a rose by any other name smell as sweet. So-called militant terms are invoked by the church and all noble enterprise, not to arouse belligerency, but to inspire necessary enthusiasm. Why deny to workmen equality in their use? Strikes and agents to observe or watch and persuade being lawful, and beyond the power of courts to forbid, in recognizing the fact it is hardly seemly to censor mere names, or to quibble over them.

Order accordingly, and effective on bond in the sum of $5,000. Either party may move to modify the order as circumstances may require.

At the hearing on August 21, 1922, pursuant to the foregoing decision of July 27, 1922, the defendants of Wolf Point and Whitefish resist extension of the temporary injunction to specifically include them. The evidence in respect to those of Wolf Point reasonably requires such extension. At least, they have been too insistent that employees attend at the unions' hall, where information, statements, argument, and manner exceeded persuasion, and savored of the abusive and menacing, calculated to incite, as was incited, fear, intimidation, and departure from plaintiff's employment and the town.

In respect to those of Whitefish it is otherwise. The only competent, material, and preponderating evidence tends to show that circulars for which defendants may be responsible are of questionable propriety; that perhaps excessive picketing was indulged, but abandoned before suit commenced; that employees have received anonymous threatening letters; that one employee was threatened by an unidentified man; and that several men, unidentified, but including one identical in name with defendant Bugg, and presumably he, orally abused a number of employees swimming in a lake, thrust some circulars upon them, and Bugg complained of them for indecent exposure and procured their arrest. The circulars are too trivial as the basis of injunction; the anonymous letters, without more, cannot be imputed to defendants; the charge of excessive picketing comes only at this hearing, and was preceded by a charge of only threatened excessive picketing; defendants appear only by counsel, and so cannot meet it, and, if a fact, was abandoned before suit commenced and not likely to be repeated; the threat is in the same category as the anonymous letters; and the alleged abuse at the lake is also first presented at this hearing, and by affidavit of one employee only, with defendants unable to meet it. The whole is little, in view of near two months of strike (the restraining order in force three weeks) and 150 men involved, and is not to be accepted as sufficient to move the discretion of the court to grant an injunction.

It is emphasized that the principles applicable to injunctions are the same in controversies between employers and employees as in any others. Injunctions go only in cases of urgent necessity, made to appear by competent, material, credible, and preponderating evidence, to guard against injuries, not merely feared by the applicant, but reasonably to be apprehended, and likely to be irreparable. They are extraordinary remedies, granted with great caution, and in the exercise of sound judicial discretion. That the applicant is annoyed, threatened, and injured will never justify a court to grant him an injunction, unless these trespasses are so great that they threaten him with irreparable injury, within the settled meaning of that term in equity.

Experience warns against injunctions upon only affidavits to vital issues, and that may surprise defendants. The evidence that may well warrant an emergency restraining order, until hearing can be had upon the application for an injunction, may fall short to justify the latter. As no one is to be subjected to injunction merely because it will not injure him (though an unwarranted injunction is an indignity, and always injurious), before he is enjoined a sufficient case must be legally made out against him.

In strikes, employers too often with little cause are quick to seek injunctions and their intimidating advantages, and courts too often likewise grant them. The consequence is a disposition to view the courts as partisans of the employers, and the judicial writs of injunction as weapons against employees however lawfully they be proceeding. And it is of this Pandora's box of obvious evils to society that the Clayton Act is designed to somewhat close the lid.

These controversies inevitably present provocative situations, and may involve fugitive encounters and disorders, for which neither party may be solely responsible. Often trivial, they do not threaten irreparable injury, and so do not warrant interposition by a court of equity, but can be adequately remedied by appeal to local authority. It may be, as contended, that near election time local administrations are disposed to neglect duty in the premises and to "play politics." But for that matter national administrations are likewise. It is of the price, as of the vice, of democracies. Nevertheless, injunctions go only in the circumstances aforesaid, and not merely to bridge gaps of administrative dereliction.

The right of employees, of men, to work (of which so much is heard during strikes, and so little other times), is but incidental, and aids plaintiff none. However much that right be infringed, plaintiff cannot complain, save to the extent that it is part of unlawful methods inflicting irreparable injury to plaintiff's property rights. The right itself is not absolute, but qualified—the right to sell labor if a buyer be found, to solicit a job (and often hopelessly and unavailingly), and to work if and as long as the buyer or job giver consents and no longer. Society has not yet progressed to insure work, or to recognize a substantial interest in a job had, though perhaps the spirit of the times, if not their necessity, even as the Clayton Act, tends in the direction of the latter at least.

In respect to the contention that the Anti-Trust Act (Comp. St. §§ 8820-8823, 8827-8830), in connection with section 16 of the Clayton Act (Comp. St. § 8835o), warrants injunction against even peaceful persuasion of employees to cease work, if the result otherwise is interruption of plaintiff's interstate transportation, it is unmaintainable. The interruption, an unintended consequence of lawful exercise of a right sanctioned by the law before and since the acts aforesaid, sanctioned by section 20 of the latter act aforesaid, is damnum absque injuria, and not within said acts, so far as injunctive relief is concerned.

In the matter of defendants' request that the order enjoin plaintiff from maintaining more guards than pickets where the latter are stationed, if and when it is made to appear that guards in any number are infringing upon defendants' rights, a corrective can be applied. The order in respect to the number of defendants' agents or pickets can be amended when necessity is made to appear, as suggested in the earlier and foregoing decision. Neither that decision nor this assumes to limit the number composing any defendants' groups for persuasion only. What is reasonable and only persuasive is a safe guide.

Order accordingly, effective on bond in the sum of $5,000.[1]

---

[1] The legality of the strike to obtain ends at variance with the decision of the Railroad Labor Board, has been sustained in Foss v. Portland Terminal Co., 287 Fed. 33 (1st cir. 1923). But that such a strike is of itself illegal under the federal laws is the necessary assumption underlying the following cases: United States v. Railway Employees' Dept., A. F. of L., 283 Fed. 479, 286 Fed. 228, 290 Fed. 978 (N.D. Ill. 1922, 1923); Michaelson v. United States, 291 Fed. 940 (7th cir. 1923), rev'd on other grounds in 266 U.S. 42 (1924); New York, N. H. & H. R. Co. v. Railway Employees' Dept., A. F. of L., 288 Fed. 589 (D. Conn. 1923); Pere Marquette Ry. Co. v. Internat'l Ass'n of Machinists, 4 Law & Labor, 304 (U.S.D.C.D.D. Mich. 1922); Great Northern Ry. Co. v. Perkins, 4 Law & Labor, 253 (U.S.D.C. W.D. Wash. (1922) For criticism of this viewpoint, see: 37 Harv. Law Rev. 486 (1924); 8 Minn. Law Rev. 323 (1924).

The strike upon an interstate railway, if unaccompanied by illegal conduct or having no other aims than the immediate ones of bettering conditions upon that railway, seems not to be regarded as a violation of the Sherman Act or the Interstate Commerce Act. But cf. Michaelson v. United States, supra. See also: Gross-

LOEWE v. LAWLOR.

Supreme Court of the United States. 208 U.S. 274 (1908).

MR. CHIEF JUSTICE FULLER delivered the opinion of the court.

This was an action brought in the Circuit Court for the District of Connecticut under § 7 of the Anti-Trust Act of July 2, 1890, c. 647, 26 Stat. 209, claiming threefold damages for injuries inflicted on plaintiffs by a combination or conspiracy declared to be unlawful by the act.

---

cup, J., in In re Charge to the Grand Jury, 62 Fed. 828 (N.D. Ill. 1894) : "Any person knowingly and willfully doing any act which contributes, or is calculated to contribute, to obstructing or hindering the mails, or who knowingly and willfully takes a part in such acts, no matter how trivial, if intentional, is guilty of violating the first of these provisions [obstructing the carriage of the mails] ; and any person who conspires with one or more persons, one of whom subsequently commits the offense, is likewise guilty of an offense against the United States. * * * The railroads carrying the mails and interstate commerce have a right to the service of each of their employes until each lawfully refuses to quit; and any concerted action upon the part of others to demand or insist, under any effective penalty or threat, upon their quitting, to the injury of the mail service or the prompt transportation of interstate commerce, is a conspiracy, unless such demand or insistence is in pursuance of a lawful authority conferred upon them by the employes themselves, and is made in good faith in the execution of such authority." Pp. 831-832. See also: In re Grand Jury, 62 Fed. 840 (N.D. Cal. 1894) ; Arthur v. Oakes, 63 Fed. 310 (7th cir. 1894).

When in pursuance of such a strike, however, the strikers resort to violence and other independently illegal conduct, the resulting conduct as a whole becomes a conspiracy in violation of the Sherman Act and/or the Interstate Commerce Act. Alaska S. S. Co. v. Longshoremen's Ass'n, 236 Fed. 964 (W.D. Wash. 1916) ; Stephens v. Ohio State Tel. Co., 240 Fed. 759 (N.D. Ohio, 1917). *Cf.* United States v. Workingman's Amalgamated Council of New Orleans, 54 Fed. 994 (C.C.E.D. La. 1893). So also the refusal of the employees of one railroad to handle equipment because of its connection with another railroad with which the union has a difficulty is regarded as an illegal conspiracy under the federal statutes. Thomas v. Cincinnati, N. O. & T. P. Ry. Co., 62 Fed. 803 (C.C.S.D. Ohio, 1894) ; United States v. Elliott, 64 Fed. 27 (C.C.E.D. Mo. 1894) ; Toledo, Ann Arbor, etc., Ry. Co. v. Pennsylvania Co., 54 Fed. 730 (C.C.N.D. Ohio, 1893) ; United States v. Cassidy, 67 Fed. 698 (N.D. Cal. 1895) ; Wabash R. R. Co. v. Hannahan, 121 Fed. 563 (C.C.E.D. Mo. 1903) ; Internat'l Brotherhood of Electrical Workers v. Western Union Tel. Co., 6 Fed.(2d) 444 (7th cir. 1925) ; Toledo Transfer Co. v. Internat'l Brotherhood of Teamsters, 7 Law & Labor, 33 (U.S.D.C. N.Y. Ohio, 1925) ; In re Lennon, 166 U.S. 548 (1897).

For the economic angle of the labor problem of public utilities, see: Morehouse, "The Background of Labor Relations of Public Utilities," 5 J. Land & Pub. Util. Econ. 275, 412 (1929) ; Marsh, "Trade Unionism in the Electric Light and Power Industry," 16 Univ. of Ill. Studies in Soc. Sci. (1928).

For the development and functioning of arbitration schemes to deal with labor relations in the railroad field, see Fisher, "Use of Federal Power in the Settlement of Railway Disputes," U. S. Dept. of Labor, Bur. Lab. Statistics Bull. No. 303 (1922) ; Ellingwood, "The Railway Labor Act of 1926," 36 Jour. Pol. Econ. 141 (1928) ; Kennedy, "Law and the Railroad Labor Problem," 32 Yale Law Jour. 553 (1923) ; Fisher, "The Railroad Labor Act; a Comparison and Appraisal" 17 Am. Econ. Rev. 177 (1927) ; Wolf, The Railroad Labor Board, (1927) ; Dixon, "Functions and Policies of the Railroad Labor Board," 10 Proc. Acad. Pol. Sci. 19 (1922) ; Magnusson and Gadsby, "Federal Intervention in Railroad Disputes," 11 Monthly Lab. Rev. 26 (1920). See also: Pennsylvania R. R. Co. v. United States R. R. Labor Board, 261 U.S. 72 (1923) ; Pennsylvania R. R., etc., Federation No. 90 v. Pennsylvania R. R. Co., 267 U.S. 203 (1925) ; Pennsylvania System Board of Adjustment v. Pennsylvania R. R. Co., 267 U.S. 219 (1925).

Upon the problem of the legality of strikes during wartime, see: Rosenwasser

Defendants filed a demurrer to the complaint, assigning general and special grounds. The demurrer was sustained as to the first six paragraphs, which rested on the ground that the combination stated was not within the Sherman Act, and this rendered it unnecessary to pass upon any other questions in the case; and upon plaintiffs declining to amend their complaint the court dismissed it with costs. 148 Fed. Rep. 924; and see 142 Fed. Rep. 216; 130 Fed. Rep. 633.

The case was then carried by writ of error to the Circuit Court of Appeals for the Second Circuit, and that court, desiring the instruction of this court upon a question arising on the writ of error, certified that question to this court. The certificate consisted of a brief statement of facts, and put the question thus: "Upon this state of facts can plaintiffs maintain an action against defendants under section 7 of the Anti-Trust Act of July 2, 1890?"

After the case on certificate had been docketed here plaintiffs in error applied, and defendants in error joined in the application, to this court to require the whole record and cause to be sent up for its consideration. The application was granted and the whole record and cause being thus brought before this court it devolved upon the court, under § 6 of the Judiciary Act of 1891, to "decide the whole matter in controversy in the same manner as if it had been brought there for review by writ of error or appeal."

The case comes up, then, on complaint and demurrer, and we give the complaint in the margin.[1]

The question is whether upon the facts therein averred and admitted by the demurrer this action can be maintained under the Anti-Trust Act.

The first, second and seventh sections of that act are as follows * * *.[2]

Bros. v. Pepper, 109 Misc. 457, 172 N.Y.S. 310 (1918), enjoining a strike for any cause whatever during the continuance of the war. Accord: Wagner Electric Manufacturing Co. v. District Lodge No. 9, 252 Fed. 597 (E.D. Mo. 1918) *semble*. *Cf.* West Va. Traction & Elec. Co. v. Elm Grove Mining Co., 253 Fed. 772 (N.D. W.Va. 1918). See: 32 Harv. Law Rev. 837 (1919). Where the direct purpose of the instigation of a strike in a munition plant was to prevent munitions from being shipped abroad to a belligerent, the United States at the time being a neutral, such conduct was deemed to be a violation of the Sherman Act. United States v. Rintelen, 233 Fed. 793 (S.D. N.Y. 1916), aff'd. *sub. nom.* Lamar v. United States, 260 Fed. 561 (2d cir. 1919). The wide-spread bituminous strike of 1919 was enjoined primarily upon the ground that it was in violation of the wartime Lever Food and Fuel Act. United States v. Hayes (unreported) (D. Ind. 1919). See: Chafee, "Progress of the Law, 1919-1920," 34 Harv. Law Rev. 388, 400 (1920); 5 Corn. Law Quar. 184 (1920). See also: Kroger Grocery & Baking Co. v. Retail Clerks Internat'l Protective Ass'n, 250 Fed. 890 (E.D. Mo. 1918). During the war, several states enacted legislation requiring able-bodied men to be gainfully employed. See 7 Monthly Lab. Rev. 1811 (1918). The constitutionality of such legislation was sustained. State v. McClure, 30 Del. 265, 105 Atl. 712 (1919). *Contra:* Ex parte Hudgins, 86 W. Va. 526, 103 S.E. 327 (1920). Upon the general handling of the labor problem during the war, see: Bing, War-Time Strikes and Their Adjustment (1921); Witte, The Government in Labor Disputes, 246-251 (1932).

[1] The complaint is omitted, the material portions of it being later set forth in the opinion.—Ed.

[2] For these sections of the Sherman Act, see *supra* pp. 495, 496.

In our opinion the combination described in the declaration is a combination "in restraint of trade or commerce among the several States," in the sense in which those words are used in the act, and the action can be maintained accordingly.

And that conclusion rests on many judgments of this court, to the effect that the act prohibits any combination whatever to secure action which essentially obstructs the free flow of commerce between the States, or restricts, in that regard, the liberty of a trader to engage in business.

The combination charged falls within the class of restraints of trade aimed at compelling third parties and strangers involuntarily not to engage in the course of trade except on conditions that the combination imposes; and there is no doubt that (to quote from the well-known work of Chief Justice Erle on Trade Unions) "at common law every person has individually and the public also has collectively, a right to require that the course of trade should be kept free from unreasonable obstruction." But the objection here is to the jurisdiction, because, even conceding that the declaration states a case good at common law, it is contended that it does not state one within the statute. Thus, it is said, that the restraint alleged would operate to entirely destroy plaintiffs' business and thereby include intrastate trade as well; that physical obstruction is not alleged as contemplated; and that defendants are not themselves engaged in interstate trade.

We think none of these objections are tenable, and that they are disposed of by previous decisions of this court.

United States v. Trans-Missouri Freight Association, 166 U.S. 290; *United States v. Joint Traffic Association,* 171 U.S. 505; and *Northern Securities Company v. United States,* 193 U.S. 197, hold in effect that the Anti-Trust law has a broader application than the prohibition of restraints of trade unlawful at common law. Thus in the *Trans-Missouri Case,* 166 U.S. 290, it was said that, "assuming that agreements of this nature are not void at common law, and that the various cases cited by the learned courts below show it, the answer to the statement of their validity is to be found in the terms of the statute under consideration;" and in the *Northern Securities Case,* 193 U.S. 331, that, "the act declares illegal every contract, combination or conspiracy, in whatever form, of whatever nature, and whoever may be the parties to it, which directly or necessarily operates in restraint of trade or commerce among the several States." * * *

The averments here are that there was an existing interstate traffic between plaintiffs and citizens of other States, and that for the direct purpose of destroying such interstate traffic defendants combined not merely to prevent plaintiffs from manufacturing articles then and there intended for transportation beyond the State, but also to prevent the vendees from reselling the hats which they had imported from Connecticut, or from further negotiating with plaintiffs for the purchase and intertransportation of such hats from Connecticut to the various places of destination. So that, although some of the means whereby the interstate traffic was to be destroyed were acts within a State, and some of them were in themselves as a part of their obvious purpose and effect beyond the scope of Federal authority, still, as we have seen, the acts must be considered as a whole, and the plan is open to condemnation, notwithstanding a negligible amount of intrastate business might be affected in carrying it out. If the purposes of the combination were, as alleged, to prevent any interstate transportation at all, the fact that the means operated at one end before physical transportation commenced and at the other end after the physical transportation ended was immaterial.

Nor can the act in question be held inapplicable because defendants were not themselves engaged in interstate commerce. The act made no distinction between classes. It provided that "every" contract, combination or conspiracy in restraint of trade was illegal. The records of Congress show that several efforts were made to exempt, by legislation, organizations of farmers and laborers from the operation of the act and that all these efforts failed, so that the act remained as we have it before us.

In an early case, *United States v. Workingmen's Amalgamated Council*, 54 Fed. Rep. 994, the United States filed a bill under the Sherman act in the Circuit Court for the Eastern District of Louisiana, averring the existence of "a gigantic and widespread combination of the members of a multitude of separate organizations for the purpose of restraining the commerce among the several States and with foreign countries," and it was contended that the statute did not refer to combinations of laborers. But the court, granting the injunction, said:

"I think the Congressional debates show that the statute had its origin in the evils of massed capital; but, when the Congress came to formulating the prohibition, which is the yardstick for measuring the complainant's right to the injunction, it expressed it in these words: 'Every contract or combination in the form of trust, or otherwise in restraint of trade or commerce among the several States or with foreign nations, is hereby declared to be illegal.' The subject had so broadened in the minds of the legislators that the source of the evil was not regarded as material, and the evil in its entirety is dealt with. They made the interdiction include combinations of labor, as well as of capital; in fact, all combinations in restraint of commerce, without reference to the character of the persons who entered into them. It is true this statute has not been much expounded by judges, but, as it seems to me, its meaning, as far as relates to the sort of combinations to which it is to apply, is manifest, and that it includes combinations which are composed of laborers acting in the interest of laborers. * * *

"It is the successful effort of the combination of the defendants to intimidate and overawe others who were at work in conducting or carrying on the commerce of the country, in which the court finds their error and their violation of the statute. One of the intended results of their combined action was the forced stagnation of all the commerce which flowed through New Orleans. This intent and combined action are none the less unlawful because they included in their scope the paralysis of all other business within the city as well."

The case was affirmed on appeal by the Circuit Court of Appeals for the Fifth Circuit.   57 Fed. Rep. 85.

Subsequently came the litigation over the Pullman strike and the decisions, *In re Debs,* 64 Fed. Rep. 724, 745, 755; S.C., 158 U.S. 564. * * *

At the risk of tediousness, we repeat that the complaint averred that plaintiffs were manufacturers of hats in Danbury, Connecticut, having a factory there, and were then and there engaged in an interstate trade in some twenty States other than the State of Connecticut; that they were practically dependent upon such interstate trade to consume the product of their factory, only a small percentage of their entire output being consumed in the State of Connecticut; that at the time the alleged combination was formed they were in the process of manufacturing a large number of hats for the purpose of fulfilling engagements then actually made with consignees and wholesale dealers in States other than Connecticut, and that if prevented from carrying on the work of manufacturing these hats they would be unable to complete their engagements.

That defendants were members of a vast combination called The United Hatters of North America, comprising about 9,000 members and including a large number of subordinate unions, and that they were combined with some 1,400,000 others into another association known as The American Federation of Labor, of which they were members, whose members resided in all the places in the several States where the wholesale dealers in hats and their customers resided and did business; that defendants were "engaged in a combined scheme and effort to force all manufacturers of fur hats in the United States, including the plaintiffs, against their will and their previous policy of carrying on their business, to organize their workmen in the departments of making and finishing, in each of their factories, into an organization, to be part and parcel of the said combination known as The United Hatters of North America, or as the defendants and their confederates term it, to unionize their shops, with the intent thereby to control the employment of labor in and the operation of said factories, and to subject the same to the direction and control of persons, other than the owners of the same, in a manner extremely onerous and distasteful to such owners, and to carry out such scheme, effort and purpose, by restraining and destroying the interstate trade and commerce of such manufacturers, by means of intimidation of and threats made to such manufacturers and their customers in the several States, of boycotting them, their product and their customers, using therefor all the powerful means at their command, as aforesaid, until such time as, from the damage and loss of business resulting therefrom, the said manufacturers should yield to the said demand to unionize their factories."

That the conspiracy or combination was so far progressed that out of eighty-two manufacturers of this country engaged in the production of fur hats seventy had accepted the terms and acceded to the demand that the shop should be conducted in accordance, so far as conditions of employment were concerned, with the will of the American Federation of Labor; that the local union demanded of plaintiffs that they should unionize their shop under peril of being boycotted by this combination, which demand defendants declined to comply with; that thereupon the American Federation of Labor, acting through its official organ and through its organizers, declared a boycott.

The complaint then thus continued:

"20. On or about July 25, 1902, the defendants individually and collectively, and as members of said combinations and associations, and with other persons whose names are unknown to the plaintiffs, associated with them, in pursuance of the general scheme and purpose aforesaid, to force all manufacturers of fur hats, and particularly the plaintiffs, to so unionize their factories, wantonly, wrongfully, maliciously, unlawfully and in violation of the provisions of the 'Act of Congress, approved July 2, 1890,' and entitled 'An Act to Protect Trade and Commerce Against Unlawful Restraints and Monopolies,' and with intent to injure the property and business of the plaintiffs by means of acts done which are forbidden and declared to be unlawful, by said act of Congress, entered into a combination and conspiracy to restrain the plaintiffs and their customers in States other than Connecticut, in carrying on said trade and commerce among the several States, and to wholly prevent them from engaging in and carrying on said trade and commerce between them and to prevent the plaintiffs from selling their hats to wholesale dealers and purchasers in said States other than Connecticut, and to prevent said dealers and customers in said other States from buying the same, and to prevent the plaintiffs from obtaining orders for their hats from such customers, and filling the same, and shipping said hats to said customers in said States as aforesaid, and thereby injure the plaintiffs in their property and business and to render unsalable the product and output of their said factory, so the subject of interstate commerce, in whosoever's hands the same might be or come, through said interstate trade and commerce, and to employ as means to carry out said combination and conspiracy and the purposes thereof, and accomplish the same, the following measures and acts, viz:

"To cause, by means of threats and coercion, and without warning or information to the plaintiffs, the concerted and simultaneous withdrawal of all the makers and finishers of hats then working for them, who were not members of their said combination, The United Hatters of North America, as well as those who were such members, and thereby crippled the operation of the plaintiffs' factory, and prevent the plaintiffs from filling a large number of orders then on hand, from such wholesale dealers in States other than Connecticut, which they had engaged to fill and were then in the act of filling, as was well known to the defendants; in connection therewith to declare a boycott against all hats made for sale and sold and delivered, or to be so sold or delivered, by the plaintiffs to said wholesale dealers in States other than Connecticut, and to actively boycott the same and the business of those who should deal in them, and thereby prevent the sale of the same by those in whose hands they might be or come through said interstate trade in said several States; to procure and cause others of said combinations united with them in said American Federation of Labor, in like manner to declare a boycott against and to actively boycott the same and the business of such wholesale dealers as should buy or sell them, and of those who should purchase them from such wholesale dealers; to intimidate such wholesale dealers from purchasing or dealing in the hats of the plaintiffs by informing them that the American Federation of Labor had declared a boycott against the product of the plaintiffs and against any dealer who should handle it, and that the same was to be actively pressed against them, and by distributing circulars containing notices that such dealers and their customers were to be boycotted; to threaten with a boycott those customers who should buy any goods whatever, even though union made, of such boycotted dealers, and at the same time to notify such wholesale dealers that they were at liberty to deal in the hats of any other non-union manufacturer of similar quality to those made by the plaintiffs, but must not deal in the hats made by the plaintiffs under threats of such boycotting; to falsely represent to said wholesale dealers and their customers, that the plaintiffs had discriminated against the union men in their employ, had thrown them out of employment because they refused to give up their union cards and teach boys, who were intended to take their places after seven months' instruction, and had driven their employés to extreme measures 'by their persistent, unfair and un-American policy of antagonizing union labor, forcing wages to a starvation scale, and given boys and cheap, unskilled foreign labor preference over experienced and capable union workmen,' in order to intimidate said dealers from purchasing said hats by reason of the prejudice thereby created against the plaintiffs and the hats made by them among those who might otherwise purchase them; to use the said union label of said The United Hatters of North America as an instrument to aid them in carrying out said conspiracy and combination against the plaintiffs' and their customers' interstate trade aforesaid, and in connection with the boycotting above mentioned, for the purpose of describing and identifying the hats of the plaintiffs and singling them out to be so boycotted; to employ a large number of agents to visit said wholesale dealers and their customers, at their several places of business, and threaten them with loss of business if they should buy or handle the hats of the plaintiffs, and thereby prevent them from buying said hats, and in connection therewith to cause said dealers to be waited upon by committees representing large combinations of persons in their several localities to make similar threats to them; to use the daily press in the localities where such wholesale dealers reside, and do business, to announce and advertise the said boycotts against the hats of the plaintiffs and said wholesale dealers, and thereby make the same more effective and oppressive, and to use the columns of their said paper, The Journal of the United Hatters of North America, for that purpose, and to describe the acts of their said agents in prosecuting the same."

And then followed the averments that the defendants proceeded to carry out their combination to restrain and destroy interstate trade and commerce between plaintiffs and their customers in other States by employing the identical means contrived for that purpose; and that by reason of those acts plaintiffs were damaged in their business and property in some $80,000.

We think a case within the statute was set up and that the demurrer should have been overruled.

Judgment reversed and cause remanded with a direction to proceed accordingly.[3]

LAWLOR v. LOEWE.

Supreme Court of the United States. 235 U.S. 522 (1915).

Mr. Justice Holmes delivered the opinion of the court.

This is an action under the act of July 2, 1890, c. 647, § 7, 26 Stat. 209, 210, for a combination and conspiracy in restraint of commerce among the States, specifically directed against the plaintiffs (defendants in error), among others, and effectively carried out with the infliction of great damage. The declaration was held good on demurrer in *Loewe* v. *Lawlor,* 208 U.S. 274, where it will be found set forth at length. The substance of the charge is that the plaintiffs were hat manufacturers who employed non-union labor; that the defendants were members of the United Hatters of North America and also of the American Federation of Labor; that in pursuance of a general scheme to unionize the labor employed by manufacturers of fur hats (a purpose previously made effective against all but a few manufacturers), the defendants and other members of the United Hatters caused the American Federation of Labor to declare a boycott against the plaintiffs and against all hats sold by the plaintiffs to dealers in other States and against dealers who should deal in them; and that they carried out their plan with such success that they have restrained or destroyed the plaintiff's commerce with other States. The case now has been tried, the plaintiffs have got a verdict and the judg-

---

[3] Upon the question of the "intent" of Congress to exclude labor unions from the operation of the Sherman Act, see: Berman, Labor and the Sherman Act. 3-54 (1930); Mason, Organized Labor and the Law, 122 *et seq.* (1925); Emery, "Labor Organizations and the Sherman Law," 20 Jour. Pol. Econ. 599 (1912); Landis, "Book Review," 44 Harv. Law Rev. 875 (1931); Mason, "Book Review," 25 Am. Pol. Sci. Rev. 461 (1931).

ment of the District Court has been affirmed by the Circuit Court of Appeals. 209 Fed. Rep. 721; 126 C.C.A. 445.

The grounds for discussion under the statute that were not cut away by the decision upon the demurrer have been narrowed still further since the trial by the case of *Eastern States Retail Lumber Dealers' Association v. United States*, 234 U.S. 600. Whatever may be the law otherwise, that case establishes that, irrespective of compulsion or even agreement to observe its intimation, the circulation of a list of "unfair dealers," manifestly intended to put the ban upon those whose names appear therein, among an important body of possible customers combined with a view to joint action and in anticipation of such reports, is within the prohibitions of the Sherman Act if it is intended to restrain and restrains commerce among the States.

It requires more than the blindness of justice not to see that many branches of the United Hatters and the Federation of Labor, to both of which the defendants belonged, in pursuance of a plan emanating from headquarters made use of such lists, and of the primary and secondary boycott in their effort to subdue the plaintiffs to their demands. The union label was used and a strike of the plaintiffs' employés was ordered and carried out to the same end, and the purpose to break up the plaintiffs' commerce affected the quality of the acts. *Loewe v. Lawlor*, 208 U.S. 274, 299. We agree with the Circuit Court of Appeals that a combination and conspiracy forbidden by the statute were proved, and that the question is narrowed to the responsibility of the defendants for what was done by the sanction and procurement of the societies above named.

The court in substance instructed the jury that if these members paid their dues and continued to delegate authority to their officers unlawfully to interfere with the plaintiffs'-interstate commerce in such circumstances that they knew or ought to have known, and such officers were warranted in the belief that they were acting in the matters within their delegated authority, then such members were jointly liable, and no others. It seems to us that this instruction sufficiently guarded the defendants' rights, and that the defendants got all that they were entitled to ask in not being held chargeable with knowledge as matter of law. It is a tax on credulity to ask anyone to believe that members of labor unions at that time did not know that the primary and secondary boycott and the use of the "We don't patronize" or "Unfair" list were means expected to be employed in the effort to unionize shops. Very possibly they were thought to be lawful. See *Gompers v. United States*, 233 U.S. 604. By the Constitution of the United Hatters the directors are to use "all the means in their power" to bring shops "not under our jurisdiction" "into the trade." The by-laws provide a separate fund to be kept for strikes, lockouts, and agitation for the union label. Members are forbidden to sell non-union hats. The Federation of Labor with which the Hatters were affiliated had organization of labor for one of its objects, helped affiliated unions in trade disputes, and to that end, before the present trouble, had provided in its constitution for prosecuting and had prosecuted many what it called legal boycotts.⎤ Their conduct in this and former cases was made public especially among the members in every possible way. ⎣If the words of the documents on their face and without explanation did not authorize what was done, the evidence of what was done publicly and habitually showed their meaning and how they were interpreted.⎤ The jury could not but find that by the usage of the unions the acts complained of were authorized, and authorized without regard to their interference with commerce among the States. We think it unnecessary to repeat the evidence of the publicity of this particular struggle in the common newspapers and union prints, evidence that made it almost inconceivable that the defendants, all living in the neighborhood of the plaintiffs, did not know what was done in the specific case. If they did not know that, they were bound to know the constitution of their societies, and at least well might be found to have known how the words of those constitutions had been construed in the act.

It is suggested that injustice was done by the judge speaking of "proof" that in carrying out the object of the associations unlawful means had been used with their approval. The judge cautioned the jury with special care not to take their view of what had been proved from him, going even farther than he need have gone. *Graham v. United States,* 231 U.S. 474, 480. But the context showed plainly that proof was used here in a popular way for evidence and must have been understood in that sense.

Damages accruing since the action began were allowed, but only such as were the consequence of acts done before and constituting part of the cause of action declared on. This was correct. *New York, Lake Erie & Western R. R. v. Estill,* 147 U.S. 591, 615, 616. We shall not discuss the objections to evidence separately and in detail as we find no error requiring it. The introduction of newspapers, etc., was proper in large part to show publicity in places and directions where the facts were likely to be brought home to the defendants, and also to prove an intended and detrimental consequence of the principal acts, not to speak of other grounds. The reason given by customers for ceasing to deal with sellers of the Loewe hats, including letters from dealers to Loewe & Co., were admissible. 3 Wigmore, Evidence, § 1729 (2). We need not repeat or add to what was said by the Circuit Court of Appeals with regard to evidence of the payment of dues after this suit was begun. And in short neither the argument nor the perusal of the voluminous brief for the plaintiffs in error shows that they suffered any injustice, or that there was any error requiring the judgment to be reversed.

Judgment affirmed.[1]

----

[1] "This was the final litigation, but it was not until two years later that a settlement was made with the Loewe Co. In the meantime, the hatters' union and the American Federation of Labor sought by voluntary contributions to raise the funds to pay the judgment. A 'hatters' day' was staged throughout the country, all union members being asked to contribute their wages for the day to the hatters. Through

DUPLEX PRINTING PRESS CO. v. DEERING.

Supreme Court of the United States. 254 U.S. 443 (1921).

Mr. Justice Pitney delivered the opinion of the court.

This was a suit in equity brought by appellant in the District Court for the Southern District of New York for an injunction to restrain a course of conduct carried on by defendants in that District and vicinity

---

these appeals the major portion of the amount was collected, and in the summer of 1917 the case was settled for a total of something over $234,000, of which amount the American Federation of Labor furnished $216,000." Witte, The Government in Labor Disputes, 135 (1932).

For a catalogue of the full proceedings in this case, see: Berman, Labor and the Sherman Act, 300-302 (1930). For other cases, growing out of the same boycott, see: Savings Bank of Danbury v. Loewe, 242 U.S. 357 (1917); Loewe v. California State Fed. of Labor, 139 Fed. 71 (C.C.N.D. Cal. 1905).

For comments upon the case, see: Megaarden, "The Danbury Hatters' Case: Its Possible Effect on Labor Unions," 49 Am. Law Rev. 417 (1915); Laidler, Boycotts, c. 9 (1913); Berman, op. cit., c. 5; Witte, op. cit., 134-136. For the part played by the American Anti-Boycott Association in the case, see: Merritt, History of the League for Industrial Rights, 22-35 (1925).

"Although the litigation was in its twelfth year when final judgment was affirmed by the Supreme Court, the end was not in sight. It was necessary to collect the judgment. Suits were accordingly started against the various savings banks to recover the moneys attached. Even that suit had to go to the United States Supreme Court to settle the question whether the attachment carried with it the accumulated interest as well as the principal. It was also necessary to foreclose judgment liens on the various pieces of real estate in Danbury, Bethel and Norwalk. Suits started for that purpose proceeded in due course. The advertisement of the sales of the various plots scheduled to take place in July, 1917, covered several pages in the local press. In all it was estimated that pursuing the greatest diligence, it would take two weeks to complete the numerous public auctions. The great speculation, the great trial of nerves, was whether the American Federation of Labor or the Hatters' Union would settle to save the defendants' homes from sale or whether the plaintiff would be obliged to go through the painful process of publicly selling these homes. Sensational newspapers published pictures of old men being ejected and thrown with beds and bedding into slushy streets. At the last moment a settlement was finally reached and the sale of the homes was averted by the unions coming to the rescue. * * *

"The case might well be called a *cause célèbre*. It was fourteen years in the courts. It was twice tried by a jury, four times was it before the United States Circuit Court of Appeals on appeal, and went three times to the United States Supreme Court. * * * It resulted in the complete abandonment of the unfair list by the American Federation of Labor. It demonstrated the fact that the protest of the American people against combination of this character, which had first been stimulated in 1902, was not 'idle, impudent and impotent.' Its result found its way into the platforms of at least one of the great political parties, and a great statesman who had formerly sat on the Supreme Court was publicly heckled concerning it when stumping as a candidate for President. Probably no case, except the Dred Scott decision, ever caused greater agitation in legal and political circles, and few, if any, have exercised greater influence on our industrial institutions. It forbade that the closed shop be forced by interstate boycotts." Merritt, op cit., 28-31.

With the Danbury Hatters' case should be compared an equally significant attack upon the Unfair List of the American Federation of Labor in the nation-wide boycott of the Bucks Stove & Range Company's products. Proceedings in this were not, however, grounded upon a violation of the Sherman Act, and the means chosen to combat the boycott was the injunction rather than the damage suit. See: American Federation of Labor v. Bucks Stove & Range Co., 33 App. D.C. 83 (1909), appeal dismissed as moot in 219 U.S. 581 (1911); Gompers v. Bucks Stove & Range Co., 221 U.S. 418 (1911); Gompers v. United States, 223 U.S. 604 (1914); Post v. Bucks Stove & Range Co., 200 Fed. 918 (8th cir. 1912). See also: Laidler, op cit., c. 8; Merritt, op cit., 34-50; Witte, op. cit., 119.

in maintaining a boycott against the products of complainant's factory, in furtherance of a conspiracy to injure and destroy its good will, trade, and business—especially to obstruct and destroy its interstate trade. There was also a prayer for damages, but this has not been pressed and calls for no further mention. Complainant is a Michigan corporation and manufactures printing presses at a factory in Battle Creek, in that State, employing about 200 machinists in the factory in addition to 50 office-employees, traveling salesmen, and expert machinists or road men who supervise the erection of the presses for complainant's customers at their various places of business. The defendants who were brought into court and answered the bill are Emil J. Deering and William Bramley, sued individually and as business agents and representatives of District No. 15 of the International Association of Machinists, and Michael T. Ney-land, sued individually and as business agent and representative of Local Lodge No. 328 of the same association. The District Council and the Lodge are unincorporated associations having headquarters in New York City, with numerous members resident in that city and vicinity. There were averments and proof to show that it was impracticable to bring all the members before the court and that the named defendants properly represented them; and those named were called upon to defend for all, pursuant to Equity Rule 38 (226 U.S. 659). Other jurisdictional averments need no particular mention. The District Court, on final hearing, dismissed the bill, 247 Fed. Rep. 192; the Circuit Court of Appeals affirmed its decree, 252 Fed. Rep. 722; and the present appeal was taken.

The jurisdiction of the federal court was invoked both by reason of diverse citizenship and on the ground that defendants were engaged in a conspiracy to restrain complainant's interstate trade and commerce in printing presses, contrary to the Sherman Anti-Trust Act of July 2, 1890, c. 647, 26 Stat. 209. The suit was begun before but brought to hearing after the passage of the Clayton Act of October 15, 1914, c. 323, 38 Stat. 730. Both parties invoked the provisions of the latter act, and both courts treated them as applicable. Complainant relied also upon the common law; but we shall deal first with the effect of the acts of Congress.

The facts of the case and the nature of the relief prayed are sufficiently set forth in the report of the decision of the Circuit Court of Appeals, 252 Fed. Rep. 722. The case was heard before Circuit Judges Rogers and Hough and District Judge Learned Hand. Judge Rogers, although in the minority, stated the case and the pleadings for the court (pp. 723-727) and delivered an opinion for reversal in which he correctly outlined (pp. 734-737) the facts as shown by the undisputed evidence—defendants having introduced none. Judges Hough and Hand followed with separate opinions for affirmance, not, however, disagreeing with Judge Rogers as to the facts. These may be summarized as follows. Complainant conducts its business on the "open shop" policy, without discrimination against either union or non-union men. The individual defendants and the local organizations of which they are the representatives are affiliated with the International Association of Machinists, an unincorporated association having a membership of more than 60,000; and are united in a combination, to which the International Association also is a party, having the object of compelling complainant to unionize its factory and enforce the "closed shop," the eight-hour day, and union scale of wages, by means of interfering with and restraining its interstate trade in the products of the factory. Complainant's principal manufacture is newspaper presses of large size and complicated mechanism, varying in weight from 10,000 to 100,000 pounds, and requiring a considerable force of labor and a considerable expenditure of time—a week or more—to handle, haul and erect them at the point of delivery. These presses are sold throughout the United States and in foreign countries; and, as they are especially designed for the production of daily papers, there is a large market for them in and about the City of New York. They are delivered there in the ordinary course of interstate commerce, the handling, hauling and installation work at destination being done by employees of the purchaser under the supervision of a specially skilled machinist supplied by complainant. The acts complained of and sought to be restrained have nothing to do with the conduct or management of the factory in Michigan, but solely with the installation and operation of the presses by complainant's customers. None of the defendants is or ever was an employee of complainant, and complainant at no time has had relations with either of the organizations that they represent. In August, 1913 (eight months before the filing of the bill), the International Association called a strike at complainant's factory in Battle Creek, as a result of which union machinists to the number of about eleven in the factory and three who supervised the erection of presses in the field left complainant's employ. But the defection of so small a number did not materially interfere with the operation of the factory, and sales and shipments in interstate commerce continued. The acts complained of made up the details of an elaborate programme adopted and carried out by defendants and their organizations in and about the City of New York as part of a country-wide programme adopted by the International Association, for the purpose of enforcing a boycott of complainant's product. The acts embraced the following, with others: warning customers that it would be better for them not to purchase, or having purchased not to install, presses made by complainant, and threatening them with loss should they do so; threatening customers with sympathetic strikes in other trades; notifying a trucking company usually employed by customers to haul the presses not to do so, and threatening it with trouble if it should; inciting employees of the trucking company, and other men employed by customers of complainant, to strike against their respective employers in order to interfere with the hauling and installation of presses, and thus bring pressure to bear upon the customers; notifying repair shops not to do repair work on Duplex presses; coercing union men by threatening them with loss of union cards and with being blacklisted as "scabs" if they assisted in installing the presses; threatening an exposition company with a strike if it permitted complainant's presses to be exhibited; and resorting to a variety of other modes of preventing the sale of presses of complainant's manufacture in or about New York City, and delivery of them in interstate commerce, such as injuring and threatening to injure complainant's customers and prospective customers, and persons concerned in hauling, handling, or installing the presses. In some cases the threats were undisguised, in other cases polite in form but none the less sinister in purpose and effect. All the judges of the Circuit Court of Appeals concurred in the view that defendants' conduct consisted essentially of efforts to render it impossible for complainant to carry on any commerce in printing presses between Michigan and New York; and that defendants had agreed to do and were endeavoring to accomplish the very thing pronounced unlawful by this court in *Loewe* v. *Lawlor,* 208 U.S. 274; 235 U.S. 522. The judges also agreed that the interference with interstate commerce was such as ought to be enjoined, unless the Clayton Act of October 15, 1914, forbade such injunction.

That act was passed after the beginning of the suit but more than two years before it was brought to hearing. We are clear that the courts below were right in giving effect to it; the real question being, whether they gave it the proper effect. In so far as the act (*a*) provided for relief by injunction to private suitors, (*b*) imposed conditions upon granting such relief under particular circumstances, and (*c*) otherwise modified the Sherman Act, it was effective from the time of its passage, and applicable to pending suits for injunction. Obviously, this form of relief operates only *in futuro,* and the right to it must be determined as of the time of the hearing. *Pennsylvania* v. *Wheeling & Belmont Bridge Co.,* 18 How. 421, 431-432. See, also, *United States* v. *The Schooner Peggy,* 1 Cranch, 103, 110; *Sampeyreac* v. *United States,* 7 Pet. 222, 239-240; *Mills* v. *Green,* 159 U.S. 651, 653; *Dinsmore* v. *Southern Express Co.,* 183 U.S. 115, 120; *Berry* v. *Davis,* 242 U.S. 468, 470.

The Clayton Act, in § 1, includes the Sherman Act in a definition of "anti-trust laws," and, in § 16 (38 Stat. 737), gives to private parties a right to relief by injunction in any court of the United States against threatened loss or damage by a violation of the anti-trust laws, under the conditions and principles regulating the granting of such relief by courts of equity. Evidently this provision was intended to supplement the Sherman Act, under which some of the federal courts had held, as this court afterwards held in *Paine Lumber Co.* v. *Neal,* 244 U.S. 459, 471, that a private party could not maintain a suit for injunction.

That complainant's business of manufacturing printing presses and disposing of them in commerce is a property right, entitled to protection against unlawful injury or interference; that unrestrained access to the channels of interstate commerce is necessary for the successful conduct of the business; that a widespread combination exists, to which defendants and the associations represented by them are parties, to hinder and obstruct complainant's interstate trade and commerce by the means that have been indicated; and that as a result of it complainant has sustained substantial damage to its interstate trade, and is threatened with further and irreparable loss and damage in the future; is proved by clear and undisputed evidence. Hence the right to an injunction is clear if the threatened loss is due to a violation of the Sherman Act as amended by the Clayton Act. * * *

The substance of the matters here complained of is an interference with complainant's interstate trade, intended to have coercive effect upon complainant, and produced by what is commonly known as a "secondary boycott," that is, a combination not merely to refrain from dealing with complainant, or to advise or by peaceful means persuade complainant's customers to refrain ("primary boycott"), but to exercise coercive pressure upon such customers, actual or prospective, in order to cause them to withhold or withdraw patronage from complainant through fear of loss or damage to themselves should they deal with it.

As we shall see, the recognized distinction between a primary and a secondary boycott is material to be considered upon the question of the proper construction of the Clayton Act. But, in determining the right to an injunction under that and the Sherman Act, it is of minor consequence whether either kind of boycott is lawful or unlawful at common law or under the statutes of particular States. Those acts, passed in the exercise of the power of Congress to regulate commerce among the States, are of paramount authority, and their prohibitions must be given full effect irrespective of whether the things prohibited are lawful or unlawful at common law or under local statutes.

In *Loewe* v. *Lawlor,* 208 U. S. 274, where there was an effort to compel plaintiffs to unionize their factory by preventing them from manufacturing articles intended for transportation beyond the State, and also by preventing vendees from reselling articles purchased from plaintiffs and negotiating with plaintiffs for further purchases, by means of a boycott of plaintiffs' products and of dealers who handled them, this court held that there was a conspiracy in restraint of trade actionable under § 7 of the Sherman Act, and in that connection said (p. 293) : "The act prohibits any combination whatever to secure action which essentially obstructs the free flow of commerce between the States, or restricts, in that regard, the liberty of a trader to engage in business. The combination charged falls within the class of restraints of trade aimed at compelling third parties and strangers involuntarily not to engage in the course of trade except on conditions that the combination imposes." And when the case came before the court a second time, 235 U.S. 522, 534, it was held that the use of the primary and secondary boycott and the circulation of a list of "unfair dealers," intended to influence customers of plaintiffs and thus subdue the latter to the demands of the defendants, and having the effect of interfering with plaintiffs' interstate trade, was actionable.

In *Eastern States Retail Lumber Dealers' Association* v. *United States,* 234 U.S. 600, wholesale dealers were subjected to coercion merely through the circulation among retailers, who were members of the association, of information in the form of a kind of "black list," intended to influence the retailers to refrain from dealing with the listed wholesalers, and it was held that this constituted a violation of the Sherman Act. Referring to this decision, the court said, in *Lawlor v. Loewe, 235 U.S. 522, 534*: "That case establishes that, irrespective of compulsion or even agreement to observe its intimation, the circulation of a list of 'unfair dealers,' manifestly intended to put the ban upon those whose names appear therein, among an important body of possible customers combined with a view to joint action and in anticipation of such reports, is within the prohibitions of the Sherman Act if it is intended to restrain and restrains commerce among the States."

It is settled by these decisions that such a restraint produced by peaceable persuasion is as much within the prohibition as one accomplished by force or threats of force; and it is not to be justified by the fact that the participants in the combination or conspiracy may have some object beneficial to themselves or their associates which possibly they might have been at liberty to pursue in the absence of the statute.

Upon the question whether the provisions of the Clayton Act forbade the grant of an injunction under the circumstances of the present case, the Circuit Court of Appeals was divided; the majority holding that under § 20, "perhaps in conjunction with section 6," there could be no injunction. These sections are set forth in the margin.[1] Defendants seek to derive from them some authority for their conduct. As to § 6, it seems to us its principal importance in this discussion is for what it does *not* authorize, and for the limit it sets to the immunity conferred. The section assumes the normal objects of a labor organization to be legitimate, and declares that nothing in the anti-trust laws shall be construed to forbid the existence and operation of such organizations or to forbid their members from *lawfully* carrying out their *legitimate* objects; and that such an organization shall not be held in itself—merely because of its existence and operation—to be an illegal combination or conspiracy in restraint of trade. But there is nothing in the section to exempt such an organization or its members from accountability where it or they depart from its normal and legitimate objects and engage in an actual combination or conspiracy in restraint of trade. And by no fair or permissible construction can it be taken as authorizing any activity otherwise unlawful, or enabling a normally lawful organization to become a cloak for an illegal combination or conspiracy in restraint of trade as defined by the anti-trust laws.

The principal reliance is upon § 20. This regulates the granting of restraining orders and injunctions by the courts of the United States in a designated class of cases, with respect to (a) the terms and conditions of the relief and the practice to be pursued, and (b) the character of acts that are to be exempted from the restraint; and in the concluding words it declares (c) that none of the acts specified shall be held to be violations of

---

[1] For these sections of the Clayton Act, see, *supra* p. 210.

any law of the United States. All its provisions are subject to a general qualification respecting the nature of the controversy and the parties affected. It is to be a "case between an employer and employees, or between employers and employees, or between employees, or between persons employed and persons seeking employment, involving, or growing out of, a dispute concerning terms or conditions of employment."

The first paragraph merely puts into statutory form familiar restrictions upon the granting of injunctions already established and of general application in the equity practice of the courts of the United States. It is but declaratory of the law as it stood before. The second paragraph declares that "no *such* restraining order or injunction" shall prohibit certain conduct specified—manifestly still referring to a "case between an employer and employees, * * * involving, or growing out of, a dispute concerning terms or conditions of employment," as designated in the first paragraph. It is very clear that the restriction upon the use of the injunction is in favor only of those concerned as parties to such a dispute as is described. The words defining the permitted conduct include particular qualifications consistent with the general one respecting the nature of the case and dispute intended; and the concluding words, "nor shall any of the acts specified in this paragraph be considered or held to be violations of any law of the United States," are to be read in the light of the context, and mean only that those acts are not to be so held when committed by parties concerned in "a dispute concerning terms or conditions of employment." If the qualifying words are to have any effect, they must operate to confine the restriction upon the granting of injunctions, and also the relaxation of the provisions of the anti-trust and other laws of the United States, to parties standing in proximate relation to a controversy such as is particularly described.

The majority of the Circuit Court of Appeals appear to have entertained the view that the words "employers and employees," as used in § 20, should be treated as referring to "the business class or clan to which the parties litigant respectively belong"; and that, as there had been a dispute at complainant's factory in Michigan concerning the conditions of employment there—a dispute created, it is said, if it did not exist before, by the act of the Machinists' Union in calling a strike at the factory—§ 20 operated to permit members of the Machinists' Union elsewhere—some 60,000 in number—although standing in no relation of employment under complainant, past, present, or prospective, to make that dispute their own and proceed to instigate sympathetic strikes, picketing, and boycotting against employers wholly unconnected with complainant's factory and having relations with complainant only in the way of purchasing its product in the ordinary course of interstate commerce—and this where there was no dispute between such employers and their employees respecting terms or conditions of employment.

We deem this construction altogether inadmissible. Section 20 must be given full effect according to its terms as an expression of the purpose of Congress; but it must be borne in mind that the section imposes an exceptional and extraordinary restriction upon the equity powers of the courts of the United States and upon the general operation of the anti-trust laws, a restriction in the nature of a special privilege or immunity to a particular class, with corresponding detriment to the general public; and it would violate rules of statutory construction having general application and far-reaching importance to enlarge that special privilege by resorting to a loose construction of the section, not to speak of ignoring or slighting the qualifying words that are found in it. Full and fair effect will be given to every word if the exceptional privilege be confined—as the natural meaning of the words confines it—to those who are proximately and substantially concerned as parties to an actual dispute respecting the terms or conditions of their own employment, past, present, or prospective. The extensive construction adopted by the majority of the court below virtually ignores the effect of the qualifying words. Congress had in mind particular industrial controversies, not a general class war. "Terms or conditions of employment" are the only grounds of dispute recognized as adequate to bring into play the exemptions; and it would do violence to the guarded language employed were the exemption extended beyond the parties affected in a proximate and substantial, not merely a sentimental or sympathetic, sense by the cause of dispute.

Nor can § 20 be regarded as bringing in all members of a labor organization as parties to a "dispute concerning terms or conditions of employment" which proximately affects only a few of them, with the result of conferring upon any and all members,—no matter how many thousands there may be, nor how remote from the actual conflict—those exemptions which Congress in terms conferred only upon parties to the dispute. That would enlarge by construction the provisions of § 20, which contain no mention of labor organizations, so as to produce an inconsistency with § 6, which deals specifically with the subject and must be deemed to express the measure and limit of the immunity intended by Congress to be incident to mere membership in such an organization. At the same time it would virtually repeal by implication the prohibition of the Sherman Act, so far as labor organizations are concerned, notwithstanding repeals by implication are not favored; and in effect, as was noted in *Loewe v. Lawlor,* 208 U.S. 274, 303-304, would confer upon voluntary associations of individuals formed within the States a control over commerce among the States that is denied to the governments of the States themselves.

The qualifying effect of the words descriptive of the nature of the dispute and the parties concerned is further borne out by the phrases defining the conduct that is not to be subjected to injunction or treated as a violation of the laws of the United States, that is to say: (a) "terminating any relation of employment, * * * or persuading others by peaceful and lawful means so to do"; (b) "attending at any place where any such person or persons may lawfully be, for the purpose of peacefully obtaining or communicating information, or from peacefully persuading any person to work or to abstain from working;" (c) "ceasing to patronize or to employ any party to such dispute, or * * * recommending, advising, or persuading others by peaceful and lawful means so to do"; (d) "paying or giving to, or withholding from, any person engaged in such dispute, any strike benefits * * *"; (e) "doing any act or thing which might lawfully be done in the absence of such dispute by any party thereto." The emphasis placed on the words "lawful" and "lawfully," "peaceful" and "peacefully," and the references to the dispute and the parties to it, strongly rebut a legislative intent to confer a general immunity for conduct violative of the anti-trust laws, or otherwise unlawful. The subject of the boycott is dealt with specifically in the "ceasing to patronize" provision, and by the clear force of the language employed the exemption is limited to pressure exerted upon a "party to such dispute" by means of "peaceful and *lawful*" influence upon neutrals. There is nothing here to justify defendants or the organizations they represent in using either threats or persuasion to bring about strikes or a cessation of work on the part of employees of complainant's customers or prospective customers, or of the trucking company employed by the customers, with the object of compelling such customers to withdraw or refrain from commercial relations with complainant, and of thereby constraining complainant to yield the matter in dispute. To instigate a sympathetic strike in aid of a secondary boycott cannot be deemed "peaceful and lawful" persuasion. In essence it is a threat to inflict damage upon the immediate employer, between whom and his employees no dispute exists, in order to bring him against his will into a concerted plan to inflict damage upon another employer who is in dispute with his employees.

The majority of the Circuit Court of Appeals, very properly treating the case as involving a secondary boycott, based the decision upon the view that it was the purpose of § 20 to legalize the secondary boycott "at least in so far as it rests on, or consists of, refusing to work for any one who deals with the principal offender." Characterizing the section as "blindly drawn," and conceding that the meaning attributed to it was broad, the court referred to the legislative history of the enactment as a warrant for the construction adopted. Let us consider this.

By repeated decisions of this court it has come to be well established that the debates in Congress expressive of the views and motives of individual members are not a safe guide, and hence may not be resorted to, in ascertaining the meaning and purpose of the law-making body. *Aldridge v. Williams,* 3 How. 9, 24; *United States v. Union Pacific R. R. Co.,* 91 U.S. 72, 79; *United States v. Trans-Missouri Freight Association,* 166 U.S. 290, 318. But reports of committees of House or Senate stand upon a more solid footing, and may be regarded as an exposition of the legislative intent in a case where otherwise the meaning of a statute is obscure. *Binns v. United States,* 194 U.S. 486, 495. And this has been extended to include explanatory statements in the nature of a supplemental report made by the committee member in charge of a bill in course of passage. *Binns v. United States, supra; Pennsylvania R. R. Co. v. International Coal Co.,* 230 U. S. 184, 198-199; *United States v. Coca Cola Co.,* 241 U.S.

265, 281; United States v. St. Paul, Minneapolis & Manitoba Ry. Co., 247 U.S. 310, 318.

In the case of the Clayton Act, the printed committee reports are not explicit with respect to the meaning of the "ceasing to patronize" clause of what is now § 20. (See House Rept. No. 627, 63d Cong., 2nd sess., pp. 33-36; Senate Rept. No. 698, 63d Cong., 2nd sess., pp. 29-31; the latter being a reproduction of the former.) But they contain extracts from judicial opinions and a then recent text-book sustaining the "primary boycott," and expressing an adverse view as to the secondary or coercive boycott; and, on the whole, are far from manifesting a purpose to relax the prohibition against restraints of trade in favor of the secondary boycott.

Moreover, the report was supplemented in this regard by the spokesman of the House committee (Mr. Webb) who had the bill in charge when it was under consideration by the House. The question whether the bill legalized the secondary boycott having been raised, it was emphatically and unequivocally answered by him in the negative.[2] The subject—he declared in substance or effect—was under consideration when the bill was framed, and the section as reported was carefully prepared with the settled purpose of excluding the secondary boycott and confining boycotting to the parties to the dispute, allowing parties to cease to patronize and to ask others to cease to patronize a party to the dispute; it was the opinion of the committee that it did not legalize the secondary boycott, it was not their purpose to authorize such a boycott, not a member of the committee would vote to do so; clarifying amendment was unnecessary; the section as reported expressed the real purpose so well that it could not be tortured into a meaning authorizing the secondary boycott. This was the final word of the House committee on the subject, and was uttered under such circumstances and with such impressive emphasis that it is not going too far to say that except for this exposition of the meaning of the section it would not have been enacted in the form in which it was reported. In substantially that form it became law; and since in our opinion its proper construction is entirely in accord with its purpose as thus declared, little need be added.

---

[2] Extracts from Congressional Record, vol. 51, Part 10, 63d Cong., 2d sess. (Page 9652.)

MR. VOLSTEAD. Would not this also legalize the secondary boycott? * * *

MR. WEBB. Mr. Chairman, I do not think it legalizes a secondary boycott.

MR. VOLSTEAD. Let me read the lines, if the gentleman will permit. And no such restraining order or injunction shall prohibit anyone—"from ceasing to patronize *those who* [or to] employ any party to such dispute, or from recommending, advising, or persuading others by peaceful means so to do."

Now, does not the word "others" in that instance refer to others than parties to the dispute?

MR. WEBB. No; because it says in line 15:

"From ceasing to patronize or employ any parties to such dispute."

MR. VOLSTEAD. * * * Can there be any doubt this is intended or does, in fact, legalize the secondary boycott?

MR. WEBB. I will say frankly to my friend when this section was drawn it was drawn with the careful purpose not to legalize the secondary boycott, and we do not think it does. There may be a difference of opinion about it, but it is the opinion of the committee that it does not legalize the secondary boycott and is not intended

The extreme and harmful consequences of the constructon adopted in the court below are not to be ignored. The present case furnishes an apt and convincing example. An ordinary controversy in a manufacturing establishment, said to concern the terms or conditions of employment there, has been held a sufficient occasion for imposing a general embargo upon the products of the establishment and a nation-wide blockade of the channels of interstate commerce against them, carried out by inciting sympathetic strikes and a secondary boycott against complainant's customers, to the great and incalculable damage of many innocent people far remote from any connection with or control over the original and actual dispute —people constituting, indeed, the general public upon whom the cost must ultimately fall, and whose vital interest in unobstructed commerce constituted the prime and paramount concern of Congress in enacting the antitrust laws, of which the section under consideration forms after all a part.

Reaching the conclusion, as we do, that complainant has a clear right to an injunction under the Sherman Act as amended by the Clayton Act, it becomes unnecessary to consider whether a like result would follow under the common law or local statutes; there being no suggestion that relief thereunder could be broader than that to which complainant is entitled under the acts of Congress.

There should be an injunction against defendants and the associations represented by them, and all members of those associations, restraining them, according to the prayer of the bill, from interfering or attempting to interfere with the sale, transportation, or delivery in interstate commerce of any printing press or presses manufactured by complainant, or the transportation, carting, installation, use, operation, exhibition, display, or repairing of any such press or presses, or the performance of any contract or contracts made by complainant respecting the sale, transportation, deliv-

---

to do so. It does legalize the primary boycott; it does legalize the strike; it does legalize persuading others to strike, to quit work, and the other acts mentioned in section 18 [now section 20], but we did not intend, I will say frankly, to legalize the secondary boycott.

(Page 9653.)

MR. WEBB. I will say this section was drawn two years or more ago and was drawn carefully, and those who drew this section drew it with the idea of excluding the secondary boycott. It passed the House, I think, by about 243 to 16, and the question of the secondary boycott was not raised then, because we understood so clearly it did not refer to or authorize the secondary boycott.

(Page 9658.)

MR. WEBB. Mr. Chairman, I should vote for the amendment offered by the gentlemen from Minnesota [Mr. Volstead] if I were not perfectly satisfied that it is taken care of in this section. The language the gentlemen reads does not authorize the secondary boycott, and he could not torture it into any such meaning. While it does authorize persons to cease to patronize the party to the dispute and to recommend to others to cease to patronize that same party to the dispute, that is not a secondary boycott, and you can not possibly make it mean a secondary boycott. Therefore this section does not authorize the secondary boycott.

I say again—and I speak for, I believe, practically every member of the Judiciary Committee—that if this section did legalize the secondary boycott there would not be a man vote for it. It is not the purpose of the committee to authorize it, and I do not think any person in this House wants to do it. We confine the boycotting to the parties to the dispute, allowing parties to cease to patronize that party and to ask others to cease to patronize the party to the dispute.

ery, or installation of any such press or presses, by causing or threatening to cause loss, damage, trouble, or inconvenience to any person, firm, or corporation concerned in the purchase, transportation, carting, installation, use, operation, exhibition, display, or repairing of any such press or presses, or the performance of any such contract or contracts; and also and especially from using any force, threats, command, direction, or even persuasion with the object or having the effect of causing any person or persons to decline employment, cease employment, or not seek employment, or to refrain from work or cease working under any person, firm, or corporation being a purchaser or prospective purchaser of any printing press or presses from complainant, or engaged in hauling, carting, delivering, installing, handling, using, operating, or repairing any such press or presses for any customer of complainant. Other threatened conduct by defendants or the associations they represent, or the members of such associations, in furtherance of the secondary boycott should be included in the injunction according to the proofs.

Complainant is entitled to its costs in this court and in both courts below.

Decree reversed, and the cause remanded to the District Court for further proceedings in conformity with this opinion.

MR. JUSTICE BRANDEIS, dissenting, with whom MR. JUSTICE HOLMES and MR. JUSTICE CLARKE concur.

The Duplex Company, a manufacturer of newspaper printing presses, seeks to enjoin officials of the machinists' and affiliated unions from interfering with its business by inducing their members not to work for plaintiff or its customers in connection with the setting up of presses made by it. Unlike *Hitchman Coal & Coke Co. v. Mitchell,* 245 U.S. 229, there is here no charge that defendants are inducing employees to break their contracts. Nor is it now urged that defendants threaten acts of violence. But plaintiff insists that the acts complained of violate both the common law of New York and the Sherman Act and that, accordingly, it is entitled to relief by injunction under the state law and under § 16 of the Clayton Act, October 15, 1914, c. 323, 38 Stat. 730, 737.

The defendants admit interference with plaintiff's business but justify on the following ground: There are in the United States only four manufacturers of such presses; and they are in active competition. Between 1909 and 1913 the machinists' union induced three of them to recognize and deal with the union, to grant the eight-hour day, to establish a minimum wage scale and to comply with other union requirements. The fourth, the Duplex Company, refused to recognize the union; insisted upon conducting its factory on the open shop principle; refused to introduce the eight-hour day and operated for the most part, ten hours a day; refused to establish a minimum wage scale; and disregarded other union standards. Thereupon two of the three manufacturers who had assented to union conditions, notified the union that they should be obliged to terminate their agreements with it unless their competitor, the Duplex Company, also entered into the agreement with the union, which, in giving more favorable terms to labor, imposed correspondingly greater burdens upon the employer. Because the Duplex Company refused to enter into such an agreement and in order to induce it to do so, the machinists' union declared a strike at its factory, and in aid of that strike instructed its members and the members of affiliated unions not to work on the installation of presses which plaintiff had delivered in New York. Defendants insist that by the common law of New York, where the acts complained of were done, and where this suit was brought, and also by § 20 of the Clayton Act, 38 Stat. 730, 738, the facts constitute a justification for this interference with plaintiff's business.

First. As to the rights at common law: Defendants' justification is that of self-interest. They have supported the strike at the employer's factory by a strike elsewhere against its product. They have injured the plaintiff, not maliciously, but in self-defense. They contend that the Duplex Company's refusal to deal with the machinists' union and to observe its standards threatened the interest not only of such union members as were its factory employees, but even more of all members of the several affiliated unions employed by plaintiff's competitors and by others whose more advanced standards the plaintiff was, in reality, attacking; and that none of the defendants and no person whom they are endeavoring to induce to refrain from working in connection with the setting up of presses made by plaintiff is an outsider, an interloper. In other words, that the contest between the company and the machinists' union involves vitally the interest of every person whose coöperation is sought. May not all with a common interest join in refusing to expend their labor upon articles whose very production constitutes an attack upon their standard of living and the institution which they are convinced supports it? Applying common-law principles the answer should, in my opinion, be: Yes, if as matter of fact those who so coöperate have a common interest.

The change in the law by which strikes once illegal and even criminal are now recognized as lawful was effected in America largely without the intervention of legislation. This reversal of a common-law rule was not due to the rejection by the courts of one principle and the adoption in its stead of another, but to a better realization of the facts of industrial life. It is conceded that, although the strike of the workmen in plaintiff's factory injured its business, the strike was not an actionable wrong; because the obvious self-interest of the strikers constituted a justification. See *Pickett v. Walsh,* 192 Massachusetts, 572. Formerly courts held that self-interest could not be so served. Commons, History of Labor in the United States, vol. 2, c. 5. But even after strikes to raise wages or reduce hours were held to be legal because of the self-interest, some courts held that there was not sufficient causal relationship between a strike to unionize a shop and the self-interest of the strikers to justify injuries inflicted. *Plant v. Woods,* 176 Massachusetts, 492; *Lucke v. Clothing Cutters' Assembly,* 77 Maryland, 396; *Erdman v. Mitchell,* 207 Pa. St. 79. But other courts, repeating the same legal formula, found that there was justification, because they viewed the facts differently. *National Protective Association v. Cumming*, 170 N.Y. 315; *Kemp v. Division No. 241*, 255 Illinois, 213; *Roddy v. United Mine Workers*, 41 Oklahoma, 621. When centralization in the control of business brought its corresponding centralization in the organization of workingmen, new facts had to be appraised. A single employer might, as in this case, threaten the standing of the whole organization and the standards of all its members; and when he did so the union, in order to protect itself, would naturally refuse to work on his materials wherever found. When such a situation was first presented to the courts, judges concluded that the intervention of the purchaser of the materials established an insulation through which the direct relationship of the employer and the workingmen did not penetrate; and the strike against the material was considered a strike against the purchaser by unaffected third parties. *Burnham v. Dowd*, 217 Massachusetts, 351; *Purvis v. United Brotherhood*, 214 Pa. St. 348; *Booth v. Burgess*, 72 N.J. Eq. 181. But other courts, with better appreciation of the facts of industry, recognized the unity of interest throughout the union, and that, in refusing to work on materials which threatened it, the union was only refusing to aid in destroying itself. *Bossert v. Dhuy*, 221 N.Y. 342; *Cohn & Roth Electric Co. v. Bricklayers Union*, 92 Connecticut, 161; *Gill Engraving Co. v. Doerr*, 214 Fed. Rep. 111; *State v. Van Pelt*, 136 N.C. 633; *Grant Construction Co. v. St. Paul Building Trades Council*, 136 Minnesota, 167; *Pierce v. Stablemen's Union*, 156 California, 70, 76.

So, in the case at bar, deciding a question of fact upon the evidence introduced and matters of common knowledge, I should say, as the two lower courts apparently have said, that the defendants and those from whom they sought coöperation have a common interest which the plaintiff threatened. This view is in harmony with the views of the Court of Appeals of New York. For in New York, although boycotts like that in *Loewe v. Lawlor*, 208 U.S. 274, are illegal because they are conducted not against a product but against those who deal in it and are carried out by a combination of persons not united by common interest but only by sympathy, *Auburn Draying Co. v. Wardell*, 227 N.Y. 1, it is lawful for all members of a union by whomever employed to refuse to handle materials whose production weakens the union. *Bossert v. Dhuy, supra; P. Reardon, Inc., v. Caton*, 189 App. Div. 501; compare *Paine Lumber Co. v. Neal*, 244 U.S. 459, 471. "The voluntary adoption of a rule not to work on non-union made material and its enforcement differs only in degree from such voluntary rule and its enforcement in a particular case. Such a determination also differs entirely from a general boycott of a particular dealer or manufacturer with a malicious intent and purpose to destroy the good will or business of such dealer or manufacturer." *Bossert v. Dhuy, supra*, p.

355. (Rev'd, p. 455.) In my opinion, therefore, plaintiff had no cause of action by the common law of New York.

Second. As to the anti-trust laws of the United States: Section 20, of the Clayton Act, declares,—

"Nor shall any of the acts specified in this paragraph be considered or held to be violations of any law of the United States."

The acts which are thus referred to are, whether performed singly or in concert,—"Terminating any relation of employment, or * * * ceasing to perform any work or labor, or * * * recommending, advising, or persuading others by peaceful means so to do; or * * * attending at any place where any such person or persons may lawfully be, for the purpose of peacefully obtaining or communicating information, or * * * peacefully persuading any person to work or to abstain from working; or * * * ceasing to patronize or to employ any party to such dispute, or * * * recommending, advising, or persuading others by peaceful and lawful means so to do; or * * * paying or giving to, or withholding from, any person engaged in such dispute, any strike benefits or other moneys or things of value; or * * * peaceably assembling in a lawful manner, and for lawful purposes; or * * * doing any act or thing which might lawfully be done in the absence of such dispute by any party thereto."

This statute was the fruit of unceasing agitation, which extended over more than twenty years and was designed to equalize before the law the position of workingmen and employer as industrial combatants. Aside from the use of the injunction, the chief source of dissatisfaction with the existing law lay in the doctrine of malicious combinations,[3] and, in many parts of the country, in the judicial declarations of the illegality at common law of picketing and persuading others to leave work. The grounds for objection to the latter are obvious. The objection to the doctrine of malicious combinations requires some explanation. By virtue of that doctrine, damage resulting from conduct such as striking or withholding patronage or persuading others to do either, which without more might be *damnum absque injuria* because the result of trade competition, became

---

[3] See: Ernst Freund, "Malice and Unlawful Interference," 11 Harv. Law Rev. 449, 461; Edward F. McClellan, "Rights of Traders and Laborers," 16 Harv. Law Rev. 237, 244; Jeremiah Smith, "Crucial Issues in Labor Litigation," 20 Harv. Law Rev. 429, 451; Commons and Andrews, Principles of Labor Legislation, pp. 95-116; Hoxie, Trade Unionism in the United States, p. 231; Groat, Attitude of American Courts Towards Labor Cases, pp. 76-77; 221; 246; J. W. Bryan, The Development of the English Law of Conspiracy, p. 147, *et seq.*

Report of the Industrial Commission, 1901, vol. XVII, p. cxiv, pp. 515, 556; Report of Royal Commission on Trade Disputes and Trade Combinations, 1906, p. 12; Report of Commission on Industrial Relations, 1915, p. 135; p. 377.

For attempts to reach this doctrine by legislation see also 52nd Cong., H.R. 6640, § 1; 56th Cong., H.R. 11667, § 7; 57th Cong., S. 649, § 7.

actionable when done for a purpose which a judge considered socially or economically harmful and therefore branded as malicious and unlawful.[4] It was objected that, due largely to environment, the social and economic ideas of judges, which thus became translated into law, were prejudicial to a position of equality between workingman and employer; that due to this dependence upon the individual opinion of judges great confusion existed as to what purposes were lawful and what unlawful;[5] and that in any event Congress, not the judges, was the body which should declare what public policy in regard to the industrial struggle demands.

By 1914 the ideas of the advocates of legislation had fairly crystallized upon the manner in which the inequality and uncertainty of the law, should be removed. It was to be done by expressly legalizing certain acts regardless of the effects produced by them upon other persons. As to them Congress was to extract the element of *injuria* from the damages thereby inflicted, instead of leaving judges to determine according to their own economic and social views whether the damage inflicted on an employer in an industrial struggle was *damnum absque injuria,* because an incident of trade competition, or a legal injury, because in their opinion, economically and socially objectionable. This idea was presented to the committees which reported the Clayton Act.[6] The resulting law set out certain acts which had previously been held unlawful, whenever courts had disapproved of the ends for which they were performed; it then declared that, when these acts were committed in the course of an industrial dispute, they should not be held to violate any law of the United States. In other words the Clayton Act substituted the opinion of Congress as to the propriety of the purpose for that of differing judges; and thereby it declared that the relations between employers of labor and workingmen were competi-

---

[4] See James Wallace Bryan, The Development of the English Law of Conspiracy:—
"We find little difficulty in attributing the illegality of combinations to strike or otherwise to advance the interests of labor, not to the material loss inflicted upon the employer concerned, but to the harm supposed to result from their activities to the public at large." And since the judge or jury believe the conduct socially bad and since it is admittedly done intentionally, not inadvertently, they declare that the actors are animated by malice which negatives the justification of "fair competition," e. g., Lord Bowen in Mogul S. S. Co. v. McGregor, Gow & Co., 1892 A.C. 25, "intentionally to do that which is calculated * * * to damage * * * and does damage another in his property or trade is actionable if done without just cause or excuse, and * * * is what the law calls a malicious injury."

[5] See A. V. Dicey, "The Combination Laws as Illustrating the Relation Between Law and Opinion in England During the Nineteenth Century," 17 Harv. Law Rev. 511, 532: "The very confusion of the present state of the law corresponds with and illustrates a confused state of opinion."

[6] It was said that this doctrine "completely unsettle(d) the law * * * and set up the chancellor in the midst of the labor organization at the inception of a strike as an arbiter of their conduct as well as a controller of their fates." 62nd Cong., 2nd sess. Hearings Before a Sub-committee of the Senate Committee on the Judiciary on H.R. 23635, p. 429.
Again, it was pointed out that the incorporation of this idea in the Sherman Law had "done violence to the right to strike—to cease work collectively * * * and to the right to withhold patronage and to agree to withhold patronage." Brief by Samuel Gompers, Hearings before the House Committee on the Judiciary on Trust Legislation, 63rd Cong., 2nd sess., vol, 2, p. 1808.

tive relations, that organized competition was not harmful and that it justified injuries necessarily inflicted in its course.[7] Both the majority and the minority report of the House Committee indicate that such was its purpose.[8] If, therefore, the act applies to the case at bar, the acts here complained of cannot "be considered or held to be violations of any law of the United States," and, hence, do not violate the Sherman Act.

The Duplex Company contends that § 20 of the Clayton Act does not apply to the case at bar, because it is restricted to cases "between an employer and employees, or between employers and employees, or between employees, or between persons employed and persons seeking employment, involving, or growing out of, a dispute concerning terms or conditions of employment"; whereas the case at bar arises between an employer in Michigan and workingmen in New York not in its employ, and does not involve their conditions of employment. But Congress did not restrict the provision to employers and workingmen *in their employ*. By including "employers and employees" and "persons employed and persons seeking employment" it showed that it was not aiming merely at a legal relationship between a specific employer and his employees. Furthermore, the plaintiff's contention proves too much. If the words are to receive a strict technical construction, the statute will have no application to disputes between employers of labor and workingmen, since the very acts to which it applies sever the continuity of the legal relationship. *Iron Moulders' Union v. Allis-Chalmers Co.,* 166 Fed. Rep. 45, 52-53; *Louisville, Evansville & St. Louis R. R. Co. v. Wilson,* 138 U. S. 501, 505; cf. *Rex v. Neilson,* 44 N. S. 488, 491. The further contention that this case is not one arising out of a dispute concerning the conditions of work of one of the parties is, in my opinion, founded upon a misconception of the facts.

Because I have come to the conclusion that both the common law of a State and a statute of the United States declare the right of industrial combatants to push their struggle to the limits of the justification of self-interest, I do not wish to be understood as attaching any constitutional or moral sanction to that right. All rights are derived from the purposes of

---

[7] Compare the following: "There are apparently, only two lines of action possible: First to restrict the rights and powers of employers to correspond in substance to the powers and rights now allowed to trade unions, and second, to remove all restrictions which now prevent the freedom of action of both parties to industrial disputes, retaining only the ordinary civil and criminal restraints for the preservation of life, property and the public peace. The first method has been tried and failed absolutely. * * * The only method therefore seems to be the removal of all restrictions upon both parties, thus legalizing the strike, the lockout, the boycott, the blacklist, the bringing in of strike-breakers, and peaceful picketing." Report of the Committee on Industrial Relations, 1915, p. 136.

[8] The majority declared that the section sets out "specific acts which the best opinion of the courts holds to be within the right of parties involved upon one side or the other of a trades dispute," which it has been necessary to affirm because of "the divergent views which the courts have expressed on the subject and the difference between courts in the application of recognized rules." The minority insisted that the section prescribes "a set rule forbidding under any circumstances the enjoining of certain acts which may or may not be actuated by a malicious motive or be done for the purpose of working an unlawful injury. etc." 63rd Cong., 2nd sess., House Report 627, p. 30; *id.* Part 2, Appendix A, p. 20.

the society in which they exist; above all rights rises duty to the community. The conditions developed in industry may be such that those engaged in it cannot continue their struggle without danger to the community. But it is not for judges to determine whether such conditions exist, nor is it their function to set the limits of permissible contest and to declare the duties which the new situation demands. This is the function of the legislature which, while limiting individual and group rights of aggression and defense, may substitute processes of justice for the more primitive method of trial by combat.[9]

UNITED MINE WORKERS OF AMERICA v. CORONADO COAL COMPANY.

Supreme Court of the United States. 259 U.S. 344 (1922).

This is a writ of error brought under § 241 of the Judicial Code, to review a judgment of the Circuit Court of Appeals of the Eighth Circuit. That court on a writ of error had affirmed the judgment of the District Court for the Western District of Arkansas, in favor of the plaintiffs, with some modification, and that judgment thus affirmed is here for review.

The plaintiffs in the District Court were the receivers of the Bache-Denman Coal Company, and eight other corporations in each of which the first-named company owned a controlling amount of stock. They were closely interrelated in corporate organization and in the physical location of their coal mines. These had been operated for some years as a unit under one set of officers in the Prairie Creek Valley in Sebastian County, Arkansas. In July, 1914, the District Court for the Western District of Arkansas appointed a receiver for all of the nine companies by a single decree. The receiver then appointed was Franklin Bache, whose successors as such are defendants in error here.

The defendants in the court below were the United Mine Workers of America, and its officers, District 21 of the United Mine Workers of America, and its officers, 27 local unions in District No. 21, and their officers, and 65 individuals, mostly members of one union or another, but

---

[9] For comment on the case, see: 21 Col. Law Rev. 258 (1921); 34 Harv. Law Rev. 880 (1921); 19 Mich. Law Rev. 628 (1921); 3 Minn. Law Rev. 212 (1919); 7 Va. Law Rev. 462 (1921); 1 Wis. Law Rev. 186 (1921); 25 New Republic, 245, 376 (1921). See also: Mason, "The Labor Clauses of the Clayton Act," 18 Am. Pol. Sci. Rev. 489 (1924); Powell, "The Supreme Court's Control Over the Issue of Injunctions in Labor Disputes," 13 Proc. Am. Pol. Sci. Ass'n 37, 48-54 (1928).

Compare: Paine Lumber Co. v. Neal, 244 U.S. 459 (1917), where upon a somewhat similar state of facts injunctive relief was refused upon the ground that the Sherman Act gave no right to a private party to enjoin its violation.

Accord: Columbus Heating & Ventilating Co. v. Pittsburgh Bldg. Trades Council, 17 Fed.(2d) 806 (W.D.Pa. 1927). Cf. Buyer v. Guillan, 271 Fed. 65 (2nd cir. 1921).

including some persons not members, all of whom were charged in the complaint with having entered into a conspiracy to restrain and monopolize interstate commerce, in violation of the first and second sections of the Anti-Trust Act, and with having, in the course of that conspiracy, and for the purpose of consummating it, destroyed the plaintiff's properties. Treble damages for this and an attorney's fee were asked under the seventh section of the act.

The original complaint was filed in September, 1914, about six weeks after the destruction of the property. It was demurred to, and the District Court sustained the demurrer. This was carried to the Court of Appeals on error, and the ruling of the District Court was reversed. *Dowd v. United Mine Workers,* 235 Fed. 1. The case, then came to trial on the third amended complaint and answers of the defendants. The trial resulted in a verdict of $200,000 for the plaintiffs, which was trebled by the court, and to which was added a counsel fee of $25,000, and interest to the amount of $120,600, from July 17, 1914, the date of the destruction of the property, to November 22, 1917, the date upon which judgment was entered. The verdict did not separate the amount found between the companies. On a writ of error from the Court of Appeals, the case was reversed as to the interest, but in other respects the judgment was affirmed. 258 Fed. 829. The defendants, the International Union and District No. 21, have given a supersedeas bond to meet the judgment if it is affirmed as against both or either of them.

The third amended complaint avers that of the nine companies, of which the plaintiff was receiver, and for which he was bringing his suit, five were operating companies engaged in mining coal and shipping it in interstate commerce, employing in all about 870 men, and mining an annual product when working to their capacity valued at $465,000, of which 75 per cent. was sold and shipped to customers' outside of the State. Of the five operating companies, one was under contract to operate the properties of two of the others, and four non-operating companies were each financially interested in one or more of the operating companies either by lease, by contract, or by the ownership of all or a majority of their stock. The defendant, the United Mine Workers of America, is alleged to be an unincorporated association of mine workers, governed by a constitution, with a membership exceeding 400,000, subdivided into thirty districts and numerous local unions. These subordinate districts and unions are subject to the constitution and by-laws not only of the International Union, but also to constitutions of their own.

The complaint avers that the United Mine Workers divide all coal mines into two classes, union or organized mines operating under a contract with the union to employ only union miners, and open shop or non-union mines, which refuse to make such a contract; that owing to the unreasonable restrictions and regulations imposed by the union on organized mines, the cost of production of union coal is unnecessarily enhanced so as to prevent its successful competition in the markets of the country with non-union coal; that the object of the conspiracy of the United Mine Workers and the union operators acting with them is the protection of the union-mined coal by the prevention and restraint of all interstate trade and competition in the products of non-union mines. The complaint enumerates twenty-three States in which coal mining is conducted, and alleges that the coal mined in each comes into competition in interstate commerce, directly or indirectly, with that mined in Illinois, Kentucky, Alabama, New Mexico, Colorado, Kansas, Oklahoma and Arkansas, in the markets of Louisiana, Texas, Oklahoma, Nebraska, Kansas, Missouri, Iowa and Minnesota, where, but for the defendants' unlawful interference, plaintiffs would have been engaged in trade in 1914; that the bituminous mines of the greater part of the above territory are union mines, the principal exceptions being Alabama, West Virginia, parts of Pennsylvania and Colorado, which the defendant has thus far been unable to organize.

The complaint further avers that, early in 1914, the plaintiff companies decided that the operating companies should go on a non-union or open shop basis. Two of them, the 'Prairie Creek Coal Mining Company and the Mammoth Vein Coal Company, closed down and discontinued as union mines, preparatory to reopening as open shop mines in April. They were to be operated under a new contract by the Mammoth Vein Coal Mining Company. Another of the companies, the Hartford Coal Company, which had not been in operation, planned to start as an open shop mine as soon as convenient in the summer of 1914. The fifth, the Coronado Coal Company, continued operating with the union until April 18, 1914, when its employees struck because of its unity of interest with the other mines of the plaintiffs. The plaintiffs say that in April, 1914, the defendants and those acting in conjunction with them, in furtherance of the general conspiracy, already described, to drive non-union coal out of interstate commerce, and thus to protect union operators from non-union competition, drove and frightened away the plaintiffs' employees including those directly engaged in shipping coal to other States, prevented the plaintiffs from employing other men, destroyed the structures and facilities for mining, loading and shipping coal, and the cars of interstate carriers waiting to be loaded, as well as those already loaded with coal in and for interstate shipment, and prevented plaintiffs from engaging in or continuing to engage in interstate commerce. The complaint alleges that the destruction to the property and business amounted to the sum of $740,000, and asks judgment for three times that amount or $2,220,000. Certain of the funds of the United Mine Workers in Arkansas were attached. The defendants, the United Mine Workers of America, District No. 21, and each local union and each individual defendant filed a separate answer. The answers deny all the averments of the complaint. The trial began on October 24, 1917, and a verdict and judgment were entered on November 22, following. The evidence is very voluminous, covering more than 3,000 printed pages. * * *

MR. CHIEF JUSTICE TAFT, after stating the case, delivered the opinion of the court.

There are five principal questions pressed by the plaintiffs in error here, the defendants below. The first is that there was a misjoinder of parties plaintiff. The second is that the United Mine Workers of America, District No. 21, United Mine Workers of America, and the local unions made defendants, are unincorporated associations and not subject to suit and therefore should have been dismissed from the case on motions seasonably made. The third is that there is no evidence to show any agency by the United Mine Workers of America, in the conspiracy charged or in the actual destruction of the property, and no liability therefor. The fourth is that there is no evidence to show that the conspiracy alleged against District No. 21 and the other defendants, was a conspiracy to restrain or monopolize interstate commerce. The fifth is that the court erred in a supplemental charge to the jury, which so stated the court's view of the evidence as to amount to a mandatory direction coercing the jury into finding the verdict which was recorded.

First. It does not seem to us that there was a misjoinder of parties under the procedure as authorized in Arkansas. * * *

Second. Were the unincorporated associations, the International Union, District No. 21, and the local unions suable in their names? The United Mine Workers of America is a national organization. Indeed, because it embraces Canada it is called the International Union. Under its constitution, it is intended to be the union of all workmen employed in and around coal mines, coal washers and coke ovens on the American continent. Its declared purpose is to increase wages and improve conditions of employment of its members by legislation, conciliation, joint agreements and strikes. It demands not more than eight hours a day of labor. The union is composed of workmen eligible to membership and is divided into districts, sub-districts and local unions. The ultimate authority is a general convention to which delegates selected by the members in their local organizations are elected. The body governing the union in the interval between conventions is the International Board consisting of the principal officers, the president, vice-president and secretary-treasurer, together with a member from each district. The president has much power. * * * The machinery of the organization is directed largely toward propaganda, conciliation of labor disputes, the making of scale agreements with operators, the discipline of officers, members, districts and locals, and toward strikes and the maintenance of funds for that purpose. It is admirably framed for unit action under the direction of the National officers. * * * The initiation fees and dues collected from each member are divided between the national treasury, the district treasury and that of the local. Should a local dissolve, the money is to be transmitted to the National treasury.

The rules as to strikes are important here. Section 27 of Article IX of the constitution is as follows:

"The Board shall have power between conventions, by a two-thirds vote, to recommend the calling of a general strike, but under no circumstances shall it call such a strike until approved by a referendum vote of the members."

Under Article XVI, no district is permitted to engage in a strike involving all or a major portion of its members without sanction of the International Convention or Board.

Section 2 of that article provides that districts may order local strikes within their respective districts "on their own responsibility, but where local strikes are to be financed by the International Union, they must be sanctioned by the International Executive Board."

Section 3 provides that in unorganized fields the Convention or Board must sanction strikes and no financial aid is to be given until after the strike has lasted four weeks, unless otherwise decided by the Board. The Board is to prescribe conditions in which strikes are to be financed by the International Union and the amount of strike relief to be furnished the striking members. In such cases, the president appoints a financial agent to assume responsibility for money to be expended from the International funds, and he only can make binding contracts. There is a uniform system of accounting as to the disbursements for strikes.

The membership of the union has reached 450,000. The dues received from them for the national and district organizations make a very large annual total, and the obligations assumed in travelling expenses, holding of conventions, and general overhead cost, but most of all in strikes, are so heavy that an extensive financial business is carried on, money is borrowed, notes are given to banks, and in every way the union acts as a business entity, distinct from its members. No organized corporation has greater unity of action, and in none is more power centered in the governing executive bodies.

Undoubtedly at common law, an unincorporated association of persons was not recognized as having any other character than a partnership in whatever was done, and it could only sue or be sued in the names of its members, and their liability had to be enforced against each member. *Pickett v. Walsh*, 192 Mass. 572; *Karges Furniture Co. v. Amalgamated Woodworkers Local Union*, 165 Ind. 421; *Baskins v. United Mine Workers of America*, 234 S.W. 464. But the growth and necessities of these great labor organizations have brought affirmative legal recognition of their existence and usefulness and provisions for their protection, which their members have found necessary. Their right to maintain strikes, when they do not violate law or the rights of others, has been declared. The embezzlement of funds by their officers has been especially denounced as a crime. The so-called union label, which is a quasi trademark to indicate the origin of manufactured product in union labor, has been protected against pirating and deceptive use by the statutes of most of the States, and in many States authority to sue to enjoin its use has been conferred on unions. They have been given distinct and separate representation and the right to appear to represent union in-

terests in statutory arbitrations, and before official labor boards. We
insert in the margin an extended reference,[1] furnished by the industry of
counsel, to legislation of this kind. More than this, equitable procedure
adapting itself to modern needs has grown to recognize the need of
representation by one person of many, too numerous to sue or to be
sued (Story Equity Pleadings, 8th ed., §§ 94, 97; *St. Germain v. Bakery,
&c., Union,* 97 Wash. 282; *Branson v. Industrial Workers of the World,*
30 Nev. 270; *Barnes & Co. v. Chicago Typographical Union,* 232 Ill. 402);
and this has had its influence upon the law side of litigation, so that, out
of the very necessities of the existing conditions and the utter impossibility of doing justice otherwise, the suable character of such an organization as this has come to be recognized in some jurisdictions, and
many suits for and against labor unions are reported in which no question has been raised as to the right to treat them in their closely united
action and functions as artificial persons capable of suing and being
sued. It would be unfortunate if an organization with as great power as
this International Union has in the raising of large funds and in directing the conduct of four hundred thousand members in carrying on, in a
wide territory, industrial controversies and strikes, out of which so much
unlawful injury to private rights is possible, could assemble its assets
to be used therein free from liability for injuries by torts committed in
course of such strikes. To remand persons injured to a suit against each
of the 400,000 members to recover damages and to levy on his share
of the strike fund, would be to leave them remediless.

---

[1] 1. Legalization of labor unions and labor combinations:
The Clayton Act—approved October 15, 1914, § 6, 38 Stat. 730, 731. California
—Penal Code, 1906, p. 581. Colorado—Rev. Stats. 1908, § 3924. Maryland—Supp.
Anno. Code, 1914, Art. 27, § 40. Massachusetts—c. 778, Acts & Res. approved July
7, 1914. Minnesota—c. 493, approved April 21, 1917. Nevada—Rev. Laws, 1912, §
6801. New Jersey—Comp. Stats. 1910, § 128, p. 3051. New York—Consol. Laws
1909, c. 40, § 582. North Dakota—Rev. Code 1905, § 8770. Oklahoma—Rev. Laws
1910, § 3764. Pennsylvania—Dig. Statute Law 1920, § 21247. Texas—Rev. Civ.
Stats. 1911, Arts. 5244-5246. Utah—c. 68, approved March 8, 1917; Laws of 1917,
c. 68, § 1. West Virginia—Acts of 1907, c. 78, § 19.
2. Exemption from anti-trust laws by statute or judicial decision:
California—Acts of 1909, c. 362, § 13. Iowa—Rholf v. Kasemeier, 140 Iowa 182.
Louisiana—Acts of 1892, Act No. 90, § 8; Rev. Laws, 1897, p. 205. Michigan—
Comp. Laws, 1897, § 11382. Montana—Rev. Code 1907, § 8289; Acts of 1909, c. 97,
§ 2. New Hampshire—Laws of 1917, c. 177, § 7. Nebraska—State v. Employers of
Labor, 102 Neb. 768. Wisconsin—Stats. of 1913, § 1747h.
3. Right given to labor unions to sue to enjoin infringement of registered union
label or trademark:
Arkansas—Acts of 1905, Act 309, § 7. Colorado—Mills' Supp. 1904, § 2985;
Rev. Stats. 1908, § 6848. Florida—Gen. Stats. 1906, § 3172. Idaho—Rev. Code of
1908, § 1453. Illinois—Rev. Stats. 1908, c. 140, § 4. Iowa—Code of 1897, § 5050.
Kansas—Gen. Stats. 1915, § 11657. Kentucky—Stats. 1903, c. 130, § 4750. Louisiana
—Acts of 1898, Act No. 49, § 5. Maryland—Supp. Anno. Code, 1914, Art. 27, § 53.
Montana—Rev. Code 1907, § 8455. Nebraska—Comp. Stats. 1913, § 3570. Nevada—
Rev. Laws 1912, § 4636. New Hampshire—Laws of 1895, c. 42, § 4. New York—
Consol. Laws 1909, c. 31, § 16. Oregon—Bellinger & Cotton's Anno. Stats. 1902,
§ 1845. Pennsylvania—Laws of 1901, Act No. 84, § 4; Dig. Statute Law, 1920, §
21241. Rhode Island—Gen. Laws 1909, c. 196, § 5. South Dakota—Rev. Code 1903,
§ 3194. Tennessee—Acts of 1905, c. 21, § 6. Texas—Civil Code, 1911, Art. 705.
Vermont—Laws of 1908, Act No. 121, § 5. Virginia—Code of 1904, § 1906d, par.
(5). Washington—Codes & Stats. 1910, § 9496. West Virginia—Acts of 1901, c. 5,

In the case of *Taff Vale Ry. Co. v. Amalgamated Society of Railway Servants*, [1901] A.C. 426, an English statute provided for the regis-

§ 5; Code of 1913, § 3582. Wisconsin—Stats. of 1911, c. 84a, § 1747a-5. Wyoming—Comp. Stats., 1910, c. 218, § 3441.

4. Unauthorized use of registered union label or trademark made an offense: Alabama—Code of 1907, §§ 7322, 7323. Arizona—Penal Code, §§ 355-358. Arkansas—Acts of 1905, Act No. 309 (amended by c. 131, Acts of 1909). California—Political Code, 1906, §§ 3200-3201; Penal Code, 1906, §§ 349a-351 (amended by c. 181, Acts of 1911). Colorado—Mills' Supp. 1904, § 2985-l to 2985-s; Rev. Stats. 1908, § 6844. Connecticut—Gen. Stats. 1902, §§ 4907-4912 (amended by c. 151, Acts of 1907). Delaware—Acts of 1899, c. 266. Florida—Gen. Stats. 1906, §§ 3169-3172. Georgia—Code of 1910, §§ 1989-1992. Idaho—Rev. Codes of 1908, §§ 1449-1455. Illinois—Rev. Stats. 1908, c. 140, §§ 1-7. Indiana—Anno. Stats. 1901, §§ 8693-8703; 3 Burns Anno. Stats. 1908, §§ 10453-10463. Iowa—Code of 1897, §§ 5049-5051. Kansas—Gen. Stats. 1909, §§ 9675-9680; Gen. Stats. 1915, §§ 11654-11659. Kentucky—Stats. of 1903, §§ 4749-4755. Louisiana—Acts of 1898, Act No. 49. Maine—Rev. Stats. 1903, c. 40, §§ 30-36. Maryland—Pub. Gen. Laws 1903, Art. 27, §§ 43-48. Massachusetts—Rev. Laws 1902, c. 72, §§ 7-14. Michigan—Comp. Laws 1897, §§ 11681-11686 (amended by c. 279; Acts of 1913). Minnesota—Rev. Laws 1905, §§ 5072-5076. Missouri—Rev. Stats. 1909, §§ 11789-11796. Montana—Penal Code 1907, §§ 8452-8457. Nebraska—Comp. Stats. 1911, §§ 4169-4173. Nevada—Rev. Laws 1912, §§ 4635-4637. New Hampshire—Acts of 1895, c. 42. New Jersey—Comp. Stats. 1910, pp. 1802, 5643-5648. New York—Consol. Laws 1909, c. 31, §§ 15, 16. Ohio—Gen. Code 1910, §§ 6219-6227, 13102, 13103, 13153-13155; Acts of 1911, p. 420. Oklahoma—Rev. Laws 1910, §§ 8211-8217. Oregon—Anno. Codes and Stats. 1902, §§ 1841-1848. Pennsylvania—Dig. Statute Law, 1920, §§ 21236-21243. Rhode Island—Gen. Laws 1909, c. 196. South Dakota—Political Code 1903, §§ 3190-3195. Tennessee—Acts of 1905, c. 21. Texas—Rev. Civ. Stats. 1911, Arts. 705, 706; Rev. Crim. Code, Arts. 1395, 1396. Utah—Comp. Laws 1907, §§ 2720-2723, 4482, 4483. Vermont—Pub. Stats. 1906, §§ 4962-4967; Acts of 1908, No. 121. Virginia—Code of 1904, §§ 1906d. Washington—Codes and Stats. 1910, §§ 9492-9500. West Virginia—Acts of 1901, c. 5; Hogg's Code, §§ 3578-3585; Code of 1913, § 487. Wisconsin—Stats. 1911, § 1747a. Wyoming—Comp. Stats. 1910, §§ 3439-3444.

5. Unauthorized use of union card, badge, or insignia made an offense: California—Acts of 1909, c. 331. Connecticut—Acts of 1907, c. 113, § 2. Massachusetts—Acts of 1909, c. 514, § 32. Minnesota—Rev. Laws 1905, § 5053, par. 4. Montana—Rev. Code 1907, § 8866. New York—Consol. Laws, 1909, c. 40, § 1278. Ohio—Gen. Code 1910, § 13163. Oregon—Acts of 1911, c. 73, §§ 1, 3. Pennsylvania—Dig. Statute Law 1920, § 1050. Texas—Rev. Crim. Stats. 1911, Art. 425. Virginia—Acts of 1908, c. 54, § 1.

6. Right to participate in selection of membership of boards of arbitration in labor controversies: Alabama—Acts of 1911, p. 320, § 6. Alaska—Acts of 1913, c. 70, § 2. Iowa—Acts of 1913, c. 292, §§ 1, 2. Indiana—Anno. Stats. 1901, § 7050 e, f. Idaho—Rev. Code 1909, §§ 1430, 1431. Louisiana—Rev. Stats. 1897, Act No. 139, Acts of 1894, § 1. Minnesota—Rev. Laws 1905, § 1828. Nevada—Rev. Laws 1912, § 1930. Nebraska—Rev. Stats. 1913, § 3638. Texas—Rev. Civ. Stats. 1911, Art. 71.

7. Right to have member of union on board of arbitrators: Connecticut—Gen. Stats. 1902, § 4708. Illinois—Hurd's Rev. Stats. 1906. c. 10, § 19. Indiana—Anno. Stats. 1901, § 1750b. Idaho—Rev. Code 1909, § 1427. Massachusetts—Acts of 1909, c. 514, § 10. Maine—Acts of 1909, c. 229, § 2. Missouri—Rev. Stats. 1909, § 7802. Montana—Rev. Code 1907, §§ 1670, 1671. Nebraska—Rev. Stats. 1913, § 3633. New Hampshire—Acts of 1911, c. 198, § 3, as amended by c. 186, Acts of 1913. South Carolina—Acts of 1916, Act No. 545, § 8. Utah—Comp. Laws 1907, § 1324. Vermont—Acts of 1912, Act No. 190, § 1.

8. Embezzlement of funds of labor union made a special offense: Nebraska—Rev. Stats. 1913, § 8659. New Hampshire—Pub. Stats. 1891, c. 273, § 17, as amended by Acts of 1905, c. 1. Pennsylvania Dig. Statute Law 1920, § 21252.

9. Bribery of union representative made an offense: Nevada—Rev. Laws 1912, § 6794. New Jersey—Acts of 1911, c. 94, § 1. New York—Consol. Laws 1909, c. 40, § 380.

10. All public printing to bear union label: Maryland—Pub. Gen. Laws 1911, Art. 58, § 9. Montana—Rev. Code 1907, § 254. Nevada—Rev. Laws 1912, § 4309.

tration of trades unions, authorized them to hold property through trustees, to have agents, and provided for a winding up and a rendering of accounts. A union was sued for damages growing out of a strike. Mr. Justice Farwell, meeting the objection that the union was not a corporation and could not be sued as an artificial person, said:

"If the contention of the defendant society were well founded, the Legislature has authorized the creation of numerous bodies of men capable of owning great wealth and of acting by agents with absolutely no responsibility for the wrongs that they may do to other persons by the use of that wealth and the employment of those agents."

He therefore gave judgment against the union. This was affirmed by the House of Lords. The legislation in question in that case did not create trade unions but simply recognized their existence and regulated them in 'certain ways, but neither conferred on them general power to sue, nor imposed liability to be sued. See also *Hillenbrand v. Building Trades Council,* 14 Ohio Dec. (N.P.) 628. Holland Jurisprudence, 12th ed., 341; Pollock's First Book on Jurisprudence, (2nd ed.) 125.

Though such a conclusion as to the suability of trades unions is of primary importance in the working out of justice and in protecting individuals and society from possibility of oppression and injury in their lawful rights from the existence of such powerful entities as trade unions, it is after all in essence and principle merely a procedural matter. As a matter of substantive law, all the members of the union engaged in a combination doing unlawful injury are liable to suit and recovery, and the only question is whether when they have voluntarily, and for the purpose of acquiring concentrated strength and the faculty of quick unit action and elasticity, created a self-acting body with great funds to accomplish their purpose, they may not be sued as this body, and the funds they have accumulated may not be made to satisfy claims for injuries unlawfully caused in carrying out their united purpose. Trade unions have been recognized as lawful by the Clayton Act; they have been tendered formal incorporation as National Unions by the Act of Congress, approved June 29, 1886, c. 567, 24 Stat. 86. In the Act of Congress, approved August 23, 1912, c. 351, 37 Stat. 415, a commission on industrial relations was created providing that three of the commissioners should represent organized labor. The Transportation Act of 1920, c. 91 §§ 302-307, 41 Stat. 469, recognizes labor unions in creation of railroad boards of adjustment, and provides for action by the Railroad Labor Board upon their application. The Act of Congress, approved August 5, 1909, c. 6, § 38, 36 Stat. 112, and the Act approved October 3, 1913, c. 16, subd. G(a), 38 Stat. 172, expressly exempt labor unions from excise taxes. Periodical publications issued by or under the auspices of trade unions are admitted into the mails as second-class mail matter. Act of 1912, c. 389, 37 Stat. 550. The legality of labor unions of postal employees is expressly recognized by Act of Congress, approved August 24, 1912, c. 389, § 6, 37 Stat. 539, 555. By Act of Congress, passed August 1, 1914. no money was to be used from funds therein appropriated to prosecute unions under the Anti-Trust Act (c. 223, 38 Stat. 609, 652).

In this state of federal legislation, we think that such organizations are suable in the federal courts for their acts, and that funds accumulated to be expended in conducting strikes are subject to execution in suits for torts committed by such unions in strikes. The fact that the Supreme Court of Arkansas has since taken a different view in *Baskins v. United Mine Workers of America, supra,* can not under the Conformity Act operate as a limitation on the federal procedure in this regard.

Our conclusion as to the suability of the defendants is confirmed in the case at bar by the words of §§ 7 and 8 of the Anti-Trust Law. The persons who may be sued under § 7 include "corporations and associations existing under or authorized by the laws of either the United States, the laws of any of the Territories, the laws of any State, or the laws of any foreign country" [§ 8]. This language is very broad, and the words given their natural signification certainly include labor unions like these. They are, as has been abundantly shown, associations existing under the laws of the United States, of the Territories thereof, and of the States of the Union. Congress was passing drastic legislation to remedy a threatening danger to the public welfare, and did not intend that any persons or combinations of persons should escape its application. Their thought was especially directed against business associations and combinations that were unincorporated to do the thing forbidden by the act, but they used language broad enough to include all associations which might violate its provisions recognized by the statutes of the United States or the States or the Territories, or foreign countries as lawfully existing; and this, of course, includes labor unions, as the legislation referred to shows. Thus it was that in the cases of *United States v. Trans-Missouri Freight Association,* 166 U.S. 290, *United States v. Joint Traffic Association,* 171 U.S. 505, *Montague & Co. v. Lowry,* 193 U.S. 38, and *Eastern States Retail Lumber Dealers' Association v. United States,* 234 U.S. 600, unincorporated associations were made parties to suits in the federal courts under the Anti-Trust Act without question by anyone as to the correctness of the procedure.

For these reasons, we conclude that the International Union, the District No. 21 and the twenty-seven Local Unions were properly made parties defendant here and properly served by process on their principal officers.

Third. The next question is whether the International Union was shown by any substantial evidence to have initiated, participated in or ratified the interference with plaintiffs' business which began April 6, 1914, and continued at intervals until July 17, when the matter culminated in a battle and the destruction of the Bache-Denman properties. The strike was a local strike declared by the president and officers of the District Organization No. 21, embracing Arkansas, Oklahoma and Texas. By Art. XVI of the International constitution, as we have seen, it could not thus engage in a strike if it involved all or a major part of its district members without sanction of the International Board. There is nothing to show that the International Board ever authorized it, took any part in preparation for it or in its maintenance. Nor did they or their organization ratify it by paying any of the expenses. It came exactly within the definition of a local strike in the constitutions of both the National and the District organizations. The District made the preparations and paid the bills. It does appear that the president of the National body was in Kansas City and heard of the trouble which had taken place on April 6 at Prairie Creek and that at a meeting of the International Board he reported it as something he had learned on his trip for their official information. He said that a man named Bache had demanded in a suit an accounting of the funds of the Southwestern Coal Operators' Association, that when he secured the information, he "went down to Arkansas and started to run his mine non-union. The boys simply marched in on him in a day down there and kicked his Colorado guards out of there and broke their jaws and put the flag of the United Mine Workers on top of the tipple and pulled the fires out of the boilers, and that was all there was to it, and the mines have been idle ever since. I do not say our boys did this, but I mean the people from all through that country marched in and stopped the work, and when the guards offered resistance, several of them were roughly handled but no lives were lost as I understand it." Later in May he made a long speech at a special convention of District No. 21 held at Fort Smith for a purpose not connected with this matter in which he referred especially to the Colorado and West Virginia strikes in which the International Union was engaged with all its might, but he made no specific allusion to the Prairie Creek difficulty. It does appear that in 1916, after Stewart, the president of District No. 21, had been convicted of conspiracy to defeat the injunction issued to protect the Prairie Creek mines in this conflict, and had gone to the penitentiary and was pardoned, White, the national president, wrote a letter thanking the President for this, and that subsequently he appointed Stewart to a position on a District committee. It would be going very far to consider such acts of the president alone a ratification by the International Board creating liability for a past tort. The president had no authority to order or ratify a local strike. Only the Board could do this. White's report in an executive meeting of the Board of the riot of April 6 shows sympathy with its purpose and a lack of respect for law but does not imply or prove on his part any prior initiation or indicate a desire to ratify the transaction as his work. The Board took no action on his report. He did not request it.

Communications from outsiders and editorials published in the United Mine Workers journal giving accounts of the occurrences at Prairie Creek and representing that the troubles were due to the aggression of the armed guards of the mine owners and that the action of the union men was justified because in defense of their homes against night attacks, do not constitute such ratification by the Board or the president after the fact as to make the International Union liable for what had been done.

The argument of counsel for the plaintiffs is that because the National body had authority to discipline District organizations, to make local strikes its own and to pay their cost, if it deemed it wise, the duty was thrust on it when it knew a local strike was on, to superintend it and prevent its becoming lawless at its peril. We do not conceive that such responsibility is imposed on the National body. A corporation is responsible for the wrongs committed by its agents in the course of its business, and this principle is enforced against the contention that torts are *ultra vires* of the corporation. But it must be shown that it is in the business of the corporation. Surely no stricter rule can be enforced against an unincorporated organization like this. Here it is not a question of contract or of holding out an appearance of authority on which some third person acts. It is a mere question of actual agency which the constitutions of the two bodies settle conclusively. If the International body had interfered or if it had assumed liability by ratification, different questions would have arisen.

Counsel cite § 2 of Art. XII of the constitution of District No. 21 to show that questions of all strikes must be referred by District officers to the National president for his decision, and suggest that in the absence of a showing it is to be inferred that they did so here and the strike was approved by him. They misconstrue the section. It applies only to a proposed strike which would affect two Districts and to which one District is opposed. It does not apply to local strikes like this.

But it is said that the District was doing the work of the International and carrying out its policies and this circumstance makes the former an agent. We can not agree to this in the face of the specific stipulation between them that in such a case unless the International expressly assumed responsibility, the District must meet it alone. The subsequent events showing that the District did meet the responsibility with its own funds confirm our reliance upon the constitution of the two bodies.

We conclude that the motions of the International Union, the United Mine Workers of America, and of its president and its other officers, that the jury be directed to return a verdict for them, should have been granted.

Fourth. The next question is twofold: (a) Whether the District No. 21 and the individual defendants participated in a plot unlawfully to deprive the plaintiffs of their employees by intimidation and violence and in the course of it destroyed their properties, and, (b), whether they did these things in pursuance of a conspiracy to restrain and monopolize interstate commerce.

The case made for the plaintiff was as follows:

(a) In March of 1914, when the Prairie Creek No. 4, Mammoth Vein Coal Mine, and the Coronado mines were operating with union labor and under a District No. 21 contract and scale of wages and terms which did not expire until July 1 following, Bache, the manager of all the properties, determined to run his mines thereafter on a non-union or open basis. He had his superintendent prepare a letter setting forth his reasons for the change and forwarded it to his principals in the East to justify the change of policy which he insisted would result in a substantial reduction in the cost of production. To avoid the charge of a breach of the union scale, he had a contract made between the Mammoth Vein Coal Mining Company, which he controlled, and the Prairie Creek Coal Company and the Mammoth Vein Coal Company, by which the Mammoth Vein Coal Mining Company, a corporation with $100 capital, agreed to run the mines. As it had signed no scale, he considered it free from obligation to the union. He then shut down the mines and prepared to open them on a non-union basis on April 6. He anticipated trouble. He employed three guards from the Burns Detective Agency, and a number of others to aid them. He bought a number of Winchester rifles and ammunition. He surrounded his principal mining plant at Prairie Creek No. 4 with a cable strung on posts. He had notices prepared for his former employees, who occupied the Company's houses, to vacate. He had notices warning trespassers from the premises posted at the entrance to the tract that was enclosed within the cable. He sent out for non-union men and had gathered some thirty or more at the mine by the day fixed for the opening.

The mines of the plaintiffs lie in the County of Sebastian on the west border of Arkansas, next to Oklahoma, in a hilly country. The whole country is full of coal mines. The annual coal-producing capacity of Arkansas is about 2,000,000 tons. The product is a smokeless coal like the Pocahontas of West Virginia. All the Arkansas mines but one small one were union. The towns in the neighborhood, Hartford, Huntington, Midland, Frogtown, and others were peopled by union miners and the business done in them was dependent on union miners' patronage. Hartford, a town of twenty-five hundred, was about three miles from Prairie Creek, Midland, less in size, lay about the same distance away in another direction, and Huntington was a mile or two further in still another direction. Frogtown was a small village about a mile and a half from Prairie Creek. Stewart, the president of the District No. 21, and the other officers promptly declared a local strike against the Prairie Creek and Mammoth Vein mine and the union miners who had not been discharged from the Coronado mine of the plaintiffs left. Through the agency of the officers of District No. 21 and the local unions, a public meeting was called at the school house, about a quarter of a mile from the Prairie Creek mine. The influence of the union men was exerted upon the shopkeepers of the towns above named to close their stores and attend the meeting. It was given a picnic character and women and children attended. The meeting, after listening to speeches, appointed a committee to visit the superintendent in charge of the mine. On this committee was one Sankard, a constable of the town of Hartford, and a union man, together with two other union miners. They asked the superintendent that the non-union men be sent away and the mine resume operations with union men. The committee was attended by a very large body of union miners. They were met at the entrance to the enclosure by two guards with guns carried behind them. The committee was admitted to see the superintendent and the crowd dealt with the guards. The guards had been directed not to use their guns save to defend their own lives or another's. The union miners assaulted the guards, took the guns away, and so injured a number of the employees, that four or five had to be sent to a hospital. The crowd swarmed over the premises, forced the pulling of the fires and hurled stones at the fleeing guards. The result was that all the employees deserted the mine, and it was completely filled with water which came in when the pumps stopped. One of the crowd went up to the top of the coal tipple and planted a flag on which was the legend, "This is a union man's country."

Mr. Bache, after the riot and lawless violence of April 6, secured from the Federal District Court an injunction against those union miners and others whom his agents could identify as having been present and having taken part. This included the president and secretary-treasurer of the District No. 21 and others. Bache then made preparations to resume mining. The mine was full of water and it required a considerable time to pump it out and get things into proper condition. Because of further threats, the court was applied to to send United States Deputy Marshals to guard the property, and they were sent. Meantime the work of reparation progressed, and Bache's agents were engaged in securing the coming of miners and other employees from in and out of the State to enlarge his force. The attitude of the union miners continued hostile, and constant effort was made by them to intercept the groups of men and women who were brought in by Bache from Tennessee and elsewhere, and to turn them away either by peaceable inducement or by threats and physical intimidation. The vicinage was so permeated with union feeling that the public officers did not hesitate to manifest their enmity toward the non-union men, and made arrests of the guards and others who were in Bache's employ upon frivolous charges. Rumors were spread abroad through the county that the guards employed by Bache were insulting and making indecent proposals to very young girls in and about Prairie Creek, and P. R. Stewart, the president of District No. 21, in the presence of some ten persons on the public street of Midland, in the latter part of May, denounced the guards for these insults and proposals, and said that he would furnish the guns if the people would take them. The evidence also disclosed that through the secretary-treasurer of District No. 21, some forty or more rifles were bought from the Remington Arms Company and secretly sent to Hartford for the purpose intended by Stewart. They were paid for by a check signed by Holt, the secretary-treasurer of District No. 21, and countersigned by Stewart, the president. Conversations with Stewart, which Stewart did not take the stand to deny, were sworn to, in which he announced that he would not permit the Prairie Creek mine to run "non-union" and intended to stop it. McLachlin, who was a member of the Executive Board of District No. 21, in the first week of July gathered up some of the guns, exactly how many does not appear, and shipped them sixty miles to McAlester, Oklahoma, the headquarters of District No. 21. It appeared that guns of like make and caliber were used by the assailants in the attack on the Prairie Creek mine on July 17. The United States marshals had been withdrawn from the premises of Prairie Creek Mine No. 4, before July 1, though the guards were retained.

The evidence leaves no doubt that during the month of June there was a plan and movement among the union miners to make an attack upon Prairie Creek Mine No. 4. By this time the number of men secured by Bache had increased to seventy or eighty, and preparations were rapidly going on for a resumption of mining. The tense feeling in respect to the coming attack increased. On Sunday night, July 12, about midnight, there was a fusillade of shots into the village of Frogtown, a small collection of houses, already mentioned, about a mile and a half from Prairie Creek mine. A number of people in fright at the cry that "the scabs were surrounding the town" left and went to Hartford, about two miles away, and thereafter guards were put out at Hartford to defend that town against attack by the guards at Prairie Creek. The ridiculous improbability that the guards at Prairie Creek who were engaged in protecting themselves and the property and in constant fear of attack should make this unprovoked assault upon the town of Frogtown, is manifest from the slightest reading of the evidence, and there crept in through a statement of one of the defendants, an active union man, to a witness who testified to it, that this shooting had been done by the Hartford constable Slankard, and himself, in order to arouse the hostility of the neighborhood against the men at Prairie Creek. On the night of the 16th, the union miners' families who lived in Prairie Creek were warned by friends to leave that vicinity in order to avoid danger, and at 4 o'clock the next morning the attack was begun by a volley of many shots fired into the premises. A large force with guns attacked the mining premises from all sides later on in the day.

The first movement toward destruction of property was at Mine No. 3, a short distance from No. 4, where the coal washhouse was set on fire. The occupants of the premises were driven out except a few who stayed and entrenched themselves behind coal cars or other protection. Most of the employees and their families fled to the ridges behind which they were able to escape danger from the flying bullets. The forces surrounding the mine were so numerous that by one o'clock they had driven out practically all of the defenders and set fire to the coal tipple of Mine No. 4, and destroyed all the plant by the use of dynamite and the match.

The assailants took some of Bache's employees prisoners as they were escaping, and conducted them to a log cabin behind the school house near the mine to which reference has already been made, and where the first riot meeting was held. The four or five prisoners were taken out of the cabin where they had been for a short time confined, and two of them, one a former union man, were deliberately murdered in the presence of their captors, by a man whose identity it was impossible to establish. The evidence in this case clearly shows that Slankard, the constable of Hartford, was present at the killing, and that the men who were killed were in his custody on the way, as he said, to the grand jury. He was subsequently tried before a Sebastian County jury for murder, and was acquitted on an alibi. Slankard, though a defendant and in court, did not take the stand in this case. The overwhelming weight of the evidence establishes that this was purely a union attack, under the guidance of District officers.

The testimony offered by defendants to show that it was only an uprising of the indignant citizens of the countryside really tended to confirm the guilt of the District No. 21. Its palpably artificial character showed that basis for it had been framed in advance for the purpose of relieving the officers of District No. 21 and the union miners of that neighborhood from responsibility for the contemplated execution of their destructive and criminal purpose. It is a doubtful question whether this responsibility was not so clearly established that, had that been the only element needed to justify a verdict, the court properly might have directed it. The president of District No. 21 and the union miners, including Slankard, whose agency in and leadership of this attack were fully proven, were present in the courtroom at the trial, but did not take the stand to deny the facts established. Indeed they had been previously brought to trial for conspiracy to defeat the federal administration of justice and for contempt because of these very acts, had pleaded guilty to the charges made, and had been sentenced to imprisonment, and their expenses as defendants in and out of jail had been paid by the District out of the District treasury and the disbursements approved by the District in convention.

It is contended on behalf of District No. 21 and the local unions that only those members of these bodies whom the evidence shows to have participated in the torts can be held civilly liable for the damages. There was evidence to connect all these individual defendants with the acts which were done, and, in view of our finding that District No. 21 and the unions are suable, we can not yield to the argument that it would be necessary to show the guilt of every member of District No. 21 and of each union in order to hold the union and its strike funds to answer. District No. 21 and the local unions were engaged in a work in which the strike was one of the chief instrumentalities for accomplishing the purpose for which their unions were organized. By § 1 of Art. XII of the constitution of District No. 21, it is provided that:

"When trouble of a local character arises between the members of local unions and their employer, the mine committee and officers shall endeavor to effect an amicable adjustment, and failing they shall immediately notify the officers of the district and said district officers shall immediately investigate the cause of the complaint, and failing to effect a peaceful settlement upon a basis that would be equitable and just to the aggrieved members, finding that a strike would best subserve the interests of the locality affected, they may with the consent and approval of the district officers, order a strike."

Thus the authority is put by all the members of the District No. 21 in their officers to order a strike, and if in the conduct of that strike unlawful injuries are inflicted, the District organization is responsible and the fund accumulated for strike purposes may be subjected to the payment of any judgment which is recovered.

(b) It was necessary, however, in order to hold District No. 21 liable in this suit under the Anti-Trust Act, to establish that this conspiracy to attack the Bache-Denman mines and stop the non-union employment there, was with intent to restrain interstate commerce and to monopolize the same, and to subject it to the control of the union. The evidence upon which the plaintiffs relied to establish this and upon which the judgment of the trial court and of the Court of Appeals went, consisted of a history of the relations between the International Union and the union coal operators of certain so-called competitive districts from 1898 until 1914. The miners of Ohio, Indiana and Illinois, large bituminous coal producing States, were members of the union and the coal operators of those States, in spite of strikes and lockouts from time to time, were properly classed as union operators. They met yearly in conference with the union's representatives to agree upon terms of employment from April 1st to April 1st. In these conferences the operators frequently complained that the competition of many non-union mines in Western Pennsylvania and the whole of West Virginia was ruinous to their business because of the low cost of production of coal in such mines due to the lower wages and less expensive conditions of working than in union mines, and urged that something must be done to stop this, or that the union scale of wages be reduced. By section 8 of the contract between the operators of the Central Competitive Coal Field and the United Mine Workers of America, dated Chicago, January 28, 1898, it was stipulated "That the United Mine Workers' organization, a party to this contract, do hereby further agree to afford all possible protection to the trade and to other parties hereto against any unfair competition resulting from a failure to maintain scale rates."

From this time on in every annual conference until after the controversy in the case before us in 1914, the subject recurred. It does not appear when, if at any time, wages were reduced because of this plea by the operators. Sometimes the contention of the operators as to the effect of non-union competition was conceded and greater activity in unionizing non-union territory was promised. Again pleas were made by the miners' representatives of the great amount of money expended by the union and, in one or two instances, of the sacrifice of human lives to effect this result. Again the union leaders flatly refused to be further affected by the argument and charged that the non-union competition of West Virginia, which was always the principal factor, was only possible because some of the most important union operators in Ohio and the central competitive field really were interested as non-union operators in West Virginia. There was considerable discussion as to the non-union competition of Kentucky fields as a basis for the operators' complaints. At times, there were suggestions from the miners' side that the operators ought to contribute funds to enable the campaign of unionizing to go on, but they never seem to have met with favor. * * *

In a joint conference between the union leaders and the coal operators, in 1904, Mr. Mitchell, the president of the union, spoke as follows:

"I believe the discussion of this matter should be carried on with perfect frankness and candor on both sides. I don't think we should disguise our position at all; and I want to state for our side of the house just where we are, as I understand it. We don't believe that a reduction in the mining rate will help you. We know that it will do us incalculable injury. We don't believe that a reduction in the mining rate will secure for you a larger amount of trade than you now have. We don't believe that the industry will be benefited by reducing wages. We know that in the past every reduction in wages has been given to the large consumers of coal— not to the domestic trade, not to those who can ill afford to pay high rates for coal, but to the railroad companies and the great manufacturers. We know that when the mining rate is lowest your profits have been least.

"Now, gentlemen, it has required many many years of work and effort and sacrifice to make wages at the mines compare favorably with wages in other industries. We are not going back to the old conditions; we are not going to consent to a reduction in wages. We believe the best thing to do is to renew our present wage scale; to make such modifications of internal questions as seem right, and then return and work out the coming scale year as we have the past scale year. I think we may as well understand now as at any other time that we are not going to consent to a reduced mining rate."

At the convention in 1906, a resolution that Districts 13, 14, 21, 24 and 25, be admitted to the interstate joint conferences, was adopted. This was urged by President Mitchell of the Union, and the Secretary, W. B. Wilson. The latter said:

"If I understand the principle upon which this movement is based, it is to bring into the joint conference those operators and those miners [of the Southwestern District] whose competitive business is closely related to each other; and in asking that the operators and miners of the Southwestern District be admitted to this conference, we are simply carrying out that principle. The coal mined in Western Pennsylvania comes in immediate and direct competition with Ohio; that mined in Ohio, as well as that in Pennsylvania, comes in competition with Indiana and Illinois; that mined in Illinois comes in competition with Iowa; that mined in Iowa comes in competition with Missouri, and coal mined in Missouri comes in competition with Kansas, Arkansas and the Indian Territory. They are all related to one another; they are all competitors with one another, and it is but just and fair that each of these fields should have a representation in the joint conference that sets a base for the prices of the ensuing year. This is the first conference that is held. Whatever wages are agreed upon here, whether it is an increase in wages, a decrease in wages, improved conditions or otherwise, it sets the pace for other districts, and those other districts have no voice in saying what that price shall be. In order to avoid that condition of affairs, in order to give justice to the operators and miners in other fields not represented here at the present time, we ask you, as a matter of fairness and justice, to permit those whose operators and miners are represented here, to participate in this joint conference."

In 1910, Bache, as a union operator, took part for his mines in fixing the scale of wages in District No. 21. Later on, at the time of a conference, he made a separate scale with the District No. 21 more favorable in some respects than that subsequently agreed on in the conference with the other operators, and he was for that reason expelled from the operators' association. He was permitted at a later time to rejoin it, but he had some litigation with it in respect to their funds, the nature of which is not disclosed by the record.

In 1913 and 1914, and in the years preceding, the International Union had carried on two strikes of great extent covering the Colorado fields, and the Ohio and West Virginia fields, in which very large sums of money had been expended and there was much lawlessness and violence. Its treasury had been drained and it borrowed $75,000 from District No. 21 during this period.

The foregoing will enable one to acquire a fair idea of the national situation, shown by the record, in respect to the mining and sale of coal so far as it bears upon this case and upon this state of fact. The plaintiffs charge that there has been and is a continuously operating conspiracy between union coal operators and the International Union to restrain interstate commerce in coal and to monopolize it, and that the work of District No. 21 at Prairie Creek was a step in that conspiracy for which it can be held liable under the Anti-Trust Act.

Coal mining is not interstate commerce, and the power of Congress does not extend to its regulation as such. In *Hammer* v. *Dagenhart,* 247 U.S. 251, 272, we said: "The making of goods and the mining of coal are not commerce, nor does the fact that these things are to be afterwards shipped or used in interstate commerce, make their production a part thereof. *Delaware, Lackawanna & Western R. R. Co. v. Yurkonis,* 238 U.S. 439." Obstruction to coal mining is not a direct obstruction to interstate commerce in coal, although it, of course, may affect it by reducing the amount of coal to be carried in that commerce. We have had occasion to consider the principles governing the validity of congressional restraint of such indirect obstructions to interstate commerce in *Swift & Co. v. United States,* 196 U.S. 375; *United States v. Patten,* 226 U.S. 525; *United States v. Ferger,* 250 U.S. 199; *Railroad Commission of Wisconsin v. Chicago, Burlington & Quincy R. R. Co.,* 257 U.S. 563; and *Stafford v. Wallace,* 258 U.S. 495. It is clear from these cases that if Congress deems certain recurring practices, though not really part of interstate commerce, likely to obstruct, restrain or burden it, it has the power to subject them to national supervision and restraint. Again, it has the power to punish conspiracies in which such practices are part of the plan, to hinder, restrain or monopolize interstate commerce. But in the latter case, the intent to injure, obstruct or restrain interstate commerce must appear as an obvious consequence of what is to be done, or be shown by direct evidence or other circumstances.

What really is shown by the evidence in the case at bar, drawn from discussions and resolutions of conventions and conference, is the stimulation of union leaders to press their unionization of non-union mines not only as a direct means of bettering the conditions and wages of their workers, but also as a means of lessening interstate competition for union operators which in turn would lessen the pressure of those operators for reduction of the union scale or their resistance to an increase. The latter is a secondary or ancillary motive whose actuating force in a given case necessarily is dependent on the particular circumstances to which it is sought to make it applicable. If unlawful means had here been used by the National body to unionize mines whose product was important, actually or potentially, in affecting prices in interstate commerce, the evidence in question would clearly tend to show that that body was guilty of an actionable conspiracy under the Anti-Trust Act. This principle is involved in the decision of the case of *Hitchman Coal & Coke Co. v. Mitchell,* 245 U.S. 229, and is restated in *American Steel Foundries v. Tri-City Central Trades Council,* 257 U.S. 184. But it is not a permissible interpretation of the evidence in question that it tends to show that the motive indicated thereby actuates every lawless strike of a local and sporadic character, not initiated by the National body but by one of its subordinate subdivisions. The very fact that local strikes are provided for in the union's constitution, and so may not engage the energies or funds of the National body, confirms this view. Such a local case of a lawless strike must stand on its own facts and while these conventions and discussions may reveal a general policy, the circumstances or direct evidence should supply the link between them and the local situation to make an unlawful local strike, not initiated or financed by the main organization, a step in an actionable conspiracy to restrain the freedom of interstate commerce which the Anti-Trust Act was intended to protect.

This case is very different from *Loewe v. Lawlor,* 208 U.S. 274. There the gist of the charge held to be a violation of the Anti-Trust Act was the effort of the defendants, members of a trades union, by a boycott against a manufacturer of hats to destroy his interstate sales in hats. The direct object of attack was interstate commerce.

So, too, it differs from *Eastern States Retail Lumber Dealers' Association v. United States,* 234 U. S. 600, where the interstate retail trade of wholesale lumber men with consumers was restrained by a combination of retail dealers by an agreement among the latter to blacklist or boycott any wholesaler engaged in such retail trade. It was the commerce itself which was the object of the conspiracy. In *United States v. Patten,* 226

U.S. 525, running a corner in cotton in New York City by which the defendants were conspiring to obtain control of the available supply and to enhance the price to all buyers in every market of the country was held to be a conspiracy to restrain interstate trade because cotton was the subject of interstate trade and such control would directly and materially impede and burden the due course of trade among the States and inflict upon the public the injuries which the Anti-Trust Act was designed to prevent. Although running the corner was not interstate commerce, the necessary effect of the control of the available supply would be to obstruct and restrain interstate commerce and so the conspirators were charged with the intent to restrain. The difference between the *Patten Case* and that of *Ware & Leland v. Mobile County,* 209 U.S. 495, illustrates a distinction to be drawn in cases which do not involve interstate commerce intrinsically but which may or may not be regarded as affecting interstate commerce so directly as to be within the federal regulatory power. In the *Ware & Leland Case,* the question was whether a State could tax the business of a broker dealing in contracts for the future delivery of cotton where there was no obligation to ship from one State to another. The tax was sustained and dealing in cotton futures was held not to be interstate commerce, and yet thereafter such dealings in cotton futures as were alleged in the *Patten Case* where they were part of a conspiracy to bring the entire cotton trade within its influence, were held to be in restraint of interstate commerce. And so in the case at bar, coal mining is not interstate commerce and obstruction of coal mining, though it may prevent coal from going into interstate commerce, is not a restraint of that commerce unless the obstruction to mining is intended to restrain commerce in it or has necessarily such a direct, material and substantial effect to restrain it that the intent reasonably must be inferred.

In the case at bar, there is nothing in the circumstances or the declarations of the parties to indicate that Stewart, the president of District No. 21, or Hull, its secretary-treasurer, or any of their accomplices had in mind interference with interstate commerce or competition when they entered upon their unlawful combination to break up Bache's plan to carry on his mines with non-union men. The circumstances were ample to supply a full local motive for the conspiracy. Stewart said: "We are not going to let them dig coal—the scabs." His attention and that of his men was fastened on the presence of non-union men in the mines in that local community. The circumstance that a car loaded with coal and billed to a town in Louisiana was burned by the conspirators has no significance upon this head. The car had been used in the battle by some of Bache's men for defense. It offered protection and its burning was only a part of the general destruction.

Bache's breach of his contract with the District No. 21 in employing non-union men three months before it expired, his attempt to evade his obligation by a manipulation of his numerous corporations, his advertised anticipation of trespass and violence by warning notices, by enclosing his mining premises with a cable and stationing guards with guns to defend them, all these in the heart of a territory that had been completely unionized for years, were calculated to arouse a bitterness of spirit entirely local among the union miners against a policy that brought in strangers and excluded themselves or their union colleagues from the houses they had occupied and the wages they had enjoyed. In the letter which Bache dictated in favor of operating the mines on a non-union basis, he said, "To do this means a bitter fight but in my opinion it can be accomplished by proper organization." Bache also testified that he was entering into a matter he knew was perilous and dangerous to his companies because in that section there was only one other mine running on a non-union basis. Nothing of this is recited to justify in the slightest the lawlessness and outrages committed, but only to point out that as it was a local strike within the meaning of the International and District constitutions, so it was in fact a local strike, local in its origin and motive, local in its waging, and local in its felonious and murderous ending.

But it is said that these District officers and their lieutenants among the miners must be charged with an intention to do what would be the natural result of their own acts, that they must have known that obstruction to mining coal in the Bache-Denman mines would keep 75 per cent. of their output from being shipped out of the State into interstate competition, and to that extent would help union operators in their competition for business. In a national production of from ten to fifteen million tons a week, or in a production in District No. 21 of 150,000 tons a week, 5,000 tons a week which the Bache-Denman mines in most prosperous times could not exceed, would have no appreciable effect upon the price of coal or non-union competition. The saving in the price per ton of coal under non-union conditions was said by plaintiffs' witnesses to be from seventeen to twenty cents, but surely no one would say that such saving on 5,000 tons would have a substantial effect on prices of coal in interstate commerce. Nor could it be inferred that Bache intended to cut the price of coal. His purpose was probably to pocket the profit that such a reduction made possible. If it be said that what District No. 21 feared was that, if Bache were successful, the defection among union operators would spread and ultimately the whole District field of District No. 21 in Arkansas, Oklahoma and Texas would become non-union, and interstate commerce would then be substantially affected, it may be answered that this is remote and no statement or circumstance appears in the record from which it can be inferred that the participants in the local strike had such a possibility in mind or thought they were thus protecting union operators in a control or monopoly of interstate commerce. The result of our consideration of the entire record is that there was no evidence submitted to the jury upon which they properly could find that the outrages, felonies and murders of District No. 21 and its companions in crime were committed by them in a conspiracy to restrain or monopolize interstate commerce. The motion to direct the jury to return a verdict for the defendants should have been granted.

Fifth. These conclusions make it unnecessary to examine the objection which the plaintiffs in error make to the supplemental charge of the court.

The case has been prepared by counsel for the plaintiffs with rare assiduity and ability. The circumstances are such as to awaken regret that, in our view of the federal jurisdiction, we can not affirm the judgment. But it is of far higher importance that we should preserve inviolate the fundamental limitations in respect to the federal jurisdiction.

The judgment is reversed, and the case remanded to the District Court for further proceedings in conformity to this opinion.[2]

---

[2] For comment on the case, see: Warren, Corporate Advantages without Incorporation, Bk. II, c. 9 (1929); Frankfurter, "The Coronado Case," 31 New Republic, 328 (1922); Lay, "The Coronado Coal Case and its Consequences," 8 Iowa Law Bull. 162 (1923); McDonough, "Liability of an Unincorporated Labor Union under the Sherman Law, 10 Va. Law Rev. 304 (1924); Magill and Magill, "The Suability of Labor Unions," 1 N.C. Law Rev. 81 (1922); Pester, "Liability of Labor Unions for Damages Resulting from Strikes and Violence," 1922 Kan. St. Bar Assn. Rep. 131; Roberts, "Labor Unions, Corporations—the Coronado Case," 5 Ill. Law Quar. 200 (1923); Sturgess; "Unincorporated Associations as Parties to Actions," 33 Yale Law Jour. 383 (1924); 10 Cal. Law Rev. 506 (1922); 22 Col. Law Rev. 684 (1922); 4 Law & Labor, 178 (1922); 1 Texas Law Rev. 114 (1922); 66 Univ. of Pa. Law Rev. 267 (1918); 71 Univ. of Pa. Law Rev. 48 (1922); 9 Va. Law Rev. 52 (1922); 2 Wis. Law Rev. 51 (1922); 32 Yale Law Jour. 59 (1922). See also: Brandeis, "The Incorporation of Trade Unions," 15 Green Bag, 11 (1903); Geldart, "Legal Personality," 27 Law Quar. Rev. 90 (1911); Laski, "Personality of Associations," 29 Harv. Law Rev. 404 (1916); Steffee, "The Taff Vale Case," 37 Am. Law Rev. 385 (1903); Ure, "Legal Position of Trade Unions," 16 Jurid. Rev. 20, 135 (1904); Walter, "The Incorporation of Trade Unions," 68 Alb. Law Jour. 68 (1906); Wambaugh, "Should Trade Unions Be Incorporated?" 15 Green Bag, 260 (1903); 42 Harv. Law Rev. 550 (1929).

The various stages of the Coronado litigation are reported in Dowd v. Mine Workers, 235 Fed. 1 (8th cir. 1916), certiorari denied in 242 U.S. 653 (1917); Coronado Coal Co. v. United Mine Workers, 258 Fed. 829 (8th cir. 1919), rev'd. *infra,* p. 575; Finley v. United Mine Workers, 360 Fed. 972 (8th cir. 1924). After this decision the case went back for a new trial, which resulted in disagreement. The case was then settled by the payment of $27,500 to the plaintiffs by District No. 21. A related litigation is reported in United Mine Workers v. Pennsylvania Co., 200 Fed. 965 (8th cir. 1924), 28 Fed.(2d) 851 (8th cir. 1928), commented on in 8 Ore. Law Rev. 378 (1929). For other material upon the Coronado litigation, see: Witte, The Government in Labor Disputes, 113-114, 136-138 (1932).

Prior to the Coronado decision the uniform current of authority in the United States was to the effect that, apart from statute, an unincorporated labor union could neither sue nor be sued as such. American Steel & Wire Co. v. Wire Drawers' & Die Makers' Unions, 90 Fed. 598 (C.C.N.D. Ohio, 1898); American Fed. of Labor v. Bucks Stove & Range Co., 33 App. D.C. 83 (1909), appeal dismissed in 219 U.S. 581 (1911); Grand Internat'l Brotherhood of Locomotive Engineers v. Green, 206 Ala. 196, 89 So. 435 (1921), subsequently changed by 1921 Ala. Acts, p. 14, as interpreted in s.c. 210 Ala. 496, 98 So. 569 (1923); Baskins v. United Mine Workers, 150 Ark. 398, 234 S.W. 464 (1921); District No. 21 v. Bourland, 169 Ark. 796, 277 S.W. 546 (1925); Cahill v. Plumbers, etc., Local 93, 238 Ill. App. 123 (1925); Karges Furniture Co. v. Amalgamated Woodworkers' Local Union, 165 Ind. 421, 75 N.E. 877 (1905); Diamond Block Coal Co. v. United Mine Workers, 188 Ky. 477, 222 S.W. 1079 (1920); Pickett v. Walsh, 192 Mass. 572, 78 N.E. 753 (1906); Reynolds v. Davis, 198 Mass. 294, 84 N.E. 457 (1908); Casson v. McIntosh, 199 Mass. 443, 85 N.E. 529 (1908); St. Paul Typothetae v. Bookbinders, 94 Minn. 351, 102 N.W. 725 (1905); Cleland v. Anderson, 66 Neb. 252, 92 N.W. 306 (1902); Branson v. Industrial Workers of the World, 30 Nev. 270, 95 Pac. 354 (1908); Hanke v. Cigar Makers Internat'l Union, 27 Misc. 529, 58 N.Y.S. 412 (1899); Tucker v. Eatough, 186 N.C.

UNITED LEATHER WORKERS INTERNATIONAL UNION v. HERKERT & MEISEL TRUNK CO.

Supreme Court of the United States. 265 U.S. 457 (1924).

MR. CHIEF JUSTICE TAFT delivered the opinion of the Court.

This suit was begun by a bill in equity filed in the District Court for the Eastern District of Missouri by the Herkert & Meisel Trunk Company and four others, all corporations of Missouri, engaged in

---

505, 120 S.E. 57 (1923); Citizens' Co. v. Typographical Union, 187 N.C. 42, 121 S.E. 31 (1924); Oster v. Brotherhood of Locomotive Engineers, 271 Pa. 419, 114 Atl. 377 (1921); Simpson v. Grand Internat'l Brotherhood of Locomotive Engineers, 83 W. Va. 355, 98 S.E. 580 (1919); Society Brand Clothes v. Amalgamated Clothing Workers, [1931] 3 D.L.R. 361. The one contrary American authority is Hillenbrand v. Building Trades Council, 14 Ohio Dec. N.P. 628 (1904). In a number of cases, however, trade unions had been made parties to suits, the novelty of such action having either escaped the attention of court and counsel or objection to such procedure having been made at too late a stage in the proceedings. See e.g. Coeur D'Alene Consolidated & Mining Co. v. Miners' Union, 51 Fed. 260 (C.C.D. Ida. 1892); United States v. Workingmen's Amalgamated Council of New Orleans, 54 Fed. 994 (C.C.E.D. La. 1893); Otis Steel Co. v. Local Union No. 218, 110 Fed. 698 (C.C.N.D. Ohio, 1901); Southern Ry. Co. v. Machinists Local Union No. 14, 111 Fed. 49 (C.C.W.D. Tenn. 1901); Goldfield Consol. Mines v. Goldfield Miners' Union, 159 Fed. 500 (C.C.D. Nev. 1908); Barnes & Co. v. Chicago Typographical Union, 232 Ill. 402, 83 N.E. 932 (1908); Anderson & Lind Mfg. Co. v. Carpenters District Council, 308 Ill. 488, 139 N.E. 887 (1923); United Mine Workers v. Cromer, 159 Ky. 605, 167 S.W. 891 (1914); Vegelahn v. Guntner, 167 Mass. 92, 44 N.E. 1077 (1896); Barr v. Essex Trades Council, 53 N.J. Eq. 101, 30 Atl. 881 (1894); Connett v. United Hatters, 76 N.J. Eq. 202, 74 Atl. 188 (1909); Ruddy v. United Ass'n Journeymen Plumbers, 79 N.J.L. 467, 75 Atl. 742 (1910). As to what constitutes sufficient service of process under the Coronado doctrine, see: Christian v. Internat'l Ass'n of Machinists, 7 Fed.(2d) 481 (E.D. Ky. 1925); Brown v. United States, 276 U.S. 134 (1928).

In the absence of such a doctrine of associational responsibility as that developed in the Coronado case, is there any effective means of reaching the assets of a trade union? Individual members of a trade union, who have either actually participated in or have been responsible as principals for the commission of tort, can be held individually liable for damages. Brown v. Lewis, 12 T.L.R. 455 (1896). And the scope of such liability has been extended by the application of conceptions of conspiracy beyond the bounds that an application of the principles of agency would justify. See: 42 Harv. Law Rev. 550 (1929). But considerable doubt exists as to whether the interest of the members in trade union funds is of a nature which will permit the subjection of such "shares" to the satisfaction of the established individual liability of its members. See: Sturgess, *supra,* at 386. No such proceeding seems ever to have been attempted. In contract actions, the funds of the unincorporated association can be rendered liable by a proceeding in equity against the trustees of the funds. Society of Shakers v. Watson, 68 Fed. 730 (6th cir. 1895); Van Houten v. Pine, 36 N.J. Eq. 133 (1882); Oster v. Brotherhood of Locomotive Firemen, 271 Pa. 419, 114 Atl. 377 (1921) *semble.* And some authority exists for the maintenance of such an action at law. Davis v. Bradford, 58 N.H. 476 (1878). *Contra:* Moore v. Stemmons, 119 Mo. App. 162, 95 S.W. 313 (1906). In tort actions, however, the difficulty of establishing an associational responsibility for the tort has made against resort to such a procedure. But *cf.* Linaker v. Pilcher, 70 L.J.K.B. 396 (1901). The doctrine of permitting suits against a few defendants as representative of the group, whether in equity or, as permitted by statute, at law, has not effectively overcome this difficulty, for the problem of the liability of such individuals whose interests in the common fund are sought to be reached still remains. See: Williams, "Some Developments of the Law Relating to Voluntary Unincorporated Associations," 6 Can. Bar Rev. 16 (1928). But *cf.* St. Germain v. Bakery & Confectionery Workers Union, 97 Wash. 282, 294, 166 Pac. 665 (1917). Such representative actions at law, when authorized by statute, have, however, substantially increased the ease of establishing individual liabilities against the many members of the group. Branson v. Industrial

making trunks and leather goods in St. Louis, against the United Leather
Workers Union, Local Lodge or Union No. 66, an unincorporated association, its officers and agents and a number of its members.   The bill
averred that each of the complainants had built up a valuable business in

Workers of the World, 30 Nev. 270, 95 Pac. 354 (1908) ; Ex parte Baylor, 93 S.C.
414, 77 S.E. 59 (1913) ; Medlin v. Ebenezer Methodist Church, 132 S.C. 498, 129
S.E. 830 (1925).
    Statutes have been passed in many states authorizing the maintenance of a suit
either against an unincorporated association as such or as against the official of such
association.   For a collection of such statutes, see : Warren, op. cit., 547, 557.   Such
statutes are constitutional.   United States Heater Co. v. Iron Molders' Union, 129
Mich. 354, 88 N.W. 889 (1902).   The statutes do not do away with the right to hold
the members of such an association individually responsible.   Davison v. Holden, 55
Conn. 103 (1887).   Though the group may be sued in its group name, if the action be
in equity the suit is substantially like that of an equitable action brought against representative defendants.   Armstrong v. Superior Court, 173 Cal. 341, 159 Pac. 1176
(1916).   Actions have been maintained under such statutes at law without any definite
indication either as to whether an associational responsibility is being sought to be
imposed or upon what funds execution may be levied upon a judgment obtained
against the group in its group name.   Bruns v. Milk Wagon Drivers' Union, 242 S.W.
419 (Mo. App. 1922) ; St. Louis & South Western Ry. Co. v. Thompson, 192 S.W.
1095 (Texas Civ. App. 1917) ; Patch Mfg. Co. v. Protection Lodge, 77 Vt. 294, 60
Atl. 74 (1905).   But cf. Davison v. Holden, supra, semble.   Under the New York
statute, it is clear that no action at law may be maintained to impose an associational
liability unless the action might have been maintained against all the individual members of the group.   Schouten v. Alpine, 215 N.Y. 225, 109 N.E. 244 (1915) ; People
ex rel. Solomon v. Brotherhood of Painters, 218 N.Y. 115, 112 N.E. 752 (1916) ;
Mazurajitis v. Makawyce, 93 Misc. 337, 157 N.Y.S. 151 (1916) ; Friedman & Co. v.
Amalgamated Clothing Workers, 115 Misc. 44, 188 N.Y.S. 879 (1921).   But no such
requirement has been applied in suits in equity seeking to enjoin the association in an
action against the association in the name of the required official.   Grassi Contracting
Co. v. Bennett, 174 App. Div. 244, 160 N.Y.S. 279 (1916) ; Master Horseshoers' Protective Ass'n v. Quinlivan, 83 App. Div. 459, 82 N.Y.S. 288 (1903).   But cf. Russell
& Sons v. Stampers' & Gold Leaf Local Union No. 22, 57 Misc. 96, 107 N.Y.S. 303
(1907).   Upon the metaphysical question as to whether the effect of such statutes is
to create an "entity" of the unincorporated association, see : Warren, op cit., 542-559.
    "This decision [the Coronado case] was based squarely upon grounds of public
policy, the court holding that, although no law expressly authorizes such suits and
the common-law rule is to the contrary, the recognition of unions as entities in many
statutes according them privileges requires that they should also be treated as entities
when claims are made against them.   The prestige of the U. S. Supreme Court is such
that the state courts might reasonably be expected to follow this conclusion.   No such
tendency, however, has been discernible to date."   Witte, The Government in Labor Disputes, 143-144 (1932).   "The decision [the Coronado case] did not effect a
general change in the status of such associations ; rather, it turned upon the character
of a trade union as such, especially because of its repeated recognition in statutes of
the United States as an entity.   It is to be read as applicable only to such cases."
Learned Hand, J., in United States & Cuban A.W.E. Corp. v. Lloyds, 291 Fed. 889,
891 (S.D.N.Y. 1923).   Thus, in the absence of a legislative background comparable
to that present in the United States legislation in the Coronado case or that present
in the English legislation in the Taff Vale case, other courts have refused to permit
trade unions to be sued as such upon the express ground of the different legislative
treatment according such unions in their respective jurisdictions.   Cf. District No. 21
v. Bourland, supra; Tucker v. Eatough, supra; Society Brand Clothes v. Amalgamated Clothing Workers, supra.   But see : Hansell v. Purcell, 1 Fed. (2d) 266 (6th cir.
1924), certiorari denied in 266 U.S. 617 (1924) (allowing the House of David, an
unincorporated religious association, to be made a party to a suit).
    Upon the citizenship of an unincorporated trade union for jurisdictional pur-
poses in the federal courts, see : Russell v. Central Labor Union, 1 Fed. (2d) 412
(E.D. Ill. 1924) ; Ex parte Edelstein, 30 Fed. (2d) 636 (2nd cir. 1929) ; 25 Col. Law
Rev. 104 (1925) ; 38 Harv. Law Rev. 510 (1925) ; 9 Minn. Law Rev. 282 (1925) ; 34
Yale Law Jour. 564 (1925).

making, selling and shipping in interstate commerce trunks and leather goods, that each received large quantities of raw material by interstate commerce, and employed a large number of persons, men and girls, that on February 28, 1920, defendants demanded that their shops be unionized and conducted as closed shops and announced that if complainants refused they would ruin the interstate commerce business of each of them, that on April 10, 1920, the defendants, acting individually and on behalf of the defendant union, in order to destroy the complainants' business and to prevent their employees from continuing in their employment unless complainants would yield to their demands, began a strike, assaulted and threatened complainants' employees, and intimidated them so as to force them against their wills to quit complainants' employment, and that they thereby prevented complainants from engaging in and carrying on their interstate business and interfered with and obstructed them in the manufacture and shipment of the products of their factories sold to be shipped in interstate commerce. The bill charged that defendants were carrying out their illegal conspiracy and purposes by mass picketing and intimidation, that the interference with complainants' interstate commerce was intentional and malicious and was intended to destroy it, that it was in violation of the Anti-Trust Law and the Clayton Act, and that they had already inflicted, and unless restrained would continue to inflict, irreparable injury upon such business. The bill shows that each complainant's damage threatened exceeded three thousand dollars. The prayer was for a temporary and then a final injunction to prevent the intimidation, illegal picketing and other interference with complainants' manufacturing and interstate business and with their employees or would-be employees engaged in carrying it on. Certain of the defendants answered the bill and denied the picketing, intimidation, and violence and the purpose to interfere with complainants' interstate business as charged, and averred that they and the fellow members of the Union had lawfully quit the employment of complainants because they could not agree upon the terms of a new agreement. The District Court upon preliminary hearing granted a temporary injunction and upon final hearing granted a final decree enjoining defendants as prayed. The case was taken on appeal to the Circuit Court of Appeals where the decree of the District Court was affirmed, one Judge dissenting. 284 Fed. 446. The cause now comes before us on appeal under § 241, Judicial Code.

The evidence adduced before the District Court showed that the defendant, the Local Union No. 66 of the United Leather Workers, having declared a strike against the complainants and withdrawn its members from their employ, instituted an illegal picketing campaign of intimidation against their employees who were willing to remain and against others willing to take the places of the striking employees, that the effect of this campaign was to prevent the complainants from continuing to manufacture their goods needed to fill the orders they had received from regular customers and would-be purchasers in other States, that such orders covered ninety per cent. of all goods manufactured by complainants, that the character of their business was known to the defendants, and that the illegal strike campaign of defendants thus interfered with and obstructed complainants' interstate commerce business to their great loss. There was no evidence whatever to show that complainants were obstructed by the strike or the strikers in shipping to other States the products they had ready to ship or in their receipt of materials from other States needed to make their goods. While the bill averred that defendants had instituted a boycott against complainants and were prosecuting the same by illegal methods, there was no evidence whatever that any attempt was made to boycott the sale of the complainants' products in other States or anywhere or to interfere with their interstate shipments of goods ready to ship.

The sole question here is whether a strike against manufacturers by their employees, intended by the strikers to prevent, through illegal picketing and intimidation, continued manufacture, and having such effect, was a conspiracy to restrain interstate commerce under the Anti-Trust Act because such products when made were, to the knowledge of the strikers, to be shipped in interstate commerce to fill orders given and accepted by would-be purchasers in other States, in the absence of evidence that the strikers interfered or attempted to interfere with the free transport and delivery of the products when manufactured from the factories to their destination in other States, or with their sale in those States.

We think that this question has already been answered in the negative by this Court. In *United Mine Workers v. Coronado Co.,* 259 U.S. 344, a coal mining company in Arkansas changed its arrangement with its employees from a closed shop to an open shop. The local union resented the change and the avowed purpose of the company to protect non-union employees by armed guards. Violence, murder and arson were resorted to by the union. Seventy-five per cent. of the output of the mine was to be shipped out of the State and a car of coal prepared for interstate shipment was destroyed by the mob of strikers and their sympathizers. It was contended that, as the result of the conspiracy was to reduce the interstate shipment of coal from the mines by 5,000 tons or more a week, this conspiracy was directed against interstate commerce, and triple damages for the injury inflicted could be recovered under the Federal Anti-Trust Law. But this Court held otherwise and reversed a judgment for a large amount on the ground that the evidence did not disclose a conspiracy against interstate commerce, justifying recovery under the law. * * *

This review of the cases makes it clear that the mere reduction in the supply of an article to be shipped in interstate commerce, by the illegal or tortious prevention of its manufacture, is ordinarily an indirect and remote obstruction to that commerce. It is only when the intent or necessary effect upon such commerce in the article is to enable those preventing the manufacture to monopolize the supply, control its price or discriminate as between its would-be purchasers, that the unlawful interference with its manufacture can be said directly to burden interstate commerce.

The record is entirely without evidence or circumstances to show that the defendants in their conspiracy to deprive the complainants of their workers were thus directing their scheme against interstate commerce. It is true that they were, in this labor controversy, hoping that the loss of business in selling goods would furnish a motive to the complainants to yield to demands in respect to the terms of employment; but they did nothing which in any way directly interfered with the interstate transportation or sales of the complainants' product.

We concur with the dissenting Judge in the Circuit Court of Appeals when, in speaking of the conclusion of the majority, he said: "The natural, logical and inevitable result will be that every strike in any industry or even in any single factory will be within the Sherman Act and subject to federal jurisdiction provided any appreciable amount of its product enters into interstate commerce." (284 Fed. 446, 464.)

We can not think that Congress intended any such result in the enactment of the Anti-Trust Act or that the decisions of this Court warrant such construction.

Decree reversed.[1]

MR. JUSTICE McKENNA, MR. JUSTICE VAN DEVANTER, and MR. JUSTICE BUTLER, dissent.

CORONADO COAL COMPANY v. UNITED MINE WORKERS OF AMERICA.

Supreme Court of the United States. 268 U.S. 295 (1925).

MR. CHIEF JUSTICE TAFT delivered the opinion of the Court.

This is a suit for damages for the effect of an alleged conspiracy of the defendants unlawfully to restrain and prevent plaintiffs' interstate trade in coal in violation of the first and second sections of the Federal Anti-Trust Act. The charge is that the defendants, in 1914, for the purpose of consummating the conspiracy, destroyed valuable mining properties of the plaintiffs. Treble damages and an attorney's fee are asked under the seventh section of the Act. The suit was brought in the District Court for the Western District of Arkansas. The plaintiffs are the Bache-Denman Coal Company and eight other corporations, in each of which the first named owns a controlling amount of stock. One of them is the Coronado Company, which gives the case its name. The corporations were correlated in organization and in the physical location of their mines.

---

[1] For comment on the case, see: 19 Ill. Law Rev. 351 (1925) ; 3 Texas Law Rev. 105 (1924).

Accord: Danville Local Union No. 115 v. Danville Brick Co., 283 Fed. 909 (7th cir. 1922) ; Silverstein v. Local No. 280 Journeymen Tailors' Union, 284 Fed. 833. *Cf.* Curran Printing Co. v. Allied Printing Council, 5 Law & Labor, 91 (U.S.D.C. Mo. 1923).

They had been operated for some years as a unit in the Prairie Creek Valley in Sebastian County, Arkansas. Immediately after the destruction of the property the District Court in a proper proceeding appointed receivers for the mines, and they or their successors are also parties to this suit. The original complaint was filed in September, 1914. It was demurred to, and the demurrer sustained. On error in the Court of Appeals the ruling was reversed. *Dowd v. United Mine Workers of America,* 235 Fed. 1. The case then came on for trial on the third amended complaint and the answers of the defendants. The trial resulted in a verdict of $200,000 for the plaintiffs, which was trebled by the court, and a counsel fee of $25,000 and interest to the date of the judgment were added. The Court of Appeals reversed the judgment as to interest, but in other respects affirmed it. 258 Fed. 829. On error from this Court under § 241 of the Judicial Code, the judgments of both courts were reversed, and the cause remanded to the District Court for further proceedings. The opinion is reported in 259th United States, 344. The new trial, in October, 1923, resulted in a directed verdict and judgment for the defendants, which was affirmed by the Circuit Court of Appeals. The case is here on error for a second time.

In our previous opinion we held that the International Union, known as the United Mine Workers of America, the union known as United Mine Workers, District No. 21, and the subordinate local unions which were made defendants, were, though unincorporated associations, subject to suit under the Anti-Trust Act, but that there was not sufficient evidence to go to the jury to show participation by the International Union in the conspiracy and the wrongs done. We found evidence tending to show that District No. 21 and other defendants were engaged in the conspiracy and the destruction of the property, but not enough to show an intentional restraint of interstate trade and a violation of the Anti-Trust Act. The plaintiffs contend that they have now supplied the links lacking at the first trial against each of the principal defendants. * * *

First. Is there any evidence in the present record tending to show that the International Union of the United Mine Workers participated? * * *

There were introduced at both trials long accounts of speeches and votes at national conventions of the International Union and meetings between union operators and representatives of the International Union from 1898 to 1914, revealing a constant effort on the part of the operators to force wages down to meet the competition of non-union mines, accompanied by assurances by the union representatives that they would do everything to unionize the competing non-union mines and enable the union mine operators to maintain the scale insisted on.

We thought at the first hearing and we think now that none of this evidence tends to establish the participation of the International in the Prairie Creek strike and disturbances.

The new evidence adduced for the purpose is chiefly the testimony of one James K. McNamara. He was the secretary of Local Union No.

1526 at Hartford and checkweighman at Mine No. 4 of the Central Coal & Coke Company, a union mine which was a competitor of the Bache-Denman mines and of larger capacity and business. McNamara seems to have been the field leader of the union forces at the battle of July 17, 1914. He was tried with others and convicted for violation of the injunction [1] as a conspiracy to defeat the process of the federal court, and was confined in the Leavenworth penitentiary. His testimony at the second trial was that in May, 1914, between the riot of April and the July battle, he went to Fort Smith to see Pete Stewart, the President of District No. 21, who was ill; that Stewart told him that he had been to Kansas City and had a talk with White, the International President, and that they had arranged a plan there to prevent Bache from producing coal. He said that White wished to see McNamara. Thereafter White came to Fort Smith to participate in the trial of the secretary of No. 21, already mentioned, between the 18th and 23rd of May. McNamara said he went to Fort Smith and met one Jim Slankard, who was a town marshal in Hartford, Sebastian County, and a very active promoter of union violence in this case, that Slankard told him that White wished to see him at the hotel, that he and Slankard went to White's room, that White said, "How is things at Prairie Creek?" that the witness said, "Things are a little watery in Prairie Creek No. 4, yet," referring to the pumping of the water out of the mine which was going on, to which White replied: "Yes, I have been informed on that"; and then said, "Stewart told me that they can not get enough men to operate the mine." And continued, "If they do that, we must prevent the coal from getting into the market."

Q. Did he say why? A. Yes sir.

Q. Tell it. A. He said, "because if Bache coal, scab dug coal, got into the market it would only be a matter of time until every union operator in that country would have to close down his mine, or scab it, because the union operators could not meet Bache competition."

Q. Did he say anything more after that? A. Yes sir.

Q. What did he say? A. He said, "When you go back to Hartford," he said, "I want you to tell the men what I have told you, but don't tell them I have told you."

Q. Did he say why not? A. Yes sir, he said he did not want the National Organization mixed up in this case; he said, "So far you have handled it, this part, and we have West Virginia and Colorado on our hands, and we can not bear any more fights."

Q. After that, did you go up and down the valley, as he said? A. I went back to Hartford and just quietly told the men what he said.

Q. How many of them did you tell, in a general way? A. I don't remember, I told practically everybody, I suppose.

Q. What did you tell them? A. I told them what White told me.

---

[1] Bache had obtained from the federal district court an injunction against the union miners and others taking part in lawless violence.—Ed.

Q. Tell them the reasons, as he had given them to you?   A. Yes
sir.

Q. And in pursuance of that, was that doctrine told all over the
valley?   A. Yes sir.   I told the men we wouldn't do anything until
Bache begun producing coal. * * *

Q. Now did you know what Pete Stewart did on Monday following
that convention about going around the field?   A. He came to Hartford
and made a speech.   He said he would furnish guns and ammunition
to all these men and their families in that valley, and if it was necessary
he would sacrifice his own life to prevent Bache getting coal out there.

McNamara further testified that he saw between three and four hundred guns in boxes at Hartford and that part of them were distributed to
the union miners and part returned to the secretary of District No. 21
at McAlester, Oklahoma. It was an avowed grievance of McNamara
that he had not been paid sufficient money for the sacrifices he had made
to the union cause. He said he had received $250 after the battle of July
17 from Stewart of District No. 21 to enable him to escape and avoid
arrest, and something more later, but nothing from White or the International. He volunteered in his cross-examination the statement that White
said to him at the interview: "Now you boys will not lose a day and your
expenses will be paid for every day you are in this trouble." He was
led by other questions to add that the trouble referred to by White was
his suffering in the penitentiary. When it was called to his attention that
his conversation with White in May, 1914, was before he had gone to the
penitentiary, he found it necessary to qualify his statement and in answer
to the question: "Did you have any arrangements to get money from
him then?" said: "It was generally understood that the National Organization was going to pay us for the time we lost * * *, and I thought the
only man to go to would be White to get it, because he was the National
President."   And so, he said, two years after he had finished his term at
the penitentiary, he met White at Hartford and asked him "When will
I get my money that I was promised for this work?" to which White
replied: "I will take it up with the Board as soon as I can."   But he said
he never got any money. We do not regard this as evidence that he was
promised or received money from the International either to induce or
reward his unlawful acts.

Giving the fullest credence to all that McNamara says, it is clear
that White did not intend by what he did to make the Prairie Creek difficulty a national affair. The International Board had not approved as
the constitution required that they should do in order to make it so. It
is quite true that White himself personally can be held as a defendant
if McNamara's evidence is to be believed, for urging and abetting the
destruction of the plaintiffs' property; but according to McNamara's testimony, repeated by him several times, White was particular to insist
that he did not wish to be regarded as acting for the International in the
matter or to involve it in the Prairie Creek difficulties. In our previous
opinion we held that a trades-union, organized as effectively as this

United Mine Workers' organization was, might be held liable, and all its funds raised for the purpose of strikes might be levied upon to pay damages suffered through illegal methods in carrying them on; but certainly it must be clearly shown in order to impose such a liability on an association of 450,000 men that what was done was done by their agents in accordance with their fundamental agreement of association.

As we said in our previous opinion, 259 U.S. 395:

"A corporation is responsible for the wrongs committed by its agents in the course of its business, and this principle is enforced against the contention that torts are *ultra vires* of the corporation. But it must be shown that it is in the business of the corporation. Surely no stricter rule can be enforced against an unincorporated organization like this. Here it is not a question of contract or of holding out an appearance of authority on which some third person acts It is a mere question of actual agency which the constitutions of the two bodies settle conclusively."

Again: .

"But it is said that the District was doing the work of the International and carrying out its policies and this circumstance makes the former an agent. We can not agree to this in the face of the specific stipulation between them that in such case unless the International expressly assumed responsibility, the District must meet it alone."

The action of the trial court in its direction of a verdict for the defendant, the International Union, must be affirmed.

Second. The tendency of the evidence to show that District No. 21 through its authorized leaders and agents and certain of its subordinate local unions organized and carried through the two attacks of April 6th and July 17th is so clear that it does not need further discussion. The only issue is whether the outrages, destruction and crimes committed were intentionally directed toward a restraint of interstate commerce. On the first trial we held that the evidence did not show this. The circumstances seemed amply to supply a different and a merely local motive for the conspiracy. The hostility of the head of District No. 21 and that of his men seemed sufficiently aroused by the coming of non-union men into that local community, by Mr. Bache's alleged breach of his contract with District No. 21 in employing non-union men three months before it expired, by his charged evasion of it through a manipulation of his numerous corporations, by his advertised anticipation of trespass and violence in his warning notices, in his enclosing his mining premises with a cable, and in stationing guards with guns to defend them. These preparations in the heart of a territory that had been completely unionized for years were likely to stir a bitterness of spirit in the neighborhood. Bache had himself foreseen such a spirit when he took part in the formulation of a letter to his stockholders for his superintendent to sign, in which it was said: "To do this means a bitter fight, but in my opinion it can be accomplished by proper organization." He testified that he was entering into a matter he knew was perilous and dangerous to his companies. In view of these circumstances, we said in the previous opinion:

"Nothing of this is recited to justify in the slightest the lawlessness and outrages committed, but only to point out that as it was a local strike within the meaning of the International and District constitutions, so it was in fact a local strike, local in its origin and motive, local in its waging, and local in its felonious and murderous ending."

Were we concerned only with the riot of April 6th, we should reach the same conclusion now; but at the second trial plaintiffs were able to present a large amount of new evidence as to the attitude and purpose of the leaders and members of District No. 21, shown especially in the interval between the riot of April 6th and the destruction of the mine property on July 17th following. This is attributed by counsel for the plaintiffs to the fact that the new witnesses had moved away from Sebastian County, Arkansas, and were freed from local restraint and to grievances of former union sympathizers and participants who thought themselves not sufficiently appreciated.

Part of the new evidence was an extract from the convention proceedings of District No. 21 at Fort Smith, Arkansas, in February, 1914, in which the delegates discussed the difficulties presented in their maintenance of the union scale in Arkansas, Oklahoma and Texas because of the keen competition from the non-union fields of Southern Colorado and the non-union fields of the South in Alabama and Tennessee. Stewart, the president, called attention to a new field in Oklahoma which he said would be a great competitor of union coal fields, and that District No. 21 would be forced to call a strike to bring into line certain operators in that section, and in the event that they did so the District would fight such a conflict to the bitter end regardless of cost. They also discussed a proposal to reduce the scale at the union mines at McCurtain, Oklahoma, which Stewart advocated, in order that the McCurtain operators might be put on a proper competitive basis in interstate markets with other operators. Several of the delegates at this convention took part in the riot of April 6th and the battle of July 17th following.

A new witness was one Hanraty, who was for seven years president of District No. 21, then a state mine inspector for three years, and then national organizer from 1912 to 1914, and president of District No. 21 again in 1915, but subsequently separated from the union. He testified that he had been closely associated as president of the District with Stewart as a member of the District executive board. He had been frequently in close conference with most of the leading men who had taken part in the violence at Prairie Creek. He said that he made speeches all through District No. 21 and did not remember a speech in which he did not mention the danger from non-union coal in taking the markets of union coal and forcing a non-union scale, and that it was a constant subject of discussion among the officers and members.

A leading witness among many others on this subject was a Dr. H. P. Routh, who practiced medicine at Hartford in 1914, and who lives now at Tulsa, Oklahoma. He said he was living at the Davis Hotel in Hartford in May, 1914, when the Executive Board of District No. 21 came down there for a meeting, and he heard a great deal of the conversation between the board members as to the effect of this threatened non-union Bache-Denman operation. The conclusion they reached was that its success would affect so injuriously the trade of the Central Coal & Coke Company in shipping and selling coal in the neighboring States, that this company, the largest coal producer in that section, would have to become non-union. He talked specifically to several members of the Board and of the Union who, the evidence shows, were shown to be actively engaged in the battle of July 17th.

In addition to this, the testimony of McNamara, already discussed, while ineffective to establish the complicity of the International Union with this conspiracy, contains much, if credited, from which the jury could reasonably infer that the purpose of the union miners in District No. 21 and the local unions engaged in the plan was to destroy the power of the owners and lessees of the Bache-Denman mines to send their output into interstate commerce to compete with that of union mines in Oklahoma, in Kansas, in Louisiana markets and elsewhere. It appeared that 80 per cent of all the product of the mines in Sebastian County went into other States.

New and more elaborate evidence was also introduced in the second trial as to the capacity of the Bache-Denman mines under the open shop. In our previous opinion we declined to hold that the mere elimination from interstate trade of 5,000 tons a week, which we took to be the practical limit of capacity of the plaintiffs, was significant in the total tonnage of the country or state or that its stoppage furnished a basis of itself for inferring a palpable and intentional restraint of interstate trade with which the defendants could be charged even though coal could be produced at a reduced cost under non-union conditions. The amount we assumed was based on the averments of the third amended bill in which the normal gross income from the four mines of the plaintiffs used by them, and which were destroyed, was alleged to be in good times before the trouble something more than $465,000 a year. At the price at which coal usually sold at the mine, this would make the output 5,000 tons a week. In a petition for a rehearing, plaintiffs urged upon us that this was an error and that the potential capacity of all the mines owned and leased by the Bache-Denman Company in that region, nine in number, was 5,000 tons a day rather than 5,000 tons a week. In the view we took of the evidence then before us, we had only the isolated circumstance of the reduction in shipment of the normal product of the four mines destroyed, without other evidence to show an actual intent and plan on the part of the defendants thereby to restrain interstate commerce. Whatever error therefore might have been made in stating the capacity of all the mines of the plaintiffs could not affect our conclusion, and the rehearing was denied. In the second trial, however, the total possible capacity not only of the destroyed mines but of the

other unworked mines of plaintiffs became more important, in view of
the direct testimony as to the moving purpose of District No. 21 to
restrain and prevent plaintiffs' competition. The possible total to which
their production might be brought was testified to by a number of new
expert witnesses who were familiar with the mines and the business of
mining and selling coal in the markets of the neighboring States. The
conclusion of some of these witnesses was that with the union restrictions removed and a regular demand for the coal, the capacity of
all the mines, owned and leased by the plaintiffs, those destroyed and
those uninjured, could have been increased to substantially more than
5,000 tons a day. Such conclusion was possibly subject to criticism as
exaggerated and speculative, and dependent on conditions probably not
realizable, but it was all relevant evidence for the jury to consider and
weigh as a circumstance with the rest of the new testimony in proof
of intent of the leaders of District No. 21 to prevent shipments to
neighboring States of such an amount of non-union coal at non-union
cost. There was also new evidence tending to show the knowledge by
Hanraty, Stewart and other leaders of District No. 21 of the character of
plaintiffs' mines and their capacity.

The mere reduction in the supply of an article to be shipped in
interstate commerce by the illegal or tortious prevention of its manufacture
or production is ordinarily an indirect and remote obstruction to that
commerce. But when the intent of those unlawfully preventing the
manufacture or production is shown to be to restrain or control the supply
entering and moving in interstate commerce, or the price of it in interstate markets, their action is a direct violation of the Anti-Trust Act.
United Mine Workers v. Coronado Co., 259 U.S. 344, 408, 409; *United
Leather Workers v. Herkert,* 265 U.S. 457, 471; *Industrial Association
v. United States, ante,* p. 64. We think there was substantial evidence
at the second trial in this case tending to show that the purpose of the
destruction of the mines was to stop the production of non-union coal and
prevent its shipment to markets of other States than Arkansas, where
it would by competition tend to reduce the price of the commodity and
affect injuriously the maintenance of wages for union labor in competing
mines, and that the direction by the District Judge to return a verdict
for the defendants other than the International Union was erroneous.

We affirm the judgment of the District Court and the Circuit Court
of Appeals in favor of the International Union of United Mine Workers
of America, and reverse that in favor of District No. 21 and the other
local unions and the individual defendants and remand the cause as to
them for a new trial.

Affirmed in part and reversed in part.[2]

---

[2] For comment on the case, see: 74 Univ. of Pa. Law Rev. 321 (1926); 35 Yale
Law Jour. 111 (1925).

Compare: Alco-Zander Co. v. Amalgamated Clothing Workers, 35 Fed. (2d) 203
(E.D. Pa. 1929), commented on in 15 Corn. Law Quar. 480 (1930); 24 Ill. Law Rev.

INDUSTRIAL ASSOCIATION OF SAN FRANCISCO v. UNITED STATES.

Supreme Court of the United States. 268 U.S. 64 (1925).

MR. JUSTICE SUTHERLAND delivered the opinion of the Court.

This is a suit by the United States against a number of voluntary associations, corporations and individuals, charging them with engaging, and threatening to continue to engage, in a conspiracy to restrain trade and commerce in building materials among the several states, in violation of the Anti-Trust Act of July 2, 1890, c. 647, 26 Stat. 209. The bill prays for an injunction restraining the further execution of the alleged conspiracy, for a dissolution of certain of the associations as illegal, and for other relief. After a hearing, the federal district court declined to dissolve any of the appellants or interfere with their general activities, but entered a decree enjoining them specifically from (a) requiring any permit for the purchase, sale or use of building materials or supplies produced without the State of California and coming into that state in interstate or foreign commerce; (b) making, as a condition for the issuance of any permit for the purchase, sale or use of building materials or supplies, any regulations that will interfere with the free movement of building materials, plumbers' or other supplies produced without the state; (c) attempting to prevent or discourage any person without the state from shipping building materials or other supplies to any person within the state; or (d) aiding, abetting or assisting, directly or indirectly, individually or collectively, others to do any of the foregoing matters or things. 293 Fed. 925. A reversal of this decree is sought upon the ground, mainly, that the evidence wholly fails to show any contract, combination or conspiracy in restraint of interstate or foreign trade or commerce, or a violation in any respect of the provisions of the Anti-Trust Act. Other grounds assigned in view of the conclusion we have reached, we put aside as unnecessary to be considered.

That there was a combination and concerted action among the appellants, is not disputed. The various agreements, courses of conduct and acts relied upon to establish the case for the government arose out of a long continued controversy,—or, more accurately, a series of controversies,—between employers engaged in the construction of buildings in San Francisco, upon the one side, and the building trade unions of San Francisco, of which there were some fifty in number with a combined membership of about 99% of all the workmen engaged in the building industries of that city, upon the other side.

---

925 (1930); 78 Univ. of Pa. Law Rev. 430 (1930). The injunction issued in this case is reprinted in 71 Cong. Rec. 3639-41 (Sept. 16, 1929), together with other critical comment upon the case.

Compare also: Mitchell Woodbury Corp. v. Albert Pick-Barth Co., 36 Fed.(2d) 974 (D. Mass. 1929); 41 Fed.(2d) 148 (1st cir. 1930); 57 Fed.(2d) 96 (1st cir. 1932).

Prior to February 1, 1921, the unions had adopted and enforced, and were then enforcing, many restrictions bearing upon the employment of their members, which the employers, and a large body of other citizens, considered to be unreasonable, uneconomic and injurious to the building industries, resulting, it was asserted, in decreased production, increased cost and generally retarded progress. Among the restrictions complained of, were rules limiting the number of apprentices, limiting the amount of work, limiting or forbidding the use of labor-saving devices, and interfering with the legitimate authority of the employer. The plumbers' union, for example, enforced the following, among others: no union plumber, whatever the emergency, was permitted to work on non-union material or to work overtime on Saturday without permission of the union; detailed reports were required showing the number of fixtures set each day, and men who exceeded the standard fixed by the union were disciplined; the time which any employer was permitted to stay on a job was limited to two hours a day; as many men as the union saw fit could be ordered on a job regardless of the wishes of the employer. Among the restrictions imposed by the painters' union were these; wide brushes with long handles for roof painting were probibited, and it was required that all such work should be done with a small brush; certain labor-saving devices were prohibited; and union painters declined to paint non-union lumber.

The unions rigidly enforced the "closed shop,"—that is, they denied the right of the employer to employ any workman, however well qualified, who was not a member of a San Francisco union; and this applied to a member of a labor union in another locality, who, moreover, practically was precluded from joining a San Francisco union by reason of the cost and onerous conditions imposed. They were confederated under the name of the Building Trades Council, by means of which their combined power was exerted in support of the demands and policies of each, until they had acquired a virtual monopoly of all kinds of building trade labor in San Francisco, and no building work of any consequence could be done in that city, except in subordination to these demands and policies.

Early in 1921, serious differences having arisen between the unions and the employers in respect of wages, hours and working conditions, an agreement for arbitration was made and a board of arbitrators selected. The board, after a hearing, made a tentative award reducing the scale of wages for the ensuing six months. Challenging the authority of the board to reduce wages, the unions refused to be bound by the award and repudiated and abandoned the arbitration. Strikes ensued; efforts to bring the strikers back to work failed; and building operations in San Francisco practically came to a stand-still. Thereupon, in an endeavor to find a solution of the difficulty, mass-meetings were held by representative citizens in large numbers and from all walks of life. At these meetings it was resolved that the work of building must go forward, and that if San Francisco mechanics refused to work, others must be employed from the outside. Funds were raised and placed in the hands of a committee of

the San Francisco Chamber of Commerce, and, under its direction, workmen were brought in from the outside with promises of employment
at the wages fixed by the arbitrators. Subsequently, the Industrial Association of San Francisco was organized to take the place of the committee
and carry on its work. The strikers, however, returned to work, and for
a time no objection was made to the employment of non-union workmen.
But later, demands were made by certain of the unions for the discharge
of all non-union workmen and the restoration of the "closed shop." These
demands were disregarded, and there was another strike. A boycott was
instituted and acts of violence against persons and property committed.
In the meantime, one of the appellants, the Builders Exchange of San
Francisco, with a membership of more than one thousand building contractors and dealers in building materials, in coöperation with the Industrial Association and other appellants, devised and put into effect what is
called the "American plan."

The basic requirement of the plan was that there should be no discrimination for or against an employee on account of his affiliation or
non-affiliation with a labor union, except that at least one non-union man
in each craft should be employed on each particular job as an evidence,
it is suggested, of good faith. In effect, the "American plan" and the
"open shop" policy are the same.

The principal means adopted to enforce the plan was the "permit
system," the object of which was to limit sales of certain specified kinds
of materials to builders who supported the plan. To render this restriction effective, the person concerned was required to obtain a permit from
the Builders Exchange, specifying the kinds and quantities of materials
to be furnished and the particular job on which they were to be used. The
materials specified were cement, lime, plaster, ready-mixed mortar, brick,
terra cotta and clay products, sand, rock and gravel. Substantially all of
these were California productions and were deliberately selected for that
reason, in order to avoid interference with interstate commerce. The
only material exception was plaster, which was brought in from the outside, but consigned to local representatives of the manufacturers or to
local dealers in San Francisco, and brought to rest in salesrooms and warehouses and commingled with other goods and property, before being subjected to the permit rule. A suggestion was made at one time that, if
necessary, the rule would be extended to all other materials used in the
building trades; but it does not appear that this was done. It is said that
lath of various kinds, wallboard and Keene cement also were put under
the rule; but we think the record discloses that, in fact, this was never
agreed upon or carried into effect.

There is evidence of efforts to extend the "American plan" to other
cities and states. Permits were extensively withheld in respect of buildings where the "American plan" was not adopted or not enforced. Builders and contractors were constantly urged to observe the plan and were
warned that failure to do so would result in a denial of future permits.
A check was kept upon shops and building jobs by inspectors, and daily

reports were made as to whether the plan was being observed. Whenever it appeared in any case that the plan was not being lived up to, a
warning letter was sent out. Under appropriate by-laws, members of
organizations subscribing to the plan who violated it were fined and in
some instances expelled; and other methods, not necessary to be recited,
in part persuasive and in part coercive, were adopted and enforced in order to secure a thorough-going maintenance of the plan.

With the conflict between the policy of the "closed shop" and that of
the "open shop," or with the "American plan," *per se,* we have nothing to
do. And since it clearly appears that the object of the plan was one entirely apart from any purpose to affect interstate commerce, the sole inquiry we are called upon to make is whether the means employed to effectuate it constituted a violation of the Anti-Trust Act; and, in the light
of the evidence adduced, that inquiry need be pursued little beyond a consideration of the nature of the permit system, what was done under it,
and the effect thereof upon interstate commerce.

The bases of the decree, which, in the opinion of the court below, were
established, may be briefly and categorically stated as follows:

1. Permits were required for the purchase of building materials
and supplies produced in and brought from other states into California.

2. Permits, even if limited to California produced materials, nevertheless, interfered with and prevented the free movement of building materials and supplies from other states into California.

3. Persons in other states were directly prevented or discouraged
from shipping building materials and supplies into California.

It will be well, *in limine,* to emphasize certain clearly established general facts, in the light of which these grounds must be considered. Interference with interstate trade was neither desired nor intended. On the
contrary, the desire and intention was to avoid any such interference, and,
to this end, the selection of materials subject to the permit system was
substantially confined to California productions. The thing aimed at and
sought to be attained was not restraint of the interstate sale or shipment
of commodities, but was a purely local matter, namely, regulation of
building operations within a limited local area, so as to prevent their
domination by the labor unions. Interstate commerce, indeed commerce
of any description, was not the object of attack, "for the sake of which
the several specific acts and courses of conduct were done and adopted."
Swift and Company v. United States, 196 U.S. 375, 397. The facts and
circumstances which led to and accompanied the creation of the combination and the concert of action complained of, which we have briefly set
forth, apart from other and more direct evidence, are "ample to supply
a full local motive for the conspiracy." *United Mine Workers v. Coronado Co.,* 259 U.S. 344, 411.

But it is not enough that the object of a combination or conspiracy
be outside the purview of the act, if the means adopted to effectuate it
directly and unduly obstruct the free flow of interstate commerce. The
statute is not aimed alone at combinations and conspiracies which con-

template a restraint of interstate commerce, but includes those which directly and unduly cause such restraint in fact. See *American Column Co. v. United States,* 257 U.S. 377, 400; *Eastern States Lumber Ass'n. v. United States,* 234 U.S. 600, 613.

It remains to apply these principles, in the light of the facts, to the several grounds above stated, upon which the decree rests.

First: That permits were required for the purchase of materials produced in and brought from other states. To the extent that this may imply that permits were required in respect of building materials or supplies produced outside the State of California and shipped into the state, it is not sustained by the evidence. The record contains two letters signed by the president of the Builders Exchange to the effect, in one, that there "are added," and, in the other of later date, that "it is now necessary to add to the permit system," other materials than those in the enumerated list; and the person addressed in the second is asked to govern himself accordingly. But the positive, uncontradicted evidence is that, in fact, permits were required for the originally listed materials and for nothing else. While about twenty-eight thousand permits in all were issued, there is a significant absence of evidence that any of them so issued related to other than such listed materials. Upon the proof, we reasonably cannot accept the view that these letters are enough to show a departure from the declared and established purpose of the movement on the whole to avoid interference with interstate trade by confining the permit system substantially to California produced articles.

It is true, however, that plaster, in large measure produced in other states and shipped into California, was on the list; but the evidence is that the permit requirement was confined to such plaster as previously had been brought into the state and commingled with the common mass of local property, and in respect of which, therefore, the interstate movement and the interstate commercial status had ended. This situation is utterly unlike that presented in the *Swift Case, supra,* where, the only interruption of the interstate transit of live stock being that necessary to find a purchaser at the stockyards, and this the usual and constantly recurring course, it was held (pp. 398-399) that there was thus constituted "a current of commerce among the States," of which the purchase was but a part and incident. The same is true of *Stafford v. Wallace,* 258 U.S. 495, 516, which likewise dealt with the interstate shipment and sale of live stock. The stockyards, to which such live stock was consigned and delivered, are there described, not as a place of rest or final destination, but as "a throat through which the current flows," and the sale as only an incident which does not stop the flow but merely changes the private interest in the subject of the current without interfering with its continuity. In *Binderup v. Pathe Exchange,* 263 U.S. 291, 309, a commodity produced in one state was consigned to a local agency of the producer in another, not as a consummation of the transit, but for delivery to the customer. This court held that the intermediate delivery did not end, and was not intended to end, the movement of the commodity, but merely halted it "as a convenient step in the process of getting it to its final destination."

But here, the delivery of the plaster to the local representative or dealer was the closing incident of the interstate movement and ended the authority of the federal government under the commerce clause of the Constitution. What next was done with it, was the result of new and independent arrangements.

In respect of other materials of the character of those on the selected list, brought from other states, it is enough to say that the quantities were not only of little comparative consequence but it is not shown that they were subjected to the permit rule.

Second: That the permit requirement for California produced materials interfered with the free movement of materials and supplies from other states. No doubt there was such an interference, but the extent of it, being neither shown nor perhaps capable of being shown, is a matter of surmise. It was, however, an interference not within the design of the appellants, but purely incidental to the accomplishment of a different purpose. The court below laid especial stress upon the point that plumbers' supplies, which for the most part were manufactured outside the state, though not included under the permit system, were prevented from entering the state by the process of refusing a permit to purchase other materials, which were under the system, to anyone who employed a plumber who was not observing the "American plan." This is to say, in effect, that the building contractor, being unable to purchase the permit materials, and consequently unable to go on with the job, would have no need for plumbing supplies, with the result that the trade in them, to that extent, would be diminished. But this ignores the all important fact that there was no interference with the freedom of the outside manufacturer to sell and ship or of the local contractor to buy. The process went no further than to take away the latter's opportunity to use, and, therefore, his incentive to purchase. The effect upon, and interference with, interstate trade, if any, were clearly incidental, indirect and remote,—precisely such an interference as this court dealt with in *United Mine Workers v. Coronado Co., supra,* and *United Leather Workers v. Herkert,* 265 U.S. 457.

In the *Coronado Case* there was an attempt on the part of the owners of a coal mine to operate it upon the "open shop" basis. The officers and members of a local miners' union, thereupon, engaged in a strike, which was carried on with circumstances of violence resulting in the destruction of property and the injury and death of persons. A conspiracy and an intent to obstruct mining operations were established, and it was proved that the effect thereof was to prevent a part of the product of the mine from going into interstate commerce. It was held that this would not constitute a conspiracy to restrain such commerce, in the absence of proof of an intention to restrain it or proof of such a direct and substantial effect upon it, that such intention reasonably must be inferred. It was pointed out that there was nothing in the circumstances or declarations of the parties to indicate that the strikers had in mind any interference with interstate commerce or competition, when they engaged in the attempt to break up the plan to operate the mines with non-union labor, and, conceding that the natural result would be to keep the preponderating part of the output of the mine from being shipped out of the state, the effect on interstate commerce was not of such substance that a purpose to restrain interstate commerce might be inferred.

In the *United Leather Workers Case* there was a strike, accompanied by illegal picketing and intimidation of workers, to prevent, and which had the effect of preventing, the continued manufacture of goods by a trunk company. It was held that this was not a conspiracy to restrain interstate commerce within the Anti-Trust Act, even though the goods, to the knowledge of the strikers, were to be shipped in interstate commerce to fill orders already received and accepted from the company's customers in other states, since there was no actual or attempted interference with their transportation to, or their sale in, such states. There is in this case a complete review of the prior decisions on the subject, upon which the Court concludes (p. 471) :

"This review of the cases makes it clear that the mere reduction in the supply of an article to be shipped in interstate commerce, by the illegal or tortious prevention of its manufacture, is ordinarily an indirect and remote obstruction to that commerce. It is only when the intent or necessary effect upon such commerce in the article is to enable those preventing the manufacture to monopolize the supply, control its price or discriminate as between its would-be purchasers, that the unlawful interference with its manufacture can be said directly to burden interstate commerce. * * *

"We concur with the dissenting Judge in the Circuit Court of Appeals when, in speaking of the conclusion of the majority, he said: 'The natural, logical and inevitable result will be that every strike in any industry or even in any single factory will be within the Sherman Act and subject to federal jurisdiction provided any appreciable amount of its product enters into interstate commerce.' "

In its essential features, the present case is controlled by this reasoning. If an executed agreement to strike with the object and effect of closing down a mine or a factory, by preventing the employment of necessary workmen, the indirect result of which is that the sale and shipment of goods and products in interstate commerce is prevented or diminished, is not an unlawful restraint of such commerce, it cannot consistently be held otherwise in respect of an agreement and combination of employers or others to frustrate a strike and defeat the strikers by keeping essential domestic building materials out of their hands and the hands of their sympathizers, because the means employed, whether lawful or unlawful, produce a like indirect result. The alleged conspiracy and the acts here complained of, spent their intended and direct force upon a local situation,—for building is as essentially local as mining, manufacturing or growing crops,—and if, by a resulting diminution of the commercial demand, interstate trade was curtailed either generally or in specific instances, that was a fortuitous consequence so remote and indirect as plainly to cause it to fall outside the reach of the Sherman Act.

The Government relies with much confidence upon *Loewe v. Lawlor,* 208 U.S. 274, and *Duplex Co. v. Deering,* 254 U.S. 443; but the facts there and the facts here were entirely different. Both cases, like the *Coronado* and the *United Leather Workers Cases* and the present case, arose out of labor disputes; but in the former cases, unlike the latter ones, the object of the labor organizations was sought to be attained by a country-wide boycott of the employer's goods for the direct purpose of preventing their sale and transportation in interstate commerce in order to force a compliance with their demands. The four cases and the one here, considered together, clearly illustrate the vital difference, under the Sherman Act, between a direct, substantial and intentional interference with interstate commerce and intentional interference which is incidental, indirect, remote, and outside the purposes of those causing it.

Third: That persons in other states were directly prevented or discouraged from shipping into California. In respect of the alleged instances of direct interference with interstate sales and shipments, the evidence is sharply conflicting, with the preponderance in most cases, we think, on the side of appellants. In many of them the interferences had no connection with the "American plan" or the system and efforts employed to effectuate it, but were in furtherance of independent trade policies or other isolated and disconnected purposes. One such case was that of the Golden Gate Building Material Company, consisting of five plastering contractors, where the basis of the refusal to accept orders for supplies was a protest by certain dealers that the company was buying for individual use and not for resale, and had been formed merely to obtain dealers' prices. A class of interferences strongly pressed in argument was that in respect of plumbing supplies, practically all of which were manufactured outside of the State of California. Lists of plumbing contractors who were not observing the "American plan" were sent to the plumbing supply houses, and some of them refused to sell materials to such contractors. That there was, at least, a sympathetic connection between this action and the "American plan" may be assumed, although plumbing supplies were not within the scope of the permit list. However this may be, and whatever may have been the original situation, the practice was abandoned long before the present suit was instituted, and nothing appears by way of threat or otherwise to indicate the probability of its ever being resumed. Under these circumstances, there is no basis for present relief by injunction. *United States v. U. S. Steel Corp.,* 251 U.S. 417, 444-445.

By the foregoing process of elimination, the interferences which may have been unlawful are reduced to some three or four sporadic and doubtful instances, during a period of nearly two years. And when we consider that the aggregate value of the materials involved in these few and widely separated instances, was, at the utmost, a few thousand dollars, compared with an estimated expenditure of $100,000,000 in the construction of

buildings in San Francisco during the same time, their weight, as evidence
to establish a conspiracy to restrain interstate commerce or to establish
such restraint in fact, becomes so insignificant as to call for the application of the maxim, *de minimis non curat lex*.   To extend a statute intended to reach and suppress real interferences with the free flow of commerce among the states, to a situation so equivocal and so lacking in substance, would be to cast doubt upon the serious purpose with which it was
framed.

The decree of the court below must be reversed and the cause remanded with instructions to dismiss the bill.

Decree reversed.[1]

UNITED STATES v. BRIMS.

Supreme Court of the United States. 272 U.S. 549 (1926).

MR. JUSTICE McREYNOLDS delivered the opinion of the Court.

Respondents were charged with engaging in a combination and conspiracy to restrain interstate trade and commerce contrary to inhibitions
of the Sherman Act, c. 647, 26 Stat. 209, and were found guilty by a
jury. The Circuit Court of Appeals reviewed and reversed the judgment
of conviction upon the sole ground of fatal variance between allegation
and proof, or failure of proof to support the charge. 6 Fed.(2d) 98. They
said—

"The indictment charged defendants with 'combining or conspiring
to prevent manufacturing plants located outside of the City of Chicago
and in other States than Illinois from selling and delivering their building
material in and shipping the same to said City of Chicago.' * * * The
proof, however, disclosed merely an agreement between defendants whereby union defendants were not to work upon nonunion-made millwork.
* * * The agreement which the defendants entered into merely dealt with
millwork which was the product of nonunion labor. It mattered not
where the millwork was produced, whether in or outside of Illinois, if it
bore the union label. The restriction was not against the shipment of
millwork into Illinois. It was against nonunion-made millwork produced
in or out of Illinois. We find no evidence which would support a finding

---

[1] For comment on the case, see: Powell, "Commerce, Congress and the Supreme
Court, 1922-25," 26 Col. Law Rev. 521, 545 (1926) ; 20 Ill. Law Rev. 393 (1926).

For the background of the controversy underlying the case, see: Haber, Industrial Relations in the Building Industry, c. 14 (1930) ; Ryder, "The Unions Lose San
Francisco," 7 Am. Mercury, 412 (1926) ; Ryder, "San Francisco's Fight for Industrial Freedom," 75 Rev. of Reviews 82 (1927) ; Eliel, "San Francisco, a Free City,"
12 Law & Labor 53, 83 (1930).   See also: Hooker, "Industrial War in Chicago,"
31 New Republic, 39 (1922) ; Donnelly, Industrial War in Chicago, (1922) *id.* 359;
(1921) 25 *id.* 185.

Compare: Belfi v. United States, 259 Fed. 822 (3rd cir. 1919).

that the agreement embodied in Article 3 of section 3 was not the real agreement of the parties. Wherefore, we conclude there is a fatal variance and the evidence does not sustain the indictment."

They considered no other objection to the judgment of conviction, and the cause came here by certiorari because that point seemed to require further examination. We think it was wrongly decided.

The challenged combination and agreement related to the manufacture and installation in the City of Chicago of building material commonly known as millwork, which includes window and door fittings, sash, baseboard, molding, cornice, etc., etc. The respondents were manufacturers of millwork in Chicago, building contractors who purchase and cause such work to be installed, and representatives of the carpenters' union whose members are employed by both manufacturers and contractors.

It appears that the respondent manufacturers found their business seriously impeded by the competition of material made by nonunion mills located outside of Illinois—mostly in Wisconsin and the South—which sold their product in the Chicago market cheaper than local manufacturers who employed union labor could afford to do. Their operations were thus abridged and they did not employ so many carpenters as otherwise they could have done.

They wished to eliminate the competition of Wisconsin and other nonunion mills which were paying lower wages and consequently could undersell them. Obviously, it would tend to bring about the desired result if a general combination could be secured under which the manufacturers and contractors would employ only union carpenters with the understanding that the latter would refuse to install nonunion-made millwork. And we think there is evidence reasonably tending to show that such a combination was brought about, and that, as intended by all the parties, the so-called outside competition was cut down and thereby interstate commerce directly and materially impeded. The local manufacturers, relieved from the competition that came through interstate commerce, increased their output and profits; they gave special discounts to local contractors; more union carpenters secured employment in Chicago and their wages were increased. These were the incentives which brought about the combination. The nonunion mills outside of the city found their Chicago market greatly circumscribed or destroyed; the price of buildings was increased; and, as usual under such circumstances, the public paid excessive prices.

The allegations of the bill were sufficient to cover a combination like the one which some of the evidence tended to show. It is a matter of no consequence that the purpose was to shut out nonunion millwork made within Illinois as well as that made without. The crime of restraining interstate commerce through combination is not condoned by the inclusion of intrastate commerce as well. The applicable principles have been sufficiently indicated in *Montague & Co. v. Lowry*, 193 U.S. 38; *Loewe v. Lawlor*, 208 U.S. 274; *Eastern States Lumber Association v. United*

States, 234 U.S. 600, 612; *Coronado Coal Co. v. United Mine Workers,* 268 U.S. 295, 310.

To explore the record and pass upon all other assignments of error presented to the court below would require unreasonable consumption of our time. We may properly require its view in respect of them.

An order will be entered reversing the judgment of the Circuit Court of Appeals and remanding the cause to that court for further proceedings in harmony with this opinion.

Reversed.[1]

MR. JUSTICE STONE took no part in the consideration or decision of this cause.

BEDFORD CUT STONE CO. v. JOURNEYMEN STONE CUTTERS' ASSOCIATION.

Supreme Court of the United States. 274 U.S. 37 (1927).

MR. JUSTICE SUTHERLAND delivered the opinion of the Court.

Petitioners, Bedford Cut Stone Company and 23 others, all, with one or two exceptions, Indiana corporations, are in the business of quarrying or fabricating, or both quarrying and fabricating, Indiana limestone in what is called the Bedford-Bloomington District in the State of Indiana. Their combined investment is about $6,000,000, and their annual aggregate sales amount to about $15,000,000, more than 75% of which are made in interstate commerce to customers outside the State of Indiana. The Journeymen Stone Cutters' Association of North America, sometimes called and hereinafter referred to as the "General Union," is an association of mechanics engaged in the stone-cutting trade. It has a constitution, by-laws and officers, and an income derived from assessments upon its members. Its principal headquarters are in Indiana, and it has a membership of about 5,000 persons, divided into over 150 local unions located in various states and in Canada, each of such local unions having its own by-laws, officers, and income derived from like assessments. By virtue of his membership, each member of these local unions is a member of the General

---

[1] Accord: United States v. Painters' District Council No. 14, 44 Fed.(2d) 58 (N.D. Ill. 1930), aff'd in 284 U.S. 582 (1931); United States v. Painters' District Council No. 2, 13 Law & Labor, 67 (U.S.D.C.E.D. Mo. 1930); Boyle v. United States, 259 Fed. 803 (7th cir. 1919); Decorative Stone Co. v. Building Trades Council, 13 Fed.(2d) 123 (2nd cir. 1926), 18 Fed.(2d) 333 (S.D.N.Y. 1927), 23 Fed.(2d) 426 (2nd cir. 1928), *sub. nom.* Dextone Co. v. Building Trades Council, 60 Fed.(2d) 47 (2nd cir. 1932) (the full history of the case is detailed in 13 Law & Labor, 103 (1931). *Cf.* United States v. Bricklayers', Masons' & Plasterers' Internat'l Union, 4 Law & Labor, 95 (U.S.D.C.S.D. N.Y. 1922). See also: Report of Illinois Building Com. to Gov. Small and the Legislature (1923).

For further proceedings in the Brims case, see: Brims v. United States, 21 Fed. (2d) 889 (7th cir. 1927).

Union. The members of the General Union and allied locals throughout the United States are stone cutters, carvers, curb cutters, curb setters, bridge cutters, planermen, lathemen, and carborundum moulding machine operators, engaged in the cutting, patching and fabrication of all natural and artificial stones; and the General Union claims jurisdiction over all of them.

This suit was brought by petitioners against the General Union and some of its officers, and a number of affiliated local unions and some of their officers, to enjoin them from combining and conspiring together to commit, and from committing, various acts in restraint of interstate commerce in violation of the federal Anti-Trust Act, c. 647, 26 Stat. 209, and to petitioners' great and irreparable damage. The federal district court for the district of Indiana, after a hearing, refused a preliminary injunction and, subsequently, on final hearing, entered a decree dismissing the bill for want of equity. On appeal, this decree was affirmed by the court of appeals upon the authority of an earlier opinion in the same case. 9 F. (2d) 40.

The facts, so far as necessary to be stated, follow. Limestone produced by petitioners is quarried and fabricated largely for building construction purposes. The stone is first taken in rough blocks from the earth and, generally, then cut into appropriate sizes and sometimes planed. Part of this product is shipped directly to buildings, where it is fitted, trimmed and set in place, the remainder being sold in the rough to contractors to be fabricated. The stone sold in interstate commerce comes into competition with other kinds of natural and artificial stone. The principal producers of artificial stone are unionized and are located outside of Indiana. Before 1921, petitioners carried on their work in Indiana under written agreement with the General Union, but since that time they have operated under agreements with unaffiliated unions, with the effect of closing their shops and quarries against the members of the General Union and its locals. Prior to the filing of the bill of complaint, the General Union issued a notice to all its locals and members, directing its members not to work on stone "that has been started—planed, turned, cut, or semi-finished—by men working in opposition to our organization," and setting forth that a convention of the union had determined that "members were to rigidly enforce the rule to keep off all work started by men working in opposition to our organization, with the exception of the work of Shea-Donnelly, which firm holds an injunction against our association." Stone produced by petitioners by labor eligible to membership in respondents' unions was declared "unfair"; and the president of the General Union announced that the rule against handling such stone was to be promptly enforced in every part of the country. Most of the stone workers employed, outside the State of Indiana, on the buildings where petitioners' product is used, are members of the General Union; and in most of the industrial centers, building construction is on a closed shop union basis.

The rule requiring members to refrain from working on "unfair" stone was persistently adhered to and effectively enforced against petitioner's product, in a large number of cities and in many states. The evidence shows many instances of interference with the use of petitioners' stone by interstate customers, and expressions of apprehension on the part of such customers of labor troubles if they purchased the stone. The President of the General Union himself testified, in effect, that generally the men were living up to the order and if it were shown to him that they did not do so in any place he would see that they did. Members found working on petitioners' product, were ordered to stop and threatened with a revocation of their cards if they continued; and the order of the General Union seems to have been enforced even when it might be against the desire of the local union. The transcript contains the record of a hearing upon these matters before the Colorado Industrial Commission, from which it appears that in obedience to the order of the General Union its members theretofore employed in Denver upon local building stopped work because petitioners' product was being used. The local contractor was notified merely that the men stopped work because the stone being used was "unfair." The contractor personally had no trouble of any kind with the union, and no other reason for the strike than that stated above existed. B. F. James, a member and an acting officer of the General Union testified that the local union in conducting its strike against a local builder had no choice in the matter; that they had their orders from the General Union with which they complied; that there was no difference or feeling whatever between the union and the local employer; that the fight was with the Bedford stone producers and they were trying to affect them through the local employer.

"Q. And you people have no choice in the matter, you are just complying with orders from the International [General Union]?

"A. We have no choice whatever.

"Q. Probably, if it was left up to you people here, knowing this employer as you do, why, your organization here, local organization, would not strike on this man?

"A. I don't believe we would, no.

"Q. But you have got to follow the orders of your International organization?

"A. Yes, sir."

The evidence makes plain that neither the General Union nor the locals had any grievance against any of the builders—local purchasers of the stone—or any other local grievance; and that the strikes were ordered and conducted for the sole purpose of preventing the use and, consequently, the sale and shipment in interstate commerce, of petitioners' product, in order, by threatening the loss or serious curtailment of their interstate market, to force petitioners to the alternative of coming to undesired terms with the members of these unions. In 1924, the president of the General Union said:

"The natural stone industry needs all the natural advantages it can possibly get, as there are so many kinds of substitutes to take the natural stone's place in the building material market, that it behooves the natural stone employers to do their utmost to see that no handicap is in its way, and it is a well known fact that when any material is known to have labor grievances, it retards that material in the building market, as the building public do not want the stigma on their building that it was built by 'unfair labor,' and they are also afraid of stoppage of work and unnecessary disputes while their building is in course of construction, and no one can blame them for that."

In the Colorado inquiry, the witness James further testified that the strike order did not make any allowance for stone theretofore ordered. "We were trying to affect the Bedford people through the local man."

"Q. So the only person injured would be your own local man, who is your employer, and your personal friend, is that it?

"A. In a way. If it was finished that way, he would be the only one hurt. We are not fighting on this Denver man. We are trying to force these people through the other subcontractors all over the country. * * *

"Q. You are trying to force the Bedford to employ members of your union to do this work?

"A. Yes, sir.

"Q. And irrespective of who it hurts, that is the object?

"A. That is the object. It is done from our headquarters.

"Q. Mr. Fernald, or anybody else, they have got to get out of the road, that is the object?

"A. We are trying to gain this point, irrespective of who it hurts."

From a consideration of all the evidence, it is apparent that the enforcement of the general order to strike against petitioners' product could have had no purpose other than that of coercing or inducing the local employers to refrain from purchasing such product. To accept the assertion made here to the contrary, would be to say that the order and the effort to enforce it were vain and idle things without any rational purpose whatsoever. And indeed, on the argument, in answer to a question from the bench, counsel for respondents very frankly said that, unless petitioners' interstate trade in the so-called unfair stone were injuriously affected, the strikes would accomplish nothing.

That the means adopted to bring about the contemplated restraint of commerce operated after physical transportation had ended is immaterial. *Loewe v. Lawlor,* 208 U.S. 274, 301; *Boyle v. United States,* 259 Fed. 803, 805-806. The product against which the strikes were directed, it is true, had come to rest in the respective localities to which it had been shipped, so that it had ceased to be a subject of interstate commerce, *Industrial Assn. v. United States,* 268 U.S. 65, 78-79; and interferences for a purely local object with its use, with no intention, express or implied, to restrain interstate commerce, it may be assumed, would not have been violation of the Anti-Trust Act. *Id.*, p. 77; *United Mine Workers v. Coronado Co.*, 259 U.S. 344, 410-411. But these interferences were not thus in pursuit of a local motive,—they had for their primary aim restraint of the interstate sale and shipment of the commodity. Interstate commerce was the direct object of attack "for the sake of which the several specific acts and courses of conduct [were] done and adopted." And the restraint of such commerce was the necessary consequence of the acts and conduct and the immediate end in view. *Swift & Co. v. United States*, 196 U.S. 375, 397. Prevention of the use of petitioners' product, which, without more, might have been a purely local matter, therefore, was only a part of the conspiracy, which must be construed as an entirety; and, when so regarded, the local transactions become a part of the general plan and purpose to destroy or narrow petitioners' interstate trade. *Montague & Co. v. Lowry*, 193 U.S. 38, 45-46. In other words, strikes against the local use of the product were simply the means adopted to effect the unlawful restraint. And it is this result, not the means devised to secure it, which gives character to the conspiracy.

Respondents' chief contention is that "their sole and only purpose * * * was to unionize the cutters and carvers of stone at the quarries." And it may be conceded that this was the ultimate end in view. But how was that end to be effected? The evidence shows indubitably that it was by an attack upon the use of the product in other states to which it had been and was being shipped, with the intent and purpose of bringing about the loss or serious reduction of petitioners' interstate business, and thereby forcing compliance with the demands of the unions. And, since these strikes were directed against the use of petitioners' product in other states, with the plain design of suppressing or narrowing the interstate market, it is no answer to say that the ultimate object to be accomplished was to bring about a change of conduct on the part of petitioners in respect of the employment of union members in Indiana. A restraint of interstate commerce cannot be justified by the fact that the ultimate object of the participants was to secure an ulterior benefit which they might have been at liberty to pursue by means not involving such restraint. *Anderson v. Shipowners Association*, 272 U.S. 359; *Duplex Co. v. Deering*, 254 U.S. 443, 468; *Ellis v. Inman, Poulsen & Co.*, 131 Fed. 182, 186.

The case, therefore, is controlled, not by *United Mine Workers v. Coronado Co., supra*, and *United Leather Workers v. Herkert*, 265 U.S. 457, as respondents contend, but by others presently to be discussed. * * *

With a few changes in respect of the product involved, dates, names and incidents, which would have no effect upon the principles established, the opinion in *Duplex Co. v. Deering, supra,* might serve as an opinion in this case. The object of the boycott there was precisely the same as it is here, and the interferences with interstate commerce, while they were more numerous and more drastic, did not differ in essential character from the interferences here. A short statement of the case will make this clear. * * *[1]

In cases arising outside the Anti-Trust Act, involving strikes like those here under review against so-called unfair products, there is a sharp conflict of opinion. On the one hand, it is said that such a strike is justified on the ground of self-interest; that the injury to the producer is inflicted, not maliciously, but in self-defense; that the refusal of the producer to deal with the union and to observe its standards threatens the interest of all its members and the members of the affiliated locals; and that a strike against the unfair material is a mere recognition of this unity of interest, and in refusing to work on such material the union is only refusing to aid in its own destruction. The opposite view is illustrated by such cases as *Toledo, etc., Ry. Co. v. Pennsylvania Co.*, 54 Fed. 730; *Thomas v. Cincinnati, etc., Ry. Co.*, 62 Fed. 803, 817, *et seq.; Moores v. Bricklayers' Union*, 23 Wkly. Cin. Law Bull. 48 (affirmed by the Supreme Court of Ohio without opinion); *Burnham v. Dowd*, 217 Mass. 351; *Purvis v. United Brotherhood*, 214 Pa. St. 348; *Booth & Brother v. Burgess*, 72 N.J. Eq. 181, 188, 196; *Piano & Organ Workers v. P. & O. Supply Co.*, 124 Ill. App. 353.

But with this conflict we have no concern in the present case. The question which it involves was presented and considered in the *Duplex Co. Case, supra,* as the prevailing and the dissenting opinions show; and there it was plainly held that the point had no bearing upon the enforcement of the Anti-Trust Act, and that since complainant had a clear right to an injunction under that Act as amended by the Clayton Act, it was "unnecessary to consider whether a like result would follow under the common law or local statutes."

Whatever may be said as to the motives of the respondents or their general right to combine for the purpose of redressing alleged grievances of their fellow craftsmen or of protecting themselves or their organizations, the present combination deliberately adopted a course of conduct which directly and substantially curtailed, or threatened thus to curtail, the natural flow in interstate commerce of a very large proportion of the building limestone production of the entire country, to the gravely probable disadvantage of producers, purchasers and the public; and it must be held to be a combination in undue and unreasonable restraint of such commerce within the meaning of the Anti-Trust Act as interpreted by this court. An act which lawfully might be done by one, may when done by many acting in concert take on the form of a conspiracy and become a public wrong, and may be prohibited if the result be hurtful to the public or to individuals against whom such concerted action is directed, *Grenada Lumber Co. v. Mississippi*, 217 U.S. 433, 440; and any

---

[1] After stating the facts of the Duplex case, the court also quoted from the opinions in Loewe v. Lawlor, 208 U.S. 274 (1908), United States v. Brims, 272 U.S. 549 (1926), and Gompers v. Bucks Stove & Range Co., 221 U.S. 418 (1911), in support of its position.—Ed.

suggestion that such concerted action here may be justified as a necessary defensive measure is completely answered by the words of this court in *Eastern States Lumber Ass'n v. United States,* 234 U.S. 600, 613, that "Congress, with the right to control the field of interstate commerce, has so legislated as to prevent resort to practices which unduly restrain competition or unduly obstruct the free flow of such commerce, and private choice of means must yield to the national authority thus exerted."

The record does not disclose whether petitioners at the time of bringing suit had suffered actual injury; but that is not material. An intent to restrain interstate commerce being shown, it is enough to justify equitable interposition by injunction if there be a dangerous probability that such injury will happen; and this clearly appears. The Anti-Trust Act "directs itself against that dangerous probability as well as against the completed result." *Swift & Co. v. United States, supra,* p. 396; *Vicksburg Waterworks Co. v. Vicksburg,* 185 U.S. 65, 82; *Thomson Machine Co. v. Brown,* 89 N.J. Eq. 326, 328.

From the foregoing review, it is manifest that the acts and conduct of respondents fall within the terms of the Anti-Trust Act; and petitioners are entitled to relief by injunction under § 16 of the Clayton Act, c. 323, 38 Stat. 730, 737, by which they are authorized to sue for such relief "against threatened loss or damage by a violation of the anti-trust laws," etc. The strikes, ordered and carried out with the sole object of preventing the use and installation of petitioners' product in other states, necessarily threatened to destroy or narrow petitioners' interstate trade by taking from them their customers. That the organizations, in general purpose and in and of themselves, were lawful and that the ultimate result aimed at may not have been illegal in itself, are beside the point. Where the means adopted are unlawful, the innocent general character of the organizations adopting them or the lawfulness of the ultimate end sought to be attained, cannot serve as a justification.

Decree reversed.

MR. JUSTICE SANFORD, concurring.

I concur in this result upon the controlling authority of *Duplex Company v. Deering,* 254 U.S. 443, 478, which, as applied to the ultimate question in this case, I am unable to distinguish.

The separate opinion of MR. JUSTICE STONE.

As an original proposition, I should have doubted whether the Sherman Act prohibited a labor union from peaceably refusing to work upon material produced by non-union labor or by a rival union, even though interstate commerce were affected. In the light of the policy adopted by Congress in the Clayton Act, with respect to organized labor, and in the light of *Standard Oil Co. v. United States,* 221 U.S. 1; *United States v. American Tobacco Co.,* 221 U.S. 106, 178-180, I should not have thought that such action as is now complained of was to be regarded as an unreasonable and therefore prohibited restraint of trade. But in *Duplex Printing Press Co. v. Deering,* 254 U.S. 443, these views were rejected by a majority of the court and a decree was authorized restraining in precise terms any agreement not to work or refusal to work, such as is involved here. Whatever additional facts there may have been in that case, the decree enjoined the defendants from using "even persuasion with the object or having the effect of causing any person or persons to decline employment, cease employment, or not seek employment, or to refrain from work or cease working under any person, firm, or corporation being a purchaser or prospective purchaser of any printing press or presses from complainant, * * *" (p. 478). These views, which I should not have hesitated to apply here, have now been rejected again largely on the authority of the *Duplex Case*. For that reason alone, I concur with the majority.

MR. JUSTICE BRANDEIS, dissenting.

The constitution of the Journeymen Stone Cutters' Association provides: "No member of this Association shall cut, carve or fit any material that has been cut by men working in opposition to this Association." For many years, the plaintiffs had contracts with the Association under which its members were employed at their several quarries and works. In 1921, the plaintiffs refused to renew the contracts because certain rules or conditions proposed by the Journeymen were unacceptable. Then came a strike. It was followed by a lockout, the organization by the plaintiffs of a so-called independent union, and the establishment of it at their plants. Repeated efforts to adjust the controversy proved futile. Finally, the Association urged its members working on buildings in other States to observe the above provision of its constitution. Its position was "that if employers will not employ our members in one place, we will decline to work for them in another, or to finish any work that has been started or partly completed by men these employers are using to combat our organization."

The trial court dismissed the bill. The United States Circuit Court of Appeals affirming the decree said:

"After long negotiations and failure to reach a new working agreement, the union officers ordered that none of its members should further cut stone which had been partly cut by non-union labor, with the result that on certain jobs in different states stone cutters, who were members of the union, declined to do further cutting upon such stone. Where, as in some cases, there were few or no local stone cutters except such as belonged to the union, the completion of the buildings was more or less hindered by the order, the manifest object of which was to induce appellants to make a contract with the union for employment of only union stonecutters in the Indiana limestone district. It does not appear that the quarrying of stone, or sawing it into blocks, or the transportation of it, or setting it in buildings, or any other building operation, was sought to be interfered with, and no actual or threatened violence appears, no picketing, no boycott, and nothing of that character."

If, in the struggle for existence, individual workingmen may, under any circumstances, co-operate in this way for self-protection even though the interstate trade of another is thereby restrained, the lower courts were clearly right in denying the injunction sought by plaintiffs. I have no occasion to consider whether the restraint, which was applied wholly intrastate, became in its operation a direct restraint upon interstate commerce. For it has long been settled that only unreasonable restraints are prohibited by the Sherman Law.[2] *Standard Oil Co. v. United States,* 221 U.S. 1, 56-58; *United States v. American Tobacco Co.,* 221 U.S. 106, 178-180; *Chicago Board of Trade v. United States,* 246 U.S. 231, 238; *United States v. Trenton Potteries Co.,* 273 U.S. 392, 396. Compare *United States v. Terminal Ass'n,* 224 U.S. 383; *United States v. Reading Co.,* 226 U.S. 324, 369. And the restraint imposed was, in my opinion, a reasonable one. The Act does not establish the standard of reasonableness. What is reasonable must be determined by the application of principles of the common law, as administered in federal courts unaffected by state legislation or decisions. Compare *Duplex Printing Co. v. Deering,* 254 U.S. 443, 466. Tested by these principles, the propriety of the unions' conduct can hardly be doubted by one who believes in the organization of labor.

Neither the individual stonecutters nor the unions had any contract with any of the plaintiffs or with any of their customers. So far as concerned the plaintiffs and their customers, the individual stonecutters were free either to work or to abstain from working on stone which had been cut at the quarries by members of the employers' union. So far as concerned the Association, the individual stonecutter was not free. He had agreed, when he became a member, that he would not work on stone "cut by men working in opposition to" the Association. It was in duty bound to urge upon its members observance of the obligation assumed. These cut stone companies, who alone are seeking relief, were its declared enemies. They were seeking to destroy it. And the danger was great.

The plaintiffs are not weak employers opposed by a mighty union. They have large financial resources. Together, they ship 70 per cent. of all the cut stone in the country. They are not isolated concerns. They had combined in a local employers' organization. And their organization is affiliated with the national employers' organization, called "International Cut Stone & Quarrymen's Association." Standing alone, each of the 150 Journeymen's locals is weak. The average number of members in a local union is only 33. The locals are widely scattered throughout the country. Strong employers could destroy a local "by importing scabs" from other cities. And many of the builders by whom the stonecutters were employed in different cities, are strong. It is only through combining the 5,000 organized stonecutters in a national union, and developing loyalty to it, that the individual stonecutter anywhere can protect his own job.

---

[2] The contrary view was unsuccessfully contended for by Mr. Justice Harlan, dissenting, in Standard Oil Co. v. United States, 221 U.S. 1, 85-100.

The manner in which these individual stonecutters exercised their asserted right to perform their union duty by refusing to finish stone "cut by men working in opposition to" the Association was confessedly legal. They were innocent alike of trespass and of breach of contract. They did not picket. They refrained from violence, intimidation, fraud and threats. They refrained from obstructing otherwise either the plaintiffs or their customers in attempts to secure other help. They did not plan a boycott against any of the plaintiffs or against builders who used the plaintiffs' product. On the contrary, they expressed entire willingness to cut and finish anywhere any stone quarried by any of the plaintiffs, except such stone as had been partially "cut by men working in opposition to" the Association. A large part of the plaintiffs' product consisting of blocks, slabs and sawed work was not affected by the order of the union officials. The individual stonecutter was thus clearly innocent of wrongdoing, unless it was illegal for him to agree with his fellow craftsmen to refrain from working on the "scab"-cut stone because it was an article of interstate commerce.

The manner in which the Journeymen's unions acted was also clearly legal. The combination complained of is the co-operation of persons wholly of the same craft, united in a national union, solely for self-protection. No outsider—be he quarrier, dealer, builder or laborer—was a party to the combination. No purpose was to be subserved except to promote the trade interests of members of the Journeymen's Association. There was no attempt by the unions to boycott the plaintiffs. There was no attempt to seek the aid of members of any other craft, by a sympathetic strike or otherwise. The contest was not a class struggle. It was a struggle between particular employers and their employees. But the controversy out of which it arose, related, not to specific grievances, but to fundamental matters of union policy of general application throughout the country. The national Association had the duty to determine, so far as its members were concerned, what that policy should be. It deemed the maintenance of that policy a matter of vital interest to each member of the union. The duty rested upon it to enforce its policy by all legitimate means. The Association, its locals and officers were clearly innocent of wrongdoing, unless Congress has declared that for union officials to urge members to refrain from working on stone "cut by men working in opposition" to it is necessarily illegal if thereby the interstate trade of another is restrained.

The contention that earlier decisions of this Court compel the conclusion that it is illegal seems to me unfounded. The cases may support the claim that, by such local abstention from work, interstate trade is restrained. But examination of the facts in those cases makes clear that they have no tendency whatsoever to establish that the restraint imposed by the unions in the case at bar is unreasonable. The difference between the simple refraining from work practiced here, and the conduct held unreasonable in *Duplex Printing Press Co. v. Deering*, 254 U.S. 443, appears from a recital in that opinion of the defendants' acts:

"The acts embraced the following, with others: warning customers that it would be better for them not to purchase, or having purchased not to install, presses made by complainant, and threatening them with loss should they do so; threatening customers with sympathetic strikes in other trades; notifying a trucking company usually employed by customers to haul the presses not to do so, and threatening it with trouble if it should; inciting employees of the trucking company, and other men employed by customers of complainant, to strike against their respective employers in order to interfere with the hauling and installation of presses, and thus bring pressure to bear upon the customers; notifying repair shops not to do repair work on Duplex presses; coercing union men by threatening them with loss of union cards and with being blacklisted as 'scabs' if they assisted in installing the presses; threatening an exposition company with a strike if it permitted complainant's presses to be exhibited; and resorting to a variety of other modes of preventing the sale of presses of complainant's manufacture in or about New York City, and delivery of them in interstate commerce, such as injuring and threatening to injure complainant's customers and prospective customers, and persons concerned in hauling, handling, or installing the presses." (pp. 463-4.)

The character of the acts held in *Duplex Printing Press Co. v. Deering* to constitute unreasonable restraint is further shown by the scope of the injunction there prescribed. * * *

The difference between the facts here involved and those in the *Duplex Case* does not lie only in the character of the acts complained of. It lies also in the occasion and purpose of the action taken and in the scope of the combination. The combination there condemned was not, as here, the co-operation for self-protection only of men in a single craft. It was an effort to win by invoking the aid of others, both organized and unorganized, not concerned in the trade dispute. The conduct there condemned was not, as here, a mere refusal to finish particular work begun "by men working in opposition to" the union. It was the institution of a general boycott, not only of the business of the employer, but of the businesses of all who should participate in the marketing, installation or exhibition of its product. The conduct there condemned was not, as here, action taken for self-protection against an opposing union installed by employers to destroy the regular union with which they long had had contracts. The action in the *Duplex Case* was taken in an effort to unionize an open shop. Moreover, there the combination of defendants was aggressive action directed against an isolated employer. Here it is defensive action of workingmen directed against a combination of employers. The serious question on which the Court divided in the *Duplex Case* was not whether the restraint imposed was reasonable. It was whether the Clayton Act had forbidden federal courts to issue an injunction in that class of cases. See p. 464.

In *Loewe v. Lawlor,* 208 U.S. 274; *Gompers v. Bucks Stove Co.,* 221 U.S. 418; and *Lawlor v. Loewe,* 235 U.S. 522, the conduct held unreasonable was not, as here, a refusal to finish a product partly made by members of an opposing union. It was invoking the power of the consumer as a weapon of offensive warfare. There, a general boycott was declared of the manufacturer's product. And the boycott was extended to the businesses of both wholesalers and retailers who might aid in the marketing of the manufacturer's product. Moreover, the boycott was to be effected, not by the co-operation merely of the few members of the craft directly and vitally interested in the trade-dispute, but by the aid of the vast forces of organized labor affiliated with them through the American Federation of Labor.

In *United States v. Brims,* 272 U.S. 549, the combination complained of was not the co-operation merely of workingmen of the same craft. It was a combination of manufacturers of millwork in Chicago, with building contractors who cause such work to be installed, and the unions whose members are to be employed. Moreover the purpose of the combination was not primarily to further the interests of the union carpenters. The immediate purpose was to suppress competition with the Chicago manufacturers. * * *

In *United Mine Workers v. Coronado Co.,* 259 U.S. 344; 268 U.S. 295; *United Leather Workers v. Herkert,* 265 U.S. 457; *Industrial Association v. United States,* 268 U.S. 64, as in *Hopkins v. United States,* 171 U.S. 578; *Anderson v. United States,* 171 U.S. 604; *Montague v. Lowry,* 193 U.S. 38, and *Swift & Co. v. United States,* 196 U.S. 375, the questions put in issue were not the reasonableness of the restraint, but whether the restraint was of interstate commerce.

Members of the Journeymen Stone Cutters' Association could not work anywhere on stone which had been cut at the quarries by "men working in opposition" to it, without aiding and abetting the enemy. Observance by each member of the provision of their constitution which forbids such action was essential to his own self-protection. It was demanded of each by loyalty to the organization and to his fellows. If, on the undisputed facts of this case, refusal to work can be enjoined, Congress created by the Sherman Law and the Clayton Act an instrument for imposing restraints upon labor which reminds of involuntary servitude. The Sherman Law was held in *United States v. United States Steel Corporation,* 251 U.S. 417, to permit capitalists to combine in a single corporation 50 per cent. of the steel industry of the United States dominating the trade through its vast resources. The Sherman Law was held in *United States v. United Shoe Machinery Co.,* 247 U.S. 32, to permit capitalists to combine in another corporation practically the whole shoe machinery industry of the country, necessarily giving it a position of dominance over shoe-manufacturing in America. It would, indeed, be strange if Congress had by the same Act willed to deny to members of a small craft of workingmen the right to co-operate in simply refraining from work, when that course was the only means of self-protection against a combination of militant and powerful employers. I cannot believe that Congress did so.

MR. JUSTICE HOLMES concurs in this opinion.[3]

AEOLIAN COMPANY v. FISCHER.

United States District Court for the Southern District of New York.
35 Fed.(2d) 34 (1929).

In Equity. Suit by the Æolian Company and other organ makers against Jacob Fischer, individually and as president of the Piano, Organ & Musical Instruments Workers' International Union of America and others, to enjoin defendant labor unions and persons associated with them from interfering with plaintiffs' business and good will, which now comes up for further consideration after trial of the issues upon final hearing.

For opinions in this court and in the Circuit Court of Appeals upon denial of the motion for preliminary injunction, see 29 F.(2d) 679, and 27 F.(2d) 560, where full statements of the nature of the controversy will be found.[1]

Jurisdiction is predicated both upon the ground of diversity of citizenship and upon the claim that defendants are engaged in a conspiracy in restraint of interstate trade and commerce, in violation of the Sherman Anti-Trust Act (26 Stat. 209 [15 U.S.C.A. § 1 *et seq.*]). * * *

THACHER, D.J. (after stating the facts as above): It is entirely clear from the proofs upon final hearing, as it was upon motion for a preliminary injunction, that the defendants did not conspire to exclude plaintiffs' organs from interstate trade or commerce, but only to coerce the employment of union organ workers by persuading members of other crafts to refuse to work in or upon the same building with plaintiffs' nonunion organ workers. In the Circuit Court of Appeals [29 Fed.(2d) 679, 680], it was said

---

[3] For the decree entered by the district court in accordance with the judgment of the Supreme Court, see: 9 Law & Labor, 297 (1927). Accord: Shea & Donnelly Co. v. Lambert, 3 Law & Labor, 33 (U.S.D.C.E.D. Mo. 1922).

For comment on the case, see: Powell, "The Supreme Court's Control over the Issue of Injunctions in Labor Disputes," 13 Proc. Acad. Pol. Sci. 37, 59-62 (1928); Royce, "Labor, the Federal Anti-Trust Laws, and the Supreme Court," 5 N.Y. Univ. Law Rev. 19 (1928); Witte, "The Journeymen Stone Cutters Decision," 17 Am. Lab. Leg. Rev. 139 (1927); 40 Harv. Law Rev. 1154 (1927); 26 Mich. Law Rev. 198 (1927); 1 St. Johns Law Rev. 189 (1927); Univ. Cinn. Law Rev. 497 (1927); 14 Va. Law Rev. 112 (1927); 4 Wis. Law Rev. 250 (1927); 37 Yale Law Jour. 84 (1927).

See also: Barnett, "Stone Cutters and the Stone Planer," 24 Jour. Pol. Econ. 417 (1909); Cummings, "Political and Social Philosophy of the Carpenters Union," 42 Pol. Sci. Quar. 397 (1927).

[1] A full statement of the nature of the controversy will be found in the second opinion of the Circuit Court of Appeals, *infra.*—Ed.

that the indirect result of this might be to impede the sale of plaintiffs' organs within this territory, but that such indirect interference with interstate commerce is not within the prohibition of the Anti-Trust Act, and in support of this statement *Industrial Ass'n v. United States,* 268 U.S. 64, 77, 45 S. Ct. 403, 69 L. Ed. 849, and *United Mine Workers v. Coronado Co.,* 259 U.S. 344, 411, 42 S. Ct. 570, 66 L. Ed. 975, 27 A.L.R. 762, were cited. But the court added: "Therefore the appellants must establish, if they would show themselves entitled to an injunction under the Federal Statutes, that the work of setting up their organs in New York or New Jersey—such work being what the defendants seek to monopolize—is itself interstate commerce because part of the interstate commerce involved in sending the organ from another state."

This question is quite clearly answered by the proofs upon final hearing, from which it appears that all of the plaintiffs, with one exception, maintain organ factories outside of this state and in the conduct of their business enter into contracts for the sale and installation of organs in buildings within the state. All of the essential parts of the organ are made in the factory, with the exception of the flues leading from the air pump to the air box or chamber. Some of the parts are temporarily assembled before shipment and are tested in the factory. But shipment is then made of the separate parts, to be installed in the premises of the purchaser. The agreement of the organ manufacturer to install is not only relevant and appropriate to the interstate sale, but is essential if an organ, as distinguished from its parts, may be sold at all. The thing sold is a musical instrument, complete in itself. The unassembled pipes, wind box, motor, console, flues, and intricate wiring cables which are shipped from the factory, are not the subject-matter of the sale, and the sale is not completed until all these parts have been installed with proper relation to one another and many intricate electrical connections have been made and adjusted so that the whole will function as a delicately tuned musical instrument. Without descending to mechanical description, it may be said that the work of installation is of the most vital importance in the construction of the completed organ, and requires in its performance not only the highest mechanical skill, but a thorough understanding of the method employed by the manufacturer in the arrangement of mechanical and electrical connections. It is more than appropriate that the manufacturer undertake this work. Without doubt he must do so if he wishes to dispose of his product at all. In order to do so, the plaintiffs maintain local organizations of skilled workmen who are engaged in the work of installation. The facts presented upon final hearing remove the necessity of drawing fine distinctions between the lightning rod, signal switch, and bridge construction cases, on the one hand, and the picture frame and ice machine cases on the other, which are cited in the opinion of the Circuit Court of Appeals. Whatever distinctions may be drawn in doubtful cases, it is clear that the instant case is governed and controlled by the decision in the ice machine case. *York Mfg. Co. v. Colley,* 247 U.S. 21, 38 S. Ct. 430, 62 L. Ed. 963, 11 A.L.R. 611. The distinction there drawn between the setting up of lightning rods (*Browning v. Waycross,* 233 U.S. 16, 34 S. Ct. 578, 58 L. Ed. 828) and the installation of an ice machine shows that the contracts here in question for the construction and installation of organs clearly involve interstate commerce not only in the manufacture and shipment of the organ, but in its installation after arrival within the state.

But from this conclusion it does not necessarily follow that the defendant unions, desirous of procuring for the union organ workers all of the local work of installation, may not consistently with federal statutes combine, and in combination refuse to work in and upon buildings where such work is performed by nonunion organ workers. In the pursuit of this local object it is true that defendants have interfered with plaintiffs' performance of contracts involving interstate commerce, but not more directly than would the strike of its factory employees accompanied by illegal picketing and intimidation intended to prevent others from taking up their work in connection with the manufacture of the same organs. Such a combination would not violate the federal statute because its effect upon interstate commerce would be indirect and incidental to the purely local purpose, by group action, to prevent the employment of nonunion labor in the manufacture of goods under contracts for delivery in interstate commerce. *United Leather Workers v. Herkert & Meisel Trunk Co.,* 265 U.S. 457, 44 S.Ct. 623, 68 L. Ed. 1104, 33 A.L.R. 566. The decisive fact being the character of the restraint imposed, no basis for decision can be found in distinctions drawn between the local work of manufacture, in the state of origin, and the local work of installation in the state of destination. The installation of the organ is quite as essentially local as building, manufacturing, mining, or growing crops. *Industrial Ass'n v. United States,* 268 U.S. 64, 82, 45 S. Ct. 403, 69 L. Ed. 849. The purpose with which men refuse to work or persuade others to do so must therefore control decision. If the purpose be to add strength to their union merely by refusing and persuading others to refuse to work with nonunion men, the restraint upon the performance of contracts involving interstate commerce is incidental and indirect, and this is quite as truly the effect whether their employment is the preparation of goods for interstate shipment or the installation of machinery after shipment is completed. The rule defining illegal combinations of workmen employed in each of these tasks, when judged from the standpoint of commercial restraint, must be the same. *Industrial Ass'n v. United States, supra.* In the latter case it was said (268 U.S. 82, 45 S. Ct. 407):

"If an executed agreement to strike, with the object and effect of closing down a mine or a factory, by preventing the employment of necessary workmen, the indirect result of which is that the sale and shipment of goods and products in interstate commerce is prevented or diminished, is not an unlawful restraint of such commerce, it cannot consistently be held otherwise in respect of an agreement and combination of employers or others to frustrate a strike and defeat the strikers by keeping essential domestic building materials out of their hands and the hands of their sympathizers, because the means employed, whether lawful or unlawful, produce a like indirect result. The alleged conspiracy and the acts here complained of, spent their intended and direct force upon a local situation—for building is as essentially local as mining, manufacturing or growing crops —and if, by a resulting diminution of the commercial demand, interstate trade was curtailed either generally or in specific instances, that was a fortuitous consequence so remote and indirect as plainly to cause it to fall outside the reach of the Sherman Act."

The vital difference under the Sherman Act "between a direct, substantial, and intentional interference with interstate commerce and an interference which is incidental, indirect, remote, and outside the purposes of those causing it," was said in that case to be clearly illustrated by the decisions in *United Mine Workers v. Coronado Co.*, 259 U.S. 344, 42 S. Ct. 570, 66 L. Ed. 975, 27 A.L.R. 762, *United Leather Workers v. Herkert & Meisel Trunk Co., supra,* and *Industrial Ass'n v. United States, supra,* on the one hand, and *Loewe v. Lawlor,* 208 U.S. 274, 28 S. Ct. 301, 52 L. Ed. 488, 13 Ann. Cas. 815, and *Duplex Co. v. Deering,* 254 U.S. 443, 41 S. Ct. 172, 65 L. Ed. 349, 16 A.L.R. 196, on the other. See, also, *Bedford Co. v. Stone Cutters' Ass'n,* 274 U.S. 37, 47 S. Ct. 522, 71 L. Ed. 916, 54 A.L.R. 791. But in the latter cases "the object of the labor organizations was sought to be attained by a country-wide boycott of the employer's goods for the direct purpose of preventing their sale and transportation in interstate commerce in order to force a compliance with their demands."

The distinction thus so sharply drawn in *Industrial Ass'n v. United States,* and so clearly applied in the *United Leather Workers'* case, is controlling here, and I am constrained to conclude that the collective refusal of local workmen to work either upon or in the same building where nonunion workmen are employed in the installation of plaintiffs' organs was at most an incidental, indirect, remote restraint upon interstate commerce, which was entirely outside of the purposes sought to be accomplished; *i. e.,* the local employment of union labor in such work.

Basing federal jurisdiction upon diversity of citizenship, plaintiffs claim that they are entitled to relief under state law. As stated upon denial of the motion for preliminary injunction [27 Fed. (2d) 560], decision turns upon whether the defendants and those who co-operated with them were justified in what they did by honest motives to advance self-interest, or were moved by malicious intent to injure the business and good will of the plaintiffs. *Exchange Bakery & Restaurant, Inc., v. Rifkin,* 245 N.Y. 260, 157 N.E. 130; *Interborough Rapid Transit Co. v. Lavin,* 247 N.Y. 65, 159 N.E. 863; *Nat'l Fireproofing Co. v. Mason Builders' Ass'n,* 169 Fed. 259, 26 L.R.A. (N.S.) 148 (C.C.A. 2d). Refusal by the members of a craft to work, either upon nonunion products or with nonunion men, in order to procure for themselves or for those associated with them in the same craft all work in which the craft is engaged, is not actionable if injury results to the employer of nonunion men. *Bossert v. Dhuy,* 221 N.Y. 342, 117 N.E. 582, Ann. Cas. 1918D, 661; *Nat'l Protective Ass'n v. Cumming,* 170 N.Y. 315, 63 N.E. 369, 58 L.R.A. 135, 88 Am. St. Rep. 648; *Paine Lumber Co. v. Neal,* 244 U.S. 459, 471, 37 S. Ct. 718, 61 L. Ed. 1256; *Gill Engraving Co. v. Doerr* (D.C.) 214 Fed. 111. In *Duplex Co. v. Deering,* 254 U.S. 443, 41 S. Ct. 172, 65 L. Ed. 349, 16 A.L.R. 196, the majority of the court gave no consideration to the common law, but, in a dissenting opinion by Brandeis, J., in which two members of the court concurred, the modern development of the common law on this subject was carefully considered. From this consideration of the law it will be seen that the conception of self-interest sufficient to justify group action in refusing to work has expanded with the growth of organized industry in recognition of changing conditions which have warranted the extension of justifiable collective action by organized labor groups in refusing to work under conditions prejudicial to the interests of the group. Nor are the efforts of the group illegal when extended beyond the employment of its members to conditions affecting the employment of others in the same trade or business. *Exchange Bakery & Restaurant, Inc. v. Rifkin, supra.* In the case at bar it cannot be said that the members of the allied crafts who refused to work on the construction of buildings or in theaters where plaintiffs' nonunion men were at work were not influenced by justifiable self-interest in their collective action. If it be lawful, as seems to be plainly implied in the *Bakery* Case, to attempt to unionize, by collective refusal to work, the various trades engaged in a large industrial plant and in all plants in the same industry, there can hardly be objection to similar efforts to unionize all the trades at work on a building in course of construction or in a theater. The employees of different contractors engaged in work on the same building, although belonging to different crafts, have many interests in common arising in connection with the prosecution of the work and the conditions of employment under which it is to be performed, and union men may well refuse to work side by side with nonunion men who are not in sympathy with the aims and purposes of their organization. The situation is much the same in a theater or on any other premises where the presence of nonunion men may properly be regarded as a condition of employment unsatisfactory to the members of a union. Such situations are plainly distinguishable from conditions approaching a general strike, carried on by persons not united by any common interest, as in *Auburn Draying Co. v. Wardell,* 227 N.Y. 1, 124 N.E. 97, 100, 6 A.L.R. 901. What was condemned in that case was a combination by fear and coercion to compel third persons to refrain from having any business relations with the plaintiff. What the plaintiff's actual and prospective customers feared was not any voluntary self-initiated movement of their own employees to quit, but that they would quit contrary to their own desires and only because they were ordered to do so, and the court was careful to state that the contest did not arise in the ordinary and natural exercise by the unions of the right to control their own labor and of the right of association. Thus the decision in that case comes to this:

That, where defendants induce men to quit work by compulsion and coercion, contrary to their own desires and interests, and by threat of such compulsion induce their employers to withdraw their patronage from another, the consequent injury to that other's business is actionable and may be enjoined. No limitation upon the right of association was intended. Indeed, any such limitation was disclaimed, for it was said:

"The rights, in virtue of which the defendants would justify the interference and the injury, are: (a) That of laborers to associate; (b) to bring within the labor organizations as members all laborers; (c) through the coherent and solidified power and influence flowing from association and united efforts to secure for all laborers higher wages, shorter hours, arbitration of labor disputes, and better working conditions. Beyond question those rights exist. Labor unions are, and for a long time have been, recognized by the courts of this country as a legitimate and useful part of the industrial system. Associations of laborers, to accomplish lawful objects by legal means, have been always recognized and protected by the law of this state. The organizations of the defendants were as lawful as the incorporation of the plaintiff. Their members might and should have promoted their strength, welfare, and their intelligent and salutary influence and control. Rights that are lawful and purposes that are useful and just cannot, however, be effectuated and accomplished by unlawful means."

In this case there is no evidence sufficient to justify a finding that the unions whose members refused to work on premises where nonunion organ workers were employed were compelled or coerced to do so against their own desires and interests. On the contrary, these men were themselves unwilling to work with the plaintiffs' nonunion employees. Nor was it in any sense illegal for the Organ Workers' Union, desirous of procuring work for its own members, to call to the attention of other trades engaged in various buildings the presence of nonunion organ workers there, and to persuade them, without coercion or compulsion, to refuse to work side by side with nonunion men. For a court to compel these members of other crafts, against their will, to work on the same premises with other men personally objectionable to them, would be a serious invasion of their right to work for and with whom they please, so long as their right to do so is not collectively exercised with malicious purpose to injure another. The clash of equal rights is obvious, and the plaintiffs, though injured, are without remedy. *National Fireproofing Co.* v. *Mason Builders' Ass'n, supra; Gill Engraving Co.* v. *Doerr, supra.*

The bill must accordingly be dismissed, with costs.

AEOLIAN CO. v. FISCHER

United States Circuit Court of Appeals for the Second Circuit.
40 Fed. (2d) 189 (1930).

Before MANTON, AUGUSTUS N. HAND, and CHASE, C.J.
MANTON, C.J.

The appellants appeal from a decree dismissing the bill of complaint after final hearing. The suit seeks to restrain the appellees, labor unions and individuals associated with them, from combining to restrain interstate commerce and destroying the business of the appellants by calling strikes or threatening to call strikes in building trades employed on buildings where the appellants were installing their organs, sold and shipped in interstate commerce. The case was here before, *Aeolian Co. v. Fischer*, 29 Fed. (2d) 679, where we affirmed an order denying the application for a preliminary injunction.

All the appellants but one are foreign corporations, and are organ manufacturers selling their product in interstate commerce to moving picture theaters, churches, and for private uses. The contracts are interstate in their nature, and provide for the building, shipping, erection, and sale of the completed organ in the house of installation.

The record differs in one aspect from that which we considered when it was here before. At final hearing, it was established and found by the court below, that the appellants were engaged in interstate commerce in the sale, shipment, and installation of its organs. * * *

With this conclusion we agree.

The only work performed by the purchaser is hoisting the organ parts, if unduly bulky, installation of high-voltage electrical connections, furnishing and installing the wind trunking between the blower room and the organ chamber, and the furnishing of light, heat, and electric power required for the erecting, tuning, and completion of the instrument. The other work of installation was performed by the appellants' skilled workers.

Labor troubles developed in the industry because of demands made by Organ Workers' Local No. 9 relative to wages and working conditions and the employment of men in New York City. This related to installation work. A general strike was called by that union, which lasted for fourteen weeks in 1925. In September, 1927, a delegate of the Organ Workers' Local No. 9 presented a form of union contract for signature to the appellant Wurlitzer Company, which made provision for the employment of none but union men and women. This contract was not signed by this appellant, and some of the men who were members of the union left the union. Organ Workers' Union No. 9 became affiliated with the Building Trade Council through the representation of its delegate, and the council consisted of various building trade unions of New York City. Its constitution forbids "their members to work with a nonunion man, or with members of a dual or hostile body to any industry represented." This co-operation on the part of the unions made it impossible for an employer or contractor engaged in the building trades to do his work with nonunion men, and the record shows that it is impossible for a building to be erected in this city without the exclusive employment of union labor. It resulted in having the force and effect of the Building Trades Council in back of the efforts of the Organ Workers' Local No. 9 to force unionism upon appellants' non-union organ workers. It may be questioned whether installation of an organ is the work of erecting a building, for, when it is installed, the organ is still a musical instrument.

Organ Workers' Local No. 9 is also affiliated with the Combined Amusement Crafts, an association of stage hands and theater operators whose sympathetic support it had threatened to use. In February or March, 1928, Local No. 9 had a membership of about ninety men, and its delegate endeavored to get the nonunion men to join. His purpose was to unionize fully the outside work of erecting organs in New York and other parts of the country and then to unionize the factories by the requirements that all organs erected in a building where union labor is employed must be manu-factured by union men and bear the union label. In order to prevent non-union men working in the building where the appellants were installing organs, the delegate of Local No. 9 told purchasers of organs that he would call out all the trades on strike if the particular organ was installed by non-union men. This threat was made to one Hammerstein, a purchaser of an organ for the Hammerstein Temple of Music, and to an owner who pur-chased an organ for the Plaza Theatre. In the Elks Club, Brooklyn, one of the appellants' (the Aeolian Company) men were locked out from the building. At the Plaza Theatre in Linden, N.J., workers were secretly substituted for the Wurlitzer men in violation of the terms of the contract of installation, and, after these men had been discovered and removed, it became necessary for the Wurlitzer Company to work at night in order to avoid interference with the building trades. The Wurlitzer Company men were driven from the work at the Ritz Theatre, Lindenhurst, N.J., and were off the job for a week until the electricians and other building trades had completed their work. Another instance of interference was a delay of from two to four days at the Castle Hill Theatre. Men were assaulted at the Marble Hill Theatre, and the entire force had to be removed and stayed away for about six weeks. The Wurlitzer men were arrested for trespassing at the Oxford Theatre, Little Falls, N.J., after the general contractor had been served with a general strike order. The owner of the Pythian Theatre was threatened with a general strike, and he paid to have the organ workers reinstated in the union so that they might finish the work unmolested. One contract, between the appellant Estey Organ Company and the Capital Theatre for additions and repairs to an organ was canceled after threats to call out the theatrical trade, and the work was finished by union men not in the employ of the Estey Organ Company. The Austin Organ Company's workmen were taken off the installation of a theater at Mt. Vernon, N.Y., after threats made by a union delegate and were not permitted to return until after they had been unionized at the company's expense. The Skinner Organ Company was given three days of grace to unionize its men at the Colony Theatre, and they were only allowed to go on with the work after they had joined the Local No. 9 at the expense of that company. Other acts of interference with the appellants' interstate commerce consisted of threats to strike and unjustified claims of right of the sheet metal workers' delegate to do the wind trunking within the organ as well as without; also threats were made by the riggers' union delegate that the organ would have to be taken out of the building because it was rigged by nonunion men. In one instance a switchboard was nailed up and the electric wires cut by an electrician on the Universal Theatre job. The Electricians' Union Local No. 3 refused to do the wiring on the organ installed in the Church of the Redeemer in Brooklyn, and a general strike followed there.

These interferences with the appellants' business have seriously affected their good will, for organ purchasers are fearful of contracting with them, feeling that they would have difficulty in installing their instruments and also with the building trades unions. This interference stands uncontradicted, although the delegate of Union No. 9 was a witness for the defense. * * *

The undoubted purpose of the appellees was to monopolize the work with which the appellants were concerned, that is, the installation of organs, and require only their membership or union workers for each job. It restricted the liberty of employers and employees to engage in interstate commerce, whenever the employment of nonunion members is involved, and is an interference with interstate commerce. It is immaterial whether the combination is unlawful because it interferes with the right of nonunion men to engage in such part of interstate commerce or with the right of employers of nonunion men to so engage; the result is the same. If the combination is illegal for either reason, the person or corporation injured in its or his property rights is entitled to relief. *Chattanooga Foundry & Pipe Works v. City of Atlanta*, 203 U.S. 390, 27 S. Ct. 65, 51 L. Ed. 241; *U. S. v. Colgate & Co.*, 250 U.S. 300, 39 S. Ct. 465, 63 L. Ed. 992, 7 A.L.R. 443; *Loewe v. Lawlor*, 208 U.S. 274, 28 S. Ct. 301, 52 L. Ed. 488, 13 Ann. Cas. 815; *U. S. v. Patten*, 226 U.S. 525, 33 S. Ct. 141, 57 L. Ed. 333, 44 L.R.A. (N.S.) 325. The inquiry is not as the court below conceived it to be, whether or not there was a combination to exclude the appellants' organs from interstate trade or commerce. It is as much a violation of the Sherman Act, as amended by the Clayton Act (15 U.S.C.A. § 1 *et seq.*), for combinations to exclude individuals from work in interstate commerce. Finding that the installation of the organ was work in interstate commerce and that there was a combination directly to restrict and obstruct that work, the opportunities of engaging therein was work of interstate commerce. But the interference with this interstate commerce was not confined to preventing workmen from engaging in the employment of the appellants as nonunion men. There was a combination to obstruct and interfere with the appellants in carrying out their interstate trade and commerce in their usual and practical way which, of itself, was a violation of the act. It is not material or important whether the restraint operates upon this interstate commerce at the point of origin or at the point where it comes to rest. *Bedford Cut Stone Co. v. Journeymen Stone Cutters' Ass'n,* 274 U.S. 37, 47 S. Ct. 522, 71 L. Ed. 916, 54 A.L.R. 791; *Binderup v. Pathe Exchange, Inc.,* 263 U.S. 291, 44 S. Ct. 96, 68 L. Ed. 308; *Ramsay Co. v. Associated Bill Posters,* 260 U.S. 501, 43 S. Ct. 167, 67 L. Ed. 368; *Duplex Printing-Press Co. v. Deering,* 254 U.S. 443, 41 S. Ct. 172, 65 L. Ed. 349, 16 A.L.R. 196. The combination formulated by the appellees to curtail the liberty of the appellants and their employees to engage in the phase of the interstate commerce involving installation was a violation of the anti-trust laws, and their refusals to permit nonunion men to work and striking to interfere with the work of the appellants in installing organs was a violation of the anti-trust acts. *Duplex Printing-Press Co. v. Deering, supra; Bedford Cut Stone Co. v. Journeymen Stone Cutters' Ass'n, supra.*

The organs involved were not part of the building construction, and there is no evidence of any community of interest between the erectors of these organs and the numerous and various trades engaged in erecting a building. There was no evidence of close contact between these groups, but the evidence is ample and undisputed that the purpose of the appellees was to secure for the organ workers' union a complete monopoly of the work of installing organs in New York and Northern New Jersey and to bring about a condition which would impose upon the craftsmen in the trade, for refusing to join their union, an impossibility of employment in their trade and thereby gaining a livelihood.

The appellee Meller made clear upon his examination that he was a member of the Building Trades Council and I "have something behind me." This he described as full sympathetic support, and, as he said, "no organ will be erected in New York City unless they erect it by union labor, as the building trades will not work with any non-union workers." The courts have condemned such interference. *Hitchman Coal Co. v. Mitchell,* 245 U.S. 249, 38 S. Ct. 65, 62 L. Ed. 260, L.R.A. 1918C, 497, Ann. Cas. 1918B, 461; *Bitterman v. Louisville & Nashville R. Co.,* 207 U.S. 205, 28 S. Ct. 91, 52 L. Ed. 171, 12 Ann. Cas. 693; *Central Metal Products Corp. v. O'Brien* (D.C.) 278 Fed. 827; *Hodge v. Meyer* (C.C.A.) 252 Fed. 479; *Amer. Malting Co. v. Keitel* (C.C.A.) 209 Fed. 351; *Irving v. Joint District Council* (C.C.) 180 Fed. 896; *Lehigh Structural Steel Co. v. Atlantic Smelting & Refining Works,* 92 N.J. Eq. 131, 111 A. 376; *McCord v. Thompson-Starrett Co.,* 129 App. Div. 130, 113 N.Y.S. 385.

In thus preventing the appellants and their employees from carrying on their business because the workmen do not belong to the union, there was formed a combination having for its primary purpose the obstruction of the appellants in carrying on their interstate business. The injury to them is not merely incidental; the direct and immediate purpose is to oust the appellants and their employees from the conduct of their business in New York and its vicinity unless they submit. The means adopted to declare a labor boycott of all the trades on the buildings, within the affected area where the appellants carry on their business, and by their control of the building business, make it impossible for the owners, contractors, or architects to do business in this area with the appellants. Such combination is a secondary boycott. *Duplex Printing-Press Co. v. Deering, supra; O'Brien v. Fackenthal* (C.C.A.) 5 Fed.(2d) 389. In such a combination against an employer there is every suggestion of coercion, attempted monopoly, and deprivation of livelihood and remoteness of the legal purpose of the union to better its members' condition. *American Steel Foundries v. Tri-City Council,* 257 U.S. 184, 42 S. Ct. 72, 66 L. Ed. 189, 27 A.L.R. 360; *Hitchman Coal & Coke Co. v. John Mitchell,* 245 U.S. 229, 38 S. Ct. 65, 62 L. Ed. 260, L.R.A. 1918C, 497 Ann. Cas. 1918B, 461; *Iron Molders' Union v. Allis-Chalmers Co.* (C.C.A.) 166 Fed. 45, 20 L.R.A. (N.S.) 315.

The record before us justified a decree in favor of the appellants for an injunction.

Decree reversed.

AUGUSTUS N. HAND, C.J., (concurring).

I concur with the majority because of the controlling decisions of the Supreme Court in *Duplex Printing-Press Co. v. Deering,* 254 U.S. 443, 41 S. Ct. 172, 65 L. Ed. 349, 16 A.L.R. 196, and *Bedford Cut Stone Co. v. Stone Cutters' Association,* 274 U.S. 37, 47 S. Ct. 522, 71 L. Ed. 916, 54 A.L.R. 791.

The District Judge relied on *United Mine Workers v. Coronado Coal Co.,* 259 U.S. 344, 42 S. Ct. 570, 66 L. Ed. 975, 27 A.L.R. 762, *United Leather Workers' Union v. Herkert & Meisel Trunk Co.,* 265 U.S. 457, 44 S. Ct. 623, 68 L. Ed. 1104, 33 A.L.R. 566, and *Industrial Association v. United States,* 268 U.S. 64, 45 S. Ct. 403, 69 L.Ed. 849. But these decisions do not, in my opinion, support the conclusion reached. Mining is not interstate commerce. *United Mine Workers v. Coronado Coal Co., supra.* Manufacturing is not interstate commerce. *United Leather Workers' Union v. Herkert & Meisel Trunk Co., supra.* Building is not interstate commerce. *Industrial Association v. United States, supra.* In all of these cases the interference was at a point where interstate commerce was not in operation, and not, as here, at a point where in contemplation of law it continued to exist.

The fact that the installation of the organs was interstate commerce required that such installation (in the same way as transportation) should be free from unlawful interference. Because of the decisions in *Duplex*

Printing-Press Co. v. Deering, and *Bedford Cut Stone Co. v. Stone Cutters'
Association, supra,* we must hold that the interference here was unlawful
and was a violation of the Sherman Anti-Trust Law (15 U.S.C.A §§ 1-7,
15).[2]

SECTION 7 (a) OF THE NATIONAL INDUSTRIAL RECOVERY ACT.

Act of June 16, 1933. 48 Stat. 198.

SEC. 7. (a)   Every code of fair competition, agreement, and license
approved, prescribed, or issued under this title shall contain the following
conditions: (1) That employees shall have the right to organize and
bargain collectively through representatives of their own choosing, and
shall be free from the interference, restraint, or coercion of employers of
labor, or their agents, in the designation of such representatives or in self-
organization or in other concerted activities for the purpose of collective
bargaining or other mutual aid or protection; (2) that no employee and
no one seeking employment shall be required as a condition of employment
to join any company union or to refrain from joining, organizing, or
assisting a labor organization of his own choosing; and (3) that employers
shall comply with the maximum hours of labor, minimum rates of pay,
and other conditions of employment, approved or prescribed by the President.[1]

EXECUTIVE ORDER.

No. 6511.   December 16, 1933.

By virtue of the authority vested in me under title I of the National
Industrial Recovery Act approved June 16, 1933 (Public, No. 67, 73d
Cong.), and in order to effectuate the purposes of said act, it is hereby
ordered as follows:

(1) The National Labor Board, created on August 5, 1933, to "pass
promptly on any case of hardship or dispute that may arise from interpre-

---

[2] For comment on the case, see: 43 Harv. Law Rev. 459 (1930); 17 Cal. Law
Rev. 424 (1929): 77 Univ. of Pa. Law Rev. 918 (1929).
   Cf. Rockwood Corp. v. Bricklayer's Local Union No. 1, 33 Fed.(2d) 25 (8th cir.
1929), certiorari denied in 280 U.S. 575 (1929); Detroit Tile & Mosaic Co. v. Mason
Contractors' Ass'n, 48 Fed.(2d) 729 (6th cir. 1931); International Brotherhood of
Electrical Workers v. Western Union Tel. Co., 6 Fed.(2d) 444 (7th cir. 1925), 46
Fed.(2d) 736 (7th cir. 1931).   See also: Palmer v. Aeolian Co., 46 Fed.(2d) 752
(8th cir. 1931).

[1] See Seiler, "The Effect of Sec. 7(a) of the National Industrial Recovery Act
upon the Rights of Employer and Employees," 11 N.Y.U.L. Quar. Rev. 237 (1933);
Twyeffort, "The United States Supreme Court and Employer-Employee Relations
under the National Industrial Recovery Act," 11 *Id.* 251; 47 Harv. Law Rev. 85, 117
(1933).

tation or application of the President's Reemployment Agreement", shall continue to adjust all industrial disputes, whether arising out of the interpretation and operation of the President's Reemployment Agreement or any duly approved industrial code of fair competition, and to compose all conflicts threatening the industrial peace of the country. All action heretofore taken by this Board in the discharge of its functions is hereby approved and ratified.

(2) The powers and functions of said Board shall be as follows:

(a) To settle by mediation, conciliation, or arbitration all controversies between employers and employees which tend to impede the purposes of the National Industrial Recovery Act; provided, however, the Board may decline to take cognizance of controversies between employers and employees in any field of trade or industry where a means of settlement, provided for by agreement, industrial code, or Federal law, has not been invoked.

(b) To establish local or regional boards upon which employers and employees shall be equally represented, and to delegate thereto such powers and territorial jurisdiction as the National Labor Board may determine.

(c) To review the determinations of the local or regional boards where the public interest so requires.

(d) To make rules and regulations governing its procedure and the discharge of its functions.

FRANKLIN D. ROOSEVELT.

EXECUTIVE ORDER.

No. 6580. February 1, 1934.

By virtue of the authority vested in me under title I of the National Industrial Recovery Act, approved June 16, 1933 (Public, No. 67, 73d Cong.), and in order to effectuate the policy of said act, I, Franklin D. Roosevelt, President of the United States, do hereby provide for and direct the enforcement of certain provisions of section 7 (a) of said act and the conditions contained therein, as incorporated in, and made a part of any code of fair competition, or agreement heretofore or hereafter approved or prescribed by me, in the following manner:

1. Whenever the National Labor Board shall determine, in such manner as it sees fit, that a substantial number (as defined in the discretion of the Board) of the employees, or of any specific group of employees, of any plant or enterprise or industrial unit of any employer subject to such a code or agreemnt, have requested the Board to conduct an election to enable them to choose representatives for the purpose of collective bargaining or other mutual aid or protection in the exercise of the rights assured to them in said section 7 (a), the Board shall make the arrange-

ments for and supervise the conduct of an election, under the exclusive control of the Board and under such rules and regulations as the Board shall prescribe. Thereafter the Board shall publish promptly the names of those representatives who are selected by the vote of at least a majority of the employees voting, and have been thereby designated to represent all the employees eligible to participate in such an election for the purpose of collective bargaining or other mutual aid or protection in their relations with their employer.

2. Whenever the National Labor Board shall have determined upon an investigation, or as the result of an election, that the majority of the employees of an employer, or the majority of any specific group of employees, have selected their representatives in accordance with the provisions of said section 7 (a), and shall have certified the names of such representatives to their employer, and thereafter upon complaint or on its own motion, the Board shall determine that such an employer has declined to recognize or to deal with said representatives, or is in any other way refusing to comply with the requirements of said section 7 (a), the Board shall report its determination promptly to the Administrator for Industrial Recovery for appropriate action.

3. The powers and duties herein conferred upon the National Labor Board are in addition to, and not in derogation of, any powers and duties conferred upon such Board by any other Executive order.

FRANKLIN D. ROOSEVELT.

EXECUTIVE ORDER.

No. 6612-A. February 23, 1934.

Executive Order No. 6580 of February 1, 1934, is hereby amended by striking out paragraph numbered 2 thereof and inserting in its stead the following paragraph:

2. Whenever the National Labor Board shall find that an employer has interfered with the Board's conduct of an election or has declined to recognize or bargain collectively with a representative or representatives of the employees adjudged by the Board to have been selected in accordance with section 7 (a) or has otherwise violated or is refusing to comply with said section 7 (a), the Board, in its discretion, may report such findings and make appropriate recommendations to the Attorney General or to the Compliance Division of the National Recovery Administration. The Compliance Division shall not review the findings of the Board but it shall have power to take appropriate action based thereon.

FRANKLIN D. ROOSEVELT.

LABOR DISPUTES LAW.

Public Resolution No. 44 (H.J. Res. 375) ; approved June 19, 1934.

Sec. 1. That in order to further effectuate the policy of title I of the National Industrial Recovery Act, and in the exercise of the powers therein and herein conferred, the President is authorized to establish a board or boards authorized and directed to investigate issues, facts, practices, or activities of employers or employees in any controversies arising under section 7a of said Act or which are burdening or obstructing, or threatening to burden or obstruct the free flow of interstate commerce, the salaries, compensations, and expenses of the board or boards and necessary employees being paid as provided in section 2 of the National Industrial Recovery Act.

Sec. 2. Any board so established is hereby empowered, when it shall appear in the public interest, to order and conduct an election by a secret ballot of any of the employees of any employer, to determine by what person or persons or organization they desire to be represented in order to insure the right of employees to organize and to select their representatives for the purpose of collective bargaining as defined in section 7a of said Act and now incorporated herein.

For the purposes of such election such a board shall have the authority to order the production of such pertinent documents or the appearance of such witnesses to give testimony under oath, as it may deem necessary to carry out the provisions of this resolution. Any order issued by such a board under the authority of this section may, upon application of such board or upon petition of the person or persons to whom such order is directed, be enforced or reviewed, as the case may be, in the same manner, so far as applicable, as is provided in the case of an order of the Federal Trade Commission under the Federal Trade Commission Act.

Sec. 3. Any such board, with the approval of the President, may prescribe such rules and regulations as it deems necessary to carry out the provisions of this resolution with reference to the investigations authorized in section 1 and to assure freedom from coercion in respect to all elections.

Sec. 4. Any person who shall knowingly violate any rule or regulation authorized under section 3 of this resolution or impede or interfere with any member or agent of any board established under this resolution in the performance of his duties, shall be punishable by a fine of not more than $1,000 or by imprisonment for not more than one year, or both.

Sec. 5. This resolution shall cease to be in effect, and any board or boards established hereunder shall cease to exist, on June 16, 1935, or sooner if the President shall by proclamation, or the Congress shall by joint resolution, declare that the emergency recognized by section 1 of the National Industrial Recovery Act has ended.

Sec. 6. Nothing in this resolution shall prevent or impede or diminish in any way the right of employees to strike or engage in other concerted activities.   Approved June 19, 1934.

WESTERN POWDER MFG. CO. v. INTERSTATE COAL CO.

District Court, Eastern District of Illinois, 1934. 5 Fed. Supp. 619.

LINDLEY, D. J.   The original bill herein, filed some years ago, resulted in the appointment of receivers for the Interstate Coal Company.   The court's administration of the property has ensued.   Among the assets is a shaft coal mine at West Frankfort known as "Mine No. 21."   Prior to the filing of the petition herein, the receivers of the coal company had by written instrument, duly authorized by the court, leased the mine and all its equipment to one Herman Rea upon a royalty basis.   Rea was, at the time of the filing of petition in possession of the property, employing a number of men who were engaged in cleaning up the mine and getting it ready for operation, and since the filing of the petition he has begun to operate it by producing coal.   Over the mine the court has no jurisdiction except such as is necessary to protect the collection of rentals from the lessee.   The receivers have no part in the operation or management of the property.

The petitioners intervening in the original suit, filed on or about December 1, 1933, their petition, which was later amended, reciting that they are employees at the mine; that the same had been closed since March 28, 1933, when an operating receiver appointed by the court ceased operation; that directly prior to the closing, the employees, including petitioners, had mined coal, some of it loaded in cars and some lying in the rooms, ready to be hoisted to the top; that the pay roll for producing same has not been paid; and that they are entitled to have said mined coal applied upon such pay roll.

Petitioners further allege that they are members of the Progressive Miners of America and have elected officers whom they have chosen to represent them in collective bargaining; that Rea, the lessee, and others, attempting to operate the mine, are violating the Code of Fair Competition for the bituminous coal industry adopted pursuant to the provisions of the National Industrial Recovery Act (48 Stat. 195), in that Rea has made a contract with the United Mine Workers of America to employ the members thereof in the mine and refuses to employ petitioners who are members of an opposing union, namely, Progressive Miners of America; that petitioners have a right to organize and bargain collectively and cannot be required, as a condition of employment, to join any company union or to refrain from joining, organizing, or assisting a labor organization of their own choosing; and that defendants have refused to permit the petitioners to work unless they would renounce their membership in the Progressive organization.

The petition seeks to restrain the receivers from disposing of the coal mined by petitioners without applying the same upon indebtedness due them; to restrain all defendants from violating the Code of Fair Competition, and especially from employing persons to take the places formerly held by petitioners; and to restrain Rea from operating until they shall have been paid what was owing them from the operating receiver under the former operation.

Thus it appears that the petition is two-fold: First, the petitioners seek a decree of this court which will direct the receivers to apply the proceeds of the coal mined to the application of the employees' debts; second, they seek to restrain the person operating the mine, namely, the lessee Rea from employing only United Mine Workers.

The United Mine Workers were allowed to intervene and become parties defendant, so that the present defendants are the receivers, the lessee Rea, and the United Mine Workers of America.

The defendants assert that two or more causes of action are joined over which the court has no jurisdiction which may be invoked in a proceeding dependent upon another equity cause; that the controversy between the petitioners and Rea as lessee is not properly the subject of a dependent or ancillary proceeding in the original cause and pertains in no way to the administration of the estate, but is a controversy wholly between persons not parties to the original suit; that the court now has no jurisdiction over the operation of the property; that the relief sought against Rea and the United Mine Workers may not be granted except upon application of the United States attorney; that the controversy involves a labor dispute between employees and employer as defined by the Norris-La Guardia Act, the conditions precedent to a court action under which have not been complied with.

The court heard evidence submitted by the parties and reserved action upon motions to dismiss until disposal of the case upon its merits.

As to the controversy between petitioners on the one hand, and the lessee Rea and the United Workers on the other, it is apparent at the threshold that there is a very serious question as to the right of petitioners to invoke the jurisdiction of the court under the provisions of the National Industrial Recovery Act. Section 3, cl. (c), of that act, 15 U.S.C.A. § 703 (c) is as follows: "The several district courts of the United States are hereby invested with jurisdiction to prevent and restrain violations of any code of fair competition approved under this chapter; and it shall be the duty of the several district attorneys of the United States, in their respective districts, under the direction of the Attorney General, to institute proceedings in equity to prevent and restrain such violations." For precedents in interpretation we turn to the decisions under the Sherman Anti-Trust Act. We find that clause (c) of the National Industrial Recovery Act above quoted is identical with section 4 of the Sherman Anti-Trust Act (15 U.S.C.A. § 4), in that both provide that the several district courts of the United States are vested with jurisdiction to prevent and restrain violations. At the end of each it is provided that: "And it shall be the duty of the several district attorneys of the United States, in their respective districts, under the direction of the Attorney General, to institute proceedings in equity to prevent and restrain such violations."

Consequently we must accept the decisions of the Supreme Court of the United States upon the Sherman Anti-Trust Act as to the right of private individuals to sue for injury for violation of that act as authoritative upon this branch of the case at bar. Without quoting from cases at length, we find that in *Minnesota v. Northern Sec. Co.,* 194 U.S. 48, 24 S. Ct. 598, 48 L. Ed. 870; *Wilder Mfg. Co, v. Corn Products Co.,* 236 U. S. 165, 35 S. Ct. 398, 59 L. Ed. 520, Ann. Cas. 1916A, 118; *General Investment Co. v. Lake Shore & Michigan Southern R. Co.,* 260 U.S. 261, 43 S. Ct. 106, 67 L. Ed. 244; *Paine Lumber Co. v. Neal et al.,* 244 U. S. 459, 37 S. Ct. 718, 61 L. Ed. 1256, the court has repeatedly held that it was the intention of Congress to limit proceedings in equity to prevent or restrain such violations of the Anti-Trust Act as caused injury, to suits instituted in the name of the United States by attorneys of the United States, acting under the direction of the Attorney General, thus securing the enforcement of the act, so far as direct proceedings in equity are concerned, according to a uniform plan operative throughout the entire country. In *Paine v. Neal, supra* there was dissenting opinion, the writer of which took the position that for an individual wrong a private citizen should have a right to bring an action in equity; but the majority of the court held to the contrary that the remedy under section 4 of the Sherman Anti-Trust Act (15 U.S.C.A. § 4), created by Congress in exactly the same language as is the cause of action in the government under the National Recovery Act, was exclusive. It follows that petitioners, as private individuals, have no right to maintain this branch of the case and that it must fail for want of proper parties.

In accordance with this conclusion is the opinion of Judge FitzHenry in the recent case of *Stanley v. Peabody Coal Co.,* 5 F. Supp. 612, in the Southern District of this state, wherein he said: "From a consideration of the construction placed upon the precise words used in paragraph (c) of section 3, of the National Industrial Recovery Act, 15 U.S.C.A. § 703 (c), when those words were used in section 4 of the Anti-Trust Act (15 U.S.C.A. § 4), we are compelled to hold that a private individual cannot maintain a suit for an injunction under paragraph (c) of section 3, especially such an injunction as is here sought."

In another recent case, *Purvis et al. v. Bazemore,* 5 F. Supp. 230, in the Southern District of Florida, Judge Akerman came to a similar conclusion. After quoting clause (c) of section 3 of the National Recovery Act, 15 U.S.C.A. § 703 (c), Judge Akerman said: "This clause, in my opinion, contemplates that actions to restrain violations of the National Industrial Recovery Act should be brought by the United States acting through its district attorneys and not by any individual members of an industry, and the district attorney is not movent here, but persons engaged in the same industry are complainants, and I do not believe they have any standing in court to ask for an injunction under the National Industrial Recovery Act."

Were it necessary, the court might well find that this branch of the case is not dependent upon the original proceeding and that the court has no jurisdiction in such a dependent proceeding to grant the relief prayed. Ordinarily the law does not enable the court in which is pending a suit within its jurisdiction to take cognizance in a dependent manner of a cause of action which is not before him. See *City of Dothan, Ala. v. First Nat. Bank of Dothan,* (C.C:A.) 61 F. (2d) 685; *General Motors v. Rubsam Corporation,* (C.C.A.) 65 F. (2d) 217. But it is not necessary to go into this phase of the question in view of the conclusion that the suit, so far as the relief hereinbefore considered is concerned, may not be invoked by private parties. For the same reason it is not necessary to discuss any question of the constitutionality of the National Industrial Recovery Act or the serious question as to whether or not the petitioners are within the category of employees as contemplated by the act.

It should be observed, however, that the National Industrial Recovery Act provides machinery for the determination of labor controversies. Administrative boards have been created for the purpose of settling such controversies, and as Judge FitzHenry pointed out in *Stanley v. Peabody Coal Co., supra,* the court has no jurisdiction of such controversies until the administrative remedies have been exhausted.

It appears that the receivers have on hand realized from the coal at the bottom of the mine at the time of the last operation $200, which represents the proceeds of sale of coal identified as coal mined by the petitioners. There was approximately 87 tons. For the production of same such of the petitioners as can be identified as having mined the same should be compensated for their labor to the extent possible. Therefore, it is only equitable that there be provision by this decree for the receivers to pay to the petitioners the sum of $200 to apply upon wages due for the production of the coal in accordance with their respective productions of coal not sold at the time the lease was made. The exact figures will appear in the exhibits offered in court. Apparently this branch of the case seeks relief dependent upon the original proceedings and involves a matter of administration of the assets. The court, therefore, has jurisdiction of the same.

It will be the order of the court, therefore, that the amended petition be dismissed for want of equity in so far as relief is prayed against Rea and the United Mine Workers, and that the $200 be paid to the petitioners in accordance with this opinion. Proper decree may be submitted.[1]

---

[1] Accord: Stanley v. Peabody Coal Co., 5 Fed. Supp. 612 (D.C.S.D. Ill. 1933). In Sherman v. Abeles, 269 N.Y.S. 849, aff'd 269 N.Y.S. 864, a labor union obtained a blanket injunction restraining an employer from abridging the rights of employees under section 7(a), pursuant to Section 3, Chap. 781, Laws 1933 Ex. Sess., a statute passed to give state cooperation in enforcing the policies of the National Industrial Recovery Act.

FRYNS v. FAIR LAWN FUR DRESSING CO.

Court of Chancery of New Jersey, 1933. 168 Atl. 862.

BIGELOW, V.C. Complainants, thirty-six in number, are members of the Needle Trades Workers' Industrial Union, lately employed by defendant in its factory at Fair Lawn. With half a dozen other men, complainants comprised all defendant's employees engaged in the actual work of dressing rabbit skins.

In August last, defendant's employees, including complainants, went on strike. Defendant immediately got in touch with a rival union, the International Fur Workers' Union, and soon agreed to hire only its members and not to recognize or deal with the union to which complainants belong. Defendant refused and still refuses to negotiate with complainants or to re-employ them unless they join the Fur Workers' Union. The same day the strike began, defendant executed the so-called re-employment agreement with the President of the United States. This agreement, by reference, embodies section 7(a) of the National Industrial Recovery Act (N. I.R.A.) of June 16, 1933, 15 U.S.C.A. § 707(a), which reads as follows: "Every code of fair competition, agreement, and license approved, prescribed, or issued under this title shall contain the following conditions: (1) That employees shall have the right to organize and bargain collectively through representatives of their own choosing, and shall be free from the interference, restraint, or coercion of employers of labor, or their agents, in the designation of such representatives or in self-organization or in other concerted activities for the purpose of collective bargaining or other mutual aid or protection; (2) that no employee and no one seeking employment shall be required as a condition of employment to join any company union or to refrain from joining, organizing, or assisting a labor organization of his own choosing; and (3) that employers shall comply with the maximum hours of labor, minimum rates of pay, and other conditions of employment, approved or prescribed by the President."

Complainants pray that defendant may be restrained from making it a condition of their employment or re-employment that complainants become members of the Fur Workers' Union or of any other body, except one of their own choice, and from interfering in any way with complainants in their right to organize and bargain collectively through representatives of their own choice.

The first question is whether the Court of Chancery has jurisdiction of the cause of action arising, as it does, out of a statute of the United States. A court of one state, in general, has jurisdiction of transitory causes of action given by the statutes of a foreign state. *Tennessee Coal, Iron & R. Co. v. George,* 233 U.S. 354, 34 S. Ct. 587, 58 L. Ed. 997, L.R.A. 1916D, 685; *Evey v. Mexican, etc., Co.,* 81 F. 294, 26 C.C.A. 407, 38 L.R.A. 387. Rights, whether legal or equitable, acquired under the laws of the United States, may be prosecuted in a state court competent to decide rights of the like character and class, subject, however, to this qualification that Congress may, if it see fit, give to the federal courts exclusive jurisdiction. Where such exclusive jurisdiction is not given or necessarily implied, resort may be had to the state court. *Claflin v. Houseman,* 93 U.S. 130, 23 L. Ed. 833; *U. S. v. Smith,* 4 N. J. Law, 37. Neither the Recovery Act nor any other statute to which I am referred vests exclusive jurisdiction, in cases like the present one, in the federal courts.

Another rule is urged by defendant: "Where the provisions for the liability is coupled with a provision for a special remedy, that remedy, and that alone, must be employed." *Pollard v. Bailey,* 20 Wall. 520, 527, 22 L. Ed. 376. Section 3(c) of the National Industrial Recovery Act (15 U.S.C.A. § 703 (c)) directs the several district attorneys of the United States to institute proceedings in equity to prevent violations of any code of fair competition approved under the act. The present suit is not brought on a code of fair competition, and no violation of such a code is charged. Hence, the special remedy given by the statute is not available to redress the alleged wrong. Complainants are properly in the Court of Chancery of New Jersey.

The next question is whether the cause of action belongs to complainants. Relief, if it be obtained, must go on the theory of contract, and complainants are not parties to the contract. "It is generally held, subject to qualifications, that a third person may sue upon a promise made to another for his benefit. Sometimes the right is placed by the courts upon provisions in codes giving the 'real party in interest' the right to prosecute suits. Sometimes it is based upon the theory of a trust; the promisor being regarded as trustee for the third party. Sometimes it is based upon the theory of agency; the promisee in the contract being considered the agent of the third party who adopts his acts in suing upon the contract. But whatever may be the correct theory, one thing is essential to the right and that is that the third person be the real promisee—that the promise be made to him in fact although not in form. It is not enough that the contract may operate to his benefit. It must appear that the parties intend to recognize him as the primary party in interest and as privy to the promise." *Pennsylvania Steel Co. v. Railway Co.,* 198 F. 721, 749, 117 C.C.A. 503, 531.

"The difficulties which presented themselves in the case of suits by third persons upon contracts made by others, were two—the want of privity, and the want of consideration moving from the third person. These difficulties have been overcome in this state, as to contracts not under seal, by decisions of the courts, * * * and, as to contracts under seal, by the statute. The only effect of the decisions and the statute is that privity of contract is not requisite in order to maintain the action, and the consideration need not move from the person for whom the contract is made. Neither the cases above cited, nor the statute, go so far as to permit a suit upon contract to be maintained by persons with whom the defendant never meant to enter into contractual relations. It is not enough that the plaintiff may be benefited by the performance of the contract. He can only maintain the action when the contract is made for him. It would be a decided novelty to hold that any one contracting with a municipal corporation is liable to an action of contract, not only by the corporation, but by every citizen of the municipality." *Styles v. F. R. Long Co.,* 70 N. J. Law, 301, 57 A. 448, 449.

. Are complainants within the rule? The first half of the re-employment contract deals with hours of work and wages. The only parties directly affected by these stipulations are the employer himself and the employees. It seems clear to me that employees are a primary party in interest to the contract; the promise, in substance, was to them. Complainants can sue thereon.

A contract is not enforceable unless supported by a valuable consideration. The re-employment agreement does not state any consideration. Its opening words are these: "During the period of the President's emergency reemployment drive, that is to say, from August 1 to December 31, 1933, or to any earlier date of approval of a code of fair competition to which he is subject, the undersigned hereby agrees with the President as follows." The agreement was made pursuant to section 4(a) of the federal statute (15 U.S.C.A. § 704(a)): "The President is authorized to enter into agreements with, and to approve voluntary agreements between and among, persons engaged in a trade or industry, labor organizations, and trade or industrial organizations, associations, or groups, relating to any trade or industry, if in his judgment such agreements will aid in effectuating the policy of this title with respect to transactions in or affecting interstate or foreign commerce, and will be consistent with the requirements of clause (2) of subsection (a) of section 3 for a code of fair competition." Defendant expressly waives, for the purpose of the present motion, doubts of the constitutionality of the statute.

The policy of the title referred to is stated in the first section thereof (15 U.S.C.A. § 701), and, among other things, "to eliminate unfair competitive practices, * * * to increase the consumption of industrial and agricultural products by increasing purchasing power, to reduce and relieve unemployment, to improve standards of labor, and otherwise to rehabilitate industry." On July 24, 1933, the President delivered a radio address dealing in part with the re-employment agreement: "We have sent out to all employers an agreement which is the result of weeks of consultation. * * * It is a plan, deliberate, reasonable and just, intended to put into effect at once the most important of the broad principles which are being established, industry by industry, through codes. Naturally, it takes a good deal of organizing and a great many hearings and many months to get these codes perfected and signed and we cannot wait for all of them to go through. The blanket agreements, however, which I am sending to every employer, will start the wheels turning now and not six months from now. * * * Those who cooperate in this program must know each other at a glance, that is why we have provided a badge of honor for this purpose; a simple design with a legend 'We do our part' and I ask that all those who join with me shall display that badge prominently. * * * And it is my purpose to keep posted in the post office of every town a roll of honor of all those who join with me. * * * While the shirking employer may undersell his competitor, the saving he thus makes is made at the expense of his country's welfare. * * * The essence of the principle is a universal limitation of hours of work per week for any individual by common consent and a universal payment of wages above a minimum, also by common consent. I cannot guarantee the success of this nation-wide plan, but the people of this country can guarantee its success."

And with the draft agreement the President sent out a statement addressed to every employer: "This agreement is part of a nationwide plan to raise wages, create employment and thus increase purchasing power and restore business; that plan depends wholly on united action by all employers. For this reason I ask you, as an employer to do your part by signing."

The agreement itself, in paragraph 10, contains this pledge: "To support and patronize establishments which also have signed this agreement and are listed as members of N.R.A. (National Recovery Administration)."

As a result of the President's appeal, thousands of employers throughout the country signed the re-employment agreement identical with that signed by defendant. What bargain did defendant make? What did it obtain as compensation for its promises? First, the blue eagle, the badge of honor of which the President had spoken, and with it the benefit of the pledge of all other members of N.R.A. to patronize their fellow members. Again, each employer who signed did so in reliance on the fact that his competitors would likewise sign and would assume the same burdens, so that the increase in his labor costs would not put him at a disadvantage, since all his competitors would be subject to a like increase. I think these considerations, slight as they are, are sufficient to support a promise of this character, intended to promote a great public endeavor. The same principle should be applied which is often found in cases dealing with subscriptions to charities: "The objection of a want of consideration for promises like the one before us has not always been regarded with favor; and judges, considering defences of that character as breaches of faith towards the public and especially towards those engaged in the same enterprise, and an unwarrantable disappointment of the reasonable expectations of those interested, have been willing, nay apparently anxious, to discover a consideration which would uphold the undertaking as a valid contract." *Barnes v. Perine*, 12 N.Y. 18, 24. See 60 C.J. 956. How slight a consideration is necessary in such cases is illustrated by *New Jersey Orthopædic Hospital & D. v. Wright*, 95 N. J. Law, 462, 113 A. 144, 145: "One inference that the jury might legitimately draw from this evidence is that Mrs. Barr raised her subscription on the agreement, first that the money, while part of the general fund, was to be specifically applied to a stated purpose, viz. the building of an operating room; secondly, that the operating room was to bear a name suggested by her; thirdly, that she would contribute if the committee would obtain the waiver by Mr. Graves of his prior claim on the room, and that they actually did obtain that waiver. Any one of these things would be a legal consideration for the promise." Defendant's agreement is supported by a sufficient consideration.

I turn to the meritorious question, whether defendant has violated his undertaking. The statutory provision embodied in defendant's contract and relied on by complainants is quoted above. Let us first consider the second clause: "That no employee and no one seeking employment shall be required as a condition of employment, to join any company union or to refrain from joining, organizing, or assisting, a labor organization of his own choosing." A company union, as I understand it, is one all of whose members are employees of a single company or group of affiliated companies. Complainants concede that the Fur Workers' Union is not a company union. It will be noted that an employer is not expressly forbidden from requiring an employee to join a union named by the employer, except it be a company union. Therefore, says defendant, it is within its rights when it requires all its employees to join the Fur Workers' Union. However, the rules of most labor unions and of the Fur Workers' Union and the Needle Trades Union are such that a workman cannot be a member of two competing unions. If they join the Fur Workers' Union, complainants must resign from the union of their own choice. And so complainants say that the action of defendant does constitute a violation. If this provision of the section stood alone, I would accept defendant's contention as correct, and would say Congress intended that, while employees should not be required by their employer to join a company union, still they might properly be required to become members of any other bona fide union designated by their employer; in other words, the employer could operate a closed shop.

The first provision of the section is this: "That employees shall have the right to organize and bargain collectively through representatives of their own choosing, and shall be free from the interference, restraint, or coercion of employers of labor, or their agents, in the designation of such representatives or in self-organization or other concerted activities for the purpose of collective bargaining or other mutual aid or protection." This enactment, embodied in the contract, gave complainants, while they were employees of defendant and constituted a majority of such employees engaged in rabbit dressing, the right to organize themselves as members of the Needle Trades Union and the right, if they so chose, to bargain collectively with defendant through the agents of that union. Defendant could not, without breach of its agreement, coerce them into a different organization or compel them to accept as their representative an agent of the Fur Workers' Union. It is true that complainants went on strike, but, even while on strike, they remained, for the present purpose, employees of defendant. I think the whole matter works out in this fashion: If a majority of the employees are members of a particular union or desire to organize within a particular union, the employer cannot dictate to them another union. But if they are not organized and are, in fact, indifferent as to how they shall be organized, or if the enterprise is just starting, then the employer may choose his union and require all his men to join it.

Defendant admits that it has made the reinstatement of complainants conditional on their joining the Fur Workers' Union. With that union only will it bargain. This, as I view the case, is a violation of the contract, and complainants may have a remedy for the wrong in this court. The irreparable injury which complainants may sustain pending final hearing is apparent. There should be interlocutory restraint in the matters above discussed.[1]

BAYONNE TEXTILE CORPORATION v. AMERICAN FEDERATION OF SILK WORKERS.

New Jersey Court of Errors and Appeals, 1934. 172 Atl. 551.

On appeal from an order of the Court of Chancery.

HEHER, J. delivered the opinion of the court. Complainant, a manufacturer of broad silks and rayon, filed a bill praying relief from the alleged unlawful interference with its property rights by defendants. It was alleged that complainant, who is the operator of a plant at the City of Bayonne on the plan technically known as the "open shop," had conformed to the provisions of the National Industrial Recovery Act, approved by the Congress on June 16, 1933 (15 U.S.C.A. Sec. 701, et seq.); that the wages paid to its employees met the standard prescribed by the act and the code adopted in accordance therewith for the government of the silk industry (which, for the time being, was the cotton textile industrial code); that defendant, American Federation of Silk Workers, a voluntary association of silk workers of national authority, with a branch in the County of Hudson, whose design and purpose with reference to complainant was to compel it to operate its plant as a "closed shop," and

---

[1] In Wisconsin State Federation of Labor v. Simplex Shoe Mfg. Co., C.C. Milwaukee County, Wisconsin, 1933, 104 C.C.H. 5215, the court, upon the theory that the President's Reemployment Agreement was a contract for the benefit of employees, granted an injunction on the application of the union, restraining an employer from interfering with the freedom of employees in designating representatives to conduct collective bargaining with defendant. On appeal to the Supreme Court of Wisconsin, the decision was affirmed but on the ground that the complaint stated a cause of action under the Wisconsin labor code, §§ 133.07 (1) and 268.18. See 104 C.C.H. 5518. Cf. Greleck v. Amsterdam, Phila. Mun. Ct., 1934, 104 C.C.H. 5422.

to coerce it into employing none but members of the defendant union, fomented a strike of complainant's employees, and conducted it in mode and manner calculated to intimidate complainant's employees, and thereby induce and compel them to leave complainant's service, or, failing that, to create such a state of fear and apprehension as to impair their efficiency and, to a substantial degree, the quality of the service rendered to complainant.

It was charged that insults, indecent and annoying language and abusive epithets were hurled at complainant's employees, by pickets acting for defendants, as they passed to and from complainant's plant; that they were threatened with physical violence if they did not withdraw from complainant's service; that windows of complainant's plant, about thirty in number, were broken by defendants, or those acting on their behalf; that defendant union, through its agents and servants, "unlawfully interfered with complainant's business in encouraging, inducing and compelling persons employed by complainant, by threats, intimidation, force or violence, to refuse to perform their duties as such employees, and to remain away from its employ"; and that, by reason of the "unlawful interference and instigation of" defendant federation, all of complainant's employees joined in the strike. It was also alleged that the strike was conducted by a strike committee of the defendant union, under the supervision of the defendants, Brown and Sacaroff, who were assisted by defendant Burn; that the picketing of complainant's plant consisted of the "personal molestation and annoyance of persons employed or willing to be employed by complainant," for the purpose of coercing them into withholding their services, and thus to terminate the plant's operations; and that, as a result of the practices pursued by defendants and those associated with them in the prosecution of the strike which they declared, there was a cessation of manufacture.

It is insisted that defendants, by this course of conduct, offended against the provisions of the National Industrial Recovery Act, and the public policy therein declared, in that they thereby hindered and hampered industrial recovery and employment, and that, additionally, they interfered with complainant's property rights to the service of its employees, and to the peaceful enjoyment of its property. It is further asserted that the strike is in violation of the Recovery Act, and the code adopted pursuant thereto, in that defendants and their co-workers did not first submit their grievances and demands to complainant through representatives of their own choosing, and did not first exhaust their remedy within the tribunals provided for in the act and code. It is also alleged that if defendants persist in the specified unlawful conduct, complainant's business will be totally destroyed, and its property will greatly diminish in value.

A restraint *pendente lite* was granted (114 N. J. Eq. 307, 168 Atl. 799), and from the order therefor defendants appeal. It is sweeping in character. It restrains not only unlawful conduct, but also that which has hitherto been regarded as lawful. It enjoins not only the intimidation and coercion of complainant's employees by violence, threats, annoyances and other unlawful practices, but the conduct of the strike itself. It prohibited defendants "from participating, promoting, encouraging, directing, or being in anywise engaged in any strike against or picketing of the complainant, its business or factory." Affirmative action on the part of the employees is expressly limited to organizing and bargaining collectively with complainant "through representatives of such employees' own choosing, from among their own number, to seek an equitable adjustment of such grievances" as they may have against complainant "relating to labor conditions in complainant's factory."

The Vice Chancellor proceeded on the assumption that the National Industrial Recovery Act outlawed strikes. The restraining order recited that the act, and the code adopted pursuant thereto, "manifest a public policy to put an end to strikes by workers employed in industry and trade. . . . by providing a forum for mediation of grievances between employers and employees." In his opinion the Vice Chancellor declared: "In view of the means afforded employees to effect mediation of alleged grievances against their employer before impartial mediators such as provided under N.R.A., it is inconceivable that they should be permitted to resort to strikes *ad libitum* against their employer. Such practices, while aims and purposes of N.I.R.A. and of N.R.A. are sought to be effected, must be regarded as taboo." He also asserted that in view of the means thus afforded "for equitable readjustments of real or fancied grievances between an employer and its employees . . . courts of equity cannot countenance strikes against employers engaged in industrial pursuits, and picketing in connection therewith, particularly by intermeddlers, where no fair effort has been made to adjust alleged grievances by employer and employees."

But in this he was clearly in error. We do not find expressed in the Recovery Act a Congressional purpose to deprive the employees of the right to strike where, as here, their demand for a wage increase is not complied with. It is fundamental that the intention and policy of Congress, as expressed in the enactment, should be effectuated. The act should receive a sensible construction—one that will not lead to injustice, oppression, or an absurd consequence. The reason and spirit of the law should prevail over its letter. *Lau Ow Bew v. United States,* 144 U.S. 47, 12 S. Ct. 517, 36 L. Ed. 340; *Jacobson v. Massachusetts,* 197 U.S. 11, 39, 25 S. Ct. 358, 49 L. Ed. 643; *United States v. Kirby,* 7 Wall. 482, 19 L. Ed 278. This statute is an emergency measure. It is so denominated. Its general object is to effect industrial recovery. The immediate objectives, in the attempted fulfillment of the general plan and purpose, are, *inter alia,* (1) to promote the organization of industry for the purpose of co-operative action among trade groups; (2) to induce and maintain united action of labor and management under adequate governmental sanctions and supervision; (3) to eliminate unfair competitive practices; (4) to promote the fullest possible utilization of the present productive capacity of industries; (5) to increase the consumption of industrial and agricultural products by increasing purchasing power; (6) to reduce and relieve unemployment; and (7) to improve standards of labor. 15 U.S.C.A., sec. 701.

The President is authorized, upon application made by one or more trade or industrial associations or groups, or upon his own motion, to "approve a code or codes of fair competition" for the government of the trade or industry in question, or any subdivision thereof, for the effectuation of the policy declared by the act. The provisions of such code shall be the standards of fair competition for such trade or industry, or subdivision thereof. *Ibid*. sec. 703. Destructive wage and price cutting are contrary to the policy of the act, and, in order to guard against such practices, the President is invested with the power to license business enterprises. *Ibid*. sec. 704.

The act, in terms, confers upon employees the right to organize and bargain collectively, *through representatives of their own choosing*. Section 7(a) (*Ibid*. sec. 707) provides that every such code of fair competition, agreement, and license approved, prescribed, or issued under the act, shall contain the following conditions:

"(1) That employees shall have the right to organize and bargain collectively through representatives of their own choosing, and shall be free from the interference, restraint, or coercion of employers of labor, or their agents, in the designation of such representatives or in self-organization or in other concerted activities for the purpose of collective bargaining or other mutual aid or protection"; and—

"(2) that no employee and no one seeking employment shall be required as a condition of employment to join any company union or to refrain from joining, organizing, or assisting a labor organization of his own choosing; . . ."

The right to organize and bargain collectively connotes the right to strike in event that such course is deemed advisable, by the employees, for their mutual aid or protection. The latter is an incident of, and imparts efficacy to, the former. It cannot be that Congress intended to reserve the right of collective action, in respect of wages, and to deprive the employees of the only weapon at their command to make its exercise effective—a lawful weapon devised to secure the enforcement of a fundamental right. A construction that would deny to the employees the privilege of striking, to enforce what they conceive to be a just demand for a wage increase, would emasculate and devitalize the clause conferring the right to organize and bargain collectively. The denial of this long-established fundamental right to strike would, in effect, compel acceptance of the scale of wages fixed by the employer. The act does not provide compulsory arbitration, in any form, of wage controversies. And "collective bargaining" is not bargaining at all, in any just sense, unless it is voluntary on both sides. *Hitchman Coal & Coke Co. v. Mitchell,* 245 U.S. 229, 38 S. Ct. 35, 62 L. Ed. 260.

The act does not empower the President to prescribe rates of pay and hours of service, binding upon employers and employees alike, nor was there any attempt here to assume such authority. Subdivision (3) of section 7(a) obliges the employers to "comply with the maximum hours of labor, minimum rates of pay, and other conditions of employment, approved or prescribed by the President." *Ibid.* sec. 707. It will be perceived that the *employers* are bound only to observe the *maximum* hours of labor, and the *minimum* rates of pay established by the President. But the act does not impose upon the employees the obligation to accept the rates of pay or the maximum hours of labor thus ordained. They are clearly at liberty to bargain, individually or collectively, for a higher rate of pay and hours of labor less the maximum so designated. This right is expressly recognized by another provision of the act. Section 7(c), which confers upon the President authority to differentiate in the exercise of the power thus granted, according to experience and skill of the employees affected, and according to the locality of the employment, enjoins "any classification according to the nature of the work involved which might tend to set a maximum as well as a minimum wage." *Ibid.* sec. 707(c).

In the permissive clause of the restraining order under review, this right of employees to organize and bargain collectively, through representatives of their own choosing, is qualified to require that such representatives be selected *"from among their own number."* This manifestly is an unwarranted attempt to modify the requirements of the act. It is a palpably unjustified interpolation. The learned Vice Chancellor evolved the theory that the Recovery Act, by the provisions in question, makes the individual plant the exclusive unit for collective bargaining, and denies to all nonemployees, termed "intermeddlers," the right of participation in such endeavors. This is obviously a misconception. The act does not, expressly or impliedly, so circumscribe the activities of the employees in striving for their mutual welfare and protection. Such a provision would run counter to a long-established federal policy in dealing with organized labor, growing out of the enforcement of the employees' constitutional guarantees. It was clearly not the purpose of Congress, as a part of the emergency program, to put collective bargaining on this parochial basis.

Many of complainant's employees joined the defendant trade union, an affiliate of the American Federation of Labor, a responsible labor organization with nationwide jurisdiction, before the strike was inaugurated. The interpretation of the act adopted by the Vice Chancellor would outlaw this organization, and prevent the affiliation of the individual unions with a body organized to promote the common aims and purposes, at least to the extent of making unlawful the rendering of aid and assistance by the principal body to secure the redress of the grievances of

employees in the individual plant, and in advancing their common interest and welfare.   The Vice Chancellor would go further.   He would
prevent the employees of the individual plant from participating in any
organization but one composed of the plant's own employees, under the
sole leadership of persons selected from its members, and limit their
activities to seeking "an equitable adjustment" of their "grievances relating to labor conditions" in their own plant.   A Congressional purpose
to effect this radical departure from a firmly established policy will not
be implied.   It must be expressed in clear and unequivocal language.

The personal liberty and right of property guaranteed by the Fifth
Amendment of the Federal Constitution embrace the right to make contracts for the purchase of the labor of others, and equally the right to
make contracts for the sale of one's own labor.   The enjoyment of these
constitutional rights is subject always to the fundamental condition that
no contract, whatever its subject-matter, can be sustained, which the law,
upon reasonable grounds, forbids as inconsistent with the public interest,
or as hurtful to the public order, or as detrimental to the common good.
Adair v. United States, 208 U.S. 161, 174, 28 S. Ct. 277, 52 L. Ed. 436;
Coppage v. Kansas, 236 U.S. 1, 14, 35 S. Ct. 240, 59 L. Ed. 441; *Hitchman Coal & Coke Co. v. Mitchell, supra.*   It would indeed be anomalous
if society, itself an organization that fosters association for the achievement of a common objective in every conceivable field of endeavor, if
not contrary to positive law or inimical to the public welfare, should bar
the union of workingmen.   The law, therefore, recognizes the right of
workingmen to unite and to invite others to join their ranks, thereby
making available the strength, influence and power that come from such
association.   By virtue of this right, powerful labor unions have been
organized.   *Gompers v. Bucks Stove & Range Co.,* 221 U.S. 418, 31
S. Ct. 492, 55 L. Ed. 797.

Labor unions, when instituted for mutual help and cooperation,
and the attainment of legitimate ends, are lawful.   They are a necessary
part of the social structure.   They are a vital force in our industrial
system, and essential for the advancement of the public welfare.   The
economic independence and security of labor are vital for the public order
and welfare.   As we have quite recently pointed out, it has long been
regarded as a proper function of the state to foster the welfare and safeguard the interests of wage-earners.   Economic and other considerations
underlie this long established state policy.   The amelioration of the condition of labor is recognized by enlightened government as a duty of
paramount importance.   And this solicitude for the wage-earners is not
alone for the members of the favored class, but for the common good.
It is conducive, if not, indeed, essential to the well-being of society that
the economic security and contentment of the class that contributes so
largely to the furnishing of its material needs be effected and sedulously

maintained. *Long v. Republic Varnish Enamel, &c., Co.,* 115 N. J. Eq. 212.[1] . . .

The legality of collective action on the part of employees, for the protection and safeguarding of their mutual interests, cannot be questioned. It is a firmly established doctrine of our federal jurisdiction that employees are entitled to organize for the purpose of securing the redress of grievances, and to promote agreements with employers relating to rates of pay and conditions of work. *Texas & N. O. R. Co. v. Brotherhood Ry. & S. S. Clerks,* 281 U.S. 548, 50 S. Ct. 427, 74 L. Ed. 1034.

And it is manifestly not essential to the legality of the combination that it be confined to the same community. That is not a requirement of the common law. The union, no matter how large or how powerful, is not an unlawful organization, nor is it an unlawful conspiracy under the common law. The law does not impose any limit upon the bargaining power which labor may acquire by union. This doctrine is given clear recognition in *Gompers v. Bucks Stove & Range Co., supra.* It is not the size of the union that taints it with illegality. It is rather the unlawful means or methods employed, or the improper conduct of the combination—the abuse of the power thereby given—that brings it within the condemnation of the law.

And the defendants cannot be regarded as "intermeddlers." They have not intruded in the legal sense. Agency indubitably existed. Employees of the complainant were members of the union when the strike was declared. The members of the defendant union and the employees of complainant, present and expectant, had a common interest in the rate of wage and the conditions of labor in the industry generally. They were not remote from any connection with or control over the matters in controversy. This was patently not a malicious interposition, but one wholly justified by the common interest in maintaining a proper standard of living. Self-interest was the motive—a yearning for the terms and conditions of labor that, in their opinion, was their due. Action of this character was justified when, in their view, the common interest was menaced. Concededly, there was no attempt to induce any of complainant's employees to leave its service in violation of any contract of employment. To render such concerted action unlawful, the object or the means used must be unlawful or exercised for the malicious purpose of injuring another; mere concert of action in and of itself, not being sufficient to render the act illegal. *N. J. Painting Co. v. Local No. 26, Brotherhood of Painters, etc.,* 96 N. J. Eq. 632, 637.[2] . . .

We do not interpret the case of *Duplex Printing Press Co. v. Deering,* 254 U.S. 443, 41 S. Ct. 172, 65 L. Ed. 349, as holding the contrary. It is not an analogous case. The question there presented was the legality of a "secondary boycott"; that is, a combination not merely to refrain

---

[1] The court here quotes at length from opinion of Taft, C.J., in American Steel Foundries v. Tri-City C. T. Council, 257 U.S. 184.

[2] The court here quotes at length from N. J. Painting Co. v. Local No. 26, Brotherhood of Painters, 96 N.J. Eq. 632.

from dealing with complainant, or to advise or by peaceful means persuade complainant's customers to refrain ("primary boycott"), but to exercise coercive pressure upon such customers, actual or prospective, in order to cause them to withhold or withdraw patronage from complainant through fear of loss or damage to themselves, should they deal with it.

This right, therefore, apart from its constitutional basis, is firmly imbedded in what has long been regarded as sound public policy in treating with labor. And it is a well-established rule that, for the purpose of determining the meaning, but not the validity, of a statute, recourse may be had to considerations of public policy. While the statute is designed to cope with the existent national emergency, said to be "productive of widespread unemployment and disorganzation of industry, which burdens interstate and foreign commerce," a purpose to disregard sound public policy must not be attributed to the lawmaking power, except upon the most cogent evidence. *Jersey City Gaslight Co. v. Consumers' Gas Co.,* 40 N. J. Eq. 427, 2 Atl. 922; *Waltham Watch Co. v. Keene,* 202 Fed. 225, 241, aff'd 209 Fed. 1007, certiorari denied, 232 U.S. 724, 34 S. Ct. 602, 58 L. Ed. 815. The natural import of the words employed in the statute, according to their common use, when applied to the subject-matter of the act, is to be considered as expressing the intention of the lawmaking body, unless the intention, so resulting from the ordinary import of the words, be repugnant to sound, acknowledged principles of national policy. And if that intention be repugnant to such principles of national policy, then the import of the words ought to be enlarged or restrained, so that it may comport with those principles, unless the legislative intention be clearly and manifestly repugnant to them. Opinion of Justices, 7 Mass.° 523. Compare *Church of the Holy Trinity v. United States,* 143 U.S. 457, 12 S. Ct. 511, 36 L. Ed. 226. There should be no greater modification of or departure from this firmly established policy than the statute expressly declares. "It is not lightly to be assumed that Congress intended to depart from a long-established policy." *Robertson v. Railroad Labor Board,* 268 U. S. 619, 45 S. Ct. 621, 69 L. Ed. 1119.

And the view that it was incumbent upon complainant's employees to resort to "mediation of (their) alleged grievances before impartial mediators such as provided under N.R.A.," is likewise untenable. The code adopted to effectuate the declared policy of the statute, and approved by President Roosevelt, prescribes a minimum wage and maximum hours of labor, and provides generally for measures calculated to preserve the balance of productive activity with consumption requirements, the stabilization of industry, and the prevention and elimination of unfair and destructive competitive prices and practices. It contains no provision for the submission to any governmental or other authority, or to arbitration, of controversies respecting wages, as a *sine qua non* of the right to strike. It provides for the submission to an industrial relations committee, chosen by the joint action of the employer and employees, and state and national industrial relations boards, constituted as therein provided, of controversies arising between the employer and employees "as to the stretch-out (or specialization) system, or any other problem of working conditions." This manifestly does not include a controversy respecting wages. *Ejusdem generis.* Even so, resort to these tribunals is not compulsory. Compare *Texas & N. O. R. Co. v. Brotherhood Ry. & S. S. Clerks, supra.* And here neither side invoked the aid of these tribunals for an adjustment of the controversy. The act provides merely that either side "may" invoke the jurisdiction of the bodies thus created. Moreover, these provisions are *ex necessitate* subject to, and the code expressly so provides, the provisions of section 7 of the Recovery Act.

It follows that, in the particulars mentioned, the learned Vice Chancellor erroneously interpreted the Recovery Act, and the injunction against a continuance of the strike was unwarranted.

If the strike itself were unlawful, as in contravention of the provisions of the Recovery Act, the restraint against picketing in any form was, of course, proper, but, inasmuch as this is not the case, it remains to consider whether the attending circumstances warrant a continuance of the restraint against picketing of a peaceable, as well as an unlawful, character. We do not think so.

True, there was evidence of unlawful acts, such as the breaking of windows of complainant's plant on one occasion, and the use, by individual participants in the strike, of abusive epithets and scurrilous and threatening language, and indulgence in other illegal practices calculated to intimidate. But there was no evidence that these unlawful acts and practices were sanctioned or acquiesced in by appellants. And there is nothing to show that the conduct of defendants tended immediately and directly to unlawful conduct by those associated with them in the common enterprise. They did not instigate, or incite the strikers and others to, violence or other illegal conduct or practices. The conduct exhibited by the affidavits is not such as to indubitably characterize the whole enterprise and course of conduct as an unlawful attempt to effect a deprivation of complainant's property rights. The unlawful occurrences were not such as to give character to the entire course of conduct, and reveal an illegal intention and purpose on the part of defendants and the pickets. On the contrary, the affidavits submitted by defendants are persuasive of an intention and purpose to refrain from picketing that would not meet the standard prescribed by law. The defendants established, by uncontradicted evidence, that they conformed, in respect of picketing, to the demands of the local police officials, and otherwise cooperated with them in their efforts to repress disorder and illegal conduct. The proofs do not establish that the pickets were grouped in such number as to constitute intimidation and obstruction. The police officials in charge permitted not more than twenty girls, ungrouped, to act as pickets at a given time, and did not allow the posting of pickets within one hundred and fifty feet of complainant's plant. Picket service was rendered by girls only.

The right to strike includes the right to use peaceable and lawful means to induce present and expectant employees to join the ranks. This rule has long been recognized in this State. It is expressly ordained by statute. 3 Comp. Stat. 3051, Sec. 128; Pamph. L. 1926, p. 348. The means employed are lawful, if peaceable, and devoid of the elements of intimidation and obstruction. *Bayer v. Brotherhood of Painters, etc.,* 108 N. J. Eq. 257; *N. J. Painting Co. v. Local No. 26, Brotherhood of Painters, etc., supra; Keuffel & Esser v. Inter. Asso. Machinists,* 93 N. J. Eq. 429; *Baldwin Lumber Co. v. Local No. 560, etc.,* 91 N. J. Eq. 240; *Jersey City Printing Co. v. Cassidy,* 63 N. J. Eq. 759, 762; *Cumberland Glass Mfg. Co. v. Glass Bottle Blowers' Ass'n,* 59 N. J. Eq. 49, 53; *Mayer v. Journeymen Stonecutters' Ass'n,* 47 N. J. Eq. 519, 531; *American Steel Foundries v. Tri-City C. T. Council,* 257 U.S. 184, 42 S. Ct. 72, 66 L. Ed. 189.

Picketing is lawful if it does not have an immediate tendency to intimidation of the other party to the controversy, or an immediate tendency to obstruct free passage such as the streets afford, consistent with the right of others to enjoy the same privilege. *Keuffel & Esser v. Inter. Asso. Machinists, supra; American Steel Foundries v. Tri-City C. T. Council, supra; Nann v. Raimist,* 225 N. Y. 307, 174 N.E. 690. The modern view is that picketing is not *per se* unlawful, and should not be enjoined, if peaceably carried on for a lawful purpose.

The general rule is that a preliminary injunction will not issue where the material facts in complainant's bill and affidavits, on which complainant's right depends, are met by a full, explicit and circumstantial denial under oath. It will issue only where the denial lacks these essential qualities, and upon the entire showing from both sides it appears reasonably probably that the complainant had the right claimed. *Ideal Laundry Co. v. Gugliemone,* 107 N. J. Eq. 108, 115.[3] . . .

Inasmuch as there was evidence of illegal acts by the pickets and their associates, it was proper to restrain defendants from a repetition of such unlawful conduct. The management of the strike was in their hands. Concededly, they formed and maintained a picket line to make the strike effective. Their insistence is that they did not direct, consent to, or acquiesce in the unlawful acts, but a restraint directed to them was nevertheless justified; for the misconduct occurred in the performance of the duties for which the pickets had been employed. The unlawful acts were done in defendants' behalf, and for their benefit, and in aid of the strike promoted by them. *Connett v. United Hatters of North America,* 76 N. J. Eq. 202, 207; *Hitchman Coal & Coke Co. v. Mitchell, supra; Local Union 313 H.R.E.I.A. v. Stathakis,* 135 Ark. 86, 205 S. W. 450,

---

[3] The court here quotes at length from Keuffel & Esser v. Inter. Asso. of Machinists, 93 N.J. Eq. 429.

6 A.L.R. 894; *Southern Ry. Co. v. Machinists' Local Union No. 14,* 111 Fed. 49, 54; *Great Northern Ry. Co. v. Local Great Falls Lodge of Inter. Asso. of Machinists,* 283 Fed. 557.

The order is modified accordingly, and, as so modified, affirmed, and the cause remanded for further proceedings in conformity with this opinion.[4]

IN THE MATTER OF THE GENERAL CIGAR COMPANY and CIGAR MAKERS INTERNATIONAL UNION OF AMERICA.

No. 163. Decisions of the National Labor Board, 1934.

A strike involving approximately 650 of the General Cigar Company, Nanticoke, Pennsylvania, employees occurred in December 1933, following the discharge of one Ambrose Lastowski, an officer of Local No. 199 of the Cigar Makers International Union, and a disagreement regarding working conditions.

The Board's attempt to mediate the dispute was not completely successful. Agreement was reached on all the differences between the parties, except the reinstatement of Lastowski. The company agreed to enter into a contract with the union, containing among other things, a provision for the collection of union dues on company property. The employer, however, refused, after extended negotiations, to reinstate Lastowski and declined to reopen its plant until the validity of his discharge had been finally determined. A hearing was accordingly held at Nanticoke, by a representative of this Board to determine the causes of Lastowski's dismissal.

Under Section 7(a) of the National Industrial Recovery Act, an employee may not be required to refrain from joining, organizing or assisting a labor organization of his own choice. The statute thus forbids the discharge of an employee for union activity. There obviously is no more effective way of interfering with the self-organization of employees than to discharge those who are active in the union of their own choosing. The statutory requirements may not be evaded by the ready reliance on other grounds for discharge. The employer, in dismissing an employee, must not be actuated in any degree whatsoever by the latter's union affiliation or activities. The statute does not impair the freedom of employers of labor to discharge their employees for infrac-

---

[4] In Rosenthal-Ettlinger Co. v. Schlossberg, 149 Misc. 210, 266 N.Y.S. 762 (1933). it was held that employees have no right to carry signs accusing an employer of having violated Section 7(a) of the National Industrial Recovery Act where there has been no hearing on the charges.

In J. & T. Cousins Co. v. Shoe & Leather Workers' Industrial Union, 150 Misc. 575, 268 N.Y.S. 547 (1933), it was held that violation by an employer of the President's Reemployment Agreement was no defense to an action by the employer to enjoin unlawful picketing by defendant union.

tions of company rules or for other proper and adequate business reasons. To safeguard the privileges conferred by the statute, however, it is imperative that the circumstances of a discharge be carefully scrutinized and that its validity be determined by the appropriate agencies of the Government entrusted with the administration and enforcement of this law.

The evidence presented at the hearing at Nanticoke is conflicting and obscure. The employment record of Lastowski reveals several infractions of company rules. Testimony was offered that he had been guilty of certain improprieties of language, but this charge was emphatically denied. No persuasive evidence was offered establishing the claim of discriminatory discharge.

The National Labor Board consequently rules that:

1. The General Cigar Company may deny the petition of Ambrose Lastowski for reinstatement.

2. The strike shall be called off immediately, the plant shall be reopened, and the workers shall return to work without prejudice or discrimination.

3. An agreement shall be made within ten (10) days between the General Cigar Company, and the Cigar Makers International Union of America, Local No. 199, covering the eleven points embodied in' the letter of the Grievance Committee, dated December 11, 1933, to the General Cigar Company.[1]

IN THE MATTER OF EDWARD F. CALDWELL & COMPANY and LIGHTING EQUIPMENT WORKERS LOCAL UNION NO. 19427.

No. 31. Decisions of the National Labor Relations Board, 1934.

This case involves the alleged violation of section 7(a) of the National Industrial Recovery Act by the Edward F. Caldwell Company of New York, which is subject to the Code of Fair Competition for

---

[1] *Cf.* H. B. Rosenthal-Ettlinger Co. v. Schlossberg, 149 Misc. 210, 266 N.Y.S. 762 (1933) : "The provisions of the National Industrial Recovery Act have made no change in the law as thus declared by the Court of Appeals. The only provision of that act which possibly affects the law as stated by the Court of Appeals, is the provision 'that no employee . . . shall be required as a condition of employment to . . . refrain from joining . . . a labor organization of his own choosing.' Section 7(a), subd. 2.

"If that means that an employer may not discharge an employee for any reason, or for no reason, and in the case of any man discharged must be prepared to show good cause for the discharge other than the union affiliations of the man discharged, all employees who are union members have been transferred to a status equivalent to that of the civil service, a result which could not have been intended. Whatever the rule of the unions may be, that is not the law of the land."

On the jurisdiction of the National Labor Board in cases of this character, see In the Matter of Tubize Chatillon Corp. & Rayon Workers Union, Case No. 254 (1934) ; In the Matter of Jersey City & Lyndhurst Bus Co. & Brotherhood of R. R. Trainmen, Case No. 235 (1934).

the Fabricated Metal Products Manufacturing and Metal Finishing and Metal Coating Industry. A strike of more than 100 employees has been in progress since May 28, 1934. The New York Regional Labor Board held hearings, both before and after the strike began, for the purpose of ascertaining the facts and of attempting to settle the original differences between the parties.

For a number of years the Edward F. Caldwell Company, manufacturers of ornamental fixtures, had had individual contracts with approximately forty of its employees. During the autumn of 1933 a majority of the company's employees made known their desire to be represented by an outside organization for the purposes of collective bargaining, and maintained this attitude thereafter. The company nevertheless, began to promote the further signature of individual contracts in April 1934, but refrained from doing so upon being advised by the New York Board that certain clauses in the agreements were inconsistent with the provisions of section 7(a) of the National Industrial Recovery Act. The objectionable clauses were withdrawn, and a new form of agreement was drafted.

On May 22 a representative of Lighting Equipment Workers Local Union No. 19427 submitted a proposed collective agreement to the company. Beginning on the very same day, and continuing until May 25, the company called every employee to the office, and requested him to sign a copy of the revised individual contract. The request was not restricted to the employees who had been parties to the original agreements. Over 100 of the 150 employees, including a majority of the union members, signed the contracts. The contracts contained express provisions covering wages and hours, as well as a clause permitting termination by either party upon thirty days' notice.

The members of the Lighting Equipment Workers Union, feeling that the circulation of the individual agreements revealed the company's unwillingness to bargain collectively, called a strike of the Caldwell Company employees. About 125 employees participated in this strike, which became effective on May 28. The company rejected a proposal of the New York Regional Labor Board for the settlement of the strike, which called for the reinstatement of all the strikers and the subsequent opening of collective bargaining negotiations. On June 20 the company wrote to those strikers who had signed the individual contracts, but not to the others, informing them that their positions would be available to them until June 26, after which time the company would hire new employees. The strikers rejected the company's subsequent offer to reinstate immediately all the employees who were parties to the individual agreements, and ten of those who were not. A few of the strikers have since returned to work and the company has employed about 75 new employees, over 40 of whom have signed individual agreements.

The union contends that the action of the company in presenting the individual contracts to its employees, when it was well aware of their desire to bargain collectively, constitutes a violation of section 7(a) of the National Industrial Recovery Act. The union also claims that the company exercised coercion to induce the employees to sign the individual agreements. The evidence of actual coercion is not impressive, and this Board considers the case on the assumption that it did not occur. Section 7(a), however, does more than prohibit employers from coercing their employees; it provides that employees shall have the right to bargain collectively through representatives of their own choosing, and it prohibits interference, as well as coercion, by employers with employees' concerted activities for the purpose of collective bargaining, or other mutual aid or protection.

An employer who, having already been informed by the representatives of his employees that they desire to bargain collectively, deliberately sets out to bargain with them individually, interferes with the right guaranteed his employees by the law. The Caldwell Company's motive is revealed by the fact that the individual contracts were presented, at the very time that the employees were attempting to negotiate collectively, to a large number of men with whom the company had not previously had similar agreements. These contracts, which covered wages and hours, the prime subjects of collective negotiation, would, if valid, empty the employees' right of collective bargaining of all significance and purpose. Since these particular agreements contain a provision which enables either party to terminate them within thirty days, the National Labor Relations Board finds it unnecessary to consider whether or not such contracts would be held by a court of competent jurisdiction to be either voidable or void, as contrary to the public policy embodied in section 7(a).

Findings. The National Labor Relations Board finds that the circulation of the individual contracts by the Edward F. Caldwell Company constituted a violation of the right of its employees to be free from the interference of the employer in their concerted activities for the purpose of collective bargaining.

Enforcement. The National Labor Relations Board rules that, in order to restore a condition in harmony with the law, the following steps should be taken:

1. The company should immediately offer reinstatement, to their former positions, to all the employees who struck on May 28 who are not now working for the company, discharging if necessary all employees hired since the strike, and terminating, according to their terms, such individual contracts as may be necessary to bring about this result. All reinstatements should be made within five days from the date of this decision, except in the case of those employees who can only be reinstated by discharging others now under contract, and in such cases the reinstatements should be made by terminating such contracts, and in any event within thirty-five days from the date of this decision.

2. The company should proceed to bargain collectively with the representatives of its employees. Should any question arise as to the

authority of Lighting Equipment Workers Local Union No. 19427 to represent the employees, an election will be conducted by this Board, or its agents, to determine the identity of their representative or representatives. Unless, within six days from the date of this decision, the company has notified the Board that it has commenced the reinstatement directed above, and within 36 days that it has completed the reinstatement and complied with paragraph 2, the case will be referred to the Compliance Division of the National Recovery Administration and to other agencies of the Government for appropriate action.

IN THE MATTER OF THE DENVER TRAMWAY CORPORATION and AMALGAMATED ASSOCIATION OF STREET AND ELECTRIC RAILWAY EMPLOYEES OF AMERICA, DIVISION 1001.

No. 149. Decisions of the National Labor Board, 1934.

On October 31, 1933 officials of the Amalgamated Association of Street and Electric Railway Employees, Division 1001, purporting to represent a majority of the employees of the Denver Tramway Corporation, a member of the Transit Code, called upon President Robertson of this company to negotiate a collective bargaining agreement. Mr. Robertson refused to deal with the delegation on the ground that the company's employees were represented by an Employees' Representative Committee selected in accordance with a plan in effect for many years. The next day the National Labor Board received the Amalgamated's complaint which was referred to Conciliator Myers of the Labor Department. The authority of the officials of the Amalgamated having been questioned, Mr. Myers proposed that an election by secret ballot be held for the selection of representatives in accordance with section 7(a) of the National Industrial Recovery Act. Mr. Robertson agreed to this proposal and cooperated in the holding of an election. The notice of the election prepared by Mr. Myers announced that it was being held to decide the question "whether the employees desire as a collective bargaining agency the Amalgamated or the present collective bargaining agency known as the Employees' Representative Committee." Of the 714 qualified voters, 36 did not vote, while 353 voted for the Amalgamated and 325 for the Committee.

Thereafter, the Amalgamated submitted to the Tramway a proposed agreement in which it was provided, among other things, that said agreement was to govern "the relations to exist during the term of this Agreement between the company and the members of the said Association." While negotiations between the Amalgamated and the Tramway upon this proposed agreement were proceeding, the Tramway continued to

deal with the Committee. The Amalgamated thereupon complained to the
Board that the company would not recognize it as the exclusive collective
bargaining agency of all the employees. A hearing was held before the
Board on this complaint.

It is the decision of the National Labor Board that the Amalgamated
Association of Street and Electric Railway Employees was selected by a
majority of those voting, both as the agency through which the employees
of the Denver Tramway Corporation would collectively bargain with
the management in negotiating an agreement and in the settlement of
any disputes which may arise between it and its employees. Any agreement reached in conformity with this decision must apply alike to all
employees of the company. The limitation to its membership in the form
of contract submitted by the Amalgamated does not meet this requirement, and must be modified accordingly.

Messrs. Green and Lewis concur in the result reached above, but do
not concur in the language of the last sentence of the opinion.

Mr. du Pont's dissenting opinion is as follows:

1.   A selection of representatives, for the purpose of collective bargaining with the employer, by the employees of the Denver Tramway
Corporation has been conducted by the National Labor Board.

2.   The ballots cast show that—

> 353 of said employees favor, as their agency for collective
> bargaining, the Amalgamated Street and Electric Railway Em-
> ployees of America.

> 325 of said employees favor, as their agency for collective
> bargaining, the Employees' Representative Committee, the plan now
> in use on the property of the Denver Tramway Corporation.

3.   The agencies above mentioned shall represent respectively the
numbers of said employees favoring them.

4.   With respect to thirty-six employees who cast no ballot, the Denver Tramway Corporation shall bargain with them individually until such
time as all or part of them shall choose representatives for collective
bargaining.[1]

---

[1] Compare the provisions of the Automobile Settlement, announced by the President March 25, 1934:

"Settlement of the threatened automobile strike is based on the following principles:

1.   The employers agree to bargain collectively with the freely chosen representatives of groups and not to discriminate in any way against any employee on the
ground of his union labor affiliations.

2.   If there be more than one group each bargaining committee shall have total
membership pro rata to the number of men each member represents.

3.   NRA to set up within twenty-four hours a board, responsible to the President
of the United States, to sit in Detroit to pass on all questions of representation, discharge and discrimination. Decision of the board shall be final and binding on
employer and employees. Such a board to have access to all payrolls and to all lists
of claimed employee representation and such board will be composed of,

    (a)   A labor representative
    (b)   An industry representative
    (c)   A neutral.

In cases where no lists of employees claiming to be represented have been dis-

IN THE MATTER OF NATIONAL ANILINE & CHEMICAL COMPANY and ALLIED CHEMICAL WORKERS LOCAL NO. 18705.

No. 234. Decisions of the National Labor Board, 1934.

This controversy between the National Aniline & Chemical Company and its employees in Buffalo comes to the National Labor Board by reference from the Buffalo Regional Board because its ruling has been disregarded by the company. The company did not sign the N.R.A. but became subject to the Code for the Chemical Industry when it went into effect on February 20, 1934.

In November, 1933, representatives of the Allied Chemical Workers' newly organized local No. 18705, to which (excluding foremen, chemists and office staff) most of the 1200 employees of the company in Buffalo belonged, held conferences with Mr. E. C. Osborn, the manager of the plant. These conferences, in which U. S. Commissioner of Conciliation Williams participated, led to an oral agreement on several points. Mr. Osborn undertook to meet a committee of workers to make a memorandum of the terms tentatively agreed on in the discussions. When the committee came at the appointed hour on November 24th, he presented to them a plant notice which embodied many, but not all, of these terms. In handing it to the committee, Mr. Osborn said, "That is all I have to say; there is nothing more to be done until the code comes through." Despite the ill feeling that this change of attitude created, the union was dissuaded from a strike by Mr. Williams and accepted postponement of further negotiations until the code should be approved. The code in February satisfied certain of the demands of the union, especially those concerning hours. But the union still wished to obtain better working conditions and especially to get by means of a collective agreement an express verbal recognition from the company of what the company by its action was already tacitly acknowledging, namely, that the union was the employees' collective bargaining agency.

---

closed to the employer, there shall be no basis for a claim of discrimination. No such disclosure in a particular case shall be made without specific direction of the President.

4. The government makes it clear that it favors no particular union or particular form of employee organization or representation. The government's only duty is to secure absolute and uninfluenced freedom of choice without coercion, restraint, or intimidation from any source.

5. The industry understands that in reduction or increases of force, such human relationships as married men with families shall come first and then seniority, individual skill and efficient service. After these facts have been considered no greater proportion of outside union employees similarly situated shall be laid off than of other employees. By outside union employees is understood a paid-up member in good standing, or anyone legally obligated to pay up. An appeal shall lie in case of dispute on principles of paragraph 5 to the Board of Three. . . ."

The National Labor Board has ruled that the right of the employees to bargain collectively implies an obligation upon the employer to negotiate in good faith and to make every reasonable effort to reach an agreement. See In the Matter of National Lock Co. and Federal Labor Union No. 18830, No. 52 (1934).

Soon after the code went into operation, the union proposed an agreement for immediate signature which embodied the tentative oral stipulations of November. The company refused to sign such an agreement. Thereupon the union, at the urging of Commissioner Williams, withdrew this so-called ultimatum and made a new proposal on March 8, postponing an immediate consideration of substantive terms of employment but obligating the company to deal with the union. This proposal was in the following words:

"It is hereby mutually understood and agreed that the National Aniline & Chemical Co., of Buffalo, New York, recognize and agree to meet and treat with the accredited officers and committee of the Aniline & Chemical Workers' Local No. 18705, affiliated with the American Federation of Labor, on all matters and grievances arising while in the employment of the National Aniline & Chemical Co., of Buffalo, N. Y.

"Regarding the Plant notice, posted by the National Aniline & Chemical Co. on November 25, 1933, the said Company agrees to meet in conference with the representatives of the above mentioned union for the purpose of adjusting any differences or grievances arising in relation to the said notice."

The company rejected the proposal and suggested an indefinite postponement of negotiations till "new legislation" was acted on by Congress. This rejection and suggestion were the immediate cause of the union's strike vote on March 16. Substantially all of the 1200 men went out the following day or as soon thereafter as they had got their operations into a condition where they could be abandoned without danger. The strike was still in effect on April 10 when the Buffalo Regional Labor Board heard the parties and ruled that the company and the union should "proceed at once to negotiate an agreement," and on May 1 when a hearing was held by the National Labor Board, following the refusal of the company to comply with the ruling of the Buffalo Board.

The company asserts that the strike was called without cause; but the union insists that there was need of a written contract with the company because the company had in November broken off negotiations rather than sign even a memorandum, and had issued a plant notice which did not carry out the understandings orally arrived at. The union, therefore, insisted on a writing which at least should recognize the union's representative capacity. The company's position is that since it has never refused to bargain collectively, there is no reason for a signed statement or contract such as that proposed on March 8.

The company maintains that it is respecting the right of employees to bargain collectively because it receives representatives of the union and discusses working conditions and grievances with them. But the right of collective bargaining means more than this. As we said recently in the Hall Baking Company case, "The objective sought by the law is the making of collective agreements." To be sure, the substance of these agreements is wholly a matter of negotiation, and is not prescribed in any respect. But an attitude of unwillingness to enter into any obligation with respect to future relations thwarts the statute, and this is the attitude of the National Aniline & Chemical Co., not only last fall but very definitely in May.

At the hearing in Washington the company's attorney unqualifiedly and repeatedly said that the company was unwilling to sign any agreement with the representatives of its employees. Nor was the company favorable to making an oral contract in the presence of witnesses. Indeed to the statement that the company appeared to be unwilling to give its employees any pledge for the future, the attorney replied, "I am inclined to think that would be the attitude of the company."

The company's refusal by word and by conduct to enter into a bilateral agreement prevents that joint regulation of conditions of employment which is the essence of the collective labor bargain. The company did not object to meeting the union, for a union organizer not employed by the company participated in many of the conferences. It did not allege that the conferees were not representative of all or some of the company's employees. Nor was there so inevitable and fixed a divergence between the parties concerning the working conditions that should exist in the plant that it could be maintained that the possibilities of collective bargaining had been exhausted. Thus, the company neither challenged the authority of the negotiators for the employees nor found it definitely impossible to agree with them as to the content of a settlement. The evidence is clear that, even if these proper persons had presented or might present acceptable demands, the company would not record, nor engage itself with them to observe, the employment code that they might jointly agree upon. If this is not a denial by the company of its employees' right to bargain collectively, the promise of section 7(a)[1] is tinsel. Congress

---

[1] Compare statement of General Johnson and Donald Richberg, N.R.A. Release No. 463 (1933):

"The plain meaning of Section 7(a) cannot be changed by any interpretation by anyone. It is the function of the Administrator and the courts to apply and to interpret the law in its administration; and no one else can assume this function and no official interpretation can be circumscribed, affected or foreclosed by any one writing his own interpretation into any code or agreement. Such an interpretation has no place there and cannot be permitted.

"The words 'open shop' and 'closed shop' are not used in the law and cannot be written into the law.

"These words have no agreed meaning and will be erased from the dictionary of the N.R.A.

"The law requires in codes and agreements that 'employees shall have the right to organize and bargain collectively through representatives of their own choosing.'

"This can mean only one thing, which is that employees can choose any one they desire to represent them, or they can choose to represent themselves. Employers likewise can make collective bargains with organized employees, or individual agreements with those who choose to act individually; provided, of course, that no such collective or individual agreement is in violation of any State or federal law. But neither employers or employees are required, by law, to agree to any particular contract, whether proposed as an individual or collective agreement.

"The law provides that employees shall be free from the interference, restraint or coercion of employers in the exercise of their rights established by the law. The conduct of employers which is here prohibited has been defined by the Supreme Court

did not write vain words, and we must not empty "the right to bargain collectively" of serious meaning.

Though there were suggestions at the hearing that the company had blacklisted certain of the strikers, the actual policy of he company has been to take on no new men during the strike but to persuade the strikers to return to work. In this the company has had a modicum of success. The jobs not so filled remain open. By refraining from recruiting a new force, the company is in a better position to reach an amicable settlement.

The National Labor Board therefore directs that, to conform with the statute, the company resume at once negotiations with the committee designated by the union, and that both parties make an earnest effort to conclude a bilateral contract concerning conditions of employment in the plant. Concurrently with the beginning of these negotiations, the strike is to be called off and the company is to reinstate all the strikers as rapidly as it has need for workmen. In so doing the company should respect seniority of service and must not exclude any man for his leadership or activity in the union or in the strike (unless violence or other improper conduct is proved against him to the satisfaction of the Buffalo Regional Labor Board). If all the employees of March 17 are not reinstated at once, the company, within ten days, should prepare and send to the Regional Labor Board a list of the employees in order of seniority still waiting employment, and, as it has need of workmen, should draw in order from this list so long as there are men on it desiring to return to work.

Mr. du Pont's dissenting opinion is as follows:

This controversy between the National Aniline & Chemical Company and its employees in Buffalo comes to the National Labor Board by reference from the Buffalo Regional Board because its ruling has been disregarded by the Company.

The National Aniline and Chemical Company did not sign the N.R.A. nor did it become subject to a Code until February 20, 1934 when the Code for the Chemical Industry went into effect.

---

in the case entitled—T. & N. O. R. R. v. Brotherhood of Railway Clerks, 281 U.S. 548. The rulings of the Supreme Court lay down the law which governs the N.R.A

"Under Section 7(a), employers are forbidden to require 'as a condition of employment' that an employee shall either 'join a company union,' or 'refrain from joining, organizing, or assisting a labor organization of his own choosing.' The law does not prohibit the existence of a local labor organization, which may be called a company union and is composed only of the employees of one company. But it does prohibit an employer from requiring, as a condition of employment, that any employee join a company union and it prohibits the maintenance of a company union, or any other labor organization, by the interference, restraint or coercion of an employer.

"If there is any dispute in a particular case over who are the representatives of the employees of their own choosing, the N.R.A. will offer its services to conduct an impartial investigation and, if necessary, a secret ballot to settle the question.

"The N.R.A. will not undertake in any instance to decide that a particular contract should be made, or should not be made between lawful representatives of employees and employers; or to decide that a contract which has been lawfully made should not be enforced.

"Cooperation in all industrial relations depends largely on the making and maintenance of agreements. The N.R.A. will promote and aid such cooperation."

Nevertheless, Mr. E. C. Osborn, manager of the Buffalo plant of the Company held conferences with representatives of the Allied Chemical Workers' Local No. 18705 during November 1933.

At these conferences U. S. Commissioner Williams participated.

Mr. Osborn undertook to meet a committee of workers to make a memorandum of the terms tentatively agreed upon at the conferences.

This meeting was held on November 24th. Mr. Osborn presented a proposed plant notice that embodied many but not all of these terms.

This notice was posted on November 25th.

Mr. Osborn stated that nothing more could be done until the Code came through.

The members of the Union, though no election to choose representatives had been held and though the Company was not obliged to deal with them, became dissatisfied and threatened to strike from which threat they were dissuaded by Mr. Williams.

The Code of the Chemical Industry which became effective in February covered some of the remaining unsettled points but the union was not satisfied concerning certain working conditions.

The union especially desired a collective agreement to the effect that the union was the employees' collective bargaining agency notwithstanding the fact that not all of the employees of the company were members of the union and would, by recognition of the union as the bargaining agency, be deprived of choice of representatives and all rights of representation.

The company refused to sign such an agreement.

Therefore, at the instance of Commissioner Williams, the union withdrew its demand and, on March 8th, made a new proposal in the following words:—

"It is hereby mutually understood and agreed that the National Aniline & Chemical Co., of Buffalo, New York, recognize and agree to meet and treat with the accredited officers and committee of the Aniline & Chemical Workers' Local No. 18705, affiliated with the American Federation of Labor, on all matters and grievances arising while in the employment of the National Aniline & Chemical Co., of Buffalo, N. Y.

"Regarding the Plant notice, posted by the National Aniline & Chemical Co., on November 25th, 1933, the said Company agrees to meet in conference with the representatives of the above mentioned union for the purpose of adjusting any differences or grievances arising in relation to the said notice."

The Company rejected the proposal and suggested an indefinite postponement of negotiations till "new legislation" was acted on by Congress. This rejection and suggestion were the immediate cause of the union's strike vote on March 16th.

The Company asserts that the strike was called without cause. Conferences had been held with the representatives of at least a part of the employees and an agreement had been reached on many of the points under discussion. The Company had not refused to continue the conferences but had suggested postponement until Congress had taken action on new legislation then pending. The Company did refuse to post the notice stating that all grievances would be taken up with the union—quite a different matter than a refusal to meet with accredited representatives of the employees.

The union insists upon a written contract.

The Company maintains that it is respecting the rights of employees to bargain collectively when it receives their representatives and discusses working conditions and grievances with them.

The law does not require written contract between employer and employee. The conferences of November 1933 resulted in terms tentatively agreed upon, many of which were embodied in the plant notice posted on November 25th.

It is not in evidence that any of these terms have been violated by the Company nor that the possibilities of collective bargaining had been exhausted. Had there been misunderstanding between the parties the Board might well be called upon to demand a definite contract but this condition of misunderstanding does not exist.

The Company has adopted a conciliatory policy and acting thereunder has taken on no new men during the strike and has tried to persuade the strikers to return to work. Jobs not so filled remain open. No new force has been recruited. . . .

IN THE MATTER OF PEOPLES PHARMACIES INC. and MARYLAND ASSOCIATION OF EMPLOYEE PHARMACISTS INC.

No. 199. Decisions of the National Labor Board, 1934.

In February 1934 the Peoples Pharmacies Inc., of Baltimore and the Maryland Association of Employee Pharmacists Inc., jointly submitted this case to the National Labor Board for arbitration. The dispute grew out of the company's refusal to sign an agreement presented by the Association. This agreement already governed other drug stores in the Baltimore area.

This Board held a hearing on February 26th, at which time the proposed contract was submitted to it. Further action was delayed pending an attempt to obtain an industry-wide settlement for the Baltimore area.

At the expiration of the time limit set and upon failure to obtain a general agreement, this Board was called upon to render a decision. At the time of the hearing the parties were in disagreement on nine of the thirty-one sections. Among the twenty-two agreed to by both parties were four which were amended by mutual consent to read as follows:

"Discharge During Trial—The employer may discharge the Employee on trial at will at any time during a period of four (4) weeks, payment to be made only during time employee is actually engaged.

"Salaries—No salaries of any employee covered by this agreement, in effect at the time of the signing of this agreement, shall be reduced. It is further agreed that all payments of salaries shall be made at the close of each working week, or on the first and fifteenth of each month where the employee is employed by the month.

"Employee's Additional Legal Rights—In the event of the violation of this agreement by the Employer, in addition to any other action taken by the Association, and without restriction because of any action taken by the Association, or which is within the Association's right to take, the Employee shall be entitled to institute and bring separate action for distinct legal and equitable relief. This agreement shall not be construed to bar the Employee from bringing any action for wages, personal injuries, or other claims, which he may have against the Employer.

"Discrimination for Association Activity—The Employer shall not discriminate against any Association members because of their Association activity outside of business hours."

In the matter of the nine contested sections, the Board is satisfied with the proposals of the Association as to the five entitled "Trial Only For Certified Association Applicants," "Hiring Deemed Steady," "Liability For Full Scale," "Vacation," and "Hostile Associations." In the remaining four the Board is of the opinion that changes are desirable, in view of the fact that this is the first collective agreement entered into by these parties. These four sections shall read as follows:

"Employ Members in Good Standing—The Employer agrees not to hire any Registered Pharmacist or Assistant, not in good standing with the Association or not a member of the Association, except that if the Association is unable to supply the Employer with the character of help which he desires, whether white or negro, male or female, Gentile or Jewish, within twenty-four hours after he has requested such help, then the said Employer may employ such persons as are available.

"No Discharge—No Employee shall be discharged, furloughed or 'vacationed,' except upon due and sufficient cause or with the consent of the Association, except as hereinbefore otherwise provided, but, in the event that the financial condition of the business is or becomes such as to demand a reduction in employment, such reduction may be made either by discharge or reduction of the hours of employment; provided the same is done in good faith and without benefiting one Employee at the expense of another.

"Discharge Compensation—An Employee shall receive two weeks' minimum notice of discharge in writing, or its monetary equivalent, except where the discharge is upon due and sufficient cause.

"*Election As Individual Contract*—The particular provisions of this agreement governing the hours of labor, wages, contract duration, and other related matters, shall enure personally to and be deemed the individual employment contract between the Employer and all Employees working for him during the period of this agreement."

The National Labor Board rules that the agreement presented by the Maryland Association of Employee Pharmacists Inc., to the Peoples Pharmacies Inc., with the changes above set forth in the four sections as amended at the hearing and the four sections as modified by the Board shall be binding on both parties from the date of signing, which shall be not later than five days from the date of this decision.[1]

IN THE MATTER OF TAMAQUA UNDERWEAR COMPANY and AMALGAMATED CLOTHING WORKERS OF AMERICA.

No. 27. Decisions of the National Labor Relations Board, 1934.

This case has been referred to the National Labor Relations Board by the Philadelphia Regional Labor Board following the failure of the employer to comply with the opinion of the Regional Board dated July 6, 1934. The employer is subject to the Code of Fair Competition for the Underwear and Allied Products Industry, effective September 18, 1933.

During April and May 1934, the Amalgamated Clothing Workers of America succeeded in enrolling in its ranks a number of employees of the Tamaqua Underwear Company of Tamaqua, Pennsylvania. On the afternoon of May 25th, Dr. J. E. Auchmuty, the general manager of the company and its guiding spirit, addressed the employees at a meeting in the

---

[1] Compare Statement of General Johnson, Administrator under the National Industrial Recovery Act, of September 4, 1933:

"Employers cannot refuse to bargain about conditions of employment with the self-chosen representatives of their workers. Employers cannot make as a condition of employment that their workers join a company union. But employers are not compelled to *agree* on any particular scale of wages or conditions of employment merely because they are bargaining with self-chosen representatives of organized workers. And no employer is denied the right to bargain individually with any worker if the worker so chooses. It is, however, the worker's choice as to whether he shall bargain individually or collectively through a representative. If any employer should make a contract with a particular organization to employ only members of that organization, especially if that organization did not have 100 percent membership among his employees, that would in effect be a contract to interfere with his workers' freedom of choice of their representatives or with their right to bargain individually and would amount to employer coercion on these matters which is contrary to the law."

In Drake Bakeries v. Bowles, Com. Pleas Ct., Cuyahoga County, Ohio, 1934. 104 C.C.H. 5357, a strike for a closed shop was held illegal because in violation of the National Industrial Recovery Act and all persuasion of workers to join the strikers was enjoined. *Cf.* Elkind & Sons, Inc. v. Retail Clerks Int. Protective Ass'n, 169 Atl. 494 (N.J. Ch. 1933) ; J. Lichtman & Sons v. Leather Workers' Industrial Union, 169 Atl. 498 (N.J. Ch. 1933).

plant which had been called and organized by several employees in supervisory positions. At this meeting, Dr. Auchmuty announced the formation of what he and all others concerned call a "company union."

On the initiative of the management and during regular plant hours, a poll of the employees was taken on May 28th, in which they were asked to state, over their signatures, whether they desired to join "our own company union" or the Amalgamated Clothing Workers of America. The results of this election, if it may be called such, do not appear in the record.

The history of immediately subsequent events is lost in the confusion of contradictory testimony. It is clear, however, that on May 28th those employees who had failed to signify their intention of joining the company union were locked out. The employees thus locked out declared a strike, but returned to work on June 6, following a settlement effected by the Philadelphia Regional Labor Board.

As a result of the efforts of the Philadelphia Regional Labor Board and under its supervision, an election was held on June 20th, in which a majority of the employees expressed a desire to be represented for the purpose of collective bargaining by the Tamaqua Employees' Union, the "company union." On June 22, Dr. Auchmuty for the company, and Allison L. Hallman, President, for the "company union," signed the following:

"It is hereby agreed that the Tamaqua Underwear Company agree to recognize the demand of the Tamaqua Employees' Union for a closed shop, beginning June 22, 1934."

On June 25, the Monday following the election, when sixty-six members of the Amalgamated came as usual to work, they were told by Dr. Auchmuty that they would be refused their old posts unless they joined the "company union." This sixty-one of them have not done and are accordingly denied employment by the company.

The facts of this case do not require us to determine, in the light of Section 7 (a) of the National Industrial Recovery Act, the validity of a closed shop agreement with a bona fide labor union resulting in the discharge of employees not joining the union. We need to decide only whether the Tamaqua Employees' Union is a company union within the intent of that part of Section 7 (a) which provides that "no employee and no one seeking employment shall be required as a condition of employment to join any company union." The hands which guided its organization were those of employees who were in an executive or supervisory capacity; and its present destinies are controlled not by the female stitchers and cutters of which almost the entire membership is composed, but by an assistant forelady, Mrs. Evans, a comparatively well-paid machinist, Hallman, and a male employee of the shipping department. If Dr. Auchmuty did not initiate the union, he has at least fostered its growth with considerable enthusiasm, by advising his employees to affiliate therewith, and by permitting it to use the plant for meetings and his office equipment for certain typing.

The character of the union is further indicated by the agreement it negotiated. A collective bargaining agreement such as this, which provides merely for the closed shop, is an oddity in the annals of labor relations. The organizers of the union, Mrs. Evans and Mr. Hallman, negotiated the closed shop agreement without, it seems, consulting the membership, and obtained the consent of Dr. Auchmuty without debate or deliberation. In this connection, the testimony of Hallman before the Board is enlightening in its lack of candor. It was Hallman who signed the agreement as President of the union. He testified at first that there was no closed shop agreement. When the existence of the agreement was put in evidence and Hallman was recalled, he stated that he was "very unfamiliar with the formation of unions, and everything else, so far as this is concerned," and that he did not even know that such an agreement was called a closed shop agreement.

In the light of all the circumstances present in this case, we are of the opinion that the Tamaqua Employees' Union is a company union within the meaning of Section 7 (a). The result is that it was contrary to the terms of the statute to dismiss those who would not join.

It is to be noted that the Philadelphia Regional Labor Board announced publicly to all voters prior to the election of June 20, that there would be no discrimination against any person participating in the election. The record is barren of evidence that this condition was unsatisfactory to the employer. And there is some evidence of assent to this condition by the leaders of the company union.

Findings. The sixty-one members of the Amalgamated Clothing Workers of America were locked out in violation of Section 7 (a).

Enforcement. Unless within ten days from the date of this decision the company has notified this Board that it has offered the aforesaid employees immediate reinstatement in their former positions with the same rights as previously enjoyed, the case will be referred to the Compliance Division of the National Recovery Administration and to other agencies of the Government for appropriate action.

CHAPTER X.

EMPLOYER INTERFERENCE WITH THE "RIGHT" TO WORK.

DICK v. NORTHERN PACIFIC RY. CO.

Washington Supreme Court. 86 Wash. 211, 150 Pac. 8 (1915).

Appeal from a judgment of the superior court for King county, Dykeman, J., entered March 5, 1914, upon sustaining a demurrer to the complaint, dismissing an action in tort. Reversed.

ELLIS, J.: This is an action for damages by reason of an alleged wrongful publication by the defendant of an untruthful statement of the cause of the plaintiff's discharge by the defendant from employment as locomotive engineer, and preventing the plaintiff from pursuing his chosen occupation.

In the first and second paragraphs of the amended complaint, the corporate capacity of the defendant, and the fact that the plaintiff was, on October 10, 1907, a capable locomotive engineer of good standing and reputation and in the defendant's employ, are alleged. The succeeding paragraphs are as follows:

"(3) That on the said day the defendant railway company, through its officers and agents, with intent to injure the plaintiff, destroy his reputation and good name, and deprive him of the confidence and esteem of his fellowmen, and for the purpose of preventing him from seeking or securing other employment with said company or any other company at all, and to ruin him in his profession as locomotive engineer, caused to be printed and published, and have ever since said time continued to print, publish and circulate, and are now publishing, printing and circulating the following false, fraudulent and defamatory instrument in writing, which is as follows, to-wit:

" 'Discharge Eng'r Dick   Livingstone, Monta.
    " 'Mr. J. R. Dick   Oct. 10, 1907.
      " 'Eng'r Livingstone.

      " 'Dear Sir: This is to advise you that you are hereby discharged from company's services for intimidating company's employees at Whitehall on the 8th inst. while in the performance of their duties.

                                  (Signed) Yours truly
" 'C-40   ————— Nelson
" 'Cy-Mk-EE   Master Mechanic.' * * *"

If the complaint states a cause of action for libel, that statement must be found in the third paragraph. The fourth and fifth paragraphs

neither state nor aid in stating such a cause. Returning then to the
third paragraph, we find no special damages alleged as resulting from
the publication of the letter there set out. To find a cause of action for
libel, therefore, we must find that the statements in the letter, which
it is alleged were false, are actionable *per se*. If they are, the plaintiff
would be entitled to such general damages for humiliation, injured feelings and mental suffering as would naturally result from the publication,
without alleging or proving any special or specific damages. *Hanson v.
Krehbiel,* 68 Kan. 670, 75 Pac. 1041, 104 Am. St. 422, 64 L.R.A. 790.
He could not recover for loss of employment, or failure to secure employment, or other specific loss by reason of the publication. These would be
special damages, and not being alleged as resulting from the publication, they cannot be proved.

Our statute defining criminal libel, Rem. & Bal. Code, § 2424 (P.C.
135 § 343), declares, among other things, that every malicious publication by writing, etc., which shall tend to expose any living person to
hatred, contempt, ridicule or obloquy, or to deprive him of the benefit
of public confidence or social intercourse or to injure him in his business
or occupation, shall be a libel. We have held that, eliminating the statutory
element of malice, actual or implied, the statutory definition meets the
essentials of libel actionable *per se* as generally recognized in civil actions
for damages. *Wilson v. Sun Publishing Co.,* 85 Wash. 503, 148 Pac. 774;
Newell, Slander & Libel (2d ed.), p. 43. It seems to us that the necessary tendency of the charge that the plaintiff had been guilty of intimidating co-employees would be to deprive him of the benefit of public
confidence, and to injure him in both social and business intercourse
with those with whom his vocation brought him in contact, and to injure him in the pursuit of his business or occupation. The language of
the letter is actionable *per se*. The third paragraph, alleging its continued publication by the defendant, therefore stated a cause of action for
libel. The complaint was open to objection for indefiniteness as to the
manner of the alleged publication, but this was not ground for demurrer
but should have been reached by a motion to make more specific.

Whether in view of the provisions of Rem. & Bal. Code, § 6565
(P.C. 291 § 159), defining blacklisting, the publication of such a statement as that here involved would under any circumstance be privileged is
a matter which we are not now called upon to decide. The plaintiff having
stood upon his amended complaint, no further amendment can be permitted. * * *

> *The judgment is reversed, and the case
> is remanded for further proceedings.*

CROW, FULLERTON, and MAIN, JJ., concur.[1]

---

[1] In Wabash R. R. Co. v. Young, 162 Ind. 102, 69 N.E. 1003 (1904), and Chicago, R. I. & P. R. Co. v. Medley, 55 Okla. 145, 155 Pac. 211 (1916), it was
held that it was not actionable to speak of an employee as an agitator creating
trouble in the ranks of the car men. See also: Cerveny v. Chicago Daily News
Co., 139 Ill. 345, 28 N.E. 692 (1891) (anarchist is libellous) ; Washington Times
Co. v. Murray, 55 App. D.C. 32, 299 Fed. 903 (1924) (secret agent of Russian

HILTON v. SHERIDAN COAL CO.

Kansas Supreme Court.   132 Kan. 525, 297 Pac. 413 (1931).

DAWSON, J.: This was an action for damages for wrongfully inducing plaintiff's employer to discharge him.

The significant facts, in brief, were these: The defendant, The Sheridan Coal Company, owned eleven coal mines in southeastern Kansas, one of which was familiarly known as No. 19 Sheridan. Defendant leased this mine to three partners, Cunningham, Giovanni and Steele, who operated it under the name of the C. & G. Coal Company. About 190 workmen were employed in and about this mine. One of these was this plaintiff, Lloyd H. Hilton, aged 25 when this lawsuit was tried. He had been a coal miner for seven or eight years. In 1925, in the course of his employment, Hilton received an injury to his right foot and ankle, and on account thereof he received compensation from his employers, the C. & G. Coal Company, of some $2,000 in cash and an award of $6 per week for permanent partial incapacity. Prior to his injury plaintiff's task in the coal mine had been "tailing a motor"— whatever that is. When he returned to work his employers gave him the job of running a motor which relieved him from standing on his injured foot and gave him better pay—$8 per day instead of $7.50, his former wages.

This defendant, notwithstanding it had leased this coal mine where plaintiff was employed to the C. & G. Coal Company, exercised a good deal of supervisory authority over the mine and over its lessees. Defendant's superintendent of mines, one Ed. Roberts, instructed the mine surveyors where entries should be made, gave directions about the employment and discharge of C. & G. workmen, repeatedly reminded the lessees that the coal operators and insurance carriers had agreed to rid the southeastern Kansas coal field of all "compensation hounds"—meaning workmen who had been hurt in the mines and had received awards therefor under the workmen's compensation act. Roberts repeatedly warned the lessees that if they employed such workmen their insurance would be canceled, and if they did not carry insurance, as their lease contract obligated them to do, their lease would be canceled by the defendant coal company.

Not long after plaintiff Hilton returned to work following his injury and award of compensation, Superintendent Roberts of the de-

---

police is libellous); Lewis v. Daily News Co., 81 Md. 473, 32 Atl. 246 (1895) (anarchist is libellous); Wilkes v. Shields, 62 Minn. 426, 64 N.W. 921 (1895) (seditious agitator is libellous); Von Gerichten v. Seitz, 94 App. Div. 130, 87 N.Y.S. 968 (1904) (anarchists is libellous); Toomey v. Jones, 124 Okla. 167, 254 Pac. 736 (1926) ("Red" is libellous). See: 51 A.L.R. 1071 (1927).

As to what constitutes a privileged occasion, see: Hebner v. Great Northern Ry. Co., 78 Minn. 289, 80 N.W. 1128 (1899); Missouri Pac. Ry. Co. v. Richmond, 73 Texas 568, 11 S.W. 555 (1889); Brown v. Norfolk & W. Ry. Co., 100 Va. 619, 42 S.E. 664 (1902); Hunt v. Great Northern Ry. Co., [1891] 2 Q.B. 189; M'Donald v. Board of Land & Works, 5 Austr. Jur. 34 (1874).

fendant company had a conversation with Cunningham, one of the lessees, employers of plaintiff. Cunningham testified:

"He said, 'How is Hilton doing?' I said, 'He is doing just fine.' So he said, 'Well, Tom, I am afraid you are going to have to get rid of him.' I said, 'Why?' He said, 'The insurance company is going to cancel your policy' He used this language: He said that, 'The state law provides that you must carry insurance.' I said 'Yes.' He said, 'We have a section in the lease that you must carry it.' I said, 'Ain't I complying with it?' He said, 'But I am telling you that you must get rid of that fellow.' He said, 'The insurance company will make you.' He said, 'The operators and the insurance companies are going to clean Kansas out of these compensation hounds.' "

Plaintiff's employers were reluctant to discharge him and his retention was the subject of repeated bickerings with Roberts. Cunningham testified:

"Mr. Roberts said * * * 'You have got that old compensation hound back here again, have you?' I said, 'The boy is suiting me all right; he is doing his work all right.' * * * About a month afterwards, he (Roberts) spoke to me about it. * * * He said, 'I see you still have young Hilton working here. Don't you know that the insurance companies won't allow you to keep him here?' I said, 'I don't see why. They settled with him and he is able to work. He is doing his work. He absolutely satisfies me. I have nothing against the boy.' * * * Roberts, Steele and I had a very heated conversation. He said if I didn't fire that man Hilton that my insurance would be taken away from me and my lease canceled. He said that he would see that the lease was canceled and that my insurance was taken away. He characterized young Hilton as a compensation hound, and he also referred to another man that I had there in the same way, and he forced me to fire another man by the name of William Brackston. * * * Every time he seen the Hilton boy, he would fly to pieces. He said that if I didn't discharge him that the Sheridan Coal Company would cancel my lease and I would also lose my insurance. * * *

"* * * He said the operators and insurance companies in Kansas were going to get rid of all the compensation hounds."

It was also shown that shortly thereafter plaintiff's employers consulted about what they must do in view of Superintendent Roberts' threats, and under his coercion they discharged plaintiff.

Thereafter the young man made persistent but unsuccessful efforts throughout the entire southeastern Kansas coal district to obtain employment. After three years' enforced idleness as a coal miner, he brought this lawsuit.

On the issues joined, the cause was tried before a jury, which returned a verdict in plaintiff's favor for $2,000 actual damages and $4,000 punitive damages.

Judgment was entered accordingly, and defendant appeals. * * *

Defendant's next contention is a much more candid one than the error based on the argument that Superintendent Roberts had no authority to speak and act for the defendant in procuring plaintiff's discharge. It is that the defendant had a right to insist on the discharge of Hilton because the insurance on its coal mine would be canceled if men drawing disability allowances were permitted to work in it, and that defendant had a right to insist that nothing be done or omitted around the mine to jeopardize its insurance coverage. To approve that argument would be to admit that employers of labor in dangerous industries have found a legitimate way to set the workman's compensation law at defiance and render nugatory its humane provisions. The legislature declares what the public policy shall be towards the employing of workmen in dangerous occupations like coal mining. It provides that injuries to workmen in that hazardous business shall be a charge upon the industry and added to the price of coal and eventually paid for by the general public who buy and burn coal. If the coal operator can get an insurance company to carry the risks of injuries to his workmen more economically than he can himself, well and good; if he cannot, the public policy does not change, but remains as the legislature declared it. The idea that the humane purposes of the workmen's compensation act can be set at naught by arbitrary action of employers and insurance carriers, or by either of them, and that unfortunate workmen who have received compensation for injuries sustained in their dangerous occupation shall be barred from reëmployment, cannot be given judicial countenance. Whatever the attitude of the insurance carriers, defendant knew that plaintiff was entitled to return to work after recovering from his injuries. It knew his employers had a right to employ him; its superintendent of mines had no right to compel its lessees to discharge him. In short, defendant must be presumed to have known that the theory underlying the entire jurisprudence of this state is that its people shall be free from vexatious oppressions and petty tyrannies such as its superintendent of mines practiced on this plaintiff, and it must have known that such a course of conduct to flout the declared legislative policy was likely to bring disagreeable consequences to those who would pursue it.

While an employer may discharge his employee not hired for a specified term for any reason or for no reason (*Coppage v. Kansas,* 236 U.S. 1), third parties have no such privilege, and they are liable in damages for such meddlesome interference if the discharge of an employee is procured thereby. In the leading case of *London Guarantee Co. v. Horn,* 206 Ill. 493, 99 A.S.R. 185, the appellant insurance company, by threatening to cancel a policy of insurance it had issued to the employer of Horn, appellee, brought about Horn's discharge. Under Horn's contract of employment he might be discharged at any time at his employer's unconstrained discretion. In the opinion affirming a judgment for damages in Horn's behalf against the insurance company, various instructive cases are reviewed, and the court said:

"We therefore conclude, both upon reason and authority, that where a third party induces an employer to discharge his employee who is working under a contract terminable at will, but under which the employment would have continued indefinitely, in accordance with the desire of the employer, except for such interference, and where the only motive moving the third party is a desire to injure the employee and to benefit himself at the expense of the employee by compelling the latter to surrender an alleged cause of action, for the satisfaction of which, in whole or in part, such third party is liable, and where such right of action does not depend upon and is not connected with the continuance of such employment, a cause of action arises in favor of the employee against the third party." (p. 507.)

In *Carter v. Coal & Coke Co. et al.,* 84 W. Va. 624, the action was against the defendant company for causing plaintiff to be discharged from the service of his employer. It was there held that one who by himself or conspiring with others induces another to break his contract of employment with a third person, to the injury of that person, is liable in damages for the injury sustained by him, whether the injury done was for the benefit of the wrongdoer or not.

United States Fidelity & Guaranty Co. v. Millonas, 206 Ala. 147, is quite similar to the case at bar. The plaintiff, John Millonas, suffered an injury to his eye while working as a sheeter for a construction company. He placed his claim for compensation in the hands of an attorney for collection. The defendant company carried the compensation insurance for the employer of Millonas. Its agent offered to settle the claim for compensation by paying a nominal sum, $50. At the same time he warned plaintiff's attorney that he would have plaintiff discharged, and stated in the presence of several witnesses that it was the policy of defendant to have the employer who had insurance with it to discharge any employee who placed his claim in the hands of an attorney. Millonas was discharged and brought this action for damages. In sustaining a judgment in his favor for actual and punitive damages (reduced to $6,000 by remittitur), the Alabama supreme court reviewed the pertinent cases, including the *Horn* case, *supra,* and noted particularly that the supreme court of the United States cited with approval the doctrine of the *Horn* case in *Truax v. Riach,* 239 U.S. 33, 60 L. Ed. 131.

In *Johnson v. Ætna Life Ins. Co.,* 158 Wis. 56, it was held that an insurance company which had insured an employer against liability for injuries sustained by the latter's workmen was not justified in causing the discharge of an employee who, after being injured, had been retained in his employment, where the purpose was to deprive the employee of his earning power so that he could not successfully carry on an action which he had brought against his employer, and in which the insurance company was defendant, to recover damages for his injury. In the opinion it was said:

"As against all others (like the appellant), the plaintiff (employee) was entitled to go his way without molestation, and if anyone assumed to meddle in his affairs he did so at his peril. There is practically little conflict in the cases on this point. (Citations.)" (p. 60.)

Other cases in accord with the *Horn* and *Millonas* cases, *supra*, are: *Railway Conductors v. Jones,* 78 Colo. 80; *Chipley v. Atkinson,* 23 Fla. 206; *Moran v. Dunphy,* 177 Mass. 485, 52 L.R.A. 115; *Clarkson v. Laiblan,* 202 Mo. App. 682; *Huskie v. Griffon,* 75 N.H. 345, 27 L.R.A., n.s., 966 and Note; *Max v. Kahn,* 91 N.J.L. 170; *Malone v. B. of L. F. & E.,* 94 N.J.L. 347; *Carmen v. Fox Film Corporation,* 198 N.Y. Supp. 766; *Cotton v. Cooper* (Tex. Com. of App., approved by supreme court), 209 S.W. 135. * * *

The judgment is affirmed.[1]

---

[1] *Accord:* United States Fidelity & Guaranty Co. v. Millonas, 206 Ala. 147, 89 So. 732 (1921); London Guarantee Co. v. Horn, 206 Ill. 493, 69 N.E. 526 (1904); Gibson v. Fidelity & Casualty Co., 232 Ill. 49, 83 N.E. 539 (1908); Hollenbeck v. Ristine, 114 Ia. 358, 86 N.W. 377 (1901); Johnson v. Aetna Life Ins. Co., 158 Wis. 56, 147 N.W. 32 (1914). In Joce v. Great Northern Ry. Co., 100 Minn. 225, 110 N.W. 975 (1907), it was held that the defendant's conduct would not be actionable if the plaintiff's claim was wholly without merit or if the defendant believed that the claim was without merit.

Accord, where the defendant procures plaintiff's discharge by garnishment of plaintiff's wages upon a fictitious claim, when defendant knows that the effect of such garnishment will result in plaintiff's discharge: Bowen v. Morris, 219 Ala. 689, 123 So. 222 (1929); 222 Ala. 703, 131 So. 909 (1930); Alabama Brokerage Co. v. Boston, 18 Ala. App. 495, 93 So. 289 (1922), aff'd in 208 Ala. 242, 94 So. 87 (1922); Southern Finance Co. v. Foster, 19 Ala. App. 109, 95 So. 338 (1923), certiorari denied in 209 Ala. 113, 95 So. 340 (1923); Lopes v. Connolly, 210 Mass. 487, 97 N.E. 80 (1912); Doucette v. Sallinger, 228 Mass. 444, 117 N.E. 897 (1917); Kennedy v. Hub Mfg. Co., 221 Mass. 136, 108 N.E. 932 (1915); Scott v. Prudential Outfitting Co., 92 Misc. 195, 155 N.Y.S. 497 (1915); Cotton v. Cooper, 160 S.W. 597 (Texas Civ. App. 1905), aff'd. in 209 S.W. 135 (Texas 1919); Evans v. McKay, 212 S.W. 680 (Texas Civ. App. 1919); Bryant v. Askin Finance Co., 146 S.C. 520, 144 S.E. 231 (1928).

Accord, where defendant prompted by other motives: Hill Grocery Co. v. Carroll, 223 Ala. 376, 136 So. 789 (1931); Chipley v. Atkinson, 23 Fla. 206, 1 So. 934 (1887); Willner v. Silverman, 109 Md. 341, 71 Atl. 962 (1909); Heffernan v. Whittsey 126 Minn. 163, 148 N.W. 63 (1914); Huskie v. Griffin, 75 N.H. 345, 74 Atl. 595 (1909); Trapp v. Du Bois, 76 App. Div. 314, 78 N.Y.S. 505 (1902); Freit v. Belmont, 132 App. Div. 723, 117 N.Y.S. 656 (1909); Jones v. Leslie, 61 Wash. 107, 112 Pac. 81 (1910). *Contra:* Holder v. Mfg. Co., 138 N.C. 308, 50 S.E. 681 (1905). *Cf* State v. Kramer, 115 Atl. 8 (Del. Gen. Sess. 1921).

In Davies v. Thomas, [1920] 2 Ch. 189, 197, Lord Sterndale, M.R., in the Court of Appeal, said: "The inducement not to employ [or to discharge where the employment is at will] is actionable only if it proceeds by illegal means. and the illegal means generally used in these cases is pressure, coercion for the purpose of injuring the third person * * * I do not think that the principle differs in the case of the inducement being effected or procured by a number of persons except to this extent, that it is much easier to infer pressure or coercion in the case of a number of persons, especially if they are in a position to make themselves objectionable if their request is not compliable with, than it is in the case of a single person"

NEW YORK, CHICAGO & ST. LOUIS R. R. CO. v. SCHAFFER.

Ohio Supreme Court. 65 Ohio St. 414, 62 N.E. 1036 (1902).

In the second cause of action the plaintiff in substance alleges that prior to the first day of January, 1895, he was in the employ of the defendant company, performing the work of a brakeman at the rate of sixty dollars per month, and that on or about the latter part of December, 1894, while in the employ of the defendant company he applied for and was granted a leave of absence for about thirty days, and that when he reported for work again on or about the first day of February, 1895, he was informed by the defendant company that he had been discharged; and he avers that he was discharged from the service of the defendant without any just cause whatever. He says that during the year 1894 there was on many of the railroads in the United States a strike which is commonly known as the A. R. U. strike, and that at the time of this strike, that is, in the summer of 1894, this plaintiff was working for the defendant company as a brakeman in the yards at Bellevue, and took no part in the strike; that he continued to work for the defendant up to the latter part of December, 1894, when he was granted a leave of absence by the defendant. He says that prior to the 6th of August, 1894, the defendant entered into a conspiracy, agreement and understanding with certain other railroad companies having lines of road running into the city of Chicago, and also other railroad companies the names of which are unknown to this plaintiff, that they would furnish to each other information as to all of the employes who had committed offenses, or were charged with having committed offenses, or who had quit work during the said strike, and also as to all their employes who were members of the American Railway Union, and that said companies entered into the further conspiracy, agreement and understanding that such employes of any and all of said companies would not be employed by any of the said companies without the release and consent from the railroad company by which the employe was last employed, commonly called by railroad men a clearance. He avers that the object and purpose of such alleged conspiracy and agreement was to maliciously and willfully interfere with such employes who had previously terminated their employment with or been discharged from the employment of either of said companies.

* * * Plaintiff says that since the conspiracy aforesaid it is impossible for anyone to secure employment unless he first presents the consent of the company for whom he last worked, or a clearance card showing that the applicant was in no way connected with the said strike; that he has repeatedly asked the officers of said company for such letters or clearance or consent, and that the company has failed and refused to furnish him therewith, and that at the time he so requested the defendant, the defendant promised and agreed to send his record to anyone employing, or desiring to employ, the defendant, but the plaintiff says that the defendant has failed and refused to furnish the record; that

since his discharge he has made application for employment to various railroad companies which have refused to consider his application unless he would first bring the consent of the defendant or a clearance as above mentioned. He further says that the defendant willfully and maliciously and in pursuance of said conspiracy, agreement and understanding, and with intent willfully and maliciously to prevent the plaintiff from securing employment, refused to give the plaintiff the said letters, consent or clearance that would enable him to secure employment in the railroad business, and because thereof, and for no other cause, he has been denied the right to contract for or take employment of any of the companies of the United States, and been prevented from obtaining employment and supporting himself by his trade or occupation. For all of which he claims to have been damaged in the sum of five thousand dollars, and asks judgment therefor. * * *

The jury returned a verdict in favor of the plaintiff in the sum of five thousand dollars on which judgment was entered by the trial court. The circuit court affirmed the judgment of the common pleas court, and this proceeding is prosecuted to reverse the judgments of the two lower courts.

DAVIS, J.: * * * Recurring to the second amended petition, upon which the case was tried, it appears that it is not alleged that the defendant agreed or conspired with other railroad companies to refuse to give to the plaintiff, or to any other discharged employe, a statement of his record, nor is there a scintilla of proof of such a combination; but on the contrary the distinct claim is that such refusal was the individual, malicious act of the defendant. It is the undoubted and unabridged natural right of every individual not to employ, or to refuse to employ, whomsoever he may wish, and he cannot be called upon to answer to the public or to individuals for his judgment. Nor can the motives which prompt his action be considered. In general terms, such right is as much inherent in corporate bodies as in natural persons. But whatever one person may lawfully do, two or more persons may join in doing. There can be no such thing as a conspiracy to do a lawful thing unless by unlawful means. If one railroad company may lawfully refuse to continue in its employ a person who has been engaged in a war upon its interests, called a strike, or who has shown himself to be negligent, incompetent, inefficient or dishonest, there does not appear to be any good reason why a number of railroad companies might not agree among themselves to not employ such a person. Indeed there are obvious reasons, public and private, why they should do so. For example, it would be very inconsistent and unjust, if while holding railroad companies to strict accountability for the negligence of their servants, we should restrict them in the natural right to protect themselves in the matter of the selection of their employes. That such a combination or agreement may be lawfully made and executed is held in the following well considered cases: *Macauley v. Tierney*, 19 R.I., 255; *Bohn Mfg. Co. v. Hollis*, 54 Minn., 223; *Brewster v. Miller*, 101 Ky., 368; *Delz v. Winfree*, 80 Tex.,

400. And see Cooley on Torts, (2 ed.) 329. If, therefore, the jury found the affirmative of the issue of fact submitted, whether the defendant combined with other companies in an agreement not to employ any person who did not furnish a statement of his record with his former employer, it would afford no basis for recovery, unless it should appear that this agreement, which is *prima facie* valid, was brought about by some illegal act of the defendant. If the defendant, by fraud, falsehood or force, had brought about a refusal to employ the plaintiff, it would have committed a positive wrong against the plaintiff which would have been actionable. Of this, however, there is not a scintilla of proof. But an agreement to tell the truth about the plaintiff, or a refusal to say anything about him would not make an otherwise legal concert of action an illegal one and authorize a recovery against the defendant. Says Field, C.J., in *Vegelahn v. Guntner,* 167 Mass., 103: "I am not convinced that to persuade one man not to enter into the employment of another, by telling the truth to him about such other person and his business is actionable at common law, whatever the motive might be." The Supreme Court of Georgia, in passing upon the constitutionality of a statute which required certain classes of corporations to communicate to their discharged employes the reasons for discharge, under heavy penalty in the name of damages, said: "A statute which undertakes to make it the duty of incorporated railroad, express and telegraph companies to engage in correspondence of this sort with their discharged agents and employes, and which subjects them in each case to a heavy forfeiture, under the name of damages, for failing or refusing to do so, is violative of the general private right of silence enjoyed in this state by all persons, natural or artificial, from time immemorial, and is utterly void and of no effect. Liberty of speech and of writing is secured by the constitution, and incident thereto is the correlative liberty of silence, not less important nor less sacred. Statements or communications, oral or written, wanted for private information, cannot be coerced by mere legislative mandate at the will of one of the parties and against the will of the other." *Wallace v. Railway Co.,* 94 Ga., 732.

The theory of the circuit court that silence, or refusal to render a statement on request, is in the nature of a slander, and, if its effect is to prevent the person from obtaining employment, it is an actionable wrong, is untenable. As stated at the outset, there was between these parties no contract for a statement, and there is no statute in Ohio requiring it; indeed it is doubtful whether one could be made that would be valid. * * *

Without pursuing this discussion further it may be said that the views of the courts below respecting the law governing this case, and as given in the charge to the jury, were entirely wrong, and that upon the facts which the jury were authorized to find upon the issues submitted to them, and which they are presumed to have found, the judgment ought to have been for the defendant.

Reversed and judgment for defendant.

Burket, Spear and Shauck, JJ., concur.

Minshall, C.J.   I concur in the judgment, and the syllabus as framed, but do not concur in the view expressed in the opinion that companies may enter into an agreement among themselves, not to employ persons who have engaged in what is known as a "strike." Such an agreement is against public policy, as tending to encourage idleness and cause poverty among working men, by depriving them of the means of earning a livelihood for themselves and their families.   Each company should be at liberty to employ such persons as in its judgment may seem best, unrestrained by any agreement with other companies.   A particular company may be disposed to employ persons, although they may have been engaged in a strike, and would do so but for the fact that it is restrained by its agreement with other companies from doing so.   It seems to me that such an agreement is clearly against public policy and should not be recognized by the courts.   To do so would, in effect, make engaging in a strike an offense punishable by exclusion from employment.   The reason I concur in the judgment and syllabus is, I fail to discern from the record that there was any evidence tending to show that the defendant had entered into an agreement with other companies not to employ persons who had been engaged in the railroad strike of 1894.   All it did was to refuse to give the plaintiff a "clearance" when requested.   This it might reasonably do for reasons stated in the opinion.[1]

WILLIS v. MUSCOGEE MANUFACTURING CO.

Georgia Supreme Court.   120 Ga. 597, 48 S.E. 177 (1904).

Simmons, C.J.: Willis brought suit for damages against the Muscogee Manufacturing Company, alleging, that the defendant had wrongfully reported him to certain other companies as having left its service in violation of one of its rules, and that, because of such report, such other

---

[1] Relief has been customarily refused where the failure to secure employment has resulted from the refusal of the original employer to furnish the employee with a clearance card.   Chicago, C. C. & St. L. Ry. Co. v. Jenkins, 174 Ill. 398, 51 N.E. 811 (1898); McDonald v. Illinois Central R. R. Co., 187 Ill. 529 (1900). The decisions refuse to recognize that there is any duty upon the part of the employer to act, in the sense of furnishing a clearance, even though such non-action results according to agreement in "blacklisting" the employee.   But cf. Handley v. Louisville & N. R. R. Co., 105 Ky. 162, 48 S.W. 429 (1898).

Upon the legality of an agreement between employers not to employ any person that had been discharged by one of their number, see: Blumenthal v. Shaw, 77 Fed. 954 (3rd cir. 1897); Baker v. Metropolitan Life Ins. Co., 23 Ky. L. 1174, 64 S.W. 913 (1901); Trimble v. Prudential L. Ins. Co., 23 Ky. L. 1184, 64 S.W. 915 (1901); Mineral Water Bottle Exchange v. Booth, 36 Ch. Div. 465 (1887).

companies had, under an agreement with the defendant, refused to give
him employment. The evidence introduced by the plaintiff was substantially as follows: In 1902 several cotton-mill companies in Muscogee
county, Georgia, among them the defendant, agreed to make and post in
their mills a rule requiring employees, when leaving the employment of
a company, to "work a six days' notice." They also agreed to report
to each other all employes who left their employment without complying with such notice, and, except in special cases, not to employ men so
reported. In pursuance of this agreement the defendant posted in its
mill the following notice: "All employees of this mill must work a six
days' notice when leaving the employ of this mill, and no employee of
any other cotton-mill of Columbus and vicinity will be employed by
this mill unless they have worked the required notice." This rule had been
in operation for several months when Willis, the plaintiff, obtained employment of the defendant. Plaintiff was perfectly familiar with the rule,
and, while he was boss in another mill, had reported other operatives
for its violation. He had worked for several of the mills which were
parties to the above-mentioned agreement, and for the defendant, prior to
1902, and had in each case, when leaving one mill for another, worked out
the required notice. Plaintiff was a "loom fixer," and as such was employed by the proper officer of the defendant. This officer agreed to employ plaintiff at $1.50 per day to repair Crompton looms, but, according
to the plaintiff's testimony, it was expressly understood that he was not
to work at that price on Crompton and Knowles looms combined. Plaintiff worked for some time on the Crompton looms, and was then directed
by an officer of the company to repair some Crompton and Knowles
looms combined. Plaintiff asked at what price, and was told that he
would receive but $1.50 per day. When he refused to work on these
looms at that price, the defendant's officer told him it was all he would
give, and that if plaintiff would not do the work for that price he could
quit. The work on these combined looms was more difficult than that
on the others, and was worth more per day. After this conversation
with the defendant's officer, plaintiff considered himself discharged. He
left and applied to other companies for employment. He was refused,
because the defendant had sent his name to the other companies on what
was called the "blacklist," in which it was stated that plaintiff had left
the service of the defendant without cause and without working the required six days' notice. Plaintiff endeavored to obtain employment from
the other companies, but failed, and, according to his contention, his
failure was the result of the report of the defendant sent to the other
companies. Finally, at a cost of some $40, he had to remove from
Columbus to Griffin, where he obtained work. There was some conflict
in the evidence as to whether the other companies refused to employ
plaintiff because of the report sent out by the defendant, or for other
reasons. At the conclusion of the evidence for the plaintiff the court
granted a nonsuit. To this judgment the plaintiff excepted.

All manufacturing companies, and as well all other persons who employ labor, have the right and power to make reasonable rules and regulations for the government of their employees. It is reasonable to require that employees shall give their employers a certain number of days' notice before leaving their service. It has been held to be reasonable to require such notice and to provide that if the notice is not given, the employee shall forfeit all wages then due him. The rule in the present case was reasonable, and one who, with knowledge of the rule, entered the service of the defendant was bound by the rule. It entered into his contract of service and became a part of it, as binding upon him as any other part of his contract. Manufacturing corporations frequently make large contracts for goods to be delivered at a specified time. In order to comply with these contracts it is necessary for them to keep the requisite number of employees in their service. If employees were allowed to leave their employment without giving any notice, it would in many cases be impossible for the employers to fill their places in time to complete the goods according to the contracts made for their delivery. With six days' notice of the intention of an employee to leave, the employer would have a reasonable time to fill his place. For these and other reasons we think that the rule was a reasonable one.

It was contended by counsel for the plaintiff in error that, while the rule may have been a reasonable one when adopted by a single corporation, it was an unlawful conspiracy for a number of corporations to join in an agreement to enforce such a rule by reporting violations of it to each other and refusing to employ any person who had been so reported. We can not see the force of the reasoning of counsel on this point. We see no reason why the officers of a dozen cotton-mills in or near the same city can not make such an agreement with each other. An employer has a right to select his employees according to what standard he may choose, though such standard be arbitrary or unreasonable. An employer certainly has a right to refuse to employ any one whom he knows to have left another employer in violation of a reasonable rule which both employers are seeking to enforce. An agreement among a number of employers to report such violations and thus assist each other in the selection of their employees is not unlawful, though coupled with an agreement to employ no one so reported, such an agreement not being binding upon the employers, and there being no allegation that it was entered into through malice. See *Baker v. Ins. Co.* (Ky.), 55 L.R.A. 271; *Brewster v. Miller's Sons* (Ky.), 38 L.R.A. 505; *Boyer v. Tel. Co.,* 124 Fed. 246; 8 Cyc. 645 *et seq.*

There are, however, limitations upon the rights of the employers in this matter. While the employee is bound by the reasonable rules of the employer, as a part of the contract of employment, and may be reported to other employers for a breach of those rules, there is a correlative duty upon the employer not to report an employee wrongfully. The rule which enters into the contract of employment is as much a part of the contract of the employer as of the employee, and both are bound by it. The employer is strictly within his rights as long as he reports no employee for a violation of the rule except such as have actually violated it. When, however, he wrongfully makes such a report and an employee is thereby damaged, such employee has a right of action.[1] While the corporations which entered into the agreement above described had a right to do so, they owed a duty to their employees not to abuse that right. If one of them falsely reported an employee, to his injury, such employee may recover for the tort. The combination of the employers was a powerful machine for the accomplishment of lawful results, but it was capable of misuse to the injury of innocent employees. When a company so misuses it, such company must take the consequences.

Our difficulty has arisen, not in coming to the above conclusions, but in applying them to the facts of the present case so as to determine whether the trial judge erred in granting a nonsuit. It was contended by counsel for the plaintiff in error that the rule as to six days' notice did not apply to the facts of this case, and that, instead of "leaving" his employer, plaintiff was discharged by defendant; that he had made a contract to do certain work on a certain kind of loom at a stipulated price, expressly excepting from the agreement work on the combined looms which he stated he would not do for the price paid for the work contracted for. Without his consent an officer of the defendant ordered him to work on the combined looms without any addition in his wages. This, he claims, was a change in his contract, to which he refused to accede, and he was then told he could quit. In consequence of this declaration by the defendant's officer, he gathered up his tools etc., and left. The other companies were then notified by defendant that plaintiff had left its employment without cause and in violation of the rule as to giving notice. On the other hand, the defendant claims that the evidence shows that the plaintiff left its service voluntarily and refused to work out the required notice, and that the defendant was, therefore, justified in reporting him to the other companies as having violated the rule. This we think was a question of fact which should have been submitted to the jury. There was enough evidence to require that the case be submitted to a jury. If the jury had found in favor of the plaintiff on this issue, he would have been entitled to recover some damages. When one promulgates an ambiguous or doubtful rule, it must be construed strictly against him. This rule of construction must be borne in mind in ascertaining whether the regulation as to notice applied to such a case as was made by the termination of the plaintiff's employment. If the employer, who promulgated the regulation, made a mistake in its construction and applied it to a state of facts which did not come within it, the employee injured by such mistake has a right to recover. The employer can not arbitrarily place an employee upon the blacklist as having violated the regulation, when in point of fact the employee's conduct did not

---

[1] In Rhodes v. Greenby Cotton Mills, 87 S.C. 18, 68 S.E. 824 (1910), the defendant was held liable for placing an employee upon an existing blacklist for a cause not within those which the blacklist by agreement covered.—Ed.

come within the terms of such regulation and he, therefore, had not violated it. On the other hand, if the plaintiff left the service of the defendant voluntarily, without cause and without giving the required notice, or if he had contracted to do all such work in his line as the company might reasonably require of him, without excepting work upon the combined looms, and then refused to work upon these looms for the agreed price per day, and left because defendant would not give him more, then the defendant had a right to report him as having left without cause and without working out the required notice. It was also contended by the plaintiff that this report to the other companies prevented his obtaining other employment, and compelled him, in order to obtain work, to remove to another city; that he thus lost time and was put to actual expense by reason of his having been reported by the defendant. The defendant claimed that the agreement between it and the other companies was voluntary and not legally binding on any of them, and that any one of the other companies could have employed plaintiff had it seen proper to do so, and that, in truth, the notice sent out to the other companies was not the real cause of the plaintiff's failure to get work. Under the evidence this was also a question for the jury, and not for determination by the court. We therefore think that the court erred in granting a nonsuit.

Judgment reversed. All the Justices concur.[2]

CORNELLIER v. HAVERHILL SHOE MANUFACTURERS' ASSOCIATION.

Massachusetts Supreme Judicial Court. 221 Mass. 554, 109 N.E. 643 (1915).

DE COURCY, J.: * * * The basis of the plaintiff's complaint is that the defendants conspired against him, and by means of a black list procured his discharge from employment. On December 12, 1912, the plaintiff, with thirty-nine other employees of the Witherell and Dobbins Company, went out on strike. He secured employment at the factory of Charles K. Fox, Inc., on December 14, began work on December 16, at 7:10 A. M., and was discharged in a summary and unusual manner about two hours later. The master finds that the cause of his discharge was the fact that he was one of the striking employees of the Witherell

---

[2] The establishment of a black list of employees because of their union affiliation has been upheld as legal in Goldfield Consol. Mines Co. v. Goldfield Miners' Union No. 220, 159 Fed. 500 (C.C. Nev. 1908); Atkins v. Fletcher Co., 65 N.J. Eq. 658, 660, 55 Atl. 1074 (1904) *semble*; Jenkinson v. Nield, 8 T.L.R. 540 (1892). *Cf.* Boyer v. Western Union Tel. Co., 124 Fed. 246 (C.C.E.D. Mo. 1903); Trollope v. London Bldg. Trades Federation, 12 T.L.R. 373 (1896); Newton v. Amalgamated Musicians' Union, 12 T.L.R. 623 (1896); Keith v. Lauder, 8 Sc. Sess. Cas. (5th ser.) 356 (1905).

and Dobbins Company, and that there existed a tacit understanding, to which the Fox Company was a party, that those striking employees should not be employed. It appears that on the day of the strike, or the day after, and at the request of the defendant Child (who was the manager of the Shoe Manufacturers' Association), Mr. Dobbins brought to a meeting of the manufacturers several lists containing the names of the employees who had gone on strike. Copies of the list were prepared and circulated by the defendants for the purpose of preventing the strikers from getting work in Haverhill and vicinity, and of forcing them to abandon the strike and return to work at the Witherell and Dobbins Company's factory against their will. The acts of the several defendants in furtherance of this combination need not be recited. The master specifically has found that Cornellier was discharged at Fox's because of this "black list." It may be said in passing that of the twenty defendants named in the bill the master finds that only the following (herein referred to as the defendants) were responsible for the acts complained of, namely, the Haverhill Shoe Manufacturers' Association, the Witherell and Dobbins Company, Gale Shoe Manufacturing Company, Charles K. Fox, Inc., Austin H. Perry, Ira J. Webster, Alwyn W. Greeley, Albert M. Child, George W. Dobbins and H. L. Webber.

Did this combination of the defendants to blacklist the striking employees of the Witherell and Dobbins Company, resulting in the discharge of and damage to the plaintiff, give him a legal cause of action? The statement of the general right of the Fox Company to terminate a workman's employment when and for what cause it chooses, where no right of contract is involved, does not carry us far. See *Coppage v. Kansas,* 236 U.S. 1. The same is true of the recognized equal rights of employers and employees to combine in associations or unions, so long as they employ lawful methods for the attainment of lawful purposes. See *Hoban v. Dempsey,* 217 Mass. 166. But it is settled that the intentional interference by even an individual, without lawful justification, with the plaintiff's right to have the benefit of his contract with his employer would be an actionable wrong. *Berry v. Donovan,* 188 Mass. 353. *Hanson v. Innis,* 211 Mass. 301. A combination to blacklist is the counter weapon to a combination to boycott, and is open to similar legal objections, when directed against persons with whom those combining have no trade dispute, or when the concerted action coerces the individual members, by implied threats or otherwise, to withhold employment from those whom ordinarily they would employ. See *New England Cement Gun Co. v. McGivern,* 218 Mass. 198, and cases cited.

It is true that in *Worthington v. Waring,* 157 Mass. 421, this court refused to enjoin the defendants from making use of a black list, stating that the rights alleged to be violated were personal and not property rights, and that there were no approved precedents in equity for issuing an injunction against the grievance there complained of. In the light of more recent decisions of the court recognizing that the right to labor and to its protection from unlawful interference is a constitutional as well as a common law right there appears to be no sound reason why it should not be adequately protected under our present broad equity powers. As intimated in *Burnham v. Dowd*, 217 Mass. 351, 359, the case of *Worthington v. Waring* cannot well be reconciled with our later decisions. It must be considered as no longer binding as an authority for the doctrine that equity will afford no injunctive relief against an unlawful combination to blacklist. * * *

Assuming that, if this were an action at law, the plaintiff could recover for the damages caused by the unlawful combination of the defendants to blacklist him, the question remains whether he is entitled to prevail in the present suit. He has brought these proceedings in a court of equity. Under the established maxim that "he who comes into equity must come with clean hands," the court will not lend its active aid to him if he has been in equal wrong with the defendants touching the transaction as to which relief is sought, but will leave him to his remedy at law. The strike at the Witherell and Dobbins factory in which he joined is intimately connected with the black list of which he complains. The plaintiff individually was free, under his contract at will, to terminate his employment for any reason that he deemed sufficient. He had an undoubted right to join a labor organization. The employer as an individual had similar rights. But while each had a right to organize with others, it by no means follows that the organizations lawfully could do everything that the individual could do. See *Martell v. White*, 185 Mass. 255, 260; *Pickett v. Walsh*, 192 Mass. 572, 582. An act lawful in an individual may be the subject of civil conspiracy when done in concert, provided it is done with a direct intention to injure another, or when, although done to benefit the conspirators, its natural and necessary consequence is the prejudice of the public or the oppression of individuals. 5 R.C.L. 1093. * * *

It is clear from the findings of the master, however, that the Witherell and Dobbins strike was conducted by unlawful means; that laws were violated and the well established rights of others invaded. On several occasions crowds of strikers paraded in front of the factory, cheering and shouting "Come out," and occasionally adding the names of men who remained at work; once at least one hundred or more paraded in front of the factory, two by two in one direction and two by two in the opposite direction, so that there were four persons abreast most of the time, and the operatives leaving the factory had difficulty in breaking through the line. Some of the employees were intimidated and followed by crowds, others had to be escorted home by police officers, and four or five were assaulted by strikers or their sympathizers because they took the place of striking employees. One serious attack, characterized by the master as cowardly and unprovoked, was made on an employee named Mills, as he was going home after dark at the conclusion of his day's work. And while the persons who committed the assaults were not identified, the union and its officials made no effort to stop or control

them; and the union men who were present when Mills was assaulted
and rendered unconscious made no effort to give any aid or to pursue
the man who struck the blow. The strike was carried on in a manner
that reasonably caused the average employee to be apprehensive for his
personal safety. The plaintiff cannot avoid responsibility for some, at
least, of these acts. The strike, which was pending for more than three
months after the bill was filed * * * was maintained under the direction
of the union to which he belonged, and for the recognition of which he
went on strike. He took part in the picketing and in at least one of
the parades, and otherwise aided and encouraged it. See *Lawlor v.
Loewe*, 235 U.S. 522.

The conduct of the plaintiff and the acts of others with whom he
was legally identified preclude him from obtaining the active aid of
a court of equity. For any damage caused by the black list which the
defendants maintained he must seek his redress, if any, at law. * * *

For the reasons herein set forth a decree is to be entered overruling the exceptions, confirming the master's report, and dismissing
the bill of complaint.

Decree accordingly.[1]

PRUDENTIAL INSURANCE COMPANY OF AMERICA v. CHEEK.

United States Supreme Court. 259 U.S. 530 (1922).

MR. JUSTICE PITNEY delivered the opinion of the court.

Robert T. Cheek sued the Prudential Insurance Company of America
in the Circuit Court of St. Louis to recover damages upon a cause of
action set forth in two counts: First, that the company being a New Jersey
corporation conducting a life insurance business in Missouri under license
of the insurance department of that State, and plaintiff having been for
more than ten years continuously employed in its service, and having re-
signed said employment and left the company's service, plaintiff demanded
of defendant's superintendent a letter setting forth the nature and character
of the services rendered by him to said corporation and the duration thereof, and truly stating for what cause plaintiff had quit said service; that
defendant, acting through its superintendent, without just cause refused to
give to plaintiff such a letter, as provided by statute, and because of this
plaintiff had been unable to secure employment and had suffered substantial damages. The second count was based upon an alleged unlawful agreement between defendant and two other companies, the Metropolitan Life
Insurance Company and the John Hancock Mutual Life Insurance Company, said companies having a monopoly of the industrial life insurance
business in St. Louis, to the effect that neither would for a period of two

---

[1] Accord: Mattison v. L. S. & M. S. Ry. Co., 3 Ohio Dec. 526 (1895).

years after his leaving the employ of either company employ any man who for any reason had left the service of or had been discharged by either of the other companies, by which means plaintiff had been rendered unable to secure employment and had sustained substantial damages.

The first count was based upon § 3020, Missouri Revised Statutes, 1909, which reads as follows: "Whenever any employe of any corporation doing business in this State shall be discharged or voluntarily quit the service of such corporation, it shall be the duty of the superintendent or manager of said corporation, upon the request of such employe (if such employe shall have been in the service of said corporation for a period of at least ninety days), to issue to such employe a letter, duly signed by such superintendent or manager, setting forth the nature and character of service rendered by such employe to such corporation and the duration thereof, and truly stating for what cause, if any, such employe has quit such service; and if any such superintendent or manager shall fail or refuse to issue such letter to such employe when so requested by such employe, such superintendent or manager shall be deemed guilty of a misdemeanor, and shall be punished by a fine in any sum not exceeding five hundred dollars, or by imprisonment in the county jail for a period not exceeding one year, or by both such fine and imprisonment."

A general demurrer interposed to each count was sustained by the trial court, and, plaintiff declining to plead further, judgment was rendered for defendant, from which plaintiff appealed to the Supreme Court of the State. That court, construing § 3020, held that it imposed a duty not upon the superintendent or manager personally but upon the corporation acting through its superintendent or other proper officer, to issue the letter; that the statute having imposed this duty for the public benefit and also for the benefit of the employees of corporations, the public remedy by fine or other penalty was not exclusive and the plaintiff as a party injured was entitled to recover his damages; overruled various constitutional objections raised by defendant to the validity of § 3020, among others that it deprived the corporation of liberty of contract without due process of law and denied it the equal protection of the laws, in violation of the Fourteenth Amendment; held that the agreement or combination alleged in the second count gave the corporations a monopoly in their business, contrary to the law and public policy of the State, and if it prevented plaintiff from obtaining employment entitled him to recover his damages caused thereby; sustained both counts on all points, reversed the judgment, and remanded the cause for trial. 192 S.W. 387.

Defendant thereupon answered the petition, reiterating in its plea to the first count the constitutional objections to § 3020, and its plea to the second count averring that to permit a recovery against it by reason of the alleged agreement between the companies would deprive defendant of its property and its right to contract without due process of law in violation of the Fourteenth Amendment.

On the issues so made up, the case went to trial and resulted in a verdict in favor of plaintiff upon both counts. Defendant having reserved its constitutional points, appealed from the resulting judgment to the Supreme Court, which, however, refused to take jurisdiction on the ground that all constitutional questions had been decided on the former appeal and that the verdict, being for only $1500, was less than the jurisdictional amount required by statute; and hence transferred the cause to the St. Louis Court of Appeals for final disposition. 209 S.W. 928. Defendant, treating this decision of the Supreme Court as a final judgment reviewable by writ of error from this court, sued out such a writ, and upon the ground that the judgment was not final under the state law the cause was dismissed March 8, 1920. 252 U.S. 567. Thereafter it was submitted to the St. Louis Court of Appeals, which in conformity to the former opinion of the Supreme Court affirmed the judgment (223 S.W. 754), overruled a motion for rehearing and refused an application for certification of the case to the Supreme Court. A writ of error from this court to the St. Louis Court of Appeals followed, under § 237, Judicial Code, as amended by Act of September 6, 1916, c. 448, 39 Stat. 726. * * *

The argument in support of the contention that the Service Letter Act is repugnant to the due process of law clause of the Fourteenth Amendment in brief is that at common law an employer is under no obligation to give a testimonial of character or clearance card to his employee; that no man is compelled to enter into business relations with another unless he desires to do so, and upon the dissolution of such relations no man can be compelled to divulge to the public his reasons for such dissolution; that it is a part of every man's civil rights that he be at liberty to refuse business relations with any other person, whether the refusal rests upon reason or is the result of whim, caprice or malice, and with his reasons neither the public nor third persons have any legal concern; and that in the absence of a contract either employer or employee may sever the relation existing between them for any reason or without reason and may not be compelled to divulge the reason without material interference with his fundamental rights. Assuming the rules of the common law to be as stated, it is obvious that to say they have an unqualified and universal application unalterable by statute, begs the question at the outset.

Section 3020 of the Revised Statutes of Missouri, now a part of the general corporation laws of the State, was derived from an Act of April 14, 1905 (Mo. Laws 1905, p. 178), entitled "An Act for the protection of laboring men by requiring employing corporations to give letter showing service of employe quitting service of such corporation, and providing penalty for violation of this act." In giving its genesis the Supreme Court declared (192 S.W. 389) : "Prior to the enactment of this statute a custom had grown up in this state, among railroad and other corporations, not to employ any applicant for a position until he gave the name of his last employer, and upon receiving the name, it would write to said former employer, making inquiry as to the cause of the applicant's discharge, if discharged, or his cause for leaving the service of such former company. If the information furnished was not satisfactory, the applicant was refused employment. This custom became so widespread and affected such vast numbers of laboring people it became a public evil, and worked great injustice and oppression upon large numbers of persons who earned their bread by the sweat of their faces. The statute quoted was enacted for the purpose of regulating that custom, not to destroy it (for it contained some good and useful elements, enabling the corporations of the state to ascertain the degree of the intelligence as well as the honesty, capacity, and efficiency of those whom they wished to employ, for whose conduct they are responsible to the public and their fellow employees), and thereby remedy the evil which flowed therefrom." And again, (p. 392): "The statute under consideration imposes no unjust burden or expense upon the respondent or other corporations doing business in this state. It was designed to protect the public interests as well as the wage-earner, against an injurious custom given birth to and fostered by said corporations. That a foreign corporation has no inherent right to exist or to do business in this state is no longer an open question. It derives those rights from the state, impressed with such conditions and burdens as the state may deem proper to impose, and when such a corporation comes into this state to do business, it must conform to the laws of this state, and will not be heard to complain of the unconstitutionality of our police regulations."

That freedom in the making of contracts of personal employment, by which labor and other services are exchanged for money or other forms of property, is an elementary part of the rights of personal liberty and private property, not to be struck down directly or arbitrarily interfered with, consistently with the due process of law guaranteed by the Fourteenth Amendment, we are not disposed to question. This court has affirmed the principle in recent cases. *Adair v. United States,* 208 U.S. 161, 174; *Coppage v. Kansas,* 236 U.S. 1, 14.

But the right to conduct business in the form of a corporation, and as such to enter into relations of employment with individuals, is not a natural or fundamental right. It is a creature of the law; and a State in authorizing its own corporations or those of other States to carry on business and employ men within its borders may qualify the privilege by imposing such conditions and duties as reasonably may be deemed expedient in order that the corporation's activities may not operate to the detriment of the rights of others with whom it may come in contact.

The statute in question is of this character; in it the legislature has recognized that, by reason of the systematic methods of engaging and dismissing employees that employing corporations themselves established, "letters of dismissal," or something of the kind, are not only customary but a matter of necessity to those seeking employment, as well as to the corporations themselves, perhaps more necessary to those seeking employment, because of their want of organization, than to the corporations.

Can it be called an unreasonable or arbitrary regulation that requires an employing corporation to furnish to an employee, who after having served it for a time is discharged or voluntarily quits the service, a letter signed by the superintendent or manager setting forth the nature, character and duration of the service rendered and for what cause, if any, he left the service? It does not prevent the corporation from employing whom it pleases on any terms that may be agreed upon. So far as construed and applied in this case it does not debar a corporation from dismissing an employee without cause, if such would be its right otherwise, nor from stating that he is dismissed without cause if such be the fact. It does not require that it give a commendatory letter. There is nothing to interfere, even indirectly, with the liberty of the corporation in dealing with its employee, beyond giving him, instead of what formerly was called a "reference" or "character," a brief statement of his service with the company according to the truth, a word of introduction to be his credentials where otherwise the opportunity of future employment easily might be barred or impeded.

That statutes having the same general purpose, though sometimes less moderate provisions, have been adopted in other States attests a widespread belief in the necessity for such legislation. Indiana Rev. Stat. 1901 (Horner), § 5206r; Acts 1911, c. 178; Acts 1915, c. 51; Montana Rev. Codes 1907, §§ 1755-1757; Nebraska Rev. Stat. 1913, §§ 3572-3574; Oklahoma Rev. Laws 1910, § 3769; Texas Rev. Civil Stat. 1911, Art. 594. Fifty years ago, in an act for the protection of seamen, Congress established and still maintains a provision that upon the discharge of any seaman, or upon payment of his wages, the master shall sign and give him a certificate of discharge, specifying the period of his service and the time and place of discharge, in a prescribed form which calls for numerous identifying particulars and permits a statement of the seaman's character and capacity. Act June 7, 1872 c. 322, § 24, 17 Stat. 262, 267, 280; Rev. Stats. § 4551; Table B, p. 896.

Plaintiff in error places much reliance upon expressions of opinion contained in a number of cases in the state courts, chiefly the following: * * *[1]

We have examined the opinions referred to with the care called for by the importance of the case before us; and are bound to say that, beyond occasional manifestations of a disinclination to concede validity to acts of legislation having the general character of Service Letter Laws, we have found nothing of material weight; no well-considered judgment, much less

---

[1] The court here reviewed the cases of Wallace v. Georgia, C. & N. Ry. Co., 94 Ga. 732, 22 S.E. 579 (1894); Atchison, T. & S. F. Ry. Co. v. Brown, 80 Kan. 312, 102 Pac. 459 (1909); St. Louis & Southwestern Ry. Co. v. Griffin, 106 Texas 477, 171 S.W. 703 (1914), holding unconstitutional under the federal or state constitution letter of service legislation within those states, and the advisory opinion of the Massachusetts Supreme Judicial Court regarding as unconstitutional a statute requiring railroad corporations to give an employee an opportunity to make a statement before he was discharged upon information furnished by another person. Opinion of the Justices, 220 Mass. 627, 108 N.E. 807 (1915).—Ed.

a formidable body of opinion, worthy to be regarded as supporting the view that a statute which, like the Missouri statute, merely requires employing corporations to furnish a dismissed employee with a certificate setting forth the nature and character of the service rendered, its duration, and for what cause, if any, the employee has left such service, amounts to an interference with freedom of contract so serious and arbitrary as properly to be regarded a deprivation of liberty or property without due process of law, within the meaning of the Fourteenth Amendment.

The cases cited from Georgia, from Kansas, and from Texas place material dependence upon provisions of the several state constitutions guaranteeing freedom of speech, from which is deduced as by contrast a right of privacy called the "liberty of silence"; and it seems to be thought that the relations between a corporation and its employees and former employees are a matter of wholly private concern. But, as we have stated, neither the Fourteenth Amendment nor any other provision of the Constitution of the United States imposes upon the States any restrictions about "freedom of speech" or the "liberty of silence"; nor, we may add, does it confer any right of privacy upon either persons or corporations.

Previous decisions of this court are far from furnishing support for the contentions of plaintiff in error. *Allgeyer v. Louisiana,* 165 U.S. 578, related to legislation of a wholly different character and contains nothing that bears upon this. *Lochner v. New York,* 198 U.S. 45, dealt with a statute concededly valid if enacted in the interest of the public health, and held it void on the ground that in truth it was not, within the fair meaning of the term, a health law but was an illegal interference with the right of individuals to make contracts upon such terms as they might deem best. *Adair v. United States,* 208 U.S. 161, 174-175; *Coppage v. Kansas,* 236 U.S. 1, 17, dealt with statutes—the former with an act of Congress making it criminal for a common carrier in interstate commerce to discharge an employee because of his membership in a labor organization; the latter with a state law making it criminal to prescribe as a condition upon which one might secure or retain employment that the employee should agree not to become or remain a member of any labor organization while so employed; and this in the absence of contract between the parties, coercion on the part of the employer, or incapacity or disability on the part of the employee. In accord with an almost unbroken current of authority in the state courts holding statutes of that character to be invalid, this court came to a like conclusion. In the latter case there was a direct interference with freedom in the making of contracts of employment not asserted to have relation to the public health, safety, morals or general welfare beyond a purpose to favor the employee at the expense of the employer, and to build up the labor organizations, which we held was not properly an exercise of the police power. This statute, in making it criminal, as it did upon the construction adopted and applied, for an employer to prescribe as a condition of employing or retaining a man competent and willing to assent to the condition, that he should agree not to become or remain a member of a labor organization while so employed, the employee being subject to no incapacity or disability, but on the contrary free to exercise a voluntary choice, in effect made it a compulsory and unwelcome term of the employment that the employee *must* be left free to join a labor union; membership in which reasonably might be expected to interfere materially with the member's fidelity to his employer.

As has been shown, the Missouri statute interposes no obstacle or interference as to either the making or the termination of contracts of employment, and prescribes neither terms nor conditions. The Supreme Court of the State, having ample knowledge of the conditions which gave rise to the particular legislation, declares with an authority not to be denied that it was required in order to protect the laboring man from conditions that had arisen out of customs respecting employment and discharge of employees introduced by the corporations themselves. It sustains the act as an exercise of the police power, but in truth it requires no extraordinary aid, being but a regulation of corporations calling for an application of the familiar precept, *sic utere tuo,* etc., in a matter of general public concern. Except by consent of the State the corporation, foreign or domestic, would have no right to employ laborers within its borders. A foreign corporation does not, as intimated by the court below, waive any constitutional objection by coming in (see *Terral v. Burke Construction Co.,* 257 U.S. 529). But it has no valid objection to such reasonable regulations as may be prescribed for domestic corporations similarly circumstanced. The State with good reason might regulate the terms and conditions of employment, including the methods of accepting and dismissing employees, so as to prevent the corporations from producing undue detriment to the individuals concerned, either while employed or when afterwards they are called upon to seek other employment. In our opinion, no danger of "blacklisting" is necessary to justify legislation requiring that corporations dismissing employees furnish them with a certificate stating the period of the service, its nature and character, and the cause, if any, that led to its termination. It might be recognized that in the highly organized conditions of industry now prevailing—largely developed by the corporations themselves and to which their success is greatly due—it is not to be expected that unemployed men can obtain responsible employment without some credentials proceeding from a former employer. The legislature might believe it to be well understood that a period of employment by a corporation—notably so in the case of insurance companies—is a test of capacity, fidelity and the other qualities that go to make efficiency; that such a corporation may operate as a training school fitting employees not only for its own but for other lines of employment. Such a training may almost inevitably produce effects upon the individuals in forming both character and reputation— effects that cannot be brought to an end at the will of the employee or of the corporation or both of them combined, although the employment may be terminated at the will of either; but may continue while the employee lives; his employment with the corporation remains a part of what is called his "record," by which he must be judged whenever afterwards he may be in search of employment. The reputation of the dismissed employee is an essential part of his personal rights—of his right of personal security (1 Black. Com. 129; 3 *id.* 119). Even the common law regarded a man's public repute as a fact having a bearing upon his ability to earn a livelihood; looked upon a good reputation in a particular trade or calling as having special pecuniary value; regarded a prospective employer as privileged to make inquiries about what his would-be employee had done in a former place of employment; conferred upon the former employer a privilege to communicate the truth in reply. What more reasonable than for the legislature of Missouri to deem that the public interest required it to treat corporations as having, in a peculiar degree, the reputation and well-being of their former employees in their keeping, and to convert what otherwise might be but a legal privilege, or under prevailing customs, a "moral duty," into a legal duty, by requiring, as this statute does, that when an employee has been discharged or has voluntarily left the service it shall give him, on his request, a letter setting forth the nature and character of his service and its duration, and truly stating what cause, if any, led him to quit such service.

It is not for us to point out the grounds upon which the state legislature acted, or to indicate all the grounds that occur to us as being those upon which they may have acted. We have not attempted to do this; but merely to indicate sufficient grounds upon which they reasonably might have acted and possibly did act to show that it is not demonstrated that they acted arbitrarily, and hence that there is no sufficient reason for holding that the statute deprives the corporation of its liberty or property without due process of law.

The argument under the "equal protection" clause is unsubstantial. As we are assured by the opinion of the Supreme Court, the mischiefs to which the statute is directed are peculiarly an outgrowth of existing practices of corporations and are susceptible of a corrective in their case not so readily applied in the case of individual employers, presumably less systematic in their methods of employment and dismissal. There is no difficulty, therefore, in sustaining the legislature in placing corporations in one class and individuals in another. See *Mallinckrodt Chemical Works v. St. Louis,* 238 U.S. 41, 55-56. And the act applies to all corporations doing business in the State, whether incorporated under its laws or not.

It is assigned for error, aside from the statute, that the decision of the Missouri court sustaining the cause of action under the second count amounts to depriving plaintiff in error of property without due process of law. * * *

The pith of the objection to the second count is that to permit a recovery against plaintiff in error on account of the agreement said to have been made between it and two other companies having a monopoly of the industrial life insurance business in the City of St. Louis, to the effect that neither of the three would within two years employ any man who had left the service of or been discharged by either of the others, was equivalent to depriving it of property without "due process of law." The Supreme Court held (192 S.W. 393), that the corporations had no lawful right to enter into a combination or agreement the effect of which was to take from them the right to employ whomsoever they deemed proper, and at the same time deprive former employees of their constitutional right to seek employment. It seems to us clear that the State might, without conflict with the Fourteenth Amendment, enact through its legislative department a statute precisely to the same effect as the rule of law and public policy declared by its court of last resort. And for the purposes of our jurisdiction it makes no difference, under that Amendment, through what department the State has acted. The decision is as valid as a statute would be. No question of "equal protection" is raised here.

The judgment under review must be and is

Affirmed.

The CHIEF JUSTICE, MR. JUSTICE VAN DEVANTER and MR. JUSTICE McREYNOLDS dissent.[2]

ANDERSON v. SHIPOWNERS ASSOCIATION OF THE PACIFIC COAST.

United States Supreme Court. 272 U.S. 359 (1926).

MR. JUSTICE SUTHERLAND delivered the opinion of the Court.

This is a suit to enjoin the respondents from maintaining a combination in restraint of interstate and foreign commerce in violation of § 1 of the Anti-Trust Act, c. 647, 26 Stat. 209, and to recover damages. Such a suit is authorized by §§ 4 and 16 of the Clayton Act, c. 323, 38 Stat. 730, 731, 737. *Duplex Co. v. Deering,* 254 U.S. 443, 464-465. Upon respondents' motion, the district court dismissed the bill of complaint, apparently upon the merits, and the circuit court of appeals affirmed the decree. 10 Fed.(2d) 96. The only question necessary to be considered here is whether the bill states a case within the Anti-Trust Act.

The bill is not concisely drawn and the application of its allegations is to some degree obscured by references to acts of Congress regulating com-

---

[2] Accord: Chicago, R. I. & P. R. R. Co. v. Perry, 259 U.S. 548 (1922). For a collection of other authorities upon the constitutionality of the service letter laws, together with a collection of such legislation, see: 36 Harv. Law Rev. 195 (1922).

Similar to this legislation was the Hackney Carriage License Act, 6 & 7 Vict. c. 86 (1843), which required proprietors to indorse the fact of and reasons for the discharge upon the license of hackney drivers, the drivers also being required to produce these licenses in order to secure re-employment. The proprietor was liable for indorsing a false ground of discharge. Hurrell v. Ellis, 2 C.B. 295 (1845) ; Rogers v. Macnamara, 14 C.B. 27 (1853). *Cf.* Seward v. Receivers of Seaboard Air Line Ry., 159 N.C. 241, 75 S.E. 34 (1912).

merce, other than the Anti-Trust Act. For present purposes the pertinent allegations, shortly stated, are as follows: Petitioner is a seaman and has followed that calling for more than twenty years on ships engaged in the carrying trade among the states on the Pacific Coast and with foreign countries. He is a member of the Seaman's Union of America, having a membership of about 10,000 seamen engaged in various forms of maritime service in the same field; and he sues on their behalf as well as his own. The members of the respondent associations own, operate or control substantially all the merchant vessels of American registry engaged in interstate and foreign commerce among the ports of the Pacific Coast and with foreign countries. These associations and their members have entered into a combination to control the employment, upon such vessels, of all seamen upon the Pacific Coast, and to that end the associations have established and maintain offices in San Francisco and San Pedro, California, where seamen are engaged and supplied to the operators of the vessels. Among other requirements, every seaman seeking employment is compelled to register, receive a number and await his turn according to the number, before he can obtain employment, the result of which is that seamen, well qualified and well known, are frequently prevented from obtaining employment at once, when, but for these conditions, they would be able to do so. A certificate is issued to each seaman which he is obliged to carry and present in order to obtain employment. The certificate, in part, recites that no person will be employed unless registered; that the certificate must be delivered to the master of the vessel upon articles being signed; that the certificate is the personal record of the seaman and the basis of his future employment. At the same time, two cards are issued,—one to the seaman, assigning him to a specified employment, and another to the ship, reciting the capacity in which the seaman is to be employed, with the statement that "he must not be employed on your ship in any capacity unless he presents an assignment card, grey in color, issued by us and addressed to your vessel designating the position to which we have assigned him." The associations fix the wages which shall be paid the seamen. Under the regulations, when a seaman's turn comes, he must take the employment then offered or none, whether it is suited to his qualifications or whether he wishes to engage on the particular vessel or for the particular voyage; and the officers of the vessels are deprived of the right to select their own men or those deemed most suitable. Without a compliance with the foregoing requirements, no seaman can be employed on any of the vessels owned or operated by members of the associations.

It is further alleged that the petitioner sought employment through the San Francisco office of the associations and was refused registration because he failed to produce a discharge book. At a later time, he was employed by the mate of a vessel engaged in coastwise interstate traffic, but was required by the mate to apply at the office of the associations for assignment as a sailor; that upon application being thus made such assignment was refused; that, nevertheless, he was directed by the mate to report on board for duty; that he did report, but was informed by the mate that he had been ordered to take no seamen except through the office of the associations, and in consequence petitioner lost the employment to his damage in a sum stated.

From these averments, the conclusion results that each of the shipowners and operators, by entering into this combination, has, in respect of the employment of seamen, surrendered himself completely to the control of the associations. If the restraint thus imposed had related to the carriage of goods in interstate and foreign commerce—that is to say, if each shipowner had precluded himself from making any contract of transportation directly with the shipper and had put himself under an obligation to refuse to carry for any person without the previous approval of the associations—the unlawful restraint would be clear. But ships and those who operate them are instrumentalities of commerce and within the Commerce Clause no less than cargoes. *Second Employers' Liability Cases,* 223 U.S. 1, 47-49. And, as was said by this Court in *United States v. Colgate & Co.,* 250 U.S. 300, 307, "The purpose of the Sherman Act is to prohibit monopolies, contracts and combinations which probably would unduly interfere with the free exercise of their rights by those engaged, or who wish to engage, in trade and commerce—in a word to preserve the right of freedom to trade." That the effect of the combination now under consideration, both as to the seamen and the owners, is precisely what this language condemns, is made plain by the allegations of the bill which we have just summarized. The absence of an allegation that such was the specific intent is not important, since that is the necessary and direct consequence of the combination and the acts of the associations under it, and they cannot be heard to say the contrary. *United States v. Patten,* 226 U.S. 525, 543. It is not important, therefore, to inquire whether, as contended by respondents, the object of the combination was merely to regulate the employment of men and not to restrain commerce. A restraint of interstate commerce cannot be justified by the fact that the object of the participants in the combination was to benefit themselves in a way which might have been unobjectionable in the absence of such restraint. *Duplex Co. v. Deering, supra,* p. 468; *Ellis v. Inman, Poulsen & Co.,* 131 Fed. 182, 186.

Respondents rely on *Industrial Association v. United States,* 268 U.S. 64; *United Leather Workers v. Herkert,* 265 U.S. 457, and *United Mine Workers v. Coronado Co.,* 259 U.S. 344; but these cases are not in point. The conspiracies or combinations in all three related to local matters—the first, to building in San Francisco, the second, to manufacturing, and the third, to mining operations—and the effect upon interstate commerce was held to be purely indirect and secondary. Neither the making of goods nor the mining of coal is commerce; and the fact that the things produced are afterwards shipped or used in interstate commerce does not make their production a part of it. Nor is building commerce; and the fact that the materials to be used are shipped in from other states does not make building a part of such interstate commerce. In the *Industrial Association Case,* after a reference to the two earlier decisions, pp. 80-82, it was said (p. 82) : "The alleged conspiracy and the acts here complained of, spent their intended and direct force upon a local situation,—for building is as essentially local as mining, manufacturing or growing crops,—and if, by a resulting diminution of the commercial demand, interstate trade was curtailed either generally or in specific instances, that was a fortuitous consequence so remote and indirect as plainly to cause it to fall outside the reach of the Sherman Act." Here, however, the combination and the acts complained of did not spend their intended and direct force upon a local situation. On the contrary, they related to the employment of seamen for service on ships, both of them instrumentalities of, and intended to be used in, interstate and foreign commerce; and the immediate force of the combination, both in purpose and execution, was directed toward affecting such commerce. The interference with commerce, therefore, was direct and primary, and not, as in the cases cited, incidental, indirect and secondary.

Taking the allegations of the bill at their face value, as we must do in the absence of countervailing facts or explanations, it appears that each shipowner and operator in this widespread combination has surrendered his freedom of action in the matter of employing seamen and agreed to abide by the will of the associations. Such is the fair interpretation of the combination and of the various requirements under it, and this is borne out by the actual experience of the petitioner in his efforts to secure employment. These shipowners and operators having thus put themselves into a situation of restraint upon their freedom to carry on interstate and foreign commerce according to their own choice and discretion, it follows, as the case now stands, that the combination is in violation of the Anti-Trust Act.

Decree reversed and cause remanded to the district court for further proceedings in conformity with this opinion.

MR. JUSTICE STONE took no part in the consideration or decision of this case.[1]

___

[1] Upon the new trial, the allegations made in the bill were deemed not proven and judgment was given for the defendant. Andersen v. Shipowners' Ass'n, 31 Fed.(2d) 539 (9th cir. 1929), certiorari denied in 279 U. S. 864 (1929). *Cf.* Tilbury v. Oregon Stevedoring Co., 7 Fed.(2d) 1 (9th cir. 1925).

"So far as I am aware, this is the only Supreme Court decision in which workingmen have successfully invoked the Sherman and Clayton Acts on their own behalf * * *." Powell, "The Supreme Court's Control Over the Issue of Injunctions in Labor Disputes," 13 Proc. Acad. Pol. Sci. 37, 60 (1928).

JOHNSON v. OREGON STEVEDORING CO.

Oregon Supreme Court. 128 Ore. 121, 270 Pac. 772 (1928).

This is an action for damages based upon the alleged blacklisting and publishing of plaintiff with the intent and for the purpose of preventing him from engaging in or securing employment as a longshoreman or in similar work. The pertinent allegations of the complaint, briefly stated, are as follows:

Some time prior to October 12, 1922, the defendants unlawfully and maliciously conspired to blacklist and publish any employee discharged by any one of the defendants, with the intent and for the purpose of preventing such discharged employee from securing other employment in the Port of Portland and Columbia River ports. Pursuant to such unlawful conspiracy the defendants established a hiring hall where longshoremen engaged in such employment would be employed and appointed one J. O'Neil as their agent. On June 3, 1925, the defendants, in the execution of their unlawful conspiracy, blacklisted and published the plaintiff with the intention of preventing him from securing similar or other employment, by causing their agent to strike plaintiff's name from the list of persons eligible to secure employment in stevedoring or longshoring in the Port of Portland and the Columbia River ports, and by communicating to each of the defendants the information that plaintiff's name had been stricken from such list, and by refusing to permit plaintiff to enter into the hiring hall maintained by defendants, and by publishing to each of the defendants a list of persons who were to be refused employment in such occupation, which list contained plaintiff's name. The complaint further charges that the defendants named therein constitute substantially all of the employers of labor in the calling in which plaintiff was engaged in the Port of Portland and Columbia River ports; that, by reason of such conspiracy, the plaintiff has been refused employment in the Port of Portland and the Columbia River ports and is wholly unable to obtain employment as a stevedore or longshoreman in such ports, and thereby has been damaged in the sum of $15,000.

The answer admitted the establishment of a hiring hall in charge of J. O'Neil as an employing agent, where defendants hired their labor, but denied the existence of the alleged conspiracy, or malice, or blacklisting, or damage to plaintiff.

The trial resulted in a judgment of $4,500 for the plaintiff. The defendants appeal, assigning error in the refusal of the trial court to grant a judgment of nonsuit or to direct a verdict, and in the giving of certain instructions and refusing other instructions requested by the defendants.
* * *

BROWN, J.: * * * The act upon which plaintiff bases his cause is entitled:

"An Act to prevent blacklisting of mechanics, unskilled laborers, and other employees."

It provides:

"Sec. 1. No corporation, company, or individual shall blacklist or publish, or cause to be blacklisted or published, any employee, mechanic, or laborer, discharged by such corporation, company, or individual, with intent and for the purpose of preventing such employee, mechanic, or laborer from engaging in or securing similar or other employment from any other corporation, company, or individual.

"Sec. 2. If any officer or agent of any corporation, company, or individual, or other person, shall blacklist or publish, or cause to be blacklisted or published, any employee, mechanic, or laborer, with intent and for the purpose of preventing such employee, mechanic, or laborer from engaging in or securing similar or other employment from any corporation, company, or individual, or shall, in any manner, conspire or contrive, by correspondence or otherwise, to prevent such discharged employee from securing employment, he shall be deemed guilty of a misdemeanor, and upon conviction thereof shall be fined in a sum not less than $50 nor more than $250, or imprisoned in the county jail not less than 30 nor more than 90 days, or both, at the discretion of the court." Gen. Laws Or., 1903, p. 137; codified as Or. L., §§ 2179, 2180.

The defendants assert that the foregoing enactment is unconstitutional and void for uncertainty. There is no merit in this contention. This statute does not offend against Section 1 of the Fourteenth Amendment to the Constitution of the United States by depriving the defendants, or either of them, of their liberty and property without due process of law, nor does it deny to them, or either of them, the equal protection of the law. It makes no attempt to regulate the liberty of the employer, either in the selection or in the discharge of an employee. Moreover, this statute, like the common law, recognizes the fundamental right of every man to seek employment unhampered by the act of a former employer. Employment for the laboring man means meat and drink; clothing and shelter. The matter of the employment of the laborer in honest toil is pre-eminently of public concern; and public policy requires that his rights shall not be violated. So, with a full realization of the paramount need for protecting the toiler in his honest endeavor to seek a livelihood, a majority of the states of the Union have enacted statutes similar to the one quoted above, denouncing as a crime the blacklisting of employees by a former employer. For a list of such statutes, see compilation of labor laws of the United States by the United States Department of Labor, Bureau of Labor Statistics.

As to man's legal right to seek employment unhindered, we quote the following from the treatment of the subject by Judge COOLEY, whose work has long been recognized as the established standard authority on the question:

"It is a part of every man's civil rights that he be left at liberty to refuse business relations with any person whomsoever. * * * With his reasons, neither the public nor third persons have any legal concern. It is also his right to have business relations with anyone with whom he can make contracts, and if he is wrongfully deprived of this right by others, he is entitled to redress. Thus, if one is prevented by the wrongful act of a third party from securing some employment he has sought, he suffers a legal wrong, provided he can show that the failure to employ him was the direct and natural consequence of the wrongful act." Cooley on Torts (2 ed.), p. 328.

Under the head of "Malicious Interference With one's Occupation," we find in Webb's Pollock on Torts, at page 406:

"There may be other malicious injuries not capable of more specific definition, 'where a violent or malicious act is done to a man's occupation, profession or way of getting a livelihood.'

"The fundamental right involved in this case is the right of every individual to seek any legal employment he may. One of the aims of the common law has been to protect every person against the wrongful acts of every other person, whether committed alone or in combination with others, and to this end it has provided an action for injuries done by disturbing a person in the enjoyment of any right or privilege which he has. See *Walker v. Cronin,* 107 Mass. 562."

In the case of *Mattison v. Lake Shore Ry. Co.,* 3 Ohio Dec. 526, 531, PRATT, J., wrote the following pertinent matter relating to the laboring man's right to seek employment:

"It is for the public interest and for the public good that the right of a man to seek his own employment in any honest work which he may seek should not be interfered with or violated. This, of course, does not interfere at all with the right of a company or of a man to judge himself who he will have work for him; and it makes no difference whether he refuses to let a man work for him because he is incompetent, or because he dislikes him; he has a right to seek his employees, but, as is frequently said, one man's right ends where another man's commences, and the right of the employer to discharge ends with his own employment, and he must not trench upon the right of the employee to seek other employment by which he may support himself and his family, and it is for the public interest that the largest liberty to seek employment should be before every man, whatever may be his employment, or whatever may be his business, trade or occupation."

A number of statutes denouncing blacklisting of employees by former employers are collected in a note to 4 L.R.A.(N.S.) 1123; and the editor of the note, in a discussion of the subject of blacklisting, said, among other things:

"The inevitable effect of this practice, when developed on a large scale, must be the subjection of a constantly increasing number of employees to disabilities and restrictions scarcely less oppressive than those to which servants were formerly subjected in England by statutory provisions long since obsolete."

The Minnesota statute prohibiting blacklisting is much like our own, and in the case of *State ex rel. Scheffer v. Justus,* 85 Minn. 279 (88 N.W. 759, 89 Am. St. Rep. 550, 56 L.R.A. 757), that statute was held to be constitutional.

The defendants say the legislature failed to define the term "blacklisting" as used in the statute. The foregoing statute is a criminal law and must show with reasonable certainty what acts or omissions the legislature intended to prohibit and punish. But reasonable definiteness, in view of conditions, is all that is required: *State v. Bailey,* 115 Or. 428 (236 Pac. 1053). The statute assailed is not indefinite. It prohibits any person from blacklisting or publishing any employee with intent and for the purpose of preventing such employee from engaging in or securing similar or other employment, or from conspiring to prevent a discharged employee from securing employment. Some of the older decisions, as do the defendants, complain likewise that the term "blacklisting" is not defined in the dictionaries. That term is found in all modern dictionaries. From Black's Law Dictionary we take the following:

"Black list. A list of persons marked out for special avoidance, antagonism, or enmity on the part of those who prepare the list or those among whom it is intended to circulate."

This definition was quoted with approval in the case of *Dick v. Northern Pac. R. Co.,* 86 Wash. 211 (150 Pac. 8, Ann. Cas. 1917A, 638), and appears, in substance, in Webster's New International Dictionary, Funk and Wagnall's Dictionary of the English Language, and in Cogley on Strikes and Lockouts, page 293. * * *

By reason of the court's instructions on the question of exemplary damages, this case should be reversed. It is so ordered.

Reversed.

RAND, C.J., and BEAN and BELT, JJ., concur in the result.[1]

---

[1] Accord: State v. Justus, 85 Minn. 279, 88 N.W. 759 (1902). *Cf.* Wabash R. R. Co. v. Young, 162 Ind. 102, 69 N.E. 1003 (1904).

For a collection of anti-blacklisting statutes, see: Witte, The Government in Labor Disputes, 213 (1932).

For cases as to the scope of such statutes, see: Cleary v. Great Northern Ry. Co., 147 Minn. 403, 180 N.W. 545 (1920) ; Goins v. Sargent, 196 N.C. 478, 146 S.E. 131 (1929) ; O'Brien v. Western Union Tel. Co., 62 Wash. 598, 114 Pac. 441 (1911).

CHAPTER XI.

EMPLOYER INTERFERENCE WITH THE "RIGHT" TO TRADE.

DEON v. KIRBY LUMBER CO.

Supreme Court of Louisiana. 162 La. 671, 111 So. 55 (1927).

ROGERS, J.: This is a suit for the recovery of damages for the alleged violation of the provisions of Act 11 of Ex. Sess. 1915 and, alternatively, under Civ. Code, art. 2315. Defendants' exceptions of no cause of action were overruled, and they appealed. The appeals are permissible, under section 13 of the statute.

Plaintiff, in his petition, sets forth, substantially, that the Kirby Lumber Company, one of the defendants, is a Texas corporation, operating a large sawmill plant and general merchandise store near the plant, at Merryville, in the parish of Beauregard. That O. E. Johnson, the other defendant, is the general manager in charge of its sawmill and store, with power to employ and discharge employees and to direct all activities, of whatsoever nature, connected with or incidental to the operation of the company.

It is alleged that some time prior to May 27, 1926, the petitioner purchased a lot of ground near the sawmill plant, erected a building thereon, stocked it with merchandise, and then opened it as a general mercantile store for business with the public.

It is alleged that a few days prior to the date on which petitioner opened his store for business, the defendant company, acting by and through its general manager and also through various foremen in charge of its various departments, and the defendant O. E. Johnson, individually, in a mass meeting called and held for the purpose, publicly notified and caused to be notified all the employees of the company that they were prohibited from purchasing any goods or wares at petitioner's store, and, further, warned said employees that any of them who dealt or traded with petitioner or who visited his store or family would be immediately discharged.

It is alleged that the defendant company did, in fact at various times discharge a number of its employees for trading with and visiting petitioner's store or family; that it reduced the wages of other employees for so doing, and threatened to discharge a number of others if they persisted in dealing with petitioner.

It is alleged that the acts of the defendants amounted to and were a conspiracy and contract to boycott petitioner, were in restraint of

688

trade on the part of the company's employees, and in violation of Act 11 of 1915. That said acts were done for the purpose of and succeeded in suppressing competition and in monopolizing the business of the locality, by forcing the employees of the defendant company to purchase articles of necessity and commerce exclusively from the company's commissary.

It is alleged that the conduct, threats, commands, acts of coercion, and intimidation set forth were done by and at the direction of the said Johnson in the course of his employment, and by the said defendant company, and with the full knowledge, consent, and active assistance of the company.

It is alleged that, as a result of defendants' actions, petitioner's business was totally ruined as it was entirely dependent upon the trade of the employees of the lumber company.

It is alleged that the acts of defendants, as set forth in the petition, have caused petitioner great annoyance and humiliation by reason of the notoriety thereby obtained in the neighborhood and the practical ostracism of himself and his family from the society of their friends, neighbors, and acquaintances.

In the alternative, petitioner averred that, if the acts complained of were not committed for the purpose of monopolizing the business and trade of the company's employees and did not amount to a conspiracy in restraint of trade, then the said acts were done with the wanton and malicious intent and desire on the part of the defendants to injure him in his business, social standing, property rights, and character.

The petition contains the necessary allegations as to the damages sustained, and the prayer is in accordance with the averments.

Plaintiff's contention, based on the facts alleged, is that three separate and distinct causes of action are set out in his petition, viz.:

First. That the defendants conspired to restrain trade, in violation of section 1 of Act 11 of 1915.

Second. That defendants' acts were done for the purpose of and succeeded in suppressing competition in handling the necessities of life, thus creating a monopoly in such commodities, in violation of section 2 of Act 11 of 1915.

Third. In the alternative, that defendants' acts were wanton and malicious and were committed for the purpose of injuring petitioner and to ruin his business, character, and social standing.

The court below overruled defendants' exceptions, holding that plaintiff's petition showed a cause of action under the first ground of his contention. The court did not pass upon plaintiff's other alleged causes of action.

Act 11 of 1915 was enacted to protect trade and commerce against unlawful restraints, combinations, conspiracies, and monopolies; to provide remedies against, punishment for, and to allow a cause of action in favor of persons injured by such acts.

Section 1 of the statute provides, in part:

"That every contract, combination in the form of trust or otherwise, or conspiracy, in restraint of trade or commerce in the state of Louisiana is hereby declared to be illegal."

Section 2 of the legislative act provides, in part:

"That every person who shall monopolize, or attempt to monopolize, or combine or conspire with any other person or persons to monopolize any part of the trade or commerce within the state of Louisiana, shall be deemed guilty of a misdemeanor," etc.

The question before us under the exceptions to the principal demands of plaintiff is whether the acts of the defendants complained of in the petition constituted a conspiracy to restrain trade or stifle competition, or to create a monopoly, so as to make them violative of and actionable under the public policy of this state, as expressed in the statute declared upon by plaintiff. * * *

The statute itself, in so far as it confers on the injured party a civil action for the recovery of damages for his injuries, is nothing more than the legislative sanction of the legal principle that any injury to a lawful business, whether the result of an unlawful conspiracy or other wrongful act, is actionable.

It may be regarded as settled by the weight of authority that, while an act of an individual may not create a civil liability, the same act may be unlawful and actionable, if committed by two or more persons in concert. Nevertheless, it is equally well settled that where an act would be lawful if done by an individual, it will also be lawful if committed by a combination, provided they have no unlawful object in view. The carrying out of the object of such combination will not furnish ground for a civil action, if the element of malice, that is, the absence of just cause or excuse, is not present. If the object of the combination is to further its own fair interest or advantage and not to injure another, its members are not liable for injuries merely incidental thereto. See 12 C.J. pp. 583, 584, and authorities cited.

The test therefore to be applied to the acts complained of is whether they were done by the defendants, in concert or singly, with malice, or with the intention of injuring plaintiff without just cause or excuse.

In applying this test, it may be observed that every one has the right to enjoy the fruits and advantages of his own enterprise, industry, skill, and credit. But this right cannot be extended so as to protect him against lawful competition, even though that competition be successfully directed to drive him out of business.

It may also be observed that there is no law which compels a man to part with his property; hence, in this state, at least, an employer who is engaged in mercantile business may, without making himself civilly liable therefor, induce his employees to discontinue their patronage of competing mercantile establishments and give it entirely to him, by appeals, persuasion, and creating a fear that they would be discharged from their employment, if his requests were not complied with. *Lewis v. Huie-Hodge Lumber Co.*, 121 La. 658, 46 So. 685; *cf. McGee v. Collins*, 156 La. 291, 100 So. 430, 34 A.L.R. 336.

A fair construction of all the averments of plaintiff's petition leads to the inescapable conclusion that competition in mercantile business existed between him and the defendants Kirby Lumber Company and its general manager, and that the acts complained of were not done maliciously to injure plaintiff, but for the purpose of securing to the defendants the trade of certain customers whose patronage they could command. Plaintiff had no superior right to the trade of these customers or of any other person. If he was injured, as alleged, his injury was the result of lawful competition and is *damnum absque injuria.*

Plaintiff argues that, in any event, the alleged restraint of trade and monopoly complained of were unlawful, under the provisions of Act 188 of 1916.

Defendants contend, first, that the statute is inapplicable, and, second, that it is unconstitutional, in that it embraces two objects both in title and in body.

It is unnecessary to discuss the constitutionality *vel non* of the legislative act, since we do not find it affects the issue presently before us.

The statute merely denounces certain acts as criminal and provides penalties therefor. It does not, in its provisions, create a right of action for the recovery of damages against the wrongdoer. The case at bar is not a proceeding necessitating the punishment of the defendants for an infraction of the law. It will be time enough to determine the legal effect of the legislative act whenever one of the class of individuals, for whose benefit and protection it was enacted, complains of its violation. The rule of law referred to in *State v. Liquidation*, 136 La. 571, 67 So. 370, is appropriate here, viz.:

"Wherever an action is brought for a breach of duty imposed by statute, the party bringing it must show that he had an interest in the performance of the duty, and that the duty was imposed for his benefit. But where the duty was created or imposed for the benefit of another, and the advantage to be derived to the party prosecuting, by its performance, is merely incidental and no part of the design of the statute, no such right is created as forms the subject of an action."

Our conclusion is that plaintiff has failed to set forth a cause of action under its principal demands. Nevertheless, if he has failed to show an unlawful conspiracy and monopoly, he has under his alternative demand shown a cause of action to recover damages from either or both of the defendants.

The allegations of the petition on this point are, substantially, omitting the alleged injury to his business and property rights, that the defendants acted maliciously and with the intent of injuring plaintiff's social standing and character, in forbidding and preventing the employees of the defendant company and their families from visiting plaintiff and his family, and in depriving petitioner and his family of the society of their friends and neighbors, amounting to the practical ostracism of plaintiff and his family.

These acts, if true, and we must accept them as true for the purpose of this discussion, are not justifiable on the theory that they were necessary for the legitimate self-interest of the defendant. It is the legal right of every man to enjoy social relations with his friends and neighbors. He is entitled to visit them and their families and to have them visit him and his family. The free and unhampered exercise of the right is necessary to his happiness, comfort, and well-being. If he be unlawfully deprived of that right by others, he is entitled to redress.

For the reasons assigned, the judgment overruling defendants' exceptions is affirmed at defendants' costs. [1]

HACKNEY v. FORDSON COAL COMPANY.

Kentucky Court of Appeals. 230 Ky. 362, 19 S.W.(2d) 989 (1929).

OPINION OF THE COURT BY JUDGE DIETZMAN—Affirming.

A demurrer having been sustained to the petition of the appellant, who was the plaintiff below, and he having declined to plead further, the court dismissed his petition, and from that judgment he appeals.

By his petition the appellant substantially averred that he was running a general store in Pike county near the mines of the appellee; that he was in no wise connected with the appellee, but on the contrary was in substantial competition with the appellee's commissary for the trade and custom of the appellee's employees; that he had enjoyed a large and lucrative trade among these employees; that on September 1, 1927, the appellee, which had theretofore been paying its employees in cash, posted a notice in which it stated that for the convenience of its employees it would thereafter issue scrip up to an amount not exceeding 70 per cent.

---

[1] Accord: Guethler v. Altman, 26 Ind. App. 587, 60 N.E. 355 (1901); Lewis v. Huie-Hodge Lumber Co., 121 La. 658, 46 So. 685 (1908); Heywood v. Tillson, 75 Me. 225 (1883); Dagostino v. Rogers, 68 Pa. Super. Ct. 284 (1917); Payne v. Western, etc., R. R. Co., 13 Lea 507 (Tenn. 1884); Robison v. Texas Pine Land Ass'n, 40 S.W. 843 (Texas Civ. App. 1897); Reding v. Kroll, Sirey, 1898, 416 (Trib. Luxembourg, 1896). *Contra:* Graham v. St. Charles St. R. R. Co., 47 La. Ann. 214, 16 So. 806 (1895) (defendant's conduct purely malicious); Webb v. Drake, 52 La. Ann. 290, 26 So. 791 (1899) (defendant's conduct purely malicious); Wesley v. Native Lumber Co., 97 Miss. 814, 53 So. 346 (1910) (defendant's conduct purely malicious); International & G. N. Ry. Co. v. Greenwood, 21 S.W. 559 (Texas Civ. App. 1893); Dapsens v. Lambret, Sirey, 1890, (Cour d'Appel, Liege, 1888) (defendant motivated by political hatred). *Cf.* Union Labor Hospital Ass'n v. Vance Redwood Lumber Co., 158 Cal. 551, 112 Pac. 886 (1910); Peek v. Northern Pacific Ry. Co., 51 Mont. 295, 152 Pac. 421 (1915).

For a discussion of the social implications of the company store, see: Hinrichs, "The United Mine Workers and the Non-Union Coalfields," 110 Col. Univ. Studies in History, Econ. and Public Law, c. 4 (1923).

of each employee's earnings. The notice concluded thus: "Any employee passing scrip to an outsider, so that it will require the company to redeem the same, will be discharged."

Appellant further averred that after this notice was posted the employees of the appellee no longer traded with him, as they drew scrip and they were afraid of being discharged if they used their scrip in dealing with any store other than those maintained by the appellee, and that by reason of this loss of trade he had been damaged in the sum of $3,000. Appellant pitched his claim on sections 2738s1 and 466 of the Kentucky Statutes, which read:

"Sec. 2738s1. It shall be unlawful for any person or persons, association, company or corporation employing others, as described in section 1, either directly or indirectly, to coerce or require any such servant or employee to deal with or purchase any article of food, clothing or merchandise of any kind whatever, from any person, association, corporation or company, or at any place or store whatever. And it shall be unlawful for any of such employers as described in the first section to exclude from work, or to punish or blacklist any of said employees for failure to deal with any other or to purchase any article of food, clothing or merchandise whatever from any other or at any place or store whatever."

"Sec. 466. A person injured by the violation of any statute may recover from the offender such damage as he may sustain by reason of the violation, although a penalty or forfeiture for such violation be thereby imposed."

Appellee makes some contention that section 2738s1, *supra,* has been repealed by section 4758b1, which is chapter 71 of the Acts of 1924. Without passing on that question, we are of opinion that the lower court properly sustained the demurrer of the appellee to the appellant's petition, because, although by section 466 a right of action is given to any person who is damaged or injured by the violation of a statute, yet this section is confined to those persons for whose benefit the statute, the violation of which has given rise to complaint, was passed.

Section 466 of the Statutes was passed to remove any doubt that might arise as to the right of a person for whose protection a statute was passed to recover for a violation of that statute, where the statute was penal in its nature, or where by its terms the statute did not prescribe the remedy for its enforcement or violation. It is settled that "a duty created by the statute is also measured by the statute, and will not be extended beyond the terms of the act, and the right of action exists only in favor of those for whose benefit the duty is imposed." 1 C.J. 952. In *Lepard v. Michigan Central R. Co.,* 166 Mich. 373, 130 N.W. 668, 40 L.R.A. (N.S.) 1105, the court said: "It is a well-established principle that the violation of a statutory duty is the foundation of an action in favor of such persons only as belong to the class intended by the Legislature to be protected by such statute." In 40 L.R.A.(N.S.) 1105, may be found a note collecting some of the authorities supporting this principle.

Section 466 of our Statutes was not intended to overturn this principle, but only to make certain that those for whose benefit a statute was passed should have a cause of action for any damages they sustained by its violation. Section 2738s1, *supra*, was passed for the benefit of employees, to the end that they should not be coerced into trading at the commissary of their employer, where they might be subject to extortion and all manner of unfair dealing. The section was never intended to protect those merchants who were in competition with the employer for the trade of his employees. Therefore, although an employee of the appellee may have a right of action for the violation of this statute, if it has been violated, a point we need not determine, yet, as the appellant was not an employee, or one for whose benefit the statute was passed, he has no cause of action for its violation.

An examination of the authorities cited by the appellant discloses that in each instance the statute, whose violation was in question, was held or assumed, without discussion, to have been passed for the benefit of those who were seeking to recover for its violation. Illustrative of the former category of cases are *Illinois Central R. Co. v. McIntosh,* 118 Ky. 145, 80 S.W. 496, 81 S.W. 270, 26 Ky. Law Rep. 14, 347; *Louisville & N. R. Co. v. Haggard,* 161 Ky. 317, 170 S.W. 956.

> *The judgment of the lower court being in accord with these views, it is affirmed.*[1]

---

[1] Upon the constitutionality of legislation similar to the Kentucky statute, see: Owen v. Westwood Lumber Co., 22 Fed.(2d) 992 (D. Ore. 1927), appeal dismissed in 278 U.S. 665 (1929); Frorer v. People, 141 Ill. 171, 31 N.E. 395 (1892); State v. Fire Creek C. & C. Co., 33 W. Va. 188, 10 S.E. 288 (1889).

Numerous states by statute forbid an employer to coerce his employees to trade with him or with some other person. See: 1931 Cal. Gen. Laws (Deering) Art. 4717; 1921 Colo. Comp. Laws, § 4170; 1927 Fla. Gen. Laws, §§ 7168, 7169; 1932 Idaho Code, § 43-602; 1926 Ind. Stat. (Burns) §§ 9346-9349; 1930 Ky. Stat. (Carroll) § 2738r-2 (limited to mine operators); 1932 La. Gen. Stat. (Dart.) § 4961; 1929 Mich. Comp. Laws, §§ 8517-8519 (limited to coercion relative to the taking out of life or accident insurance); 1921 Mont. Rev. Code, §§ 11223-11224 (limited to coercion by the employer to compel the employee to board at a company boarding house); 1929 Nev. Comp. Laws, § 10472; 1910 N.J. Comp. Stat. p. 3047, § 105 (limited to making illegal withholding of wages of employees longer than usual in order thereby to compel them to trade with company store); 1929 N. Mex. Stat. §§ 88-626, 618, 619; 1932 Ohio Code (Page) §§ 12944, 12946; 1930 Ore. Code, § 14-861; 1917 Porto Rico Acts, No. 91, § 2; 1932 Tenn. Code, § 11361 (limited to making illegal the withholding of wages of employees longer than usual in order thereby to compel them to trade with company store); 1925 Texas Pen. Code, Art. 1620; 1917 Utah Comp. Laws, § 8513; 1933 Wash. Rev. Stat. (Remington) § 10504 (limited to forbidding railroads to exert pressure with regard to the purchase by employees of uniforms); 1932 W. Va. Code, § 2354.

Connecticut makes it unlawful for an employer to exact more than a reasonable sum for merchandise sold his employees. 1930 Conn. Gen. Stat. § 5209. Massachusetts makes it illegal for employers engaged in public works to require as a condition of employment that their employees shall trade at a particular place. 1932 Mass. Gen. Laws, c. 149, § 25. Virginia forbids a company store from selling to employees at unreasonable prices. 1930 Va. Code, § 1820.

A few states prohibit employers from maintaining company stores. 1924 Md. Code (Bagby) Art. 23, § 248 (limited to railroad and mining companies); N.Y. Consol. Laws, c. 36, § 10 (limited to employers carrying on public works under contract); 1930 Pa. Stat. (Purdon) c. 15, §§ 1574, 1575 (all mining and manufacturing companies included).

INDEX

AFFIDAVITS
credence given to, in trade disputes,
225
of union's intent, 463
used in contempt hearings for violation of injunction, 288
used in trade dispute, 238

AGREEMENTS
See Contracts

ANTI-TRUST ACT
See Sherman Act

ANTI-UNION CONTRACTS
criticized by U. S. Coal Commission, 181
employee contracts to be non-union,
174
in general, 181-184
where used, 181n

APPEAL
by certiorari, 141
by strikers to others, 196
in what manner allowable, 196
to Federal Court under Fourteenth
Amendment, 268

APPRENTICE
master's control regulated by gild, 1

BLACKLIST
See Boycott
boycotting employees failing to
work out notice period, 666
defined, 687
of employees because of union affiliations, 669
of employees discharged, 684
published as means of boycott, 435
published during boycott, 441
securing discharge of employee, 669

use abandoned by A. F. of L., 532n
violating Sherman Act, 537
within prohibitions of the Sherman
Act, 530

BONDS
forfeiture for violation of contract,
388, 393

BOYCOTTS
See Strikes; Picketing
accomplished by publications, 435
affecting a person not party to trade
agreement, 427
as injuring member of union which
entered into trade agreement, 429
as interference with trade, 408n
by persons not employees, 444
by publishing statements, 441
by threats of loss, 534
by union labor as interference with
interstate commerce, 615
by union labor to force employer to
have closed shop, 434
by use of signs, 411
classes of: (1) backward, (2) forward, (3) lateral, (4) transportation, 404
coercing others to boycott trader,
688
conduct amounting to threat of
others, whether legal, 432
decisions on legality in conflict, 465
defined, 262n, 403
forms of pressure, 404
fought by damage suit, 521, 529
fought by injunction, 532n
furthering union interests, in general, 403
inducing breach of contract, 438
inducing dealers not to supply goods,
426

695

BOYCOTTS (Cont.)

inducing persons not to trade with others, 419

injunction to restrain, 433

legality depending on considerations of public policy, 466n

legality determined by acts involved, 451

legality questioned, 286n

legality recognized, 286n

majority judicial opinion against, 286

not necessarily illegal, 465

not unconstitutional to authorize, 279

of employers of non-union men, 473

of materials handled by non-union employees, 594

of materials of non-union shop interfering with interstate commerce, violating Sherman Act, 597

of one trader by others, when lawful or not, 417, 418n

primary, 408n

primary and secondary distinguished, 286n

publishing blacklist, 435

publishing list of "unfair" persons, 453, 462

purpose, 404

secondary, 408n

secondary, as illegal coercion, 437n. 536

to coerce employer to unionize shop, 527

to compel unionization, 462

to enforce compliance with union order, 430

to prevent work being done, 438

to restrain interstate trade, 443

to secure employment of union men only, 466

union men refusing to work, 438

unlawful as secondary, 635

using publication stating employer "unfair," 407

when conduct unlawful, 436

when unlawful, 408n

withdrawal of patronage, 454

within prohibitions of Sherman Act, 530

CARRIERS

in interstate commerce, 167

CAUSE OF ACTION

arising from discharge due to blacklist, 670

exercising legal right resulting in damage to another, 321

for interference with trade, 690

for money had and received, 330

for wrongfully blacklisting employee, 668, 668n

refusing letter of clearance as ordered by statute, 674

CERTIORARI

method of review, 141n

CLAYTON ACT

applied to trade dispute, 214, 318

authorizing suit for injunction, 680

compared to English statute, 226

congressional intent not followed by judiciary, 233

constitutional, 231

construction of § 20, 277, 538, 539, 546

decisions under, 231

difference of opinion under, 543

doctrine of Duplex case, 532

includes injunctive relief for violation of anti-trust law, 535

irreparable injury needed to gain injunction, 229, 232

judicial abuse by use of Sherman Act, 231

legalizing trade associations, 210

limiting use of injunction in trade dispute, 210, 538-540

not authorizing secondary boycotts, 541, 541n

object of, 215

providing for number of pickets, 519

provision for ex-employees, 517

provisions, 140, 210

trade dispute as condition precedent to conduct of strikers, 233

whether applicable to certain persons, 444

whether prevents issuing injunction in boycott case, 537

who are employees, 215n

CLEARANCE CARD
employer need not furnish, 664, 665n
explanation, 664

CODE OF FAIR COMPETITION
to be approved by President, 632

COERCION
by boycott, 403
by union orders benefiting members, 451
by union to force one to coerce another, 471
enjoined, 103
inducing employer to unionize, 456
inducing others not to act, 457
insurance company threatening cancelation unless employee discharged, 659
of persons to agree not to join union to obtain employment, 374
of persons to agree to join union to obtain employment, 375
on employees as to where to trade, 694
on employer to unionize shop, 527
restraint of mind sufficient, 307
through combination compelling third person to act, 458
to employ union men by refusing to work with non-union labor, 605
to unionize, 127
when by-law providing for expulsion is coercive, 418
whether by-law empowering committee to suspend was coercive, 417

COLLECTIVE BARGAINING
agreements by employees, 150, 159
as crime of conspiracy, 30, 30n
attitude of English law towards, 5-9, 9n, 15
employees choose representatives under NIRA, 632
legality of, by employees, 635
legality of object, 127
made illegal, 4
necessarily voluntary on both sides, 117
prosecutions because of, 5-10
right to, recognized by NIRA, 616

thwarted by employer refusing to enter contract, 647
under Combination Act of 1824
rights of employees, 16, 17
Under Act of 1825
legality depended on means employed, 17, 17n

COMBINATIONS
See Conspiracy
affecting conduct of others, 202
against an employee by a union, 221
as a conspiracy, 455, 480
as not an offense, 13n, 16
as offense, 12
can not do everything one can do, 316, 317
for mutual protection recognized, 350
illegal combination defined, 46
in pursuit of trade objects, 66
in restraint of interstate commerce violating Sherman Act, 524
judicial attitude toward, 10, 11, 34
lawful objectives, 155
lawful, though trying to gain at expense of fellowmen, 310
legality depending on test of objective, 13, 33, 480
legislative attitude, 34
of employers, 421
prohibited by statute, 5-10
refusal to work with non-union men lawful, 609
restrained when obstructing interstate commerce, 536
right to preserve, 325
Sherman Act, 495
to advance interests of union and members, 322
to cease working until wages increased, 421
to do what individual may do, 323, 335
to interfere by coercion, 71
to obtain monopoly of employment, 472
to procure breach of contract, 71, 120
to regulate conduct, 202
to secure "closed shop," 459, 534
to strike or picket, 145, 324
when within prohibitions of Sherman Act, 524, 530

698 INDEX

COMMON-LAW

attitude against collective bargaining relaxing, 20
conspiracy illegal, 11
dealing with labor contract, 1
doctrine of conspiracy, 11

COMPETITION

right of others to compete, 59, 60
when union not a competitor, 121
whether lawful or not, 45-48

CONDUCT

amounting to a threat, whether lawful, 238, 432, 516
amounting to interference with interstate commerce, 535
amounting to irreparable injury, 239
amounting to unreasonable restraints, 603
by one union against another being malicious and unlawful, 304
by trade union, whether interference or not, 557
example of unlawful conduct, 251, 252
libelous and abusive attacks on reputation enjoined, 272
not amounting to conspiracy to restrain interstate trade, 569
of one union injuring another restrained, 308
of pickets authorized by statute, as depriving one of due process and equal protection, 274
of pickets not unlawful, 637
of strike, 209
of strikers, orderly or not, 190, 191, 193n, 194
of union in destroying business of another as determining legality of acts, 318
regulated by combination, 202
whether union participated in strike, 559, 576

CONSPIRACY

See Combinations
abstaining from handling non-union materials, 594
acts in furtherance of, enjoined, 501

as a crime influenced by consideration of public policy, 204
as a tort, 24
as illegal gradually restricted, 19
between unions to boycott employer, 432
causing loss of business, 65
combinations as, 10-15, 29
common-law doctrine, 4, 11
common law restored by Act of 1825, 17
definition, 68, 422, 480
doctrine in Tubwomen v. Brewers case, 11
doing what each could do, not unlawful, 664
effect of, to do lawful act, 345
employers agreeing not to hire employees who do not furnish record, 663
enjoined, 132
in restraint of trade, 111
indictment for, replaced by use of injunction, 36
intent important in, 75, 76
intent to injure third party, 63
liability for, 68
maliciously inducing breach of contract, 77
mere combination not criminal, 31
motive, 80
not to employ strikers, 670
not unlawful since trade dispute existed, 344
overt act not necessary, 4
restraining interstate commerce, violating Sherman Act, 574
resulting from moral coercion, 270
Sherman Act, 495
statutory effect on, as crime, 4
to blacklist employees, 684
to boycott employees who did not work out the notice period, 667
to boycott trader, 688
to coerce complainant, 516
to combine, illegal, 10, 11, 12, 12n
to compel discharge of certain employees, 311
to corner trade, 42
to deprive person of property, 89
to extort money by strike, 331
to further a strike enjoined, 262

CONSPIRACY (Cont.)

to induce breach of contract, 77, 84, 87

to injure, 65, 68n, 89, 91, 106, 107, 166, 270

to injure business of another, 436

to injure business of employer not using union labor, 459

to interfere with interstate trade violating Sherman Act, 575

to interfere with trade, 420

to make union men join another union, 302

to prevent employment of non-union men, 459

to prevent sale of material, 426

to procure abstainance from entering contract, 84

to procure discharge of employee by publishing blacklist, 669

to raise wages, 4

to restrain trade, 136, 513

to restrain trade by injuring engines, 513

to secure discharge of an employee unless he joined union, 385

to unionize miners, 110, 126

trade association not in restraint of trade under Clayton Act, 210

when act done within jurisdiction of court, 512

when existent to violate Sherman Act, 567

when justified, 204

when not enjoined in Federal Court, 295

when unlawful, 132

venue in, 512

violating Sherman Act, 137, 512

CONSTITUTIONAL LAW

Clayton Act valid, 231

Congress can not interfere with liberty of contract, 169

due process
   constitutionality of legislation restricting equity jurisdiction in labor disputes, 266-279, 291

service letter laws, 680n

State cannot interfere with liberty of contract, 175

statute ordering employer to issue clearance card, 674

statute preventing blacklisting, 687

statute prohibiting employer preventing employee joining union, 326

statutes concerning employment, 181n

validity of Erdman Act, 169

validity of statutes regulating interstate commerce, 503

CONTEMPT PROCEEDINGS

for violation of injunction, 131n, 288

hearing for contempt as criminal case without rights generally given a criminal, 288

imprisonment for violation of injunction, 501, 577

power of Congress over proceedings in criminal contempt, 501, 503

proceedings used as substitute for criminal trial, 507

trial for, demand for new judge, 298

trial provisions of Federal statute, 297

violation of injunction by strangers, 412n

CONTRACTS

See Statute of Laborers; Trade Agreements

action for enticement, 7

action for money had and received, 330

action to recover money paid to union as a fine, 329

agreement enforceable by one not a party to contract, 364

arbitration committee provision, 342

between company and one union excluding men of others, 377

between employer and employee, 165

between employers
   not to hire men violating rules of other employers, 665

between union and member, 150, 159, 165

breach by employee, 401

breach by employer, 401

breach by intimidation, 55

CONTRACTS (Cont.)
breach of contract
    civil liability, 2, 2n
    criminal liability, 2, 2n
breach caused by picketing, 98
by employees for union to arbitrate,
    159
consideration for re-employment
    agreement, 627
distinguished from trade agreement,
    361
enjoining inducing breach of con-
    tract, 134
enticing laborer away a criminal of-
    fense, 14, 15
freedom to contract, 429
freedom to contract extends to trade
    agreements, 390
freedom to, interfered with by Erd-
    man Act, 171, 172
freedom to, not affected by statute
    ordering letter of clearance, 676
in restraint of trade, 19, 47
inducing breach by union punishable,
    25
inducing breach of, 49, 77, 87, 91, 103,
    106, 128, 136, 137, 153
inducing breach of, by boycott, 438
inducing breach of, with justifica-
    tion, 95
inducing employer to discharge em-
    ployee, giving rise to cause of ac-
    tion, 660
inducing violation of, 165
injunction against inducing breach
    of contract, 103
interference by union representative,
    49
interference with by a third person,
    148, 416
interference with, by union represen-
    tative, 370
interference with contract of employ-
    ment by third party, 670
interfering with contract relation-
    ship, 160
labor contract
    common law, 1-3
    national law, 1-3
legislative interference with anti-
    union contracts
        crime to discharge employee of

interstate carrier merely for
    belonging to union, 168
liberty of contract, 175
liberty to, 170, 417
maliciously inducing breach, 53
not interfered with, 338
not to be member of union, 243
not to subcontract work affecting a
    third party, 478
not to unionize, 130n
of employer association with labor
    union binding employer, 358
persuading employee to leave, 128
persuading persons not to enter em-
    ployment, 128
procuring breach, 111, 134, 200
refusal of employer to contract
    thwarts right to collective bar-
    gaining, 647
requirement of quitting notice as
    part of contract, 667
restraining interference with con-
    tractual relations, existing or pro-
    posed, 110, 202, 259
right of subcontractor when union
    calls strike against general con-
    tractor, 467
right to induce termination by law-
    ful means, 157
right to make contracts guaranteed
    by Federal Constitution, 634
right to terminate, 49
threat to terminate, 145
to disable engines as in restraint of
    trade, 513
to employ only members of certain
    union amounting to coercion, 652n
to employ union labor only, under
    NIRA, 653
trade agreement not part of em-
    ployee's contract, 369
union inducing breach of contract by
    employer, 311
when breached, 2
when not interfered with by strike,
    323
when refusal to work not breach of,
    341
whether justifiable interference with,
    118
whether strike breaches contract to
    arbitrate, 343

CONTRACTS (Cont.)

who can sue on contract of re-employment, 626

yellow-dog contract

employee coerced to be non-union, 174

not effective in Federal court, 183

statute prohibiting held unconstitutional, 326

CORPORATIONS

ordered to issue clearance card by statute, 676

COUNTERFEIT

of union label, 483

DAMAGES

recovered by employee for discharge caused by union, 380

wrongfully inducing employer to discharge employee, 657

DEFINITIONS

blacklist, 687

boycott, 403

conspiracy, 422, 480

injure, 43

malice, 417

maliciously, 43

"unfair," 406

wrongfully, 43

DUE PROCESS

rights guaranteed by Federal Constitution, 169

rights safeguarded by the due process clause, 273

state determines by what processes legal rights may be asserted, 292

whether statute denying injunction deprives one of property without due process, 282

whether statute violated "due process" clause, 174

EMPLOYEE

agreement between Association and Union not part of his contract, 369

and employer, when relation exists, 107

breach of contract by, 401

blacklisted because of union affiliations, 669

can bargain individually or through representative, 652n

can select own labor organization, 639

coerced as to trading place, 694, 694n

discharge for union activity, forbidden by NIRA, 639

discharge of, 363

discharged at request of union, 380

discharged when name on blacklist, 669

enforcing trade agreement made for his benefit, 364

exercising legal right causing injury to another, 321

freedom to elect with whom he will work, 474, 475

hired for indefinite term can be discharged at will without cause, 363

locked out contra to statute, 654

members of striking union acting on own volition, 516

no cause of action where unemployed because clearance card refused him, 665n

persons included under NIRA, 633

recovered for unlawful interference with "right" to work, 658

refused clearance letter by employer contra to statute, 674

refusing to work with non-union labor not restraint of trade, 607

right to choose employer, 340, 410

right to elect representatives, 644, 647n

right to preserve organization, 325

right to refuse to work, 335, 340

right to seek work unhindered, 685

right to use persuasion, 518

rights under trade agreement, 360n

seeking damages for wrongful discharge, 361

seeking enforcement of trade agreement, 361

seeking redress in equity without clean hands, 672

suing on basis of re-employment agreement, 626

under Clayton Act, 215n

vigorous methods allowable, 518

EMPLOYEE (Cont.)

when discharged has no right to demand reason for discharge, 664

when necessary to ratify trade agreement, 365

who can sue on contract of re-employment, 626

EMPLOYER

agreeing not to hire employees who
do not furnish record, 663

agreement not to hire employees
discharged by others, 684

and employee, when relation exists,
107

bound by agreement made by association, 358

bound by re-employment agreement,
627

breach of contract by, 401

can specify employees shall be non-
union, 179, 243

cannot wrongfully cause blacklist of
employee, 667

challenging act of union as ultra
vires, 334

coerced to use union labor, 456

coercing employees to join another
union, 628

combining to resist demands of employees, 423, 424

denying right to bargain collectively
by refusing to contract, 647

enjoined from abridging rights of
employee under NIRA, § 7 (a),
623n

excluded from business by union,
458

fined by labor union, 348

interfering with "right" to work, 655

need not state cause of discharge,
664

not enjoined from violating trade
agreement, 400

refusing employee clearance letter
as ordered by statute, 674

refusing to bargain collectively as
violating § 7 (a) of NIRA, 642

refusing to comply with NIRA,
§ 7 (a), 618

refusing to give discharged employee consent to work for another railway, 663

right to discharge a union worker,
170

right to discharge employee, 162, 176

right to discharge employee under
NIRA, 639, 640n

right to keep open shop, 132, 134,
167

right to refuse to employ, 667

right to specify employees and how
to operate, 410

rights under trade agreement, 360n

saying employee an agitator not actionable, 656n

seeking recovery of money paid to
union as fine, 329

threatening discharge of employees
if trade with certain merchant, 691

when shop open or closed, 459n

writing that employee intimidated
others actionable per se, 656

EMBEZZLEMENT

of union funds an offense, 555n

ENTICEMENT

See Contracts

as criminal offense, 15

elements essential for cause of action, 221

of servant from master's employ, 107

statutory material, 102n

Tenn. statute on, 101

to terminate contract
illegal by Tenn. statute, 101
in general, 101, 106

EQUITY

doctrine of "clean hands," 671

lack of power to order return to
work, 345, 346

mandatory order refused, 345, 346

rule 38 permitting suits against representative of class of people, 533

will aid union as well as employer,
397

will not enjoin crimes, 506

ERDMAN ACT

power to regulate interstate commerce, 171

relating to interstate carriers and employees, 167

EVIDENCE

supporting indictment, 513

EXECUTIVE ORDER

creating National Labor Board and its powers, 616

directing enforcement of NIRA, § 7 (a), 617

punishing employer refusing to comply with NIRA, § 7 (a), 618

EXTORTION

intent to extort, 41n

of money by means of strike, 329

FEDERAL GOVERNMENT

as proper party seeking injunction, 504, 505

authorized to prevent interference with interstate commerce, 502

powers of, 509

FORFEITURE

of cash bond for violation of trade agreement, 388, 393

of property under Sherman Act, 496

GILDS

municipal regulations superseding, 1n

HEBERT, SENATOR

favoring confirmation of Parker, 144

HUME, JOSEPH

influence on legislation, 16

IDENTIFICATION

of defendants by naming representatives of class when numerous, 412

INDICTMENT

charging violation of Sherman Act, 512

INDUCING BREACH OF CONTRACT

See Contracts

INJUNCTION

acts not subject to restraining orders, 186

against all picketing, 149

against commission of crimes, 506

against conspiring to further a strike, 264

against interference with business, 103

against interference with scabs, 103

against libel, 270

against making public the fact of a dispute, refused, 267

against persons not employees of complainant, 534

against "persuasion," not upheld, 212

against picketing, 103, 212

against picketing, when not justified, 124

against railroad making clerks withdraw from union, 173n

against union for unauthorized acts of members, 517

against union includes members, 412n

against unlawful conduct, 638

against unlawful picketing, 134

against violence in picketing, 199

anti-injunction statute of Illinois, 224n

as improper relief to individual for statutory violation, 479

as method of enforcing business law, 464

as not proper relief for individuals under statutes, 622

as remedy against alleged wrongful act, 42

as remedy for boycott, 533

as remedy for conspiracy to injure interstate trade, 533

based only on affidavits, 520

conditions precedent to issuance in Federal court, 297

considerations in granting, 152, 153

contempt proceedings for violation of, 501, 577

criticized as based on untrustworthy proof, 226

discretion of court to grant, 253

discussion of Hitchman case injunction, 143, 222

INJUNCTION (Cont.)

discussion of the Red Jacket injunction, 143

doctrine of Hitchman case, 110

Duplex case discussed, 222

effect of, 142, 142n

effect on right to issue, when acts are criminal, 509

enjoining use of union funds for prohibited purposes, 265

Federal court in Debs case, 500

for inducing patrons to cease patronage, refused, 267

futility of, 232

government by, 511n

grant of, in Federal court, limited, 183

in labor controversies, 37

inducing termination of contract by lawful means not restrained, 157

issuance of, in U. S. and England compared, 226

issued to restrain conduct amounting to coercion, 239

jurisdiction to grant, 147

limited in Debs case, 509

mandatory injunction to restrain violation of trade agreement, 399

motive for seeking, 288

need not protect all property rights by injunction, 292, 293

not available to individual for violation of Federal statute, 478

not proper relief for private party for violation of statute, 464

objection to, as not being obeyed, 232

ordering return to work not granted, 345

peaceful persuasion permitted, 260

persons bound, 412n

power to grant, not inherent, 188

proceedings under, stayed, 402

prohibiting acts inducing breach of contract, 103

prohibiting picketing, 97

prohibition of, as raising question of due process, 282

relief based on violation of Sherman Act, to private suitors, 535

relief granted, 122

replacing indictment for conspiracy, 36

restraining action inducing employees to leave, 152

restraining acts inducing or causing breach of contract, 97

restraining acts inducing persons not to deal with others, 185

restraining acts of violence, 260, 264

restraining boycotting by signs, 411

restraining calling of strike against railroads, 500

restraining coercion, 103

restraining combinations obstructing free flow of commerce, 536

restraining commission of a crime, 202

restraining counterfeiting of union label, 494

restraining employer from abridging rights of employees under NIRA, § 7 (a), 623n

restraining enforcement of union orders, 455

restraining guards injuring pickets, 236

restraining interference with business, 97, 134, 259, 683

restraining interference with contract, 89

restraining interference with contract relationships, 110, 123, 259, 263

restraining interference with employees, 132, 262

restraining interference with operation of railroad, 262

restraining interference with person's business, 132

restraining interference with persons not yet bound by contract, 202, 203

restraining interference with railroads in Debs case, 500

restraining libelous and abusive attacks, 272

restraining one union from interfering with business of another, 252

restraining one union from interfering with members of another, 300

restraining order in Great Northern Ry. case, 235

INJUNCTION (Cont.)

restraining peaceful picketing interfering with trade, 207

restraining persons from procuring breach of contract, 69

restraining persuasion to breach existing contracts, 200

restraining picketing, 37, 264

restraining pickets from interference with customers, 246

restraining publication of words, 251, 255, 255n, 265

restraining refusal to work under Federal statutes, 604

restraining strike for closed shop as violating NIRA, 652n

restraining strike to force men to join union, 36, 317n

restraining "threat, violence or intimidation," 129

restraining unauthorized use of union label, 490, 494

restraining union efforts persuading members not to work, 349

restraining union from disciplining members, 349

restraining union from threatening strike so as to injure members of another union, 308

restraining union interference with business of employer, 348

restraining unionization, 133

restraining unionizing employees, 131

restraining unlawful acts of union members acting on own volition, 516

restraining unlawful interference, 458

restraining unnecessary loitering near entrances, 263

restraining use of union label denied, 487

restrictions on issuance under Clayton Act, 538

restrictions on use sought, 288, 289

resulting from conspiracy, 132

resulting from trespass, 149

right of government to ask such relief, 504

sought by employees against union, 320

temporary restraining orders in Federal court, 296

strike as violating NIRA not enjoined, 631

to prevent interference with interstate commerce, 502

to prevent irreparable injury, 214

to prevent violation of code of fair competition, 621

to prevent lockout in violation of contract, 397

to prevent lockout of union laborers, 396

to prevent strike in violation of contract, 397

to prohibit laborers from ceasing work refused, 353

to protect property rights, 147

to restrain boycotting, 433, 436

to restrain conspiracy, 91, 583

to restrain displaying "unfair" sign before place of business refused, 404

to restrain enforcement of union labor regulation, 336

to restrain interference with interstate commerce under Sherman Act, 594

to restrain interference with trade agreement, 380n

to restrain persons from inducing breach of contract, 84

to restrain union from enforcing rule, 333

to restrain union from seeking discharge of certain employees, 311

to restrain union labor strike, 340

to restrain union placing contractor on unfair list, 348

to restrain union seeking discharge of complainants by strike, 320

to restrain unionizing, 134

to restrain wrongful use of trade mark, 484

under re-employment agreement restraining employer interfering with employees concerning representatives, 629

union prohibiting members handling non-union material not restrained, 450

use in America, 287

INJUNCTION (Cont.)
use in England, 287
views of Hebert, Senator, 144
views of Jones, Senator, 144
views of Mitchell, Attorney General.
144
views of Wagner, Senator, 143
violations of, heard by court of equity, 288
what Federal courts can enjoin, 296
what Federal courts cannot enjoin.
294, 295
when court will grant it, 296, 520
when not to issue in trade dispute.
210
when too broad, 203, 254
whether issuance prohibited by Clayton Act, 537
whether issued or not under Clayton Act, 214, 215
will not compel performance of personal service contract, 345
word "scab" not prohibited, 256, 256n

INTERFERENCE
See Contracts
between master and servant, 104
by a combination of persons, when not competition, 372
by employer, with "right" to work, 655
by legislative act with freedom to contract, 171, 172
by picketing, 201
by third party procuring discharge of employee, 659, 660
by union in contract between employer and employee, 311
causing persons to stop dealing with a third party, 61
Congress prohibited from interfering with liberty of contract, 175
effect of justification, 128, 371
in contractual relations by third person, 40
inducing breach of contract, 77, 87, 91
inducing persons not to trade with others, 420

justifiable refusal to handle material of another, 544
maliciously by third person with business of another, 417
right to be free from, 304
state, prohibited from interfering with liberty of contract, 175
though injurious, only incidental to right to contract, 482
through exercise of a legal right not a cause of action, 321
to force unionization, 458
union ordering members not to work on non-union material, 447, 452
when actionable, 610
whether justification for, 118
whether union participated in unlawful interference, 559
with a right may be justified, 281
with an organization by an outsider, 155
with coal mining not interference with interstate commerce, 566
with contract, 49, 104
with contract of employment by union representative, 371
with contract relation by union striking against third party, 471
with contract relations, 71, 82, 111
with contract relationship not justified by object of inducing laborer to join union, 373, 374
with contract relationships by union, when justified, 372
with employees enjoined, 132, 137
with interstate commerce, 500, 513
    by order not to handle non-union material, 597
    by refusal to work with non-union labor, 606
    by strike, 516
with interstate trade of products of a factory, 534
with right of employees to select representatives, 173n
with right to do business, 71
with "right" to trade, 688, 692
with "right" to work, 660, 661n, 670, 686

INTERSTATE COMMERCE

Act in relation to, 167

affected by agreement to work on union products only, 591, 592

affected by union order not to handle non-union material, 595

carriers and employees, 167

conspiracy to restrain, 443

decisions as to what is within Sherman Act, 615

does not include coal mining, 566

intent to control supply and price as violating Sherman Act, 582

interference with, as a crime, 233

interference with factory products, 534

interference with goods in transit and stationary, 515n

national government authorized to prevent interference with, 502

not interfered with by illegal picketing, 589

not interfered with by strike against manufacturer, 574

not regulated by Erdman Act, 171

not restrained by refusal to work with non-union labor, 605

power to regulate, 171

restrained by acts disabling engines, 513

Sherman Act, 495

unlawful interference by union seeking monopoly of the employment, 613

validity of Federal statutes, 503

when interfered with, 582

when interfered with by reducing supply of materials, 574, 582

when interfered with under Sherman Act, 608

when only incidentally interfered with, 588

whether affected by union plan requiring permit to handle materials, 586

INTIMIDATION

as interference with trade, 420

as unlawful conduct depends on method used, 205

by number of pickets, 217

by picketing, 241

by union members acting on own volition, 516

conduct amounting to, 210n, 516

defined, 27

not dependent on numbers, 241, 242

right to be protected against, 518

through boycott, 435

through publications, 435

what it includes, 201

INTERVENTION

by third person in contractual relations, 41

with use of property, 39

IRREPARABLE INJURY

See Injunctions

JOURNEYMAN

master's control regulated by gild, 1

JUDICIARY

abuse of power, in disregarding Clayton Act, 231

action against union for act of member, forbidden, 25

discretion to grant injunction, 407

equitable relief in Federal courts restricted, 294, 295

exercising quasi-legislative functions, 287

Federal court, when not bound by state court decision, 268

relaxing attitude against combinations in favor of laborers, 15

view of courts differs from intent of Congress in re Clayton Act, 233

wide discretion in contempt hearings, 288

JURISDICTION

Federal court

admitting Fourteenth Amendment involved, 268

based on diversity of citizenship, 138, 138n, 533

based on interstate commerce clause, 533

based on provisions of the NIRA, 621

JURISDICTION (Cont.)
    based on Sherman Act, 138, 495,
        496, 605
    to grant injunctions, limited,
        183
    to grant injunctive relief under
        NIRA, 622
    trade union citizenship for pur-
        poses of Federal court juris-
        diction, 572n
    what was withdrawn from Fed-
        eral courts, 187
    judicial discretion in exercising pow-
        er, 163
    lack of, over persons not served, 184
    of court in equity, in case of crim-
        inal contempt, 507
    to grant injunction, 147
    State court
        case based on Federal statute,
            624

JURY TRIAL
    not necessary under Act of 1799, 15

LABOR CONTRACT
    See Contracts

LABOR DISPUTES LAW
    provisions of, 619

LABOR UNIONS
    See Trade Unions

LABORERS
    liable civilly and criminally, 21
    resentment against statutes prohib-
        iting combinations, 16

LEGAL CONCEPTS
    effect of Statutes of Laborers, 3

LEGALITY
    of acts destroying business of an-
        other, 318

LEGISLATION
    English
        Act of 1799, 14
        Act of 1800, 15
        attitude toward Ireland, 10
        Bill of Conspiracies of Victual-
            lers and Craftsmen, 6

        Combination Act of 1824, 13, 16
        Combination Act of 1825, 16
        concerning labor contracts, 282,
            283, 283n
        Conspiracy and Protection Act
            of 1875, 23
        criminal offenses under Act of
            1799, 15
        effect of, 227
        Master and Servant Act of 1867,
            21
        Molestation of Workmen Act of
            1859, 18
        Ordinance of Laborers, 1
        Reform Act of 1832, 21
        7 Geo. 1, c. 13, 11
        Statute of Elizabeth, 6
        Statute of Laborers, 1
        Trade Disputes Act of 1906, 26
        Trade Disputes Act of 1927, 26
        Trade Union Act, 1871, 21
        relaxing rigors against combi-
            nations, 15
    United States
        Act of March 23, 1932, 183, 294
        Clayton Act, 140, 210
        constitutionality of Erdman Act,
            169
        effect of, 227
        employees allowed to choose
            representatives without inter-
            ference by union or employ-
            er, 173n
        Erdman Act, 167
        in re interstate commerce, 502,
            502n, 503
        Labor Disputes Law, 619
        limiting use of injunction by
            Federal court, 183
        National Industrial Recovery
            Act, 616
        Sherman Act, 495
        Transportation Act, 1920, 232
    By States
        Arizona
            anti-injunction statute in labor
                disputes, 266
            anti-trust statute extended field
                of equitable relief, 278
        California
            anti-picketing ordinance, 197

EGISLATION (Cont.)
  Illinois
    anti-injunction statute, 224n
  Kansas
    penalty for coercing persons
      seeking employment, 174
  New York
    anti-monopoly statute, 479
  Tennessee
    Tennessee Code, 1932, 101
  affecting common law conspiracy,
    423
  affecting right to combine, 5-11, 14
  aim of, in restricting use of injunc-
    tions, 289
  by judiciary, 287
  changing common law rule relat-
    ing to strikes, 544
  classification of persons, 275
  dealing with labor contract, 1
  denying injunction still valid though
    curtails remedy, 188
  interfering with anti-union contract,
    167, 174
  limiting injunctions, affecting rem-
    edy and not property rights, 188
  limiting use of injunction in Fed-
    eral court, 186, 187, 294
  limiting use of injunction not appli-
    cable when strike for wrongful
    purpose, 244
  of British Dominions concerning la-
    bor disputes, 284, 284n
  ordering letter of clearance, 676-679
  ordinary remedies at law or equity
    not lost by Act of March 23, 1932,
    297
  preventing blacklisting of employ-
    ees, 685
  protection against wrongful use of
    label, 493
  restraining interference with trade
    as criminal, 690
  restricting use of injunction, 289
  state cannot deprive one of liberty
    of contract, 177
  unlawful to coerce employee not to
    belong to union, 174
  violated, when giving individual a
    cause of action, 693
  violation of, as not giving rise to
    injunctive relief, 464

  when one is involved in a labor dis-
    pute, 298
  when trade dispute exists, 298

LIBEL
  accusations amounting to libellous
    publications, 657n
  accusing one of being an anarchist,
    656n
  by employer against employee, 656

LOCKOUT
  injunction will issue if contract be-
    ing violated, 397
  of union men by employers, 426

MASTER
  control of apprentice regulated by
    gild, 1
  control of journeyman regulated by
    gild, 1
  liable civilly, 21

MASTER AND SERVANT
  differs from lord and villein, 1
  right of Congress to regulate, 172
  when relation exists, 107

MONOPOLY
  Sherman Act, 495

MOTIVE
  does not make unlawful a lawful
    act, 305
  may determine whether act lawful
    or not, 305
  not excusing strike interfering with
    interstate trade, 598

NATIONAL INDUSTRIAL
  RECOVERY ACT
  employee can select own labor or-
    ganization, 639
  employees choose representatives
    for collective bargaining, 632
  employees locked out contra to
    statute, 654
  employer and employee can still
    contract for wages and hours, 633
  employer refusing collective bargain-
    ing under § 7 (a), 642
  employer requiring employee to join
    certain union, 624

NATIONAL INDUSTRIAL
  RECOVERY ACT (Cont.)
forbids discharge of employee for
  union activities, 639
identical with Sherman Act to enjoin violations, 621
Labor Board supervision of election
  of employees' representatives, 644
mediation as condition precedent to
  right to strike, 636
policy furthered by Labor Disputes
  Law, 619
President prescribing conditions of
  employment, 616
provisions every code of fair competition must contain, 616
purpose of, 631
special remedy to redress a wrong,
  625
when union is a "company union"
  within meaning of § 7 (a), 654
where injunctive relief not remedy
  for individual, 622

NATIONAL LABOR BOARD
arbitrating disputed points between
  employer and employee, 650
created by executive order, 617
powers of, 617, 618
supervising election of employee
  representatives, 643, 653

NUISANCES
picketing, 202
public or private, 506

OBJECT
as justification of strike, 309

OPEN SHOP
right by employer to keep, 132, 134,
  167

ORDINANCE OF CONSPIRA-
  TORS
conspiracies, 4

ORDINANCE OF LABORERS
See Statute of Laborers
effect on contracts, 1, 2
effect on legal concepts, 3
features, 1

PARKER, JOHN J.
confirmation favored by Hebert, 144
confirmation favored by Jones, 144
confirmation opposed by Wagner,
  143
nominated to U. S. Supreme Court,
  141
rejection by U. S. Senate, 141

PARTIES
defendants, proper joinder of, 412n,
  552
defendants, sued as representatives
  of a class, 533
Federal government as party seeking injunction, 504, 505
individuals as not proper parties
  asking for injunctive relief under
  statutes, 622
naming representative of a class
  when numerous, 411n
who bound by injunction, 412n

PATROLLING
See Picketing

PERSONAL SERVICE
See Contracts

PERSUASION
See Picketing

PICKETING
acts allowable, 199
acts enjoined, 199
allowable limits under Act of 1875,
  23
appeal to others, 196, 197
as a nuisance, 194n
as illegal, 285n
as interfering with trade enjoined,
  207
as intimidation, 241
as never peaceful, 208n
as private nuisance, 202
as violation of ordinance forbidding
  unlicensed street meetings, 198n
by a mass, 250n
by mass illegal, 27
by strikers, peacefully, 192
causing breach of contract, 98
coercive picketing unlawful, 19, 249

PICKETING (Cont.)

conduct amounting to an unlawful annoyance, 270

display of "unfair" sign, when lawful, 407

displaying signs, when intimidation, 410

diversity of views regarding, 290

enjoined, 97, 103, 134, 208n

in absence of strike, 244n

in itself illegal, 16, 17, 240, 287n

intimidating, not interfering with interstate commerce, 589

intimidation merely by large number of pickets, 217

lawful if peaceful, 287n

legality depending on circumstances, 247

legality depending on purpose or manner, 239

limiting number of pickets, 218, 219n

majority judicial opinion favors peaceful, 287

New Jersey rule of no picketing, 240

not per se unlawful, 291

number of pickets allowable, 519

patrolling as intimidation, 201

peaceful, 97, 247

peaceful picketing legalized, 26, 26n

requiring pickets to be citizens and English-speaking, 219n

right to picket recognized by Arizona court, 266

rule in Tri-City case, 218, 218n

rule of reasonableness determining legality, 209

signs in foreign language, 98

standard of lawful or unlawful, 208

unlawful when blocking exit and entrance, 229, 239

violating anti-picketing ordinances, 198n

what is lawful patrolling, 200

when conduct is lawful, 218

when conduct was unlawful interference, 247

when disorderly, 195

when not enjoined, 110-123

where conduct not unlawful, 637

whether lawful depends on circumstances, 213, 217, 218

whether motive justifies, 202

PLACE, FRANCIS

influence on legislation, 16

POLICE

activities in trade disputes, and strikes, 228n

POLICE POWER

restraining disorderly picketing, 195

POST-OFFICE DEPARTMENT

non-mailable propaganda. 194

PROCEEDINGS

under injunction, stayed, 402

PROPERTY RIGHT

includes manufacturing and disposing of products, 535

PROSECUTIONS

because of collective bargaining, 5-10

for conspiracy, 12, 29, 29n, 30, 35

for violation of labor code, 7

PUBLIC POLICY

agreement not to hire employee who struck, 665

frowns on insurance company barring injured men from being re-employed, 659

PUBLICATIONS

as instrument of boycott, 442, 443

RECEIVERS

strike restrained against railroad in charge of receiver, 230

RE-EMPLOYMENT AGREEMENT

between President and employer, 626

binding on employer, 627

consideration for, 627

REGISTRATION

of trade unions, 22

REMEDY

determined by legislature, 292n

REPEAL

movement for, of Combination Act, 16

RESTRAINT OF TRADE

See Interstate Commerce
agreement to hire only men sent by association, 683
agreements illegal but not criminal, 20
agreements in, unenforceable, 19
by disabling engines, 513
combinations in, not necessarily criminal, 19
common law prior to 1825, 19
conspiracy to restrain trade, 111, 136, 443
distinguished from criminal conspiracy, 19
doctrine of as applied to combinations of laborers, 19
early English conception of groups as combinations in, 1-6
interference resulting in, 134
Sherman Act, 495
trade agreement in restraint, 389
union by-law determining wages held valid, 35
union not in restraint, 338
union under Clayton Act not in, 210

RESTRICTIONS

on combinations, 3, 3n

REVIEW

by Federal court, 268
of English labor background, 282, 283, 283n

SHERMAN ACT

See Interstate Commerce
affected by agreement to work on union products only, 591, 592
anti-trust law not violated, 338
applies only to interstate commerce, 524
combinations in restraint of interstate trade illegal, 525
decisions under, 524
doctrine of Hatters' case, 521
doctrine of Paine lumber case, 549n
examples of violations due to restraint of interstate commerce, 604
giving Federal court jurisdiction, 533
identical with NIRA, 621
includes combinations not contemplating but actually restraining interstate commerce, 587
making interference with interstate commerce a crime, 134, 233
not violated by refusal of union men to work with non-union labor, 605
prohibiting boycott, 530
prohibits only unreasonable restraints, 601
providing for damages for unlawful conspiracy, 523
provisions of, 495
restraining strikes as violating, 231
trade unions suable, 557
"unfair list" within prohibitions of the Act, 530
violated by blacklist, 537
violated by combination restraining interstate trade, 524
violated by union order not to handle non-union material, 597
violated by union striking for monopoly of the employment, 613
violation charged, 512
what it aims at prohibiting, 524
when case within the statute set up, 527, 528
when combination a conspiracy within Act, 530
when unlawful interference with interstate commerce exists, 608

SPECIFIC PERFORMANCE
See Contracts

STATUTE OF LABORERS

effect on contracts, 1, 2
effect on legal concepts, 3
features of, 1

STRIKE

See also Wages; Strikers
affecting price of commodity in interstate trade violates Sherman Act, 567
after vote by members, 321
against decision of Railroad Labor Board illegal of itself, 515-521, 521n
against employer, reducing supply for interstate trade, 589
against one person, injuring another, as unlawful interference, 471

STRIKE (Cont.)

agreement not to, pending hearing of complaint, 396

arising from refusal to bargain collectively, 646

as bargaining element, 206

as lawful instrument, 221

as threat in exacting fines, 332

as threat to enforce rule of union, 334

as unlawful, 285n

by employees, whether violating Sherman Act as interfering with interstate trade, 574

by union against another injuring employer, 471

by union against employer of labor of other union, 258n

by union as a general right, 314

by union may be illegal, 314

causing breach of contract, 469, 477

combination to, 145

common law in relation to, changed by statutes, 544

concerning wages, 112, 114, 135, 211, 336, 419, 440

conduct of, 209

conflict of cases as to legality of object, 324

conflicting views on right to, when interstate commerce interfered with, 598

defined, 322

definition of intimidation, 18n

definition of peaceful persuasion, 18

definition of threat, 18n

difference between English and American backgrounds, 226, 227

displaying "unfair" sign, when lawful, 407

employer refusing to pay a fine levied by union, 329

Federal intervention, 35

for benefit of union, injuring subcontractor, 469

for better conditions, 325

for closed shop violating NIRA, 652n

for recognition of union is illegal, 310n

history of, 228

in England
coercion illegal, 22, 22n
peaceful persuasion legal, 18
sympathetic, 27
when conspiracy, 17

when illegal, 27

when not conspiracy, 17

in violation of trade agreement, 341, 347n, 426

injuring subcontractor, though called against another, 469

interfering with interstate commerce, when not unlawful, 516

intimidation at, 149

justification as depending on object, 309

lawful when interruption of interstate commerce an unintended consequence, 521

legality determined by acts involved, 451

legality of, during wartime, 523n

motive no excuse when interstate trade interfered with, 598

mutual, when employer locks out employees, 516

not unconstitutional to authorize, 279

not violating NIRA, 631

notice of, not intimidation, 476

notification of strike to be called for employing non-union labor as unlawful, 285n

objects for which men may strike

obstructing carrying of the mails illegal, 522n

old viewpoint of, as being wicked, 206

on railway, whether interference with interstate commerce, 516

refusal to work with non-union labor, 321

restrained when against receiver appointed by court, 230

right to, recognized, 230, 324

right to, under NIRA, 632

secondary boycott, 271

state intervention, 35

statute limiting use of injunction, does not apply when strike for wrongful purpose, 244

threat to, coupled with intimidation, 303

threatened, as instrument of coercion, 461

to advance interests of union and members, 322

to cause general contractor to employ union men, 469

STRIKE (Cont.)

to coerce employer to join an association benefiting employees, 352

to compel employer to run shop against his will, 340

to control supply and price in interstate trade violates Sherman Act, 582

to enforce rule requiring certain number in orchestra as object of strike, 334

to enforce trade agreement, 347n

to force employer to pay a fine, 329

to force men to join union enjoined, 317n

to force unionization to help union shops, 567

to force unionization, when not in restraint of trade under Sherman Act, 607

to injure business, unlawful, 354

to keep non-union laborers from getting employment enjoined, 314

to promote interest of union members, 357

to secure closed shop, 327n, 433, 630

to secure discharge of non-union labor, 316, 320, 321, 343

to secure employment of union men only, 466, 475

to secure monopoly of employment interfering with interstate trade, 613

to secure work others were doing, 311

to strengthen and preserve a union, 310n, 325

when not interfering with contract, 323

whether contract to arbitrate breached or not, 343

whether union participated or not, 559, 578

STRIKERS

See also Strike; Wages

anti-picketing ordinances, 194

blacklisted by employers, 670

breach of peace defined, 191

injured by blacklist, coming into equity without clean hands, 672

picketing peacefully, 192

requisite of common interest among strikers, 545

right to appeal to others, 196, 197

whether conduct orderly or not, 190, 191, 193n, 194

THREATS

See Strike

by group, 38

TORTS

by union members making funds of union liable, 24

civil conspiracy, 24

to recover money, 331

TRADE AGREEMENT

as contract between employer and union, 390

as in restraint of trade, 389

between association and employer to hire only laborers sent by the association, 682

between association and union prohibiting subcontracting, 476

between company and a union
excluding men of others, 375
for supplying labor, 379
that employees belong to union, 386
to employ only men of the union as long as available, 381

between employer and union, valid, 382

between employers' association and union when order by union is oppressive, 394

between employers
not to employ strikers, 670
not to hire persons leaving employ of the others, 673
whether lawful, 424

between railway association and union not part of employee's contract, 369

between union and association concerning wages, 425

between unions and members not to work with non-union labor, 473

boycott under, affecting a person not party to, 427

coercing others to join a union, 391

defendant not member of association making contract, 360n

TRADE AGREEMENT (Cont.)

distinguished from contract, 361n

enforceable by member of union a party to the agreement, 365

giving all work to union men, 383

giving preference in employment of workmen, 382

interference with contract not justified by, 372

limiting right to employ laborers not against public policy, 390

not to employ men violating rules of company, 665

not to hire employees who did not furnish record, 663

not to hire employees who engaged in strike, against public policy, 665

not to hire men of other unions valid, 375

not to strike or lockout pending hearing complaints, 396

not to subcontract as benefiting union members, 481

plaintiff not member of union which made agreement, 360

provision to pay employee during plant shut down, 358

ratification by employee, when required, 365

requiring employee work out notice period or be blacklisted, 666

resulting in monopoly, 425n

rights of employer and employee under, 360n

states conditions of employment, 361n

that employees join union after working a certain period or be discharged, 388

that employees must join union, as illegal, 393

to employ only union labor, when legal, 395n

to hire only union members, when oppressive and when not, 370, 394, 396

to hire only union men of good standing, and discharge others, 388, 392

to employ union labor only, under NIRA, 653

to run at capacity for a definite period, and use union labor only, 399

where not applicable to employee, 372

wrongfully causing employee to be blacklisted, 667

TRADE DISPUTES

activities of armed guards in, 228n

as condition precedent to conduct of strikers under Clayton Act, 233

between two unions, 250

defined, 27n, 298

law of British Dominions concerning, 284, 284n

lawful to tell public that non-union labor employed, 248

modification of common law principles in U. S., 285

peaceful acts not enjoined, 295

term "unfair" defined, 406

when existing under Federal statute, 298

when one is involved in a labor dispute, 298

TRADE UNIONS

See Combinations

acting where no dispute between employer and employee, 242

adopting rules which affect others, 449

against an employee, 221

agreements excluding men of other unions, 375

agreements not to unionize, 130n

allowable under NIRA, 633

as bargaining power, 221

as intermediary, 322

as political force, 23n, 25, 26

assets of unions reachable or not. 571n

boycotting to compel unionization, 462

by-law of union penalizing member accepting less wages held valid, 35

cannot do everything each member can do, 316, 317

causing discharge of employee refusing to join, 386

TRADE UNIONS (Cont.)

causing discharge of non-union employee, 370, 380

certain aspects legalized, 21

chosen by employees, whether can contract for union labor only, 653

citizen for purpose of Federal jurisdiction, 572n

coercion of persons to agree not to join to secure employment, 374

coercion of persons to agree to join to secure employment, 375

coercion to form, 127

compelling employer to run shop against his will, 340

conduct by, whether interference with business or not, 557

control over members, 451

criminal liability for activities removed, 21, 22

delegation of authority to officials assumed, 530

destroying business of another, 318

development in U. S., 28-37

disciplinary measures against members, 27

embezzlement of union funds, 555n

employees being coerced to join other union, 629

exempt from anti-trust statutes, 554n

increasing membership, 139

inducing breach of contract punishable, 25

fines exacted by threat of strike, 332n

forcing unionization so as to help other union shops, 567

funds liable for torts of members, 24

general right to strike, 314

inability to control members, 516

inducing employer to use closed shop policy, 456

inducing persons not to deal with third party, 61

larceny of funds by member, 20

lawful methods in unionizing, 139

lawful objects, 146, 315

legality under Federal Anti-Trust Act, 125

legality under law of West Virginia, 125

legalized, 554n

members acting on own volition, 516

members need not accept employment, 338

not against any public policy, 386

not allowing union members to work with non-union men, 447

not "intermeddlers" in collective bargaining, 635

not liable for act of a member, 25

not prohibited by the NIRA, 648n

not responsible for acts of people not associated with them, 517

obligations of, 156

obtaining agreements for preference in employment, 383

officers of, as outsiders, 285n

one union has as much right as another, 304

order not to work on non-union material, 447

ordering employer to do certain acts, 394

persuading members to terminate contract, 148

protection of union funds, 20

publishing statements as intimidation, 411

purpose of, 145

referring to men of other unions as non-union men, 302

refusal to work with non-union men lawful, 609

refusing to abide by decision of arbitration board, 584

refusing to handle materials, 545

registered, 22

relaxing of common-law attitude against, 20

requiring union men to do the work as interference with interstate trade, 613

responsibility for acts of members, 517

restrained from obstructing interstate commerce, 536

right to enjoin enfringement of registered label or trademark, 554n

right to have member on board of arbitration, 555n

right to penalize members, 338

TRADE UNIONS (Cont.)

right to preserve organization, 325

right to specify what kind of workmen shall compose union, 319

right to sue, 554, 554n

seeking discharge of certain employees, 311

seeking discharge of non-union labor, 343

seeking discharge of non-union men distinguished from refusing to work with non-union labor, 318

seeking monopoly of employment, 472

social and political considerations influencing U. S. view, 33

soliciting discharge of employee, 380

soliciting membership, 143

striking against general contractor, affecting others, 470

strike to enforce rule as lawful object, 334

striking to secure work others had, 311, 319n

subject to suit, 552, 553, 554, 556, 570n

subject to suit though unincorporated, 576

union orders as coercion, 451

unionizing a mine, 126n

unionizing employees, 126n

unionizing without employer's consent, 126

when forcing unionization would violate Sherman Act, 567

when not a business competitor, 121

when seeking unionization not an interference with interstate trade, 607

when shop open or closed, 459n

when union a "company union" within meaning of § 7 (a), NIRA, 653, 654

whether conduct imputed to union, 559

whether union participated in strike, 576

whether union participated in unlawful interference, 559

TRADE MARK

exclusive use of, 483

union label as, 483

TRIAL

constitutional right to jury trial not abridged by contempt suit, 507

for contempt under Act of March 23, 1932 regulated, 297

for contempt, without jury, 288

ULTRA VIRES

whether action of union ultra vires or not, 334

UNION

See Trade Unions

UNION LABEL

as trade mark, 483, 488

counterfeit of, 483, 488, 492, 494

distinguished from trade mark, 484, 485

exclusive right to use, 483, 489

not applied to a vendible article, 486, 487

not property, 485

registration as trade mark refused, 485n

unauthorized use of, an offense, 555n

unauthorized use of enjoined, 490, 494, 554n

use of without authority injures union labor, 490

use protected by statutes, 493

UNITED STATES COAL COMMISSION

report, 181

VESTED PROPERTY RIGHT

business as "property," 270, 279

business as property right, 270

esteem of public not a vested right, 266

WAGES

See Strike; Strikers
as cause for strike, 211
as lawful objectives of combination,
   16, 18
as object of strike, 309, 341
as unlawful objectives of combination, 2-14
minimum rate only prescribed, 633
not fixed by President, 633
strike concerning, 112, 135

WAGNER, SENATOR

opposing confirmation of Parker,
   143

WORKMEN'S   COMPENSATION
ACT

paying injured men, 659

YELLOW-DOG CONTRACTS

affected by NIRA, 616
criticized, 181
employee had to contract to remain
   non-union, 174
not enforceable in Federal courts,
   183

Supplement to

LANDIS'

CASES ON LABOR LAW

1934-1937

By

NATHAN WITT

Assistant General Counsel
National Labor Relations Board

Chicago
THE FOUNDATION PRESS, INC.
1937

INTRODUCTION

The rapid march of events has made desirable, if not necessary, the publication of a supplement to my Cases on Labor Law. It is apparent that the corpus that has been called "Labor Law" is being subjected to one major operation after another. Thus, during the past three years we have witnessed the passage of drastic anti-injunction legislation in State after State, and the constitutional validation of such legislation by the courts; the decline of the yellow-dog contract and the emergence of the sit-down; the enactment of the National Labor Relations Act, constitutional attacks made upon it, and the rise of a movement for parallel legislation in the States. The doubt cast upon the efficacy of traditional legal remedies in this field, manifested by the creation of administrative tribunals, makes an understanding of methods of approach to the various problems in labor law as important and as necessary as a grasp of legal doctrine.

Like other fundamental changes in the law important social movements and pressures are here reflected, primarily labor's drive, much intensified in the past few years, for organization in the economic and political fields: When it is remembered that we have yet to feel the full legal consequences of the split in the labor movement, it is well to begin to assay in terms of law the direction in which these social pressures are taking us.

I am indebted to Mr. Nathan Witt for the preparation of this Supplement. As Assistant General Counsel to the National Labor Relations Board, not only has he had the occasion to keep in touch with the day-by-day developments in labor law, but he has had the opportunity of partaking in some of the most significant of these. His choice of materials and the additional references that he has embodied will, I know, make this volume essential to those who wish for themselves and their students an adequate introduction to the events of the past few years.

J. M. LANDIS

Washington, D. C.,
August, 1937

iii

TABLE OF CONTENTS

	Page
INTRODUCTION	iii
Chapter I. The Courts, and Labor's Aims and Tactics	1
Chapter II. The Legislatures and the Injunction	44
Chapter III. The Legislatures and the Right to Organize	71

v

TABLE OF CASES

(Reference is to pages)

Algonquin Printing Company and United Textile Workers of America, Local No. 1044, In the matter of, 153

Aluminum Company of America and Aluminum Workers Union No. 19104, In the matter of, 150

Ansin Shoe Manufacturing Company and Shoe Workers' Protective Union, Local No. 80, In the matter of, 164

Dubinsky v. Blue Dale Dress Co., 37

General Motors Corporation v. International Union United Automobile Workers, 19

Globe Machine and Stamping Co., and Metal Polishers Union, Local No. 3, et al., In the matter of, 142

Goldfinger v. Feintuch, 30

International Harvester Company and Local Union No. 57, International Union, United Automobile Workers of America, In the matter of, 160

Jeffery-DeWitt Insulator Company v. National Labor Relations Board, 129

Keith Theatre v. Vachon, 1

Motor Transport Company and General Chauffeurs, Teamsters & Helpers, Local Union No. 200, In the matter of, 140

National Labor Relations Act, 87

National Labor Relations Board v. Jones & Laughlin Steel Corporation, 97

Remington Rand, Inc. and Remington Rand Joint Protective Board, In the matter of, 169

St. Joseph Stock Yards Company and Amalgamated Meat Cutters and Butcher Workmen of North America, In the matter of, 134

Senn v. Tile Layers Protective Union, 44

Service Wood Heel Co. v. Mackesy, 25

United Electric Coal Companies v. Rice, 59

Virginian Railway Company v. System Federation No. 40, 71

vii

CHAPTER I

THE COURTS, AND LABOR'S AIMS
AND TACTICS

KEITH THEATRE v. VACHON

Supreme Judicial Court of Maine, 1936. 134 Maine 392, 187 Atl. 692.

HUDSON, JUSTICE. The plaintiff, lessee and operator of Keith's Theatre in the city of Portland, complains in equity against eight men of Portland, two men of South Portland (all union officials), three local unions, to wit, Local No. 458 of the International Alliance of Theatre Stage Employees and Moving Picture Machine Operators of the United States and Canada, the Portland Stage Employees Union No. 114, and the American Federation of Labor of Musicians Local Union No. 364 (voluntary and unincorporated labor organizations in Portland), and seeks injunctive relief from the picketing of its theatre by the defendants, their agents and servants. Hearing upon bill, answer, and replication was had before a single justice of this court, who refused to issue an injunction. The case now is before us on appeal and exceptions, the plaintiff excepting to the rulings of law as made by the Presiding Justice and appealing from his decision. The appeal and exceptions permit of one discussion.

The evidence as presented is not before us for the reason that the plaintiff is content to accept "the Court's findings of facts. . . ."

These findings may be thus summarized:

1. When the plaintiff started to operate its theatre, conferences were held with union representatives at which were discussed the adoption of the union wage schedule and operation of the theatre as a "closed shop," but no agreement for either was made.

2. The plaintiff conducted its theatre as an "open shop."

3. The wages it paid were materially lower than those of the union schedule, while the latter were considerably higher than the manager said the plaintiff could "afford to pay and live."

1

4. The plaintiff's employees were entirely satisfied with the wages they received. They neither struck nor picketed. They had no grievance against the plaintiff.

5. While the plaintiff did not have in its employment members of any unions, yet it did not refuse to employ union help. It would not consent, however, to employ only union laborers.

6. The picketing complained of commenced in August, 1935, and the court found that it was "for the sole purpose of compelling the plaintiff to adopt the so-called closed shop agreement and the union schedule of wages."

7. The picketing consisted mostly of walking "back and forth in front of the theatre with signs on which was printed a statement to the effect that Keith's Theatre is unfair to organized labor, that it does not employ union stage hands, musicians and operators, and urging the public not to patronize the house." For a time the same sentiments were expressed by word of mouth. It also is conceded that the musicians' union passed a vote fining any of its members $10 who attended the theatre, and that this fine was imposed in at least two cases.

8. The single justice stated "with the exception of the action of the musicians' union, which involved only its own members, I find no evidence of any boycott, any threat, any intimidation of either the public or employees. The activities of the pickets have been an annoyance; but the pickets have not accosted patrons or employees; and their actions have not resulted in the collection of any crowds, which have blocked the entrances of the theatre or the approaches thereto. When they have talked in too loud a voice, they have stopped on being admonished. The evidence indicates that the public has paid very little attention to them; and there is nothing to show what, if any, effect their efforts have had in reducing the patronage of the theatre."

Having thus found the facts, the justice then said: "The problem in this case resolves itself into the simple issue whether the picketing of this theatre by these defendants as carried on should be restrained. An injunction should be granted, if, first, the end sought to be gained is unlawful, or, second, if the means used are oppressive," and then held that the end sought was lawful and the means employed not oppressive, to both of which rulings the plaintiff excepted, and from the decision based on such rulings it appealed.

In this state we have been remarkably free from labor conflicts which might foment strikes, boycotts, and picketing. Common sense, control of temper, and application of the Golden Rule upon the part of both employers and employees have made possible peaceable adjustments of their difficulties, so that until now this court has never had occasion to consider or discuss the use of the injunction in labor disputes. From other states, as well as federal courts, have come down many able opinions, displaying much lack of unanimity in labor law. This court, then, both unaided and un-hampered by prior Maine decisions, but well served by the reasoning of other courts, is free to declare as law herein that which it considers best calculated in accordance with legal principles to effect justice.

Many of the older opinions dealt with questions about which now there seems to be no particular controversy. Not many years ago it was claimed that labor unions were illegal, and the Court of Queen's Bench, in the case of Hornby v. Close [1867], 2 L.R. 2 Q.B. 153, decided that a trade union was illegal, even though it existed only to secure higher wages and shorter working hours, because it was in restraint of trade. This continued to be the law in England until changed by an Act of Parliament in 1871. In this country, the courts have held fairly uniformly that labor unions, "when instituted for mutual help carrying out their legitimate objects," are lawful organizations. Yates Hotel Co., Inc., v. Meyers et al. (Sup.) 195 N.Y.S. 558; American Steel Foundries v. Tri-City Central Trades Council et al., 257 U.S. 184, 42 S. Ct. 72, 66 L. Ed. 189, 27 A.L.R. 360.

A trade union or labor organization has been defined to be "a combination of workmen usually, but not necessarily, of the same trade or [of several] allied trades, for the purpose of securing by united action, the most favorable conditions of as regards wages, hours of labor, etc., for its members." Stone v. Textile Examiners & Shrinkers Employers' Association, 137 App. Div. 655, 122 N.Y.S. 460.

"Workingmen may combine for their mutual benefit and protection and to improve their economic and social condition, including the improvement of working conditions, the obtaining of such wages as they choose to demand, and the establishment of a standard of wages throughout the country, without incurring either criminal or civil liability, even though they know that their action will necessarily cause loss to their employers, or to other persons." Oakes, Organized Labor and Industrial Conflicts, sec. 3, and cases cited thereunder.

The performance of work is vitally necessary to existence. Usually it is a matter of contract between employer and employee. Without question, fair and just compensation should always be paid for the work performed. The ideal contract is one in which the parties are able to determine and agree upon a wage that shall fairly and justly compensate the employee.

But the contracting parties are not always in exact equality in education and experience, influence and mentality, so that one of them may not have an advantage over the other in the making of the contract. Freedom to contract plays an important part. One who has no choice, but must work at whatever wage he can obtain, is an easy prey for an unfair and unjust employer.

Thus, inequality of position between the employer (and often it is a corporation of vast power) and a single employee, is sufficient justification for the creation of trade unions.

Work being necessary, the labor market should be as free as possible, both to employer and employee.

". . . The right freely to contract with one's fellow-men without interference other than may arise from the exercise by others of some equal or superior right" should be granted in a free labor market. Oakes, supra, page 406.

"The right to the free flow of labor is not an absolute right; it is limited by the right of employes to combine for purposes which in the eye of the law justify interference with the plaintiff's right to a free flow of labor. A combination which interferes with a plaintiff's right to a free flow of labor is legal if the purpose for which it is made justifies the interference with that right. On the other hand, it is illegal if that purpose does not justify the interference (which ensues from the making and enforcing of the combination in question) with the plaintiff's right to a free flow of labor." Haverhill Strand Theatre, Inc., v. Gillen, et al., 229 Mass. 413, 118 N.E. 671, 673, L.R.A. 1918C, 813, Ann. Cas. 1918D, 650.

A strike has been defined to be "a combined effort among workmen to compel the master to the concession of a certain demand, by preventing the conduct of his business until compliance with the demand." Farmers' Loan & Trust Co. v. Northern Pac. R. Co. et al. (C.C.) 60 F. 803, 821, 25 L.R.A. 414.

A strike may be legal or not, depending upon its purpose.

"Whether the purpose for which a strike is instituted is or is not a legal justification for it is a question of law to be decided by the court. To justify interference with the rights of others the strikers must in good faith strike for a purpose which the court decides to be a legal justification for such interference. To make a strike a legal strike it is necessary that the strikers should have acted in good faith in striking for a purpose which the court holds to have been a legal purpose for a strike." De Minico v. Craig et al., 207 Mass. 593, 598, 94 N.E. 317, 319, 42 L.R.A. (N.S.) 1048.

A strike necessarily assumes the existence of a grievance. To right the asserted wrong is its purpose. No one is known ever to have struck because his wage is too high or his work day too short. Only such strikes as are called for the purpose of obtaining that which is lawful are lawful strikes. Strikes to accomplish certain ends are lawful, although they hamper the employer and put him to financial loss. While out on strike it is not considered that the strikers have abandoned their employment, but rather have only ceased from their labor.

"Neither strike nor lockout completely terminates, when this is its purpose, the relationship between the parties. The employees who remain to take part in the strike or weather the lockout do so that they may be ready to go to work again on terms to which they shall agree—the employer remaining ready to take them back on terms to which he shall agree. Manifestly, then, pending a strike or a lockout, and as to those who have not finally and in good faith abandoned it, a relationship exists between employer and employee that is neither that of the general relation of employer and employee, nor again that of employer looking among strangers for employees, or employees seeking from strangers employment." Iron Molders' Union v. Allis-Chalmers Co. (C.C.A.) 166 F. 45, 52, 20 L.R.A.(N.S.) 315.

As the free flow of labor is subject to interruption by a lawful strike, so is it by picketing by employees if they refrain from threats, coercion, intimidation, force, and violence. A controversy having arisen between the employer and its employees, whether it has resulted in cessation of labor or not, that to be accomplished is to end the dispute either by a resumption of their former contractual relationship, or, if that be impossible, by an accepted modification of it. The end sought is reconciliation. Strikes and picketing are simply means to that end.

"It is the right of every man, unless bound by contract to serve for a definite period, to leave at any time an employment which for any reason is distasteful to him; and this right is as perfect and complete as the correlative right of all men to seek employment wherever they can find it. . . . A strike is not therefore, in itself an unlawful act, even though its effect is to cause loss to the employer. The legality or illegality of a strike depends, first, upon the purpose for which it is maintained, and, second, upon the means employed in carrying it on. The fact that the combination is for a lawful purpose does not render it less unlawful where the end is to be attained by the employment of improper means, and a strike for an unlawful purpose may not be carried on by means that otherwise would be legal." Oakes, supra, sec. 312, page 419.

With these general observations we come now to the case at bar. The justice held that the end sought by this picketing was lawful. As to what that end was is not in dispute, for it is conceded that it had a two-fold purpose, first, to compel the plaintiffs to adopt the so-called "closed shop" agreement, and, second, to adopt the union schedule of wages.

"Without question a strike for both a legal and an illegal purpose is an illegal strike. . . ." Baush Machine Tool Co. v. Hill et al., 231 Mass. 30, 36, 120 N.E. 188.

Then, were both of these purposes lawful? Unquestionably
employees have a lawful right to strike to obtain an increase in
wages, and we think so even though as increased they are on a level
with the union schedule.

The other, and no doubt the principal, purpose inducing this
picketing was to compel the plaintiff "to adopt the so-called closed
shop agreement." Was this a lawful purpose justifying even peaceable picketing by the defendants? Here it becomes necessary to
call particular attention to the fact that this picketing was not
done by the plaintiff's employees, who were entirely satisfied with
their employment still pursued, but by agents and servants of the
defendant unions who had no contract nor relationship, direct or
indirect, either with the plaintiff or the plaintiff's employees. Had
there been a grievance and had a strike by the plaintiff's employees
resulted from it, even if it were held that they could picket peaceably to secure unionization for their own benefit, non constat that
these defendants, their agents and servants, could picket though
peaceably. While we need not go so far in this case as to hold that
the employees themselves could not picket peaceably or strike to
secure unionization, yet there is much eminent authority to that
effect.

"Strikes to secure recognition of the union, to force discharge
of non-union men, or to effect a closed shop have been held illegal.
Plant v. Woods, 176 Mass. 492, 57 N.E. 1011, 51 L.R.A. 339, 79
Am. St. Rep. 330; Berry v. Donovan, 188 Mass. 353, 74 N.E. 603,
5 L.R.A. (N.S.) 899, 108 Am. St. Rep. 499, 3 Ann. Cas. 738; Folsom
v. Lewis, 208 Mass. 336, 94 N.E. 316, 35 L.R.A. (N.S.) 787; W. A.
Snow Iron Works, Inc., v. Chadwick, 227 Mass. 382, 388, 389, 116
N.E. 801, L.R.A. 1917F, 755; Baush Machine Tool Co. v. Hill, 231
Mass. 30, 120 N.E. 188; Folsom Engraving Co. v. McNeil, 235 Mass.
269, 276, 277, 126 N.E. 479; Moore Drop Forging Co. v. McCarthy,
243 Mass. 554, 137 N.E. 919." Stearns Lumber Co. v. Howlett et
al., 260 Mass. 45, 60, 61, 157 N.E. 82, 87, 52 A.L.R. 1125.

"The question whether the closed shop is a legitimate subject
of industrial dispute is one of considerable difficulty. In the majority of cases it has been held that, on account of its tendency to give
union labor a monopoly, it is not a legitimate aim." Oakes, supra,
Sec. 292, page 392.

Many cases pro and con are collated in Oakes, supra, and appear in footnotes 71, 72, and 73 to section 292, on pages 392 to 397
inclusive.

In Sarros et al. v. Nouris et al., 15 Del. Ch. 391, 138 A. 607, 611,
the court said:

"The real object of the strike being as I have said to compel
the complainants to unionize their business by subjecting it to
control and domination by the labor organization, an object which

the law does not recognize as legitimate, the complainants are entitled to protection against the continued picketing of their place of business by the defendants or their agents. If it is lawful for the defendants to destroy a part of the complainants' business by the picketing and its incidental boycott, it would be lawful for them if possible to destroy it in toto. As I read the authorities, their weight is to the effect that such çalamitous consequences can not be visited upon the complainants as punishment for their refusal to surrender the right which is theirs to employ nonunion labor if they choose. This being true, the picketing which has been going on is unlawful, whether peaceful or otherwise. I am not, therefore, called upon to go into the question of whether picketing if peacefully conducted is permissible in labor controversies, for if the object of the picketers is unlawful, piçketing of all kinds is likewise so."

Also, Elkind & Sons, Inc., et al. v. Retail Clerks' International Protective Ass'n et al., 114 N.J. Eq. 586, 169 A. 494; George Jonas Glass Co. v. Glass Blowers' Ass'n et al., 77 N.J. Eq. 219, 79 A. 262, 41 L.R.A. (N.S.) 445; Hughes et al. v. Kansas City Motion Picture Machine Operators et al., 282 Mo. 304, 221 S.W. 95; Goldberg, Bowen & Co. v. Stablemen's Union, 149 Cal. 429, 86 P. 806, 8 L.R.A. (N.S.) 460, 117 Am. St. Rep. 145, 9 Ann. Cas. 1219; Pierce v. Stablemen's Union, 156 Cal. 70, 103 P. 324; McMichael v. Atlanta Envelope Co., 151 Ga. 776, 108 S.E. 226, 26 A.L.R. 149; Levy & Devaney, Inc., v. International Pocket Book Workers' Union, 114 Conn. 319, 158 A. 795, 796; Sterling Chain Theaters, Inc., v. Central Labor Council, 155 Wash. 217, 283 P. 1081; St. Germain et ux. v. Bakery, etc., Union, 97 Wash. 282, 166 P. 665, L.R.A. 1917F, 824; Music Hall Theatre v. Moving Picture Machine Operators et al., 249 Ky. 639, 61 S.W. (2d) 283; Jefferson & Indiana Coal Co. v. Marks, 287 Pa. 171, 134 A. 430, 47 A.L.R. 745; Citizens' Co. v. Asheville Typographical Union, 187 N.C. 42, 121 S.E. 31; Lehigh Structural Steel Co. v. Atlantic Smelting & Ref. Works, 92 N.J. Eq. 131, 111 A. 376.

In an article in the Yale Law Journal, entitled "Labor and the Courts," vol. 39, page 683 on page 696, it is stated: "Courts are hopelessly divided as to whether a strike to unionize a shop or in pursuance thereof to compel the discharge of a nonunion employee is legal or illegal. New York, Illinois, California, Minnesota, and a substantial group of other states hold such a strike legal. But there are important states, such as Massachusetts, Pennsylvania, and New Jersey, which hold the strike to unionize a shop illegal. The holding of such a strike illegal seems manifestly unjust. Under the existing law it is clear that employers have the unquestioned right, acting singly or in association, to discharge employees because they belong to a union. If the employers have this right, why should the employees not possess an exactly similar right, acting singly or in association, to cease working for an employer because he runs a non-union shop? In other words, employees should be as free to strike as the employer is free, under the existing law, to discharge, in order to accomplish the unionization or the de-unionization of a shop, trade, or industry."

What would appear to be the fallacy in the above reasoning, it would seem, is that equality results. It seems to us that it does not, for the employee upon his discharge may work for whomsoever he chooses, while the employer, after compulsory unionization, is restricted to the employment of only union help. Besides, the employer has an established business which should have the right of continued existence, if conducted lawfully. The fact of ownership of property and responsibility therefor should give the owner all reasonable rights of control and management in order to preserve it, else in the end the right to have and to hold property will be seriously impaired.

"The right to conduct a lawful business is a property right, protected by the common law and guaranteed by the organic law of the state. See L. D. Willcutt & Sons Co. v. Driscoll, 200 Mass. 110, 117, 85 N.E. 897, 23 L.R.A. (N.S.) 1236." Godin v. Niebuhr, 236 Mass. 350, 351, 128 N.E. 406, 407.

Different reasons are given for the conclusion reached that unionization is an unlawful purpose, but chief among them, it would seem, is the fact that to hold otherwise would give union labor a monopoly which is against public policy. Public policy, it is said, demands free competition. To restrict the field of competition by exclusion of nonunion labor would not only destroy in large measure freedom of contract, but deny to nonunion labor its lawful right to earn its subsistence as it desires. The laborer, whether union or not, in the absence of contract to the contrary, should be accorded the right to work where and for whom he pleases, provided the work be lawful and agreement be reached upon terms of employment. This is not saying that laborers may not unite in their efforts to obtain their lawful rights. It simply means that those who do not see fit to unite may have preserved to them their freedom to contract.

But be it as it may (as to whether employees themselves can lawfully strike or picket peaceably to secure unionization), we do not think that it was lawful for these defendants to picket even peaceably to secure unionization by the employer of its satisfied and nonstriking employees.

"When necessary to prevent irreparable injury, an injunction will be granted to prevent third persons having no connection with employer or employees, and no interest in the relations existing between them, from inciting or coercing strikes among employees who are not dissatisfied with the terms of their employment and are not seeking an increase of wages." 32 C.J., sec. 225, p. 164, and cases cited in Foot Note 57.

Reasons urged are (1) that "persons who have no agency for the employees of the company can not set up any rights that the employees might have. The right of the latter to strike would not give to the defendants the right to instigate a strike. The difference is fundamental. Hitchman Coal, etc., Co. v. Mitchell, 245 U.S. 229, 38 S. Ct. [65] 190, 62 L. Ed. 260 (L.R.A. 1918C, 497, Ann. Cas. 1918B, 461). (2) Also, the fact that employees were at liberty to quit the employment at pleasure did not deprive the employer of its right to injunctive relief against interference with its employees by third persons seeking to unionize them. Eagle Glass, etc., Co. v. Rowe, 245 U.S. 275, 38 S. Ct. 80, 62 L. Ed. 286." Foot Note 57a, 32 C.J. 164.

The employer's right to carry on its lawful business cannot be interfered with without just cause or excuse. As to its own employees, it may be said to have opened the door to negotiations with them, and the door is not closed, even after they have gone out on strike. Having taken them into its employment, it may be said to have consented by implication to reasonable discussion of their disagreements and possibly even to peaceable picketing, but it contravenes the fact, express or implied, to say that it has made any such concession or surrender to strangers.

In this case the picketers not only had no grievances of their own against the plaintiff, but were not picketing by permission of the employees or any one else, whether belonging to a union or not, who had any relationship with the theatre company. They were simply attempting to advance the cause of trade unions generally by forcing unionization. That effected, might result not only in the incurrence of indebtedness that the business would not warrant, but in giving to strangers at least substantial partial control and management of the plaintiff's business. These picketers, instead of attempting by their conduct to reconcile a difference that had already arisen between the plaintiff and its employees, sought to create trouble between them to the end that the union might indirectly derive a benefit from such newly created trouble. They were not content simply to display the signs stating that the plaintiff was unfair to organized labor, of which there is no proof in the case, but urged the public not to patronize the theatre.

What justification or excuse is there for such interference? The defendants cannot justify as agents of the plaintiff's employees, for they had no authority. Their belief that it would be better for these employees to join the union, even if true, gives them no right to compel the employees to accept such an alleged better-

ment. Their intentions might be most laudable, but still freedom
of thought and action upon the part of the employees is their right
without dictation from those of different opinion. The Legislature,
if it acts constitutionally, may enact law that will compel all employers to unionize; but that result should not be obtained by the
compulsory act of strangers. While these defendants no doubt
believed that these employees should join the union, the employees
themselves were of a different mind, as well as the employer. The
plaintiff and his employees had as much right to their views as
had these defendants. We do not think it equitable to compel the
employees and their employer, all satisfied that no wrong exists
between them, to adopt and put into effect the desire of these defendants, who have no property or contractual rights to lose, as
have the employer and its employees, if the injunction be denied.
Unionization obtained, these employees would lose their jobs unless they joined the union. This court should neither deprive a
laborer of his lawful employment nor force him to join a union
at the behest of them who by some courts are called "intermeddlers."

"Defendants set up, by way of justification or excuse, the right
of working men to form unions, and to enlarge their membership
by inviting other working men to join. The right is freely conceded, provided the objects of the union be proper and legitimate,
which we assume to be true, in a general sense, with respect to
the union here in question. Gompers v. Buck's Stove & Range Co.,
221 U.S. 418, 439 (31 S. Ct. 492, 55 L. Ed. 797, 34 L.R.A. (N.S.)
874). The cardinal error of defendants' position lies in the assumption that the right is so absolute that it may be exercised
under any circumstances and without any qualification; whereas
in truth, like other rights that exist in civilized society, it must
always be exercised with reasonable regard for the conflicting
rights of others. Brennan v. United Hatters, 73 N.J. Law, 729,
749 (65 A. 165, 9 L.R.A. (N.S.) 254, 118 Am. St. Rep. 727, 9 Ann.
Cas. 698)." Hitchman Coal & Coke Co. v. Mitchell, supra, 245 U.S.
229, at pages 253 and 254, 38 S. Ct. 65, 73, 62 L. Ed. 260, L.R.A.
1918C, 497, Ann. Cas. 1918B, 461.

"The strike agitators were mere volunteers. They sought
mainly to advance their own personal interests by demonstrating
to their superiors their usefulness in inciting strikes and their
ability to enforce their demands. They assumed the role of those
aptly characterized by Vice Chancellor Fallon in Bayonne Textile
Corporation v. American Federation of Silk Workers et al., 114
N.J. Eq. 307, 168 A. 799, 803, as 'intermeddlers.'" Elkind & Sons,
Inc., et al. v. Retail Clerks' International Protective Ass'n et al.,
114 N.J. Eq. 586, 169 A. 494, 496.

In Harvey v. Chapman et al., 226 Mass. 191, 115 N.E. 304,
L.R.A. 1917E, 389, it was held that a provision dealer was entitled

to an injunction against officers and members of a labor union with whom he had no trade dispute from boycotting his business by means of a false statement that the plaintiff's employees were out on a strike and from seeking by picketing, by displaying banners and by the distribution of circulars to compel the plaintiff to discharge his employees or to coerce them into paying fees demanded of them by the defendant association. The court said (226 Mass. 191, at page 195, 115 N.E. 304, 305, L.R.A. 1917E, 389): "It needs no discussion to show that such intentional and harmful interference with the plaintiff's business renders the defendants liable, unless there appears a legal justification for their conduct. No such justification is disclosed. There was no real trade dispute between the parties. As there was in fact no strike at the plaintiff's store at any time since July 9, 1915, it is unnecessary to consider what the defendants properly might do under a legal strike." Also, Cornellier v. Haverhill Shoe Mfrs.' Ass'n, 221 Mass. 554, 109 N.E. 643, L.R.A. 1916C, 218; M. Steinert & Sons Co. v. Tagen, 207 Mass. 394, 93 N.E. 584, 32 L.R.A. (N.S.) 1013.

Harvey v. Chapman, supra, has been cited with approval many times, as in Olympia Operating Co. v. Costello et al., 278 Mass. 125, on page 130, 179 N.E. 804; Stearns Lumber Co. v. Howlett, supra, 260 Mass. 45, on page 65, 157 N.E. 82, 52 A.L.R. 1125; Moore Drop Forging Co. v. McCarthy, supra, 243 Mass. 554, on page 563, 137 N.E. 919; Godin v. Niebuhr, supra, 236 Mass. 350, on page 352, 128 N.E. 406. In the latter case the court said, 236 Mass. 350, on page 351, 128 N.E. 406, 407: "One who interferes with another's business, for the purpose of compelling present or prospective customers to withhold their patronage, is responsible for the harmful consequences, unless he shows a legal justification for such interference and to constitute such justification, it must appear not only that the interference was in pursuance of a lawful purpose, like trade competition, but that it was carried on by lawful means. The harmful circulation of libelous statements for the purpose of injuring the business of another is a malicious interference with that other's property rights, for which the wrong doer is answerable in damages." Also, Martineau et al. v. Foley et al., 231 Mass. 220, 120 N.E. 445, 1 A.L.R. 1145.

In the recent case of Driggs Dairy Farms, Inc., v. Milk Drivers' & Dairy Employees' Local Union No. 361, et al., 49 Ohio App. 303, 197 N.E. 250, 252, decided January 28, 1935, it was held that injunctive relief would be given to a wholesale and retail marketer of milk, restraining the officers and members of a labor union with whom it had no trade dispute from picketing its place of business and the places of business of its customers and from boycotting them by displaying banners and circulating handbills bearing false statements and by other methods. In that case no controversy had arisen between the plaintiff and its own employees. The picketers were strangers, members of a union. They displayed banners on which it was stated that the plaintiff company was unfair to organized labor, that it had violated the provisions of National Industrial Recovery Act (48 Stat. 195), and it contained an earnest solicitation for support of the purchasing public to refuse to purchase any products which the plaintiff company distributed, the concluding sentence of which was, "Patronize only those men who display a union button." The court, while granting the injunction against picketing as not justified, did say that the injunction should not "prevent the defendants from reasonable and peaceable persuasion, using only the truth." No doubt by "reasonable and peaceable persuasion" the court meant fair argument that might successfully carry its appeal to and convince the mind without the use of coercion of any sort.

The defendants rely strongly upon the decision in American Steel Foundries v. Tri-City Central Trades Council, 257 U.S. 184, 42 S. Ct. 72, 78, 66 L. Ed. 189, 27 A.L.R. 360, in which the opinion was written by the late Chief Justice Taft. In that case the justice in his opinion asked the question: "Is interference of a labor organization by persuasion and appeal to induce a strike against low wages, under such circumstances without lawful excuse and malicious?" And he answered it: "We think not." Clearly Justice Taft was not generalizing, but speaking of the facts in that particular case. He had just said: "Each case must turn on its own circumstances." The facts therein were quite different from those in this case. In that, unionization was not involved. There was a lawful strike by the employees because of the reduction of their wages, while in this case there not only was no strike, but no controversy between the employer and its employees. Furthermore, in that case the defendants represented the strikers, while here the defendants are complete strangers. Speaking of the right of communication between the employees on the job and the defendant picketers, some of whom were ex-employees, Justice Taft said (257 U.S. 184, on page 204, 42 S. Ct. 72, 76, 66 L. Ed. 189, 27 A.L.R. 360): "How far may men go in persuasion and communication and still not violate the right of those whom they would influence? In going to and from work, men have a right to as free a passage without obstruction as the streets afford, consistent with the right of others to enjoy the same privilege. We are a social people and the accosting by one of another in an inoffensive way and an offer by one to communicate and discuss information with a view to influencing the other's action are not regarded as aggression or a violation of that other's rights. If, however, the offer is declined, as it may rightfully be, then persistence, importunity, following and dogging become unjustifiable annoyance and obstruction which is likely soon to savor of intimidation. From all of this the person sought to be influenced has a right to be free and his employer has a right to have him free."

Thereafter the Justice said (257 U.S. 184, on page 206, 42 S. Ct. 72, 77, 66 L. Ed. 189, 27 A.L.R. 360) : "A restraining order against picketing will advise earnest advocates of labor's cause that the law does not look with favor on an enforced discussion of the merits of the issue between individuals who wish to work, and groups of those who do not, under conditions which subject the individuals who wish to work to a severe test of their nerve and physical strength and courage. . . . Regarding as primary, the rights of the employees to work for whom they will, and, undisturbed by annoying importunity or intimidation of numbers, to go freely to and from their place of labor, and keeping in mind the right of the employer incident to his property and business to free access of such employees, what can be done to reconcile the conflicting interests?"

Then, dealing with the facts in that case (from which it appeared that at capacity the plant employed 1600 people,) the court permitted "the strikers and their sympathizers" to have "one representative for each point of ingress and egress in the plant or place of business" and it enjoined all others "from congregating or loitering at the plant or in the neighboring streets by which access is had to the plant, that such representatives should have the right of observation, communication and persuasion, but with special admonition that the communication, arguments and appeals shall not be abusive, libelous or threatening, and that they shall not approach individuals together but singly, and shall not in their single efforts at communication or persuasion obstruct an unwilling listener by importunate following or dogging his steps. This is not laid down as a rigid rule, but only as one which should apply to this case under the circumstances disclosed by the evidence and which may be varied in other cases."

In the later case of Truax et al. v. Corrigan et al., 257 U.S. 312, 42 S. Ct. 124, 132, 66 L. Ed. 254, 27 A.L.R. 375, Justice Taft commented on his decision in the Tri-City Case and said that it held "it was lawful for ex-employees on a strike and their fellows in a labor union" to picket peaceably. We see no warrant for construing that decision as holding that complete strangers, without any relationship to the employees still on the job, could picket, though peaceably, to obtain accomplishment of a purpose, as here unionization, not desired by the employees themselves and contrary to the wishes of their employer.

In addition to American Steel Foundries v. Tri-City Central Trades Council, supra, the justice, in denying the issue of the injunction in this case, relied on the decision in Bomes v. Providence Local No. 223, 51 R.I. 499, 155 A. 581, 582, and from it quoted this language: "The respondents have the right to persuade the public by any lawful means to patronize or to refuse to patronize complainant's theater. But this right is not superior to the right of complainant to conduct his business free from unlawful interference. The attempt to unionize complainant's theater may result in actual injury to complainant, but it is not a legal injury unless the damage resulting therefrom is caused by a violation of a legal right of the complainant. There is a violation of such a legal right when the methods used are coercive."

Certain distinctions are to be noted between the Bomes Case and the one at bar, for in the former the theatre's former employees were not only members of the defendant union, but that union had had a contract with the complainant whereby the complainant had agreed to employ only union help, and so the union, it may be said, was speaking with some authority for ex-employees of the complainant. The union in reality by the picketing was attempting to secure a renewal of the former contract in behalf of union members who had previously been employed by the complainant. And yet in that case the judgment appealed from by which the injunction had been granted was affirmed and Chief Justice Stearns said: "In the circumstances and in view of the deliberate violation by respondents of the rights of complainants, we think that to now permit any picketing in the limited space near the theater would inevitably result in the obstruction of the public use of the street and sidewalk and an added injury to complainant. For the reason stated, we are of the opinion that the injunction was warranted in this case."

In Stillwell Theatre, Inc. v. Kaplan, 259 N.Y. 405, 182 N.E. 63, 84 A.L.R. 6, cited by defendant's counsel, the picketers were not only ex-employees, but there had been a contract whereby the employer had agreed to employ only members of their union. The theatre company made a new contract of like effect with another union so the real controversy was between the two unions. There did not enter into it the question of unionization. It was simply a question whether the union and its members who had been employees under the contract not renewed could picket to the end that they might be re-employed. The court held that it would not decide such a controversy and enjoin the picketing unless it were shown that violence, deceit, or misrepresentation was employed to bring about the desired results.

New York is one of the states that holds a strike to unionize is lawful, but as we understand the Stillwell Case, it does not go so far as to hold that strangers who have had no contractual relationship either with the employer or the employees have the right to picket, though peaceably. That the New York court might so hold is indicated by its fairly recent decision in Julie Baking Co., Inc., et al. v. Graymond et al., 152 Misc. 846, 274 N.Y.S. 250, in which, although it was a case not involving organized labor, it was held that members of a neighborhood organization could peaceably picket against a bakery in protest of alleged extortionate prices for necessities. Still, the same court granted an injunction in A. S. Beck Shoe Corporation v. Johnson, 153 Misc. 363, 274 N.Y.S. 946, enjoining picketing by some negroes who by their picketing were attempting to compel the shoe corporation to employ a certain percentage of negro help in place of white persons. In the latter case, the court having commented on its decisions revealing the history of that state's judicial attitude toward labor injunction, said, on page 952 of 274 N.Y.S.: "In other words, this broad liberal policy permitting concerted action to interfere with the business of employers is specifically limited to labor disputes."

As indicated in the note to the Beck Case in Harvard Law Review, volume 48, page 691, it is difficult to justify such a distinction.

Counsel for the defendants have cited other cases which have been carefully examined, but in no one of them do we find authority for denying the issue of the injunction under the facts in this case, unless we take the ultraliberal view (and there is no evidence in this case to support it) that social values and necessities justify such interference upon the part of strangers.

"In determining whether this justification exists, the social value of the ends sought and the necessity for picketing to secure them should be weighed against the prospective injury to both the public and the person picketed." Harvard Law Review, vol. 48, p. 691.

Are the ends sought of sufficient social importance to justify peaceable picketing by these strangers under the facts in this case? We do not feel that they are.

Picketing is defined in Bouvi. Law Dict., Baldwin's Century Edition, page 935, and (Rawle's 3rd Rev.) page 2590 as "posting members at all the approaches to the works struck against for the purpose of reporting the workmen going to or coming from the works; and to use such influence as may be in their power to prevent the workmen from accepting work there."

In Jones v. Van Winkle Gin & Machine Works, 131 Ga. 336, 62 S.E. 236, 238, 17 L.R.A. (N.S.) 848, 127 Am. St. Rep. 235, it is said that "The very word 'picket' is borrowed from the nomenclature of warfare, and is strongly suggestive of a hostile attitude towards the individual or corporation against whom the labor union has a grievance."

In Union Pacific Railroad Co. v. Ruef et al. (C.C.) 120 F. 102, 121, it is declared that " 'picketing' has been condemned by every court having the matter under consideration. It is a pretence for 'persuasion,' but is intended for intimidation. Gentlemen never seek to compel and force another to listen to the art of persuasion. To stop another on the street, get in his road, follow him from one side of the street to another, pursue him wherever he goes, stand in front of his residence, is not persuasion."

Even peaceable picketing is not intended to affect only the employer and its employees. Its purpose is also to involve the public in the controversy. It seeks to use the public as a cudgel. Besides desiring to secure its approval on the merits of the issue, its particular purpose is so to arouse and inflame it that it will not patronize the employer unless under compulsion the employer accedes to the demands of the picketers. Fair argument failing, loss of patronage by its incited customers must make the employer abandon its lawful right to manage, control, and perhaps save its business. If public opinion thus obtained, resulting beneficially to union labor, affected adversely only the employer and employees, it would not be quite so harmful, but the natural tendency of such public opinion, created in a forge of white heat, is to manifest itself in ways decidedly against the best interests and welfare of society itself.

Sir Basil Thomson, author of "The Story of Scotland Yard," in speaking of riots (natural products of bitter labor conflicts) has quoted from an American writer, Mr. Melville Lee, as follows: "When this moment arrives all self-control is repudiated; decent and orderly men become desperadoes; cowards are inspired by a senseless bravado; the calm reason of common sense gives place to the insanity of licence, and unless the demoralizing tendency is checked, a crowd rapidly sinks to the level of its most degraded constituent. The explanation of these phenomena is probably to be found in an excessive spirit of emulation, aroused under conditions of excitement, which makes a man feel that the responsibility of his actions is no longer to be borne by himself but will be shared by the multitude in which he has merged his identity."

Peaceable picketing, so called, is conceived in battle; its real purpose is to conquer. It would compel acquiescence, not induce it by mere persuasion. Unquestionably its tendency is always militant. Then is it really in the interest of society to foster it? Disregarding its effect upon the contractual and property rights of the picketed and conceding its efficacy as an aid to unions in securing victories in labor conflicts, are the ends thus obtained of sufficient social value to justify it? Peace and contentment between employer and employee are to be recognized, commended, and safeguarded. There were such between this plaintiff and its employees.

The interests of society do not require their termination at the hands of these nonrelated defendants. This interference, even if it had not reached the stage of threats, intimidation or coercion, force or violence, cannot be justified as society-required.

We do not wish to be understood as denying the right of the representatives of the unions by proper speech and persuasive argument to attempt the conversion of any employer to their belief that unionization is best; we would not so limit freedom of speech; but we see a distinction between peaceable persuasion by speech and peaceable picketing. True, the latter is said not to have in it force or violence, threats, intimidation, or coercion, yet in all picketing there is an element not appearing in fair argument and a reasonable appeal for justice.

The picketer, in this case, however peaceable, in effect says to the employer: "Here I am at the entrance of your theatre and here I shall remain until you accede to my demands. I shall brand you as unfair to labor, and so prejudice the public and your present satisfied employees against you and your business that you must choose between submission and its possible destruction."

Recently a Maine writer of distinction has truly stated: "Justice, defined correctly, . . . is the largest measure of individual liberty consistent with the rights of others."

Would we give the right to picket peaceably to the employer's own employees (and this we do not decide), we cannot grant it to these defendants without destroying that consistency of rights absolutely essential to effect justice.

Social welfare does not demand that nonrelated persons or organizations shall have the right, even by peaceable picketing, to attempt to break down and destroy a satisfactory relationship between an employer and its employees in order to supplant it by another whose terms are satisfactory only to the dictators of it. To permit such an enforced and unwanted substitution would violate that right of contract and freedom of action that in large part have made possible the industrial development of this nation. It would tend to thwart ambition and destroy initiative. It would be taking a long step toward socialistic control of private business and industry. To allow any organization, whether a union or not, without warrant of constitutional legislative action, to dictate the business policy of an industry, whether owned by an individual or a corporation, even though that which is dictated would benefit the members of the organization compelling it, there being no relationship between the organization and the employer and its employees, nor labor dispute, nor strike, would tend to destroy very materially that liberty which under our democratic form of government the people are entitled to have and retain.

Appeal and exceptions sustained. Decree below reversed. Bill
sustained. Case remanded for issue of writ of injunction.[1]

---

[1] Accord, in holding that a strike for the closed shop will be enjoined:
International Ticket Co. v. Wendrich, C.C.H. Labor Law Serv., par. 16402
(Ct. of Chancery, N.J., July 16, 1937, unreported); 218-220 Market St.
Corp. v. Delicatessen & Cafeteria Workers', 118 N.J. Eq. 448, 179 Atl. 689
(1935); Wasilewski v. Bakers Union, 118 N.J. Eq. 349, 179 Atl. 284 (1935).
But see Four Plating Co. v. Metal Polishers, etc., Union, Ct. of Chancery, N.J.,
September 14, 1937. See also the interesting opinion by Bigelow, V.C., in Feller
v. Local 144 C.C.H. Labor Law Serv., par. 16250 (Ct. of Chancery, N.J., May
4, 1936, unreported), aff'd, C.C.H. Labor Law Serv., par. 16370 (Ct. of Errors
and Appeals, N.J., March 24, 1937, unreported), with which compare Restful
Slipper Co. v. United Shoe & Leather Union, 116 N.J. Eq. 521, 174 Atl. 543
(1934). For an explanation of the New Jersey cases in terms of the differing
attitudes of the Chancellor and Vice-Chancellors, see: Konvitz, "Labor and the
New Jersey Courts," 4 Mercer Beasley L. Rev. 1 (1935); 4 I.J.A. Bull. No.
11a, 4 (1936).
    Cf. Freed & Co. v. Doe, 154 Misc. 644, 278 N.Y.S. 68 (1935), holding that
picketing for a closed shop covering retail salespeople will be enjoined because
the closed shop should be restricted to occupations which are standardized.
But cf. later opinions in the same case, 283 N.Y.S. 186 (N.Y. Sup. Ct., 1935),
and N. Y. Law Journal, March 1, 1936, unreported. See also: Wise Shoe Co. v.
Lowenthal, 266 N.Y. 264, 194 N.E. 749 (1935), 35 Col. L. Rev. 454 (1935);
Krips Holding Co. v. Canavan, 159 Misc. 3, 288 N.Y.S. 468 (1936), bringing
musicians within the definition of "occupation" in the N. Y. Anti-Injunction
Act, post, p. 58, note 8.
    Compare also the cases involving union disciplinary action which im-
pede the employer's access to a free labor market: Robinson v. Bryant, 184
S.E. 298 (Ga., 1936); Yankee Network v. Gibbs, 3 N.E. (2d) 288 (Mass.,
1936).
    The opinions in the cases which refuse to give recognition to the right
of picketing in "non-labor" disputes also contain provocative discussion of
first principles: New Negro Alliance v. Sanitary Grocery Co., C.C.H. Labor
Law Serv., par. 16400 (App. D.C., 1937); Green v. Samuelson, 178 Atl. 109
(Md., 1935) (injunction granted forbidding picketing by Negroes against racial
discrimination in employment); People v. Kopezak, 153 Misc. 187, 274 N.Y.S.
629 (N.Y. Ct. Spec. Sess., 1934), aff'd without opinion, 266 N.Y. 565, 195 N.E.
202 (1935) (picketing by tenants demanding fireproof conditions held to constitute disorderly conduct); Beck Shoe Corp. v. Johnson, 153 Misc. 363, 274
N.Y.S. 94 (1934) (injunction granted forbidding picketing by Negroes against
racial discrimination in employment). Contra: Julie Baking Co. v. Graymond,
152 Misc. 846, 274 N.Y.S. 250 (1934) (injunction denied against consumers
picketing in protest against the price of bread). See: 48 Harv. L. Rev. 691
(1935).
    Compare the main case with those delimiting and permitting "peaceful
picketing": Lisse v. Local Union No. 31, 41 Pac. (2d) 314 (Calif., 1935); International L. G. W. Union v. Dorothy Frocks Co., 95 S.W. (2d) 1346 (Tex. Civ.
App., 1936); Kimbel v. Lumber, etc., Workers Union No. 2575, 65 Pac. (2d)
1066 (Wash., 1937). See also: Cooper, "The Fiction of Peaceful Picketing,"
35 Mich. L. Rev. 73 (1936); Eskin, "The Legality of 'Peaceful Coercion' in
Labor Disputes," 85 U. of Pa. L. Rev. 456 (1937).
    On picketing in labor disputes as a breach of the peace or as disorderly
conduct, see: State v. Perry, 196 Minn. 330, 265 N.W. 302 (1936) (picketing
home of non-striker as breach of peace); People v. Quesada, 154 Misc. 152,
276 N.Y.S. 711 (N.Y. Ct. Spec. Sess., 1935), 4 I.J.A. Bull. No. 6, 1 (1935). Cf.
Ex parte Harder, 49 Pac. (2d) 304 (Calif. App., 1935), holding anti-picketing
ordinance invalid because of failure to define "picketing." See also: State v.
Nield, Md. App., August 12, 1937.

GENERAL MOTORS CORPORATION v. INTERNATIONAL UNION UNITED AUTOMOBILE WORKERS

Circuit Court, Genesee County, Michigan, 1937. (C.C.H. Labor Law Serv., par. 16354.)

PAUL V. GADOLA, CIRCUIT JUDGE. This proceeding involves a simple legal question that would be of relatively little importance except to the litigants involved, other than that it is of great public interest because of the relationship existing between the parties litigant at the present time and as they affect the general public and welfare of all of our people. The question involved is solely as to the right of the defendants to occupy the premises involved in this litigation described in the amended bill of complaint of the plaintiff.

It is proper that this matter should finally be brought before a court of competent jurisdiction for decision. If two individuals were in difference, the law would not permit them to take their grievance or wrongs in their own hands and attempt to redress them by their own actions. Because a great number of people are involved, there is no difference, and the courts are the proper forum to redress wrongs and protect rights.

If the plaintiffs in this action are legally entitled to possession of the premises in question, they could, by appropriate action, seek the assistance of this Court in the protection of their right of possession. The defendants, if they are right, could apply to this Court and be assisted by the injunctive process of this Court in maintaining their position of possession.

These defendants have not seen fit to do that, but on the contrary, the plaintiffs have sought the assistance of this Court. It makes no difference, however, which side to the controversy first seeks the assistance of the Court. The Court must fairly and impartially interpret and administer the law relative to the question involved, namely the right of possession of the premises. . . .

At the outset of the argument on behalf of the defendants, counsel stated that we were now not operating under the laws of 1898, but were operating under the clear mandate of the people as expressed in 1936, probably referring to the election of 1936.

This Court has previously stated he must take the law as he finds the law, and he must interpret and follow that law. If there is to be a change in the laws it is legislative function to make these changes, and the Court perforce must follow the mandates of the legislature relative thereto, but the Court cannot legislate, the Court can but interpret and enforce.

The question involved here as to the right of possession of the premises in question seems to have been clearly settled by the law through the Supreme Court of our State.

In Lane v. AuSable, 181, at page 26, the Court took occasion to pass upon the rights of a striker in and to premises that he occupied as his residence. The opinion of the Court is very clearly stated relative to those rights, and reads as follows:

"This suit is brought by William Lane to recover damages which he alleges he sustained by reason of an unlawful eviction of himself and his family from certain premises located in the city of Muskegon Heights, owned by defendant. The plaintiff was chief operator of the sub-station of the defendant at Muskegon Heights when a strike came on."

Then, after quoting at length from the testimony, the Court goes to its decision and used this language:

"The relation of landlord and tenant between the parties did not exist. It was the relation of employer and employed; the plaintiff being in possession of property belonging to the employer by virtue of his employment. When the plaintiff voluntarily severed the relationship which entitled him to the use of the property, that moment he ended his right to its use. Suppose a maid servant was employed at a monthly wage of $20 and the use of a furnished room in the house of her employer, and should then go on a strike and refuse to do any work, could she still insist upon the right to use the furnished room? A statement of the proposition shows its unreasonableness and yet it is like the instant case in principle.

"The language used in Bowman v. Bradley, 181 Pa. 351 (24 Atl. 1082, 17 L.R.A. 213), is pertinent here:

"If the possession of the house be regarded as an incident of the hiring, the incident must fall with the principal. If it be regarded as part of the compensation stipulated for, then the right to the compensation ceased when the labor was discontinued.

"Bowman had the same right to insist on the payment of the cash part of his wages as on that part which provided his family a place to live. His right under the contract of hiring was like that of the porter to the possession of the porter's lodge; like that of the coachman to his apartments over the stable; like that of the teacher to the rooms he or she may have occupied in the school buildings; like that of the domestic servants to the rooms in which they lodge in the house of their employers. In all these cases, and others that might be enumerated, the occupancy of the room or house is incidental to the employment. The employee has no distinct right of possession, for his possession is that of the employer, and it cannot survive the hiring to which it is incidental, or under which it is part of the contract price for the services performed . . . when his contract ended, his rights in the premises were extinguished, and it was his duty to give way to his successor. . . . The case seems to have been begun, and tried, by the plaintiff on the theory that his right to the possession of the house was superior to his right to remain in the defendant's service. . . . When the labor ceased on the 19th of July, the plaintiff ceased to pay for his occupancy by ceasing to labor without remonstrance or objection, he must be held to acquiesce in the defendant's right to terminate the contract for labor. If that contract was rightfully terminated, then the plaintiff's right to the house was at an end, and he could be lawfully put out of possession. . . . It is not necessary that occupation of a house, or apartment, should be a necessary incident to the service to be performed in order that the right to continue in possession should end with the service. It is enough, if such occupation is convenient, for the purposes of the services, and was obtained by reason of the hiring.

"To the same effect is Heffelfinger v. Fulton, 25 Ind. App. 33 (56 N.H. 688), and Trustees v. Froislie, 37 Minn. 447 (35 N.W. 260)."

The latter case is a case of a pastor of a church, and the question of the right of the administrator of the pastor's estate to keep possession of the premises after the decease of the pastor.

The main case, Lane v. AuSable Electric Company, has never been reversed in Michigan, has never been so much as cited since its adoption by the Supreme Court of the State of Michigan, and remains and is the law of the State of Michigan today. It did not go back to 1898, or to any of those dates. It is a case of 1914, and was decided by our Court at that time.

Now, as to the right of injunctive relief. Hall v. Nestor, 22 Mich. at 141, which, in the opinion of this Court, provides the right under our law to injunctive relief. Quoting at great length from a great many authorities, but particularly from Pomeroy, in his Equity Jurisprudence, at Section 1357,

"If a trespass to property is a single act, and is temporary in its nature and effects, so that the legal remedy of an action at law for damages is adequate, equity will not interfere. The principle determining the jurisdiction embraces two classes of cases, and may be correctly formulated as follows:

"(1) If the trespass, although a single act, is or would be destructive, if the injury is or would be irreparable,—that is, if the injury done or threatened is of such a nature that, when accomplished, the property cannot be restored to its original condition, or cannot be replaced by means of compensation in money,— then the wrong will be prevented or stopped by injunction.

"(2) If the trespass is continuous in its nature, if repeated acts of wrong are done or threatened, although each of these acts, taken by itself, may not be destructive, and the legal remedy may, therefore, be adequate for each single act if it stood alone, then, also, the entire wrong will be prevented or stopped by injunction on the ground of avoiding a repetition of similar actions. In both cases the ultimate criterion is the inadequacy of the legal remedy. All the cases, English and American, have professed to adopt the inadequacy of legal remedies as the test and limit of the injunctive jurisdiction, but in applying this criterion the modern decisions, with some exceptions among the American authorities, have certainly held the injury to be irreparable, and the legal remedy inadequate in many instances and under many circumstances where Chancellor Kent would probably have refused to interfere. It is certain that many trespasses are now enjoined which, if committed, would fall short of destroying the property or of rendering its restoration to its original condition impossible. The injunction is granted not merely because the injury is essentially destructive, but because being continuous or repeated, the full compensation for the entire wrong cannot be obtained in one action at law for damages. While this same formula is employed by the courts of equity in defining their injunction, the jurisdiction itself has practically been enlarged. Judges have been brought to see and to acknowledge,—contrary to the opinion held by Chancellor Kent,—that the common law theory of not interfering with persons until they shall have committed a wrong, is fundamentally erroneous, and that remedy which prevents a threatened wrong is in its essential nature better than a remedy which permits the wrong to be done, and then attempts to pay for it by the pecuniary damages which a jury may assess. The ideal remedy in any perfect system of administering justice would be that which absolutely precludes the commission of a wrong, not that which awards punishment or satisfaction for a wrong after it is committed."

Likewise, in the case of Ideal Mfg. Co. v. Wayne Circuit Judge, 139 Mich. 92, which opinion the Court read yesterday in denying the motion on the part of the defendants, the law clearly established that real grounds are set up in a bill of complaint for equitable relief by injunction asking for temporary relief, that is in the duty of the Court, when the statements in the bill of complaint set up sufficient grounds to issue a temporary injunction, and that an order to show cause is not essential, is not necessary, and really is not the proper procedure, so that the order to show cause in this case was merely a matter of courtesy, more or less, so that the parties might be heard here in court.[1] . . .

This Court cannot take the mandate of 1936. As expressed, this Court must follow the law as established by the Supreme Court of the State of Michigan.

---

[1] The court here cites and discusses the following Michigan authorities to the effect that peaceful picketing may be enjoined; Beck v. Railway Teamsters' Protective Union, 118 Mich. 497, 77 N.W. 13 (1898); Ideal Manufacturing Co. v. Ludwig, 149 Mich. 133, 102 N.W. 372 (1907); Baltic Mining Co. v. Houghton Circuit Judge, 177 Mich. 632, 144 N.W. 209 (1913); Clarage v. Luphringer, 202 Mich. 612, 168 N.W. 440 (1918).—Ed.

It therefore follows that the relief asked for by plaintiffs in this action must be granted. The injunction shall be issued out of this Court commanding the defendants that have appeared, and all defendants, and all persons operating through, under or by virtue of any contact with these defendants, to evacuate the premises in question, and further that they shall be restrained from picketing the plants of the plaintiff.[2]

This order further provides that the sheriff of this county shall read the order of the Court in the premises described to the parties therein, and that shall be sufficient notice of the order of the Court to all parties involved. And further providing that the evacuation shall be done within 24 hours from this time. . . .

(Injunction)

Whereas, it has been represented to us in the Circuit Court for the County of Genesee, in Chancery, on the part of General Motors Corporation, a Delaware Corporation, plaintiff, that it has lately exhibited its amended bill of complaint against you, the said defendants and the others above mentioned, to be relieved, touching the matters therein complained of; in which amended bill of complaint it is stated; among other things, that you are combining and confederating with others to injure the said plaintiff, touching the matters set forth in the said amended bill of complaint, and that your actings and doings in the premises are contrary to equity and good conscience; and whereas, a hearing has been had in open court touching the matters set forth in said amended bill of complaint, and whereas the Court has decided that the plaintiff is entitled to the temporary injunctive relief prayed for in its said amended bill of complaint; WE THEREFORE, in consideration thereof, and of the particular matters in the said amended bill of complaint set forth; do strictly command you, the said defendants, and all the persons hereinbefore mentioned, and each and every one of you, and all to whom knowledge of this in-

---

[2] Accord, Chrysler Corp. v. International Union United Automobile Workers, C.C.H. Labor Law Serv., par. 16358 (Circuit Ct. Wayne Co., Mich., 1937); Plecity v. Local No. 27, C.C.H. Labor Law Serv., par. 16357 (Sup. Ct. Los Angeles Co., Calif., 1937). See also Apex Hosiery Co. v. Leader, 90 F.(2d) 155 (C.C.A. 3d, 1937), post, p. 127, note 14.

Two states have declared the sit-down strike unlawful by statute: 1937 Tenn. Laws, c. 160; 1937 Vt. Laws, c. 210. The State Labor Relations Act in Massachusetts makes the sit-down strike an unfair labor practice (1937 Laws, c. 436, sec. 8 A, post, p. 96, note 4). No penalty or method of enforcement is provided, except, semble, that a cease-and-desist order may issue.

In the course of the Congressional debates which took place while the wave of sit-down strikes was at its height early in 1937, Representative Coffee of Washington defended the legality of the sit-down strike with an analysis of the authorities. (81 Cong. Rec., March 30, 1937, at 3730.) Cf. Garrison, "Government and Labor: The Latest Phase," 37 Col. L. Rev. 897 (1937), 904 et seq.—Ed.

junction shall come, under the penalty of Fifteen Million Dollars, to be levied on your lands, goods and chattels, to our use, that you and every one of you do:

1. On or before 3 o'clock P.M., February 3, 1937, cease and desist from further occupying any portion of the property and premises of the plaintiff known as Plant No. 1 Fisher Body Division of General Motors Corporation, located on South Saginaw Street in the City of Flint, Michigan, and Plant No. 2 of Fisher Body Division of General Motors Corporation, located on Chevrolet Avenue in the City of Flint, Michigan, (Plant No. 1 being bounded on the north by the Pere Marquette Railroad, on the south by Hemphill Avenue, on the west by Culbertson, and on the east by South Saginaw Street; and Plant No. 3 located on Chevrolet Avenue, lying between Hasselbring Avenue and Flint River, in the City of Flint, Michigan), and from interfering with the plaintiff's possession and use thereof.

2. On or before 3 o'clock P. M., February 3, 1937, depart from and vacate the premises of the plaintiff described in the preceding paragraph hereof without damaging or injuring the same, or any of the contents thereof in any manner whatsoever.

3. On and after 3 P. M., February 3, 1937, absolutely desist and refrain from continuing or being in, on, upon, or going upon the premises and plants aforesaid, of plaintiff.

4. Absolutely desist and refrain from interfering with the plants aforesaid, the machinery and property of the plaintiff aforesaid, and plaintiff's use and possession thereof, and from continuing to trespass thereupon; and from carrying out any conspiracy whatsoever to unlawfully deprive or interfere with plaintiff's possession of its said property and business.

5. Absolutely desist and refrain from picketing the premises of the plaintiff hereinbefore described, or loitering at or near the approaches of the factory buildings of said plants, or upon the public streets or highways leading to said plants, or at any places where the non-striking employees of the plaintiff desiring to work for plaintiff enter or alight from conveyances en route from or to said plants.

6. Absolutely desist and refrain from in any manner interfering with the non-striking employees of the plaintiff, by way of threats, personal violence, intimidation, or any other unlawful means calculated or intended to prevent such persons from entering or continuing in the employment of the plaintiff, or calculated or intended to induce any such person or persons to leave the em-

---

3 The injunction issued in Chrysler Corporation v. International Union United Automobile Workers (Circuit Ct. Wayne Co., Mich., 1937), supra, note 2, included a clause providing for a penalty of $10,000,000.—Ed.

ployment of the plaintiff, and from addressing any threatening or insulting, or abusive language to employees of the plaintiff, who may desire to work in said plants for plaintiff.

7. Absolutely desist and refrain from in any manner interfering with the free access of non-striking employees of the plaintiff to plaintiff's premises hereinbefore described and located in the City of Flint, Michigan, and from in any manner interfering with the free return of said employees to their place of employment or to their homes or elsewhere.

8. Absolutely desist and refrain from protecting, aiding or assisting any person or persons in the commission of any of the acts herein prohibited.

9. Absolutely desist from unlawfully conspiring, confederating or combining directly or indirectly for the purpose of doing any of the acts hereinbefore prohibited. Until the further order of this Court.

You are hereby notified that the order of the Court entered in this cause on February 2nd, 1937, authorizing the issuance of this injunction, provides that the reading of this injunction by the Sheriff shall constitute sufficient service thereof upon all persons to whom the same shall be read, and you and each of you to whom notice of this injunction shall come, by the reading thereof, by the Sheriff to you, are ordered to depart forthwith from the premises of the plaintiff hereinbefore described, and you and each of you are hereby commanded to observe each and every provision of this injunction.

SERVICE WOOD HEEL CO. v. MACKESY

Supreme Judicial Court of Massachusetts, 1936. 199 N.E. 400.

RUGG, CHIEF JUSTICE. This is a suit by a manufacturer of wood heels to enjoin the defendants, officers and members of the United Shoe & Leather Workers Union, from doing acts to prevent sales by the plaintiff to shoe manufacturers. The case was referred to a master, whose report contains the facts. No appeal was taken from an interlocutory decree confirming the report. The bill was filed July 18, 1934, and the master's report was dated August 1, 1934. The case is here on appeal from a final decree entered October 6, 1934, dismissing the bill with costs. The pertinent facts as found by the master are these: Early in March, 1934, there was a general strike by the defendant union involving virtually all the shoe manufacturers in Haverhill. After many conferences, the strike was terminated on April 9, 1934, by written agreements between the several manufacturers and the defendant union. These agreements provided for closed shops and fixed wages and hours of employment, and contained a clause that after June 1, 1934, all "wood heels placed on shoes of all types must be made by Union heel makers." The principal inducements motivating the defendant union in entering into these agreements were to secure for its members the labor included in the actual shoe manufacturing operations and also the work of manufacturing the wood heels supplied to the shoe manufacturers. One of the locals of the defendant union in Haverhill comprised those engaged in making wood heels. One of the shoe manufacturers signing such agreements with the defendant union was a copartnership known as the Simon Shoe Company. In accordance with such agreement, that company employs only union operatives. That company, during nearly all of the seven years it had been in business, had purchased its finished wood heels from the plaintiff, a corporation engaged in Lawrence in the manufacture and finishing of such heels. It had been customary for the plaintiff to agree orally with the Simon Shoe Company, at first annually and more recently semiannually, on terms for the sale and delivery of wood heels. Early in 1934, they had made such an agreement for the manufacture by the plaintiff and purchase by the Simon Shoe Company, for the ensuing six months, of a specified number of cases of wood heels. The strike reduced production by the Simon Shoe Company during the first part of 1934, and it was therefore agreed that the plaintiff would sell and the Simon Shoe Company purchase, after the expiration of the six months' period, until the agreed number of heels had been delivered.

The plaintiff employs about one hundred and thirty persons; they have no connection with the defendant union. In the spring of 1934, the officers and employees of the plaintiff, fearing loss of business arising from the Haverhill agreements, organized a company union having no affiliation with the defendant union. The plaintiff's officers and the Haverhill manufacturers knew that the defendant union would not recognize heels made by members of a company union as made by union heel makers within the meaning of the agreement of April 9, 1934. The master found that this organization was a bona fide company union. In June, 1934, an officer of the defendant union told the Simon Shoe Company in substance that it would have to get another heel manufacturer that its contract for the purchase of heels from the plaintiff would not be recognized and that it must secure union made heels. In the following month, the union made it clear to the Simon Shoe Company that, unless it secured and used at its factory union made heels, there would be a strike or walkout. Thereupon, the Simon Shoe Company ceased to do business with the plaintiff and has since bought heels of another manufacturer. The Simon Shoe Company signed the agreement of April 9, 1934, with the defendant union freely and voluntarily. The arrangements between the plaintiff and the Simon Shoe Company for the sale and purchase of wood heels were voluntarily made and mutually satisfactory, and but for the interference of the defendant union the plaintiff would still be making and delivering wood heels to the Simon Shoe Company. That company acted reasonably in supposing that, if it continued to deal with the plaintiff, the defendant union would by strike or walkout compel the cessation of its business with the plaintiff. The unexpired agreement between the plaintiff and the Simon Shoe Company under which sales of wood heels were made by the plaintiff to that company was entered into before the agreement of April 9, 1934, between the defendant union and the Simon Shoe Company. The officers of the union, before the execution of the agreement of April 9, 1934, and ever since up to the time the Simon Shoe Company ceased to buy of the plaintiff, knew that the plaintiff was supplying all the wood heels used by that manufacturer under some arrangement although they did not know its details or its duration in time. The final essential findings of the master are to the effect that the members of the defendant "union are acting in concert to deprive the plaintiff of selling its goods to the Simon Shoe Company and that as a result of the action" of the defendant union the shoe company has ceased taking any more heels from the plaintiff; that the shoe company was satisfied to continue its business arrangements with the plaintiff and the plaintiff was satisfied to continue selling heels to the shoe company, and "that these two concerns would still be operating under their oral agreement made early in 1934 but for the acts of the respondent union, which have caused this shoe company to breach its agreement with the plaintiff and to cease taking the plaintiff's goods."

On the facts, the plaintiff has suffered a wrong and appears to be entitled to some relief. The plaintiff had a contract for the manufacture and sale to the Simon Shoe Company of a certain number of cases of shoe heels. The contract had not expired when the contract of April 9, 1934, between the defendant union and the Simon Shoe Company was made. It was in force in July, 1934, when the coercive force of the defendant union was put forth which caused that "shoe company to breach its agreement with the plaintiff and to cease taking the plaintiff's goods." The agreement of April 9, 1934, between the defendant union and the Simon Shoe Company, having been made voluntarily, was legal between the parties. Hoban v. Dempsey, 217 Mass. 166, 169, 104 N.E. 717, L.R.A. 1915A, 1217, Ann. Cas. 1915C, 810; Shinsky v. O'Neil, 232 Mass. 99, 102, 121 N.E. 790; Pickett v. Walsh, 192 Mass. 572, 584, 78 N.E. 753, 6 L.R.A. (N.S.) 1067, 116 Am. St. Rep. 272, 7 Ann. Cas. 638. That agreement, however, does not justify the defendants in putting forth their power to compel the Simon Shoe Company to break its existing contract with the plaintiff by ceasing to do business with the plaintiff. This point is explicitly covered by the decision in A. T. Stearns Lumber Co. v. Howlett, 260 Mass. 45, 157 N.E. 82, 52 A.L.R. 1125. One question involved in that case was whether a strike was lawful to enforce an agreement made by an employer with a union to furnish its employees with union made materials by compelling the employer to break an existing contract for the purchase of material not made by the union. It was not expressly found as a fact in that case that such agreement between the employer and the union was entered into voluntarily, but for the purposes of that decision it was assumed that such agreement was entered into voluntarily. It was decided (260 Mass. 45, at pages 66, 67, 157 N.E. 82, 89, 52 A.L.R. 1125) that "it is clear that such an agreement could not affect existing contracts for the purchase of non-union made material," and that "the rights to which the plaintiffs [seeking to uphold existing contracts for the purchase of nonunion made material against a strike by the union:] were entitled under the decisions previously cited, could not thereby be destroyed." The decisions there previously cited include Berry v. Donovan, 188 Mass. 353, 74 N.E. 603, 5 L.R.A. (N.S.) 899, 108 Am. St. Rep. 499, 3 Ann. Cas. 738; Pickett v. Walsh, 192 Mass. 572, 78 N.E. 753, 6 L.R.A. (N.S.) 1067, 116 Am. St. Rep. 272, 7 Ann. Cas. 638; Beekman v. Marsters, 195 Mass. 205, 80 N.E. 817, 11 L.R.A. (N.S.) 201, 122 Am. St. Rep. 232, 11 Ann. Cas. 332; Burnham v. Dowd, 217 Mass. 351, 104 N.E. 841, 51 L.R.A. (N.S.) 778; New England Cement Gun Co. v. McGivern, 218 Mass. 198, 105 N.E. 885, L.R.A. 1916C, 986; and W. A. Snow Iron Works, Inc., v. Chadwick, 227 Mass. 382, 389, 116 N.E. 801, L.R.A. 1917F, 755. See, also, Armstrong Cork & Insulation Co. v. Walsh, 276 Mass. 263, 177 N.E. 2. In A. T. Stearns Lumber Co. v. Howlett, 260 Mass. 45, 157 N.E. 82, 52 A.L.R. 1125, a strike to compel the breaking of such existing contracts by refraining from buying nonunion made material was held to be illegal and was enjoined. That decision is authoritative in favor of the plaintiff with respect to its contract with the Simon Shoe Company.

It is recited in the master's report that the plaintiff in open court waived any claim for damages against the defendant union. That cannot rightly be construed as waiver of right to strictly equitable relief. The breaking of its contract with the plaintiff by the Simon Shoe Company affected not only the plaintiff but its employees; it may have injured the plaintiff in other ways. The contract between the plaintiff and the Simon Shoe Company made in the early part of 1934 was to continue for six months. Because of the interruption caused by the strike, the Simon Shoe Company at the expiration of that six months had not taken as many heels as it had agreed to buy of the plaintiff. Thereafter, it was agreed that the plaintiff should continue under the oral agreement until it had manufactured and delivered to the Simon Shoe Company the total number of cases agreed upon earlier in the year. It was a mere extension as to time of performance of the original oral agreement. This appears to have been a reasonable arrangement in view of unforeseen interferences with the original agreement and was not designed to circumvent the agreement of April 9, 1934. It is not found by the master to be tainted with illegality. It stands with reference to the rights of the plaintiff on the same footing as the original contract. It was not limited as to time. No ground is disclosed on the record why it should not be completed now. There is nothing in the record to justify the inference that the right of the plaintiff to complete its contract with the Simon Shoe Company was not valuable to it. The plaintiff has established that a wrong has been done it by the defendant union. "Every subject of the commonwealth ought to find a certain remedy, by having recourse to the laws, for all injuries or wrongs which he may receive in his person, property, or character." Article 11 of the Declaration of Rights of the Constitution. The time for affording relief seemingly has not gone by, as in cases like Brown v. City Council of Cambridge (Mass.) 194 N.E. 88, and Blume v. William Shenkel & Sons Co., 266 Mass. 15, 164 N.E. 618.

It does not appear that the right of the plaintiff which has been violated is so trivial or insubstantial as not to be proper for injunctive relief. The rule of cases like A. Doykos & T. Pappas, Inc., v. Leventhal (Mass.) 195 N.E. 348, is not applicable. While there is a certain element of discretion in according injunctive relief, that principle cannot be invoked to support a decree dismissing a suit in equity where a contractual right of the plaintiff has been invaded and the only relief available is by way of injunction.

The contention of the defendant union that the action of the plaintiff in co-operating with its employees to form a company union, when it knew that the defendant union would not recognize wood heels made by such union as union made under the agreement of April 9, 1934, was so reprehensible as to bar relief in equity, cannot be supported. The doctrine that equity will not aid one guilty of illegal or inequitable conduct in the matter with regard to which relief is sought is well recognized. New York, New Haven & Hartford Railroad Co. v. Pierce Coach Lines, Inc., 281 Mass. 479, 482, 183 N.E. 836; New England Wood Heel Co. v. Nolan, 268 Mass. 191, 197, 167 N.E. 323, 66 A.L.R. 1079; Taylor v. Ashe, 284 Mass. 182, 188, 187 N.E. 548. The conduct of the plaintiff does not fall under the condemnation of that doctrine. The company union is found to have been formed in good faith.

If the contention of the plaintiff was unsound that its products
were union made, such as the Simon Shoe Company could buy and
use under its agreement of April 9, 1934, that contention did not
mislead the defendant union and on the facts found involved no
moral turpitude.

The decree dismissing the bill is reversed and a decree with
costs is to be entered in favor of the plaintiff with respect to its
contract made early in 1934 with the Simon Shoe Company and
to its extension.

Ordered accordingly.[1]

GOLDFINGER v. FEINTUCH

New York Supreme Court, New York County, 1936. 159 Misc. 806,
288 N.Y.S. 855.

COLLINS, JUSTICE. This case concerns the legality of the conduct of the defendant union which the plaintiff claims constitutes
an unlawful secondary boycott.

For some years the plaintiff has operated a retail delicatessen
store on the lower east side of Manhattan. In addition to Kosher
delicatessen provisions he sells other foodstuffs and conducts a
luncheonette business. One of the brands of Kosher provisions he
sells is Ukor, a nonunion made product manufactured by a copartnership consisting of Walter and Irving Blumenthal. The Blumenthals operate the only nonunion plant in the city of New York
manufacturing Kosher meats. The defendant union has been endeavoring to unionize the Blumenthal nonunion oasis. Having
failed in its direct negotiations with the Blumenthals towards
unionization, the union has carried its campaign to Blumenthal's
customers, among them the plaintiff. The union's committee in-
terviewed the plaintiff in an effort to procure the plaintiff to abstain from selling Ukor products and to patronize only union
manufacturers. The plaintiff says that his installation of another
product, union made, with the consequent retailing of such other
product, along with Ukor products, did not satisfy the union, but
that the union demanded that the plaintiff sell union made products solely.

The salesmen of Kosher meat manufacturers are likewise
unionized, and the plaintiff asserts that the defendant union went
to the extent of procuring the salesmen's union to effect the refusal by a union manufacturer to sell its products to the plaintiff.
The two unions, so the plaintiff claims, have joined forces to compel the plaintiff to sell only union merchandise. The plaintiff pro-

---

[1] For comment on the case, see: 20 Minn. L. Rev. 838 (1936); 45 Yale
L.J. 1310 (1936).

Addendum

Goldfinger v. Feintuch, 288 N.Y.S. 855, which appears on page 30 of this supplement was reversed without opinion in 295 N.Y.S. 753 (App. Div. 1937).

Provision Company is unfair to union labor. Please buy union made delicatessen only." A Ukor sign is displayed in plaintiff's window. The plaintiff's testimony is that on two or more occasions customers were accosted by a picket with the warning, "Scab merchandise. Don't buy here." The plaintiff appealed to the police and they caused the pickets to leave without making an arrest, but with the departure of the police the picketing was resumed and persists to this day. The plaintiff insists that the picketing has reduced his receipts about $100 a week.

The defendant maintains that the picketing is peaceful, and, therefore, lawful. It contends that in this litigation the plaintiff is but a pawn of the Blumenthals, that the plaintiff is only a nominal party; the real interested parties being the Blumenthals. To support that theory the defendant points to the facts, first, that the plaintiff's attorneys were retained and are being paid by the Blumenthals, and, second, that the Blumenthals sought directly to restrain the union from prosecuting its unionization campaign, and, having failed in that attempt, are now utilizing the plaintiff as the ostensible damaged party. Blumenthal v. Feintuch, 153 Misc. 40, 273 N.Y.S. 660; Blumenthal v. Weikman, 154 Misc. 684, 277 N.Y.S. 895, affirmed without passing on the question of secondary boycott, 244 App. Div. 721, 279 N.Y.S. 966.

The defendant's theory that the Blumenthals are the real parties in interest and that the plaintiff is but a nominal party does not impress me as possessing validity. Of course the Blumenthals are interested in the litigation; whether the plaintiff is being boycotted because he handles Ukor products is of great concern to the manufacturer of those products. But it does not follow that the plaintiff is unharmed by the boycott. He, too, is interested, vitally so. He is suffering a decrease of business. Seemingly, the boycott is effective, otherwise the union would not be pursuing it. It is immaterial that the Blumenthals are defraying the expenses of the litigation; that they are doing so is quite understandable and lawful. It does not affect the plaintiff's rights.

The fundamental question is the legality of the Union's conduct in picketing the plaintiff's store.

Undeniably, there is no strike in the plaintiff's store, nor has the union any grievance against the plaintiff other than that he is selling Ukor products. Indeed, the plaintiff can have no labor trouble because he employs no labor; he has no clerks; his is a one-man store; and that the union may lawfully picket the Blumenthal plant is conceded. But has the union the right to picket the store of a Blumenthal customer? May the union carry its grievance against Blumenthal to the doorstep of a third party for the sole reason that the third party sells Blumenthal goods?

To propound the question more broadly: Are the activities of a union restricted to the employer against whom the union has a grievance, or may the activities be extended so as to include and affect neutrals?

The general right of a union to picket peacefully is indubitable. The existence of a strike is not essential. "Picketing without a strike is not more unlawful than a strike without picketing." Exchange Bakery & Restaurant v. Rifkin, 245 N.Y. 260, 263, 157 N.E. 130, 132.[1] Nor are the acts of the union limited to picketing. When the object is lawful, reasonable means to achieve it may be pursued.

"Where the acts of an employee or employees . . . are reasonably and directly calculated to advance lawful objects, they should not be restrained by injunction." Bossert v. Dhuy, 221 N. Y. 342, 365, 117 N.E. 582, 587, Ann. Cas. 1918D, 661; Paine Lumber Co. v. Neal, 244 U.S. 459, 37 S. Ct. 718, 61 L. Ed. 1256.

That the object here sought is lawful is not controvertible. The legality of unionization is no longer an issue. Admittedly, the union is striving to drive the Blumenthals into the union camp. The efforts are proper. "Conversion to the employee's cause by peaceful persuasion or picketing is an instrumentality both salutary and lawful." Nann v. Raimist, 255 N.Y. 307, 174 N.E. 690, 73 A. L.R. 669; Aberon Bakery Co., Inc. v. Raimist, 141 Misc. 774, 776, 254 N.Y.S. 38, 41.

"When men attempt to assert what they claim to be their rights in good faith, in a decent, orderly way without resort to violence and within the law, their interests are as sacred as those of the plaintiff, and a court of equity should see to it that they are not improperly interfered with by the writ of injunction." Reardon, Inc. v. Caton, 189 App. Div. 501, 511, 178 N.Y.S. 713, 719.

Stillwell Theatre, Inc., v. Kaplan, 259 N.Y. 405, 182 N.E. 63, 84 A.L.R. 6, does not present a precisely parallel situation, but

---

[1] Cf. Keith Theatre v. Vachon, 134 Maine 392, 187 Atl. 692 (1936), supra, p. 1; cases arising under anti-injunction statutes, cited post, p. 47, note 5 and p. 48, note 6.—Ed.

the language there employed is pertinent in answering the plaintiff's argument that even peaceful picketing is tantamount to coercion, and thus forbidden. Said the court 259 N.Y. 405, at page 412, 182 N.E. 63, 66, 84 A.L.R. 6: "The collateral result of the attempted persuasion of the public not to patronize the theatre while it employed the members of the rival union might make it unprofitable for the employer to go on with the contract, but to state fairly and truly to the public that the conduct of the employer is socially objectionable to a labor union is no persuasion to break a contract. This court has never undertaken to restrain such conduct, although it has had the opportunity. It has been at pains to avoid doing so." [2]

Here, the conduct complained of as "socially objectionable" is that "of the employer" and the statement is made "to the public." More, the statement is fair and true. But instead of being made "to the public" at the employer's plant, where the objectionable social conduct is being practiced, it is made "to the public" elsewhere, where the employer's goods are marketed.

It has been held that the picketing of customers by members of the Window Cleaners Union was permissible so long as the picket signs omitted mention of the customer's name. (Spanier Window Cleaning Co., Inc. v. Awerkin, 225 App. Div. 735, 232 N.Y.S. 886). The signs here complained of do not bear the plaintiff's name. In a later case a ruling by Mr. Justice Shientag denying injunctive relief to a window cleaning contractor against the picketing of the contractor's customers (N. Y. Law Journal, February 21, 1934, p. 879) was affirmed (Tri-Boro Window Cleaning Co., Inc. v. Krat, 241 App. Div. 799, 270 N.Y.S. 921).

Frankfurter and Green, in their work on the Labor Injunction, p. 45, say: "A strike or threat to strike may be brought to bear upon neutrals, provided that the neutrals thus used as a lever are within the same industry as those in whose coercion the union is primarily interested."

In Bossert v. Dhuy, supra, it was decided that union carpenters were within their rights in refusing to work on a building where certain of the building material came from a mill employing non-union labor. It was said 221 N.Y. 342, at pages 364, 365, 117 N.E. 582, 587, Ann. Cas. 1918D, 661: "When it is determined that a labor organization can control the body of its members for the purpose of securing to them higher wages, shorter hours of labor and better relations with their employers, and as a part of such control may refuse to allow its members to work under conditions

---

[2] See Edjomac Amusement Corp. v. Empire State M. P. O. Union, 156 Misc. 856, 283 N.Y.S. 6 (1935), in which the picketing union was permitted to display signs announcing that plaintiff did not employ its members only on condition that the signs also stated that plaintiff "employs Union labor." The case is criticized in 4 I.J.A. Bull. No. 7, 10 (1936).—Ed.

unfavorable to it, or with workingmen not in accord with the sentiments of the labor union, the right to refuse to allow them to install nonunion made material follows as a matter of course, subject to there being no malice, fraud, violence, coercion, intimidation or defamation in carrying out their resolutions and orders."

Similar results were reached in Willson & Adams Co. v. Pearce, 240 App. Div. 718, 265 N.Y.S. 624, affirmed 264 N.Y. 521, 191 N.E. 545, and more recently in New York Lumber Trade Association v. Lacey, 245 App. Div. 262, 281 N.Y.S. 647, affirmed 269 N.Y. 595, 199 N.E. 688.

The principle of the above cases is that a labor union may present its cause to the public and solicit public support to the extent of urging the public not to purchase nonunion made goods or not to patronize nonunion shops. Of course, the campaign must be free from fraud, duress, intimidation, coercion, malice, violence, or defamation. If the object is lawful and peaceful methods are pursued and the truth is adhered to, the courts should not interfere. To do so would place the courts on the side of the employer, against the employee. The policy of the law is one of neutrality, to aid neither side unless, of course, the clear violation of an established right compels intervention.

The plaintiff insists that the picketing of his store transgresses peaceful persuasion and constitutes coercion or intimidation. But if to picket a neutral is coercion or intimidation, then picketing the offending nonunion employer would be equally coercive or intimidating. To inform the public by peaceful means that a store sells nonunion goods is not, as I understand the cases, coercion or intimidation within the condemned and prohibited sense.

The fundamental invalidity of the plaintiff's position is his insistence that persuasion is necessarily coercive; that picketing per se implies or effects coercion. Once it is seen that peaceful methods of persuasion are not synonymous with coercive methods, the fallacy of the plaintiff's position is exposed. The plaintiff's doctrine that picketing is a species of coercion and intimidation is dogma long since discarded. " 'Picketing' connotes no evil." Exchange Bakery & Restaurant Co. v. Rifkin, supra, 245 N.Y. 260, at page 263, 157 N.E. 130, 133.

"But wanton or malicious picketing, picketing by coercion, terror, threats, trespass, intimidation or violence, or by false or deceptive utterance, is odious to justice and offends the law. The scope of freedom is not so unbridled and limitless as to sanction transgression of another's conflicting rights." Aberon Bakery Co., Inc. v. Raimist, supra.

The plaintiff's complaint that as a neutral he should not be caused to suffer because of the union's grievance against the Blumenthals, is perfectly understandable. And it appeals to the sympathies. But for innocents to suffer in labor controversies is by no means uncommon. It is unfortunate that one not an immediate party to a dispute, and whose conduct did not provoke it, should be dragged into it. But this result is an incident, though a regrettable one, of our economic and social system. If this plaintiff has rights, so have the members of the defendant union. The plaintiff is not prohibited from dealing in Ukor products. The law does not assume to dictate what products he should or should not handle. He is at liberty to handle nonunion goods. But neither does the law forbid the defendant from peacefully and truthfully informing the public that the plaintiff sells nonunion delicatessen. Not infrequently what serves as an advantage to one operates to the detriment of another. When one loses, another usually gains. Quite obviously, it is to the disadvantage of the plaintiff that his store be picketed; but it is equally obvious that the defendant union might be done a greater injury if the picketing is forbidden. As the plaintiff applies for equitable relief, the equities are to be weighed and measured, and judgment rendered accordingly.

In those cases where injunctions were granted the factual situations were different than the situation here. National House Cleaning Contractors v. Bobaluc, 243 App. Div. 699, 277 N.Y.S. 966; affirming, Law Journal Dec. 20, 1934, p. 2489; Grandview Dairy Inc. v. O'Leary, 158 Misc. 791, 285 N.Y.S. 841; George F. Stuhmer & Co. v. Korman. 241 App. Div. 702, 269 N.Y.S. 788, affirmed 265 N.Y. 481, 193 N.E. 281; Commercial House & Window Cleaning Co. v. Awerkin, 226 App. Div. 734, 233 N.Y.S. 728, reversing, 138 Misc. 512, 240 N.Y.S. 797; Auburn Draying Co. v. Wardell, 227 N.Y. 1, 5, 124 N.E. 97, 99, 6 A.L.R. 901. In each of the cases last cited. there was present some element of fraud or coercion or intimidation. In none of them was it held that mere peaceful picketing, which, as I perceive it, is but a medium of persuasion, is sufficient to constitute a basis for injunctive relief.

In Duplex Printing Press Co. v. Deering, 254 U.S. 443, 466, 41 S. Ct. 172, 176, 65 L. Ed. 349, 16 A.L.R. 196, a condemned secondary boycott was characterized as: "A combination not merely to refrain from dealing with complainant, or to advise or by peaceful means persuade complainant's customers to refrain ('primary boycott'), but to exercise coercive pressure upon such customers, actual or prospective, in order to cause them to withhold or withdraw patronage from complainant through fear of loss or damage to themselves should they deal with it."

Patently, therefore, if the combination is merely "to refrain from dealing with complainant, or to advise or by peaceful means persuade complainant's customers to refrain," the combination is lawful. It becomes unlawful when "coercive pressure upon such customers, actual or prospective," is exercised.

In the Auburn Draying Case, supra, there were "notices, warnings and declarations." The action complained of was "affirmative and aggressive." Coercion was resorted to. It appeared that: "The defendants are intentionally attempting to coerce the plaintiff to unionize its business by aggressively inducing its established and potential customers to ignore its existence in order to be free from the loss and injury which the action of the defendants would otherwise bring to those customers."

Thus, we see that the test is the means employed to attain the end. The factor that the picketed person is a neutral is not decisive.

In my judgment it makes no difference whether the so-called boycott is primary or secondary; if the medium be peaceful persuasion only, then the boycott is lawful. But if the medium goes beyond peaceful persuasion, then it is unlawful even though the conduct bears on a primary boycott.

The plaintiff is correct in declaring that violence is not a necessary element of coercion. Coercion may assume various forms. But certainly peaceful picketing alone does not amount to coercion. Coercion is forbidden in all cases; it is never lawful. So that if mere peaceful picketing were in and of itself coercion, there could never be peaceful picketing in any case, whether the picketed be the employer or a neutral. "Lawful persuasion or inducing" is not coercion. It is perfectly lawful to "appeal to the sympathetic aid of would-be customers by a simple statement of the fact . . . and a request to withhold patronage." Truax v. Corrigan, 257 U. S. 312, 327, 42 S. Ct. 124, 128, 66 L. Ed. 254, 27 A.L.R. 375. The Truax opinion also contains this terse definition of an illegal secondary boycott: "A secondary boycott of this kind is where many combine to injure one in his business by coercing third persons against their will to cease patronizing him by threats of similar injury."

Once more we see that without coercion or some other unlawful force a secondary boycott is not banned. Again, I hold, it is the method and not the relationship between the parties, that supplies the test of lawfulness.

My conclusion, therefore, is that what was done here is lawful and will not be restrained. Blumenthal v. Feintuch, supra; Blumenthal v. Weikman, supra.

From what has been written it becomes unnecessary to determine the applicability of section 876-a of the Civil Practice Act to this case. I rest my decision on the ground that such coercion or other means as the law condemns has not been established. But that section tellingly indicates the policy of this state concerning injunctions in labor disputes. Since its enactment and the passage of the Norris-LaGuardia Act, 29 U.S.C.A. secs. 101-115, many of the old precedents have become outmoded. They mark a new era in the domain of labor injunctions. More and more the tendency is to permit the parties to compose their differences without resort to injunction. The old order was injunction first, the new is injunction last.

Although there is, as observed, some testimony of coercion and intimidation, it is not of sufficient robustness to warrant a finding to that effect. But the defendant is warned that it must conduct its persuasion in a peaceful manner. No coercion, fraud, intimidation, persecution or threats will be tolerated. Nor is the plaintiff to be interfered with in his dealings with manufacturers or others. There is to be no manifestation of malice. The conduct of the plaintiff's business is not to be interrupted. No one is to be molested.

Application for injunction denied, without prejudice to renewal in the event the warning herein given is violated. Findings and conclusions passed upon. Submit decision and judgment accordingly.[3]

DUBINSKY v. BLUE DALE DRESS CO.

New York Supreme Court, New York County, 1936.
162 Misc. 177, 292 N.Y.S. 898.

McCOOK, JUSTICE. In February, 1936, the Popular Priced Dress Manufacturers Group, Inc., an association of employers (hereinafter called the Association), made a collective agreement with the plaintiffs' international and joint board, the latter representing five local unions. This contract was to run for nearly three years and purported to make effective a desire for co-operation in establishing for the industry a living wage and fair and reasonable conditions of labor and to provide methods for fair and peaceful adjustment of disputes so as to secure uninterrupted operation and general stabilization. The field was the business of manufacturing dresses which sold at the wholesale price of $4.75 or less. Hours,

---

[3] But cf. American Gas Stations v. Doe, 293 N.Y.S. 1019 (App. Div., 1937).

For comment on the case, see: 14 N.Y.U.L.Q. Rev. 83 (1936).

For unsuccessful efforts by the Blumenthals to enjoin the union from picketing their customers, see: Blumenthal v. Feintuch, 153 Misc. 40, 273 N.Y.S. 600 (1934), 35 Col. L. Rev. 456 (1935); Blumenthal v. Weikman, 154 Misc. 684, 277 N.Y.S. 895 (1935), aff'd in memorandum opinion, 244 App. Div. 721, 279 N.Y.S. 966 (1935).

For other cases on the boycott, see: Perfect Laundry Co. v. Marsh, 120 N.J. Eq. 508, 186 Atl. 470 (1936); Grandview Dairy v. O'Leary, 158 Misc. 791, 282 N.Y.S. 332 (1935); Hydrox Ice Cream Co. v. Doe, 159 Misc. 642, 289 N.Y.S. 683 (1936), aff'd in memorandum opinion, 293 N.Y.S. 1013 (App. Div., 1937); Driggs Dairy Farms v. Milk Drivers, etc., Local Union No. 361, 49 Ohio App. 303, 197 N.E. 250 (1935). See also: Feinberg, "New York Law of Secondary Boycott," 6 Brooklyn L. Rev. 209 (1936).

wage scales, union shops, and equitable division of work were dealt
with and agreed upon by definition. Removal of factories beyond
the 5-cent fare carrier limit was forbidden. The union was to
have access to the books of the Association members and the
right of visits to shops. It was sought to prevent such incidents
as strikes, stoppages, and lockouts or alleviate them by provisions
for submission of complaints, grievances, and disputes by either
side to the other, with joint investigation by the manager of the
Association and the manager of the union or their deputies, and on
the failure of agreement by these, reference to a trial board, consisting of a representative of each organization and an impartial
chairman.

By application for membership in the Association, representation in writing to the plaintiffs, and other acts, the defendants Blue
Dale Dress Company, Inc., and its subsidiary, Blue Fox Dress Company, Inc., are to be deemed members of the Association from
April 25, 1936, and bound by all the terms of the collective agreement.

The plaintiffs charge that the defendants Fishman, the chief
officers and substantially the proprietors of the Blue Dale and
Blue Fox Corporations, conspiring with the defendant Goldstein,
locked out all their workers, members of the plaintiff unions, and
removed their factories from No. 253 West Thirty-Fifth street,
New York City, where they operated on two floors as separate
units, to Archbald, near Scranton, Pa., and continue to lock their
employees out and threaten to operate instead a nonunion shop
at Archbald, thereby violating the collective agreement in two important particulars and causing great and irreparable damage to
plaintiffs and their members, for which various forms of relief
are sought. The two portions of the agreement particularly applicable read as follows:

"Moving Shops. Twenty-fourth: No member of the association shall, during the term of this agreement, move his shop or
factory from its present location to any place beyond which the
public carrier fare is more than 5 cents."

"Strikes—Stoppages—Lockouts. Twenty-seventh: During the
term of this agreement, there shall be no general lockout, general
strike, individual shop lockout or individual shop strike or shop
stoppage for any reason or cause, but work shall proceed in operation subject to the determination of any dispute or grievance as
hereinafter provided, except where garments are not settled in the
manner provided for in this agreement or wages are not paid on
their due date, as provided for herein. There shall be no individual
lockout, strike or stoppage pending the determination of any complaint or grievance, except in the cases aforementioned. Should the
employees of any shop or factory cause a stoppage of work or shop

strike, or should there result in any shop or factory a stoppage of work or shop strike for reasons other than those aforementioned, notice thereof shall be given by the Association to the Union. The latter obligates itself to return the striking workers and those who have stopped work to their work in the shop within twenty-four hours after the receipt by the Union of such notice, except in the cases aforementioned, and until the expiration of such time it shall not be deemed that the striking workers have abandoned their employment. In the event of a substantial violation of this clause on the part of the Union, the Association shall have the option to terminate this agreement. The existence or non-existence of such substantial violation shall be determined by the Trial Board, as constituted under this contract, on all the facts and circumstances.

"Should any member of the Association cause a lockout in his or its shops or factory, notice thereof shall be given by the Union to the Association. The Association obligates itself, within twenty-four hours after the receipt of such notice, to terminate the lock-out and to cause its members to re-employ the workers, and until the expiration of such time, it shall not be deemed that the employer has forfeited his rights under the agreement. In the event of a substantial violation of this clause on the part of the Association, the Union shall have the option to terminate this agreement. The existence or non-existence of such substantial violation shall be determined by the Trial Board on all the facts and circumstances."

Defendants deny the charges and upon the trial have attempted to prove that the plaintiffs did not faithfully perform their part of the agreement, but violated the same by strikes, stoppages, and otherwise, so that the defendants were justified in regarding the agreement as at an end. From such facts they seek to draw the conclusion that plaintiffs have not come into equity with clean hands and must be denied any relief.

In their briefs the defendants appear to have abandoned an earlier contention that the collective agreement was void for want of mutuality, a defense which a growing body of authority rejects "as inapplicable to collective agreement cases." See Simpson on "Fifty Years of American Equity," Harv. Law Review for December, 1936, p. 121, at 201 top, and cases cited. It is consistent with the principle of mutuality to anticipate unauthorized stoppages by groups of employees and, by providing for the adjustment of such complaints, to deprive the employer of the right to treat these incidents as an excuse for abrogating the contract.

There are three issues of fact: (1) Was there a lockout on the last days of November and the first days of December of its employees by defendants? (2) Did defendants move their factory from New York City to Pennsylvania with intention to save money by operating a nonunion shop and thus to deprive plaintiffs' members of their employment? (3) Did the plaintiffs so abuse their power in relation to the defendants as to render the further doing of business in New York a practical impossibility?

The court finds a lockout occurred on October 29. The formal labor complaint filed by plaintiffs, joined in by the managers of the Association and the union through their deputies, and the manner of its reception by the Fishmans, make that clear; the resignation of the corporations from the Association on October 31, and the secret removal of the machines the same night from New York to Archbald complete the picture.

At the outset defendants contended that the taking of the lease in Archbald was the act of Goldstein as an individual. After the latter admitted on the stand that he was a nephew of the Fishmans, that he was financially irresponsible, and that he and Abraham Fishman had conversed with the visitor from Archbald, Pa., it could no longer be doubted that he was merely a dummy for his uncles and their corporations. From the admissions of the Fishmans and regarding the siutation as a whole, it is equally clear that the intention was at one stroke to get rid of the obligations of the contract and to obtain cheaper nonunion labor in a more indulgent community. The court finds in favor of the plaintiffs on this point also.

There is a close relation, in law as well as fact, between the second and third points. The date of the Archbald lease was October 10. The earliest New York cases accept the principle, now regarded as elementary, that a party contemplating rescission must elect between that remedy and the course of pursuing his contract rights; that he may not accept acts insisted on as performance by the other party and then be permitted to rescind. Genet v. President, etc., of Delaware & H. Canal Co., 28 App. Div. 328, 51 N.Y.S. 377. The principle was expressly extended to labor union cases by this court in Schlesinger v. Quinto, 117 Misc. 735, 192 N.Y.S. 564, affirmed 201 App. Div. 487, 194 N.Y.S. 401, where Wagner, J., said, in commenting on a somewhat similar situation: "It therefore, as far as the purposes of this motion are concerned, becomes unnecessary and immaterial to decide whether, prior to June 3, 1921, either of the parties had violated or breached the conditions of the agreement. Whatever had before occurred was to all intents waived by both." (117 Misc. 735, 743, 192 N.Y.S. 564, at page 568.)

Apart from this principle of law, the significance of the date of the signing of the lease, October 10, lies in its relation to the date of the alleged general strike, October 19. The court finds from all the facts that no general strike or any strike occurred on or about that date, and is of opinion that the claim was put forward by defendants to becloud the issue by meeting in advance the plaintiffs' claim of waiver.

There was a strike, or stoppage of work, on July 24, conducted spontaneously by the shop girls of Blue Dale in sympathy with defendants' shipping clerks then on strike. It was disavowed by the union, and the girls returned to work the same afternoon. There was a strike of cutters on July 29, attributable to their belief that the Fishmans were themselves violating the agreement by cutting at night. It was called by the union, contrary to the agreement. The Fishmans appealed to the principle of arbitration and were sustained by the impartial chairman. The union promptly notified the cutters to return to work but, partly because they were informed of the decision on a Friday afternoon with two nonworking days to follow, partly perhaps through the dissatisfaction of the men themselves, their return was delayed until the following Tuesday or Wednesday. However, the defendants did not complain of noncompliance nor, as they had the right to do under the agreement, hire other cutters. Apparently the explanation is that the Fishmans had plenty of work already cut in advance so did not care. At all events the defendants invoked in each of these two cases their rights under the contract and in each instance obtained substantial justice from the arbitral machinery they had themselves set going.

There is considerable conflict as to other incidents after the cutters' strike and before the signing of the Pennsylvania lease. Defendants charge that the girls again struck in August, but the court accepts the testimony of the employees supported by that of the Association's manager against the Fishmans and finds no such strike occurred. There followed complaints of assault, insult, stoppages, inferior workmanship, and unequal distribution, now by one side, now by the other, but all these disputes were, so far as the record shows, adjusted informally. The July episodes got the parties off to a bad start and thereafter honors were about even on settlements and decisions. The unfortunate result seems attributable to a head-on collision between a union conscious of power and an employer with an unenviable business record, an aggressive personality, and a determination to make a success this time at all costs. The important difference between the methods adopted by the two sides is that the plaintiffs continued content with the collective agreement, while the defendants grew more and more dissatisfied with it, and when they found themselves unable to obtain its modification took the law into their own hands through the radical and conclusive step of making the Archbald lease. Their conduct thereafter has already been sufficiently discussed.

Defendants have seen fit to criticize the officers of the Association for subserviency to the union and indifference to their own members, the defendants, but these officials seem on the face of things to have done their duty. If they were not ardent defenders of these particular members an explanation simpler than disloyalty presents itself. There were other members of the Association. One of the chief objects of joining was protection against unfair competition. If plaintiffs' charges are true, it is not natural to suppose that defendants' general popularity in the Association would grow by reason of their attitude, nor could its officers be expected to register great enthusiasm for the Fishmans individually. At any rate, some of the most important assertions made by the latter as witnesses were flatly contradicted by the Association's manager and the impartial chairman. The court is unable to find evidence of any such conduct on the part of the plaintiffs as would disqualify them, on any recognized equitable theory, from asserting and maintaining their rights in the premises under the collective agreement.

It follows that defendant should be directed, so long as they remain in this industry, to comply with the terms of the collective agreement, specifically by putting all the members of plaintiffs' union whom they locked out on October 29 and thereafter back to work, or as many of them as they may have work for, anywhere; by moving back within the agreed area in New York City all the machinery and other effects hitherto removed to Archbald, since they cannot be made to abide by the contract in Pennsylvania. The language of the agreement is clear, a proper occasion is presented, and so far as any precedent exists it favors the remedy. Farulla v. Ralph A. Freundlich, Inc., 152 Misc. 761, 274 N.Y.S. 70; Id., 153 Misc. 738, 277 N.Y.S. 47, and Id., 155 Misc. 262, 279 N.Y.S. 228. The logic of the situation calls for application of strong measures. With the end of NRA (48 Stat. 195) appeared a new need for such contracts as the one in suit. Without a remedy as wide as that need, unscrupulous employers of labor will be tempted to play one community off against another, unlawfully depriving New York City of her business and her inhabitants of their livelihood. For a discussion of the entire subject, see "Legal Problems Raised by the Relocation of Industry: The Runaway Shop," 36 Col. Law Rev. 776.

It has been suggested that this court may lack jurisdiction or find that a thoroughgoing decree cannot be enforced. Neither objection appears to possess substance or validity. The Fishmans have appeared and defended, and so has their agent Goldstein. Between them they own or control the stock of both corporations, the lease in New York and the lease outside the state. The Blue Dale and Blue Fox alike are New York corporations, which still maintain offices at the old address in Manhattan. All the parties therefore who are found to have acted in concert to create the lockout and effect the removal are before the court and subject to its mandate.

The defendants also should be compelled to account to the plaintiffs by reason of the lockout, and a referee will be appointed to compute the compensatory damages sustained by members of the plaintiff union.

Settle decree accordingly.[1]

---

[1] For comment on the case, see: 50 Harv. L. Rev. 700 (1937); 5 I.J.A. Bull. 97 (1937).

For cases enforcing closed shop agreements, see: Mississippi Theatres Corp. v. Hattiesburg Local Union, 174 Miss. 439, 164 So. 887 (1936); De Agostina v. Parkshire Ridge Amusements, Inc., 155 Misc. 518, 278 N.Y.S. 662 (1935), with which compare De Agostina v. Holmden, 157 Misc. 819, 285 N.Y.S. 909 (1935), and New York cases cited Landis 101, n. 6. See also Wasserstein v. Beim, 294 N.Y.S. 439 (N. Y. Sup. Ct., N. Y. Co., 1936), enforcing trade agreement and rejecting defense based on strike as duress. Cf. Upholsterers', etc., International Union v. Essex, etc., Co., 12 N.J. Misc. 637, 174 Atl. 207 (1934), in which the union was denied enforcement of a closed shop agreement as tending to monopoly by virtue of the fact that similar agreements had been made with 52 of 80 employers in the area. But see: Farulla v. Freundlich, 152 Misc. 761, 763, 274 N.Y.S. 70 (1934); American Fur Mfgrs. Ass'n v. Associated etc. Mfgrs., 161 Misc. 246, 291 N.Y.S. 610 (1936), aff'd in the Appellate Division, N.Y.L.J., May 15, 1937, 2453, Col. 6.

On the extended litigation in Farulla v. Freundlich, 155 Misc. 262, 279 N.Y.S. 228 (1935), see Note, "Legal Problems Raised by the Relocation of Industry: The Runaway Shop," 36 Col. L. Rev. 776 (1936), and for the sequel, see In the Matter of Ralph A. Freundlich, Inc., and Max Marcus, Case No. C-78, 2 N.L.R.B. ...... (1937).

For the remedial action which the National Labor Relations Board requires the "runaway" employer to take, see: In the Matter of S. & K. Knee Pants Co. and Amalgamated Clothing Workers, Case No. C-106, 2 N.L.R.B. ...... (1937). Cf. In the Matter of Remington Rand and Remington Rand, etc., Board, Case No. C-145, 2 N.L.R.B. ...... (1937), post, p. 169.

See also: Fuchs, "Collective Labor Agreements," 35 Col. L. Rev. 493 (1935); Simpson, "Fifty Years of American Equity," 50 Harv. L. Rev. 171 (1936) 193 et seq.

The theory that the relation of the individual employee to the trade agreement applying to his employment is that of a third party beneficiary (Johnson v. American Ry. Express Co., 163 S.C. 198, 161 S.E. 473 (1931), Landis 361) is apparently gaining ground in the cases: Rentschler v. Missouri Pac. R., 126 Neb. 493, 253 N.W. 694 (1934); Youmans v. Charleston & W. C. Ry., 175 S.C. 99, 178 S.E. 671 (1935); Dierschow v. West Suburban Dairies, Inc., 276 Ill. App. 355 (1934); Volquardsen v. Southern Amusement Co., 156 So. 678 (La., App., 1934); see Beatty v. Chicago, B. & Q. R., 49 Wyo. 22, 52 P.(2d) 404 (1935), with which compare Lambert v. Georgia Power Co., 183 S.E. 814 (Ga., 1936), and Louisville & N. Ry. v. Bryant, 263 Ky. 578, 92 S.W. (2d) 749 (1936). However, the doctrine that the trade agreement merely establishes a usage (Moody v. Model Window Glass Co., 145 Ark. 197, 224 S.W. 436 (1920), Landis 358) is still followed: Burton v. Oregon-Washington R. & Nav. Co., 148 Ore. 648, 38 P.(2d) 72 (1934); Unkovich v. N. Y. Central R. R., 117 N.J. Eq. 20, 174 Atl. 876 (1934). See also: Donovan v. Travers, 285 Mass. 167, 188 N.E. 705 (1934); Mueller v. Chi. & N. W. Ry., 194 Minn. 83, 259 N.W. 798 (1935); Yazoo & M. V. R. R. v. Mitchell, 161 So. 860 (Miss., 1935); Anderson, "Collective Bargaining Agreements," 15 Ore. L. Rev. 229 (1933); Christenson, "Seniority Rights Under Labor Union Working Agreements," 11 Temp. L.Q. 355 (1937).

CHAPTER II

THE LEGISLATURES AND THE INJUNCTION

SENN v. TILE LAYERS PROTECTIVE UNION

Supreme Court of the United States, 57 S. Ct. 857 (1937).

MR. JUSTICE BRANDEIS delivered the opinion of the Court.

This case presents the question whether the provisions of the Wisconsin Labor Code which authorize giving publicity to labor disputes, declare peaceful picketing and patrolling lawful and prohibit granting of an injunction against such conduct, violate, as here construed and applied, the due process clause or equal protection clause of the Fourteenth Amendment.

The Labor Code occupies sections 103.51 to 103.63 of the Wisconsin Statutes, 1935 (Wis. Laws, 1931, c. 376; Laws, 1935, c. 551, sec. 5). But only the following provisions of section 103.53 are directly involved on this appeal:

"(1) The following acts, whether performed singly or in concert, shall be legal: . . .

"(e) Giving publicity to and obtaining or communicating information regarding the existence of, or the facts involved in, any dispute, whether by advertising, speaking, patrolling any public street or any place where any person or persons may lawfully be, without intimidation or coercion, or by any other method not involving fraud, violence, breach of the peace, or threat thereof. . . .

"(1) Peaceful picketing or patrolling, whether engaged in singly or in numbers, shall be legal.[1]

"(2) No court, nor any judge or judges thereof, shall have jurisdiction to issue any restraining order, or temporary or permanent injunction which, in specific or general terms, prohibits any person or persons from doing, whether singly or in concert, any of the foregoing acts."

On December 28, 1935, Senn brought this suit in the Circuit Court of Milwaukee County, against Tile Layers Protective Union,

---

[1] Subsections (h), (i) and (k) are likewise relevant to the present issue, as supplementing subsections (e) and (1), but do not require special discussion.

44

Local No. 5, Tile Layers Helpers Union, Local No. 47, and their business agents, seeking an injunction to restrain picketing, and particularly "publishing, stating or proclaiming that the plaintiff is unfair to organized labor or to the defendant unions"; and also to restrain some other acts which have since been discontinued, and are not now material. The defendants answered; and the case was heard upon extensive evidence. The trial court found the following facts:

The journeymen tile layers at Milwaukee were, to a large extent, members of Tile Layers Protective Union, Local No. 5, and the helpers, members of Tile Layers Helpers Union, Local No. 47. Senn was engaged at Milwaukee in the tile contracting business under the name of "Paul Senn & Co., Tile Contracting." His business was a small one, conducted, in the main, from his residence, with a showroom elsewhere. He employed one or two journeymen tile layers and one or two helpers, depending upon the amount of work he had contracted to do at the time. But, working with his own hands with tools of the trade, he performed personally on the jobs much work of a character commonly done by a tile layer or a helper. Neither Senn, nor any of his employees, was at the time this suit was begun a member of either union, and neither had any contractual relations with them. Indeed, Senn could not become a member of the tile layers union, since its constitution and rules require, among other things, that a journeyman tile setter shall have acquired his practical experience through an apprenticeship of not less than three years, and Senn had not served such an apprenticeship.

For some years the tile laying industry had been in a demoralized state because of lack of building operations; and members of the union had been in competition with non-union tile layers and helpers in their effort to secure work. The tile contractors by whom members of the unions were employed had entered into collective bargaining agreements with the unions governing wages, hours and working conditions. The wages paid by the union contractors had for some time been higher than those paid by Senn to his employees.

Because of the peculiar composition of the industry, which consists of employers with small numbers of employees, the unions had found it necessary for the protection of the individual rights of their members in the prosecution of their trade to require all employers agreeing to conduct a union shop to assent to the following provision:

"Article III. It is definitely understood that no individual, member of a partnership or corporation engaged in the Tile Contracting Business shall work with the tools or act as Helper but that the installation of all materials claimed by the party of the second part as listed under the caption 'Classification of Work' in this agreement, shall be done by journeymen members of Tile Layers Protective Union Local #5."

The unions endeavored to induce Senn to become a union contractor; and requested him to execute an agreement in form substantially identical with that entered into by the Milwaukee contractors who employ union men. Senn expressed a willingness to execute the agreement provided article III was eliminated. The union declared that this was impossible; that the inclusion of the provision was essential to the unions' interest in maintaining wage standards and spreading work among their members; and, moreover, that to eliminate article III from the contract with Senn would discriminate against existing union contractors, all of whom had signed agreements containing the article. As the unions declared its elimination impossible, Senn refused to sign the agreement and unionize his shop. Because of his refusal, the unions picketed his place of business. The picketing was peaceful, without violence, and without any unlawful act. The evidence was that the pickets carried one banner with the inscription "P. Senn Tile Company is unfair to the Tile Layers Protective Union," another with the inscription "Let the Union tile layer install your tile work."[2]

The trial court denied the injunction and dismissed the bill. On the findings made, it ruled that the controversy was "a labor dispute" within the meaning of section 103.62; that the picketing, done solely in furtherance of the dispute, was "lawful" under section 103.53; that it was not unlawful for the defendants "to advise, notify or persuade, without fraud, violence or threat thereof, any person or persons, of the existence of said labor dispute; . . .

"That the agreement submitted by the defendants to the plaintiff, setting forth terms and conditions prevailing in that portion of the industry which is unionized, is sought by the defendants for the purpose of promoting their welfare and enhancing their own interests in their trade and craft as workers in the industry.

---

[2] The complaint as to certain action of defendants other than the picketing was disposed of by defendants' agreement to discontinue the same, and is not now in question. It had been shown that, with a view to picketing Senn's jobs, the unions had caused his automobile to be followed from his place of business to the jobs where he and his men were working. It had also been shown that, some months earlier, the unions had sent letters to local architects and contractors requesting them not to patronize Senn because he was conducting a non-union shop and threatening to picket them if they did so but that there had been no picketing of any architect or contractor and no such steps had been taken by the unions. Through counsel, the unions agreed: (1) That thereafter they would not pursue plaintiff's automobile from his residence to his jobs; and (2) that they would refrain from sending any further letters to architects or contractors, and would not indulge in any acts or conduct referred to in the letters theretofore sent. The court treated this agreement by counsel as disposing of the claim for relief on this ground.

"That Article III of said agreement is a reasonable and lawful rule adopted by the defendants out of the necessities of employment within the industry and for the protection of themselves as workers and craftsmen in the industry."

Senn appealed to the Supreme Court of the state, which affirmed the judgment of the trial court and denied a motion for rehearing, two judges dissenting. 222 Wis. 383, 268 N.W. 270, 274, 872. The case is here on appeal.

First. The defendants moved to dismiss the appeal for want of jurisdiction. They contend that the federal question presented is not substantial. And friends of the court suggest that the appeal should be dismissed because the decision below was based upon non-federal grounds, or that there was an alternative, independent non-federal ground broad enough to sustain the judgment; that the challenge here is not to a statute, but to a judicial decision based upon principles of general law which have been approved by some judges and disapproved by others;[3] and that there is nothing to show that the provisions of the Wisconsin Labor Code here questioned are not merely declaratory of the common law of Wisconsin as it existed prior to the statute. But it sufficiently appears that the provisions of the Labor Code were relied upon; that their validity under the Fourteenth Amendment was duly challenged below; and that the rulings by the state courts were based ultimately on the Labor Code. Whether the statute as construed and applied violates the Fourteenth Amendment presents issues never expressly passed upon by this Court. We deny the motion to dismiss.

Second. The hearings below were concerned mainly with questions of state law. Senn insisted there that the statute was no defense, because the controversy was not a "labor dispute" within the meaning of section 103.62.[4] The courts ruled that the controversy was a "labor dispute";[5] and that the acts done by the de-

---

[3] Compare Zaat v. Building Trades Council, 172 Wash. 445, 20 F.(2d) 589; Roraback v. Motion Pictures Operator's Union, 140 Minn. 481, 168 N.W. 766, 169 N.W. 529, 3 A.L.R. 1290; Hughes v. Motion Pictures Machine Operator's Union, 282 Mo. 304, 221 S.W. 95; Finke v. Schwartz, 28 Ohio N.P. 407. See Thompson v. Boekhout, 249 App. Div. 77, 291 N.Y.S. 572.

[4] That section provides:

"The term 'labor dispute' includes any controversy concerning terms or conditions of employment, or concerning the association or representation of persons in negotiating, fixing, maintaining, changing, or seeking to arrange terms or conditions of employment, or concerning employment relations, or any other controversy arising out of the respective interests of employer and employe, regardless of whether or not the disputants stand in the proximate relation of employer and employe."

[5] Accord, in holding that a case involves or grows out of a labor dispute within the meaning of the Norris-LaGuardia Act (47 U.S. Stat. 70, c. 90) and state anti-injunction statutes, infra, note 8, even though none of plaintiff's employees are members of defendant union: Cinderella Theatre Co. v. Sign Writers' Local Union, 6 F. Supp. 164 (E.D. Mich., 1934); Dean v. Mayo, 8 F. Supp. 73 (W.D. La., 1934), injunction granted on amended bill, 9 F. Supp. 459 (1934), aff'd, sub. nom. Mayo v. Dean, 82 F.(2d) 554 (C.C.A. 5th, 1936); S. S. Kresge Co. v. Amsler, C.C.H. Labor Law Serv., par. 16393 (E.D. Mo.,

fendant were among those declared "lawful" by section 103.53.
See, also, American Furniture Co. v. I. B. etc. Chauffeurs etc. General Local No. 200, 222 Wis. 338, 268 N.W. 250, 106 A.L.R. 335.[6]
Those issues involved the construction and application of the statute and the Constitution of the state. As to them the judgment of its highest court is conclusive. The question for our decision is whether the statute, as applied to the facts found, took Senn's liberty or property or denied him equal protection of the laws in violation of the Fourteenth Amendment. Senn does not claim broadly that the Federal Constitution prohibits a state from authorizing publicity and peaceful picketing. His claim of invalidity is rested on the fact that he refused to unionize his shop solely because the union insisted upon the retention of article III. He contends that the right to work in his business with his own hands is a right guaranteed by the Fourteenth Amendment and that the state may not authorize unions to employ publicity and picketing to induce him to refrain from exercising it.

The unions concede that Senn, so long as he conducts a non-union shop, has the right to work with his hands and tools. He may do so, as freely as he may work his employees longer hours and at lower wages than the union rules permit. He may bid for contracts at a low figure based upon low wages and long hours. But

---

1937); Miller Parlor Furniture Co. v. Furniture Workers' Industrial Union, 8 F. Supp. 209 (D.N.J., 1934); George B. Wallace Co. v. International Association of Mechanics, 63 P.(2d) 1909 (Ore., 1936); see Starr v. Laundry, etc., Workers' Local Union No. 101, 63 P.(2d) 1104, 1110 (Ore., 1936); Dr. Lietzman v. Radio Broadcasting Station W. C. F. L., 282 Ill. App. 203 (1935); Restful Slipper Co. v. United Shoe & Leather Union, 116 N.J. Eq. 521, 174 Atl. 543 (1934). But cf. cases cited infra, note 6, and Thompson v. Boekhout, 273 N.Y. 390, 7 N.E. (2d) 674 (1937): "The application of section 876-a of the Civil Practice Act is confined to injunctions in cases 'involving or growing out of a labor dispute.' The Legislature has in the same section defined 'labor disputes.' That definition makes clear the intent of the Legislature to subject injunctions issued in disputes involving or growing out of the relations of employer and employee to special regulations deemed appropriate to the nature of such disputes. Where the owner of a small business seeks to avoid 'labor disputes' as defined in the statute, by running his business without any employees, an attempt to induce or coerce him to hire an employee or employees, upon terms and conditions satisfactory to persons associated in such attempted inducement or coercion is not a 'labor dispute' within the letter or spirit of the statutory definition. We hold that the statute has no application in this case." See similar cases arising in absence of statute cited Landis 244, n. 1. See also: Jensen v. St. Paul M. P. O. Union, 194 Minn. 58, 59 N.W. 811 (1935); Samuel Hertzig Corp. v. Gibbs, 3 N.E. (2d) 831 (Mass., 1936).—Ed.

[6] In the case cited, the court denied an injunction against picketing for a closed shop agreement with an employer none of whose employees belonged to the picketing union. Contra: Lauf v. Shinner, 82 F.(2d) 68 (C.C.A. 7th, 1936), 90 F.(2d) 250 (C.C.A. 7th, 1937); Colonial Baking Co. v. Hatenbach, C.C.H. Labor Law Serv., par. 16051, (E.D. Tenn., 1934); Safeway Stores v. Retail Clerks' Union, 184 Wash. 322, 51 P.(2d) 322 (1935), arising under statute later declared unconstitutional in Blanchard v. Golden Age Brewing Co., 63 P.(2d) 397 (Wash., 1936). Cf. New Negro Alliance v. Sanitary Grocery Co., C.C.H. Labor Law Serv., par. 16400 (App. D.C., 1937); Donnelly Garment Co. v. International L. G. W. Union, (W.D. Mo., August 13, 1937). See comments: 31 Ill. L. Rev. 688 (1937); 35 Mich. L. Rev. 340 (1935); 84 U. of Pa. L. Rev. 771, 1027 (1936); 46 Yale L.J. 1067 (1937).—Ed.

the unions contend that, since Senn's exercise of the right to do so is harmful to the interests of their members, they may seek by legal means to induce him to agree to unionize his shop and to refrain from exercising his right to work with his own hands. The judgment of the highest court of the state establishes that both the means employed and the end sought by the unions are legal under its law. The question for our determination is whether either the means or the end sought is forbidden by the Federal Constitution.

Third. Clearly the means which the statute authorizes—picketing and publicity—are not prohibited by the Fourteenth Amendment. Members of a union might, without special statutory authorization by a state, make known the facts of a labor dispute, for freedom of speech is guaranteed by the Federal Constitution. The state may, in the exercise of its police power, regulate the methods and means of publicity as well as the use of public streets. If the end sought by the unions is not forbidden by the Federal Constitution the state may authorize working men to seek to attain it by combining as pickets, just as it permits capitalists and employers to combine in other ways to attain their desired economic ends. The Legislature of Wisconsin has declared that "peaceful picketing and patrolling" on the public streets and places shall be permissible "whether engaged in singly or in numbers" provided this is done "without intimidation or coercion" and free from "fraud, violence, breach of the peace or threat thereof." The statute provides that the picketing must be peaceful; and that term as used implies not only absence of violence, but absence of any unlawful act. It precludes the intimidation of customers. It precludes any form of physical obstruction or interference with the plaintiff's business. It authorizes giving publicity to the existence of the dispute "whether by advertising, speaking, patrolling any public street or any place where any person or persons may lawfully be"; but precludes misrepresentation of the facts of the controversy. And it declares that "nothing herein shall be construed to legalize a secondary boycott." See Duplex Printing Press Co. v. Deering, 254 U.S. 443, 466, 41 S. Ct. 172, 176, 65 L. Ed. 349, 16 A.L.R. 196. Inherently, the means authorized are clearly unobjectionable. In declaring such picketing permissible Wisconsin has put this means of publicity on a par with advertisements in the press.

The state courts found that the unions observed the limitations prescribed by the statute. The conduct complained of is patrol with banners by two or four pickets. Compare American Steel Foundries v. Tri-City Central Trade Council, 257 U.S. 184, 207, 42 S. Ct. 72, 77, 66 L. Ed. 189, 27 A.L.R. 360. The picketing was peaceful. The publicity did not involve a misrepresentation of

fact; nor was any claim made below that relevant facts were suppressed. Senn did not contend that it was untruthful to characterize him as "unfair," if the requirement that he refrain from working with his own hands was a lawful one. He did not ask that the
banners be required to carry a fuller statement of the facts. Compare American Furniture Co. v. I. B. etc. Chauffeurs etc. General
Local No. 200, 222 Wis. 338, 340, 347, 268 N.W. 250, 251, 255, 106
A.L.R. 335. Moreover, it was confessedly open to Senn to disclose
the facts in such manner and in such detail as he deemed desirable,
and on the strength of the facts to seek the patronage of the public.

Truax v. Corrigan, 257 U.S. 312, 42 S. Ct. 124, 128, 66 L. Ed.
254, 27 A.L.R. 375, is not applicable. The statute there in question
was deemed to have been applied to legalize conduct which was not
simply peaceful picketing, not "lawful persuasion or inducing," not
"a mere appeal to the sympathetic aid of would-be customers by a
simple statement of the fact of the strike and a request to withhold patronage." It consisted of libelous attacks and abusive epithets against the employer and his friends; libelous and disparag-
ing statements against the plaintiff's business; threats and intimidation directed against customers and employees. The means employed, in other words, were deemed to constitute "an admitted
tort," conduct unlawful prior to the statute challenged. See 257
U.S. 312. at pp. 327, 328, 337, 346, 42 S. Ct. 124, 127, 128, 131,
134, 66 L. Ed. 254, 27 A.L.R. 375. In the present case the only
means authorized by the statute and in fact resorted to by the
unions have been peaceful and accompanied by no unlawful
act. It follows, that if the end sought is constitutional—if the
unions may constitutionally induce Senn to agree to refrain from
exercising the right to work in his business with his own hands,
their acts were lawful.

Fourth. The end sought by the unions is not unconstitutional.
Article III, which the unions seek to have Senn accept, was found
by the state courts to be not arbitrary or capricious, but a reasonable rule "adopted by the defendants out of the necessities of employment within the industry and for the protection of themselves
as workers and craftsmen in the industry." That finding is amply
supported by the evidence. There is no basis for a suggestion that
the unions' request that Senn refrain from working with his own
hands, or their employment of picketing and publicity, was malicious; or that there was a desire to injure Senn. The sole purpose of the picketing was to acquaint the public with the facts and,
by gaining its support, to induce Senn to unionize his shop. There
was no effort to induce Senn to do an unlawful thing. There was
no violence, no force was applied, no molestation or interference,
no coercion. There was only the persuasion incident to publicity.
As the Supreme Court of Wisconsin said:

"Each of the contestants is desirous of the advantage of doing business in the community where he or they operate. He is not obligated to yield to the persuasion exercised upon him by respondents. . . . The respondents do not question that it is appellant's right to own his own business and earn his living in any lawful manner which he chooses to adopt. What they are doing is asserting their rights under the acts of the Legislature for the purpose of enhancing their opportunity to acquire work for themselves and those whom they represent. . . . The respondents' act of peaceful picketing is a lawful form of appeal to the public to turn its patronage from appellant to the concerns in which the welfare of the members of the unions is bound up."

The unions acted, and had the right to act as they did, to protect the interests of their members against the harmful effect upon them of Senn's action. Compare American Steel Foundries v. Tri-City Central Trades Council, supra, 257 U.S. 184, 208, 209, 42 S. Ct. 72, 78, 66 L. Ed. 189, 27 A.L.R. 360. Because his action was harmful, the fact that none of Senn's employees was a union member, or sought the union's aid, is immaterial.

The laws of Wisconsin, as declared by its highest court, permits unions to endeavor to induce an employer, when unionizing his shop, to agree to refrain from working in his business with his own hands—so to endeavor although none of his employees is a member of a union. Whether it was wise for the state to permit the unions to do so is a question of its public policy—not our concern. The Fourteenth Amendment does not prohibit it.

Fifth. There is nothing in the Federal Constitution which forbids unions from competing with nonunion concerns for customers by means of picketing as freely as one merchant competes with another by means of advertisements in the press, by circulars, or by his window display. Each member of the unions, as well as Senn, has the right to strive to earn his living. Senn seeks to do so through exercise of his individual skill and planning. The union members seek to do so through combination. Earning a living is dependent upon securing work; and securing work is dependent upon public favor. To win the patronage of the public each may strive by legal means. Exercising its police power, Wisconsin has declared that in a labor dispute peaceful picketing and truthful publicity are means legal for unions. It is true that disclosure of the facts of the labor dispute may be annoying to Senn even if the method and means employed in giving the publicity are inherently unobjectionable. But such annoyance, like that often suffered from publicity in other connections, is not an invasion of the liberty guaranteed by the Constitution. Compare Pennsylvania Railroad Co. v. United States Railroad Labor Board, 261 U.S. 72, 43 S. Ct.

278, 67 L. Ed. 536.[7] It is true, also, that disclosure of the facts may prevent Senn from securing jobs which he hoped to get. But a hoped-for job is not property guaranteed by the Constitution. And the diversion of it to a competitor is not an invasion of a constitutional right.

Sixth. It is contended that in prohibiting an injunction the statute denied to Senn equal protection of the laws, and Truax v. Corrigan, supra, is invoked. But the issue suggested by plaintiff does not arise. For we hold that the provisions of the Wisconsin statute which authorized the conduct of the unions are constitutional. One has no constitutional right to a "remedy" against the lawful conduct of another.

Affirmed.

MR. JUSTICE BUTLER dissenting. Plaintiff is a tile layer and has long been accustomed to work as a helper and mechanic in that trade. The question presented is whether, consistently with the due process and equal protection clauses of the Fourteenth Amendment, the state may by statute authorize or make it lawful for labor unions to adopt and carry into effect measures intended and calculated to prevent him from obtaining or doing that work. The decision just announced answers that question in the affirmative. The facts are not in controversy. Let them disclose the concrete application of the legislation now held valid.

Plaintiff lives and works in Milwaukee. Since the latter part of 1931 he has been engaged in performing small tile laying jobs. He has personally performed almost half the manual labor required. He usually employs a tile setter and helper; occasionally he has more than one of each. He has never been a member of the tile layers union. Though a competent mechanic in that trade, he is excluded from membership because he takes contracts and because he has not served the apprenticeship required by union rules. In 1935 he had about 40 jobs. His net income was $1,500 of which $750 was attributed to his own labor. The balance, constituting his profit as contractor, was not enough to support him and family.

Defendant Local No. 5 is composed of tile layers. Its membership, 112 in 1929, had fallen to 41 at the time of the trial in January, 1936. Early in 1935 it proffered to all local contractors including plaintiff a contract fixing wages, hours and the like. About half of them signed; the others did not. It contained the following: "It is definitely understood that no individual, member

---

[7] The state has, of course, power to afford protection to interests of personality, such as "the right of privacy." The protection by decision or statute of such interests of personality rests on other considerations than are here involved. See Moreland, The Right of Privacy Today, (1931) 19 Ky. L.J. 101; Lisle, The Right of Privacy, 19 Ky. L.J. 137; Green, The Right of Privacy, (1932) 27 Ill. L. Rev. 237, 238.

of a partnership or corporation engaged in the Tile Contracting Business shall work with the tools or act as Helper, but that the installation of all materials claimed by the party of the second part [Local No. 5] as listed under the caption 'Classification of Work' in this agreement, shall be done by journeymen members of Tile Layers Protective Union Local #5." Because of that provision plaintiff declined to sign. But repeatedly he declared to representatives of the union that he was willing to employ its members and to comply with its rules as to wages, hours, and working conditions; he assured them that, when his business was sufficient to permit, he would refrain from manual labor, and explained that without personally working he could not now continue in business. Conceding the truth of that statement, the union nevertheless persistently declined to modify its demands.

The president of Local No. 5 testified that, if plaintiff did not sign the contract, it would do everything "to harass and put things in his way"; that it intended to announce to the world that he is a nonunion contractor and on that account should not be patronized, to picket his place of business, to ascertain where he had jobs and to picket them and in that way bring pressure to bear upon him to become a union contractor, to put him in the category of a non-union contractor unless he agrees to lay aside the tools of the trade. The program so declared corresponds with what the unions had already done against him.

In July, 1935, Local No. 5 sent to all contractors and architects letters stating: "Some time ago we presented to each individual tile contractor in the city a copy of our new agreement [this refers to the one plaintiff was called on to sign] in which we specified what constitutes a bona fide contractor and who should install the work. Not having heard from some of these so called tile contractors in a given time, we beg of you to contact the list of fair contractors listed below in awarding the tile work in your building operations. If in two weeks time anyone outside this list is awarded tile work we will then picket such jobs, contractors' or architects' offices, or employ other lawful means to help us in our fight to better the conditions of our trade." Plaintiff's name was not on the list approved by the union. Therefore the letter meant that, in order to prevent him from working, the union would apply the described pressure to him, his work, the jobs of which his tile laying was a part, the contractors and the architects from whom he got work.

Commencing December 6, 1935, it put in front of his house two men carrying signs, one being: "P. Senn Tile Company [meaning the plaintiff] is unfair to the Tile Layers Protective Union," and the other: "Let the Union tile layers install your tile work." And regularly from 8 in the morning until noon and from 1 to

4 in the afternoon it carried on picketing of that sort, sometimes using four men. They refrained from speaking to plaintiff
or others and committed no breach of the peace. In that sense
they carried on "peaceful picketing." The union sent men in automobiles to follow plaintiff when going from his home to his work,
and instructed all its members to discover where he had jobs in
order to picket them.

To justify the elimination of plaintiff, counsel told the court
that "because of the demoralized condition of the trade, the union
decides it does not want a contractor, whether he be skilled in the
trade or unskilled, to work with the tools of the trade with the
men because there is not enough work to go around." And on the
witness stand the president of Local No. 5 expressed the idea that,
if the contractors did not work, members of the union would be
taken off relief.

The trial court found the picketing peaceful and lawful; it did
not pass on other acts constituting pressure put on plaintiff. But
the unions themselves deemed unlawful much that they had
threatened and done to coerce him. The findings say that "the
defendants, by their counsel, have stated in open court that they
will not pursue the automobile of the plaintiff from his place of
business to his jobs; that they will refrain from sending any further letters to architects or contractors, and will not indulge in
any acts or conduct referred to in said letters towards said contractors and architects." The trial court held plaintiff not entitled
to relief. The supreme court affirmed. 222 Wis. 383, 268 N.W. 270,
872. Following its decision in American Furn. Co. v. I. B. of T. C.
& H., 222 Wis. 338, 268 N.W. 250, 106 A.L.R. 335, construing section 103.62, it held that within the meaning of that section a "labor
dispute" existed between plaintiff and defendants and that under
section 103.53 the picketing was legal.

The clauses of the Fourteenth Amendment invoked by plaintiff are: "No State shall . . . deprive any person of life, liberty,
or property without due process of law; nor deny to any person
within its jurisdiction the equal protection of the laws." Our decisions have made it everywhere known that these provisions forbid state action which would take from the individual the right
to engage in common occupations of life, and that they assure
equality of opportunity to all under like circumstances. Lest the
importance or wisdom of these great declarations be forgotten or
neglected, there should be frequent recurrence to decisions of this
court that expound and apply them.

"While this Court has not attempted to define with exactness
the liberty thus guaranteed, the term has received much consideration and some of the included things have been definitely stated.
Without doubt, it denotes not merely freedom from bodily restraint

but also the right of the individual to contract, to engage in any of the common occupations of life, to acquire useful knowledge, to marry, establish a home and bring up children, to worship God according to the dictates of his own conscience, and generally to enjoy those privileges long recognized at common law as essential to the orderly pursuit of happiness by free men." Meyer v. Nebraska, 262 U.S. 390, 399, 43 S. Ct. 625, 626, 67 L. Ed. 1042, 29 A.L.R. 1446.

"The right to follow any of the common occupations of life is an inalienable right. It was formulated as such under the phrase 'pursuit of happiness' in the Declaration of Independence, which commenced with the fundamental proposition that 'all men are created equal, that they are endowed by their Creator with certain inalienable rights; that among these are life, liberty and the pursuit of happiness.' . . . I hold that the liberty of pursuit—the right to follow any of the ordinary callings of life—is one of the privileges of a citizen of the United States." Concurring opinion of Mr. Justice Bradley in Butchers' Union Co. v. Crescent City Co., 111 U.S. 746, 762, 4 S. Ct. 652, 657, 28 L. Ed. 585, approvingly quoted in Allgeyer v. Louisiana, 165 U.S. 578, 589, 17 S. Ct. 427, 41 L. Ed. 832.

"Included in the right of personal liberty and the right of private property—partaking of the nature of each—is the right to make contracts for the acquisition of property. Chief among such contracts is that of personal employment by which labor and other services are exchanged for money or other forms of property. If this right be struck down or arbitrarily interfered with, there is a substantial impairment of liberty in the long-established constitutional sense. The right is as essential to the laborer as to the capitalist, to the poor as to the rich; for the vast majority of persons have no other honest way to begin to acquire property, save by working for money." Coppage v. Kansas, 236 U.S. 1, 14, 35 S. Ct. 240, 243, 59 L. Ed. 441, L.R.A. 1915C, 960.

"It requires no argument to show that the right to work for a living in the common occupations of the community is of the very essence of the personal freedom and opportunity that it was the purpose of the Amendments to secure." Truax v. Raich, 239 U.S. 33, 41, 36 S. Ct. 7, 10, 60 L. Ed. 131, L.R.A. 1916D, 545, Ann. Cas. 1917B, 283.

"Under that amendment, nothing is more clearly settled than that it is beyond the power of a state, 'under the guise of protecting the public, arbitrarily [to] interfere with private business or prohibit lawful occupations or impose unreasonable and unnecessary restrictions upon them.'" New State Ice Co. v. Liebmann, 285 U.S. 262, 278, 52 S. Ct. 371, 374, 76 L. Ed. 747.

"The Fourteenth Amendment . . . undoubtedly intended not only that there should be no arbitrary deprivation of life or liberty, or arbitrary spoliation of property, but that equal protection and security should be given to all under like circumstances in the enjoyment of their personal and civil rights; that all persons should be equally entitled to pursue their happiness and acquire and enjoy property; that they should have like access to the courts of the country for the protection of their persons and property, the prevention and redress of wrongs, and the enforcement of contracts; that no impediment should be interposed to the pursuits of any one except as applied to the same pursuits by others under like circumstances; that no greater burdens should be laid upon one than are laid upon others in the same calling and condition." Barbier v. Connolly, 113 U.S. 27, 31, 5 S. Ct. 357, 359, 28 L. Ed. 923.

"For the very idea that one man may be compelled to hold his life, or the means of living, or any material right essential to the enjoyment of life, at the mere will of another, seems to be intolerable in any country where freedom prevails, as being the essence of slavery itself." Yick Wo v. Hopkins, 118 U.S. 356, 370, 6 S. Ct. 1064, 1071, 30 L. Ed. 220.

The legislative power of the state can only be exerted in subordination to the fundamental principles of right and justice which the guaranties of the due process and equal protection clauses of the Fourteenth Amendment are intended to preserve. Arbitrary or capricious exercise of that power whereby a wrongful and highly injurious invasion of rights of liberty and property is sanctioned, stripping one of all remedy, is wholly at variance with those principles. Truax v. Corrigan, 257 U.S. 312, 327, 42 S. Ct. 124, 127, 66 L. Ed. 254, 27 A.L.R. 375.

It may be assumed that the picketing, upheld in virtue of the challenged statute, lawfully might be employed in a controversy between employer and employees for the purpose of persuading the employer to increase pay, etc., and dissuading nonunion workers from displacing union members. The right of workers, parties to a labor dispute, to strike and picket peacefully to better their condition does not infringe any right of the employer. American Foundries v. Tri-City Council. 257 U.S. 184, 209, 42 S. Ct. 72, 78 L. Ed. 189, 27 A.L.R. 360; United Mine Workers v. Coronado Co., 259 U.S. 344, 386, 42 S. Ct. 570, 574, 66 L. Ed. 975, 27 A.L.R. 762; Wolff Packing Co. v. Industrial Court, 262 U.S. 522, 540, 541, 43 S. Ct. 630, 634, 635, 67 L. Ed. 1103, 27 A.L.R. 1280; Dorchy v. Kansas, 264 U.S. 286, 289, 44 S. Ct. 323, 324, 68 L. Ed. 686. But strikes or peaceful picketing for unlawful purposes are beyond any lawful sanction. The object being unlawful, the means and end are alike condemned. Dorchy v. Kansas, 272 U.S. 306, 311, 47 S. Ct. 86, 87, 71 L. Ed. 248; Toledo, A. A. & N. M. Ry. Co. v. Pennsylvania Co., (C.C.) 54 F. 730, 737-739, 19 L.R.A. 387. And see Truax v. Corrigan, supra, 257 U.S. 312, 327, 42 S. Ct. 124, 127, 66 L. Ed. 254, 27 A.L.R. 375; Exchange Bakery & Restaurant, Inc., v. Rifkin, 245 N.Y. 260, 262, 263, 157 N.E. 130.

The object that defendants seek to attain is an unlawful one.

Admittedly, it is to compel plaintiff to quit work as helper or tile layer. Their purpose is not to establish on his jobs better wages, hours, or conditions. If permitted, plaintiff would employ union men and adhere to union requirements as to pay and hours. But, solely because he works, the unions refuse to allow him to unionize and carry on his business. By picketing, the unions would prevent him working on jobs he obtained from others and so destroy that business. Then, by enforcement of their rules they would prevent him from working as a journeyman for employers approved by the union or upon any job employing union men. Adhering to the thought that there is not enough work to go around, unquestionably the union purpose is to eliminate him from all tile laying work. And highly confirmatory of that purpose is the failure of the contract proposed by the union to permit plaintiff personally to do work in the performance of jobs undertaken by him for prices based upon union rates of pay for all labor, including his own.

The principles governing competition between rival individuals seeking contracts or opportunity to work as journeymen cannot reasonably be applied in this case. Neither the union nor its members take tile laying contracts. Their interests are confined to employment of helpers and layers, their wages, hours of service, etc. The contest is not between unionized and other contractors or between one employer and another. The immediate issue is between the unions and plaintiff in respect of his right to work in the performance of his own jobs. If as to that they shall succeed, then will come the enforcement of their rules which make him ineligible to work as a journeyman. It cannot be said that, if he should be prevented from laboring as helper or layer, the work for union men to do would be increased. The unions exclude their members from jobs taken by non-union employers. About half the tile contractors are not unionized. More than 60 per cent. of the tile layers are non-union men. The value of plaintiff's labor as helper and tile layer is very small—about $750 per year. Between union members and plaintiff there is no immediate or direct competition. If under existing circumstances there ever can be any, it must come about through a chain of unpredictable events making its occurrence a mere matter of speculation. The interest of the unions in the manual labor done by plaintiff is so remote, indirect, and minute that they have no standing as competitors. Berry v. Donovan, 188 Mass. 353, 358, 74 N.E. 603. Under the circumstances here disclosed, the conduct of the unions was arbitrary and op-

pressive. Roraback v. Motion Picture Machine Operators' Union,
140 Minn. 481, 486, 168 N.W. 766, 169 N.W. 529, 3 A.L.R. 1290;
Hughes v. Motion Picture Machine Operators, 282 Mo. 304, 221
S.W. 95.

Moreover, the picketing was unlawful because the signs used
constitute a misrepresentation of the facts. One of them declared
plaintiff "unfair" to the tile layers union and, upon the basis of
that statement, the other sign solicited tile work for union tile
layers. There was given neither definition of the word nor any
fact on which the accusation was based. By the charge made,
there was implied something unjust or inequitable in his attitude
toward labor unions. But there was no foundation of fact for any
such accusation. There was no warrant for characterizing him as
"unfair" or opposed to any legitimate purpose of the tile layers
union or as unjust to union men. There is no escape from the
conclusion that the unions intended by the picketing they carried
on to misrepresent plaintiff in respect of his relation to, or dealing
with, the tile layers union and by that means to deprive him of his
occupation. The burden may not justly be held to be on him, by
counter-picketing or otherwise, to refute or explain the baseless
charge.

The judgment of the state court, here affirmed, violates a principle of fundamental law: That no man may be compelled to hold
his life or the means of living at the mere will of others. Yick Wo
v. Hopkins, ubi supra. The state statute, construed to make lawful
the employment of the means here shown to deprive plaintiff of his
right to work or to make lawful the picketing carried on in this
case, is repugnant to the due process and equal protection clauses
of the Fourteenth Amendment. Truax v. Corrigan, supra, 257 U.S.
312, 328, 42 S. Ct. 124, 128, 66 L. Ed. 254, 27 A.L.R. 375.

I am of opinion that the judgment should be reversed.

MR. JUSTICE VAN DEVANTER, MR. JUSTICE MCREYNOLDS and MR.
JUSTICE SUTHERLAND join in this dissent.[8]

---

[8] For comment on the case, see 6 I.J.A. Bull. 1 (1937).

See Landis 183 and 186 for the provisions of the Norris-LaGuardia Act
(47 U.S. Stat. 70, c. 90). For legislation in the states generally similar to the
federal and Wisconsin statutes, see: 1933 Colo. Laws, c. 59; 1933 Idaho Laws,
c. 215; 1933 Ind. Laws, c. 12; 1934 La. Laws, c. 203; 1935 Md. Laws, c. 574;
1933 Minn. Laws, c. 416; 1935 N.Y. Laws, c. 11, secs. 298, 299, 477; 1935 N.D.
Laws, c. 247; 1933 Ore. Laws, c. 355; 1937 Pa. Laws, Act No. 308; 1933
Utah Laws, c. 15; 1933 Wash. Laws, Spec. Sess., c. 7; 1937 Wyo. Laws, c. 37.
For more limited anti-injunction legislation, see: Ariz. Rev. Code 1928, sec.
4286; 1925 Ill. Laws, p. 378; 1913 Kansas Laws, c. 233; 1935 Mass. Laws,
c. 407; 1926 N.J. Laws, c. 207.

The following cases also sustain the constitutionality of various features
and applications of statutes limiting the issuance of injunctions: Levering &
Garrigues Co. v. Morrin, 71 F.(2d) 284 (C.C.A. 2d, 1934), cert. denied, 293
U.S. 595 (1934), Landis 184; United Electric Coal Companies v. Rice, 80 F.(2d)
1 (C.C.A. 7th, 1935), cert. denied, 297 U.S. 714 (1936), infra, p. 59; Fenske
Bros. v. Upholsterers International Union, 358 Ill. 239, 193 N.E. 112 (1934),
cert. denied, 295 U.S. 734 (1935), criticized for its narrow interpretation of

UNITED ELECTRIC COAL COMPANIES v. RICE

Circuit Court of Appeals for the Seventh Circuit, 1935. 80 F.(2d) 1.

EVANS, CIRCUIT JUDGE. Appellant, a Delaware corporation, owns and operates several coal mines in Illinois. Among them is a strip mine, near Freeburg in the County of St. Clair. Appellees are for the most part miners, former employees of appellant in the Freeburg mine. They are residents of Illinois. Appellee, First District of the Progressive Miners of America, is a voluntary, unincorporated association, composed entirely of individuals who are residents of Illinois and primarily engaged in mining coal. The other local unions, also made parties to this suit, are divisions of the Progressive Miners of America, which operate in various southern Illinois counties.

The District Court denied appellant the injunctive relief which it sought against appellees, who were charged with having wilfully and forcibly prevented the operation of the mine at Freeburg and with having damaged appellant's property and interfered with the conduct of its business.

The court found the material allegations of the complaint in appellant's favor, but denied relief because of section 8 and the public policy sections 1, 2, and 3 of the Norris-LaGuardia Act (29 USCA secs. 108, 101-103). The findings cover twenty-one pages of the transcript and are too long to be here set forth in their entirety.

The real controversy is one between two unions,—The United Mine Workers of America, hereinafter called the United; and the Progressive Miners of America, hereinafter called the Progressive.

the statute in 35 Col. L. Rev. 616 (1935) and 3 I.J.A. Bull., No. 9, 7 (1935), with which compare Rosen v. United Shoe & Leather Workers Union, 287 Ill. App. 49, 4 N.E. (2d) 507 (1936); Dehan v. Hotel & Restaurant Employees, etc., Association, 159 So. 637 (La. App., 2d, 1935); Starr v. Laundry, etc., Workers' Local Union No. 101, 63 P.(2d) 1104 (Ore., 1936); George B. Wallace Co. v. International Association of Mechanics, 63 P.(2d) 1090 (Ore., 1936); see Local Union No. 26 v. Kokomo, 5 N.E. (2d) 624 (Ind., 1937); Aberdeen Restaurant Corp. v. Gottfried, 158 Misc. 785, 285 N.Y.S. 832 (1935). Contra: Blanchard v. Golden; Age Brewing Co., 63 P.(2d) 397 (Wash., 1936), 4 U. of Chi. L. Rev. 500 (1937).

On the constitutional questions, see also the authorities cited by Landis 184, n. 10; Fraenkel, "Recent Statutes Affecting Labor Injunctions and Yellow Dog Contracts," 30 Ill. L. Rev. 854 (1936); Riddlesbarger, "State Anti-Injunction Legislation," 14 Ore. L. Rev. 501 (1935); 5 Fordham L. Rev. 125 (1936); 13 N.Y.U.L.Q. Rev. 92 (1935).

For legislation making yellow-dog contracts unenforceable, see: Norris-LaGuardia Act (47 U.S. Stat. 70, c. 90); 1931 Ariz. Laws, c. 19; 1931 Colo. Laws, p. 439, sec. 1, 1933 Colo. Laws, p. 405, sec. 2; 1933 Idaho Laws, c. 215; 1933 Ill. Laws, p. 588; 1933 Ind. Laws, c. 12; 1934 La. Laws, Nos. 202, 203; 1935 Md. Laws, c. 574; 1933 Mass. Acts, c. 351; 1933 Minn. Laws, c. 416; 1935 N.Y. Laws, c. 11; 1935 N.D. Laws, c. 247; 1931 Ohio Laws, 114v. 562; 1933 Ore. Laws, c. 355; 1937 Pa. Laws, Act. No. 308; 1933 Utah Laws, c. 15; 1931 Wis. Laws, c. 376, 1935 Wis. Laws, cs. 541, 551.

It is a bitter contest. For over two years it has been fought by the officers of these two unions. Neither group has been willing to compromise. Appellant is the innocent bystander, a victim of this unabated conflict. Appellant has no dispute with its employees. The wage scales in force apparently were satisfactory to employer and employee alike. The working conditions brought no discontent. The employees were desirous of working for appellant. With them appellant wished to operate its mine. This has been prevented by the struggle between the two unions over who should represent the employees.

The focus of the conflict, the Freeburg mine, is one of several owned and operated by appellant. Over a period of many years, appellant was under contract with United to employ only United men in its several mines unless such union employees were not available. In March, 1928, such a contract (which ran four years) was again entered into. There was then no coal miners' union other than the United. The Progressive, however, came into existence shortly after this contract expired. It sought to oust the United. It demanded recognition as the representative of the local union with which appellant must contract. United disputed Progressive's right to so speak. To secure recognition, Progressive called its members from appellant's employment. When appellant sought, on several occasions, to open its mine with men who refused to strike, the Progressive picketed the property and resorted to violence. Appellant was thereby forced to suspend operations.

We take the following fact statement from the findings of the District Court. The Freeburg property consisted of about 700 acres (owned or controlled) and it annually produced over 300,000 tons of coal. It was forced to shut down by appellees. Since March 31, 1933, the mine has operated only one day. Its damages were fixed at $350,000 up to the time of trial.

Wages and employment conditions are the subject of contract between operators and miners. The operators have their association and the miners, their union. Representatives of these two organizations meet, and the contract they enter into is binding upon them throughout the State of Illinois after the miners have approved of it. Such a contract was made March 31, 1928, and expired March 31, 1932. During this period there was but one union, and the operators spoke through their representative. When the contract was about to expire, negotiations were conducted by the officers of the two organizations, and on April 1, 1932, an agreement was reached whereby the 1928 contract was continued in force until same was terminated upon thirty days' notice or until a state-wide agreement was ratified. Shortly thereafter a state-wide agreement was executed and became effective August 10, 1932, and continued until March 31, 1933. It was over the ratification of this agreement that differences arose among the miners. Ballots were stolen and counts thwarted. The officers then declared or attempted to declare the contract in force. This contract was quite similar to the preceding one and contained the same provisions respecting the employment of members of the United. It was about this time that a large number of Illinois members of the United became dissatisfied and terminated their membership in United, and organized the Progressive. This union divided the state into locals, and the mine in question was in the jurisdiction of local No. 47. Operation of the Progressive in this district was under control of one Jones. The contest for membership and control of more laborers by the two unions was extremely bitter from the start. The character of the warfare is described in the opinion written in People v. Beacham, 358 Ill. 373, 193 N.E. 205.[1]

In September, 1932, the majority of the local union at Freeburg voted to join the Progressive. They did not, however, surrender their charter granted by the United. The same officers continued. Thereafter the war became more bitter. A demand was made upon appellant to sign a working contract with the Progressive. Pickets closed the mine. On the evening of October 18, appellant and officers of the local Progressive made arrangements whereby the men returned to work and the pay-off check was made payable to the officers of the union without designating the name of the union. The mine continued to operate under such arrangement without interruption until April, 1933, when the Progressives demanded that the appellant abrogate its contract with the United and enter into a similar one with the Progressive. This demand was refused, and, on March 31, 1933, the president of the Progressive local informed the superintendent that all operations would cease at midnight, since which time the mine has been closed, save for one day. Disorder and destruction of property have followed, and when attempts were made to open the mine, the opposition evidenced by 2500 men, more or less effectively armed, threatened the miners who resumed employment with violence and even with death.

A few employees who had rejoined the United and who sought to go to work, but were not permitted to do so, filed a complaint before the Bituminous Coal Labor Board.[2] Appellant and Progressive were both made parties. A hearing was had with all parties represented by counsel. The Board held: "That the contract between United Electric Coal Company and the United Mine Workers

---

[1] See also Stanley v. Peabody Coal Co., 5 F. Supp. 612 (S.D. Ill., 1933). —Ed.

[2] This board was created under Art. 7, sec. 5, of the Code of Fair Competition for the Bituminous Coal Industry, pursuant to the National Industrial Recovery Act (Act of June 16, 1933. 48 Stat. 198).— Ed.

of America is in force for the purpose of collective bargaining in
this mine." It further directed that its decision should be in force
for the period of six months.

The Progressive refused to accept or adopt this decision and
refused to allow the mine to open. The sheriff and other local officers declined to act or to protect appellant's property. The District Court stated:

". . . It is further obvious that the sheriff of St. Clair
County and his deputies were *both unwilling and unable* to furnish
adequate protection to plaintiff's property, and, although a new
sheriff took office during the trial of this case, he and his deputies
are and will be unable to afford such protection." 9 F. Supp. 635,
636.

Violence at the mine by members of the Progressive and their
sympathizers grew. A majority of the miners working in the mine
signed a petition asking appellant to resume operation. In securing the signatures representatives of appellant accompanied the
employees and stated that it was the only way that the employees
could hope to resume work.

The District Court stated that the men to whom the petition
(which asked appellant to reopen the mine) was presented, "were
subjected to coercion and duress *by being informed, in effect,* that
the only way they could hope to resume their former jobs in the
mine was for them to become members of United Mine Workers of America; that this statement was confirmed whenever necessary by the mine manager; . . . it does not appear how many
of those who signed said petition actually joined said local. . . ."

In disposing of the case the court also said:

". . . The evidence compels two further findings:

"First. That the policy followed by plaintiff in dealing with
its employees at the Freeburg mine which gave rise to the particular labor dispute here involved has been and is in conflict with
the public policy declared in the said Norris Act in that it has in
effect denied to its striking employees at said mine, including many
of the defendants in this case, freedom of association, self-organization, and designation of representatives of their own choosing
to negotiate the terms and conditions of their employment as well
as freedom from interference, restraint, or coercion in the designation of such representatives and in self-organization and in other
concerted activities for the purpose of collective bargaining. 29
USCA secs. 101, 102 and 103.

"Second. That the plaintiff has failed to make every reasonable effort to settle the dispute here involved by negotiation. 29
USCA sec. 108."

The significance of these two findings is disclosed by the
court's observation:

"The two findings set forth in the preceding paragraph, depriving this court as they do of jurisdiction to enjoin acts and conduct on the part of the defendants which are not only destructive but legally indefensible, are of such consequence as to demand a somewhat detailed statement of the factual situation shown by the evidence and the applicable principles of law."

The District Court has stated its views in support of the conclusions reached, and they might well be set forth in full because of their clarity if a due regard for the length of this opinion did not forbid.

The statutes involved are set forth in the margin.

To reverse the decree appellant argues:

(1) That section 108, 29 USCA—the Norris-LaGuardia Act, section 8—limiting the power of a Federal court of equity to restrain threatened injuries to property, is unconstitutional.

(2) If said Act be constitutional, it is not applicable to the facts in the instant case because (a) the controversy does not involve a labor dispute, (b) the Act does not apply where injunctions are sought to prevent injury to property, (c) if a labor dispute is involved and section 108 be construed as appellees contend, then the evidence shows appellant used "reasonable effort to settle such dispute" and that it did not fail to comply with all obligations imposed upon it by law with respect to labor disputes.

(1) Inasmuch as Congress may take from, as well as confer upon, inferior Federal courts jurisdiction of cases which involve controversies between citizens of different states (Kline v. Burke Construction Co., 260 U.S. 226, 43 S. Ct. 79, 67 L. Ed. 226, 24 A.L. R. 1077; Ex parte Robinson, 19 Wall. 505, 510, 22 L. Ed. 205; Bessette v. W. B. Conkey Co., 194 U.S. 324, 24 S. Ct. 665, 48 L. Ed. 997; Sheldon v. Sill, 8 How. (49 U.S.) 441, 449, 12 L. Ed. 1147; Levering & Garrigues Co. v. Morrin (C.C.A.) 71 F. (2d) 284), we find no support for a conclusion which would deny validity of this legislation.[3]

The legislation in question took from District Courts, jurisdiction of causes involving labor dispute injunction suits between citizens of different states, in certain limited instances, and was within the power of Congress conferred by article 3, sections 1 and 2 of the United States Constitution.

(2) Do the facts present a case "growing out of a labor dispute" or which is "involved in a labor dispute," as those two phrases are used in the Act?

Looking to the purpose, as well as to the words, of the Act, we are satisfied that the term "labor dispute" should be most

---

[3] Toledo Fence & Post Co. v. Lyons (C.C.A.) 290 F. 637; Hallowell v. Commons, 239 U.S. 506, 36 S. Ct. 202, 60 L. Ed. 409. See, also, Michaelson v. United States (C.C.A.) 291 F. 940; Id., 266 U.S. 42, 45 S. Ct. 18, 69 L. Ed. 162, 35 A.L.R. 451.

broadly and liberally construed. The term "labor disputes" comprehends disputes growing out of labor relations. It infers employment—implies the existence of the relation of employer and employee. Disputes between these parties are the general subject matter of this legislation. All such disputes seem to be clearly included.

Equally clear we think must be the conclusion that the dispute referred to in the statute *must* be one between the employer and the employee or growing directly out of their relationship. It does not apply to disputes between employees or to disputes between employee unions to which employer is not a real party. The employer is not precluded from invoking the jurisdiction of a Federal court of equity unless it appears that it was in some way a party to the dispute, between two unions.

Confirmation of this conclusion may be found in the other sections of the Act which clearly indicate that the entire Act had reference to controversies over wages and conditions of employment which arise between employer and employee and result in strikes or threatened strikes which work hardships upon the innocent third party—the public.

In seeking to avoid strikes, it was to be expected that arbitration would be encouraged and resort to court proceeding discouraged. It is quite apparent that the employer has nothing to arbitrate and no use for conciliators when it and its employees are in accord. It is hard to see what sort of arbitration or conciliation was intended if the legislation referred to anything other than to strained or striking relationships between employer and employee over wages and conditions of employment. Where the difference is between two unions, each striving to contract with the employer, and there is no controversy as to terms of employment with said employer, we are unable to see where any labor dispute exists to which the employer is a party.

Of course, there may be a seeming controversy between two unions which is in reality merely a labor dispute between the employer and employees. Such a situation falls within the meaning of the term "labor dispute." The employer may not avoid inclusion in a labor dispute if he participates in union activity which directly or indirectly influences or affects employment relations.

Subsection (c) of section 113, 29 USCA defines labor dispute as follows:

"(c) The term 'labor dispute' includes any controversy concerning terms or conditions of employment, or concerning the association or representation of persons in negotiating, fixing, maintaining, changing, or seeking to arrange terms or conditions of employment, regardless of whether or not the disputants stand in the proximate relation of employer and employee."

There was no *controversy* between appellant and appellees on any subject. Appellant's employees could join any union they wished. They could change membership in one union for that of another. They could quit work, individually or collectively. But they cannot assert they have a controversy with appellant because of the existence or exercise of such rights. They could not, with no controversy with appellant at stake, change membership in unions and then demand of appellant that it break a valid contract which it had with another union and call it a controversy.

There is no evidence which would justify us in assuming that appellant, through the United, was seeking to change the labor contract with its employees. The record shows that the terms of the contract were not in dispute. The Progressives were willing to sign the same contract which had been made for them by their previous representative, the United. We cannot escape the conclusion, therefore, that the facts in this case present no labor controversy between appellant and the mine workers. On the other hand, it clearly appears that the controversy was between two unions; that appellant was not a participant therein and was interested only because it had made a contract with one union when that union represented all of its employees including most of appellees.

Did the appellant fail to make every reasonable effort to settle the dispute either by mediation or voluntary arbitration, as required by section 108, assuming the controversy to be a labor dispute?

The findings of the District Court on this issue are against the appellant. It is sufficient to say that the evidence strongly if not conclusively establishes the following facts. Appellant dealt with the United when the United represented all of the miners in the United States. Among the union miners who were thus affected were appellees—the employees of appellant. The contract thus negotiated was continued in force by mutual consent of the parties for a new months after its expiration. In making a new contract, an association of operators represented appellant and the United represented the miners, including those working at the Freeburg mine. A new contract was negotiated between the United and representatives of appellant. This was in August, 1932. At this time there was no question but that the United represented appellant's employees. It was after this contract was entered into and in the month of September, 1932, that individual members of United working for appellant joined the Progressive.

It was largely through appellant's peace negotiations that arrangements were made whereby its employees (appellees) continued to work, although they were members of the Progressive. This was accomplished by appellant's making the pay-off checks to an individual without identifying his union affiliation. This continued until April, 1933. In no respect did appellant fail thus far in its attempt to continue the employer-employee relationship. It was willing, indeed anxious, to continue this relationship. It was at this time and place that appellees insisted that appellant should break its contract with United. Appellees, not appellant, terminated the employer-employee relationship. It was terminated without any controversy or dispute between them as to wages or conditions of employment.

Thereafter repeated efforts were made to get the parties back at work and the mine opened. To accomplish this result certain employees sought the aid of a third party. The B. C. L. Board was petitioned for help. Again appellant was a neutral party at this hearing. It appeared and acquiesced in the Board's jurisdiction. It was willing to abide by its decision. At this time the validity of said Board's existence had not been successfully challenged. It was generally recognized as a neutral, impartial, outside body, not unfriendly to labor or labor unions and was created for the purpose of conciliating differences between employer and employee or among employee unions and to avoid strikes and to terminate strikes. It is fair to assume that all parties were acting in good faith in appearing before this Board. Progressive however refused to abide by its decision.

In determining whether appellant made "every reasonable effort to settle the dispute" it may be conceded that the ruling of said Board was not binding upon any of the parties and that appellees might legally repudiate its decision. Submission, however, to it on appellant's part was some evidence of good faith, as well as of an honest effort to peaceably induce its employees to return to work.

From this time on there was nothing upon which appellant could compromise or arbitrate. Not only was its contract with the United binding upon it, but even if there existed no contract it had an absolute right to make a contract with United. There is not a scintilla of evidence to justify the conclusion that the United was the appellant's—an employer-union.

However, negotiations continued to the day of the trial. When the case was on for trial appellant's president met the general counsel for appellees and the latter pronounced an ultimatum to the effect that appellant "would not be permitted to operate said mine upon any condition except under a contract with Progressive."

Just what appellant was further expected to do in the face of this pronouncement has not been suggested. Demand that one party break its valid contract and concede away its right to contract with its employees was not within the field of possible compromise. Had it broken its contract with United, it would not only have invited a strike by United at other mines, but a suit for damages and an injunction as well.

The desire to arbitrate disputes—to iron out differences with employees—is highly commendable. But it is a misnomer to designate, as an offer to arbitrate, a demand to break a contract with a third party against said party's objection and to surrender one's right to employ individuals because they happen to belong to a union—a bona fide employees' union—other than that to which the demander belongs. Such a demand permanently closed the door of mediation. It was a demand for an unconditional surrender. Its acceptance was as impossible as the demand was arrogant. If taken as expressive of appellees' only terms of negotiation, it closed the door to further conciliation or arbitration.

The court concluded that appellant had not made "every reasonable effort" to settle the dispute because it did not meet the officers of the Progressive after receiving the communication bearing date of October 2, 1933, which reads as follows:

"The undersigned, being the representative of the membership composing Local Union No. 47, located at Freeburg, Illinois, Progressive Miners of America, hereby demand and request of you as such representatives, the replacement of all of the membership of said Local Union as employees of your Company who are now on strike by reason of your refusal to recognize the Organization and the representatives of the Organization of said employees' own choosing, to-wit: the Progressive Miners of America. In the name of said employees we make this demand and request and hereby notify you that each of said employees is ready and willing to return to his employment with your Company under the terms and conditions of the Bituminous Coal Code as provided for in the National Industrial Recovery Act, approved June 16, 1933."

This demand by the Progressives was not unlike the ultimatum which appellees' counsel issued to appellant's president. Regarding it the District Court observed that if appellant ". . . could not, or believed it could not, accede to such demands, . . . this did not relieve it of the duty to negotiate. The purpose of negotiation and often the result, is to obtain modification of demands."

This conclusion, however, does violence to the terms of appellees' demand. The parties had been haggling over this single issue for more than a year. Appellees were not negotiating or trying to settle a difference with appellant. They were striking at a rival union, the United, through appellant. The blow was aimed at United, but it hit appellant, an innocent third party.

Appellees' position as stated in their demand was not that they were willing to compromise or negotiate with appellant, but they consistently and defiantly asserted that members of the United must not be employed. They had not only made such pronouncement before, but in violation of the law of Illinois, as well as the Federal government, and in destructive defiance of the rights of appellant, they had intimidated the local authorities and threatened death to those who sought to operate the mine without becoming Progressives.

Our conclusion is that the finding that appellant failed to make reasonable efforts to settle the dispute is not supported by the evidence.

Another contention which goes to the merits of this case, even upon appellees' construction of the statute, involves the meaning and application of section 108. Appellant contends that it was entitled to enter a Federal court of equity and seek an injunction to protect its property against *wilful* acts of trespass, as well as against acts of violence, committed by its employees during a strike regardless of the stage of the peace negotiations. To support its views appellant cites the Congressional Reports leading up to the passage of the Act. The Act is called the Norris-LaGuardia Act. Senator Norris was one of its sponsors. It was intended as he said to abolish "yellow dog" contracts. The question of its scope was naturally a matter of vital importance. In its report in the Senate, the committee said:

"It is not sought by this bill to take away from the judicial power any jurisdiction to restrain by injunctive process unlawful acts, or acts of fraud or violence."

In explaining its terms and their limitations, the sponsors said before the House:

"Gentlemen, this bill does not—and I cannot repeat it too many times—this bill does not prevent the court from restraining any unlawful act. . . ."

"Contrary to the belief of some people, this bill does not attempt to take away from the Federal courts all power to restrain unlawful acts or acts of fraud or violence in labor disputes."

"The public is amply protected as the bill is now drawn. It is a mistaken notion that some have that all injunctions are proscribed. There still is left to the Federal courts the right to issue injunctions when there are unlawful acts threatened or committed, when substantial and irreparable injury to complainant's property is done—and when there is no adequate remedy at law in all those cases, the Federal courts will still have the right to issue injunctions. When there is fraud, when there is violence, and when there is crime injunctions may issue. When any of those things are threatened or committed injunctions may ensue."

The intention of Congress was thus clearly expressed. It was evidently not intended to take from courts of equity, jurisdiction of suits to restrain *unlawful* acts or acts of *violence*.

Appellees, however, argue that although such may have been
the intention of Congress it unfortunately did not express its intention and its enactment actually withdrew from the Federal
courts all jurisdiction to grant injunctions in all cases growing
out of labor disputes.

The premise to appellees' argument cannot be gainsaid. Cases
without number may be cited which hold committee reports, con-
gressional debates, etc., will not be considered where the words of
the statute are unambiguous and their meaning clear. Standard
Fashion Co. v. Magrane-Houston Co., 258 U.S. 346, 42 S. Ct. 360, 66
L. Ed. 653; United States v. Shreveport Grain & Elevator Co., 287
U.S. 77, 53 S. Ct. 42, 77 L. Ed. 175; Caminetti v. United States, 242
U.S. 470, 37 S. Ct. 192, 61 L. Ed. 442, L.R.A. 1917F, 502, Ann. Cas.
1917B, 1168; Stafford v. Wallace, 258 U.S. 495, 42 S. Ct. 397, 66
L. Ed. 735, 23 A.L.R. 229; Duplex Printing Press Co. v. Deering,
254 U.S. 443, 41 S. Ct. 172, 65 L. Ed. 349, 16 A.L.R. 196.

There seemingly is no canon of statutory construction better
settled than the one which forbids reference to Congressional Records or to statements of legislators except in cases where the language of the statute is doubtful, uncertain or ambiguous. Such
references may never be used to create doubt. 25 Ruling Case
Law, pp. 1037, 1038.

It is difficult for us to assume that the section is free from
doubt in view of the positive statements of its sponsors to the
contrary. In fact, it is argued by appellant that appellees have
not been able to create a doubt as to the unsoundness of the position by them taken. In other words the parties are hopelessly at
variance over the breadth of the construction of the words of section 108. It appears to us that the doubt is not over the meaning
of the words, but of their applicability and Senator Norris's statement as to the nonapplicability of the section to *acts of fraud* and
violence should be considered, and when considered they exclude
from the scope of section 108 acts of fraud and acts of violence
which destroy or damage the employer's property.

Every reason would seem to support the position taken by
the sponsors of this Act. Refusal to protect property from wilful
destruction by others is so contrary to our individual and collective sense of justice that it is quite impossible to extend the meaning of language so as to exclude such protection without affirmative and specific words to that effect.[4]

[4] Upon what constitutes "governmental machinery of mediation or voluntary arbitration" (47 U.S. Stat. 70, c. 90, sec. 8) see: Mayo v. Dean, 82 F.(2d)
554 (C.C.A. 5th, 1936); Cole v. Atlanta Terminal Co., 15 F. Supp. 131 (N.D.
Ga., 1936). See also: Cinderella Theatre Co. v. Sign Writers' Local Union, 6 F.
Supp. 164 (E.D. Mich., 1934); Dean v. Mayo, 8 F. Supp. 73 (W.D. La., 1934).
As to the necessity of a showing of compliance "with any obligation imposed
by law which is involved in the labor dispute in question" as required by the
same section, see Lauf v. Shinner, 82 F.(2d) 68 (C.C.A. 7th, 1936). As to

The decree is reversed, with instructions to enter one consistent with the views expressed in this opinion.[5]

what constitutes "every reasonable effort" by the plaintiff to settle the dispute by negotiation, see Grandview Dairy v. O'Leary, 158 Misc. 791, 285 N.Y.S.
841 (1936); Canvas Glove Mfg. Works v. Doe, C.C.H. Labor Law Serv., par.
16163 (N.Y. Sup. Ct., 1935), with which compare findings relative to same dispute, In the Matter of Canvas Glove Mfg. Works and International Glove
Makers Union, 1 N.L.R.B. 519 (1936).

As to who are "public officers" (47 U.S. Stat. 70, c. 90, sec. 7(e)), see:
Newton v. Laclede Steel Co., 80 F.(2d) 636 (1935); Cole v Atlanta Terminal Co., 15 F. Supp. 131 (N.D. Ga., 1936). Upon the requirement generally in
anti-injunction legislation, see Dean v. Mayo, 9 F. Supp. 459 (W.D. La., 1934),
aff'd sub. nom. Mayo v. Dean, 82 F.(2d) 554 (C.C.A. 5th, 1936); Grandview
Dairy v. O'Leary, supra; cases cited by Landis 189, n. 11.

For a doubtful reading of the provision limiting responsibility of officers
and members of trade unions (47 U.S. Stat. 70, c. 90, sec. 6) see: Mayo v.
Dean, 82 F.(2d) 554 (C.C.A. 5th, 1936). Cf. Cinderella Theatre Co. v. Sign
Writers' Local Union, supra.

On whether pending suits are affected by the passage of anti-injunction
legislation, see: Micamold Radio Corp. v. Beedie, 156 Misc. 390, 282 N.Y.S. 77
(1935); Kronowitz v. Schlansky, 156 Misc. 717, 282 N.Y.S. 564 (1935); Aberdeen Restaurant Co. v. Gottfried, 158 Misc. 785, 285 N.Y.S. 832 (1935); National House Cleaning Contractors v. Bobaluc, 296 N.Y.S. 673 (App. Div.
1937). See also Levering & Garrigues Co. v. Morrin, 71 F.(2d) 284 (C.C.A.
2d, 1934), Landis 184.—Ed.

[5] Certiorari was denied, sub. nom. Rice v. United Electric Coal Companies, 297 U.S. 714, 56 S. Ct. 590 (1936). For comment on the case, see:
50 Harv. L. Rev. 1295 (1937); 36 Col. L. Rev. 157 (1936); 4 I.J.A. Bull. No.
11, 1 (1936); 45 Yale L.J. 1320 (1936).

The court has extended the doctrine of the case in the subsequent cases
of Newton v. Laclede Steel Co., 80 F.(2d) 636 (1935), where the court found
that the pickets were not "for the most part" employees of the complainants
(at 636), and that the complainants had "the support of the great majority
of their employees" (at 638); Lauf v. Shinner, 82 F.(2d) 68 (1936), 90 F.(2d)
250 (1937); Scavenger Service Corp. v. Courtney, 85 F.(2d) 825 (1936). In
the first two cases, there were in existence at the time of the controversies
labor organizations apparently restricted in membership to employees of the
complainants—an "Employees Representation Plan" in the Newton case (at
638), and an alleged "company union" in the Lauf case (at 74). See also:
Hedges-Walsh-Weidner Co. v. Duffy, C.C.H. Labor Law Serv., par. 16C66
(E.D. Tenn., 1934); Safeway Stores v. Retail Clerks Union, 184 Wash. 322,
51 P.(2d) 322 (1935).

See In re Cleveland & Sandusky Brewing Co., 11 F. Supp. 198 (N.D.
Ohio, 1935), deciding that the Norris-LaGuardia Act does not deprive the
bankruptcy court of its power to prevent interference with property under its
jurisdiction, and also intimating that no "labor dispute" was involved because
of the jurisdictional struggle between two unions (at 205). The case is criticized in 35 Col. L. Rev. 1140 (1935), 49 Harv. L. Rev. 341 (1935), 45 Yale L.J.
372 (1935). Cf. Russell v. United States, 86 F.(2d) 389 (C.C.A. 8th, 1936),
50 Harv. L. Rev. 1302 (1937).

See also La Rose v. Possehl, 156 Misc. 476, 282 N.Y.S. 332 (1935), to the
effect that a suit to restrain a union from refusing to recognize plaintiff as a
member does not grow out of a "labor dispute" as defined in the New York
Anti-Injunction Act, supra, p. 58, note 8; Beatty v. Chicago, B. & Q. R. R., 49
Wyo. 22, 52 P.(2d) 404 (1935).

Chapter III

THE LEGISLATURES AND THE RIGHT TO ORGANIZE

VIRGINIAN RAILWAY COMPANY v. SYSTEM FEDERATION No. 40

Supreme Court of the United States, 1937. 300 U.S. 515.

Mr. Justice Stone delivered the opinion of the Court.

This case presents questions as to the constitutional validity of certain provisions of the Railway Labor Act of May 20, 1926, c. 347, 44 Stat. 577, as amended by the Act of June 21, 1934, c. 691, 48 Stat. 1185, 45 U.S.C. secs. 151-163, (45 U.S.C.A. secs. 151-163), and as to the nature and extent of the relief which courts are authorized by the Act to give.

Respondents are System Federation No. 40, which will be referred to as the Federation, a labor organization affiliated with the American Federation of Labor and representing shop craft employees of petitioner railway, and certain individuals who are officers and members of the System Federation. They brought the present suit in equity in the District Court for Eastern Virginia, to compel petitioner, an interstate rail carrier, to recognize and treat with respondent Federation, as the duly accredited representative of the mechanical department employees of petitioner, and to restrain petitioner from in any way interfering with, influencing, or coercing its shop craft employees in their free choice of representatives, for the purpose of contracting with petitioner with respect to rules, rates of pay, and working conditions, and for the purpose of considering and settling disputes between petitioner and such employees.

The history of this controversy goes back to 1922, when, following the failure of a strike by petitioner's shop employees affiliated with the American Federation of Labor, other employees organized a local union known as the "Mechanical Department Association of the Virginian Railway." The Association thereupon entered into an agreement with petitioner, providing for rates of pay and working conditions, and for the settlement of disputes

71

with respect to them, but no substantial grievances were ever presented to petitioner by the Association. It maintained its organization and held biennial elections of officers, but the notices of election were sent out by petitioner and all Association expenses were paid by petitioner.

In 1927 the American Federation of Labor formed a local organization, which, in 1934, demanded recognition by petitioner of its authority to represent the shop craft employees, and invoked the aid of the National Mediation Board, constituted under the Railway Labor Act, as amended, to establish its authority. The Board, pursuant to agreement between the petitioner, the Federation, and the Association, and in conformity to the statute, held an election by petitioner's shop craft employees to choose representatives for the purpose of collective bargaining with petitioner. As the result of the election, the Board certified that the Federation was the duly accredited representative of petitioner's employees in the six shop crafts.

Upon this and other evidence, not now necessary to be detailed, the trial court found that the Federation was the duly authorized representative of the mechanical department employees of petitioner, except the carmen and coach cleaners; that the petitioner, in violation of section 2 of the Railway Labor Act, (45 U.S.C.A. secs. 151a, 152), had failed to treat with the Federation as the duly accredited representative of petitioner's employees; that petitioner had sought to influence its employees against any affiliation with labor organizations other than an association maintained by petitioner, and to prevent its employees from exercising their right to choose their own representative; that for that purpose, following the certification, by the National Mediation Board, of the Federation, as the duly authorized representative of petitioner's mechanical department employees, petitioner had organized the Independent Shop Craft Association of its shop craft employees, and had sought to induce its employees to join the independent association, and to put it forward as the authorized representative of petitioner's employees.[1]

---

[1] The court found that after the certification by the Mediation Board "the defendant, by and through its officers, agents and servants, undertook by means of the circulation of a petition or petitions addressed to the National Mediation Board to have the certification of the National Mediation Board aforesaid altered, changed or revoked so as to deprive its Mechanical Department employes of the right to representation by said System Federation No. 40, Railway Employes Department of the American Federation of Labor, so designated as aforesaid, and thereafter did cause to be organized the Independent Shop Crafts Association by individual Mechanical Department employes by circulating or causing to be circulated applications for membership in said Independent Shop Crafts Association notwithstanding the certification as aforesaid by the National Mediation Board of said System Federation No. 40, Railway Employes Department of the American Federation of Labor, as the authorized representative of its Mechanical Department employes, . . ."

Upon the basis of these findings the trial court gave its decree applicable to petitioner's mechanical department employees except the carmen and coach cleaners. It directed petitioner to "treat with" the Federation and to "exert every reasonable effort to make and maintain agreements concerning rates of pay, rules and working conditions, and to settle all disputes, whether arising out of the application of such agreements or otherwise . . ." It restrained petitioner from "entering into any contract, undertaking or agreement of whatsoever kind concerning rules, rates of pay or working conditions affecting its Mechanical Department employees, . . . except . . . with the Federation," and from "interfering with, influencing or coercing" its employees with respect to their free choice of representatives "for the purpose of making and maintaining contracts" with petitioner "relating to rules, rates of pay and working conditions or for the purpose of considering and deciding disputes between the Mechanical Department employees" and petitioner. The decree further restrained the petitioner from organizing or fostering any union of its mechanical department employees for the purpose of interfering with the Federation as the accredited representative of such employees. (D.C.) 11 F. Supp. 621.

On appeal the Court of Appeals for the Fourth Circuit approved and adopted the findings of the district court and affirmed its decree. 84 F.(2d) 641. This Court granted certiorari to review the cause as one of public importance. 299 U.S. ......, 57 S. Ct. 43, 81 L. Ed. ....

Petitioner here, as below, makes two main contentions: First, with respect to the relief granted, it maintains that section 2, Ninth, of the Railway Labor Act, (45 U.S.C.A. sec. 152, subd. 9), which provides that a carrier shall treat with those certified by the Mediation Board to be the representatives of a craft or class, imposes no legally enforcible obligation upon the carrier to negotiate with the representative so certified, and that in any case the statute imposes no obligation to treat or negotiate which can be appropriately enforced by a court of equity. Second, that section 2, Ninth, in so far as it attempts to regulate labor relations between petitioner and its "back shop" employees, is not a regulation of interstate commerce authorized by the commerce clause because, as it asserts, they are engaged solely in intrastate activities; and that so far as it imposes on the carrier any obligation to negotiate with a labor union authorized to represent its employees, and restrains it from making agreements with any other labor organization, it is a denial of due process guaranteed by the Fifth Amendment. Other minor objections to the decree, so far as relevant to our decision, will be referred to later in the course of this opinion.

The concurrent findings of fact of the two courts below are not shown to be plainly erroneous or unsupported by evidence.

We accordingly accept them as the conclusive basis for decision, Texas & N. O. R. Co. v. Brotherhood of Railway & S. S. Clerks, 281 U.S. 548, 558, 50 S. Ct. 427, 429, 74 L. Ed. 1034; Pick Mfg. Co. v. General Motors Corporation, 299 U.S. 3, 4, 57 S. Ct. 1, 2, 81 L. Ed. ......, and address ourselves to the questions of law raised on the record.

First. The Obligation Imposed by the Statute. By Title III of the Transportation Act of February 28, 1920, c. 91, 41 Stat. 456, 469, (45 U.S.C.A. secs. 131-146), Congress set up the Railroad Labor Board as a means for the peaceful settlement, by agreement or by arbitration, of labor controversies between interstate carriers and their employees. It sought "to encourage settlement without strikes, first by conference between the parties, failing that, by reference to adjustment boards of the parties' own choosing, and if this is ineffective, by a full hearing before a national board . . ." Pennsylvania R. Co. v. United States Railroad Labor Board, 261 U.S. 72, 79, 43 S. Ct. 278, 281, 67 L. Ed. 536. The decisions of the Board were supported by no legal sanctions. The disputants were not "in any way to be forced into compliance with the statute or with the judgments pronounced by the Labor Board, except through the effect of adverse public opinion." Pennsylvania Railroad System & Allied Lines Federation v. Pennsylvania R. Co., 267 U.S. 203, 216, 45 S. Ct. 307, 311, 69 L. Ed. 574.

In 1926 Congress, aware of the impotence of the Board, and of the fact that its authority was generally not recognized or respected by the railroads or their employees, made a fresh start toward the peaceful settlement of labor disputes affecting railroads, by the repeal of the 1920 Act and the adoption of the Railway Labor Act (44 Stat. 577). Report, Senate Committee on Interstate Commerce, No. 222, 69th Cong., 1st Sess. Texas & N. O. R. Co. v. Brotherhood of Railway & S. S. Clerks, supra, 281 U.S. 548, 563, 50 S. Ct. 427, 431, 74 L. Ed. 1034. By the new measure Congress continued its policy of encouraging the amicable adjustment of labor disputes by their voluntary submission to arbitration before an impartial board, but it supported that policy by the imposition of legal obligations. It provided means for enforcing the award obtained by arbitration between the parties to labor disputes. Section 9 (45 U.S.C.A. sec. 159). In certain circumstances it prohibited any change in conditions, by the parties to an unadjusted labor dispute, for a period of thirty days, except by agreement. Section 10 (45 U.S.C.A. sec. 160). It recognized their right to designate representatives for the purposes of the Act "without interference, influence, or coercion exercised by either party over the self-organization or designation of representatives by the other." Section 2, Third, 44 Stat. 577. Under the last-mentioned provision this Court held, in the Railway Clerks case, supra, that employees were free to organize and to make choice of their representatives without the "coercive interference" and "pressure" of a company union organized and maintained by the employer; and that the statute protected the freedom of choice of representatives, which was an essential of the statutory scheme, with a legal sanction which it was the duty of courts to enforce by appropriate decree.

The prohibition against such interference was continued and made more explicit by the amendment of 1934.[2] Petitioner does not challenge that part of the decree which enjoins any interference by it with the free choice of representatives by its employees, and the fostering, in the circumstances of this case, of the company union. That contention is not open to it in view of our decision in the Railway Clerks case, supra, and of the unambiguous language of section 2, Third, and Fourth, of the Act, as amended (45 U.S. C.A. sec. 152, subds. 3, 4).

But petitioner insists that the statute affords no legal sanction for so much of the decree as directs petitioner to "treat with" respondent Federation "and exert every reasonable effort to make and maintain agreements concerning rates of pay, rules, and working conditions, and to settle all disputes whether arising out of the application of such agreements or otherwise." It points out that the requirement for reasonable effort to reach an agreement is couched in the very words of section 2, First (45 U.S.C.A. sec. 152, subd. 1), which were taken from section 301 of the Transportation Act, (45 U.S.C.A. sec. 132), and which were held to be without legal sanction in that Act. Pennsylvania Railroad System & Allied Lines Federation v. Pennsylvania R. Co., supra, 267 U.S. 203, 215, 45 S. Ct. 307, 310, 69 L. Ed. 574. It is argued that they cannot now be given greater force as reenacted in the Railway Labor Act of 1926, and continued in the 1934 amendment. But these words no longer stand alone and unaided by mandatory provision of the statute as they did when first enacted. The amendment of the Railway Labor Act added new provisions in section 2, Ninth (45 U.S.C.A. sec. 152, subd. 9), which makes it the duty of the Mediation Board, when any dispute arises among the carrier's employees,

---

[2] Section 2 of the Act, as amended in 1934, (45 U.S.C.A. sec. 151a), declares that its purposes, among others, are "(2) to forbid any limitation upon freedom of association among employees or any denial, as a condition of employment or otherwise, of the right of employees to join a labor organization" and "(3) to provide for the complete independence of carriers and of employees in the matter of self-organization and to carry out the purposes of this Act [chapter]." The section was also amended to provide that "neither party shall in any way interfere with, influence, or coerce the other in its choice of representatives," section 2, Third (45 U.S.C.A. sec. 152, subd. 3), and that "it shall be unlawful for any carrier to interfere in any way with the organization of its employees, or to use the funds of the carrier in maintaining or assisting or contributing to any labor organization . . . or to influence or coerce employees in an effort to induce them to join or remain or not to join or remain members of any labor organization," section 2, Fourth (45 U.S.C.A. sec. 152, subd. 4).

"as to who are the representatives of such employees," to investigate the dispute and to certify, as was done in this case, the name of the organization authorized to represent the employees. It commands that "Upon receipt of such certification the carrier shall treat with the representative so certified as the representative of the craft or class for the purposes of this Act [chapter]."

It is, we think, not open to doubt that Congress intended that this requirement be mandatory upon the railroad employer, and that its command, in a proper case, be enforced by the courts. The policy of the Transportation Act of encouraging voluntary adjustment of labor disputes, made manifest by those provisions of the Act which clearly contemplated the moral force of public opinion as affording its ultimate sanction, was, as we have seen, abandoned by the enactment of the Railway Labor Act. Neither the purposes of the later Act, as amended, nor its provisions when read, as they must be, in the light of our decision in the Railway Clerks case, supra, lend support to the contention that its enactments, which are mandatory in form and capable of enforcement by judicial process, were intended to be without legal sanction.[3]

Experience had shown, before the amendment of 1934, that when there was no dispute as to the organizations authorized to represent the employees, and when there was willingness of the employer to meet such representative for a discussion of their grievances, amicable adjustment of differences had generally followed and strikes had been avoided.[4] On the other hand, a prolific source

---

[3] The 1934 amendment imposed various other obligations upon the carrier, to which criminal penalties were attached [section 2, Tenth (45 U.S.C.A. sec. 152, subd. 10)] e.g., prohibitions against helping unions, by contributions of funds, or assistance in the collection of dues, section 2, Fourth (45 U.S.C.A. sec. 152, subd. 4); against requiring employees to promise to join or not to join a labor union, section 2, Fifth (45 U.S.C.A. sec. 152, subd. 5); against changing rates of pay, etc., without specifying a conference upon thirty days' notice, section 2, Seventh (45 U.S.C.A. sec. 152, subd. 7); and see the requirement that the carrier post notices that all disputes will be determined in accordance with the Act, section 2, Eighth (45 U.S.C.A. sec. 152, subd. 8).

[4] In the first two years after the enactment of the Railway Labor Act of 1926, 363 cases concerning rates of pay, rules, or working conditions were submitted to the United States Board of Mediation, and about 25 per cent. of these were withdrawn by the parties. Yet, during the same period, more than 600 direct and voluntary settlements were negotiated. See United States Board of Mediation, First Annual Report, For the Fiscal Year Ended June 30, 1927, pp. 10, 11; Second Annual Report, For the Fiscal Year Ended June 30, 1928, pp. 11, 58, 59. Compare National Mediation Board, Second Annual Report, For the Fiscal Year Ended June 30, 1936, at p. 1: "For every dispute submitted to . . . these Boards, there were many others considered and settled in conferences between representatives of carriers and of the employees as required by section 2, second, of the Act."

See, also, testimony of William M. Leiserson, Chairman of the National Mediation Board until February 1, 1937, at Hearing by National Labor Relations Board in the case of Jones & Laughlin Steel Corporation [No. 419, October Term, 1936]: "If we have a threat of a strike now [on the railroads] it might be on a big fundamental question, like wages and hours, and we usually find we can settle those by arbitration or otherwise . . . But if the

of dispute had been the maintenance by the railroads of company unions and the denial by railway management of the authority of representatives chosen by their employees. Report of House Committee on Interstate and Foreign Commerce, No. 1944, 73rd Cong., 2d Sess., pp. 1-2.[5] Section 2, Ninth, of the amended Act (45 U.S.C. A. sec. 152, subd. 9), was specifically aimed at this practice. It provided a means for ascertaining who are the authorized representatives of the employees through intervention and certification by the Mediation Board, and commanded the carrier to treat with the representative so certified. That the command was limited in its application to the case of intervention and certification by the Mediation Board indicates not that its words are precatory, but only that Congress hit at the evil "where experience shows it to be most felt." Keokee Consol. Coke Co. v. Taylor, 234 U.S. 224, 227, 34 S. Ct. 856, 857, 58 L. Ed. 1288.

Petitioner argues that the phrase "treat with" must be taken as the equivalent of "treat" in its intransitive sense, as meaning "regard" or "act towards," so that compliance with its mandate requires the employer to meet the authorized representative of the employees only if and when he shall elect to negotiate with them. This suggestion disregards the words of the section, and ignores the plain purpose made manifest throughout the numerous provisions of the Act. Its major objective is the avoidance of industrial strife, by conference between the authorized representatives of employer and employee. The command to the employer to "treat with" the authorized representative of the employees adds nothing to the 1926 Act, unless it requires some affirmative act on the part of the employer. Compare the Railway Clerks case, supra. As we

---

issues involved were discrimination or discharge of men because they had joined the organization, or the question would be the right of the organization to represent them, we could not have settled those strikes." See Governmental Protection of Labor's Right to Organize, National Labor Relations Board, Division of Economic Research, Bull. No. 1, August, 1936, pp. 17-18.

[5] See, also, Statement by Representative Crosser, in charge of the bill on the floor, in Hearings, House Committee on Rules, 73d Cong., 2d Sess., on H.R. 9861, pp. 10-11, 13: "The purpose of the bill is . . . [inter alia] to outlaw the attempt that has been made in numerous instances by employers who control alleged labor unions, and thereby, to use a slang phrase, to 'gum up the works.' . . . We have had 8 years of operation of this act, and we have prevented any strikes. But strikes have been threatened because of the defects which have been found in this bill."

Under the 1926 Act disputes over the designation of employee representatives could be dealt with by the old United States Mediation Board only by agreement of the parties. The carriers agreed to an election conducted by the Board but nine times in six years, see testimony of William M. Leiserson, Chairman of National Mediation Board until February 1, 1937, at Hearing by National Labor Relations Board in the case of Jones & Laughlin Steel Corp. [No. 419, October Term, 1936]; Governmental Protection of Labor's Right to Organize, National Labor Relations Board, Division of Economic Research, Bull. No. 1, August, 1936, p. 50. The 1934 amendment was followed by a large increase in the number of representation disputes submitted to the National Mediation Board. See infra, Note 7.

cannot assume that its addition to the statute was purposeless, we must take its meaning to be that which the words suggest, which alone would add something to the statute as it was before amendment, and which alone would tend to effect the purpose of the legislation. The statute does not undertake to compel agreement between the employer and employees, but it does command those preliminary steps without which no agreement can be reached. It at least requires the employer to meet and confer with the authorized representative of its employees, to listen to their complaints, to make reasonable effort to compose differences—in short, to enter into a negotiation for the settlement of labor disputes such as is contemplated by section 2, First (45 U.S.C.A. 152, subd. 1).

Petitioner's insistence that the statute does not warrant so much of the decree as forbids it to enter into contracts of employment with its individual employees is based upon a misconstruction of the decree. Both the statute and the decree are aimed at securing settlement of labor disputes by inducing collective bargaining with the true representative of the employees and by preventing such bargaining with any who do not represent them. The obligation imposed on the employer by section 2, Ninth (45 U.S. C.A. sec. 152, subd. 9), to treat with the true representative of the employees as designated by the Mediation Board, when read in the light of the declared purposes of the Act, and of the provisions of section 2, Third and Fourth (45 U.S.C.A. sec. 152, subds. 3, 4), giving to the employees the right to organize and bargain collectively through the representative of their own selection, is exclusive. It imposes the affirmative duty to treat only with the true representative, and hence the negative duty to treat with no other. We think, as the Government concedes in its brief,[6] that the injunction against petitioner's entering into any contract concerning rules, rates of pay, and working conditions, except with respondent, is designed only to prevent collective bargaining with anyone pur-

---

[6](Note 35a.) "The Government interprets the negative obligations imposed by the statute and decree as having the following effect:

"When the majority of a craft or class has (either by secret ballot or otherwise) selected a representative, the carrier cannot make with anyone other than the representative a collective contract (i.e., a contract which sets rates of pay, rules, or working conditions), whether the contract covers the class as a whole or a part thereof. Neither the statute nor the decree prevents the carrier from refusing to make a collective contract and hiring individuals on whatever terms the carrier may by unilateral action determine. In hirings of that sort the individual does not deal in a representative capacity with the carrier and the hiring does not set general rates of pay, rules, or working conditions. Of course, as a matter of voluntary action, not as a result of the statute or the decree, the carrier may contract with the duly designated representative to hire individuals only on the terms of a collective understanding between the carrier and the representative; but any such agreement would be entirely voluntary on the carrier's part and would in no sense be compelled.

"If the majority of a craft or class has not selected a representative, the carrier is free to make with anyone it pleases and for any group it pleases contracts establishing rates of pay, rules, or working conditions."

porting to represent employees, other than respondent, who has been ascertained to be their true representative. When read in its context, it must be taken to prohibit the negotiation of labor contracts, generally applicable to employees in the mechanical department, with any representative other than respondent, but not as precluding such individual contracts as petitioner may elect to make directly with individual employees. The decree, thus construed, conforms, in both its affirmative and negative aspects, to the requirements of section 2.

Propriety of Relief in Equity. Petitioner contends that if the statute is interpreted as requiring the employer to negotiate with the representative of his employees, its obligation is not the appropriate subject of a decree in equity; that negotiation depends on desires and mental attitudes which are beyond judicial control; and that since equity cannot compel the parties to agree, it will not compel them to take the preliminary steps which may result in agreement.

There is no want of capacity in the court to direct complete performance of the entire obligation; both the negative duties not to maintain a company union and not to negotiate with any representative of the employees other than respondent and the affirmative duty to treat with respondent. Full performance of both is commanded by the decree in terms which leave in no uncertainty the requisites of performance. In compelling compliance with either duty it does far less than has been done in compelling the discharge of a contractual or statutory obligation calling for a construction or engineering enterprise, New Orleans, Mobile & Texas Ry. Co. v. Mississippi, 112 U.S. 12, 5 S. Ct. 19, 28 L. Ed. 619; Wheeling Traction Co. v. Board of Com'rs., (C.C.A.) 248 F. 205; see Gas Securities Co. v. Antero & Lost Park Reservoir Co., (C.C.A.) 259 F. 423, 433; Board of Com'rs v. A. V. Wills & Sons, (D.C.) 236 F. 362, 380; Jones v. Parker, 163 Mass. 564, 40 N.E. 1044, 47 Am. St. Rep. 485, or in granting specific performance of a contract for the joint use of a railroad bridge and terminals, Joy v. St. Louis, 138 U.S. 1, 11 S. Ct. 243, 34 L. Ed. 843; Union Pacific Ry. Co. v. Chicago, R. I. & P. Ry. Co., 163 U.S. 564, 16 S. Ct. 1173, 41 L. Ed. 265; cf. Prospect Park & Coney Island R. Co. v. Coney Island & Brooklyn R. Co., 144 N.Y. 152, 39 N.E. 17, 26 L.R.A. 610. Whether an obligation has been discharged, and whether action taken or omitted is in good faith or reasonable, are everyday subjects of inquiry by courts in framing and enforcing their decrees.

It is true that a court of equity may refuse to give any relief when it is apparent that that which it can give will not be effective or of benefit to the plaintiff. Equity will not decree the execution of a partnership agreement since it cannot compel the parties to remain partners, see Hyer v. Richmond Traction Co., 168 U.S. 471,

482, 18 S. Ct. 114, 42 L. Ed. 547, or compel one to enter into performance of a contract of personal service which it cannot adequately control, Rutland Marble Co. v. Ripley, 10 Wall. 339, 358,
19 L. Ed. 955; Karrick v. Hannaman, 168 U.S. 328, 336, 18 S. Ct.
135, 42 L. Ed. 484; Tobey v. Bristol, Fed. Cas. No. 14,065; Weeks v.
Pratt, (C.C.A.) 43 F.(2d) 53, 57; Railway Labor Act, sec. 2, Tenth
(45 U.S.C.A. sec. 152, subd. 10). But the extent to which equity
will go to give relief where there is no adequate remedy at law is
not a matter of fixed rule. It rests rather in the sound discretion
of the court. Willard v. Tayloe, 8 Wall. 557, 565, 19 L. Ed. 501;
Joy v. St. Louis, supra, 138 U.S. 1, 47, 11 S. Ct. 243, 34 L. Ed. 843;
Morrison v. Work, 266 U.S. 481, 490, 45 S. Ct. 149, 153, 69 L. Ed.
394; Curran v. Holyoke Water Power Co., 116 Mass. 90, 92. Whether
the decree will prove so useless as to lead a court to refuse to
give it, is a matter of judgment to be exercised with reference
to the special circumstances of each case rather than to general
rules which at most are but guides to the exercise of discretion.
It is a familiar rule that a court may exercise its equity powers,
or equivalent mandamus powers, United States ex rel. Greathouse
v. Dern, 289 U.S. 352, 359, 53 S. Ct. 614, 617, 77 L. Ed. 1250, to
compel courts, boards, or officers to act in a matter with respect to
which they may have jurisdiction or authority, although the court
will not assume to control or guide the exercise of their authority.
Interstate Commerce Commission v. United States ex rel. Humboldt
S. S. Co., 224 U.S. 474, 32 S. Ct. 556, 56 L. Ed. 849; United States
ex rel. Louisville Cement Co. v. Interstate Commerce Commission,
246 U.S. 638, 38 S. Ct. 408, 62 L. Ed. 914; see Work v. United States
ex rel. Rives, 267 U.S. 175, 184, 45 S. Ct. 252, 255, 69 L. Ed. 561;
Wilbur v. United States ex rel. Kadrie, 281 U.S. 206, 218, 50 S. Ct.
320, 324, 74 L. Ed. 809.

In considering the propriety of the equitable relief granted
here, we cannot ignore the judgment of Congress, deliberately expressed in legislation, that where the obstruction of the company
union is removed, the meeting of employers and employees at the
conference table is a powerful aid to industrial peace. Moreover,
the resources of the Railway Labor Act are not exhausted if negotiation fails in the first instance to result in agreement. If disputes
concerning changes in rates of pay, rules, or working conditions,
are "not adjusted by the parties in conference," either party may
invoke the mediation services of the Mediation Board, section 5,
First (45 U.S.C.A. sec. 155, subd. 1), or the parties may agree to
seek the benefits of the arbitration provision of section 7 (45
U.S.C.A. sec. 157). With the coercive influence of the company union ended, and in view of the interest of both parties in
avoiding a strike, we cannot assume that negotiation, as required
by the decree, will not result in agreement, or lead to successful

mediation or arbitration, or that the attempt to secure one or another through the relief which the district court gave is not worth the effort.

More is involved than the settlement of a private controversy without appreciable consequences to the public. The peaceable settlement of labor controversies, especially where they may seriously impair the ability of an interstate rail carrier to perform its service to the public, is a matter of public concern. That is testified to by the history of the legislation now before us, the reports of committees of Congress having the proposed legislation in charge, and by our common knowledge. Courts of equity may, and frequently do, go much farther both to give and withhold relief in furtherance of the public interest than they are accustomed to go when only private interests are involved. Pennsylvania v. Williams, 294 U.S. 176, 185, 55 S. Ct. 380, 385, 79 L. Ed. 841, 96 A.L.R. 1166; Central Ky. Natural Gas Co. v. Railroad Commission of Kentucky, 290 U.S. 264, 270-273, 54 S. Ct. 154, 156, 157, 78 L. Ed. 307; City of Harrisonville v. W. S. Dickey Clay Mfg. Co., 289 U.S. 334, 338, 53 S. Ct. 602, 603, 77 L. Ed. 1208; Beasley v. Texas & Pac. Ry. Co., 191 U.S. 492, 497, 24 S. Ct. 164, 48 L. Ed. 274; Joy v. St. Louis, supra, 138 U.S. 1, 47, 11 S. Ct. 243, 34 L. Ed. 843; Texas & Pac. Ry. Co. v. Marshall, 136 U.S. 393, 405, 406, 10 S. Ct. 846, 34 L. Ed. 385; Conger v. New York, West Shore & Buffalo R. Co., 120 N.Y. 29, 32, 33, 23 N.E. 983. The fact that Congress has indicated its purpose to make negotiation obligatory is in itself a declaration of public interest and policy which should be persuasive in inducing courts to give relief. It is for similar reasons that courts, which traditionally have refused to compel performance of a contract to submit to arbitration, Tobey v. Bristol, supra, enforce statutes commanding performance of arbitration agreements, Red Cross Line v. Atlantic Fruit Co., 264 U.S. 109, 119, 121, 44 S. Ct. 274, 275, 276, 68 L. Ed. 582; Marine Transit Co. v. Dreyfus, 284 U.S. 263, 278, 52 S. Ct. 166, 170, 76 L. Ed. 282.

The decree is authorized by the statute and was granted in an appropriate exercise of the equity powers of the court.

Second. Constitutionality of Section 2 of the Railway Labor Act (45 U.S.C.A. secs. 151a, 152). (A) Validity Under the Commerce Clause. The power of Congress over interstate commerce extends to such regulations of the relations of rail carriers to their employees as are reasonably calculated to prevent the interruption of interstate commerce by strikes and their attendant disorders. Wilson v. New, 243 U.S. 332, 347, 348, 37 S. Ct. 298, 61 L. Ed. 755, L.R.A. 1917E, 938, Ann. Cas. 1918A, 1024. The Railway Labor Act, Section 2 (45 U.S.C.A. sec. 151a), declares that its purposes, among others, are "to avoid any interruption to commerce or to the operation of any carrier engaged therein," and "to provide for the prompt and orderly settlement of all disputes concerning rates of pay, rules, or working conditions." The provisions of the Act and its history, to which reference has been made, establish that such are its purposes, and that the latter is in aid of the former. What has been said indicates clearly that its provisions are aimed at the settlement of industrial disputes by the promotion of collective bargaining between employers and the authorized representative of their employees, and by mediation and arbitration when such bargaining does not result in agreement. It was for Congress to make the choice of the means by which its objective of securing the uninterrupted service of interstate railroads was to be secured, and its judgment, supported as it is by our long experience with industrial disputes, and the history of railroad labor relations, to which we have referred, is not open to review here.[7] The means chosen are appropriate to the end sought

---

[7] There was evidence available to Congress that the labor policy embodied in the Railway Labor Act had been successful in curbing strikes. In the eight years subsequent to the passage of the 1926 Act, there were only two small railroad strikes. Since the 1934 amendment, there has been but one. See National Mediation Board, First Annual Report, For the Fiscal Year Ended June 30, 1935, p. 8; Second Annual Report, For the Fiscal Year Ended June 30, 1936, p. 1.

In the water transportation and motor transportation fields, there were frequent strikes. A table submitted by the United States [see Respondent's Brief, Associated Press v. National Labor Relations Board, No. 365, October Term, 1936, p. 57], and derived from United States Department of Labor, Bureau of Labor Statistics, Bulletins No. R. 339 (1936), p. 4; No. R. 389 (1936), p. 4; Monthly Labor Review (May-September, 1936), Monthly "Analysis of Strikes," shows the following:

Man-days of idleness due to labor strikes.

	1933	1934	1935	(1936 Jan.-May)
Water Transportation	32,752	1,068,867	749,534	119,820
Motor Transportation	155,565	859,657	202,393	46,054
Railroads	0	0	56	0

Yet there were many disputes between rail carriers and their employees. Apart from the more trivial grievances and differences of opinion in the interpretation of agreements, 876 disputes, principally over changes in rates of pay, rules or working conditions, were referred to the United States Board of Mediation between 1926 and 1934. The following table, derived from its Eighth Annual Report, For the Fiscal Year Ended June 30, 1934, pp. 4-5, indicates the success of the mediation and arbitration machinery set up by the Railway Labor Act.

Fiscal Year Ending June 30,—

Manner of Disposition	1927	1928	1929	1930	1931	1932	1933	1934	Total
Mediation Agreements	57	84	46	25	24	45	23	17	321
Withdrawn by Parties	24	45	43	20	21	69	20	26	268
Arbitration Agreements	27	14	10	4	2	4	3	9	73
Closed Account:									
Refusal to Arbitrate	0	0	9	3	1	47	39	50	149
Retired or closed,									
other causes	3	2	21	10	5	5	10	9	65

But statistics show that many more labor disputes were settled by direct negotiation, supra, footnote 4, and Congress might reasonably have feared that the action of certain railroads in negotiating only with unions dominated by

and hence are within the congressional power. See Railway Clerks case, supra, 281 U.S. 548, 570, 50 S. Ct. 427, 433, 74 L. Ed. 1034; Railroad Retirement Board v. Alton R. Co., 295 U.S. 330, 369, 55 S. Ct. 758, 771, 79 L. Ed. 1468.

But petitioner insists that the Act as applied to its "back shop" employees is not within the commerce power since their duties have no direct relationship to interstate transportation. Of the 824 employees in the six shop crafts eligible to vote for a choice of representatives, 322 work in petitioner's "back shops" at Princeton, W. Va. They are there engaged in making classified repairs, which consist of heavy repairs on locomotives and cars withdrawn from service for that purpose for long periods (an average of 105 days for locomotives and 109 days for cars). The repair work is upon the equipment used by petitioner in its transportation service, 97 per cent. of which is interstate. At times a continuous stream of engines and cars passes through the "back shops" for such repairs. When not engaged in repair work, the back shop employees perform "store order work," the manufacture of material such as rivets and repair parts, to be placed in railroad stores for use at the Princeton shop and other points on the line.

The activities in which these employees are engaged have such a relation to the other confessedly interstate activities of the petitioner that they are to be regarded as a part of them. All taken together fall within the power of Congress over interstate commerce. Baltimore & Ohio R. Co. v. Interstate Commerce Commission, 221 U.S. 612, 619, 31 S. Ct. 621, 55 L. Ed. 878; cf. Pedersen v. Delaware, Lackawanna & Western R. Co., 229 U.S. 146, 151, 33 S. Ct. 648, 57 L. Ed. 1125, Ann. Cas. 1914C, 153. Both courts below have found that interruption by strikes of the back shop employees, if more than temporary, would seriously cripple petitioner's interstate transportation. The relation of the back shop to transportation

them would prevent such settlements and lead to strikes. See supra, footnote 5. That there were many disputes, apparent and latent, for which the 1926 Act had not provided adequate machinery, is shown by the large number of representation disputes (more than 230) referred to the National Mediation Board in the first two years of its existence, see First Annual Report, For the Fiscal Year Ended June 30, 1935, p. 9; Second Annual Report, For the Fiscal Year Ended June 30, 1936, pp. 5, 7.

It is the belief of the National Mediation Board that peace in the railroad industry is largely due to the 3,485 collective agreements covering rates of pay, rules, and working conditions, which were filed by June 30, 1936 [see National Mediation Board, Second Annual Report, For the Fiscal Year Ended June 30, 1936, p. 26]. In its First Annual Report, For the Fiscal Year Ended June 30, 1935, it concluded (p. 36): "The absence of strikes in the railroad industry, particularly during the last two years when wide-spread strikes, the usual accompaniment of business recovery, prevailed throughout the country, is to be explained primarily not by the mediation machinery of the Railway Labor Act, but by the existence of these collective labor contracts. For, while they are in existence, these contracts provide orderly, legal processes of settling all disputes as a substitute for strikes and industrial warfare."

is such that a strike of petitioner's employees there, quite apart
from the likelihood of its spreading to the operating department,
would subject petitioner to the danger, substantial, though possibly indefinable in its extent, of interruption of the transportation service. The cause is not remote from the effect. The relation between them is not tenuous. The effect on commerce cannot
be regarded as negligible. See United States v. Railway Employees
Department of the American Federation of Labor (D.C.) 290 F.
978, 981, holding participation of back shop employees in the nation-
wide railroad shopmen's strike of 1922 to constitute an interference
with interstate commerce. As the regulation here in question is
shown to be an appropriate means of avoiding that danger, it is
within the power of Congress.

It is no answer, as petitioner suggests, that it could close its
back shops and turn over the repair work to independent contractors. Whether the railroad should do its repair work in its
own shops, or in those of another, is a question of railroad management. It is petitioner's determination to make its own repairs
which has brought its relations with shop employees within the
purview of the Railway Labor Act. It is the nature of the work
done and its relation to interstate transportation which afford
adequate basis for the exercise of the regulatory power of Congress.

The Employers' Liability Cases, 207 U.S. 463, 498, 28 S. Ct.
141, 52 L. Ed. 297, which mentioned railroad repair shops as a
subject beyond the power to regulate commerce, are not controlling here. Whatever else may be said of that pronouncement, it is
obvious that the commerce power is as much dependent upon the
type of regulation as its subject matter. It is enough for present
purposes that experience has shown that the failure to settle, by
peaceful means, the grievances of railroad employees with respect
to rates of pay, rules or working conditions, is far more likely to
hinder interstate commerce than the failure to compensate workers who have suffered injury in the course of their employment.

(B) Validity of section 2 of the Railway Labor Act Under
the Fifth Amendment. The provisions of the Railway Labor Act
applied in this case, as construed by the court below, and as we
construe them, do not require petitioner to enter into any agreement with its employees, and they do not prohibit its entering into
such contract of employment as it chooses, with its individual
employees. They prohibit only such use of the company union as,
despite the objections repeated here, was enjoined in the Railway
Clerks case, supra, and they impose on petitioner only the affirmative duty of "treating with" the authorized representatives of its
employees for the purpose of negotiating a labor dispute.

Even though Congress, in the choice of means to effect a permissible regulation of commerce, must conform to due process,

Railroad Retirement Board v. Alton R. Co., supra, 295 U.S. 330, 347, 55 S. Ct. 758, 761, 79 L. Ed. 1468; Chicago, R. I. & P. Ry. Co. v. United States, 284 U.S. 80, 97, 52 S. Ct. 87, 92, 76 L. Ed. 177; see Louisville Joint Stock Land Bank v. Radford, 295 U.S. 555, 589, 55 S. Ct. 854, 863, 79 L. Ed. 1593, 97 A.L.R. 1106, it is evident that where, as here, the means chosen are appropriate to the permissible end, there is little scope for the operation of the due process clause. The railroad can complain only of the infringement of its own constitutional immunity, not that of its employees. Erie R. Co. v. Williams, 233 U.S. 685, 697, 34 S. Ct. 761, 58 L. Ed. 1155, 51 L.R.A. (N.S.) 1097; Jeffrey Mfg. Co. v. Blagg, 235 U.S. 571, 576, 35 S. Ct. 167, 59 L. Ed. 364; Rail & River Coal Co. v. Yaple, 236 U.S. 338, 349, 35 S. Ct. 359, 59 L. Ed. 607; cf. Hawkins v. Bleakly, 243 U.S. 210, 214, 37 S. Ct. 255, 61 L. Ed. 678, Ann. Cas. 1917D, 637. And the Fifth Amendment, like the Fourteenth, see West Coast Hotel Co. v. Parrish, 300 U.S. 379, 57 S. Ct. 578, 81 L. Ed. ......, decided this day, is not a guarantee of untrammeled freedom of action and of contract. In the exercise of its power to regulate commerce, Congress can subject both to restraints not shown to be unreasonable. Such are the restraints of the Safety Appliance Act (45 U.S.C.A. sec. 1 et seq.), Johnson v. Southern Pac. Co., 196 U.S. 1, 25 S. Ct. 158, 49 L. Ed. 363; of the act imposing a wage scale on rail carriers (45 U.S.C.A. secs. 65, 66); Wilson v. New, supra; of the Railroad Employers' Liability Act (45 U.S.C.A. sec. 51 et seq.), Second Employers' Liability Cases, 223 U.S. 1, 32 S. Ct. 169, 56 L. Ed. 327, 38 L.R.A. (N.S.) 44; of the act fixing maximum hours of service for railroad employees whose duties control or affect the movement of trains (45 U.S.C.A. secs. 61-64), Baltimore & Ohio R. Co. v. Interstate Commerce Commission, supra; of the act prohibiting the prepayment of seamen's wages (46 U.S. C.A. sec. 599), Patterson v. Bark Eudora, 190 U.S. 169, 23 S. Ct. 821, 47 L. Ed. 1002.

Each of the limited duties imposed upon petitioner by the statute and the decree do not differ in their purpose and nature from those imposed under the earlier statute and enforced in the Railway Clerks case, supra. The quality of the action compelled, its reasonableness, and therefore the lawfulness of the compulsion, must be judged in the light of the conditions which have occasioned the exercise of governmental power. If the compulsory settlement of some differences, by arbitration, may be within the limits of due process, see Hardware Dealers Mutual Fire Ins. Co. v. Glidden Co., 284 U.S. 151, 52 S. Ct. 69, 76 L. Ed. 214, it seems plain that the command of the statute to negotiate for the settlement of labor disputes, given in the appropriate exercise of the commerce power, cannot be said to be so arbitrary or unreasonable as to infringe due process.

Adair v. United States, 208 U.S. 161, 28 S. Ct. 277, 52 L. Ed. 436, 13 Ann. Cas. 764, and Coppage v. Kansas, 236 U.S. 1, 35 S. Ct. 240, 59 L. Ed. 441, L.R.A. 1915C, 960, have no present application. The provisions of the Railway Labor Act invoked here neither compel the employer to enter into any agreement, nor preclude it from entering into any contract with individual employees. They do not "interfere with the normal exercise of the right of the carrier to select its employees or to discharge them." See the Railway Clerks case, supra, 281 U.S. 548, 571, 50 S. Ct. 427, 434, 74 L. Ed. 1034.[8]

. . . Petitioner assails the decree for its failure to conform to the requirements of Section 9 of the Norris-LaGuardia Act (29 USCA sec. 109), which provides: "Every restraining order or injunction granted in a case involving or growing out of a labor dispute shall include only a prohibition of such specific act or acts as may be expressly complained of in the bill of complaint or petition filed in such case and as shall be expressly included in . . . findings of fact made and filed by the court." The evident purpose of this section, as its history and context show, was not to preclude mandatory injunctions, but to forbid blanket injunctions against labor unions, which are usually prohibitory in form, and to confine the injunction to the particular acts complained of and found by the court. We deem it unnecessary to comment on other similar objections, except to say that they are based on strained and unnatural constructions of the words of the Norris-LaGuardia Act, and conflict with its declared purpose, Section 2 (29 USCA sec. 102), that the employee "shall be free from the interference, restraint, or coercion of employers of labor, or their agents, in the designation of such representatives or in self-organization or in other concerted activities for the purpose of collective bargaining or other mutual aid or protection."

It suffices to say that the Norris-LaGuardia Act can affect the present decree only so far as its provisions are found to conflict with those of Section 2, Ninth, of the Railway Labor Act (45 USCA sec. 152, subd. 9), authorizing the relief which has been granted. Such provisions cannot be rendered nugatory by the earlier and more general provisions of the Norris-LaGuardia Act. See the Railway Clerks case, supra, 281 U.S. 548, 571, 50 S. Ct. 427, 434, 74 L. Ed. 1034; cf. Callahan v. United States, 285 U.S. 515, 518, 52 S. Ct. 454, 455, 76 L. Ed. 914; City of Walla Walla v. Walla Walla Water Co., 172 U.S. 1, 22, 19 S. Ct. 77, 43 L. Ed. 341; International Alliance v. Rex Theatre Corp., (C.C.A.) 73 F.(2d) 92, 93.

Affirmed.[9]

---

[8] The portion of the opinion dealing with the challenge to the validity of the certificate of the National Mediation Board because it failed to state the number of eligible voters in each craft or class is omitted.—Ed.

[9] In Brotherhood of Railroad Shop Crafts v. Lowden, 86 F.(2d) 458 (C.C.A. 10th, 1936), cert. denied, 57 Sup. Ct. 435 (1937), the constitutionality

NATIONAL LABOR RELATIONS ACT

Act of July 5, 1935. 49 Stat. 449.

Findings and Policy

SECTION 1. The denial by employers of the right of employees to organize and the refusal by employers to accept the procedure of collective bargaining lead to strikes and other forms of industrial strife or unrest, which have the intent or the necessary effect of burdening or obstructing commerce by (a) impairing the efficiency, safety, or operation of the instrumentalities of commerce; (b) occurring in the current of commerce; (c) materially affecting, restraining, or controlling the flow of raw materials or manufactured or processed goods from or into the channels of commerce, or the prices of such materials or goods in commerce; or (d) causing diminution of employment and wages in such volume as substantially to impair or disrupt the market for goods flowing from or into the channels of commerce.

The inequality of bargaining power between employees who do not possess full freedom of association or actual liberty of contract, and employers who are organized in the corporate or other forms of ownership association substantially burdens and affects the flow of commerce, and tends to aggravate recurrent business depressions, by depressing wage rates and the purchasing power

---

of the clause in Section 2, Fourth, of the Railway Labor Act which makes the "check-off" of union dues unlawful was sustained.

In Matter of R. C. A. Manufacturing Co. and United Electrical & Radio Workers, Case No. R-39, 2 N.L.R.B., ... (1936), the National Labor Relations Board, after indulging the presumption that Congress intended to apply the same principles to the fields covered by the respective statutes, interpreted Section 9(a) of the National Labor Relations Act (infra, p. 90), the analogue to Section 2, Fourth, of the Railway Labor Act, to require certification of the union which received a majority of the votes cast, although a majority of the eligibles had failed to vote. In so doing, the Board refused to follow the decision of the District Court in the main case (11 F. Supp. 621 (E.D. Va., 1935)) with respect to the carmen and coach cleaners. See also: Railway Employes' Dept. v. Nashville, C. & St. L. Ry., C.C.H. Labor Law Serv., par. 16279 (M.D. Tenn., 1936).

On questions of eligibility in elections conducted by the National Mediation Board, see: Brotherhood of Locomotive Firemen & Enginemen v. Kenan, 87 F.(2d) 651 (C.C.A. 5th, 1937) (furloughed employees); Brotherhood of Railroad Trainmen v. National Mediation Board, 88 F.(2d) 757 (App. D.C., 1936) (part-time employees); Lane v. Union Terminal Co., 12 F. Supp. 204 (N.D. Tex., 1935). See also: Association of Clerical Employees v. Brotherhood of Ry. & S. S. Clerks, 85 F.(2d) 152 (C.C.A. 7th, 1936) (blank ballots).

See: National Mediation Board, First Annual Report, For the Fiscal Year Ended June 30, 1935, and Second Annual Report, for the Fiscal Year Ended June 30, 1936. For an excellent review of the work of the National Railroad Adjustment Board, created by Section 3 of the Railway Labor Act, as amended, see: Garrison, "The National Railroad Adjustment Board: A Unique Administrative Agency," 46 Yale L.J. 567 (1937).

of wage earners in industry and by preventing the stabilization of competitive wage rates and working conditions within and between industries.

Experience has proved that protection by law of the right of employees to organize and bargain collectively safeguards commerce from injury, impairment, or interruption, and promotes the flow of commerce by removing certain recognized sources of industrial strife and unrest, by encouraging practices fundamental to the friendly adjustment of industrial disputes arising out of differences as to wages, hours, or other working conditions, and by restoring equality of bargaining power between employers and employees.

It is hereby declared to be the policy of the United States to eliminate the causes of certain substantial obstructions to the free flow of commerce and to mitigate and eliminate these obstructions when they have occurred by encouraging the practice and procedure of collective bargaining and by protecting the exercise by workers of full freedom of association, self-organization, and designation of representatives of their own choosing, for the purpose of negotiating the terms and conditions of their employment or other mutual aid or protection.

DEFINITIONS

SEC. 2. When used in this Act—

(1) The term "person" includes one or more individuals, partnerships, associations, corporations, legal representatives, trustees, trustees in bankruptcy, or receivers.

(2) The term "employer" includes any person acting in the interest of an employer, directly or indirectly, but shall not include the United States, or any State or political subdivision thereof, or any person subject to the Railway Labor Act, as amended from time to time, or any labor organization (other than when acting as an employer), or anyone acting in the capacity of officer or agent of such labor organization.

(3) The term "employee" shall include any employee, and shall not be limited to the employees of a particular employer, unless the Act explicitly states otherwise, and shall include any individual whose work has ceased as a consequence of, or in connection with, any current labor dispute or because of any unfair labor practice, and who has not obtained any other regular and substantially equivalent employment, but shall not include any individual employed as an agricultural laborer, or in the domestic service of any family or person at his home, or any individual employed by his parent or spouse.

(4) The term "representatives" includes any individual or labor organization.

(5) The term "labor organization" means any organization of any kind, or any agency or employee representation committee or plan, in which employees participate and which exists for the purpose, in whole or in part, of dealing with employers concerning grievances, labor disputes, wages, rates of pay, hours of employment, or conditions of work.

(6) The term "commerce" means trade, traffic, commerce, transportation, or communication among the several States, or between the District of Columbia or any Territory of the United States and any State or other Territory, or between any foreign country and any State, Territory, or the District of Columbia, or within the District of Columbia or any Territory, or between points in the same State but through any other State or any Territory or the District of Columbia or any foreign country.

(7) The term "affecting commerce" means in commerce, or burdening or obstructing commerce or the free flow of commerce, or having led or tending to lead to a labor dispute burdening or obstructing commerce or the free flow of commerce.

(8) The term "unfair labor practice" means any unfair labor practice listed in section 8.

(9) The term "labor dispute" includes any controversy concerning terms, tenure or conditions of employment, or concerning the association or representation of persons in negotiating, fixing, maintaining, changing, or seeking to arrange terms or conditions of employment, regardless of whether the disputants stand in the proximate relation of employer and employee.

(10) The term "National Labor Relations Board" means the National Labor Relations Board created by section 3 of this Act.

(11) The term "old Board" means the National Labor Relations Board established by Executive Order Numbered 6763 of the President on June 29, 1934, pursuant to Public Resolution Numbered 44, approved June 19, 1934 (48 Stat. 1183), and reestablished and continued by Executive Order Numbered 7074 of the President of June 15, 1935, pursuant to Title I of the National Industrial Recovery Act (48 Stat. 195) as amended and continued by Senate Joint Resolution 133 [1] approved June 14, 1935. [2]

RIGHTS OF EMPLOYEES

SEC. 7. Employees shall have the right to self-organization, to form, join, or assist labor organizations, to bargain collectively

---

[1] So in original. The correct reference is to Senate Joint Resolution 113.—Ed.

[2] Sections 3-6, creating the Board, providing for its appointment and for the appointment of its employees, making provision for its expenses, etc., and giving it authority to make rules and regulations, are omitted.—Ed.

through representatives of their own choosing, and to engage in concerted activities, for the purpose of collective bargaining or other mutual aid or protection.

SEC. 8. It shall be an unfair labor practice for an employer—

(1) To interfere with, restrain, or coerce employees in the exercise of the rights guaranteed in section 7.

(2) To dominate or interfere with the formation or administration of any labor organization or contribute financial or other support to it: *Provided,* That subject to rules and regulations made and published by the Board pursuant to section 6 (a), an employer shall not be prohibited from permitting employees to confer with him during working hours without loss of time or pay.

(3) By discrimination in regard to hire or tenure of employment or any term or condition of employment to encourage or discourage membership in any labor organization: *Provided,* That nothing in this Act, or in the National Industrial Recovery Act (U.S.C., Supp. VII, title 15, secs. 701-712), as amended from time to time, or in any code or agreement approved or prescribed thereunder, or in any other statute of the United States, shall preclude an employer from making an agreement with a labor organization (not established, maintained, or assisted by any action defined in this Act as an unfair labor practice) to require as a condition of employment membership therein, if such labor organization is the representative of the employees as provided in section 9 (a), in the appropriate collective bargaining unit covered by such agreement when made.

(4) To discharge or otherwise discriminate against an employee because he has filed charges or given testimony under this Act.

(5) To refuse to bargain collectively with the representatives of his employees, subject to the provisions of section 9 (a).

REPRESENTATIVES AND ELECTIONS

SEC. 9. (a) Representatives designated or selected for the purposes of collective bargaining by the majority of the employees in a unit appropriate for such purposes, shall be the exclusive representatives of all the employees in such unit for the purposes of collective bargaining in respect to rates of pay, wages, hours of employment, or other conditions of employment: *Provided,* That any individual employee or a group of employees shall have the right at any time to present grievances to their employer.

(b) The Board shall decide in each case whether, in order to insure to employees the full benefit of their right to self-organization and to collective bargaining, and otherwise to effectuate the policies of this Act, the unit appropriate for the purposes of collective bargaining shall be the employer unit, craft unit, plant unit, or subdivision thereof.

(c) Whenever a question affecting commerce arises concerning the representation of employees, the Board may investigate such controversy and certify to the parties, in writing, the name or names of the representatives that have been designated or selected. In any such investigation, the Board shall provide for an appropriate hearing upon due notice, either in conjunction with a proceeding under section 10 or otherwise, and may take a secret ballot of employees, or utilize any other suitable method to ascertain [3] such representatives.

(d) Whenever an order of the Board made pursuant to section 10 (c) is based in whole or in part upon facts certified following an investigation pursuant to subsection (c) of this section, and there is a petition for the enforcement or review of such order, such certification and the record of such investigation shall be included in the transcript of the entire record required to be filed under subsections 10 (e) or 10 (f), and thereupon the decree of the court enforcing, modifying, or setting aside in whole or in part the order of the Board shall be made and entered upon the pleadings, testimony, and proceedings set forth in such transcript.

PREVENTION OF UNFAIR LABOR PRACTICES

SEC. 10 (a) The Board is empowered, as hereinafter provided, to prevent any person from engaging in any unfair labor practice (listed in section 8) affecting commerce. This power shall be exclusive, and shall not be affected by any other means of adjustment or prevention that has been or may be established by agreement, code, law, or otherwise.

(b) Whenever it is charged that any person has engaged in or is engaging in any such unfair labor practice, the Board, or any agent or agency designated by the Board for such purposes, shall have power to issue and cause to be served upon such person a complaint stating the charges in that respect, and containing a notice of hearing before the Board or a member thereof, or before a designated agent or agency, at a place therein fixed, not less than five days after the serving of said complaint. Any such complaint may be amended by the member, agent, or agency conducting the hearing or the Board in its discretion at any time prior to the issuance of an order based thereon. The person so complained of shall have the right to file an answer to the original or amended complaint and to appear in person or otherwise and give testimony at the place and time fixed in the complaint. In the

---

[3] So in original.—Ed.

discretion of the member, agent or agency conducting the hearing or the Board, any other person may be allowed to intervene in the said proceeding and to present testimony. In any such proceeding the rules of evidence prevailing in courts of law or equity shall not be controlling.

(c) The testimony taken by such member, agent or agency or the Board shall be reduced to writing and filed with the Board. Thereafter, in its discretion, the Board upon notice may take further testimony or hear argument. If upon all the testimony taken the Board shall be of the opinion that any person named in the complaint has engaged in or is engaging in any such unfair labor practice, then the Board shall state its findings of fact and shall issue and cause to be served on such person an order requiring such person to cease and desist from such unfair labor practice, and to take such affirmative action, including reinstatement of employees with or without back pay, as will effectuate the policies of this Act. Such order may further require such person to make reports from time to time showing the extent to which it has complied with the order. If upon all the testimony taken the Board shall be of the opinion that no person named in the complaint has engaged in or is engaging in any such unfair labor practice, then the Board shall state its findings of fact and shall issue an order dismissing the said complaint.

(d) Until a transcript of the record in a case shall have been filed in a court, as hereinafter provided, the Board may at any time, upon reasonable notice and in such manner as it shall deem proper, modify or set aside, in whole or in part, any finding or order made or issued by it.

(e) The Board shall have power to petition any circuit court of appeals of the United States (including the Court of Appeals of the District of Columbia), or if all the circuit courts of appeals to which application may be made are in vacation, any district court of the United States (including the Supreme Court of the District of Columbia), within any circuit or district, respectively, wherein the unfair labor practice in question occurred or wherein such person resides or transacts business, for the enforcement of such order and for appropriate temporary relief or restraining order, and shall certify and file in the court a transcript of the entire record in the proceeding, including the pleadings and testimony upon which such order was entered and the findings and order of the Board. Upon such filing, the court shall cause notice thereof to be served upon such person, and thereupon shall have jurisdiction of the proceeding and of the question determined therein, and shall have power to grant such temporary relief or restraining order as it deems just and proper, and to make and enter upon the pleadings, testimony, and proceedings set forth in such transcript a decree enforcing, modifying, and enforcing as so modified, or setting aside in whole or in part the order of the Board. No objection that has not been urged before the Board, its member, agent or agency, shall be considered by the court, unless the failure or neglect to urge such objection shall be excused because of extraordinary circumstances. The findings of the Board as to the facts, if supported by evidence, shall be conclusive. If either party shall apply to the court for leave to adduce additional evidence and shall show to the satisfaction of the court that such additional evidence is material and that there were reasonable grounds for the failure to adduce such evidence in the hearing before the Board, its member, agent, or agency, the court may order such additional evidence to be taken before the Board, its member, agent, or agency, and to be made a part of the transcript. The Board may modify its findings as to the facts, or make new findings, by reason of additional evidence so taken and filed, and it shall file such modified or new findings, which, if supported by evidence, shall be conclusive, and shall file its recommendations, if any, for the modification or setting aside of its original order. The jurisdiction of the court shall be exclusive and its judgment and decree shall be final, except that the same shall be subject to review by the appropriate circuit court of appeals if application was made to the district court as hereinabove provided, and by the Supreme Court of the United States upon writ of certiorari or certification as provided in sections 239 and 240 of the Judicial Code, as amended (U.S.C., title 28, secs. 346 and 347).

(f) Any person aggrieved by a final order of the Board granting or denying in whole or in part the relief sought may obtain a review of such order in any circuit court of appeals of the United States in the circuit wherein the unfair labor practice in question was alleged to have been engaged in or wherein such person resides or transacts business, or in the Court of Appeals of the District of Columbia, by filing in such court a written petition praying that the order of the Board be modified or set aside. A copy of such petition shall be forthwith served upon the Board, and thereupon the aggrieved party shall file in the court a transcript of the entire record in the proceeding, certified by the Board, including the pleading and testimony upon which the order complained of was entered and the findings and order of the Board. Upon such filing, the court shall proceed in the same manner as in the case of an application by the Board under subsection (e), and shall have the same exclusive jurisdiction to grant to the Board such temporary relief or restraining order as it deems just and proper, and in like manner to make and enter a decree enforcing, modifying, and enforcing as so modified, or setting aside in whole or in part the order of the Board; and the findings of the Board as to the facts, if supported by evidence, shall in like manner be conclusive.

(g) The commencement of proceedings under subsection (e) or (f) of this section shall not, unless specifically ordered by the court, operate as a stay of the Board's order.

(h) When granting appropriate temporary relief or a restraining order, or making and entering a decree enforcing, modifying, and enforcing as so modified or setting aside in whole or in part an order of the Board, as provided in this section, the jurisdiction of courts sitting in equity shall not be limited by the Act entitled "An Act to amend the Judicial Code and to define and limit the jurisdiction of courts sitting in equity, and for other purposes," approved March 23, 1932 (U.S.C., Supp. VII, title 29, secs. 101-115).

(i) Petitions filed under this Act shall be heard expeditiously, and if possible within ten days after they have been docketed.

INVESTIGATORY POWERS

SEC. 11. For the purpose of all hearings and investigations, which, in the opinion of the Board, are necessary and proper for the exercise of the powers vested in it by section 9 and section 10—

(1) The Board, or its duly authorized agents or agencies, shall at all reasonable times have access to, for the purpose of examination, and the right to copy any evidence of any person being investigated or proceeded against that relates to any matter under investigation or in question. Any member of the Board shall have power to issue subpenas requiring the attendance and testimony of witnesses and the production of any evidence that relates to any matter under investigation or in question, before the Board, its member, agent, or agency conducting the hearing or investigation. Any member of the Board, or any agent or agency designated by the Board for such purposes, may administer oaths and affirmations, examine witnesses, and receive evidence. Such attendance of witnesses and the production of such evidence may be required from any place in the United States or any Territory or possession thereof, at any designated place of hearing.

(2) In case of contumacy or refusal to obey a subpena issued to any person, any District Court of the United States or the United States courts of any Territory or possession, or the Supreme Court of the District of Columbia, within the jurisdiction of which the inquiry is carried on or within the jurisdiction of which said person guilty of contumacy or refusal to obey is found or resides or transacts business, upon application by the Board shall have jurisdiction to issue to such person an order requiring such person to appeal before the Board, its member, agent, or agency, there to produce evidence if so ordered, or there to give testimony touching the matter under investigation or in question; and any failure to obey such order of the court may be punished by said court as a contempt thereof.

(3) No person shall be excused from attending and testifying or from producing books, records, correspondence, documents, or other evidence in obedience to the subpena of the Board, on the ground that the testimony or evidence required of him may tend to incriminate him or subject him to a penalty or forfeiture; but no individual shall be prosecuted or subjected to any penalty or forfeiture for or on account of any transaction, matter, or thing concerning which he is compelled, after having claimed his privilege against self-incrimination, to testify or produce evidence, except that such individual so testifying shall not be exempt from prosecution and punishment for perjury committed in so testifying.

(4) Complaints, orders, and other process and papers of the Board, its member, agent, or agency, may be served either personally or by registered mail or by telegraph or by leaving a copy thereof at the principal office or place of business of the person required to be served. The verified return by the individual so serving the same setting forth the manner of such service shall be proof of the same, and the return post office receipt or telegraph receipt therefor when registered and mailed or telegraphed as aforesaid shall be proof of service of the same. Witnesses summoned before the Board, its member, agent, or agency, shall be paid the same fees and mileage that are paid witnesses in the courts of the United States, and witnesses whose depositions are taken and the persons taking the same shall severally be entitled to the same fees as are paid for like services in the courts of the United States.

(5) All process of any court to which application may be made under this Act may be served in the judicial district wherein the defendant or other person required to be served resides or may be found.

(6) The several departments and agencies of the Government, when directed by the President, shall furnish the Board, upon its request, all records, papers, and information in their possession relating to any matter before the Board.

SEC. 12. Any person who shall willfully resist, prevent, impede, or interfere with any member of the Board or any of its agents or agencies in the performance of duties pursuant to this Act shall be punished by a fine of not more than $5,000 or by imprisonment for not more than one year, or both.

LIMITATIONS

SEC. 13. Nothing in this Act shall be construed so as to interfere with or impede or diminish in any way the right to strike.

SEC. 14. Wherever the application of the provisions of section 7 (a) of the National Industrial Recovery Act (U.S.C., Supp. VII, title 15, sec. 707 (a)), as amended from time to time, or of section 77 B, paragraphs (l) and (m) of the Act approved June 7, 1934, entitled "An Act to amend an Act entitled 'An Act to establish a uniform system of bankruptcy throughout the United States' approved July 1, 1898, and Acts amendatory thereof and supplementary thereto" (48 Stat. 922, pars. (l) and (m)), as amended from time to time, or of Public Resolution Numbered 44, approved June 19, 1934 (48 Stat. 1183), conflicts with the application of the provisions of this Act, this Act shall prevail: *Provided,* That in any situation where the provisions of this Act cannot be validly enforced, the provisions of such other Acts shall remain in full force and effect.

SEC. 15. If any provision of this Act, or the application of such provision to any person or circumstance, shall be held invalid, the remainder of this Act, or the application of such provision to persons or circumstances other than those as to which it is held invalid, shall not be affected thereby.

SEC. 16. This Act may be cited as the "National Labor Relations Act." [4]

---

[4] See: National Labor Relations Board, First Annual Report, For the Fiscal Year Ended June 30, 1936; Governmental Protection of Labor's Right to Organize, National Labor Relations Board, Division of Economic Research, Bulletin No. 1, August, 1936; Green and Others: Labor's Charter of Rights (1937); Bernheim and Van Doren (eds.): Labor and the Government (1935); Lorwin and Wubnig: Labor Relations Boards (1935); Garrison, "Government and Labor: The Latest Phase," 37 Col. L. Rev. 897 (1937); Magruder, "Half Century of Legal Influence Upon the Development of Collective Bargaining," 50 Harv. L. Rev. 1071 (1937).

See also: Latham, "Legislative Purpose and Administrative Policy Under the National Labor Relations Act," 4 Geo. Wash. L. Rev. 433 (1936); Legis., "The Wagner Labor Disputes Act," 35 Col. L. Rev. 1098 (1935); Comment, "The National Labor Relations Act—Constitutional and Statutory Problems," 30 Ill. L. Rev. 884 (1936).

See also: Decisions and Orders of the National Labor Relations Board: Volume 1, December, 1935, to July, 1936; Volume 2, July, 1936, to July, 1937 (cited as N.L.R.B.); Chamber of Commerce of the U. S., Labor Relations Board's Decisions 1935-1937 (1937); Despres and Myer, "The National Labor Relations Board—Decisions of its First Year," 4 U. of Chi. L. Rev. 97 (1936); Note, "Employer Interference With Lawful Union Activity," 37 Col. L. Rev. 816 (1937).

Five states have enacted labor relations acts, all of which are closely patterned after the National Act: 1937 Mass. Laws, c. 436; 1937 N.Y. Laws, c. 443; 1937 Pa. Laws, Act No. 294); 1937 Utah Laws, c. 55; 1937 Wis. Laws, c. 51. The Pennsylvania and Utah statutes do not vary in any material detail from the National Act. The Massachusetts Act qualifies the right to strike by declaring that a sit-down strike is an unfair labor practice. (Sec. 8A.) The New York and Wisconsin Acts make the practices of labor espionage and blacklisting specifically unfair, and inhibit in greater detail than does the National Act employer domination of and interference with "company unions." (N.Y., sec. 704; Wis., sec. 111.08.) The New York Act empowers the Board to select not only the employer, craft, or plant unit for the purposes of collective bargaining, but also "any other unit"; however, "where the majority of employees of a particular craft shall so decide the board shall designate such craft" as the appropriate unit. (Sec. 705.) The Wisconsin Act specifically permits a closed shop agreement to be made with any labor organization not a "company union," whether it represents a majority of the employees or not

NATIONAL LABOR RELATIONS BOARD v. JONES & LAUGHLIN STEEL CORPORATION

Supreme Court of the United States, 1937. 301 U.S. 1.

MR. CHIEF JUSTICE HUGHES delivered the opinion of the Court.

In a proceeding under the National Labor Relations Act of 1935,[1] the National Labor Relations Board found that the respondent, Jones & Laughlin Steel Corporation, had violated the Act by engaging in unfair labor practices affecting commerce. The proceeding was instituted by the Beaver Valley Lodge No. 200, affiliated with the Amalgamated Association of Iron, Steel and Tin Workers of America, a labor organization. The unfair labor practices charged were that the corporation was discriminating against members of the union with regard to hire and tenure of employment, and was coercing and intimidating its employees in order to interfere with their self-organization. The discriminatory and coercive action alleged was the discharge of certain employees.

The National Labor Relations Board, sustaining the charge, ordered the corporation to cease and desist from such discrimination and coercion, to offer reinstatement to ten of the employees named, to make good their losses in pay, and to post for thirty days notices that the corporation would not discharge or discriminate against members, or those desiring to become members, of the labor union. As the corporation failed to comply, the Board petitioned the Circuit Court of Appeals to enforce the order. The court denied the petition holding that the order lay beyond the range of federal power. 83 F.(2d) 998. We granted certiorari. 299 U.S. 534, 57 S. Ct. 119, 81 L. Ed. ......[2]

The procedure in the instant case followed the statute. The labor union filed with the Board its verified charge. The Board thereupon issued its complaint against the respondent alleging that its action in discharging the employees in question constituted unfair labor practices affecting commerce within the meaning of section 8, subdivisions (1) and (3), and section 2, subdivisions (6) and (7) of the Act. Respondent, appearing specially for the purpose of objecting to the jurisdiction of the Board, filed its answer. Respondent admitted the discharges, but alleged that they were

---

(Sec. 111.07.) The Wisconsin Act requires the Board to maintain a register of labor organizations; to be eligible for the register a labor organization must "persuade the board that it is not a company union." (Sec. 111.06 (2).) The Wisconsin Act also provides for separate committees of employers and union officials to investigate and make reports on complaints of labor practices other than unfair labor practices, and gives the Board authority to arbitrate and conciliate. (Secs. 111.15; 111.12; 111.16.) See: Feinsinger and Rice: The Wisconsin Labor Relations Act (Bull. U. of Wis., 1937).

[1] Act of July 5, 1935, 49 Stat. 449, 29 U.S.C. 151.

[2] The portion of the opinion outlining the scheme of the Act is omitted.—Ed.

made because of inefficiency or violation of rules or for other good reasons and were not ascribable to union membership or activities. As an affirmative defense respondent challenged the constitutional validity of the statute and its applicability in the instant case. Notice of hearing was given and respondent appeared by counsel. The Board first took up the issue of jurisdiction and evidence was presented by both the Board and the respondent. Respondent then moved to dismiss the complaint for lack of jurisdiction and, on denial of that motion, respondent in accordance with its special appearance withdrew from further participation in the hearing. The Board received evidence upon the merits and at its close made it findings and order.

Contesting the ruling of the Board, the respondent argues (1) that the Act is in reality a regulation of labor relations and not of interstate commerce; (2) that the Act can have no application to the respondent's relations with its production employees because they are not subject to regulation by the federal government; and (3) that the provisions of the Act violate section 2 of article III and the Fifth and Seventh Amendments of the Constitution of the United States.

The facts as to the nature and scope of the business of the Jones & Laughlin Steel Corporation have been found by the Labor Board and, so far as they are essential to the determination of this controversy, they are not in dispute. The Labor Board has found: The corporation is organized under the laws of Pennsylvania and has its principal office at Pittsburgh. It is engaged in the business of manufacturing iron and steel in plants situated in Pittsburgh and nearby Aliquippa, Pa. It manufactures and distributes a widely diversified line of steel and pig iron, being the fourth largest producer of steel in the United States. With its subsidiaries— nineteen in number—it is a completely integrated enterprise, owning and operating ore, coal and limestone properties, lake and river transportation facilities and terminal railroads located at its manufacturing plants. It owns or controls mines in Michigan and Minnesota. It operates four ore steamships on the Great Lakes, used in the transportation of ore to its factories. It owns coal mines in Pennsylvania. It operates towboats and steam barges used in carrying coal to its factories. It owns limestone properties in various places in Pennsylvania and West Virginia. It owns the Monongahela connecting railroad which connects the plants of the Pittsburgh works and forms an interconnection with the Pennsylvania, New York Central and Baltimore & Ohio Railroad systems. It owns the Aliquippa & Southern Railroad Company which connects the Aliquippa works with the Pittsburgh & Lake Erie, part of the New York Central system. Much of its product is shipped to its warehouses in Chicago, Detroit, Cincinnati and Memphis,—to the last two places by means of its own barges and transportation equipment. In Long Island City, New York, and in New Orleans it operates structural steel fabricating shops in connection with the warehousing of semi-finished materials sent from its works. Through one of its wholly-owned subsidiaries it owns, leases, and operates stores, warehouses, and yards for the distribution of equipment and supplies for drilling and operating oil and gas mills and for pipe lines, refineries and pumping stations. It has sales offices in twenty cities in the United States and a wholly-owned subsidiary which is devoted exclusively to distributing its product in Canada. Approximately 75 per cent. of its product is shipped out of Pennsylvania.

Summarizing these operations, the Labor Board concluded that the works in Pittsburgh and Aliquippa "might be likened to the heart of a self-contained, highly integrated body. They draw in the raw materials from Michigan, Minnesota, West Virginia, Pennsylvania in part through arteries and by means controlled by the respondent; they transform the materials and then pump them out to all parts of the nation through the vast mechanism which the respondent has elaborated."

To carry on the activities of the entire steel industry, 33,000 men mine ore, 44,000 men mine coal, 4,000 men quarry limestone, 16 000 men manufacture coke, 343,000 men manufacture steel, and 83,000 men transport its product. Respondent has about 10,000 employees in its Aliquippa plant, which is located in a community of about 30,000 persons.

Respondent points to evidence that the Aliquippa plant, in which the discharged men were employed, contains complete facilities for the production of finished and semi-finished iron and steel products from raw materials; that its works consist primarily of a by-product coke plant for the production of coke; blast furnaces for the production of pig iron; open hearth furnaces and Bessemer converters for the production of steel; blooming mills for the reduction of steel ingots into smaller shapes; and a number of finishing mills such as structural mills, rod mills, wire mills, and the like. In addition, there are other buildings, structures and equipment, storage yards, docks and an intraplant storage system. Respondent's operations at these works are carried on in two distinct stages, the first being the conversion of raw materials into pig iron and the second being the manufacture of semifinished and finished iron and steel products; and in both cases the operations result in substantially changing the character, utility and value of the materials wrought upon, which is apparent from the nature and extent of the processes to which they are subjected and which respondent fully describes. Respondent also directs attention to the fact that the iron ore which is procured from mines in Minnesota and Michigan and transported to respondent's plant is stored

in stock piles for future use, the amount of ore in storage varying
with the season but usually being enough to maintain operations
from nine to ten months; that the coal which is procured from the
mines of a subsidiary located in Pennsylvania and taken to the
plant at Aliquippa is there, like ore, stored for future use, approximately two to three months' supply of coal being always on
hand; and that the limestone which is obtained in Pennsylvania
and West Virginia is also stored in amounts usually adequate to
run the blast furnaces for a few weeks. Various details of operation, transportation, and distribution are also mentioned which for
the present purpose it is not necessary to detail.

Practically all the factual evidence in the case, except that
which dealt with the nature of respondent's business, concerned its
relations with the employees in the Aliquippa plant whose discharge
was the subject of the complaint. These employees were, active
leaders in the labor union. Several were officers and others were
leaders of particular groups. Two of the employees were motor
inspectors; one was a tractor driver; three were crane operators;
one was a washer in the coke plant; and three were laborers. Three
other employees were mentioned in the complaint but it was withdrawn as to one of them and no evidence was heard on the action
taken with respect to the other two.

While respondent criticises the evidence and the attitude of the
Board, which is described as being hostile toward employers
and particularly toward those who insisted upon their constitutional rights, respondent did not take advantage of its opportunity
to present evidence to refute that which was offered to show discrimination and coercion. In this situation, the record presents no
ground for setting aside the order of the Board so far as the facts
pertaining to the circumstances and purpose of the discharge of the
employees are concerned. Upon that point it is sufficient to say
that the evidence supports the findings of the Board that respondent
discharged these men "because of their union activity and for the
purpose of discouraging membership in the union." We turn to
the questions of law which respondent urges in contesting the
validity and application of the Act.

First. The Scope of the Act.—The Act is challenged in its entirety as an attempt to regulate all industry, thus invading the reserved powers of the States over their local concerns. It is asserted that the references in the Act to interstate and foreign
commerce are colorable at best; that the Act is not a true regulation of such commerce or of matters which directly affect it
but on the contrary has the fundamental object of placing under
the compulsory supervision of the federal government all industrial labor relations within the nation. The argument seeks support in the broad words of the preamble (section 1) and in the
sweep of the provisions of the Act, and it is further insisted that

its legislative history shows an essential universal purpose in the light of which its scope cannot be limited by either construction or by the application of the separability clause.

If this conception of terms, intent and consequent inseparability were sound, the Act would necessarily fall by reason of the limitation upon the federal power which inheres in the constitutional grant, as well as because of the explicit reservation of the Tenth Amendment. Schechter Corporation v. United States, 295 U.S. 495, 549, 550, 554, 55 S. Ct. 837, 851, 853, 79 L. Ed. 1570, 97 A.L.R. 947. The authority of the federal government may not be pushed to such an extreme as to destroy the distinction, which the commerce clause itself establishes, between commerce "among the several States" and the internal concerns of a state. That distinction between what is national and what is local in the activities of commerce is vital to the maintenance of our federal system. Id.

But we are not at liberty to deny effect to specific provisions, which Congress has constitutional power to enact, by superimposing upon them inferences from general legislative declarations of an ambiguous character, even if found in the same statute. The cardinal principle of statutory construction is to save and not to destroy. We have repeatedly held that as between two possible interpretations of a statute, by one of which it would be unconstitutional and by the other valid, our plain duty is to adopt that which will save the Act. Even to avoid a serious doubt the rule is the same. Federal Trade Commission v. American Tobacco Co., 264 U.S. 298, 307, 44 S. Ct. 336, 337, 68 L. Ed. 696, 32 A.L.R. 786; Panama R. R. Co. v. Johnson, 264 U.S. 375, 390, 44 S. Ct. 391, 395, 68 L. Ed. 748; Missouri Pacific R. R. Co. v. Boone, 270 U.S. 466, 472, 46 S. Ct. 341, 343, 70 L. Ed. 688; Blodgett v. Holden, 275 U.S. 142, 148, 276 U.S. 594, 48 S. Ct. 105, 107, 72 L. Ed. 206; Richmond Screw Anchor Co. v. United States, 275 U.S. 331, 346, 48 S. Ct. 194, 198, 72 L. Ed. 303.

We think it clear that the National Labor Relations Act may be construed so as to operate within the sphere of constitutional authority. The jurisdiction conferred upon the Board, and invoked in this instance, is found in section 10(a), 29 U.S.C.A. sec. 160(a), which provides:

"Sec. 10(a). The Board is empowered, as hereinafter provided, to prevent any person from engaging in any unfair labor practice (listed in section 8 [section 158]) affecting commerce."

The critical words of this provision, prescribing the limits of the Board's authority in dealing with the labor practices, are "affecting commerce." The Act specifically defines the "commerce" to which it refers (section 2(6), 29 U.S.C.A. sec. 152(6)):

"The term 'commerce' means trade, traffic, commerce, transportation, or communication among the several States, or between the District of Columbia or any Territory of the United States and any State or other Territory, or between any foreign country and any State, Territory, or the District of Columbia, or within the District of Columbia or any Territory, or between points in the same State but through any other State or any Territory or the District of Columbia or any foreign country."

There can be no question that the commerce thus contemplated by the Act (aside from that within a Territory or the District of Columbia) is interstate and foreign commerce in the constitutional sense. The Act also defines the term "affecting commerce" (section 2(7), 29 U.S.C.A. sec. 152 (7)):

"The term 'affecting commerce' means in commerce, or burdening or obstructing commerce or the free flow of commerce, or having led or tending to lead to a labor dispute burdening or obstructing commerce or the free flow of commerce."

This definition is one of exclusion as well as inclusion. The grant of authority to the Board does not purport to extend to the relationship between all industrial employees and employers. Its terms do not impose collective bargaining upon all industry regardless of effects upon interstate or foreign commerce. It purports to reach only what may be deemed to burden or obstruct that commerce and, thus qualified, it must be construed as contemplating the exercise of control within constitutional bounds. It is a familiar principle that acts which directly burden or obstruct interstate or foreign commerce, or its free flow, are within the reach of the congressional power. Acts having that effect are not rendered immune because they grow out of labor disputes. See Texas & N. O. R. Co. v. Railway & S. S. Clerks, 281 U.S. 548, 570, 50 S. Ct. 427, 433, 434, 74 L. Ed. 1034; Schechter Corporation v. United States, supra, 295 U.S. 495, at pp. 544, 545, 55 S. Ct. 837, 849, 79 L. Ed. 1570, 97 A.L.R. 947; Virginian Railway Co. v. System Federation, No. 40, 300 U.S. 515, 57 S. Ct. 592, 81 L. Ed. ......, decided March 29, 1937. It is the effect upon commerce, not the source of the injury, which is the criterion. Second Employers' Liability Cases (Mondow v. New York, N. H. & H. R. Co.), 223 U.S. 1, 51, 32 S. Ct. 169, 56 L. Ed. 327, 38 L.R.A. (N.S.) 44. Whether or not particular action does affect commerce in such a close and intimate fashion as to be subject to federal control, and hence to lie within the authority conferred upon the Board, is left by the statute to be determined as individual cases arise. We are thus to inquire whether in the instant case the constitutional boundary has been passed.

Second. The Unfair Labor Practices in Question.—The unfair labor practices found by the Board are those defined in section 8, subdivisions (1) and (3). These provide:

"Sec. 8. It shall be an unfair labor practice for an employer—

"(1) To interfere with, restrain, or coerce employees in the exercise of the rights guaranteed in section 7 [section 157 of this title]. . . .

"(3) By discrimination in regard to hire or tenure of employ-ment or any term or condition of employment to encourage or dis-courage membership in any labor organization."

Section 8, subdivision (1), refers to section 7, which is as fol-lows:

"Section 7. Employees shall have the right to self-organization, to form, join, or assist labor organizations, to bargain collectively through representatives of their own choosing, and to engage in concerted activities, for the purpose of collective bargaining or other mutual aid or protection."

Thus, in its present application, the statute goes no further than to safeguard the right of employees to self-organization and to select representatives of their own choosing for collective bargain-ing or other mutual protection without restraint or coercion by their employer.

That is a fundamental right. Employees have as clear a right to organize and select their representatives for lawful purposes as the respondent has to organize its business and select its own of-ficers and agents. Discrimination and coercion to prevent the free exercise of the right of employees to self-organization and repre-sentation is a proper subject for condemnation by competent legis-lative authority. Long ago we stated the reason for labor organi-zations. We said that they were organized out of the necessities of the situation; that a single employee was helpless in dealing with an employer; that he was dependent ordinarily on his daily wage for the maintenance of himself and family; that, if the em-ployer refused to pay him the wages that he thought fair, he was nevertheless unable to leave the employ and resist arbitrary and unfair treatment; that union was essential to give laborers oppor-tunity to deal on an equality with their employer. American Steel Foundries v. Tri-City Central Trades Council, 257 U.S. 184, 209, 42 S. Ct. 72, 78, 66 L. Ed. 189, 27 A.L.R. 360. We reiterated these views when we had under consideration the Railway Labor Act of 1926, 44 Stat. 577. Fully recognizing the legality of collec-tive action on the part of employees in order to safeguard their proper interests, we said that Congress was not required to ignore this right but could safeguard it. Congress could seek to make appropriate collective action of employees an instrument of peace rather than of strife. We said that such collective action would be a mockery if representation were made futile by inter-ference with freedom of choice. Hence the prohibition by Congress of interference with the selection of representatives for the purpose of negotiation and conference between employers and employees, "instead of being an invasion of the constitutional right of either, was based on the recognition of the rights of both." Texas & N. O. R. Co. v. Railway & S. S. Clerks, supra. We have reasserted the same principle in sustaining the application of the Railway Labor Act as amended in 1934 (45 U.S.C.A. sec. 151 et seq.). Virginian Railway Co. v. System Federation, No. 40, supra.

Third. The Application of the Act to Employees Engaged in Production.—The Principle Involved.—Respondent says that, whatever may be said of employees engaged in interstate commerce, the industrial relations and activities in the manufacturing department of respondent's enterprise are not subject to federal regulation. The argument rests upon the proposition that manufacturing in itself is not commerce. Kidd v. Pearson, 128 U.S. 1, 20, 21, 9 S. Ct. 6, 32 L. Ed. 346; United Mine Workers v. Coronado Co., 259 U.S. 344, 407, 408, 42 S. Ct. 570, 581, 582, 66 L. Ed. 975, 27 A.L.R. 762; Oliver Iron Co. v. Lord, 262 U.S. 172, 178, 43 S. Ct. 526, 529, 67 L. Ed. 929; United Leather Workers v. Herkert & Meisel Trunk Co., 265 U.S. 457, 465, 44 S. Ct. 623, 625, 68 L. Ed. 1104, 33 A.L.R. 566; Industrial Association v. United States, 268 U.S. 64, 82, 45 S. Ct. 403, 407, 69 L. Ed. 849; Coronado Coal Co. v. United Mine Workers, 268 U.S. 295, 310, 45 S. Ct. 551, 556, 69 L. Ed. 963; Schechter Corporation v. United States, supra, 295 U.S. 495, at page 457, 55 S. Ct. 837, 850, 79 L. Ed. 1570, 97 A.L.R. 947; Carter v. Carter Coal Co., 298 U.S. 238, 304, 317, 327, 56 S. Ct. 855, 869, 875, 880, 80 L. Ed. 1160.

The Government distinguishes these cases. The various parts of respondent's enterprise are described as interdependent and as thus involving "a great movement of iron ore, coal and limestone along well-defined paths to the steel mills, thence through them, and thence in the form of steel products into the consuming centers of the country—a definite and well-understood course of business." It is urged that these activities constitute a "stream" or "flow" of commerce, of which the Aliquippa manufacturing plant is the focal point, and that industrial strife at that point would cripple the entire movement. Reference is made to our decision sustaining the Packers and Stockyards Act.[3] Stafford v. Wallace, 258 U.S. 495, 42 S. Ct. 397, 66 L. Ed. 735, 23 A.L.R. 229. The Court found that the stockyards were but a "throat" through which the current of commerce flowed and the transactions which there occurred could not be separated from that movement. Hence the sales at the stockyards were not regarded as merely local transactions, for, while they created "a local change of title" they did not "stop the flow," but merely changed the private interests in the subject of the current. Distinguishing the cases which upheld the power of the state to impose a non-discriminatory tax upon property which the owner intended to transport to another state, but which was not in actual transit and was held within the state subject to the disposition of the owner, the Court remarked:

---

[3] 42 Stat. 159.

"The question, it should be observed, is not with respect to the extent of the power of Congress to regulate interstate commerce, but whether a particular exercise of state power in view of its nature and operation must be deemed to be in conflict with this paramount authority." Id., 258 U.S. 495, at page 526, 42 S. Ct. 397, 405, 66 L. Ed. 735, 23 A.L.R. 229. See Minnesota v. Blasius, 290 U.S. 1, 8, 54 S. Ct. 34, 36, 78 L. Ed. 131. Applying the doctrine of Stafford v. Wallace, supra, the Court sustained the Grain Futures Act of 1922[4] with respect to transactions on the Chicago Board of Trade, although these transactions were "not in and of themselves interstate commerce." Congress had found that they had become "a constantly recurring burden and obstruction to that commerce." Board of Trade of City. of Chicago v. Olsen, 262 U.S. 1, 32, 43 S. Ct. 470, 476, 67 L. Ed. 839; compare Hill v. Wallace, 259 U.S. 44, 69, 42 S. Ct. 453, 458, 66 L. Ed. 822. See, also, Tagg Bros. & Moorhead v. United States, 280 U.S. 420, 50 S. Ct. 220, 74 L. Ed. 524.

Respondent contends that the instant case presents material distinctions. Respondent says that the Aliquippa plant is extensive in size and represents a large investment in buildings, machinery and equipment. The raw materials which are brought to the plant are delayed for long periods and, after being subjected to manufacturing processes "are changed substantially as to character, utility and value." The finished products which emerge "are to a large extent manufactured without reference to pre-existing orders and contracts and are entirely different from the raw materials which enter at the other end." Hence respondent argues that, "If importation and exportation in interstate commerce do not singly transfer purely local activities into the field of congressional regulation, it should follow that their combination would not alter the local situation." Arkadelphia Milling Co. v. St. Louis, Southwestern R. Co., 249 U.S. 134, 151, 39 S. Ct. 237, 63 L. Ed. 517; Oliver Iron Co. v. Lord, supra.

We do not find it necessary to determine whether these features of defendant's business dispose of the asserted analogy to the "stream of commerce" cases. The instances in which that metaphor has been used are but particular, and not exclusive, illustrations of the protective power which the Government invokes in support of the present Act. The congressional authority to protect interstate commerce from burdens and obstructions is not limited to transactions which can be deemed to be an essential part of a "flow" of interstate or foreign commerce. Burdens and obstructions may be due to injurious action springing from other sources. The fundamental principle is that the power to regulate commerce is the power to enact "all appropriate legislation" for its "pro-

_____
[4] 42 Stat. 998.

tection and advancement" (The Daniel Ball, 10 Wall. 557, 564, 19
L. Ed. 999) ; to adopt measures "to promote its growth and insure
its safety" (County of Mobile v. Kimball, 102 U.S. 691, 696, 697,
26 L. Ed. 238) ; "to foster, protect, control, and restrain." (Second
Employers' Liability Cases, supra, 223 U.S. 1, at page 47, 32 S. Ct.
169, 174, 56 L. Ed. 327, 38 L.R.A. (N.S.) 44). See Texas &
N. O. R. Co. v. Railway & S. S. Clerks, supra. That power is plen-
ary and may be exerted to protect interstate commerce "no matter
what the source of the dangers which threaten it." Second Employers' Liability Cases, 223 U.S. 1, at p. 51, 32 S. Ct. 169, 176,
56 L. Ed. 327, 38 L.R.A. (N.S.) 44; Schechter Corporation v.
United States, supra. Although activities may be intrastate
in character when separately considered, if they have such a close
and substantial relation to interstate commerce that their control
is essential or appropriate to protect that commerce from burdens
and obstructions, Congress cannot be denied the power to exercise
that control. Schechter Corporation v. United States, supra. Undoubtedly the scope of this power must be considered in the light
of our dual system of government and may not be extended so as
to embrace effects upon interstate commerce so indirect and remote
that to embrace them, in view of our complex society, would
effectually obliterate the distinction between what is national and
what is local and create a completely centralized government. Id.
The question is necessarily one of degree. As the Court said in
Board of Trade of City of Chicago v. Olsen, supra, 262 U.S. 1, at
p. 37, 43 S. Ct. 470, 477, 67 L. Ed. 839, repeating what had
been said in Stafford v. Wallace, supra: "Whàtever amounts to
more or less constant practice, and threatens to obstruct or unduly
. to burden the freedom of interstate commerce is within the regulatory power of Congress under the commerce clause and it is
primarily for Congress to consider and decide the fact of the danger
and to meet it."

That intrastate activities, by reason of close and intimate relation to interstate commerce, may fall within federal control is
demonstrated in the case of carriers who are engaged in both interstate and intrastate transportation. There federal control has
been found essential to secure the freedom of interstate traffic from
interference or unjust discrimination and to promote the efficiency
of the interstate service. The Shreveport Case, (Houston, E. & W.
T. R. Co. v. United States), 234 U.S. 342, 351, 352, 34 S. Ct. 833,
58 L. Ed. 1341; Railroad Commission of Wisconsin v. Chicago, B.
& Q. R. Co., 257 U.S. 563, 588, 42 S. Ct. 232, 237, 66 L. Ed. 371, 22
A.L.R. 1086. It is manifest that intrastate rates deal *primarily*
with a local activity. But in ratemaking they bear such a
close relation to interstate rates that effective control of the one
must embrace some control over the other. Id. Under the Trans-

portation Act, 1920,[5] Congress went so far as to authorize the Interstate Commerce Commission to establish a state-wide level of intrastate rates in order to prevent an unjust discrimination against interstate commerce. Railroad Commission of Wisconsin v. Chicago, B. & Q. R. R. Co., supra; Florida v. United States, 282 U.S. 194, 210, 211, 51 S. Ct. 119, 123, 75 L. Ed. 291. Other illustrations are found in the broad requirements of the Safety Appliance Act (45 U.S.C.A. secs. 1-10) and the Hours of Service Act (45 U.S.C.A. secs. 61-64). Southern Railway Co. v. United States, 222 U.S. 20, 32 S. Ct. 2, 56 L. Ed. 72; Baltimore & Ohio R. R. Co. v. Interstate Commerce Commission, 221 U.S. 612, 31 S. Ct. 621, 55 L. Ed. 878. It is said that this exercise of federal power has relation to the maintenance of adequate instrumentalities of interstate commerce. But the agency is not superior to the commerce which uses it. The protective power extends to the former because it exists as to the latter.

The close and intimate effect which brings the subject within the reach of federal power may be due to activities in relation to productive industry although the industry when separately viewed is local. This has been abundantly illustrated in the application of the federal Anti-Trust Act (15 U.S.C.A. secs. 1-7, 15 note). In the Standard Oil and American Tobacco cases (Standard Oil Co. v. United States), 221 U.S. 1, 31 S. Ct. 502, 55 L. Ed. 619, 34 L.R.A. (N.S.) 834, Ann. Cas. 1912D, 734; (United States v. American Tobacco Co.), 221 U.S. 106, 31 S. Ct. 632, 55 L. Ed. 663, that statute was applied to combinations of employers engaged in productive industry. Counsel for the offending corporations strongly urged that the Sherman Act had no application because the acts complained of were not acts of interstate or foreign commerce, nor direct and immediate in their effect on interstate or foreign commerce, but primarily affected manufacturing and not commerce. 221 U.S. 1, at page 5, 31 S. Ct. 502, 55 L. Ed. 619, 34 L.R.A. (N.S.) 834, Ann. Cas. 1912D, 734; 221 U.S. 106, at p. 125, 31 S. Ct. 632, 65 L. Ed. 663. Counsel relied upon the decision in United States v. Knight Co., 156 U.S. 1, 15 S. Ct. 249, 39 L. Ed. 325. The Court stated their contention as follows: "That the act, even if the averments of the bill be true, cannot be constitutionally applied, because to do so would extend the power of Congress to subject dehors the reach of its authority to regulate commerce, by enabling that body to deal with mere questions of production of commodities within the States." And the Court summarily dismissed the contention in these words: "But all the structure upon which this argument proceeds is based upon the decision in United States v. E. C. Knight Co., 156 U.S. 1, 15 S. Ct. 249, 39 L. Ed. 325. The view, however, which the argument takes of that case, and the

---

[5] Secs. 416, 422, 41 Stat. 484, 488; Interstate Commerce Act, sec. 13 (4).

arguments based upon that view have been so repeatedly pressed
upon this court in connection with the interpretation and enforcement of the Anti-Trust Act, and have been so necessarily and
expressly decided to be unsound as to cause the contentions to be
plainly foreclosed and to require no express notice" (citing cases).
221 U.S. 1, at pp. 68, 69, 31 S. Ct. 502, 519, 55 L. Ed. 619, 34 L.R.A.
(N.S.) 834, Ann. Cas. 1912D, 734.

Upon the same principle, the Anti-Trust Act has been applied
to the conduct of employees engaged in production. Loewe v. Lawlor, 208 U.S. 274, 28 S. Ct. 301, 52 L. Ed. 488, 13 Ann. Cas. 815;
Coronado Coal Co. v. United Mine Workers, supra; Bedford Cut
Stone Co. v. Stonecutters' Association, 274 U.S. 37, 47 S. Ct. 522,
71 L. Ed. 916, 54 A.L.R. 791. See, also, Local 167 International
Brotherhood of Teamsters v. United States, 291 U.S. 293, 297,
54 S. Ct. 396, 398, 78 L. Ed. 804; Schechter Corporation v. United
States, supra. The decisions dealing with the question of that
application illustrate both the principle and its limitation. Thus,
in the first Coronado case, the Court held that mining was not interstate commerce, that the power of Congress did not extend to
its regulation as such, and that it had not been shown that the
activities there involved—a local strike—brought them within the
provisions of the Anti-Trust Act, notwithstanding the broad terms
of that statute. A similar conclusion was reached in United Leather
Workers' v. Herkert & Meisel Trunk Co., supra, Industrial Association v. United States, supra, and Levering & Garrigues v. Morrin,
289 U.S. 103, 107, 53 S. Ct. 549, 550, 77 L. Ed. 1062. But in the
first Coronado case the Court also said that "if Congress deems
certain recurring practices though not really part of interstate
commerce, likely to obstruct, restrain or burden it, it has the
power to subject them to national supervision and restraint." 259
U.S. 344, at page 408, 42 S. Ct. 570, 582, 66 L. Ed. 975, 27 A.L.R.
762. And in the second Coronado Case the Court ruled that, while
the mere reduction in the supply of an article to be shipped in
interstate commerce by the illegal or tortious prevention of its
manufacture or production is ordinarily an indirect and remote
obstruction to that commerce, nevertheless when the "intent of
those unlawfully preventing the manufacture or production is
shown to be to restrain or control the supply entering and moving
in interstate commerce, or the price of it in interstate markets,
their action is a direct violation of the Anti-Trust Act." 268 U.S.
295, at page 310, 45 S. Ct. 551, 556, 69 L. Ed. 963. And the existence of that intent may be a necessary inference from proof of the
direct and substantial effect produced by the employees' conduct.
Industrial Association v. United States, 268 U.S. 64, at page 81,
45 S. Ct. 403, 407, 69 L. Ed. 849. What was absent from the evidence in the first Coronado Case appeared in the second and the
Act was accordingly applied to the mining employees.

It is thus apparent that the fact that the employees here concerned were engaged in production is not determinative. The question remains as to the effect upon interstate commerce of the labor practice involved. In the Schechter Case, supra, we found that the effect there was so remote as to be beyond the federal power. To find "immediacy or directness" there was to find it "almost everywhere," a result inconsistent with the maintenance of our federal system. In the Carter Case, supra, the Court was of the opinion that the provisions of the statute relating to production were invalid upon several grounds,—that there was improper delegation of legislative power, and that the requirements not only went beyond any sustainable measure of protection of interstate commerce but were also inconsistent with due process. These cases are not controlling here.

Fourth. Effects of the Unfair Labor Practice in Respondent's Enterprise.—Giving full weight to respondent's contention with respect to a break in the complete continuity of the "stream of commerce" by reason of respondent's manufacturing operations, the fact remains that the stoppage of those operations by industrial strife would have a most serious effect upon interstate commerce. In view of respondent's far-flung activities, it is idle to say that the effect would be indirect or remote. It is obvious that it would be immediate and might be catastrophic. We are asked to shut our eyes to the plainest facts of our national life and to deal with the question of direct and indirect effects in an intellectual vacuum. Because there may be but indirect and remote effects upon interstate commerce in connection with a host of local enterprises throughout the country, it does not follow that other industrial activities do not have such a close and intimate relation to interstate commerce as to make the presence of industrial strife a matter of the most urgent national concern. When industries organize themselves on a national scale, making their relation to interstate commerce the dominant factor in their activities, how can it be maintained that their industrial labor relations constitute a forbidden field into which Congress may not enter when it is necessary to protect interstate commerce from the paralyzing consequences of industrial war? We have often said that interstate commerce itself is a practical conception. It is equally true that interferences with that commerce must be appraised by a judgment that does not ignore actual experience.

Experience has abundantly demonstrated that the recognition of the right of employees to self-organization and to have representatives of their own choosing for the purpose of collective bargaining is often an essential condition of industrial peace. Refusal to confer and negotiate has been one of the most prolific causes of strife. This is such an outstanding fact in the history of labor disturbances that it is a proper subject of judicial notice and requires no citation of instances. The opinion in the case of Virginian Railway Co. v. System Federation, No. 40, supra, points out that, in the case of carriers, experience has shown that before the amendment, of 1934, of the Railway Labor Act, "when there was no dispute as to the organizations authorized to represent the employees and when there was a willingness of the employer to meet such representative for a discussion of their grievances, amicable adjustment of differences had generally followed and strikes had been avoided." That, on the other hand, "a prolific source of dispute had been the maintenance by the railroads of company unions and the denial by railway management of the authority of representatives chosen by their employees." The opinion in that case also points to the large measure of success of the labor policy embodied in the Railway Labor Act. But, with respect to the appropriateness of the recognition of self-organization and representation in the promotion of peace, the question is not essentially different in the case of employees in industries of such a character that interstate commerce is put in jeopardy from the case of employees of transportation companies. And of what avail is it to protect the facility of transportation, if interstate commerce is throttled with respect to the commodities to be transported!

These questions have frequently engaged the attention of Congress and have been the subject of many inquiries.[6] The steel industry is one of the great basic industries of the United States, with ramifying activities affecting interstate commerce at every point. The Government aptly refers to the steel strike of 1919-1920 with its far-reaching consequences.[7] The fact that there appears to have been no major disturbance in that industry in the more recent period did not dispose of the possibilities of future and like dangers to interstate commerce which Congress was entitled to foresee and to exercise its protective power to forestall. It is not necessary again to detail the facts as to respondent's enterprise. Instead of being beyond the pale, we think that it presents in a most striking way the close and intimate relation which a manufacturing industry may have to interstate commerce and we have no doubt that Congress had constitutional authority to safeguard the right of respondent's employees to self-organization and freedom in the choice of representatives for collective bargaining.

---

[6] See, for example, Final Report of the Industrial Commission (1902), vol. 19, p. 844; Report of the Anthracite Coal Strike Commission (1902), Sen. Doc. No. 6, 58th Cong., Spec. Sess.; Final Report of Commission on Industrial Relations (1916), Sen. Doc. No. 415, 64th Cong., 1st Sess., vol. 1; National War Labor Board, Principles and Rules of Procedure (1919), p. 4; Bureau of Labor Statistics, Bulletin No. 287 (1921), pp. 52-64; History of the Shipbuilding Labor Adjustment Board, U. S. Bureau of Labor Statistics, Bulletin No. 283.

[7] See Investigating Strike in Steel Industries, Sen. Rep. No. 289, 66th Cong., 1st Sess.

Fifth. The Means Which the Act Employs.—Questions Under the Due Process Clause and Other Constitutional Restrictions.— Respondent asserts its right to conduct its business in an orderly manner without being subjected to arbitrary restraints. What we have said points to the fallacy in the argument. Employees have their correlative right to organize for the purpose of securing the redress of grievances and to promote agreements with employers relating to rates of pay and conditions of work. Texas & N. O. R. Co. v. Railway & S. S. Clerks, supra; Virginian Railway Co. v. System Federation, No. 40. Restraint for the purpose of preventing an unjust interference with that right cannot be considered arbitrary or capricious. The provision of section 9(a) that representatives, for the purpose of collective bargaining, of the majority of the employees in an appropriate unit shall be the exclusive representatives of all the employees in that unit, imposes upon the respondent only the duty of conferring and negotiating with the authorized representatives of its employees for the purpose of settling a labor dispute. This provision has its analogue in section 2, Ninth, of the Railway Labor Act, as amended (45 U.S.C.A. sec. 152, subd. 9), which was under consideration in Virginian Railway Co. v. System Federation, No. 40, supra. The decree which we affirmed in that case required the Railway Company to treat with the representative chosen by the employees and also to refrain from entering into collective labor agreements with anyone other than their true representative as ascertained in accordance with the provisions of the Act. We said that the obligation to treat with the true representative was exclusive and hence imposed the negative duty to treat with no other. We also pointed out that, as conceded by the Government,[8] the injunction against the company's entering into any contract concerning rules, rates of pay and working conditions except with a chosen representative was "designed only to prevent collective bargaining with anyone purporting to represent employees" other than the representative they had selected. .It was taken "to prohibit the negotiation of labor contracts, generally applicable to employees" in the described unit with any other representative than the one so chosen, "but not as precluding such individual contract" as the company might "elect to make directly with individual employees." We think this construction also applies to section 9(a) of the National Labor Relations Act (29 U.S.C.A. sec. 159(a)).

The Act does not compel agreements between employers and employees. It does not compel any agreement whatever. It does not prevent the employer "from refusing to make a collective contract and hiring individuals on whatever terms" the employer "may by

---

[8] See Virginian Railway Co. v. System Federation, No. 40, 300 U.S. 515, 57 S. Ct. 592, 600, 81 L. Ed. ......, note 6, decided March 29, 1937.

unilateral action determine." [9] The Act expressly provides in
section 9(a) that any individual employee or a group of employees shall have the right at any time to present grievances
to their employer. The theory of the Act is that free opportunity for negotiation with accredited representatives of employees
is likely to promote industrial peace and may bring about the
adjustments and agreements which the Act in itself does not
attempt to compel. As we said in Texas & N. O. R. Co. v. Railway & S. S. Clerks, supra, and repeated in Virginian Railway Co. v.
System Federation, No. 40, the cases of Adair v. United States,
208 U.S. 161, 28 S. Ct. 277, 52 L. Ed. 436, 13 Ann. Cas. 764, and
Coppage v. Kansas, 236 U.S. 1, 35 S. Ct. 240, 59 L. Ed. 441, L.R.A.
1915C, 960, are inapplicable to legislation of this character. The
Act does not interfere with the normal exercise of the right of the
employer to select its employees or to discharge them. The employer may not, under cover of that right, intimidate or coerce its
employees with respect to their self-organization and representation, and, on the other hand, the Board is not entitled to make
its authority a pretext for interference with the right of discharge
when that right is exercised for other reasons than such intimidation and coercion. The true purpose is the subject of investigation with full opportunity to show the facts. It would seem that
when employers freely recognize the right of their employees to
their own organizations and their unrestricted right of representation there will be much less occasion for controversy in respect
to the free and appropriate exercise of the right of selection and
discharge.

The Act has been criticised as one-sided in its application; that
it subjects the employer to supervision and restraint and leaves
untouched the abuses for which employees may be responsible;
that it fails to provide a more comprehensive plan,—with better
assurances of fairness to both sides and with increased chances
of success in bringing about, if not compelling, equitable solutions
of industrial disputes affecting interstate commerce. But we are
dealing with the power of Congress, not with a particular policy or
with the extent to which policy should go. We have frequently
said that the legislative authority, exerted within its proper field,
need not embrace all the evils within its reach. The Constitution
does not forbid "cautious advance, step by step," in dealing with
the evils which are exhibited in activities within the range of legislative power. Carroll v. Greenwich Insurance Co., 199 U.S. 401,
411, 26 S. Ct. 66, 50 L. Ed. 246; Keokee Coke Co. v. Taylor, 234
U.S. 224, 227, 34 S. Ct. 856, 58 L. Ed. 1288; Miller v. Wilson, 236
U.S. 373, 384, 35 S. Ct. 342, 59 L. Ed. 628, L.R.A. 1915F, 829;

---

[9] See Note 8.

Sproles v. Binford, 286 U.S. 374, 396, 52 S. Ct. 581, 588, 76 L. Ed. 1167. The question in such cases is whether the Legislature, in what it does prescribe, has gone beyond constitutional limits.

The procedural provisions of the Act are assailed. But these provisions, as we construe them, do not offend against the constitutional requirements governing the creation and action of administrative bodies. See Interstate Commerce Commission v. Louisville & Nashville R. Co., 227 U.S. 88, 91, 33 S. Ct. 185, 57 L. Ed. 431. The Act establishes standards to which the Board must conform. There must be complaint, notice and hearing. The Board must receive evidence and make findings. The findings as to the facts are to be conclusive, but only if supported by evidence. The order of the Board is subject to review by the designated court, and only when sustained by the court may the order be enforced. Upon that review all questions of the jurisdiction of the Board and the regularity of its proceedings, all questions of constitutional right or statutory authority are open to examination by the court. We construe the procedural provisions as affording adequate opportunity to secure judicial protection against arbitrary action in accordance with the well-settled rules applicable to administrative agencies set up by Congress to aid in the enforcement of valid legislation. It is not necessary to repeat these rules which have frequently been declared. None of them appears to have been transgressed in the instant case. Respondent was notified and heard. It had opportunity to meet the charge of unfair labor practices upon the merits, and by withdrawing from the hearing it declined to avail itself of that opportunity. The facts found by the Board support its order and the evidence supports the findings. Respondent has no just ground for complaint on this score.

The order of the Board required the reinstatement of the employees who were found to have been discharged because of their "union activity" and for the purpose of "discouraging membership in the union." That requirement was authorized by the Act. Sec. 10(c), 29 U.S.C.A. sec. 160(c). In Texas & N. O. R. Co. v. Railway & S. S. Clerks, supra, a similar order for restoration to service was made by the court in contempt proceedings for the violation of an injunction issued by the court to restrain an interference with the right of employees as guaranteed by the Railway Labor Act of 1926. The requirement of restoration to service of employees discharged in violation of the provisions of that Act, was thus a sanction imposed in the enforcement of a judicial decree. We do not doubt that Congress could impose a like sanction for the enforcement of its valid regulation. The fact that in the one case it was a judicial sanction, and in the other a legislative one, is not an essential difference in determining its propriety.

Respondent complains that the Board not only ordered reinstatement but directed the payment of wages for the time lost by the discharge, less amounts earned by the employee during that period. This part of the order was also authorized by the Act. Sec. 10(c). It is argued that the requirement is equivalent to a money judgment and hence contravenes the Seventh Amendment with respect to trial by jury. The Seventh Amendment provides that "In suits at common law, where the value in controversy shall exceed twenty dollars; the right of trial by jury shall be preserved." The Amendment thus preserves the right which existed under the common law when the Amendment was adopted. Shields v. Thomas, 18 How. 253, 262, 15 L. Ed. 368; In re Wood, 210 U.S. 246, 258, 28 S. Ct. 261, 52 L. Ed. 1046; Dimick v. Schiedt, 293 U.S. 474, 476, 55 S. Ct. 296, 79 L. Ed. 603, 95 A.L.R. 1150; Baltimore & Carolina Line v. Redman, 295 U.S. 654, 657, 55 S. Ct. 890, 891, 79 L. Ed. 1636. Thus it has no application to cases where recovery of money damages is an incident to equitable relief even though damages might have been recovered in an action at law. Clark v. Wooster, 119 U.S. 322, 325, 7 S. Ct. 217, 30 L. Ed. 392; Pease v. Rathbun-Jones Engineering Co., 243 U.S. 273, 279, 37 S. Ct. 283, 61 L. Ed. 715, Ann. Cas. 1918C, 1147. It does not apply where the proceeding is not in the nature of a suit at common law. Guthrie National Bank v. Guthrie, 173 U.S. 528, 537, 19 S. Ct. 513, 43 L. Ed. 796.

The instant case is not a suit at common law or in the nature of such a suit. The proceeding is one unknown to the common law. It is a statutory proceeding. Reinstatement of the employee and payment for time lost are requirements imposed for violation of the statute and are remedies appropriate to its enforcement. The contention under the Seventh Amendment is without merit.

Our conclusion is that the order of the Board was within its competency and that the Act is valid as here applied. The judgment of the Circuit Court of Appeals is reversed and the cause is remanded for further proceedings in conformity with this opinion.

It is so ordered.

MR. JUSTICE MCREYNOLDS delivered the following dissenting opinion.

MR. JUSTICE VAN DEVANTER, MR. JUSTICE SUTHERLAND, MR. JUSTICE BUTLER and I are unable to agree with the decisions [10] just announced.

We conclude that these causes were rightly decided by the three Circuit Courts of Appeals and that their judgments should be affirmed. The opinions there given without dissent are terse, well-

[10] In National Labor Relations Board v. Fruehauf Trailer Co., 301 U.S. 49 (1937), and National Labor Relations Board v. Friedman-Harry Marks Clothing Co., 301 U.S. 58 (1937), cases companion to the main case, application of the Act to a manufacturer of commercial trailers and to a manufacturer of men's clothing, respectively, with respect to employees engaged in production, was sustained. The dissenting opinion of Mr. Justice McReynolds contains further facts in both cases.—Ed.

considered and sound. They disclose the meaning ascribed by experienced judges to what this Court has often declared and are set out below in full.

Considering the far-reaching import of these decisions, the departure from what we understand has been consistently ruled here, and the extraordinary power confirmed to a Board of three, the obligation to present our views becomes plain.

The Court as we think departs from well-established principles followed in Schechter Poultry Corporation v. United States, 295 U.S. 495, 55 S. Ct. 837, 79 L. Ed. 1570, 97 A.L.R. 947 (May, 1935), and Carter v. Carter Coal Co., 298 U.S. 238, 56 S. Ct. 855, 80 L. Ed. 1160 (May, 1936). Upon the authority of those decisions, the Circuit Courts of Appeals of the Fifth, Sixth and Second Circuits in the causes now before us have held the power of Congress under the commerce clause does not extend to relations between employers and their employees engaged in manufacture, and therefore the Act conferred upon the National Labor Relations Board no authority in respect of matters covered by the questioned orders. In Foster Bros. Mfg. Co. v. National Labor Relations Board, 85 F.(2d) 984,[11] the Circuit Court of Appeals, Fourth Circuit, held the Act inapplicable to manufacture and expressed the view that if so extended it would be invalid. Six District Courts, on the authority of Schechter's and Carter's cases, have held that the Board has no authority to regulate relations between employers and employees engaged in local production.[12] No decision or judicial opinion to the contrary has been cited, and we find none. Every consideration brought forward to uphold the Act before us was applicable to support the Acts held unconstitutional in causes decided within two years. And the lower courts rightly deemed them controlling.

By its terms the Labor Act extends to employers—large and small—unless excluded by definition, and declares that, if one of

---

[11] In the case cited, the company is engaged in the manufacture and distribution of beds, couches, and related products and equipment. Eighty per cent of the raw materials used in the manufacture of its products are obtained from outside of the State, and slightly more than 50 per cent of its finished products are shipped to other states. In 1935, the average number of employees was 125, and the company's sales totaled $390,000. Cf. Renown Stove Company v. National Labor Relations Board, 90 F.(2d) 1017 (C.C.A. 6th, 1937), in which a petition to set aside an order of the Board was dismissed on the authority of the main case. The company manufactures and distributes gas stoves and heaters, and incidental parts and accessories. "Considerably over" 50 per cent of its raw materials are secured by the company from states other than Michigan, where it is located, and approximately 55 per cent of its stoves are shipped to other states. It employs from 175 to 250 workers, and in 1935 the value of its sales was $508,000. For these and other facts see In the Matter of Renown Stove Company and Stove Mounters' International Union, and International Brotherhood of Foundry Employees, Case No. C-79, 2 N.L.R.B. ...... (1936). See also Jeffery-DeWitt Insulator Co. v. National Labor Relations Board, 91 F.(2d) 134 (C.C.A. 4th, 1937), post, p. 129.—Ed.

[12] All the cases referred to arose on applications for injunctions to restrain administrative proceedings of the Board.—Ed.

these interferes with, restrains, or coerces any employee regarding his labor affiliations, etc., this shall be regarded as unfair labor practice. And a "labor organization" means any organization of any kind or any agency or employee representation committee or plan which exists for the purpose in whole or in part of dealing with employers concerning grievances, labor disputes, wages, rates of pay, hours of employment or conditions of work.

The three respondents happen to be manufacturing concerns—one large, two relatively small. The Act is now applied to each upon grounds common to all. Obviously what is determined as to these concerns may gravely affect a multitude of employers who engage in a great variety of private enterprises—mercantile, manufacturing, publishing, stock-raising, mining, etc. It puts into the hands of a Board power of control over purely local industry beyond anything heretofore deemed permissible.[13] . . .

V.

In each cause the Labor Board formulated and then sustained a charge of unfair labor practices towards persons employed only in production. It ordered restoration of discharged employees to former positions with payment for losses sustained. These orders were declared invalid below upon the ground that respondents while carrying on production operations were not thereby engaging in interstate commerce; that labor practices in the course of such operations did not directly affect interstate commerce; consequently respondents' actions did not come within Congressional power.

Respondent in No. 419 is a large, integrated manufacturer of iron and steel products—the fourth largest in the United States. It has two production plants in Pennsylvania where raw materials brought from points outside the state are converted into finished products, which are thereafter distributed in interstate commerce throughout many states. The Corporation has assets amounting to $180,000,000, gross income $47,000,000, and employs 22,000 people—10,000 in the Aliquippa plant where the complaining employees worked. So far as they relate to essential principles presently important, the activities of this Corporation, while large, do not differ materially from those of the other respondents and very many small producers and distributors. It has attained great size; occupies an important place in business; owns and operates mines of ore, coal, and limestone outside Pennsylvania, the output of which, with other raw material, moves to the production plants. At the plants this movement ends. Having come to rest, this material remains in warehouses, storage yards, etc., often for months, until the process of manufacture begins. After this has been completed,

[13] Sections II, III, and IV of the opinion, setting forth in full the opinions of the Circuit Courts of Appeal in the three cases, are omitted.—Ed.

the finished products go into interstate commerce. The discharged employees labored only in the manufacturing department. They took no part in the transportation to or away from the plant; nor did they participate in any activity which preceded or followed manufacture.

Our concern is with those activities which are common to the three enterprises. Such circumstances as are merely fortuitous—size, character of products, etc.—may be put on one side. The wide sweep of the statute will more readily appear if consideration be given to the Board's proceedings against the smallest and relatively least important—the Clothing Company. If the Act applies to the relations of that Company to employees in production, of course it applies to the larger respondents with like business elements although the affairs of the latter may present other characteristics. Though differing in some respects, all respondents procure raw materials outside the state where they manufacture, fabricate within and then ship beyond the state.

In Nos. 420, 421 the respondent, Michigan corporation, manufactures commercial trailers for automobiles from raw materials brought from outside that state, and thereafter sells these in many states. It has a single manufacturing plant at Detroit and annual receipts around $3,000,000; 900 people are employed.

In Nos. 422, 423 the respondent is a Virginia corporation engaged in manufacturing and distributing men's clothing. It has a single plant and chief office at Richmond, annual business amounting perhaps to $2,000,000, employs 800, brings in almost all raw material from other states and ships the output in interstate commerce. There are some 3,300 similar plants for manufacturing clothing in the United States, which together employ 150,000 persons and annually put out products worth $800,000,000.

VI.

The Clothing Company is a typical small manufacturing concern which produces less than one-half of one per cent. of the men's clothing produced in the United States and employs 800 of the 150,000 workmen engaged therein. If closed today, the ultimate effect on commerce in clothing obviously would be negligible. It stands alone, is not seeking to acquire a monopoly or to restrain trade. There is no evidence of a strike by its employees at any time or that one is now threatened, and nothing to indicate the probable result if one should occur.

Some account of the Labor Board's proceedings against this Company will indicate the ambit of the Act as presently construed.

September 28, 1935, the Amalgamated Clothing Workers of America, purporting to act under section 10(b) of the National Labor Relations Act, filed with the Board a "Charge," stating that the Clothing Company had engaged in unfair labor practices within the meaning of the Act—section 8(1) (3), 29 U.S.C.A. sec. 158 (1, 3)—in that it had, on stated days in August and September, 1935, unjustifiably discharged, demoted or discriminated against some twenty named members of that union and, in other ways, had restrained, interfered with and coerced employees in the exercise of their right of free choice of representatives for collective bargaining. And further "that said labor practices are unfair labor practices affecting commerce within the meaning of said Act."

This "Charge" contained no description of the Company's business, no word concerning any strike against it past, present or threatened. The number of persons employed or how many of these had joined the union is not disclosed.

Thereupon the Board issued a "Complaint" which recited the particulars of the "Charge," alleged incorporation of the Company in Virginia, and ownership of a plant at Richmond where it is continuously engaged in the "production, sale and distribution of men's clothing"; that material is brought from other states and manufactured into clothing, which is sold and shipped to many states, etc.,—"all of aforesaid constituting a continuous flow of commerce among the several states." Also that while operating the Richmond plant the Clothing Company discharged, demoted, laid off or discriminated against some twenty persons "employed in production at the said plant . . . for the reason that all of the said employees, and each of them, joined and assisted a labor organization known as the Amalgamated Clothing Workers of America, and engaged in concerted activities with other employees for the purpose of collective bargaining and other mutual aid and protection," etc. Further, that the Company circulated among its employees and undertook to coerce them to sign a writing expressing satisfaction with conditions; induced some members of the union to withdraw; did other similar things, etc.—all of which amounted to unfair labor practices affecting commerce within the meaning of section 8 (1) (3) (4) and section 2 (6) (7) of the Labor Act. "The aforesaid unfair labor practices occur in commerce among the several states, and on the basis of experience in the aforesaid plant and others in the same and other industries, burden and obstruct such commerce and the free flow thereof and have led and tend to lead to labor disputes burdening and obstructing such commerce and the free flow thereof." The complaint says nothing concerning any strike against the Clothing Company past, present or threatened; there is no allegation concerning the number of persons employed, how many joined the union, or the value of the output.

The respondent filed a special appearance objecting to the Board's jurisdiction, which was overruled; also an answer admitting the discharge of certain employees, but otherwise it generally denied the allegations of the "Complaint."

Thereupon the Board demanded access to the Company's private records of accounts, disclosure of the amount of capital invested by its private owners, the names of all of its employees, its payrolls, the amounts and character of all purchases and from whom made, the amounts of sales and to whom made, including the number and kind of units, the number of employees in the plant during eight years, the names and addresses of the directors and officers of the Company, the names and addresses of its salesmen, the stock ownership of the Company, the affiliation, if any, with other companies, and the former occupations and businesses of its stockholders.

During hearings held at Richmond and Washington, unfettered by rules of evidence, it received a mass of testimony—largely irrelevant. Much related to the character of respondent's business, general methods used in the men's clothing industry, the numbers employed and the general effect of strikes therein. The circumstances attending the discharge or demotion of the specified employees were brought out.

Following this the Board found—

The men's clothing industry of the United States ranks sixteenth in the number of wage earners employed, with more than 3,000 firms and 150,000 workers engaged. The steps in the typical process of manufacture are described. Raw material is brought in from many states, and after fabrication the garments are sold and delivered through canvassers and retailers. "The men's clothing industry is thus an industry which is nearly entirely dependent in its operations upon purchases and sales in interstate commerce and upon interstate transportation."

The Amalgamated Clothing Workers of America is a labor organization composed of over 125,000 men and women employed in making clothing. Members are organized in local unions. Before recognition of this union by employers long and bitter strikes occurred, some of which are described. The union has striven consistently to improve the general economic and social conditions of members. Benefits that flow from recognizing and co-operating with it are realized by manufacturers.

Description is given of the Clothing Company's operations, the sources of its raw material (nearly all outside Virginia), and the method used to dispose of its output. Eighty-two per cent. is sold to customers beyond Virginia. It is among the fifty largest firms in the industry, and among the ten of that group paying the lowest average wage.

In the summer of 1935 the employees at the Richmond plant formed a local of the Amalgamated Clothing Workers and solicited memberships. The management at once indicated opposition and declared it would not permit employees to join. Hostile acts and the circumstances of the discharge or demotion of complaining employees are described. It is said all were discharged or demoted because of union membership. And further that "Interference by employers in the men's clothing industry with the activities of employees in joining and assisting labor organizations and their refusal to accept the procedure of collective bargaining has led and tends to lead to strikes and other labor disputes that burden and obstruct commerce and the free flow thereof. In those cases where the employees have been permitted to organize freely and the employers have been willing to bargain collectively, strikes and industrial unrest have gradually disappeared, as shown in Finding 19. But where the employer has taken the contrary position, strikes have ensued that have resulted in substantial or total cessation of production in the factories involved and obstruction to and burden upon the flow of raw materials and finished garments in interstate commerce."

The number of employees who joined the union does not appear; the general attitude of employees towards the union or the Company is not disclosed; the terms of employment are not stated —whether at will, by the day or by the month. What the local Chapter was especially seeking at the time we do not know.

It does not appear that, either prior or subsequent to the "Complaint," there has been any strike, disorder or industrial strife at respondent's factory, or any interference with or stoppage of production or shipment of its merchandise. Nor that alleged unfair labor practices at its plant had materially affected manufacture, sale or distribution; or materially affected, burdened or obstructed the flow of products; or affected, burdened or obstructed the flow of interstate commerce, or tended to do so.

The Board concluded that the Clothing Company had discriminated in respect to tenure and employment and thereby had discouraged membership in the union; that it had interfered with, restrained and coerced its employees in violation of rights guaranteed by section 7 of the National Labor Relations Act; that these acts occurred in the course and conduct of commerce among the states, immediately affect employees engaged in the course and conduct of interstate commerce, and tend to lead to labor disputes burdening and obstructing such commerce and the free flow thereof.

An order followed, March 28, 1936, which commanded immediate reinstatement of eight discharged employees and payment of their losses; also that the Company should cease and desist from discharging or discriminating against employees because of connections with the union, should post notices, etc. On the same day the Board filed a petition asking enforcement of the order in the United States Circuit Court of Appeals (Second Circuit) at New York, which was denied July 13, 1936. National Labor Relations Board v. Friedman-Harry Marks Clothing Co., 85 F.(2d) 1.

VII.

The precise question for us to determine is whether in the circumstances disclosed Congress has power to authorize what the Labor Board commanded the respondent to do. Stated otherwise, in the circumstances here existing could Congress by statute direct what the Board has ordered? General disquisitions concerning the enactment are of minor, if any, importance. Circumstances not treated as essential to the exercise of power by the Board may, of course, be disregarded. The record in Nos. 422-423—a typical case —plainly presents these essentials and we may properly base further discussion upon the circumstances there disclosed.

A relatively small concern caused raw material to be shipped to its plant at Richmond, Va., converted this into clothing, and thereafter shipped the product to points outside the State. A labor union sought members among the employees at the plant and obtained some. The Company's management opposed this effort, and in order to discourage it discharged eight who had become members. The business of the Company is so small that to close its factory would have no direct or material effect upon the volume of interstate commerce in clothing. The number of operatives who joined the union is not disclosed; the wishes of other employees is not shown; probability of a strike is not found.

The argument in support of the Board affirms: "Thus the validity of any specific application of the preventive measures of this Act depends upon whether industrial strife resulting from the practices in the particular enterprise under consideration would be of the character which Federal power could control if it occurred. If strife in that enterprise could be controlled, certainly it could be prevented."

Manifestly that view of Congressional power would extend it into almost every field of human industry. With striking lucidity. fifty years ago, Kidd v. Pearson, 128 U. S. 1, 21, 9 S. Ct. 6, 10, 32 L. Ed. 346, declared: "If it be held that the term [commerce with foreign nations and among the several states] includes the regulation of all such manufactures as are intended to be the subject of commercial transactions in the future, it is impossible to deny that it would also include all productive industries that contemplate the same thing. The result would be that Congress would be invested, to the exclusion of the states, with the power to regulate, not only manufacture, but also agriculture, horticulture, stock raising, domestic fisheries, mining,—in short, every branch of human industry." This doctrine found full approval in United States v. E. C. Knight Co., 156 U. S. 1, 12, 13, 15 S. Ct. 249, 253, 39 L. Ed. 325; Schechter Poultry Corp. et al. v. United States, supra, and Carter v. Carter Coal Co., et al., supra, where the authorities are collected and principles applicable here are discussed.

In Knight's Case Chief Justice Fuller, speaking for the Court, said: "Doubtless the power to control the manufacture of a given thing involves, in a certain sense, the control of its disposition, but this is a secondary, and not the primary, sense; and, although the exercise of that power may result in bringing the operation of commerce into play, it does not control it, and affects it only incidentally and indirectly. Commerce succeeds to manufacture, and is not a part of it . . . It is vital that the independence of the commercial power and of the police power, and the delimitation between them, however sometimes perplexing, should always be recognized and observed, for, while the one furnishes the strongest bond of union, the other is essential to the preservation of the autonomy of the states as required by our dual form of government; and acknowledged evils, however grave and urgent they may appear to be, had better be borne, than the risk be run, in the effort to suppress them, of more serious consequences by resort to expedients of even doubtful constitutionality."

In Schechter's Case we said: "In determining how far the federal government may go in controlling intrastate transactions upon the ground that they 'affect' interstate commerce, there is a necessary and well-established distinction between direct and indirect effects. The precise line can be drawn only as individual cases arise, but the distinction is clear in principle . . . But where the effect of intrastate transactions upon interstate commerce is merely indirect, such transactions remain within the domain of state power. If the commerce clause were construed to reach all enterprises and transactions which could be said to have an indirect effect upon interstate commerce, the federal authority would embrace practically all the activities of the people, and the authority of the state over its domestic concerns would exist only by sufferance of the federal government. Indeed, on such a theory, even the development of the state's commercial facilities would be subject to federal control."

Carter's Case declared—"Whether the effect of a given activity or condition is direct or indirect is not always easy to determine. The word 'direct' implies that the activity or condition invoked or blamed shall operate proximately—not mediately, remotely, or collaterally—to produce the effect. It connotes the absence of an efficient intervening agency or condition. And the extent of the effect bears no logical relation to its character. The distinction between a direct and an indirect effect turns, not upon the magnitude of either the cause or the effect, but entirely upon the manner in which the effect has been brought about. If the production by one man of a single ton of coal intended for interstate sale and shipment, and actually so sold and shipped, affects interstate commerce indirectly, the effect does not become direct by multiplying the tonnage, or increasing the number of men employed, or adding to the expense or complexities of the business, or by all combined."

Any effect on interstate commerce by the discharge of employees shown here would be indirect and remote in the highest degree, as consideration of the facts will show. In No. 419 ten men out of ten thousand were discharged; in the other cases only a few. The immediate effect in the factory may be to create discontent among all those employed and a strike may follow, which, in turn, may result in reducing production, which ultimately may reduce the volume of goods moving in interstate commerce. By this chain of indirect and progressively remote events we finally reach the evil with which it is said the legislation under consideration undertakes to deal. A more remote and indirect interference with interstate commerce or a more definite invasion of the powers reserved to the states is difficult, if not impossible, to imagine.

The Constitution still recognizes the existence of states with indestructible powers; the Tenth Amendment was supposed to put them beyond controversy.

We are told that Congress may protect the "stream of commerce" and that one who buys raw material without the state, manufactures it therein, and ships the output to another state is in that stream. Therefore it is said he may be prevented from doing anything which may interfere with its flow.

This, too, goes beyond the constitutional limitations heretofore enforced. If a man raises cattle and regularly delivers them to a carrier for interstate shipment, may Congress prescribe the conditions under which he may employ or discharge helpers on the ranch? The products of a mine pass daily into interstate commerce; many things are brought to it from other states. Are the owners and the miners within the power of Congress in respect of the latter's tenure and discharge? May a mill owner be prohibited from closing his factory or discontinuing his business because so to do would stop the flow of products to and from his plant in interstate commerce? May employees in a factory be restrained from quitting work in a body because this will close the factory and thereby stop the flow of commerce? May arson of a factory be made a Federal offense whenever this would interfere with such flow? If the business cannot continue with the existing wage scale, may Congress command a reduction? If the ruling of the Court just announced is adhered to, these questions suggest some of the problems certain to arise.

And if this theory of a continuous "stream of commerce" as now defined is correct, will it become the duty of the federal government hereafter to suppress every strike which by possibility may cause a blockade in that stream? In re Debs, 158 U.S. 564, 15

S. Ct. 900, 39 L. Ed. 1092. Moreover, since Congress has intervened, are labor relations between most manufacturers and their employees removed from all control by the state? Oregon-Washington R. Co. v. Washington (1926) 270 U.S. 87, 46 S. Ct. 279, 70 L. Ed. 482.

To this argument Arkadelphia Milling Co. v. St. Louis Southwestern Railway Co., et al., 249 U.S. 134, 150, 39 S. Ct. 237, 63 L. Ed. 517, affords an adequate reply. No such continuous stream is shown by these records as that which counsel assume.

There is no ground on which reasonably to hold that refusal by a manufacturer, whose raw materials come from states other than that of his factory and whose products are regularly carried to other states, to bargain collectively with' employees in his manufacturing plant, directly affects interstate commerce. In such business, there is not one but two distinct movements or streams in interstate transportation. The first brings in raw material and there ends. Then follows manufacture, a separate and local activity. Upon completion of this and not before, the second distinct movement or stream in interstate commerce begins and the products go to other states. Such is the common course for small as well as large industries. It is unreasonable and unprecedented to say the commerce clause confers upon Congress power to govern relations between employers and employees in these local activities. Stout v. Pratt (D.C.) 12 F. Supp. 864. In Schechter's Case we condemned as unauthorized by the commerce clause assertion of federal power in respect of commodities which had come to rest after interstate transportation. And, in Carter's Case, we held Congress lacked power to regulate labor relations in respect of commodities before interstate commerce has begun.

It is gravely stated that experience teaches that if an employer discourages membership in "any organization of any kind" "in which employees participate, and which exists for the purpose in whole or in part of dealing with employers concerning grievances, labor disputes, wages, rates of pay, hours of employment or conditions of work," discontent may follow and this in turn may lead to a strike, and as the outcome of the strike there may be a block in the stream of interstate commerce. Therefore Congress may inhibit the discharge! Whatever effect any cause of discontent may ultimately have upon commerce is far too indirect to justify Congressional regulation. Almost anything—marriage, birth, death —may in some fashion affect commerce.

VIII.

That Congress has power by appropriate means, not prohibited by the Constitution, to prevent direct and material interference with the conduct of interstate commerce is settled doctrine. But the interference struck at must be direct and material, not some mere possibility contingent on wholly uncertain events; and there must be no impairment of rights guaranteed. A state by taxation on property may indirectly but seriously affect the cost of transportation; it may not lay a direct tax upon the receipts from interstate transportation. The first is an indirect effect, the other direct.

This power to protect interstate commerce was invoked in Standard Oil Co. v. United States, 221 U.S. 1, 31 S. Ct. 502, 55 L. Ed. 619, 34 L.R.A. (N.S.) 834, Ann. Cas. 1912D, 734, and United States v. American Tobacco Co., 221 U.S. 106, 31 S. Ct. 632, 55 L. Ed. 663. In each of those cases a combination sought to monopolize and restrain interstate commerce through purchase and consequent control of many large competing concerns engaged both in manufacture and interstate commerce. The combination was sufficiently powerful and action by it so persistent that success became a dangerous probability. Here there is no such situation, and the cases are inapplicable in the circumstances. There is no conspiracy to interfere with commerce unless it can be said to exist among the employees who became members of the union. There is a single plant operated by its own management whose only offense, as alleged, was the discharge of a few employees in the production department because they belonged to a union, coming within the broad definition of "labor organization" prescribed by section 2(5) of the Act. That definition includes any organization in which employees participate and which exists for the purpose in whole or in part of dealing with employers concerning grievances, wages, etc.

Section 13 of the Labor Act (29 U.S.C.A. sec. 163) provides— "Nothing in this Act [chapter] shall be construed so as to interfere with or impede or diminish in any way the right to strike." And yet it is ruled that to discharge an employee in a factory because he is a member of a labor organization (any kind) may create discontent which may lead to a strike and this may cause a block in the "stream of commerce"; consequently the discharge may be inhibited. Thus the Act exempts from its ambit the very evil which counsel insist may result from discontent caused by a discharge of an association member, but permits coercion of a nonmember to join one.

The things inhibited by the Labor Act relate to the management of a manufacturing plant—something distinct from commerce and subject to the authority of the state. And this may not be abridged because of some vague possibility of distant interference with commerce.

IX.

Texas & New Orleans Railroad Co., et al. v. Brotherhood of Railway & Steamship Clerks et al., 281 U.S. 548, 50 S. Ct. 427, 434,

74 L. Ed. 1034, is not controlling. There the Court, while considering an act definitely limited to common carriers engaged in interstate transportation over whose affairs Congress admittedly has
wide power, declared: "The petitioners invoke the principle declared in Adair v. United States, 208 U.S. 161, 28 S. Ct. 277, 52 L.
Ed. 436, 13 Ann. Cas. 764, and Coppage v. Kansas, 236 U.S. 1, 35 S.
Ct. 240, 59 L. Ed. 441, L.R.A. 1915C, 960, but these decisions
are inapplicable. The Railway Labor Act of 1926 does not interfere
with the normal exercise of the right of the carrier to select its
employees or to discharge them. The statute is not aimed at this
right of the employers but at the interference with the right of
employees to have representatives of their own choosing. As the
carriers subject to the Act have no constitutional right to interfere
with the freedom of the employees in making their selections, they
cannot complain of the statute on constitutional grounds."

Adair's Case, supra, presented the question—"May Congress
make it a criminal offense against the United States—as by the 10th
section of the act of 1898 [30 Stat. 428] it does—for an agent or officer of an interstate carrier, having full authority in the premises
from the carrier, to discharge an employee from service simply because of his membership in a labor organization?" The answer was
no. "While, as already suggested, the right of liberty and property
guaranteed by the Constitution against deprivation without due
process of law is subject to such reasonable restraints as the common good or the general welfare may require, it is not within the
functions of government—at least, in the absence of contract between the parties—to compel any person, in the course of his business and against his will, to accept or retain the personal services
of another, or to compel any person, against his will, to perform
personal services for another. The right of a person to sell his
labor upon such terms as he deems proper is, in its essence, the
same as the right of the purchaser of labor to prescribe the conditions upon which he will accept such labor from the person offering
to sell it. So the right of the employee to quit the service of the
employer, for whatever reason, is the same as the right of the employer, for whatever reason, to dispense with the services of such
employee. It was the legal right of the defendant, Adair,—however
unwise such a course might have been,—to quit the service in which
he was engaged, because the defendant employed some persons
who were not members of a labor organization. In all such particulars the employer and the employee have equality of right, and
any legislation that disturbs that equality is an arbitrary interference with the liberty of contract which no government can
legally justify in a free land." "The provision of the statute under
which the defendant was convicted must be held to be repugnant
to the Fifth Amendment and as not embraced by nor within the

power of Congress to regulate interstate commerce, but, under the guise of regulating interstate commerce, and as applied to this case, it arbitrarily sanctions an illegal invasion of the personal liberty as well as the right of property of the defendant, Adair."

Coppage v. Kansas, following the Adair Case held that a state statute, declaring it a misdemeanor to require an employee to agree not to become a member of a labor organization during the time of his employment, was repugnant to the due process clause of the Fourteenth Amendment.

The right to contract is fundamental and includes the privilege of selecting those with whom one is willing to assume contractual relations. This right is unduly abridged by the Act now upheld. A private owner is deprived of power to manage his own property by freely selecting those to whom his manufacturing operations are to be entrusted. We think this cannot lawfully be done in circumstances like those here disclosed.

It sems clear to us that Congress has transcended the powers granted.[14]

---

[14] See comments on the case and its companion cases: 37 Col. L. Rev. 860 (1937); 32 Ill. L. Rev. 196 (1937); 5 I.J.A. 125 (1937). See also: Garrison, "Government and Labor: The Latest Phase," 37 Col. L. Rev. 897 (1937).

In Washington, Virginia and Maryland Coach Co. v. National Labor Relations Board, 301 U.S. 142 (1937), the Court unanimously sustained the application of the Act to an interstate motor bus carrier in its relations with drivers and mechanics. Accord: National Labor Relations Board v. Tidewater Express Lines, 90 F.(2d) 301 (C.C.A. 4th, 1937); National Labor Relations Board v. Pacific Greyhound Lines, C.C.H. Labor Law Serv., par. 16398 (C.C.A. 9th, 1937); National Labor Relations Board v. Pennsylvania Greyhound Lines, C.C.H. Labor Law Serv., par. 16388 (C.C.A. 3d, 1937). In the last two cases cited, the Court refused to enforce certain portions of the Board's order. See infra, p. 167, note 1. In Agwilines, Inc. v. National Labor Relations Board, 87 F.(2d) 146 (C.C.A. 5th, 1936), the Act was held applicable to a coastwise steamship company in its relations with its longshoremen. See also National Labor Relations Board v. Delaware-New Jersey Ferry Co., 90 F.(2d) 520 (C.C.A. 3d, 1937); National Labor Relations Board v. Bell Oil & Gas Co., C.C.H. Labor Law Serv., par. 16397 (C.C.A. 5th, 1937).

In Associated Press v. National Labor Relations Board, 301 U.S. 103 (1937), the Court held that the Act was applicable to a press association in its relations with a rewrite man. Mr. Justice Sutherland delivered a dissenting opinion, in which Mr. Justice Van Devanter, Mr. Justice McReynolds, and Mr. Justice Butler concurred, on the ground that such application abridged the freedom of the press guaranteed by the First Amendment to the Constitution. But in National Labor Relations Board v. Mackay Radio & Telegraph Company, 87 F.(2d) 611 (C.C.A. 9th, 1937), in which the decision antedated the main case, the Court, with Garrecht, C.J., dissenting, refused to enforce an order of the Board, Wilbur, C.J., holding that the Act violates the Fifth Amendment to the Constitution, and Mathews, C.J., finding the order of the Board technically defective. In so far as the decision is based on the opinion of Wilbur, C.J., it is no longer law. Cf. National Labor Relations Board v. Pacific Greyhound Lines, supra; National Labor Relations Board v. Santa Cruz Fruit Packing Co., C.C.H. Labor Law Serv., par. 16401 (C.C.A. 9th, 1937).

In National Labor Relations Board v. National N. Y. Packing & Shipping Co., 86 F.(2d) 98 (C.C.A. 2d, 1936), the Court enforced an order of the Board directed against a New York company engaged in the consolidating and arranging for transportation of packages, 90 per cent of which are already on an interstate journey pursuant to a contract of sale between the seller in New York and the buyer elsewhere. The company acts as agent for the out-of-state buyers, the purpose being to obtain more favorable freight rates on bulk shipments.

In Apex Hosiery Co. v. Leader, 90 F.(2d) 155 (C.C.A. 3d, 1937), an injunction under the Sherman Act was granted against a sit-down strike in a large hosiery mill. The Court said: "In the Jones and Laughlin case, which was brought under the Wagner Act, the Supreme Court declared what conduct in relation to interstate commerce comes within federal control and gives federal courts jurisdiction. It makes no difference, so far as jurisdiction is concerned, whether that conduct violates the provisions of the Sherman Act or the Wagner Act. The Sherman Act provides that every combination or conspiracy in restraint of trade or commerce among the several states is declared to be illegal. It is undisputed in the case at bar that there was a combination, a conspiracy, which actually restrained trade, and interstate commerce. The Supreme Court in the Jones & Laughlin Case has defined commerce among the several states and the facts in the present case bring it within that definition. Hosiery of the value of $600,000, as above stated, had been manufactured and made into the finished product from raw materials imported from the southern states and from a foreign nation, had been sold and was ready to be shipped out of the commonwealth when the factory was seized. The defendants by combination and conspiracy have been holding possession of this merchandise ever since the unlawful seizure and have thus restrained it from going into the stream of interstate commerce. This and other conduct clearly violate the provisions of the Sherman Act.

. . . a strike if lawfully conducted is in itself lawful and its lawfulness now has statutory recognition. There could be no conspiracy under the Sherman Act or otherwise because of doing a lawful thing. It could not become a conspiracy unless the means employed were unlawful. It may be that the ultimate intent of the conspirators in this case was to force the plaintiff to sign an agreement for a closed shop. This would be perfectly all right if the defendants had used lawful means to bring it about, but when they used unlawful means—the commission of crimes and the restraint of interstate commerce—they knew exactly what they were doing and must have intended, as rational beings, to do exactly what they did. The ultimate object which they had in view in no way exculpates them from the violation of the Sherman Act." (At 159-160.)

In Cushman Co. v. Mackesey, C.C.H. Labor Law Serv., par. 16372 (Me., 1937), the Court based a temporary injunction against activities in connection with a strike resulting from the employer's refusal to bargain collectively on the ground, inter alia, that when the union called the strike, it did not represent a majority of the employees. See also: Grace Co. v. Williams, (W.D. Mo., July 6, 1937); Magruder: "Half Century of Legal Influence Upon the Development of Collective Bargaining," 50 Harv. L. Rev. 1071, 1107 (1937). But cf. Lund v. Woodenware Workers Union, 19 F. Supp. 607 (D. Minn., 1937); In the Matter of Charles Cushman Co. and United Shoe Workers of America, Case No. R-161, August 30, 1937.

For other cases arising under the Federal Anti-Trust Laws, but not involving the National Labor Relations Act, see: Mayo v. Dean, 82 F.(2d) 554 (C.C.A. 5th, 1936); Hicks v. Bekins Moving & Storage Co., 87 F.(2d) 583 (C.C.A. 9th, 1937); Kolkin v. Gotham Sportswear, Inc., 10 F. Supp. 682 (S.D. N.Y., 1935); United States v. Needle Trades Workers' Industrial Union, 10 F. Supp. 201 (S.D.N.Y., 1935). See also New York Lumber Trade Associtaion v. Lacey, 245 App. Div. 262, 281 N.Y.S. 647 (1935), aff'd without opinion, 269 N.Y. 595, 199 N.E. 688 (1935), 269 N.Y. 677, 200 N.E. 54 (1936), cert. denied, 298 U.S. 684 (1936), holding that inasmuch as the United States Shipping Board has regulatory powers with respect to a conspiracy between defendant shipping companies and trade unions not to accept freight delivered by non-union teamsters, the state courts will not grant an injunction. See comments: 35 Col. L. Rev. 1312 (1935); 45 Yale L.J. 367 (1935).

JEFFERY-DeWITT INSULATOR COMPANY v. NATIONAL LABOR RELATIONS BOARD

Circuit Court of Appeals for the Fourth Circuit, 1937.
91 F.(2d) 134.

PARKER, C.J.[1] . . . The contention that the Board was without jurisdiction to afford relief to the union, on the ground that members of the union were not employees at the time of the unfair labor practices complained of, proceeds upon the assumption that that relationship was severed when the employees continued on strike and refused to return to work when the company resumed operations on June 20, 1935 [2] and that, as this was prior to the passage of the Wagner Labor Relations Act on July 5, 1935, the provisions of that Act are not effective to preserve the rights of employees as a basis for action on the part of the Board. We think, however, that this takes too narrow a view both of the rights of employees and of the purpose of the statute. It has long been recognized by the law, as well as in common understanding, that the relationship existing between employer and employee is not necessarily terminated by a strike.[3] . . .

Irrespective of the statute, therefore, the strike did not of itself result in a complete severance of the relationship which had been established between the company and its employees. They were employees on strike because of the labor dispute which existed; and this situation was not materially changed by the resumption of operations on June 20th, even though the company announced that those employees who desired to work must go to work on that day. . . . The strike continued and resulted for a considerable period in greatly hampering the operations of the company. The June factory payroll was 67 per cent. below that of May and the August payroll 50 per cent. below it. No inventories were taken at the end of the calendar months June, July and August in accordance with the company's custom because of the disorganized state of its business. The existence of the dispute between the company and its employees was recognized by the department of labor of both the state and the nation, and conciliators came upon the scene and attempted to adjust it. The company recognized its existence when its general manager stated to the conciliators that it "would be very fine" "for the men to call the strike off and come back to work."

It is not necessary to go into detail as to the respective rights of the company and its employees after the resumption of work

---

[1] The statement of the case is omitted.—Ed.
[2] The strike was declared on June 15th, and negotiations continued until June 20th.—Ed.
[3] The review of the authorities is omitted.—Ed.

on June 20th or to decide at precisely what point the relationship between a company and its striking employees is completely terminated so as not to be further subject to the regulatory power of Congress over the interstate commerce in which the company is engaged. It is sufficient for the case in hand that at the time the conciliators came upon the scene the strike was still in progress and a labor dispute within any fair meaning of that term existed between the company and its striking employees.

To such a situation we think the Act was clearly applicable. It provides that "the term 'employee' . . . shall include any individual whose work has ceased as a consequence of, or in connection with, any current labor dispute . . . and who has not obtained any other regular and substantially equivalent employment." Sec. 2(3), 29 USCA 152 (3). And the term "labor dispute" is defined as including "any controversy concerning terms, tenure or conditions of employment, or concerning the association or representation of persons in negotiating, fixing, maintaining, changing, or seeking to arrange terms or conditions of employment, regardless of whether the disputants stand in the proximate relation of employer and employee." Sec. 2(9), 29 USCA 152(9). Here there was clearly a current labor dispute within the above definition and the striking employees were persons whose work had ceased because of it. It is an unfair labor practice within the meaning of the act for an employer to refuse to bargain collectively with representatives of his employees. Sec. 8(5), 29 USCA 158(5). The Board is empowered to prevent any person from engaging in an unfair labor practice affecting commerce as defined in the Act; and it is required to take jurisdiction of a labor dispute when it is charged that any person has engaged in an unfair practice within its meaning. Sec. 10(a) (b), 29 USCA 160(a) (b).

It is argued, however, that the Act, which was not passed until July 5th, must be given a prospective operation and not be applied to disputes which had their origin prior to its passage. It is a sufficient answer to this that the dispute was current at the time of the passage of the Act and that, under the principles of law theretofore recognized, the relationship between the company and its striking employees had not been so completely terminated as to have no further connection with the company's business or the commerce in which it was engaged. The action of the Board was not predicated upon anything that occurred prior to the passage of the Act, but upon an unfair labor practice which occurred ten days after its effective date, i.e. upon the refusal to bargain collectively with the representative of the employees, which occurred July 15th. The mere fact that the labor dispute had commenced prior to the passage of the Act does not withdraw the parties or the dispute from the regulatory power of Congress as to acts sub-

sequently occurring. The Act is highly remedial in character and
is entitled to a broad and liberal construction; and it is hardly
to be presumed that Congress should have intended its provisions,
designed as they are for the promotion of industrial peace, to
have no application to pending disputes. Certainly the unfair labor
practices forbidden by the Act would tend to prolong such disputes, and there was just as much reason to forbid them in existing labor disputes as in disputes which might subsequently arise.
So long as there was an existing relationship between the company
and its striking employees affecting commerce as defined in the
Act, this relationship was subject to the regulatory power of Congress; and the Act is given a prospective operation when applied
to subsequent unfair labor practices affecting such relationship,
notwithstanding they may have occurred in the course of a labor
dispute which had its origin before the Act was passed. Cf. George
v. City of Asheville (C.C.A. 4th) 80 F.(2d) 50, 55.

The company's second contention is that it was not guilty of
an unfair labor practice in refusing to bargain with the union on
and after July 15th, for the reason that efforts to bargain with it
prior to June 20th had resulted in failure and an impasse in the
negotiations had been reached. The answer to this is that nearly a
month of "cooling time" had elapsed since the negotiations of June
15th to 20th, the status of the controversy had undergone considerable change as a result of the operation of the plant, the striking
employees after nearly a month of idleness were doubtless willing
to make concessions to compromise the matters in difference and
conciliators had arrived upon the scene for the purpose of trying
to secure an adjustment. It is true that the Act does not require
the parties to agree but merely to negotiate with each other; but
it is based upon the idea that negotiations honestly entered into will
generally result in the settlement of differences, and commands
negotiation for that reason. Statistics show the reasonableness
of the hope upon which it proceeds.[4] Of 14,889 disputes handled
by the United States Conciliation Service between 1915 and 1936,
11,421 disputes, or over 76 per cent, were satisfactorily adjusted.
During the fiscal year ending June 30, 1936 the Conciliation Service
intervened in 1012 disputes and secured settlement of 805 of them.
The experience under the Railway Labor Act demonstrates that
negotiation is the most effective method yet devised of settling
differences between employer and employee and avoiding industrial
conflict. Virginian Ry. Co. v. System Federation No. 40, 300 U.S.
515, 57 S. Ct. 592, 598.

Whether the refusal to negotiate further in this case was unreasonable under the circumstances of the case and on that ac-

[4] See Annual Report of Secretary of Labor for fiscal year ending June
30, 1936, pages 23 and 26.

count an unfair labor practice, was a question of fact as to which we are bound by the finding of the Board, if it has substantial support in the evidence. We think that it has such support. We cannot say that the failure of negotiations to result in agreement in June so clearly precluded the possibility of agreement in July under the changed circumstances then existing that the finding by the Board, to the effect that the refusal to negotiate was unreasonable and grew out of a desire to be rid of the union, is unsupported by the record. On the contrary we think that the finding is a reasonable one upon the facts. If an employer in the presence of a strike could rid himself of the obligation to negotiate by declaring further negotiations to be useless and refusing to recognize as employees those failing to return to work on his terms, the statute enjoining collective bargaining would largely fail of its purpose. We do not think that it can be brushed aside so easily.

The company's third contention is ruled against it, we think, by the decision of the Supreme Court in the case of National Labor Relations Board v. Friedman-Harry Marks Clothing Co., 301 U.S. 58, 57 S. Ct. 645. The relationship of the company's business to interstate commerce cannot be distinguished on any principle with which we are familiar from the relationship of the business involved in the Friedman-Harry Marks Clothing Company case. Both with respect to its purchase of raw materials and its sale of finished product, the company is engaged in interstate commerce; and its share of this commerce will be substantially burdened and interfered with by strikes among its employees, even though these employees are engaged in manufacturing. It is within the power of Congress, therefore, to regulate the relationship between the company and its employees so as to avoid the burden and interference. National Labor Relations Board v. Jones & Laughlin Steel Corp., 301 U.S. 1, 57 S. Ct. 615.

For the reasons stated, the petition of the company to set aside the order of the Board will be denied, and decree will be entered enforcing it pursuant to the provision of Sec. 10(f) of the Act, 29 USCA 160(f).

Decree Accordingly.

NORTHCOTT, CIRCUIT JUDGE, dissenting: I do not agree with the majority of the court in the conclusions stated in the opinion. Disputes had arisen between the company and the union in October, 1933 and March, 1934. These disputes were settled. Again on June 15, 1935, the union declared a strike and on June 20, 1935, the employees were notified positively that their demands would not be met and the company began operation of the plant with employees other than the strikers. While the business was carried on with a greatly depleted force the plant was running, and gradually getting back to a normal condition.

The law under which the National Labor Relations Board acted was passed by the Congress of the United States to become effective July 5, 1935. At the time the law went into effect there was no current labor dispute at the plant of the company and nothing that the law could affect with respect to the already settled dispute between the company and its former employees. This dispute had been finally and definitely settled on June 20.

The employees had made certain demands and gone on a strike. These demands were rejected by the company on June 20 and the plant reopened without the striking employees. When the law became effective there was no dispute that would justify any action on the part of the Labor Board. The finding of the Board to the effect that there was such a dispute has no support in the evidence as shown in the record in the case and we are not bound by such a finding unless there is substantial evidence to support it.

It can not be the law that strikes will be regarded as settled only when the strikers admit that they are settled or that no action by an employer will terminate a strike no matter how definite or positive such action may have been. Such a holding is unfair to the employer and cannot, in my opinion, be justified. Certainly Congress can never have intended, in the passage of the Act, that consideration be given to one party only to a controversy. Both sides should receive fair consideration.

There was no current labor dispute when the Act became effective and there was nothing to which the jurisdiction of the Board could possibly attach. The order of the Board was without authority and based upon no substantial evidence.[5]

---

[5] See further as to the effect of a strike on the employer's duty to bargain: In the Matter of Allen & Co. and Federal Labor Union Local No. 18526, 1 N.L.R.B. 714 (1936); In the Matter of Birge & Sons Co. and United Wall Paper Crafts, 1 N.L.R.B. 731 (1936); In the Matter of Columbian Enameling & Stamping Co. and Enameling & Stamping Mill Employees Union, 1 N.L.R.B. 181 (1936). On when a strike terminates, see: Hertzig v. Gibbs, 3 N.E. (2d) 83 (Mass., 1936), 4 U. of Chi. L. Rev. 340 (1937), 31 Ill. L. Rev. 691 (1937), 21 Minn. L. Rev. 344 (1937). See also authorities cited by Landis 244, n. 1.

As to whether the demand for a closed shop modifies the duty to bargain, see: In the Matter of Columbian Enameling & Stamping Co. and Enameling & Stamping Mill Employees Union, supra; In the Matter of International Filter Co. and International Association of Machinists, 1 N.L.R.B. 489, 498 (1936).

In National Labor Relations Board v. Delaware-New Jersey Ferry Co., 90 F.(2d) 520 (C.C.A. 3d, 1937), after the Board had made its order requiring the company to bargain collectively with the union which represented a majority of the employees at the time of the hearing, the company secured the appointment of a committee of three employees, and entered into an agreement with the committee directly. (See In the Matter of Delaware-New Jersey Ferry Co. and Marine Engineers' Beneficial Association, Case No. C-4, Supplemental Decision, 2 N.L.R.B. ...... (1936)). The Court, with Biggs, C.J., dissenting, held that the existence of the agreement with the committee was a bar to the enforcement of the Board's order.

IN THE MATTER OF ST. JOSEPH STOCK YARDS COMPANY
and AMALGAMATED MEAT CUTTERS AND BUTCHER
WORKMEN OF NORTH AMERICA

Case No. C-43. Decisions of the National Labor Relations Board,
1936. 2 N.L.R.B. ....

. . . The issue is precise: is the refusal by an employer to
enter into an agreement, oral or written, with the proper representatives of his employees after an understanding has been
reached on the terms of the agreement by discussion and negotiation, an unfair labor practice within the meaning of Section 8?
The two subdivisions of that Section pertinent in a consideration
of this issue are subdivision (1)—it shall be an unfair labor practice for an employer to interfere with or restrain his employees in
the exercise of the rights guaranteed in Section 7, among which
is the right to bargain collectively—and subdivision (5)—it shall
be an unfair labor practice for an employer to refuse to bargain
collectively with the representatives of his employees.

The issue presented is not novel. The old National Labor Relations Board, in a series of decisions that gave substance to the
"right to bargain collectively" in Section 7(a) of the National
Industrial Recovery Act,[1] dealt with the problem. In In the Matter
of Houde Engineering Corporation that Board said:

"Collective bargaining, then, is simply a means to an end. The
end is an agreement. And, customarily, such an agreement will
have to do with wages, hours and working conditions, and will
have a fixed duration. The purpose of every such agreement has
been to stabilize, for a certain period, the terms of employment,
for the protection alike of employer and employee. By contrast,
where all that transpires is a demand by employees for better terms
and an assent by the employer, but without any understanding as
to duration, there has been no collective agreement, because neither
side has been bound to anything.

"Section 7(a) must be construed in the light of the traditional
practices with which it deals, and the traditional meanings of the
words which it uses. When it speaks of 'collective bargaining' it
can only be taken to mean that long-observed process whereby
negotiations are conducted for the purpose of arriving at collective agreements governing terms of employment for some specified

---

[1] "Sec. 7(a). Every code of fair competition, agreement, and license approved, prescribed, or issued under this title shall contain the following conditions: (1) That employees shall have the right to organize and bargain collectively through representatives of their own choosing, and shall be free
from the interference, restraint, or coercion of employers of labor, or their
agents, in the designation of such representatives or in self-organization or in
other concerted activities for the purpose of collective bargaining or other
mutual aid or protection; . . ."

period. And in prohibiting any interference with this process, it must have intended that the process should be encouraged, and that there was a definite good to be obtained by promoting the stabilization of employment relations through collective agreements." [2]

The exact point was passed upon in In the Matter of National Aniline & Chemical Company. As a result of conferences between the employer and representatives of its employees, tentative understandings were reached with respect to certain proposals submitted by the latter. However, instead of embodying those understandings in a written memorandum, the employer simply posted a plant notice which purported to contain the terms agreed upon. It later refused to sign an agreement containing those terms. Relying upon the Houde decision, the old Board held that the employer's conduct was at variance with the statute:

"Section 7(a) . . . requires employers to go further than merely to receive the duly constituted representatives of their employees, to give ear to their demands, and to assent to such demands if they are satisfactory. The statute imposes duties consistent with its purpose. It contemplates that the demands, or modifications of such demands, if acceptable to the employer, be embodied in an agreement, and that such an agreement bind both parties for a certain period of time. If such an agreement did not run for a definite period of time it would be without legal validity as an agreement. The collective bargaining requirement in Section 7(a), if it did not contemplate the embodiment of mutually satisfactory terms in a legally valid agreement, would be empty of significance." [3]

The National Aniline and Houde decisions were followed in numerous cases, all of which affirmed the proposition that the duty to bargain collectively demanded of the employer that he negotiate with a sincere desire to reach an understanding and that he enter into an agreement embodying the understanding if one

---

[2] In the Matter of Houde Engineering Corporation, 1 National Labor Relations Board Decisions (1934) 35, 35-36. The Board cited numerous decisions of the National Labor Board and the Petroleum Board that held the same view of collective bargaining.

[3] In the Matter of National Aniline & Chemical Company, 1 National Labor Relations Board Decisions (1934) 114, 116. The decision further stated: "In view of the argument of the Union that a collective agreement, under Section 7(a), must necessarily be reduced to writing, we desire to state, without touching on the applicability of the Statutes of Frauds of the several States, that a collective oral agreement is not necessarily invalid. However, the proposals originally submitted by the Union in this case included detailed provisions covering wages, hours and a variety of working conditions. If an employer assents to most or all of such proposals, the resulting agreement, unless reduced to writing, will be so impractical of enforcement and so fruitful of disputes concerning terms that an insistence by an employer that he will go no further than to enter into an oral agreement may be evidence, in the light of other circumstances in the case, of a denial of the right of collective bargaining." (At 116.)

is achieved.[4] As pointed out previously in this decision, the doctrine was applied in a case involving the employer now before us where, as here, it had refused to enter into any agreement with the Union.[5]

Coming to the present Act, we find that its terminology in Section 7 with respect to the right to bargain collectively is practically identical with that of Section 7(a) of the N.I.R.A. In addition the present Act in Section 8, subdivision (5) makes express what was implied in the former statute—it is an unfair labor practice for an employer to refuse to bargain collectively with the representatives of his employees. In view of the numerous decisions of the old Board interpreting the duty to bargain collectively as demanding of the employer that he make every reasonable effort to arrive at an understanding which, if reached, must be embodied in an agreement, it is only reasonable to assert that the Congress in Section 7 and Section 8, subdivision (5) of the Act intended its language to carry the same obligation. Similarly, since that interpretation formed the basis for the old Board's declaration of the majority rule principle, the adoption of that principle in Section 9(a) of the Act may likewise be regarded as an acceptance of the underlying reasoning.

The Reports of the Congressional Committees on the Act confirm our view. The House Report states with respect to Section 8, subdivision (5): "The fifth unfair labor practice, regarding the refusal to bargain collectively, rounds out the essential purpose of the bill to encourage collective bargaining and the making of agreements."[6] In the discussion of the majority rule principle, we find these words: "As has frequently been stated, collective bargaining is not an end in itself; it is a means to an end, and that end is the making of collective agreements stabilizing employment relations for a period of time, with results advantageous both to the worker and the employer."[7] The decision of the old Board in the Houde case was relied upon to support the principle. The Senate Report in connection with Section 8, subdivision (5) states:

"It seems clear that a guarantee of the right of employees to bargain collectively through representatives of their own choos-

---

[4] In the Matter of Atlanta Hosiery Mills, I National Labor Relations Board Decisions (1934) 144; In the Matter of Colt's Patent Fire Arms Manufacturing Co., II National Labor Relations Board Decisions (1935) 155; In the Matter of Denver Towel Supply Company, II National Labor Relations Board Decisions (1935) 221; In the Matter of Federal Mining and Smelting Company, II National Labor Relations Board Decisions (1935) 481; In the Matter of Square D Company, II National Labor Relations Board Decisions (1935) 430.

[5] In the Matter of St. Joseph Stockyards Co., II National Labor Relations Board Decisions (1935) 112.

[6] House of Representatives, Report of the Committee on Labor, 74th Congress, 1st Session, Report No. 1147, at p. 20.

[7] Ibid, at p. 20.

ing is a mere delusion if it is not accompanied by the correlative duty on the part of the other party to recognize such representatives as they have been designated (whether as individuals or labor organizations) and to negotiate with them in a bona fide effort to arrive at a collective bargaining agreement." [8] And again, in the section dealing with the majority rule, we find language similar to that in the old Board decisions: "The object of collective bargaining is the making of agreements that will stabilize business conditions and fix fair standards of working conditions." [9]

In the light of the above, we can only conclude that the issue raised by the respondent must be determined against it on the basis of authority and precedent. But even if the issue be regarded as a de novo matter, we feel a similar conclusion is inescapable. An assertion that collective bargaining connotes no more than discussions designed to clarify employer policy and does not include negotiation looking toward the adoption of a binding agreement between employer and employees is contrary to any realistic view of labor relations. The development of those relations had progressed too far when the Act was adopted to permit the conclusion that the Congress intended to safeguard only the barren right of discussion. The protection to organization of employees afforded by the first four subdivisions of Section 8 can have meaning only when the ultimate goal is viewed as the stabilization of working conditions through genuine bargaining and agreements between equals. That such is the goal is made clear in Section 1 of the Act, wherein the policy of the United States is stated to be the protection of self-organization of workers and the designation of their representatives for the purpose of negotiating the terms and conditions of their employment.

The same conclusion is reached by another approach. The respondent presses upon us its willingness at all times to receive and discuss the collective demands presented to it and to state its decision on those demands. But it asserts that it is enough that any acquiescence in those demands be made tangible by their adoption as part of its business policy and argues that it is not required to enter into an agreement embodying the understanding reached. Such confirmation through agreement is said to be unnecessary, for its employees have been informed that the respondent intends to continue the business policy thus inaugurated or already in existence. But in asking protection against unforeseen changes in the respondent's personnel and other uncertainties of the future, the employees are only acting as would any reasonable and prudent business man. To this the respondent replies

---

[8] Senate, Report of the Committee on Education and Labor, 74th Congress, 1st Session, Report No. 573, at p. 12.
[9] Senate, Report of the Committee on Education and Labor, 74th Congress, 1st Session, Report No. 573, at p. 13.

that its policy is not to sign agreements or make agreements. Certainly we cannot take such a statement literally. It would be preposterous to claim that all of respondent's multifarious activities are based not upon the customary contracts of commerce but solely upon the hope that the policies of the concerns and individuals participating in those activities will continue unaltered. The respondent's statement simply means that its policy is not to enter into agreements with labor organizations representing its employees.

The solution of the problem lies in the recognition of that attitude. Such an attitude grows out of an antipathy toward organization of workers and a refusal to concede that the policy of the United States shall be the policy of the respondent. It is designed to thwart and slowly stifle the Union by denying to it the fruits of achievement. It is based upon the knowledge that in time employees will grow weary of an organization which cannot point to benefits that are openly credited to its aggressiveness and vigilance and not to an employer's benevolence that on the surface may appear genuine but in truth is forced upon the employer by the organization. To many this unwillingness to enter into an agreement with a labor organization may seem no more than a harmless palliative for the employer's pride and to amount only to a petty refusal to concede an unimportant point purely as a face-saving device. But the frequency with which the old Board was compelled to denounce such a policy on the part of employers indicates its potency as a device subtly calculated to lead to disintegration of an employee organization. Viewed from the other side, the main objective of organized labor for long has been the collective agreement and the history of organization and collective bargaining may be written in terms of the constant striving for union recognition through agreement. In many cases employees have left their employment and struck solely because of the employer's refusal to enter into a collective agreement. An objective that has been so bitterly contested by employer and employee, that has been the cause of many long and costly strikes, must be evaluated in the light of the conflict it has produced. The respondent's persistent adherence to the policy of not entering into agreements with labor organizations representing its employees must be regarded as an intentional and effective interference with the employees' exercise of the rights guaranteed in Section 7 of the Act.

We therefore conclude that the Act imposes upon employers the duty to meet with the duly designated representatives of their employees, to bargain in good faith with them in a genuine attempt to achieve an understanding on the proposals and counterproposals advanced, and, finally, if an understanding is reached to embody that understanding in a binding agreement for a definite term. Here the respondent and the Union had in the course of their negotiaticns achieved a meeting of the minds upon four points. The Union then requested that the respondent enter into an agreement containing these four points. In our view of the Act, the minds of the parties having met, it imposed upon the respondent a definite obligation to embody the understanding in an agreement. The respondent's failure to do so constituted an unfair labor practice, within the meaning of Section 8, subdivisions (1) and (5).

We must not be considered as holding that an employer is obligated by the Act to accede without more to the terms of a contract presented to him by the representatives of his employees. The Act does not so provide and we make no such interpretation. The Senate Report is clear on this point: "The committee wishes to dispel any possible false impression that this bill is designed to compel the making of agreements or to permit governmental supervision of their terms. It must be stressed that the duty to bargain collectively does not carry with it the duty to reach an agreement, because the essence of collective bargaining is that either party shall be free to decide whether proposals made to it are satisfactory." [10] Thus, an employer is not required to sign the specific agreement presented to him by representatives of his employees. Nor is he obligated to agree to any of their demands solely for the sake of reaching some agreement when genuine accord is impossible although both sides are acting in good faith. But the line between these privileged areas and the duty imposed by the Act is distinct; the employer must negotiate in good faith in an endeavor to reach an understanding, and that understanding if eventually achieved must be incorporated into an agreement if the representatives of the employees so request. Even that duty does not require that the employer enter into an unalterable obligation for an extended period of time, since many collective agreements contain a clause permitting termination or modification by either party upon prescribed notice. The duration of the agreement, like any of its substantive terms, is a matter for negotiation between the parties.[11] . . .

---

[10] Senate, Committee on Education and Labor, 74th Congress, 1st Session, Report No. 573, at p. 12.
[11] The Conclusions of Law and the Order are omitted.—Ed.

IN THE MATTER OF MOTOR TRANSPORT COMPANY and
GENERAL CHAUFFEURS, TEAMSTERS & HELPERS,
LOCAL UNION NO. 200

Case No. R-113. Decisions of the National Labor Relations Board,
1937. 2 N.L.R.B. ....

. . . The company is a corporation organized and existing
under the laws of the State of Wisconsin. Its principal office and
place of business is in Milwaukee, Wisconsin, where it operates
as a local cartage carrier, and as a contract and common carrier
of freight in interstate commerce. In the latter phase of its business it is subject to and is registered under the Federal Motor
Carriers Act, 49 Stat. 543. In the conduct of its business the
company owns and operates 67 single unit trucks, 41 tractors
and 65 trailers. These are operated by 147 drivers and helpers
employed by the company. Seventeen dock-men and helpers participate in the unloading of trucks and the preparation of freight
for loading at terminals owned and operated by the company in
Milwaukee, Racine, Kenosha, Waukesha, Burlington, Watertown
and Sheboygan, in the State of Wisconsin. At Milwaukee, Wisconsin the company also employs nine mechanics and mechanics'
helpers and a clerical force of 10 persons. Besides the terminals,
the company has warehouse facilities and stations in approximately
50 other cities and towns in the State of Wisconsin, and in North
Chicago, Waukegan, Winthrop Harbor, Beech, Zion and South
Beloit in the State of Illinois.
. . . Local 200 suggested that the unit should consist of
drivers, drivers' helpers, dock-men and dock-men's helpers in
Milwaukee County, Wisconsin, employed by the company. The
U.P.U.E. differed from Local 200 in that it would also include in
the unit mechanics, mechanics' helpers and office personnel, and
moreover would embrace employees of the company outside of
Milwaukee County, Wisconsin wherever situated.

The status and function of the office force is completely different from that of other employees of the company engaged in or
about the transportation of freight, with the result that there is
not that community of interest regarding wages, hours and working conditions which makes for an appropriate collective bargaining unit. We therefore find that the employees engaged in the office
of the company shall not be included in the appropriate unit.

The mechanics and mechanics' helpers are of course more
closely related to the actual transportation process, and barring
other considerations their inclusion in the unit in question would
not necessarily be regarded as inappropriate. However, traditionally mechanics have organized into labor organizations apart from

other employees in the freight transportation industry, and have set up their own standards of working conditions. This condition exists in Milwaukee County, Wisconsin as well as in other parts of the United States. Furthermore, the mechanics employed by the company have themselves expressed no desire to be included in the unit under consideration. For these reasons we hold that the mechanics employed by the company shall not be included in the appropriate unit.

The remaining problem is whether all the drivers, drivers' helpers, dock-men and dock-men's helpers employed by the company, or only those engaged in Milwaukee County, Wisconsin, constitute an appropriate unit. Here again, were this presented as an original matter, the question would not be free of doubt. The issue is posed, however, years after drivers and dock-men in the industry generally and in Milwaukee County, Wisconsin had adopted the procedure of bargaining in individual units covering employees in local communities only. Thus Local 200 has jurisdiction over employees in Milwaukee County, Wisconsin only.[1] This practice has arisen from the collective experience of drivers and dock-men the country over influenced by variations in the cost of living, wage scales, working conditions, and standards of living from community to community, and by the desirability of obtaining maximum participation in the affairs of the labor organization by members wherever situated. The form of organization thus voluntarily chosen and retained for many years by employees in the industry generally is necessarily entitled to great weight in determining the unit in question. Moreover, it appears that 59 of the 80 drivers, drivers' helpers, dock-men and dock-men's helpers employed by the company in Milwaukee, Wisconsin, exclusive of supervisory employees, desire that the appropriate unit be defined in keeping with the practice in the industry. Although 53 other employees of the company signed a petition requesting that the unit should embrace all employees of the company, it is significant that not one of the signers was employed in Milwaukee County, Wisconsin. The Board is loath to combine in one unit employees of the company engaged in and outside of Milwaukee County, Wisconsin, knowing that a majority of the former prefer to bargain as a separate unit.

It was contended by the union that friction and antagonisms may result between those employed in Milwaukee County, Wisconsin and those engaged by the company elsewhere, in the event that the former were declared to constitute an appropriate unit. This argument is not convincing for two reasons: (1) It is based on the assumption that an appropriate unit consisting of the Mil-

---

[1] Other locals of the International Brotherhood of Teamsters, Chauffeurs, Stablemen and Helpers admit to membership employees situated outside of Milwaukee County, Wisconsin.

waukee County, Wisconsin employees must necessarily result in a choice of rival labor organizations to represent the employees in and outside of Milwaukee County, Wisconsin, which is a non sequitur; and (2) employees of the company belonging to the U.P.U.E. and to Local 200 are working together harmoniously at the present time despite the rivalry between the two labor organizations.

We therefore find that the drivers, drivers' helpers, dockmen and dock-men's helpers, in Milwaukee County, Wisconsin, employed by the company, constitute a unit appropriate for the purposes of collective bargaining.[2] . . .

IN THE MATTER OF GLOBE MACHINE AND STAMPING CO., and METAL POLISHERS UNION, LOCAL No. 3, et al.

Case Nos. R-178, R-179, R-180. Decisions of the National Labor
Relations Board. August 11, 1937.

STATEMENT OF CASE

On May 13, 1937, Metal Polishers Union, Local No. 3, herein called the Polishers Union, International Association of Machinists, District No. 54, herein called the I. A. M., and Federal Labor Union 18788, herein called the Federal Local, filed separate petitions with the Regional Director for the Eighth Region (Cleveland, Ohio), alleging that questions affecting commerce had arisen concerning the representation of employees of The Globe Machine and Stamping Co., Cleveland, Ohio, herein called the Company, and requesting the National Labor Relations Board, herein called the Board, to conduct an investigation pursuant to Section 9 (c) of the National Labor Relations Act, 49 Stat. 449, herein called the Act. On May 19, 1937, the Board, acting pursuant to Section 9 (c) of the Act, and Article III, Section 3 of National Labor Relations Board Rules and Regulations—Series 1, as amended, authorized the Regional Director to conduct an investigation and to provide for an appropriate hearing; and the Board further ordered, pursuant to Article III, Section 10 (c) (2) of the Rules and Regulations—Series 1, as amended, that the three cases be consolidated for the purposes of

---

[2] The Conclusions of Law and the Certification of Representatives are omitted.

Accord, as to the weight given to the established practice in the particular industry: In the Matter of Birge & Sons Co. and United Wall Paper Crafts, 1 N.L.R.B. 731 (1936); In the Matter of International Mercantile Marine Co. and International Union of Operating Engineers, 1 N.L.R.B. 384 (1936).

For a decision as to what is a "craft or class" as used in Section 2, Fourth, of the Railway Labor Act, as amended (supra, p. 71), see: Brotherhood of Ry. & S. S. Clerks v. Nashville, C. & St. L. Ry., C.C.H. Labor Law Serv., par. 16248 (D. Tenn., 1936).

the hearing. On June 17, 1937, the Regional Director issued a notice of hearing to be held at Cleveland, Ohio, on June 24, 1937, copies of which were duly served upon the Company, upon the three petitioning unions, and upon the United Automobile Workers of America, herein called the U. A. W. A., a labor organization named in the petitions as claiming to represent the Company's employees.

Pursuant to the notice, a hearing was held at Cleveland, Ohio, on June 24 and 25, 1937, before Charles E. Persons, the Trial Examiner duly designated by the Board. The Board, the Company, the Polishers Union, and the I. A. M. were represented by counsel, and the U. A. W. A. was represented by two of its officers. All participated in the hearing. The Federal Local did not appear and took no part in the proceedings. Full opportunity to be heard, to examine and to cross-examine witnesses, and to introduce evidence bearing on the issues was afforded all parties appearing. Objections to the introduction of evidence were made during the course of the hearing by counsel for the parties. The Board has reviewed the rulings of the Trial Examiner, and finds that no prejudicial errors were committed. The rulings are hereby affirmed.

Upon the entire record in the case, the Board makes the following:

FINDINGS OF FACT

I. THE BUSINESS OF THE COMPANY

The Company is a corporation, organized in 1902 under the laws of Ohio, with its principal office and place of business located in Cleveland, Ohio. Its plant is also located in Cleveland. It is engaged principally in the manufacture of radiator grilles for automobiles. It has a registered trade-mark for use in interstate commerce.

In 1936, the volume of the Company's business was $2,500,000, of which $2,495,300, or about 98 per cent, was done without the State of Ohio. Delivery is made by the Company at the purchaser's plant, shipment being made by railroad and independent trucking companies. Most of the product is sent to Michigan. The total amount of purchases made by the Company in 1936 amounted to $1,103,000, of which amount $714,000, or 65 per cent, was made without the State of Ohio. The principal raw material is steel, which comes chiefly from Pennsylvania.

The number of the Company's employees fluctuate greatly, having been as high as 750 and as low as 500 during the first six months of 1937. This fluctuation is apparently due to the fact that the Company, being an auto parts plant, is subject, in accentuated form, to the seasonal variations of the automobile industry.

II. THE ORGANIZATION INVOLVED

A. *The Petitioning Unions*

The three unions who filed petitions in this proceeding are all labor organizations affiliated with the American Federation of Labor. Local No. 3 of the Polishers Union includes members who are working in various plants in Cleveland. It claims jurisdiction over the polishers and buffers at the Company's plant. The I. A. M. limits its jurisdiction to the punch press operators. Its members at the Company's plant are in five or six different locals, all within District No. 54. The Federal Local claims the balance of the production and maintenance workers. Its membership is apparently restricted to men working at the Company's plant.

B. *The United Automobile Workers of America*

The U. A. W. A. is a labor organization affiliated with the Committee for Industrial Organization. It admits to membership all of the employees of the Company who are included within the three groups claimed by the petitioning unions. It appears to have a separate Local, No. 243, for employees of the Company.

III. THE QUESTION CONCERNING REPRESENTATION

A. *The Background of Organization at the Company's Plant*

In 1933, there were at the Company's plant, a chapter of the Mechanics Educational Society of America, herein called the M. E. S. A., which included tool and dye workers only; a specialists local of the I. A. M., which included the men working in the punch press room; and the Federal Local, which included all other employees engaged in production and maintenance. There is some evidence in the record that for a time, the I. A. M. local included welders and other workers at the plant, and that after some conflict, the membership in that local was restricted to punch press men.

During the period from 1933 to late in 1936, practically all of the employees engaged in production and maintenance were in one of the three unions. While it does not appear that the plant was a closed shop, it is clear that most men who worked there joined one of the unions shortly after they started working, if they were not already members. Although no signed agreements were reached at any time with the Company, there were continuous and friendly negotiations which resulted in oral agreements covering hours, wages, and grievances. It would appear, however, that these agreements were in no sense formal, since the members of the unions were only informed of their terms orally by the members of the negotiating committee, and the terms were never embodied in an agreement or otherwise made the subject of formal memoranda. Negotiations were conducted by a joint committee at least for the A. F. of L. unions and the product of these negotiations was termed a "federated agreement."

In December, 1936, the polishers at the plant were transferred from the Federal Local into the petitioning local of the Polishers Union. There were 60 polishers at this time employed at the plant and most of them joined in a body on December 16, 1936. Thereafter, negotiations for the polishers, which theretofore had been conducted by the Federal Local, were conducted by the Polishers Union.

Shortly before the transfer of the polishers, the tool and dye men in the M. E. S. A. voted to go over to the Committee for Industrial Organization. Just how formal that action was does not appear, and it would seem that the U. A. W. A. did not begin its organizational drive at the plant until some months thereafter. Nevertheless, there is evidence that at this time, and during the following months, there was considerable sentiment among the men to change their form of organization and to affiliate with the C. I. O. The U. A. W. A. began its drive at the plant in February, and on March 6, 1937, it called a meeting of all the men, the attendance at which was between 550 and 650. No formal check-up was made of those attending the meeting. There was a door guard who had worked for the Company for about 16 years and who knew all of the men at the plant. He admitted only those who he knew were employed by the Company. In addition a witness who testified for the U. A. W. A., who had worked at the plant for 14 years, testified that a majority from every department of the plant, including the polishing and punch press departments, were present, and a representative of each department stood up at the meeting and attested the fact that a majority was present from his department. This meeting unanimously decided to join the U. A. W. A. The U. A. W. A. witness stated that 85 per cent of the men then working were present, and that the remaining 15 per cent endorsed the action during the following days.

During the succeeding months the U. A. W. A. attempted to negotiate with the Company, and finally on May 17, 1937, called a strike which was effective in causing a complete shut-down of the plant. It does not appear in the record how many men and what departments participated in this strike. The strike was settled three days later, on May 20, 1937, by a signed agreement between the Company and the U. A. W. A., which provided, among other things, for a flat eight cents an hour raise for all employees, with somewhat higher raises for lower paid employees. The agreement was to remain in force until May 19, 1938, "unless terminated prior thereto by any decision of the National Labor Relations Board."

B. *The Present Situation*

The Polishers Union, the I. A. M., and the U. A. W. A. placed membership lists in evidence. No list was submitted by or for the Federal Local. The Polishers Union list includes members in good standing who were working for the Company, as of the beginning of 1937. It has 59 names. The I. A. M. list contains 95 names of members who were working at the plant on May 13, the date of the petitions. The U. A. W. A. list includes all paid up members of the local at the Company's plant. It lists 35 polishers, and 119 in the press room. The total for all departments is 687. It should be noted that the Polishers Union list was made up as of a time when there was a production peak. At the time the petitions in this case were filed, there were only about 35 polishers working at the plant.

Since the Company employed not more than 750 men at any time during the first six months of 1937, it is obvious that there are many duplications in these lists. The exact number is difficult to ascertain due to inaccuracy in the copying of names. However, the names of most of the men in both the polishing and punch press departments appear on two lists. Thus it can be seen that the men who were in the petitioning unions at the beginning of the year signed up almost unanimously in the U. A. W. A. during its organizational drive in February and March. However, there is evidence of a subsequent swing back to the Polishers Union and the I. A. M. Several of the witnesses for these two unions testified that they were among those who had joined the U. A. W. A. while still holding membership in one of the petitioning unions, and stated further that they now preferred the latter. At the present time it is impossible to find which of the contending groups is favored by a majority of the polishers and of the punch press operators.

C. *The Present Controversy*

The petitioning unions claim that there are three separate units for collective bargaining in this plant. The U. A. W. A. contends that the plant cannot be subdivided as claimed and that it should be treated as one unit. All parties are agreed that there should be an election. They are also all agreed that eligibility should be based on the payroll for the week including May 13, 1937, the date of the petitions, and such a payroll has been supplied by the Company.

IV. THE APPROPRIATE UNIT

The Company's plant has numerous departments, major and minor, through which its products flow in the course of production. A representative of the Company testified that all products go through at least three departments and that a tie up of one department would tie up the whole plant. A classification list which was placed in evidence shows that many different types of work are done at the plant.

Both polishing [1] and punch press work are done at the plant of the Company in separate, clearly-defined areas; the former in two rooms on separate floors, and the latter all in one room. There is evidence that men are shifted about from department to department and that they may be taken from assembly and put onto polishing or punch press work. There is little evidence, however, that men ever return from polishing or press room work to other departments.

There is a great deal of testimony as to the degree of skill required for polishing and press room work. With regard to polishing it appears that some degree of skill is required for the work done at the Company's plant, although the operations are relatively simple and can be learned rather quickly. A man may become sufficiently adept at the tasks required in the plant without becoming an all-round polisher. However polishers are paid higher wages than are men on the assembly line, and in general, when taking on new men, experienced polishers are sought. Much the same applies to the punch press men. They are termed specialists by the I. A. M. They are not all-round machinists, but rather operators of a particular kind of machine. There was testimony to the effect that a new man would have to work very slowly and the product of his early labor would not be worth very much. There was also evidence, however, that a specialist at one machine within the press room would not necessarily be able to operate any other punch press machine.

In view of the facts described above, it appears that the Company's production workers can be considered either as a single unit appropriate for the purposes of collective bargaining, as claimed by the U. A. W. A., or as three such units, as claimed by the petitioning unions. The history of successful separate negotiations at the Company's plant, and also the essential separateness of polishing and punch press work at that plant, and the existence of a requirement of a certain amount of skill for that work are proof of the feasibility of the latter approach. The successful negotiation of a plant-wide agreement on May 20, 1937, as well as the interrelation and interdependence of the various departments at the Company's plant, are proof of the feasibility of the former.

---

[1] The Polishers Union claims jurisdiction over polishers and buffers. The record is not clear, but it seems that the same men do both polishing and buffing at the plant. Throughout this opinion, polishing may be taken to include buffing.

In such a case where the considerations are so evenly balanced, the determining factor is the desire of the men themselves.[2] On this point, the record affords no help. There has been a swing toward the U. A. W. A. and then away from it. The only documentary proof is completely contradictory. We will therefore order elections to be held separately for the men engaged in polishing and those engaged in punch press work. We will also order an election for the employees of the Company engaged in production and maintenance, exclusive of the polishers and punch press workers and of clerical and supervisory employees.

On the results of these elections will depend the determination of the appropriate unit for the purposes of collective bargaining. Such of the groups as do not choose the U. A. W. A. will constitute separate and distinct appropriate units, and such as do choose the U. A. W. A. will together constitute a single appropriate unit.

V. THE EFFECT OF THE QUESTIONS OF REPRESENTATION ON COMMERCE

On May 17, 1937, there was a strike at the Company's plant which caused a complete stoppage and shut-down during its three-day duration. A representative of the Company testified that the strike had repercussions outside of the state in which the Company is located.

We find that the questions concerning representation which have arisen, occurring in connection with the operations of the Company described in Section I above, have a close, intimate, and substantial relation to trade, traffic, and commerce among the several States, and have led and tend to lead to labor disputes burdening and obstructing commerce and the free flow of commerce.

CONCLUSION OF LAW

Upon the basis of the above findings of fact, the Board makes the following conclusion of law:

Questions affecting commerce have arisen concerning the representation of the employees of The Globe Machine and Stamping Co., within the meaning of Section 9 (c) and Section 2, subdivisions (6) and (7) of the National Labor Relations Act.

---

[2] This factor was held to be of significance in Matter of Atlantic Refining Co., 1 N.L.R.B. 359; Matter of Chrysler Corporation, 1 N.L.R.B. 164; Matter of International Mercantile Marine Co. et al., 1 N.L.R.B. 384; and in Matter of New England Transportation Co. and International Association of Machinists, 1 N.L.R.B. 130.

DIRECTION OF ELECTIONS

By virtue and pursuant to the power vested in the National Labor Relations Board by Section 9 (c) of the National Labor Relations Act, 49 Stat. 449, and pursuant to Article III, Section 8 of National Labor Relations Board Rules and Regulations—Series 1, as amended, it is

DIRECTED that, as part of the investigations authorized by the Board to ascertain representatives for collective bargaining with The Globe Machine and Stamping Co., elections by secret ballot shall be conducted within fifteen (15) days from the date of this Direction, under the direction and supervision of the Regional Director for the Eighth Region, acting in this matter as agent for the National Labor Relations Board, and subject to Article III, Section 9 of said Rules and Regulations, among those employees of The Globe Machine and Stamping Co. who fall within the groups described below who were on the payroll of the Company for the week which included May 13, 1937:

a. Those engaged in polishing and buffing to determine whether they desire to be represented by the Metal Polishers Union, Local No. 3, affiliated with the American Federation of Labor, or the United Automobile Workers of America, affiliated with the Committee for Industrial Organization, for the purposes of collective bargaining.

b. Those engaged in the press room in the operation of punch press machines to determine whether they desire to be represented by International Association of Machinists, District No. 54, affiliated with the American Federation of Labor, or the United Automobile Workers of America, affiliated with the Committee for Industrial Organization, for the purposes of collective bargaining.

c. All other employees engaged in production and maintenance, except supervisory and clerical employees, to determine whether they desire to be represented by Federal Labor Union 18788, affiliated with the American Federation of Labor, or the United Automobile Workers of America, affiliated with the Committee for Industrial Organization, for the purposes of collective bargaining.[5]

---

[5] See also: In the Matter of City Auto Stamping Company and International Union, United Automobile Workers of America, Local No. 12, Case No. R-203, August 11, 1937.

IN THE MATTER OF ALUMINUM COMPANY OF AMERICA
and ALUMINUM WORKERS UNION No. 19104

Case No. R-4. Decisions of the National Labor Relations Board,
1936. 1 N.L.R.B. 530.

. . . Taking the petition in this case at its face value, the Board is only asked to investigate and certify, pursuant to Section 9(c) of the Act, the "name or names of the representatives that have been selected" by the employees at the Alcoa plants. Ordinarily, such a request would involve (1) a decision as to whether the employees at those plants constitute an appropriate bargaining unit within the meaning of Section 9(b); (2) if they do constitute such unit, the holding of an election to determine whom the employees desire as their representatives for collective bargaining; and (3) the certification of the name or names of the representatives chosen at such an election. Normally, such cases arise from situations in which the only organization claiming to represent the employees contends that it represents a majority of the employees in an appropriate unit but the employer refuses to bargain with it on the ground that such representation is not established, or in which each of two or more competing organizations claims a majority. The machinery of Section 9(b) and 9(c) is thus designed to complement and make workable the principle of the majority rule declared in Section 9(a). Its purpose is simply to resolve, by means of an election or other suitable method, any doubts concerning which, if any, organization can claim the exclusive right to bargain collectively for certain employees.

As stated above, on its face the instant petition appears to present the normal situation described above: one organization, Aluminum Workers Union No. 19104, claims to represent a majority of the employees at the Alcoa plants of the Company. It asserts that another body, the Council,[1] contests this claim. It in effect requests an election to resolve the issue thus created. However, the foregoing brief summary of the facts in the case indicates that the issues here are of an essentially different character. A short statement of the real issues in the case makes it clear that under the guise of a petition for certification the parties are presenting entirely different questions to this Board for its decision.

Assuming for the purposes of the argument that the Alcoa plants constitute an appropriate bargaining unit, as the Union contends, an election would be necessary to establish the strength of the Union. If the Union received a majority vote in such an election, the Board would then certify it as the representative of

---

[1] The National Council of Aluminum Workers, composed of representatives of local unions of aluminum workers.—Ed.

the employees at Alcoa. But such certification would in no way conclude this controversy since the underlying question here is not whether the Union shall represent the employees, but rather, who shall represent the Union in its dealings with the Company. The solution of that question is far from simple. Wetmore, the president of the Union, contended before the Board that he speaks for the Union in all matters, including its dealings with the Company. He claims that his contention is supported by the actual wishes of the members of the Union. With equal vigor, Williams asserted that the applicable rules of the American Federation of Labor demand that the Alcoa Union bargain only in concert with the other unions through the Council which he heads and that consequently that body and not Wetmore speaks for the Alcoa Union in its dealings with the Company. It may be observed, so as further to point the problem, that the rules of the American Federation of Labor as applied to this case are by no means free from doubt. The Alcoa Union is a Federal Labor Union directly chartered by the American Federation of Labor. The Constitution of the Federation in Article XIV provides as follows:

"Sec. 2. The Executive Council (of the Federation) is authorized and empowered to charter Local Trade Unions and Federal Labor Unions, to determine their respective jurisdictions not in conflict with National and International Unions, to determine the minimum number of members required, qualifications for membership and to make rules and regulations relating to their conduct, activities and affairs from time to time and as in its judgment is warranted or deemed advisable."

While this section was referred to by Williams, he did not offer evidence of any action by the Executive Council itself directed to the instant case or any delegation of authority to President Green, but introduced only the ruling of the latter. While it might be said that a strict and technical view would therefore make that ruling of President Green inapplicable, it must be remembered that Wetmore and the organization he represents are still, and voluntarily, parts of a larger organization and that Green is its president. It is possible that the unwritten law of tradition and custom makes his rulings binding within the Federation until altered. However, as hereinafter appears in our view of the case it becomes unnecessary to resolve these opposing contentions.

The course and conduct of the future bargaining of the Alcoa Union is thus bound up with the question of who shall speak for that Union. The real question is therefore who represents and speaks for the Alcoa Union and not whether that Union represents a majority of the employees at Alcoa. The Board feels that the question is not for it to decide. Such a question, involving solely and in a peculiar fashion the internal affairs of the American Federation of Labor and its chartered bodies, can best be decided by the parties themselves. The availability of the Board as a convenient forum for the airing of such problems would induce the parties to present them to the Board without first having made any real attempt to compose their differences among themselves. The consequent accumulation of cases on its docket would considerably hamper the work of the Board. Nor do we feel that the petitioner itself after a full consideration of the implications of its request would desire the Board to pass judgment upon such matters.

It is preferable that the Board should not interfere with the internal affairs of labor organizations. Self-organization of employees implies a policy of self-management. The role that organizations of employees eventually must play in the structure established by Congress through that Act is a large and vital one. They will best be able to perform that role if they are permitted freely to work out the solutions to their own internal problems. In its permanent operation the Act envisages cohesive organizations, well-constructed and intelligently guided. Such organizations will not develop if they are led to look elsewhere for the solutions to such problems. In fine, the policy of the National Labor Relations Act is to encourage the procedure of collective bargaining and to protect employees in the exercise of the rights guaranteed to them from the denial and interference of employers. That policy can best be advanced by the Board's devoting its attention to controversies that concern such fundamental matters. The petition for certification is accordingly dismissed.[2]

---

[2] For an extension of the doctrine to cases in which one of the unions may have no members among the employees involved, see: In the Matter of Standard Oil Co. and International Association of Oil Field, etc., Workers, 1 N.L.R.B. 530 (1936). In Matter of Interlake Iron Corp., Case No. R-149, 2 N.L.R.B. ...... (1937), the Board refused to apply the doctrine to a case involving a union affiliated with the American Federation of Labor, on the one hand, and a union affiliated with the Committee for Industrial Organization, on the other, saying: ". . . although technically both the contending unions may be said to be affiliated with the same organization, the American Federation of Labor, we should be blind indeed to the facts of common knowledge if we therefore concluded that both unions would submit to the authority of that body. Since the action by the Executive Council of the American Federation of Labor on September 5, 1935, suspending the international unions affiliated with the Committee for Industrial Organization, if not for a long time before, those unions have ceased to obey the orders of the Federation." For an analysis of the legal problems raised by the suspension, see The C.I.O. Controversy, 5 I.J.A. Bull. 15 (1936).

The Board's construction of the Act was approved in California State Brewers' Institute v. International Brotherhood of Teamsters, etc., (N.D. Calif., June 25, 1937), a case growing out of the bitter and widespread jurisdictional contest between the Brewers' Union and the Teamsters' Union. For other aspects of the same struggle, see: In re Cleveland & Sandusky Brewing Co., 11 F. Supp. 198 (N.D. Ohio, 1935); Blanchard v. Golden Age Brewing Co., 63 P.(2d) 397 (Wash., 1936). For the attitude of the courts, see also: Horan v. Barrett, C.C.H. Labor Law Serv., par. 16265 (N.Y. Sup. Ct., 1936); Touraine Knitwear Co. v. Hillman, C.C.H. Labor Law Serv., par. 16266 (N.Y. Sup. Ct., 1936).

IN THE MATTER OF ALGONQUIN PRINTING COMPANY and UNITED TEXTILE WORKERS OF AMERICA, LOCAL No. 1044.

Case No. C-7. Decisions of the National Labor Relations Board, 1936. 1 N.L.R.B. 264.

. . . *Relations Between the Respondent and the Union.* The Union is a local of the United Textile Workers of America and is a labor organization of textile workers. The Union was organized in August, 1933. Textile workers in various mills in Fall River are eligible for membership. Very shortly after its formation the Union secured a membership of about 80 per cent. of the workers in the respondent's plant and continues to have that membership. The Union and the respondent, through its superintendent, Mr. Harley, came to an oral understanding on the method to be used in adjusting grievances. Under this arrangement the Union was to have a steward in each department of the plant who would take up grievances with the foreman of the department. If the steward was unable to settle a grievance, he would report to the Shop Chairman. The Shop Chairman would talk with the foreman of the department in question. If he did not succeed with the foreman, he would talk with the superintendent. Failing there, he would place the matter in the hands of the Union's business agent.

In April, 1934, there was a strike in the plant. The duration of the strike does not appear from the record. In September, 1934, the plant was closed as a result of the general strike throughout the textile industry. Shortly thereafter the Union members walked out of the plant for one day as a protest against the employment of six or seven workers who had continued working during the general strike. These six or seven men had been led by one Mahoney, who, prior to the general strike, had been a Union member and who shortly thereafter sought to form a union restricted to plant members. This attempt at organization seems to have come to nothing. In January, 1935, Thomas Joyce became superintendent of the Algonquin plant. He refused to deal with the Union officials in respect to the settlement of disputes. In May the Union brought a case of alleged discharge for union activity before the Textile Labor Relations Board. About this time the National Industrial Recovery Act was held unconstitutional, and the Textile Board did not render a decision in that case. Mr. Jennings, the treasurer of the respondent, admitted on cross-examination that he resented the difficulties caused by union activity, that his attitude toward the Union and its officials was not a friendly one, that he was more friendly toward those workers who had continued at work during the general strike, that the Union officials were more responsible than the rank and file for employee dissatisfaction, that he had expressed resentment to Mr. Bishop, the Union's business agent, both in connection with the Union's appeal to the Textile Labor Relations Board and with other activities of Mr. Bishop among the employees.

Manuel Madeiros. Mr. Madeiros hàd worked for the respondent since 1921, with the exception of two three-month intervals. He worked for two years at various jobs, earning at first $14.00 and later $16.00 per week, until finally he was promoted to the job of back-tender at increased pay. He worked as back-tender until July 19, 1935.˙ His immediate foreman testified that his work was as satisfactory as that of any other back-tender, and there is no evidence or suggestion to the contrary.

Madeiros was known as a vigorous Union officer. He joined the Union in August, 1933. He became a member of the executive board. In December, 1933, he was made Shop Chairman; he continued in this position as long as he was employed by the respondent. During his incumbency he presented 75 to 100 grievances to the management; many of them he carried to the superintendent. In June, 1935, Madeiros was elected vice-president of the Union to fill an unexpired term; in November he was elected vice-president for a full term. He became thereby the highest ranking Union officer in the plant, the president of the Union being employed in another plant. Madeiros was the spearhead of Union activity in the respondent's plant. He did not limit himself to the formal matter of presenting grievances. When Mahoney began to organize a plant union, Madeiros protested.

On June 17, 1935, the plant was shut down. Final liquidation of the respondent was being seriously considered. The respondent had (and still has) 15 printing machines available for use in its plant. Each machine in use is manned by a printer. Each printer has a back-tender to assist him in the operation of the machine. In addition, nine or more spare hands would be carried if all 15 machines were in use. At the time of the shutdown there were 14 printers, 15 back-tenders (one not working) and 11 spare hands carried on the payrolls. The plant reopened for the two weeks ending July 13 and July 20, 1935. In the first week there were employed 8 printers, 8 back-tenders and 4 spare hands; in the second there were 6 printers, only 5 back-tenders and 4 spare hands. Mr. Madeiros was employed the first week but not the second; he was told that it was his turn to loaf. The plant was reopened again for the week ending August 24, 1935, and at the date of the hearing was still running. In the week of August 24th there were 8 printers, 8 back-tenders and 7 spare hands. In the following week there were 10 printers, 12 back-tenders and 7 spare hands. The 2 extra back-tenders were apparently used as spare hands. The following week there were 12 printers, 13 back-tenders (one was working as a spare hand) and 7 spare hands (exclusive of the back-tender working as such).

Mr. Madeiros applied for work the day of the reopening in August, to Mr. Blake, a sub-foreman in the printing department (known as a second hand) who was taking the applications of the back-tenders and spare hands. Blake told him: "I haven't got you on the list. You had better see the boss." "The boss" was Mr. Snell, foreman of the printing department. Mr. Snell told Madeiros: "I haven't got anything for you, I am carrying out my orders from the office." A week later Madeiros again presented himself to Snell and was given the same answer. About three weeks after the plant reopened, Bishop, the business agent of the Union, spoke to Snell on behalf of Madeiros. Snell told him that he had orders not to reemploy Madeiros. Bishop spoke to Jennings, the respondent's treasurer, requesting him to stagger the work so that Madeiros and Lauretta Rawston might be reemployed. Jennings replied that they no longer cared to stagger the work.

Mr. Blake, the second hand, testified that when the plant reopened he employed all of the old back-tenders except Madeiros, ten for the position of back-tender, four as spare hands. When Madeiros arrived, Blake testified, all of the jobs he had to give out had been filled. Later those back-tenders working as spare hands were shifted to their regular positions and he "called back" the regular spare hands to fill the vacancies. Even if Blake's recollection of the facts was correct, it would still cause very real suspicion of discrimination against Madeiros: the respondent employs every available back-tender except Madeiros, even supplanting four of the regular spare hands to make jobs for them; more men are "called back"; Madeiros has, in the interim, again sought employment, but still no work can be found for him; instead the regular spare hands are now used.

The facts, however, as revealed by the respondent's employment records, show a somewhat different situation. In the first week of the reopening only eight of the back-tenders appear on the rolls. They were apparently all used as back-tenders since there were eight printers employed that week. The following week 12 of the back-tenders appear on the rolls, 2 being used, apparently, as spare hands, since there are only 10 printers. Five of these were men not employed in the previous week, one from the previous week having dropped out for one week. In the following week there are 13 back-tenders, one serving as spare hand. One of the regular back-tenders had been employed elsewhere, but in the week ending October 19 we find him on the payroll, first as a spare hand, then in his regular position. At later periods some one or other of the back-tenders serves as spare hand or truckman.

The situation then is this: Mr. Madeiros presents himself during the week ending August 24th and is told there is no work. He returns the next week; again he is told there is no work. Yet in that week all of the available remaining 5 back-tenders are reemployed, work being made for two or three of them as spare hands And most significant of all, in that same week there appears on the rolls a new spare hand, J. Robello, who has never appeared there at all. Thus it appears that with the single and persistent exception of Madeiros, the respondent has reemployed all of the old back-tenders, and that when they could not be used as back-tenders, has found other work for them. In a week when Madeiros was applying for employment and when two of his fellow back-tenders were taken on as spare hands, an entirely new spare hand was taken; yet there was no work for Madeiros.

Mr. Madeiros was a good worker. His seniority was superior to at least four of the back-tenders and most of the spare hands. Mr. Jennings testified that he bore no ill feeling against Madeiros. Yet, with respect to employment, the discrimination against him is beyond doubt, and this discrimination is explicable only on the ground of his prominence in Union activity. It has already been shown above that the respondent harbored resentment against the Union. Madeiros, the Shop Chairman, was the constant and visible symbol of the Union and its claims.

The respondent maintains that the work of Madeiros did not cease as a consequence of a current labor dispute but by reason of the closing of the plant due to depressed business conditions. The intended implication is that under those circumstances a refusal to employ him at a later date cannot be a violation of the Act. This defense is in line with the statement which Bishop testified Mr. Jennings made to him, that "everyone was hired from week to week and that they didn't have to take everyone back." The respondent no doubt has in mind the definition of an employee under Section 2, subdivision (3), providing that the term "employee" shall include one whose work has ceased as a consequence of a current labor dispute. But Section 8, subdivision (3) in forbidding discrimination in employment, is not limited to those who are employees at the time of the discrimination. It forbids discrimination in regard "to hire" generally. The purpose of the provision is, it is true, to protect employees in their right to self-organization. But surely a refusal by an employer to rehire a former employee because of his union activities which are well known to his former fellow workers discourages the latter and so restrains them in the exercise of their right to self-organization.

Lauretta Rawston. Mrs. Rawston was a "doubler." Doubling is the process of folding the cloth double and winding it on a cardboard spool for shipping. She had been employed by the respondent for 18 years, off and on. She was out five years because of sickness, and was laid off in 1933 or 1934 by an efficiency expert because she was a married woman. Before the shutdown in June, eight doublers were employed. During the temporary operations in July, Mrs. Rawston was not employed. When the plant was reopened five of the doublers were reemployed. Two did not apply, and Mrs. Rawston on applying was told that she would be sent for when she was wanted. She has never been sent for nor has she been reemployed. Two new doublers have since been employed.

Mrs. Rawston joined the Union in January, 1934. Shortly afterwards she became a shop steward. In the early part of 1935 she was elected financial secretary to fill an unexpired term; and in the fall was elected financial secretary for a full term.

The respondent claims that Mrs. Rawston was refused employment because she was not efficient. On April 1, 1935, the respondent employed Thomas Riley as overseer of packing. Mr. Riley inaugurated a policy of taking day-to-day records of the output of the doublers. He noted the number of "short" and "regular" pieces of cloth handled by each doubler. Pieces vary from 10 to 40 yards. Those between 10 and 20 yards are known as short pieces; over 20 yards as regular pieces. Regular pieces average 30 yards. The short pieces are more easily and quickly handled than the regular pieces.

On the basis of these records, the respondent maintains that Mrs. Rawston was among the three most inefficient of the doublers, and points out that none of these three has been reemployed. This argument is offered to show that the verdict of inefficiency was not devised solely to keep out Mrs. Rawston. The other two girls, however, did not apply for reemployment. Further doubt is cast on this argument by the fact that, even accepting the records at their full value, one of the girls, Dais, has a higher total for the period of the records than at least one of those who was taken back. It thus still remains to be explained that of the whole group of doublers Mrs. Rawston alone was refused reemployment.

We have studied these production records carefully and we have come to the conclusion that they are so inadequate and show a situation so peculiar that the respondent could not from the records have formed any opinion of Mrs. Rawston's efficiency. The respondent's judgment as to her efficiency is based on the fact that she has handled the next to the smallest total number of pieces. The records cover a period of nine weeks. The number of pieces do not, at least over so short a period, provide a common and constant factor of comparison. The pieces vary from 10 to 40 yards; the amount of time consumed in handling these pieces varies, the shorter the piece, the less the time consumed. The respondent has made no study of the amount or rate of variation.

The respondent has made no time analysis of this or any other element of work involved in the doubling process. The respondent has never on the basis of experiment or experience established a standard of expectable performance based on actual elements of work content. Mr. Riley testified that he had decided on a minimum of 400 long or 500 short pieces per day. Yet, during the nine weeks when the records were kept, no worker ever handled anything like that number.

Mr. Riley testified that the existence of these undefined and unanalyzed variations did not impair the usefulness and reliability of the record, because on the average all workers would receive an equal number of short and long pieces. If it is the normal practice in the plan to even up the long and short pieces among all the workers, then the facts shown by the records are surprising indeed; for it appears that of the total pieces done by each of three workers, Mrs. Rawston being one of them, 88 per cent., 88.6 per cent. and 88.9 per cent. respectively, were long pieces—the highest percentage is Mrs. Rawston's; whereas the percentage of long pieces for the six other workers is 59, 43.4, 51.2, 46.8, 47.6 and 40.1, respectively. It should be further pointed out that the three workers having the highest percentage of long pieces were on all of the nine weekly record sheets listed first in the order: Wilcox, M. Rogers and Rawston, reading left to right. From these facts it is clear that these three workers were deliberately being given one kind of work, the other six another. Why this was so we do not know. It may be because these were the oldest and most experienced workers and this work was considered more difficult. But what is very clear is that it utterly destroys the usefulness of the records in rating these nine workers. To the already completely inadequate analysis of time factors upon which the record is based, there is added the fact that the nine workers were not even doing the same work. We credit the respondent's officers and foremen with the normal intelligence and experience to be found among those who for many years have been engaged in this industry. We cannot believe that on such a record kept for nine short weeks the respondent concluded that a worker employed by it for eighteen years was inefficient to the point that she alone of all those applying for work should be refused.

The pattern of facts in Mrs. Rawston's case is strikingly like that in Mr. Madeiros'. Each had worked many years for the respondent, each had become in 1935 an important union officer—the only union officer reemployed by the respondent was a sergeant-at-arms—each was the only one in his or her group who, applying for reemployment, was refused.

We found that respondent's hostility to the Union, particularly to its officers, accounts for its refusal to reemploy Mr. Madeiros. That consideration is equally relevant in the case of Mrs. Rawston. Standing together the two cases reinforce the conclusion which we have drawn from each case separately: that the respondent by striking at the leadership of the Union was seeking to discourage Union membership and activity. Therefore we find that the respondent has discriminated against Lauretta Rawston and Manuel Madeiros with respect to terms of employment for the purpose of discouraging membership and activity in the union among its employees and has interfered with, restrained and coerced its employees in the exercise of the rights guaranteed in Section 7 of the Act.[1]

---

[1] The Conclusions of Law and the Order are omitted.

For other cases illustrating the technique adopted by the Board for evaluating evidence of inefficiency as the alleged motivating reason for the discharge, see: In the Matter of Atlanta Woolen Mills and Local No. 2307, U.T.W.A., 1 N.L.R.B. 316 (1936) (textile mill hands; defense of inefficiency rejected as to four employees, sustained as to one); In the Matter of General Industries Co. and Hobart Flenner et al., 1 N.L.R.B. 678 (1936) (plastic moulders; defense of inefficiency rejected as to three employees, sustained as to one); In the Matter of Hearst and American Newspaper Guild, Case No. C-136, 2 N.L.R.B. ...... (1937) (newspaper photographer; defense of inefficiency rejected); In the Matter of Pacific Greyhound Lines and Brotherhood of Locomotive F. & E., Case No. C-134, 2 N.L.R.B. ...... (1936) (bus drivers; defense of inefficiency rejected), reinstatement order enforced, National Labor Relations Board v. Pacific Greyhound Lines, C.C.H. Labor Law Serv., par. 16398 (C.C.A. 9th, 1937); In the Matter of Pennsylvania Greyhound Lines and Local Division No. 1063; 1 N.L.R.B. 1 (1935) (automobile mechanics; defense of inefficiency rejected as to five employees, sustained as to four), reinstatement order enforced, National Labor Relations Board v. Pennsylvania Greyhound Lines, C.C.H. Labor Law Serv., par. 16388 (C.C.A. 3d, 1937); In the Matter of Quidnick Dye Works and Federation of Dyers, etc., of America, Case No. C-149, 2 N.L.R.B. ...... (1937) (folder of textiles; defense of inefficiency rejected); In the Matter of Willard, Inc., and Hotel & Restaurant Employees Alliance, Case No. C-164, 2 N.L.R.B. ...... (1937) (waiter; defense of inefficiency rejected).

In Agwilines, Inc. v. National Labor Relations Board, 87 F.(2d) 146 (C.C.A. 5th, 1936), the court refused to enforce the order of the Board as to three of seven longshoremen whom the Board had ordered reinstated. As to two of the three, the Board had found that they had been discharged for union activities and not, as claimed by the employer, for carelessness. The court was of the opinion that the Board's findings were not supported by evidence. (See National Labor Relations Act, sec. 10(e), supra, p. 92.)

For other typical discrimination cases, see: National Labor Relations Board v. Jones & Laughlin Steel Corp., 301 U.S. 1 (1937); National Labor Relations Board v. Fruehauf Trailer Co., 301 U.S. 49 (1937); National Labor Relations Board v. National N. Y. Packing & Shipping Co., 86 F.(2d) 98 (C.C.A. 2d, 1936); In the Matter of Oregon Worsted Co. and United Textile Workers, 1 N.L.R.B. 915 (1936); In the Matter of Protective Motor Service Co. and Twenty-five Employees, 1 N.L.R.B. 639 (1936); In the Matter of United Aircraft Mfg. Corp. and Industrial Aircraft Lodge No. 119, 1 N.L.R.B. 236 (1936).

For cases of discrimination against strikers upon application for reinstatement, and for the nature of the Board's orders in such cases, see: In the Matter of Allen & Co. and Federal Labor Union Local No. 18526, 1 N.L.R.B. 714 (1936); In the Matter of Mackay Radio & Telegraph Co. and American Radio Telegraphists' Ass'n, 1 N.L.R.B. 201 (1936), petition to enforce denied on constitutional grounds, 87 F.(2d) 611 (C.C.A. 9th, 1937), supra, p. 127, note 14; In the Matter of Remington Rand and Remington Rand Joint Protective Board, Case No. C-145, 2 N.L.R.B. ...... (1937), infra, p. 169; In the Matter of Timken Silent Automatic Co. and Ormsbee, 1 N.L.R.B. 335 (1936).

IN THE MATTER OF INTERNATIONAL HARVESTER COMPANY and LOCAL UNION No. 57, INTERNATIONAL UNION, UNITED AUTOMOBILE WORKERS OF AMERICA

Case No. C-41. Decisions of the National Labor Relations Board, 1936. 2 N.L.R.B. ....

. . . . We may now turn to a consideration of the legality of the Plan under the National Labor Relations Act in the light of the facts found above. Section 8, subdivision (2) declares that it shall be an unfair labor practice for an employer "to dominate or interfere with the formation or administration of any labor organization or contribute financial or other support to it."

At the outset it must be remembered that the respondent conceived of the Plan, formulated it and caused it to be put into operation. It started out as the respondent's Plan—not the employees'. It has continued to be the respondent's Plan. Its entire upkeep, all its expenses, are defrayed by the respondent. The persons who are charged with the task of representing employees are reimbursed by the respondent for the work they perform in such capacity. The respondent admitted such financial support but contended it was not contrary to the Act for the following reasons: (1) the proviso of Section 8, subdivision (2), properly construed, permits the practice of allowing employee representatives to perform all of their duties without loss of pay. Consequently, they may be compensated at their regular rate of pay for time spent in activities in connection with the Plan, such as contacting constituents, meeting among themselves, etc., even though such activities do not involve at the time conferences with management, since such activities enable the representatives later to confer intelligently with management. But the clear words of the proviso negate any such construction—"an employer shall not be prohibited from permitting employees *to confer with him* during working hours without loss of time or pay" (italics ours). The Senate Committee Report speaks of the "right to receive normal pay *while conferring*," and it is manifest that the proviso goes no further than permitting such conferences directly with management to occur without loss of pay to the employee representatives; (2) The respondent further contended that Section 8, subdivision (2) does not prohibit the respondent from giving financial support to the Plan and bearing the expenses incidental to its operation since the Plan is not a labor organization and the Section only prohibits the contribution of financial support to a "labor organization." The Plan is said not to be a labor organization in that it is not a membership society capable of acting as a legal entity—it has no members, no existence of any kind as an artificial person but is merely an aggregate of practices. In relation to the efficacy of the Plan as a collective bargaining mechanism, this admission is significant. As an argument, however, it borders on the frivolous in view of the language of Section 2, subdivision (5) defining the term "labor organization" as used in the Act to include *"any agency* or employee representative committee or *plan* in which employees participate and which exists for the purpose, in whole or in part, of dealing with employers" (italics ours). It is obvious that the term "labor organization" is not used in its ordinary meaning but in a special and technical sense solely for the purpose of statutory draftsmanship and to make the prohibition of Section 8, subdivision (2) all inclusive. That prohibition was intended to apply to any device which would tend to displace, or masquerade as, a genuine labor organization, whether it was itself such a genuine organization or not. In short, the term "labor organization" was so defined to avoid the very contention that the respondent now urges upon us.

The respondent's contributions are not limited to financial support. Its President, Vice-Presidents, Manager of Industrial Relations, Superintendents—in fact its whole executive and supervisory force—unceasingly extoll the virtues of the Plan. The employee whose economic life is at the mercy of those who sing such praises will not fail to comprehend their significance. And, such economic considerations aside, the praises of such business leaders at the very least are certain to commend the Plan to many an employee and his family—"Approbation from Sir Hubert Stanley is praise indeed." In another field, by careful manipulation and scrupulous adherence to the outward forms of collective bargaining, the respondent has so interwoven the Plan into the numerous beneficial activities designed to improve the welfare and morale of the employees and thus increase their efficiency—vacation plan, Credit Union, Athletic Association, pension plan, safety measures, etc.—that the Plan receives credit for many of these benefits in the eyes cf the employees. This association of things intrinsically beneficial to the employees with a system of collective bargaining which in reality has played little or no part in their creation or functioning constitutes "restraint" upon the employees to adhere to the Plan and "support" for the Plan. The impropriety would hardly be more obvious if the respondent were to inaugurate the practice of Christmas bonuses and allot them to the employee representatives for distribution.

With equal skill and subtlety the respondent controls the procedure of the Plan. Its Industrial Relations Department sits at the controls, keeping constant watch. The normal operations of the Plan can be steered in any direction by means of the many checks carefully established—preliminary meetings, management officials as Chairman and Secretary, appeals to higher executives, etc. Now this change will be made, now that change, if the management so "wishes to record its desire."

The Plan is thus entirely the creature of the management. The respondent in its relation to the employees may be conceived as a holding company—the Athletic Association, pension plan, vacation plan are the subsidiary operating companies. The Harvester Industrial Council Plan is merely one of these subsidiary concerns controlled by the respondent. In so controlling it the respondent is beyond question acting contrary to Section 8, subdivision (2), and interfering with, restraining and coercing employees in the exercise of the rights guaranteed in Section 7 of the Act.

We find that the aforesaid acts of the respondent tend to lead to labor disputes burdening and obstructing commerce and the free flow of commerce.

The respondent has controlled the Plan at its Fort Wayne Works ever since its inception in 1927, and such control today is a violation of the Act. To terminate that violation and to insure to the employees at the Fort Wayne Works the right to self-organization and the free choice of representatives for collective bargaining guaranteed to them by the Act, the Board will order that the respondent shall withdraw all recognition from the Plan as an agency for collective bargaining at the plant and completely disestablish it as a representative of its employees. Such disestablishment is the only effective remedy in the case. In the Matter of Pennsylvania Greyhound Lines, Inc., decided December 7, 1935; In the Matter of Clinton Cotton Mills, decided December 31, 1935; In the Matter of Wheeling Steel Corporation, decided May 12, 1936; In the Matter of Ansin Shoe Manufacturing Company, decided June 12, 1936.[1]

CONCLUSIONS OF LAW

Upon the basis of the foregoing findings of fact the Board makes the following conclusions of law:

1. The plan of employee representation and collective bargaining at the Fort Wayne Works known as the "Harvester Industrial Council Plan" is a labor organization, within the meaning of Section 2, subdivision (5) of the Act.

---

[1] This form of order was reviewed in National Labor Relations Board v. Pennsylvania Greyhound Lines, C.C.H. Labor Law Serv., par. 16388 (C.C.A. 3d, 1937), and National Labor Relations Board v. Pacific Greyhound Lines, C.C.H. Labor Law Serv., par. 16398 (C.C.A. 9th, 1937). In both cases, the court refused to enforce the order in so far as it required withdrawal of recognition and disestablishment, on the ground that such action may be required only upon the formal designation of some other labor organization as the representative for purposes of collective bargaining. Cf. Virginian Railway Co. v. System Federation No. 40, 300 U.S. 515 (1937), supra, p. 71.—Ed.

2. By its domination and interference with the administration of such "Harvester Industrial Council Plan," and by its contribution of financial and other support thereto, the respondent has engaged in and is engaging in unfair labor practices, within the meaning of Section 8, subdivision (2) of the Act.

3. By the conduct set forth above, the respondent has interfered with, restrained and coerced its employees in the exercise of the rights guaranteed in Section 7 of the Act, and has engaged in and is engaging in unfair labor practices, within the meaning of Section 8, subdivision (1) of the Act.

4. The aforesaid unfair labor practices are unfair labor practices affecting commerce, within the meaning of Section 2, subdivisions (6) and (7) of the Act.

ORDER

On the basis of the findings of fact and conclusions of law, and pursuant to Section 10, subdivision (c) of the National Labor Relations Act, the National Labor Relations Board hereby orders that the respondent, International Harvester Company, and its officers and agents, shall:

1. Cease and desist from in any manner interfering with, restraining or coercing its employees in the exercise of their rights to self-organization, to form, join or assist labor organizations, to bargain collectively through representatives of their own choosing, and to engage in concerted activities for the purpose of collective bargaining or other mutual aid or protection;

2. Cease and desist from dominating or interfering with the formation or administration of any labor organization of its employees or contributing financial or other support thereto.

3. Take the following affirmative action, which the Board finds will effectuate the policies of the Act:

(a) Withdraw all recognition from the "Harvester Industrial Council Plan" as representative of its employees at the Fort Wayne Works for the purpose of dealing with respondent concerning grievances, labor disputes, wages, rates of pay, hours of employment, or conditions of work; and completely disestablish the "Harvester Industrial Council Plan" as such representative;

(b) Post notices in conspicuous places throughout all departments of the Fort Wayne Works stating (1) that the "Harvester Industrial Council Plan" is so disestablished, and that respondent will refrain from any recognition thereof, and (2) that such notices will remain posted for a period of at least thirty (30) consecutive days from the date of posting.

IN THE MATTER OF ANSIN SHOE MANUFACTURING COMPANY and SHOE WORKERS' PROTECTIVE UNION, LOCAL NO. 80

Case No. C-26. Decisions of the National Labor Relations Board, 1936. 1 N.L.R.B. 929.

. . . the Ansin and Anwelt Companies[1] announced that they were going to leave Athol. Prominent citizens organized a banquet at which Ansin, upon invitation, spoke. A Citizens' Committee was formed. This committee addressed a letter to Charles McAdams, clerk of the Union, and requested that "a committee of workers from the Ansin and Anwelt Factories be appointed" to meet with the Citizens' Committee. The following day, the Reverend Barker, chairman of the Citizens' Committee, asked McAdams which workers had been chosen to meet with the Committee. McAdams named, among others, David Carey, the organizer. The Reverend Barker stated that they would refuse to sit with the union committee if Carey were on it. An employee of Anwelt was selected in place of Carey. A group of non-union employees also was called to the meeting, and finally, Sidney Ansin, who knew that invitations had been extended to the union and non-union groups. During the period of the meetings and negotiations considered below the Reverend Barker called upon Ansin a number of times. Ansin reports the purpose of his calls as follows: "He wanted to know if the directors (of the two companies) would continue to stay in business there, if he could definitely determine from the workers that we (the companies) were going to be permitted to work harmoniously and continue operations there without having legal agreements unjustly broken."

At a meeting in which all committees and Ansin were present, a Mr. Pregent of Keene, New Hampshire, read and explained an agreement in force in that city between a shoe factory and its employees, who were organized on a one-plant basis. Ansin said that with few minor changes, the agreement would be satisfactory to him. At a meeting the following day Ansin read the Keene agreement with substantial variations proposed by him. He had added a provision for collecting dues for the union—whatever union it was to be—by shop stewards in the factory. To this there was objection: dues, it was said, should be collected by a business agent of the union. Ansin said that the dues collector must be responsible; that if his workers were forced to pay dues he wanted to know who was taking them, and what they were going to be

---

[1] The business of the Anwelt Company was conducted in conjunction with that of the Ansin Company. See the companion case, In the Matter of Anwelt Shoe Manufacturing Co. and Shoe Workers' Protective Union, 1 N.L.R.B. 939 (1936).—Ed.

used for. He suggested instead a check-off by the companies. During this conversation, in which Ansin participated, there was an assumption that a new union would be formed. A question arose as to the choice of business agent. Ansin insisted that the business agent must be a resident of Athol. He would not tolerate Carey or Nolan, the president of the International. These "outsiders" were "interferers." "Our relations with our employees," Ansin testified at the hearing, "were always very harmonious. We never had any trouble in the life of our two-year contract that amounted to anything, and all differences were adjusted until August of this year, when Mr. Nolan came to Athol and told the workers that by having 51 per cent. of those workers he could have a closed shop." McAdams was suggested as a business agent. Ansin approved the suggestion. McAdams, himself, made no comment.

Ansin testified at the hearing that whether the companies stayed in Athol depended upon "the success of the plan," which was discussed at these meetings. Ansin at this time offered $1,000 to start a hospitalization and welfare fund for the employees. This fund, too, depended upon the assurance to the companies that they could get along without "interference." Similarly, Ansin stated that he would take back the four discharged Anwelt workers, if the agreement were accepted.

The Citizens' Committee called a mass meeting of Anwelt and Ansin workers on Tuesday, November 11. At this meeting printed ballots appeared. There were two sets of ballots. One carried the names of candidates for officers of a new organization. Among these candidates was McAdams for business agent. McAdams had not given anyone authority to use his name in this manner. He was told that the Committee and the shop workers had picked him and that this was agreeable to Mr. Ansin. He insisted that these ballots be destroyed. The second set of ballots carried the question of choice between the existing Union and a new organization.

The Reverend Barker presided. He told the workers that Ansin would contribute a sum of money to start off the new organization. At the beginning of the meeting about 400 were present— there were about 1,000 employees in both factories, though at this time the Ansin plant was idle. The question of choosing between organizations was put to a vote. By this time only about 250 persons remained in the meeting. Of these a majority voted for a new organization. The vote was loosely conducted, without a check-list or identification of voters. Someone suggested that a Mr. Austin, an employee, take the chair, which he did. Meanwhile, Mr. Tyler, a member of the Citizens' Committee, telephoned to Ansin with respect to a question which had arisen concerning the proposed agreement. A disagreement arose between Ansin and Tyler and at the suggestion of the Citizens' Committee, the meeting was adjourned to the following Friday. During the entire meeting the Citizens' Committee was present, though its members, after the vote in favor of the new organization, had announced that "they had done their duty" and that they would retire from the hall and leave the workers to carry on their business. Mr. Ansin's secretary was also present taking notes; an employee noted her presence; upon request she withdrew.

A second meeting was held on the following Friday. About 250 persons were present. Austin continued as chairman. He read the proposed agreement. It contained a provision permitting a 50 hour work week. McAdams objected that the State law forbade more than 48 hours work for women. After more of the agreement had been read, Ferris, an Anwelt employee, protested that the agreement was "nothing more or less than a company union" and he moved that "the thing be torn up and discarded." The motion was carried by a large vote. The following Tuesday McAdams and Ferris [2] were laid off and have not yet been reemployed.

Some days after the Friday meeting, a mass meeting was held of Ansin workers alone. At this meeting about 100 persons were present. The Reverend Barker opened the meeting. "You people are suffering the consequences of the trouble in the Anwelt Department." He suggested the formation of an independent organization of Ansin workers. After 25 or more workers left the hall, the remainder agreed to form a new organization, the "Progressive Shoe Workers' Union." Officers were then nominated and elected from the floor. The Reverend Barker and one Barnes, an Ansin employee, approached Ansin and asked him if the new union might meet in the factory. Previously Ansin had refused to allow the use of his factory, but he now permitted it and two meetings of the new organization were held in the factory. Respondent and the Progressive signed an agreement. Article I read: "The purposes of our organization will be to promote a better understanding between the employer and the employees of the Ansin Shoe Manufacturing Company." Respondent checks-off the Progressive dues—10 cents per week—from the wages of employee-members. The pay envelope has a printed item noting the deduction. The agreement contains a provision for a "union shop": after two weeks employment it is compulsory for the employee to become a member of the Progressive union. The new union takes as members only employees of the Ansin Company. The Progressive union is a labor organization.

The charge against respondent is that it dominated and interfered with the formation and dominates and interferes with the administration of the Progressive union and contributes financial and other support to it. Sidney Ansin, testifying at the hearing,

---

[2] These two men are among those whose lay-off has given rise to the case against the Anwelt Company.

sought consistently to give the impression that respondent was purely passive in all the events described above; it did not call the meetings, write the by-laws, or propose the form of the new organization. It did not, in other words, actively take a part in initiating or forming the specific organization here attacked.

We do not so narrowly interpret Section 8, subdivision (2) of the Act, as to require this direct and immediate link between the employer and the outlawed organization. This section does not stand alone; its meaning is derived not solely from its words but from related Sections and from the purposes of the Act. This Section makes specific one of the ways in which an employer can interfere with the broad right of the employees under Section 7 to bargain collectively through representatives of "their own choosing," and is to be construed so as to further the intention of Section 7. Its object is to protect the rights of employees from being hamstrung by an organization which has grown up in response to the will and the purposes of the employer, an organization which would not be, in the sense of Section 7, an organization of the employees' choice. The workers may be aware of their employer's antipathy to union organization and seek to propitiate him by acceptable conduct. This may be unavoidable. But the employer can be prevented from engaging in overt activity calculated to produce that result. If labor organizations are to be truly representative of the employees' interest, as was the intention of Congress as embodied in this Act, the words "dominate and interfere with the formation of any labor organization" must be broadly interpreted to cover any conduct upon the part of an employer which is intended to bring into being, even indirectly, some organization which he considers favorable to his interests.

Of such conduct by respondent the record is full. When the president of the International announced, as Sidney Ansin says, that the Union would seek a closed shop, respondent countered with a threat to leave town. It is quite possible that Ansin did not arrange the intervention of the Citizens' Committee; that may have been quite unnecessary. Ansin had laid down an ultimatum: if we are to stay here, see to it that our labor relations are satisfactory. Thus advised of their danger, the employees and even more the business interests of the community, whose primary interest was to keep the factories in town on any terms, might well be expected to seek an acceptable solution. But Ansin's intervention did not stop at this point. He participated in the meetings between the Committee and his employees: meetings which were in essence labor organization meetings. His alleged role at these meetings was that merely of negotiator of the labor contract. This position is disingenuous. Though Ansin may have made very few suggestions as to the form which the organization was to take, his positive insistence that the business agent of the new organization be a resident of Athol revealed his demand that the new organization must not be a national organization; and the Committee's statement to McAdams that Carey, the outside organizer, must not be on the Union delegation showed at the very least that the Committee comprehended Ansin's views and that the whole problem of these meetings was to find a labor organization acceptable to Ansin. Ansin's vague offer of $1,000 for hospitalization, which in the speech of the Reverend Barker to the mass meeting became an offer of funds to the new Union—an offer which up to the time of the hearing had never been fulfilled in any form—was both a further pressure, and an attempt to give all of this pressure a benevolent aspect.

The "lay-off" of McAdams and Ferris after they had thwarted the organization of the combined Ansin-Anwelt workers was a pointed reminder of what the employees were expected to do. Thereupon 75 out of 500 Ansin workers formed, under the Reverend Barker's auspices, the new union. With this newly formed organization, Ansin signed an agreement embodying the "union-shop," an arrangement almost as drastic as the "closed shop," the suggestion of which by Nolan had caused Ansin to announce that the companies would leave Athol.

Thus has Ansin's original ultimatum borne fruit. Cautiously and discreetly reinforced from time to time by a suggestion, a show of power easily understood—yet combined always with the forms of aloofness and disinterestedness—it has brought forth a union restricted in membership to respondent's employees, and by the "union shop" clause, has ousted the old Union and its membership from the plant. This outcome does not flow from that free choice which our Act is designed to foster and protect. It is the result of fear deliberately provoked and a sufficient suggestion as to how the displeasure might be appeased. We find that respondent has dominated and interfered with the formation of the Progressive Shoe Workers' Union. . . .[3]

---

[3] The Conclusions of Law and the Order are omitted.

Cf. In the Matter of Lion Shoe Co. and United Shoe & Leather Workers' Union, Case No. C-92, 2 N.L.R.B. ...... (1937). For other typical cases arising under Section 8, subdivision (2) of the Act, see: In the Matter of Atlas Bag & Burlap Co. and Milton Rosenberg, 1 N.L.R.B. 292 (1936): In the Matter of Clinton Cotton Mills and Local No. 2182, 1 N.L.R.B. 97 (1935); In the Matter of Oregon Worsted Co. and United Textile Workers, 1 N.L.R.B. 915 (1936); In the Matter of Remington Rand and Remington Rand Joint Protective Board, Case No. C-145, 2 N.L.R.B. ...... (1937), infra, p. 169: In the Matter of Wheeling Steel Corp. and Amalgamated Association, 1 N.L.R.B. 698 (1936); and cases cited supra, p. 162, note 1.

IN THE MATTER OF REMINGTON RAND, INC. and REMINGTON RAND JOINT PROTECTIVE BOARD

Case No. C-145. Decisions of the National Labor Relations Board, 1937. 2 N.L.R.B. ....

. . . From the thousands of pages of testimony in this proceeding there may be distilled two very plain facts: the unwavering refusal of the respondent to bargain collectively with its employees and the cold, deliberate ruthlessness with which it fought the strike which its refusal to bargain had precipitated. If the provisions of the Act ever required justification, one need go no further than the facts of this case. Over 6,000 employees, with their families and dependents, are subjected to the miseries of a prolonged strike, the people of six communities experience the economic hardships that inevitably result when an accustomed source of income is suddenly withdrawn, these same communities are turned into warring camps and unreasoning hatreds are created that lead to abuses alien to a sane civilization—all because the respondent refused to recognize the rights of six thousand employees. A decent respect for the rights of human beings demands that no employer be free to ignore his employees in such fashion, but that, as provided by the Act, they be entitled through the procedure of collective bargaining to have a voice in shaping their destinies. Human rights aside, even a calculating dollars and cents approach to the situation would require that an employer confer with the representatives of his employees, for here six manufacturing plants are rendered idle and the channels of commerce dislocated, at a cost of millions of dollars, simply because the respondent could not bring itself to meet with its employees. In the legal phraseology of the Act the respondent, from April, 1936 to the strike on May 26, and again from the strike to the time of the hearings in this case, has continuously refused to bargain collectively with the representatives of its employees as required by Section 8, subdivision (5). In the language of the average person, the respondent, through Rand, its President, has exhibited a callous, imperturbable disregard of the rights of its employees that is medieval in its assumption of power over the lives of men and shocking in its concept of the status of the modern industrial worker.

To draw attention from its determined refusals to bargain collectively with the representatives of its employees and as part of its "back to work" movements, the respondent secretly formed Employees' Associations which it exhibited to the public as genuine employee organizations dealing with the respondent at arm's length. Those Associations—the Middletown Remrand Employees'

Back-to-Work Association, the Ilion Typewriter Employes Protective Association, and the Syracuse Employes' Independent Association—were "labor organizations" within the technical definition given that phrase in Section 2, subdivision (5) of the Act, for they were organizations in which employees participated and which existed for the purpose of dealing with employers concerning labor disputes and conditions of work, here the reopening of the plant. In view of that status, the respondent was forbidden by Section 8, subdivision (2) to dominate or interfere with their formation or administration or to contribute financial or other support to them. From the facts found above, the conclusion is inescapable that the respondent has deliberately flouted that provision of the Act. All three Associations were nothing more than dummy organizations operated by the respondent to further the "back to work" movement and break the strike. All three Associations operated in an identical manner—advertisements, offices, telephone numbers, requests to the respondent to open the plant, mass meetings and celebrations of employees at such openings. In each city where the Associations operated the advertisements were in the same pattern—and moreover, were skillfully written. Moreover, in Norwood, where the respondent did not choose to create such an Association but instead conducted the "back to work" movement entirely in its own name, the mechanics were nevertheless identical. The appearance of each Association coincided with a drive on the respondent's part to create a "back to work" breach in union ranks and they were admirably suited to that end. The use of telephones, while permitting the respondent to ascertain the number of employees ready to return to work, as pointed out before also enabled it to keep secret the number of such employees, and through the fear occasioned by such secrecy prompt many more to telephone. In addition, the very presence of these Associations would induce the public to believe that there was a large body of employees who did not belong to the unions and that the strike was supported by only a small minority of employees. The Associations also offered a basis for requests for heavy police protection and a medium for the dissemination of propaganda which if handed out by the respondent in its own name might be held suspect by the public. It is apparent that these Associations had many expenses—offices, telephones, advertisements, printed literature, offers of trips to Ilion, etc. Yet there is no indication of any means whereby the Associations themselves obtained the large funds necessary to defray such expenses. There were no dues, no requests for contributions. The money obviously came from the respondent. Bergoff's testimony in regard to the Ilion Association and Ellis' activities on behalf of the Middletown Association would in themselves indicate that these Associations were alter egos of the respondent. It should be noted that at the Board's hearing in this case, Ellis was introduced by Simson as the "Attorney for the Remington Rand at Middletown." Ellis had, as pointed out above, represented both strikebreakers employed by the respondent and the respondent itself in legal proceedings arising during the strike, so that his intimate relationship to the respondent is beyond question. Yet we also find Ellis preparing application blanks for the Middletown Association and attempting to secure office space for it. We therefore find that the respondent organized and operated these Associations and defrayed their expenses in violation of Section 8, subdivision (2). At Ilion, and later at Middletown, there was an attempt to capitalize on the results of these "back to work" Associations by using them as a basis in the formation of company-controlled organizations among the employees that had returned to work. The successor organizations are tainted with the illegality of their predecessors and are likewise in violation of the Act.

We turn to a consideration of the other unfair labor practices. The strike was caused by the respondent's unqualified and determined refusal to meet with the representatives of its employees. Thus when the strike came the respondent knew it was not to be settled by collective bargaining or mediation. Outside agencies, unaware of the quality of the respondent's determination, and seeing only a costly and bitter strike, would make efforts to mediate the dispute. Governors, Industrial Commissioners, Mayors, State Mediation Boards, Federal Conciliators would attempt in turn to end the strike by the peaceful method of conferences. But all were predestined to failure in the face of that unyielding resolve to fight the strike rather than to compromise ever so little through the concession of a conference. And in the execution of that resolve the respondent exhibited even a greater disregard for human rights and values than that which characterized its earlier refusals to bargain. It immediately engaged not one, but four strikebreaking agencies and with their aid charted its campaign. That campaign, as we have shown, was built around "back to work" movements, created systematically by the respondent and operated for the most part through Associations formed by it, which culminated in some cases in reopenings of the plants attended by celebrations and the return of massed groups of employees or thugs masquerading as such. These movements were built up through an intensive propaganda drive, openly in advertisements and news articles, covertly through the work of "missionaries." They were buttressed by threats to move the plants, and in some cases by actual movements of machinery, designed to create fear of loss of employment on the part of employees and fear of economic starvation on the part of whole communities. These threats presented a bewildering maze to both the employee

and the man in the street—the Norwood and Syracuse plants were
moving to Ilion, yet the Ilion plant was for sale. The Tonawanda
and Middletown plants were also to be moved, and yet where
could they be moved to if the other plants were also in the process
of being transferred? The answer of course is that such confusion
best served the respondent's interests, for no one community could
feel sure of not being the victim. Keeping pace with these "back
to work" movements was the respondent's constant drive to obtain
the presence of large forces of police and guards, not only for the
intimidation that their presence would work upon the average
employee, but also because of the psychological effect such forces
possess to turn the average citizen against a strike and the tendency of police and guards to indulge in excesses of force and
arrest against employees on strike. Where the "back to work"
movements did not result in inducing a sufficient number of employees to return, the respondent hired thousands of strikebreakers
to operate its plants, describing them to the public as "loyal employees."

Such was the main attack. It was supported by a variety of
manoeuvres and devices. Spies were planted in the various towns.
The company attempted to bribe union leaders and to influence
public officials. Individual bargaining was resorted to through
bonuses, personal telegrams, and visits of foremen and "missionaries" in order to undermine the solidarity of the union members.
Union leaders were discharged and others arrested for the
purpose of demoralizing the union. We have previously discussed
in detail these discharges of union leaders at Ilion, Syracuse and
Tonawanda. All of the individuals discharged, whose names appear in the Conclusions of Law, were discharged because of their
union membership and activity, and their discharges, and each
of them, thus constitute discrimination in regard to hire and tenure
of employment to discourage membership in a labor organization
contrary to Section 8, subdivision (3) of the Act. These individuals, who were employees at the time of their discharge, thus
ceased work as a consequence of unfair labor practices on the
part of the respondent and therefore continued to be employees
of the respondent within the meaning of the Act. Scenes of disorder and violence, to be described to the public as riots, were
staged so that they could serve as the basis for injunctions, requests for police protection and "law and order" tirades in the
press. In the planning of these disorders, the respondent exhibited
the small value it placed on human life, for with even-handedness
it stood willing to sacrifice the lives of the men whom it hired to
break the strike as well as those of the strikers. Likewise, in
having its agents commit acts of violence in such a fashion as to
ascribe the guilt to the strikers and in its deliberate provocation of

disorders by the strikers, it was not deterred by the knowledge that innocent men would be arrested and fined, that a citizenry, made almost hysterical through the respondent's subtle playing on its emotions and thoughts, would inflict excessive punishment upon men acting under infuriating provocation. Nor did the respondent stop at making dupes of the civil authorities or the leading citizens, as at Ilion, so that they would do the job for the respondent.

But all of these stratagems demanded for their success a public opinion favorable to the respondent and opposed to the strikers. The respondent appreciated that today the success or failure of a strike of such magnitude may ultimately depend upon the reaction of the public. It also recognized that a public fully informed of the tactics the respondent was employing and of its firm refusal to meet with its employees would in all probability condemn their use. Finally, it realized that the public is nearly entirely dependent upon the press and the radio for its information. Consequently, the respondent proceeded to wage a publicity campaign designed both to cloak its ruthlessness toward its employees and the public and to swing opinion against the unions. To this end numerous advertisements in the names of the respondent and its "back to work" associations were inserted in which the facts were distorted or completely falsified, the unions and their leaders maligned and the communities' dependence upon the respondent's payrolls stressed. Radio speeches of the same nature were made at frequent intervals. Release after release was handed out by the respondent from its executive offices and from its various plants, such practice to be varied at times by suddenly shutting off that source of news and forcing the papers to turn to the advertisements or to the Associations when such sources better served the respondent's immediate needs. Harding kept constant watch over the various press association reports so that the respondent could remedy impressions in the reports contrary to its ends or supply through releases and advertisements information which it thought the public should be handed and which those reports did not carry. Replies to offers of mediation were so framed as to be no more than a means of conveying to the public some particular item of propaganda that the respondent was desirous of spreading. Aspects that were sure to evoke a desired response were continually stressed, such as violence and threats of the likelihood of loss of a particular plant through closing and moving elsewhere.

It must be remembered that by striking the employees did not sever their status as such with the respondent. Section 2, subdivision (3) of the Act defines the term "employee" to include "any individual whose work has ceased as a consequence of, or in connection with, any current labor dispute or because of any unfair labor practice." Here the strike was caused by the respondent's refusal to bargain collectively and hence the employees ceased work as a consequence of an unfair labor practice. Moreover, the strike was obviously a "labor dispute" within the meaning of Section 2, subdivision (9) of the Act, since it was a controversy concerning conditions of employment and the association and representation of persons seeking to arrange terms and conditions of employment, and hence the employees also ceased work in connection with a current labor dispute. Thus, those employees who have not returned to work but who have remained on strike and who have not obtained employment elsewhere, between three and four thousand at the time of the hearing, have been since May 26 and still are the employees of the respondent in view of the unfair labor practice that caused the strike and the currency of the labor dispute. These employees were, of course, within their rights in striking, for Section 13 of the Act declares that "Nothing in this Act shall be construed so as to interfere with or impede or diminish in any way the right to strike." Under Section 8, subdivision (1) of the Act, the respondent was forbidden to interfere, restrain or coerce these employees in the exercise of their rights guaranteed in Section 7—among others, to bargain collectively and to engage in concerted activities for that purpose and for mutual aid and protection. The activities of the respondent which we have described in detail, were all designed to and did in fact interfere with, coerce and restrain its employees in the exercise of their rights. To put it concisely, those activities were employed to defeat the strike, to end the strike by breaking it rather than by settling it through collective bargaining. As the strike was in the first instance directly caused by the respondent's refusal to bargain collectively in violation of Section 8, subdivision (5) and was thereafter perpetuated through further refusals also in violation of that section, all of those activities must be regarded as contrary to Section 8, subdivision (1). While many, if not all, of those activities would likewise constitute unfair labor practices even though the strike and its continuation were not themselves the results of unfair labor practices, such a determination need not be made in this proceeding. Here, by its illegal refusal to bargain collectively, the respondent caused and perpetuated a strike and consequently any activities on its part designed to end that strike by defeating it, in contrast to settling it by the method of collective bargaining, are in violation of Section 8, subdivision (1). Each step taken so to defeat the strike constituted an assertion that the respondent would illegally continue to refuse to settle the strike through collective bargaining as provided by the Act—they were but the opposite faces of the same coin. We find that by its refusal to bargain collectively, and by its other acts, the respondent interfered with, coerced and restrained its employees in the exercise of the rights guaranteed in Section 7 of the Act.

Our previous decisions point the general remedy for these illegal acts. We have required in cases of strikes caused by a refusal to bargain collectively that the employer both bargain collectively with the representatives of his employees and restore as far as possible the status quo that existed at the time of the strike. Normally such restoration of the status quo is accomplished by the reinstatement of all employees on the payroll at the time of the strike, any new employees hired since that date to be dismissed if such action is necessary. If, because of curtailed production or other reasons, there are not a sufficient number of positions available to take care of all of the employees on the payroll at the time of the strike, the initial reinstatement is to be made on the basis of seniority by classifications, and those not reinstated are to be placed, on a similar basis, on a preferential list.[1] However, the respondent's acts of closing one of its plants, the Norwood plant, opening another, the Elmira plant, and shifting the equipment of still other plants, have introduced factors which make solution of the problem more difficult. While the total number of individuals now employed is approximately equal to the number employed at the date the strike was called, there has been a radical alteration in the location of the jobs for these employees. Thus, the Norwood plant has been closed and its equipment moved to the Ilion and Elmira plants so that while no jobs are available at Norwood, additional jobs are available at Ilion and Elmira. Similarly, 45 per cent. of the Syracuse operations and a substantial percentage of the Middletown operations have been transferred to Elmira, so that although the number of available positions in Syracuse and Middletown has been greatly reduced, a corresponding number of positions is now available at Elmira. Consequently, if all of the employees on the payroll of May 26, 1936 are to be reinstated, many will find it necessary to move from their present homes to other towns where positions are available. With nearly 4,000 employees to be reinstated under such conditions, the complexity of the problem created by the respondent's acts is readily realized.

The respondent will be ordered to reinstate all those production and maintenance employees involved who were employed on May 26, 1936 and who have not since received regular and substantially equivalent employment elsewhere. As the first step in

---

[1] Matter of Columbian Enameling & Stamping Co. and Enameling & Stamping Mill Employees Union, No. 19694, 1 N.L.R.B. 181; Matter of Rabhor Company, Inc., a Corporation, and International Ladies Garment Workers Union, 1 N.L.R.B. 470; Matter of S. L. Allen & Company, Incorporated, a Corporation, and Federal Labor Union, Local No. 18526, 1 N.L.R.B. 714.

carrying out this general order, such production and maintenance employees shall be reinstated to their former classifications, on the basis of seniority by classifications, where positions in such classifications are now open or have been filled by individuals employed since May 26, 1936 who were not employed on that date, the respondent dismissing such individuals if that is necessary to accomplish the reinstatement so ordered. In this fashion as far as possible employees will be reinstated in the plants in their own towns and will not be required to move elsewhere. But after such reinstatement there will still be a large group of employees, composed almost exclusively of Norwood, Syracuse and Middletown employees, who will have to move to other cities in order to obtain reinstatement. Consequently, all such production and maintenance employees not reinstated in the plant in their own towns shall be grouped together, regardless of the plant in which they were previously employed, on a single preferential list on the basis of seniority by classifications, to be offered the positions at the Elmira plant, and any positions still available at any of the other plants after those who struck at such plants have been reinstated. At Elmira, as well as elsewhere, individuals employed since May 26, 1936 who were not employed on that date must be dismissed if such action is necessary to effectuate such reinstatement. Thereafter, this list shall be drawn upon whenever further employees are needed at any of the plants involved, including the Elmira plant, preference being given to employees on the list then residing in the locality in which employment is available. The respondent will be ordered to pay the transportation expenses of any employee and his family who is forced to move in order to obtain reinstatement under these conditions.[2] As can be gathered, the Board has attempted to keep such moving to a minimum by ordering that available positions at each plant be filled by employees residing in the locality. Finally, as many of the employees who had prior to the strike designated the Joint Board as their representative for collective bargaining will thus be reinstated to the Elmira plant instead of to the plants where they had worked on May 26, 1936, we will include the Elmira plant together with the other plants in the unit which we have found to be appropriate for collective bargaining.

The employees who were individually discharged will be reinstated to their former positions and in addition be awarded back pay on the following basis: (1) those who were discharged

---

[2] The respondent in a statement to the Securities and Exchange Commission stated that among the expenses it suffered because of the strike were those "incident to the moving of machinery, materials and the families of employees, and the re-establishment of operations in the new locations," indicating that it recognized an obligation to employees thus forced to move their homes.

when they sought reinstatement during the continuance of the strike, designated as Group A in the Conclusions of Law, will receive back pay from the date of such discharge; (2) those who were discharged before the strike commenced or during the continuance of the strike but not as a consequence of applications for reinstatement, designated as Group B in the Conclusions of Law, will receive back pay from the date of discharge to the date of the strike if the plant was operating in that period, and again from the date on which operations in their department began after the reopening of the plants involved to the date of offer of reinstatement.[3]

---

[3] The Conclusions of Law and the Order are omitted.

In Remington Rand v. Crofoot, 248 App. Div. 356, 289 N.Y.S. 1025 (1936), the court affirmed an order granting the company a temporary injunction against the union in Syracuse, incidentally expressing a doubt that the case involved a "labor dispute" as defined in the New York Anti-Injunction Act, supra, p. 58, note 8.

For other cases involving labor espionage by private detectives, see: National Labor Relations Board v. Fruehauf Trailer Co., 301 U.S. 49 (1937); In the Matter of Fashion Piece Dye Wks. and Federation of Silk & Rayon Dyers, etc., 1 N.L.R.B. 285 (1936); In the Matter of Pennsylvania Greyhound Lines and Local Division No. 1063, 1 N.L.R.B. 1 (1935). For the form of order in such cases, see: In the Matter of Fruehauf Trailer Co. and United Automobile Workers, 1 N.L.R.B. 68 (1935); cf. Magruder, "Half Century of Legal Influence Upon the Development of Collective Bargaining," 50 Harv. L. Rev. 1071 (1937) 1096 et seq.

For other cases concerning interference with the right of self-organization by local and state agencies, see: In the Matter of Carlisle Lumber Co. and Lumber & Sawmill Workers' Union, Case No. C-93, 2 N.L.R.B. ...... (1936) (State Police); In the Matter of J. Freezer & Son and Amalgamated Clothing Workers, Case No. C-105, July 26, 1937 (Chamber of Commerce); In the Matter of Jones & Laughlin Steel Corp. and Amalgamated Association, 1 N.L.R.B. 503 (1936), order enforced, National Labor Relations Board v. Jones & Laughlin Steel Corp., 301 U.S. 1 (1937), supra, p. 97 (local police); In the Matter of Oregon Worsted Co. and United Textile Workers, Case No. C-167, July 16, 1937 (State Board of Conciliation); In the Matter of Fainblott and International L. G. W. Union, 1 N.L.R.B. 864 (1936) (Mayor; Sheriff).

A federal statute prohibits the interstate importation of strikebreakers and other persons for the purpose of interfering with the right of self-organization. Public No. 776, 74th Cong., 2d Sess. (1936), Legis. 85 U. of Pa. L. Rev. 406 (1937). See U. S. v. Bergoff, C.C.H. Labor Law Serv., par. 16396 (D. Conn., 1937).

Generally, as to labor espionage, strikebreakers, "back to work" movements, and the use of violence to interfere with the right to organize, see: Levinson, I Break Strikes: The Technique of Pearl L. Bergoff (1935); Calkins, Spy Overhead (1937); Huberman, The Labor Spy Racket (1937); Hearings before Subcommittee of the Committee on Education and Labor on S. Res. 266, 74th Cong., 2d Sess. (1936-1937), Preliminary Report of the Subcommittee (S. Rep. No. 46, 75th Cong., 1st Sess. (1937)); Report of the Subcommittee, "The Chicago Memorial Day Incident" (S. Rep. No. 46, Pt. 2, 75th Cong., 1st Sess. (1937)); Note, "Employer Interference With Lawful Union Activity," 37 Col. L. Rev. 816 (1937); Legis, 85 U. of Pa. L. Rev. 406 (1937); Landis 223 et seq. and notes.

On the use of the military in labor disputes, see: Strutwear Knitting Co. v. Olson, 13 F. Supp. 384 (D. Minn., 1936); Comment, "Use of Military Force in Domestic Disturbances," 45 Yale L.J. 879 (1936).